Twentieth-Century Literary Criticism

Guide to Gale Literary Criticism Series

For criticism on	Consult these Gale series
Authors now living or who died after December 31, 1959	*CONTEMPORARY LITERARY CRITICISM (CLC)*
Authors who died between 1900 and 1959	*TWENTIETH-CENTURY LITERARY CRITICISM (TCLC)*
Authors who died between 1800 and 1899	*NINETEENTH-CENTURY LITERATURE CRITICISM (NCLC)*
Authors who died between 1400 and 1799	*LITERATURE CRITICISM FROM 1400 TO 1800 (LC)* *SHAKESPEAREAN CRITICISM (SC)*
Authors who died before 1400	*CLASSICAL AND MEDIEVAL LITERATURE CRITICISM (CMLC)*
Black writers of the past two hundred years	*BLACK LITERATURE CRITICISM (BLC)*
Authors of books for children and young adults	*CHILDREN'S LITERATURE REVIEW (CLR)*
Dramatists	*DRAMA CRITICISM (DC)*
Hispanic writers of the late nineteenth and twentieth centuries	*HISPANIC LITERATURE CRITICISM (HLC)*
Native North American writers and orators of the eighteenth, nineteenth, and twentieth centuries	*NATIVE NORTH AMERICAN LITERATURE (NNAL)*
Poets	*POETRY CRITICISM (PC)*
Short story writers	*SHORT STORY CRITICISM (SSC)*
Major authors from the Renaissance to the present	*WORLD LITERATURE CRITICISM, 1500 TO THE PRESENT (WLC)*

ISSN 0276-8178

Volume 67

Twentieth-Century Literary Criticism

**Excerpts from Criticism of the
Works of Novelists, Poets, Playwrights,
Short Story Writers, and Other Creative Writers
Who Lived between 1900 and 1960,
from the First Published Critical
Appraisals to Current Evaluations**

Scot Peacock
Editor

Thomas Ligotti
Associate Editor

GALE

DETROIT • NEW YORK • TORONTO • LONDON

STAFF

Scot Peacock, *Editor*

Thomas Ligotti, *Associate Editor*

Marlene S. Hurst, *Permissions Manager*
Michele Lonoconus, Maureen Puhl, *Permissions Associates*
Jeffrey Hermann, *Permissions Assistant*

Victoria B. Cariappa, *Research Manager*
Michele P. LaMeau, Tamara C. Nott, Tracie A. Richardson, Cheryl L. Warnock,
Research Associates
Alfred A. Gardner, I, Sean R. Smith, *Research Assistants*

Mary Beth Trimper, *Production Director*
Deborah L. Milliken, *Production Assistant*

Sherrell Hobbs, *Macintosh Artist*
Randy Bassett, *Image Database Supervisor*
Robert Duncan, *Imaging Specialist*
Pamela Hayes, *Photography Coordinator*

Library of Congress Catalog Card Number 76-46132
ISBN 0-7876-1166-2
ISSN 0276-8178

Printed in the United States of America
10 9 8 7 6 5 4 3 2 1

Contents

Preface vii

Acknowledgments xi

Gertrude Bell 1868-1926 1
  English nonfiction writer and archaeologist

Nikolai Berdyaev 1874-1948 20
  Russian philosopher

Robert Byron 1905-1941 84
  English travel writer, art critic, and historian

R. G. Collingwood 1889-1943 92
  English philosopher and historian

V. I. Lenin 1870-1924 198
  Russian political leader and theorist

Rachilde 1860-1953 267
  French critic, autobiographer, and novelist

Literary Criticism Series Cumulative Author Index 341

Literary Criticism Series Topic Index 423

TCLC Cumulative Nationality Index 431

Preface

Since its inception more than fifteen years ago, *Twentieth-Century Literary Criticism* has been purchased and used by nearly 10,000 school, public, and college or university libraries. *TCLC* has covered more than 500 authors, representing 58 nationalities, and over 25,000 titles. No other reference source has surveyed the critical response to twentieth-century authors and literature as thoroughly as *TCLC*. In the words of one reviewer, "there is nothing comparable available." *TCLC* "is a gold mine of information—dates, pseudonyms, biographical information, and criticism from books and periodicals—which many libraries would have difficulty assembling on their own."

Scope of the Series

TCLC is designed to serve as an introduction to authors who died between 1900 and 1960 and to the most significant interpretations of these author's works. The great poets, novelists, short story writers, playwrights, and philosophers of this period are frequently studied in high school and college literature courses. In organizing and excerpting the vast amount of critical material written on these authors, *TCLC* helps students develop valuable insight into literary history, promotes a better understanding of the texts, and sparks ideas for papers and assignments. Each entry in *TCLC* presents a comprehensive survey of an author's career or an individual work of literature and provides the user with a multiplicity of interpretations and assessments. Such variety allows students to pursue their own interests; furthermore, it fosters an awareness that literature is dynamic and responsive to many different opinions.

Every fourth volume of *TCLC* is devoted to literary topics. These topic entries widen the focus of the series from individual authors to such broader subjects as literary movements, prominent themes in twentieth-century literature, literary reaction to political and historical events, significant eras in literary history, prominent literary anniversaries, and the literatures of cultures that are often overlooked by English-speaking readers.

TCLC is designed as a companion series to Gale's *Contemporary Literary Criticism,* which reprints commentary on authors now living or who have died since 1960. Because of the different periods under consideration, there is no duplication of material between *CLC* and *TCLC*. For additional information about *CLC* and Gale's other criticism titles, users should consult the Guide to Gale Literary Criticism Series preceding the title page in this volume.

Coverage

Each volume of *TCLC* is carefully compiled to present:

- criticism of authors, or literary topics, representing a variety of genres and nationalities

- both major and lesser-known writers and literary works of the period

- 6-12 authors or 3-6 topics per volume

- individual entries that survey critical response to each author's work or each topic in literary history, including early criticism to reflect initial reactions; later criticism to represent any rise or decline in reputation; and current retrospective analyses.

Organization of This Book

An author entry consists of the following elements: author heading, biographical and critical introduction, list of principal works, excerpts of criticism (each preceded by an annotation and a bibliographic citation), and a bibliography of further reading.

- The **Author Heading** consists of the name under which the author most commonly wrote, followed by birth and death dates. If an author wrote consistently under a pseudonym, the pseudonym will be listed in the author heading and the real name given in parentheses on the first line of the biographical and critical introduction. Also located at the beginning of the introduction to the author entry are any name variations under which an author wrote, including transliterated forms for authors whose languages use nonroman alphabets.

- The **Biographical and Critical Introduction** outlines the author's life and career, as well as the critical issues surrounding his or her work. References to past volumes of *TCLC* are provided at the beginning of the introduction. Additional sources of information in other biographical and critical reference series published by Gale, including *Short Story Criticism, Children's Literature Review, Contemporary Authors, Dictionary of Literary Biography,* and *Something about the Author,* are listed in a box at the end of the entry.

- Some *TCLC* entries include **Portraits** of the author. Entries also may contain reproductions of materials pertinent to an author's career, including manuscript pages, title pages, dust jackets, letters, and drawings, as well as photographs of important people, places, and events in an author's life.

- The **List of Principal Works** is chronological by date of first book publication and identifies the genre of each work. In the case of foreign authors with both foreign-language publications and English translations, the title and date of the first English-language edition are given in brackets. Unless otherwise indicated, dramas are dated by first performance, not first publication.

- Critical excerpts are prefaced by **Annotations** providing the reader with information about both the critic and the criticism that follows. Included are the critic's reputation, individual approach to literary criticism, and particular expertise in an author's works. Also noted are the relative importance of a work of criticism, the scope of the excerpt, and the growth of critical controversy or changes in critical trends regarding an author. In some cases, these annotations cross-reference excerpts by critics who discuss each other's commentary.

- A complete **Bibliographic Citation** designed to facilitate location of the original essay or book precedes each piece of criticism.

- **Criticism** is arranged chronologically in each author entry to provide a perspective on changes in critical evaluation over the years. All titles of works by the author featured in the entry are printed in boldface type to enable the user to easily locate discussion of particular works. Also for purposes of easier identification, the critic's name and the publication date of the essay are given at the beginning of each piece of criticism. Unsigned criticism is preceded by the title of the journal in which it appeared. Some of the excerpts in *TCLC* also contain translated material. Unless otherwise noted, translations in brackets are by the editors; translations in parentheses or continuous with the text are by the critic. Publication information (such as footnotes or page and line references to specific editions of works) have been deleted at the editor's discretion to provide smoother reading of the text.

■ An annotated list of **Further Reading** appearing at the end of each author entry suggests secondary sources on the author. In some cases it includes essays for which the editors could not obtain reprint rights.

Cumulative Indexes

■ Each volume of *TCLC* contains a cumulative **Author Index** listing all authors who have appeared in Gale's Literary Criticism Series, along with cross references to such biographical series as *Contemporary Authors* and *Dictionary of Literary Biography*. For readers' convenience, a complete list of Gale titles included appears on the first page of the author index. Useful for locating authors within the various series, this index is particularly valuable for those authors who are identified by a certain period but who, because of their death dates, are placed in another, or for those authors whose careers span two periods. For example, F. Scott Fitzgerald is found in *TCLC,* yet a writer often associated with him, Ernest Hemingway, is found in *CLC.*

■ Each *TCLC* volume includes a cumulative **Nationality Index** which lists all authors who have appeared in *TCLC* volumes, arranged alphabetically under their respective nationalities, as well as Topics volume entries devoted to particular national literatures.

■ Each new volume in Gale's Literary Criticism Series includes a cumulative **Topic Index,** which lists all literary topics treated in *NCLC, TCLC, LC 1400-1800,* and the *CLC* yearbook.

■ Each new volume of *TCLC,* with the exception of the Topics volumes, includes a **Title Index** listing the titles of all literary works discussed in the volume. In response to numerous suggestions from librarians, Gale has also produced a **Special Paperbound Edition** of the *TCLC* title index. This annual cumulation lists all titles discussed in the series since its inception and is issued with the first volume of *TCLC* published each year. Additional copies of the index are available on request. Librarians and patrons will welcome this separate index; it saves shelf space, is easy to use, and is recyclable upon receipt of the following year's cumulation. Titles discussed in the Topics volume entries are not included *TCLC* cumulative index.

Citing *Twentieth-Century Literary Criticism*

When writing papers, students who quote directly from any volume in Gale's literary Criticism Series may use the following general forms to footnote reprinted criticism. The first example pertains to materials drawn from periodicals, the second to material reprinted from books.

[1]William H. Slavick, "Going to School to DuBose Heyward," *The Harlem Renaissance Re-examined,* (AMS Press, 1987); excerpted and reprinted in *Twentieth-Century Literary Criticism,* Vol. 59, ed. Jennifer Gariepy (Detroit: Gale Research, 1995), pp. 94-105.

[2]George Orwell, "Reflections on Gandhi," *Partisan Review,* 6 (Winter 1949), pp. 85-92; excerpted and reprinted in *Twentieth-Century Literary Criticism,* Vol. 59, ed. Jennifer Gariepy (Detroit: Gale Research, 1995), pp. 40-3.

Suggestions Are Welcome

In response to suggestions, several features have been added to *TCLC* since the series began, including annotations to excerpted criticism, a cumulative index to authors in all Gale literary criticism series, entries devoted to criticism on a single work by a major author, more extensive illustrations, and a title index listing all literary works discussed in the series since its inception.

Readers who wish to suggest authors or topics to appear in future volumes, or who have other suggestions, are cordially invited to write the editors.

Acknowledgments

The editors wish to thank the copyright holders of the excerpted criticism included in this volume and the permissions managers of many book and magazine publishing companies for assisting us in securing reprint rights. We are also grateful to the staffs of the Detroit Public Library, the Library of Congress, the University of Detroit Mercy Library, Wayne State University Purdy/Kresge Library Complex, and the University of Michigan Libraries for making their resources available to us. Following is a list of the copyright holders who have granted us permission to reprint material in this volume of *TCLC*. Every effort has been made to trace copyright, but if omissions have been made, please let us know.

COPYRIGHTED EXCERPTS IN *TCLC*, VOLUME 67, WERE REPRINTED FROM THE FOLLOWING PERIODICALS:

Archaeology, v. 44, July/August, 1991. Copyright (c) 1991 by the Archaeological Institute of America. All rights reserved. Reproduced by permission of the author.—*CLIO*, v. 14, Fall, 1984 for "Solzhenitsyn's Portrait of Lenin" by Paul N. Siegel. (c) 1984 by Robert H. Canary and Henry Kozicki. Reproduced by permission of the author.—*History and Theory*, v. XXIX, 1990. Both reproduced by permission.—*International Affairs*, v. 46, No. 3, July, 1970 for "A Centenary View of Lenin" by Arnold Toynbee. Reproduced by permission of International Affairs and the author.—*L'Esprit Createur*, v. 32, Winter, 1992. Copyright (c) 1992 by L'Esprit Createur. Reproduced by permission.—*Michigan Romance Studies*, v. 9, 1989. Copyright 1989 Michigan Romance Studies. Reproduced by permission.—*Nineteenth-Century French Studies*, v. XVI, Fall, 1987 & Winter, 1988. (c) 1987 by T. H. Goetz. Reproduced by permission.—*Performing Arts Journal*, v. 7, Spring, 1983. (c) copyright 1983 Performing Arts Journal. Reproduced by permission of Johns Hopkins University Press.—*Philosophy*, v. LXIV, October, 1989 for "Collingwood on Art and Fantasy" by Peter Lewis. (c) The Royal Institute of Philosophy 1989. Reproduced by permission of the publisher and the author.—*Philosophy*, v. XXXV, April, 1960 for "From Facts to Thoughts: Collingwood's Views on the Nature of History" by Nathan Rotenstreich. (c) The Royal Institute of Philosophy 1960. Reproduced by permission of the publisher and the author.—*Review of Metaphysics*, v. V, June, 1952. Copyright 1952 by the Review of Metaphysics. Reproduced by permission.—*Revista Hispanica Moderna: Columbia University Hispanic Studies*, v. XLVI, June, 1993. Reproduced by permission.—*Romance Studies*, n. 18, Summer, 1991. Reproduced by permission.—*Science and Society*, v. XXIX, Winter, 1965. Copyright 1965 by S & S Quarterly, Inc. Reproduced by permission.—*Slavic Review*, v. 30, March, 1971 for "Lenin's Utopianism: 'State and Revolution'" by Rodney Barfield. Copyright (c) 1971 by the American Association for the Advancement of Slavic Studies, Inc. Reproduced by permission of the publisher and the author.—*Slavic Review*, v. 46, Spring, 1987 for "Rereading Lenin's 'State and Revolution'" by Alfred B. Evans. Copyright (c) 1987 by the American Association for the Advancement of Slavic Studies, Inc. Reproduced by permission of the publisher and the author.—*The Australasian Journal of Philosophy*, v. XXVI, September, 1948. Reproduced by permission.—*The Journal of Aesthetics and Art Criticism*, v. XL, Summer, 1982. Copyright (c) 1982 by The American Society for Aesthetics. Reproduced by permission.—*The Journal of Aesthetics and Art Criticism*, v. XLVI, Winter, 1987. Copyright (c) 1987 by The American Society for Aesthetics. Reproduced by permission.—*The Journal of Religion*, v. 49, July, 1969 for a review of "Faith and Reason: Essays in the Philosophy of Religion" by Julian Hartt. (c) 1969 by The University of Chicago. Reproduced by permission of the author.—*The Midwest Quarterly*, v. XXIX, Spring, 1988. Copyright, 1988, by The Midwest Quarterly, Pittsburgh State University. Reproduced by permission.—*The Philosophical Quarterly*, v. 1, April, 1951. (c) The Philosophical Quarterly 1951. Reprinted by permission.—*The Russian Review*, v. 40, January, 1981. Copyright 1981 by The Russian Review, Inc. Reproduced by permission.—*The Russian Review*, v. 53, October, 1994. Copyright 1994 The Ohio State University Press. Reproduced by permission.—*The Times Literary Supplement*, n. 4813, June 30, 1995. (c) The Times Supplements Limited 1995. Reproduced from The Times Literary Supplement by permission.

COPYRIGHTED EXCERPTS IN *TCLC*, VOLUME 67, WERE REPRINTED FROM THE FOLLOWING BOOKS:

Gertrude Bell

1868-1926

(Full name Gertrude Margaret Lowthian Bell) English nonfiction writer and archaeologist.

INTRODUCTION

Bell was one of the first Western women to travel and do archaeological research in the deserts of the Middle East. She wrote extensively on the ancient cultures of the region, and documented the daily experience of her travels as a prolific letter writer. Bell also established and was the first director of the State Museum for Antiquities in Baghdad, Iraq.

Biographical Information

Bell was born into an upper-class family in county Durham, England. Her father was a knighted industrialist; her mother died when Bell was two. Bell's stepmother, Florence Eveleen Eleonore Olliffe, was a noted dramatist, novelist, and nonfiction writer. After graduating from Oxford in 1888 with honors in history, Bell was forbidden by her parents from marrying Harry Cadogan, a man she apparently loved and who died a year later. In 1892 she visited Persia—now Iran—for the first time, and inaugurated a peripatetic life devoted to the study of ancient cultures and the preservation of antiquities. Her accomplishments include traveling around the world twice, attaining fluency in Arabic and Persian, climbing the Swiss Alps, and conducting major explorations of the Middle Eastern deserts, many never before visited by a Westerner. She was also made a Commander of the British Empire and a Fellow of the Royal Geographic Society. With her travels restricted by the events of World War I, Bell worked first for the Red Cross as a tracker of missing persons, and then for the British intelligence service out of Cairo, Egypt. After the war, she worked with Thomas Edward Lawrence—immortalized as "Lawrence of Arabia"—helping to establish the nation of Iraq. An accomplished and seemingly independent woman, Bell was a founding member of the Woman's Anti-Suffrage League, believing that strident feminism, symbolized by the right to vote, was a hindrance to the progress of women in English society.

Major Works

Bell's first work, *Safar Nameh* (1894), a book of essays on her travels in Persia, was first published anonymously; she was not happy with the quality of the work at the time. It was subsequently published under her name, with an introduction in which she somewhat disclaims the book as a youthful effort. *Safar Nameh* has been praised for evoking the natural beauty of what is now Iran, and for conveying the romantic enthusiasm of the author. Her first major work, *Syria: The Desert and the Sown* (1907), is an account of her first serious expedition in the Middle East, started in 1905, during which she journeyed through Syria, Turkey, and Yemen. The title of the book comes from Omar Khayyam's *The Rubaiyat* (eleventh-twelfth century), in Edward Fitzgerald's 1859 translation; "The strip of herbage strown that just divides the desert from the sown." In *Amurath to Amurath* (1911) Bell describes her experiences during a 1909 journey that took her along the Euphrates river from Aleppo to Hit, then to Karbala and Baghdad. During this trek she met with Kurdish tribesman and visited the castle at Ukhaidir, considered a superlative example of Sassanian architecture and reminiscent of pre-Muhammadan buildings. This book was criticized by some commentators at the time for emphasizing architectural detail and history over the narrative of her trip. *Palace and Mosque at Ukhaidir* (1914) describes her return to this site, and is copiously illustrated with Bell's drawings and photographs.

PRINCIPAL WORKS

Safar Nameh. Persian Pictures. A Book of Travel (nonfiction) 1894; also published as *Persian Pictures*, 1928
Poems from the Divan of Hafiz (translation) 1897
Syria: The Desert and the Sown (nonfiction) 1907
The Thousand and One Churches [with Sir William Ramsay] (nonfiction) 1909
Amurath to Amurath: A Study in Early Mohammadan Architecture (nonfiction) 1911
Palace and Mosque at Ukhaidir (nonfiction) 1914
The Arabs of Mesopotamia (nonfiction) 1917
The Civil Administration of Mesopotamia (nonfiction) 1920
*The Letters of Gertrude Bell (letters) 1927
†The Earlier Letters of Gertrude Bell (letters) 1937
The Arab War: Confidential Information for General Headquarters (nonfiction) 1940
‡Gertrude Bell: A Selection from the Photographic Archive of an Archaeologist and Traveler (photographs) 1976

*This work was edited by Lady Florence Bell.
†This work was edited by Elsa Richmond.
‡This work was edited by Stephen Hill.

CRITICISM

Elizabeth Robins (essay date 1911)

SOURCE: "A New Art of Travel," in *Fortnightly Review,* Vol. 95, No. 8, March 1, 1911, pp. 470-92.

[*In the following essay, Robins recounts a trip she took with Bell to Arabia and discusses Bell's writings on Arabia.*]

There is a natural freemasonry among travellers. Even he whose journeying has been brief, and scarce beyond the borders of his native land, will nevertheless come home with a better knowledge, not of other places only, but of his own relation to his fellow-man; so little can the best-equipped carry with him, so much at every turn does he find himself in need of the knowledge and good-will of those he meets.

No amount of couriers or maps will relieve the traveller of dependence upon those, he goes amongst. The situation in which he finds himself, abroad, sets in a high, clear light certain facts that only the stay-at-home may disregard.

I am moved to these reflections by a journey I have just made under conduct of the person whose name is at the head of this paper. The lands through which she led me were as strange to me as they could be to any pilgrim. That they are strange no longer, that I know my way now to new sources of beauty and refreshment, that I come home with a sense of exhilaration so keen, bringing memories of adventure in the desert and *Arabian Nights* entertainment in Khans and Palaces, I owe to the two volumes named in my sub-title.

Now, the world is yet more full of books than the earth's surface is of roads and bye-paths and blind alleys. "Show me the way," says one traveller. "What shall I read?" says another.

In the name, then, of that confessed freemasonry I am constrained to constitute myself on this occasion a kind of guide-post.

I am here to say: This is the way—and a right good way it is.

The journey in **The Desert and the Sown** begins where so much else began, at Jerusalem—with a ride round the walls of the Holy City on a stormy February morning. Is your ardour chilled by the strong west wind that comes sweeping in from the Mediterranean? The leader of the expedition says, "No one with life in his body could stay in on such a day." The alternative to "staying in" is to set forth on a journey of many weeks over mountain, river and desert in a land asserted by the local authorities, and reported by special correspondents to *The Times,* to be unsafe for the European traveller. At dawn

the muleteers Miss Bell brought with her from Beyrout had been sent forward with tents and a month's supplies. The only one of her servants with her at the start is Mikhail, native of the Lebanon, engaged as cook, upon the recommendation of "not caring twopence whether he lives or whether he is killed."

That qualification sets the note.

The conversation of this desert *chef* would seem to bear out his "character." He tells his new employer how with his last he was shipwrecked on Lake Van: "We were as near death as a beggar to poverty, but your excellency knows a man can die but once."

And so, past groups of Russian pilgrims to the Mount of Olives, these two gallop down the road that winds through the wilderness of Judea. They escape out of those slime pits of Genesis to catch up with the caravan on the slope of the last hill which overlooks Jordan valley and the Dead Sea—"backed by the misty steeps of Moab." The first halt is by the Holy River, near what Miss Bell calls "the most inspiring piece of architecture in the world."

Now we have heard that, amongst other things, Miss Bell has been twice round the world. She has visited

> "The awful ruins of the days of old:
> Athens and Tyre and Balbec, and the waste
> Where stood Jerusalem, the fallen towers
> Of Babylon, the eternal pyramids,
> Memphis and Thebes. . . ."

We are given, therefore, some measure of what lies before us when we hear that no one of these other wonders is so inspiring as—a wooden bridge across the River Jordan, "because it is the Gate of the Desert." In this tremendous neighbourhood the tents are pitched that first night, and a bonfire lit of tamarisk and willow. In the light of it one of the little handful who shares the solitude of the Turkish toll-taker, dances and lifts his voice out of the babel of Syrian dialect to tell the stranger the latest gossip of the desert.

As by Jordan Bridge you are prepared in some sort for the desert, so are you promptly given a measure of the human experience that lies before you. Your acquaintance in **The Desert and the Sown** ranges, even in these early hours, from a ragged and renegade Arab recruit, to persons of consideration, like the family at Salt. The region where they dwell on the hem of the desert, has been famed, you are told, since the fourteenth century for its gardens. Not only in the matter of grapes and apricots would the ancient order seem still to be upheld. A magnificent old man in full Arab dress comes out to meet the stranger, who had been commended to his good offices by his kinsman. Habib Faris takes the horse by the bridle; he, and no other, he declares shall offer the lady hospitality. In the guest chamber, where floor and divan are covered with thick carpets, she is soon established before an excellent supper. Others of the family (one she calls "an old acquaintance") come in to "honour themselves" with an evening of talk. "God forbid," says she, "the honour is mine." And so they seat themselves to drink the bitter black coffee of the Arabs, which is better than any nectar. The cup is handed with "deign to accept," you pass it back empty, murmuring "May you live!" As you sip, someone ejaculates, "A double health," and you reply, "Upon your heart."

Presently she introduces her business: How was she to elude the vigilance of the authorities and make her way to the Druze mountains?

It is hers to tell that story, and all that befell in the circuitous route she follows to Damascus, turning aside wherever there were castles or ruined villages to inspect, or sheikhs to gossip with over the coffee cups.

From Damascus she makes her way to Heliopolis, skirting anti-Lebanon to Homs, then with a wide detour westward to the Nosairiyych, and so back to the Orontes at Hama; thence northward to Aleppo, and after that following an irregular course westward, by way of Antioch, to the sea. When in a tea-shop of Damascus she calls for her score, the red-bearded Persian *patron* answers: "Your Excellency is known to us. For you there is never anything to pay." At Serjilla, Sheikh Yunis presents her with a palace and its adjacent tomb, that she may live and die in his neighbourhood.

Small wonder when, all unwilling, she left unvisited that mysterious castle east of the Rubbeh and the Sheikh of Ghiath had said, "When you next return, oh lady—" she answered promptly, "Yes, when I return."

Her new book shows how she kept the spirit of that pact, and how she did much more.

The advance made in the volume just published is one of the most interesting things about it. *Amurath to Amurath* is not only better written. It is better thought. It is more than a spirited record of wandering in the East interspersed with random notes on archeology. The traveller comes home from her last five months in the cities and waste-places of Syria and Mesopotamia with an archæological feather in her cap that alone would proclaim her journey memorable.

Miss Bell has been the first to make a scientifically-ordered report of that castle-fortress in the desert which, on first seeing its vast mass against the sky-line, she took for a natural feature of the landscape. She, and now the learned world as well, have come to know it for the finest example of Sassanian architecture which has yet been discovered.

"Of all the wonderful experiences that have fallen my way," she says, "the first sight of Kheidir is the most memorable. It reared its mighty walls out of the sand, almost untouched by time, breaking the long lines of the waste with its huge towers, steadfast and massive, as

though it were, as I had at first thought it, the work of nature, not of man. We approached it from the north, on which side a long low building runs out towards the sandy depression of the Wâdy Lebay'ah. A zaptieh caught me up as I reached the first of the vaulted rooms, and out of the northern gateway a man in long robes of white and black came trailing towards us through the hot silence.

"'Peace be upon you,' said he.

"'And upon you peace, Sheikh 'Ali,' returned the zaptieh. This lady is of the English.'

"'Welcome, my lady Khân,' said the sheikh."

And so she enters one of those "palaces, famous in pre-Mohammedan tradition, whose splendours had filled with amazement the invading hordes of the Bedouin, and still shine with a legendary magnificence, from the pages of the chroniclers of the conquest. Even for the Mohammedan writers they had become nothing but a name."

The sheikh who welcomed her was himself in some sort a guest, having, with his friends and followers, taken refuge there upon some political disturbance in his native Nejd. "He and his brothers passed like ghosts along the passages, they trailed their white robes down the stairways that led to the high chambers where they lived with their women, and at night they gathered round the hearth in the great hall where their forefathers had beguiled the hours with tale and song in the same rolling tongue of Nejd. Then they would pile up the desert scrub till the embers glowed under the coffee-pots, while Ma'ashi handed round the delicious bitter draught which was the one luxury left to them. The thorns crackled a couple of oil wicks placed in holes above the columns, which had been contrived for them by the men-at-arms of old, sent a feeble ray into the darkness, and Ghânim took the rebâbah and drew from its single string a wailing melody to which he chanted the stories of his race."

So little of the significance of that singing was lost upon his English guest that she could cap his verses with one from his own poet:

> We wither away but they wane not, the stars that
>   above us rise;
> And the mountains remain after us, and the
>   strong towers when we are gone.

For all the distinguished entertainment offered, she works at her plans of the vast edifice from sunrise until dark—just as later, she turns from contemplation of the glittering domes of that little town of Samarra, "set down like a child's toy upon the waste"—and descending from the spiral tower of the ruined Abbasid city, she sets to work upon the mosque. "To measure a wall would not seem to be a complicated business, yet I do not care to remember how many hours I spent upon the mosque."

A peasant comes to her among the ruins of the elder city, whose bazaars and palaces in the bygone days stretched without a break along the Tigris for one-and-twenty miles. The modern representative of this departed glory comes asking, would she like to see a picture he had just unearthed? It proves to be a beautiful piece of plaster work, doomed to destruction that the bricks behind it might be removed. A reward is offered for any further specimens, and these are duly brought. In the same way the peasants supply the traveller with basketsful of patterned potsherds, innumerable examples of which she drew and photographed.

At Tell Ahmar, where she found a Hittite epigraph cut in basalt, "The whole village turned out to help in the work of masking moulds of the inscriptions, those who were not actively employed with brush and paste and paper sitting round in an attentive circle."

She tells the Arabs at Abu Sáîd what is the origin of the stones they use to mark the graves of their dead. For these bits of basalt are the ancient hand-mills in which the living, long ago, were used to grind their corn.

Near one of Layard's pits at Nimrûd she comes across a stone statue projecting "head and shoulders out of the ground, the face of the king or god which it represents being already terribly battered. The number of Assyrian statues known to us is exceedingly small—not more than seven or eight have been brought to light—yet this splendid example is allowed to fall into decay for want of a handful of earth wherewith to cover it." Not so perhaps, for with fair words and with bakhshish she extracts a promise of a sheikh of the Jebbûr that he would bury it.

And so with those "seeing eyes," that do not fail to note any such resemblance as may exist between Mar Behnam beyond Nineveh and the Coptic Monasteries of Egypt—with the stored mind familiarised by the Orient Gesellschaft with the pictures of Ashur before ever she sets foot in Assyrin, on she goes, skirting in the Tûr Abdin the ancient battle-ground of Persian and Byzantine.

"Into this country I came, entirely ignorant of its architectural wealth, because it was entirely unrecorded. None of the inscriptions collected by Pognon go back earlier than the ninth century; the plans which had been published were lamentably insufficient and were unaccompanied by any photographs. When I entered Mâr Yakûb at Salah and saw upon its walls mouldings and carved string courses which bore the sign manual of the Græco-Asiatic civilisation I scarcely dared to trust the conclusions to which they pointed. But church after church confirmed and strengthened them. The chancel arches, covered with an exquisite lacework of ornament, the delicate grace of the acanthus capitals, hung with garlands and enriched with woven entrelac, the repetition of ancient plans and the mastery of constructive problems which revealed an old architectural tradition, all these assure to the churches of the Tûr Abdin the recognition of their honourable place in the history of the arts."

Work so thorough as that recorded in these pages is not achieved without a price. The archæologist relieves her feelings on one occasion by frankly calling the measuring and planning a "labour of hatred."

Such an outburst emboldens the lay mind to hope that her pursuit of mathematical exactitude was enlivened by the resultant ability to point out the inaccuracies of other folk. If to do this is, as Theodore Hook maintains, the business of a traveller, Miss Bell is not the person to fail him. Kiepert himself she catches out now and then, though she is usually found singing his praises. Herzfeld's plans, on the other hand, are discovered to be "exceedingly inaccurate and his architectural observations seldom to be trusted." Even Ammianus Marcellinus is caught tripping in his march down the Euphrates with the Emperor Julian. Miss Bell discovers at Carrhæ that his account is "irreconcilable with the facts of geography"—which dictum, if he hears of it, must a little disconcert the Græco-Roman shade accustomed for a matter of fifteen centuries to see his authority unquestioned.

Miss Bell's disposition to examine testimony and to try conclusions brings her home, then, with something more than a collection of traveller's tales, however aptly told; something more than an addition to existing stores of archæological knowledge.

In sum, her achievement is that she has developed a new art of travel.

It is an art at which only the dry-as-dusts may cavil, and only because this new kind of traveller returns with other spoils in her saddlebags, besides the notebooks, full of plans and measurements, many hundred photograph films, the rubbings of fading inscriptions and moulds of decoration motif, faint perhaps and crumbling fast—doomed to oblivion but for the timely rescue—yet so full of significance for the instructed eye, that it is traceries such as these that yield up the age-long secrets, telling of the great race movements, of an unguessed efflorescence of human glory, of its blight and ruin.

But these are matters for the expert.

From the point of view of the general reader, *Amurath to Amurath* is, first and foremost, a many-sided study of a people—or rather of that medley of races, faiths and problems bound up in the Ottoman Empire. This part of the book seems to be offered as a contribution towards Western understanding of the unprecedented political crisis through which the Turks have newly come. In *The Desert and the Sown* the traveller makes her way through Syria amused by the picture of contemporary life, and quick to seize upon vestiges of a many-storied past. In *Syria* she was the spectator. In *Amurath to Amurath* she is friend and partisan.

The motif of the new book is Freedom.

Freedom for the Young Turk, and through him freedom, or some semblance of it, for the motley populations which have hitherto been harried and robbed in the name of the Sultan, and in his name, or his despite, done equal deeds of blood and ruth. Freedom is the immediate jewel, it appears, even of the soul of a Turk. He must be free, we are told, to bring back fertility to his abandoned fields—free to govern without passion, soberly, wisely, as his statecraft-loving soul dictates.

Miss Bell makes out a striking case for the bad economy of social disorder. We hear continually of cornlands lying waste, of folk not daring even to drive the goats to pasture, of every man in the district sitting with his loaded rifle across his knees on watch for the coming of the raiders. Amongst the sorry wealth of similar pictures we have such as this, catching desolation in the act: "Shetâteh is an oasis of 160,000 palms. The number is rapidly diminishing, and on every side there are groups of headless trunks from which the water has been turned off. This is owing to the iniquitous exactions of the tax-gatherers, who levy three and four times in the year the moneys due from each tree, so that the profits on the fruit vanish and even turn to loss."

Finding corn at famine prices, and no fresh meat obtainable for man, nor grass for beast, she is haunted by a sense of that majestic presence of "the river in the midst of uncultivated lands, which, with the help of its waters, would need so little labour" to make those lands productive. That vast tracts of the desert used formerly, and might be made again, to blossom as the rose, is the hopeful reminder reiterated from page to page.

Towards the end of her journey, coming upon the village of Shahr, she finds "its sheltered fields covered with corn, its gardens planted with fruit-trees, but the streets and houses were no less ruined than the temples of the Great Goddess. The hot breath of massacre had passed down the smiling vale and left Shahr a heap of ashes. I found the inhabitants huddled together on a bluff where half a dozen of their dwellings had escaped destruction. A young school-master from the American college of Tarsus told me the story."

For my last extract upon the theme of bad economy in social disorder take this: Miss Bell's caravan is passing through a well-watered valley. "The deep grass through which we journeyed, both on this day and on the next, is looked upon as a sore peril, since it tempts the Kurds down into the lowland pastures. To avoid this annual reign of terror, the peasants are wont to set it on fire as soon as it ripens, leaving but a small patch round each village. For a week the plain is wrapped in flame and

smoke, and the stifling heat of the burning rises up to the hill-top monastery of Mâr Yakûb, where the Catholic priests are witnesses to the appalling destruction of what might have been a rich harvest, and to the bitter oppression which turns the bounty of nature into a recurring threat. Jûsef, whose imagination is not to be roused except by considerations of a soundly practical character, cast his eye over the fields and observed thoughtfully: 'The muleteers of Baghdad must starve this year to buy fodder for their cattle, yet here is enough to feed all the Jezîreh.'"

Few things in modern politics are more striking than the evidence that, even in Asia, there is a growing disposition to weary of that old liberty to waste and to be wasted. "No sooner had I landed in Beyrout," says Miss Bell, "than I began to shed European formulas and to look for the Asiatic value of the great catch-words of revolution." Her acquaintance with the Turkey that came into being in July, 1908, she dates from the time of her arrival in Aleppo—that Aleppo which she loves for its architecture and for being the Gate to Asia.

It was there, "sitting at the feet of many masters, who ranged down all the social grades, from the high official to the humblest labourer for hire," that she learnt of the outburst of enthusiasm which had greeted the granting of the constitution—of some of the disappointments that followed, and of their cause. "The Government," she says with a fine discrimination, "was still to the bulk of the population a higher power, disconnected from those upon whom it exercised its will. You might complain—just as you cursed the hailstones that destroyed your crops, but you were in no way answerable for it, nor would you attempt to control or advise it, any more than you would offer advice to the hail-cloud." "Many a time," she says, "I searched for some trace of the Anglo-Saxon acceptance of a common responsibility in the problems that beset the State." She goes through village after village, listening to the echoes of revolution while she looks at tombs and shrines.

Already among the Weldeh tribe she has heard the plaint: "We have neither camels nor sheep, for the Government has eaten all!" Then one asks about the new Government—and "liberty, what is that?"

About an hour from Bâb her caravan was joined by a Circassian "wrapped in a thick black felt cloak, which, with the white woollen hood over an astrachan cap, skirted coat with cartridges ranged across the breast, and high riding-boots, is the invariable costume of these emigrants from the north."

She asks him about the recent elections and finds that he takes a lively interest in the politics of the day. They ride along together, discussing the Arab view of franchise.

And so, past Roman milestones, one bearing the name of the Emperor Septimius Severus, by mosque and pool she follows towards Hieropolis, the same road travelled by that faithful Apostate of whom Anatole France says: "Nourri dans la violence romaine et dans la cruauté byzantine, il semble n'avoir appris que le respect de la vie humaine et le culte de la pensée."

Near Manbij, two days later, she hears a chance-met traveller asking one of her party the meaning of hurrîyeh (liberty). For his part, if it means the right to vote, he has no use for it. He thanks God that no one there is "and el hukûmeh" (on the official register). For to be upon the list of voters is to be compelled to do military service, and too often in Turkey to be marked down for official extortion as well.

In collecting the opinions of all sorts and conditions, Miss Bell has not only at her service the gift of tongues, she has the knack of grasping instantly who (from her point of view) are the people, as well as the things, best worth seeing. She had these advantages already in working order several years ago at Hamah. Without loss of time she learns which are the most powerful Mohammedan families of the town. She has pleasant experience of their feudal hospitality, and on her way home encounters in the street an aged Afghan, with whom she discusses English foreign relations. It might be supposed an aged Afghan would know little of such matters. this one showed himself as well, possibly better, informed than the average Briton. Miss Bell found him cognizant even of the then recent interchange of visits and civilities between Kabul and Calcutta. Here, and later, she is apt at drawing the moral: "The East is one vast sounding-board." Varying the symbol to iterate the truth: "All Asia," she says, "is linked together by fine chains of relationship"—the bond between the western and central parts being the faith of Islam.

That may account, in part, for the fact that she found, even among the intractable hordes in the remote fastnesses of the desert, men as ready to take an interest in Egyptian finance as was the Arab to whom she explained the principles of the Fellahin Bank in Cairo. When she had finished he inquired if such an institution might not be introduced into Syria. Five years earlier still, a similar question had been put in the mountains of the Hauran. "The Druze sheikhs of Kanawat had assembled in my tent under shadow of night, and after much beating about the bush, asked whether, if the Turks again broke their treaties with the Mountain, the Druzes might take refuge with Lord Cromer in Egypt, and whether I would not charge myself with a message to him."

On this later journey, as she rides toward Tell esh Shaïr, the zaptieh and she began to talk of the prospects of good administration under the new order. Mahmud placed great confidence in the Young Turks, and said that every one except the effendis was in favour of the dastur (the constitution). "The effendis fear liberty and justice, for these are to the advantage of the poor. But they, being corrupt and oppressors of the poor, set themselves in secret against the dastur, and because of this we have confusion everywhere."

After being two weeks without news she goes to certain friends of hers at Deir, Mahommedan gentlemen of good birth and education. "They told me that the Grand Vizir, Kiamil Pasha, had fallen, which was true; and that the Mejlis had quarrelled with the Sultan and were about to depose him, which was only prophetic. They made me realise how different an aspect the new-born hopes of Turkey wore on the Bosphorus, or even on the Mediterranean, from that which they presented to the dwellers on the Euphrates: I had already passed beyond the zone that had been quickened by the enthusiasm of European Turkey into some real belief in the advent of a just rule. One of my friends had received an invitation to join the local committee, but he had refused to do so. 'I am lord over much business,' said he, 'but they are the fathers of idle talk.' All thinking men in Deir were persuaded that a universal anarchy lay before them; the old rule was dead, the new was powerless, and the forces of disorder were lifting their heads."

At Baghdad light is shed upon the power of the Press to check corrupt practices. And again, at Baghdad the traveller is impressed that "He who holds the irrigation canals, holds the country," is a maxim which can be applied as well to Mesopotamia as it was to Egypt. An irrigation system, justly administered, would, by general admission, be a better means of control than an army corps.

On the way to examine the ruins of Khmeida Miss Bell discusses with a couple of Arabs the incidence of the sheep-tax—a passage of significance.

If she has to wait for the boat in which to cross the Euphrates she goes into a neighbouring coffee house and joins the circle. The talk is of ravage and extortion and the hopeless failure of the old Government as administered by the fourteen different Kaimmakams they had had in six years.

The English stranger reminds the circle that the new Government was sending them a new Kaimmakam to administer according to juster laws. The new Kaimmakam was on his way. But the information was neither new nor altogether cheering. One of the coffee-drinkers explained that "When the telegram came last summer telling of liberty and equality, the people had assembled before the seràya, the Government house, and bade the Kaimmakam begone, for they would govern themselves. Thereat came orders from Baghdad that the people must be dispersed; and the soldiers fired upon them, killing six men. And we do not know what the telegram about liberty and brotherhood can have meant."

Stopping at Kal' at Sergât, where the Germans are excavating the mound of Ashur, she gets news not only of how things went on in the Parthian period, in the late

Assyrian, and in those earlier times without a name. She has news of nearer happenings—all the more disquieting because as yet nothing but rumour. "Constitutional Government had foundered suddenly, and it might be for ever. The members of the Committee had fled from Constantinople, the Liberals were fugitive upon their heels, and once more Abd ul Hamid had set his foot upon the neck of Turkey."

At Mangul she meets an Effendi on horseback with an escort of zaptiehs.

"What tidings have you from Constantinople?" she asks.

The Effendi drew his brows together.

"We hear that troops from Salonica have entered the town and captured two barracks."

As she approached Mosul—"a sound that made our hearts stand still." The boom of cannon. They meet an old man and ask, "Why are they firing cannon in Mosul?"

"God knows," he answered, and wrung his hands together.

The whole passage is extraordinarily well done. For contrast see the page where the traveller, after many adventures, lies down on the clover underneath a hawthorn bush to wait for the Tigris boat. "It was here," she says, "that we were to bid a final farewell to the Greeks who had accompanied us from the outset of the journey." She finds the passage: "'So at length we parted, and Cheirosophus in advance with the light-armed troops scaled the hills of the Finik and led slowly forward, leaving Xenophon to bring up the rear with the heavy-armed men. Their shields and corselets glittered upon the steep they climbed, and reached the summit of the ride, and disappeared . . .'

"'Effendim!' Fattûh broke into my meditations. 'Effendim, the boat is ready.'

"'Oh, Fattûh,' said I, 'the Greeks are gone.'

"Fattûh looked vaguely disturbed.

"'The Greeks of old days, who marched with us down the Euphrates,' I explained. Fattûh can neither read nor write, but he searched his memory for fragments of my meaningless talk.

"'Those?' he said. 'God be with them!'"

If a large portion of Miss Bell's last book embodies a plea that the Turk shall (under the blessings of representative government) be left free to stay at home and cultivate his lands, both books celebrate the joy in the writer's own freedom to wander at will over the wide earth.

I find myself wondering as I read her pages, what do these Turks, Arabs, Chaldeans, Devil-worshippers and the rest, what do they think of this fair-haired apparition out of the West, this woman equally concerned about current politics and Hittite inscriptions? What, for instance, was in the mind of Hassan Beg Na'i that day Miss Bell interrupted his coffee party? He, unlike most of the men she met, conducted her forthwith to the ladies of his house and left her with them. We can well believe that this was luck for the harem, since "Hassan Beg is a strict master, and neither his wife nor his mother, nor any woman that is his is allowed to put her nose out of doors." One would like to know what the harem thought of Miss Bell. But most of all one wonders at the indiscretion of Hassan Beg. Surely his ladies might have walked abroad from dawn till "evening prayer," and never once encountered so instructive an example of all that the Hassan Begs most fear and deprecate. But what looks like daring may be but the measure of a sore perplexity.

The Guardian of the Tomb of the Shi'ah sanctuary was a more liberal soul. To this charming and cheerful Mullah in the long robes and white turban the traveller must needs apply for permission to explore the sacred precincts.

"Not only did he grant my request; but he presented me with a bunch of pomegranate flowers and entertained me with coffee and sherbet.

"'Why,' said he, 'do you travel so far?'

"I replied that I had a great curiosity to see the world and all that lay therein.

"'You are right,' he answered. 'Man has but a short while to live, and to see everything is a natural desire. But few have time to accomplish it—what would you? We are but human.' And he drew his robe round him and sipped contentedly at the sherbet."

His impressions would also be of interest.

But I am bound to admit that Miss Bell does not seem to share my curiosity on this theme. She is too full of what she thinks about it all to bother about what others think of her. As she hastened over broken lava into that "ghostly stronghold of a world of ghosts," the ruined fortress of Kal' at el Beida, the one or two Arabs she finds sauntering there are noted with less concern than if they were *Iris susiana* growing in the stony courts. The turbans, too, without doubt, added the indigenous touch, but they gave her no more pause than would the antlered heads of deer above a crag in Anti-Taurus. The discreet turbaned figures paid, she thinks, "as little attention to me as I to them," and instantly she concentrates upon the matter in hand. "Who reared this famous citadel that guards a dead land from an unpeopled?" "Whose art fashioned the flowing scrolls on doorpost and lintèl; whose eyes kept vigil from the tower?" She balances one learned speculation against another. "The fact remains that we are not certain of its origin—the desert may give up its secrets, the history of the Safa and the Ruhbeh may be pieced together from the lettered rocks, but much travel must be accomplished first, and much excavation on the Syrian frontier, in Hira, perhaps, or in Yemen."

And, meanwhile, I, in my limited way, keep wondering what was going on underneath those turbans.

All the gravity and reserve of the East is not proof at times against the speculation, the stark bewilderment she must constantly have roused.

Once, in the valley of the Orontes, her tents were pitched in a favoured spot where a great Persian water-wheel filled the air with pleasant rumbling. A coffee maker came and set up his brazier by the edge of the road. A sweetmeat seller spread his wares by the water side. On a stretch of grass ". . . in the delicious sun . . . some gaily dressed youths galloped and wheeled Arab mares." It turned out to be a holiday, and the un-mounted rabble, to the tune of many hundreds, kept the festal day by surrounding and watching every movement in the lady's camp. The men were bad enough, she says, the women were worse, and the children worst of all. The excitement of the populace was further stimulated by the coming of the richest dweller in the district, bringing the Kadi to call upon the stranger. When later she reciprocated their polite attention, her progress to the Pasha's house was impeded by an escort of at least three hundred people.

"Please God," says the Pasha, "the populace does not trouble your Excellency; for if so we will order out a regiment of soldiers."

She admits that her refusal of this drastic measure was half-hearted. So obviously so, the great man added that the Kaiser "when he was in Damascus gave orders that no one was to be forbidden to come and gaze on him." And so with an ill grace she submits to the tyranny of august example. Two years later, at Tomarza, her interest in Cappadocian ruins was held by her Armenian host to be the thinnest of cloaks wherewith, in his opinion, she was trying to cover some political purpose. "By all Tomarza I was regarded as an itinerant missionary collecting evidence with regard to the massacre." Beyond doubt, she was less plagued than most would have been—by reason of her sure knowledge of when to apply the extinguisher to a curiosity grown flagrant. She seems to have dealt gently with the Druze who questioned her upon her social status—what was the extent of her father's wealth, and did she, at home, ride with the King? But another of that tribe found his catechism cut short:—

"'Listen, oh you! I am not "thou," but Your Excellency.' He laughed," she says, "and understood, and took the rebuke to heart."

All the same, one must needs sympathise with the bewilderment of priest and pasha, sheikh and zaptiech, at a young woman as able to give as to demand information, whether about the new laws or the ancient inscriptions built at hazard into the mosques—a traveller able to cap their quotations from their own classics, able to check their account of their own roads and mountain ranges, by comparing what they say, now with the map of Kiepert, now with *"le doux Ammian,"* and now with Xenophon. In an effort to adjust one's focus to catch a glimpse of the traveller as she passes before Eastern eyes, one recalls the two young Seijari women, "wonderfully beautiful, wearing blue cloths hanging from their heads fastened with heavy gold ornaments like the plaques of the Mycenæan treasure, one behind either temple." They walked with the English stranger through the ruins of the castle, but when they reached the great outer gate they stopped: "Allah," said one, "you go forth to travel through the whole world, and we have never been to Hamâh."

Even the men-folk, and guides professed, offered in vain their symbolic warning: "Wallah, we have never heard of anyone who wished to go by that road." Our traveller is quite ready to be the first foot there. But, unlike those who would dissuade her, she has heard of the others who went that way. And in spirit she bears them company—I shall dare say to their honour.

If any tell me that I rate too highly the achievements of this traveller, it will be one who has not read her books. I may not speak of Miss Bell's technical accomplishments. I am ready, however, to maintain that she belongs not merely to the little groups of the learned in this land or in that. As one loving well the earth and the sun, a swift horse and a storm, a knotty problem in politics or the nice conduct of caravans, creature of quick humour and infinite resource, teller of tales and painter of memorable pictures, she belongs to the larger world.

Significant of many things is the picture she herself presents taking her caravan to and fro across the ruin-chequered waste, taking her eager challenging mind into citadel, palace and shrine, discussing the revolution with great officials; talking of liberty with judges, prisoners, and beggars; of religion with Armenian, Nestorian, and Moslem; of domestic life with jealously guarded wives; of the psychology of the raid with Bedouins, Arabs, and Druze robbers. Then at the end of the day sitting down in her tent, after ten hours in the saddle, to compare her march with that of the Ten Thousand.

Miss Bell's own record (apart from accounts of burning farms and decimated villages) is too honest to be all pleasant reading. Following hard upon that wonderful picture of the ride in the rain to the Crusader fortress, is a scene that might have served Euripides for his Trojan women. Late in the day the traveller leaves her caravan to follow the road, and with one of the Kaimmakams horsemen she climbs the steep bridle-path. "And so at sunset we came to the Dark Tower and rode through a splendid Arab gateway into a vaulted corridor built over a winding stair. It was almost night within; a few loop-holes let in the grey dusk. . . . At intervals we passed doorways leading into cavernous blackness. The stone steps . . . were much broken; the horses stumbled and climbed over them as we rode up and up—and passed gateway after gateway, until the last brought us out into the courtyard in the centre of the keep." The lord of the castle is a man of letters, but he heaved a sigh of relief at her salutation. "Praise be to God, your Excellency speaks Arabic!" and thereupon the talk and the hospitality flowed in generous flood. At dinner the family party was augmented by the introduction of an ancient dame—"a friend who has come to gaze upon your Excellency."

Later, when the ladies were alone, the aged guest refused to sit on the divan, being more accustomed, as she said, to the floor, where she sat close to the brazier, holding her wrinkled hands above the coals. She was clad in black, and her head was covered by a thick white linen cloth bound closely above her brow—giving her the air of some aged prioress of a religious order. Outside the turret room the wind howled, the rain beat against the single window—and the talk turned naturally, we are told, to deeds of horror. A recent family tragedy was the theme: "The ancient dame rocked herself over the brazier and muttered, 'Murder is like the drinking of milk here! God! There is no other but Thou!' A fresh gust of wind swept round the tower and another woman took up the tale. 'This Khanum,' said she, nodding her head towards the figure by the brazier, 'knows also what it is to weep. Her son was but now murdered in the mountains. They found his body lying stripped by the path.'

"The mother bent anew over the charcoal and the glow was on her face: 'Murder is like the spilling of water!' she groaned. 'Oh Merciful!'"

As she says in another place, "How many thousand years this state of things has lasted those who shall read the earliest records of the inner desert will tell us, for it goes back to the first of them, but in all the centuries the Arab has bought no wisdom from experience."

The worst of it is the Arab has so many to bear him company.

Of all these scenes the one most significant, certainly the one most haunting, is one most lightly touched. With her police escort the traveller is riding towards Damascus, past Brak, where there is a military post. "Just before we reached it we met a little Druze girl, who cowered by the roadside and wept with fear at the sight of us. 'I am a maid!' she cried. 'I am a maid!'" One echoes the traveller's comment: "Her words threw an ominous shadow upon the Turkish *régime*." In the mind of the most defenceless, with what nameless hor-

rors must be associated those guardians of the peace, the much-belauded soldiers of the Sultan!

When I see that I have come thus far without mention of theft and pursuit of Miss Bell's note-books, photographs, and money, with no whisper of her raid upon the Palace of the Khalifs, or even her visit to the Devil-worshippers, I recognise the hopelessness of trying to do more than fall back upon my original *rôle*. But if, in my capacity of guide-post, I proclaim to man or woman footing it on the dusty road: This is the way to Regions *Quellenreich* (as the best map of the desert has it); if I call out to the passer-by: "Here is refreshment and down yonder Romance"—I must not fail to set up some red triangle or other masonic sign adapted to new needs of warning.

These are not books to be lightly recommended. There's a spell in them. They are like to conjure holes in those stout walls behind which the town-dweller sits at his task; and in the breach, lo! pictures "steeped in the magic of sunset, softly curving hollows to hold the mist, softly swelling slopes to hold the light, and over it all the dome of the sky which vaults the desert as it vaults the sea." How shall eyes be kept on ledgers or on butcher's books when happier folk are turning their faces towards the wilderness. "I looked back upon the ancient mound of Hît, the palm groves, and the dense smoke of the pitch fires rising into the clear air. . . . Now no one rides into the desert, however uncertain the adventure, without a keen sense of exhilaration. The bright morning sun, the wide clean levels, the knowledge that the problems of existence are reduced on a sudden to their simplest expression, your own wit and endurance being the sole determining factors—all these things brace and quicken the spirit. The spell of the waste seized us as we passed beyond the sulphur marches; Hussein Onbâshi held his head higher, and we gave each other the salaam anew, as if we had stepped out into another world that called for a fresh greeting."

"At the pleasant hour of dusk I sat among the flowering weeds by my tent door while Fattûh cooked our dinner in his kitchen among the rocks, Sfâga gathered a fuel of desert scrub, Fawwâz stirred the rice-pot, and the bubbling of Hussein's narghileh gave a note of domesticity to our bivouac. My table was a big stone, the mares cropping the ragged grass round the tent were my dinner-party; one by one the stars shone out in a moonless heaven, and our tiny encampment was wrapped in the immense silences of the desert, the vast and peaceful night."

I repeat there's magic in these books. I have seen sober, anchored folk made strangely restless by these pages—seen them for the first time in my knowledge pulling at the chains of custom and duty. At moments when they should have been concerned with domestic routine, or the right administration of the Poor Law—behold them speculating, what would it be like . . . to go wandering in the desert till one chanced upon deserted palaces?

What like to come, in the land of the Devil-worshippers, upon Shalmaneser's kings and lion-mounted gods beside a flower-starred pool; and with that mighty procession for companioning to go swimming in the brown water that looked a disc of polished bronze in a setting of enamel—green and white and scarlet.

Who can count on safety against impressions that shall touch you like a flame? Take the end of the scene beginning: "The coffee beans were roasted and crushed, the coffee pots were simmering in the ashes, when there came three out of the East and halted at the open tent." The talk of Arab and Druze, of feud and raiding, is interrupted by the coming of this other guest: "A tall young man, with a handsome, delicate face, a complexion that was almost fair, and long curls that were almost brown. As he approached, Nahar and the other sheikhs rose to meet him, and before he entered the tent, each in turn kissed him upon both cheeks. Namrud rose also and cried: 'Good, please God. Who is with you?' The young man raised his hand and replied, 'God.'"

"He was alone," says the traveller out of the West.

Again among the tents of Hamri: "The coffee was ready when I arrived, and with the cups the talk went round to desert politics and the relation of this sheikh with that, all through the Weldeh camps. The glow of sunset faded, night closed down about the flickering fire of thorns, a crescent moon looked in upon us and heard us speaking of new things. Even into this primeval world a rumour had penetrated, borne on the word Liberty." "The thin blue smoke of the morning camp fires rose out of the hollows, and my heart rose with it, for here was the life of the desert, in open spaces under the open sky, and when once you have known it, the eternal savage in your breast rejoices at the return to it."

Here, then, are some of the reasons. I say, flatly, these are books I shall not have it on my conscience to recommend to all. Rather will I maintain they should be put upon the Index. Not only are they beyond precedent "unsettling." They do not so much as pretend that any one of the traveller's rash and daring deeds has its proper evil following. Eloquent celebrant as she is of the necessity of strict obedience to the law, the Fates permit her to set authority at defiance from Babylon to Anti-Taurus—and no one a penny the worse! She will kidnap a zaptieh or two as soon as eat curds. She will join a raid, and if there isn't one handy she will invent one. If she compliments the Turkish official, it is as like as not for the way he accepts her refusal to obey his orders. When you set them aside, as, she says airily, "you must from time to time," the Turkish officials "conceal their just annoyance and bear you no ill-will for the trouble you have caused them."

She congratulates herself on having handled matters with a firm hand at Rakkah. An official telegram came to the Mudir from headquarters directing that Miss Bell's progress down the left bank of the Euphrates should be arrested.

"The Vali commanded that I should be turned back across the river and conveyed carefully from guardhouse to guardhouse along the highroad."

I need hardly say this traveller did not alter her itinerary to please the Vali of Aleppo. She gets the bewildered Rakkah Mudir to send a telegram of remonstrance to his chief, inviting him to cancel his commands. The charming part of the story is that Miss Bell did not even wait to hear whether this recommendation found favour with the Vali. She pursued her journey, concerned only to remember at her next camp that somewhere near here Julian must have received his Arab reinforcements. Her meditations—historic and archæologic—are broken in upon by a breathless zaptieh from Rakkah, bringing an answer to the telegram. It sets forth the Vali's flat refusal to rescind his orders. His subordinate, the Mudir, also sends word by the same hand that if Miss Bell does not instantly return he will be obliged to recall the escort she had induced him to allow her. Her comment upon this is: "I fear that even those who cannot properly be numbered among the criminal classes catch an infection from the lawless air of the desert, but whatever may be the true explanation of our conduct, we never contemplated for a moment the alternative of obedience, and bidding a regretful farewell to friend Mahmud, we went on down the defile."

With pleasing effect comes her information a little later: "The region which we now entered is particularly lawless."

The flouting of authority on the part of this apostle of Law and Order is no matter of chance or sudden caprice. In the older book she tells how she faced the probability of the Government's refusing her permission to penetrate the country of the Druzes. If for a moment she hesitates, it is because on the road she means to travel there is a military post certain to be primed and ready to resist the progress of those who defy the Powers that Be. She weighs the chances: "At Bosra they knew me; I had slipped through their fingers five years before, a trick difficult to play a second time *from the same place*." But she evolves a plan. Yusef's two small sons sit, listening, open-eyed. One, discerning in her a kindred spirit, brings her a scrap of advertisement bearing on it—the map of America! It is a far cry. But she understands him perfectly, and reciprocates the attention, showing the children her maps, and telling them how big the world is, "and how fine a place." What use to tell her in return that "parts of it" are unfit for her consumption? Mere waste of breath to sound their epitomised warning. If they have "never known anyone to go that road before!"—what's that but reason the more for her going? The escort is often hard to find. There was that difficulty in penetrating the remote region in the Syrian desert reputed waterless. At last the traveller induces a man of the reckless Deleim to join her, with an escort of five armed horsemen, in return for a handsome reward. We are less surprised that "the handsome reward" failed to keep the gentleman to his word when we read what the country looked like even to the person keen to travel it:

"The heavy smoke of the pitch fires hung round Hit, and the sulphur marshes shone leprous under the sun—a malignant landscape that could not be redeemed by the little shrines which were scattered like propitiatory invocations among the gleaming salts.

"'It is the road of death,' said Hussein Onbâshi, stuffing tobacco into the cup of his narghileh.

"'Wallah!' said another, 'if the water-skins leak between water and water, or if the camel fall lame, the rider perishes.'

"'By the truth, it is the road of death,' repeated Hussein. 'Twice last year the Deleimi robbed the mail and killed the bearer of it.'"

Miss Bell had by this time spread out Kiepert's map.

"Inform me," said the ruthless Englishwoman, "concerning the water."

"If this account is exact," she sums up the situation, "there must be four days of waterless desert on the road of death."

Do you think she turned aside? The Deleimi did. Not she.

The whole of the astonishing passage may be commended to the reader. As she says, it is only town-dwellers like Fawwâz who fear the desert. All the same, it has an effect of being none too tranquil.

It must be admitted that Miss Bell's servants gave her gallant support, though there was one whose 'arak bottle she was obliged on occasion to smash upon a stone.

But Fattûh was a pearl. Cheerful, unfailing, a man who, in Heine's phrase, *"das Herz auf der linken Seite hat, auf der liberalen,"* was as ready for adventure as his lady Khân.

"The soldiers of Musheidah," she says, "though they were unexceptionable as hosts, were inefficient as guides. When I announced that I wished to ride by the old Tigris bed, they exclaimed in horror that it was unsafe to leave the highroad. At this Fattûh laughed outright, remarking that we had travelled over many a worse desert."

The magnificent carelessness of that "many a worse desert" would be hard to beat. One hopes that in the "character" she gave Fattûh Miss Bell did not forget to say he was a mine of stories and delight. Fattûh it was

who visited in prison the thief who had stolen all his money—yes, and lent him some more, "for he was very poor—and we ate together."

"Did you see him again?" Miss Bell asked.

"Eh, wallah!" replied Fattûh. "I met him in Deir, and there I feasted him in the bazaar. And now he lives in Deir, and I go to his house whenever I pass through the town, for we are like brothers. But he has not returned me the pound I lent him while he was in prison," added Fattûh regretfully.

In his estimate of the Western woman, Fattûh leaves the most "advanced" panting in his rear. Moreover, he seems to have no difficulty in getting other men to follow his spirited lead. When the craven Deleimi refused to risk himself and his horsemen on "the road to death," Fattûh, Miss Bell tells us, suggested that he should see what could be done with the Mudir. She, having a lively confidence in Fattûh's diplomacy, entrusted him with her passports and papers, and sent him forth with plenipotentiary powers. He returned triumphant.

"Effendim," said he, "that Mudir is a man." This is ever the highest praise that Fattûh can bestow, and my experience does not lead me to cavil at it. "When he had read your buyuruldehs he laid them upon his forehead and said, 'It is my duty to do all that the effendi wishes.' I told him," interpolated Fattûh, "that you were a consul in your own country. He will give you a zaptieh to take you to Kebeisah, and if you command, the zaptieh shall go with you to Kal'at Khubbàz."

All our cherished ideas of the impossibility of making the Oriental accept, or so much as comprehend, the Western view of woman—they are blown to the winds in these books. Of a hundred surprises on this head there is the case of the Mullah at Dûr. He refused to unlock the door of the shrine. One of Miss Bell's attendants took the old gentleman aside, "and explained that I was employed by the Government as a surveyor; upon which the mullah, with perhaps a silent reflection on the laxity of the age in the matter of official appointments, threw open the door and bade me enter."

Yet, despite the modernness of Miss Bell's attitude and her actions, there is more than a touch of the mediæval in her mind. These books show her accepting, with no misgiving, the old idea of what constitutes glory. They show her under the spell of that faith so frayed and so discredited—faith in the power of ruling caste.

Elaborate ceremonial (other people's), fear and dread of kings, these are not to her a survival of the childishness of the average man, but proof of the power of the exceptional man. It naturally follows that she is open to all the old-time associations that gathered about the panoply of war. She thrills like a schoolboy at the name of Nero, at the thought of conquest by arms. She is profoundly stirred even at a petty raid over stolen cattle amongst tribes without a name. "I, too," she exclaims in that moment of exaltation, "thank God I, too, come of a fighting race." "My soldiers have told me," she says in one place, speaking of her police escort. Had one opened at the page by chance and read the phrase apart from context, one would think it either a fragment of military memoir or the words of some queen uttered in the Middle-Ages.

But why not "Queen?" as the Sayyid called her.

"If I see truly, I am king of what I see." Let her account of what she sees be read by any reddest republican alive, and he will justify the Sayyid's vocative. In that it came so readily to his lips, we have but one reason the more why Miss Bell (apart from her equipment of language and history) was precisely the person to go amongst Orientals. They will hardly outdo her love of stately ceremonial, or her faith in the efficacy of the aristocratic idea. Her Eastern friends could not have dealt so understandingly with a more democratic mind. They found her meeting their Vali and their princes—hardly as equals, indeed, since she swept them and their edicts aside whenever she saw fit. Her way of ranging herself on the side of the ruling class was to do a little ruling in her own right. She passes judgment on their judges; she measures their Kadi and their Mudir as she measures their castles and their mosques. She sets down Ghishghash boastful, foolish, "extremely talkative, though all that he said was not worth one of Faiz's sentences."

She compliments the Kaimmakam of Drekish upon his use of Syrian Arabic; and Reshid Agha, she says with decision, is the chief magnate and also the chief villain of Salkin.

Yet you would be wrong to think she has forgotten that the forefathers of these folk "watched the stars before the English had begun to keep pigs." Nor must anyone do her the injustice of interpreting her attitude as one of mere personal arrogance. The power she thinks she conjures with is the power of the English. Her eager national pride treasures every sign of deference to Great Britain. In other matters, critical beyond most, she can take as simple-minded delight in a Moslem's compliment to her race as though the Oriental, with his habit of courtesy, would not have turned a flattering phrase as easily for Teuton, Gaul, or Japanese. So far from such inconsistencies making the subject of this study a less interesting figure, any sketch of her would be incomplete that did not give some indication of the very human side of one whose reach and grasp are so much farther, and firmer, than that of most women or of most men. For the grave student is a lover of mountains; the severe critic is a good laugher. She not only thrills and waxes eloquent at sight of the Euphrates, she jibes at it for not being "a good table water."

Of the road to Saleh, she says in a burst: "I continue to call it a road for want of a name bad enough for it"—

and when we have travelled with her for a space we are ready to share Muhammad's surprise:

"Oh lady, you have not laughed once, not when I showed you the ruins, nor when I told you the name of the hills."

To have deserved that reproach how often must she have betrayed the rapture with which she neared the high places, or set herself to study history on the spot where it was made.

If you think, therefore, to escape caring for her on one count, behold she will trip you up with its opposite.

Law-lover and law-breaker, she is a reactionary passionate for freedom.

Is there not something of all this in her name? I lay myself open to the charge of childishness in admitting that for me the queenly "Gertrude" falls fittingly on the ear like a ceremonious introduction. Wholly inconceivable that in her case the name should ever have been "nicked" or shortened. But hard upon the heels of this formal "Gertrude" comes Lowthian, with its music of Border ballad and its echo of Border raid; and finally, your wandering fancy is called smartly to attention by the last staccato note of the Bell.

Gertrude Lowthian Bell!

You are not of my camp nor of my nation—and yet, Wallah! in the words of the Sheikh of the Amarat, "if you come to my tents, welcome and kinship."

Sir E. Denison Ross (essay date 1928)

SOURCE: Preface to *Persian Pictures* by Gertrude Bell, Boni and Liveright, 1928, pp. 5-11.

[*In the following preface to* Persian Pictures, *Ross discusses Bell's early impressions of Persia and includes a lengthy excerpt from a letter Bell wrote to her cousin Horace Marshall.*]

The letters of Gertrude Lowthian Bell are so fresh in the public mind, and seem so clearly destined to become a classic, that there is little need in this place for biographical details. It will suffice to say that she was born on July 14, 1868, at Washington Hall, Durham, then the residence of her grandfather, the late Sir Lowthian Bell. In 1885 she entered Lady Margaret Hall, Oxford, and in 1887 took a brilliant First in History. During her student days in Oxford, when she indulged in games with no less zeal than in her studies, she seems to have caught the fever of the Orient, so that when in 1891 her uncle Sir Frank Lascelles was appointed Minister in Teheran we find her declaring that the great ambition of her life was to visit Persia. Thus it came about that in the spring of 1892 Gertrude Bell set out for Teheran with Lady Lascelles, and the little book now re-issued was the fruit of this her first excursion into the East. Part of it was written on the spot and part of it after her return to England. In a letter dated 1892 (presumably in December) she writes, 'Bentley wishes to publish my Persian things, but wants more of them, so after much hesitation I have decided to let him and I am writing him another six chapters. It's rather a bore and what's more I would vastly prefer them to remain unpublished. I wrote them you see to amuse myself and I have got all the fun out of them I ever expect to have, for modesty apart they are extraordinarily feeble. Moreover I do so loathe people who rush into print and fill the world with their cheap and nasty work—and now I am going to be one of them. At first I refused, then my mother thought me mistaken and my father was disappointed and as they are generally right I have given way. But in my heart I hold very firmly to my first opinion. Don't speak of this. I wish them not to be read.'

It is interesting to hear that Gertrude Bell had so poor an opinion of her first essay in literature, and it is also interesting to learn that the last six chapters were, so to speak, written to order: for I think it must be conceded that there is a something in those chapters which were written in Persia which is wanting from the later ones, in spite of their charm of style and characterization. In the end the little book appeared anonymously, and thus a compromise was effected between the wishes of her parents and her own modesty.

It may suitably be recalled that a somewhat similar fate attended another book of Persian travel, namely Edward G. Browne's *Year Amongst the Persians,* which appeared a year before **Persian Pictures**. Neither Edward Browne nor his publisher seems to have realized the exceptional qualities of this book, which was never reprinted until after the death of that great scholar in 1925.

Miss Bell's little book is of course slight in comparison with Browne's, and whereas Browne took with him to Persia a first-class knowledge of the language and literature of that country, Miss Bell had only studied Persian for a few months previously to her departure for Teheran. In that brief space she had, however, learnt to read with some degree of fluency, and she no doubt understood a great deal of what was said to her in conversation, though she refers to the constant use of an interpreter.

There is a peculiar magic in the air of Persia which inspires all who visit her with poetry and romance: and this is not easily to be explained: for Persia today is a country in which very few traces remain to remind the traveller of her past glories. The cities of old Iran have been built and destroyed in the course of her long history, and nature and man seem to have combined to place Persia in our day under the ban of neglect. A score of cities have in turn been royal capitals, and as such have received all the embellishments that powerful monarchs could bestow on them, only to be abandoned and finally left in ruins, and even the ruins have often been ruthlessly destroyed. The country itself is full of vast desolate tracts. In spite of all this Persia casts her spell on every traveller, a spell worked by marvellous sunsets over the undulating deserts, by the glorious gardens the Persians love so well, and, last but not least, of the subtle charm of the Persians themselves, who are all poets and philosophers of nature, whether prince or muleteer. Like Kinglake's *Eöthen,* this little book is free from all details of geographical discovery or antiquarian research, from all political disquisitions and from all useful statistics. It is a book of travel to be classed with that choice group of English works which include Young's *Travels* and Borrow's *Bible in Spain.* Only in the chapter entitled 'A Murray of the First Century' do we get a foretaste of Miss Bell's later work in the field of archæology which earned for her a world-wide fame among scholars. The mention of *Eöthen* reminds us of the famous chapter in which Kinglake describes the plague in Cairo, and it was a curious coincidence that took Miss Bell to Persia when a cholera epidemic was at its height, and gave her the opportunity of observing the behaviour of the Persian populace in the face of this dread disease, just as Kinglake had watched the Egyptians nearly eighty years earlier.

This little book was published by Bentley in 1894 under the title of **Safar Nameh. Persian Pictures. A book of travel,** without the author's name. It was favourably received and then quickly forgotten. The only copy known to me is that from which the present edition is being made. In 1897 Miss Bell published her **Poems from the Divan of Hafiz,** under her name. In this she gave evidence not only of the scholarly knowledge of Persian she had by this time acquired, but also of a rare poetic gift. This book also was well received, but did not attain the wide publicity it deserved, and, like the **Persian Pictures,** it is only being reprinted after Gertrude Bell's death. Not till 1907 did Miss Bell produce her first work on a large scale, **The Desert and the Sown,** which at last brought her due recognition as a scholar and a traveller, went through two editions and was translated into German.

It is a matter of great regret that her letters from Persia, of which there were a good many, cannot be found. One, however, addressed to her cousin Horace Marshall and dated Gulahek, June 18, 1892, has been preserved and was printed in the **Letters of Gertrude Bell.** Seeing that it makes so characteristic a supplement to the **Persian Pictures,** the opportunity has been taken of reproducing it in this place.

Are we the same people I wonder when all our surroundings, association, acquaintances are changed? Here that which is me, which womanlike is an empty jar that the passer by fills at pleasure, is filled with such wine as in England I had never heard of, now the wine is more important than the jar when one is thirsty, therefore I conclude, cousin mine, that it is not the person who danced with you at Mansfield St. that writes to you today from Persia.—Yet there are dregs, English sediments at the bottom of my sherbet, and perhaps they flavour it more than I think. Anyhow I remember you as a dear person in a former existence, whom I should like to drag into this one and to guide whose spiritual coming I will draw paths in ink. And others there are whom I remember yet not with regret but as one might remember people one knew when one was an inhabitant of Mars 20 centuries ago. How big the world is, how big and how wonderful. It comes to me as ridiculously presumptuous that I should dare to carry my little personality half across it and boldly attempt to measure with it things for which it has no table of measurements that can possibly apply. So under protest I write to you of Persia: I am not me, that is my only excuse. I am merely pouring out for you some of what I have received during the last two months.

Well in this country the men wear flowing robes of green and white and brown, the women lift the veil of a Raphael Madonna to look at you as you pass; wherever there is water a luxuriant vegetation springs up and where there is not there is nothing but stone and desert. Oh the desert round Teheran! miles and miles of it with nothing, *nothing* growing; ringed in with bleak bare mountains snow crowned and furrowed with the deep courses of torrents. I never knew what desert was till I came here; it is a very wonderful thing to see; and suddenly in the middle of it all, out of nothing, out of a little cold water, springs up a garden. Such a garden! trees, fountains, tanks, roses and a house in it, the houses which we heard of in fairy tales when we were little: inlaid with tiny slabs of looking-glass in lovely patterns, blue tiled, carpeted, echoing with the sound of running water and fountains. Here sits the enchanted prince, solemn, dignified, clothed in long robes. He comes down to meet you as you enter, his house is yours, his garden is yours, better still his tea and fruit are yours, so are his kalyans (but *I* think kalyans are a horrid form of smoke, they taste to me of charcoal and paint and nothing else). By the grace of God your slave hopes that the health of your nobility is well? It is very well out of his great kindness. Will your magnificence carry itself on to this cushion? Your magnificence sits down and spends ten minutes bandying florid compliments through an interpreter while ices are served and coffee, after which you ride home refreshed, charmed, and with many blessings on your fortunate head. And all the time your host was probably a perfect stranger into whose privacy you had forced yourself in this unblushing way. Ah, we have no hospitality in the west and no manners. I felt ashamed almost before the beggars in the street—they wear their rags with a better grace than I my most becoming habit, and *the* veils of the commonest women (now the veil is the touchstone on which to try a woman's toilette) are far better put on than mine. A veil should fall from the top of your head to the soles of your feet, of that I feel convinced, and it should not be transparent.

Say, is it not rather refreshing to the spirit to lie in a hammock strung between the plane trees of a Persian garden and read the poems of Hafiz—in the original mark you!—out of a book curiously bound in stamped leather which you have bought in the bazaars. That is how I spend my mornings here: a stream murmurs past me which Zoroastrian gardeners guide with long handled spades into tiny sluices leading into the flower beds all around. The dictionary which is also in my hammock is not perhaps so poetic as the other attributes—let us hide it under our muslin petticoats!

This also is pleasant: to come in at 7 o'clock in the morning after a two hours' ride, hot and dusty, and find one's cold bath waiting for one scented with delicious rose water, and after it an excellent and longed for breakfast spread in a tent in the garden.

What else can I give you but fleeting impressions caught and hardened out of all knowing? I can tell you of a Persian merchant in whose garden, stretching all up the mountain side, we spent a long day, from dawn to sunset, breakfasting, lunching, teaing on nothing but Persian foods. He is noted for his hospitality: every evening parties of friends arrive unexpectedly, "he goes out, entertains them," said the Persian who told me about it, "spreads a banquet before them and relates to them stories half through the night. Then cushions are brought and carpeted mattresses and they lie down in one of the guest-houses in the garden and sleep till dawn when they rise and repair to the bath in the village." Isn't it charmingly like the Arabian Nights! but that is the charm of it all and it has none of it changed; every day I meet our aged kalendars and ladies who I am sure have suits of swans' feathers laid up in a chest at home, and some time when I open a new jar of rose water I know that instead of a sweet smell, the great smoke of one of Suleiman's afreets will come out of its neck.

In the garden there are big deep tanks where in the evenings between tennis and dinner I often swim in the coldest of cold water. Before we left Teheran when it was too hot to sleep, I used to go out at dawn and swim under the shadow of the willows. We were very glad to leave Teheran though we like the house there. It began to be very stuffy and airless: here, though we are only 6 miles away, there is always air, except perhaps between two and four in the afternoon when one generally sleeps. We are much higher up and much nearer the hills and all round us are watered fields where the corn is almost ripe for cutting. The joy of this climate! I don't think an English summer will be very nice after it.

I learn Persian, not with great energy, one does nothing with energy here. My teacher is a delightful old person with bright eyes and a white turban who knows so little French—French is our medium—that he can neither translate the poets to me nor explain any grammatical difficulties. But we get on admirably nevertheless and spend much of our time in long philosophic discussions carried on by me in French and by him in Persian. His point of view is very much that of an oriental Gibbon, though with this truly oriental distinction, that he would never dream of acknowledging in words or acts his scepticism to one of his own countrymen. It would be tacitly understood between them and their intercourse would be continued on the basis of perfect agreement. Now this is a great simplification and promotes, I should imagine, the best of good manners. . . .

This letter reminds us of the magic influence which the *Arabian Nights* exercises over us all and which for every traveller colours the Islamic East with romance. It is sufficient that he should have read the *Nights* for him to find at every turn the scenario of familiar tales or an approximate setting for imaginary adventures.

The debt of the world to old Galland, who discovered and translated the *Nights* at the end of the seventeenth century, cannot be over-estimated. Gertrude Bell was drawn to the East by this spirit of romance; she found what she sought, and everything she saw on her first journey was coloured by the pictures she had previously conceived as a result of her reading of Persian poetry and the Arabian tales. Not till later in her life was she to find herself confronted with the East as a modern reality—as an element in world politics; and compelled by necessity to treat these picturesque and romantic denizens of Oriental towns and deserts as ordinary mortals.

The strenuous years in Baghdad, where most of her work was far from romantic, never wrought any change in her enthusiasm for the East, and it was perhaps fitting that she should end her days—though alas! all too soon—in the land she knew and among the people she loved with so much understanding.

Michael Swan (essay date 1957)

SOURCE: "The Emma of the Desert," in *A Small Part of Time: Essays on Literature, Art and Travel,* 1957. Reprint by Dufour Editions, 1961, pp. 129-37.

[*In the following essay, Swan discusses a volume of published letters Bell wrote to her father and stepmother from abroad.*]

There is evidently some special quality in the British national character which has produced so long a succession of indomitable women travellers; it is almost impossible to imagine a Lady Mary Wortley Montagu from France recounting her lively stories of adventure in the harems of Stamboul, or a Lady Hester Stanhope from Italy dominating the caravanserais of the Syrian desert. The Latin mind must find lives so adventurous as theirs alarmingly unfeminine; the Moorish invasion of Spain and those Saracenic raids on the littorals of Italy left behind them the indelible mark of female sequestration.

All the same, it seems to have been the achievement of our women travellers rarely to lose their feminity, to produce, in fact, an often delightful form of hermaphroditism: they will gossip as women but outmarch the strongest man; they will show feminine will by insisting on reaching a desert ruin before sunset, but show a masculine appetite for scholarship when the time comes to make the account of the journey. In this century we have had two great descendants in the line from Lady Mary and Lady Hester; Miss Freya Stark and Gertrude Bell, both women whose deepest passions were enflamed by the ancient and mysterious civilizations of the Arab world.

When Gertrude Bell died quietly in her sleep, at Baghdad, she was only fifty-seven, a woman celebrated as a traveller but perhaps more famous as a colonial administrator, one of the dominant forces behind the creation of Iraq. In 1927, the year after her death, two large volumes of her letters to her father and stepmother were published. The fact that no letters to any other correspondents were printed gives the book unity, but it is a pity that one is still unable to see her in all her aspects as a letter-writer. Even so, these letters do put her whole character and career into perfect perspective. And what a remarkable woman she was! Here is the pretty young girl with the Titian colouring, the finely chiselled nose and the determined mouth, who loved fine clothes, bubbling with zest and gaiety at Oxford, taking a brilliant First in Modern History in spite of telling her distinguished examiner during the viva that she had never been able to agree with his view of Charles I; here, later, is the frequenter of Europe's embassies, learning Latin in her spare hours to fill a lacuna in her education, making history by climbing the Finsteraarhorn, the flirter with the First Secretary at the British Legation in Teheran, the traveller across the Syrian desert to the mountain of Jebel Druze, the Arabic scholar, the archaeologist, the fine photographer, the accurate measurer of the desert ruins. . . . Her talents were prodigious and, blessed with curiosity, she spared herself nothing to satisfy her enthusiasms. Her work for the British Government in Iraq was the last of her great enthusiasms—she knew the Arab intimately and her advice was taken by the Government—but even during those last, hard-driving years she devoted hours to the Museum of Antiquities and portioned out the various findings at Ur.

Apart from all other interests, Gertrude Bell's letters to her parents are documents of family love and unity, though her own mother died when she was three. It seems clear that her almost extreme integration of personality and her various charms—not to mention her wilfulness—derived from her love of her family. At the age of fifty she wrote to her father, a Northumbrian ironmaster and colliery owner: 'Goodbye, darling father, I think and think of you. However long I'm away from you, your love and mother's is like the solid foundation on which all life rests.' Family love was all the love she seems to have needed, and she had little wish to marry, although the flirtation in Teheran took a deeper turn, and might have ended in marriage had the First Secretary, Henry Cadogan, not died. Her friend, Janet Courtney, mysteriously says that this brief romance was 'neither the first nor the last in her life', but of these affairs the letters say nothing.

Much of Gertrude Bell's independence of spirit came from her upbringing, which was by no means typically Victorian. Her father was a liberal-minded, free-thinking intellectual, and he believed in giving his daughter her freedom in every way; without his money and encouragement she would have been unable to make her desert journeys. The atmosphere in which she was brought up might have turned her into the perfect New Woman of the nineties, but bloomers, bicycles and votes for women did not claim her; indeed, during the suffragette disturbances she worked actively against the movement, believing that it would destroy all the gradually won achievements of the professional woman. It was one of her many charms that in spite of doing so well many things that had always been in man's province she never lost her femininity. The young girl who had burst into Janet Courtney's room with 'I've got a hat, Janet, but a hat!' never lost her love of clothes, and from a goat's-hair tent at Wadi el Asibiyeh might send home detailed instructions for a new evening dress to be made by Marthe, her Sloane Street dressmaker. And although she was proud of her work in Iraq during and after the 1914 war, she thought of herself as only the assistant to such men as Sir Percy Cox and Sir Henry Dobbs, the real architects of the protectorate.

The figure of Gertrude Bell is so attractive from such countless aspects that the predatory cynic in us may begin to look for the catch in her character, the price she paid for her happiness. The catch cannot be defined, only felt vaguely—and perhaps unjustifiably. After reading all her work, one is forced to say that in spite of her extraordinary array of talents hers was fundamentally a conventional mind, and that although she had brilliant talent she had neither great intellect nor the sensibility of the artist. One reads the letters with delight and is thrilled by her superb description of the two days on the Finsteraarhorn, but how rarely one wants to mark a passage that is memorable for that piercing intuition, that unique vision of a special mind. In her lifetime she was sometimes called 'the Diana of the Desert', but after reading her letters one might prefer to call her 'The Emma of the Desert', for she has so many of Miss Woodhouse's characteristics.

Whenever there was a question of fear she seems, paradoxically, to lose her femininity. One expects her, one wants her, to shrink behind her guard of soldiers during her frequent dangerous encounters in the desert, but instead she is always well to the fore. Her only comment when asked what she had felt like during the two terrible nights on the Finsterrerhorn was: 'Oh, it was rather chilly.' In all her writings—letters and books—there is not a line to show that she had ever known the

meaning of fear. It is an element which one misses, its presence would have given a special humanity to her work. There are other indications of a kind of insensibility. Her agnosticism, which bordered on atheism, prevented her from writing with any religious sympathy for the Arab's all-enveloping reverence for the godhead. She learned to speak the languages of the people she loved with a feeling for all their nuances and subtleties, and her Arabs loved her. She understood entirely their way of thinking, but her own feet were so firmly planted in the desert sand that the Arab way of believing completely defied her understanding. Many Arabian travellers have been compelled by some mystique of the desert and its monuments of the past, but a mystique in any form was contrary to Gertrude Bell's nature, although that is not to say that she was not compelled by an irresistible joy in the life of the desert; in *The Desert and the Sown* (1907) she writes: 'To wake in that desert dawn was like waking in the heart of an opal. The mists lifting their heads out of the hollows, the dews floating in ghostly wreaths from the black tents, were shot through first with the faint glories of the eastern sky and then with the strong yellow rays of the risen sun. We climbed the Jebel el Alya and crossed the wide summit of the range, the landscape was akin to that of our own English border country . . . the glorious cold air intoxicated every sense and set the blood throbbing. See the desert on a fine morning and die—if you can.'

That passage is typical, in its sense of joy, of *The Desert and the Sown* which, with *Amurath to Amurath* (1911), are the only general books she wrote, with the exception of *Persian Pictures,* an immature little book which she wrote when she was twenty-four. It is perhaps right that her letters have proved her literary memorial, but her two books deserve to be better known, for they are classics of their kind. Incidents which are treated cursorily in the letters appear with all their possibilities exploited and, far more than in the letters, one is given a sense of the adventure of this attractive girl setting off with her muleteers and her guide into the unexplored wastes, and feeling, with the poet Mutanabbï, that 'the most exalted seat in the world is the saddle of a swift horse'. Not a morning or an afternoon passes without an encounter: Russian pilgrims with long beards and crinkly kneeboots on their way to Jerusalem; a Christian encampment out of the Acts of the Apostles; a band of nomadic bedouin bearing down on her camp furiously firing their rifles (in welcome, as it turned out); the nights sitting by the sage-bush fire in the tent of a desert sheikh, drinking the bitter coffee she so loved and discussing the ways of the desert and the beauties of Arabic poetry. Or, during the long hours of the journey, there were the enchanting conversations with Namrud the guide, from whom she coaxed such stories and observations of wisdom; it was Namrud who told her that the Arabs believed there was a strong racial connection between themselves and the Japanese.

An interesting feature of both *The Desert and the Sown* and *Amurath to Amurath* is the large number of photographs taken by Gertrude Bell herself, many of which are masterpieces of travel photography, and make one realize how enormously the value of a travel book is enhanced by really adequate illustration.

Perhaps, of all the desert moments, those that gave Gertrude Bell her purest excitement were those when suddenly, above the rim of the desert, would appear the ruined towers of Ukheidir, or the remains of the fabulous palace of Ctesiphon, with its astonishing vaulted roof, unchanged from the time when it protected Chosroes and his court. She was no 'virtuoso' who came merely to see and enjoy; she would camp for days at the ruins, measuring them and making accurate plans, taking rubbings and pressings of inscriptions. She was an amateur archaeologist but she did nothing without professional zeal, and there is no doubt that she added much to the knowledge of Arabic cultures. In 1905, during a visit to the ruins of Bin Bir Kilisse, she recorded an inscription which later produced an entirely new line of inquiry. Two years later she and Sir William Ramsay measured and mapped the ruins, and together they published a formidable volume called *The Thousand and One Churches,* whose *Arabian Nights* echo is misleading. 'It will be a very dull book, you understand,' she wrote to her stepmother, but she was always ready to accept the fact that dullness could be worthwhile.

In *The Desert and the Sown* she mixes the archaeological with the human in perfect proportion; one of the problems of writing a travel book is to know exactly when to stop in the description and discussion of mere stones—an author's personal enthusiasms need to be kept under control. In this book Gertrude Bell never offers more than her readers can take, but in *Amurath to Amurath* she is less inclined to assist the uninitiated reader, printing plans and giving lists of the exact measurements of the fluted niches at Ukheidir. Nevertheless it is a book which in the main lives up to the high intentions of its preface: 'In that spacious hour when the silence of the embracing wilderness was enhanced rather than broken by the murmur of the river, and by the sounds, scarcely less primeval, that wandered round the camp-fire of my nomad hosts, the task broadened into a shape which was in keeping with the surroundings. I would attempt to record the daily life and the speech of those who had inherited the empty ground whereon empires had risen and expired.'

Amurath to Amurath, alas, was Gertrude Bell's last book, except for a little guide to Mesopotamia which she produced for the British Government during the 1914-18 War. Her desert journeys were now over; she had learnt the lesson of the Arabs, and now she could devote her knowledge to their welfare. In 1919 she, with Prince Feisal and T. E. Lawrence, was at the Paris Conference to plead the cause of the Arabs. Her friends, who had not seen her for four years, remarked that she looked as if she had turned into finely tempered steel, and her strength was tried during the next years of intense work.

When her task was nearly done, it was suggested to her that she should return to England and stand for Parliament. The anti-suffragette, the un-masculine feminist wrote in a letter: 'I haven't the quickness of thought and speech which could fit the clash of Parliament. I can do my own job in a way, and explain why I think that the right way of doing it, but I don't cover a wide enough field, and my natural desire is to slip back into the comfortable arena of archaeology and history.' Was she planning, for that retirement of which death cheated her, a last desert journey? Did she want to wake once more in the heart of an opal and taste the bitter coffee? Did she want to know, again, days like that morning when she had come across some poor Arabs in the desert who had been robbed by members of the Deleim tribe: 'Their tale filled me with futile anger so that I desired nothing so much as to catch and punish the thieves, and without waiting to consider whether this lay within our power I galloped on in the direction indicated by the peasants . . . we searched the sandhills without success, but when we came down to the Euphrates, there were five armed men strolling unconcernedly along the bank. . . . Now you do not wander with a rifle in your hand in unfrequented parts of the Euphrates bank for any good purpose, and we were persuaded that these black-browed Arabs were the five we sought. . . . Unfortunately we had no proof against them . . . and though we spent some minutes in heaping curses upon them, we could take no steps of a more practical kind. My soldier was in an agony of nervous anxiety lest we should relieve them of their rifles. He looked forward to a journey alone to Baghdad, and it is not good for a solitary man to have an outstanding quarrel with the Deleim. Finally I realized that we were wasting breath in useless bluster. . . . If we were to concern ourselves with the catching of thieves we might as well abandon all other pursuits in Turkey.'

No passage in her works could express better the heart of this remarkable woman.

Brian Fagan (essay date 1991)

SOURCE: "Bell of Baghdad," in *Archaeology,* Vol. 44, No. 4, July/August, 1991, pp. 12, 14, 16.

[*In the following essay, Fagan discusses Bell's influence on archeological expeditions in Persia as well as her important role in the creation of the Iraq Museum.*]

For all its troubles in recent months, Baghdad's Iraq Museum remains one of the world's great repositories of antiquities. Like so many other major museums, it owes its existence to the vision and drive of an inspired archaeologist, in Baghdad's case the indefatigable Gertrude Bell. Born in 1868, the daughter of a wealthy English industrialist, Bell was accustomed to having her way. She entered Oxford at the age of 18 at a time when female students were not allowed outside the college precincts unchaperoned. It is said that she had the un-heard-of temerity to disagree with her examiners during her orals, a portent of things to come.

After leaving Oxford in 1892, she set out on the first of her many travels, which included a seven-month stay in Jerusalem. The literary reviews were quick to take notice of her writings, among them some poetry and a travel book on Persia. She had the luxury of ample means and could afford to take her time. In Jerusalem, she improved her Arabic and had her first taste of desert travel, enduring "tents with earwigs and black beetles, and muddy water to drink." She acquired an addiction to the desert and the Near East. "One doesn't keep away from the East when one has got into it this far," she wrote prophetically. It was while she was in the Holy Land that she developed a passion for archaeology, taking more than 600 photographs of monuments near Jerusalem. Inspired by the beauty of these ancient sites, she spent the next few years studying archaeology in Rome and Paris. Although she initially concentrated on the Byzantine period, publishing a major work on the *Thousand and One Churches* at Birbinkilise in Turkey in 1909, her mind always turned toward her first love, the desert.

When Gertrude told friends she planned a journey to the walled, eighth-century Abbasid palace of Ukhaidir in the central Arabian desert, they were horrified. Sweeping their objections aside, she set off through the territory of the hostile Deleim Arabs. For four days, she photographed and surveyed the huge castle with its walled enclosure, tripping over her soldier escorts, who never let their rifles out of their hands as they held her measuring tapes. "I can't persuade them to lay down the damnable things for an instant," she complained. Her account of this extraordinary journey, *Amurath to Amurath,* established Gertrude as a traveler and archaeologist of the first rank. By this time, she was literally intoxicated by desert travel, as much by the people as by the fascinating archaeological sites. She often traveled at night. "Can you picture the singular beauty of these moonlit departures?" she wrote. "The frail Arab tents falling one by one, leaving the camp fires blazing into the night; the dark masses of the kneeling camels, the shrouded figures binding up the loads, shaking the ice from the water skins, or couched over the hearth for a moment's warmth before mounting." She spent hours talking with the local sheikhs and nomadic tribesmen and was one of the first Europeans to detect the stirrings of deep-felt Arab nationalism. Her strong opinions gained her some enemies. As one contemporary wrote:

> From Trebizone to Tripolis
> She rolls the Pashas flat
> And tells them what to think of this
> And what to think of that.

In 1911, she visited the Hittite excavations at Carchemish, on the Turkish-Syrian border, hoping to catch the irascible but competent David Hogarth, legendary for his expertise in Minoan archaeology and for his bad temper before breakfast. He had already gone home, so her host was the young T. E. Lawrence, soon to become the legendary Lawrence of Arabia. Soon after her arrival, Bell informed the Carchemish archaeologists that their methods were "prehistoric" compared to those of the Germans. She was probably right, but the archaeologists counter-attacked with what Lawrence called "a display of erudition." According to Lawrence, she was "taken (in five minutes) over Byzantine, Crusader, Roman, Hittite, and French architecture." Lawrence and his colleagues discoursed on "prehistoric pottery, telephoto lenses, Bronze Age metal techniques, Meredith, Anatole France, and the Octobrists." They even told her about German excavation methods on the Baghdad railroad, being built only a few miles away. By all accounts Gertrude retreated in some disarray. "Gerty has gone back to her tents," Lawrence wrote to Hogarth with glee. As gifted an archaeologist as the opinionated Gertrude was, she was not beloved.

Bell might have gone down in history as little more than a bold desert traveler had World War I not broken out. Her knowledge of the Arabian desert was invaluable to British intelligence in 1914. The only female political officer in an all-male establishment, she became a power broker in Baghdad when the war ended and the British ruled over a former province of the Ottoman Empire that was soon to become Iraq. She flattered tribal leaders, interviewed them, and gave them presents. These actions gained her the reputation of being pro-Arab, which she undoubtedly was, for she shared with Lawrence and a few others the gift of being able to communicate with desert people. "When they talk of tribes of sheikhs, or watering places, I don't need to ask where they are," she wrote. "I know . . . I see again the wide Arabian horizon." She lived a hectic but lonely life, where the respect and companionship of her colleagues were paramount. She was eclectic in her interests: dogs, photography, mountaineering, languages, and, above all, people. She became a champion of Arab independence, and of their cultural heritage.

The early 1920s were heady days in Baghdad, a time of makeshift government and individual initiative. One priority was antiquities legislation. The first law to control excavation and regulate the export of archaeological material was passed in 1922. There were many foreign expeditions anxious to work between the Tigris and the Euphrates and eager to export their finds. The Germans wanted to take the remains of the Ishtar Gate, which they had excavated at Babylon before the war. The gate was eventually taken to Berlin, where it was put on display. The Americans and the British were pressing for excavations at Ur. With these requests, and many others on her desk, Gertrude sat down to organize the Department of Antiquities and the Iraq Museum. The museum's first home was a shelf in her house, the second a few humble rooms near the palace of King Faisal I. In 1926, however, the government gave her "a real museum like the British Museum only a little smaller." Within her new quarters, Bell busied herself ordering shallow pottery drawers and negotiating with foreign expeditions.

Her most formidable adversary was Leonard Woolley, who presided over the joint University of Pennsylvania-British Museum expedition to Ur of the Chaldees. "He's a tiresome little man, but a first class digger and an archaeologist after my own heart," she wrote. Her visits to Ur at the end of each season were dreaded for their long hours and epic bargaining. "We had to claim the best things for ourselves," she wrote. Woolley fought hard, but she always took an impartial referee along to arbitrate over prize objects. Sometimes the arguments were ferocious, "but we have no cause for complaint," wrote Woolley, after his second season in 1924, "though I would not say that to Miss Bell . . ." "Who decides if we disagree?" another archaeologist once asked. "I do," Gertrude Bell promptly replied—and she did.

More than 60 years later, it is hard for us to imagine what it must have been like administering archaeology in a country that was really on the frontier in 1925. In addition to working with numerous foreign expeditions, each conducting large-scale excavations, Gertrude was overseeing pre-Sumerian, Sumerian, Babylonian, Assyrian, and spectacular later sites, all with a limited budget. In the end, the burden and the pitiless summer heat undermined her health. Lonely and politically discredited by the British as pro-Arab, she committed suicide in 1926 at the age of 58.

Bell's reputation in Iraq is somewhat tarnished today, for many Iraqi scholars believe that she gave away too much. This remarkable woman, however, trod an intellectual and moral tightrope in Iraq. On the one hand, she strove to preserve the interests of the new nation and its patrimony. On the other, Bell the intellectual wanted to place the interests of science, and its wealthy backers, above those of pure nationalism. Her vision and drive, combined with a dedicated and honest outspokenness, are qualities that often seem lacking today.

FURTHER READING

Biography

Burgoyne, Elizabeth. *Gertrude Bell: From Her Personal Papers, 1889-1914.* London: Ernest Benn, 1958, 320 p.
  Early biography of Bell. The volume includes many of her letters and other autobiographical writings.

Hill, Stephen. "Gertrude Bell." *Antiquity* 50, Vols. 199-200 (September-December 1976): 190-93.
  Overview of Bell's life and work.

Kamm, Josephine. *Daughter of the Desert: The Story of Gertrude Bell.* London: The Bodley Head, 1956, 191 p.
  Sympathetic account of Bell's life and career.

Winstone, H. V. F. *Gertrude Bell.* London: Jonathan Cape, 1978, 322 p.
  Examination of Bell's life that makes use of material unavailable to previous biographers. Winstone claims his portrait of Bell is less one-sided than earlier accounts.

Criticism

Review of *Persian Pictures,* by Gertrude Bell. *Life and Letters* 1, No. 4 (September 1928): 318-20.
  Positive assessment of an early work. The reviewer also praises Bell's *Poems from the Divan of Hafiz,* a volume of poems by the fourteenth-century Persian mystic Hafiz that Bell translated, and for which she wrote an extended historical introduction.

Review of *Persian Pictures,* by Gertrude Bell. *The London Quarterly* XXXV (1928): 272-73.
  Brief, favorable review.

Tinling, Marion. "Gertrude Bell: Persian Treasures." In *Women into the Unknown: A Sourcebook on Women Explorers and Travelers,* pp. 39-46. New York: Greenwood Press, 1989.
  Overview of Bell's life, focusing on her travels and literary career.

Nikolai Berdyaev

1874–1948

Russian philosopher.

INTRODUCTION

Berdyaev is ranked among the foremost Christian philosophers of the twentieth century. Although his early philosophical leanings were toward Marxist materialism, his mature thought is primarily concerned with the possibilities for human freedom and creativity in a Christian context. Berdyaev viewed history as a manifestation of God's plan for the ultimate perfection of humanity. He thus interpreted the biblical fall as humanity's descent into objectification and the end of history as the inauguration of a divine kingdom that would transcend the limitations of objective, material reality. Berdyaev's concern with individual freedom led to his critiques of Marxism, capitalism, socialism, and other developments in modern history that he considered profance and dehumanizing. His moral system, in addition, is based on the Christian ethic of redemption, in which evil must be overcome and material restrictions surmounted so that a kingdom of God founded on love and compassion might be created.

Biographical Information

Berdyaev was born in the town of Lipky, near Kiev, on March 6, 1874. His parents were of noble birth—his mother was a Russian princess and his father a military officer who saw to it that his son joined the Corps of Cadets as a youth. Showing little interest in a military life, Berdyaev later attended the University of Kiev, where he embraced Marxism and became involved with the Social Democrats. In 1898 Berdyaev was expelled for his connection with the Marxist revolutionary movement and two years later was banished to Vologda in northern Russia until 1903. The following year he married Lydia Troucheva and moved with her to St. Petersburg. By this time Berdyaev had broken with the Marxists and embraced Christianity, becoming a lifelong member of the Russian Orthodox Church. Over the course of the next two decades, Berdyaev undertook an intense study of philosophy and rose to prominence among the intelligentsia in St. Petersburg and Moscow. In 1920, three years after the Bolsheviks had seized power in Russia—and in part due to his youthful socialist leanings—Berdyaev was appointed professor of philosophy at the University of Moscow. In 1922, however, he was again exiled, this time for his public criticism of the new Soviet regime, and in September of that year he left Russia for Berlin, where he founded the Academy of Philosophy and Religion. His stay in Berlin was brief and lasted only until 1924, at which time he moved to

Paris to continue his literary activities. That year Berdyaev realized fame in Europe with the publication of *Novoe srednevekov'e* (*The End of Our Time*). In 1925 he founded the periodical *Put'* ("The Way"), which he edited until 1939. Over the course of these years in Paris his fame grew into international prominence. During World War II his writings stirred some antipathy among the occupying Nazis in France, but he was never arrested. Following the war, Berdyaev was awarded an honorary doctorate from Cambridge University. In 1948 he died of a heart attack in Paris.

Major Works

Berdyaev's philosophical writings follow a line of development from Marxism and social philosophy toward idealism and the evolution of his system of religious metaphysics. As part of this process, many of his early writings demonstrate an interest in the historical movements that have brought about what Berdyaev perceived to be a crisis of individual freedom in society. In *Sub'ektivizm i individualizm v obshchestvennoi filosofii*, his first significant philosophical work, Berdyaev attempted to find harmony between Marxism and precepts of modern idealism. *Dukhovnyikrizis inteligentsii* and *Filosofiia svobody* represent his early explorations of a religious philosophy. The latter is Berdyaev's theodicy—his statement on God's existence in spite of the hard reality of suffering and evil in the world. *Smysl tvorchestva: Opyt opravdaniia cheloveka* (*The Meaning of the Creative Act*) is an investigation of the possibilities for human freedom and creativity achieved by the collaboration of God and man. Berdyaev's exploration of the historical factors contributing to human religious development begins with *Smysl istorii: Opyt filosofii cheloveckestkoi sud'by* (*The Meaning of History*). Originally a series of lectures, the work outlines Berdyaev's eschatological view of history as a process moving toward the end of secular time and ending in the creation of the kingdom of God on earth. In *The End of Our Time*, Berdyaev prophesies an end to liberalism and humanism in the post-World War I era, and the birth of a "New Middle Ages" accompanied by a return to the emphasis on spirituality that characterized that earlier epoch. *Filosofiia svobodnogo dukha* (*Freedom and the Spirit*) is a critique of the overt rationalism and abstract metaphysics that are hallmarks of modern philosophical inquiry. Considered one of Berdyaev's most enduring philosophical works, *O naznachenii cheloveka : Opyt paradoksal'noi etiki* (*The Destiny of Man*), contains his ethical system and thoughts on good, evil, compassion, anguish, war, and redemption. *Sud'ba cheloveka v sovremennom mire* (*The Fate of Man in the Modern*

World) is largely a revision of Berdyaev's theories in *The End of Our Time* and confronts the issue of dehumanizing political and economic forces in the twentieth century, among which Berdyaev included capitalism, communism, fascism, nazism, and the rise of technology. Ths idea is further elucidated in *O rabstve i svobode cheloveka : Opyt personalisticheskoi filosofii* (*Slavery and Freedom*). In *Dukh i real'nost'* (*Spirit and Reality*) Berdyaev links ethical concerns to his conception of the "spirit." According to Berdyaev, the surmounting of evil, suffering, and objectification, as well as the realization of freedom and creativity, are all realized in the liberation of the human spirit. Berdyaev further illustrates his eschatological view of history in *Russkaia ideia* (*The Russian Idea*) and *Au seuil de la nouvelle époque* (*Towards a New Epoch*); both works look to a transformation and perfecting of modern man and the role that Russia has played and will play in this process. Among his three posthumously published works, Berdyaev's *Samopoznanie: Opyt filosofskoi avtobiografii* (*Dream and Reality: An Essay in Autobiography*) departs from his other writings in that it delves into the important events in the author's personal life and their relation to the development of his existential philosophy. *Istina i otkrovenie* (*Truth and Revelation*) presents a summary of Berdyaev's thoughts on Christian revelation in conjunction with science, history, theology, and reason. *Tsarstvo Dukha i isarstvo kesaria* (*The Realm of Spirit and the Realm of Caesar*)—published from an unfinished manuscript found after Berdyaev's death—contains the philosopher's final reflections on Marxism, socialism, freedom, and world government, and proclaims his belief in the eventual "victory of the realm of Spirit over that of Caesar."

Critical Reception

Since the mid 1920s, and particularly after his death in the late 1940s, Berdyaev's writings have continued to be read worldwide. Influenced by Leo Tolstoy, Friedrich Nietzsche, and Fyodor Dostoevsky, Berdyaev is thought to continue the tradition of these and writers in exploring the existential problems that have occupied philosophers of the modern era, such as alienation, objectification, and the loss of freedom. The central concerns of Berdyaev's philosophy—freedom, creativity, community, and spirituality in society, the existence of God, the nature of human personality, and the goal of history—are the enduring questions of humanity, and are approached by Berdyaev, scholars have noted, in his consistently aphoristic and systematic style.

PRINCIPAL WORKS

Sub'ektivizm i individualizm v obshchestvennoi filosofii: Kriticheskii etiud o N. K. Mikhailovskom (philosophy) 1901

Novoe religioznoe sozdanie i obshchestvennost' (philosophy) 1907

Sub Specie Aeternitatis: Opyty filosopkie, sotsial'nye i literaturnye, 1900-1906 (essays) 1907

Dukhovnyi krizis intelligentsii (philosophy) 1910

Filosofiia svobody (philosophy) 1911

Aleksei Stepanovich Khomiakov (biography) 1912

Dusha Rossii (nonfiction) 1915

Smysl tvorschestva: Opyt opravdaniia cheloveka [*The Meaning of the Creative Act*] (philosophy) 1916

Nationalizm i imperializm (essay) 1917

Nationalizm i messianizm [*Nationalism and Messianism*] (essay) 1917

Krizis iskusstva (philosophy) 1918

Sud'ba Rosii: Opyty po psikhologii voiny i natsional'nosti (nonfiction) 1918

Filosofiia Dostoevskogo [*Dostoevskii: An Interpretation*] (criticism) 1921

Konets renessansa (philosophy) 1922

Filosofiia neravenstva: Pis'ma k nedrugam po sotsial'noi filosofii (philosophy) 1923

Smysl istorii: Opyt filosofii cheloveckestkoi sud'by [*The Meaning of History*] (philosophy) 1923

Novoe srednevekov'e. Razmyshlenie o sud'be Rossii i evropy [*The End of Our Time, Together with an Essay on the "General Line" of Soviet Philosophy*] (nonfiction) 1924

Konstantin Leont'ev [*Leontiev*] (biography) 1926

Filosofiia svobodnogo dukha. 2 vols. [*Freedom and the Spirit*] (philosophy) 1927-28

O dostoinstve krhistianstva i nedostoinstve khristian (nonfiction) 1928

Marksizm i religiia. Religiia, kak orudie gospodstva i ekpluatatsii (nonfiction) 1929

Krhistianstvo i klassovaia bor'ba [*Christianity and Class War*] (nonfiction) 1931

O naznachenii cheloveka: Opyt paradoksal'noi etiki [*The Destiny of Man*] (philosophy) 1931

The Russian Revolution: Two Essays on Its Implications in Religion and Philosophy (essays) 1931

Russkaia religioznaia psikhologiia i kommunisticheskii ateizm (nonfiction) 1931

O samoubiistve. Psikhologischeskii etiud (nonfiction) 1931

The Bourgeois Mind, and Other Essays (essays) 1934

Ia i mir ob'ektov: Opyt filosofii odinochestva i obshcheniia [*Solitude and Society*] (philosophy) 1934

Sud'ba cheloveka v sovremennom mire [*The Fate of Man in the Modern World*] (philosophy) 1934

Dukh i real'nost'. Osnovy bogochelovecheskoi dukhovnosti [*Spirit and Reality*] (philosophy) 1937

O rabstve i svobode cheloveka: Opyt personalisticheskoi filosofii [*Slavery and Freedom*] (philosophy) 1939

Russkaia ideia: Osnovnye problemy russkoi mysli XIX veka i nachala XX veka [*The Russian Idea*] (philosophy) 1946

Au seuil de la novelle époque [*Towards a New Epoch*] (philosophy) 1947

Ekzistentsiial'naia dialektika bozhestvennago i chelovecheskogo [*The Divine and the Human*] (philosophy) 1947

Opyt eskhatologicheskoi metafiziki: Tvorchestvoi ob'tivatsiia [*The Beginning and the End: An Essay on Eschatological Principles*] (philosophy) 1947

Samopoznanie: Opyt filosofskoi avtobiografii [*Dream and Reality: An Essay in Autobiography*] (autobiography) 1949

Tsarstvo Dukha i isarstvo kesaria [*The Realm of Spirit and the Realm of Caesar*] (philosophy) 1949

Istina i otkrovenie: Prolegomeny k kritike otkroveniia [*Truth and Revelation*] (philosophy) 1953

Istoki i smysl russkogo kommunizma [*The Origin of Russian Communism*] (nonfiction) 1955

Christian Existentialism: A Berdiaev Anthology (essays) 1965

CRITICISM

Evgueny Lampert (essay date 1945)

SOURCE: "God-Manhood," in *Nicolas Berdyaev and the New Middle Ages,* James Clarke & Co., Ltd., 1945, pp. 33-58.

[*In the following excerpt, Lampert elucidates the concept of "God-Manhood" in Berdyaev's thought.*]

[The idea of God-Manhood] summarizes the quintessence of Berdyaev's thought. He begins and ends his reasoning not with God or man, but with God *and* man, with the God-man, with Christ and God-manhood. This defines both the content and "style" of his thought. Without bearing this in mind it is hardly possible to discern the inner motives and trace the complex thread of his argument. "Both philosophy and theology should start neither with God nor with man, but rather with the God-man. The basic and original phenomenon of life is the meeting and interaction of God and man, the movement of God towards man and of man towards God" (***Freedom and the Spirit***).

Men have seldom been able to realize fully the fundamental fact of religion, namely, that God is both the wholly "Other One," transcendent and utterly beyond the world and man; and yet creates and reveals himself to man, enters into him and becomes the inmost content of man's very existence. How can that which is transcendent to man be equally immanent in him, and consequently in so far not transcendent at all? How can that which is immanent in man be transcendent and wholly beyond him? In face of such a dilemma there seems to be no other solution than to reject either the one alternative, viz., God-in-the-world and man (this view is sometimes called *dualism*); or the other, viz., God-beyond-the-world and man (*monism*)—with all the far-reaching and disastrous consequences of both points of view.

This paradox indicates how the problem of religion presents itself to Berdyaev. Both points of view he regards as a witness to the limits and impotence of discursive reasoning, which is incapable of comprehending the mystery of the living correlation of God and man, of the transcendent and the immanent, of the absolute and the relative, of the one and the many, of the whole and the part, and so forth. If we understand all these concepts as static and immovable entities, as it were congealed into logical crystals, then God himself must needs appear to be a sheer misunderstanding, evident to anyone familiar with the elements of logic: he is, so to say, hot ice, bitter sugar or a round square. Yet logical contradiction and impossibility is no evidence of actual impossibility. Life itself is such a contradiction and impossibility to Berdyaev; and these contradictions, which he seeks to bring to light and to transcend in all their implications, point to the mystery of God-manhood, to the mystery of the vital meeting and all-pervading mutual penetration of God and man. God-manhood is in fact that *coincidentia oppositorum* (to speak in the terms of the mediaeval theologian Nicolas of Cusa), the coincidence and unification of opposites, of God and man and God and the world, which unites what discursive reasoning is incapable of uniting, and renders every moment and atom of life and being a witness to the supreme simultaneous oneness and duality of God and man.

Berdyaev's intention is not to propound a metaphysical doctrine; he wants to describe as it were intuitively a mystery which belongs to the very depth of being and is revealed in existence itself. The mystery of God-manhood is, indeed, unfathomable, irrational, inexpressible in terms of the objectivized world, where one object displaces the other, where all things are extraneous to one another and mutually exclusive. And only in as much as the grip of this objectivized world is loosened, only in so far as man is freed from the world of divided and isolated things and objects, can he become aware of true life in its unity and multiplicity, in its absoluteness and relativity, in its transcendence and immanence, in its agony and bliss—in other words, in its God-manhood.

The idea of God-manhood is clearly of primary importance for Berdyaev's teaching about God and man, on which we shall dwell in more detail presently. But it has also more general implications. It does not merely denote a special understanding of the relation between God and man, but in general expresses a particular feeling for an *ethos* of life; an *ethos* which above all finds itself up against any static attitude to life where everything tends to become fixed, divided and "extrinsic"; where all things remain impenetrable substances, opposing unsurmountable barriers to one another and creating estrangement and limitations. God-manhood is to Berdyaev the revelation of the way out of the isolated state of the "natural world." It gives birth to striving for the infinite, for fullness and boundlessness of life, where nothing is external or "extrinsic," as in the world of lifeless things and objects, but all is *within* and all is known from within. In fact, for Berdyaev nothing in life is "objective" at all, but all is profoundly "subjective," *i.e.,* all is inherent in the knowing, experiencing and living subject; in other words all is *existential.*

Thus the idea of God-manhood leads us to those elements in Berdyaev's thought which he himself describes as "existential," partly under the influence of certain modern philosophical currents.

So-called existential philosophy, as well as theology, goes back on the one hand to the phenomenological school (Husserl), and on the other to Soren Kierkegaard, and is without doubt one of the most significant movements in contemporary thought. To begin with, it breaks with the abstract tendency of philosophical thinking and seeks a more immediate, concrete, "intuitive" vision of life. We have already noted that this was the concern of the Russian philosophical tradition in the early twentieth century and before, with its radical criticism of West-European abstract, idealistic thought and its claim to a more realistic, intuitive world-outlook. Modern existential philosophy moves on the same lines. Its main concern is to view the essence of being not in general, abstract principles and ideas, but immediately in man's own personal existence. The unusual categories with which it operates—anxiety, fear, anguish, triviality, death—are taken from the experience of human life and replace the categories of substance, cause, quality, quantity, etc., which are ultimately mere abstractions. Yet phenomenological and existential philosophy as it is expressed by its most brilliant representatives, like Hartmann and Scheler, either denies man, his activity and creativeness (*cf.,* Scheler's *Vom Ewigen im Menschen*)—the same, though in a different sense, applies to the school of so-called dialectical theology, which to some extent derives its origin from the "existential" movement—or denies God and is openly atheistic (*cf.,* Heidegger's sensational book *Sein und Zeit,* whose popularity, however, is due more to fashion than to real appreciation). Berdyaev is pre-eminently a *Christian.* Christ the God-man is the vital pivot of his thought. Furthermore he is a *humanist,* in the deepest and true sense of the word. He believes in and seeks for the truth of man.

. . . . .

In the first place it is important to elicit how Berdyaev's existential philosophy states the problem of knowledge. How do we approach reality? What is the relation between "thought" and "being?" Berdyaev's answer may be summarized in the following way: as long as the knowing subject and the known object are conceived as divided, as long as reality presents itself to us "objectively," or rather in an objectivized way, so long must knowledge needs remain inadequate to reality, *i.e.,* a knowledge pertaining to disparate, disintegrated being (*cf.,* **Solitude and Society,** the title of whose Russian original is **I and the World of Objects.**) True cognition presupposes unity or oneness of "being" and "thought,"

a unity which transcends the very differentiation and opposition of subject and object. And this unity is initially present in the creative act of knowledge. Moreover, Berdyaev seems to deny the very problem of traditional epistemology in as much as it is concerned with the question as to whether one should or should not recognize the known object as a primary independent reality. As is well known, this problem finds its classical expression on the one hand in scholastic and Thomist "realism," for which the known object must have a primacy over the knowing subject; and on the other hand, in "Idealism," which tends to deny objective reality and reduce it to concepts or sensations arising in the mind of the knowing subject.

Berdyaev. does not admit that knowledge is at all determined by the opposition of "subject" and "object," or of "thought" and "being," in as much as they face each other in an extraneous way. The very fact of cognition is for him an event in being, a revelation of its ontological nature. Being can never be objectivized or exteriorized, whether in theory or in practice; it is revealed in man's very existence, from within; it is co-inherent and co-existent in man.

We are naturally inclined to identify reality with objectivity; and to prove the reality of something usually means to prove its objectiveness and extrinsicality. While this may be true to some extent (in fact, to a very limited extent) of purely external things accessible to our empirical perceptions, it cannot be applied at all to spiritual realities. "The discovery of reality," says Berdyaev, "depends on the activity of the spirit, on its intensity and ardour. We cannot expect that spiritual realities will be revealed to us in the same way as objects of the natural world, presented to us externally, such as stones, trees, tables, chairs, or such as the principles of logic . . . In the realm of spirit reality is not extraneous, for it proceeds from the spirit itself" (***Freedom and the Spirit***). Thus it is not objectivity which is the criterion of reality, but, paradoxically enough, the criterion is the reality itself as revealed in man's existence.

In this way Berdyaev hopes to guard knowledge from "ossification," from the conversion of its content into static "things," which to a large extent has come about in so-called scientific thought. He regards cognition as an integral, creative act of the spirit, which does not know anything external at all, for which everything is its own life, everything is *within,* "in the depth."

The question however arises as to whether such a theory of knowledge does not render cognition objectless altogether, and consequently devoid of content. Is it not threatened by "evacuation," and thus by becoming a knowledge of nothing at all? Does not Berdyaev assume that there is nothing transcendent to and beyond man, or if so, only as an "object" or "thing," *i.e.,* as something ultimately false and unreal? The inner logic of his thought in no way suggests such an inference, although some of his utterances, particularly in the discussion of the more practical implications of his epistemology, might lead to such conclusions. Berdyaev's theory of knowledge is indeed "objectless," in the sense that the object of knowledge is not fixed into "thinghood," that its content does not denote a "something" which exists on its own account, in isolation, out of vital relation with concrete human existence. But it is surely not objectless in the sense that it precludes anything but the knowing subject, which is actually one of the worst forms of Idealism and subjectivism, and which, as we have seen, Berdyaev explicitly repudiates. Moreover, his existentialism even presupposes man's self-transcendence—to God, to other men and to the world. Yet such self-transcendence is an *inward* process, not an outward one into the world of isolated, extraneous things. Man becomes aware of other reality than himself only in awareness of its relation to his own being, in self-awareness; and this latter is the initial fact of his self-determination to anyone or anything. The relation of man to God and to man is an event within his very existence, in his inmost profundity; it is an inherent part of his own destiny. "Return into oneself and self-awareness," says Berdyaev, "imply out-going to the other one and self-transcendence" (*The Meaning of Creativeness*). Such is the Copernican discovery of his existentialism, not less significant than the "Kopernikanische Tat" of Kant.

All this makes the fundamental difference of Berdyaev's thought from every kind of psychologism and solipsism. Psychology regards man as cast into the objectivized world: the "soul," *"psyche,"* remains a solitary, self-contained unit, an unrelated and isolated being. To this Berdyaev opposed what he calls *pneumatology,* which considers man above all as a spirit, equally personal, free and self-determining, yet always open, continually surpassing itself, and vitally correlated with God, other men and the world at large. "Man's spirit is not an inert substance, self-contained and self-sufficient" (*Freedom and the Spirit*). In fact Berdyaev does not recognize it as a "substance" at all, if substance means a limitable, finished, static reality. "Spirit is existence," *i.e.,* a reality which transcends all limitations and divisions, all fixity and immobility.

This theory of knowledge has far-reaching implications for Berdyaev's religious outlook and his philosophy of the Christian revelation.

In the first place, his existentialism precludes a thorough distinction between so-called natural and supernatural knowledge. This distinction in itself he regards as a product of objectivized thinking, in as much as it implies that men can think of God out of direct relation with and so to say in abstraction from, the Christian revelation. If the Christian revelation is an event within human existence, in the very depth of being, which it is indeed pre-eminently, it must be recognized as intensely relevant at the initial stage of our knowledge of God and the ultimate meaning of life. An act of faith is thus implied not only in the realm of "supernatural" revelation, but in all true knowledge. Only return to the ultimate depth of being renders philosophical thinking a possibility at all. The two ends of the chain of human thought must be integrated into a single existential intuition. "One cannot arrive at God, to him there are ultimately no 'ways'; one can only go out from God; he is not merely at the end: he is at the beginning" (**"The Russian Religious Idea"** in *Problems of Russian Religious Consciousness*). "I am the way, the truth and the life" (John xiv. 6).

In this sense Berdyaev almost identifies philosophy with mysticism. Their difference is as it were of a quantitative rather than qualitative nature. The true difference lies not so much between mystical and philosophical knowledge, as between what he calls the "mysticism of perfection," or "elevation of the soul to God," and the mysticism of penetration into the mysteries of being, of divine and human life, or of philosophical *gnosis,* a kind of second-sight or insight into the supreme meaning of all things. In this latter sense Berdyaev regards as mystics such men as Jacob Böhme, Baader, Dostoevsky, Solovyev, Léon Bloy, who were, however, all more or less far from being "perfect." He even defines mysticism as "knowledge which has its source in vital and immediate contact with the ultimate reality . . . It is derived from the word 'mystery,' and must therefore be regarded as the foundation and source of all creative movement" (*Freedom and the Spirit*).

The other religious implication of Berdyaev's existentialism is his belief in the reciprocity of every act of God's revelation to man. "In as much," he says, "as revelation is an event within man, in the very depth of human destiny, it presupposes not only the one who reveals, but the one to whom the revelation is made too; in other words, it implies man's active and creative participation. Revelation cannot operate on man automatically and mechanically, independently of who and what he is" (*The Meaning of Creativeness*. Cf., *Freedom and Spirit*).

Berdyaev repudiates the traditional theological view that revelation is based on belief in the "moderately normal," unchangeable, natural human being, who belongs to an eternal natural order. Any idea of finiteness, of a finished objective order, be it supernatural or natural and social, he regards as primarily responsible for the false and disastrous conservatism of certain forms of Christian consciousness, wherein man is left with only one task—to conform to and obey this order, the very permanence of which is considered to be a preordained condition of revelation. Moreover, revelation itself is believed to be an entirely "objective" act, independent of any creative participation of man in it. To this view Berdyaev opposes the idea of man's free creative relation to God and his call to interaction with him. Such opposition to any fixed permanence of both the "supernatural" and "natural" orders marks Berdyaev's revolutionary, dynamic, and active Christian consciousness, which looks to the things to come and expects man to change creatively the outer and inner conditions of life.

. . . . .

The idea of divine-human interaction brings us back to the fundamental assumption of Berdyaev's philosophy, that of God-manhood, which we shall now endeavour to analyse in its main elements.

It has already been noted that Berdyaev is not concerned to frame a rational doctrine of God and man, and that he does not attempt to co-ordinate or synthesize the divine and human principles in a rational system. He thinks of God-manhood not conceptually, but rather *mythologically*. "Christianity is entirely mythological, as indeed all religion is; and Christian myths express the deepest and most central realities of the spiritual world. It is high time to cease being ashamed of Christian mythology and trying to strip it of myth. No system of theological or metaphysical concepts can destroy Christian mythology and it is precisely the myths of Christianity which constitute its greatest reality; for it becomes an abstraction as soon as it is freed from them" (*Freedom and the Spirit*). And he adds that materialism and positivism equally live by myths, whether they be those of material nature or of scientific knowledge.

What, then, is the content of the myth of God-manhood? This is described by Berdyaev as the "drama of love and freedom between God and man; the birth of God in man and the birth of man in God." "Spiritual experience shows us that man longs for God, and that God longs for man and yearns for the birth of man who shall reveal his image." This fact finds its fullest and most concrete expression in Christianity, in which "the humanity of God is revealed and the divine image of man." Berdyaev sees the depth of true life in this primordial divine-human mystery, in the meeting and mutual relatedness of God and man. He does not conceive of religious life (just as in his analysis of knowledge) as a confrontation of an unchangeable, static and ultimately lifeless religious "subject" with an equally changeless and static religious "object," and is in consequence compelled to recognize a reciprocal relation and interaction between God and man, that is, precisely "the birth of God in man and the birth of man in God, and the revelation of God to man and of man to God."

Within the depth of spiritual life there is unfolded before us the religious drama of God's dealings with man and man's with God. Without God and within human nature alone there can be no spiritual life. That quality of life which is called spiritual can only exist in man if there is something to deepen his life, something to which he can transcend himself . . . On the other hand, if there were nothing but the divine nature, if God had, as it were, no other self except himself, there would be no original phenomenon in spiritual life, and all would disappear into an abyss of divine selfhood and undifferentiated abstraction. God

must limit himself and go out into the other self, that is into the being of man.

Berdyaev distrusts all systems of rational theology; he accuses them of disregarding the problem of God-manhood and thus leading to an objectivized, "idolatrous" conception of the relation between God and man. He describes in rather horrifying words the notion of God prevalent in some of these systems:

God conceived as a metaphysical transcendent being, as an immutable inert substance, represents the latest form of idolatry in the history of the human spirit. Monotheism can in fact be a form of idolatry . . . Man in bondage to the objectivized world conceives of God as a great exterior force, as a "super-natural" power in every respect comparable to a "natural" power. God is merely the highest and most perfect of all forms of power, or in other words a projection of natural being. This supreme power demands to be appeased. The transcendent God avenges himself like the gods and man of the fallen world.

But Christianity appeared in the world to conquer decisively both idolatry and servitude. It affirmed the religion of the Trinity, in which God revealed himself as Love and the Beloved.

Berdyaev, then, does not think of God except in relation to man. Surely this does not imply that God *per se* is not at all, or that man supplies something which is lacking in God. Yet since God is Creator, since he created man, the living personal being related to him who is the living personal Creator, he cannot but be himself supremely related to man, for every living and personal act becomes real only in this relatedness. The fact that God "longs for man, for his other one, for the free response of his love," shows not that there is any insufficiency or absence of fullness in the being of God, but on the contrary the superabundance of his plenitude and perfection (cf., *Freedom and the Spirit*). Just because God's life is "agreement of contraries," he embraces both the perfection of his eternal transcendent being and the distinct and vital experience of man's relation to him. In this sense every act of God's revelation to man, and of man's participation in it, does not concern and affect man alone but also God, *i.e.*, it is an essentially divine-human act. Berdyaev is even bold enough to refer to the amazing words of the Catholic mystic, Angelus Silesius, who says, "I know that without me God could not endure for a moment. Were I brought to naught, he would yield up the ghost for lack of me" (*Der Cherubinische Wandersmann*)—words which may well disturb and alarm us. But this utterance expresses for Berdyaev a truth of innermost spiritual experience—an existential truth, not a metaphysical proposition. As such it does not necessarily lead to pantheism (which has become the bogy of rationalist theologians). Hence the abundance of symbolic and mythological language in his theology, which is "safer" and indeed more adequate to express the mysteries of divine-human life than abstract metaphysics. "To speak of God-manhood, of God's reciprocal relation to man, is a mythological representation and not a philosophical proposition; it is to speak the language of the prophets of the Bible rather than that of the Greek philosophers."

. . . . .

Three fundamental problems are bound up in Berdyaev's thought with the idea of God-manhood: the problems of *creativeness,* of *freedom,* and hence of *evil.*

God-manhood is the call to mankind to manifest the image of the Creator in human life. *Man is a creator,* in virtue of his divine-human (theandric) nature and of the image and likeness of God in him. This is the ontological and ethical basis of Berdyaev's teaching about man. And he takes on the task of discovering, defining and justifying the image of the Creator in man. In the world to-day, in which the image of man is threatened with destruction, man-creator is and must become the supreme Christian ideal. Berdyaev is no doubt justified in his profound dissatisfaction with the traditional Christian attitude to this problem. Christians have too often reduced the whole issue to a mere submission of the creative act of man in all spheres of cultural and social life to religion and religious authority. Here the creative act—whether cognitive, artistic, ethical, social or technical—was regarded as of essentially secondary significance, as of inferior quality and even harmful from the religious point of view. A sharp distinction was drawn between the "sacred" and the "profane," which resulted to begin with in Christians living in two different rhythms, the religious rhythm of the Church, governing a limited number of days and hours in their life, and the unreligious rhythm of the world, governing a greater number—in other words in secularization; and finally this involved man's rise against religion as a tyranny, in an attempt to establish autonomy for his creative dignity and achievements. To the idea of a mere subordination of the creative act of man to a hierarchically superior power, Berdyaev opposes the idea of the *intrinsic* religious value of this act in its free realization, the idea of its existential meaning. "God expects from man a free creative act," for truly "My Father worketh hitherto and I work," and "the works that I shall do he [man] shall do also; and greater works than these shall he do" (John v. 7; xiv. 12).

It must be understood that Berdyaev's apologia for creativeness has little or nothing in common with the modern ideas of "activism." The technical and economic processes of our civilization demand of man that he should always be "doing" something: a perpetual frenzied activity and the use of every moment of time for action. Such activism threatens to eliminate all contemplation from life. This means that man will cease to *pray,* that he will have no longer any relation to God, that he will no longer believe in the possibility of disinterested knowledge of truth. Yet man is determined in relation not only to time, but also to eternity. He cannot be absorbed in the flux of time, in a ceaseless actualiza-

tion of every instant, in the mad precipitancy of the temporal process. Man is called to recollect and to bethink himself in utter silence, to realize the depth of life revealed in his relatedness to life eternal. In as much, then, as the creativeness of modern activism is a denial of life eternal, in as much as it *binds* man in time, Berdyaev rejects such creativeness. No doubt man is called to activity and work—he cannot and should not remain simply a contemplative, for neither God nor the world is a spectacle: he must continue God's own original creative act; he must transform and organize the world. Yet man is above all a meeting-point of two converging worlds, the eternal and the temporal, and hence is not only vitally related to time but also to eternity. This, too, pertains to the supreme existential truth about man. When man is turned into the tool or object of an impersonal activistic process in this world he is no longer a free personal human being; in fact, he ceases to be creative. For true creativeness frees man from the flux of time; it turns his gaze to Heaven, it reunites human existence with its sources in God-manhood, and modifies the natural configuration of things.

Many are alarmed and repelled by Berdyaev's exaltation of creativeness, and objections have been raised from all sides to the very understanding of man as creator and as called to creativity. It may seem however that his critics, who accuse him of over-valuing and divinizing man, of "titanism" and humanism, have largely misunderstood the particular way in which he posits the whole problem. After all, to have a high idea of man as creator and as called to participate in God's creative action is in itself far from being an invitation to proud and egocentric independence, for man bears primordially and irrevocably the seal of God's creative power who made him "in the beginning." "It is strange to think," says Berdyaev, "that God could have created something small and insignificant as the crown of his creation. It is impious and blasphemous to have a low opinion of God's idea, and to hold it in contempt as despicable and of no account" (*The Meaning of Creativeness*). Man's creativeness is therefore not his autonomous right or claim, but rather his duty before God and the fulfilment of his will: not to be creator and not to live creatively, not to take part in God's unceasing creative action in the world, is disobedience to God, and in the last resort rebellion against him. Such is Berdyaev's approach to the problem. It may be asked whether Christianity has freed Prometheus from his fetters, or has chained him still more heavily. I believe that it has freed him, for he was chained not by God, but by the demons of nature with whose power he was wrestling.

Berdyaev himself wrote a great deal about the falsehood of humanism, in which man has asserted himself without and against God and has gradually cut himself off from the sources of being; moreover he has shown that this led in its turn to a denial and destruction of man, for "Humanism has destroyed itself by its own dialectic" (*The End of Our Time;* cf., *The Meaning of History*). But to the question as to where the falsehood of humanism lies, why it is impotent, why it is experiencing such an overwhelming crisis to-day, he answers not that it has overstressed the dignity and calling of man to creativeness, but that it has not done this enough, and so has in fact resulted in man's degradation and denial. It did not give man his full dignity, which reaches to the heavens, to God, and this fatally under-estimated him. Berdyaev wants to overcome humanism, not against man, in order to degrade him, but in the name of the God-man, and hence in the name of man. Most of the anti-humanistic tendencies of to-day, on the other hand, imply derogation of man and dehumanization of life and thought. So-called dialectical theology (Karl Barth, E. Brunner and others, *see* above) is particularly interesting and significant in this respect. It has shown not only an acute and just reaction against humanism, but also a revolt, an almost demonic revolt, against any link and vital relation between the creature and his Creator: hence a revolt against the eternal mystery of God-manhood, which is revealed in Christ and must be revealed in Christ's humanity.

Berdyaev stands firm in his conviction that Christianity is *human,* that, in fact, herein lies its distinctness, though many Christians have maintained, and continue to maintain, the contrary. His vision of man in the light of the mystery of God-manhood has rendered his thought essentially and profoundly Christian.

The most important works of Berdyaev are devoted to the problems of ethics; and he once said that he considered his ethics to be Christian in as much as he has succeeded in showing them to be human. Even the **Destiny of Man,** one of his most abstruse, complex books, which is largely inspired by the themes of eschatology, by the agony of pondering on the problem of evil and Hell, is actually about the simple truth of *being human,* which many modern theologians are so much inclined to despise. He has shown the emergence of a morality which paves man's way to Hell, paves it by its devotion to the "good," to moral principles and ideals, and heralds a path which would free man from this hell of goodness. And he is ready to place himself beyond good and evil in order to ask whether that which has long been held to be good and evil is really good and evil.

. . . . .

We turn to the second problem connected with the idea of God-manhood, that of *freedom*. This problem in general, as well as in the particular context of Berdyaev's philosophy, is bound up with very complex metaphysical presuppositions and implications, which in view of the nature of the present essay cannot be expounded: I shall therefore confine myself simply to a few hints as to how Berdyaev formulates the problem.

In common speech, and even in philosophies, the concept of freedom has two different connotations. There is freedom as a way, freedom as choice, choice between good and evil, freedom by which truth or God is recognized and accepted, but which in itself is undetermined by anything or any one. And there is freedom as an aim to be achieved, freedom in the truth, freedom that is in God and a gift of God. When we say that man has acquired freedom because his higher nature has conquered the lower, because reason has come to control his passions, we are speaking of freedom in the latter sense. It is the freedom of which the gospel says, "Ye shall know the truth, and the truth shall make you free" (John viii. 32). Here truth brings freedom, and freedom is as it were not first but second. When, on the other hand, we say that man freely chose the path of life and in freedom came to truth, we are speaking of freedom in the former sense, of freedom which is "first" and not "second."

Now this first kind of freedom may issue not only in good, but in evil as well. It bears no guarantee of goodness, no certainty that man will follow the right path and will come to God. Moreover, as Berdyaev says, this freedom has a "fatal tendency to destroy itself, to turn into its opposite and precipitate man into anarchy, which in its turn brings slavery and tyranny" (***Philosophy of Freedom***). "We know in our own experience that the anarchy of passions and the lowest impulses of our nature, which live each for its own ends, bring us into a real state of slavery, deprive us of the freedom of the spirit, and end in disintegration" (***Freedom and the Spirit***). This applies equally to personal and social life. Freedom which remains "formal," objectless, incapable of positive choice, indifferent to truth, leads to the disintegration of man and of the world. Thus, taken in itself, the first kind of freedom is powerless to preserve and maintain true freedom, and always threatens man with destruction.

Berdyaev maintains the distinction between the two freedoms. But the defectiveness, or rather the potential defectiveness, of the first kind of freedom does not lead him to an unqualified upholding of freedom in the second sense, of freedom that is in truth and goodness, of freedom which is regarded as identical with truth and reasonableness. For him the will to self-determination must have the primacy over reason. He is aware that a mere freedom of reasonableness too may destroy itself, may bring about the power of compulsory goodness and give rise to a religious and social life in which freedom turns out to be a child of necessity. If the first kind of freedom may lead to anarchy, the second may lead to theocratic or "totalitarian" despotism. This is witnessed to by innumerable pyres lit by Christians and non-Christians alike to burn heretics in the name of truth and its liberating power. Such freedom does not know what Dostoevsky expressed in the striking words of the Great Inquisitor to Christ: "Thou hast desired the free love of man. The freedom of his faith has been dearer to thee than anything else . . . In place of the hard and ancient law, man was to decide for himself, in the freedom of his heart, what is good and what is evil." In these words Berdyaev's own faith may be discerned. Like Dostoevsky, he rejects "miracle" and "authority" as violations of human conscience, as the denial to man's spirit of his freedom.

> "I can receive the supreme and final freedom from truth alone, but the truth cannot force or compel me: my acceptance of the truth pre-supposes my freedom, my free movement in it. Freedom is not only an aim but a path. . . . Freedom has brought me to Christ, and I know no other path leading to him. Nor am I the only one who has passed through this experience. No one who has left a Christianity based on authority can return to anything but a Christianity which is free . . . I admit that it is grace which has brought me to faith, but it is grace experienced by me as freedom. Those who have come to Christianity through freedom bring to it that same spirit of freedom" (*Freedom and the Spirit*). "A man who has achieved a definite victory over the seductive temptations of humanism, who has discovered the hollow unreality of the divinization of man by man, can never hereafter abandon the liberty which has brought him to God, nor the definite experience which has freed him from the power of evil" (*ibid.*).

And finally:

> When man returns to God after an experience of apostasy, he knows a freedom in his relations with him untasted by one who has passed his life in the peace and security of his traditional faith, and who has remained within the confines of his spiritual inheritance (*ibid.*).

What, then, is Berdyaev's answer to the question of the relation between the two forms of freedom? Sometimes their relation appears to him a continuous irreducible conflict, for "man moves from the first kind of freedom to the second, and from the second to the first, but everywhere freedom is poisoned from within and dies" (*Freedom and the Spirit*). Life itself is a proof of such constant conflicts. In fact there is no solution *save in the coming of Christ the God-man.* "Only the New Adam can take from freedom its deadly effect without compromising freedom itself . . . The grace of Christ is the illumination of freedom from within and hence knows no outward restraint or coercion. It differs from the truths of this world and from the truths of the 'other world' as understood by sinful man, which all seek to organize life by constraint and end by depriving him of the freedom of the spirit. The light of Christ illuminates the dark irrationality of freedom, without, however, imposing limitations upon it." The very nature of Christ's grace is shown by Berdyaev as both divine and human, for it proceeds not only from God but from the God-man, from God's eternal God-manhood. Hence man has a part in it and shares it freely. In the power of the mystery of God-manhood God meets the beloved creature, and the reciprocation of his love is infinitely and supremely free. (It may be noted in parenthesis that this view has nothing in common with Pelagianism, which seems to be a typically Western heresy: its very

approach to the problem of the relation between God and man is alien to Berdyaev, being as it is the result of an incipient disintegration of the Christian myth of God-manhood.)

Here are a few truly inspiring passages from *Freedom and the Spirit* where Berdyaev presents his Christian interpretation of freedom:

> It is Christianity alone which can comprehend the fundamental mystery of human freedom, which is inseparably linked with the union of two natures in Christ the God-man; a union which, however, does not in any way annul their distinction. The source of man's freedom is in God, and that, not in God the Father, but in God the Son, while the Son is not only God but man . . . that is, Eternal Man. The freedom of the Son is that in which and by which the free response to God is effected. It is the source of the freedom of the whole human race, for this freedom is not only that of the old Adam but also of the spiritual Adam, that is, of Christ. It is in the Son that the free response is given to the call of divine love and to God's need of his other one, a response which is heard in the heavenly and spiritual sphere and which is re-echoed upon earth and in the natural world . . . The whole generation of Adam is in the Son of God, and it finds in him the inner source of its liberty, which is not only a freedom like God's, but freedom in relation to God and in its attitude towards him. To receive the freedom of Christ is not only to receive the freedom of God but to receive also, by partaking of Christ's human nature, that freedom which enables man to turn to God." And further, speaking about the Cross: "God the Son, veiled beneath the form of a crucified slave, does not force recognition of himself upon anyone. His divine power and glory are manifested in the act of faith and free love. The Crucified speaks to the freedom of the human spirit, for without a free act on the part of the spirit there can be no recognition of him as God. A crucified God is hidden as well as revealed. The constraint exercised by the natural world wholly disappears in the act of divine revelation, for everything turns on the existence of inner freedom. Man, obsessed by the forces of the external world, sees nothing in the Crucified but a human being suffering torture and humiliation, and the consequent defeat and annihilation of truth so far as this world is concerned. Divine truth seems to be powerless . . . But the religion of truth crucified is the religion of the freedom of the spirit; it possesses no logical or juridical power of compulsion and is revealed as love and liberty.

The mystery of freedom, then, and the solution of its inherent tragedy must be sought for in the Christian revelation of God-manhood, in Christ the God-man, crucified and risen.

Nonetheless the light that proceeds from Christ and illuminates all the paths of human freedom does not render Berdyaev in any way insensitive to the overwhelming power of evil, sin and suffering born from this free-dom, and does not make him content and happy in an easy-going optimism. In fact, as we have already seen, awareness of evil and sin in the world and the capacity for suffering and compassion are for him preeminent signs of a true Christian spirit. "Man is a creature who suffers and is compassionate, who is sensitive to pity, who in these ways proves the dignity of human nature" (*Spirit and Reality*). In the face of the evil and agonies in the world Berdyaev refuses to accept any conception of God's providence which establishes a rational or moral expediency and "final causality." "In this world there are irreconcilable good and evil, unjust suffering, the tragic destiny of great and just men. It is a world in which prophets are stoned and unjust men, the persecu-tors and crucifiers of the just, are triumphant. It is a world in which innocent children and innocent animals have to suffer. It is a world in which death, evil and anguish reign supreme. Is Divine Providence effective in this world?" (*ibid.*).

. . . . .

In this very question we feel Berdyaev's deep awareness of that terrible age-long action brought for their suffer-ings by stricken mankind against God—a challenge to the Hidden God to reveal himself. At one time Berdyaev was a convinced atheist; but, like many other people who have seriously and deeply questioned about the meaning of life and have sought the truth, he was an atheist, not because of intellectual difficulties which stood in the way of his belief in God, but for moral reasons, because spiritually he could not solve the ago-nizing problem of theodicy, *viz.,* of the "justification" of God in face of the tragic strickenness of the world and man. And may it not be that the overwhelming fact of boundless evil and innumerable sufferings in the world is indeed the only serious objection to faith in God? This is surely why, among the rebels against God, there are people of a deeply sensitive conscience, imbued with the thirst for truth and justice. The historical destiny of the Russian people is a striking witness to this.

Thus no optimistic teleology is capable of facing, not to speak of solving, the problem of evil. To solve it one must first of all taste the tragedy of evil; evil must be lived through, or rather lived out from within; one must experience all the paths and possibilities of freedom. "Good," says Berdyaev, "is revealed and triumphs through the ordeal of evil." He answers the argument against God from the existence of evil in the world by affirming that the very existence of evil is a proof of the existence of God. "If the world consisted wholly and solely of goodness and righteousness there would be no 'need' for God, for the world itself would be God. God is, because evil is. And that means that God is because freedom is" (*Dostoevsky;* cf., *Freedom and the Spirit*).

Berdyaev as it were offers man the way to light through darkness, through the abyss and chasms of freedom. It almost seems that he, not unlike Dostoevsky and other

Russians, wants to *know* evil, so that in the experience of this knowledge it may be overcome. This is a danger-ous truth (and what truth is not dangerous!); it is a truth only for the really free and spiritually mature. Only a slave or a spiritual infant could understand it to mean that one must consciously take the path of evil in order to be enriched and to arrive happily at the good. Berdyaev is no evolutionist for whom evil is but a mo-ment in the development of good—such a point of view is fundamentally untragic and optimistic (besides being morally vicious), and for this reason alone quite alien to him. "Only the unmasking of evil, only deep suffering from evil, can raise man to greater heights. It is pre-cisely self-satisfaction in evil which means utter ruin . . . Evil is the tragic path of man, his destiny, the trial of his freedom. But it is not a necessary moment in the evolution of good . . . Man may be enriched by the experience of evil, become more acutely conscious; but for this he must suffer, realize the horror of perdition, expose evil, cast it into the fire of Hell and expiate his guilt" (*Dostoevsky*).

Evil, then, is overcome from within, through living it out, through deep inward awareness of its meaning, through inner illumination—in other words, existen-tially. "And the light shineth in the darkness; and the darkness comprehendeth it not" (John i. 5). This is the path of Christ's redemption. God who came down to earth and became man shared the destiny of stricken and sinful humanity, and in this sharing redeemed it. "Christ has died, and we must freely accept death as the way to life and as an interior moment of it" (*Freedom and the Spirit*). The cross of Christ is the revelation of the meaning of evil and suffering, and the only adequate answer to the question, "Is Divine Providence effective in the world?" God does not explain or justify the an-guish of life, but takes it on himself, tastes its full hor-ror, and in so doing illuminates it. Thus the problem of evil points as well to the twofold mystery with which life is bounded—to God-manhood, in whose power tragic existence becomes and is Christian existence.

"The transfiguration of the life of the world into eternal life is the supreme goal of all things. The way which leads to it involves the free acceptance of the cross, suffering, and death. Christ is crucified above the dark abyss in which being and non-being blend one with the other. The light which shines from the Crucified is a light shining in the darkness. It is this light which both illuminates the shadows of being and overcomes the darkness of non-being" (*op. cit.*).

Pitirim A. Sorokin (essay date 1950)

SOURCE: "Nikolai Berdyaev," in *Social Philosophies of an Age of Crisis*, The Beacon Press, 1950, pp. 137-44.

[*In the following essay, Sorokin focuses on the social and historical concerns and implications of Berdyaev's philosophy.*]

Berdyaev is the author of many works in philosophy, social science, political economy and ethics: *The Meaning of Creativeness* (1916), *The Meaning of History* (1923), *Philosophy of Inequality* (1922), *The New Middle Ages* (1924), *Christianity and Class Struggle* (1931), *Solitude and Society* (1930), and many others. Most of Berdyaev's books have been translated into several languages.

Omitting the metaphysical part of Berdyaev's philosophy of history, the following empirical points of his reading of historical events should be mentioned.

(1) Methodologically, a mere description of singularistic historical events, persons, and objects only results in a dead corpse of history. "When one reads a scientific book on, say, ancient peoples, one clearly feels that from the history of cultures of these peoples their soul, their inner life are removed and one gets instead only a sort of external photograph or picture"—which does not in the least explain the why, wherefore, or even the how of all these events and persons. In order to understand these whys and wherefores, the soul and the inner logic of history, it is necessary "not only that the object-matter of history be historical, but also that the cognizing subject of historical study experience and unfold in himself 'the historical.'" It is necessary that the cognizing subject and cognized object of history become one, that the subject himself live history, not merely look on historical events from the outside. On this point Berdyaev, like Spengler and Northrop, insists on a direct intuitional identification of the cognizing subject with the cognized object, without which no adequate understanding of anything, especially of historical and socio-cultural processes, is possible.

(2) Like all the other authors under consideration Berdyaev rejects all forms of the linear interpretation of historical process and all linear theories of progress in its unilinear, oscillating, spiral, and branching varieties. Theories of progress are not tenable either metaphysically, logically, factually, or ethically.

(3) All great cultures are simultaneously mortal and immortal in their existence within the limits of empirical history itself. They contain temporal as well as eternal principles. Each of the cultures experiences moments of emergence, florescence, and ups and downs, and eventually declines as a unity; at the same time, each of the great cultures survives in its perennial, eternal values. Graeco-Roman culture did not disappear entirely at the time of its fall. Its perennial values, such as Roman law, Greek art, Greek philosophy, and so on, did not die; they were incorporated into the culture of the Middle Ages, Arabian culture, and are still living a vigorous life. In other words, the temporal elements or values of a culture die; the perennial ones persist and live as long as human history goes on. Even after its empirical end the transfigured perennial values will, in some transcendental, mystical way, pass beyond the empirical end of history into the "transcendental great beyond."

Here Berdyaev points, in general terms, to what I call the lasting and dying elements in culture, with their indefinitely long and limited life-durations, a point that has so far been overlooked by social scientists and philosophers of history.

(4) Independently of—and possibly even earlier than—Spengler, Berdyaev regarded the Western culture as already having passed its Barbaric, Medieval-Christian, and modern Humanist-Secular phases. Its Medieval-Christian phase was over in the thirteenth century, and its Humanist phase ended in about the nineteenth century. To Berdyaev the twentieth century is the transitory period from the dying Humanist phase to the emerging phase of the "New Middle Ages."

The main task of the medieval phase of Christian-Western culture, according to Berdyaev, was to discipline, manifoldly develop, and spiritualize man, or an accumulation of the "spiritual fission-forces" in the developed personality and the Western culture. Monkhood and knighthood fulfilled this function by disciplining and spiritualizing man. The images of a monk and a knight are veritably types of a disciplined, integrated, and manifold personality, spiritually free, unafraid of anything external, with enormous concentration on the inward through tense "fission-forces" centered around the Kingdom of God. This medieval phase had to end and did end because it did not supply a sufficient channel for releasing the enormously concentrated forces for a free, creative transformation of the empirical reality. The Middle Ages end with the marvelous Christian mystical Renaissance of the thirteenth century that serves as a bridge to the subsequent Humanist phase. Joachim of Floris, St. Francis of Assisi, Dante, Giotto, and St. Thomas Aquinas are the brilliant stars of this wonderful Renaissance, which is the summit and the end of the Medieval phase.

Then follows the largely non-Christian, even increasingly anti-Christian, phase of Western culture's secular Humanism. Humanism puts man in the center of the universe, makes him the measure of all things and the highest value. Its main function was to release and develop the free, creative forces of man: man's trial and test in freedom, unhampered by anything except man's own sense, reason, and self-control. It was, therefore, the period of man's liberation from all "super-human" controls, and deconcentration of his concentrated inner forces, the period in which he spent the creative funds accumulated in the medieval period, and abandoned the religious central value of the Middle Ages; the period of secularization and external freedom. These tasks were accomplished in the course of some six centuries. Humanist culture spent most of the funds accumulated in the previous periods and exhausted its creative power. As a result in the nineteenth century this Humanist culture immanently produced the ever-increasing germs of its own destruction. The Medieval-Christian and the Humanist-Modern phases both dialectically led to their own decay.

The Medieval-Christian culture aspired only to the Kingdom of God and denied value to the empirical City of Man. But instead of becoming absorbed in the City of God, it ended—dialectically—by becoming enmeshed in the City of Man. The Christian Church itself grew into the most powerful empirical organization in entire Medieval Europe. Humanist culture aspired to man's glory, power, and creativity, and sought to make him both self-master and master of the empirical world. It finished by utterly demoralizing man, disintegrating the man-made universe and exhausting man's creative forces:

> Here the dialectics of history consists of the self-affirmation of man that has led to his self-extermination, and the development of the free play of purely human forces, not connected with the super-human high purpose, that led to the exhaustion of purely human creative resources. . . . The passionate striving towards a creation of beauty and perfection of form, which marks the advent of the Humanist-Renaissance phase, led to the destruction and distortion of the perfection of form. . . . The more proudly Humanist man relied upon himself, and the more he moved away from the Christian, Divine, Medieval foundations of personality, the less creative, less powerful, and less self-controlling he grew progressively.

The Humanist period opens with man full of joy and self-confidence. It ends with a deep disillusion in all the dreams, strivings, and illusions of the Humanist man and culture. None of the great expectations were realized.

The crisis and end of the Humanist phase was already quite apparent in the nineteenth century. The entrance of the machine and technology into man's historical existence dealt a mortal blow to Humanism. Increasing loss of man's control over the human race's machine-made universe, decreasing self-control and mastery of the lower, animal propensities in man, a growing distortion of the very image of a true humanist man in favor of a demoralized human mechanism and human animal so different from humanist man—these are some of the signs that mark the end of the Humanist phase. The emergence and successful growth of anti-Humanist philosophies and ideologies are further signs. Nietzsche's final verdict, "Man is a shame and disgrace; man must be overcome and transcended"—Humanism must be ended in order to open the way for the superman—is one example of this. Marx also sacrifices man and humanism on the altar of the inhuman, superpersonal kingdom of collectivism. Similarly, even the philosophies and ideologies of Kant, Comte, Spencer, right up to Husserl, are anti-humanistic. Likewise, Humanist ethics and aesthetics, politics and economics, either developed into non-humanist forms or else disintegrated into

fragmentary atoms, devoid of power, form, and control. Many mystic, explicitly anti-Humanist currents appeared. In the nineteenth century, socialism, anarchism, capitalism, futurism, "modernism" and theosophy all revolted against, and mortally weakened, the Humanist culture. At the present time the Humanist phase is largely over and mankind is entering the "New Middle Ages."

(5) In discussing the reason why all great cultures eventually disintegrate as unities (surviving, however, in their perennial values), and why their creative power eventually declines, Berdyaev makes a highly suggestive generalization. "Culture is not a realization of a new *life,* of a new way of existence, but a realization of new *values.* All achievements of culture are symbolic rather than realistic."

At its creative period culture creates not for the practical purpose of a utilitarian or hedonistic improvement of the empirical life, but for the sake of the values themselves. It creates truth for the sake of truth and cognition, beauty for the sake of beauty, goodness for the sake of goodness. In all this there is little of "real, practical life," of the passionate "will to live," of the intense desire to organize "life," to enjoy "life." There is little of practical utility.

Having created the values, however, culture immanently changes its direction and passes beyond culture into the Spenglerian "civilization." Created values cannot help entering real life and changing it; with the change the culture itself changes. It now tends towards a practical realization of its power, towards a practical organization of life, towards a diffusion of its applied results. A mere blossoming of the arts and sciences, a deepening and refinement of thought, the highest flare-ups of artistic creativity, the contemplation of the kingdom of God and of genius—all these now cease to be experienced as real life, cease to inspire as the highest goal. Instead, there grows an intense will to live, to enjoy the "full, real life," to master, improve, and transform this life. This lust for "real life" eventually undermines the creative genius of culture. A period of cultural blossoming presupposes a severe limitation of the will to "live"; it demands an unselfish, somewhat ascetic transcendence over the passionate "gluttony for life." When such a "gluttony for life" develops in the masses, then this "life," and not the cultural creativity, becomes the supreme end. Since they are always aristocratic, cultural creativity and culture cease to be the supreme self-values and become mere means for the "practical improvement of life," for "prosperity and happiness." With this degradation of culture and of pure creativity to the level of third class means-values, the will for culture and disinterested creativeness weakens and eventually dies. With it dies the will for creative genius, and genius becomes increasingly scarce. Under these conditions culture cannot stay at its high level; it is bound to slide down; its quality tends to be replaced by quantity; a sort of social entropy develops and culture turns into an uncreative "civilization." Culture immanently declines and crumbles because it deviates from the purposes and tasks that were born at its creative phase.

This explains why the highest cultural blossoming of Germany at the end of the eighteenth and beginning of the nineteenth centuries—when within a period of a few decades the world saw Lessing, Herder, Goethe, Schiller, Kant, Fichte, Hegel, Schelling, Schleiermacher, Schopenhauer, Novalis, Mozart, Handel, Haydn, Beethoven, and dozens of other first-class "stars"—occurred in the period when the real life of Germany was poor, difficult, depressing, and bourgeois. Similarly, Italy's real life of the Renaissance period was miserable and unenviable. Even the practical life of the great creators themselves—be it Mozart or Beethoven, Leonardo or Michelangelo—was painful and tragic. "Culture has always been a great failure with respect to life." There is a kind of oppositeness between culture and life. When life becomes "civilized," "happy and prosperous," then the creativity of culture declines and culture is replaced by "civilization." "Culture is unselfish and disinterested in its highest achievements; civilization is always utilitarian and interested." Such is the dialectic of the decline of creative culture into uncreative civilizations.

Although it is fairly general, this degradation of culture into civilization is not a creative culture's only destiny. Culture can take another way—the way of religious transfiguration of life, and through that the realization of genuine existence (being). Such was the course that the declining Graeco-Roman culture followed. It resulted in the emergence and growth of Christianity. At its heroic and truly Christian period, Christianity led to the religious transfiguration of life and the creation of a great Christian Medieval culture. Eventually Christianity ceased to be truly religious and became largely verbal, ritualistic, an economic and political machinery; as such it lost its transfiguring power. It is possible that the West's transitional culture will choose this religious way of transfiguring life in order to perpetuate its perennial values and bring humanity closer to a genuine creative life.

Russia may play an important role in this pilgrimage of culture; however, this role still remains problematic and uncertain. Berdyaev is much less complimentary towards Russia than are Schubart, Danilevsky, and Spengler. "The traditions of culture have always been weak in Russia. We have built a rather ugly civilization. Barbarian forces have always been strong with us. Even our will towards a religious transfiguration of life has been infected by a sort of sickly day-dreaming." Under these conditions only Russia's potential religiosity, together with the most intense suffering and a consciousness of the epochal crisis, may help Russia find the way of religious transfiguration of life instead of decaying into an uncreative civilization or barbarism.

V. V. Zenkovskii (essay date 1953)

SOURCE: "F. M. Dostoyevsky, V. Solovyov, and N. A. Berdyayev," in *Russian Thinkers and Europe,* translated by Galia S. Bodde, American Council of Learned Societies, 1953, pp. 154-87.

[*In the following essay, Zenkovskii provides an assessment of Berdyaev as a specifically Russian thinker.*]

Berdyayev has gone through a complex and signal spiritual evolution from critical idealism to a religious *Weltanschauung,* and his books reflect various stages of Russian seekings for the truth. Centered, however, in all his ideology and creative work lie the problems of history. By examining these we can best clarify for ourselves both the evolution of Berdyaev's thought and its general principles. Of essential interest are his following works: **The Meaning of History** (1923), **The Destiny of Russia** (a collection of articles, 1918), and **The New Middle Ages** (1924). Some relevant material can also be obtained from his two other books: **The Meaning of Creative Work** (1916), and **Philosophy of Inequality** (1923).

The basic and characteristic trait of Berdyayev's thought is his genuine Christian universalism, seemingly inherited from Vladimir Solovyov. Having achieved a religious viewpoint and come to a definite support of Orthodoxy—the philosophy of which Berdyayev constantly strives to build—he remains equally aloof from the anti-Catholic tendency of Dostoyevsky and the pro-Catholic thought of Solovyov. He has a high regard for the Catholic world, and devotes several essays to its general study; he also possesses a good knowledge of Catholicism in its various currents. Like other Russian thinkers, he knows less, and is rather superficially conscious of Protestantism, which he identifies too closely with the humanistic culture of Europe. Yet despite his realization of Russia's national originality and the earnestness of his messianic mood (as especially revealed in his wartime collection of articles entitled **The Destiny of Russia**), Berdyayev is completely free from anti-Westernism, as well as from a straight-laced Slavophilism. His writings give us the feeling of possessing a synthetic spirit that is comprehensively and inwardly organic, free and genuine. Although his works are saturated with polemics, he has a pronounced capacity for adjusting himself to the moods of others and is not averse to borrowing ideas that are congenial to him. The synthetic power of his concepts is thus very great; as if forming a musical chord, there sound various motifs which have inspired the Russian mind, yet without suppressing or creating discords with one another. Thus we are able to trace in him the influence of the most diverse Russian thinkers, yet this does not prevent him from preserving his own originality.

As regards the relationship between Russia and Europe, Berdyayev to some extent comes close to the synthesizing ideas of Dostoyevsky and Solovyov. He goes considerably beyond these men, however, having been fruitfully activated in this regard by the influence of the Great War. He frees himself entirely from all historical and spiritual provincialism, and in some ways has a broader and deeper outlook than even Vladimir Solovyov. Thus in Berdyayev we find a conclusion brought to the entire period following the Crimean War, and perhaps the beginning of a new period in the history of Russian consciousness.

Let us examine, first of all, Berdyayev's critique and appraisal of the West. In *The Meaning of Creative Work* (1916) he writes: "The victory of the bourgeois spirit led in the nineteenth and twentieth centuries to a false and mechanical civilization, profoundly antagonistic to any genuine culture."

"This mechanical civilization—which levels, depersonalizes, and devaluates everything—with its devilish technology closely resembling black magic, is a pseudo-being, a spectral, inside-out sort of being. Bourgeois civilization marks the depths of the non-cosmic world; man's inner self perishes in it and is replaced by an external automatic kind of man. Civilization has created an enormous technical energy which was designed to usher in the reign of man over nature. However, these technical forces now reign over man himself. They make him a slave and kill his soul . . . It is as if, within this colossal technical civilization, the demons of evil have been released so as to revenge themselves upon fallen men. Civilization fails to realize the kingly dream of man." The transition of European culture into civilization, according to Berdyayev, came as a result of a change in man's relationship to nature, and in particular, of the appearance of the machine. "Civilization," he writes, "has not a natural, nor a spiritual, but a mechanical basis. It is, first of all, technical. In it technology triumphs over the spirit, over the organism; in civilization the thought itself becomes technical" (*The Meaning of History*.) "The spirit of civilization," we read in the same work, "is that of the petty bourgeoisie. The civilization of Europe and the United States has created an industrial capitalistic system, which is the exterminator of the spirit of eternity, the spirit of holiness. The capitalistic civilization of modern times is killing God and is the most godless of civilizations . . . The processes of barbarization and coarsening begin to show themselves in it."

"In modern history," we read in another book, *The New Middle Ages,* "the center of gravity in life is displaced from the spiritual to the material milieu, and from the internal to the external. Not the Church, but the stock market becomes the dominating and regulating force in life. The civilization of the nineteenth and twentieth centuries rejects the sacred symbolism of culture and craves for a life as realistic as possible; it wishes to master and transform life and creates for this purpose this powerful technology . . ."

"The exclusive preoccupation of Europe with social questions," we read in another book, *The Destiny of Russia,* "is a sign of the downfall of humanity." "The economic basis of the civilization of the nineteenth century," he writes again (*The New Middle Ages*), "has distorted the hierarchical order of society and generated an economic materialism, which [in turn] has faithfully reflected the reality of the nineteenth century . . . The worship of Mammon instead of God is natural both to capitalism and socialism." "Modern history," we read in the same book, "has created an objectless culture and an objectless society, which does not know for what it lives . . . Modern man is not free in spirit . . . He is in the power of a master unknown to him, a superhuman and non-human force which is conquering human society and does not wish to know the Lord's Truth."

Berdyayev also notes that "the individualistic civilization of the nineteenth century, with its democracy, materialism, technology, public opinion, the press, the stockmarket, and parliament, has contributed to the decline and withering of the individual, to its levelling and a general amalgamation . . ." "We have gone beyond," we read elsewhere, "the foundations of an entire historical epoch. The entire basis of life is shattered, and the falsity and rottenness of the foundations on which civilized society of the nineteenth and twentieth century has rested have become apparent . . . We are entering an epoch of terrible revelations. Vainly do people dream of a return to the bourgeois civilization of the nineteenth century. The catastrophes of wars and revolutions as yet unheard of have been laid in the foundations of this civilization. The tragic nature of the contemporary crisis lies in the fact that, at the bottom of his soul, no one believes in any political forms or any social ideologies." Let us, finally, stress another point in Berdyayev's analysis of contemporary reality in which he repeats the thoughts of Strakhov and others. "The creative will," he writes, "cannot be satisfied with separate, autonomous spheres of culture. On the contrary, it is directed toward unity and integration. But in this epoch of ours a visible and acknowledged spiritual center of intellectual life does not exist. The spiritual center of the coming epoch may be only the Church, as it was in the Middle Ages."

In his book on the meaning of history, Berdyayev treats in an interesting way the problem of the historical roots of the decay which has been manifesting itself in Europe in recent times. The analysis of the Renaissance and of Humanism which he gives in this book brings into the foreground the "providentially inevitable great test of human freedom." We shall not develop this theme here, but will pass on to Berdyayev's interpretation of Russia, which will bring us to his understanding of the present crisis of Europe.

With a typical tendency for generalizations, Berdyayev speaks at length of the profound antinomies in the Russian soul, and explains them by the preponderance of the feminine principle and under-development of masculinity in the Russian character. However, it is just these traits which determine the peculiarity of Russia's destiny and its place in the approaching crisis in world history. "Russia," he writes, "has never been able to accept humanistic culture as a whole, with its rationalistic consciousness, its formalized logic and formal law, its religious neutrality, and its secular middle-of-the-road tendency. Russia has never completely left the Middle Ages and the sacral epoch." "The Russian people," we read elsewhere, "cannot create a middle-of-the-road humanistic realm. They do not want a state based on law in the European sense of the word. They want either the kingdom of God and a brotherhood in Christ, or a comradeship in Antichrist who is the king of this world. In the Russian people there has always been a unique detachment that is unknown to the peoples of the West . . . The peoples of the West are chained by their very virtues to an earthly life and its blessings, while the Russian people by their virtues stand detached from this earth and direct themselves to Heaven."

The originality of Russia is also revealed by Berdyayev in his analysis of Westernism and Slavophilism. "Neither Westerners nor Slavophiles," he remarks, "could understand the mystery of the Russian soul. In order to understand the mystery, one has to view it from still another, a third point; one has to rise above the contra-distinction between the two principles: Eastern and Western. In God's plan, Russia is a great and united 'East and West,' whereas in its actual state it is an unsuccessful and mixed East and West.'" "The end of Slavophilism," he writes elsewhere," is also the end of Westernism, and of the inherent contradistinction between East and West. There has been particularism, provincialism, and the absence of universal spirit in Westernism too. Russian consciousness cannot be either Slavophilistic or Westernistic." "The World War will lead to a surmounting of the old approach to the question of Russia and Europe, and of the East and West. It will put an end to the internal dispute between Slavophiles and Westerners, by eliminating both Slavophilism and Westernism as provincial ideologies . . . Today . . . the provincialism of the mind is being overcome, . . . and by the will of fate we are being led forth into the vast reaches of world history." And in the same work we read: "While the end of the provincially isolated life of Europe is approaching, that of Russia approaches even faster. Russia must go forth into the world's vastness. The end of Europe will see the appearance of Russia as a determining spiritual force on the arena of world history . . . Russia, occupying the place of a mediator between the East and West, and being itself 'East and West,' has been called to play a great role in uniting humanity. The World War brings us to the problem of Russian messianism."

Extremely curious is the revival in the above quoted passages of the themes—now presented in somewhat different tones—which occupied Russian thought throughout the course of the nineteenth century. Berdyayev gives a new treatment to the motif, already familiar to us, of Russia's peculiar historical develop-

ment. Especially interesting is the revival of the early "soil" ideas, which are inevitably brought to mind when we read, for example, that "Russia is to proclaim its new word to the world during the coming epoch." In a later book (*The New Middle Ages*) Berdyayev again returns to these thoughts: "Russia, placed midway between East and West, is achieving—although in a terrible and catastrophic way—a constantly growing world significance." Likewise, in the coming era of world culture which Berdyayev defines as a "new Middle Ages," he says that "a quite special place will belong to Russia."

However, while "Russia's involvement in world affairs signifies the end of its isolated provincial existence, and of its slavish subjection to the ideologies of Slavophilism and Westernism," the World War is "leading Europe, too, out of its isolation, and is exposing radical contradictions within Europe itself." In this respect, even imperialism, "no matter how frequently base are its motives and evil its tactics, nevertheless tends to give egress from an isolated national existence, and permits passage beyond the borders of Europe into the vastness of the world."

"The most powerful feeling produced by the World War is the realization that this war marks the end of Europe as a monopolizer of culture, and as an isolated province of the globe claiming to be the universe. The World War has drawn all races and parts of the globe into the world orbit, and brings East and West into a close proximity heretofore unknown in history . . . This world aim now looms more acutely before mankind than the internal aims of crystallised European states and cultures. This historical turning point had been inwardly prepared for by a spiritual crisis in European culture, and by the collapse of positivism and materialism in the modern European mind . . . Europe has for a long time striven to overcome itself and to go beyond its limits. It is not the ideal of culture in general; it is itself provincial. In Europe there has long since existed a secret, inward attraction toward the East . . . Social and political thought will now face the vastness of the world, the problem of controlling and governing the whole surface of the globe, the problem of the intermingling of all types and cultures, the unification of humanity through struggle, and the mutual interaction and communion of all races. Culture ceases to be European and becomes universal. Europe will have to relinquish her position as a monopolizer of culture . . . Our aim is that the end of Europe and the new turning point in history should be experienced with spiritual penetration and religious understanding."

Extremely characteristic in this passage is the combining of Christian universalism with the universal historical approach, which is now freed from the "monopoly" of Europe. This brings Berdyayev close to Leontyev and the Eurasians, while it also definitely separates him from Solovyov. "A process of world unification is taking place," he writes, "which is vaster than a mere European unification. The spirit of universalism must be awakened in Christian peoples, and the will for a free universalism must be revealed." Berdyayev gives Russia a particularly important place in this task of world unification: "Of all peoples, that of Russia is the most pan-human and universal in its spirit: this is a part of its national make-up. The task of the Russian people is to be that of creating a world unification and forming a single Christian spiritual cosmos." Berdyayev links this idea with that of a "new Middle Ages," which he defines as follows: "I call the process directed toward the overcoming of national isolation and the creation of universal unity that of the end of modern history and the beginning of a new Middle Ages."

Michael Alexander Vallon (essay date 1960)

SOURCE: "An Evaluation: 'My Ways Are Not Your Ways,'" in *An Apostle of Freedom: Life and Teachings of Nicolas Berdyaev,* Philosophical Library, 1960, pp. 292-313.

[*In the following excerpt, Vallon offers a critical appraisal of the salient concepts of Berdyaev's religious philosophy.*]

> It is no longer I who live, but Christ who lives in me; and the life I now live in the flesh I live by faith in the Son of God.
>
> —Galatians 2:20

Berdyaev described his philosophy as "existential" to indicate that his thought was rooted not in discursive reason, but in life experience. He never related himself, however, to any of the existential schools, and least of all to the atheistic variety represented by Jean-Paul Sartre which often is erroneously identified with existentialism *par excellence*. He shares in the basic conviction of all existentialists, namely, that existence precedes essence, but he differs from most of them in that he derives his primary insights into philosophy and religion mainly from Boehme, Khomyakov, and Dostoyevsky instead of Kierkegaard.

Existential philosophy permeates the whole of Berdyaev's thinking. Its starting point is not an abstract concept, but the concrete person. Without keeping this in mind one cannot understand his teaching at all. To help, therefore, in performing an evaluation of his philosophical and theological work we shall turn briefly to the chief characteristics of his existentialism. Berdyaev affirms the primacy of subject in opposition to the object and the objective world. The subject alone exists and is truly real. The object is secondary, not real, but a mere symbol of reality. Subject is connected with the noumenal realm of spirit and freedom; object is related to the world of nature and determinism. Berdyaev, therefore, places personality, the existent subject, in extreme contrast to being which he regards as a product of thought. Being has no existence; only personality

exists. Spirit can be experienced only in personality, in subject, not in being, in object. It follows that the former alone, not the latter, represents the criterion of truth.

Berdyaev's existentialism should in no way be confused with egocentricity. It is personalism, not individualism. "Personalism does not mean, as individualism does, an egocentric isolation." Egocentricity and egoism are the product not of the personality, but of the Ego." Ego is the enemy of personality. Indeed, the realization of personality necessarily involves the destruction of Ego. "Personality presupposes a going out from self to another and to others, it lacks air and is suffocated when left shut up in itself." "The personal needs another. . . . Communion belongs to the realm of freedom and means liberation from slavery," both to himself and the world.

Neither should Berdyaev's understanding of spirit be mistaken for subjectivism. It is not a state of individual consciousness, nor is it consciousness itself. Spirit is not subjective, although it exists in subject. Spirit is rather a reality transcending subject and independent from it; but at the same time it is immanent in subject whereby alone it can be apprehended. Spirit is freedom, and activity. It is opposed not to matter which, according to Berdyaev, possesses no "autonomous reality," but to necessity of the objectified world which it attempts to set free by a process of transfiguration.

Since the world of objects is deprived of reality, the identification of the "objective" with the "real" as recognized in positivist world outlooks, is unwarranted and erroneous. It is, Berdyaev observes, precisely the result of objectivisation, namely, the substitution of symbols for the realities they are supposed to represent. In the process the world of natural objects, social institutions, and intellectual conceptions tend to become accepted as realities while true primal reality, that of spirit, is lost. For this reason scientific knowledge cannot discover the ultimate truth. Science deals exclusively with objects. In this respect it is justified and useful. But science has nothing to say about their meaning; this is imparted by the existential subject alone. Science is descriptive, not explanatory. It describes the order of becoming, not the source of being. It indicates means, not ends. It depicts the "how," not the "why" of things. The latter is found only by personality in a creative act. It is the true knowledge.

Berdyaev's epistemology, then, is anthropocentric, active, and existential. It is rooted in the concrete reality of life-spiritual not natural. This is so, in his judgment, because man, a spiritual being, is not alien to noumenal reality; on the contrary, he is wholly immersed in it. "I, the knower, abide in reality from the very first and am an inalienable part of it. I know reality in and through myself, as man. Only an existent can know existence." Knowledge, therefore, is not merely a passive intellectual information "about something," but an intuitive dynamic "something," a creative spiritual experience involving man's whole self. It is an event within the existential subject revealing the reality of the spirit. It is a communion between the knower and the known. "Knowledge of truth is communion with truth and life in it."

Such are, then, the distinctive characteristics of Berdyaev's thought. It is existential, personalistic, and intuitive. It presupposes activity and freedom. But first and foremost, it postulates the spirit as the alpha and omega of all that exists. We shall now, against the above outlined background, proceed to a critical appraisal of Berdyaev's teaching [according to the following pattern: 1) God; 2) man; 3) God-Man; 4) Ethics; and 5) Philosophy of History]. We shall conclude by singling out Berdyaev's perennial contribution to Western and Christian thought.

1) *God*. . . . [The] foundation of Berdyaev's world-view lay not an intellectual concept but a mystical intuition—the intuition of the unfathomable *Ungrund*. The term designates the Godhead, the *Mysterium Magnum* from which are realized both the triune God and Freedom. The creation of the world by God-the-Creator is a secondary act. In this regard three questions might be raised. First, is the mystical apprehension valid? Second, what is the nature of creation? And third, is the idea of "uncreated freedom" Christian?

The first question apparently calls for an affirmative answer. Mysticism is too old and too common an experience to be dismissed as merely a psychological aberration or as the fruit of unbridled imagination. "Mysticism," writes Rufus M. Jones, "is as old as humanity, is not confined to any one racial stock, is undoubtedly one of the original grounds of personal religion." As to the character of mysticism, the same writer defines it as an "immediate experience of a divine-human intercourse and relationship." William James also believes that "personal religious experience has its root and centre in mystical states of consciousness." In other words, "to be a mystic is simply to participate here and now in that real and eternal life."

Two facts in connection with mysticism are undeniable, whatever it may be, and whatever part it is destined to play in the unveiling of truth and reality. On the one hand, it is the leading characteristic of some of the greatest religious personalities of the world—the founders of the Eastern Religions; Plotinus and Francis of Assisi; Eckhart and Bruno; Catherine of Siena and John of the Cross; Jacob Boehme and George Fox; Brother Lawrence, William Blake, and William Wordsworth. On the other, all the mystics, whatever their time, or personal, mental, and physical constitution, alike strongly declare that in their experiences they transcend the created world and attain direct knowledge of ultimate reality—namely, God. Moreover, they all predicate God as the unity underlying diversity, as the *coincidentia oppositorum* in whom antitheses co-exist in a harmonious synthesis. This knowledge, they maintain, is based not on revelation, logic or reason, or demonstrated facts, but on intuitive, immediate apprehension of the divine in an I-Thou encounter.

Berdyaev's religious existentialism is obviously mystical. To him, too, mysticism is the source of true religious knowledge. "Mysticism," he writes, "understood as a mode of knowledge rather than a finished product, has always exercised my imagination. I believe in the existence of a universal mystical experience." This means "a penetration into the innermost recesses of the spiritual world, where . . . nothing is external to me, everything is in me and with me, within the depths of myself." This knowledge is possible, he believes, because human nature is endowed with a godlike quality, namely, the spirit. As the intellect is given man to perceive natural things, so the spirit is given him to apprehend spiritual things. It is in and through the spirit that the human-divine encounter is made possible.

Berdyaev's attitude, I think, is both correct and Christian. Christianity has always been an inexhaustible source of mystical experience. The vast and uninterrupted flow of Christian mystics, and the compelling earnestness of their messages, bear witness to the authenticity of their basic ecstasies and visions. It might also be noted that Jesus' own psychology, as illustrated in the Gospels, is analogous to that of the mystics. "In its pains and splendors," writes Underhill, "its dual character of action and fruition, it reflects their experience upon the supernatural plane of more abundant life."

Furthermore, is not the main point of Christian epistemology as a whole that we know incomparably more and better through faith, hope, and love than by means of intellect? And what else are the three New Testament virtues if not precisely the channels of intuitive cognition? Such cognition, or rather the possibility of it, is by no means the exclusive appanage of the mystics. I am inclined to think that each human being carries within himself the seed of mysticism. Of course, few undertake the continuous, painstaking training of will and spiritual concentration requisite in achieving an insight which could be identified as mystical. But the fact that all through the ages the rank-and-file of Christians have faithfully and repeatedly responded to the message of the mystics seems to prove the existence of an intimate kinship between the two groups.

Berdyaev, then, may definitely be placed in the category of the Christian mystics. He regarded himself primarily as a *homo mysticus* rather than a *homo religiosus*. His awareness of God is founded on spiritual revelation first, and only then confirmed by the revelation in the Scriptures. It should be noted, however, that Berdyaev's mysticism is not of the monistic type so current both in Eastern and Western Christianity. He rejected the neoplatonic mysticism of the One which from Plotinus was carried over into Christian life by Pseudo-Dionysius the Areopagite. Monistic mysticism is necessarily hostile toward man, his freedom and personality. It obliterates all distinction between the divine and the human and postulates the final absorption of the latter by the former. Berdyaev is, of course, on solid ground when he argues from Boehme's point of view that, for Christian metaphysics, the relation between the Creator and the creature is one of partnership, and not absorption. Christian revelation recognizes and maintains the distinction between God and man. Christ the Crucified Lord constitutes the meeting, not a blending, ground of the divine and human personalities. He symbolizes the dialectic of freedom and love between God and man. Christian mysticism, then, is dualistic, not monistic.

Berdyaev's religious experience lends itself to an interesting comparison with Martin Buber's theological thought. The Jewish philosopher likewise is the representative and one of the main sources of religious existentialism. The core of his teaching is that "all real living is meeting." The meeting, according to Buber, is based on two types of relations expressed in "primary words" I-Thou and I-It. These refer not to the object of the relation, but to the nature of the relation itself. The I-Thou locution indicates a relation of person to person, of subject to subject, and implies the commitment of one's whole being. The term I-It, on the other hand, designates a relation of a person to a thing, of subject to object, and involves not a total, but only a partial commitment of one's being. Naturally the I-Thou relation takes priority over the subject-object relation. Indeed, it is only within the I-Thou relation that personality is realized: "Through the *Thou* a man becomes *I*." The I-Thou relation introduces man in dialogue mainly, though not exclusively, with other men and with God. Now God is the eternal Thou in whom "the extended lines of relations meet." Thus, "every particular Thou is a glimpse through to the eternal Thou; by means of every particular Thou the primary word addresses the eternal Thou." God is the true Thou of a man's life, "which cannot be limited by another Thou, and to which he stands in a relation that gathers up and includes all others."

The human-divine encounter, Buber insists, does not annihilate the I. Man before God remains forever a "Single One,"—a distinctive, independent personality—"praying and serving and loving, such as is possible only by an I to a Thou." Like Berdyaev, Buber rejects the monistic, absorptionist type of mysticism. "All doctrine of absorption," he writes, "is based on the colossal illusion of the human spirit that is bent back on himself," while actually the Ego has no real existence outside of its relationship with the Thou. Buber's conclusion on the subject is of a piece with that of Berdyaev. "Not before a man can say I," he declares, "in perfect reality—that is, finding himself—can he in perfect reality say Thou—that is, to God."

To ascertain the validity of Berdyaev's existential mysticism is no problem when attempted in the light both of the time-honored tradition of Christian mysticism and the modern religious existentialism. But when we be-

come concerned with the content of his mystical experience, then difficulties begin to arise in the shape of striking antinomies. Thus in regard to the question of the nature of creation, Berdyaev's answer reveals vagueness and contradiction. Granted that God-the-Creator and the meonic freedom proceed from the transcending divine Ungrund; granted again that the former creates out of the latter a spiritual world and man; yet nothing is said which clarifies the nature of that creation. Was it similar to the Platonic pattern of the world of Ideas? At first view such an approximation might seem plausible. Berdyaev, it has been noted, declares that man is capable of "remembering" things he had seen in the lost paradise, prior to his earthly life. But a closer examination proves the comparison preposterous. Plato's noumenal world represents a static, ontological scheme of things. Not so Berdyaev's. To him the world of spirit denotes a voluntaristic character; it is dynamic. The one spells immutability, the other involves changeableness.

Further, was it the abode of one or many spirits? Every man's spiritual pre-existence should support the second supposition. Berdyaev's continuous stress on the One who consents to creation, however, would rather suggest the existence in the spiritual world of only one human spirit, the archetype and the source of all other individual souls. If it be so, how does the passage from the one to the many take place? Moreover, Berdyaev says that God-the-Creator made the world out of meonic stuff. But at the same time he affirms that the Other is none else than the Second Person of the Trinity—the divine manhood. If the Other's response to God requires the use of meonic freedom, as Berdyaev suggests, then the world would be the result of no creation at all, for a "response" evidently cannot be identified with "creation." And even if, contrary to elementary coherence, such identification were forcibly assumed, the initiative for creation should be ascribed not to God but to the Other. In case, however, God did create the world out of the meonic stuff, it still remains to explain what relation the "response" of the Other bears to creation. If none, as might be advanced, then the creation of the world would appear not as a free response of "no-thingness" to the call of God, but a deliberate manifestation of God's incentive and omnipotence—a thesis diametrically opposed to Berdyaev's understanding of God's nature and character. Finally, it might be observed, in spite of all Berdyaev's reservations and qualifications, the meonic freedom conveys much more the idea of "something-ness" rather than "no-thingness."

The main criticism, however, has been voiced not against Berdyaev's confused picture of creation, but against his conception of "uncreated freedom." It is argued that if man's freedom is not created and given to him by God, but proceeds from another non-divine source, then ontological dualism becomes inescapable. The theory might, so the commentators contend, indicate Zoroastrianism or Manicheism, but assuredly it does not express the Christian point of view. Evgeny Lampert, for example, calls it "the most disastrous conclusion in his [Berdyaev's] whole philosophy; and one which seems in fact in no way warranted by his own fundamental presuppositions." Matthew Spinka also agrees with this judgment. The reasons for his dissent from Berdyaev on the subject are, in his enumeration, the following: first, God's endowment of man with freedom does not make Him "responsible for man's abuse of that freedom"; second, the "'uncreated freedom' . . . does not free God from responsibility for at least consenting to use the 'meonic' stuff in creation, although he knew it contained freedom," that is, the possibility of evil; and finally, the whole idea, Spinka believes, is gnostic not Christian.

Lampert and Spinka's remarks are quite typical of the common criticism formulated against Berdyaev's view. We shall, therefore, dwell shortly upon them. Proceeding with the above mentioned argument, only in reverse order, we may first underscore that, with regard to the subject under discussion, Berdyaev can scarcely pass for a gnostic. Of course, his teaching on the pre-existence of souls and man's falling away from a higher realm of goodness and freedom into a lower world of phenomena and necessity is related to gnosticism. But his representation of God-the-Creator has nothing in common with the gnostic Demiurge fashioning the world in subordination to the Supreme Being. Berdyaev's theogony—the realization of the divine Trinity in the *Ungrund*—does not mean that God has a beginning: the theogenoic process is eternal; and so is God.

The next objection concerning God's responsibility for using the meonic stuff in engendering the world is met by Berdyaev with the assumption that God, as it were, could not help it. Since the very essence of His nature is creativity, He must create whatever way there is in the unfathomable mystery of primeval spiritual reality. But God is not only the creator, He is also the Redeemer. If He cannot help creating, He does redeem the creation. The Incarnation is precisely an act of divine redemption whereby men are called to become the partners of God in gaining victory over meonic evil, nay, in realizing the transformation of evil into good.

The third objection apparently presents a real difficulty. Evidently God cannot be held responsible for man's abuse of freedom. Berdyaev was well aware of that. In fact, his whole philosophy, in accord with the Christian tradition, hinges on man's direct responsibility for his own destiny. Although his explanation of that responsibility is, as we have seen, at variance with the one commonly held by the Christian churches. He contends, in effect, that man is responsible for himself because he stands absolutely free in relation to God. A freedom created and given by God should, in Berdyaev's belief, signify only one thing, to wit, that God is the Lord and Controller of Freedom. The doctrine inevitably leads to metaphysical monism, on the one hand, and predestinarianism, on the other. It also eliminates the insight of divine tragedy, and imposes instead the idea of a farce God is playing to Himself

Lampert's argument to the effect that the theory of "uncreated freedom" is both a "disastrous conclusion" of Berdyaev's philosophy and "unwarranted by his own fundamental presuppositions" is the least acceptable of all four. Fielding Clarke rightly questions its validity when he declares that Berdyaev's idea of "uncreated freedom" is "the very reverse of a conclusion. How can it be unwarranted by Berdyaev's 'fundamental presuppositions' when it is quite obviously itself one of those very same 'fundamental presuppositions'?" It must be reiterated that without grasping Berdyaev's fundamental metaphysical presuppositions no understanding of his thought can ever be achieved. God and "uncreated freedom" do not constitute an ontological dualism. Berdyaev admitted himself that the manner of his thinking may have contributed to the misunderstanding of his philosophy. But then he ceaselessly insisted that terms such as "Ungrund," "God-the-Creator," and "Uncreated Freedom" are not rational concepts but descriptive symbols. They are not susceptible to rationalization. All one can do, in his view, is to interpret them in the light of one's experience. Berdyaev's own interpretation might be formulated as follows: I apprehend the ultimate reality neither in terms of monism nor of dualism but *as if* there were at the root of existence a basic antithesis, to wit, between God and uncreated freedom both of which, however, are transcended in the final mystery of the divine Godhead. He who will adapt this approach to Berdyaev's thought will alone gain access to its depth and significance.

2) *Man.* Next to "uncreated freedom" Berdyaev's passionate emphasis on the supreme value of man is the most characteristic feature of his philosophy. He regards the human person primarily as the bearer of the image of God and eternity, and not of time and the world. Each man is an absolute end in himself. Each human being is rooted in God. Each individual shares with God a part of divine nature. Berdyaev's staunch belief in man drew upon him much criticism from the Orthodox, Catholics, and Protestants alike. Yet he never abated an inch. He summed up his position in the following words: "It is not possible for my faith to be shaken by man, however low he may sink; for this faith is grounded not on what man thinks about man, but on what God thinks about him."

Accordingly, Berdyaev predicated man not so much as a sinful creature, as one who is destined to creativity and transformation. The final truth about man is not his sin, but a creative ascent. He declared that,

> Religious meaning of life and being is not wholly a matter of redemption from sin, but that life and being have positive, creative purposes. . . . Salvation from sin, from perdition, is not the final purpose of religious life: salvation is always *from* something and life should be *for* something. Many things unnecessary for salvation are needed for the very purpose for which salvation is necessary—for the creative upsurge of being. Man's chief end is not to be saved but to mount up,

creatively. For this creative upsurge salvation from sin and evil is necessary. From the religious viewpoint the epoch of redemption is subordinated to the epoch of creativeness.

Berdyaev's understanding of human nature at this point may appear both dangerously individualistic and biblically unwarranted. However, it is neither. It has already been pointed out that Berdyaev professed personalism not individualism. Indeed, he drew a sharp distinction between the two. Individuality is of nature; personality, of the spirit. The one belongs to the world of phenomena; the other is related to the noumenal order. Nevertheless, they are not alien to each other. A realized personality is the harmonious integration of both with the spiritual principle "having the mastery over all the powers of man's soul and body." The accent on spiritual supremacy should necessarily absolve Berdyaev of all suspicion of individualism.

Further, his teaching finds justification also in the Scripture. Of course, the Old and New Testaments alike repeatedly insist on the idea that man is a sinner. And so he is. But then he equally reflects the image of God. Of the two terms determining the source of human inner polarity, namely, "the Image of God" and "the Fall," the living reality and final truth can be attributed to the former alone. John's story of Jesus and the adulteress affords an excellent illustration of the case in point. The Master is depicted as facing a woman taken in adultery, dragged before him as a guilty sinner, indicted by the law of Moses, and condemned to death by stoning. But when her accusers dissolved and left Christ alone with her, he directed his appeal not to her sinfulness, but to something deeper, something the crowd of Pharisees, blinded by the jurisprudential awareness of sin, could not see—the image of God in her. "Jesus looked up and said to her, 'Woman, where are they? Has no one condemned you?' She said, 'No one, Lord.' And Jesus said, 'Neither do I condemn you; go, and do not sin again.'"

This particular instance is in no way exceptional. The New Testament repeatedly indicates a high estimate of man. Certainly, men are foolish and wicked. And yet, the ultimate truth about man penetrates deeper than his sinfulness: he is first of all a son of God; fallen, but not rejected; wounded by the fall, but not depraved. Paul wrote to the Thessalonians: "You are all sons of light"; to the Galatians: "Because you are sons, God has sent the Spirit of his Son into our hearts"; to the Corinthians: "We are the temple of the living God"; to the Romans: "It is the Spirit himself bearing witness with our spirit that we are children of God". To Paul's insight into human nature the writer of the First Letter of John adds his own testimony: "We are God's children now; it does not yet appear what we shall be."

It should be noted, however, that the evangelical stress on Godlike dignity and worth of man is not laid upon him as an independent creature. He is of a supreme value only when viewed in the light of Christ. Such is

also Berdyaev's anthropology. It is in Christ and through Christ, he affirms, that the wound caused by the Fall is healed, that the sins are forgiven, and redemption achieved. "Man cannot forgive himself his sins," he writes, "he is unable to forget his evil past. But Christ has taken upon Himself the sins of the world, and He can take away our sin and forgive it. It is only in and through Christ that the past can be forgiven and forgotten." The redeemed man is a free and transformed man whom God illuminates from within and inducts into the divine life. Whereupon man achieves his creative ascent. The conclusion of the matter is that Berdyaev's emphatic anthropodicy or defence of the infinite value of man is both scriptural and Christian.

3) *God-Man.* . . . [The] concept God-Manhood, as incarnated in Jesus Christ, the Son of God and the Son of Man, summarizes the quintessence of Berdyaev's thought. Berdyaev is incontestably one of the most Christ-centered philosophers. Indeed, his very emphasis on man's freedom points inescapably in the direction of Christ. "Freedom has brought me to Christ," he writes, "and I know of no other path leading to Him." What has been said about Spinoza may *mutatis mutandis* be equally applied to Berdyaev: he was a Christ intoxicated Christian. His too loudly heralded anthropomorphism is actually a Christomorphism. Indeed, Christ, as Fielding Clarke rightly observes, constitutes the "inner consistency" of Berdyaev's thought. In the British commentator's words,

> Of Berdyaev it may be said that he is the most literally Christian of all Christian thinkers, for Christianity did not start as a philosophy but as the 'Way.' It begins in a meeting with Christ, the God-Man, and everything—theology, prayer, sacraments, the Church, the life and witness of Christians in the world spring out of this meeting. . . .

[To] Berdyaev Christ is the fullest and most concrete expression of the fundamental and dramatic mutual relatedness of God and man. He is the fulfillment of the I-Thou human-divine encounter. In Christ not only God reveals Himself to man, but man also is revealed to God. Through Christ man is recognized as divine, and God as human. The presence of the divine in man is disclosed in God's image in him and in his capacity for love and creativity. The appearance of the human in God is displayed in His need for man, for man's love and response.

Compared with traditional Christologies of rational theology Berdyaev's comprehension of Christ might seem exceedingly bold and almost irreverent. Does it not obliterate the distinction between the creature and the Creator? Does it not place both of them on the same level of necessity and impotence? Do not they emerge as eternal victims of the meonic freedom? There is some confusion here, so much so that, as was previously noted, Berdyaev makes a double assertion which is logically contradictory. On the one hand, he construes mankind in terms of the Second Person of the Trinity, and on the other, he affirms that God created man out of the meonic stuff. Accordingly, it is not clear whether, besides God-the-Creator, Christ reveals God-the-Son or the fallen meonic humanity, or both. If the first is true, then how is it possible for Christ to reveal the fallen nature of man, since obviously the Second Person of the Trinity cannot be conceived in terms of the Fall. If the second is correct, then again it is not easy to see the sinless Christ (and Berdyaev accepts Him as such) disclosing the sinfulness of human nature. Finally, if the third supposition is true, the question still remains unanswered concerning the reciprocal relation within Christ of the two natures, not human and divine, but fallen and unfallen.

The above mentioned objections, correct as they may be from the logical standpoint, are, however, scarcely applicable to Berdyaev's picture of Christ. In fact, he would reject them as just so many instances of rational objectification incapable of seizing the truth of a religious experience. To him the term God-man does not at all designate an intellectual concept. It is a myth, that is, a verbal description, necessarily inadequate, of the primordial divine-human mystery as he apprehends it in the depth of his spirit. Berdyaev's idea of God-manhood stands closer to the Eastern Orthodox than to Roman Catholic and Protestant traditions, although it is not alien to the West. Eckhart, Tauler, and Silesius commonly expressed it. But it was Vladimir Solovyev who, the first, developed it systematically. Difficult as it may appear to the rank-and-file of Christians, the whole idea affords, however, spiritual justification. The Bible continuously discloses God's need of man. God needs man for the realization of His purposes. If He is active in nature, yet more so is He within human souls and hearts.

Berdyaev's doctrine of God-Man actually drives home the simple and fundamental truth of the centrality of Christ—the God-Man—in history and the personal destiny of man. He is the great Liberator. He Himself threw light upon the nature of His earthly mission by deliberately quoting Isaiah at the threshold of His ministry: "The Spirit of the Lord is upon me," Christ declared in His first recorded sermon, "because he has anointed me. . . . He has sent me to proclaim *release* to the captives . . . to set at *liberty* those who are oppressed." At the close of His ministry the message was the same: "So if the Son makes you *free,* you will be *free* indeed."

Christ sets man free from the slavery of sin; and there is no sin which He cannot wipe out and forgive. He liberates the human being from slavery to himself—to his passions, pride, and egotism; from slavery to nature, its necessity and determinism; from slavery to society, its pretense for primacy and dominion; and from slavery to life's evils, suffering, and futility. But most of all, Christ's freedom raises man to the glory of inner rebirth and spiritual transformation. This represents the highest human-divine achievement in man whereby, in Paul's words, "it is no longer I who live, but Christ who lives in me."

It is in the light of man transformed through Christ into a new creature that Berdyaev's view on the Church should also be considered. He is right in affirming that the Kingdom of God is not, and never can be, associated with the existence of any particular church, not even with all the churches combined. The true Christian Church is the invisible *koinonia* of those who live in Christ and in whom Christ lives. Her scope is ecumenical for she cuts across all national and racial barriers to reach with her saving touch of grace every human being under the sun. Her purpose is cosmic for, beyond the salvation of the individual believer, she tends to the transformation of society and the world as a whole. Her distinctive quality, when fully manifested, is *sobornost,* that is, a divinely enlightened spiritual communion wherein the entire creation—animate and inanimate—is brought under the light of Christ "in whom all things hold together."

4) *Ethics*. Berdyaev's moral teaching stems directly from the substance of his existential philosophy: Man, God, and Freedom. It is, in my estimation, the finest attainment of his thought. Moreover, it is rooted in the Christian experience and justified by the Holy Writ. The ethics of law is directed toward the dualism between good and evil and the moral destitution of the sinful state of man. In the fallen world of vindictiveness, tyranny, greed, lust, and envy; of interminable conflicts between values and tragic contradictions in life, the law is necessary. Although it is oppressive, it is also protective. It restrains unruly instincts, controls offensive behavior, and creates social order. Without external compulsion and legalistic norms no social life could be possible. Lawlessness would inevitably spell license and anarchy. It was with this insight in mind that Paul admonished the Christians in Rome to make certain each of them remains a loyal "subject to the governing authorities. . . . For rulers are not a terror to good conduct, but to bad." The Christians, therefore, are not despisers of law, but its respecters. They realize the importance of the normative function of the state and act in accordance with the rules and regulations of their respective lawful government.

It is obvious, however, that large areas of human experience in virtue of their very nature are amenable to no juridical compulsion. Intellectual and emotional life, for instance, are barely affected by law. The fear of prison can prevent me from stealing or murdering, but not from brooding over ill thoughts. No law is ever capable of wiping out my past, forgiving my sins, or making me good and just. Law is powerless to change my inner mental and spiritual condition. Moreover, the ethics of Law, as Berdyaev accurately underlines, assumes rather a negative character. The "do not" provides no automatic clue to what I positively should do. Life issues are far from being always as clear and defined as black versus white. My moral problems are not necessarily confined to the telling of right from wrong. There are circumstances in life far more complex and troublesome which involve my choice, not between an act distinctly good and one manifestly bad, but between two acts each of which is either bad or good.

In other words, to achieve insight, wisdom, and purity which make for a wholesome personality; to convert pride and egocentricity into humility and theocentricity which alone characterize the unfallen state of man; and finally to receive the forgiveness of my sins and a spiritual rebirth I need not the law, but a redeemer. Berdyaev's ethics of redemption comes straight from the pages of the Gospel. In a language burning with faith in Christ, the great Orthodox Christian preaches the reconciliation of man to God wrought in the Revelation, the liberation from sin, the acquisition of new power through the Redeemer, the victory of hope, faith, and love over despair, darkness, and pain. Time and again he directs our attention to the abiding truth that we are the Sons of God, not of Satan; of spirit, not of matter, meant for fellowship and life with our Creator. Accordingly, he invites us to affirm each man in God and focus our love, not on an abstract, non-existent humanity, but on each concrete, living human being. In the light of Christ all men are brothers; toward that light they are all called. In it also is disclosed the infinite love of God for His estranged children, and His suffering awaiting of their return. "For God so loved the world that he gave his only Son, that whoever believes in him should not perish but have eternal life."

Redemption, however, is not God's final end for man. Its positive significance consists in creativity. Man is redeemed from sin and the law in order to create. It has already been noted that the New Testament repeatedly insists on man's creative vocation. Berdyaev's summoning the world to creativity, particularly in the moral sphere, is moving and inspiring. Creativity, he rightly reminds us, penetrates deeper than the distinction between evil and good; even deeper than the obligation to struggle against evil and promote the good; actually it signifies the transformation of evil into good. Is not this the idea Paul wanted to convey when he wrote: "Do not be overcome by evil, but overcome evil with good"? The Kingdom of God is precisely life regenerated in which there is left no trace of evil, because, through man's moral creativity, and with the grace of Christ, it was overcome and turned into good.

Berdyaev's teaching of universal salvation is the logical development of the doctrine of cosmic transfiguration. It admits of Christ's final victory over all aspects of Antichrist. It testifies that the Kingdom of God—the realm of love, goodness, and righteousness—will eventually be established. Hence, naturally, Berdyaev repudiates the concept of eternal hell. "If hell is eternal," he exclaims, "then I am an atheist." This viewpoint stands in rather sharp contrast to the one traditionally held by the majority of the Christian divines whether Catholic, Orthodox, or Protestant. All three denominations admit the existence of external torments of hell along with eternal bliss of heaven. On whose side is the truth?

The point in question, of course, is to know which of the two sides is actually borne out by scriptural justification. A critical examination of the New Testament seems at first to indicate that Christ believed and taught that the doom of the finally impenitent will be eternal. In effect, He frequently warned His hearers against the danger of incurring final reprobation. He also spoke of the "eternal fire" into which the hardened sinners will be thrown. Yet a closer scrutiny of Jesus' figurative sayings discloses no sufficient evidence to support the belief in eternal damnation. Many of these passages, if not arbitrarily taken out of context, must as Schleiermacher justly suggests, "allude to some earlier event." Others are couched in the conditional tense which seems to cast doubt as to the eventual realization of the possibility of irremediable doom. Others again, intimate universalism. Consider the following: "[God] desires all men to be saved and to come to the knowledge of truth." "[God] is the Savior of all men, especially of those who believe." "For the Son of man came to save the lost." He is "indeed the Savior of the world." He was sent by the Father "not to condemn the world, but that the world might be saved through him." Thus the scriptural conclusion on the matter appears more likely on the side of Berdyaev than on that of Augustine, Luther, and Calvin. "The New Testament references," writes Schleiermacher in the vein of Berdyaev's thought, "forbid us to think of the definitive victory of evil over one part of the human race, and from which we must rather infer that before the general resurrection evil will have been completely overcome." In the end, then, all creation will be gathered with its creator, and God will be "everything to every one."

Not only Scripture, but human consciousness at its best also seems to issue no warrant for the doctrine of everlasting hellfire: an endless suffering is deeply felt as unjust whatever men may have done. Even the human law punishes the offender, primarily not from the motive of retribution or self-protection, but with a view toward his reformation. There is hope of making him again a useful member of society such as he was before the offense. An endless punishment in hell would defeat its own purpose. It would rob the sinner from benefiting by the punishment and turning his evil ways into steps leading to God. But the truth is different. The Shepherd never abandons his flock. On the contrary, he is always out in the search for the lost sheep, and when he finds it, "he rejoices over it more than over the ninety-nine that never went astray."

Berdyaev's radiant vision of universal salvation is unfortunately blurred with vexatious inconsistencies. His affirmation that man does not possess immortality as an endowment, but that he must win it appears to contradict his idea of the pre-existence of the spirit. On the other hand, the annihilation of the self which he conceives to be the alternative to salvation is both opposed to universality and scarcely more ethical than eternal hell. In the first case, salvation precludes all concept of universality as long as there are spirits who disintegrate into nothingness; in the second, the final determination either of eternal life or of eternal death, within the framework of a man's three score and ten odd years of blunders and mistakes, without any chance for a new start, looms as fantastic and immoral as the idea of the everlasting punishment itself. Finally, Berdyaev seems to speak of resurrection as well as immortality. Although he formulates the former in terms of Paul's spiritual, not fleshly, body, yet it does not appear wholly consistent with the latter. Is the spiritual body formed immediately after death? If so what happens to it before the resurrection? Is it raised on the eve of the judgment day? But then its status meanwhile is likely to resemble one of total annihilation. Can anything be resurrected out of nothing? Despite the above mentioned discrepancies one is left, after a long and assiduous study of Berdyaev's thought, with the impression of his believing that negative assumptions will never reach fulfillment. He remains to the last confident in the destiny of man and in the final human-divine encounter. Indeed, Berdyaev is a metaphysical optimist.

5) *Philosophy of History.* Berdyaev's understanding of history preserves to a striking degree a biblical flavor, though not quite as it is commonly accepted. His basic conviction that "nothing seems to succeed in history and yet all things are significant in it," is strongly supported by scriptural references. History acquires significance on account of God's active presence within it. He created the world, in the first place, which also means that history was intended by Him for a purpose; He must therefore attach a deep interest to the historical happenings whereby the destiny of the world is carried out. Hence "all things are significant in it." The Hebrew Psalmist expressed the same conviction when he uttered that "the earth is the Lord's and the fullness thereof, the world and those who dwell therein." But the world is also a fallen world. Within the framework of its objectified, unredeemed state it has no permanent stability. Everything in it is of necessity inconstant, fleeting, forever unachieved. It is, as the same Psalmist noted, "founded upon the seas, and established upon the rivers." Such a floating world cannot have solid foundations in time. For this reason "nothing seems to succeed in history."

No wonder, then, that Berdyaev's sense of history should engender a twofold experience: "the experience of history's hostile and alien character and of my implication in it." The early Christians felt very much in like manner. They were, in John's words, "not of the world," but only "out of the world." Yet they were also aware of their high calling as "ambassadors for Christ" appointed to go into the world "and make disciples of all nations." What resolves the tragic polarity of history is, as Berdyaev saw it in the light of the Gospel, that history has an end. This is also what imparts the supreme meaning to the historical process. The Kingdom of God, then, cannot be attained in the world of time and history. It can be realized only beyond time in the eternal order of the spirit.

Berdyaev's eschatology, however, has no relation with any sort of apocalypticism. The establishment of the Kingdom is not a unilateral proposition—from God to man—but rather a human-divine achievement. As Spinka justly comments, "this is the creative, dynamic understanding of Christian eschatology. A passive expectation of the end is more likely to bring about God's terrible judgment than the Kingdom of God." Actually, according to Berdyaev, there is a foretaste of the Kingdom in every present creative act. "Every moral act of love, of mercy, and of sacrifice brings to pass the end of the world where hatred, cruelty, and selfishness reign supreme. Every creative act entails . . . the promise of a new, an 'other' world, where God's power is revealed in freedom and in love." This is the language of the Christian faith.

Nobody more than Berdyaev himself was conscious of the logical inconsistencies of his thought. To explain these he pointed out that,

> The inconsistencies and contradictions which are to be found in my thought are expressions of spiritual conflict, of contradictions which lie at the very heart of existence itself, and are not to be disguised by a façade of logical unity. True integrality of thought, which is bound up with integrality of personality, is an existential, not a logical, unity. . . . The philosopher is guilty of treason if the basic themes of his philosophical thinking are altered, the fundamental *motifs* of his thought, the groundwork of his scale of values. One can change one's view about where and how freedom of the spirit is realized. But if love of freedom is replaced by love of servitude and violence, then treason is the result.

Berdyaev preferred to remain faithful to his intuitions rather than to logical coherence. He made no attempt to formulate a system of philosophy. In fact, he was just the opposite of a systematic philosopher. "My vocation," he acknowledged, "is to proclaim not a doctrine but a vision." Yet this vision in its entirety is less affected with logical error than many another systematic exposition. His philosophy is all of one piece. Its main themes—God, man, Christ, objectification, freedom, creativity, eschatological solution of the dualism of the noumenal and phenomenal worlds—preserve a remarkable internal coherence. Each of these themes postulates the next one and, in turn, can be deduced from it. Put together they form a harmonious whole—a whole which gives expression to one of the deepest and most majestic spiritual experiences of the divine, and in which faith borrows the language of philosophy, and philosophy becomes an act of faith.

Matthew Spinka (essay date 1962)

SOURCE: "Nicolas Berdyaev, the Philosopher of Personalism," in *Christian Thought from Erasmus to Berdyaev,* Prentice-Hall, Inc., 1962, pp. 214-24.

[*In the following essay, Spinka traces Berdyaev's development as a thinker.*]

Among those who repudiate our secularist civilization most consistently, comprehensively, and vehemently is the Russian religious philosopher, Nicolas A. Berdyaev. Since his acceptance of the Christian world-view he had been a man in revolt against a world in revolt against God. Having rejected God, our era is now in the process of repudiating man, as far as his spiritual nature is concerned. This is seen in such movements as fascism and communism; for having rejected God, we are now renouncing man.

Berdyaev was born in Kiev of an old aristocratic family, and although in opposition to it, he retained the best features of his aristocratic upbringing throughout his life. His father, a retired officer in the Cavalier Guard, placed him in the Pages' Corpus. But soldiering was not Nicolas' chosen career; he was a serious, studious youth, eager to learn the meaning of life. Thus philosophy was his most congenial study. After graduating from the military school, he entered Kiev University. Previously, he had read philosophy "on his own." At fourteen he had already read Kant, Schopenhauer, and Hegel. He bears witness to the potent influence exerted on him during his later life by the biblical prophets, Job, the Greek tragedies, Cervantes, Shakespeare, Goethe, Byron, Dickens, Balzac, Ibsen, Dostoevsky, Tolstoy and Tyutchev. At the University he fell under the spell of Marx and played a prominent part as leader of the student Marxist circle. He was consequently expelled from the University and exiled for three years to the Vologda province, although during the last year he was allowed to reside at Zhitomir. But he affirms that he never was an orthodox Marxist, nor a materialist or a positivist. He writes in his spiritual autobiography:

> During a certain period of my life I have been an atheist, if one understands by that term an anti-theist, the rejection of the traditional religious notions about God. But I have not been an atheist, if by that term one understands the rejection of the supreme spiritual principle of spiritual values independent of the material world. I have not been a pantheist.

But the deterministic, anti-humanist character of orthodox Marxism, the doctrinaire denial of the ethical nature of man, soon compelled Berdyaev to part company with his fellow-revolutionaries. He had learned from Kant that the highest value in the world is the human personality, and this conviction remained fundamental to his creed throughout his whole life. He had supposed in joining the Marxist circle that the new revolutionary gospel was humanistic. But a closer acquaintance with the movement convinced him of the contrary; he saw with grief that among the Marxists there was no more respect for personality than among the bourgeoisie. It was this that caused him to break with the revolutionaries and gradually turn to, and accept, the essentially

Christian interpretation of the meaning of human existence. Dostoevsky's influence contributed mightily to this change, particularly his concept of Christianity as depicted in "The Grand Inquisitor," to which Berdyaev never tires of referring. Nevertheless, he insists in his autobiography that he never experienced a "conversion" as that occurrence is commonly understood: "I did not experience the crisis of conversion perhaps for the reason that my spiritual life consists of crises." His religious goals have been twofold: "the search for meaning and the search for eternity. The search for meaning was my first search for God, while the search for eternity was my first search for salvation." ". . . I am more a *homo mysticus* than a *homo religious.*" Nevertheless, he remained all his life opposed to the "official" Orthodoxy of the Russian Church, at times even violently criticizing it:

> I never pretended that my religious thought had a churchly character. I sought the truth and experienced as truth that which was revealed to me. The historic Orthodoxy has appeared to me insufficiently ecumenical and limited, almost sectarian. I am not a heretic [he had been so accused] and least of all a sectarian; I am a believing free-thinker.

During the First World War he published an article severely denouncing the Holy Governing Synod. He was to be tried in court as a "blasphemer"—a crime punishable by permanent exile to Siberia. But the trial was postponed on account of the War and was never resumed. Because of his individualist interpretation of Christianity, he is not to be regarded as a typical representative of Russian Orthodoxy. That purpose could be served far better by Father Sergius Bulgakov, who likewise had passed from Marxism to Christianity, but became a priest and in the end—as dean of the Orthodox Academy in Paris—the outstanding theologian of his Church. Berdyaev at best represents the free, lay character of Russian religious thought.

When the First World War broke out, and particularly after the victory of the Bolshevik Revolution in October of 1917, Berdyaev found himself violently opposed to the new regime. In a book written during that time, but not published until later when he was already abroad, Berdyaev savagely denounced the secularist and atheistic intellectuals of Russia for the "treason" they had committed against the Russian people that revenged itself upon them in such a ghastly fashion in the Revolution. But he likewise condemned the Revolution. And although he was appointed by the faculty of the University of Moscow to the chair of philosophy, a man of his convictions could not long retain the post. He was twice arrested and jailed, and finally in 1922 was expelled from Russia along with seventy like-minded members of the intelligentsia. At first, he lived in Berlin, but two years later he moved to Paris, where he remained the rest of his life. The books he wrote during this period of exile brought him to the attention of the world. But, as he has recorded in his spiritual autobiography, "I am not satisfied with any of the books I have written, or any word I have spoken."

Berdyaev is the philosopher of freedom *par excellence.* As a Kantian, he learned from his master that human personality is of the highest value, and he spent a lifetime elaborating that thesis. Dostoevsky taught him the religious significance of spiritual freedom, a lesson Berdyaev enforced in all his books. But before he was able to affirm and expound his own religious convictions, he had to establish them philosophically. For he was a religious philosopher, not a theologian. In his estimation, most modern philosophy since Kant has been anti-religious—particularly that of Marx and Nietzsche. They denied the authentic personality of man—Berdyaev's cardinal tenet. Consequently, he repudiated them.

For a long time he also struggled with Kantian epistemology, which had dug an impassable gulf between the phenomenal and the noumenal worlds. But in the end he returned to his first love, Kant, and placed him, along with Plato, on the highest pinnacle of philosophical fame. For Kant as a dualist affirmed the existence of the noumenal, as well as the phenomenal, world, thus placing the spiritual world upon a sure and certain foundation. And although Kant himself did not successfully blaze a path to the apprehension of the spiritual world, he prepared the way for others to do so. Berdyaev writes of him: "Among the philosophers Kant possesses the greatest significance. The philosophy of Kant is philosophy of freedom."

Berdyaev is one of those who, following in the footsteps of Kant, blazed a path to the spiritual realm by his Christian personalism, or existentialism. He defines the latter as ". . . the knowledge of the human existence and the knowledge of the world through the human existence." He classified himself as belonging to that type of philosophy which is nowadays called "existential" (not that of Heidegger and Jaspers, but of Augustine, Pascal, Kierkegaard and Nietzsche). "The principal characteristic of my philosophical type consists above all in *having placed at the basis of philosophy not being, but freedom.* Not one other philosopher has done that, it seems, in such a radical form." For him, then, personality, the existent subject, is primary, while being, the ontological object, is secondary. Being denotes matter, existence stands for the spiritual entities. Accordingly, "existence is not essence, is not substance; it is a free act." He therefore inverts the Cartesian dictum, "I think, therefore I am," and asserts instead, "I am, therefore I think." Thought cannot exist by itself, in isolation, any more than the grin of the Cheshire cat can persist "on the vacant air," after the cat has disappeared. Thought necessarily presupposes a thinker. Reality does not exist before the perceiving subject but after it. Only the existential subject is real and free; the object is contingent and determined. Consequently, the identification of the "objective" with the "real" as made in "scientific" thinking, is an error. Scientific knowledge deals exclusively with objects, things; as such it is eminently justified within its own proper limits, and even is immensely beneficial and useful. But there are no meanings in objects; therefore, science cannot find or yield any meanings, whether positive or negative. Nor is there meaning in any mechanical contrivance, no matter how ingenious, save the function which its designer built into it. Meanings are created solely by persons, by subjects capable of a purposeful action; hence, meanings are subjective, not objective. Accordingly, apart from the reality of the spirit or of persons, there exist no meanings.

As a deduction from this radical form of his existentialist philosophy, which affirms the subject as the only real existent, Berdyaev chose the concept of objectification for his special emphasis.

> I do not believe in the solidity and durability of the so-called 'objective' world, [he writes], the world of nature and history. Objective reality does not exist, it is only an illusion of apprehension; only the objectification of reality exists which is born of a certain direction of the spirit.

> In the last years I have formulated that problem [subject-object relationship] as an estrangement, by the process of objectification, of the solely real subjective world. The objective world is the product of objectification, it is a fallen, shattered, and fettered world. . . . Reality for me is not at all identical with being and even less with objectivity. The subjective and personalist world is the only genuinely real one.

Stated as simply as possible, objectification means converting a subject—a spiritual entity, into an object—a thing or a commodity. The commonest and the most reprehensible of such cases is that of treating a man as a thing—an inveterate and almost instinctive practice in family, social, industrial, and national relations. When one spouse regards the other as a convenience, the value of which consists primarily in the use he or she may be made of; when in society human beings are looked upon primarily as laborers or professionals or judged by the size of their bank account; when industry looks upon employees as mere "hands," a commodity to be hired for the sake of profitable production of goods; when a political ruling system uses men as means to power, as cannon fodder for the purpose of imperialistic expansion; "in short, wherever man is used as a means rather than an end, objectification takes place."

Accordingly, all present-day civilization, since it represents man's creation, is thus "objectified," for in it men deal with one another not in the personal "I-Thou," but the impersonal "I-It" relationship (to use Martin Buber's phrase).

> The spirit in culture, religion, morals, science, art, and law is the objective spirit. . . . The objectified culture . . . is as indifferent and harsh toward human personality, as lacking in perception

of the inward existence, as is history and all the rest of the objectified world. . . . Thus making an idol of culture is as inadmissible as is its barbaric rejection. It is necessary to accept and endure the tragic conflict. . . . It is necessary to accept history, to accept culture, to accept that fearsome, tortuous, fallen world. But the last word does not belong to this objectification. That word is spoken by another order of existence. The objective world will be extinguished in eternity—eternity enriched by the experienced tragedy.

The results of objectification are destructive of human personality, dehumanizing. Any genuinely personal communion on that basis is impossible. Consequently, social relations assume a lower, impersonal level, because community is not possible without communion.

This leads to Berdyaev's concept of human personality, which he regards as of the greatest value. He asserts that he accepted Christianity because he found in it a much more firm ground for his faith in man's supreme destiny than anywhere else. Man partakes of both the bodymind organism and of the spirit. Thus he is a microcosm, the meeting point of two disparate elements, but comprising a unitary being. Since our natural and social scientists and psychologists by and large ignore or deny the spiritual nature of man, this failure of theirs constitutes the greatest danger to our culture, which thus becomes depersonalized. But Berdyaev vehemently protests against it by insisting that man is both a body-soul organism and spirit, both an object and a subject. In so far as he is the body-soul entity, he is an object in bondage to the laws governing all matter. Within this physical realm he is determined and therefore unfree. He may, and often does, live predominantly in this realm—in the Pauline phrase, he is of the flesh. Berdyaev's term for such a man is that he is an individual, but not a person. Only as man develops his spiritual nature and makes it the dominant element in his life does he become a person. He writes:

> Personality is not the same thing as the individual. An individual belongs to the natural, biological category. Not only the animal and the plant, but also the diamond, the glass, the pencil are of this category. Personality, however, belongs to the spiritual, not the natural, category. . . . It is a break-through of the spirit into nature. Personality is not attained without an effort of the spirit over the psychical and physical nature of man. A man may have a brilliant individuality without being a person.

This for Berdyaev is no mere theoretical datum. For him as an existentialist it is of immense personal concern. It is not a matter of indifference whether or not a man is a person. It is his duty; if he is a slave to anything, whether external or inward, he has failed in the supreme task of life.

But how does an individual attain the status of a person? Or in Christian terms, how is man saved from his "fallen" condition, in which he is alienated from God by his own self-assertion—the original sin (an act which Berdyaev places in the pre-existent realm)? By God's grace, man can be saved; for despite his "fall," he still possesses free will. His destiny is bound up with the freedom of choice which is within his power. For God has provided in Jesus Christ a way of redemption. The unique doctrine of Incarnation reveals the divine plan of salvation of all mankind, if mankind chooses to accept it. For Christ is not only the supreme revelation of what God is, but also of what man may and ought to be. God the Word became man, the Godman. Thus "God was in Christ, reconciling the world unto Himself." Man, too, may experience a basic transformation of his "fallen" nature into that of the son of God. Berdyaev speaks of this spiritual transformation as theanthropy, the attainment of the divine-human personality, which in his estimation is the only proper concept of personality. In this he follows the ancient Eastern Christian tradition (formulated principally by Irenaeus that "the Logos of God, our Lord Jesus Christ, who, on account of his great love became what we are that he might make us what he is himself"), but uses the more modest and more accurate term, the "divine-human." The result of redemption is the freedom of the sons of God: "Man ought to be free, he dares not be a slave, for he ought to be man. Such is the will of God."

Since man is a free spirit, capable of apprehending God's revelation of Himself, Berdyaev asserts the necessity of such a revelation. It takes many forms, but it is always a spiritual experience. The Father reveals Himself in nature, but were we to depend on this revelation alone, our knowledge of God would certainly be inadequate and even erroneous. One may see this result in the recent "naturalistic theology." It is only in the Son that the deepest spiritual levels of divine revelation are reached. But in the end, only when the human spirit meets the Divine Spirit in an existential encounter is there an immediate, intuitive apprehension of God. This is the work of the Holy Spirit. For Berdyaev, such an experience is the only adequate "proof" of the existence of God; hence, along with Kant, he rejects the traditional ontological "proofs" such as those of Thomas Aquinas. "God is not Being and the categories of being are not applicable to Him, but belong ever to thought. He exists—is the Existent—and one can think of Him only existentially and symbolically." God is never an object, but a subject.

> Our knowledge of God is, therefore, basically intuitive, subjective, experiential, or, if you will not blanch at the word, mystical. It is neither exclusively intellectual, emotional, volitional, nor intuitional, but rather integral, combining all these four together with the indefinable additional element which results from this integral approach.

But just because man is a free ethical agent he is capable not only of responding voluntarily to God's love, but also of repudiating it, rebelling against it and falling away from God. This results in his misery and suffering. God does not inflict it; man causes it to himself. Striving to affirm himself, to become man-god, he destroys himself, often involving others in his ruin. Hence, society is involved in destruction brought upon itself by its own choices. Modern secularism denies the spiritual nature of man and thus depersonalizes him. Berdyaev sees in this our supreme danger; he describes the results of the process as follows:

> The living sources of creation, both human and superhuman, dry up; the aim and object of creation, which are also superhuman, disappear; and the result is man's complete disintegration. For, when man follows the path of self-affirmation, ceases to respect the higher principle and asserts his self-sufficiency, he exterminates and denies his true self according to the laws of an inexorable dialectic. . . . he becomes the slave of the baser processes, disintegrating with the elements of his own nature and becoming the victim of the artificial nature of the machine he has conjured up into life, and these de-personalize, weaken, and finally annihilate him.

The Christian ethic of redemption is contrary to the worldly standards of value. For it, man as a spiritual being, and not a high standard of living and of economic well being, is of the highest value. "Man shall not live by bread alone," even though it is of concern to Christians that mankind lack not bread. The aim of the Christian ethic is the renewal of the spiritual mainsprings of human personality—the spiritual transformation of men and women. A civilization is Christian only to the degree to which it subserves this aim. For there can be no good society without good men and women. All improvements—technological, political, economic, or cultural—if they exclude this kind of basic transformation, are superficial and wholly inadequate.

This, then, is the primary and paramount task of the Christian Church—the transformation of human motivation by subjecting it to the will of God. It cannot be effected forcibly, for the life of the spirit is the life of freedom. God compels no one, forces no one; but to reject Him is to choose evil and its consequent suffering. To charge Christianity with failure to impose salvation upon society after the pattern of the "Grand Inquisitor," or of communism, is to misunderstand the Christian redemptive ethic completely. The "failure of Christianity" is chargeable only to the failure of Christians.

Because the method of Christianity is solely that of persuasion by word and life, the demand for an imminent transformation of the world is a symptom of misunderstanding of its character. Such a demand rests either on a mistaken notion of the apocalyptic hope or, more commonly, on the identification of Christianity with the secularist "progress." Thus the radical doctrine of Berdyaev that man "has a right to hell, as it were," has a direct bearing on his view of history. Berdyaev is not a historian in the accepted professional sense of the

word; rather he is a philosopher of history, concerned with discerning its meaning. In the first place, then, he affirms that history can have no meaning except on a religious basis; to him, history is a process wherein the human drama of redemption from sin is played, is a return of the fallen man to God. He thus recurs to Origen's conception of history even to the extent of affirming the pre-existent phase in which both Origen and Berdyaev have placed the "fall" of man. The central point of history, conceived as a redemptive process of the fallen man, is the coming of Christ. Historically, it had been the principal task of the Christian Church to witness to the fact of the Incarnation of the Word and the consequent possibility of the theandric transformation of man. But unfortunately, the Church had on the whole been unfaithful to its task and had compromised with the world; the Western Church became a papal caesarism while the Byzantine Church became caesaro-papism. In the modern era it has not sufficiently withstood the corroding influence of secularism.

Furthermore, history has meaning because it tends toward a God-appointed goal. Berdyaev thus not only rejects Nietzsche's notion of the "eternal recurrence," but even more vehemently repudiates the secularist concept of automatic and inevitable "progress." No such mechanical concept can have authentic meaning, because it lacks true teleology—an end toward which it aims. Such "progress' is not going anywhere; therefore, it is essentially meaningless. Men cannot determine the cosmic goal, since they themselves are the product of, and determined by, the cosmic forces. For all mechanical forces as conceived by the natural sciences are determined by natural laws and therefore purposeless. Only God can purpose an end and thus impart meaning to history; for this end will be triumph of meaning. Thus the meaningfulness of history is possible only to those who believe in God and His purpose for the world.

This eschatological faith cannot be realized within human history, within time: it extends beyond time into eternity. However, a believer in God need not await it passively, as if it were an event wholly outside and beyond the possibility of his cooperation in bringing it about. In fact, he has a duty to cooperate with God in bringing it about; for although it is an event primarily determined and wrought by God, man may contribute to its accomplishment. Since "The end of history is the end of that exteriorization and objectification, a return to inwardness," man has a part to play in it. For he can surely do his share; in fact, without such an effort on his part, "the Kingdom would be delayed."

And the ultimate goal is the Kingdom of God, when He will be all in all, and when all evil will be vanquished. "The final victory of God over the forces of Hades cannot be accomplished by the division into two kingdoms—divine and diabolic, the saved and those damned to eternal suffering—it can be attained only as one kingdom." But how that can be done without violating man's freedom Berdyaev does not say.

Robert Paul Mohan (essay date 1965)

SOURCE: "Nicholas Berdyaev, Captive of Freedom," in *Twentieth-Century Thinkers: Studies in the Work of Seventeen Modern Philosophers,* edited by John K. Ryan, Alba House, 1965, pp. 205-12.

[*In the following essay, Mohan provides an overview of Berdyaev's life and thought.*]

Reinhold Niebuhr once referred to Nicholas Berdyaev as the outstanding religious personality of our time. Evelyn Underhill and the late Goeffrey Francis Fisher, Archbishop of Canterbury, echoed this sentiment. He has also been called the "supreme Russian philosopher," passionately interested in the moods and ideas of his time. *The London Times* said that in a lifetime he had accepted and denied with equal vehemence more ideas than most men even fleetingly dream of. The *New York Times* called him the most exciting writer on contemporary religious themes. He was a man as pugnacious as Léon Bloy in his search for the Absolute, but agonizingly aware of freedom and its responsibilities, a "naysayer" to life at one moment, and boldly assertive the next; exhibiting an almost neurotic sensitivity at one time, and at another a stoic courage.

This spiritual anarchist, as he described himself, gives us a great insight into his personality in his *Dream and Reality*. He tells his autobiography is not to be a diary in the sense of André Gide's *Journal* or the confessions of Jean Jacques Rousseau and St. Augustine, but rather a philosophical autobiography of what he calls a "history of spirit and self knowledge".

There is an almost Kierkegaardian anxiety in Berdyaev—a persistent feeling of alienation and aloneness despite his constant political and social and ideological involvements. As he once phrased it: "Nothing is my own and all things are mine". He tells that as a child he was never conscious of belonging to his parents, and was repelled by family ties. Even family resemblances he considered an affront to the dignity of the individual human person.

Berdyaev was born in Kiev, the first center of Christianity in Russia, in 1874. He died an expatriate in Paris in March 1948, much to the relief of his fellow emigrés. As a twenty-year old youth Berdyaev turned to Marxism, was arrested twice in the next four years by Tsarist police, and later exiled to Vologda for two years. After the October revolution he was twice arrested by the Soviets, as by this time he had become disenchanted with Marxism, and was not hesitant in saying so. Despite his dislike of Marxism he taught at the University of Moscow, but was eventually exiled to Berlin and later moved on to Paris.

Berdyaev's family, though of Muskovite origin, belonged to the aristocracy of the southwest, and were strongly influenced by the West. French was the language of the home. His mother was a beautiful, aloof aristocrat who was never quite convinced that the Berdyaev family into which she had married was normal. His aunt owned a hundred and fifty thousand acres in Kiev, and had palaces in Warsaw, Paris, Nice, and Rome.

As a child of fourteen, the young Berdyaev was devouring Kant, Hegel, and Schopenhauer. Surprisingly enough, he attributes his religious awakening, not to the Bible, nor to the Orthodox Church, but to Schopenhauer, who also brought home to him the tragic sense of the pain of human sensitivity. From his earliest years he was deeply conscious of what was believed to be the destiny of the Russian people; he was conscious of remaining a nobleman even as he sought justice for the oppressed in revolutionary activity.

Through his childhood Berdyaev nursed resentment against the semi-feudal society of his parents, and the Church, which he felt to be a political tool. But although on occasion extremely critical of orthodoxy, Berdyaev seems to have been considerably influenced by the Orthodox Church, and affiliated himself as an expatriate only with those congregations that were linked to the Moscow patriarchate. Basic to his worship was the concept of 'sobornost', a unity born of voluntary togetherness, a common mind of the assembled faithful. His early bias against the church was probably derived from his father's free-thinking tendencies and Voltairean scepticism. It was probably to Voltaire, discovered in his father's library, that Berdyaev himself owed his lifelong interest in the philosophy of history. His studies in history led him to this conclusion that nothing seems to succeed in history, but that all things acquire their significance in it.

Berdyaev was not aware of a specific moment of conversion, although he had no great reluctance for dramatizing his many great decisions. Philosophically, Kant was a great influence in his life, and the one whom he regarded as the philosopher of freedom *par excellence*. Yet he says in the same breath, "I have never complied with *any* philosophical tradition". Even Karl Marx in his later days is said to have remarked, "I am not a Marxist." Berdyaev too, even when he saw in Marxism an articulate protest against the inequities of his world, never admitted himself to be completely a Marxist. Not only would his anarchic spirit resist the relentless restraints on human personality, but idealism was the philosophy he represented himself as embracing at this period.

This realism was not the idealism opposed to realism in the traditional philosophic sense; neither does it seem to represent any abstract metaphysics.

His *Destiny of Man* contains praise of Kant, but he rejects the Kantian noetic, and actively opposed the neo-Kantianism of the Russian intelligentsia which he felt reduced authentic Kantianism thought to a kind of ethical moralism. Kant's greatest contribution in Berdyaev's opinion was his conviction that true morality was within and not empirically arrived at.

Berdyaev's disenchantment with Marxism was by no means based on a regard for capitalism, which he considered the greater evil, and one doomed to destruction. No party or system could long interest this restless spirit who was really interested in a personalistic socialism, free of both collective and individual restraints.

Of enormous influence on Berdyaev was Dostoevsky, whose character Stavrogin, in *The Possessed,* he longed to be identified with as a young man. He loved to dramatize himself as the aristocrat of the Revolution, "the dark haired nobleman gleaming with life, and wearing the mask of cold aloofness." Dostoevsky he considered the artist of terror who gave artistic utterance to the anguish and sense of alienation which Berdyaev never completely lost. He says: "The heroes in Tolstoy's and Dostoevsky's novels were of greater importance for me than philosophical and theological schools of thought, and it was at their hands that I received Christianity." It is indeed quite questionable, as will be indicated later, how much Christianity Berdyaev actually accepted. His mystical anarchism is well-expressed in the words of Dostoevsky's Ivan Karamazov: "I accept God, but I do not accept His world."

It is perhaps to Dostoevsky that Berdyaev owes his belief in a spiritual freedom in Christianity which is free of restraint from either God or man. In his book on Dostoevsky, Berdyaev states that his turning to Christ was not a turning to the Christ of the Gospels, but to the image of Christ as contained in the story of the Grand Inquisitor.

Tolstoy's influence was perhaps less significant, although his background was more like Berdyaev's own. Tolstoy, a count, was also a member of the repentant, breast-beating aristocracy, deeply disturbed by the social irresponsibility of the landed gentry and the general pointlessness of life as he saw it.

One might concentrate on two particular aspects of Berdyaev's thought which are of more than average importance: his concept of the divine and his concept of freedom.

Reference has already been made to his independent Dostoevskian approach to the majesty of God. Berdyaev never accepted the concept of a transcendent God in the Christian sense. Berdyaev sees God not as Lord, but as Liberator from the slavery of the world.

He says:

> "It is unfortunate that Christians have come to speak or drone in the language of meek obsequiousness called humility, and to conduct themselves accordingly, for this belies the Christian conception of man as a God-like spiritual being."

Berdyaev is a believer in God because he is primarily a believer in man. His is a metaphysics of freedom not of being, for freedom is more ultimate than being itself. His God is a limited God, a God who knows needs and suffering, and who can be enriched by human creativeness. "God has need of man, of his creative response to a divine summons." Or again: "God desires a free creative daring in man."

He accepted as a motto for his book, *The Meaning of the Creative Act,* the motto from Angelus Silesius: "I know that without me God cannot exist for a single second. If I cease to be, He too, must necessarily cease to be."

God is not reached by reason but by mysticism, and the greatest of the mystics to him was Jakob Boehme from whom the rather bizarre theory of the *Ungrund* is derived. From the primordial Absolute itself God the creator comes. Freedom is not dependent on God, but externally exists in the primordial nothing out of which God creates. It is, in a sense, anterior to God himself. God is powerless over the anterior realm and is thus exonerated from responsibility for evil. As in Whitehead, creativity is strongly emphasized, but there is no theory or analogy by which meaningful parallels of human and divine creativity may be drawn. God to the degree that He is known, is known in the language of symbolism.

Lacking a theory of analogy, Berdyaev's anthropomorphism is one of concept not merely of idiom or methodology. Both the theory of freedom and his theory of the divine result from his agony of being unable to resolve the problem of evil. Berdyaev rejects categorically the idea of Providence, stating that if God is present in evil and suffering, in destruction and misery, in plague and cholera, then faith is impossible and rebellion justified. God reconciles man to the suffering of creation not because he reigns, but because he suffers. All theological attempts to resolve the problem of evil Berdyaev sees as intolerable rationalizations. Evil springs from indeterminacy which Providence itself cannot banish.

Berdyaev also expresses horror at the notion of God's seeing from all eternity the outcome of human history. Man is not merely a creature, but self-creative, and in creating self, creates deity. Hell is rejected as totally incompatible with the notion of divinity. He proclaims with much heat that if hell is a reality than he is an atheist.

Berdyaev describes himself as a seeker of truth, a rebel desirous of freedom to the bondage of life, to things, objects, abstractions, ideologies, and the fatalism of history. His search was for an anti-hierarchical personalism—and he phrases it eloquently:

> "As the result of a long spiritual and intellectual journey I have arrived at a particularly keen awareness of the fact that every human person-

ality, the personality of the least significant of men, bearing as it does within itself the image of the highest existence, cannot be a means to any end whatever."

He summarizes his views of the anti-freedom forces in his theory of objectivization. As Spengler's civilization is a sclerosed culture that has lost its creative power, so Berdyaev's objectivized man is a destroyed personality. Objectivization is defined as an operation whereby man is brought to servitude, alienation, law, hostility, impersonality, and death. Personality to him is prior to being itself, for being as conceptualized becomes an abstraction—and consequently an enslaving factor.

Personality, as essentially spiritual, exists in the world of freedom, a subjective force in the world of objects. It is not even caused by God—for this to Berdyaev would be a form of objectivization. Objectivization is impersonality, the "ejection of man into the world of determinism." It creates the sociological realities of community, state, nation, and church and imposes restrictive laws of universal obligation. Man's duty is the duty of "transcension", the by-passing of the world of objectivization to the inner core of existence which is the meeting ground with the reality of God, other people, and interior values.

The vague reality of transcension is defined by Berdyaev as an "active dynamic process", an immanent aloofness from depersonalizing society, a realm of freedom where one achieves alike, strength against catastrophe and a direct confrontation of life's supreme personal values. Transcension thus becomes the realization and fulfillment of personality as objectivization is its negation.

Personality as an "individually unrepeatable form" is forever unique as opposed to the world which emphasizes the restricting common aspect of things.

It is indeed important to note that objectivization extends not only to the material conditions of existence but to any systematized or organized rationalization—hence the existentialistic dislike for any systematic philosophy. Moreover, "the criteria of truth is found in the subject and not in the object." And again: "It is expressly in subjectivity and not in objectivity that primary reality is found."

Objectivization is most obvious in the form of society itself which imposes relationships and restrictions inimical to personality. Especially in organic theories of society is man considered a mere subjected part of a whole.

In culture too human nature is seen by Berdyaev as objectivized, exteriorized, and depersonalized. Creativity and artistic genius is inhibited by the "congested and crystallized conditions of culture."

The state is similarly a great depersonalizing agent, possessing no ontological validity other than the exteriorization of the people themselves, ever ready to encroach upon the rights of the human person.

It would be an oversimplification to see in Berdyaev's thought a simple antithesis between spiritual and natural values, since man's slavery may be to himself as well as to nature, war, nationalization, the bourgeois spirit, collectivism, eroticism, aesthetics, and even history.

Berdyaev remains something of a paradox: a philosopher who despised discursive reason; a cadet who hated the military; a fearful hypochondriac who worked calmly through revolution and bombardment; a lover of God who was never quite at home in God's world. Berdyaev was indeed a man of great religious sensibility, but though he believed that a philosophy of personality could be worked out only on a Christian basis, he was hardly a Christian in any recognizably orthodox sense of the term. A man of great insights and great prejudices, he nevertheless, as has been said, underscored and emphasized the fact of freedom when much of the world was ready to forget it.

Fuad Nucho (essay date 1967)

SOURCE: "Freedom and Necessity (The Paradox)," in *Berdyaev's Philosophy: The Existential Paradox of Freedom and Necessity,* Victor Gollancz Ltd., 1967, pp. 47-97.

[*In the following excerpt, Nucho explicates the significance of such concepts as freedom, necessity, and personality in Berdyaev's thought.*]

FREEDOM AND NECESSITY

(The Paradox)

1 A CONCEPTION OF MAN

Berdyaev's entire thinking is anthropocentric. The structure of his existential philosophy is erected on the foundation of his philosophical anthropology. His preoccupation with the problem of freedom arises out of his deep interest and personal involvement in man's predicament and destiny. Man is the chief object of his concern. At the heart of his thought lies a persistent attempt to understand what it means to be a person. Berdyaev's philosophy of freedom begins and ends with man.

> The essential and fundamental problem is the problem of man—of his knowledge, his freedom, his creativeness. Man is the key to the mystery of knowledge.

Berdyaev's philosophical anthropology is thoroughly existential. It deals with man not as a concept but as a living person. The stress on man as an existing entity often leads Berdyaev to switch suddenly to the first person singular as in the following passage:

> Man cannot be left out of knowledge . . . I, a
> man, want to know reality, and the knowledge
> which may be attained in non-human realms is
> nothing to me. I, the knower, abide in reality . . .
> I know reality in and through myself, as man.
> Only an existent can know existence.

What Berdyaev had come to know about existent man,
chiefly through firsthand experience, constitutes both
the sounding board and the springboard of his existential thinking. The very problem of freedom, the pivot of
his philosophical thought, issues out of his conception
of man, man's nature and man's destiny. For this reason, the first question that must be answered is: What is
man according to Berdyaev?

For Berdyaev, man is a complex being with a dual nature. Man belongs at one and the same time to, and is
the meeting place of, two worlds. He is both divine and
human, heavenly and earthly, the child of God and the
product of nature. Man is the point where two spheres
intersect, the place at which they meet. He belongs to
two different orders. "There is a spiritual man and there
is a natural man, and yet the same individual is both
spiritual and natural." Man is conscious of the duality of
his nature. He is aware of both his greatness and his
worthlessness. "He knows himself as the image of God
and as a drop in the ocean of the necessities of nature."

The two natures in man are constantly in a state of war,
both hot and cold, and man himself is the battleground.
Now one of these natures, now the other seems to prevail.

Berdyaev does not claim originality in what he asserts
about the duality of man's nature. "All deep thinkers
have felt this," he says. He is especially cognizant, in
this respect, of his affinity to Pascal, who "understood
that the whole of Christianity is related to this duality of
man's nature." Berdyaev echoes the familiar words of
Pascal:

> What a chimera is man! What a novelty! What a
> monster, what a contradiction, what a prodigy!
> Judge of all things, imbecile worm of the earth;
> depository of truth, a sink of uncertainty and error;
> the pride and refuse of the universe . . . know
> then, proud man, what a paradox you are to
> yourself!

When he writes:

> What a strange being—divided and of double
> meaning, having the form of a king and that of a
> slave, a being at once free and in chains, powerful
> and weak, uniting in one being glory and worth-
> lessness, the eternal with the corruptible.

The duality of man's nature is for Berdyaev the micro-
scope through which he diagnoses man's predicament,
and the telescope through which he attempts to discern
man's destiny. Obviously, this dualism in man can be
traced back to the Platonic doctrine of the two worlds,
the world of phenomena and the world of ideas, which
Berdyaev adopted in its Kantian revised version where
the world of phenomena is equated with the world of
necessity and the world of ideas or *things-in-themselves*
is identified as the world of freedom.

In Berdyaev's view of man, we also find a Neo-Platonic
flavor tempered with Boehme's mysticism. Despite his
dualism, man is nevertheless a microcosm. He is himself
a small universe and not a fractional part of it. Man and
the cosmos measure their forces against each other, as
equals.

But man is not merely a microcosm. He is also a
microtheos. This is so because "man is not only of this
world but of another world; not only of necessity, but of
freedom." Belonging to two worlds, man is, therefore,
"a self-contradictory and paradoxical being, combining
opposite poles within himself."

The thorny paradox of freedom and necessity grows out
of Berdyaev's dualistic anthropology. Because of his
dual nature, there are *two intentions* in man's "conscious mind, one which leads to the enslaving world of
objects and to the realm of necessity, the other which is
directed towards the truly existent world, the realm of
freedom."

Berdyaev's diagnosis of man's condition reveals that
man has followed the first of the two intentions, namely,
that which leads to the enslaving world of necessity.
"The human spirit," he writes, "is in prison. Prison is
what I call this world, the given world of necessity."

This is the fundamental problem which confronts Berdyaev, demanding a positive solution. Man is a prisoner
of necessity and he desperately needs to see the light
and breathe the air of freedom. Berdyaev approached
this dilemma with concern and enthusiasm. He made it
his lifework to help bring about the liberation of man
from the chains of necessity. And it is man as a living
person, man as an existent being, who needs to be set
free. In the task which Berdyaev sets for himself, he
himself is existentially involved. "My sense of uprooted-
ness and disestablishment in the world . . . is at the
heart of my whole world outlook."

What is the nature of the prison in which the human
spirit is held captive, the prison which Berdyaev calls
"this world, this given world of necessity"? The answer
to this question may be discerned by discussing the four
realms in which the paradoxical antithesis of freedom
and necessity operates: nature, society, civilization, and
history.

2 THE DETERMINISM OF NATURE

Necessity rules relentlessly in the realm of nature. Man
is a natural being and is bound by many ties to the
cosmos. He finds himself under the rule of natural necessity. His body is governed by natural processes, and

is dependent on the soil, water, air, and sunshine for its very existence. Man is both nourished and destroyed by nature. He dies and his physical body is dissolved. Natural forces kill man, if not suddenly, then slowly. Nature is an order of determinism. Its laws demand obedience and submission. Man experiences natural necessity within himself and outside himself. He has to wrestle constantly with natural necessity and the power of his mind is his chief weapon.

Berdyaev distinguishes four periods in man's relationship to nature and the cosmos. The first is that of man's submersion in cosmic life, when he was completely dependent on nature. In this primitive period, man's relation to nature was dominated by myth and magic. The second stage is characterized by man's partial liberation from the power of cosmic forces through the development of a primitive economy. Here also, he is freed from the superstitions concerning the demons in nature. In the third period, the mechanization of nature and its scientific and technical control take place. Industry is also developed and with it appears the complex problem of labor and management. Finally, there is the disruption of cosmic order in the discovery of the infinitely great and the infinitely small, the tremendous power of man over nature, and his enslavement by his own discoveries. Berdyaev foresaw a fifth period in the relationship between man and nature, when man's still greater control of nature's forces will be realized, and when man will also have control over his own technics and mechanization.

It is true, says Berdyaev, that the Renaissance witnessed a truce between man and nature. Nature was discovered, and man sought its many blessings. He became learner in its school, felt the enchantment of the outward appearance of nature, and was attracted by the joys of the natural life. It is quite true that man gave up the struggle against nature which medieval man had waged. The Renaissance was concerned with a scientific as well as with an artistic discovery of nature. But that was not all. This early truce with nature was short-lived. In order to harness and utilize nature's forces, man was forced into war with nature itself which modern man has continued to carry on through his technology. Nature is still man's enemy. It still rules with its laws of necessity. "Nature, in its fallen state," says Berdyaev, "is wholly subject to causal determination and, as such, is the figure of necessity."

It should be pointed out here that what Berdyaev means by nature is not limited to the physical universe. For him, nature has a much wider and deeper connotation. He explicitly states that by nature he does not mean "animals, plants, minerals nor stars, forests and seas." Berdyaev does not use the term nature exclusively as an antithesis to civilization or even to the supernatural, nor as the cosmos or the creation, nor even as the world of matter and space. "To me," he explains, "nature is above all the contradiction of freedom; the order of nature is to be distinguished from the order of freedom."

If nature means the antithesis of freedom, then, by the same token, it is also the antithesis of personality and spirit. "Nature, in this sense, is the world of objectification, that is to say, of alienation, determinability, impersonality." The slavery of man to nature is a slavery to that objectification, to that alienation, to that determinability. Often Berdyaev seems to use the term *nature* as equivalent to the *world* of the New Testament which is to be considered as hostile, as sinful. "This natural world is but the child of hatred and division, which in its turn engenders bondage and servitude." "The natural world, 'this world,'" he also writes, "is the servitude, the enchainment of existence."

Man's slavery to the world of things, to material necessity, is a crude form of slavery which can easily be detected. But there are other forms of man's slavery to nature, says Berdyaev, which are "more refined and less noticed." He mentions, for instance, what he calls "the lure of the cosmos." Berdyaev believes that there is in man a deep-seated desire to return to mother earth. This desire is often awakened and intensified by the overwhelming pressures of civilization and the heartaches and headaches of personal existence. Man seeks temporary relief by responding to "the lure of the cosmos." He turns to nature as a refuge from the demands of reason and the enslaving standards of civilization. Berdyaev does not mean here the occasional and recreational enjoyment of the beauty of nature. What he is referring to is the attempt to experience a fusion with cosmic life with the underlying assumption that nature itself is sacred. There are periods in history which are characterized by a return to nature as a guide and as a lost paradise. This is what the romantics of all time try to do. The outstanding figure of the French Enlightenment, Jean Jacques Rousseau (1712-78) deified nature and thought that man came from it good and pure and that he had been alienated by civilization from his true nature. This "degeneration," according to Rousseau, could be stopped and eventually overcome and man would reach a state of perfection if he were given full freedom to develop according to his natural necessity. The tendency to return to nature or to do things "according to nature" as well as the belief in the existence of a world-soul with which man may seek union may be observed in people seeking release from the demands and tensions of civilized life through exaltation of, and reliance on, such ties as those to race, soil, blood and sex.

Berdyaev rejects a teleological, a mechanical, as well as a naturalistic interpretation of the world process on the ground that they all lead to an "ideal spiritual determinism." This results in the loss of man's freedom and the enslavement of his personality. All attempts to realize freedom through fusion with cosmic life, such as those of all orgiastic cults, are founded on the belief in the possibility of "an ecstatic emergence beyond the boundaries of personal existence into the cosmic element," and on "the hope of entering into communion with this primary element." Such attempts are based on illusions and deprive man of his personality and dignity. "Fusion with cosmic life does not emancipate personality, it brings about dissolution and annihilation."

3 THE RULE OF SOCIETY

Man is not only a natural being. He is also a social being. He must, therefore, find self-realization in social life. He finds it necessary to live within a society. On society he must depend in his struggle for life against nature. Berdyaev thinks that man feels his relatedness to society even more keenly than his relation to nature.

The paradox of freedom and necessity operates in every social environment. Society both enriches and enslaves the life of man. It enriches when it seeks to establish unity among people and when the common struggle for survival and well-being is carried out by cooperative efforts. Society is a blessing to man when it is conceived as a free union of men in the spirit of brotherhood. Society contributes to man's spiritual health and promotes his freedom when it takes the form of a religious togetherness, a *sobornost,* and when it is guided by the conviction that "the final goals of man's life are not social, but spiritual."

Unfortunately, the influence of society's necessity upon man is much greater than that of its freedom. In his social relations, man often submits to the voice of necessity in society, which addresses him:

> You are my creation; everything that is best in you has been put there by me, and therefore you belong to me and you ought to give your whole self back to me.

Even in its noble objective to induce and introduce cooperation and unity, society often uses coercive and unjust means. Having within himself not merely the need for bread, the symbol of the means of human existence, but also the longing for world-wide unity, for fraternal association, man follows those who promise prosperity and security. The paradox of freedom and necessity persists in the kind of world we have, with its evil, strife, and war. "How can one combine the solution of the problem of bread for everyone," Berdyaev asks, "a problem on which human life depends, with the problem of freedom, on which human dignity depends?"

We understand the paradox of freedom and necessity in society more clearly, and begin to see our way to its solution more distinctly, when we remember that there are two ways of conceiving society and two paths that society follows. Society, according to Berdyaev, may be interpreted either as *nature* or as *spirit.* As nature, society is ordered in accordance with the laws of nature, with the rule of necessity as the guiding principle, and the struggle for eventual predominance and mastery as the primary motives, and force and compulsion as the executive means. As spirit, society rests on the principle of personality with a quest for freedom as its motivating goal and a passion for love and mercy as its basic

means. In actual experience, society is both nature and spirit. Both principles, that of necessity and that of freedom, are at work in it. But we cannot deny the obvious fact that the natural in society predominates over the spiritual, necessity over freedom, coercive objectivity over free personality, the will to power and mastery over love and mercy. The tragedy of man's predicament is partly due to this fact.

The conception of society as nature has been expressed in what might be termed organic theories and organic interpretations. The organic interpretation of society is invariably hierarchical. Society is thought of in terms of a higher personality that stands over and above the personality of the individual man, a larger personality that engulfs the individual one. Thus the primacy of society over the human personality is asserted, and man finds himself enslaved. The criterion of value is sought in the organism of society, which supposedly stands on a higher level than the human personality.

Berdyaev vehemently objects to the organic interpretation of society. He denies the existence of an organic principle for the organization of society. To claim the existence of such a principle is to give a false character of sacredness to things that are only relative. The organic in society is nothing but an illusion. As nature is partial, so is society partial. Not society, but man, is an organism. Society is an organization based on cooperation and coordination. As Berdyaev puts it, "man is the organism and society is his organ . . . The organic theory of society is a mere game in biological analogy."

It is true, Berdyaev reminds us, that within society itself there are organic formations, such as the family, the tribe, as there are mechanical formations, like the club, the labor union. Both the organic and mechanical types of formations enslave man, the former more than the latter because it often claims sacredness. Berdyaev mentions a third kind of human association within society which is spiritual in nature, namely, the church. "Only a spiritual community liberates man." Unfortunately, because "some of the aspects of this spiritual life may be expressed in social forms . . . religion tends to become a social phenomenon and the Kingdom of God a social institution."

The conflict of freedom and necessity in society arises out of the fact that man must live in a social environment, where law, order and authority are necessary, and yet his personality "can never be a part of society, because it can never be a part of anything." On the one hand, "society is an infinitely more powerful thing than the personality"; and on the other hand, "personality affirms its supreme value even in the sphere of social life." In this paradoxical situation man finds himself and it causes him much pain and suffering.

4 THE DOMINATION OF CIVILIZATION

The battle between freedom and necessity is also fought in the world made by man, the very civilization he creates for the purpose of liberating himself from natural necessity. In this man-made domain, the paradox of freedom and necessity appears in a more frightening form.

What Berdyaev means by civilization and the distinction he makes between it and culture must be borne in mind. This is important because civilization is commonly taken to mean culture as well. He stresses the fact, first of all, that "in a certain sense civilization is older and more primitive than culture, culture takes shape later. The invention of technical equipment, even of the most elementary tools by primitive man is civilization, just as civilization is the whole socializing process." According to Berdyaev, civilization is concerned with man's physical survival, while culture aims at his intellectual and spiritual development. Civilization is closer to nature and necessity, and culture is nearer to spirit and freedom.

> By civilization must be meant a process which is more social and collective, by culture, a process which is more individual and which goes deeper.
>
> Civilization indicates a higher degree of objectification and socialization, whereas culture is more closely linked with personality and spirit. Culture indicates . . . the victory of form over matter.

Man creates a civilization in order to set himself free from the forces of nature and their enslaving necessity. Civilization was initiated by the invention of primitive tools which man continued to improve and increase. The conquest of nature stimulated the cooperative effort of men and called for organization of their lives.

The most revolutionary event in the history of civilization is the emergence of a technological knowledge with the triumphant advance of the machine. The whole structure of civilization was remolded by the technological progress. Through his technical skill, man has been able to harness the forces of nature and subordinate them to his own purposes. The splitting of the atom and man's initial thrust into outer space are only the beginning of a cosmic revolution which is the fruit of modern civilization.

It would seem rather banal and quite unnecessary, says Berdyaev, to enumerate the blessings of civilization in all its various provinces. He has no quarrel with the positive aspect of our technological civilization. But he does stubbornly take issue with its negative results.

> Civilization promises to emancipate man and there can be no dispute that it provides the equipment for emancipation; but it is also the objectification of human existence and, therefore, it brings enslavement with it. Man is made the slave of civilization.

Civilization is the theme of man's struggle with, and triumph over, the tyranny of natural necessity. But pe-

riodically, as it has already been noted, man has returned to nature seeking liberation from civilization which, after freeing him from the chains of nature, shackled him with glittering fetters of its own. Civilization arose as a means, but soon it was turned into an end. It has become a tremendous power which controls man. Man himself has become a means for the realization of the technical and industrial process of civilization. The continuous growth of the multiplicity of things in daily life crushes man. Who has not felt the powerful grip of things!

> Technical progress testifies not only to man's strength and power over nature; it not only liberates man but also weakens and enslaves him; it mechanizes human life and gives man the image and semblance of a machine.

Like most existentialists, Berdyaev deplores the mechanization of life and the enslavement of man by the very machine he created. It is the machine that replaced man and thus plagued him with unemployment. "The machine has a crushing effect on the human soul, it damages emotional life first of all, thus shattering the integrity of the human personality."

Machinery has destroyed the unity of human life. Modern technology has placed in man's hands a fearful instrument of destruction and has, therefore, surrounded his existence with an atmosphere of fear and anxiety. Our overorganized civilization demands of man an evergrowing activity, but by this demand it enslaves him and turns him into a mechanism. This is partly due to the change in man's relation to time.

Through the conquest of time by the machine, time itself has undergone an acceleration to which the rhythm of human life must respond. Our civilization is entirely oriented toward the future. Each moment is but a means to the succeeding moment. Our world is a world of mathematical time measured by the calendar and the clock.

Swept away by the torrent of time, man does not have adequate time to assert himself as the free creator of his future. Applied to economic life, the new conception of time gives rise to a utilitarian estimate of man. Man's value is dependent upon his productivity within a given time. This leads slowly but surely to the destruction of man's personality.

One of the most unfortunate results of modern technological and industrial civilization is the appearance of vast impersonal masses of people. It is the negative effects of civilization that produce the mass man, to whatever class he may belong. The main characteristics that distinguish the man who belongs to the masses are

> a lack of expressed personality, the absence of personal originality, a disposition to swim with the current of the quantitative force of any given moment, an extraordinary susceptibility to mental contagion, imitativeness, repeatability.

The mass man, in Berdyaev's view, appropriates the technical side of civilization, but is able to assimilate spiritual culture only with difficulty and reluctance, if at all. "The masses in the present transitional period," says Berdyaev, "are devoid of all spiritual culture." This is another way of saying that the masses of today are chained by modern technology and are enslaved by its necessity. They have surrendered their freedom as a price for materialistic satisfactions; and without freedom there can be no spiritual culture.

What adds intensity to the seriousness of man's predicament is the fact that culture itself, which is meant to be an agent of freedom, is gravely endangered by a "process of democratization and leveling-down, by the domination of the mass." The crisis of culture in our times lies in the stress on quantity at the expense of quality. It is increasingly demanded of culture that it be watered down to correspond to the needs and desires of the masses. "The mass determines what shall be the accepted culture, art, literature, philosophy, science, even religion." Culture is undergoing such drastic changes, says Berdyaev, that it needs a new name. Besides this process of "democratization" of culture and its resultant mass production, there is also the danger arising out of the tendency in man to idolize his own cultural creations and to become a slave to his own cultural values. And whenever and wherever that happens, man finds himself behind the bars of necessity. Thus in the sphere of civilization and despite the cultural creativeness of man, the paradox of freedom and necessity remains unresolved. Its tension continues to plague man.

5 THE GRIP OF HISTORY

A head-on collision between freedom and necessity takes place in history. In the realm of the historical, Berdyaev discerns the most paradoxical form of man's predicament. This is so because "without freedom there is no history but only the realm of nature. Yet at the same time history suppresses the freedom of man; it subordinates him to its own necessities."

We shall address ourselves first to the first part of this paradox, namely, that "history presupposes freedom," which receives in Berdyaev's books generous reiteration but inadequate interpretation. Perhaps the key that might unlock Berdyaev's meaning is found in his statement: "History postulates the freedom of man. The determinism of nature cannot be transferred to history." Nature does not presuppose freedom, as far as man is concerned, because it existed before man and man is not the maker of nature. Man's relation to history with respect to freedom, however, is different. History presupposes man's existence and, therefore, his freedom. It is the result of the creative or destructive activity of his freedom. It is true that man is a historical being, born into a historical epoch and must realize himself in history, but it is also true that "it is man that makes history . . . and that it is to be supposed that he makes history for his own sake." "History is also my history. I have

indeed had a share in its happening." Again, Berdyaev states, "I accept history not because I am part of history but because history is part of me. That means that I accept it not as an obedient slave but as a free man."

It is one of the fundamental tenets of Berdyaev's philosophy of history that the freedom of the spirit belongs to him who does not conceive of history "as an exterior imposition" but rather "as an interior event of spiritual significance, that is, the expression of freedom." "Only in such a free and emancipating view," Berdyaev goes on to say, "can history be understood as the expression of man's inner freedom."

It might add more light to what Berdyaev means by the words "history postulates the freedom of man" to mention also that, in his opinion, there are two major elements in history: the conservative and the creative. The first refers to the tie with the past through its heritage, the second is identified with man's dynamic and creative drive toward self-fulfillment. No historical process is possible without the union of these two elements. "The absence of either of these two elements invalidates the postulate of history." Man's debt to the past must be translated into a duty toward the future, a duty which expresses itself in free creative activity that becomes a part of history.

As a historical being, man must live in time which, according to Berdyaev, has three dimensions: cosmic time, historical time, and existential time. Cosmic time may be symbolized by the circle. It is the time which is related to the movement of the earth, and is divided into years, months, days, hours, minutes, and seconds. This is, so to speak, nature's time, and as a natural being, man lives in cosmic time.

Man lives also in historical time. History is also subject to cosmic time. It is measured by centuries and years, but it has its own historical time which is the result of the movement and change of man and society. Historical time may be symbolized by the straight line reaching into the past and into the future. Its direction is toward the future. It is true that in historical time there is also return and repetition as is the case in cosmic time. There are strong resemblances between certain periods of history. But, nevertheless, the novel element dominates. Every event in historical time is in a sense unique; and every year, decade, and century introduces a new life and new happenings. Historical time has a closer connection with human activity than cosmic time.

There is also existential time. This should not be thought of in complete isolation from cosmic and historical time. The symbol of existential time is the point. This kind of time is not computed mathematically. It is not summed up nor divided into parts. Existential time, writes Berdyaev, is "the irruption of eternity into time . . . It is the time of the world of subjectivity . . . A moment of existential time is an emergence into eternity." Man's creative activity, for instance, is performed in existential time and is merely projected into historical time. It is this projection, this *objectification,* which results in the tragic conflict between man and history.

History, whether it studies the universe or man, is an interpretation of what has been but is no more. As such, it is primarily an objective process insofar as it investigates the past as an object. It is, consequently, relegated, like nature, to the objective world. By virtue of its objective nature, history is indifferent to man and his personality. This indifference is potentially capable of turning man into a tool for the actualization of history. When this happens, he becomes a statistical unit in historical events and records.

Never before has man been more at the mercy of the processes at work in history than he is in our times. No person escapes the effect of the historical event of today. The fatality of history tends to reduce all men to a common level. History does not give man any promises or guarantees. "History needed man as its material, but has not recognized him as her purpose."

What adds to man's misery in and through history is the fact that often he himself deifies history and regards its processes as sacred. Not infrequently, he is willing to bow his head and knee to historical necessity, which thus itself becomes a criterion of values; and obedience to this necessity is regarded as the only freedom he possesses.

Berdyaev allocates a substantial amount of blame for man's predicament in history to Hegel who considered all history as sacred. Hegel also thought of history as the victorious march of the Spirit toward freedom. The concept of freedom occupies a prominent place in Hegel's philosophy, but it is a freedom within the frame of necessity. For Hegel, necessity, *Notwendigkeit,* has two different meanings: the one is identical with external motivation, and the other is equated with internal self-regulation. The latter kind of necessity Hegel calls freedom.

> Necessity . . . in the ordinary acceptation of the term in popular philosophy means determination from without only—as in finite mechanics, where a body moves only when it is struck by another body, and moves in the direction communicated to it by the impact. This, however, is a merely external necessity, not the real inward necessity which is identical with freedom.

Like Kierkegaard and Dostoyevsky before him, Berdyaev protested against Hegel's idea of a universal Spirit revealing itself in history. Hegel wanted to sacrifice man and his human existence on the altar of his philosophy of history. To history, Hegel subordinated not only man but also God, who, in his view, is the creation of history itself. The implications of Hegelian philosophy would be the unconditional surrender and obedience to the conquerors in history and the acknowledgment of them as instruments for the realization of the Spirit which, according to Hegel, is freedom. Hegel's freedom is the freedom of the universal and not of the individual. Hegel's philosophy of freedom actually denied freedom by acknowledging it as the product of necessity and, at times, necessity itself.

There is something in man, says Berdyaev, which makes him rebel against being converted into a means employed by a pitiless and inhuman historical process.

> On the one hand I accept history as my path, the path of man, and on the other hand I indignantly tear the mask from it and rebel against it . . . History has set its ineffaceable stamp upon me. Yet at the same time I am a free spirit, a person who bears the image and likeness of God, not only the image of the world . . . One must preserve one's freedom in the realm of necessity.

History is then an arena of the unresolved conflict between freedom and necessity. Man himself makes history, but history takes no account of him and often uses him as fuel in the struggle between classes, nations, faiths, and ideas. The clash between history and human personality is never resolved within historical time because man cannot cease to be a historical being. Men try to escape this paradox through historical pessimism. They surrender to irrational fate, but find that the chains of their slavery have become heavier. More often, the escape takes the direction of historical optimism. Men are lured by the mirage of progress and are moved by dreams of Utopia but sooner or later find themselves stranded in the scourging desert of disillusionment. For Berdyaev, the solution of the paradox of freedom and necessity does not lie within history. He cannot rest his faith on the uncertain facts of historical time. "Many a soul has lost its faith on the shifting sand of these historical facts."

. . . . .

FREEDOM AND PERSONALITY

(The Implications)

1 THE DYNAMICS OF PERSONALITY

Berdyaev's anthropology is strictly personalistic, and so is his philosophy, which he sometimes describes as a philosophy of personalism. His *summum bonum* is the human personality, its self-realization, its development and progress in the attainment of truth and beauty. Everything is seen from the viewpoint of personality. Everything is evaluated by the nature of its effect on the human personality.

But man's personality, Berdyaev immediately insists, can exist only in the spiritual climate of freedom. Its self-fulfillment is realized in and through freedom. Freedom is, as it were, the diet on which personality feeds and the oxygen it breathes. In the words of Berdyaev,

> The personality is not only related to freedom but cannot exist without it. To realize the personality is therefore to achieve inner freedom, to liberate man from all external determination.

This vital relationship between freedom and personality makes a study of Berdyaev's concept of personality a prerequisite to the understanding of his philosophy of freedom.

What is personality according to Berdyaev? Personality is not a biological or a psychological, but rather an ethical entity. It is not a natural but a spiritual category. By nature, man is an individual; by spirit, he is a personality. We may say of a man that he lacks personality, but we cannot deny him individuality. Personality is not the soul as distinct from the body. Berdyaev rejects the dualism of soul and body and advocates a "vital unity of soul and body in man." Soul and body mutually permeate each other. The dualism for him exists not between soul and body, but between spirit and nature, between freedom and necessity; and personality is a certain condition which exists between the opposites of this dualism, namely, "the victory of the spirit over nature, of freedom over necessity."

Personality, therefore, belongs to an entirely different order than that of soul and body. It is "not born of a father and mother . . . Personality in man is not determined by heredity, biological and social." Personality is rather and "above all an 'axiological' category: it is the manifestation of an existential purpose." It should not be conceived in substantial terms but should be understood as "the absolute existential centre" which determines itself from within.

The definition of personality by Max Scheler as the union of our acts and their potentialities seems to appeal to Berdyaev. Yet, personality is more than that. Berdyaev writes:

> When confronted with the personality, I am in the presence of a Thou. It is not an object, a thing, or a substance; nor is it an objectified form of psychic life—the object of psychology.

Here Berdyaev echoes Martin Buber's I-Thou relationship. But in his contrast of personality with *thing,* he reflects the influence of William Stern, a contemporary psychologist and philosopher, whose personalist philosophy rests on the assumption that the person is a psychological unity, characterized by purposiveness and individuality. Berdyaev refers to Stern's contribution and finds in this thinker's antithetical terms *Person und Sache,* person and thing, a distinction which replaces the traditional one between spirit and matter.

Stern defines personality as that existential entity which, despite its multiplicity, is capable of constituting "a unity possessed of originality and value," and of forming, despite the multiplicity of its functions, "a unity endowed with independence and finality."

The essential quality of personality is its *unitas multiplex*. As such, it is an integral whole, not a sum of parts. It is an end in itself, unlike the thing, which is a means to an end. A fundamental characteristic of the personality is its capacity to be a free agent.

Berdyaev goes along with Stern up to this point. He disagrees with him as soon as Stern begins to elaborate a whole hierarchy of overlapping personalities into which he admits collectives such as the nation. For Berdyaev, this elaboration is anathema and unforgivable. In his view, it makes Stern's supposedly personalistic philosophy too rationalistic and, therefore, it "cannot claim to be strictly existential."

Berdyaev goes beyond Stern to state "another most important property" in which the personality radically differs from the thing, namely, "being able to experience joy and suffering" and being endowed with "the sense of a unique and indivisible destiny." "Personality is my whole thinking, my whole willing, my whole feeling, my whole creative activity."

In an effort to clarify his concept of personality, Berdyaev calls attention to the fact that the Latin word *persona* signifies a *mask* and has theatrical associations. "The personality is essentially a mask. Man employs it not only to disclose himself to the world, but also to defend himself from its importunity." This should be understood in a positive way. Personality as a mask implies "a task to be achieved." Its pulse is the creative act. Its aim is the triumph over all sorts of determinations.

> Personality is activity, opposition, victory over the dragging burden of the world, the triumph of freedom over the world's slavery. The fear of exertion is harmful to the realization of personality. Personality is effort and conflict, the conquest of self and of the world, victory over slavery, it is emancipation.

As a task to be accomplished, as a creative activity, personality is constantly in a process of change. It requires time for the actualization of its potentialities. But with the change there is also the element of immutability in personality. This accounts for its paradoxical nature. This paradox in personality expresses itself also in the fact that, on the one hand, personality is potentially universal, and, on the other hand, it is a distinct, unrepeatable, irreplaceable being, unique in every respect. "The secret of the existence of personality lies in its absolute irreplaceability, its happening but once, its uniqueness, its incomparableness."

Personality is a religious and spiritual category. Seen in the Christian context, it is "the image and likeness of God in man and this is why it rises above the natural life." As such, personality is not a part of something but a unity possessing absolute worth. Its value is intrinsic and cannot be reduced to a common denominator. Man's worth is the personality within him.

Personality is the reflection of the divine image and likeness, and, consequently, it is the true path leading to God. Man is given the power to become a personality. He must be afforded every opportunity of achieving this. But the process requires great efforts on his part. The struggle to become a personality, integrated and consolidated, is a painful process. This is so because strong resistance is constantly encountered and a conflict with the enslaving power of the world ensues. But it is precisely in the heat of the struggle that the fruits of freedom ripen. The quest for freedom, and personality is freedom, inevitably involves suffering and a "capacity to bear pain."

The path of the realization of personality is paved with love and sacrifice. Love and sacrifice constitute the relationship of one personality to another. They are the means by which the personality is freed from the prison of self. They are the channels by which the personality identifies itself with another personality. Sacrifice is the medium through which the uniqueness is respected. This means that the personality grows and expands only in relation to another personality. The recognition of each personality's uniqueness, that it constitutes a Thou, is essential to our understanding of the mystery of love.

> To be in love with another's personality is to perceive the identity and unity underlying its perpetual change and division; it is to perceive its nobility even in the midst of utter degradation.

From the point of view of ethics, Berdyaev reminds us, personality is linked with character. A strong personality implies a strong character; and a strong character signifies the victory of the spiritual principle in man. True morality begins with power over oneself and ends with triumph over slavery to oneself. This must precede any victory over the enslavement to this world. "Character is conquest and attainment; it presupposes freedom." A good character is an indication that a person has established distinctions, is not indifferent, but has made his choice. Such a person is neither blind nor enslaved to the status quo or to conventions. The personality of such a man is free.

Despite his stress on the close relationship between personality and morality, Berdyaev registers his disagreement with Kant, who passes over from the intellectual to the ethical conception of personality. According to Kant, "morality alone makes the person a person, the self a self." In the Kantian sense, and as Professor Kroner put it,

> That which is called "character" in the strictly moral sense is not identical with the "nature" of an individual, but it depends upon the free decisions and actions of the person. I am responsible for my character; I myself am its author.

Because of this fact, personality is not just a phenomenon among other phenomena. Personality is an end in itself, not a means to an end; it exists through itself. "Nevertheless," concludes Berdyaev, "Kant's doctrine of personality is not true personalism because the value of personality is defined by its moral and rational nature, which comes into the category of the universal."

According to Berdyaev, the existence of the human personality with its loves and fears, with its hopes and anxieties, with its unique and unrepeatable destiny, is a paradox in the world of nature and within the confines of society, civilization, and history. Personality is unceasingly faced with an environment which is alien to it. The human personality with its aspirations, and the conditions of existence in this world are contradictory to each other and cannot but clash. In the process of its self-realization, personality must constantly struggle against the forces of estrangement and exteriorization, against what Berdyaev calls the principle of objectification which enslaves man by its chains of necessity and threatens his freedom with the fetters of causality. What Berdyaev means by this term is the next question for discussion.

2 THE PRINCIPLE OF OBJECTIFICATION

Objectification is a fundamental concept in Berdyaev's philosophy. It is a principle that operates in the "'objective world', i.e. the world of our natural and historical environment." Objectification is the process by which a subject is converted into an object. The most common and easily recognizable objectification takes place whenever a person, a spiritual entity, is treated as a thing, as an object, as a commodity. Whenever a human being is used as a means rather than as an end, objectification occurs. Everything, including God, may be, and generally is, liable to be objectified.

The principle of objectification occupies a vital role in Berdyaev's dualistic world. It is a one-way bridge leading from the higher and real world, the realm of freedom, to the lower and unreal world, the realm of necessity. "Objectification is a symbolical description of the fallen state of a world in which man finds himself subservient to necessity and disunion."

The bridge of objectification on which spiritual realities, *things-in-themselves,* slide down into the ocean of necessity, into the world of phenomena, is itself located in man's mind and is constructed on wrong social and spiritual attitudes of hatred and injustice, of disdain and prejudice. Operating through abstraction, objectification invariably leads to the burning fires of dehumanization, depersonalization and degradation. It prevails in most social relations, which are characterized by superficial and impersonal contacts and in which the person's spiritual status is not recognized. Berdyaev often alludes to the world in which such conditions exist as the "fallen world." It is the world in which society is no longer knit by spiritual ties. It is a world in which the I-Thou relationship has been replaced by the I-It relationship.

People practice the principle of objectification more than they realize. Often, objectification becomes their second nature and they begin to think of it as quite normal. When that happens, they become spiritually bankrupt and self-alienated. Objectification is a disease which drains off man's spiritual qualities. Man ceases to be self-directed and becomes other-directed. Life degenerates into mere accommodation to what is common and average. It becomes geared to external norms and standards. Inner motivation disappears and its function is taken over by social customs and conventions, by the rule of expediency and convenience. Man is no longer a creator but an imitator. He loses his freedom and becomes a slave. To use Berdyaev's own words, "in the process of objectification the subjective spirit loses its identity."

> Objectification is the ejection of man into the external, it is an exteriorization of him, it is the subjection of him to the conditions of space, time, causality and rationalization.

To sum up, Berdyaev considers the following to be the main characteristics of objectification:

1 The estrangement of the object from the subject.

2 The absorption of the unrepeatably individual and personal in what is common and impersonally universal.

3 The rule of necessity, of determination from without, the crushing of freedom and the concealment of it.

4 Adjustment to the grandiose mien of the world of history, to the average man, and the socialization of man and his opinions, which destroys distinctive character.

The process of objectification operates not only in society and people but also in nature and things. Berdyaev makes a distinction between the creative activity and the created product. While the former is a part of the noumenal world and is free from objectification, the latter is a part of the phenomenal world and is affected by objectification. The symphony which a composer creates, for instance, is a part of the objectified world, but the creative activity by which the symphony was composed is part of the world of spirit and freedom. It is in this sense that Berdyaev also equates objectification with materialization of spiritual entities. Man has a tendency to worship the product of his creation. This results in his enslavement to and by the things he produces. This explains the fact, Berdyaev points out, that property can be on the one hand a source of freedom and independence, and, on the other hand, an agent of man's slavery. Exploitation and abuse of natural resources lead to their objectification. Living exclusively by and for the power of money and the things that power can buy objectifies man's spirit. As a result, man is no longer defined by what he is but by what he has.

Berdyaev makes a deductive statement that "the world of appearance is the outcome of objectification." Objects are all created by subjects. The "fallen world," in other words, is man-made. It must be noted that the attempt to understand "the world as a product of spirit, to comprehend even the corporeal world with all its phenomena as essentially intellectual or spiritual in its origin and content," as Windelband has shown, is nothing new. It was the "final result of ancient philosophy" to conceive the world in this manner.

In his theory of objectification, Berdyaev has a close affinity to the German idealists who thought that the world is *my idea* or, as Schopenhauer often called it, a "phenomenon of the brain." Schopenhauer, who identified Kant's *thing-in-itself* with the Will, but who denied any causal relation between the *thing-in-itself* and the world of phenomena, nevertheless regarded phenomenal nature as objectification, that is, "as the perceptional and conceptional mode of representation of the will or the immediately real." It may be noted in passing, as Matthew Spinka has pointed out, that Karl Marx, during his early period, formulated his basic concept of "social injustice in terms of *Verdinglichung* (objectification), i.e., as the treatment of the proletarians as things, as a commodity."

But Berdyaev differs from the German idealists in his assertion that the agent of objectification is not the supra-personal Spirit or Absolute Idea but the human spirit itself. The objectification of the world through human manipulation turns the freedom of noumena into the necessity of phenomena. In other words, it results in the loss of freedom.

For Berdyaev, the objectified world is not the true and real world. It is only a symbol of the real world of the spirit. But the awareness that anything in this world is merely a symbol of another world has a positive function. It helps in liberating man from a slavish dependence on this world. This theory will be developed in detail later.

In the area of knowledge, objectification implies that the knower and the known are mutually alien. Applied to persons, it means *knowing about* them rather than *knowing them*. In this respect there is an essential difference between natural sciences and the humanities. In natural sciences, objectification does not destroy the object of knowledge, since nature itself is the result of objectification. In the humanities and in the realm of the spirit, objectification leads to the destruction of the reality which we seek to know.

Through the process of objectification, the true Church, as a non-authoritarian spiritual entity, as a spiritual union and communion in love and freedom, is transformed into an authoritarian social institution with conflicts within and without and with worldly ambitions. No wonder that the visible and historic church often alienates people from God. Fortunately, the earnest and faithful Christian can always transcend the objectified church and can be a part of the life of the true Church, the *sobornost,* which is sustained by the indwelling Spirit of the risen Lord.

> The historical Church reminds one of other historical bodies, is very similar to the State, to the kingdom of Caesar . . . It also is subject to the power of necessity. But the Church is also metahistorical; another world beyond this world is disclosed in it. It is a spiritual society; the realm of freedom is in it.

3 DEPERSONALIZATION AND DEHUMANIZATION

The process of objectification is the chief enemy of man, his personality and his freedom. It lies at the heart of the dehumanization of modern man and the depersonalization of his personality. The principle of objectification, Berdyaev thinks, accounts for the crumbling of civilizations. This principle, by which subjects are turned into objects, operates in man's own mind.

Berdyaev underscores, first of all, the overturning of the hierarchy of values as the most dangerous and most consequential product of objectification. Those values which rank high, such as truth, beauty, goodness, and freedom are brought lower, and those which are at the bottom of the scale, such as expediency, usefulness, exploitation, and violence are elevated to the top. Putting the matter in terms of means and ends, the means in man's life, such as economics and politics, become ends in themselves. "The means take central place, and the ends are either forgotten, or become purely rhetorical."

Berdyaev convincingly shows how this reversal of values is characteristic of our times. The real aims of human life have been displaced. Man's life is filled with an abundance of the means of living but has been alarmingly emptied of the ends which make life worth living. Man has forgotten the *why* of living and is preoccupied with the *know-how.* He is too busy to think about the meaning and the purpose of life. For him the means have an immediate reality but the aims, which he has deposited in the attic of his mind, have no reality at all.

Behind this displacement of values is a pragmatic outlook, itself the outcome of objectification, which makes the usefulness of a thing or a being determine its place on the scale of values. In determining the value of entities, their qualities and quantities, the element of truth is totally ignored. "One of the worst evils," warns Berdyaev, "is a utilitarian attitude toward truth." Man has the devious illusion that the truth is his servant. There is no awareness that he has been called to serve the truth.

Berdyaev notes that part of the same confusion in values is the widespread prevalence of the principle that the end justifies the means. Evil means are being used to achieve good ends, means which contradict the very

ends sought. Christianity is no exception. Its history is checkered with dark means and bright ends. In Europe, the attempt was made to spread the Christian message of love and forgiveness by blood and violence. The phantom of the professional Christian inquisitor darkens many decades of church history. Evil means have weakened rather than strengthened the church. The noble ends of the French Revolution were lost in the terror and violence of the guillotine.

Berdyaev cites with bitter criticism "the dehumanization and bestialization" of our times, the "barbaric forms of cruelty" of our modern society, and, with sarcasm, the "bestialism" which "is something quite different from the old, natural, healthy barbarism; it is barbarism within a refined civilization." "Here," he continues, "the atavistic, barbaric instincts are filtered through the prism of civilization, and hence they have a pathological character." The ABC of bestialism is that everything is permissible: "Man may be used in any way desired for the attainment of inhuman and antihuman aims." Objectification leads, with reliable regularity, to a denial of the value of the human personality. Man is depersonalized and dehumanized by its operation. He loses his personality and his humanity when he is used as a means for whatever ends. Our modern world is not moved by the values of the spirit, the value of the human personality, the value of human freedom, the value of eternal truth. It is moved by such values as power, wealth, nation, class, race. All these and many others are put above man by man himself. Power ranks high in man's estimation, even higher than his own personality. The quest for power leads him to sacrifice his humanity and thus he becomes inhuman to his fellow man. The process of depersonalization and dehumanization, Berdyaev regretfully declares, has indeed penetrated all phases of human life.

A conspicuous picture of man's dehumanization and the loss of his personal freedom may be observed in the field of economics. Personality is made to depend on what a man possesses. Property is considered the guarantee of man's freedom and security. But the freedom and security conferred by property vanish with the loss of that property. Money, "the great enslaver of a man and of mankind," is "symbol of impersonality."

Berdyaev does not hesitate to pass judgment on both Capitalism and Communism as powerful agents of depersonalization and dehumanization. As an economic system, Capitalism is the breeding of money by money for money's sake. Production exists for the purpose of making profits, and man exists to keep the wheels of production turning. No wonder such a system sees nothing wrong with destroying large quantities of food supplies for purely economic interests at a time when millions are starving. Man does have the duty to develop himself economically, but, Berdyaev cautions,

> The divorce of economy from life, the technical interpretation of life, and the fundamental cap-

italist principle of profit, transform man's economic life into a fiction. The capitalist system is sowing the seeds of its own destruction by sapping the spiritual foundation of man's economic life.

Berdyaev's verdict on Communism is equally severe, but it takes a different direction. On the whole, he had no economic nor even political quarrels with Communism. He was in favor of its objectives of putting an end to the exploitation of man by man, and of terminating the class struggle and giving birth to a classless society. He commended the communist dream of creating a world organization that would abolish war. But he vigorously opposed both Marxism and Communism on spiritual grounds. In Marxism, he discerned an economic variation of the Hegelian theme. In his book, *The Realm of Spirit and the Realm of Caesar,* Berdyaev devotes a chapter to an analysis of "The Contradictions in Marxism." "The contradiction in Marxism lies also in the fact that the realm of freedom . . . will be the inevitable result of necessity . . . This is essentially a denial of freedom." Marx subjected man "to historic necessity, to the point of deifying this necessity." He thought of the present as nothing but means to the future; and thus, as Berdyaev writes, "the value of human life for itself in the present is denied." The system that set out to humanize society produced "a process of dehumanization," for "Marx's atheism . . . results from his exclusion of one very important phase, of man as a spiritual being."

Berdyaev was convinced that today's Communism has deviated from the original economic philosophy of Marxism and has become a form of "State Capitalism." He recognized soon after the Russian Revolution that "Communism . . . imperils the living principle of freedom and personality." In his book, *The Origin of Russian Communism,* Berdyaev has clearly shown how "only that sort of freedom, freedom for the collective construction of life in the general direction of the communist party, is recognized in Soviet Russia." Furthermore, hostility to religion belongs to the very essence of Communism. It denies the freedom of choice and the freedom of conscience and thus it crushes with its materialistic fist man's individual personality and personal liberty. Its denial of God naturally leads to its denial of the human personality.

Having to work with and through machines, man is finding that slowly but surely his emotional life is being damaged. The machines were invented for the purpose of freeing man from slavery to nature and time, and were supposed to lighten the burden of his labor, but instead they have become his mute yet noisy slave driver and not infrequently invoke upon him the curse of unemployment. Through the mechanization of life, man is mercilessly forced to degenerate into a machine. Confronted with "almighty technics," man is dissolved into certain functions. His personality, his freedom, his real center, all disappear. Closely related to the towering achievements of modern technology are the amazing discoveries of modern science, which likewise have a hand in the process of dehumanization.

Berdyaev recognizes the symptoms of dehumanization also in modern literature and philosophy. Particularly in the novel, he finds that man is decomposed and that his whole imagination is distorted. His real image can no longer be discerned. In the psychological novel, which is concerned with the analysis of the subconscious life, man appears to be dissolved into one or a few of his component elements. "Modern novelists almost completely lack creative imagination, they are either preoccupied with themselves, or simply picture the evil realities with which they are burdened." Often, the characters disappear beneath their sadistic instincts or are lost in the blind alleys of their sex life. No doubt, admits Berdyaev, the modern novel contains much of the truth about man and about what is happening to him in the present age.

In philosophic thought, the depersonalization and alienation of the human personality is a more complex process. It may be detected in such movements as empiricism, idealism, naturalism and materialism. Modern philosophy, particularly Existentialism, although it stresses the question about man, his existence and freedom, has nevertheless betrayed signs of disintegration and degradation. In Heidegger's ontology of Nothing, Berdyaev finds a philosophy of pessimism and despair in which man is hopelessly lost in a metaphysical jungle of fear, worry, and death. Jaspers, whom Berdyaev regarded as "a far more authentic existentialist than Heidegger and Sartre," shows a modified tendency toward the same thinking as Heidegger even though he did not admit "an ontological knowledge by means of concepts" and accepted only "the possibility of metaphysics as symbolic knowledge." Berdyaev severely criticizes Sartre's philosophy, "which debases man and denies every higher principle in him," and he wonders how it "can possibly be linked with the *rôle* of freedom in human life, and the possibility of creating a new and better way of life." He finds Sartre's concept of freedom and his emphasis that "man is condemned to freedom" too negative, too empty, and devoid of any connection with truth. And what metaphysics is there in Freud except the metaphysics of death and nothingness? According to Freud, says Berdyaev, man is torn between the instinct of sex and the instinct of death. He also mentions the "dehumanization of Christianity" by some modern religious thinkers such as Karl Barth in whose "dialectic theology . . . the image of God in man is shattered."

Throughout his books, Berdyaev discusses with existential flavor the dehumanizing operations which are characteristic of "the realm of Caesar," the state. He agrees with Nietzsche that "the state is the most cold-blooded of monsters." There is in man a natural disposition to dominate others. He finds it hard to resist the temptation to develop and exercise sovereignty over his fellow men.

Unfortunately, says Berdyaev regretfully, Christians have not followed the example of Christ. They have responded to the claims of sovereigns by genuflecting without reflection. The words of Christ "Render unto Caesar the things that are Caesar's and unto God the things that are God's" have commonly been misunderstood and misinterpreted. They have often been taken as a justification for reconciling the kingdom of Caesar and the Kingdom of God. But these words of the Master, Berdyaev explains, do not imply evaluations and do not give Caesar and his realm a religious connotation. They were not meant to abolish the conflict between the two kingdoms. Was not the life of Christ precisely this conflict carried out till the end with earnestness and without flinching?

The clash between the Kingdom of God and the kingdom of Caesar is here to stay because under the conditions of this world the function of the state is necessary. It will always remain so. In philosophical terms, this is the conflict between freedom and necessity, between the spirit and the objectified world. What must be rejected is the state's claim of sovereignty. "Sovereignty belongs to no one: it is only one of the illusions of objectification." Caesar is the product and the agent of the objectified world and therefore cannot hold the right of sovereignty. "The relationships between church and state have been, and always will be, contradictory and they present an insoluble problem."

The tragic fact is that the cult of sovereignty is, nevertheless, practiced in the kind of world we live in, and the poison of imperial authority runs in the veins of human rulers. The state itself, especially the totalitarian state, never refrains from attempting, and never gives up pretending, to act as if it were a church in giving meaning to the lives of men, and thus exercises domain over their souls, minds, and hearts. The state has continuously shown the tendency and desire to trespass the limits of control and authority and power to which it is lawfully entitled. The totalitarian state voices and defends the arrogant and erroneous claim that man exists for its own sake. Instead of being the guardian of man's rights and the protector of his freedom, it stamps upon his rights and tramples his temple of freedom. Consequently, man is dehumanized and his personality is paralyzed by the state's hypnotic power. He surrenders his freedom at the altar where the mystifying and stultifying sacrament of imperial authority is administered. Knowingly or unknowingly, the state is inclined to be guided by the expedient principle that prevailed at the trial of Jesus: "It is better for us that one man should die for the people than the whole nation should perish." But Berdyaev is not unaware of the complexity caused by the fact that the people themselves are not always innocent but often find their own deceitful dreams come true in the actions and transactions of the state.

> The state is, of course, a projection, an exteriorization, an objectification of a condition of the people themselves . . . and there lies the chief evil and a source of human slavery.

The greatest threat confronts man, Berdyaev argues, when the state is conceived as a personality, as an organism, having its own existence apart from the people. It is then that its depersonalizing mechanism operates on a larger and more dangerous scale. It is then that "the prince of this world" is already at the helm of the state steering it to totalitarianism and, with it, to self-destruction. But regardless of the uniform he wears and the flag he flies, Caesar has an irresistible tendency to demand not only what is properly his own, but also what is God's; he wants the whole of man to be subject to himself. And in this lies the greatest tragedy of history, that of freedom and necessity, of human fate and historic destiny.

Douglas K. Wood (essay date 1982)

SOURCE: "The Twentieth-Century Revolt against Time: Belief and Becoming in the Thought of Berdyaev, Eliot, Huxley, and Jung," in *The Secular Mind: Transformations of Faith in Modern Europe*, edited by W. Warren Wagar, Holmes & Meier Publishers, Inc., 1982, pp. 197-219.

[*In the following essay, Wood considers Berdyaev along with T. S. Eliot, Aldous Huxley, and C. G. Jung as representative of modern thinkers whose works express a "revolt against time."*]

Time the leech; time the destroyer; time the bloody tyrant; portrayed in a thousand forms, hypostatized in a thousand metaphors, described in a thousand symbols. From the dawn of civilization to the present, the same lament continues: time is a devious slayer, a traitorous provider who gives only to take away; a patron of life who wears the black cowl of death beneath a disguise of light and laughter. As an Elizabethan poet has said:

> Even such is Time, which takes in trust
> Our Youth, and joys, and all we have;
> And pays us but with age and dust,
> Which, in the dark and silent grave,
> When we have wandered all our ways,
> Shuts up the story of our days. . . .

MUTABILITY TRADITION

In the twentieth century the lament against the eroding power of time endures and frequently appears to increase in its intensity. On occasion it clearly resembles the melancholy protest of the Elizabethans. Dylan Thomas, for example, bitterly describes the "Grief Thief of Time" who sets "its maggot" on our track and, in another poem, the destructive "force that through the green fuse drives the flower"—a force which he equates with "The lips of time," which "leech to the fountainheads" of youth. Or again, in "Variations on a Time Theme" the Scottish poet Edwin Muir registers his dismay with the apparently meaningless "sad stationary journey" of time which consumes each successive generation. Such expressions of hopelessness, of protest and impotent rage "against the dying of the light" inevitably wrought by time are not uncommon in any age: they are representative of the "mutability tradition" in literature. When Muir and Thomas recoil in horror or sadness at the spectacle of temporal decay, they are giving contemporary expression to a sentiment that can be traced in the primitivist poetry of antiquity, the verse of Lorenzo de Medici, or the stanzas of Lord Herbert of Cherbury. According to this tradition, time is synonymous with change, the process that exhausts life-forms and insures the eventual decomposition of every sentient and inanimate object in the universe. It is the principal enemy whose very omnipotence often inspires a spirit of resistance. Thus, for instance, Muir and Thomas, like Shakespeare or other twentieth-century writers (e.g., Edward Thomas, Walter de la Mare, Robert Graves, Rupert Brooke, James Joyce, Nikos Kazantzakis, and C. Day Lewis), admit that they would like to "Make war upon this bloody tyrant, Time." But—and here is the rub—they also realize that, in the last resort, "nothing 'gainst Time's scythe can make defence." A private mythology, an exaltation of love and life, an *amor fati* or a deliberate flaunting of death may enable the individual to reconcile himself to nothingness, but they are not enough, in Edwin Muir's phrase, to "put all Time's display to rout."

THE REVOLT AGAINST TIME

While the vitality of the "mutability tradition" is maintained in twentieth-century European literature, it does not represent the only protest against the destructive characteristics of the temporal process. For in fact this century has witnessed a far more dramatic and significant protest against mutability—an attack on time that not only laments the ravages of contingency, but demands and tries to achieve the transcendence and abolition of the temporal process. Whereas Thomas and Muir helplessly lament the passage of time, the major proponents of the twentieth-century revolt against time not only denounce the sad waste of the temporal process, but try to accomplish either a permanent or temporary destruction of time itself. Their rallying cry is that of the hero of Kazantzakis's novel *The Rock Garden:* "I declare war on time! I declare war on time!" Yet their protest—their desire, in the Greek author's words, to turn "the wheel back" and resuscitate the dead—is not simply a product of romantic sentimentalism—a spontaneous reaction of the heart. For while it may be exemplary of Everyman's objection to the inexorable cycle of life and death, it represents a confident and determined assault on the process of temporal corruption; a thoroughgoing and self-conscious attempt to eliminate the flux of events.

VARIETIES OF TIME

Four of the most outstanding protagonists of the twentieth-century revolt against time—namely, the Russian religious eschatologist Nicolas Berdyaev (1874-1948),

the British poet T. S. Eliot (1888-1965), the British novelist Aldous Huxley (1894-1963), and the Swiss psychologist C. G. Jung (1875-1961)—aim their respective attacks on temporal process primarily against the time of human *experience*—against what Georges Poulet has called *le temps humain,* i.e., psychological, qualitative, or subjective time. This is not to say that they are not also at war with what they regard to be *scientific time;* they are. Indeed, they wish to eliminate or surmount the *ontological dimension of time* itself whether it be viewed from a "human" or "scientific" perspective. But, it is important to note at the outset, they approach the problem of time in a different way from the scientist. The latter—as opposed, say, to the poet or novelist—is principally interested in constructing an "objectively" valid system of measurement. The quartet I have selected for study, however, are also concerned with the problems of measuring time, especially *historical time,* another form of temporality they yearn to transcend or destroy. Yet their methods of periodizing historical time are decidedly different from those the scientist employs when he attempts to measure *cosmic time.* For while it is undeniable that scientific concepts of time contain subjective elements and that some scientists have rebelled against "objective" conceptions of temporal process, it is nevertheless true that most scientists try to remove their ideas of time from the subjective foundations of individual experience. Instead of being concrete their conception of time is *abstract;* it is quantitative rather than qualitative, public rather than private or personal. In other words, the scientist is generally preoccupied with the measurement of physical events, while the poet, novelist, or speculative philosopher of history—or again the philosopher of physics—is chiefly concerned with the *nature* of time. The scientist is intent upon discovering an empirically verifiable concept of time that will enable him to calculate cosmic events—to construct a universal metric from which "calendars" and "clocks" can be derived—while the individual who, like Berdyaev, Eliot, Huxley, and Jung, ultimately bases his notion of time upon personal or subjective experience, is concerned with the *meta*physical dimensions of temporality—with the ultimate meaning as well as the ontological and axiological nature of time.

SPATIALIZATION

Now although it is true that Berdyaev, Eliot, Huxley, and Jung derive their concepts of time from personal experience—and, concomitantly, that they direct their attacks on temporality primarily against subjective time (*le temps humain* or *Ich-Zeit*) and secondarily against what they understand as scientific time—it is equally true that they believe in the objective validity of their own notions of time. When Berdyaev refers to the Beginning and End of historical time, when Eliot describes the cyclical revolutions of the temporal process, or again, when Huxley discusses the dance of Shiva, or Jung the cycle of aeons, each is referring to an objective structure or pattern of events that he considers to be a universal aspect or condition of human existence. Such claims of objectivity are not uncommon. Individuals who shape their time-concepts on the foundations of personal experience usually extend their immediate perceptions of time (i.e., of succession, change, motion, supercession, simultaneity, and/or transitional intervals) by either interpreting time as a linear progression or as a cyclical repetition. Linear time-concepts no doubt arise from the ability to anticipate or remember events—circular (or spiral) concepts of temporal process, from the observance of enduring and repetitive aspects of human experience. Yet in both cases, the ability to extend the "blooming, buzzing confusion" of time as an immediate datum of consciousness through the use of a symbolic form (circle, spiral, line) provides the individual at once with an "objective" model with which to interpret, order, and control events, as well as a spatial diagram of time that may eventually enable him to destroy the temporal process itself.

The interrelation between the desire to abolish or transcend time and the transformation of experiential time into an objective (yet unscientific) dimension of human experience through the use of spatial symbols is a typical feature of Berdyaev's, Eliot's, Huxley's, and Jung's approach to the time-problem. Not only do they share a common and aggressively antipathetical *attitude* toward time; not only, that is to say, do they regard time as an enemy who must be surmounted or destroyed; but they also employ (spatial) *concepts* of time to annihilate the temporal process. They transform their subjective feelings about time into a personal concept of time (which purportedly has universal validity), and use their spatialized or pictorial representations of temporal process to eliminate time. As Milic Capek has observed, "The elimination of time and its spatialization are closely related." For in imposing a graphic symbol upon time or "in contemplating a spatial diagram of temporal process it is easy and psychologically natural to forget its underlying dynamic meaning." Spatialization of time transforms succession into juxtaposition, and presents uncompleted moments of time as a completed or simultaneous whole. It represents time statically and deprives it of its inherent momentum. In Capek's view, this "Eleatic" tendency can be discovered in early interpretations of Einstein's theory of relativity as well as idealistic trends in contemporary metaphysics. Yet (as Capek himself realizes) the use of spatial symbols to order, control, and destroy the temporal process is an extremely ancient practice—a practice that can be found in archaic as well as modern societies, in the presuppositions of the *Enuma Elish* or in the writings of Berdyaev, Eliot, Huxley, and Jung.

When Berdyaev, Eliot, Huxley, and Jung use the verbal equivalents of spatial images to describe the time-process, they not only retrace the path of a venerable tradition—a tradition, by the by, that was not seriously challenged until the end of the nineteenth century—but they also achieve the same "epistemological" result as, for instance, "archaic man," the medieval eschatologist, the advocate of the idea of progress, or the champion of

dialectical materialism. By imposing, in other words, a graphic symbol upon their immediate experience of time, they delimit the temporal process and establish its boundaries. This epistemological act (which orders and, in some cases, establishes direct control over the temporal process) in turn permits them to invest time with a teleological meaning, or to formulate a sharp distinction between the time-process and eternity that may eventually precede and ultimately facilitate the transfiguration of time into timelessness. Expressed concretely, when Berdyaev imposes a circle on cosmic time, a line on the historical process, and a point on existential time (i.e., that period of timeless time that precedes the destruction of the phenomenon of time itself and the return to eternity); or, analogously, when Eliot describes "The time of the seasons and the constellations/The time of milking and the time of harvest" as well as the time "of Heaven" that, in the last twenty centuries, has brought "us farther from God and nearer to the Dust" as a series of cycles, each is using a spatial image to clarify and focus the realities of the time-process. Yet their use of time-symbols does not end here. For once they have interpreted time in terms of spatial images, they are prepared to destroy or transfigure the temporal process. Berdyaev, for example, gives the linear structure of historical time a "Beginning" and an "End," and, by making history finite and cosmic time subordinate to history (i.e., the unfolding of the divine-human drama) achieves the inevitable and irreversible abolition of every kind of time (cosmic, historical, and existential). On the other hand Eliot—who, unlike Berdyaev, rarely appears to examine the nature of time under the aspect of eschatology, especially apocalyptic eschatology—uses the circular structure that he imparts to astronomical, biological, and "moral" time to formulate a relationship between timelessness and time. This relationship (that is, the relationship between the "still point" and the "turning world") is then employed to reconcile the temporal process and eternity. By introducing a third term, namely, his notion of the "dance" (which is a poetic transcription of Bradley's concept of the Absolute), Eliot not only reconciles time and eternity but transforms the temporal process into a "pattern / Of timeless moments."

ETERNITY IMAGES

Eliot's use of the circle demonstrates the way in which time-symbols are frequently transformed into eternity-images or symbols of timelessness. It is not only, as Capek observes, psychologically natural to eliminate time by portraying it as a spatial pattern; it is equally natural to suppose that the symbolic structure that makes time static and deprives it of its dynamic meaning must be related to, if not synonymous with, timelessness. The oldest symbol that has been employed to portray *both* time and eternity has been the circle. This popularity is no doubt ascribable to the basic and traditional function of the circle as an "ordering symbol." It must be remembered that the perfect geometrical structure of the circle (all points equidistant from the center) has not only been used to clarify and order the temporal process. Indeed, it can also be found demarcating the sacred precincts of a temple *(temenoi),* delimiting the world-order (frequently in combination with a square representing the cardinal points of the compass), describing the movement of the planets (for instance, in Aristotle's "celestial world"), protecting man from inimical forces (as, for example, in the case of the magic circle), harmoniously rationalizing man's position in the universe (i.e., establishing the microcosm-macrocosm relationship), giving concrete expression to the emotions of a mental patient, or again, objectifying an individual's concept of eternity. Yet while the evidence suggests the ubiquity and preeminence of the circle as an ordering symbol (and here we are primarily interested in its capacity as a time-symbol and eternity-image), it is obviously but one of many symbols (and, in fact, types of symbols) that are used by human beings to order their realities.

NONDISCURSIVE SYMBOLS AND TIME

As a time-symbol the circle, like the straight line and its variants (e.g., what Berdyaev occasionally refers to as the "undulating line" of history), is what Ernst Cassirer and Susanne Langer would call a nonlinguistic or nondiscursive symbolic form. Nondiscursive forms of symbolism (viz., ritual, myth, religion, and art) articulate or objectify feelings or emotional concepts, rather than rational or discursive thoughts (such as the concepts of mathematics). Their meaning or import is essentially connotative (as opposed to denotative) because they lack the syntax or grammatical structure of linguistic symbolisms. But it is not just the circle or line—the graphic symbol or its verbal equivalents—that is nondiscursive, for often the prose used to elucidate a philosophy of history or idea of time is itself non-discursive. In other words, although a description of the temporal process may be expressed in verbal symbols, in words that constitute a "language," their significance or import may be nondiscursive because the meaning conveyed by their language is metaphorical. It is undeniable that many linguistic treatises dealing with the problem of time often revert to a nondiscursive level, either to use the verbal equivalent of a pictorial symbol to express their philosophy (or, perhaps more accurately, their myth) of time, or to employ metaphorical or poetic symbols (poetry is defined as a nondiscursive form of symbolism) to articulate feelings they have about time that cannot be expressed with the verbal precision or grammatical rigidity of analytical thought. A dramatic example of the use of nondiscursive prose to describe the time-process is provided by Berdyaev's numerous works on the philosophy of history. For not only does he use spatial images to describe the time-process, but again and again, under the ecstasy of an overwhelming vision of man's destiny, he reverts to a metaphorical level of expression to convey the meaning of his apocalyptic interpretation of history. Underneath his discourses on Kantian epistemology, below the rational threshold of his examination of the problem of objectification lies the

eschatological vision that permeates and unifies every strand of his thought. And his eschatology, like all eschatology, is created out of nondiscursive symbols—images that belong to the world of myth, rather than to the realm of logic and science. The linear pattern of Western eschatology probably rests upon an extremely ancient structure of feeling—a structure of feeling that, like the emotions associated with the circular notion of temporal process, may ultimately be derived from the birth-death-rebirth pattern of primitive initiations, from what the Dutch anthropologist Van Gennep has called "the rites of passage." At any rate, Berdyaev's language is shot through with an emotional terminology (a vocabulary that is strikingly reminiscent of primitive initiation rites), and, like Eliot, he relies on graphic symbols to order, control and eliminate time.

The same can be said of Huxley and Jung. They too appreciate the epistemological function of time-symbols, and, like Berdyaev and Eliot, use nondiscursive images of temporal process to express a group of interrelated ideas that they associate with the meaning of man's existence in time. According to Huxley and Jung, time is equivalent to physical change, to perpetual perishing and becoming—a process of growth and decay that conforms to the symbolic structure of a circular form. Thus while, like Eliot, they recognize the existence of different historical ages, they tend to de-emphasize or ignore the linear pattern of historical time. Their reason for not stressing the past-present-future structure of historical time lies partially in their conception of a homogeneous human nature. Like Thucydides (and T. S. Eliot) Huxley and Jung infer a cyclical movement of the temporal process from the constancy of human nature. If man is the same *in esse* (as he is assumed to be), he will act essentially the same throughout time. Therefore, human time, like cosmic and biological time—or again, the changes experienced by societies or civilizations—necessarily repeats the same fundamental pattern. *Corso i ricorso:* or almost, since Huxley, Jung, and Eliot recognize that although the formal pattern of the temporal process (what W. H. Auden calls the "general average way" of time) is constant, particular events—say, an individual's life history—may not be identical in detail. An individual possesses the potential of imposing his own signature upon the repetitive rhythm of the cyclical process. Yet on occasion Eliot, for example, even appears to deny this limited definition of (individual) novelty. And it is not impossible to find him describing human activity as a result of divine predestination. This deterministic streak runs throughout his later poetry and all of his plays, and it helps to elucidate his conception of what may be termed "moral time." Because of Original Sin, Eliot assumes, man—natural man, man living in the fallen time of creation—remains essentially the same throughout history. The repudiation of the concept of a plastic human nature (coupled with the notion of primordial sin) implies that all historical periods are essentially identical. Yet identical only in the sense that they are equally corrupt or morally inadequate. Thus antiquity, the era of the metaphysical poets, and the twentieth century are fundamentally the same because, in Eliot's view, Original Sin precludes moral progress *sub specie temporis.* But again this does not mean that every temporal situation repeats itself in exactly the same manner ad infinitum. For there is a difference between, for instance, the Middle Ages and our own age. Indeed Eliot (like Berdyaev and Jung) believes that modern civilization has declined since the Middle Ages (particularly the Age of Dante, or what Berdyaev and Jung refer to as the Age of Mystic Italy or the Age of Joachim of Flora), and that contemporary Western culture represents a tragic departure from the integrated society of medieval Europe. Even the grandson of "Darwin's bulldog," Aldous Huxley, can be caught looking back nostalgically to an age of mystics that, he poignantly regrets, disappeared in the cannon smoke of seventeenth-century power politics. Yet in spite of their recognition of historical or contingent differences between cultures past and cultures present, in spite of their belief that we are, as a waggish Huxleyan mouthpiece says in *Eyeless in Gaza,* well on in the third volume of Gibbon, they tend to ignore particular differences and insist that, since human nature is constant, time is cyclical (or spiral).

Initially puzzling as it may seem, Berdyaev—the linear eschatologist par excellence—also examines the rise and fall of civilizations under the aspect of circular time. Yet his concept of cyclical process (which he, like Hegel, also employs to interpret cosmic time) cannot be used to describe the general pattern of history. For, in Berdyaev's view, history is essentially a divine-human drama—a soteriological mystery play—that unfolds in a linear progression. But the pattern of cultural events— the history of individual civilizations—follows a spiral course.

Approaching the problem from the standpoint of analytical psychology, C. G. Jung arrives at a concept of cultural (or historical) transformation that bears a family resemblance to Berdyaev's. According to the Swiss psychologist, all time (biological, astronomical, and historical) is cyclical. The lives of individual men, the processes of nature, and the rise and fall of civilizations all follow a circular course. Yet whereas astronomical and biological time perennially recapitulate the same pattern, historical time allows for minor variations: its cycles never repeat themselves exactly, and therefore history develops as a series of spirals.

Although the implications of his theory of history are never fully developed, the end result of Jung's psychological interpretation of history—his law of *enantiodromia* or compensation that controls (without actually causing) the succession of historical aeons—is quite similar to Berdyaev's apocalyptic vision. Like Berdyaev, Jung gives the apparently meaningless process of growth and disintegration a meaning by assimilating the cyclical course of cultural history (or the history of civilizations) into an inclusive pattern of universal history.

Civilizations, like human beings, may inevitably be born only to die; but (by imposing nondiscursive symbols upon the phenomenon of temporal flux) it is possible to see that they perish for a purpose. In Jung's schema the helix of historical time is transformed into the circle of timeless perfection—into a psychological condition (symbolized by the *mandala* [Sanskrit: circle] or the astrological symbol of Aquarius) that is homologous with what Teilhard de Chardin would call "point Omega." In Berdyaev's system, on the other hand, the jagged line of history eventually smashes the cycle of cultural and cosmic time by reaching its appointed End. It resolves the antinomies of the historical process, and accomplishes the return to timelessness—to eternity, which Berdyaev (like Jung, Eliot, and Huxley) describes as a timeless and spaceless circle.

If Jung had been asked to interpret Aldous Huxley's concept of time, he would undoubtedly begin by observing the similarity between his own notion of temporal process and that of the Englishman. For, like Jung, Huxley also imagines time and eternity as a circle. The Swiss psychologist may even (especially in later life) have agreed with Huxley's view—which he derived from Hindu and Buddhist sources—that the phenomenon of time is actually an illusion *(maya)* perceived by minds alienated from reality. In any case, Jung would probably have concluded his remarks about Huxley's concept of time with a discourse on the nature of mandala symbolism because Huxley's cones and circles (like Yeats's gyres or Eliot's still point and turning world, or again, Berdyaev's spaceless and timeless circle of eternity) perform all of the major functions that Jung ascribes to the mandala. That is, they impose order on the chaotic flux of experience, clarify the psychological relationship between the individual and (in this instance) the time-process, and (most significantly from Jung's point of view) represent the final achievement of man under the aspect of time—namely, the establishment of a permanent or at least temporary relationship between the individual and eternity. It is impossible to say whether Huxley, who was familiar with Jung's theories, ever recognized that his time-symbols and eternity-images could be interpreted as mandalas. Nevertheless his occasional (nondiscursive) descriptions of the relationship between the temporal process and timeless Reality appear to correspond to Jung's definition of the mandala or image of psychic wholeness. (Actually, it should be observed parenthetically, Jung and his followers would regard most time-symbols and all eternity-images as mandalas or, what one disciple has called, circles of the psyche—i.e., symbols that are analogous to but one step removed from genuine mandalas.) Sidestepping the issue, however, of whether Huxley's pictorial descriptions of time and eternity are really mandalas or not, it is important to point out that his use of graphic symbols to portray the temporal process offers a dramatic example of the intimate connection between the spatialization and destruction of time, on the one hand, and the transformation of time into eternity, on the other.

In his first full-blown mystical novel, *Eyeless in Gaza,* for example, Huxley describes time and eternity as two cones that share a common apex. The temporal world (represented by the first cone) culminates in a point—a point that, like Berdyaev's point of existential time, Eliot's still point, or Jung's point or center of the mandala, marks the end of time and the commencement of eternity. As the world of time (or the first cone) converges on its apex, it is gradually transfigured into timelessness. The second cone in its turn expands toward a base whose circle is equated with the ground of all being, eternal Reality, or timelessness. This intricate image, which is reminiscent of Yeats's famous description of time and eternity in *A Vision,* is directly related to another symbol that Huxley uses to describe the temporal process: viz., the dance. For like Eliot (whose concept of the dance reconciles the still point with the turning world by transforming time into "a pattern/Of timeless moments") Huxley uses the dance of Shiva Nataraja to explain the mysterious connection between perpetual perishing and eternal stillness. Shiva represents becoming and timelessness: he is at once the spinner of the cosmic illusion and the pattern of unmoving movement or eternity. Unfortunately, however, the vast majority of human beings do not realize that the annihilating force of time is merely a product of their egocentric visions of reality. If only mankind could cast off the straitjacket of its collective ego, if only it could gain the experience of the mystic, it could see that time and eternity, *samsara* and *nirvana,* are one and the same—that Shiva or Reality is an eternal dance or process of timelessness.

MYSTICISM

Huxley's concept of "scientific religion"—his emphasis upon mysticism and empirical theology—is also found in the works of Berdyaev, Eliot, and Jung. In fact *mysticism is as important to the twentieth-century revolt against time as spatialization.* Together they form the prongs of the offensive: they provide the essential method or epistemological procedure by which Berdyaev, Eliot, Huxley, and Jung (as well as other twentieth-century antitemporalists, e.g., Charles Williams, W. B. Yeats, and Hermann Hesse) achieve their victory over the temporal process. But, the question naturally arises, what is mysticism? Is it universally identical? And does it assume the same *degree* of importance, say, in Berdyaev's thought as it does in Huxley's, in Eliot's work as it does in Jung's?

According to William James (who realized that the words "mysticism" and "mystical" have a bewildering variety of connotations in common parlance), there are "four marks" that characterize an experience as mystical: viz., ineffability, noetic quality, transiency, and passivity. That is, a mystical experience defies expression, exemplifies a nondiscursive form of knowledge, lasts for a short while, and occurs only in passive states of mind—i.e., when the subject (or individual mystic) "feels as if his own will were in abeyance," or "as if he were grasped and held by a superior power." Now while it is undeniable that these "four marks" characterize all

forms of mystical phenomenology (including the mysticism of Berdyaev, Eliot, Huxley, and Jung), James's definition of mysticism remains incomplete. For he leaves unmentioned the most typical, fundamental, and pervasive element or constituent of mystical experience: namely, the transcendence of time—the feeling of rising above or being liberated from the powers of temporality. And it is this archetypal characteristic of mysticism—more than any other single feature of preternatural experience—that receives by far the greatest emphasis in the writings of Berdyaev, Eliot, Huxley, and Jung. Eliot, for example, recognizes that the purest and most direct apprehension of Reality can be achieved only during a timeless state of mystical consciousness. For "Time past and time future / Allow but a little consciousness. / To be conscious is not to be in time." Aldous Huxley also believes that "Deliverance is out of time into eternity," and that "Men achieve their Final End in a timeless moment of conscious experience." Again, Berdyaev, while insisting upon an eschatological interpretation of human destiny, feels that in "creative" ecstasy man discovers "a way out from the time of this world, historical time and cosmic time." And finally, Jung, who believes that man's end is self-awareness—a state of psychic wholeness attained only after the arduous integration of the "temporal" conscious and the "eternal" unconscious—confides that the richest moments of his life were nontemporal states of consciousness.

Given this amendment of James's definition, however, is it possible to say that this mysticism is universally the same? For even though reports of mystical experiences appear to be unanimous in stressing James's "four marks," temporal transcendence, and (to amend James's definition once again) the achievement of unity or communion with a supernatural Reality, is it accurate to say that mysticism is always identical in form and content? The answer is no, for while all mystics may, for example, wish to transcend time, their methods of attaining liberation—as well as their concepts of Reality—often differ. In a provocative book written in response to Aldous Huxley's *Doors of Perception,* R. C. Zaehner maintains that there are three fundamental types of mystical experience, viz., pan-en-henic, monistic, and theistic. Ignoring for the moment both the Oxford don's axe-grinding and the probability that there may be other varieties of preternatural experience, it is possible to use two of Zaehner's categories to contrast the mysticism of Eliot, Berdyaev, and Jung, on the one hand, and that of Huxley, on the other. Eliot and Berdyaev, for instance, are definitely theistic mystics. Their goal—the final cause of their spiritual quests—is to achieve personal communion with God in a timeless moment of consciousness or "creative" ecstasy. While Berdyaev is a fairly consistent dualist and Eliot—especially in later life—a convinced monist, both agree that the personality is not destroyed during mystical experience. As they see it, the mystic (and it should be recalled that both of these men believed to the marrow that they had actually transcended time during moments of mystical contemplation) establishes, in Martin Buber's phrase, an "I-

Thou" relationship with God. God and man are joined together—united—but *ex hypothesi;* their communion precludes the elimination of their respective identities. They are one yet separate, united yet distinct. Aldous Huxley, on the other hand, denounces the "personalist" emphasis of Western theology, for he believes that it represents a disguised form of egotism. Behind the admonitions to worship the personality of Christ—behind the eloquent orations on the dignity of the human personality lies the narcissistic self-image of Western man. In opposition to the theist's concept of communion Huxley proposes the perennial philosophy's notion of nonpersonal union with the divine Ground. When, according to Huxley, the genuinely "theocentric" mystic establishes direct contact with eternity, his ego (as well as his "personality") is dissolved in the timeless and all-consuming depths of the Absolute (Brahman). He realizes that his individuality—his self—is an indissoluble and indistinguishable part of a larger and all-encompassing Self (Atman) and that, like time, the personality is an illusion that separates man from the divine Ground of all being. Huxley's mysticism is obviously monistic: he ultimately reduces every thing and every soul in the universe to One spiritual principle, Reality, the divine Ground, or eternity.

In contrast, C. G. Jung, while appreciating and recognizing the similarities between his own analytical psychology and Eastern religious thought, repudiates the notion of annihilating the personality. The psyche must be transformed but not eliminated. A balance, a dynamic equilibrium, should be established between consciousness and unconsciousness—an equilibrium that Jung calls the self, i.e., that condition of psychic wholeness symbolized by the mandala. During his middle years, and especially in later life, Jung regarded individuation (or the attainment of psychic integration) as an experience of timelessness. According to the Swiss psychologist, the collective unconscious and its contents (i.e., the archetypes) represent a spaceless and timeless mode of being. This statement is more than a hypothesis, for, in Jung's view, the intrinsic space-timelessness of the objective psyche has been proved by J. B. Rhine's ESP experiments. The existence of telepathic phenomena, however, not only establishes the space-timelessness of the lower depths of the psyche, but indicates that there is another form of being behind the veil of the archetypes. Thus when a person becomes individuated, he not only participates in the timeless dimension of the collective unconscious but is provided with evidence of an "absolute object" upon which everything depends for its existence.

While Jung's mysticism may stand in complicated yet necessary relation to his general approach to the time-problem—i.e., to his concepts of archetypal configuration and synchronicity—his peculiar variety of mysticism appears to be closer to the theistic category of preternatural experience than either to the pan-en-henic or the monistic. Like the theist, for example, Jung not only defends the integrity of the personality but stresses

the notion of conscious communion or participation in a timeless reality. In spite of these similarities, however, there remain two significant differences that preclude Jung's complete entrance into the theistic ranks: namely, his belief that Christ is a symbol of the self and his opinion that individuation is a psychological experience. And yet, it cannot be forgotten that Jung never denied the validity of Christianity, and that he not only believed that he had transcended time in a state of "completed individuation" but that the unconscious impinges upon a form of existence outside space and time. Professor Zaehner tries to explain monistic and pan-en-henic mysticism (i.e., nature mysticism) in terms of Jungian psychology (thus, by implication, equating monistic and nature mysticism with genuine or incompleted individuation and, by explication, emancipating theistic mysticism from psychology). But it is obvious that Jung's kind of mysticism defies exact classification, and that, if it were to be categorized at all, it would be more accurate to place it on the fringes of the theistic variety of preternatural experience.

Although it is obvious that mysticism plays a cardinal role in Jung's relentless attack on the temporal process—a role that exceeds either synchronicity or myth in its importance—what priority does mysticism assume in the thought of Eliot, Huxley, and Berdyaev? For Eliot and Huxley, mysticism—the direct experience of eternity here and now—represents the most significant method of overcoming time. While (as both authors state explicitly in several of their essays on aesthetics) creativity may afford the individual a way of destroying time, mystical consciousness (even if it is only what Catholic theologians call "gratuitous graces" as opposed to full-blown mystical experiences) is by far the most exalted mode of liberation from the flux of events. Time the destroyer can be eliminated by the artist—or again by the mythologist who, for instance, may, like Eliot in "The Waste Land," transform the chaos of temporal existence into an ordered pattern by using the timeless themes of myth and legend. But it remains for the mystic to achieve the highest and most comprehensive triumph over the temporal process. It is true that it is occasionally possible to detect an undercurrent of what appears to be eschatological expectation in the works of Huxley and Eliot. And yet neither author relies on eschatology to destroy time. Indeed, both Eliot and Huxley spurn eschatological visions of man's destiny, and, if they seem to refer to the future in apocalyptic terms, it is not in a spirit of exultation but of despair. Berdyaev, on the other hand, does not interpret the apocalypse pessimistically. He regards it as the noblest creation of the divine-human partnership—the consummation of the story of man's estrangement from eternity. Mystical communion with God may allow the individual to escape the power of time for an ephemeral moment in eternity (or to anticipate the eventual resolution of the conflicts of history in the Age of the Spirit), but mysticism cannot destroy the phenomenon of time itself. It enables the individual to *transcend* time, but it does not, it cannot, assure mankind of a final victory over the temporal process. The only way, Berdyaev insists, to *abolish* time irrevocably is to create a metaphysic of history—to accept the apocalyptic hope, the fervent belief, of an approaching End to the historical process that will destroy every kind of time and restore man to his former "theandric" status (or Godmanhood). The difference between the thrust of Berdyaev's argument, however, and that of Eliot, Huxley, and Jung should not obscure the fundamental importance of their mutual agreement on the necessity of overcoming time. Not only do they use spatial symbols to order, control, and destroy time, not only do they base their belief that time can be eliminated on personal mystical experience but they insist unanimously that man can only achieve redemption and save the world from suicide by grounding his life in eternity.

THE HISTORICAL IMPORTANCE OF TWENTIETH-CENTURY
ANTITEMPORALISM

"Spatialization" and "mysticism," "time-symbols" and "eternity-images," "apocalyptic eschatology," "creativity," and "the direct experience of eternity"—each of these terms, each of these phrases, is representative of ancient and yet enduring responses to the problem of transcending or abolishing time. And yet, if these patterns of reaction—if these epistemological procedures and methods—are merely symptomatic or exemplary of traditional responses to the problem of mastering and overcoming the time of human experience, is there anything unusual about the twentieth-century revolt against time? In other words, what is the historical and sociological importance of twentieth-century hostility toward time? In the first place (and this should be stressed), this study is not simply concerned with four exceptional individuals (rare birds or intellectual freaks) who yearn to transcend or abolish time: such individuals—and this should be obvious by now—can be found in almost any age. And while it is important to note the antiquity and pervasive continuity of the desire to transcend time, it is equally important to recognize the unusual configurations this desire has assumed in the twentieth century. Berdyaev, Eliot, Huxley, and Jung, for example, were all at one time agnostics, atheists, or sceptics who believed in the intrinsic value of temporal civilization and endorsed some form of "time-philosophy", that is, a philosophy in which time—real duration or historical time—is substituted for eternity and in which reality is equated with time or becoming, such as Bergsonism (Eliot), the liberal idea of Progress (Huxley and Jung), and Marxism (Berdyaev). Yet shortly before or after the First World War and the Russian Revolution, these (and many other) intellectuals began to reconsider their metaphysical presuppositions, and, as a consequence, they eventually repudiated their secular world views. This reappraisal (to draw a succinct and systematic summary) ultimately took the form of: (1) a strong reaction or revulsion from the time of human experience, expressing itself in (a) a revolt against time-philosophy in all its protean shapes, and (b) a refusal to accept the identification of time with Reality; and (2) a denial of a previously held agnosticism, atheism, or scepticism, as well as a "conversion" to a traditional form of religious phenomenology, namely, mysticism (the entire quartet), and/or an acceptance of the dogma of an institutional religion (Eliot and, to some extent, Berdyaev).

This comprehensive reversal of attitudes (which in itself is an extraordinary phenomenon) exemplifies the experience, not only of my quartet, but of religious antitemporalists in general. For the majority of the thinking men and women who revolted against time in the early decades of this century did so by attacking time-philosophies and by discovering (or returning to) religion. They rebelled against the secularization of modern consciousness by challenging the hegemony of the idea of (temporal) change in contemporary thought. Thus their "conversions-in-reverse" were a direct reaction against the "Great Substitution" of the previous century; they rejected out of hand the *Ersatzreligionen* that had substituted time for eternity, history or becoming for timelessness. It is worth recalling here that "the word *secularization* came to mean what we now mean when we use it"—namely, "a growing tendency in mankind to do without religion, or to try to do without religion"—in the forty or more years following the publication of the *Origin of Species* (1859). This was the period, rather than the late seventeenth century or the Enlightenment, that witnessed the *secularization of the European mind*—a fact that underscores the revolutionary nature of the antitemporalists' dramatic change in outlook. They stood the secular movement on its head and proceeded to build a *Weltanschauung* that had its roots in a prescientific age. And while it is not unusual to find intellectuals in various historical periods who criticize their societies for lacking spiritual values, it is striking to discover so many who, at the close of an era recognized for its optimistic appraisal of human affairs, abandon their secular world views to adopt a hostile attitude toward time, history, and culture. Yet it is on this last point, more than any other, that the twentieth-century revolt against time distinguishes itself from other efforts to transcend temporality in the modern era. Not only, in other words, do the religious antitemporalists attack the ontological limitations of time and condemn all varieties of time-philosophy; they also single out "time" as a symptom of the "disease" afflicting Western civilization. Or, to put it another way, they couple their personal desire to transcend or abolish time with an attack on the (secular or time-obsessed) values of Western culture. In particular, they frequently criticize the preeminent value placed in an advanced industrial civilization on "clock time" and its economic correlative, expressed in Benjamin Franklin's aphorism "Time is money." Their cultural criticism is thus indicative of the broad-scale protests against the increasing complexity and materialization of modern life.

THE LATE NINETEENTH-CENTURY BACKGROUND

Protests against the dehumanization of life are obviously not unique to the twentieth century, and in fact, recent denunciations of the mechanization of human existence have their origin in different (yet related) currents of nineteenth-century thought. It is important to be aware of this background to the twentieth-century revolt against time. For although, in most cases, nineteenth-century protests against the materialization of life do not involve a concomitant attack on temporal process, they nevertheless exemplify a significant change in attitude toward Western culture that (especially in the years following World War I) eventually culminated in a repudiation of the overwhelming value placed on time by the optimists of *la belle époque*.

A CHANGE IN THE SPIRIT OF EUROPE

By a striking coincidence, the period of the nineteenth century (1871-1900) that demonstrated the greatest confidence in "materialism"—i.e., in an attitude toward life characterized by a pride in material accomplishments, a this-worldly pragmatism, and a "philosophy" dominated by material and mechanistic conceptions—was also a period of growing dissatisfaction with the development of Western culture in general, and the quality of nineteenth-century life in particular. Yet the chorus of criticism—which gradually increases in volume from the depression years of the 1870s onward—had already announced itself prior to the commencement of what Carlton J. H. Hayes has called *A Generation of Materialism*. Karl Marx and Charles Kingsley, for instance, excoriated the established classes for exploiting the poor laborer, Honoré de Balzac satirized the crass materialism of the bourgeoisie, John Henry Newman attacked the religious and political "liberalism" of his contemporaries, and Matthew Arnold noted the deracination and anarchy, the confusing whirligig of new and ever-swarming ideas, in nineteenth-century culture—all before 1870. Still, as Benedetto Croce once observed, there is an important "change in the public spirit of Europe" after 1870—a change that represents an acceleration of the critique of nineteenth-century life already inaugurated by such men as Newman, Marx, and Arnold.

The "change" described by Croce represents an intellectual and political response to the long-range effects (to use E. J. Hobsbawm's terminology) of the "dual revolution"—the Democratic Revolution and the Industrial Revolution—as well as the dramatic growth of Europe's population, the subsequent birth of the "masses," and the increase in the rivalries among "nations" and "classes." The growing standardization of life coupled with the rapid materialization of middle-class values, the depreciation of the "inner world" of the spirit and the glorification of the machine, the burgeoning discontinuity and dissociation of European culture as well as the dangerously naive equation of technological advancement with human "progress"—all features of nineteenth-century life criticized by such men as Baudelaire, Carlyle, Dostoievski, Nietzsche, Burckhardt, Samuel Butler, and Alfred de Vigny—intensified the perplexities and dissatisfactions of intellectuals living during the three decades after the Franco-Prussian War.

REVOLT AGAINST POSITIVISM

The growing antagonism toward nineteenth-century culture reached its apogee during the 1890s. This is not to say that by the last decade of the century the majority of educated Europeans had renounced their "materialism" or their confidence in the future. On the contrary, most Europeans seem to have remained steadfastly loyal to their faith in the inventiveness and productivity of Western civilization until 1916. Some, such as Walter Mehring's father, even thought that the turn of the century would bring the millennium. Nevertheless, the decade of the 1890s inaugurated an intensive reevaluation of the direction and purpose of European civilization—a reappraisal that was marked not only, as H. Stuart Hughes has pointed out, by a "revolt against positivism," but by a new preoccupation with "spiritism" or the "occult."

In Germany, France, Italy, and England the renunciation of positivism took the form of "a growing awareness of the things of the spirit." The protest was registered in the works of philosophers, sociologists, historians, and poets, in the writings of intellectuals such as Wilhelm Windelband (who issued a "declaration of war against positivism"), Henri Bergson (who attacked the quantitative and ratiocinative "fallacies" of modern thought), Max Weber (who stressed the priority of ideas in shaping the origin and development of "material" events, for example, modern capitalism), Benedetto Croce (who tried to emancipate history from science), or again George Meredith (who championed the life of the senses and defended the achievements of the spirit at the expense of positivism). Yet the desire to "escape from materialism" (of which the revolt against positivism is representative) was not limited to a repudiation of nineteenth-century "scientism." For there is another current of thought in the 1890s—the "discovery" of spiritism—which also marks a change, although perhaps a minor change, in the spirit of *fin de siècle* Europe. As early as 1875, the world-traveling Russian occultist Madame (Helena) Blavatsky founded the Theosophical Society in New York City. She and her successor Annie Besant were able to create a religious organization that continued to influence European intellectuals (either directly or indirectly, positively or negatively) into the twentieth century (e.g., Nicolas Berdyaev, T. S. Eliot, Aldous Huxley, W. B. Yeats, and Charles Williams). This new concern for mysticism and the occult (which finds its counterpart in two currents of twentieth-century thought, the Anthroposophical movement of Rudolf Steiner and the vogue of Eastern and Western mysticism) was given further impetus by the "spiritual" interest of Sir Oliver Lodge and Alfred Russel Wallace, as well as the founding of the Society for Psychical Research in 1882—a society that, through its investigation and research activities, anticipated some of the results of J. B. Rhine's ESP experiments in the 1930s.

While there may have been attempts to "escape from materialism" during the generation of materialism, while there may have been protests against the state of nineteenth-century culture, against the increasing "multitudinousness," "sick hurry," complexity, and mechanization of life—the protests and attempted escapes were not indicative of a widespread dissatisfaction with the "bourgeois century." On the contrary, they were generally made by a minority of exceptional, often hypersensitive, individuals. Yet not only were the limits of the protest circumscribed, but, most significantly, the protesters themselves failed to isolate "time" in their diagnoses as an essential ingredient of the "modern malady." This point is important, for it is not until shortly before or after the First World War and the Russian Revolution that the critique of modern life—conducted, particularly after 1916, by a dramatically expanding spectrum of intellectuals—singles out "time" as a symptom of the "disease" affecting Western civilization.

THE IMPACT OF WORLD WAR I

Now the correlation between the outbreak of the revolt against time, on the one hand, and the waning years of the nineteenth century and the commencement of World War I, on the other, is not an accident. Europe, it should be recalled, had not known a war that could compare in magnitude with the wars of the Napoleonic period for nearly a century when the guns of August shattered the *pax Victoriana* in 1914. Of course, there had been the Franco-Prussian War in 1870 and the Crimean fiasco sixteen years earlier, but, as of summer 1914—four years after what became the real "Recessional" of Edward VII's funeral—Great Britain and the Continent had experienced a hundred years of relative peace. The absence of a major war, however, could not disguise the existence of serious social, economic, and political problems—of the wretched plight, for example, of most of the working classes, of political revolution, of many-faceted "Decadence," or of the violent growth of nationalism. And yet (and this is a striking point) while they were evidently aware of the gravity and complexity of these conditions, three members of my quartet (C. G. Jung, T. S. Eliot, and Aldous Huxley), for instance, did not begin to translate their dissatisfaction with Western culture into an attack on time until the First World War. Berdyaev, on the other hand, had become sufficiently unsettled before the war by what he considered the decadence of nineteenth-century culture to advocate an idealistic version of Marxist revolution. But even Berdyaev, who had joined the Russian Orthodox church in 1912, continued (like Jung, Eliot, and Huxley) to maintain a positive attitude toward historical time until the war and (although he is ambivalent on this issue) perhaps as late as the Bolshevik assumption of power.

The delay in the commencement of their revolt against time can perhaps be partially explained by the fact that Berdyaev, Eliot, Huxley, and Jung (like antitemporalists in general) all came from the established classes of society. That is to say: although they were dissatisfied with the state of Western society, they tended to view the future with confidence or indifference because of the

secure positions their families occupied in the social hierarchy. Thus, if this hypothesis is correct, the experience of an enormous catastrophe (the war or, in Berdyaev's case, the failure of the Russian Revolution) was necessary before these men could renounce their allegiance to time-philosophy. There would, however, seem to be another reason for the delay, and that is, quite simply, the factor of age. Whereas Berdyaev and Jung were nearing middle age at the beginning of the War, Huxley and Eliot were respectively twenty and twenty-six. In other words, it might be supposed that what appears to be a common (if not coordinated) effort to revolt against time could not have taken place until the younger members of the quartet had reached a greater maturity. But, as an examination of their life-histories demonstrates, these discrepancies in age are not crucial. And in fact, only a few years (and in some instances perhaps no more than a few months) actually separate the independent development of their antagonistic attitudes toward time, and their identification of their attack on temporal process with an attack on Western culture.

THE ENGAGEMENT OF A QUARTET

The importance that Berdyaev, Eliot, Huxley, Jung, and other prominent religious antitemporalists ascribe to mysticism—perhaps even more than that which they accord to "spatialization" or the quest for timelessness in myth—has encouraged critics to regard the twentieth-century revolt against time as an example of sheer escapism—a manifestation of an invalid, if not cowardly, reluctance to confront the challenging complexities of modern life. Their attempt to transcend the ontological dimensions of time; their vigorous effort to move beyond history, time-philosophy, and the idea of Progress; and their equally forceful struggle to overcome religious scepticism by "re-creating" the concept of eternity from the images and metaphors of symbolic language have been too quickly interpreted as indications of a concerted endeavor to avoid the anxieties generated by a civilization in crisis. Yet it would be a mistake to view the protagonists of the twentieth-century revolt against time as escapists. For rather than experiencing a "failure of nerve," or withdrawing, like Koestler's yogi, from active participation in the affairs of the world, antitemporalists like Berdyaev, Eliot, Huxley, and Jung have responded energetically to the problems facing our time. It might be true that they have, to borrow Charles Frankel's phrase, "re-discovered sin," or the constancy of human imperfection, and they have abandoned the optimistic anthropology of the nineteenth century. But their abandonment of the facile anthropocentric optimism of the previous century does not mean that they have abandoned humanity. For while they question the validity of Western culture, and while they are directly concerned with their own attempts to transcend or abolish time, they also suggest positive measures by which to improve the sad state of the West (and, by implication, the entire world). They refuse to accept the role of ivory-tower philosophers, for they are vitally concerned with man's fate in the modern world. This *engagement* should not be depreciated, for although they believe that man's greatest achievement is the transcendence of time in mystical intuition or the eschatological destruction of the temporal process, they would like every person to establish contact with reality. Thus they stressed the necessity of a massive reorientation of human values, a universal endorsement of the belief in spiritual reality, and a thorough-going denial of the ultimate importance of things in time. But they were not always confident that man would change the structure of his consciousness, effect a spiritual revolution, or transform the nightmare of history into sweetness and light. And yet, Berdyaev, Eliot, Huxley, and Jung persisted in diagnosing what they thought were the causes of twentieth-century ills; they continued to suggest remedies. For they never gave up trying to convince human beings of their higher calling and spiritual dignity—they never stopped insisting that man's final end lay outside the ontological limitations of the ephemeral universe in an eternal reality that could be apprehended by human beings in time.

Robert M. Randolph   (essay date 1988)

SOURCE: "The Possibilities of Creativity: Nicholas Berdyaev and Robert Bly," in *The Midwest Quarterly,* Vol. XXIX, No. 3, Spring, 1988, pp. 321-32.

[*In the following essay, Randolph examines the spiritual significance that Berdyaev attached to human creativity, using the work of American poet Robert Bly to exemplify Berdyaev's criteria for genuine creativity in works of art.*]

In *D. H. Lawrence: Novelist,* F. R. Leavis writes of Lawrence:

> It is plain from the letters and other sources that he went forward rapidly once he had started on an enterprise, writing long stretches in remarkably little time as the creative flow carried him on. The first draft written, he revised, not by correcting locally or re-working parts, but by re-writing the whole with the same kind of creative *elan* as had gone into the earlier version (and this he habitually did yet again).

In "Symbol and Reality in Nicolas Berdyaev," Robert D. Knudsen writes of Berdyaev, "He says that he composed his writing quickly, even in a state of dizziness, not disturbing the cascade of his thought even by the consultation of books." Berdyaev himself writes in his autobiography, *Dream and Reality,* "Only in the white heat of creative ecstasy, when none of the divisions into subject and object had yet arisen, did I experience moments of fulfillment and joy."

Although integrity of structure is contained in unbroken impulse for both Lawrence and Berdyaev, Lawrence is working toward a form while Berdyaev is experiencing a state of being. It is the necessary casting of one's

creativity into a form which Berdyaev terms as tragic, yet inherent, in our world. Form, Berdyaev says, was never a goal of his and was, in fact, the cause of agony and embarrassment:

> An artist must needs be concerned with the adequacy and effectiveness of his finished work. For my part, I have, so far as I can remember, never been concerned with these things, and I have no claim whatsoever to artistic perfection in my writings. . . . When I see my work done within the objective world and standing over against me as a fixed and irrevocable object, I suffer agonies of discontent and embarrassment. . . . Creative works are within time, with its objectifications, discords and divisions, but the creative act is beyond time: it is wholly within, subjective, prior to all objectification.

In *The Destiny of Man,* as in many other places, Nicholas Berdyaev acknowledges his indebtedness to the thinking of Jakob Boehme. Berdyaev accepts Boehme's idea of the "Ungrund," a primordial condition of non-being from which, Boehme and Berdyaev say, God came. Freedom is an inherent condition of the Ungrund, so that both God and freedom came from it. The creation of the world by God is, therefore, a secondary act, preceded by the coming forth of God:

> Out of the Divine Nothing . . . God the Creator is born. . . . From this point of view it may be said that freedom is not created by God: it is rooted in the Nothing, in the Ungrund from all eternity. Freedom is not determined by God; it is part of the nothing out of which God created the world.

God created "man," who was an androgynous being, according to Boehme and Berdyaev, but God did not (could not) create freedom. In fact, God created "man" hoping to find a "friend" to help hold back non-being through creativity. Berdyaev writes that God "longs for his other, his friend, freedom in man."

Freedom is part of the "material" from which God made man, by a creative act. Berdyaev sees God as "the greatest of artists," able to make man without altering the freedom in the material from which man is made. God is able to keep back non-being within God's self through creativity. God's work with regard to people, however, is tremendous: "The divine self-crucifixion must conquer evil meonic freedom by enlightening it from within without forcing it, without depriving the created world of freedom." God must overcome the state of "meonic" (mé, not; on, being) freedom of the Ungrund, which is non-objective dynamism underlying being and from which being and existence come. God has power over being but not over freedom; but to permit being is to permit freedom. The problem that God faces is to turn freedom to creativity and to turn people away from a sense of obedience with regard to God, to a sense of co-creatorship with God. God wants people "to answer the call to enter the freedom of the divine life and participate in God's creative work of conquering non-being. God does not answer His own call: the answer is from freedom which is independent of Him."

According to Berdyaev, the androgynous Adam was free. There must have been freedom of choice, he argues, for the Fall to have taken place. Adam's "sin" was not disobedience but disbelief. As a result of the Fall, humanity opted to learn of good and evil through experience rather than "escaping" good and evil through creativity. Even after the coming of Christ, who showed that creativity existed in humanity and that creativity led to transcendent being, human beings still seek obedience rather than creativity. "The slavery of the creature," Berdyaev writes, "is connected with a monarchic conception of God—the conception of God as an autocratic master":

> The static conception of God as *actus purus* having no potentiality and completely self-sufficient is a philosophical, Aristotilian, and not a biblical conception. In the Bible God has affective emotional states, dramatic developments in His inner life characteristic of all life.

The urge to obedience denies the possibility of creativity. It arises from the fear of tragedy in one's life and the possibility of avoiding pain through obeying God, but not only is true "obedience" found, paradoxically, in creativity, but also there is no way to avoid tragedy because tragedy is inherent in life, in freedom. God cannot limit freedom without limiting being. Therefore, "without destroying freedom, the potency of evil cannot be conquered." Nevertheless, we can reconcile ourselves to tragedy in the world "because God suffers in it too." Tragedy exists within the divine life itself and it is "impossible to moralize about tragedy because it is inherent in freedom."

In creating "man" in his own image, God made "man" a creator too, "calling him to free spontaneous activity and not to formal obedience to His power." This creativity is "the achievement of being" outside of good and evil, "through a free act." It is the *freedom* and *creativity* in Christ's human nature which matters to us, and which is the lesson from God.

If, however, God "longs for His other, His friend, freedom in man," and God suffers with people (God "shares his creatures' destiny," Berdyaev says), God's hope and happiness would seem to lie in human creativity.

Berdyaev discusses creativity in *Dream and Reality*. "Creativity," he writes, "stands in no need of justification from the religious or any other point of view; it is its own justification in virtue of the very existence of man; it is that which constitutes man's relation and response to God." Any understanding of creativity having to do with culture, cultural values and products of culture, he argues, involves a secondary meaning of creativity. As Berdyaev writes about it, creativity has to do with process, not with works.

Berdyaev calls the creative act an "ek-stasis, a breaking through to eternity." It is eminently a movement of self-transcendence, reaching out to what is higher than oneself." The creative act transforms, and is the opposite of, self-sufficiency. It is a change in being. Redemption, Berdyaev argues, consists in changing one's being through creativity, transforming the self and responding to God's call to create in God's image, in freedom. Indeed, Berdyaev points out that "creativity is possible only on account of freedom, which is not determined by anything, not even by Being."

Humanity cannot create without a medium in which to work, writes Berdyaev,

> and yet the basic characteristic of a creative act consists in not being wholly determined by its medium, and that it comprises something new, something which cannot be derived from the external world in which it is embodied, or indeed from some fixed repository of ideal forms which press upon the creator's imagination.

In that way, being arises out of non-being, not out of a "re-distribution of being." One who could complete the creative act and make something new, not "derived from the external world in which it is embodied," would seem to be the "friend" for whom God longs—the one to help hold back non-being.

Berdyaev says that there can be no redemption and no salvation without humanity's creative response to God. "The ultimate fulfillment of redemption and the coming of God's kingdom comprises a creative act on the part of man." In that sense, "the creative act is eschatological."

If true creativity would be "God's Kingdom," a perpetual dynamic creative state of being, then created works could only be static symbols of creativity, which Berdyaev says they are, and not what he calls "realistic creativity." Realistic creativity, he says, would be the making of new being, not derived from the world in which it is embodied by a re-distribution of being. To mistake works for realistic creativity is "a temptation," and also "the betrayal of creativity." Realistic creativity would be the victory of reality over the symbol. It would be the creation of reality. However, Berdyaev asks, is it possible to pass from symbol to reality or is it just a "tormenting dream?"

He says that Gogol, Tolstoy, Dostoevsky, Nietzsche, Ibsen, and "the Symbolists" have "striven to transcend art," but they have not transcended it. "No doubt," writes Berdyaev, "even to raise the problem is tantamount to demanding a miracle from man." However, he argues, "a miracle is already involved in the very act of creation which conforms to no order the laws of which are known, and demands for its explanation an agency transcending the possibilities of a given and determinate world." It would seem that while a miracle is involved in art, especially in the art of those artists named, it is not the miracle of "realistic creativity," since art itself is not transcended in their work.

A characteristic of the "Kingdom of God," according to Berdyaev, is that the symbolic nature of works of art would be transcended. His idea of this Kingdom is depicted in part in ***The Meaning of the Creative Act:***

> The dawn of the creative religious epoch also means a most profound crisis in man's creativity. The creative act will create new being rather than values of differentiated culture; in the creative act life will not be quenched. Creativity will continue creation; it will reveal the resemblance of human nature to the Creator. In creativity the way will be found for the subject to pass into object, the identity of the subject with object will be restored.

Berdyaev says, then, "literature ceases to be only literature; it would be new being," and when that occurs,

> art is transformed into theurgy, philosophy into theosophy, society into theocracy. The norms of classicism are overthrown, according to which beautiful art, true philosophy and a just social order are supposed to be created. Symbolism in art passes beyond the boundaries and norms of classical art, reveals the final limits of the creative artistic act, and leads to theurgy.

The "new being" of literature somehow, in Berdyaev's thinking, has "final limits," even though the "identity of the subject with the object will be restored."

Berdyaev says that all the great Russian writers (naming Gogol, Dostoevsky and Tolstoy) have the "impulse to a final and other kind of being." Because, however, "the creative ecstasy shatters the whole of man's being" and "is an out-breaking into another world," the impulse to seek another kind of being can be threatening. "Creativity," Berdyaev says, "is always sacrificial" (Lowrie).

In summary of Berdyaev's argument as it has been presented in this essay, then: both freedom and God came from a primordial state of non-being, called the Ungrund. God created androgynous "man," but freedom was part of the material from which "man" was made. "Man" fell, indicating that freedom of choice was involved, and opted to learn about good and evil through experience instead of transcending those categories through creativity. People seek obedience to God, which is a wrong turning leading to objectification and systematization. People should instead seek creativity within the freedom originating in the Ungrund, which leads to being. Christ's message of redemption was that freedom and creativity found in human nature, as well as in God, lead to new being and transcendent being. Works of creativity in culture are symbols of the possibility for new being, but are themselves finally betrayals of that possibility if accepted as, within themselves, transcendent. God awaits humanity's creativity, to co-create the "Kingdom of God." In that Kingdom, works of art will

lose their symbolic nature, but will nevertheless be restricted by the "final limit" of creativity.

Consideration of the "final limit" of creativity, in this paper, will follow consideration of the concern with creativity of the poet Robert Bly, who seems to be trying to do what Berdyaev says is impossible—to transcend the symbolic nature of art to the extent of producing forms of being—to, as Berdyaev might see it, create the Kingdom of God.

Robert Bly's first book of poems, *Silence in the Snowy Fields,* contains an epigraph from Jakob Boehme: "We are all asleep in the outward man." Bly acknowledges his interest in Boehme in several places in his writing. In a book of essays about Bly entitled, *Robert Bly: When Sleepers Awake,* William V. Davis briefly discusses the value of Boehme's philosophy to Bly and includes a quotation from Berdyaev in explanation of one of Boehme's points.

Davis argues that *The Man in the Black Coat Turns* (1981), "describes the end of the journey which Silence *[Silence in the Snowy Fields]* began." Davis calls it a "self-referential elegy," a "turn toward home." He argues, moreover, that the turn toward home is a turn toward darkness, the darkness of the Ungrund, and Davis quotes Boehme:

> Freedom is and resides in darkness, it turns away from the desire for darkness toward the desire for light, it seizes the darkness with its eternal will; and darkness tries to seize the light for freedom and cannot attain it, for darkness closes in again upon itself with its desires, and transforms itself back into darkness.

Davis sees Bly's turning toward darkness as turning toward the power of source, a movement from Bly's first two books, *Silence in the Snowy Fields* and *The Light Around the Body,* to the darkness in *The Man in the Black Coat Turns.* Davis uses a line from the prose poem, "The Ship's Captain Looking Over the Rail," contained in *The Man in the Black Coat Turns,* to make the point: "When a man steps out at dawn," the line reads, "and breathes the air, it seems to him that he has lived his whole life to create something dark!" Bly, Davis says, is the ship's captain, and he goes on to point out that seeking the dark is a seminal concern of Bly's.

According to Berdyaev's thinking, if Bly wants to "create something dark," such as the Ungrund, Bly is on dangerous ground for three reasons. First, the dark cannot be created since meonic darkness predates being. Second, intending to create some form embodying "realistic creativity" is a "betrayal of creativity," since true creativity is process. Bly would be seeking form where process should be. And finally, there could be sacrifice of some sort involved.

An essay that Bly wrote in 1963 entitled, "A Wrong Turning in American Poetry," provides a clear statement of his philosophy, one which continues to inform the reader about his latest work. It concerns the connection between poet and poem, subject and object, in which Bly's poetry organically grows. In that essay, Bly sets the "1917 generation" of poets, Eliot, Pound and Williams, against the stream of influence from Spanish and German poets, notably Lorca, Machado, Neruda and Rilke, and sees a sort of betrayal of creativity in the "1917 generation," for much the same reasons that Berdyaev might find them to have missed the mark. Bly's argument can be understood in this passage:

> Eliot, Pound, Moore, and Williams, all born within five years of each other, form a poetic generation we might call the generation of 1917. They support certain ideas with great assurance. Eliot's support of the idea of the "objective correlative" is an example. His phrasing of the idea is as follows: "The only way of expressing emotion in the form of art is by finding an 'objective correlative,' in other words a set of objects, a chain of events which shall be the formula of that particular emotion." The tone is final but the statement is not true. . . . These men have more trust in the objective outer world than in the inner world. As poets, they want to concern themselves with objects. The word "formula" above suggests that *objects* are essential in a poem. He wants to arrange them in a formula, as a scientist would, so that the controlled experiment can be repeated any number of times.

Clearly, in the landscape of this paper, the echo can be heard of Berdyaev's statement that being does not arise from a "re-distribution" of objects. This idea of Eliot's, says Bly, is completely unlike Lorca's idea of poetry. "For Lorca there is not time to think of a cunning set of circumstances that would carry the emotion in a dehydrated form to which the reader need only add water." The "Lorcan" tradition sees the poem as an "infinite concentration of personality," the goal of which is to "make men more and more inward until they stop admiring objects, at which point they will be able to see them clearly, if they wish to." Such a poem is finally indistinguishable from the personality of the poet. Bly writes:

> The great poets of this century have written their poems in exactly the opposite way from the generation of 1917. In the poems of Neruda, Vallejo, Jiminez, Machado, Rilke, the poem is an extension of the substance of the man, no different from his skin or his hands. The substance of the man who wrote the poem reaches far out into the darkness and the poem is his whole body, seeing with his ears and his fingers and his hair.

In Berdyaev's terms, Bly sees the poets named above as having been unable to keep united subject and object. They have been able to do what the Russian writers named by Berdyaev were not able to do; they have been able to transform literature into self. They have transcended the "temptation" of art forms by creating being,

not symbols of being, making the poet and the poem one personality, one "skin," through creativity.

There are strong parallels in the thinking of Berdyaev and Bly: Both see creativity as, in some sense, redemptive. Both see the dark (Ungrund) as the source of energy, and both see obedience to objects as the path away from creativity. There is, however, a striking difference between them with regard to the question of the "final limits" of creativity.

Bly seems to say that in the blend of poet and poem into one skin, the limits of creativity are the same as the limits of human being, the poem being no more "symbolic" than the poet. Berdyaev, however, were he alive and conversant with Bly, might feel moved to warn him thus:

> Created beings do not create beings—these are created only by God. . . . Such an attempt is always demonic—it is black magic. Only God has the power to create living being, personality. . . . Substance cannot be created in the creative process. Every attempt to understand creativity as the reproduction of new living beings, rather than as an increase in energy, as growth and upswing created by God, is both godless and demonic. The tendency in this direction leads to the production of an automatic and mechanical being, devoid of life. This is the creativity of the fallen angel. (*Creative Act*)

A further danger beyond these statements but drawn from the thinking of Berdyaev, could be that if a poet were to succeed in creating something dark, it might be himself. The new being of the poem might be his own new being as well, in the union of subject with object. One wonders if the dark a poet might create would release him. Berdyaev has said that only God can create humanity from the Ungrund; perhaps that is the element of "sacrifice" involved in creativity.

What the poet might be sacrificing might be his own being. Bly seems to know this. The last line of *The Man in the Black Coat Turns* is: "I fight—it's time—it's right—and am torn to pieces fighting." What could be the motive for such a risk?

In the prose poem, "Eleven O'Clock at Night," Bly writes, "I am aware of the consciousness I have, and I mourn the consciousness I do not have," and he adds a few lines later, "now more and more I long for what I cannot escape from" (*Coat*): Bly seems aware of the danger involved in what Berdyaev terms the "ek-stasis" of the creative act and is nevertheless seeking it in order to achieve new consciousness.

From Berdyaev's perspective, Bly is surely a "religious" poet. Despite his probable admonitions to Bly concerning the "godlessness" of trying to create being, Bly would surely be Berdyaev's poet in another sense—in trying to achieve new being by risking his own being in creativity, and by trying to be the friend that God seeks.

Brian Horowitz (essay date 1994)

SOURCE: "A Jewish-Christian Rift in Twentieth-Century Russian Philosophy: N. A. Berdiaev and M. O. Gershenzon," in *The Russian Review,* Vol. 53, No. 4, October, 1994, pp. 497-514.

[In the following essay, Horowitz details the reasons for the ideological conflict between Berdyaev and his long-time friend M. O. Gershenzon.]

> My philosophy has always been a philosophy of conflict.
>
> (Nikolai Berdiaev about himself)

> The erudite "Kulturtrèger" several times showed me the power of the elemental forces living within him.
>
> (Andrei Belyi about Mikhail Gershenzon)

The Bolshevik Revolution of October 1917 found the two friends, religious philosopher Nikolai Berdiaev and historian and philosopher M. O. Gershenzon, on different sides of the conflict. Berdiaev's vehement opposition to the Revolution ostensibly caused him to sever relations with the sympathizer Gershenzon. In 1952, Gershenzon's daughter, Nataliia Mikhailovna Gershenzon-Chegodaeva, wrote in her memoirs that her father's and Berdiaev's friendship "ended badly. During the days of the October Revolution, when my dad was completely aflame, passionately awaiting and welcoming the new, they suddenly severed relations, disagreeing over political convictions. Several painful letters remain which reflect the break."

The sudden end to the relationship between two of Russia's most creative thinkers of this century is usually attributed to their differences of opinion about the October Revolution. In fact, however, the politics at the time of the Revolution was only a catalyst for the break; the real cause of their estrangement lay in their unresolvable philosophical debates and their emotional conflicts arising from their Christian and Jewish backgrounds. They clashed philosophically because Berdiaev favored an idiosyncratic Christian philosophy, while Gershenzon adhered to a pantheist religion of the "cosmos." Their personal dispute, which revolved around anti-Semitism, arose because of Berdiaev's exclusive attachment to Christianity. These differences are evident in their respective attitudes toward the Russian intelligentsia, Slavophilism, World War I and the October Revolution.

Although scholars have shed light on the life and work of Nikolai Berdiaev, little is known about Gershenzon. Mikhail Osipovich Gershenzon was born of Jewish parents in 1869 in Kishinev in the Pale of Settlement. Although he excelled at Moscow University, winning a gold medal for his work on ancient Greek history, Gershenzon was prevented from pursuing an academic career due to his status as a Jew. In spite of cultural anti-Semitism, Gershenzon finally achieved fame with his critical articles and monographs about Russian literature and culture.

Gershenzon's multifaceted oeuvre, which ranges from scholarship on Russian thinkers of the nineteenth century to critical works on contemporary Russian literature and Pushkin, earned him the acclaim of critics and fellow writers. Vasilii Rozanov proclaimed him "Russia's best historian," while N. Kotliarevskii helped Gershenzon to win the Academy of Science's Akhmatovskii award for the best historical work of 1909. In addition, readers called him the "Russian Carlyle" and many praised Gershenzon as a "master" of Russian prose. For Gershenzon, popularity was essential because he lived most of his life without a secure income, depending on the sale of his books and articles for his livelihood.

Gershenzon was also an active observer of Russia's political life. He edited and contributed to *Landmarks,* the 1909 collection of essays criticizing the Russian revolutionary intelligentsia, and coauthored the famous ***Correspondence from Two Corners*** with the poet Viacheslav Ivanov. Despite Gershenzon's ideological irreconcilability to the Soviet regime, he held important offices in the literary bureaucracy. He was the first president of the Moscow Union of Writers, and from 1922 to 1925 served as the head of the Literary Section of the Soviet Academy of Sciences. He died in Moscow from heart failure in 1925.

Several descriptions of the close friendship between Berdiaev and Gershenzon are available from such first-hand witnesses as Fedor Stepun, Evgeniia Gertsyk, Andrei Belyi, Nataliia Baranova-Shestova and Gershenzon's daughter. The latter remembered Berdiaev as a constant visitor:

> In 1914-15 my parents were very close with Berdiaev and not only with him, but also with his wife, the beautiful and dignified woman (sort of a poet), Lidia Iudifovna, and her sister Evgeniia Iudifovna. . . . The Berdiaevs lived on Saint Vasil'evskii Street and at one time interaction between our houses was frequent. They did domestic errands for each other. And our cabinet with the glass doors covered with colored paper depicting fantastic little lions remains as a memory of the Berdiaevs. My parents somehow bought it from the Berdiaevs especially for us, for our books and toys.

Although Berdiaev and Gershenzon began their friendship in 1909 while collaborating on *Landmarks,* their circle of friends and set of interests had been drawing them together earlier. They befriended the same individuals (S. Frank, S. Bulgakov, V. Ivanov and P. Struve) and wrote for the same journals (*Voprosy filosofii i psikhologii, Russkaia mysl'* and *Nauchnoe slovo*). Just as many other Russian *intelligenty* in the

early twentieth century had done, Berdiaev and Gershenzon turned away from the nineteenth-century preoccupations with the political struggle against the autocracy and with the well-being of the peasants, embracing
philosophical idealism and the search for personal metaphysics. Concretely, Berdiaev and Gershenzon were affected by Friedrich Nietzsche and the metaphysical interpretation of his teachings as a guide to the spiritual
realization of the individual. In addition, Fedor Dostoevsky, Vladimir Solov'ev and Lev Tolstoy influenced
them intellectually and emotionally. These native sources helped Berdiaev and Gershenzon to discover their
roles as secular religious thinkers and to create their
own perspectives on the difficult social, political and
religious questions facing Russia.

The first decade of the twentieth century was a transitional period for Berdiaev. He followed the same trajec-
tory as Frank, Bulgakov and Struve, leaving the camp of
Critical Marxism and heading toward philosophical idealism. In 1902, Berdiaev contributed an article to *Problems of Idealism,* a volume which served as a *profession
de foi* of the idealists, and during this period he attacked
the philosophical premises of his old idols, Legal Marxism and Neo-Kantianism. In essays published five years
later in **Sub specie aeternitatis,** Berdiaev exposed the
anti-individualist content of Marxist thinking and the
deceptive epistemology of neo-Kantianism. He claimed
that Kantian idealism proclaimed certainties it could not
defend. Real certainty, Berdiaev was coming to realize,
could not be attained by philosophy, but only by religion, which treated man not as an isolated brain, but as
a full person living in the world.

Berdiaev's practical work also reflects his transition to
idealism. From 1905-6 he served as editor of *Voprosy
zhizni,* the journal associated with the Symbolist movement, and soon after he served on the editorial board of
a journal, *Put',* devoted to the study of philosophy and
religion. He was also involved in the establishment of
the Moscow Psychological Society and the Moscow Re-
ligious-Philosophical Society. These practical affairs
attest to Berdiaev's organization skills and his broad
association with a large variety of different individuals
and intellectual movements.

In contrast, Gershenzon arrived at an antipositivist perspective in relative isolation. His idealist philosophy
seems to have been formed from various sources: his
study of antipositivist methods in pedagogy, German
romantic literature, the Slavophiles and Symbolist poetry. In particular, in Russian Symbolism Gershenzon
discovered his ideal of an egoistic individual who used
his spiritual strength to transform reality. While Gershenzon admired powerful individuals, he claimed that
spiritual accomplishments were more valuable than
achievements in society. His unwavering faith in the
primary value of the individual as an anarchistic destroyer of society's encrusted values aligned him intellectually with Symbolists such as Andrei Belyi,

Viacheslav Ivanov, Fedor Sologub and Dmitrii Merezhkovskii. His conviction that real freedom could only be
achieved in the spirit, meanwhile, aligned him with
religious philosophers such as Lev Shestov, S. Bulgakov
and V. Ern.

In addition to initiating his friendship with Berdiaev,
Landmarks was a breakthrough for Gershenzon because
it brought him into close contact with the leading philosophers of the day. In its structure and neoreligious
perspective, this volume of essays by seven non-Marxist
thinkers was conditioned by its predecessor, *Problems of
Idealism.* But *Landmarks* was a very different endeavor.
It was not merely a manifesto of the Neo-Idealist movement, as was *Problems of Idealism;* more importantly, it
was a critique of the ideological mainsprings of the
intelligentsia in the aftermath of the unsuccessful 1905
Revolution. Thus it carried a discreet political message.
Landmarks not only disparaged the mentality of the
revolutionaries, it expressed the common sentiment of
an entire group of thinkers who had resolutely turned
away from revolution. According to the editor
Gershenzon, writing in his introduction, the contributors expressed their shared belief in the superiority of
the spiritual or "internal" life over its political or "external" facade and the need for each individual to perfect himself before taking up the task of perfecting society.

Since the contributors were calling for comprehensive
changes in the intelligentsia's basic orientation, *Landmarks* elicited an enormous storm of criticism. The
strong response was uplifting for the contributors, since
it convinced them that there was a potentially large
interest in religious ideas. More importantly for the
contributors themselves, however, *Landmarks* set a tone
of sibling comradery, but it also created emotional and
intellectual expectations from those new friendships that
could not be fulfilled. In the case of Gershenzon and
Berdiaev, *Landmarks* gave the deceptive impression of a
unity that did not really exist.

Although once *Landmarks* appeared in print there was
an immediate fallingout among the contributors (B.
Kistiakovskii and A. Izgoev repudiated Gershenzon's
introduction because they advocated external changes,
such as legal reform), Berdiaev was ideologically
closest to Gershenzon and did not take issue with the
introduction. Regardless of other points of dispute
with Gershenzon, he could unconditionally agree that
political change had to take a back seat to the transformation of the individual. As a solution to the political
problems of tsarist injustice and leftist intransigence,
Berdiaev emphasized the efficacy of education in the
development of moral individuals who would take the
lead in improving society. In tandem, Gershenzon professed his belief that society could be reformed only
through the spiritual perfection of its individual members. For both thinkers, the reform of political institutions was to follow and serve the internal growth of
individuals.

Despite their agreement on the primacy of the spiritual sphere of human life, Berdiaev had significant differences with Gershenzon. In fact, Berdiaev had a completely opposite view of the intelligentsia and its role in Russia's future. While Berdiaev merely wanted to change the intelligentsia's values, leaving its basic structure intact, Gershenzon envisioned all change to occur through individuals. Thus, he did not consider the intelligentsia of any positive importance.

In his *Landmarks* article, "Creative Self-Consciousness," Gershenzon claims that the 1905 Revolution failed because of an unfortunate severing of "consciousness" and "will" in each individual member of the intelligentsia. Such severing was caused by the negligence of an individual's own personal life. For all too long the individual *intelligent* had subordinated personal goals to those of the collective, becoming a "cripple," physically, mentally and politically unhealthy. In order to rectify the situation, Gershenzon advised a return to individual interests.

In contrast to what we would usually consider "individual interests," Gershenzon suggests that these are spiritual endeavors. Spirituality here means the dictates of the cosmos that people follow their individual "wills." Will, in contrast to reason, is that absolutely personal (*lichnoe*) part of the individual, the spirit, which perceives the natural union or "holism" (*tsel'nost'*) between a person and the universe. Gershenzon explains that will, not "supra-personal" reason, should rule the individual because it is connected with an individual's real feeling and thus is the "inner motor of his whole life." Unlike the "pure-cerebral" idea, which is "essentially dead," will is an "idea-feeling" or an "idea-passion." According to Gershenzon, the individual must avoid rational thinking because being is organically grounded in spirituality, which is manifested by the pantheistic feeling that the individual is part and parcel of the universe.

Gershenzon's counsel for a return to personal life, to an internal spirituality achieved through the union of the individual with the cosmic whole, implicitly requests the complete elimination of the intelligentsia. The individual would not congregate for the purpose of changing the world or reforming the state; rather, an individual's radicalism is the transformation of his own psyche. Gershenzon probably arrived at his individualism out of pessimism about political organizations. In Russia every organized group—the intelligentsia, the government and the political parties—was tained by moral laxity or worse with regard to the Jews and their struggle to achieve elementary civil rights. Gershenzon's own experience had shown that only individuals treated the members of other nationalities without discrimination.

Compared with Gershenzon's maximalism, Berdiaev comes across as a moderate in *Landmarks*. His goal is not the ultimate destruction of the intelligentsia, but a sensible reform of its priorities. Admiring the intelligentsia's traditional search for truth and justice, he takes issue with its strategy. Finding its constant subordination of moral absolutes to the relative exigencies of day-to-day politics wrong and destructive, he concludes that the intelligentsia should seek its purpose in eternal truths: God, religion and philosophy. In his *Landmarks* article, "Philosophical Truth and the Truth of the Intelligentsia," Berdiaev writes that even today "the young people in our intelligentsia cannot recognize the independent significance of science, philosophy, education, universities," and subordinate them "to the interests of politics, the parties, tendencies and circles."

Despite these flaws, Berdiaev did not regard the intelligentsia as a useless and dangerous association. On the contrary, he ascribes a great potential to it. The intelligentsia's venerable history as the embodiment in Russia of the eternal values of education and social progress shows its virtuous high regard for philosophy and the values of absolute truth. Although its basic attitude toward changing the world should remain the same, it must modify its consciousness toward religion. "All the historical and psychological facts say that the Russian intelligentsia can move to a new consciousness only on the basis of a synthesis of knowledge and faith," he argued. That synthesis should be one that "positively satisfies the intelligentsia's valuable need for an organic union of theory and practice, and 'truth-absolute' and 'truth-justice.'"

Although before the appearance of *Landmarks* Berdiaev and Gershenzon struggled against logical positivism and rationalism in the defense of religious feeling, by 1910 their thinking had radically diverged, as Berdiaev shifted markedly toward Christianity. Berdiaev was nonecumenical and religious in a broad manner. Making no distinction between religion or metaphysics, he had lauded any honest attempt to penetrate the spiritual mysteries and religious purpose of life. In this respect his attitude toward religion paralleled that of the other major secular religious thinkers of Russia of the time, Merezhkovskii, Bulgakov, Ivanov, Rozanov and Shestov. In *Sub specie aeternitatis,* for example, Berdiaev supported such non-Christian spiritual ideas as "Mystical Anarchism," Dmitrii Merezhkovskii's idiosyncratic "Religion of the Third Testament," and the sociological theories of F. Lassale and R. Avenarius.

By 1910, however, Berdiaev turned from his nonecumenicalism and began arguing for a social reconstruction of society on specifically Christian principles. Only Christianity, he now believed, could give an ultimate significance to man's past, present and future and determine the unique role of every individual in history. In this way, Berdiaev trod the same evolutionary path to Christianity that the other former Legal Marxists, Sergei Bulgakov and Semen Frank, traversed. Like them, Berdiaev found in idealism only a way-station on the road to Christianity.

Berdiaev first offered his ideas on Christian freedom and election and the purpose of Christian communal life in *The Intelligentsia's Spiritual Crisis* (1910). Although the Christian views he expressed in this work were not strongly felt in his contribution to *Landmarks,* both works contain Berdiaev's conviction that the issues of politics and religion must be addressed together. In *The Intelligentsia's Spiritual Crisis,* Berdiaev claims that Christianity had been wrong to reject politics. Christians, he claims, must use the inherent freedom given by God in an active way to free humanity from the unfreedom of nature and human institutions. Humanity must participate as God's son in the voluntary construction of an anarchistic, Christian theocracy—a political-religious utopia. This vision of a theocratic world allowed Berdiaev to uphold the tsarist state as a temporary good, even though overcoming the state was his ultimate goal. "The state is not the final goal of social development, this aim lies in the free power of God and in anarchy, but only through the state and its power is this aim achieved. One should conditionally sanction the state in order to overcome it absolutely."

In *The Philosophy of Freedom* (1911), Berdiaev offers an epistemological basis for Christianity, arguing that at base every philosophy is founded on an unprovable premise, that is, faith, but only one philosophy is founded on freedom. Since every philosophy is inevitably subjective, Christianity is no less "rational" than Kant's idealism or Hume's empiricism. In fact, Berdiaev claims that Christianity is more rational because it treats the whole human being in the world with individual religious feelings and religious knowledge. Rationalism and empiricism deal merely with rationally verifiable matter. Thus, they wrongly give no consideration at all to the entire part of human's being that cannot be verified—religious belief.

Christianity, according to Berdiaev, is the only philosophy which provides humanity with freedom. Through resurrection of the body, the Christian is freed from the material world and is no longer a slave to bodily destruction. This lifts humanity's vision from the world of the body to the world of the spirit. Moreover, in Berdiaev's view this freedom is not and cannot be coercive, it must be chosen voluntarily. For this reason, God brought his son to earth in the form of a pauper, so that man would not be tempted by material gain and thereby be forced to believe. The idea of freedom takes precedence even over the idea of perfection because, as he confesses in his autobiography, "it is impossible to accept obligatory, enforced perfection."

Perfection, for Berdiaev, is humanity's fulfillment of Christ's promise to return to earth at the end of time. Since history is the road that must be traveled to arrive at the end, Christianity posits human history as a story of divine purpose. In Christ is the secret of humanity's freedom, the secret of the beginning and end of history and the secret of resurrection. In *The Philosophy of Freedom,* Berdiaev explains:

> At the center of the tragedy stands the divine Man—Christ. The historical movement of the tragedy goes to and from Him. Christ is the absolute center of the cosmos, and He became embodied as a man and appeared on the earth. Therefore humanity acquired a cosmic significance, in Him the soul of the world returned to God. . . . Christianity is not even faith in the immortality of the soul, in its natural transformation, but faith in resurrection, which must be conquered universally, prepared historically, must be a task of the entire cosmos.

Human history—the evolution from the beginning of the world to its return to God—is a specifically Christian task in which all must participate. From this claim, one can understand Berdiaev's belief that the Jews' renunciation of Christ was historically incorrect and that they must join the religion of Christ in order to participate in the divine plan: "That Christ turned the history of the world upside-down is a fact which the whole world is forced to accept; not only the Christian world, but also the world foreign to Christ and antagonistic to Him."

Berdiaev's increasing attachment to Christianity underlay the conflict that erupted between him and Gershenzon, for that attachment suffused Berdiaev's views on many other issues, over some of which he and Gershenzon clashed vigorously. Take, for example, their attitudes toward Slavophilism. Few Russians understood the importance of Slavophilism in the early twentieth century, especially since it was regarded as politically retrograde. Berdiaev and Gershenzon agreed on the importance of Slavophile thought, in its own right and for its application to contemporary philosophical problems. But they approached the Slavophiles from different sources and therefore emphasized different aspects of the teaching. Berdiaev, as did Frank and Bulgakov, came upon the Slavophiles from an examination of Vladimir Solov'ev and found in them eloquent spokesmen for Russian Orthodoxy. In contrast, Gershenzon discovered the Slavophiles from his historical studies of such Westernizers as Herzen, Ogarev and Chaadaev, and he juxtaposed the two groups. Gershenzon interpreted the Slavophiles as spokesmen of a universal spiritual psychology. Needless to say, he was isolated in his viewpoint.

In *Historical Sketches* (1910), Gershenzon explored the biographies and philosophies of Ivan Kireevskii, Iurii Samarin and Nikolai Gogol in order to shed light on three aspects of Slavophile thought. And by binding them together he hoped to show that Slavophilism was a united, whole philosophical system. In addition, he wanted to reveal the main differences between the Slavophile and Westernizer philosophies and demonstrate why Slavophile thought was superior. And, finally, as he admitted when responding to Petr Struve's criticisms of *Historical Sketches,* Gershenzon wrote the book because he

> wanted to tell how the (philosophical) break came about, how one of the doctrines presented here,

the rationalist, was completely mastered by the huge majority of society, and the other, religious, was distorted already in its infancy and with time became more and more distorted; how they struggled at first, how their struggle became more complicated, and finally, what were the profound consequences for the individual and society due to the domination of the former and the neglect and distortion of the latter.

According to Gershenzon, the victory of the Westernizers was a tragedy for Russia because their reliance on rationalism and intellectual sources for humanity's happiness contradicts man's true religious nature. The Slavophiles' universal philosophy better corresponds to human psychological needs and thus would have served Russia better.

Berdiaev, who was himself working on the Slavophiles at this time, held a mixed opinion of *Historical Sketches*. In 1912, when working on a book about the theologian Aleksei Stepanovich Khomiakov, he was able to write that "I highly value Gershenzon's works." He thought Gershenzon was "very sensitive to the religious motivation of the Slavophiles and their psychological features" and regarded him as one of "the first to see in Slavophilism an example of Russian national self-consciousness and not just one movement among others." At the same time, however, he vehemently disapproved of Gershenzon's idiosyncratic and unfounded interpretation of the Slavophiles as teachers of a universal spirituality whose importance lies primarily outside the context of Russian Orthodox religious life. As early as 1910 he complained that "Gershenzon gives an individualistic interpretation of the essence of Slavophilism and in this lies his one-sidedness."

What irritated Berdiaev most of all was the intentional exclusion from *Historical Sketches* of Khomiakov, whom Gershenzon believed a mere imitator of Kireevskii. This, in Berdiaev's eyes, was a fundamental flaw in Gershenzon's understanding of Slavophilism, for Berdiaev regarded Khomiakov as the central figure of the Slavophile group. "Khomiakov was above all a Russian Orthodox theologian, a Christian thinker, a cavalier of the Russian Orthodox Church," Berdiaev wrote in 1912. "Gershenzon clearly does not like Khomiakov and ignores him to the same extent to which he loves Kireevskii to a passion. This attitude toward Khomiakov prevents Gershenzon's evaluation of Slavophilism in its entirety, destroys historical perspective."

Gershenzon believed he had good reason for ignoring Khomiakov. Unlike Berdiaev, he did not want to investigate or construct a Russian Orthodox theology or even examine the religious content of Slavophilism; rather, he sought to extract from Slavophilism an ahistorical, universal spirituality, "to husk the authentic core, the eternal religious truth, to cleanse it of its Slavophile skin which had strongly grown onto it, and clearly to explain it as simply as possible." But Berdiaev regarded

Gershenzon's attempt to universalize the Slavophiles as methodologically dubious and historically unacceptable:

> He takes from Slavophilism merely that which is dear to him, clearly perceives in Slavophilism merely that which is visible from the position on which he stands. One can cleanse Slavophilism of the rotten idealism of the backward forms of life, of assigning an absolute significance to the reigning form of government, but it is impossible to cleanse Slavophilism of the universal truth of Christianity.

The vehemence of Berdiaev's criticisms is understandable, given the special interest he had in the theological significance of Slavophilism and his focus on Khomiakov, who is manifestly a Russian Orthodox thinker. But there is a sense in which they are overstated. Berdiaev's objection to Gershenzon's separation of Slavophilism and Russian Orthodoxy seems a bit unfair when one considers that even Berdiaev admitted the scholar's right to remove from Slavophilism the ugly remnants of contemporary ideological and political institutions. As a reinterpretation of Slavophilism for its time, Gershenzon's work is a valid and significant contribution to the literature. But if Gershenzon's task is, as he himself defined it, "historical" in nature—the objective investigation of the ideas in the historical context they were created—then Gershenzon cannot be excused in completely purifying Slavophilism of its Russian Orthodox elements, and Berdiaev's criticisms, while one-sided in favor of a Russian Orthodox interpretation, are justified.

The disagreement over the Slavophiles recalls the essential differences in their thinking: the pointedly Russian Orthodox focus of Berdiaev's thinking and Gershenzon's idea of religion as a general human urge or psychological necessity. Of course, their disparate philosophical backgrounds and interests help to explain their attitudes toward Slavophilism. Despite the influence of his free-thinking Voltarian father, Berdiaev was brought up a member of the Russian Orthodox Church, and his works proclaim the preeminence of Christianity as the sole religion of salvation. In contrast, Gershenzon tried to find a personal religion of the cosmos to replace his Judaism, which he believed was tainted by the provincialism and backwardness of the Pale of Settlement.

In this way, while Berdiaev interpreted the Slavophiles as intellectual catalysts for his own return to Russian Orthodoxy, Gershenzon used the Slavophiles as timeless spokesmen of a nondenominational spirituality, one which satisfies the individual's psychological needs for religion without forcing membership in any religious institution. This latter requirement was especially important for Gershenzon because he had strong personal reasons for not wanting to renounce Judaism. With pogroms and expulsions of Jews from the capitals fairly ordinary events in Russia at that time, Gershenzon's knowledge that Berdiaev's aggressively Christian argumentation could justify anti-Semitic activity probably exacerbated the ideological conflict. Although Gershenzon was not a practicing Jew and was completely assimilated to Russian culture, he was sensitive to ideologies that promulgated racial or religious superiority or incited anti-Jewish feeling.

The outbreak of World War One obscured Berdiaev's and Gershenzon's different religious perspectives and brought the two into temporary agreement. Despite their limitless objection to the slaughter and destruction, both found redeeming features in the horrors of war: bourgeois society had revealed a hidden propensity for self-annihilation; people were tired of the old world and yearned for change. Berdiaev hoped that the war would usher in a new, religious world. The war was "providential and unavoidable," he wrote to Gershenzon in 1914, "and I believe that we and the whole world will emerge from it reborn. The genuine world can only be reached through war. The bourgeois world isn't worth a thing, it was a lie. Now my whole soul desires Russia's victory over the Germans." Gershenzon revealed much the same beliefs in a 1915 article, "The Second Year of War":

> It turns out first of all that nobody thinks about personal property, not only us, but even the greedy Germans: blossoming, rich industry, wonderfully established trading contacts, comfort and loveliness—let them get ruined and disappear, they are not worth a cent! Who could have expected such scorn for the things of this world from a European? Or in the depth of his soul did he really not cherish them before the war as well, as it would seem; that is, he pretended to cherish them, but not in the absolute, but with a certain hidden reservation to himself, that this is only until a better thing comes along, and so that nothing else pushed itself in meanwhile?

As the war progressed, their positions gradually diverged. Under the influence of events, Berdiaev developed his ideas concerning the essence and purpose of the nation, viewing the forces of imperialism and messianism with utopian hopefulness. In articles of this period Berdiaev expressed a new optimism. The war, he asserted, had contributed to the positive, dialectical process of preserving the self-identity of each separate nation, while secretly encouraging the unity of all nations. As he put it in 1916, humanity's contemporary history was undergoing a "dual process":

> a process of universalism and a process of individualization, unification into large bodies and dissolution into smaller bodies. Nationalism is the beginning of individualization, imperialism— the beginning of universalism. At the same time that nationalism is inclined to isolation, imperialism desires an exit into the world expanse. These beginnings are of differing quality, but do not exclude each other, they coexist.

At his highest point of delusion here, Berdiaev announced, moreover, that "through struggle and discord, imperialism all the same promotes the unification of humanity."

Berdiaev's optimism during the war appears to be connected with his idea of "Creativity," a concept he culled from Nietzsche but then transformed and applied to Christianity. In *The Meaning of Creativity,* published in 1916, although written a few years earlier, Berdiaev promotes creativity as the means for the realization of the Christian purpose and each individual's spiritual perfection. The goal of the relationship between humanity and God, Berdiaev claims, is the fusion of humanity and God in bringing about the principle eschatological purpose of Christianity—eternal life beyond the confines of history. In describing this relationship, Berdiaev writes that "God's final mystery is the birth of man in God. And this mystery is a unique mystery. For man not only needs God, but God also needs man. In this is Christ's mystery, the mystery of the God-man."

In this philosophy Jesus Christ plays the most significant role, since he is the model of the creative individual who successfully accomplished what each person is intended to do: he joined with God and creatively moved humanity closer to its goal—the end of history, perfection beyond historical time. The secret of Christ and his instruction for man was his exercise of free will, his free acceptance of the crucifixion. His freedom is the life of the spirit and not of the body, the surpassing of this life and the revelation of eternal life. In a letter to Gershenzon from June 1915 Berdiaev wrote that "Christianity is above all a revelation of freedom in the spirit."

> The suffering and torture of life, the horror of death enters inside and becomes experienced as a free Golgotha and not as an imposed and enforced necessity. Christ defeated death because he experienced it not as an external, enforced fact of the natural order, but as an internal moment of life itself, as the free acceptance of the crucifixion.

In Berdiaev's conception, the crucifixion exemplifies creativity. It stands for man's control of his own destiny for the sake of the realization of the eschatological aim of Christianity. In this sense, man no longer has to accept life as he finds it, but must work to change its course. Creativity, which is man's "overcoming of himself" in a monumental act of self-becoming, permits humanity the freedom to direct history.

Berdiaev's early optimism about the war can thus be explained by his philosophical ideas of the time. The same self-becoming which Berdiaev knew philosophically, he probably thought he espied mystically in the depths of the violent armed conflict. He was convinced that current events corresponded to the imagined course of Christian teleology. Beneath the overt destruction of material life Berdiaev saw free, creative individuals eagerly transforming the world. Christians, Germans and Russians would join together in overcoming the body (was war not a rejection of the body?) and fulfill the imperative of realizing the Christian eschatology. Berdiaev, who had often fallen prisoner to his own esoteric concepts, did not fully notice the cleft between his ideas and reality. Only in 1917 did he understand the full scope of his mistake; at that time he renounced the war, strongly fearing that a Communist seizure of power was about to take place.

In contrast to Berdiaev, Gershenzon rejected institutional religion, relying on cosmic thinking in formulating his own solution to the war. Gershenzon suggested that individuals who employ "will" and not "reason" would reject the war, since war was caused by rationalism. Rationalism had propagated an epistemology based on the individual's adherence to supra-individual reason, and this epistemology was not new but had merely found its most authentic expression in war. In contrast to the world founded on reason, Gershenzon dreamed of a new world which he hoped could be engendered through the "triple image of perfection": the perfect image of the self, the perfect image of society and the perfect image of oneself in society.

In his 1918 treatise, *The Triple Image of Perfection,* Gershenzon claimed that for humanity to reaffirm its own existence, it has learned to utilize other beings for its own ends; it has discovered and perfected an epistemology based on the division and reduction of things. The rationale is that complete individuals provide no utility; only by breaking them up into pieces can one use them. Gershenzon used a tree as an example: useless while alive and whole, when cut down and broken into pieces it could be used to a variety of ends or fashioned into innumerable things. So it was with other beings, which humanity once saw as complete individuals, but no longer. Now it sees in them only faceless members of a class, group or race from which can be exacted utility. Gershenzon explains:

> Man creates his things in this way. He creates them all from their innate bodies. But each innate body is individual; taken in the living wholeness of its individual qualities, it is useless for man. In order to gain possession of it, one must first of all rip it out from the powerful unity of nature, and this means to kill its personality, that is, to cut down or rip out a tree; a corpse is made: man's first victory.

The problem, however, is that by affirming one's individuality, a person destroys the image of perfection within.

There is only one way of overcoming the illness of rational thinking, and that is the realization of one's image of perfection. In this case, the individual returns to the original state of "holism" in which is perceived the unity of the whole of being and one's perfect place in the universe. According to Gershenzon, through love the individual's warped perception of the world can be corrected. In *The Triple Image of Perfection* he writes, "The image of perfection of he who loves is excited to action: either he realizes himself through the loved one, or at least he actively reaffirms himself through guarding the loved one; he who is loved, only through the affirmation of the loved one, is he taught to know in

himself his image of perfection." Gershenzon is speaking of spiritual love, not erotic love; love in which the person perceives the other as a complete individual and an end in itself, not as a means toward an end. This "holistic" perception heals the spiritual wounds caused by the person's former way of thinking. Through the perception of the other as a whole, you yourself become whole as well.

In Gershenzon's view a "holistic" worldview would solve all the intractable problems caused by rationalism and its epistemology of "divide and conquer." It must be added that Gershenzon rarely, if ever, dealt with the real issues of an actual commonwealth. He seems to have believed that if all individuals possessed a holistic consciousness, the problems of society and even conflicts between countries would resolve themselves. Although such a personalist morality reflects the influence of Tolstoyan ethics, such abstract thinking was highly detached given the critical political situation at the time.

Incidentally, their differences concerning the war refer to their original divisions in *Landmarks:* Just as before, so too in 1914, Berdiaev entrusted man's fate to organized institutions, in this case the Church, while Gershenzon placed his faith solely in secular individuals detached from any organized groups. In addition, while Berdiaev put his faith in Christianity as the vehicle of salvation, Gershenzon placed his hope in a pantheistic personal religion.

The final catalyst for the break in Berdiaev's and Gershenzon's already tense relationship was a disagreement over political affiliation in September 1917. Perhaps this disagreement would not have severed their relationship in normal times, but the political radicalism of the moment demanded that each individual choose between two and only two camps: for or against the Bolsheviks. In his final letter to Gershenzon, written on 29 September, Berdiaev attacked him for his apparent allegiance to Bolshevism. Like the other contributors to *Landmarks,* Berdiaev felt Gershenzon had made a large ideological shift to the left, becoming in his eyes a political enemy:

> Have you finally really forgotten that you were one of the important initiators of "Landmarks," that the most critical article against the revolutionary intelligentsia belongs to you, and you expressed disgust at its sincere cast of mind. This obligates you. How could it be, that at the moment of the revolution, when the former forces have been unchained and those same ideas and feelings which you mercilessly criticized have been thrown to the dark masses, when the enormous spiritual values have been exposed to danger, you have lost all your spiritual baggage, swim with the current and use street language foreign to you? And you began to cry out the words about "the bourgeois," "counter-revolution," "without annexation and indemnity" and so forth, although these words are empty and filled with a terrible lie. It is painful to watch. It is awful that the best

writers in Russia have shown so little spiritual independence and have not found their own words at this most difficult minute of all history.

Responding to Berdiaev the next day, in a letter which would be his last to his former collaborator, Gershenzon explains the essential difference between the two camps and the reasons he chose to support the revolution:

> I believe that the best people in Russia have separated into two parties: the party of the heart and the party of the idea, ideology; the first feel pain for the living person, for those in need and burdened, the other, and you among them, feel no less pain for the values—statehood, holism and the might of Russia. People of the heart also have their ideology—internationalism and so on; and one against the other two ideologies have risen, one for the happiness and freedom of the individual person, the other for the preservation of supra-personal values. On the one and the other side are the best, the most spiritual and honest people of Russia. Mercenary, morally empty people have attached themselves to both groups: to Lenin—those who are greedy, seeking to rip for themselves a piece of "happiness," to Struve and you—those who are awaiting the "happiness," which has already been won to return, the industrialists and landowners. The workers and the peasants pillage Russia in the name of the individual, Riabushinskii and P. N. L'vov destroy it in the name of national values! I repeat: the heart and psychology have their own ideology and for that you should respect them.

Gershenzon was torn. Although he identified with the "humiliated, tortured people, in whom the feeling of the human pride, honor and dignity of the individual had so violently appeared," Gershenzon also knew "the importance and beauty of values, their necessity and not only in their own right, but . . . also for each individual person." Despite Gershenzon's confession of ambivalence, however, it is a fact that the old intelligentsia was surprised by what they regarded as Gershenzon's outward change. In 1918, when Petr Struve was inviting the contributors to *Landmarks* to participate in the publication of *From the Depth,* he pointedly excluded Gershenzon, "who had become politically foreign to us," as unsuitable for a volume in which the contributors "were going to give a principled foundation for their negation of Bolshevism." But Gershenzon thought Berdiaev and the others were "terribly mistaken" in their judgment about his stance. In his final letter to Berdiaev he had plaintively pointed out that "during the whole period of the revolution I have not written one newspaper article. And I have not written because my feeling is contradictory, because at one and the same time I rejoice and I am horrified."

In light of his confessed inability to decide between the warring groups, is it certain that Gershenzon had become a sympathizer of Bolshevism? The case is at least more complex that Berdiaev believed. Gershenzon did not want to choose between the cultural values of "state-hood" (*gosudarstvennost'*) and the "concrete individual now living," understanding the importance of both. The dispute, he wrote to Berdiaev, was "natural and beneficial," and he believed that after "the individual and the values fight once again as they have many times before," they would reach a "temporary *modus vivendi* on which they will calm down for a moment and then splendidly blossom until a new confrontation." But Gershenzon had no desire to embrace one side or lend his voice in such a way that would aggravate tensions: "Russia's situation is so terrible that one side has got somehow to cede to the other and find a compromise."

Clearly, then, Gershenzon and Berdiaev had their own distinct perceptions of the political landscape in September 1917. Berdiaev perceived the choice as one between liberalism and radicalism even before the Bolshevik Revolution. He thereby excluded the Socialist Revolutionaries as a realistic force. Gershenzon still thought the center would hold and a compromise could be found. In this case, Berdiaev was more perceptive, foreseeing that the middle would fold and the two political extremes would be left to fight for ultimate dominance.

As the whirl of events engulfed Berdiaev, he no longer remained optimistic about the course of history. In the face of Russia's fall, the inevitable defeat by Germany and the impending victory of Bolshevism, he could not remain patient. The image of Berdiaev in 1917 is that of a headstrong fighter, an uncompromising conservative. An unpublished letter from Lev Shestov to Gershenzon, written on 19 August 1917, supports this picture. He described Berdiaev as "drowned in politics. From morning till night at meetings. He is extremely indisposed to all leftists."

Berdiaev was indeed active politically with former tsarist generals and conservative intellectuals. In 1917 he contributed to and sat on the editorial board of the political journal *Narodopravstvo,* which devoted itself mainly to the war with Germany and which supported the Provisional Government's call for "war until a victorious end." Because this journal carried the mildly anti-Semitic articles of a certain Boris Kremnev, a pseudonym, it was thought, for the journal's editor, Georgii Chulkov, Gershenzon felt Berdiaev was guilty by association, even though his own articles were not anti-Semitic.

Judging from his later articles, it seems fair to say that Berdiaev was not a bigot. More likely, the crisis of 1917 prompted him to behave in less than absolutely justifiable ways, swallowing a dose of anti-Semitism larger than he normally would have accepted in exchange for the political support of conservatives. In *Self-Knowledge,* Berdiaev acknowledged the errors he committed during this period and recalled them with a mixture of regret and shame. "I had a heavy impression when the rout of the Russian army from the front began," he wrote in 1949. "Surely, the traditional feelings burst within me, connected with the fact that I belong to a military family and my ancestors were Georgievskii generals of the old army; all this, generally speaking, is completely alien to me."

Berdiaev's refusal to compromise over the issue of the Revolution effectively ended whatever chances remained for him and Gershenzon to reconcile their differences and misunderstandings. For Berdiaev, the Revolution was not simply a political matter: it was also a "straight-forward religious question" because the atheistic Bolsheviks intended to create a Russia, guided by the philosophy of dialectical materialism, in which the Church would be suppressed. Berdiaev had always spoken out against atheism as one of the temptations of material life and as the main opponent of Christianity. In contrast, for Gershenzon the Revolution promised to redress old injustices, end racial discrimination against Jews and perhaps even create a society without the former harmful institutions of culture.

A look back over Berdiaev and Gershenzon's relationship shows that the disagreements over individual ideas actually point to a more general clash caused by differences in philosophy and personal temperament. While Berdiaev based his views on his Nietzschean conception of Christianity, Gershenzon held steady to his ecumenical, cosmic spirituality. Moreover, Berdiaev's ever greater attachment to Christianity conflicted with Gershenzon's metaphysical beliefs and offended his Jewish sensibilities, while Gershenzon's pantheism ran counter to Berdiaev's vision of Russian and world history.

The epilogue to this relationship is not very long. Although they were fated to meet many more times, Gershenzon and Berdiaev never renewed their friendship. Gershenzon encapsulates his relationship to Berdiaev in the postrevolutionary era in a 1922 letter to Lev Shestov:

> The Berdiaevs live the same way they used to, and not too badly. Both women work and earn a lot. He writes a great deal—in these years he has written, it seems, five large books; and just as before on Tuesdays they have "Church comealongs," as I called them, with lectures on mystical, Church and national themes. I exchange a few words with him when I see him, but only.

On Berdiaev's side one finds a touching reminiscence accompanied by regret and self-criticism. Berdiaev writes in *Samopoznanie:* "I broke my relationship with my old friends, V. Ivanov and M. Gershenzon, because I saw in their behavior accommodation and cooperation. I think now that I was not completely right, especially toward M. Gershenzon. The Soviet structure at that time was still not completely worked out and organized, it was impossible yet to call it totalitarian and in it there were many contradictions."

Gershenzon, it appears, was right; after the Revolution their thinking was almost completely at odds. While Berdiaev moved further in the direction of his existentialist Christianity, Gershenzon held tenaciously to his ideas of cosmic harmony. Philosophy, which had played such a great role in solidifying their friendship, played a no less important role in destroying it. Their mutual interests in Russian history, Slavophilism and idealistic metaphysics could not hide the fundamental differences in their thinking. In the end they let their relationship disintegrate rather than try to repair the chasm between them.

FURTHER READING

Allen, E. L. *Freedom in God: A Guide to the Thought of Nicholas Berdyaev.* New York: The Philosophical Library, Inc., 1951, 43 p.
    Brief introductory study of Berdyaev's philosophy.

Lowrie, Donald A. *Rebellious Prophet: A Life of Nicolai Berdyaev.* New York: Harper & Brothers, 1960, 310 p.
    Comprehensive biographical and critical study of Berdyaev.

Wernham, James C. S. *Two Russian Thinkers: An Essay in Berdyaev and Shestov.* Toronto: University of Toronto Press, 1968, 118 p.
    Examines Berdyaev's thought in relation to theology, Existentialism, Marxism, and Scripture.

Additional coverage of Berdyaev's life and career is contained in the following source published by Gale Research: *Contemporary Authors,* **Vol. 120.**

Robert Byron

1905–1941

English travel writer, art critic, and historian.

INTRODUCTION

A journalist for London's *Daily Express*, Byron is largely remembered for his travel narratives, including *The Road to Oxiana* (1937), which many critics consider to be his masterpiece. This work represents the culmination of Byron's somewhat fictionalized travel diaries that record expeditions through Europe, the Middle East, and Asia in the 1920s and 1930s. In *The Road to Oxiana* and similar works, Byron—primarily a Byzantinist—exercised his proclivity to examine and comment on the beauty of local architecture and art. His findings on ancient structures and the modern incarnations of the cultures that produced them are among his most enduring contributions. Somewhat eccentric and idiosyncratic in his presentation of these themes, Byron is nevertheless recognized by critics for his carefully perceived and good-humored recollections of Europe and the East between the First and Second World Wars.

Biographical Information

Byron was born in Wiltshire, at the town of Wembley, on February 26, 1905. Though his family was distantly related to Lord Byron, his parents were solidly middle class. He grew up, with two sisters, near Salisbury in Savenake Forest and, despite his family's modest financial means, attended Eton and later Merton College, Oxford. In 1925, while still an undergraduate, Byron and two companions undertook an automobile tour of Europe and eventually made their way to Greece. He recorded that excursion in his first travel book, *Europe in the Looking-Glass*, published in 1926. The same year he left Oxford with a third class degree in history. Byron returned to Greece twice soon after, once in 1926 and again in 1927, visiting Mt. Athos and examining the many frescoes contained in Greece's centuries-old churches and monasteries. These voyages resulted in his second travelogue, *The Station. Athos: Treasures and Men* (1928), *The Byzantine Achievement* (1929), and *The Birth of Western Painting* (1930), a collaborative work undertaken with the help of David Talbot Rice, one of his traveling companions. In 1929 Byron began his career in journalism, traveling to India as a correspondent for the *Daily Express*. The result, *An Essay on India*, was published two years later. Byron recorded his travels during the years 1931-32 in his next travel book, *First Russia, then Tibet* (1933). A tour in Persia with his close friend Christopher Sykes during the years 1933-34, followed by almost three years of writing and traveling in China and the Far East, culminated in the

publication of his most widely acclaimed work, *The Road to Oxiana*. By 1936, however, he had returned to London and was experiencing the mounting tensions surrounding the Nazi domination of Europe. By the time war was declared by Great Britain in 1939, Byron was engaged as a special correspondent for the British Broadcasting Company Overseas News Department. While en route to Cairo for the news service in February of 1941, he was drowned when his ship was sunk by a torpedo.

Major Works

Of Byron's nine works written without collaboration, nearly all were drafted in the form of travel diaries which examine the peculiarities of culture and architecture in Mediterranean Europe, the Middle East, and Asia. Critics have observed that these writings describe a steady development in terms of Byron's overall style. His earliest travel books, *Europe in the Looking-Glass* and *The Station,* are thought to be of less consequence than his more mature writings, though both illustrate Byron's wit, erudition, and hint at the studied awareness of setting that characterize his later works. Marred by what Paul Fussell called Byron's occasional "massiveness of expression" and "polemical disposition," these books nevertheless demonstrate the author's essentially good-natured and comic tone, a quality he maintained throughout his writings. In his third book, *The Byzantine Achievement*, Byron added a new dimension, providing a detailed history of the art and culture of the Byzantine east along with his personal travel narrative. In *An Essay on India*, Byron explores political factors more fully than in his earlier writings, evaluating the successes and failures of British colonialism in the region. Byron voices his disdain for the inelegant ideology of the Soviet Union, while delighting in the beauty of its architecture in *First Russia, then Tibet*; he goes on to detail his exploits in the largely untouched and alien culture of Tibet. The title of *The Road to Oxiana*, Byron's penultimate travelogue, refers to the Amus Darya river, called the Oxus, which runs through northeastern Afghanistan. The story is both a quest for a glimpse of the river and a search for the sources of Moslem architecture and civilization. Critics of the work have almost universally praised its artful evocations of scene and manner, as well as Byron's masterful recreation of what appears to be a completely spontaneous travel diary—despite the fact that it was carefully constructed over the course of three years of thought and revision. In his brief *How We Celebrate the Coronation: A Word to London's Visitors* (1937), one of his last works published before the outbreak of war, Byron demonstrates his sardonic sense of humor, decrying the materialism and profit-mongering of real-estate developers in England.

PRINCIPAL WORKS

Europe in the Looking-Glass (travelogue) 1926
The Station. Athos: Treasures and Men (travelogue) 1928
The Byzantine Achievement (art criticism) 1929
The Birth of Western Painting [with David Talbot Rice] (art criticism) 1930
An Essay on India (travelogue) 1931
The Appreciation of Architecture (art criticism) 1932
First Russia, then Tibet (travelogue) 1933
How We Celebrate the Coronation: A Word to London's Visitors (essay) 1937
Imperial Pilgrimage (travelogue) 1937
The Road to Oxiana (travelogue) 1937

CRITICISM

Graham Greene (essay date 1937)

SOURCE: "The Byronic East," in *The London Mercury,* Vol. XXXVI, No. 212, June, 1937, pp. 195-96.

[*In the following review of* The Road to Oxiana, *Greene discusses what he considers the book's strengths and shortcomings.*]

"Samarcand, for the last fifty years, has attracted scholars, painters, and photographers. Thus the setting of the Timurid Renaissance is conceived as Samarcand and Transoxiana, while its proper capital, Herat, remains but a name and a ghost. Now the position is reversed. The Russians have closed Turkistan. The Afghans have opened their country. And the opportunity arrives to redress the balance. Strolling up the road towards the minarets, I feel as one might feel who has lighted on the lost books of Livy or an unknown Botticelli."

It is this mixture of scholarship and romanticism that gives Mr. Byron's account of a journey through Persia and Afghanistan [*The Road to Oxiana*] its unusual and agreeable flavour: the poetic imagination which evokes a personal East so vividly—the roses stuck in the rifles of Afghan soldiers, the opium flowers "glowing in the dusk like lamps of ice," the dead wolf under a wild fruit tree in pink blossom—is strengthened by the architectural detail, so that at their best his descriptions have the merits of two worlds. Take, for example, his account of the doorways in Persepolis:

> Other architectural features are the stairs, the platform, and the palace doors. The stairs are fine because there are so many of them. The platform is fine because its massive blocks have posed, and solved, an engineering problem. Neither has any art. But the doorways have. They, and they alone, boast a gleam of true invention; they suggest ideas, they utter a comment, with regard to other doorways. Their proportions are narrow and thick, thus inviting a perpetual to and fro; whereas our doors ask the figure to pause and frame itself.

And this of the ruins of Balkh:

> And from these acred cerements, first on the north and then on the south of the road, rose the worn grey-white shapes of a bygone architecture, mounds, furrowed, and bleached by the rain and sun, wearier than any human works I ever saw: a twisted pyramid, a tapering platform, a clump of battlements, a crouching beast, all familiars of the Bactrian Greeks, and of Marco Polo after them. They ought to have vanished. But the very impact of the sun, calling out the obstinacy of their ashen clay, has conserved some inextinguishable spark of form, a spark such as a Roman earthwork or a grass-grown barrow has not, which still flickers on against a world brighter than itself, tired as only a suicide frustrated can be tired.

Occasionally—that last comparison is an example—Mr. Byron's romanticism runs uncomfortably riot: a more serious complaint which has to be made against an admirable book is a kind of unsteadiness of approach, as if the author had been in some doubt in what quarter he was going to find his public. The firm vivid writing edges away at one end into a rather smart, cheap, unsympathetic superiority to his surroundings, as when, against the Persian custom, he turned his muleteers from his room: "I answered that I also have customs, and one of them is not to be inconvenienced by the pipe or presence of muleteers in my own employ"; at the other to a text-book dryness: "The dome of the middle chamber is some fifteen feet higher than the other two. Higher still is the elliptical cupola which separates it from the front dome, and which roofs the passage between the middle chamber and the outer ruined one. The passage is divided into two storeys," etc. This type of description demands photographs or drawings to illustrate it: mathematical and not visual it will appeal only to specialists, who may find the humour and romanticism of the rest of the book tiresome; nor are the pages of Persian and Afghan history always transformed into personal material. We are left with three books, one a little gossipy and knowing with private jokes, the second almost too dryly instructive, the third among the best books of Eastern travel since Kinglake.

G. M. Young (essay date 1948)

SOURCE: "Cities and Harvests," in *Daylight and Champaign,* revised edition, Rupert Hart-Davis, 1948, pp. 28-34.

[In the following essay, Young praises Byron's display of insight and adept prose style in The Road to Oxiana.]

A diary is not to be judged like other books, because in real life incidents will not happen in the right order, or observe their proper artistic balance. Mr. Byron's objective was the Oxus: his route was by Cyprus, Jerusalem, and Damascus into Persia; and thence by Afghanistan and the Khyber to Peshawar. But though his appeal to the Minister of the Interior of Turkestan might have melted a stone—a stone being assumed to have no appreciation of irony—he was not allowed to see the stream which, as he gracefully informed His Excellency, had been celebrated by the sacred pen of Matthew Arnold. So it was not the Oxus but Mr. Byron that proved to be the foiled circuitous wanderer. But one disappointment, in a region which seems to be half-crazy with adolescent nationalism and the frontier-complex, is not much to set against such a harvest of things observed and felt. I divide travel books into those which make me want to go there, and those which make me thankful that someone else has gone for me. *The Road to Oxiana* is of the latter class. I trust I shall always be young enough to giggle consumedly over motor breakdowns and funny foreigners, but in the flesh I find them merely tiresome. And I would rather see the garden at Kavar through Mr. Byron's eyes than my own, because they see so much more. It reminded me of another garden, one which Virgil knew, 'below the castled crag of Oebalia'.

Even finer is the journey across the steppe to the Tower of Kabus, itself alone worth many journeys.

> As plans of cities are inset on maps of countries, another chart on a larger scale lay right beneath our wheels. Here the green resolved, not into ordinary grass, but into wild corn, barley, and oats, which accounted for that vivid fire, as of a life within, in the green. And among these myriad bearded alleys lived a population of flowers, buttercups, and poppies, pale purple irises and dark purple campanulas, and countless others, exhibiting all the colours, forms and wonders that a child finds in its first garden. Then a puff of air would come, bending the corn to a silver ripple, while the flowers leaned with it; or a cloud shadow, and all grew dark as for a moment's sleep, though a few feet off there would be no ripple and no darkness; so that this whole inner world of the steppe was mapped on a system of infinite minute recessions, having just those gradations of distance that the outer lacked.

Of prose like that I can say nothing. Mr. Byron's references to childhood are always apt, as another passage will indicate:

> The sound of the machinery became apocalyptic, clanking and fizzing without any sort of rhythm till at last, with a final deafening cannonade, it ceased altogether, and Abbas beamed at us with the expression of a conductor laying down his baton at the end of an applauded symphony. A

sympathetic report from the near hind tyre, though a beat late, announced that it too needed rest. There was no spare tyre. Gathering up the shreds of the outer cover, Abbas produced a patching outfit. The afternoon shadows were lengthening. It remained to bring the engine to life. But this was accomplished with a few random blows of a hammer, as one beats a child.

The power of making every situation yield all it contains of comedy and beauty at once is the best gift of a mature culture to its elect children. On this theme I should like some day to expatiate, with illustrations from the *Birds* of Aristophanes, from the *Misanthrope,* and, last and finest fruit of the insolent humanism of the eighteenth century, the verse and prose of another pilgrim who died one hundred and thirteen years ago. It is to this tradition that Mr. Byron adheres. By humanism I mean a determination of the mind to maintain its own poise, and to view the world in its own perspective: and I call it insolent for the readiness with which it turns to aggression if its poise is disturbed by sectarian clamour or its perspective blurred by fashionable sentiment. Kinglake had it, but in Kinglake I am always aware of an uneasy self-consciousness which prevents him from ever surrendering completely to the scene before him, or to his own emotions; while I do not suppose that Mr. Byron has ever struck out an adjective for fear that someone might call it sentimental, or mitigated a single impertinence lest someone should call it indiscreet. I am sure, too, that my most earnest representations will never stop him writing such sentences as—

> Dawn, like a smile from the gallows, pierced the gusty, drizzling night.

And how, not being bootblacks, poppies manage to 'shine their leaves', I ask with no expectation of an answer.

How will the humanist approach Jerusalem?

> The buildings are wholly of stone, a white cheese-like stone, candid and luminous, which the sun turns to all tones of ruddy gold. Charm and romance have no place. All is open and harmonious. The associations of history and belief, deep-rooted in the first memories of childhood, dissolve before the actual apparition . . . Set in this radiant environment, the Church of the Holy Sepulchre appears the meanest of churches . . . The visitor is in conflict with himself. To pretend to detachment is supercilious; to pretend to reverence, hypocritical. The choice lies between them. Yet for me that choice has been averted. I met a friend in the doorway, and it was he who showed me how to cope with the Holy Places. . . .
>
> Stepping through the Franciscans as though they were nettles, Gabriel dived into a hole three feet high, from which came a bright light. The inner chamber was about seven feet square. At a low slab of stone knelt a Frenchwoman in ecstasy. By her side stood another Greek monk.

'This gentleman has been to Mount Athos,' announced Gabriel to his crony, who shook hands with me across the body of the Frenchwoman. 'It was six years ago—and he remembers Synesios' cat. This is the Tomb'—pointing to the slab of stone—'I shall be in here all day to-morrow. There isn't much room, is there? Let's go out.'

I should like also to quote Baalbek—which, incidentally, tried Kinglake a little above his powers—

and the stone peach-coloured, with a marmoreal texture, not transparent, but faintly powdered, like bloom on a plum. . . .

The stars came out and the mountain slopes grew black. I felt the peace of Islam. And if I mention this commonplace, it is because in Egypt and Turkey that peace is now denied, while in India Islam appears, like everything else, uniquely and exclusively Indian. In a sense it is so; for neither man nor institution can meet that overpowering environment without a change of identity. But I will say this for my own sense: that when travelling in Mohammedan India without previous knowledge of Persia, I compared myself to an Indian observing European classicism, who had started on the shores of the Baltic instead of the Mediterranean.

The idea is new to me; I have no knowledge of my own with which to verify it; and it is less the originality or correctness of the observation that impresses me than the range of historic reflection which it implies. But the traveller among the monuments of Timarid magnificence and power has much to reflect upon, and the history of that astonishing race, who, ruling in Samarcand and Herat, made themselves felt from Pekin to Byzantium, furnishes the bony structure of Mr. Byron's narrative. It is a story to go to the heart of the humanist, when he reads, in the words of the Emperor Babur, how in Herat—as in Florence—

whatever work a man took up he aimed and aspired to bring it to perfection:

and it seems to reach its artistic climax in the mausoleum of Timur's daughter-in-law, Gohar Shad, whose history Mr. Byron has at last pieced together and elucidated.

Educated at Eton and one of the larger Oxford colleges, Mr. Byron finds it easy to assume the habits of a lower-middle-class Persian, and in that guise he was able to penetrate into her mosque. What follows I shall quote, because it conveys more completely than any other passage in the book the spirit in which Mr. Byron's pilgrimage was made.

Turbaned Mullahs, white-robed Afghans, vanished like ghosts between the orbits of the lamps, gliding across the black pavement to prostrate themselves beneath the golden doorway. A sound of chanting was heard from the sanctuary, where a single tiny figure could be seen abased in the dimness, at the foot of its lustred mihrab. Islam! Iran! Asia! Mystic, languid, inscrutable!! One can hear a Frenchman saying that, the silly fool—as if it was an opium den in Marseilles. We felt the opposite: that is why I mention it. Every circumstance of sight, sound, and trespass conspired to swamp the intelligence. *The message of a work of art overcame this conspiracy, forcing its way out of the shadows, insisting on structure and proportion, on the impress of superlative quality, and on the intellect behind them.*

'Please blow your nose,' whispered our guide.

'Why?'

'I ask you, blow it, and continue to blow.'

Without the aesthetic apprehension, a man loses three parts of life: without the comic apprehension he is in danger of losing his head as well. But to the humanist, to the observer with a classical tradition behind him, it is not enough for the world to be lovely and amusing: it must be intelligent. Of Malcontenta, Mr. Byron writes:

Outside, people argue over the sides and affect to ignore the back. The front asks no opinion. It is a precedent, a criterion. You can analyse it—nothing could be more lucid; but you cannot question it. Europe could have bidden me no fonder farewell than this triumphant affirmation of the European intellect.

'You can analyse it, but you cannot question it': that is classicism. No room here for good intentions, or adumbrations, or compliances with what other people think you ought to think. The artist has said what he meant to say. Romantic art, and romantic criticism, is always hinting at the things left unsaid, and, too often, when you ask point blank: What are they? well, it just does not know. None of my readers, I hope, will suppose I think lightly of Ruskin if I confess that, every now and then, in reading him, I catch myself saying, like the Arab whom Palgrave charged two dirhems for an eyewash, 'I say, Mister, remember God!' Far too much modern writing, I mean of the descriptive and analytic kind, seems to me to derive from the looser Victorian Romanticism, with the added demerit that the writers have taken their eye off the object, and are trying to squint simultaneously at their own subconscious and someone else's style.

Of the Omayad Mosque, and the mosaic landscapes of the Grand Arcade, Mr. Byron says:

For all their Pompeian picturesqueness, their colonnaded palaces and crag-bound castles, they are real landscapes, more than mere decoration, concerned inside formal limits with the identity of a tree or the energy of a stream.

If he had brought back nothing else, that lesson would be enough. But it is the lesson of the whole book. Identity and energy within formal limits, that is style, that is reason, that is freedom. I doubt if there was ever a time when had we more cause to be grateful for those who have the courage to assert their necessity, and the genius to exemplify their virtue.

Bruce Chatwin   (essay date 1981)

SOURCE: Introduction to *The Road to Oxiana* by Robert Byron, Pan Books, 1981, pp. 9-15.

[*In the following essay, Chatwin expresses his admiration for* The Road to Oxiana.]

Anyone who reads around the travel books of the thirties must, in the end, conclude that Robert Byron's **The Road to Oxiana** is the masterpiece. Byron was a gentleman, a scholar and an aesthete, who drowned in 1941 when his ship to the Mediterranean was torpedoed. In his short life he travelled as far as China and Tibet, and to most of the countries nearer home. In 1928 he published **The Station,** an account of a visit to the monasteries of Mount Athos, and followed it up with two pioneering volumes on Byzantine civilization, which, at that time, received scant consideration from academic circles. He had some lively prejudices. Among the targets of his abuse were the Catholic (as opposed to the Orthodox) Church; the art of Classical Greece; the paintings of Rembrandt; Shakespeare—and when his Intourist guide protested that the plays could never have been written by a grocer from Stratford-upon-Avon, he murmured, 'They are exactly the sort of plays I would expect a grocer to write.' In 1932, attracted by the photo of a Seljuk tomb-tower on the Turkoman steppe, he set out on a quest for the origins of Islamic architecture. And if it is fair to place his earlier books as the work of a dazzlingly gifted young amateur, it is equally fair to rank **The Road to Oxiana** as a work of genius.

I write as a partisan, not as a critic. Long ago, I raised it to the status of 'sacred text', and thus beyond criticism. My own copy—now spineless and floodstained after four journeys to Central Asia—has been with me since the age of fifteen. Consequently, I am apt to resent suggestions that it is a 'lost book' or in need of being 'rescued from the library shelves'. By a stroke of luck, it was never lost on me.

Because I felt the death of Robert Byron so keenly, I sought out his friends and pestered them for their reminiscences. 'Very cross,' they said. 'An awful tease.' 'Surprisingly tough.' 'Abrasive.' 'Incredibly funny.' 'Fat.' 'Rather hideous . . . eyes like a fish.' 'Wonderful imitation of Queen Victoria.' By the time I was twenty-two, I had read everything I could—by and about him—and that summer set out on my own journey to Oxiana.

In 1962—six years before the Hippies wrecked it (by driving educated Afghans into the arms of the Marxists)—you could set off to Afghanistan with the antici-

pations of, say, Delacroix off to Algiers. On the streets of Herat you saw men in mountainous turbans, strolling hand in hand, with roses in their mouths and rifles wrapped in flowered chintz. In Badakhshan you could picnic on Chinese carpets and listen to the bulbul. In Balkh, the Mother of Cities, I asked a fakir the way to the shrine of Hadji Piardeh. 'I don't know it,' he said. 'It must have been destroyed by Genghiz.'

Even the Afghan Embassy in London introduced you to a world that was hilarious and strange. Control of the visa section rested with a tousle-haired Russian emigré giant, who had cut the lining of his jacket, so that it hung, as a curtain, to hide the holes in the seat of his pants. At opening time, he'd be stirring up clouds of dust with a broom, only to let it settle afresh on the collapsing furniture. Once, when I tipped him ten shillings, he hugged me, lifted me off the floor and bellowed: 'I hope you have a very ACCIDENT-FREE trip to Afghanistan!'

No. Our journeys were never quite accident-free: the time a soldier lobbed a pick-axe at the car; the time our lorry slid, with gentle resignation, over the cliff (we had time to jump off); the time we were whipped for straying into a military area; the dysentery; the septicaemia; the hornet sting; the fleas—but, mercifully, no hepatitis.

Sometimes, we met travellers more high-minded than ourselves who were following the tracks of Alexander or Marco Polo: for us, it was far more fun to follow Robert Byron. I still have notebooks to prove how slavishly I aped both his itinerary and—as if that were possible—his style. Take this entry of mine for 5 July 1962 and compare it with his for 21 September 1933:

> In the afternoon we called on Mr Alouf the art dealer. He took us to an apartment filled with french-polished 'French' furniture, most of it riddled with worm and upside down. He had recently converted to Catholicism and, on showing us a signed photograph of Pope Pius XII, crossed himself fervently and rattled his dentures.

> From a cupboard he produced the following:

> A Roman gold pectoral set with blue glass pastes. A forgery.

> A Neolithic marble idol with an erect phallus, on an accompanying perch. The perch was genuine, the idol not.

> Thirty Syro-Phoenician funerary bone dolls.

> A 'Hittite' figure, bristling with gold attributes, perhaps the one Byron saw in 1933. A fake.

> Various worrying gold objects.

> A collection of Early Christian glasses (genuine). 'I have many glasses,' said Mr Alouf, crossing himself, 'covered with crosses. But they are in the bank.'

Finally, a marble head of Alexander the Great. 'I have refuse twenty-thousand dollars for this piece. TWENTY THOUSAND DOLLARS! All arch-aeologists agree mine is the only genuine head of Alexander: Look! The neck! The ears!' Perhaps—but the face was entirely missing.

From the Levant we would go on to Teheran. There was more money about than in Byron's day and many more Europeans after it. But the Shah was a pale copy of his father and already he, too, looked pretty silly, and the men around him, queasy. One day we went to see HE Amir Abbas Hoveyda in his office at the Iranian Oil Company (he was not yet Prime Minister): 'A man with big eyes and despairing gestures. He seemed trapped behind the enormity of his desk. He offered us the use of his helicopter in case we should need it.'

Once Byron gets to Iran, his search for the origins of Islamic architecture really gets under way. But to con-struct, out of stone and brick and tile, a prose that will not only be readable but carry the reader to a pitch of excitement requires talents of the highest calibre. This is Byron's achievement. His paean of praise for the Sheikh Lutf'ullah Mosque in Isfahan must put him at least in the rank of Ruskin. One afternoon, to see how it was done, I took **The Road to Oxiana** into the mosque and sat, cross-legged, marvelling both at the tilework and Byron's description of it.

Now the 'experts' will carp that, while Byron may have had lyrical powers of description, he was not a schol-ar—and, of course, in their sense he wasn't. Yet, time and again, he scores over sound scholarship with his uncanny ability to gauge the morale of a civilization from its architecture, and to treat ancient buildings and modern people as two facets of a continuing story.

Already in *The Byzantine Achievement,* written at twenty-five, there is a haunting passage that tells in four sentences as much about the schism of the Western and Eastern Churches as any number of portentous volumes:

> The existence of St Sophia is atmospheric; that of St Peter's, overpoweringly, imminently substan-tial. One is a church to God; the other a salon for his agents. One is consecrated to reality, the other, to illusion. St Sophia, in fact, is large, and St Peter's is vilely, tragically small.

On the subject of Iran, he is even more clairvoyant. On reading *The Road to Oxiana* you end up with the im-pression that the Iranian plateau is a 'soft centre' that panders to megalomaniac ambitions in its rulers without providing the genius to sustain them.

As is well known, the late Shah-in-Shah saw in the ruins of Persepolis a mirror image of his own glory and, for that reason, held his coronation binge about a mile from the site, in tents designed by Jansen of Paris, where a riff raff of royalty could dine with the ghosts of his *soi-disant* predecessors.

Read, therefore, Byron's comments on Persepolis in the light of the pretensions and downfall of the Pahlevi Dynasty:

> The stone, owing to its extreme hardness, has proved impervious to age; it remains a bright smooth grey, as slick as an aluminium saucepan. This cleanness reacts on the carving like sunlight on a fake old master; it reveals, instead of the genius one expected, a disconcerting void . . . My involuntary thought as Herzfeld showed us the new (newly excavated) staircase was: 'How much did this cost? Was it made in a factory? No, it wasn't. Then how many workmen for how many years chiselled and polished these endless figures?' Certainly, they are not mechanical fig-ures; nor are they guilty of elaboration for their own sake; nor are they cheap in the sense of lacking technical skill. But they are what the French call *faux bons*. They have art, but not spontaneous art . . . Instead of mind or feeling, they exhale a soulless refinement, a veneer a-dopted by the Asiatic whose own artistic instinct has been fettered and devitalized by . . . the Mediterranean.

Now if you pursue this vein, you will find that, under the bravura passages, Byron is expounding a very seri-ous thesis—and one of crucial importance for under-standing our own time. All he finds most admirable in Persian art—the tower at Gumbad-i-Kabus, the Seljuk Mosque in Isfahan, the incomparable mausoleum of the Mongol Khan Uljaitu, or the buildings of Gohar Shad—results from a fusion (one could say, a chemical explo-sion) between the old Iranian civilization and the peoples of nomad stock from the Oxus Basin and be-yond. You even feel that Byron's favourite character, Shir Ahmad Khan, the Afghan Ambassador to Teheran, belongs among these first-rate monuments: in other words, genius visits Iran from the north-east.

Certainly—in Byron's day, and mine—to cross the Af-ghan frontier, after the lowering fanaticism of Meshed, was like coming up for air. 'Here at last,' he wrote of Herat, 'is Asia without an inferiority complex.' And it is this moral superiority of the Afghans, together with a fear of the centrifugal forces spinning in Central Asia, that has scared the Russians and the bunch of seedy traitors who have sold their country. (May they boil in Gehenna!) So when I read that the Heratis have been sending women's dresses and cosmetics to the cowards of Kandahar, I think back to a dress I once saw flapping in the old clothes bazaar in Herat—a gown of flamingo crêpe with sequined butterflies on the hips and the label of a boutique in Beverly Hills.

Even in Kabul, the unlikely was always predictable: the sight of the King's cousin Prince Daud at a party, the old 'Mussolini' blackshirt, with his muddy smile and polished head and boots, talking to—who?—Duke Ellington, who else? The Duke in a white-and-blue spotted tie and a blue-and-white spotted shirt: he was on his last big tour. And we know what happened to Daud—shot, with his family, in the palace he usurped.

I can guess what's happened to the crippled Nuristani boy, who brought us our dinner from his village up the mountain. We had camped by the river, and he came down the rock face, swinging his crutch and his withered leg and, somehow, hanging on to the dish and a lighted firebrand. He sang while we ate—but they have bombed the village and used gas on the inhabitants.

I can guess, too, what happened to Wali Jahn. He took me to safety when I got blood-poisoning. He carried me on his back through the river, and bathed my head, and made me rest under the ilexes. But when we came back, five years later, he was coughing, deep retching coughs, and had the look of someone going down to the cold.

But what have they done to Gul Amir the Tadjik? He was ugly as sin with an unending nose and silver earrings. You never saw anyone so devout. Every time he wanted a rest, 'There was no God but God . . .' but as he bowed his face to Mecca, he would squint out sideways and, when I fell in the river trying to cast a trout fly, God was forgotten in a peal of girlish giggles.

Where is now the Hakim of Kande? We stayed in his summer-house under a scree of shining schist and watched the creamy clouds coming over the mountain. In the evening we saw a girl in red creeping out of a maize field: 'The corn is high,' he said. 'In nine months there will be many babies.'

What's become of the trucker who admired my earlobes? We left him in the middle of the road. His carburettor had clogged and his hashish pipe had clogged, and the pieces were all mixed up, on the road, and we were in a hurry.

Or the houseboy at the Park Hotel in Herat? He wore a rose-pink turban and, when we asked for lunch, said:

'Yessir! Whatyoulike? Everything!'

'What you got?'

'No drink. No ice. No bread. No fruit. No meat. No rice. No fish. Eggs. One. Maybe. Tomorrow. YES!'

Or the man in Tashkurgan who took me to his garden? It was a very hot and dusty afternoon and Peter was looking for traces of the Bactrian Greeks. 'Go and find your Greeks,' I said. 'Give me your Marvell and I'll find a garden'—where I really did stumble on melons as I passed and had green thoughts in a green shade.

Or the mad woman in Ghazni at the Tomb of Mahmud? She was tall and lovely and she stared gloomily at the ground and rattled her bracelets. When they opened the doors, she flung herself on the wooden balustrade, and flapped her crimson dress and cawed like a wounded bird. Only when they let her kiss the tomb did she fall silent. And she kissed the inscription, as if each white marble letter contained the cure for her sickness.

How could she know what Byron wrote of it? 'I have enjoyed many examples of it [kufic lettering] in the last ten months. But none can compare with these tall rhythmic ciphers, involved with dancing foliage, which mourn the loss of Mahmud, the conqueror of India, Persia and Oxiana, nine centuries after his death in the capital where he lived.'

This is the year—of all years—to mourn the loss of Robert Byron, the arch-enemy of Appeasement, who said, 'I shall have warmonger put on my passport,' when he saw what the Nazis were up to. Were he alive today, I think he would agree that, in time (everything in Afghanistan takes time), the Afghans will do something quite dreadful to their invaders—perhaps awaken the sleeping giants of Central Asia.

But that will not bring back the things we loved: the high, clear days and the blue icecaps on the mountains; the lines of white poplars fluttering in the wind, and the long white prayer-flags; the fields of asphodels that followed the tulips; or the fat-tailed sheep brindling the hills above Chakcharan, and the ram with a tail so big they had to strap it to a cart. We shall not lie on our backs at the Red Castle and watch the vultures wheeling over the valley where they killed the grandson of Genghiz. We will not read Babur's Memoirs in his garden at Istalif and see the blind man smelling his way around the rose bushes. Or sit in the Peace of Islam with the beggars of Gazar Gagh. We will not stand on the Buddha's head at Bamiyan, upright in his niche like a whale in a dry-dock. We will not sleep in the nomad tent, or scale the Minaret of Jam. And we shall lose the tastes—the hot, coarse, bitter bread; the green tea flavoured with cardamoms; the grapes we cooled in the snow-melt; and the nuts and dried mulberries we munched for altitude sickness. Nor shall we get back the smell of the beanfields; the sweet, resinous smell of deodar wood burning, or the whiff of a snow leopard at 14,000 feet. Never. Never. Never.

FURTHER READING

Fussell, Paul. "Sancte Roberte, Ora pro Nobis." In *Abroad: British Literary Traveling between the Wars*, pp. 79-112. Oxford University Press, 1980.

Fussell offers an overview of Byron's life and literary career.

Grant, A. T. K. Review of *First Russia, then Tibet. International Affairs* 13, No. 1 (January-February 1934): 447.
  Discusses Byron as a "somewhat self-consciously unconventional traveller" in a largely positive assessment of this travelogue.

Sykes, Christopher. "Robert Byron." In *Four Studies in Loyalty,* pp. 95-146. William Sloane Associates, Inc., 1948.
  Provides a survey of Byron's works. Sykes accompanied Byron on the travels described in *The Road to Oxiana.*

Young, Vernon. "Road Show." *American Scholar* 52, No. 1 (Winter 1982-83): 138-40.
  Brief account of Byron's career occasioned by a reprinting of *The Road to Oxiana.* Young praises the author's ability to evoke settings in the work, while criticizing its overall style.

R. G. Collingwood

1889–1943

(Full name Robin George Collingwood) English philosopher and historian.

INTRODUCTION

Both an acknowledged authority on the archaeology of Roman Britain and a renowned philosopher of history, Collingwood is remembered for his philosophical system in which he analyzed the relationships between art, religion, science, history, and philosophy. First outlined in his *Speculum Mentis; or, The Map of Knowledge* and later revised and expanded in subsequent works, the bases of this system are several of Collingwood's most well-known theories of knowledge. The first of these, the basic tenet of his historical theory, states that the historian can only achieve knowledge by recreating prior acts of thought. Another of his central ideas is the convertibility of history and philosophy, a concept which implies that a thorough study of either discipline will ultimately lead to the same end. A third element of Collingwood's philosophy is his Theory of Presuppositions. According to this theory, every form of science (which includes historical inquiry) seeks to achieve truth by posing and then answering questions. This complex of questions, however, must finally rest upon a system of presuppositions—accepted absolutes that can be deemed neither true nor false.

Biographical Information

Collingwood was born in Cartwell Fell, Lancashire, on February 22, 1889. His father was a painter and archaeologist who passed his interest in Roman archaeology on to his son. Raised in a relatively poor family with three sisters, Collingwood was educated at home under the tutelage of his father and mother until the age of thirteen. He spent five years at Rugby beginning in 1903, assisted financially by a wealthy family friend. Although he disliked the school, he continued there and later matriculated at University College, Oxford. He earned his bachelor's degree in 1912, and was thereafter granted a fellowship from Pembroke College as Tutor in Philosophy. He began working on his *Religion and Philosophy* at this time, and served as a tutor until the outbreak of World War I. During the hostilities he joined the Admiralty Intelligence Division of the British Armed Forces, employing his considerable knowledge of foreign languages. After the war Collingwood returned to writing and teaching as a professor-lecturer at Pembroke College between 1921 and 1928 and later at Oxford until 1935. During this period he developed his mature philosophical system, which he constantly revised throughout his career. In 1932 he suffered a stroke that forced him to take an extended leave of absence from teaching. In the interim he continued to focus attention on his writing, and later resumed teaching. In 1934 Collingwood was named Waynflete Professor of Metaphysical History and in 1938 received an honorary doctorate from St. Andrews University, Scotland. Continued strokes devastated his health over the course of the decade, however, forcing him to resign his post in 1941, and eventually leading to his death on January 9, 1943.

Major Works

In one of his earliest works, *Religion and Philosophy*, Collingwood defined many of the problems that would characterize his philosophical career. In it, he stated that in order to understand the nature of knowledge the human mind must be examined historically rather than psychologically and that history and philosophy were identical disciplines, an idea that he later retracted, although he continued to acknowledge deep affinities between these two fields of study. By 1924 he had formulated his Theory of Presuppositions—outlined, he later noted, in a destroyed manuscript of 1917, but not published until 1940 in *An Essay on Metaphysics*—and realized his goal of developing a philosophical system. The result was his *Speculum Mentis*, in which Collingwood delineated five types of experience and their guiding principles. These five—ranging from those that rely on imagination to those that most closely approach concrete truth—were experiences relating to art, religion, science, history, and philosophy. Thus, art involves an imaginative experience guided by a perception of beauty, while philosophy renders truth through self-knowledge and the awareness of the limitations of the other four forms of experience. In his later works, Collingwood refined, reevaluated, and in some cases rescinded these evaluations. In *Faith and Reason* he dropped his former idea that religion was a symbolic form of experience reliant upon imagination and inferior to philosophy. *The Philosophy of History* and *The Idea of History* prsented Collingwood's conception of history as a form of scientific inquiry, along with his notion that the historian must reenact ways of thinking peculiar to various periods of the past in order to attain knowledge of human history. This elevation of religious and historical experience led Collingwood to expand his definition of philosophy in *An Essay on Philosophical Method*, calling it not only an awareness of the limitations of natural science, religion, and art, but also a source of true knowledge, both categorical and universal, achieved through "critical reflection" on these other disciplines. In the field of aesthetics Collingwood had adopted a language-based theory of art by the late 1930s, a position which led him to view artistic creation as a phenomenon of expression as well as one of imagination. He documented this revised conception in *The Principles of Art*. In *The New Leviathan; or Man, Society, Civilization and Barbarism*, the last book he published during his lifetime, Collingwood discarded many of his doctrines of an earlier period and stated the precepts of his ethical and political theories. As part of the former he defined three types of ethical thought—utilitarian ethics, concrete ethics, and absolute ethics—while in his political philosophy he attempted to construct a twentieth-century version of Thomas Hobbes' "classical politics."

Critical Reception

While Collingwood was criticized during his lifetime for his adoption of the precepts of traditional idealism, and later for his rejection of those ideas, more recent critics have perceived both of these stages as integral to his philosophy. Ater his death, Collingwood was labeled a neo-idealist and his philosophy described as a "systematic synthesis of British empiricism and post-Kantian idealism." Nevertheless, although the overall significance of his work remains a matter of contention among scholars, Collingwood is generally acknowledged for his important contribution to the philosophy of history, and critics continue to evaluate his thought on the subjects of aesthetics, metaphysics, and the philosophy of science.

PRINCIPAL WORKS

Religion and Philosophy (philosophy) 1916
Ruskin's Philosophy (criticism) 1920
Roman Britain (history) 1923
Ambleside Roman Fort (history) 1924
Speculum Mentis; or, The Map of Knowledge (philosophy) 1924
The Roman Signal Station on Castle Hill, Scarborough (history) 1925
A Guide to the Chesters Museum (history) 1926
A Guide to the Roman Wall (history) 1926
Outlines of a Philosophy of Art (philosophy) 1926
Faith and Reason (philosophy) 1928
Roman Eskdale (history) 1929
The Archaeology of Roman Britain (history) 1930
The Book of the Pilgrimage of Hadrian's Wall, July 1st to 4th, 1930 (history) 1930
The Philosophy of History (philosophy) 1930
An Essay on Philosophical Method (philosophy) 1933
The Historical Imagination (philosophy) 1935
Human Nature and Human History (philosophy) 1936
Roman Britain and the English Settlements [with J. N. L. Myres] (history) 1936
The Principles of Art (philosophy) 1938
An Autobiography (autobiography) 1940

An Essay on Metaphysics (philosophy) 1940
The Three Laws of Politics (philosophy) 1941
The New Leviathan; or, Man, Society, Civilization and Barbarism (philosophy) 1942
The Idea of Nature (philosophy) 1945
The Idea of History (philosophy) 1946
Essays in the Philosophy of Art (philosophy) 1964
Essays in the Philosophy of History (philosophy) 1965

CRITICISM

G. Buchdahl (essay date 1948)

SOURCE: "Logic and History: An Assessment of R. G. Collingwood's Idea of History," in *The Australasian Journal of Philosophy*, Vol. XXVI, No. 2, September, 1948, pp. 94-113.

[*In the following essay, Buchdahl focuses on Collingwood's approach in* The Idea of History *to the problematic nature of historical facts and historical knowledge.*]

This article is not concerned with everything Collingwood has had to say about history, but only some interesting parts of certain passages in his ***Idea of History***. The problem dealt with in those passages is: How can we give an account of historical facts, how can there be historical knowledge? And this may (without perhaps prejudging the issue too much) be divided into: (a) how much can we discover as having occurred? (b) what is the best explanation that can be given of these occurrences?

I say I do not want to prejudge the issue by subdividing our question into one concerning the detail of historical facts on the one hand, and one concerning their connection on the other, because (at least if Collingwood is right) it is not quite clear whether there *are* indeed two questions, nor in which order these ought to be asked. Many people, for instance, would probably agree that they are at least interdependent in the sense in which scientific data and scientific theories are. Scientific data, they would say, gain their meaning only within the framework of a certain theory; often their acceptance or rejection depends upon the sort of theory we have. And it is of course obvious that these theories, in turn, depend on the data.

In order to bring out Collingwood's views as clearly as possible I shall first of all mention some of the objections he urges against those whom he considers his opponents. Broadly speaking, Collingwood is engaged in "a running fight with what may be called a positivistic conception (of history) . . . as the study of successive events lying in a dead past, events to be understood as the scientist understands natural events, by classifying them and establishing relations between the classes thus defined" (228). [Numbers in brackets refer to page-numbers of R. G. Collingwood's *Idea of History*. Oxford, 1946.] This, Collingwood says, is the correct procedure of Natural Science. For its data are given by perception; they are "mere particulars" (222), "observed but not understood". To understand them, we must discover "relations between general types of them" (ibid.). Now if we wanted to apply this procedure to history, this would assume that there *are* "given" historical facts, capable of being digested unchewed (to adapt a metaphor of Bradley's); and secondly, that we could order these facts into classes. Take the last point first. Collingwood does not think that we *can* order historical facts into classes very easily; people who try to do this (he quotes Vico, Hegel, Comte, Marx, Spengler and Toynbee—describing their work as "pigeon-holing" [263]) have never achieved anything of "value for science" (265). For he thinks that a necessary pre-requisite for a satisfactory pattern of this sort would be that it should "impress itself as inevitable" upon the facts (ibid.). None of these patterns do, he says. What is his reason for this?

Briefly his reason seems to be this. The positivists assume that the data, the facts, which they might attempt to correlate into a uniform pattern are, to borrow an expression of Russell's, "hard", i.e., given, perceived, incorrigible. But actually they are not; on the contrary, they are always open to criticism, emendation, even rejection. Therefore the normal constructive account or theory, whereby we attempt to connect and understand our facts will not only, like all scientific hypotheses, be open to the objection that it does not connect the facts necessarily (e.g., that alternative hypotheses are always thinkable); it also will itself vitally affect what we shall in fact accept *as* an historical fact, and what we shall reject. Now to put the matter somewhat graphically, this view has the effect of loosening the facts from a solid background whilst at the same time apparently throwing all the weight upon the constructive account of the historian. But as so often is the case, philosophers who thus seem to destroy the fetters of necessity, immediately proceed to replace them by more solid chains. To this end, Collingwood attempts two things: (a) to convey the impression that it is possible for the historian to construct an "a priori necessary" account; (b) to show that his ideal of necessity is of a special kind: namely that of internal, quasi-organic connection. Only if the facts are "internally connected" (whatever that may mean) are they necessarily connected. Hence he asserts that the material for the historian is thought. "Thought", you will find, is the model making the assertion of internal connection plausible. And this for two reasons, one, because thought is the "inner" side of events, and then again, because thought, he says, is the only thing that, whilst created at a particular instant in time, yet lives forever, is carried on in the course of history, the only thing that is both now and always.

Like most philosophers, Collingwood is not too clear on the nature and content of his ideals, is not clear how

what he feels as a deficiency determines the choice of his ideal. To make up for this lack of philosophical self-consciousness, I will try and bring this out into the open by quoting a passage from Bradley's *Appearance and Reality,* Bradley being the man who, on Collingwood's admission, probably influenced him most and comes the closest to his general views (apart perhaps from Kant and Croce). "The failure of what is called 'explanation' lies in the difficulty that the principles taken up are not merely in themselves not rational but, being limited, remain external to the facts to be explained" (*Appearance and Reality,* Second edition, p. 502). And ". . . if the terms from their inner nature do not enter into the relation, then, so far as they are concerned, they seem related for no reason at all, and so far as they are concerned, the relation seems arbitrarily made" (p. 514, ibid.). Unless their *inner* nature connects the terms, the relation is an arbitrary one: this objection, and, per contra, the ideal behind it, determine Collingwood's doctrine in a far-reaching way and are the clue to an understanding of his thought; they supply us, as it were, with an insight into the mental atmosphere surrounding Collingwood's work. Like Bradley, what he wants are very much "tighter" relations than science would seem to be able to furnish.

To see this more clearly, let us now return to Collingwood's *first* point of attack, that on the positivistic notion of historical fact. "The historian, investigating any event in the past, makes a distinction between what may be called the outside and the inside of an event" (213). The "outside" is, for example, Caesar's action in crossing the Rubicon. The inside is the thought that motivated him. Now here Collingwood's argument goes as follows: In giving the causation of an event in history, it is not enough to assign the "cause" in the "scientific sense", i.e., by assigning the event to a class of events as one of their members and thus forming a law. This is all that science can do and need do: for it "merely perceives" events from the outside, as it were (214), and the further search for its cause is then conducted by assigning it to a class. (To use a Kantian phrase: The "objects" of science are "mere appearances" which we do not know in themselves, from within, but merely from without.) Now "for history the object to be discovered is not the mere event but the thought expressed by it" (214). This thought we never perceive, but reach by indirect methods, using circumstantial evidence, as we commonly call it; and this involves theory and construction. Hence "to discover that thought is already to understand it". (Because, I presume, in trying to discover it, we use circumstantial reasoning, theory and construction; that is to say, we connect the thought with others, checking it against them. But this sort of activity is what we *mean* by "understanding".) "After the historian has ascertained the facts, there is no further process of inquiring into their causes. When he knows what happened, he already knows why it happened" (214).

But why should we be so *sure* that we have *understood* the thought correctly any more when we have discovered it, albeit by roundabout methods, than any ordinary event? Remember that the ideal of understanding is to get our facts into relations (often called "laws"); and Collingwood's ideal is nothing short of necessary, and to *him* this means internal, relations. Now I suggest that he allowed himself to be misled by the metaphorical use of the adjective "inner". Remembering the passage from Bradley, quoted above, I think it is clear that Collingwood was searching for "inner connections", "internal relations". And once having distinguished an inner and an outer side of events, the inner side being the thought behind the event, he must have argued that through the thought we know the event from within, and hence also are capable of seeing how it points to and connects up with other thoughts, and through this with other events. It is easy to make this slide, because we often do say: if I had known what he *thought,* I would have understood the way in which he acted. But it seems to me that in the end the other person's thought, particularly when this thought, by admission, is re-constructed, is just as much reached from the "outside", or to use Kant's expression again, is as much "an appearance" as anything else. That Collingwood did not realise this may be due, among other things, to his peculiar view of thought, to which we shall return later. At present I am merely concerned with showing what, he thinks, hangs on his rejection of the positivistic conception of fact. Thoughts are the facts which we require for an understanding of history, because they alone enable us to get to the inside of the historical fabric. But thoughts are never given. Hence they must be reconstructed. And this reconstruction will have to be carried on by indirect means, since we never have direct access to them (for the thoughts as reported in documents, for instance, may be false, misleading, and so on).

Let us now look a little more closely at this process of construction and its implications. The historian does not deal with directly perceived events, as science may be said to do (doubtfully so, perhaps), but only with those that lie in the past (233). Thus, inference plays a major part in history. But there is a more important aspect to this matter. The historian, in the course of his researches, carries on a three-fold activity: that of selection, interpolation (i.e., construction), and criticism. We need not say too much about the meaning of these terms, since this will be fairly obvious. The historian clearly has to select from a multitude of facts and documentary material (primary and secondary sources) those items that appear to him to be the most authentic, the best suited, to act as evidence for a plausible account. He has to interpolate, because no matter how fully the events with which he is dealing may be reported, quite clearly there will be gaps that have to be filled in. Finally, he will have to subject his sources to internal and external criticism. He will have to compare the reported statement of the case with others from different writers; he will have to attempt an evaluation of the main tendencies of the religious and political thought of the time, for instance, in order to be able to "weight" the statements in his hands and allow for idiosyncrasies of lan-

guage in the writer concerned. One thing he cannot do: simply accept what is offered to him as a report of what happened.

Collingwood is rather struck by the aspect of criticism and its implications: for it seems to give to the historian the power to accept or reject a certain statement. "Suetonius (for example) tells me that Nero at one time intended to evacuate Britain. I reject this statement, not because any better *authority* flatly contradicts it, for of course none does; but because my reconstruction of Nero's policy based on Tacitus will not allow me to think that Suetonius is right" (244-5). In other words, selection and interpolation appear to imply that there are certain facts to select from, and to interpolate between; that there are certain definite facts which may be connected and thus explained (although alternative explanations may well be possible). But on the view that these facts, as reported, may themselves be rejected in the light of a criticism based upon a construction or reconstruction of these very facts,—in the light of this we see that we really have not got any solid, hard facts to go on. Indeed, these facts may become modified or rejected in the process of construction for which they were originally to serve as the "raw material". Hence all the weight is now thrown on to the construction. "The web of imaginative reconstruction is something far more solid and powerful than we have hitherto realized" (244). This realisation is what Collingwood calls the "Copernican Revolution in the theory of History" (236). It amounts to saying, according to him, that in all these activities the historian acts "autonomously", and that since there are no hard data, "historical thought gives itself its data" (244)—a somewhat queer summing up of the situation.

Of course, this sounds somewhat harsh, paradoxical. It looks as if it amounted to "the rejection of all the testimony that has come down to us, and the substitution for it of a dream spun out of the critic's brain"—as Charles Peirce once put the matter in a similar context. (In "Scientific Attitude and Fallibilism"—*The Philosophy of Peirce,* p. 25.) But I think that last statement of Collingwood's, quoted above, is perhaps really no more than a somewhat challenging summing up of a perfectly sensible observation that no historian merely collects "sources", merely works with "scissors-and-paste", as Collingwood puts it, but selects and interprets. Had he merely said: the historian interprets, he formulates "constructive descriptions" in the light of which he accepts or rejects certain facts, I think his theory would not have sounded very revolutionary. Nevertheless, making it so sound has the advantage of perhaps drawing attention to certain difficulties into which it may be well to inquire more closely.

Collingwood's strong point seems to be this: All historical facts are non-perceptible. The "evidence" for them, in the shape of documents, etc., may be said to be perceptible, but not the facts for which these *are* the evidence. For this reason alone we may expect a certain amount of inferential reasoning and circumstantial argument. Historians want to know whether certain facts took place and whether these facts can be suitably correlated with others. Collingwood's thesis is that not only are the connections between the facts not given (i.e., not only do we have to *construct* the most plausible account that will connect given facts), but neither are the facts themselves. The facts are "soft" (not hard), and the evidence proposed in their favour may always conceivably be rejected. Any such facts will be rejected if they do not fit a known law, or situation alleged or known to possess a unity of a certain sort.

To fix the matter, let us take an example. Let us take up Fisher's *History of Europe*. Opening the book at random we find the following statement: Laud was the founder of New England. We will not take this too literally, but shall content ourselves with letting it imply that the Puritans were mainly responsible for the colonisation of New England. The evidence for this is that certain fairly large numbers of so-called Puritans did go to New England. What we *assume* is that religious issues were decisive at that time; in the light of this we would probably be inclined to lay little stress on the fact that there were also some non-Puritans who immigrated into New England, e.g., merchants and farmers. This evidence would not fit very well into the general picture. But now we will decide to choose another theory. We undertake an analysis of the economico-sociological composition of the population and make the assumption that economic issues were decisive in regulating the flow of immigration. This will make us not only look for further evidence for non-Puritan immigration and colonisation: it will cause us to play down, to say the least, the element of Puritanism. Actual figures, statistics, of course, on the whole cannot be rejected: we must not understand Collingwood to do this. But they can be played down. And in the final statement, masquerading as a proposition of fact, as the one reported above, the other evidence will simply disappear.

We may perhaps with advantage contrast this situation with another one encountered in, say, one of the physical sciences. The "facts" with which we deal in the latter are in a slightly different category in that a fairly large number of them are perceivable, or nearly incorrigible. Whereas there are no such perceivable facts in history which, as such, have to be accepted, and also fewer nearly incorrigible statements. Now I can easily conceive of an objection that might be raised against this last statement. One might insist on the similarity between the historical and the scientific situation by saying that all *scientific* facts are corrigible or soft, too. I think we must, however, try and understand this objection rightly. A datum of perception in science may, of course, be rejected because it is subsequently found to have been an erroneous perception (through repetition of the experiment). Or it may be corrigible in the sense that it is true subject to experimental error. Nevertheless, given a fact and a theory, and faced with a choice between them (due to a clash), we do not—assuming

that we wish in this instance to retain the theory—reject the fact as such, as reported, if it is an item of observation. We may reject it because we say: if you look again you will find an error in your observations and calculations somewhere. This is what Newton might have said when his theory led to a value for the Moon's distance from the Earth different from that "observed". The observation eventually yielded to the theory. Or we may reject it because we think that we can *explain* the contradiction by further hypotheses or occurrences which do not clash with the theory in question. Thus it is a consequence of Maxwell's Electro-Magnetic Theory that the Refractive Index of light is equal to the square-root of the Dielectric Constant. When independent measurements are made of these two constants, it is, however, found that with decreasing wave-lengths large discrepancies appear. Again we do not reject the theory. But neither do we reject our measurements of the two constants as such. We merely maintain that the observations do not invalidate the theory because the discrepancy can be accounted for by making certain further assumptions concerning the composition of matter. (We must, of course, make sure that these additional assumptions do not conflict with the theory we are discussing.) We are thus enabled to retain a theory which on other grounds manages to correlate a large number of observations. But a clash between one fact and another, or a fact and a theory, may in history lead to the rejection of that fact, because the latter is never perceived, but based on evidence which may be defective. In the "scientific" case the matter lies differently, because the "evidence" is perceptible evidence, or better: is *about* a perceptual situation that may in principle be repeated (by means of an experiment). Hence the evidence, here, and as such, must stand, although I don't want to give the impression that the distinction is a rigid one. Collingwood uses this state of affairs, first, to throw all the weight on the construction, i.e., the theory. Second, in order to show that you only know that you have an unimpeachable so-called datum, when you have also got your construction. Once again, knowing your facts and understanding them go hand in hand.

Now we *might* say that it does not really seem to follow that *all* historical data are equally soft, at any particular instant at which an historical enquiry is made. I think that this is obviously not the case, and that some data are rather better authenticated than others. It would then follow that the historian was not equally free to handle all his data "autonomously" as Collingwood puts it. Also, it might well be the case that we simply accept that construction which embraces the largest *number* of the best authenticated data. But Collingwood does not seem to be satisfied with this kind of coherence theory and insists, as we shall see presently, that there is a special sort of way in which we can "understand the thought of the past".

The historian, then, acts autonomously (237). As with Kant and the Idealists, we are given the impression that the centre of gravity has shifted into the creative Self, the individual. What, then, is now to become of our criterion of truth? The historian cannot write arbitrarily—that cannot be meant. However much we may be "struck by this power to reject something explicitly told by our authorities and to substitute something else" (237), there must somewhere exist a guarantee that our story is not fiction, not an arbitrary selection and collection of material. Collingwood gives us a clue by reminding us of the answer that Bradley had given to the same question, after carrying out a similar analysis of the status of historical knowledge. Bradley had said (in his essay on "The Presuppositions of Critical History") that the historical narrative must be agreeable to the historian's "experience". This meant, I suppose, that the story had to be a "possible" one. Collingwood's objection to this is that such a criterion would be the same as that of any good fiction writer. Further, the use of the word "possible" suggests that the story is accepted as plausible because it mentions a situation that is *similar* to others. But according to Collingwood this is to confuse history with science, whereas in the former you do not encounter repeat-situations. (This objection would seem to be at the same time directed against those who think, like Hempel, that the only way to explain a particular situation *is* through showing it to be a term in a universal cause-effect situation. But I shall return to this point presently.)

At this stage Collingwood introduces Kant's concept of the Imagination—a concept he has already used extensively in his ***Principles of Art***. We construct with the help of the imagination, but if our construction is not to be an altogether arbitrary one, it must be "genuinely necessitated", it must be that which "operating not capriciously as fancy but in its a priori form, does the entire work of the historical construction" (241). Why does he call it "a priori"? The term is used in a sense directly corresponding to that employed by Kant in his deduction of the categories. It is autonomous, creative, non-derivative, yet "necessary", necessitated. The construction must develop from a sort of "internal necessity" (242), and its characters must be "possible" characters. Collingwood leaves it at that. There is no "proof" (transcendental or otherwise) of this character of necessity-cum-autonomy, and indeed there could not be one. The notion of spontaneity is, after all, introduced in order to free the historian from the chains of his material. (Cf. 278, where the doctrine of the arbitrary spontaneous selection of material by the historian is recommended, because it frees the historian from the tremendous burden of the wealth of material that has accumulated.) Collingwood could therefore quite possibly have gone on to say that it was a matter for "decision" on the part of the competent historian to select the most plausible material and integrate it in the light of certain overriding considerations.

Collingwood prefers an apparently safer path. The expression of necessity is introduced in order to tie the historian down again, in order to have a starting point, in order to escape the apparent circle of fact presupposing theory and theory presupposing fact. (We must also remember that what is being reconstructed is the *thought* of the past, and I have already indicated how this suggests the feeling of getting inside the historical flux and thus gives us internal, that is, necessary connections.) The situation is here very similar to that encountered in the ethical system of Kant: we must be free, yet necessitated; we must have necessary freedom. Unfortunately the hints Collingwood gives us about this concept and its verification are not very precise. The only clue given, that of "internal necessity", which connects the historian's material, still looks very much like Bradley's and like the artist's, the novelist's criterion. Collingwood is acutely aware of this fact and therefore adds what looks like a further criterion, intended to make the construction—as he puts it—a "true" one. In order that the construction may be true, it must satisfy the following set of criteria: (a) it must be localised in space and time; (b) it must be consistent within itself and with other parts of historical constructions. These two criteria don't take us much further. The first, unless it means that we have independent ways of establishing the truth of an historical assertion, throws us back on to the second. And the second we have already dealt with and merely reiterates the remarks made concerning the sort of "internal necessity" that connects the elements of the historian's material. And the third criterion? (c) An historically true statement must "stand in a peculiar relation to something called evidence" (246)! This certainly looks a bit like a circle. The whole point of the theory had been to supply a way out of the difficulty that we have no "hard" data, and now we are apparently thrown back on to what is here called "evidence".

Of course, from a psychological point of view, there may be no need to be worried at all. We encounter similar situations in science, and two writers at least, who characterise it as a circular one, are not at all worried. Thus Cohen and Nagel, in their *Introduction to Logic and Scientific Method* (p. 396) write as follows: "The method of science is thus essentially circular. We obtain evidence for principles by appealing to empirical material, to what is alleged to be 'fact'; and we select, analyse, and interpret empirical material on the basis of principles". However, Collingwood is rather disturbed by this difficulty, and tries to make the position appear less circular by playing down this notion of evidence. "Evidence", as he conceives it, certainly does not consist in any incorrigible data or sources. There are no intrinsically bad and good sources. "Everything is evidence which the historian can use as evidence" (247). We shall accept that as evidence which fits most adequately into the imaginative account (279-80). So, after all, "there is nothing other than historical thought itself, by appeal to which its conclusions may be verified" (243).

We are then, I think, left somewhat in doubt as to just how far we are to take this notion of "evidence" seriously. If we do, then Collingwood's account, despite all its bravado, boils down to something very much like that of his opponents, the "positivistic historians".

Hempel, for instance, also admits that the historian, although he attempts to discover general laws that fit the facts of history, proceeds mostly by way of what Hempel calls "explanation sketches" (op. cit., 5.4). "Such a sketch consists of a more or less vague indication" of what is considered relevant, and if the data, the "evidence" fit it, we shall accept it. I think the main difference of approach lies in this: Hempel, apart from never questioning the hardness of *some* data at least, is rather more concerned with how we come to formulate such "sketches" and with the independent evidence which we can put forward in their favour. Collingwood, so far as I can see, never in the least discusses the necessity for such a search into general explanations, and he cannot, of course, openly do this, because he has locked the door, as we have seen, by asserting that there *are* no regularities which we could use here. Nevertheless, he has introduced this notion by the back door. And this comes out in the following way: Evidence becomes evidence to the historian, says Collingwood, in so far as he can use it. "And he cannot use it unless he comes to it with the right kind of historical knowledge" (247). In so far as he is "master of his craft" (238) he can treat his evidence in such a way as to give an adequate account.

But what are we to understand by "historical knowledge"? And how does this knowledge help us integrate our facts? We are not told. But I think we may take it that it will be of a kind that insures that a certain situation *must* have occurred, because the situation in question has generally been found to exist in other similar circumstances. For that is what we *mean* by "explaining" the facts belonging to such a situation. But how do we know what is generally the case? Surely only through having—inductively—discovered certain regularities. And this is precisely Hempel's standpoint. Of course, we may not be certain as yet of the general situations that hold, we may not yet have discovered any recurrent patterns, or we may not yet be in the possession of sufficiently well tested sociological and economic laws—we have seen Hempel admit this, and we also find that Collingwood admits it. Only, we find Collingwood interpreting this very same state of affairs as being further evidence in favour of his own doctrine. History is a living thing, he tells us; no history written is ever final, each generation writes its own. And thus the account that is most adequate will gradually emerge. This is his answer to the charge that for aught we know our constructions may be quite arbitrary. But when a fact such as this can be brought to support two opposing theories, it is best not to attribute too much importance to it.

The situation is, broadly speaking, this: both sides, of course, want explanations which more or less necessarily connect the alleged historical facts. But whereas Hempel looks for a universal, for a law, for some sort of regularity, which is to serve as a major premiss in an historical argument, Collingwood seems to look in principle for a unique situation (a picture), which is to do

the work of connection. He does this, as we have seen, for a variety of reasons, not the least for this: that he thinks that no historical situation is repetitive. However, in that case the difficulty arises of having to make good the claim that such a unique situation *would* necessarily account for the facts; and I cannot see how this can be done except at the very least, on an analogy with other situations which the one which allegedly accounts for the facts in our case, is assumed to resemble in relevant respects. Now Collingwood admits this, I say, because he admits that only the historian who is a master of his craft, and who has the "requisite knowledge" (of such situations) will interpret the facts rightly. Having said this, he passes on, not telling us how the historian gains such knowledge, nor what sort of knowledge it is to which he is here referring. And I think he passes on because he has a theory at the back of his mind amounting to this: the historian's thought is heir to the thought of the past. The thought of the past, as it were, comes to life in him again; there is a sort of organic development of thought going on all the time—this at least was the theory put forward in his *Autobiography*. I shall return to this presently.

The misleading aspect of Collingwood's doctrine, I contend, lies on the one hand in slurring over the way in which constructions are arrived at; on the other, in giving the impression that constructions both *can* be and *are* the final arbiters. But they *are* not the final court of appeal; for I think that on his own admission it would seem that "evidence" (however understood) holds equal place with the construction. And the latter *cannot* be the final judge, because he has not made good the claim that these constructions are *necessary* ones, which is what he set out to do.

Why then is Collingwood so sure that his constructions do not, in the end, hang in the air? To understand this, we must recall what we said at the beginning of this article. We there showed that Collingwood holds that the historian's peculiar job is to reconstruct, to re-enact the *thought* of the past (thought being somehow viewed as the *inner* side of events). I said *before,* that he rather exaggerates the importance of thought, because the aspect of the "internality" of thought (the thought behind, inside events) suggests internality of relations. (And I would stress again, it suggests but does not entail it.) *Now* I want to say that Collingwood chooses the thought metaphor for the further reason that he thinks that thought is, in principle, the only thing of the past that *can* be recaptured, literally re-enacted. It will be noticed that construction is now being turned into reconstruction, and this into re-enactment. You may remain for ever outside the actions that constituted the consequences of the motivating thought. But if you should somehow be able to reconstruct, to re-live, that thought, then you will have recaptured the exact flow of the connected tissue of events. Here again, I think, Collingwood is once more a little misled by a somewhat drawn-out proof to the effect that literally the same act of thought can be re-enacted (albeit in principle only, I suppose). He therefore slurs over the difficulty as to how we are in fact to re-enact it.

He discusses two possible objections to the thesis that we re-enact the thought of the past. If we mean by this phrase thinking a thought *like* the past one, then we seem to be involved in a sort of correspondence theory of truth. And Collingwood does not like correspondence theories. They, to him, involve something like this: You first have the original thought, and then you have this thought reconstructed in the mind of the present-day historian. And the content of this present thought would be said to be "true" if it *mirrored* that of the original one. Now this account conceives the "mirroring relation" as a sort of "external relation" (as indeed it has been understood, e.g., by Moore and Russell and the Wittgenstein of the *Tractatus*). This, Collingwood seems to think, implies that the terms of this relation are conceived of in "atomic" fashion, given, complete, independent. From this it is then inferred that no means exist, in principle, of knowing these atomic data, in so far as they lie in the past. For knowing such a datum involves a kind of internal relation between knower and known. And this is, as we have seen, excluded by hypothesis. Hence he asserts that for such a theory the past thought is dead, that we can never know it as it was, in principle. We would therefore at once be involved in all the difficulties of having to reconstruct this thought by roundabout methods, a task which his "re-living" doctrine was supposed to make possible.

Should we say, then, that literally the same thought lives again? Collingwood hesitates. If there were complete identity (i.e., if not only the "content" of the original thought were mirrored in the present thought, but if the very same thought were re-lived) then we would seem to be involved in a dilemma. On the one hand, since the original thought process took place in a definite psycho-physical context, an insistence on complete identity would make it impossible ever to think the thought again. But on the other hand, if you insisted on the possibility of this feat, there would seem to be nothing but a sort of everliving present (somewhat on the lines of Croce's doctrine). Strictly taken, this ought to involve "oblivion of myself", as Collingwood says (301), and he does not want this to happen either. (The difficulty here seems to be this: you want a distinction, so that you can talk of past and present, and the moment you are presented with it you reject it and complain that nothing short of identity is knowledge. This is the sort of situation that has arisen in the history of philosophy on a number of occasions.)

It is rather difficult to present Collingwood's thought here at all coherently. One thing is certain, that the minimum demanded by him is to have the thought of the past carried over into the present. Thus he writes: ". . . the historian's own mind is heir to the past and has come to be what it is through the development of the past into the present, so that in him the past is living in the present" (171). How this is to be achieved by normal

means he nowhere tells us in these pages. He finally suggests, somewhat lamely, that whilst the actual physical and psychological context within which the original thought occurred can, of course, not be revived, yet the thought as such, in so far as it is *true*, the thought which not only the original thinker, but any one *could* have, nay, *must* have experienced, if he was to talk sense— that can be revived. I cannot see how this carries conviction. The thought as anyone *could* think it, quite apart from any difficulties as to how we are to discover that thought, is this not the old criterion of possibility again? Collingwood himself rejected this criterion in his criticism of Bradley, as we have seen. To make his position more convincing, he has recourse to rather a queer example, the reconstruction of Plato's thought. He must have reasoned that since Plato, in order to make *sense*, must have thought *truly*, whatever the context may have been then, *if* we only now reconstruct a *sensible* argument, we may be sure that we have also *correctly* reconstructed Plato's thought. This, however, is giving Plato quite a lot of credit; perhaps he did not always think sensibly in the sense demanded by the argument. In any case, it is not likely that the thought of the past has been overmuch occupied with the Eternal Verities!

In fact it is not at all obvious what use we can make of this theory of re-enactment, unless it is put forward in order to console us in certain difficulties. We are first of all expressly told that the historian *constructs autonomously*, so why now this attempt to give the impression that he *re-lives* the real past? We notice here a familiar opposition of conflicting ideals, which very often occur together in a philosopher's doctrines. On the one hand we have Autonomy, on the other Necessity. On the one hand Construction, on the other Reconstruction.

We shall not say much about the difficulties that surround the notion of the miraculous power whereby we can, as it were, slide into the thought of the past. The *picture* that Collingwood has conjured up in the ***Autobiography*** appears to be that of the thought of the past surging on, carried by the living stream of the historical current and springing forth in the creative construction of the present-day historian. But this is perhaps a sort of poetic description of an ideal—it is certainly not very good logic, nor even sound practical advice.

Let us try and summarise the main trends of Collingwood's position. There are no "hard" facts in history. This makes them dependent upon the constructive account of the historian, it gives the historian complete freedom to create an account embodying what he accepts as the most adequate evidence. What is to count as adequate evidence will depend progressively upon how much the historian knows about his subject, the more he "gets the feel" of his subject.

This is Collingwood the individualist, the creative artist. But there is also Collingwood the man who thirsts after a knowledge which will impress itself as necessary upon the facts. This side is accommodated by the use of the concept of the construction that is a priori, of the a priori imagination—although nothing like a "transcendental deduction" is attempted. This side of Collingwood's intellectual desires is further accommodated by the doctrine that the material for the reconstruction of the past is thought, the thought that lies behind the events. By thus getting inside the events we may hope actually to "see" how they are connected (connected internally, that is to say). On the other hand, past thoughts, not being perceptible now, must certainly be reconstructed. Collingwood is concerned to show that they are reconstructed in a very important sense, viz., they are re-enacted. There is an aspect of thought that lives forever and becomes reembodied in the mind of the present-day thinker. How this is to be done in practice, Collingwood does not discuss in this book. (A not very satisfactory attempt to do this had been made in the *Autobiography* with his "encapsulation" theory, which amounted to saying that contemporary thought can "re-enact" that of the past because it contains it.) The general tenor of his doctrine will, however, be apparent by now. On the one hand, artistic creativeness, autonomy, freedom. On the other we actually enter into the necessary flux of history—indeed, we are part of it.

The negative merits of this work seem to me to lie in the honesty with which Collingwood allows conflicting ideals to come to the fore, bravely resisting the temptation to suppress either at the expense of the other. More positively, Collingwood manifests a very fine feeling for some of the more practical and artistic aspects of historical writing. But these merits are severely offset by what I consider an important defect: the playing down of the importance of the discovery of generalisations for the purpose of understanding history, even its particular situations. Collingwood brushes off the necessity for this by invoking the concept of free yet necessitated constructions; further, by vaguely referring to the fact that the historian must be a master of his craft, must bring the right kind of historical knowledge to his work and must know how to ask the right kind of questions. How all this is to be achieved he does not tell us in detail.

I will not add anything concerning the metaphysics of these pages. I have perhaps given the impression that his artistic outlook and individualism follow deductively from his doctrine. In fact, it is just as likely that the converse is true. Nevertheless, I believe that by studying his metaphysics critically we may gain a certain amount of insight into a writer's practical ideals.

Errol E. Harris (essay date 1951)

SOURCE: "Collingwood on Eternal Problems," in *The Philosophical Quarterly,* Vol. 1, No. 3, April, 1951, pp. 228-41.

[*In the following essay, Harris discusses Collingwood's ideas on the possibility of an "ultimate standard" of philosophical truth.*]

The notion of eternal truth is as old as philosophy itself, and, surely, of all things, truth can hardly be subject to alteration. The standard by which we judge must be an ultimate standard, for, if it were not, no claim even to relative truth could be justified; and no such standard could be changeable, for, if it were, the claims of the successive competitors for our allegiance would be utterly baseless. The attempt, so often made, to base them on psychological needs is in the highest degree question-begging, for the theory, which determines those needs and the relation to them of the supposed standards, itself lacks authority unless it can be substantiated by reference to some criterion exempt from the psychological conditioning which it claims to have discovered.

Yet the belief is very prevalent today that this ancient idea of an eternal truth is unfounded. Not only are there those who canvass a conventional standard of truth which may be arbitrarily changed to suit our convenience, but there are others less extreme who nevertheless find it hard to believe in an absolute criterion. 'It may be well to inquire,' writes Basil Willey, 'not with Pilate "What is Truth?" but what was *felt to be* "truth" and "explanation"' (at the period under review). Explanation, he says, cannot be defined absolutely; one can only say that it is a statement which satisfies the demands of a particular time and place. If it is to satisfy, 'its terms should seem ultimate' but that again depends upon certain assumptions the source of which is said to be 'sub-logical'—'not, that is, a "conviction" resulting from an intellectual process, but a quite simple set of the whole being towards a particular way of life'.

Here we have a typical modern attitude to truth; a doctrine which, tested by its own criterion, must be regarded at best as something *purely* modern and local, in that it can only be temporary and provisional, satisfying the demands only of a particular place and time; and if its source is something 'sub-logical,' on what grounds can it claim to be taken seriously?

Closely bound up with our notion of truth are the conceptions we entertain of the nature of philosophical problems and the method by which they are to be studied. If there is a body of eternal truth, the problems which beset the philosopher in his search for it will always be relevant to the same objective and there will be a sense in which they may be called eternal also. But, in calling them so we may mean one of two things: a problem may be eternally insoluble and so, like the poor, always with us; or it may be logically related to an eternal truth (its solution), so that even when solved it would still be characteristic of a necessary phase in the process of thought required for the attainment of that truth. In the second meaning, even a mathematical problem, like that of the Pythagoreans about the incommensurability of the diagonal, would be eternal in so far as it must always be faced and surmounted by the student of mathematics at some stage in his progress. But if philosophical problems are relative to eternal or ultimate truths, they will be eternal in both these senses, for the knowledge of ultimate truth implies omniscience, short of which the problem must remain unsolved; yet an ideal solution may be presumed and some progress towards it may be made even by finite minds.

It is, however, notorious that solutions of philosophical problems offered in one generation, or by one type of theory, fail to satisfy universally, and what appeals in one period or intellectual *milieu* is unacceptable in others. Does this mean that the problem is really different in each case, with the corollary that the truth to which it is relevant is different; or is it only that the proffered solution is false and requires correction or total replacement?

Many modern philosophers scout the ideas of eternal truth and eternal problems, though they do not deny that certain true propositions (notably those of mathematics) are tenseless. They deny the existence of so-called ultimate realities, if only because they are beyond the reach of the senses. Truth, for some, is what is empirically verifiable and such verification does not seem to require omniscience (though, on closer examination it does seem to require omnisentience); nor could it properly be called eternal, for verification by means of sense-perception is a momentary matter and no proposition can be sensuously verified once and for all, but ought strictly to be tested afresh every time it is called in question; nor is there any guarantee, on the principles adopted by philosophers who think in this way, that empirical observation will always give the same result. Similarly, a problem is held either to be soluble by the application of certain accredited methods of investigation—a logistic calculus, or an experimental method, or both—or else to be insoluble altogether; and in neither case should it be called eternal, for in neither case does it remain with us. Either it is filed away and pigeon-holed in the stock of acquired knowledge as solved, or it is rejected as meaningless, for a question that can have no answer is held to be a senseless question.

But we should, surely, be somewhat too self-confident if we assumed that simply because we could not discover the answer to a question it therefore had none. A problem may well be insoluble for me, even with the help of the most modern techniques, but that gives me no right to the comforting belief that it is absolutely insoluble, and so does not exist. Doctrines which deny the existence of philosophical problems for such reasons smack rather too much of wishful thinking. Moreover, if we have no stable criterion of truth, the 'accepted' methods of investigation may only be provisionally valid and the view which discredits eternal problems may itself pass into disrepute.

But there are others who deny the existence of eternal problems for historical rather than for epistemological

reasons. Willey, whom I have quoted, is one of these, for he points out that the seventeenth century shift from scholasticism to 'the new science' was a shift of interest from the 'why?'—the final cause—to the 'how?'—the manner of causation. It was a change in the nature of the question. So T. D. Weldon, also, writes that 'to suppose that there is a "problem of causality" or "a problem of the inter-relation of mind and body" which presents itself unaltered to succeeding generations of human beings is mere moonshine. The verbal form of the question may be identical but that is all.'

It should follow from all this that the historical treatment of a philosophical problem is valueless. For if the problem is not the same, except in verbal form, in the various periods when it is discussed, and if a problem of contemporary interest, which is or may be similarly stated, is nevertheless a different question, the answer proposed in the past can give no guidance and can throw no light upon the solution demanded in the present. Yet, oddly enough, the writers who are most emphatic about the impermanence of truths and of problems are usually those who insist most strongly upon historical treatment. Those I have quoted are examples of this curiously contradictory attitude and a similar contradiction can be traced in the philosophy of Collingwood. He is equally emphatic about the non-existence of eternal problems: 'Was it really true, I asked myself, that the problems of philosophy were, even in the loosest sense of that word, eternal? Was it really true that different philosophies were different attempts to answer the same questions? I soon discovered that it was not true; it was merely a vulgar error, consequent on a kind of historical myopia which, deceived by superficial resemblances, failed to defect profound differences.' At the same time he is tirelessly insistent that philosophy is an historical study and maintains that this very discovery of the impermanence of philosophical problems makes the history of philosophy philosophically important.

The question whether or not there are eternal problems in philosophy is, then, after all an epistemological question even when it arises from historical considerations, for if succeeding generations of philosophers are called upon to meet the same problems, or problems which have persisted in some recognisable and identifiable form from the past, the study of the work of their predecessors will be of primary importance in their attempts both to understand and to answer the question with which they are faced. But if there are no such problems the nature and the method of philosophy will be different, it will be concerned with matters of only immediate interest and the philosopher will be like Professor A. J. Ayer's journeyman who works piecemeal at rather special questions in a field of more or less exact science, where once a problem is solved it is finally disposed of.

Collingwood is quite clear that the question is one of method and in his view it is only when the method of philosophy is misconceived that we are deceived into believing in the existence of eternal problems. His first account of the matter is stated in his *Autobiography,* where he condemns the methods of those whom he calls 'realists.' They imagine, he says, that all philosophers in all ages have raised the same questions and it is simply their answers which have differed, so that it would be sensible and relevant to ask which of two answers to a given question was the right one. To do this one must find out first whether the proposed answer is self-consistent, for should it contradict itself it will have proved to be false. The method of philosophy, in consequence, would consist mainly of the analysis of propositions into other propositions in order to detect whether or not they contradict one another. To this process the history of philosophy would be secondary. If the object is to discover the 'right' answer to an 'eternal' question, it is not of immediate importance to know what answers others have given in the past and our interest in other philosophers will be limited to ascertaining whether their answers are 'right.' To do so it will obviously be necessary to find out what those answers were and that is the work of the historian of philosophy, but it is useful only as a guide leading us by examples of other men's trial and error towards the goal which we seek—the 'right' answer.

Now all this, Collingwood maintains, is fundamentally mistaken and is based upon a false logic which commits the error of thinking that truth and falsehood belong to propositions as such—an error not confined to 'realists' but shared with them by 'idealists' and symbolic logicians. Collingwood believes that it is impossible to determine whether or not a proposition is true without knowing what question it is meant to answer and the discovery of that requires historical investigation. We have no right to assume or to jump to the conclusion that a given philosopher's theories are intended as answers to a stock set of eternal questions without valid evidence that these actually were the questions he had in his mind. But we can only acquire the evidence by means of historical research. It follows, therefore, that the work of the historian of philosophy is an integral part of the work of evaluating the theories of the philosopher under consideration. More than this, when we know the question to which a theory is the answer, whether it is the right answer or not depends simply upon whether it 'enables us to get ahead with the process of questioning and answering,' not (it would seem) on conformity to any absolute standard of eternal truth.

When we turn to Collingwood's second account of the matter in the *Essay on Metaphysics,* we see why this is so and we learn, further, that the historian's work is not only essential to the philosopher's quest but that it is the whole of it—at least, so far as it is the quest of the metaphysician. For metaphysics, according to Collingwood, is the science of 'absolute presuppositions' and its method is to analyse the thought of, for example, the natural scientist with the object of unearthing these presuppositions and determining whether or not they are absolute. If they prove to be the answers to prior questions, they are only relative and it is legitimate to ask concerning them whether they are right or wrong. But if they are absolute they are themselves prior to all questions and to ask whether or not they are true is a nonsensical question.

The subject-matter of metaphysics, accordingly, is a certain class of historical facts and the preliminary training of the metaphysician should be historical, for the proper method of metaphysics is the historical method—not the out-dated and inefficient method of 'scissors and paste' history, but that of scientific research, by which evidence is sifted, marshalled and systematized and the facts are determined, not merely on hearsay or authority, but by direct scientific investigation.

Consequently, though metaphysics is a systematic study, it is not the study of a closed system. Its task is not system-building. The metaphysician should not and cannot aim at completeness; he is not faced with a repertory of problems which are *the* problems of metaphysics and of which the answer to one determines the answer to the rest, and he cannot, therefore, adopt a deductive or quasi-mathematical procedure similar to that attempted by Spinoza. It will follow also that there are no 'schools' associated with eminent philosophers whose adherents are constantly at loggerheads about the 'truth' or 'falsehood' of their masters' doctrines. For the masters are not maintaining any doctrine except the historical one that such-and-such absolute presuppositions are made by the scientists and scholars of their time.

When the metaphysician realises that this is really what he is doing and when he studies the metaphysical results obtained by his predecessors in past ages, he will soon become aware that there are no eternal problems; that the questions raised in one generation are not the same, despite superficial likenesses, as those of the next. They change continually and continuously and so far as they are alike their sameness is not that of a 'universal' and their differences those between instances of the universal. The sameness is that of an historical process and the difference that 'between one thing which in the course of that process has turned into something else, and the other thing into which it has turned.'

The contradiction, which I earlier attributed to the historicists, implied in their denial of eternal problems concurrently with their insistence upon the importance of the history of philosophy seems here to have been avoided. Eternal problems are certainly denied, and just as it would be futile, therefore, to try to discover their solutions, so, Collingwood would as certainly have held, it would be futile to seek to trace the history of past attempts to solve them. His emphasis on the importance of the history of philosophy has a different ground. Yet it is one which I hope to show presently only re-establishes the contradiction.

(i) If the metaphysician is to display the presuppositions of the science of a particular period he will find evidence in the work of the metaphysicians of that period, who were engaged on the work of unearthing those very presuppositions. But his attitude towards such evidence will not be simply to take it at its face value. He will have to check it, by himself examining and analysing the propositions of the contemporary science, to discover whether the contemporary metaphysician had successfully revealed its absolute presuppositions—for *his* analysis may have been faulty.

(ii) But the historian-metaphysician's interest in doing this is directed primarily towards the absolute presuppositions of science themselves, and only secondarily towards the account given of them by the philosophers of the day; and it is so directed because his real object is to trace the processes of change of the 'constellations' of absolute presuppositions which are at the basis of scientific thought from one period to the next. In doing so, as has been said, he will discover the impermanence of problems and the stupidity of imagining that they can be eternal, but his attention will also be directed to the more fascinating, more difficult and more important question 'Why do they change?' In answer to this question, Collingwood declares, no reason can be given which makes sense except an historical reason. There are stresses and strains in the intellectual systems of every age which render their presuppositions (in Collingwood's terminology) 'consupponible' only under pressure, and as those strains increase so the constellations break down and must be replaced by others. But what is abandoned does not altogether disappear; it persists in suspension (as it were), or as Collingwood says 'incapsulated in a context of present thoughts which, by contradicting it, confine it to a plane different from theirs.'

The essential aim of the true metaphysicians' study, therefore, is to discover the strains which give rise to the changes—it is what one might call (borrowing a word from Bernard Bosanquet) the 'morphology' of the absolute presuppositions of knowledge.

This view of the nature of metaphysics is not lightly to be brushed aside, but in the last analysis it will not survive criticism. In the first place, the doctrine of absolute presuppositions as expounded by Collingwood is, I think, unsound. That all philosophy is concerned with the uncovering of latent presuppositions is hardly to be disputed and that some body of these might be described as absolute in the sense that they are ultimate—that unless they are presupposed no science, no inference, no thinking in short, would be possible—this too cannot in the end be denied. It is true also that these presuppositions are not the same in every historical period any more than the conceptions of the natural sciences remain the same as those sciences progress and develop. But the account which Collingwood gives of such absolute presuppositions, of their relations to one another and to the questions which arise from them, is,

in my opinion, faulty, though he himself, as I hope to show presently, provides the means of correcting the error.

Collingwood states his case in such a way as to suggest that absolute presuppositions are something quite contingent—something which, on analysis of the propositions of science, we just find to be so-and-so. The stresses and strains to which they are said to be subject are never explained. What is their source? In what sort of tension do they result? It would seem not to be due to logical inconsistency, for Collingwood says that absolute presuppositions cannot be deduced one from another (though they must be 'consupponible'—whatever that may mean) and if this is so it will likewise be impossible to deduce the contradictory of any one of them from any other. The strains remain a mystery and the 'unstable equilibrium' in which they result is a metaphor to which no literal meaning is given. Consequently, when the historian-metaphysician discovers the absolute presuppositions of science in successive periods and traces the series of their changes, he has no means of explaining that series. For it is not sufficient to say that the changes are due to internal strains if it is not known what sort of strains to look for. Yet we are told that no sensible answer can be made to the question 'Why do absolute presuppositions change?' except an historical answer and we now see that historical answer there is none.

The history which is metaphysics should, if we follow this account of it, be a purely descriptive study stating the presuppositions of science in each successive period baldly side by side, and all Collingwood's impassioned protests that history 'is concerned not with "events" but with "processes"' come to naught, for the process has been reduced to a mere series of events. Such a study would be devoid of philosophical interest and would bear little resemblance to the work of the great metaphysicians of the past which Collingwood claims as examples of the method he is advocating.

The contradiction thus remains between the rejection of eternal problems and the insistence upon the historical method. For if the problems are not the same from one period to the next, the historical method can enlighten us very little. It can tell us what they have been in the past; it can give us a chronological list of the presuppositions made in succeeding ages; but if it cannot explain their continuity it can throw no light upon the present in which our immediate interest lies. On the other hand, if the historical method is of real value; if the past remains 'incapsulated' in the present so that the present cannot be properly understood without it; if the historical process is really continuous and the historian can really explain the changes involved in it, then there must be an identity running throughout its course which will justify our inclination to call the problems of one age the same problems as those of another—there will be *some* sense in which problems are eternal.

The contradiction is the result of the unsatisfactory account we have been given of absolute presuppositions and to this we must first turn our attention. If absolute presuppositions are to give rise to questions they must have some implications and if they are to be 'consupponible' the implications of one must, at least in part, be identical with those of another (to say that they must be mutually consistent means no more nor less than this). Consequently, absolute presuppositions must be in some way mutually implicated. Collingwood denies this because, he says, they would then be relative and not absolute, but, as we shall presently see, the disjunction is based upon a fallacy. Once it is realised that to be consupponible is to have compatible implications it becomes clear that the source of internal strains in any constellation of absolute presuppositions will be some logical incompatibility and we should have to examine the implications of the presuppositions in order to discover this. So we should be led to the investigation of a matter which Collingwood always passes over in silence. He tells us that the logical efficacy of a supposition is that it causes questions to arise, but just how questions arise and what makes suppositions give rise to them he never inquires. What is the relation between absolute presuppositions and the science that they underlie and are said to render possible? Questions such as these demand nothing less than a logic of science and, in the light of *that* the study of the morphology of absolute presuppositions would become a philosophical history of thought on the lines of Hegel's history of philosophy, demonstrating that it is throughout a dialectical process—whether or not the principle of the dialectic were Hegelian. A good deal of what Collingwood has written seems to support such a conception both of metaphysics and of history, but if this conception is to be taken seriously his repudiation of eternal problems in philosophy cannot stand.

The questions involved in the study of absolute presuppositions are, therefore, not all of them historical and, though what I have called the morphology of absolute presuppositions is certainly in one aspect an historical study, it follows a method which, if universal in history (as Collingwood seems at times to be implying), would make history a philosophical study rather than vice versa.

It is astonishing that Collingwood, in the *Essay on Metaphysics,* should so far have obfuscated what seven years earlier he had so lucidly explained. For in his *Essay on Philosophical Method* he gives a profound and convincing account of the relation of philosophy to its history and provides by implication an admirable answer to the question of eternal problems. In the earlier work Collingwood points out that the distinguishing feature of philosophical thinking, which marks it off from the natural sciences, is the principle which he calls 'the overlap of classes.' In science, a universal concept or genus is specified into mutually exclusive classes or species, whereas in philosophy the universal, though it may be specified, is such that the species overlap. 'The overlap,' he writes, 'is not exceptional, it is normal; and

it is not negligible in extent, it may reach formidable dimensions.' By numerous and convincing examples he shows that this is the case and the principle proves to be fundamental, explaining all the features of philosophical method subsequently discussed. Neglect of the principle leads to what he calls the fallacy of false disjunction and its alternative applications, the fallacy of precarious margins and the fallacy of identified coincidents. Those who fail to recognise the overlap of classes imagine that the instances of a philosophical universal can be rigidly divided into separate groups corresponding to the division of the universal into species, whereas any instance, owing to the overlap, may belong to two (or more) such groups at once. The proposition that it belongs either to one or to another of two species is, therefore, a false disjunction. If, on the other hand, observing the overlap, we seek to identify two species altogether, we fail to make a necessary distinction and falsely identify what are only coincident. The attempt to steer a middle course, to ignore the area of overlap as one of ambiguity and to confine our attention to that part of the subject-matter in which the overlap is not apparent, would be to ignore those instances which are philosophically most important and so to commit the error of attending only to precariously marginal examples.

But if philosophical species overlap, the classes of presupposition distinguished in the *Essay on Metaphysics* should likewise display this propensity. And this is just what we find when we examine their character more closely. An absolute presupposition is logically prior to every question and every proposition of the science in which it is presupposed. It is not the answer to any question raised in that science and so it cannot be scientifically 'justified.' A relative presupposition, on the other hand, is the answer to a prior question and it is therefore possible to justify it as the right answer or to reject it as wrong. But when they are raised to what Collingwood calls 'the philosophical phase,' it becomes apparent that absolute presuppositions are no more than the basal hypotheses of the sciences, and the philosopher's task is not only to discover what they are, but, as Plato maintained, to cancel or remove them by revealing their merely hypothetical character in the light of a more comprehensive and fundamental conception which is not a mere hypothesis but is capable of maintaining and justifying itself. The presuppositions which are absolute for science prove to be relative when viewed philosophically. Using Kantian instead of Platonic language we may say that they are empirically absolute but transcendentally relative. Empirically (or scientifically) it does not make sense to question their validity, but transcendentally they can be *deduced,* an account can be given of them in a theory the subject-matter of which is not hypothetical but is categorical, a philosophical theory making no assumptions and following a method whereby we can at once establish our starting-point by reasoning and check the principles of the reasoning by experience, a method not strictly deduction nor strictly induction but having something in common with both.

Collingwood's contention in the later essay that metaphysics is the science of absolute presuppositions may, therefore, be correct, but his description of its aim and method certainly is not; for it does not confine itself to determining what those presuppositions are. The scientist himself is able, often enough, to do as much as that (and Collingwood holds that the more scientific he is the more clearly will he be aware of what he presupposes). The metaphysician's object is to go further and to criticise those presuppositions—a task which, in his later work, Collingwood declares to be impossible. Yet the very process of discovery is already the beginning of criticism. What Collingwood calls 'metaphysical analysis,' the process of discovering what question is presupposed as prior to a given proposition and again what that question presupposes, is a method of criticism. It is a process of developing the implications of a proposition and displaying its connections with others in some systematic body of knowledge the structure of which becomes apparent as we proceed. Collingwood is, therefore, right to insist on its continuity with scientific analysis. But this process cannot go on *in vacuo*. Only on the basis of a total experience, in the light of which the given proposition from which we begin has meaning and significance, and only by reference to that, can we develop its implications and so discover what it presupposes. And what comes to light as we do so is the systematic structure of that experience itself. Yet, as the system grows, so experience develops and is modified. What was before confused and obscure becomes, by the operation of thought upon it, definite and articulated (and let us not forget that thought is no mere 'armchair' occupation but may, on occasion, require considerable practical activity by way of observation and experiment); so that what was before 'known' only vaguely and 'in dim forecast' becomes known precisely and in its explicit relations to the rest of experience. The process by which initial confusions are clarified and consequent contradictions removed may properly be called criticism; and it is just this process, by which the systematic structure of experience is elucidated, that reveals what in our thinking is derived from what presuppositions. It is, moreover, this process that, in an unselfconscious manner, is going on throughout the development of science; but when we come to reflect upon it, when it becomes selfconscious or (as Collingwood says) raised to its philosophical phase, it becomes the philosophical method—the critical method elaborated (though not originated) by Kant.

The metaphysician, therefore, discovers the absolute presuppositions of science (its '*a priori* principles') by reflection upon the nature of the experience which the science investigates. The form of his argument (as in Kant's first *Critique*) is 'If our experience is to be such as it is and if such-and-such propositions are to be made in science, then such-and-such presuppositions (e.g., that all perceptible things have extensive magnitude, or that all change is supported by a permanent substratum) are necessarily implied.' But the principles he discloses, though *a priori* for the scientist (absolutely presupposed

by him), are so only because of the admitted nature of experience. Experience, as we have it, is prior to the absolute presuppositions and is presupposed in them. If our experience were other than it is the *a priori* elements in science would be different. Accordingly, the presuppositions which are absolute for science are for philosophy relative to experience. They are the defining characteristics of experience or, as Hegel expressed it, provisional 'definitions of the Absolute.'

It follows that as science advances and as knowledge grows, the nature of our experience is modified. The manner in which we interpret it at one stage, at a later stage will not serve, and absolute presuppositions change. These changes, exhibited in the course of scientific progress, are the changes incident upon and inherent in the development of knowledge. The series of changes, like the development, is continuous—it is an historical process—and the continuity running through it is as important as the differences which display themselves *seriatim* within it.

Collingwood, therefore, is right to maintain that metaphysics is an historical study, but the important point is the nature of the historical process, which turns out to be a critical (or, as I called it before, a dialectical) process, and the historical method adopted accordingly may not be simply descriptive but must also be dialectical. The scientific historian, sifting and weighing his evidence, may still content himself, when he has drawn his conclusions, with a description of facts and events. But, for the metaphysician, description, however necessary, is not enough (and we may question whether it is enough even for the historian). The dynamic of the process of historical change must be investigated and analysed, and this dynamic is the dialectical principle running through the process. History and metaphysics, as branches of knowledge, overlap.

Seven years after the *Essay on Philosophical Method* Collingwood had so far forgotten what he had written as to distinguish rigidly between history and metaphysics, apparently forgetting that these are specifications of the philosophical concept, Knowledge, and then, discovering that they overlap, he identified them entirely, committing the fallacy of false disjunction issuing in the false identification of coincidents, to which he had himself earlier drawn attention. He failed to see that though both the specific forms may be exemplified in the same instances, yet they remain two. The Aristotelian formula . . . applies here as elsewhere in philosophy. . . . Consequently, he is led into further confusion from which his own earlier warnings might have saved him. Let us therefore return to his exposition in the earlier work.

The specification of the philosophical universal into overlapping classes is further explained by showing that it always takes the form of an ascending scale. The overlapping classes cannot be mere differences in kind, for that is the characteristic of non-philosophical species; nor can they be mere differences in degree, for even such differences are mutually exclusive. But if these two sorts of difference are combined (if they overlap), we have a generic concept specified into a scale of forms such that each embodies a variable element in a specific degree, the distinctions between the species occurring at critical points on the scale of gradations. But it further transpires that the variable element and the generic essence are the same thing—the principle of overlap applies here as elsewhere—and the scale is one throughout which the generic essence is successively displayed by the specific forms in continuously increasing fulness. Moreover, the specific forms prove to be both opposites and distincts, so that the scale consists of a gradation of forms, each embodying the generic essence more fully than the last, each distinct from every other and each the opposite of its predecessor in the scale; just as goodness and badness are at once distinct and opposite moral conditions and gradations in a scale of moral worth.

Now a scale of forms of this kind is a development, and if it occurs in time it is an historical process. When, therefore, we compare the philosophical theories of different generations, as Collingwood does in the *Autobiography,* and we find that, while they have a certain sameness, they differ both as to the questions raised and the answers offered, and when we discover, as Collingwood does, that these differences and this sameness are those of an historical process, should we not realise that the theories are phases in a scale of forms which is the specification of a philosophical universal? This, indeed, is exactly what Collingwood himself maintains in Chapter IX of the *Essay on Philosophical Method* where the history of philosophy is given as an example of such a scale. What, then, are we to make of his assertion in the *Autobiography* that the sameness of and difference between two philosophical theories are *not* 'the sameness of a "universal" . . . and the difference between two instances of that universal' but *are* 'the sameness of an historical process and . . . the difference between one thing which in the course of that process has turned into something else, and the other thing into which it has turned'? Again the principle of the overlap of classes has been forgotten along with the teaching that the philosophical universal specifies itself into a scale of forms.

But if we accept the earlier statement of Collingwood's theory, we find good reason for saying that the problems with which philosophers deal are in every age the same, as well as for saying (as he does in his later works) that they are not. Philosophies differ, it is true, in degree and in kind; they are also opposed to one another, so as to give rise to argument and dispute, but they are nevertheless the specifications of one and the same philosophical universal and so their differences and oppositions are only the normal characteristics of the phases in a scale of forms. What is still more significant is the fact that such a scale is always an ascending scale. The phases embody progressively more and more fully the generic essence, and such a progression implies a completion, a

summit to the ascent, an acme—that which throughout the gamut of gradations, informs the particulars and makes them *its* particulars and yet does so in varying degrees, so that none of them except the last fully typifies the universal. When these phases or gradations, then, are the successive notions of a philosophical problem and its solution, each of them indeed will differ from the last, will even in a sense be in opposition to it, yet each will be a fuller and a truer account of that eternal problem and that eternal truth which all are attempting to express with varying degrees of success. The eternal problems are relative to the philosophical universals which in the history of philosophy are specified in a scale of forms, and accordingly the method of philosophy is at once historical and dialectical. It must trace the scale of forms throughout its length in order to achieve its goal (a goal of which the best achievements of the human intellect fall far short), but the method it adopts must nevertheless always be critical and even, to a certain extent, eristic.

The metaphysician, accordingly, *must* be a system-builder; but his system being a philosophical system will display itself as a scale of forms. And it will be one that, among its various methods of self-manifestation, expresses itself in an historical process the course of which the metaphysician must study. He will, therefore, also be an historian tracing the series of differing and opposing doctrines in which the universal he is seeking to characterise has, in the past, revealed its specifications.

Thus the implication of contradiction in the doctrine of the *Essay on Metaphysics* is avoided in the *Philosophical Method* and the contradiction itself can be resolved by the application of the principles there expounded. And, for all that he says in the later work, these principles must surely be regarded as fundamental to Collingwood's whole position, for he is emphatic in his assertion that there is a continuity of development in historical changes, and when he maintains that metaphysics is an historical study he insists at the same time that its essential interest lies in the manner of and the reasons for the changes in absolute presuppositions from one period to the next. He insists, also, that the understanding of the past is indispensable to the proper understanding of the present, whether we are dealing with absolute presuppositions or with other historical matters. And to admit all this is to admit, after all, that there is a sense—not loose or indefinite, but precise—in which the problems of philosophy are eternal; not the sense in which any historical fact can be called eternal because it has happened once and for all, but that in which it is true to say (with Kant) that only the permanent can change. The new form which a problem takes is only a new *form,* but the problem is still the same. Its form is new because new material relevant to it has come to hand, because new evidence has been discovered and new interpretations have been made. All this has certainly modified it, but it has not sheerly changed; it has developed and grown, which it could not have done if it had been replaced by an utterly different question. We cannot, therefore, refuse to call philosophical problems eternal, at least in *this* sense, for if the resemblances between those of one generation and those of another were purely superficial and deceptive, we should have to believe that these resemblances had deceived the philosophers themselves who raised the questions and must consequently have falsified their attempted solutions. They must have mistaken one problem for another entirely different and so have been ignorant of the questions they were trying to answer. For, clearly, the philosophers of the past believed themselves to be discussing the same problems as had been tackled by their predecessors and they built upon foundations which their predecessors had laid. The denial of eternal problems, in *this* sense, then, would make nonsense of the whole history of philosophy and would render contemporary thought completely unintelligible.

To support this conclusion we may call Collingwood himself as witness, for, writing of the history of philosophical thought, he says: 'It is a genuine history in so far as the events contained in it lead each to the next: so far, that is, as each philosopher has learnt his philosophy through studying the work of his predecessors. For in that case each is trying to do what his predecessors did—to philosophize; but to do it better by doing it differently; assimilating whatever seems true, rejecting whatever seems false, and thus producing a new philosophy which is at the same time an improved version of the old. His successor in turn stands in this same relation to himself, and thus the entire history of thought is the history of a single sustained attempt to solve a single permanent problem, each phase advancing the problem by the extent of all the work done on it in the interval, and summing up the fruits of this work in the shape of a unique presentation of the problem.'

Leo Strauss   (essay date 1952)

SOURCE: "On Collingwood's Philosophy of History," in *Review of Metaphysics,* Vol. V, No. 4, June, 1952, pp. 559-86.

[In the following essay, Strauss studies the relationship between philosophy and history in Collingwood's works.]

(I)

R. G. Collingwood's **The Idea of History** "is an essay in the philosophy of history." Philosophy of history, as Collingwood understood it, is of very recent origin. It emerged as a sequel to the rise of "scientific history" which took place in the latter part of the nineteenth century (254). If one assumes that "scientific history" is the highest or final form of man's concern with his past, the understanding of what the "scientific historian" does, or epistemology of history, may become of philosophic interest. And if the older or traditional branches

of philosophy cannot make intelligible the "new historical technique" or solve the problems "created by the existence of organized and systematized historical research"; if, in other words, "the traditional philosophies carry with them the implication that historical knowledge is impossible" (5-6), epistemology of history becomes of necessity a philosophic concern or a philosophic discipline. But philosophy of history must be more than epistemology of history. In the first place, epistemology of history is likely to be of vital concern only to certain technicians, and not to men as men. Above all, thought about historical thought must be thought about the object of historical thought as well. Hence philosophy of history must be both epistemology of history and metaphysics of history (3, 184). Philosophy of history comes then first to sight as an addition to the traditional branches of philosophy. But philosophy hardly permits of mere additions. Certainly philosophy of history cannot be a mere addition: philosophy of history necessarily entails "a complete philosophy conceived from an historical point of view" (7, 147). For the discovery on which philosophy of history is based concerns the character of all human thought; it leads therefore to an entirely new understanding of philosophy. In other words, it was always admitted that the central theme of philosophy is the question of what man is, and that history is the knowledge of what men have done; but now it has been realized that man is what he can do, and "the only clue to what man can do" is what he has done (10); therefore, "the so-called science of human nature or of the human mind resolves itself into history" (220, 209). Philosophy of history is identical with philosophy as such, which has become radically historical: "philosophy as a separate discipline is liquidated by being converted into history" (x).

Collingwood was prevented by his death from elaborating his philosophy of history in the full sense of the term. He believed that he could do no more than to attempt "a philosophic inquiry into the nature of history regarded as a special type or form of knowledge with a special type of object" (7). Since philosophy of history in the narrower sense admittedly points to philosophy of history in the comprehensive sense, it might seem that Collingwood unjustifiably postponed the discussion of the fundamental issue. But it is perhaps fairer to say that philosophy of history in the comprehensive sense presupposes philosophy of history in the narrower sense, or that the fusion of philosophy and history presupposes the soundness or adequacy of "scientific history": if the historical understanding of the last four or five generations is not decisively superior to the historical understanding that was possible in the past, the conversion of philosophy into history loses its most convincing, or at least its most persuasive, justification.

Scientific history, being "now a thing within the compass of everyone" (320), is the cooperative effort of a very large number of contemporaries which is directed toward the acquisition of such knowledge as "ideally" forms part of "a universal history" or of knowledge of "the human past in its entirety" (27, 209). It is a theoretical pursuit; it is "actuated by a sheer desire for truth" and by no other concern (60-61). The attitude of the scientific historian, however, is not that of a spectator. Knowledge of what men have done is knowledge of what men have thought: "All history is the history of thought" (215, 304). Scientific history is thought about thought. Past thought cannot be known as such except by being re-thought, or re-enacted, or re-lived, or re-produced (97, 115, 218). For the scientific historian, the past is not something foreign, or dead, or outside his mind: the human past is living in his mind, though living as past. This does not mean that the entire past can be re-enacted by every scientific historian; there must be a kind of sympathy between the historian's thought and his object; and in order to be truly alive, "the historian's thought must spring from the organic unity of his total experience, and be a function of his entire personality with its practical as well as its theoretical interests" (305). Since "all thinking is critical thinking" and not a mere surrender to the object of thought, re-thinking of earlier thought is identical with criticism of earlier thought (215-16, 300-01). The point of view from which the scientific historian criticizes the past is that of the present of his civilization. Scientific history is then the effort to see the human past in its entirety as it appears from the standpoint of the present of the historian's civilization (60, 108, 215). Yet history will not be self-knowledge if the historian sees the past in the light of the present of his civilization without making that present his primary theme. The scientific historian's task is therefore to show how the present of his civilization, or the mind of the present-day, or that "determinate human nature" which is his civilization, has come into existence (104, 169, 175, 181, 226). Since scientific history is a peculiarity of modern Western thought, it may be described as the effort of present-day Western man to understand his peculiar humanity and thus to preserve it or enrich it.

Since genuine knowledge of the past is necessarily criticism and evaluation of the past from the point of view of the present, it is necessarily "relative" to the present, *i.e.,* to the present of a given country or civilization. The point of view of a given historian is "valid only for him and people situated like him" (60, 108). "Every new generation must rewrite history in its own way" (248). Objectivity in the sense of universal validity would then seem to be impossible. Collingwood was not disturbed by this danger to "scientific" history (cf. 265). There were two reasons for his confidence. In the first place, the belief in progress, and hence in the superiority of the present to the past, still lingered on in his thought. He could therefore believe that if historical knowledge is relative to the present, it is relative to the highest standpoint which has ever existed. To see that the belief in progress survived in Collingwood's thought, it almost suffices to look at the Table of Contents of his book: he devoted more space to Croce, to say nothing of other present-day thinkers, than to Herodotus and Thucydides. He took it for granted that the historian can and must

distinguish "between retrograde and progressive elements" in the phenomena which he is studying (135). More than half of his book is devoted to a comparison of the modern scientific conception of history with "the medieval conception of history with all its errors" (56) and the classical conception with its grave "defects" (41-42). The second reason why Collingwood was not disturbed by the "relativity" of all historical knowledge was his belief in the equality of all ages. "The present is always perfect in the sense that it always succeeds in being what it is trying to be," or the present has no standard higher than itself (109). There are no ages of decline or of decay (164). Augustine looked at Roman history from the point of view of an early Christian, and Gibbon did so from that of an enlightened eighteenth century Englishman: "there is no point in asking which was the right point of view. Each was the only possible for the man who adopted it" (xii). The historian who sees the past from the point of view of a present must not be worried by the prospect of a future progress of historical knowledge: "the historian's problem is a present problem, not a future one: it is to interpret the material now available, not to anticipate future discoveries" (180). Being thus protected against the surprises which the future may have in store, the scientific historian can be satisfied that the historical knowledge which is relative to the present, and is based on the material accessible at present, fulfills all the requirements of certainty or science. The fact that all historical knowledge is relative to the present means that it is relative to the only standpoint which is possible now, to a standpoint which is in no way inferior to any standpoint which was possible in the past or which will be possible in the future. Regardless of whether or not Collingwood found a way for reconciling the two different reasons indicated, each of them, if sound, would justify him in assuming that understanding of the past from the point of view of the present is unobjectionable, and in fact inevitable.

The procedure which we have just outlined is characteristic of *The Idea of History*. Collingwood moved consciously and with enthusiasm toward a goal which most of his contemporaries were approaching more or less unconsciously and haltingly, that goal being the fusion of philosophy and history. But he was not very much concerned with examining the means by which he tried to reach his goal. He vacillated between two different views of history, the rationalistic view of Hegel, and a non-rationalistic view. He never clearly realized that these two views are mutually incompatible. The historical reason for this failure was his lack of acquaintance with Nietzsche's epoch-making critique of "scientific history."

There is a tension between the idea of universal history and the view that in history "the mind of the present day apprehends the process by which this mind itself has come into existence through the mental development of the past" (169). If the modern Western historian studies Greek civilization, he may be said to re-enact the genesis of his own civilization, which has formed itself "by reconstructing within its own mind the mind of the Hellenic world" and thus to enter upon the possession of his inheritance (163, 226-27); he may be said to attempt to understand himself as modern Western man, or to mind his own business. But the case of the modern Western historian who studies Chinese or Inca civilization is obviously different. Collingwood did not reflect on this difference. He justly rejected Spengler's view that "there is no possible relation whatever between one culture and another." But he failed to consider the fact that there are cultures which have no actual relations with one another, and the implications of this fact: he dogmatically denied the possibility of "separate, discrete" cultures because it would destroy the dogmatically assumed "continuity of history" as universal history (161-64, 183).—According to one view held by Collingwood, the idea of scientific history, "the idea of an imaginary picture of the past [is], in Kantian language, *a priori* . . . it is an idea which every man possesses as part of the furniture of his mind, and discovers himself to possess in so far as he becomes conscious of what it is to have a mind" (248); scientific history is therefore the actualization of a potentiality of human nature. According to another view also held by Collingwood, one cannot speak of the furniture of the human mind, and not even of *the* human mind, which as such would be subject to "permanent and unchanging laws"; the idea of scientific history is not, in principle, coeval with the human mind but is itself "historical"; it has been acquired by Western man on the basis of his unique experience (of the Christian experience in particular); it is rooted in modern Western thought and its needs; it is meaningful only for modern Western thought (xii, 12, 48-49, 82, 224, 226, 255).—Collingwood regarded history as a theoretical pursuit, but he also said that the historian's thought must be "a function of his entire personality with its practical as well as its theoretical interests."—All history, Collingwood repeatedly said, is the history of thought or of rational activity or of freedom (215, 304, 315, 318): one cannot abandon "Hegel's belief that history is rational" without abandoning history itself (122); by speaking of "the contingency of history," the historian "expresses [the] final collapse of his thought" (151). Accordingly, Collingwood held that understanding of the thought of the past is not only compatible with criticism of thought of the past from the point of view of the present, but inseparable from it. On the other hand, however, he tended to believe that the ultimate facts of history are free choices which are not justifiable by rational activity; or that the ultimate facts of history are mere beliefs; and hence that history is not rational or that it is radically contingent or that it is, so to speak, a sequel of different original sins. Accordingly, he tended to hold that the historian cannot criticize the thought of the past but must remain satisfied with understanding it (cf. 316-18).

Collingwood's failure to clarify his position sufficiently can be explained in part by the need which he felt "to engage in a running fight" with positivism or naturalism (*i.e.,* "the confusion between historical process and natural process") (228, 181-82). His main preoccupation was with vindicating "the autonomy of history" against the claims of modern natural science. The view that historical knowledge is partly dependent on modern natural science was based on the fact that man's historical life is dependent on nature; and man's knowledge of nature is not identical with modern natural science. Collingwood was therefore driven to assert "the autonomy of history" without any qualification: "the historian is master in his own house; he owes nothing to the scientist or to anyone else," for "ordinary history," rightly understood, "contains philosophy inside itself" (155, 201). History does not depend upon authority nor on memory (236-38). ". . . in history, just as there are properly speaking no authorities, so there are properly speaking no data" (243). "Freed from its dependence on fixed points supplied from without, the historian's picture of the past is thus in every detail an imaginary picture, and its necessity is at every point the necessity of the *a priori* imagination. Whatever goes into it, goes into it not because his imagination passively accepts it, but because it actively demands it" (245). It is because of its "autonomy" that history must be universal history (246): truth is totality. Collingwood should not have hesitated to call this view "idealistic" (cf. 159). It is indeed not a solipsistic view: historical thought is both autonomous and objective; the historian's house "is inhabited by all historians" (155). More precisely, it is inhabited by all present day historians. It is a house without windows: the mind of the present day is autonomous or master in its own house because it cannot understand the thought of the past without criticizing it, *i.e.,* without transforming it into a modification of present day thought, or because it is not disturbed by problems which it cannot solve ("To ask questions you see no prospect of answering is the fundamental sin in science"—281) or because it is not disturbed by the possibilities of the future ("the only clue to what man can do is what man has done"—10, 180). A particularly noteworthy consequence of Collingwood's idealism is the banishment of biography from history: the limits of biography are "biological events, the birth and death of a human organism: its framework is thus a framework not of thought but of natural process" (304). This decision had the additional advantage of keeping the subjectivity of scientific history within limits which, for Collingwood, were reasonable. If the "biographical" is sub-historical, it will as little go into the making of the subject which acquires or possesses historical knowledge, as it will become an element of the object of historical knowledge. Historical knowledge will not become relative to the individual historian. It will retain its objectivity by being relative to "the mind of the present day." A difficulty is created by the circumstance that "the historian's thought must spring from the organic unity of his total experience," which experience, being total, could be thought to include his "immediate experience with its flow of sensations and feelings" and those "human emotions [which] are bound up with the spectacle of [his] bodily life" (304): "total experience" would seem to include the most "personal" experiences.

To do justice to Collingwood's idea of history, one must examine his practice as a historian. The largest part of his book is devoted to a history of historical knowledge. That history is on the whole conventional. In studying earlier thinkers, Collingwood never considered the possibility that the point of view from which the present day reader approaches them, or the questions which he addresses to them, might be in need of a fundamental change. He set out to praise or blame the earlier thinkers according to whether they helped or hindered the emergence of scientific history. He did not attempt to look at scientific history, for once, from the point of view of the earlier thinkers. What is not quite conventional in Collingwood's history, are some of his judgments: he had the courage to wonder whether Thucydides and Tacitus deserve the title of historians (29, 38-39). Furthermore, his history of historical knowledge is somewhat obscured by an ambiguity which he did not consistently avoid. His discussion of "Human nature and human history" culminated in the assertion that historical knowledge is coeval with the historical process, because the historical process is a process in which man inherits the achievements of the past, and historical knowledge is the way in which man enters upon the possession of that inheritance (226-27; cf. 333-34). In this crucial context Collingwood thus identified historical knowledge with accepting a tradition or living in a tradition. As a rule, however, he assumed that historical knowledge is not coeval with historical life but is an "invention" made at a certain time in Greece (19) and developed later on by the heirs of the Greeks.

The most revealing section of Collingwood's history of historical knowledge is his statement about the Greek conception of history. The Greeks created scientific history. This fact is paradoxical, for Greek thought was based "on a rigorously anti-historical metaphysics" (18-20). The "chief category" of that metaphysics "is the category of substance," and "a substantialist metaphysics implies a theory of knowledge according to which only what is unchanging is knowable" (42). "Therefore history ought to be impossible," *i.e.,* impossible as a science; history must be relegated to the realm of "opinion." Yet the very view that what is truly, or what is truly knowable, is the permanent, implied a fundamental distinction between the permanent and the changeable, and hence the insight that change is necessary: the Greeks' pursuit of the eternal presupposed "an unusually vivid sense of the temporal." In addition, they lived in a period of rapid and violent change: hence their "peculiar sensitiveness to history." For this reason however "their historical consciousness" was of a peculiar kind: it was "not a consciousness of age-long tradition molding the life of one generation after another into a uniform pattern; it was a consciousness of . . . catastrophic changes from one state of things to its opposite . . ." (22; cf. 26, 34). But since they believed that only the permanent is knowable or intelligible, they regarded "these catastrophic changes in the condition of human life" as unintelligible. They did not deny "that in the general pattern of these changes certain antecedents normally led to certain consequents," and that these sequences can be established by observation; but they could not tell why "certain antecedents normally led to certain consequents": "There is here no theory of causation." "This conception of history was the very opposite of deterministic": the sequences of antecedents and consequents are not necessary; they can be modified by the men who know of them; "thus the Greeks had a lively and indeed a naïve sense of the power of man to control his own destiny." Since the Greeks were compelled to consider history "as, at bottom, not a science, but a mere aggregate of perceptions," they had to identify "historical evidence with the reports of facts given by eye witnesses of these facts." They did not uncritically accept those reports. But their criticism could not go beyond making quite certain whether the eye witness really told what he had seen, and reaching a decision as to which of various conflicting reports deserved to be accepted. This conception of historical evidence limited history to the study of "events which have happened within living memory to people with whom [the historian] can have personal contact"; it made impossible scientific history of the remote past: the historian cannot be more than "the autobiographer of his generation" (22-27).

Some critical remarks seem to be necessary. When asserting that thinking historically and thinking in terms of substance are incompatible, Collingwood presupposed that "it is metaphysically axiomatic that an agent, being a substance, can never come into being and can never undergo any change of nature" (43). Did the Greeks then not know that human beings, for example, come into being? Or is it necessary to refer to Aristotle's statement that coming into being simply is said only of substances? Why then should the Greeks have been unable to observe and to describe the coming into being of substances and their changes? Collingwood asserted that in "substantialist" classical historiography "all the agencies that appear on the stage of history have to be assumed ready-made before history begins" (45) and that the classics therefore regarded nations and cities as substances, "changeless and eternal" (44). He did not even attempt to prove that the classics conceived of cities and nations as substances. But even if they did, their almost daily experience would have convinced them that cities at any rate are not "changeless and eternal" substances, that they are founded and grow and decay and perish, to say nothing of other changes which they undergo. Why then should the Greeks have been unable to observe and describe the coming into being and the changes of cities? To say nothing of the fact that it is safe to infer what men could do from what they did. ". . . the Greeks could not even contemplate the possibility of raising the problem which we should call the problem of the origin of the Hellenic people" (34). But, to take the most obvious case, were there no Greek thinkers who taught that the human race had come into being, that in the beginning men roamed in forests, without social bonds of any kind and in particular without language, and hence without the Greek language? Certainly these thinkers did not merely contemplate the possibility of raising the problem of the origin of the Hellenic people, but they did raise it and, according to their lights, solved it. Collingwood did not see that the reflections of the Greek philosophers on the nature and origin of language are equivalent to reflections on the nature and origin of nations. If they did not attempt to give historical accounts of the genesis of this or that nation, or of any nation, they had reasons like these: They did not have at their disposal historical evidence of events of this kind; they regarded the city as a higher form of society than the nation; and they thought that societies in their full vigor and maturity were more instructive regarding the highest possibilities of man than are societies newly coming into being. There may be a connection between these views and "substantialism." It suffices to note that Collingwood did not even try to reveal that connection. Prudence would have dictated to Collingwood to refrain from speaking of "substantialism" and to limit himself to saying that the classics were, for whatever reason, more concerned with the permanent and hence with the recurrent than with what is merely temporal and local, or that they believed that the unique can ultimately be understood only in the light of the permanent or recurrent. From this he could legitimately have concluded that from the point of view of the classics, history is inferior in dignity to philosophy or science. To prove his thesis, it would have been necessary for him to show, in addition, that the primacy of the concern with the permanent or recurrent precludes or endangers serious concern with what happens here and now or what happened there and then. He did not show this. To say nothing of other considerations, one may be chiefly concerned with the permanent or recurrent and yet hold that a given unique event (the Peloponnesian War, for example) supplies the only available basis for reliable observation which would enable one to form a correct judgment about certain recurrences of utmost importance. A man who held this view would of course study that unique event with utmost care, and, assuming that he was a superior man, he might have surpassed as a historian, *i.e.*, as a man who understands actions of men, all the scientific historians of the nineteenth and twentieth centuries.

Collingwood held that the Greeks had a "historical consciousness" of a particular kind: it was "not a consciousness of age-long tradition molding the life of one generation after another into a uniform pattern," but a consciousness of "catastrophic changes" (22). This statement is, to say the least, very misleading. "The Greeks" were perfectly conscious of the existence of "age-long traditions molding the life of one generation after another into a uniform pattern." But they believed, or at any rate Plato believed or suggested, that Greek life—in contradistinction especially to Egyptian life—was not dominated by such traditions: "you Greeks are always children . . . you are, all of you, young in soul; for you do not possess in your souls a single ancient opinion

transmitted by old tradition nor a single piece of learning that is hoary with age." The Greeks were less dominated by age-long traditions than were other nations because there lived in their midst men who had the habit of questioning such traditions, *i.e.*, philosophers. In other words, there was a greater awareness in Greece than elsewhere of the essential difference between the ancestral and the good. On the basis of this insight there existed in classical Greece "a historical consciousness," not merely of "catastrophic changes" but also of changes for the better, of progress, and this consciousness was a consciousness not merely of progress achieved but also of the possibility of future progress. Collingwood did not even allude to this element of "the Greek conception of history." He apparently never tried to understand "the historical consciousness" which expresses itself in the first book of Aristotle's *Metaphysics,* for example. Consideration of this book alone would have sufficed to make him hesitate to write that "the Greek historian was only the autobiographer of his generation" (27).

But let us concede that a man like Thucydides was primarily concerned with "catastrophic change" rather than with long periods in which practically no change, or only slow changes for the better, took place; and let us assume that Collingwood has given an account, based on Thucydides' work, of this preference, although Collingwood did not even attempt to do this. Was he entitled to say that the Greeks were forced to regard catastrophic changes as unintelligible, *i.e.*, as in no way traceable to determinate causes? The mere fact that he could not help censoring Thucydides for being "the father of psychological history" which is "natural science of a special kind" (29) would seem to prove that there was at least one Greek who regarded catastrophic change as intelligible. According to Collingwood, the Greeks regarded the change from a state of extreme wealth or power to a state of extreme poverty or weakness, as a mysterious rhythm; "the universal judgment that very rich men, as such, fall . . . is, in Aristotle's view, only a partially scientific judgment, for no one can say why rich men should fall" (24). If Collingwood had considered the analysis of the characters of the rich and the powerful in the second book of the *Rhetoric,* or the analysis of tyranny and dynastic oligarchy in the *Politics,* he could have told us that Aristotle had a good explanation for the fall of rich and powerful men if they are not virtuous or lucky. Collingwood mistook for no theory of causation what is in effect a theory of causation that includes chance as a cause of historical events.

Only because Collingwood disregarded, among other things, what the classics have to say about the power of chance, could he confidently assert that "the Greeks had a lively and indeed a naïve sense of the power of man to control his own destiny" (24) or that for Hellenic thought "selfconsciousness [was] a power to conquer the world" (36) or that classical thought implied "that whatever happens in history happens as a direct result of the human will" (41). It taxes the imagination to understand how the same man could have written these sentences a few pages after he had written "that these catastrophic changes in the condition of human life which were to the Greeks the proper theme of history, were unintelligible" (22).

As for Collingwood's remark that, for the Greeks, history was "at bottom . . . a mere aggregate of perceptions" (24), it suffices to say that one page later he noted that men like Herodotus and Thucydides succeeded in calling up a fairly "coherent" "historical picture" of the events which they studied. In his discussion of the Greek conception of historical evidence, he was silent about the basic distinction between seeing with one's own eyes and hearsay, and the use which the classical historians made of that distinction for evaluating traditions or reports. In particular, he did not consider that seeing with one's own eyes includes understanding of the nature of man and of the nature of political things, an understanding which fulfills in Greek history approximately the same function which "historical imagination" fulfills in Collingwood's "scientific history."

Collingwood's account of the classical conception of history, which had to be "in every detail an imaginary picture" in order to conform with his standards of historical truth (cf. 245), indirectly reveals more about "the idea of history" than do all the subsequent sections of his book. The idea of history is more than the view that knowledge of what men have done or thought is possible or necessary. It is the view that such knowledge properly understood is identical with philosophy or must take the place of philosophy. The idea of history thus understood is indeed alien to classical thought. According to Collingwood, it could not emerge before classical "substantialism" was abandoned and classical "humanism" was profoundly modified. If history is the account, or the study, of what men have done, and philosophy is the study of something which is presupposed by all human doings, the idea of history requires in the first place that the apparent presuppositions of all human doings be resolved into products of human doings: this is what Collingwood meant by the need for abandoning "substantialism." The apparent presuppositions of all human doings are objects of human knowledge, as distinguished from the products or results of human action. The first step in the direction of the idea of history was therefore that the distinction between knowledge and action or between theory and practice be questioned. Knowledge had to be conceived as a kind of making or production. Collingwood referred in the usual manner to Vico's *verum et factum convertuntur* (64). But he failed to go back to Vico's source, *i.e.,* to Hobbes, and hence he could rest satisfied with the conventional way of describing the genesis of the idea of history. Now, if the thinker or maker is man as man, or every individual regardless of time and place, philosophy remains "unhistorical." If there is to be an essential connection between thought, or the content of thought, and time and place, what we know or think must be such a making as is essentially dependent on the making of earlier men, or rather of earlier men who lived "here," and yet it

must be different from earlier thought. It cannot be different from earlier thought if it could have been anticipated, *i.e.,* thought, by earlier men: it must be the unforeseen and unforeseeable outcome of earlier thought. It is this requirement which Collingwood had in mind when he demanded the abandonment or radical modification of Greek "humanism" which attributed "far too little to the force of a blind activity embarking on a course of action without foreseeing its end and being led to that end only through the necessary development of that course itself" (42), *i.e.,* without being led to that end by the plan of a god or of nature (55, 57, 58, 81, 104). He described the requirement in question somewhat more accurately when he contrasted Greek thought with the determinism of seventeenth century natural science which laid the foundation for conceiving of thought as such, and of every "stage" of thought, as the necessary and unintended "product of a process" (23, 57, 58, 81, 87). For the reason indicated, he failed, however, to raise the question regarding the connection between the conception of thinking as making and the peculiar "determinism" of modern natural science. He thus failed to see that the basic stratum of "the idea of history" is a combination of the view that thinking is making, or "creative," with the need, engendered by that view, of giving a "deterministic" account of thinking, or such a "genetic" account as presupposes at no point anything except "motion" or "process." Collingwood's "idealism" prevented him from looking beyond the antagonism of "idealism" and "naturalism" or from seeing that "history" and "scientific materialism" are inseparable from each other. (Compare, however, the remark on p. 269 about the kinship between scientific history and Baconian natural science.)

II

Collingwood did not prove "by deed" the superiority of scientific history to the common-sense type of history which prevailed, on the most different levels, in the past. His most important statements are errors which competent men in earlier times would not have committed simply because they were more careful readers than we have become. Scientific history is based on the assumption that present day historical thought is the right kind of historical thought. When it is confronted with the fact that earlier historical thought is different from present day historical thought, it naturally concludes that earlier historical thought is defective. And no one can be blamed if he does not study very carefully such doctrines or procedures as he knows in advance to be defective in the decisive respect. Collingwood wrote the history of history in almost the same way in which the eighteenth century historians, whom he censored so severely, are said to have written history in general. The latter condemned the thought of the past as deficient in full reasonableness; Collingwood condemned it as deficient in the true sense for history.

This is not to deny that Collingwood also believed in the equality of all ages and that he therefore tended to regard the historical thought of any one period as equally sound as that of any other period. One might think that to the extent to which he held that belief, he would have tried to understand the historical thought of each period of the past on its own terms, without measuring it by the standard of scientific history. Yet the belief in the equality of all ages leads to the consequence that our interpretation of the thought of the past while not superior to the way in which the thought of the past interpreted itself, is as legitimate as the past's self-interpretation and, in addition, is the only way in which we today can interpret the thought of the past. Accordingly, there arises no necessity to take seriously the way in which the thought of the past understood itself. In other words, the belief in the equality of all ages is only a more subtle form of the belief in progress. The alleged insight into the equality of all ages which is said to make possible passionate interest in the thought of the different ages, necessarily conceives of itself as a progress beyond all earlier thought: every earlier age erroneously "absolutized" the standpoint from which it looked at things and therefore was incapable of taking very seriously the thought of other ages: hence earlier ages were incapable of scientific history.

The two beliefs which contended for supremacy in Collingwood's thought implied that earlier thought is necessarily relative to earlier times. "The *Republic* of Plato is an account, not of the unchanging ideal of political life, but of the Greek ideal as Plato received it and reinterpreted it. The *Ethics* of Aristotle describes not an eternal morality but the morality of the Greek gentleman. Hobbes' *Leviathan* expounds the political ideas of seventeenth century absolutism in their English form. Kant's ethical theory expresses the moral convictions of German pietism . . ." (229). Collingwood understood then the thought of a time in the light of its time. He did not then re-enact that thought. For to re-enact the thought which expresses itself in Plato's *Republic,* for example, means to understand Plato's description of the simply good social order as a description of the true model of society with reference to which all societies of all ages and countries must be judged. Collingwood's attitude towards the thought of the past was in fact that of a spectator who sees from the outside the relation of an earlier thought to its time.

The deficiencies of Collingwood's historiography can be traced to a fundamental dilemma. The same belief which forced him to attempt to become a historian of thought, prevented him from becoming a historian of thought. He was forced to attempt to become a historian of thought because he believed that to know the human mind is to know its history, or that self-knowledge is historical understanding. But this belief contradicts the tacit premise of all earlier thought, that premise being the view that to know the human mind is something fundamentally different from knowing the history of the human mind. Collingwood therefore rejected the thought of the past as untrue in the decisive respect. Hence he could not take that thought seriously, for to

take a thought seriously means to regard it as possible that the thought in question is true. He therefore lacked the incentive for re-enacting the thought of the past: he did not re-enact the thought of the past.

We draw the conclusion that in order to understand the thought of the past, one must doubt the view which is at the bottom of scientific history. One must doubt the principle which is characteristic of "the mind of the present day." One must abandon the attempt to understand the past from the point of view of the present. One must take seriously the thought of the past, or one must be prepared to regard it as possible that the thought of the past is superior to the thought of the present day in the decisive respect. One must regard it as possible that we live in an age which is inferior to the past in the decisive respect, or that we live in an age of decline or decay. One must be swayed by a sincere longing for the past.

Collingwood had to face this necessity when he had to speak of Romanticism. According to him, Romanticism is in danger of developing into "a futile nostalgia for the past," but "that development was checked by the presence in Romanticism of . . . the conception of history as a progress" (87). This remark lacks precision. Its deficiency is partly due to Collingwood's insufficient familiarity with the German intellectual movement around the year 1800. For instance in his statement on Friedrich Schiller (104-105), he limited himself to a survey of Schiller's lecture on the value of universal history without taking any notice of Schiller's essay on naïve and sentimental poetry. Similarly he asserted that "Hegel wrote the first sketch of his philosophy of history in the Heidelberg *Encyclopædia*" (111). The romantic soul, we prefer to say, is characterized by longing, by "futile" longing, by a longing which is felt to be superior to any fulfillment that is possible "now," *i.e.,* in post-revolutionary Europe. A perfect expression of Romanticism is *Madame Bovary*: the dead Emma, who, in spite of, or because of, the fact that she had an "esprit positif," had spent her life in a longing that led to nothing but failure and degradation, is more alive than the contemporary representatives of the ancient faith and the modern faith who, with the corpse of Emma between them, engage in a noisy disputation, *i.e.,* share between themselves the rule over the nineteenth century. True Romanticism regards the highest possibility of the nineteenth or twentieth century, "futile" longing, as the highest possibility of man, in so far as it assumes that the noble fulfillments of the past were based on delusions which are now irrevocably dispelled. True Romanticism believes that while the past was superior to the present as regards "life" or "culture" or "art" or "religion" or the nearness of God or gods, the present is superior to the past as regards the understanding of "life" or "culture," etc. It believes therefore that the present is superior to the past in regard to knowledge of the decisive truth, *i.e.,* in the decisive respect. It therefore never submits its notions of "life" or "culture" or "art" or "religion" to a criticism which is enlightened by what the assumed models of "life" or "culture," etc., explicitly thought about these themes. Hence Romanticism perpetuates the belief in the superiority of modern thought to earlier thought, and Romantic history of thought is fundamentally as inadequate, or as "un-historical," as non-romantic, progressivist history of thought.

Collingwood believed that "in history as it actually happens there are no mere phenomena of decay: every decline is also a rise" (164). This sanguine statement cannot be reconciled with his remark that if we abandoned scientific history, "we should be exemplifying and hastening that downfall of civilization which some historians are, perhaps prematurely, proclaiming" (56). Here Collingwood admitted that a decline which is not "also a rise" is possible. Yet this momentary insight did not bear fruit in his understanding of earlier thought. He blamed Tacitus for representing history "as essentially a clash of characters, exaggeratedly good and exaggeratedly bad," and he blamed the philosophies of Tacitus' age as "defeatist philosophies which, starting from the assumption that the good man cannot conquer or control the wicked world, taught him how to preserve himself unspotted from its wickedness" (39-40). Since Collingwood dogmatically excluded the possibility of unqualified decay, he could not imagine that there might be ages in which virtuous political action is impossible, and "defeatist" withdrawal is the only sane course of action; he could not consider the possibility that such ages may allow of an excess in wickedness in tyrannical rulers, and of a heroic virtue in their victims, for which there are no parallels in happier epochs. His "historical consciousness" or historical imagination did not leave room for the possibility which Tacitus assumes to have been a fact. His historical consciousness could not be broadened by a study of Tacitus because scientific history recognizes no authority, but is master in its own house: it is not guided by a presumption in favor of the judgments which the wise men of old passed on their own times.

Collingwood was forced to admit the possibility of decline when he discussed the conditions under which progress is possible. For to admit that progress is possible and not necessary means to admit the possibility of decline. But it is precisely his discussion of the conditions of progress which shows how largely he remained under the spell of the belief in necessary progress or how far he was from understanding the function of historical knowledge. Progress, he said, "happens only in one way: by the retention in the mind, at one phase, of what was achieved in the preceding phase" (333). The retention of earlier achievements is "historical knowledge" (326). It is therefore "only through historical knowledge that [progress] comes about at all" (333). Collingwood assumed that "what was achieved in the preceding phase" has merely to be retained: he did not consider the possibility that it may have to be recovered because it had been forgotten. Accordingly, he identified historical knowledge, not with the recovery of earlier

achievements, but with their retention: he uses Aristotle's knowledge of Plato's philosophy, and Einstein's knowledge of Newtonian physics, as examples of historical knowledge (333-34). He further assumed that progress requires the integration of earlier achievements into a framework supplied by the later achievement. He did not consider the possibility that progress may consist in separating recent achievements from their present framework and integrating them into an earlier framework which must be recovered by historical knowledge proper. But whatever might be true of progress, certainly the awareness of progress requires that the thought of the past be known as it actually was, *i.e.,* as it was actually thought by past thinkers. For, if to understand the thought of the past necessarily means to understand it differently from the way the thinkers of the past understood it, one will never be able to compare the thought of the present with the thought of the past: one would merely compare one's own thought with the reflection of one's own thought in ancient materials or with a hybrid begotten by the intercourse of one's own thought with earlier thought. What we might be inclined to regard as decisive insights alien to the thought of the past may in fact be delusions produced by the oblivion of things known to the thinkers of the past. Awareness of progress presupposes the possibility of understanding the thought of the past "as it really has been." It presupposes the possibility of historical objectivity.

Collingwood implicitly denied the possibility of historical objectivity by asserting that criticism of the thought of the past from the point of view of the present is an integral element of understanding the thought of the past (215). The historian is forced to raise "such questions as: Was this or that policy a wise one? Was this or that economic system sound? Was this or that movement in science or art or religion an advance, and if so, why?" (132). Such questions cannot be answered except from the standpoint of the historian's time (60, 108). This conclusion depends in the first place on the premise that there are no unchangeable standards for judging human actions or thoughts. But it depends also on the further premise that the historian's primary task is to pass judgment on the past. Yet before one can pass judgment on the wisdom of, for example, a given policy, one must establish the character of that policy. "For example, to reconstruct the history of a political struggle like that between the Roman emperors of the first century and the senatorial opposition, what the historian has to do is to see how the two parties conceived the political situation as it stood, and how they proposed to develop that situation: he must grasp their political ideas both concerning their actual present and concerning their possible future" (115). The primary task of the political historian would then seem to consist in understanding a given situation and given ends as they were understood by those who acted in the situation. The contemporaries of a struggle that is similar to the contest between the Roman emperors and the senatorial opposition have an easier access to that historical phenomenon than have people who lack experience of this particular kind of politics. But this does not make the understanding of the phenomenon in question relative to different situations: the difference in regard to the length and the difficulty of the way towards the goal does not affect the goal itself. In addition, "historical imagination" liberates the historian from the limitations caused by the experiences peculiar to his time.

It may be objected that the very selection of the theme implies the inescapable subjective element: the reason for the historian's interest in a given situation is different from the reason for the actors' interest in it. The reason for the historian's interest in a historical phenomenon expresses itself in the questions which he addresses to the phenomenon concerned and hence to his sources, and this question is in principle alien to his sources. "The scientific historian no doubt spends a great deal of time reading . . . Herodotus, Thucydides, Livy, Tacitus, and so forth . . . , but he reads them . . . with a question in his mind, having taken the initiative by deciding for himself what he wants to find out from them . . . the scientific historian puts them to the torture, twisting a passage ostensibly about something quite different into an answer to the question he has decided to ask" (269-70). There is no doubt that one may use the classical historians as a quarry or as ruins, to supply oneself with materials for erecting the edifice called the economic history of classical antiquity, for example. In doing this one makes the assumption that economic history is a worthwhile enterprise, and this assumption is indeed apparently relative to the preoccupations of the nineteenth and twentieth centuries, and alien to the classical historians. An intelligent or conscientious use of the classical historians for a purpose alien to them requires, however, a clear recognition of the fact that that purpose is alien to them and of the reason for that being so. It therefore requires that the classical historians first be understood on their own terms, *i.e.*, as answering their own questions, and not the questions with which the modern historian tortures them. Collingwood admitted this necessity in his way: "The question [the scientific historian] asks himself is: 'What does this statement mean?' And this is not equivalent to the question 'What did the person who made it mean by it?' although that is doubtless a question that the historian must ask, and must be able to answer" (275). But this admission is much too weak. The answer to the question "What did the person who made the statement mean by it?" must precede the answer to the question "What does this statement mean within the context of my question?" For "the statement" is the statement as meant by the author. Before one can use or criticize a statement, one must understand the statement, *i.e.*, one must understand it as its author consciously meant it. Different historians may become interested in the same statement for different reasons: that statement does not alter its authentic meaning on account of those differences.

Collingwood severely criticized "the scissors-and-paste historian" who reads the classical historians "in a purely receptive spirit, to find out what they said" and "on the understanding that what they did not tell him in so many words he would never find out from them at all" (269). But he did not realize that both "the scissors-and-paste historian" and the scientific historian make the same mistake: they use the classical historians for a purpose alien to the latter before having done justice to the purpose of the classical historians. And both make this identical mistake for the same reason: they take "history" for granted. Whatever may be the stand-point or the direction of interest or the guiding question of the present day historian, he cannot use his sources properly if he does not, to begin with, rigorously subordinate his question to the question which the author of his sources meant to answer, or if he does not, to begin with, identify his question with the question consciously raised by the author whose work he intends to use. The guiding question of the historian who wants to use Herodotus, for example, must become, for some considerable time, the question as to what question was uppermost in Herodotus' mind, *i.e.,* the question of what was the conscious intention of Herodotus, or the question regarding the perspective in which Herodotus looked at things. And the question regarding Herodotus' guiding intention, as well as the answer to it, is in no way affected by the diversity of questions with which modern historians approach Herodotus. In attempting to answer the question regarding Herodotus' intention, one must not even assume that Herodotus was a "historian." For in making this assumption one is likely to imply that he was not a "philosopher" and thus to exclude without examination the possibility that Herodotus' intention cannot be understood without a complete revision of our "categories." Collingwood did not merely fail duly to appreciate the fact that the historian must provisionally subordinate his own question to the questions which the authors of his sources meant to answer. He likewise failed to consider the possibility that the historian may eventually have to retract his own question in favor of the questions raised by the authors of his sources.

Yet while the critical function of the historian may not become noticeable most of the time, or ever, the historian is, nevertheless, necessarily a critic. He selects a theme which he believes to be worthwhile: the critical judgment that the theme is worthwhile precedes the interpretation. He provisionally subordinates his question to the question guiding his author: eventually the historian's own question re-asserts itself. Nor is the interpretation proper—the activity which follows the reasoned selection of the theme and which is coextensive with the subordination of the historian's question to the question guiding his author—separable from criticism. As Collingwood put it, it is a "self-contradictory task of discovering (for example) 'What Plato thought' without inquiring 'Whether it is true'" (300). One cannot understand a chain of reasoning without "re-enacting" it, and this means without examining whether or not it is valid. One cannot understand premises without understanding them as premises, *i.e.*, without raising the question whether they are evident or intrinsically necessary. For if they are not evident, one must look for the supporting reasoning. The supporting reasoning, a crucial part of the teaching of the author as the author understood it, might easily pass unnoticed if one failed to look for it, and one is not likely to look for it unless one is prompted to do so by a realization of the in-evident character of the premises concerned. Therefore the establishment of the fact (if it is a fact) that an author makes a dogmatic assumption may be said to be inseparable from the interpretation of the author in question.

But the fact that the historian is necessarily a critic does not mean, of course, that his criticism necessarily culmi-nates in partial or total rejection; it may very well cul-minate in total acceptance of the criticized view. Still less does it mean that the historian necessarily criticizes the thought of the past from the point of view of present day thought. By the very fact that he seriously attempts to understand the thought of the past, he leaves the present. He embarks on a journey whose end is hidden from him. He is not likely to return to the shores of his time as exactly the same man who departed from them. His criticism may very well amount to a criticism of present day thought from the point of view of the thought of the past.

The fact that interpretation and criticism are in one sense inseparable does not mean that they are identical. The meaning of the question "What did Plato think?" is different from the meaning of the question "Whether that thought is true." The former question must ulti-mately be answered by a reference to texts. The latter question cannot possibly be settled by reference to texts. Every criticism of a Platonic contention implies a dis-tinction between the Platonic contention, which must be understood as such, and the criticism of that contention. But interpretation and criticism are not only distin-guishable from each other. To a certain extent they are even separable from each other. Plato's thought claims to be an imitation of the whole; as such it is itself a whole which is distinguished from the whole simply. It is impossible to understand the imitation without look-ing at the original. But it is possible to look at the original in compliance, or without compliance, with the directives supplied by the imitation. To look at the original in compliance with the directives supplied by the imitation means to try to understand the whole as Plato understood it. To understand the whole as Plato understood it is the goal of the interpretation of Plato's work. This goal is the standard which we presuppose, and to which we ultimately refer, whenever we find someone's interpretation of Platonic doctrine defective: we cannot find an interpretation defective without hav-ing "seen" that goal. The attempt to understand Plato's thought as Plato understood it is inseparable from criti-cism, but that criticism is in the service of the striven-for understanding of Plato's thought. History as history, as quest for the understanding of the past, necessarily presupposes that our understanding of the past is incom-plete. The criticism which is inseparable from interpre-tation is fundamentally different from the criticism which would coincide with the completed understand-ing. If we call "interpretation" that understanding or criticism which remains within the limits of Plato's own directives, and if we call "criticism" that understanding or criticism which disregards Plato's directives, we may say that interpretation necessarily precedes criticism because the quest for understanding necessarily precedes completed understanding and therewith the judgment which coincides with the completed understanding. The historian who has no illusions about the difference of rank between himself and Plato will be very skeptical in regard to the possibility of his ever reaching adequate understanding of Plato's thought. But what is impos-sible for most men is not therefore intrinsically impos-sible. If one denies the legitimacy of the goal which we called adequate understanding of Plato's thought, *i.e.,* if one denies the possibility of historical objectivity, one merely substitutes a spurious right of subjectivity and of arbitrary assertions for the honest confession that we are ignorant of the most important facts of the human past.

It is then indeed a "self-contradictory task of discover-ing 'What Plato thought' without inquiring 'Whether it is true'." It is indeed impossible to understand a line of Plato if one is not concerned with what Plato was con-cerned with, *i.e.,* the truth about the highest things, and hence if one does not inquire whether what Plato thought about them is true. It is indeed impossible to understand what Plato thought without thinking, *i.e.,* without articulating the subjects about which Plato thought. Thinking about Plato's subjects cannot be lim-ited by what Plato said or thought. It must take into consideration everything relevant, regardless of whether Plato seems to have considered it or not. That is to say, trying to understand Plato requires remaining loyal to Plato's guiding intention; and remaining loyal to Plato's intention means to forget about Plato and to be con-cerned exclusively with the highest things. But Col-lingwood assumed that we must not forget about Plato in spite, or rather because, of the fact that we must aim at no other end than the truth regarding the highest things. This assumption is legitimate and is not defeated by its consequences, if it means that we may have to learn something from Plato about the highest things which we are not likely to learn without his guidance, *i.e.,* that we must regard Plato as a possible authority. But to regard Plato as a possible authority means to regard him for the time being as an actual authority. We must, indeed, ourselves articulate the subjects about which Plato thought, but in doing this we must follow Plato's indications as to the manner in which these subjects should be articulated. If Plato took something for granted which we are in the habit of doubting or even of denying, or if he did not push the analysis of a given subject beyond a certain point, we must regard it as possible that he had good reasons for stopping where he stopped. If it is necessary to understand Plato's thought, it is necessary to understand it as Plato himself understood it, and therefore it is necessary to stop where he stopped and to look around: perhaps we shall gradually understand his reasons for stopping. As long as we have not understood Plato's thought, we are in no position to say "Whether it is true." The "historian of philosophy" is a man who knows that he has not yet understood Plato's thought and who is seriously concerned with understanding Plato's thought because he suspects that he may have to learn from Plato something of utmost importance. It is for this reason that Plato's thought cannot become an object, or a spectacle, for the historian. It is to be feared that Collingwood underestimated the difficulty of finding out "What Plato meant by his statements" or "Whether what he thought is true."

History, *i.e.,* concern with the thought of the past as thought of the past, takes on philosophic significance if there are good reasons for believing that we can learn something of utmost importance from the thought of the past which we cannot learn from our contemporaries. History takes on philosophic significance for men living in an age of intellectual decline. Studying the thinkers of the past becomes essential for men living in an age of intellectual decline because it is the only practicable way in which they can recover a proper understanding of the fundamental problems. Given such conditions, history has the further task of explaining why the proper understanding of the fundamental problems has become lost in such a manner that the loss presents itself at the outset as a progress. If it is true that loss of understanding of the fundamental problems culminates in the historicization of philosophy or in historicism, the second function of history consists in making intelligible the modern notion of "History" through the understanding of its genesis. Historicism sanctions the loss, or the oblivion, of the natural horizon of human thought by denying the permanence of the fundamental problems. It is the existence of that natural horizon which makes possible "objectivity" and therefore in particular "historical objectivity."

Nathan Rotenstreich (essay date 1960)

SOURCE: "From Facts to Thoughts: Collingwood's Views on the Nature of History," in *Philosophy,* Vol. XXXV, No. 133, April, 1960, pp. 122-37.

[In the following essay, Rotenstreich provides an analysis of Collingwood's views regarding history as a set of facts and as an object of knowledge.]

I

There is a common distinction between two aspects of history: history as the object dealt with and history as the way of dealing with the object. Within the "objective" aspect of history one may distinguish between the attempt to define the object as man and the attempt to define it as process. Within the "subjective" aspect there is the prevailing tendency to put forward the nature of the conceptual method as one employing individual concepts.

Collingwood's view of the nature of history, in spite of the many-sided development it underwent, can hardly be classified in accordance with these distinctions. He dealt with the two aspects of history mentioned above, although he did not sharply distinguish them. In the first steps he made as a systematic thinker, he attempted to define the nature of history through the nature of the historical object. But since consideration of the nature of history was included from the outset in a *Speculum Mentis,* which is, and perhaps was meant to be, a kind of "Phenomenology of Mind", he could hardly ignore the problem of knowledge and its relation to the nature of the object. Let us therefore consider how he approached this problem in the first period of his development.

"History is that which actually exists." "The object of history is fact as such." The obvious tendency of this approach is to define the nature of history by stating that historical knowledge has necessarily a given object, namely fact. History is not defined as a branch of knowledge dealing with a fact in *time,* nor as dealing with the facts of human life, etc. It is just attachment to fact that it is considered as the essence of history. Even the fact that historical knowledge deals with the past is not derived from any particular relationship between this knowledge and time in its dimensions. The nature of a fact is a sufficient guide, according to Collingwood, in determining the relation between history and the past: "the historian's business is with fact; and there are not future facts". The aspect of time is certainly secondary on this view. It is an outcome of the nature of facts and not an independent factor.

There is one further characteristic feature of the nature of the historical object *qua* fact, viz. its individuality. Nothing new is added through this feature, since "matter of fact" and "individuality" might be considered as synonymous. Collingwood does not determine the meaning of "individuality", at this point, e.g. whether or not the historical fact occurs only once. One may be permitted to wonder whether this would be the meaning he attached to individuality, since this meaning carries with it from the outset the aspect of time, which is not the aspect stressed by Collingwood in the first place. Individuality connotes matter of fact, that is to say, the impossibility of a deduction of the fact from a hypothesis or from a systematic setting. Once we assume deducibility, the deduced element ceases to be individual and becomes a variable in a set or in a manifold of replaceable elements. A fact is bound to be individual, since we are bound to accept it as it is, because it is given.

The relationship between individuality and historical knowledge has been extensively discussed in modern philosophy, and Collingwood himself participated in this discussion. The purpose of this discussion was to point to the nature of the historical method and its conceptual apparatus. Collingwood does not consider individuality to be a feature of this apparatus, since he considers it as the nature of the object itself. He assumes that the nature of the object itself guides historical knowledge in employing conceptual ways and means to square with the object.

The cognitive attitude adequate to the object as fact is *assertion*. Assertion suggests the acceptance of the object as it is, and because it is. An assertion is a categorical statement, the admission that something exists as concrete and given. Historical knowledge is assertive, and in this capacity it is opposed to scientific knowledge, which is hypothetical. In a way Collingwood arrives here at a paradoxical conclusion: historical knowledge, being related at its objective pole to facts and at its subjective pole to assertion, must be a naïve knowledge, a receptive one. This conclusion may be considered as an indication of Collingwood's form of idealism in his early period. Constructions, as manifested in science, are according to Collingwood a lower stage in the development of the forms of mind and reality than assertions of the given concreteness. Once we reach the stage of concreteness there is no legitimate room for constructions. Constructions indicate the gap between the knowing subject and the known object and therefore they are bound to remain abstract. Once we reach a meaningful reality we have but to recognize it as such, that is to say, to assert it. It goes without saying that this systematic presupposition of Collingwood's view blocked the way towards an analytic understanding of the nature of historical knowledge. The very fact that Collingwood eliminates hypothetical statements from history and confines historical statements to assertions indicates that he does not do justice to historical reasoning: every historical inference is hypothetical, being from given data to their causes. As a passage from data to their causes it is hypothetical and there is no room here for mere assertion of causes. It is clear in terms of the history of ideas that Collingwood wanted to step across the boundaries of historical knowledge as outlined by Bradley, but he did not succeed in doing it.

This consideration of history as related to facts on the one hand, and to the assertive act on the other leads Collingwood to a paradoxical historical conclusion. Philosophy of History in its manifestation in Vico was explicitly anti-Cartesian. Descartes has been blamed for being abstract; hence philosophical prominence has been given to history as a concrete creation. But Collingwood, although deeply rooted in the Viconian tradition, considers the main achievement of Descartes to be precisely in the discovery of history. "Descartes, in his cogito ergo sum, laid down that historical fact was the absolute meaning of knowledge." Only because Collingwood gives history a generic meaning as a knowledge of ultimate irreducible facts can he identify historicity with the objective of Descartes. "Cogito ergo sum" in his view expresses a fact; hence the nature of the statement of Descartes is a historical one. Here Collingwood's tendency becomes clearly apparent: history deals with facts; hence where one finds an attitude of *hypotheses non fingo* there one finds history. Indirectly

Collingwood meets here the criticism of the Cartesian tradition as expressed in Vico. As a matter of fact Descartes—this is Collingwood's view—does not assume a self-sustained abstract knowledge. "Descartes meant what he said, and what he said was that the concrete historical fact, the fact of my actual present awareness, was the root of science. . . . Science presupposes history and can never go behind history: that is the discovery of which Descartes' formula is the deepest and the most fruitful expression." Vico, on this view, did not realize the concrete, historical-factual basis of the Cartesian abstraction.

The structure of the Cartesian system is an example of the nature of the dependence of science upon history and a further means to clarify the nature of history. If history employs assertions and is categorical, science employs suppositions and is hypothetical. Collingwood tried to show that each supposition presupposes at least one assertion, the assertion that there is supposition here. In other words science as a texture of suppositions presupposes history as a body of assertions. We may sum up the logic of Collingwood's conception of the relation between science and history in these two points: (1) there is no possibility of an infinite regression of suppositions. The end of the chain of suppositions implies an assertion of fact. (2) Thus a chain of suppositions ultimately leads to fact, which is the domain of history. Science henceforth implicitly presupposes history, while the realm of history proper is the explicit manifestation of the implicit presupposition. In this period of his development, Collingwood tried to overcome the duality of science and history through a dialectical device: he made the two realms stages in the manifestation of Mind, giving each of them its relative justification. This dialectical justification of the various stages of development of Mind was possible on the basis of the underlying assumption, that is to say that the difference between the stages is one of *modality* of assertions and not one of *material* content or *ontological* realm. "The abstract cannot rest upon the more abstract, but only on the concrete", and history is the first acknowledgement of concreteness.

The elimination of any construction in history leads Collingwood at this stage to assume an inner relation between the historical attitude and philosophical realism. "Fact as something independent of my own or your knowledge of it". "The historical form of dogmatism is that represented by modern realism . . . which results from discovering the concept of fact". This is one of the most remarkable traits in Collingwood's entire development: history is thought to be connected with epistemological realism, since history rests on the very assertion of given facts. It is precisely here that the fundamental change occurred in the later stage of his thought: history will then be connected with an anti-realistic attitude, as against the realism expounded by the "minute philosophers". But this change was made possible only by a change in Collingwood's entire philosophical attitude. Collingwood in the period of **Speculum Mentis** employs a clear cut dichotomy: hypothesis on the one hand and assertion on the other. Assertion was considered as characteristic of a higher cognitive level than hypothesis. The entire system, including the relation of history to philosophy, is based on this primary assumption. This dichotomy in turn was based on the consideration of concreteness as the ideal goal of knowledge, parallel to the consideration of concreteness as the ultimate stage of the manifestation of Mind. One may say that here the Hegelian attitude becomes apparent, as the knowing subject becomes submerged in the object; the view of epistomology itself is a sign of the alienation between subject and object, an alienation which must be overcome. Once concreteness is the ideal there is no room for cognitive *activity,* on the part of the subject. The appropriate attitude towards concreteness is the ideal there is no room for a cognitive *activity.* As against this dichotomy in the early stage another dichotomy is put forward in the mature stage of Collingwood's system, that of *questioning* against *assertion.* With this new dichotomy a new understanding of history emerges.

This clinging to the given facts is the first point to be stressed in terms of the limitations of history as a form of Mind. The very possibility that history may lead to a dogmatic attitude indicates the weakness of history. Dogmatism is rooted in the assertion of something as ultimate though really it is provisional only. Historical knowledge assumes that what is asserted as a fact is a real fact; it does not recognize its own immanent limitations. It considers its own facts to be recognized as given and hence as the real facts. But these facts cannot be real since they are set in a partial context only. Facts included in an all-embracing context, Collingwood therefore argued, are facts known by philosophy and not by history. The aim of history is to know the facts but it does not reach this goal since the context of history is always incomplete. If we do not know the complete context, we do not even know the single fact, according to the Hegelian maxim that the truth is the whole. "If history exists, its object is an infinite whole which is unknowable and renders all its parts unknowable" . . . "we must claim access to the fact as it really was. This fact . . . is inaccessible. History as a form of knowledge cannot exist." Historical knowledge thus condemns the knowing subject to a passive position of sheer assertion. In the last resort there is no meaningful room within the historical domain, as the domain of an assertion of facts, for the status of the knowing subject. If, however, the subject is eliminated there is no justification of the claim of historical knowledge to be a knowledge of the concrete. There is only one legitimate meaning of the notion of concreteness, that of totality. But totality is outside the scope of historical knowledge. Totality as the all embracing context is a philosophical concept and not an historical one. Thus history is only on the threshold of philosophy, since it intends to reach concreteness but does not reach it. Philosophy requires the victory of history over science since it presupposes the establishment of the striving towards concreteness. But philosophy ultimately overcomes history, just as an objective

arrived at overcomes the sheer strife for and the formulation of it. History ends with its own breakdown, but this is a positive, that is to say, a dialectical breakdown, since out of the debris of history philosophy emerges.

In an earlier book, Collingwood had formulated the relation between history and philosophy as one of identity which became later on a "Leitmotif" of Collingwood's system: "history a parte objecti—the reality which historical research seeks to know—is nothing else than the totality of existence; and this is also the object of philosophy. History a parte subjecti—the activity of the historian—is investigation of all that has happened and is happening; and this is philosophy too. History and Philosophy are therefore the same thing". This emphasis on the identity of the two realms certainly does not reappear in *Speculum Mentis.* But we may perhaps see the difference in the attitudes between *Religion and Philosophy* (1916) and *Speculum Mentis* (1923) as a difference in point of view only and not as a fundamental one: the claim of history is to be philosophy. But this claim does not succeed because of the immanent limitation of history as the knowledge of given facts. *Religion and Philosophy* stresses the identity of history and philosophy in terms of the *program,* while *Speculum Mentis* stresses the difference between the two realms in terms of the *realization* of the common program. In both works the intermediary between history and philosophy is the striving towards concreteness, which in turn implies totality. The connection of history with the aspect of totality and concreteness did not leave room for the dimension of time. On the contrary: since concrete totality is self-contained, the problem had to be raised whether or not time is included in the all-embracing totality. According to Collingwood history does not deal with data in time, but with data as such. Hence the problem of the relation between data and time has not been raised. But the time aspect appears in *Speculum Mentis* indirectly, though it does not fit organically into the entire conception as outlined in this book. The time aspect appears in connection with the problem of novelty in history on the one hand and of permanence on the other. "It is process in which method or regularity does not exclude novelty; for every phase while it grows out of the preceding phase, sums it up in the immediacy of its own being and thereby sums up implicitly the whole of the previous history. Every such summation is a new act, and history consists of this perpetual summation of itself." Here at once the aspect of process comes to the fore, although this aspect had not been stressed when the nature of history had been considered in terms of its status in the chain of manifestations of Mind. It goes without saying that there is no sense in considering the aspect of novelty and summation unless we presuppose the background of time. But the relation of history to time remains a riddle in Collingwood's system in all its phases and is one of the paradoxes of his entire conception. Collingwood aims to consider history *sub specie acternitatis* and thus expel time from history. Collingwood was so eager to stress the identity of history with philosophy that he tried to abstract history from its real milieu and to deal with history without dealing with time. This is like Hamlet without the Prince of Denmark.

2

The conception of history as outlined in *Speculum Mentis* underwent various fundamental changes. Between the earlier conception and the later there is an intermediate one which is expounded in a paper of 1925. In this paper Collingwood emphasized not so much the *factuality* of history as the *individuality* of historical events; yet this might be considered as a change in terminology only. But this change has certainly some basis in Collingwood's explicit criticism of history, since he tries now to show that history is in the end an unachievable task: "the alleged facts upon which it builds its inductions are actually never secure enough to bear the weight that is put on them". Collingwood criticized history in *Speculum Mentis* as being pretentious, as attempting to reach totality which is beyond its power. There was no question as to facts, and therefore Descartes' "cogito" as an isolated fact or a statement of a fact was not put in doubt. To be sure, no fact could be understood unless placed in the context of totality, and this context was thought to be set by philosophy and not by history. The question could be raised in the context of *Speculum Mentis* whether a fact can be considered as being a fact when isolated from its context, or whether we may still assume the existence of the fact and stress the importance of the context only for the understanding of its full meaning. The realistic trend involved in history would refer to the independent *existence* of the given fact while a full *understanding* of the fact would necessarily overstep the scope of the fact as such. Unless I am mistaken, the paper of 1925 marks the emergence of his understanding of the relation between the two aspects of history. Facts are no longer considered as confined to themselves apart from their being understood: ". . . inductive study is itself based on ascertained facts, but these facts in their turn can never at any given moment finally be ascertained, for instance the discovery of this Roman villa may bring into question doctrines hitherto generally accepted as to the provenance and date of some kinds of pottery". Here Collingwood explicitly accepts the standard of "the truth as the whole" as the inner standard of history too. Yet this standard eventually shows the finitude of historical knowledge. Collingwood does not distinguish any more between the fact as such which is ascertained in its giveness and the meaning of the fact which places the fact in a context. Here he assumes only one legitimate context—that of totality. To be sure, the historical fact, even when placed in the total context, does not lose its individuality; it might be for this reason that Collingwood stressed in this stage of his doctrine the trait of individuality in the nature of the historical object more than the trait of factuality.

The cognitive act which characterized history in *Speculum Mentis* was assertion. In the paper of 1925 Collingwood writes of the act of perception. Perception as Collingwood understands it now is an activity on the part of the knowing subject. He stresses the aspect of activity in perception by putting to the fore the *judgment* implied in perception: "in all perceptions we are making a judgment, trying to answer the question what it is that we perceive, and all history is simply a more intense and sustained attempt to answer the same question". Collingwood criticizes the dichotomy of sensation and thought, and tries to show that sensation itself involves an act of thought. If sensation implies thought then perception also implies thought in its shaped form as judgment. The aspect of judgment is brought to the fore in perception through a very important notion, which is to occupy a central position in Collingwood's later system. Even perception, he argues, is an act of answering a question. The x is not sensed as such. Perception interprets the x and determines its nature and meaning and this determination is certainly an activity. "History is perception raised to its highest power, just as art is imagination raised to its highest power." Thus from two points of view the former conception of history undergoes a far-reaching criticism. From the point of view of the object, factuality ceases to be understood in a naïve way as something merely given. From the point of view of the subject historical knowledge is no longer just assertion; it is perception and as such a manifestation of a cognitive activity. These two angles of criticism are interrelated: since the fact is not given it is in a way created, through the act of perception. The object of history is not defined as independent of the knowledge of it: "The historian's data consist of what he is able to perceive".

The criticism of the shortcomings of historical thought as outlined in the system of *Speculum Mentis* was based on the assumption that historical thought does not establish the total context. One of the expressions of the partiality of the historical context was the fact that the historian himself was left outside the context of his thought. The gulf between object and subject was an indication of the inherent weakness of history in its unrealizable pretension to be concrete. This criticism is restated in the article on **"The Nature and Aims of a Philosophy of History"**, but the context of the criticism is now different. The relation between history and philosophy is no longer that of a formulation of a program and the fulfilment of it. History is "object-centred" thinking, it "asks questions only about its own object, not about the way in which it comes to know that object". The fact that the historian is not included in the setting of his thought is an outcome of the very trend of historical thought. This trend may be stated in the following way: historical thought is a *perceptive* thought but not a *reflective* one. ". . . he [i.e. the historian] is always the spectator of a life in which he does not participate: he sees the world of fact as it were across a gulf which, as an historian, he cannot bridge." Here again this shift in Collingwood's understanding of history becomes clear: history is finite not only because its subject-matter is partial and, as partial, can never be definite. It is finite because the subject or the knower remains on a plane different from that of his object. The finitude of history lies in the very duality of subject and object. To put it in other words: within the system of *Speculum Mentis* factuality was regarded as an advantage of history as against the hypothetical nature of science, which is based on a chain of suppositions. The problem of the alienation between subject and object was hinted at but was only a secondary feature rooted in the incompleteness of history. In terms of assertion on the part of the knower there was no room to point to the gulf between the knower and his object. Once the active nature of the subject has been brought to the fore the whole perspective changed: in perception considered as judgment, or act of thought, the knower is separated from his object. Against the totality of facts, objectively considered, a new totality is hinted at, comprising both subject and object. In both works the main concept in Collingwood's understanding of history is that of totality. In *Speculum Mentis* history had a realistic feature. Totality was realistic at least in its claim: a totality of facts placed in an all-embracing context of facts. In the paper of 1925 the new aspect of history comes to the fore: history as an activity of thought. Totality here is understood as containing both the subject and his object. The relation between history and philosophy in *Speculum Mentis* is one of a program and its fulfilment, while the relation between history and philosophy in the paper of 1925 is one between naïve thought which is object centred, and reflective thought. Reflective thought is understood in terms of Hegel's conception of self-consciousness as an identity of subject and object.

The change in the meaning of totality might perhaps be tied up with the change in the whole systematic approach. *Speculum Mentis* is a kind of Phenomenology of Mind, a study in the progressive manifestations of Mind. History is one of the forms of Mind: it is Mind as it manifests itself in factuality. The later phases of Collingwood's philosophy were at least more modest— or to put it in other words—not phenomenological, but epistemological. History is no longer understood as a manifestation of Mind, but as a form of knowledge. Philosophy of history is mainly a theory of historical knowledge and not a theory of the status of history in the progressive manifestations of Mind. Therefore the problem of totality arises within the scope of historical consciousness and not within the scope of historical facts. From this point of view the article of 1925 is at least an anticipation of the new approach as it was to be formulated in the mature system.

3

In the course of time Collingwood's view of the nature of history changed still more. There is in the first place an assumption which might be considered trivial when detached from the earlier view, or from the far-reaching conclusion derived from it in the mature view: history is "knowledge of the world of human affairs". The neutral object of history as fact becomes now a specific object, within the human realm.

What is the background of this new understanding of the nature of history? It seems as if Collingwood himself gives us a clue to the hidden motives which led him towards this change. In the first place, the deeper understanding of the nature of fact accomplishes the first change: "facts is a name for what history is about: *facta, gesta,* things done . . . deeds". Here Collingwood uses still the first meaning of the term "facts" which indicates their giveness. But "facts has also a secondary sense, . . . 'things made'. A making is a deed, a thing made is the result of a deed. To know about deeds is to know about their results." "The historical method involves studying both deeds and their results in this case, both mental activities and their results, for example concepts". There is here a kind of regress carried out from facts *qua* results to the process creating them. Historical method is interested both in the results and in their background. In dealing with historical facts *qua* results, Collingwood performs a reduction from facts to motives. History does not deal with facts, as events; it deals with events as actions, and the term action is intended to connote both the aspect of motive and that of results. Since the historical concern has been clearly placed in the human realm, the historical fact which was in the first place the ultimate datum, ceases to be ultimate. It necessarily points to its background within the human realm, to motives, thoughts and purposes expressing themselves in acts. This new view which we may call, for sake of convenience, the *anthropological* view of history. There emerges now the new conception which explicitly does not identify events with historical objects: "I mean more than he [sc. S. Alexander] does by the word 'historicity'. For him to say that the world is 'a world of events' is to say 'the world and everything in it is historical.' For me, the two things are not at all the same."

This shift to the human realm carries with it a new understanding of the individuality of the historical object. There is no longer an attribution of individuality to a neutral object; individuality has now a *human* meaning. It means a human being whose deeds are understood in terms of historical method. History in its shift from events to thoughts studies individuals. Individuality ceases to be a mark of the given object on the one hand or else a conceptual device on the other, and is held to reside in the very nature of the specific object of the research. Yet this confinement of individuality to the human sphere is the source of a new problem in Collingwood's system. Since the historical individual expresses himself in thoughts which in turn lead to results, individuality cannot be "monadic". "Because individuality is the vehicle of a thought which because it was actually theirs, is potentially everyone's." Here we have to point out that this new change undermines the clear connection of history with individuality, which was so much stressed in the former view. The individual nature of the historical object is a fact in itself. But there is no essential connection between the object of history *qua* thought or purpose and the individual who personally was the bearer of the thought. The connection between the real object of history *qua* actions rooted in thoughts, and the human individuals in whom these actions actually did occur is accidental. Indeed, Collingwood comes back here to the Hegelian conception of the "cunning of Reason", and views individuals as embodiments and agents of the Reason of history. Individuals cease to be considered as ultimate self-sufficient entities.

A further significant change occured in the shift from knowledge based on the sole ascertaining of facts to a knowledge based on questioning. In Collingwood's approach to history there is an increasing share of activity "a parte subjecti"; from an assertion which indicates the sole acceptance of the fact he moved to perception which contains the activity of judgment; from this he moves further to the "Baconian understanding of history", viz. challenging the given circumstances by putting questions to them. The difference of this from assertion is stressed in the following passage: "The questioning activity, as I called it, was not an activity of achieving a compresence with, or apprehension of something; it was not preliminary to the act of knowing, it was one half, the other half being answering the question of an act which in its totality was knowing".

4

The Baconian approach to history points to the purposive nature of history, while the purposive nature of the historical action makes the questioning activity possible, that is to say, altogether meaningful. Thus there is in Collingwood's mature system a double contraction of the realm of thought. History proper, in Collingwood's view, becomes history of *thought*. Thought is not understood as just content or meaning. Thought receives from the outset a connotation which is intended to make it suitable for the historical context: thought is *purpose,* either purpose as the driving force of an action or purpose as the end the action is aiming at. Thought is understood as intentionality towards the future and as moving towards it. The purpose of historical understanding is to discover from the results the action which created that result. "Political theory is the history of political thought: not 'political theory', but the thought which occupies the mind of a man engaged in political work: the formation of a policy, the planning of means to execute it, the attempts to carry it into effect, the discovery that others are hostile to it". This example taken from the field of political history is certainly a clue to Collingwood's entire system of historical knowledge: Collingwood could place history in the realm of purposive activities since in the late phase of his development he did not take into account the objective circumstances in which the purposive activity takes place, for instance, the geographical data essential for purposive planning of an action, or the stamina and endurance of a people or a society which is called upon to act, etc. Collingwood—and this is the main criticism of his view with reference to his contraction of history to purposive activities—placed the activity, as it were, in a

vacuum; he understood it as having meaning only when related from the outset to meaningful activity. The only meaningful activity which he took into account was that of sponsoring an action with a purpose in view. But in history there are meanings assigned to given facts through what may roughly be called in Toynbee's terminology responses to circumstances: an earthquake, although by no means a purposive activity created within the human realm, certainly has a historical meaning through its impact on the human realm, that is to say through the meaning connected with this disaster after the event and not in anticipation of it. This is another indication of the anthropological view of history as set out by Collingwood: man is a being who projects the future, a being to whom the future is not given but is rather created through his own deeds. Hence history as an understanding of human affairs has to discover this essential feature of human existence. But Collingwood detached human activity from its given environment and took into account only the meanings created by a purposive action and those anticipating the forthcoming results.

Historical research, however, does not deal with thoughts within the realm of one's own life. Thought creates results, and unless it does so it is inaccessible to the historian. The first condition for a historical object *qua* thought to be known is, that thought has to express itself in the realm of facts. Collingwood here remains faithful to his original understanding of the nature of the historical object *qua* fact, but goes beyond the realm of mere facts by rooting them in the realm of thought. This is the first condition which makes historical knowledge possible "a parte objecti". But there is another condition "a parte subjecti": "the historian must be able to think over again for himself the thought whose expression he is trying to interpret". One wonders what kind of condition is brought to the fore in this formulation. The first condition is certainly an epistemological condition: unless it has results there is no way of knowing the thought itself. The second condition, that "a parte subjecti", sounds like a psychological condition: one has to be a mathematician, at least a potential one, in order to understand mathematics, or one has to be able to reconstruct the plan of a political action in order to understand a historical political action. But actually this condition has been provided for in the very fact that historical knowledge deals with thought, and thought is not confined to the individual existence, since it has a universal meaning. Furthermore the fact that history deals with thoughts makes it a priori understandable for a historian. The condition formulated as to the ability of the historian to rethink the investigated thought sounds like a condition stated for a philologist to be able to read the script of the text he is dealing with.

There is a clear epistemological advantage implied in this shift towards thought. There is no room for a sheer ascertaining of thoughts, as if they were meaningless facts. Since we move in the realm of meaning, the ascertaining of the fact of thought is "eo ipso" an understanding of it. "*To discover* that thought is already to understand it. After the historian has ascertained the facts there is no further process of inquiring into their causes. When he knows what happened, he already knows why it happened." The ontological nature of the historical realm *"qua"* thought leads to some clear epistemological consequences: towards thoughts there is only one possible attitude: that of a thoughtful activity. "A parte subjecti" this activity means understanding of the motives, since thought "a parte objecti" means motives and purposes expressed in deeds. To *know* a thought means to *understand* it.

This line in Collingwood's thought was expressed in an earlier article: "what happens, happens for a good reason, and it is the business of history to trace the reason and to state it. And that means to justify the event". This line in Collingwood's thought can be understood in the light of his later development: since every historical act is an outcome of a purposive action, every act is understandable and as understandable it is justifiable. Justification does not mean approval of the act but detection of its motives. Collingwood rejects explicitly the moral approval of every act, once we understand it in its motive. ". . . this truth is grossly distorted if it is twisted into the service of the vulgar optimism which takes it for the whole truth." The half truth hinted at in this statement refers to the feature of the understanding as an *intellectual* act and not as *moral* approval. It seems that to regard the nature of historical knowledge as the understanding of a thought does not lead to the Leibnizian optimism which Collingwood rejects, but rather to a tolerance, the nature of which he formulated in connection with Ruskin's view: ". . . tolerance: the activity to live one's own life and yet to admire and to love people who live by the systems which one rejects".

We have considered above what Collingwood understood as the second condition of historical consciousness, i.e. the mind of the historian. This condition has been regarded as trivial, since it puts forward the psychological disposition of the historian and not the objective essence of historical consciousness as such. Collingwood would certainly reject this interpretation because of the main subjectivistic trend of his new system. History shifts in his view from the domain of the understanding of the specific nature of the object to the emphasis of the meeting between object and subject. This is a subjectivistic interpretation of the saying: "Die Weltgeschichte is das Weltgericht". ("The history of the world is the world's bar of judgment.") This saying, in Hegel's context pointed to the trial within the actual historical process, where the superseding events determine the success and the value of the previous events. Collingwood put into this saying a new content: "*die Weltgeschichte is das Weltgericht:* and it is true, but in a sense not always recognized. It is the historian himself who stands at the bar of judgment, and there reveals his own mind in its strength and weakness, its virtues and its vices". How could Collingwood attribute to the old saying this subjectivist connotation? The starting point

of Collingwood's new understanding of history lies in the assumption that all history is the history of thought. Thus history is, of necessity, from the outset a meaningful realm. This is a kind of an axiomatic assumption of his entire view. If so, then it is the task of the historian to detect the meaning of the realm he is investigating. If he fails in that his failure is an indication of his own weakness, and not of the absence of meaning in the events as such. As a matter of principle the historical events as such are understandable since they are events in the realm of thought. The failure to understand them is henceforth a psychological or spiritual weakness on part of the man who tries to understand them. This is a mitigated version of the former trend: although historical events are not justified they are understandable. Again the spiritual nature of history comes to the fore: within the system of **Speculum Mentis** the spiritual nature of history was inherent in the status of history as one of the forms of Mind, although Mind manifested itself in neutral *prima facie* non-spiritual, phenomena of facts. Within the later system, the spiritual nature of history appears in the very content of the historical object. However, there remains the question of how Collingwood could attribute this fundamental status to the strength or to the weakness of the mind of the historian. If historical events are meaningful in themselves, since they are placed within the domain of thought, how is it that the historian can fail to understand them? "The historical process is itself a process of thought, and it exists only in so far as the minds which are parts of it know themselves for parts of it." The mind of the historian is a part of the process and how is it that *it* stands at the bar of judgment and not the mind which exhibits itself in the events investigated? One may put this critical observation in the following way: either the mind of the historian has an independent standing and thus there is no self-evident identity between history as *res gestae* and their narration, or else it is a part of the historical realm and hence there cannot be a problem of principle connected with the mind of the historian, which is fundamentally a part of the objective realm.

5

There is a lack of symmetry in Collingwood's theory of history, because the status of the mind of the historian is by no means as essential as the status of the object of his mind as thought. But Collingwood, for systematic reasons, wanted to emphasize the parallel status of the historical object and the historical subject and even made this parallelism the main point in his criticism of the German school's approach to history on the one hand, and that of the contemporary French philosophical school on the other: . . . "whereas the German movement tries to find the historical process objectively existing outside the thinker's mind, and fails to find it there just because it is not outside, the French movement tries to find it subjectively inside the thinker's mind, and fails to find it because, being thus enclosed within the subjectivity of the thinker, it ceases to be a process of knowledge and becomes a process of immediate experience: it becomes a merely psychological process, a process of sensations, feelings, sentiments. The root of the error in both cases is the same. The subjective and the objective are regarded as two different things, heterogeneous in their essence, however intimately related . . . it is wrong in the case of history, where the process of historical thought is homogeneous with the process of history itself, both being processes of thought". The error of both schools lies in their one-sidedness; only Croce, as Collingwood observes, grasped the synthetic nature of history. But Collingwood is actually closer to the German school than he himself was aware of: although he tries to establish the synthesis between thought as object and the mind of the historian, the mind of the historian has a secondary status only since the meaningful event is bound to be understood, precisely because it is meaningful. The mind of the historian may have value as an example of the height human understanding is able to reach, but according to the principles of Collingwood's own view it cannot have an ontological status. Although Collingwood strove in his later conception of history towards a well-balanced synthesis of object and subject he still retains a conception which attributes a preponderance to the historical object.

Alan Donagan (essay date 1964)

SOURCE: Introduction to *Essays in the Philosophy of Art* by R. G. Collingwood, edited by Alan Donagan, Indiana University Press, 1964, pp. ix-xx.

[*In the following essay, Donagan offers an overview of Collingwood's theoretical writings on art.*]

R. G. Collingwood is generally acknowledged to have contributed more to the philosophy of art and the philosophy of history than any other British philosopher of his time. His *Principles of Art* (1938) and *Idea of History* (1946) are readily obtainable and widely studied. Yet, despite his beautiful and vigorous prose style, neither of these important books is fully intelligible by itself. You must go to *The New Leviathan* (1942) if you would understand the philosophy of mind that he partly developed in *The Principles of Art*; and you will probably misinterpret the methodology of *The Idea of History* if you neglect his impassioned but revealing *Autobiography* (1939).

In order fully to master Collingwood's philosophy of art you must go even farther afield: to the writings, all of them published in the years from 1922 to 1929, which are reprinted in [*Essays in the Philosophy of Art*]. Except for the passages on art in his general philosophical works, for reviews, and for a chapter on "Aesthetic" contributed to a collaborative work, *The Mind,* edited by R. J. S. McDowall, they include everything Collingwood wrote about aesthetics before *The Principles of Art*. In them, you can follow his thought in the process of formation.

In the earliest of them, *Ruskin's Philosophy,* the philosopher whom Collingwood praised with least reserve was Hegel. His debt to Hegel is obvious in the dialectical structure of the second and third chapters of *Outlines of a Philosophy of Art*. It is also obvious, although less directly, in its sixth chapter, which summarizes the "phenomenology of mind" which Collingwood had elaborated a year before in *Speculum Mentis*. According to that phenomenology, art is the first of the five activities of the whole human spirit: the others are, in order, religion, science, history, and philosophy. They constitute a scale of forms, in which the more advanced both contain and correct the more primitive. Art, the most primitive of the five, is purely imaginative, and interested only in its internal coherence. Most works of art have meaning, but not as such: as works of art they are windowless monads which do not even know that they are windowless. Religion, which is also imaginative, includes art: but it transcends art in dogmatically affirming that its imagery conveys truth. In turn, religion requires a higher activity to transcend it, because it cannot comprehend that it conveys truth only metaphorically, and so cannot inquire what that truth is. It would be superfluous to pursue the dialectic by which Collingwood elucidates the higher phases of mental life: science, history, and philosophy. Every phase, he declared, is "a nisus towards self-consciousness," which is finally fulfilled in philosophical insight.

This impressive scheme has paradoxical consequences for art which Collingwood did not try to conceal. If artists as artists are unaware of what their work means, then it follows, as he conceded in *Speculum Mentis,* that they cannot do well even as artists unless "they are more than artists." He expressed the same paradox in the *Outlines,* when he wrote that "we may value art for what it says, because what it says is beautiful; or for what it means, because what it means, but does not say, is true." Since he did not deny that the meaning of a work of art partly determines its value, he could not escape the conclusion that its value partly lies outside itself: "the value of art as a form of experience," he confessed, "is . . . its self-transcendence" (*Speculum Mentis*). Alas, his account in the *Outlines* of the self-transcendence of art was disastrous.

> As art actually exists [he wrote] it exists not in . . . isolation, but in the closest union with thought [i.e. the four higher phases of mental life]; what has by thought been grasped becomes expressive, because immediate, in the form of art, *and thus every . . . other phase of the spiritual life passes into art,* there to be focused into a luminous point *from which it can reissue into the explicitness of thought* (my italics).

Collingwood's position here is, on the one hand, that you can only "grasp," or be aware of, what is "immediate" or "luminous," i.e. art; and, on the other hand, that you cannot express what you mean without mediacy, i.e. thought. From this the absurdity follows that nobody can become aware of what he thinks. Even if a thought should "pass into" art (becoming an object of awareness, but ceasing to say what it means), and then "reissue" into thought (coming again to say what it means, but ceasing to be an object of awareness), it would not at any point become an awareness of a thought. In the same way, if a surface is painted black all over, and then white all over, it does not at any time become black *and* white all over.

To escape this absurdity Collingwood found it necessary to modify his position slightly but profoundly. Whereas in the *Outlines* he had held that art, or imagination, always exists "in the closest union with thought," which transcends it, in *The Principles of Art* he recognized that imagination is a necessary element in every act of thought. To think is not to transcend imagination, but to put imagination to work in a specific way.

Although the dialectical phenomenology in the *Outlines*, like an unwieldy suit of armour, may once have afforded protection against adversaries long forgotten, it now only conceals the shape of Collingwood's thought. Its place in his philosophy of art, as he himself had written of a Lockean doctrine in Ruskin's *Modern Painters*, "is not structural but ornamental." Stripped of ornamentation, Collingwood's aesthetic can be seen to have owed little to Hegel, and almost everything to Ruskin and Croce.

As the first chapter of his *Autobiography* shows, Collingwood was bred from childhood in the practice of art as Ruskin conceived it. He had himself received the training he prescribes in his essay **"Art in Education"**; and he received it at home, from his father, W. G. Collingwood, Ruskin's disciple, friend, and biographer. What above all Collingwood owed to Ruskin's influence was the conviction that in all its manifestations each human mind is a unity. In *Ruskin's Philosophy*, he acknowledged his debt for the principle; and he also followed Ruskin in some of his applications of it. For example, when he wrote that a painter "paints in order to see" (*Outlines*) and described "drawing, painting and modelling" as "the training of the eye" (**"Art in Education,"** p. 202), he was repeating Ruskin's lesson in *Oxford Lectures on Art* that the power to draw is inseparable from the power to see. Ruskin, indeed, went further, holding "fine technical work" to be a proof of "every other good power." Again, when Collingwood wrote that "if we are to recover the artistic sanity of the Greeks and the Middle Ages and the Renaissance, we must first recover the conviction that nothing can be beautifully made unless it is efficiently made, nothing efficiently made unless it is beautifully made" (**"Art in Education,"** p. 194), he was repeating another of Ruskin's dicta: "from highest to lowest, health of art has first depended on reference to industrial use" (*Oxford Lectures*, IV 117, p. 108).

Collingwood nevertheless conceded that on one point Ruskin had misapplied his principle. In *Two Paths* Ruskin had written that "the period in which any given people reach their highest power in art is precisely that in which they appear to sign the warrant of their own ruin . . ." (*Ruskin's Philosophy*). Attributing public ruin to moral decay, he had gone on to infer that art flourishes when morality withers, which contradicts his inference from the principle of the unity of the human mind that "the manual arts are as accurate exponents of ethical state, as other modes of expression; first, with absolute precision, of that of the workman; and then with precision, disguised by many distorting influences, of that of the nation to which it belongs" (*Oxford Lectures*, III 71, pp. 77-8).

Ruskin twice attempted, but without success, to escape this contradiction. First, he denied that an art which flourishes when morality decays can be a true art, on the ground that it is not naturalistic. But the art of Michelangelo and Tintoretto was naturalistic. Later, he explained that "the great art-periods of the past were fatal to national life because art has always been in the service of a rich and proud nobility, careless of the misery in which its less fortunate neighbours lay" (*Ruskin's Philosophy*). This explanation implies of Tintoretto's art either that it is proud and callous, which Ruskin did not think, or that its quality is not an exponent of the morality of Tintoretto's nation, which contradicts Ruskin's hypothesis.

Collingwood found an explanation of the impermanence of artistic styles in Browning's line, "What's come to perfection perishes." "[T]he perfection of any one artistic style . . . lays a dilemma before the human spirit: either . . . become merely imitative, or else launch out into the void, feeling for a new style . . . and acquiescing in the death of the old." But why should not art become merely imitative? In answering this question Collingwood could get no help from Ruskin or Browning. He had to look beyond them, to Croce.

Collingwood's relations with Croce were very close. He translated into English two of Croce's books (the first of them in 1913), and two articles, one of them the important "Aesthetic" for the *Encyclopaedia Britannica* (14th ed.). In a letter to Croce written in 1921 Collingwood referred to himself as "a friend and disciple of your philosophy," and Croce's influence on his philosophy of art grew with the years. Of *The Principles of Art* (1938), he was to write to Croce that "the doctrine taught in it is in all essentials your own." Yet, even allowing for grateful hyperbole, he could not have written so about his earlier *Outlines*. He did, indeed, acknowledge in his Preface that the "general conception" of art expounded in the *Outlines* was "already familiar from the works of Coleridge, Croce, and many others." But in elaborating that general conception he diverged considerably from Croce.

The *Outlines* follows Croce in defining art generically as a mental activity, and specifically as imaginative. It also follows Croce in describing imagination as unconcerned with the reality or unreality of the objects it creates. Furthermore, in it Collingwood adopted Croce's distinction between sensation and imagination: sensation yields only "impression," which fall short of full awareness; it is imagination that raises sense-impressions to the level of consciousness, creating what Croce called "intuitions." Although Collingwood eschewed Croce's terminology, he clearly drew Croce's distinction in passages like the following. "[A] painter paints . . . in order to see. . . . A person who does not draw has only a dim and vague feeling of the look of things, and at no single point has he a clear or accurate grasp of their appearance. . . . Similarly, the practice of music is a sharpening of our discrimination with regard to the pitch, intensity, quality and inter-relations of sounds; the drama and the novel perform the same function with regard to human nature." It may be observed that, in the final sentence of this passage, Collingwood implicitly extended the province of art to every level of consciousness: "human nature" is not an object of sensation.

In reformulating Croce's analysis of imagination, Collingwood gave it a Ruskinian tincture. Although Croce maintained that every imaginative creation has a physical counterpart, he also maintained that properly a work of art exists in the mind, its physical counterpart being no more than an "externalization" produced, not by art, but by "technique." Croce's proposition that art is not the exercise of a technique was accepted by Collingwood (*Outlines*); nor is it, taken by itself, inconsistent with Collingwood's Ruskinian proposition that technique, while primarily a matter of muscular control, is "secondarily . . . a training not of the muscles but of the eye and ear, or, more precisely, of the imagination . . ." (*Outlines*). Croce did not deny that you cannot imagine visually unless you learn to draw; indeed, he expressly stated that you do not imagine clearly what a thing looks like unless you can draw it. But he did not emphasize it. Following Ruskin, Collingwood did.

The definition of art as imaginative enabled Collingwood to answer the question, "Why should art not be merely imitative?" If art is imaginative, it is the activity by which we become conscious of our impressions; but *our* impressions are not those of previous generations. "The transformations which art undergoes in the course of its history are the expression not of a self-contained life of art . . . , but of the life of the spirit as a whole" (*Outlines*). As conditions of life change art must change; and the art of the past can only be appreciated by an effort of historical imagination.

Since he held that every mental activity has a conative or "practical" and an emotional side, as well as a cognitive one, Collingwood could not accept as complete the definition of art as imagination, which refers only to its cognitive side. A complete definition must take account of its practical and emotional sides.

Practically, Collingwood maintained, art attempts to achieve beauty; and emotionally, it is the enjoyment of beauty, so far as beauty is achieved. And, repudiating the notion that any activity of mind can properly be judged by a criterion outside itself, he went on to conclude that beauty, as the criterion by which art is practically judged, must be defined in terms of art itself, i.e. of imagination. He therefore defined it as "the unity or coherence of the imaginary object" (*Outlines*).

This definition can hardly fail to appear circular. Art, i.e. imagination, attempts to achieve beauty, i.e. the unity or coherence possessed by whatever is imagined. But what unity or coherence is that? You may even be tempted to close the book in disgust when you find Collingwood impeccably deducing that "it is impossible to imagine anything that is not beautiful," and that "all ugliness, so far as it does actually exist, is not the ugliness of an object imagined but the ugliness of an object not imagined" (*Outlines*). Attempting to achieve beauty is attempting to imagine well: but in trying to imagine well, what are we trying to achieve?

Two answers to this question may be dismissed at once. It will not do to say that we are simply trying to achieve clear awareness. It is true that Collingwood held that imagination is the activity by which we become aware of things; but we do not try to become aware of anything and everything. Of what does an artist try to become aware? Nor will it do to say that he tries to become aware of what it is useful to be aware of. Even if in education the aim of art is to enable a child to be practically efficient when he grows up, that aim is external to art. It is not the function of art *in itself*. What is that function?

Croce answered his question in a paper of 1908, which was included as an appendix to Ainslie's 1909 English translation of *Aesthetic,* and in *Problemi di Estetica* (1910). Although it is in the last degree improbable that Collingwood had not read these works, they left little or no mark on his *Outlines*. But in **"Form and Content in Art"** . . . , he showed signs of assimilating their teaching; and when he wrote *The Principles of Art* he had wholly done so.

Briefly, Croce argued that art is the attempt to express emotion. In his terminology, artistic intuition is "lyrical." As Croce wrote: "what confers coherence and unity upon the intuition is emotion . . . an intuition is truly such when it represents an emotion, and can rise only from it and above it. . . . Not the idea, but the emotion is what confers upon art the ethereal lightness of the symbol: a longing enclosed within the circumference of an image: that is art. . . ." Croce would have rejected as absurd the question, "Why does the artist try to express his emotion?" By its very nature, emotion strives towards expression.

In **"Form and Content in Art"** Collingwood identified the content of art with what he called its "romantic element," to which he variously referred as "the connexions that bind art to the rest of life," "emotion," "consciousness of a sincere interest," and "conviction".

And he argued that a work of art can be created only when this romantic element goes together with a "classical element," which he identified with "the artist's formal or formative power." Despite his carelessly anti-Crocean use of the word "technique," what in this paper he described as the formal or classical element in art clearly corresponds to what Croce called "intuition," and what he described as the romantic element in art corresponds to what Croce called its "lyrical" character. The following remarks from the penultimate paragraph of Collingwood's essay anticipate the thought and even the phrasing of his later, fully Crocean, doctrine in *The Principles of Art,* "[U]ntil he has learnt to speak, [the artist] has nothing to say. He may have feelings working within him, but they are only obscure emotional perturbations, and do not take the shape of . . . a conviction . . . brought clearly before himself."

Why did not Collingwood from the first embrace the conception of art as the expression of emotion? Any answer must be conjectural. But it is significant that the *Outlines* diverges most strikingly from Croce's *Aesthetic* in giving a central place to the concept of beauty. In this he followed Ruskin and the German idealists. It is true that by defining beauty in terms of a Crocean concept of imagination, he emptied it of the content it had for them. But was he aware of this? Echoing Hobbes, I make bold to submit that the theory of beauty in the *Outlines* is the ghost of the Ruskinian conception sitting crowned upon the grave thereof. In **"Form and Content in Art"** Collingwood made no use of the concept of beauty; and in *The Principles of Art* he argued that "aesthetic theory is the theory not of beauty but of art," and that the theory of beauty belongs with the theory of love.

William M. Johnston   (essay date 1967)

SOURCE: "Benedetto Croce as a Foil to R. G. Collingwood," in *The Formative Years of R. G. Collingwood,* Martinus Nijhoff, 1967, pp. 68-80.

[*In the following excerpt, Johnston focuses on the philosophical career of Benedetto Croce in relation to Collingwood's development as a philosopher.*]

(1) CROCE AND COLLINGWOOD: A COMPARISON

Benedetto Croce is the contemporary thinker whom early Collingwood most resembles. As we shall see, this is true especially of Croce's writings from 1901 to 1910. Whether the resemblance is owing to Croce's direct influence upon Collingwood or to Vico's influence upon both Croce and Collingwood is one of those problems of affiliation which are so elusive in the case of Collingwood (and also of Croce). That Collingwood felt a certain affinity with Croce is abundantly clear. In 1921, for example, Collingwood wrote to Croce:

This I say because some things in the paper look like the observations of a hostile critic, and I

should like you to know that that is very far from being the character they were intended to bear. I have no time to write about work to which I feel hostile: I only write about the people whom I most closely agree with.

As one reads *Speculum Mentis* (1924), the language, the type of distinctions used, and the categories accepted as ultimate remind one of Croce's works written between 1901 and 1910. Although Collingwood seldom cites any explicit sources for his ideas, he does indicate a wide familiarity with Croce's works. In *The Idea of History,* the fifteen pages on Croce (written probably in 1936) show a profound grasp of Croce's development and are among the best brief treatments of the Italian philosopher.

On the other hand, if one were guided solely by Collingwood's interpretations of Croce, one would get a very one-sided view of the Neapolitan's achievements. This is due partly to a habit which Collingwood shares to some extent with Croce, namely a reluctance to cite specific sources for his ideas and interpretations. In a letter of April 20, 1938 to Croce, Collingwood explains his reluctance to use footnotes and to cite authorities as being "in accordance with a method of writing which I inherit from a long line of English philosophers . . ." Like Croce in the historical portions of his *Estetica, Logica, Pratica,* and *Storiografia,* Collingwood seldom writes any work which offers a conspectus of a man's whole thought. Rather in articles and books like *The Idea of History,* he selects those themes which fit a general scheme which he is developing. Although there can be no doubt that Collingwood could have written a brilliant monograph on Croce, and especially on Croce's relationship to Vico, he chose to write portions of *The Idea of History* instead. In fact, Collingwood's only extensive monograph on a single thinker is the essay *Ruskin's Philosophy.*

In contrast to this, Croce wrote a large quantity of monographs, both in his early "philological" period (1888-1894) and throughout his career. Not a few of Croce's critics and admirers have pointed out to what extent he was the complete bibliophile and *erudito.* A study has even been made of the books in his personal library. As Luigi Salvatorelli puts it:

To read old records, to leaf through pages of an archive, to go in search of the unpublished fact, of the quaint detail, patiently to reconstruct a chronology of events, a *curriculum vitae,* a family genealogy, was for Croce an inborn vocation, an exquisite pleasure, from his early youth to his advanced old age.

Croce himself testifies to his love for books from his earliest days, and pleads that at least up to 1915 this penchant disqualified him to be a man of action.

Unlike Croce, Collingwood never ventured into literary criticism, political history, or the narrative history of modern Europe. In Collingwood, a similar breadth of interests was taken up by pursuit of the arts. Collingwood painted, drew Roman inscriptions, and played music, activities which so far as I know were remote from Croce's interests. Indeed, Collingwood's oft-repeated insistence that no man can write an aesthetic without having practiced one or preferably more of the arts is quite absent from Croce. As Collingwood says:

> Looking at pictures and reading books about them qualifies nobody for discussing the philosophy of art. For that, one must spend much time and trouble in the actual practice of the arts, or at least one of them, and learn to reflect on the experience so gained.

Croce may have had more varied research interests, but Collingwood engaged in a greater variety of artistic pursuits.

It is this important difference which suggests that Croce's influence on Collingwood may have been less profound than a comparison of their works would suggest. Although Collingwood may have borrowed much terminology from Croce, as well as from Vico and Gentile, the Englishman's basic inspiration came from elsewhere. Enough has already been said about Ruskin to indicate that he was the chief source of R. G. Collingwood's aims and inspirations. Collingwood used the philosophical terminology of the Italians to import precision to the formulation of problems which Ruskin's example had pressed upon him. This, I believe, is why Collingwood could express great sympathy with Croce, and yet feel that he was not a disciple of the Italian. He was not a disciple, because his inspiration came from another source, but he was pursuing an enterprise similar to part at least of Croce's.

(2) CROCE VERSUS MICHAEL OAKESHOTT AS A FOIL TO COLLINGWOOD

Besides Croce, the other contemporary who most resembles early Collingwood is Michael Oakeshott (1901-). After studying at Cambridge University, in 1933 Oakeshott published *Experience and Its Modes,* a work which discusses history, science, and practical activity as "modes" of experience. According to Oakeshott, experience in its pure form is grasped only by philosophy.

It is significant that in **The Idea of History** Collingwood devotes nine pages to the discussion of this work. Not only does he praise Oakeshott as "the high-water mark of English thought upon history," but he accords to only three other thinkers an equally lengthy treatment in **The Idea of History**. These three thinkers are Kant, Hegel, and Croce. As we shall see, Hegel and Croce are Collingwood's two chief predecessors in delineating forms of experience, and there is reason to believe that Oakeshott is his principal successor.

Like Collingwood, Oakeshott is chary about acknowledging intellectual debts, using even fewer footnotes than Collingwood. In the Introduction to *Experience and Its Modes,* he says merely that he has received the most help from Hegel's *Phänomenologie des Geistes* and from F. H. Bradley's *Appearance and Reality.* Although Oakeshott does not mention Collingwood, E. W. F. Tomlin is of the opinion that **Speculum Mentis** exercised considerable influence over *Experience and Its Modes.* A comparison of the two works reveals striking similarities both in general conception and detailed exposition. It is just possible that *Experience and Its Modes* is the only major work in philosophy to have been profoundly influenced by **Speculum Mentis**.

It seems better, however, to expound Collingwood's early thought around Croce and Ruskin rather than around Oakeshott, and this for two reasons. First, generally it is preferable in intellectual history to interpret a thinker in the light of his predecessors rather than of his successors. Too often successors have a vested interest in how the thought of their precursors is to be construed. And they tend to stress those elements in a precursor which reinforce their own point-of-view, as in the classic cases of the followers of Hegel and of Marx. Indeed, one of the most useful correctives for the pleas *pro domo* of a thinker's followers is to examine his predecessors. In our case, then, Collingwood would make a plausible point of departure for study of Oakeshott, but the road runs less easily the other way. Second, because at this writing Oakeshott is still living there is the chance that he may develop further in his thinking. He has already evolved enormously since he published *Experience and Its Modes* in 1933, and his work after 1945 shows less evidence of affinity with Collingwood than does his earlier writing. Rather than introduce problems of interpreting a contemporary, it seems preferable to omit Oakeshott from further discussion.

(3) CROCE'S EARLY CAREER (1866-1900)

Benedetto Croce was born February 25, 1866, of an old, well-to-do Neapolitan family. In politics his father was conservative, preserving loyalty to the ousted Bourbon monarchy and never reconciled to the Kingdom of Italy. Croce relates in his *Autobiography* that his family never discussed politics so that he grew up in an intellectual atmosphere barren of political issues. The same is true of R. G. Collingwood.

Croce's parents owned a vast library, and Croce's remotest memory of his father pictures him shut up in his study. At an early age Croce himself became a bibliophile, so that at the age of six or seven he was enthralled by book-stores and by the vision of the past which they afforded.

Although Croce's parents were devout Roman Catholics, who sent their eldest son to be educated by nuns and Jesuits, Croce soon underwent a religious crisis, which he strove to conceal from his family. Gradually he outgrew his religious beliefs, with the result that in his later philosophy of culture he accords religion scant place. Herein he differs significantly from Collingwood, who all his life regarded religion as a necessary, even indispensable component of culture.

A further difference from Collingwood is that in 1883 at age seventeen Croce suffered a cataclysmic loss of his family. Both his parents and his only sister were killed in the earthquake of Casamicciola. Only a brother survived. This blow caused young Croce several years of nervous depression, and it may have contributed to the relatively late age of thirty-five at which he found his vocation as philosopher. Collingwood, on the other hand, found his vocation as early as age twenty.

From 1883 to 1886 Croce stayed in Rome befriended and adopted by his father's former protégé, and later rival, Silvio Spaventa. Here the orphan received his first exposure to political life, since Spaventa's guests included many politicians. Croce enrolled in the Faculty of Law, without completing the course. In fact, he who was to become one of his country's most learned men, never took a university degree! At Rome came Croce's first experience of formal philosophy in the lectures of Antonio Labriola (1843-1904). In his *Autobiography,* Croce reports that his *Pratica,* written almost twenty years later, derives from musings on Labriola's Lectures on ethics delivered in 1884-1885.

In 1886, Croce returned to Naples to the life of an independent scholar. For six years, he devoted himself to research in archives and church libraries of his native city. He wrote several books on Neapolitan history, notably on the Revolution of 1799. In many ways, these six years of archival research, scarcely interrupted by mundane concerns, were to exert decisive influence on Croce. As his original calling in life, archival research held him in its spell during the formative period of his early twenties. Only later, in an effort to broaden his horizon beyond antiquarian research, did Croce embark upon the philosophy of history. Croce's later identification of history and philosophy seems but an articulation of the motive which had animated him in the archives.

Croce's first major undertaking in the philosophy of history was a series of articles on Marxism written between 1895 and 1900. Here again it was Labriola who inspired the young Neapolitan to engage in philosophy. Croce's approach to Marx is characteristic of much of his later thought. As a self-educated man, Croce possessed a remarkable capacity for learning from scratch the fundamentals of a subject. As a result, he could not help seeing economics as part of a larger whole which embraced history and philosophy. Already he was wondering about the relationship of economics to other "modes of operation" of the mind. Croce's interest in Marxism at this important stage in his career marks a further difference from Collingwood. The latter never had a profound interest in Marx, nor more than a pass-

ing interest in economics. In the guise of "utilitarian action," Croce, on the other hand, was to elevate economics into one of four basic modes of experience.

Above all what Croce retained from his involvement with Marxism was a commitment to

> the essential assertion of historicism: "Men themselves make history, but they do it in a particular given environment based on pre-existent, real conditions. . . ."

It would be a mistake, however, to believe that at the turn of the century Croce's chief concern was with history, or with its claims to be all-pervasive. This young scholar of Neapolitan antiquities had another enthusiasm, which played an equally decisive role in his development: the theory of art or, as he, following German tradition, called it, aesthetic.

Unlike Collingwood, Croce was not an avid practitioner of any of the arts. He did not paint or compose or even, so far as we know, write verses. His approach to art was strictly that of the connoisseur, the cabinet scholar. What distinguished him from the mere art critic was his interest in, and appreciation of, all forms of artistic expression: painting, sculpture, architecture, music, and above all, literature. He tells us in *An Autobiography* that he first came to appreciate painting in the churches where he accompanied his mother as a boy: the pictures and tombs fascinated him and helped to arouse in him interest in the past. Echoes of Ruskin!

Croce's philosophy of culture began to take shape when around 1900 he turned from Marxism to aesthetics. About that time, he abandoned any further effort to exert political influence. Rather he set himself the task of trying to spell out the chief "modes of operation" of the mind or spirit. It is this "philosophy of spirit" which Croce evolved over the next ten years which is of special importance for the study of Collingwood.

(4) CROCE'S PHILOSOPHY OF CULTURE (1901-1915)

Between 1902 and 1912 Croce published a series of works which expound his conception of the spheres of experience. The best-known of these books are the *Estetica* (1st ed. 1902), the *Logica* (1st ed. 1905), and the *Pratica* (1st ed. 1909). The difficulty of tracing Croce's development is compounded by the fact that he revised each of these works several times and that for each work, at least one of the revisions included alteration of major themes. For our purpose it will be sufficient merely to sketch Croce's vision of the spheres of experience.

The key conception, which Croce first enunciated in the *Estetica* of 1904, is that experience is divided into two spheres: theoretical activity and practical activity. Each of these has two layers, a higher and a lower. In the case of theoretical activity, the lower layer is called aesthetic, and the higher layer is called logic. In the case of practical activity, the lower layer is called economic, and the higher layer is called morality. As one may infer from their titles, the *Estetica* and *Logica* deal respectively with the two layers of theoretical activity, while the *Pratica* deals in one volume with the two layers of practical activity.

Philosophy is defined as the activity which characterizes the other activities, describing the proper sphere of each. Philosophy does not have a sphere of its own, apart from its boundary-making function. This, however, is a large task, so large in fact that Croce can consider all three volumes as contributions to philosophy. These three volumes comprise the trilogy of *Filosofia dello Spirito*: Philosophy of the Spirit.

Croce assigns a curious place to religion in his philosophy of culture. Whereas he sees art and science as distinct forms of experience, religion he subsumes under morality as a species of practical activity. Croce does not consider religion to be an autonomous form of experience.

Croce's discussion of the forms of experience goes beyond the first three volumes of the *Filosofia dello Spirito*. Three other works written between 1905 and 1916 are of special importance for Croce's conception of the spheres of experience. The first of these is the *Saggio sullo Hegel* (1906). In this work, Croce advances a notion which is crucial to his critique of Hegel and which will serve as the basis for the total revision of the *Logica* in its second edition of 1909. This notion is the distinction between two types of opposition: opposites and what Croce calls "distincts." Opposites are concepts which exclude each other, like hot and cold. Distincts are concepts, which though contrary, yet imply each other, like one and many or body and spirit. To use Collingwood's terms, the distincts are "distinct but not separate." Croce contends that Hegel erred in constructing his dialectic because he treated all forms of opposition as opposites. This led him to forced conclusions about the relationship of concepts which are really distincts. Hegel failed to see, says Croce, that the one and the many comprise a single whole, just as do the spirit and body. This notion of concepts which form distinct yet inseparable parts of a larger whole comprises the basic logical doctrine of Collingwood's **Speculum Mentis**.

A second work by Croce which analyses and evaluates another thinker is his *Filosofia di Giambattista Vico* (1911). This book marks a shift in Croce's attitude toward the place of history in his schema of the spheres of experience. In the *Pratica* (1909), history was regarded as the study of practical activity at both its levels: economic activity and morality. Philosophy, on the other hand, was seen as the activity which characterizes these and the other spheres of experience. As such, philosophy is not identifiable with any one of them, and it comes closest not to history, but to logic. In the *Filosofia di Giambattista Vico,* however, Croce endorses Vico's view that history is co-extensive with philosophy and that philosophy is best studied as a branch of history, that is an expression of the spirit in past epochs.

Since 1912, the learned world has linked with Croce's name the thesis that philosophy resolves without remainder into history. A corollary of this view holds that history expands to include the study of all other forms of thought. Croce states this "historicism" openly for the first time in the *Teoria e Storia della Storiografia* (1917). Given the relative lateness (1911) with which Croce states the thesis of the convertibility of history and philosophy, it is surprising that it should be almost unanimously regarded as the hallmark of his contribution to philosophy. When critics speak of Collingwood's debt to Croce, they usually have in mind their joint espousal of this thesis.

In actuality Croce's greater significance for the early Collingwood lies in Croce's effort from 1902 to 1912 to describe the four spheres of experience. Croce's conception of theoretical and practical spheres, which are divided respectively into aesthetic and logic and into economic and morality, has tended to be forgotten in the wake of his later so-called "historicism." But at least for Croce's friend and colleague, Giovanni Gentile (1875-1944), the effort to spell out the characteristics of the spheres of experience was a far greater inspiration than the historicism. Likewise, what Croce meant for the early Collingwood was to serve above all as an example of how to go about describing the spheres of experience.

Collingwood was, to be sure, severely critical of what he called the "rigid and abstract formalism" of the schema of four forms of experience offered in the *Filosofia dello Spirito*. But Collingwood made that remark in the same year (1923) as he was writing **Speculum Mentis,** in which he tries to improve upon Croce's doctrine of the four forms of experience. This stricture came shortly after Collingwood had confided in a letter to Croce that he had written his article, **"Croce's Philosophy of History"** (1921), not on:

> the hundred points on which I agree with your view of history but . . . on the hundred and first where I find myself differing from you. . . .

In particular, the point on which Collingwood agreed with Croce was that history could best be characterized by comparing it with art, religion, science, and philosophy. This is what Collingwood was to attempt in **Speculum Mentis**. In some ways, that work continues Croce's Philosophy of the Spirit. Collingwood has made many modifications, he elevates religion to the status of a form of experience, and he demotes economics and morality. Nevertheless, if one searches the annals of early twentieth century philosophy for a figure who preceded Collingwood in the enterprise of describing forms of experience, Croce looms largest. Gentile, to be sure, had made some modifications in Croce's thesis which

Collingwood adopted, and of course Hegel lies behind the whole undertaking. But it was Croce who resurrected this approach in the twentieth century, and that is his supreme contribution to the work of the early Collingwood.

(5) CROCE'S INTRODUCTION INTO ENGLAND (1907-1920)

The two men who introduced Croce into England, Douglas Ainslie and J. A. Smith, were of unequal philosophic talent. Douglas Ainslie (1865-1948) was an amateur aesthetician, a disciple of Walter Pater (1839-1894), who stumbled upon Croce's *Estetica* in 1907. As he himself says, he believed that in Croce he had discovered a new world of philosophic insight, which he wished to bring to English readers. The result was a series of translations of Croce's major works in the field of philosophy of culture. The *Aesthetic* appeared first (in 1909), *The Philosophy of the Practical* in 1913, *What is Living and What is Dead in the Philosophy of Hegel* in 1915, and the *Logic* in 1917.

Ainslie did not attempt to write even a short interpretation of Croce's thought. His contribution was solely as a translator, and his work in this capacity has received scathing criticism. It has become a commonplace of Croce-studies that the Ainslie translations are not to be relied upon, and if used at all, must be followed in the original text. Yet this judgement is excessively harsh, due perhaps to the fact that those who can read philosophical Italian well enough to judge Ainslie's work are few in number and may be inclined to exaggerate the importance of that attainment.

A more balanced verdict on Ainslie's translations may be found in two reviews of them written by Bernard Bosanquet (1848-1923) in 1914 and 1918. Bosanquet, who was patrician enough not to preen himself on his knowledge of Italian, found that Ainslie did slip into inaccuracies and occasionally into mistranslations. The chief fault he found in the fact that Ainslie "did not appreciate the inconvenience of expressions that lack precision in a logical treatise." Nevertheless, although Bosanquet recommended that those who could, should consult the Italian in conjunction with Ainslie's rendering of it, he found the bulk of Ainslie's work serviceable and a genuine help to the English-speaking reader. He did not feel that Croce had been betrayed by his translator.

Besides Ainslie, the other man chiefly instrumental in bringing Croce to the attention of the philosophical public in England was John Alexander Smith (1863-1939), almost invariably known as J. A. Smith. Smith was Collingwood's predecessor in the chair of the Waynflete Professorship of Metaphysical Philosophy, which he held from 1909 to 1934. Although a brilliantly gifted polymath, who reminds one a bit of Collingwood in the breadth of his intellectual and research interests (ranging from fine points of Aristotle Scholarship to the philosophy of mathematics), Smith differed from Collingwood in that he was never able to write anything longer than an article or a book review. Collingwood mentions in his *Autobiography* that he pleaded with Smith to put his ideas on paper in a systematic form, but to no avail. Collingwood saw in Smith's literary paralysis a sign of the senescence of Oxford idealism.

However that may be, it was Smith who first introduced the Oxford community to the ideas of Croce. Smith relates in his brief philosophical autobiography that he discovered Croce while vacationing at Naples, prior to returning to Oxford to take up his duties as Waynflete Professor. In Naples in 1910, Smith noticed that books by a man named Croce were displayed prominently on bookstands all over the city. Finally he decided to investigate who this Croce was, and he became so enthralled by the Italian's thought that he made his Inaugural Lecture at Oxford an exposition of portions of the *Estetica* and *Pratica*.

It is difficult to estimate the extent of Smith's influence on his contemporaries. He was renowned among undergraduates for his prowess as an interpreter of Aristotle, and candidates for "Greats" found him an inspiration in this portion of their preparation. One gathers that his lectures on Croce and Gentile created little stir. As always, Collingwood is chary of admitting to having been influenced, and he refers to Smith simply as "my friend." There is no way to tell whether it was Smith, or someone else, who first set Collingwood to reading Croce. Collingwood had already taught himself Italian at Rugby, so that he could read Dante. In any event, he must have made Croce's acquaintance while still an undergraduate because in 1913 there appeared Collingwood's first venture of any sort into print, a translation of Croce's *The Philosophy of Giambattista Vico*.

As we have seen, the Italian text of this work had been published just two years before, and it marks something of a turning point in Croce's development. It is regrettable that we have no record of how Collingwood made the acquaintance of this work or of who induced him to undertake the translation. The latter appeared without any preface or introduction, save a brief "Translator's Note."

There is still a third figure at Oxford who may have had a share in introducing the young Collingwood to the Italian philosopher. This is Collingwood's undergraduate tutor at University College, E. F. Carritt (1878-), who at this writing is still living and remains possibly the last survivor in philosophy of his generation at Oxford.

In *An Autobiography,* however, Collingwood paints a rather unflattering portrait of Carritt as "another prominent member of the 'realist' school." By the "realist" school, Collingwood means notably Cook Wilson (1849-1915) and "his followers," H. A. Prichard (1871-1947) and H. W. B. Joseph (1867-1943). Collingwood credits

Carritt with having introduced him to the "realist" logic which was supplanting the idealism of T. H. Green (1836-1882) and F. H. Bradley (1846-1924) at Oxford. It was the Lockean epistemology of the "realists" which was to dominate Oxford philosophy during Collingwood's entire tenure there, isolating him from his colleagues in philosophy. On the other hand, he professes gratitude to Carritt for having given him sound foundation in this philosophy. It was from this realist foundation that he was to move on to develop his own approach, which in his view was neither "realist" nor "idealist":

> At that time [the 1920's], any one opposing the "realists" was automatically classified as an "idealist", which meant a belated survivor of Green's school. There was no ready-made class into which you could put a philosopher who, after a thorough training in "realism", had revolted against it and arrived at conclusions quite unlike anything the school of Green had taught.

During Collingwood's time as an undergraduate, Carritt was preparing a book entitled *The Theory of Beauty*. It contains a lengthy chapter on the aesthetic of Benedetto Croce. This suggests that Collingwood may have had opportunities to discuss Croce with his tutor. But if Carritt did help introduce Collingwood to Croce, the younger man did not wish to remember it in his *Autobiography*. One cannot be entirely convinced by this omission, however, because as an undergraduate Collingwood was not so opposed to the school of Cook Wilson and E. F. Carritt as he later became.

Carritt too is not so critical of Croce's aesthetic as Collingwood's labels might lead one to expect. Carritt devotes to Croce as lengthy a treatment as he accords to any other aesthetician, and he praises him as a man of great philosophical talent. In particular, he esteems Croce for discarding all discussion of the problem of *genres* in art, a problem which Carritt believes is a useless leftover from the eighteenth century. On the other hand, Carritt criticizes Croce's identification of intuition with expression, the same identification which Collingwood was to make in his concept of art as imagination. Carritt also criticizes Croce's identification of expression with beauty and his definition of ugliness as non-expression.

Whatever part Carritt may have had in introducing Croce to Collingwood, there can be little doubt that Carritt influenced Collingwood's views on aesthetics. Later the younger man termed Carritt's *The Theory of Beauty* "the best general introduction to the subject in English," and much of Carritt's terminology reappears in Collingwood's writings on aesthetics. Nevertheless, while Carritt may have shaped the language in which Collingwood reflected on art, it was Croce who influenced the way Collingwood approached the relationship of art to other forms of experience.

Julian Hartt (essay date 1969)

SOURCE: Review of *Faith and Reason: Essays in the Philosophy of Religion,* in *The Journal of Religion,* Vol. 49, No. 3, July, 1969, pp. 280-94.

[*In the following essay, Hartt provides an analysis of Collingwood's religious thought.*]

I

Mr. Rubinoff's subtitle is excessively modest. In the Editor's Introduction [to *Faith and Reason: Essays in the Philosophy of Religion* by R. G. Collingwood], and in the introductions to each of the major divisions of the Collingwood material he presents in this volume, he mounts an interesting and important argument about the consistency of Collingwood's philosophy, early and late. He says: "According to my interpretation . . . Collingwood's thought should be regarded as a gradually developing scale of forms which admits of differences as well as similarities. And such differences as may appear either as a series of irreconcilable inconsistencies or as evidence of significant changes of outlook will emerge, when so regarded, as systematic differences which perform a dialectical function in the system as a whole." Thus he takes the field against such interpreters of Collingwood as T. M. Knox and Alan Donagan who argue that Collingwood's thought suffers from grave inconsistencies (see particularly Donagan, *The Later Philosophy of R. G. Collingwood* [Oxford, 1962]). To make his thesis stick against such meticulous and formidable critics, Mr. Rubinoff will surely need to apply his thesis to Collingwood's later philosophy, since *Faith and Reason* does not carry Collingwood into the extraordinarily creative period of the 1930's. More than that, Rubinoff will have to show that the "gradually developing scale of forms" is the actual internal structure of Collingwood's overall philosophy rather than a hermeneutical device externally applied to his thought in order to render it consistent as well as dialectical.

I should say now that I do not intend in this essay to enter the lists either for or against Mr. Rubinoff's thesis; or otherwise deport myself as though I had the credentials to speak authoritatively on the appropriate questions concerning the development of Collingwood's philosophy. Rather, I wish to focus attention upon some elements of Collingwood's philosophy that have shown remarkable staying power, both in philosophy and in theology, though particularly, for my purposes, in theology. Rubinoff's selection of material from the "early Collingwood," and his clear and even-handed interpretation of this material, have considerable merit for this purpose.

II

Collingwood has been spared the formation of a cult dedicated to the apotheosis of its hero. Even so sympathetic a friend and interpreter as T. M. Knox insists that

Collingwood did not achieve the stature of such luminaries of the first magnitude as Alexander and Whitehead, though he had the promise. And Alan Donagan, who has mounted the most telling argument so far about Collingwood's consistency, is quite ready to sustain the best in Collingwood against the poorer. So also Louis Mink, who has recently provided a striking and cogent interpretation of Collingwood's philosophy of mind. These are hardly to be regarded as so many efforts, along with Rubinoff's, to refurbish an image damaged by major attack or obscured by the mists of time. It is, rather, the case that Collingwood was a remarkably seminal thinker—to use an appraisive term applied many years ago to G. H. Mead by John Dewey. Especially on such themes as Mind, Art, History, Religion, and Civilization, Collingwood said much of enduring importance. I think it may be difficult to prove that his thinking on these things can be rounded off into System, though we wish Rubinoff well as he sets himself to that task. At the very least, Collingwood traces connections among these central elements in the life of spirit. I am at the moment quite prepared to leave it to the philosophers to determine just how systematic that connective tissue is. Collingwood's theological influence flows pre-eminently from his doctrines of history. But that is not the whole story, as I shall now endeavor to indicate.

III

Collingwood was probably not the prime author of historical relativism as a theological viewpoint. I suppose that Troeltsch deserves that honor, such as it is. There is more than a tincture of relativism in Collingwood's theory of history, no doubt, and of the skepticism logically enmeshed in it. But he had his own line of resistance to the skeptical entailment; and this has not yet reached the theological relativists, perhaps because Collingwood's position is deeply involved with an uncommonly sophisticated philosophical doctrine of mind; and theologians do not usually sit in on that game, though they may cozy up to apparent winners. Yet Collingwood's philosophy of history continues to be important for theological purposes. One thinks of H. Richard Niebuhr's *Meaning of Revelation* (New York, 1942). There Niebuhr drew a distinction between inner and outer history that corresponds roughly to Collingwood's distinction between real history on the one hand and chronicle and "scissors-and-paste" history on the other. Too, Collingwood made much of the function of the historian as an interpreter of facts. He did not stop to propound a hermeneutical theory, under that label, at any rate. But he made much of the conviction that "facts" and "meanings" are not given to or found by the historian in isolation from each other. It would be hard offhand to think of a notion dearer the heart of contemporary theology than this: *Meaning* rather than *fact* is after all what *real* history is all about.

There are other sorts of theological affinities with Collingwood's philosophy. For example some theologians represent religion as a constitutive element of human life; and they can discover faith even where it is philosophically denied. So also the early Collingwood:

> Faith is the religious habit of mind. That is to say, it is the attitude which we take up toward things as a whole. There is a certain analogy to it in the attitude which we take up toward a relative or limited whole like our country. We come to know what our country is, what it means to us, by living in it, and acting and thinking as parts of it; we love it in knowing it, and certainly could not know it without loving it. Our devotion to it, our willingness to sacrifice our personal welfare and even our lives to its honor, are elements in our attitude toward it as a whole, and therefore religious elements; but in so far as it is not *the* whole but only *a* whole, that is, at bottom only a finite thing, it is at best only an earthly god and our worship of it is not pure worship but in part idolatrous.

This was written in 1928, in an essay called **"Faith and Reason."** Thus it clearly anticipates the contemporary theological discovery of (*a*) the omni-presence of the "religious element" in human life and (*b*) the polytheistic-idolatrous propensities of man,—things we thought had been discovered by Tillich and the Niebuhrs.

In this same essay Collingwood makes a claim that clearly anticipates a cardinal thesis in Schubert Ogden's philosophical theology. Collingwood writes:

> Practical faith consists in the certainty that life is worth living, that the world into which we have been unwillingly thrust is a world that contains scope for action and will give us a fair chance showing what we are made of; a world in which, if we turn out complete failures, we shall have only ourselves to blame. Practical faith means "accepting the universe," or, what is the same thing, knowing that we are free.

Here we have *in nuce* Ogden's rebuke to the philosophical nay-sayers, in *The Reality of God and Other Essays* (New York, 1966) (particularly, "The Strange Witness of Unbelief"). But we have also a clear anticipation of something Tillich was trying to uncover in the tortuous analysis of despair in *The Courage To Be* (New Haven, Conn., 1952).

Despite these theologians the very recent theological period was dominated by men who wanted no truck with universal religion or with the "religious dimension." Barth was of course the chief spokesman in the attempt to show that (but never very clearly how) Revelation puts religion out of business—at least for the Christian. This was a powerful inducement for theologians to ignore religious phenomena and to get on with the odd business of creating a "religionless Christianity." It is not terribly surprising that religious phenomena are still around. Indeed in the American scene the swinging theologians have had to become apprentice sociologists in order to track down the wonderful diversity of the religious elements in American life; in order thereafter to celebrate properly the spiritual beauties of secularized culture.

I have not yet mentioned what may well be the most important and the most interesting theological affinities with elements of Collingwood's thought. These are: (1) The relation of faith to Absolute Presuppositions. (2) The role of religion in the vicissitudes of Civilization. (3) The fate of Revelation in a systematic or comprehensive philosophy of spirit. I propose to discuss these in the order indicated.

IV

To begin, (1) hardly any element of Collingwood's philosophy has attracted as much interest or drawn as much fire as his doctrine of absolute presuppositions. His formulation of this doctrine (in *An Essay on Metaphysics*) is straightforward, relatively simple, and totally lacking any deliberate hint of mystification. The question-and-answer method of rational enquiry (developed in *An Essay on Philosophical Method*, [London, 1933] but already adumbrated in *The Philosophy of History* [1930]) makes it clear that behind every determinate question there is something already supposed—not, of course, the "answer" but something that puts the question into business. From this alone it appears to follow: (*a*) Behind the method itself lurks an assumption with which the method itself cannot cope, that is, that the world will stand still for rational probes into its meaning. Or, (*b*) any particular enquiry is grounded in something not itself the object of *that* enquiry, for example, "What is the cause of x" presupposes that we know what *cause* means (or, if that is different, how it ought to be used). But if we set out to find out what *cause* is, we should, it seems, be up against either a primordial intuition of the way the world wags, and there's an end on it, or an arbitrary stipulation, an axiom, if you prefer.

There would seem, then, little profit in trying to make something big out of (*b*). It is no doubt true; but it is not very instructive.

But is (*a*) any richer? This depends on what one means by coping with absolute presuppositions. For Collingwood this most explicitly does *not* mean that there is some way of figuring out whether an absolute presupposition, or a set of them, is true or false; for there is not. The explanation for this seems to be very simple: absolute presuppositions are not propositions. The force of this unqualified truth-disclaimer is derived very largely, if not entirely, from his identification of propositions with assertions. This hardly means that absolute presuppositions simply defy statement or expression. It means, so far, that they cannot be argued for or argued against. So with absolute presupposition we are not confronted with something so deeply buried in the psyche that once it is brought up to the light of day, it promptly disintegrates; or, to put it paradoxically, so

soon as it becomes recognizable it loses its identity. It might lose its function. But is Collingwood ready, yet, to identify the meaning of an absolute presupposition with its function?

Collingwood's doctrine does invite trivialization. It might, for instance, be taken to be a peculiarly earnest propounding of a commonplace situation: If I set out to prove x (whatever x is), I must assume that the instrument employed for that purpose is itself valid (or appropriate: in any case one would not say true). Or suppose I say, "If you don't believe the barn is red, look for yourself." I am *not* thereby calling in question either the method of ostensive signs or the reliability of visual perception. Both can be called in question; but neither is in fact called in question by asking, "Isn't the barn red, after all?" Each is actually assumed to be valid. But on Collingwood's terms, they would be relative rather than absolute presuppositions.

So let us try again. Let us say that coming to terms with absolute presuppositions is really a matter of coming to understand them. That sounds something like a hermeneutical enterprise; and the more so when it is re-enforced with the conviction that the metaphysician-historian (for the drive of *An Essay on Metaphysics* is to abolish the distinction between them) cannot smoke out his own (or his culture's?) absolute presuppositions without depriving them of their absoluteness. But set this conviction aside for the moment. What is it to understand an absolute presupposition? It is certainly not a matter of testing or evaluating; so perhaps it is a matter of seeing how such a thing functions, or did function. What is so rewarding about that? Worse yet, how does that differ at all from the history of ideas? Aristotelian science used certain conceptions of *cause*. If you understand Aristotelian science you *eo ipso* understand that absolute presupposition, cause. That is, any system of explanations (scientific, theological, or whatnot) operates with assumptions not explained by the system; but these assumptions are surely exhibited in the system; and anybody who wants to know about those assumptions need only follow out that system. He may still wonder "Well, why *those* assumptions?", but that now means only, "Well, why that system?" And I suppose the only serious answer to that question is, "It seemed to work." And that assumes that the minds or the culture for whom it worked (or seemed to: a subsequent historical judgment?) were satisfied with its answers to the questions they wanted to ask.

Surely another sort of interpretation of absolute presuppositions is conceivable. Perhaps they are pre-dispositions (or even precommitments) that live in a half-lit shadowy backward of the mind. But mind so far as it is rational distrusts shadows: it is dedicated to the illumination and perhaps the expurgation of whatever lurks there. Therefore someone must be delegated to go in after these dim but potent predispositions. And that is the metaphysician. The metaphysician becomes the dredger for absolute presuppositions.

But again something nags at us. Whose absolute presuppositions can the philosophical dredger-man bring up into clear daylight? Not, says Collingwood, his own; or, more properly, I suppose, our own. This does not mean that one cannot be made aware of the absolute presuppositions upon which one's epoch or culture is grounded. I see very little comfort in Collingwood for that kind of irrationalism. But once they are elucidated, what is more natural, indeed what is all but inevitable, but that we should proceed at once into the appraisal of these presuppositions? Something impels us to ask, "Are they true?" And as we have seen, Collingwood believes that question to be nonsense. One can ask, "Is it true?" only of a proposition; and absolute presuppositions are not propositions. But neither are they attitudes or dispositions; for if they were, the historian's task would be hopeless indeed.

Here Professor Louis Mink has come forward with a very helpful suggestion. Collingwood's absolute presuppositions are best understood as being concepts and constellations of concepts. "Like Kant, Collingwood regards a constellation of absolute presuppositions as a system of concepts which provides the formal structure of experience—which determines, that is to say, what we count as an item of experience at all." I should think we would need at once to add: concepts framed or imbedded in some kind or another of linguistic structure, for example, as the subject of a definitional (or axiomatic) sentence: "By cause we mean. . . ." Definitional and axiomatic sentences are not assertions. But they are not easily construable, either, as subrational or prerational determinations of the mind to bend the world one way rather than another or to have it one way rather than another. For in fact various conceptual systems (and probably imaginal ones too) can be constructed upon any given set of definitions.

Now one of the plainest and least avoidable of all historical generalizations is that absolute presuppositions change. But whether changes in dominant world views and in systems of explanation are the *effects* of shifts in absolute presuppositions is far from being that clear. I mean it is neither that clear in Collingwood nor in history itself. It is true for both that every so often it becomes apparent, to properly perceptive and clearheaded minds, that what was lately unquestionable is now open to question and may actually be rejected, either because it is hopelessly obscure or is otiose; or—and I don't see how we can a priori leave this out of consideration—it just seems wrong.

Here we might suppose Collingwood is right, and say that even in an age of pervasive doubt, or in a mind which begins by making doubt a methodological principle (as Descartes is supposed to have done), there has been a shift of absolute presuppositions. The new questions betoken the rise of a new age; and what makes the new questions possible, logically, is no more doubted, and is no more dubitable, than what the now discredited philosophic piety took to be both self-evident and indispensable. But is that shift, that giving-up of one set of absolute presuppositions and the discovery that another set has taken over—is that a rational process? Is it the result of a rational probe that has finally got to the bottom of a mind-set, and not merely seen through a set of axioms; and finds it dubious? Or does it just happen? Does Spirit zig and zag according to a logic of its own, the chief features of which can be made out retrodictively but none of which is available for prophecy?

It is tempting to linger longer over Collingwood's absolute presuppositions as a philosophical-historical problem. But theology is waiting in the wing. What, that is, could be more appealing (except to the hardiest of Revelationists) than to absorb absolute presuppositions into an account of faith? On several counts this seems plausible.

One. Absolute presuppositions are either accepted or rejected—as absolute. As Collingwood says, it is impossible to mount arguments in their behalf. "We must accept them and hold firmly to them; we must insist on presupposing them in all our thinking without asking why they should be thus accepted." Surely it is possible to interpret religious faith in a way very like this, that is, as a phenomenon that has some aspects of decision in it but is not, so to speak, decisively a matter of decision. Faced with threats or with seductive alternatives, the man of faith may then decide to stand fast. But what he clings to, that upon which he stands, was not created or posited by his will, and it will not vanish simply at his wilful spurning.

Two. Faith, too, seems to be something deeper and solider than beliefs, if beliefs are propositions (or assertions). For many theologians of the present age it is self-evident, or at least is indubitably the case, that faith is deeper and existentially far richer than mere belief, so far as belief, is construed propositionally. Indeed, if one had to choose between revelation and faith, it would seem that the religiously sensitive person, to say nothing of one on the alert for falsifications of existence, would ride with faith. For all sorts of other people are always asking about beliefs, "Are they true?"; or, "How would you go at convincing us that they are true?" Whereas it would seem that all a reasonable person could ask about faith is, "Do you or do you not have it?" Beyond this one might venture tentatively to give an autobiographical account both of how one came to have such a thing and of how the world looks when one has it. But it would be a serious mistake if this were understood as a concession that after all faith is about (or refers to) something in such a way that the adequacy or propriety of treating it that way could be debated clearly and fruitfully.

Three. Thus upon the foundation of faith one might weave a life-style; or perhaps even construct a massive society; or—in retrospect—form a cultural epoch. That is, in the first instance, a Christian life; and in the second, the church; and, in the third, Christendom.

Whether or not Collingwood would have approved of such theological exploitations of his theory of absolute presuppositions, I think there is something wrong with this view of faith and that is its virtual isolation from belief taken in a strong sense—the sense of intending a world that is extralinguistic and, for that matter, extra-experiential. "I believe in God" is no doubt a vote of confidence in the way the world is being run. It may also express a disposition to accept gracefully whatever descends upon one from the world beyond our disposi-tions. But a person who wanted to express so generous and withal so vague a sentiment surely would not need to use for this purpose a linguistic vehicle certain to draw the fire of the enemies of "God" rather than en-emies of the sentiment. One can deplore sentiments but one cannot refute them. But if someone tells me that God is the source of my well being and is efficaciously concerned with my ills, I should feel entitled to ask, "Is that so?" rather than merely "Why do you say such odd things?", or, "Well, certainly not many people feel *that* way any more."

So far, then, as faith carries forward some element of belief it is not to be identified with Collingwood's abso-lute presupposition. For what we are urged to hang on to, through thick and thin, is more than an attitude and it is more than a constellation of concepts devoid of assertorial intent or power. The faith to which the reli-gious man clings is a way of construing the whole of experience and the world. Here I think Collingwood, especially in the early period, is right, but only in a very general sort of way. Thereafter differences appear. The Christian believes that his life-orientation is the right one because it conforms, at least in its intent, to what God demands and makes possible of achievement. Thus in what he believes, or accepts on faith, if you prefer, he is exposed to something that judges his life-orientation and his church and his civilization and his cultural epoch. Thus "I believe in God" means that a total ref-ormation, an absolute revolution, is somewhere out there in store for me and for my world. In the meantime the faithful man is therefore faced with a double de-mand: he must make the most of the "system" that is his inheritance; but he must also be ready to see it die.

v

Thus we arrive at the second salient of this essay: (2) the role of religion in the vicissitudes of civilization.

Collingwood, both as a philosopher and as a loyal En-glishman, was gravely concerned over the state of West-ern civilization. In the last ten years of his life Germany mounted yet another barbaric assault upon Christendom. At the beginning of that period, as well as later, he had attacked philosophical trivializers and gamesmen with as much vigor, but hardly with as much coolness, as Berkeley had gone after the "minute philosophers" in his time. Leaving the question of Collingwood's health aside, we can see retrospectively an excellent reason for the difference in tonality: Berkeley had not to face the

totalitarian fanatic looking down the gun barrel at him. We may doubt that the British philosophers Collingwood attacked can be largely blamed for the incredible shortness of vision displayed by political leadership in Britain in the period 1933-40; or for the inertness of the British people as the Nazi gangsters (apparently Collingwood's favorite epithet for them, and it will do) safely inflated bluff after bluff into the ghastly nightmare of an empire of millennial boasts dripping with real blood. But we cannot doubt Collingwood's searing prescience, nor the soundness of the passions which animate that most remarkable of all his writings, *The New Leviathan*. We may, however, wonder whether his earlier concern for the integrity of religion, and for the primordial character of faith, had been diluted, or perhaps even transformed, by the mag-nitude of the threat to the human scheme he had come to believe to have transcendent value; and which he calls Christendom.

Earlier he had given a clear indication of the role of religion vis-a-vis absolute presuppositions. In *An Essay on Metaphysics* he wrote:

> The result of simply presupposing our presup-positions, clinging to them by a sheer act of faith, whether or not we know what they are, whether or not we work out their consequences, is the creation of a religion; and the institutions of a religion have this as their object, to consolidate in believers and perpetuate in their posterity the absolute presuppositions which lie at the root of their thought (p. 197).

> . . . The guardianship of the European 'scientific frame of mind' is vested in the religious in-stitutions of European civilization. . . . For if science is 'experience' interpreted in the light of our general convictions as to the nature of the world, religion is what expresses these convictions in themselves and for their own sake, and hands them on from generation to generation (p. 198).

Thus we are prepared for the conservative-defensive role of religion when Civilization is attacked by barbarians, such as the Saracens, the Turks, the Albigensi and, at last, in Collingwood's waning years, the Germans. Collingwood's account of the Albigensian business is particularly interesting. In this revival of Manichaenism he finds a flat denial of the properly dialectical view of the relation of mind and body. Collingwood does not, of course, approve of the brutality with which the Cathari sects were crushed—although there was violence enough on both sides of the struggle. But he does be-lieve that the metaphysical-moral monotheism of Chris-tian Europe indeed had to be defended against the "eristic" account of body versus mind.

But even if we were persuaded by Collingwood's claims for the religious foundation of the civilization he calls Christendom, we should have to ask what place he is prepared to assign to the prophetic-critical functions of religion in the Western world. I mean specifically the religious-ethical criticism of the social order intended to lay bare infidelity to the Covenant (however construed), rather than to rally citizens to the defense of the order against noxious heresies from within and barbaric assault from without. The prophet may indeed offer a theological interpretation of the barbaric threat: divine punishment for unshriven sin. Even so he is likely to offer a way out or a way through to health—to what Collingwood calls "Peace and Plenty" (**New Leviathan,** chap. xl) and that is a radical amendment of life, corporate and individual. "Let justice roll down like waters and righteousness like a mighty stream." So Amos, and thereafter the prophetic component in Western religion.

Ought we to interpret this religious tradition as being essentially a vivid re-presentation of the absolute presuppositions of the people of God? Or ought we to broaden our understanding of the prophetic performance to include fresh apprehensions of the will of the living God? The rhetoric of the prophet may lead us to confuse proper regard for the foundation of the covenant (again, however construed) with what the people of God (whoever they are) must do now to justify its position in the commonwealth of man. The prophetic element in Western religion is most fertile when it has made and reinforced this distinction. This does not mean that the prophet must appeal to fresh or novel revelations in order to justify his criticisms of the social order. It does mean that the God of his faith is unremittingly attentive to the predicament and the performance of the elect, whoever they are. "He that watches over Israel slumbers not nor sleeps." In this there is great comfort. And there is uncommon threat, too. For it is to this perfectly focused transcendent God to whom mankind answers for every moral flaw, and upon whom the "hope of glory" absolutely depends.

VI

Thus we arrive at the third question: (3) what is the fate of revelation in a comprehensive philosophy of spirit? Obviously the question is manageable only if two antecedent conditions are satisfactorily settled. (*a*) We must be clear about revelation. (*b*) We must come to terms with the principal features of the philosophy of spirit.

a) Revelation has not had an easy ride on the seas of philosophy for a long time. For revelation is religion's greatest offense wherever (to switch metaphors) philosophy has been installed as the grand vizier of the cognitive empire. The heart of the offense is the claim that *x* is knowledge at once of God (the ultimately and decisively real) and of man's true destiny; and this *x* is not a mode or instance of knowing of which either the content or the principle is subsumable under a general account of the cognitive enterprise. The concept of revelation can of course be used in a weaker, humbler and more generous sense, that is, as a religious label for the (not so very wonderful but yet wonderfully useful) habit

reality has of making itself available for man's cognitive appetite (à la Spinoza in *The Theological-Political Tractate*).

Where revelation is understood in the much stronger sense suggested above we can easily analyze the offense into its important parts. One of these is the offense to a comprehensive audit of all cognitive accounts; for it seems self-evident to the modern mind that the auditing system must be a native feature of the natural reason; and revelation challenges that. And then there is the realistic fear that revelation, if it came off, would give its beneficiaries (and their supernaturally appointed heirs and assigns) an enormous advantage over everybody else. One would not need to presuppose the truth of the doctrine of original sin to predict that this advantage would lead sooner or later to grand mischief against the body politic; for the mere presumption of such an advantage has in fact repeatedly done so. So it would have been immensely reassuring to the rest of mankind (or, more likely to its philosophical advocates) had God plainly warned the beneficiaries of his special dispensations against their misuse; or if he had at the same time, if not by the same stroke, appointed general advocates or monitors to protect the interests of the generality of mankind. Philosophers have commonly assumed that office. But in the modern world they have rarely claimed that their reasons for doing so stood on all fours with the special dispensations of Providence. They have, instead, characteristically appealed to the sanctions and warrants of reason as such. This has been their standard contribution to that classic impasse called reason versus revelation.

b) A philosophy of spirit might provide a way around this sterile confrontation. That has been the hope and thereafter the program of a company of philosophical theologians since the early years of the nineteenth century. However plain and grievous the disagreements between Hegel and Schleiermacher, there was a common cause bigger than both of them; and that is the philosophy of spirit. For the philosophy of spirit is a rationally systematic (in that sense scientific) effort to account for human culture as the diverse and yet unitive achievements of mind. Accordingly, philosophy of spirit begins with a phenomenology of mind in order to let its structures and powers become evident. Thereafter it ought to be possible to place (which is not at all the same as explaining) each of the realms of spirit in relation to each other: Science, art, religion, politics, and philosophy itself. It is not necessary to add to this the realm of history, since if the initial or fundamental phenomenology of mind is done adequately the processful or creative-dynamic character of spirit is fully evident from the outset.

Is it a mistake—roughly as important as egregious—to try to subsume such an undertaking under metaphysics, whether or not it is metaphysical idealism, and thereafter limit serious discussion of the matter to such questions as monistic or pluralistic. What about the external world? What about the transcendence of God? How can a thinker dare to be systematic when life everywhere bristles with paradox, absurdity, etc? This move is a patent mistake, no matter how much the later philosophy of Hegel may have fortified it (if it did), because the announced target of the philosophy of spirit is not being and its modes. The subject and the object alike is spirit, the creative potency of man, realized in the objective forms of history. So if one persists in asking, "But what about nature?", the philosopher of spirit can and must reply, "That is what science studies." Or, "But what about God as he *really* is?", can and must evoke the reply, "That is what the forms of the religious life comprehend."

Now I am inclined to think that Rubinoff is right in his thesis, that is, that Collingwood's program was consistent—persistent, rather—from the early writings on philosophy of religion, through **Speculum Mentis,** and on to the end. At the end, in **The New Leviathan,** he is still hard at work on the program; harder than ever, actually, because he could see that spirit itself had come under challenges both brutal and ultra-sophisticated. Thus in 1927 he wrote: "It is by faith that we grasp reality, whether we call that reality by the name of God or by any other name, as immediately and certainly present to us." We have already seen that this knowledge is a kind of intuitive apprehension of the world as a whole. Experience, that is, is a unitary affair, from the outset. It remains to be shown that the world is really a reflection of the mind itself, but not at all in the sense of an ego-projection (à la Fichte). Rather, the world is a spiritual process, essentially dialectical, certainly all-inclusive. Thus in **The Principles of Art** (London, 1938) Collingwood propounds an indispensable element of the program: consciousness as multi-leveled. Since he had already discerned the dialectical structure of spirit he had then to decide whether the forms and levels of spirit are to be construed after the model of a hierarchy or, to the contrary, whether the forms had each its indestructible integrity, within the unity of spirit itself. I think it is clear he opted for the latter. Accordingly, faith and reason are dialectically related to each other, but not art and science. Or, and more tellingly for our purpose, God and man are dialectically related, but not religion and civilization. This means that man as person is not *aufgehoben* into the Absolute. But it also means that "God" is not the odd name of a being existing somehow and somewhere beyond the realm of spirit. In 1916 Collingwood wrote:

> Thus God is at once immanent and transcendent; and man can be regarded as, on the one hand, a part of the universal divine spirit, and on the other, as a person separate from God and capable of opposition to him. God is immanent because all human knowledge and goodness are the very indwelling of his spirit in the mind of man; transcendent because, whether or not man attains to these things, God has attained to them; his being does not depend upon the success of human endeavor.

But lest we fall forthwith into the error of freeing this mysterious self-existence of God from the dialectical life of spirit we must note that

> just as a being really limited in time could not know of its own limitation . . . so a being really finite could not know itself as finite. The self-knowledge of man as finite is already his assertion of himself as infinite.

> God standing aloof from the drama of human sin and redemption, a mere stage manager, is no true symbol of the absolute mind in its concreteness. But this is exactly where the truth of our religious imagery shines most brilliantly. It is God who accepts the burden of error, takes upon himself the moral responsibility for the fall, and so redeems not his creature but himself.

Thus Collingwood's famous reduction of metaphysics to history (**An Essay on Metaphysics**) and the denial of access via history to simple facts of the past (**The Idea of History**) are in principle entirely consistent with the encompassing philosophy of spirit, and in fact are strict requirements of it.

It should therefore be apparent that revelation cannot survive the embrace of such a philosophical program. This is not because religion is swallowed up by an absolute philosophy. It is, rather, because such a belief as revelation expresses is itself taken up into the historical process of spirit; and any possibility of its having a trans-experiential intentionality is systematically eliminated. But, again, this is not because somebody knows that much about the constitution and behavior of reality beyond the mind (or spirit). If Collingwood is right the situation is much simpler and more decisive than that: we have no way in fact of appropriating and interpreting such knowledge that would not in principle destroy the integrity of spirit in its human realizations and aspirations. Thus from revelation we cannot build down and out into the actualities of human life in the round. Whereas from a proper account of spirit we can give the religious dimension (faith plus the supreme dedication to the defense of civilization) an honest priority of immediacy, vividness, and richness relative to the specializations of the cultural-historical forms of life.

VII

The work of Rubinoff, Mink, and Donagan is bringing Collingwood back into the scene as a philosopher of considerable magnitude. It is clear that his work as a philosophical theologian can be ignored only by thinkers who continue piously to believe that Barth (or somebody or other) demolished any and every philosophical theology as a thing of any relevance for the interpretation of the Christian faith. The third volume of Tillich's *Systematic Theology* is quite enough, by itself, to show us that that negative attitude suffers from premature closure—or, in less neutral terms, from dogmatism. It may be the case that revelation does not need and cannot profit from a philosophy of spirit. That needs to be demonstrated rather than merely asserted. I should think that Barth's *Church Dogmatics,* Vol. III ("Creation"), could only with severe difficulties be absorbed into such a demonstration.

Louis O. Mink (essay date 1969)

SOURCE: "The Dialectic of Experience," in *Mind, History, and Dialectic: The Philosophy of R. G. Collingwood,* Indiana University Press, 1969, pp. 7-58.

[*In the following excerpt, Mink discusses* Speculum Mentis *as a work that introduced and coordinated the major issues elaborated in Collingwood's later writings.*]

1   COLLINGWOOD'S PENTATEUCH OF FORMS OF EXPERIENCE: A SUMMARY

Throughout his life Collingwood occupied himself with the relations and differences among art, religion, science, history, and philosophy, regarded sometimes as ways of life, sometimes as types of experience, and sometimes as modes of knowledge. At least one of his books is devoted to each of these, as their titles indicate: *Religion and Philosophy* (1916); *Outlines of a Philosophy of Art* (1925) and *Principles of Art* (1938); *The Idea of Nature* (1945); *The Idea of History* (1946); and, of course all of these, but also the *Essay on Philosophical Method* (1933), the *Autobiography* (1939), and the *Essay on Metaphysics* (1940) occupy themselves specifically with philosophy. Only *The New Leviathan* (1942) does not discuss explicitly and at length these special forms of experience and knowledge.

Again and again he returned to the task of drawing up constitutions for the kingdom of knowledge, and although he never argued that his Pentateuch of Art, Religion, Science, History, and Philosophy is an exhaustive list, in practice it remained canonical, although the importance of Religion as a separate category became attenuated after 1928, as he came to identify his categories less with "ways of life" and more with types and methods of knowledge. In an important way this series of constitutions provides a reduced and brilliant image of the changes (or development) of his thought, which sometimes are matters of nuance or emphasis, sometimes more fundamental alterations.

But although he undertook repeatedly to distinguish history from science, or philosophy from religion (always in such a way as to describe their connections as well as their differences) it is only in *Speculum Mentis* that he drafted a complete constitution, with equal attention to each of the five areas. While in his later books many of his ideas underwent modification and change, I am convinced (and it is consistent with his own later views about historical understanding) that it is only

against the background of *Speculum Mentis* that his later views can be correctly interpreted.

Speculum Mentis deals not with a single problem but with an entire family of problems, all of which arise out of reflection on the entire range of experience. As stated in the Prologue, the progenitor of these problems is the disintegration in the modern world of the conception—or rather of the *possibility,* since the conception survives to plague us by its lack of exemplification—of a "complete and undivided life," of experience regarded as an integrated *whole,* which Collingwood took to be a characteristic virtue of the medieval outlook. This is an outlook which we could not recover if we would—an enterprise which the attempts of neo-medievalists have not made more attractive. Yet, lacking that integrity by which the diversity of human activity was hierarchically organized under the unifying principle of faith, the special problem of modern life is that an increasingly unsatisfied demand for beauty, faith, and knowledge coexists with unwanted overproduction of art, religion, and philosophy. Moreover, these are detached from each other, so that they are separately unsatisfying and collectively unrelated. One can dabble in each, but how to combine them in a single complex unity, a *life,* is not understood.

There do exist ways of life which are alien but fascinating in their single-minded exclusiveness, and which for this very reason provide rich themes for biography and fiction. It is the plunge into a single form of life which unites Thomas Merton and Gulley Jimson, but at the same time separates the religious life from the artist's life. To one who is curious about both forms of life but exemplifies neither, there are problems of understanding. What connection, if any, is there between aesthetic experience and religious experience? There are, of course, theories about this: the view that religious experience is a work of aesthetic imagination or the counterview that art is a form of religious expression—even when demonic. Both views are, as answers to such questions tend to be, reductive. Similar questions, in their most general form too well known to require listing, arise about the relation of religion to science, science to art, history to philosophy, and so on; again, answers are most often reductive, and are notable more for their number than for their cogency.

In *Speculum Mentis,* Collingwood sets out unabashedly to adjudicate the rival claims of all the major kinds of experience or "forms of consciousness." Such an ambition might appear immodest, but it is in fact what philosophers have always attempted collectively and often individually. It is sanctioned by both traditional and contemporary views of the philosopher's job, and both views are represented in the division and classification which Collingwood makes of major kinds of experience. He has two criteria for recognizing an activity as a "form of consciousness": it must in fact be capable of being regarded (even though in the end this may not be consistently possible), as a "way of life," enlisting all of one's faculties and energies, and at the same time it must be a claim to knowledge about the world or to a method of achieving knowledge. The former criterion is the older meaning of "philosophy," the sense in which both slave and emperor could be Stoic philosophers. The latter is the modern meaning of philosophy as the critique of knowledge—the sense in which Hume could give up philosophy as a young man and Whitehead could take it up as an old one. That Collingwood unites the two indicates his belief that the elucidation of experience and the critical analysis of theory can and must be done together.

These two criteria also jointly limit the possible forms of consciousness. They rule out the political and the economic lives merely as such, because utilitarian activity does not make a claim to knowledge although it may be the practical side of a form of consciousness which does. The criteria do not admit the differences between social, monastic, and reclusive life as fundamental, nor do they distinguish between types of personality or between cosmic attitudes such as pessimism and optimism. In fact, Collingwood finds only five candidates: Art, Religion, Science, History, and Philosophy. It is well to capitalize the names, as he does, not as honorific designations nor in order subtly to reify them, but as a reminder that in **Speculum Mentis** they do not necessarily refer to the professional or institutional activities called by those names in common language and by Collingwood himself in his later books. One might think of them initially as what we comfortably, if not very clearly, refer to as the aesthetic attitude, the religious life, scientific inquiry, the historical consciousness, and the philosophical temper.

Art. By "Art," Collingwood means the activity and the products of imagination suspended from all questions and claims about the reality of the objects of imagination. Art (or imagination) asserts nothing, or rather, it can suppose everything without considering the question of the coherence of different acts or products of imagination. Whether a portrait "looks like" its model is not a question for Art (although this may be difficult to explain to a sitter who has paid for a satisfactory likeness). Nor is it a flaw in Sophocles' *Antigone* that the officious Creon of that play cannot be recognized as the wise and patient Creon of *Oedipus Rex*. Hence a primary characteristic of imagination is what Collingwood calls the "monadism of art," the reference being not to Leibniz's principle that "each monad mirrors the universe" but to his description of monads as "windowless," unrelated to and unaffected by all other monads.

Now "art" here clearly means not the artifacts viewed in galleries and the compositions reproduced in concert halls, but imaginative *acts,* whether of artist or spectator. Aesthetic experience as such does not distinguish between a limited class of things called "works of art" and the rest of the world; it is a possible attitude which may be taken up toward anything. It may be illustrated by what Collingwood elsewhere called the "principle of the picture-frame," referring to the conscious act of attention by which, imaginatively, a frame can be set around part of the extended visual or auditory fields and what lies within the frame perceived as pure spectacle. Such an experiment is not difficult, and its results can be extraordinary: a bleak industrial wasteland, grimy and depressing, can take on an entirely different visual character when a segment is "framed" and regarded, so to speak, two-dimensionally rather than three-dimensionally. (Learning to draw in perspective requires a similar cultivated act of attention; in Collingwood's view it is quite right to regard this as already an imaginative act rather than a technical skill in the service of imagination.) Looked at from this standpoint, it is possible to see (although the example is not Collingwood's) the sense in which photography can be one of the *beaux-arts*. Many would deny photography the name of art on the grounds that a technical apparatus performs all of the functions usually associated with artistic creation. And so it does; but selecting a point of vantage, composing the picture within the frame, and changing the frame in the process of developing the prints are nevertheless all imaginative acts, in Collingwood's sense.

The implications of identifying art with imagination rather than with a class of artifacts, with complex human activity rather than with physical objects, were not fully worked out by Collingwood until **The Principles of Art**. But the problem at hand is a different one: the claim of Art to be a possible way of life and a form of knowledge. One might think, regarding with a disenchanted eye the excesses of a century and a half of Romanticism, that neither claim has been made good or is likely to be. But it remains to understand why this should be so. In Collingwood's view, it is because the aesthetic life is inherently unstable and the aesthetic claim to immediate and intuitive knowledge is inherently inconsistent. The instability of a life of pure imagination might be thought due to the fact that a world of physical necessities exacts ultimate penalties from anyone who tries to convert it into pure spectacle. Standing in the middle of a busy road, one might manage to regard the approaching vehicles with disinterested imagination, but not for long. And imaginatively framing a bowl of slowly rotting fruit as model for a still-life will hardly protect a painter from the pangs or the effects of hunger. But although such considerations are obvious, Collingwood's point is that the world of fact does not merely constrain the aesthetic imagination but is necessary to it; and therefore in regarding itself as rejecting the world of fact the aesthetic consciousness is deceiving itself. But imagination, as such, is incapable of reflecting on itself, and therefore cannot recognize that it is necessarily dependent on what as a form of consciousness it excludes.

The instability of the "aesthetic life," in fact, is a consequence of the impossibility of maintaining the attitude of imagination without *assertion*. This attitude is like—and in Collingwood's view it *is*—an attitude of questioning or supposing which anticipates no answer or resulting assertion. But questioning, he argues, presupposes assertions which make the questions important or relevant; and it implies the possibility of an answer. Otherwise there would be no way of distinguishing one supposal from another.

This may seem a strained and over-intellectual analogy when applied to art. It is not without relevance to representational art, the epic and the novel, drama, and narrative dance; but in what sense are absolute music and non-objective art "supposals" or "questions"? They are, of course, suspensions of assertion; but a painting by Kandinsky would seem to be a suspension of assertion in a sense quite different from Dante's *Inferno*. The latter, despite its topographical detail, does not *assert* that one will find the entrance to Hell or the Mount of Purgatory if one explores the actual surface of the world we walk. There seems a lacuna here. In part, it was recognized and developed by Collingwood in *The Principles of Art,* where by careful argument he identified imagination with expression (an identification which, he remarked in *Speculum Mentis,* Croce had unsuccessfully attempted). But even so, it would be a mistake to suppose that the attitude of "questioning" means that a work of art asks a specific question or set of questions which could be given alternative verbal formulation. It refers rather to the act of imagination in general, not to this or that act of imagination; and in this sense, an imaginative act may be considered a general supposal that its object can be isolated from all other experience—without regard to what this other experience may be.

The instability of imagination as a claim to knowledge results from the fact that this claim cannot even be made without abandoning the standpoint of the immediacy of intuition. This may seem obvious, but there is also a special argument for it which is essential to Collingwood's project of relating Art to other forms of experience. The inadequacy of any general theory of intuitive knowledge is simply that no *theory* itself is intuitive. A claim to knowledge must at least be defended by an argument whose cogency as an argument is not incompatible with the truth of its conclusions. But this is just what occurs when the deliverances of intuitive immediacy are extended to include all possible knowledge: the possibility of an *argument* for this conclusion is ruled out together with all other arguments. It is not *prima facie* self-contradictory to believe that in art truths are revealed which are not accessible in other ways, and indeed this has been widely believed. But in any case one cannot defend this view without appealing to other standards of knowledge beyond the revelations of art. In his well-known study of Beethoven, Mr. J. W. N. Sullivan claimed that Beethoven had reached heights of understanding not available to more earth-bound spirits, and had expressed these insights in his late quartets and sonatas. But how could Sullivan discover this? If by the same process, presumably we should have another quartet—by Sullivan—rather than a book. But if by some other means, then Beethoven's late works, if they do in

fact show forth a kind of knowledge, are checks for large amounts on a bank which is never open for business.

Collingwood's special argument for rejecting the claims of intuition both rests on and reveals his fundamental conception of experience, a conception whose most notable feature is the rejection of all dualisms: the dualism of data and interpretation (here he departs from empiricism), and the dualism of emotion and intellect (here he departs from rationalism in both its exigent and mitigated forms). In this case the dualism rejected is that of intuition—whether sensation or imagination—and thought. *All* experience, from the perception of a color to the logical analysis of abstract argument, Collingwood regards as both intuitive *and* conceptual; "it is all intuitive and all conceptual." The merits of this thesis may be debated later; at the moment it is its consequences that we are after. And the immediate consequence is that Art as a claim to knowledge is a claim to be merely intuitive, whereas it is at the same time implicitly conceptual although it represses its dim awareness of this fact and cannot in fact make it explicit without ceasing to be Art as such.

But to say that Art as a form of life is implicitly conceptual does not mean (as it did for Schopenhauer) that a *work of art* fleshes out a concept in vivid and particular illustration, as if every narrative must have a moral and every bit of music a "meaning." Collingwood uses the vocabulary of Hegel: intuition is "immediate," conceptual thought "mediates." But what is meant is not difficult to see: the immediacy of intuition (which still refers to imagination, regarded as a kind of knowledge) refers to the surface qualities of experience as such: the blueness of a blue patch, the pitch and timbre of a note or the legato or staccato quality of a melody. It also refers to the ease and fluency of a logical inference or to the frustrating puzzlement of a paradox; many years later, Collingwood pointed out in *The Principles of Art* that as emotion is never independent of reason, so reason is never independent of emotion, and there are "emotions of reason." "Mediation" is simply experience reflected on and become self-conscious. In Art such reflection might seem to result in the acceptance of "standards," such as correct perspective in drawing, or the Unities in drama; the aesthetics of classicism was such an attempt to subordinate imagination to abstract and even mathematical formulae. Collingwood's point is that, entirely apart from this, any conscious *control* of imagination has already imposed some standard, however implicit. So the dramatist introduces a character, the painter thumbs out a line ("A little more? There, that's it.") because the work in progress seems to demand it. It is useless to ask him why, or to try to explain why, in any theory of general application. But some standard of relevance, fittingness, or appropriateness is at work here. It is not *applied* to experience, because it is *part of* experience itself; but it is not part of intuition itself. There survives here the ancient Platonic doctrine that recognition and comparison are implicitly conceptual;

but Collingwood denies that a purely intellectual concept is being applied to a purely sensuous experience. "This blue is brighter than that" is both intuitive (so far as the blues are concerned) *and* conceptual (so far as the relation "brighter than" is concerned), and neither can be isolated from the other. Without the relation, there are not two blues; and without the blues there is no relation. Intuition and conceptual thought are not two different kinds of experience or functions of mind. Rather, intuition is that aspect of any experience which is immediate and unreflective; thought is that aspect of any experience which reflects upon itself or is capable of doing so. The form of experience called Art is precisely that aesthetic attitude which claims to be wholly intuitive; in fact, however, it is implicitly conceptual. To articulate its structure through self-reflection does not destroy the immediacy of imagination but supersedes its tacit claim to stability and exclusiveness.

Religion. The life of Art, therefore, is an error when it claims to be an exclusive possibility. But this failure is felt before it can be understood. It is felt as the failure of the imagination to assert a world of fact which it necessarily presupposes, to commit itself to a claim which it suggests in failing to make it. Art imagines but does not assert, even though imagining is a kind of supposal and supposal is a transient stage in the process leading to assertion. What carries this process to its end Collingwood calls "Religion." Religion is imagination which believes in the reality of its own products.

This definition of religion is not novel; it resembles Feuerbach's and is subject to the criticisms which have been brought against Feuerbach. It is easy to object that the definition seems designed to apply only to religions with an elaborated mythology and rules out purely ethical religions such as Confucianism. Yet no definition of religion can be made as a satisfactory inductive generalization which will simultaneously satisfy the demand of including everything ever referred to by the term and yet avoid the sterility of utter vagueness. The utility of definitions in such cases is to call attention to certain features commonly overlooked or underestimated; and in Collingwood's case it is intended to find a way of relating some, if not all, important features of religion to some, if not all, important features of art and science. From this standpoint, the relation, if arguable, is clear and memorable: Religion is Art asserting and worshipping its own object. But since this object is asserted as real, many consequences follow: where Art is monadic, hence pluralistic and tolerant, Religion claims its assertions to be *true,* hence all incompatible assertions to be false. Where the products of Art are not related at all to each other (although *we* may compare them), Religion is *cosmological,* and for the first time conceives the world as a single ordered whole; hence it is also *social,* both in the sense that it defines a community of believers and in the sense that this community must have *some* attitude toward unbelievers, for example, that "all those who are not for us are against us." Finally, it is credal,

its creed preserving, defining and encouraging the central imaginative act.

But Religion, too, is subject to an inner development of the sort which revealed the instability of Art both as a way of life and as a claim to knowledge. This comes about, again, because Religion, although a legitimate and necessary kind of experience, cannot preserve its characteristics unaltered *once it becomes conscious of them.* The special problem of religion is that the direct objects of religious consciousness are symbolic, pointing to meanings which they do not contain. Yet their efficacy as symbols depends on the fact that religious consciousness ignores this distinction, which, in Collingwood's language, is only "implicit." Hence the literal acceptance of ritual and creed is natural and inevitable, but unstable. In one of his apter metaphors, Collingwood says that Religion is "thought growing up in the husk of language, and as yet unconscious that language and thought are different things. The distinction between what we say and what we mean, between a symbol or word and its meaning, is a distinction in the light of which alone it is possible to understand religion; but it is a distinction hidden from religion itself."

Now this observation is in principle the legacy of the nineteenth century study of comparative religion and of the development of the "higher criticism" of the Old and New Testaments, which ended forever the literalist interpretation of Biblical mythology and chronicle except for sectarian groups determined to remain in a state of intellectual arrest. But Collingwood puts uncritical Religion in a novel framework in showing its development out of Art and its issue in Science. The conflict between "science and religion" can be seen in a new light: its basis is no longer a conflict between the superstitious literalism of religion and an enlightened scientific method, but a conflict between religion not yet conscious and religion become conscious of the distinction which defines it. (The historical implication is that the intellectual method of the sciences was itself a product of this religious instability; and in fact Collingwood maintained this historical thesis in *The Idea of Nature,* the *Essay on Metaphysics,* and finally in *The New Leviathan*.) Once the religious attitude has become aware that what it *says* is not what it *means,* it is a legitimate object for rational criticism, but the enlightened rationalism which points out that the concrete imagery of religion is neither historically true nor scientifically possible is using a weapon which has been forged and put into its hands by the development of Religion itself. And yet there is no return; as criticism owes its possibility to Religion itself, so in turn it produces a theology which reinterprets religious assertions to accommodate the meanings which have been uncovered. But as Collingwood observes, this reinterpretation is not a defense of Religion, but its negation. Theology cannot recover the lost innocence of the encompassing religious life, because it has recognized distinctions and accepted critical standards the *unawareness* of which is an essential characteristic of what it purports to defend.

It has, in being explicitly a mode of thinking, forfeited its chance to return to the innocence of implicit thought.

The transition from immediacy to self-consciousness within Religion is a revolution sharper than the transition from Art to Religion. That replaced supposal by assertion, this replaces language by thought, or rather by a fusion of thought and language in which the two cannot be sharply distinguished. For the first time, therefore, a logic of propositions is possible, the proposition being the meaning expressed in a statement—e.g., the meaning, unstatable in itself, of equivalent sentences. Religion, like Art, therefore, turns out to be a "philosophical error": not as worship, which is the natural state of the religious consciousness, but as theology, which introduces standards of explication of meaning and criticism of inference which are alien to the primary religious consciousness. In fact, "theology is a manifestation not of the religious spirit but of the scientific spirit," and therefore it is not a mode of experience but a transition to a different mode of experience.

Science. By "Religion" Collingwood obviously means something more limited than the extended contemporary senses of this term. On the other hand, by "Science" he means something much broader than the contemporary restriction of the term to the natural sciences. In neither case is he attempting a general description of all the things which happen to be called by a single name, but rather is identifying something like an ideal type to which a variety of instances more or less closely approximate. The first characteristic of "Science" is that is a kind of thinking aware of itself as such or "explicit"; in both Art and Religion, thought is present, but only as "implicit." The primary objects of this self-conscious kind of thinking are not concrete objects of imagination, as in both Art and Religion, but concepts, or abstract universals. "Object of imagination" is itself, for example, a concept, as is "object of thought." And so are all the terms—"imagination," "relation," "supposal," "assertion"—in which Art and Religion are *described,* but which do not appear in their own vocabularies. "Classification is the key-note of the scientific spirit; but classification is nothing but the abstractness of the scientific concept."

Collingwood's discussion of Science yields nothing in abstractness to Science itself. He is not generous with examples, but it is clear that his paradigm of science is not experimental inquiry but mathematics; it is not Faraday whom he has in mind but Plato and the Platonic insistence on the unintelligibility of phenomena, like triangles scratched in the sand, apart from the intelligibility of concepts, like the concept of triangle. In effect, he imputes Platonism to science (and not unreasonably so) when he describes Science as the "affirmation of the abstract or classificatory concept as real." (Art, it will be recalled, makes no assertions at all; Religion asserts the reality of an object, but one which is imaginative rather than conceptual.) Such a description resembles Whitehead's "fallacy of misplaced con-

creteness" (which it antedated by a year), but it is easier to bring out Collingwood's point if one remembers that he was not, like Whitehead, referring directly to contemporary physics. Otherwise some of Collingwood's statements seem simply perverse: "Sensuous experience is . . . unnecessary to the scientist, and all he has to do is to think." This is true of a mathematician if of anyone; and Collingwood emphasizes that mathematics is an exact or a priori science, the only one which is an unalloyed instance of his description. He claims, however, that the description has other applications, because it accounts for the mechanism (determinism) and materialism of empirical natural science: mechanism because physical events are regarded as indifferently comparable instances of abstractly formulated laws, materialism because the abstract universal is "indifferent to its own particulars." This is, I think, exactly the meaning of "materialism" which Russell had in mind when he said that "matter is whatever satisfies the equations of physics"; and in this sense Collingwood is quite right in saying that "mathematics, mechanism, and materialism are the three marks of all science"; but the description is less interesting than it seems because "mechanism" and "materialism" are so broadly conceived that they include what ordinarily have been regarded as alternatives to them (e.g., vitalism, since the concept of "entelechy" has the same indifference to its manifestations as an abstract universal to its instances).

Collingwood knows perfectly well that modern natural science is empirical and that scientific hypotheses are related in complex ways to statements of experimental and observational evidence. He recognizes the heuristic necessity of factual experience in *suggesting* hypotheses, even in mathematics; but, strangely, he does not discuss what contemporary philosophy of science has so exhaustively explored, the confirmation and disconfirmation of hypotheses by the facts of the case. In part, this omission is dictated by his scheme: he wishes to reserve the "realm of fact" as the proper object of "historical" rather than of "scientific" thinking. But it is not merely gratuitous, if one distinguishes between an abstract and concrete sense of "fact": what *counts* as a fact in science is nothing more than the givenness, the datum-character of properties relevant to a hypothesis: "Scientific fact is a fact purged of its crude and scientifically scandalous concreteness, isolated from its historical setting and reduced to the status of a mere instance of a rule." And, of course, it goes without saying that "concrete" fact is not just an aggregate or congeries of abstract "facts."

What Collingwood is aiming at here should now be clear: he wishes to show that what he chooses to call History emerges from Science as its development and fulfillment, as Science in its turn emerged from Religion and Religion emerged from Art. He thinks that the history of science since the Renaissance suggests this because of the introduction into sciences such as astronomy, geology, and biology of the temporal dimension: astronomy becomes the history of the universe, biology the history of species, and so on. This can hardly be taken seriously as more than an academic pun, because "history" in this case means no more than "change over time," and has nothing significant in common with what Collingwood himself means by "History." But he adverts to a second argument for the necessary passage from Science to History, namely that the framing and exploration of hypotheses itself *presupposes* the possession of an ordered body of facts, and "these facts, as actually ascertained by observation and experiment, are matter of history". That this argument is not lightly advanced is indicated by the fact that Collingwood restated it without significant change, years afterward, in the conclusion to **The Idea of Nature**.

Now this argument inverts the commonly accepted opinion that the mere observation and recording of facts belongs to an elementary "natural history" stage of science and is to a more advanced theoretical stage as butterfly-collecting, say, is to genetics. In the accepted view, it is the ordinary activities of historians which are proto-scientific, rather than the ordinary activities of scientists which are proto-historical. Collingwood surely cannot mean that what we know as science will, as it becomes more sophisticated, look more and more like what we know as history. (It has been widely held, and one can at least imagine the possibility, that future historiography will be more like present natural science—like a science of society, that is—whenever it is not merely chronology or antiquarianism. None of this has anything to do, of course, with the use of scientific methods, like chemical analysis or carbon-14 dating of artifacts, by historians.)

Yet Collingwood is not just playing Paris to History's Aphrodite. The clue to his apparent inversion of the order of thought from the unintelligible aggregation of particular facts to the intelligible unity of an explanatory theory lies, I think, in the notion, as yet unclarified, of *self-consciousness*. Science as science need not be consciously aware of what it presupposes; yet once it has become so aware, it has reached a coign of vantage beyond itself. The analogy here is not to what has earlier been said of the relation between Art and Religion but to the different relation between Religion and theology: theology (which is implicit Science) is Religion become critical of its own meanings and claims. And something like this occurs when Science becomes aware of its own activity and *simultaneously aware* that, insofar as it attempts to describe, explain, or justify itself, *this* activity is not itself scientific inquiry, but something else.

Now when Science reaches the stage of recognizing this, Collingwood claims, it is able to see how much it has taken for granted. Beginning *in medias res,* as it were, it frames hypotheses about whole classes of events which exist for it as *data,* although the events belong to the past and as such are objects of *historical* knowledge (even though this may be individual memory). Perhaps this can be accepted as a truism; but it does not seem to

justify the startling conclusion that "natural science as a form of thought exists and always has existed in a context of history, and depends on historical thought for its existence." For one thing, the form of thought which we call specifically history "did not exist before the eighteenth century." What Collingwood himself refers to in **The Idea of Nature** as science is at least as old as the Renaissance; how can it "depend for its existence on a form of thought" which it antedates by centuries?

Misunderstanding, at this crucial point, of the relation of Science and History is easy and almost inevitable, and Collingwood himself does not avoid misstating his point or obscuring it by special pleading. His argument in summary seems to be: Science as abstract, theoretical, and hypothetical presupposes a world of concrete facts to which its statements refer but which they do not exhaust. What does deal with them, at least in principle, is History. So Science as a form of thought is less adequate than and is fulfilled in History.

But as Collingwood sometimes fails to distinguish between nature and science, so here he fails to distinguish between history and the theory of history. Hence the shimmering ambiguity of a statement like this: "I venture to infer that no one can understand natural science unless he understands history: and that no one can answer the question what nature is unless he knows what history is." The word "history," in the most natural reading of this, should mean "historical thought" in the first statement and "historical reality" in the second. Yet if we interchange these, we get two entirely different statements, namely that one can understand natural science only in terms of its own (real) history, and nature itself only as the object of a science historically understood.

To bring out the same point in a different way: one should not interpret Collingwood (despite his own encouragement) to mean merely that scientists use records of past observations, and so on, and therefore in order to be complete scientists should be better historians. Rather he means: if one *reflects on* the process of scientific inquiry (and a scientist may well not do so) he becomes aware that scientific facts are classes of occasions on which certain observations have been made, and these observations are, for us, historical facts. The problem is not, except in rare cases, whether they are indeed facts; it lies in the *concept* of historical fact, and this is a matter of the theory of historical knowledge. Thus it is not that a particular piece of scientific research leads on to a specific problem of historical research, but that the scientific attitude becomes aware of itself as an historical phenomenon and raises questions which call for a *theory* of history. Why, for example, has organized science been a phenomenon of Western civilization, and cumulative science as we know it today a phenomenon of the post-Renaissance period? Can one give a satisfactory account of what natural science is without taking these questions into consideration? It is not surprising that when Collingwood came to write that part of his systematic philosophy which would deal with Science, he produced not a philosophy of science but a history of the idea of nature, and found that different concepts of nature have been the presuppositions of different (Greek, medieval, modern) ideals of scientific inquiry.

History. As Science is the assertion of abstractions (concepts, theories), History is the affirmation of fact. As a form of thought, its object is the past and the present, but it is only incidentally the "study of the past," and that because there are no future facts. But, in any case, History is not the affirmation of facts as a disjunct plurality but of the "world of fact" as a concrete unity; the former is the province of Science, because its "facts" are abstractions from the latter. It is the concreteness of fact, not its pastness, which distinguishes it as the object of History. And the emphasis on "concreteness" rather than on pastness is underlined by Collingwood when he takes *perception* to be the origin and a specific instance of historical thought. There is a faint echo in this somewhat odd use of the term "history" of Locke's "historical, plain method," a non-temporal meaning which otherwise survives today only in the term "natural history." It is clearly not Collingwood's intention merely to insist on a niggling etymological propriety; yet what is historical consciousness, apart from the fact that it is not Science, and what is the "concrete" apart from the fact that it is not the abstract?

As usual, Collingwood is less than helpful in his habit of conflating several different meanings in a single term. In this case there seem to be two main ones: with respect to knowledge, the concrete is the complete rather than the partial; with respect to the objects of knowledge, it is the independence of those objects from our ways of understanding them. Moreover, for Collingwood, Science deals only with *particulars,* artificially marked off or abstracted from the web of relations in which they actually stand; only History can deal with *individuality,* for "individuality is concreteness." (And like Spinoza and Hegel, Collingwood's final judgment is that there can be only *one* true "individual," that which appears to the incomplete perspective of History as "*the* world of fact.")

To call History "concrete" thus refers at least to our inescapable sense of the expanding web of real relations in the environing world; it is the feeling of "More!" demanded by the real world of our every attempt to capture it in description or explanation, or rather it is this feeling elevated to conscious recognition. But "concrete" may also refer to the world of fact itself, standing resolutely over against any claim to knowledge of it. Collingwood is unlikely to have committed the simple fallacy of confusing knowledge *of* something concrete with knowledge as itself concrete, even though he does often verge on the philosopher's bad habit of letting nature solve his problems for him. (Speaking of "dialectical opposites" at one point, he says, "Hold up a stick and distinguish its top and bottom; there you have a

concrete synthesis of opposites in an individual whole." But one cannot *explain* how "opposites" are "synthesized" by pointing to a natural object, as if to say, "It has solved the problem, so surely *we* can." Sticks do not have problems, nor syntheses either.) He not only recognizes the difference between historical knowledge and its object, but attributes to this difference the "breakdown of history." The *object* of history is the infinite world of facts, an indefinitely complex totality of events and relationships; historical knowledge, on the other hand, is inescapably fragmentary and specialized. Hence its "superiority" to Science lies not in its practice but in its ideal conception of itself. The theoretical concepts of Science do not exhaust the world, but scientific thought can encompass them because they are its own constructions. The ideal object of History is the concrete world itself; it explains an event not by exhibiting it as an instance of a theoretical law but by tracing out in detail its real connections with the web of real events—it seeks the genealogy of events, as it were, rather than their genetics. But this means that every piece of history is necessarily regarded as part of a universal history of which there is no historian. Collingwood's point might be put this way: Science's concept of reality is attenuated but its performance is excellent; History's concept of reality is adequate but its performance is correspondingly unsatisfactory. Science dips a wide-meshed net which brings up a fraction of the ocean's teeming life; History dips a narrow-meshed net which brings up more than anyone can enumerate and describe; it faces the terrifying plenitude of *was eigentlich gewesen ist.*

So the sense of the concrete is in jarring conflict with the limitations of inquiry: "History is an unstable attitude which leads either back into science or forward into philosophy, according as the intellectual vigour of the historian is exhausted or stimulated by his attempt to get rid of the abstractions of science." It is natural, of course, for professional historians (whose own form of experience may well be that of Science) to attempt to justify the specialization of historical inquiry by convincing themselves that historical events and processes can be isolated from one another as particular objects of inquiry; this is exemplified, for example, in periodization, although every historian will allow that there are no cut-off dates, the events earlier or later than which are of no relevance to, say, the Renaissance historian. But specialization cuts the Gordian knot only by relapsing into a pre-historical mode of experience: either it atomizes history into events which can be classified and regarded as instances of general laws, or it decomposes history into wholly unique and individual histories (e.g., biographies). The former is the atomism of Science, the latter the "Monadism" of imagination, or Art. So the historical consciousness is as unstable in its own way as the modes of experience which have preceded it. It is, in fact, the "*reductio ad absurdum* of all knowledge considered as knowledge of an objective reality independent of the knowing mind." History, as it were, makes explicit an insoluble problem which was already implicit in the religious consciousness: it is the assertion of a completely objective and independent reality which in the end turns out to permit no knowledge of such a reality sufficient even to support the initial affirmation.

Probably no one would deny that this problem—or puzzle, or impasse—is the armature on which the history of philosophy has bit by bit sculpted its own body. Such a metaphor, if a bit strained, is a not inapt reference to Collingwood's view of *mind,* however, which he regards as having, like the history of philosophy itself, continuously recreated itself out of its own substance. So the Gordian knot of History's inability to realize its own ideal can be untied only by achieving the self-conscious recognition that the problem is one *of its own creation*; but in attaining this recognition it passes over into Philosophy. In technical terms, Collingwood regards History as taking for granted an epistemological distinction between subject (the activity of knowing) and object (the object of knowledge). But this distinction is itself an abstraction, a survival, as it were, of Science in the mode of History. How could it be avoided? By recognizing that "the world of fact which is explicitly studied in history is . . . implicitly nothing but the knowing mind as such."

This may seem like solving a puzzle with a paradox; and Collingwood barely pauses to justify the identification of subject and object by the a priori argument that a mind's error about its own nature distorts its activity in a way appropriate to the error, from which it follows that no object of mental activity can be independent of the way in which it is known.

It would, I think, be a mistake to try to distill from **Speculum Mentis** alone what Collingwood might have meant by his cavalier identification of the historical *object* as the "knowing mind." The record of his succeeding books, especially **The Idea of History** and the **Essay on Metaphysics** is, as we shall see, clearly the history of his continuing attempt to explain it to himself. In **Speculum Mentis** he was bemused by the use to which he could put the formula without fully elucidating or justifying it: he could use it to good effect in bringing about the transition to Philosophy as the "self-consciousness of mind" which History achieves, at the expense of ceasing to be History once recognition is achieved; and, more importantly, he could use it as a stick with which to beat the contemporary philosophy of epistemological realism which in his **Autobiography,** with bitterness unsoftened by time, he described as a "futile parlour game" for "minute philosophers." But in exploiting the latter use he defeated the former purpose. It is not at the level of History but at the level of Philosophy that the self-knowledge of mind is relevant to the *issue* of realism; and he might better have left History at the stage of recognizing that it itself belongs to the world of fact which is its object, so that there is a history of histories, not as another field of specialization, like the history of plumbing, but as a constitutive element in the historical consciousness as such. For

Gibbon the history of the Roman Empire was a series of purely Roman events. But the history of the Roman Empire now includes Gibbon and others, at least in the sense that a contemporary historian is aware that his concept of history is ingredient in his work and itself is *part* of the history of histories of the Roman Empire. The logic of the concept of history, it is evident, is very intricate. For Collingwood it is enough to show that History passes through phases leading to an awareness of itself as part of its own object. The elucidation of this state is then no longer History but Philosophy.

Philosophy. In the series beginning with Art and continuing through Religion, Science, and History, each stage has proved to be the explicit formulation of something implicit in the earlier stage; each is an achievement but at the same time an error regarded from the standpoint of the next stage. But the error of each is not like that of a self-sealing delusory system but rather like the unstable error of self-inconsistency, which itself throws up the criterion of consistency by which it may criticize and transcend itself. At each stage, the activity of *thought* (which is a generic term comprising imagination, conceptualization, affirmation and denial, etc.) assumes itself to be distinct from its object. Thought which reaches the stage of explicit self-consciousness and has itself as its own object is Philosophy. And its object is not merely itself as a diaphanous activity, of course, but itself together with its objects. To choose an example which is not Collingwood's, it is a debatable question (at least for mathematical intuitionists, such as Brouwer and Heyting), whether the kind of inference involved in *reductio ad absurdum* proofs is a satisfactory proof, indeed whether the Principle of Excluded Middle holds at all. Now this and similar arguments about the foundations of mathematics are arguments about mathematics rather than mathematical arguments; insofar as they are about the standards of mathematical reasoning, they are also about its objects: no one ignorant of mathematics could think about mathematical thinking. So the philosophy of mathematics is not a branch of mathematics, like abstract algebra, but metamathematics (it will be remembered that mathematics is an instance of Science, in Collingwood's terms); and similarly historical thinking, conscious and critical of itself, becomes metahistory or Philosophy.

Each *direct* form of consciousness gives rise to its *reflective* form, and this reflective form may either pass over into the next form of consciousness or remain (no doubt by what C. S. Peirce called the "method of tenacity") in the dogged and repetitive affirmation of itself. As the latter, each form generates an erroneous and dogmatic philosophy. Dogmatism, in fact, is "simply the resistance which a given form of experience presents to its own destruction by an inner dialectic." Aesthetic philosophy (Collingwood obviously has Bergson in mind although he does not mention him by name) exalts feeling and "intuition" as a substitute for intellect. Religious philosophy, whether as theism or atheism, interprets the metaphorical statements of religion as literal, and undertakes to prove or disprove what the religious consciousness itself is unable even to define. Scientific philosophy is the justification, in logic and metaphysics, of the description of the world in abstract concepts. Finally, Historical philosophy is represented by epistemological realism, the view that knowledge makes no difference to its objects.

If each of these is an "error," philosophy as such (or "Philosophical philosophy") must be the vantage point from which this can be recognized and argued. But what is this vantage point? Insofar as each is or claims to be a kind of knowledge, it would be nothing more than special pleading to claim that "Philosophy" somehow knows *as they are* the *objects* which are in some distorted way grasped by Art, Religion, and the rest. Yet in some sense this is nevertheless the case, although only in the sense that "object" has for Philosophy alone a *critical* meaning. Collingwood does not mean that Philosophy is like an experimental psychologist's comparing with what he *sees* to be a circle the reports that it is elliptical by subjects wearing distorting goggles. Rather it is like a psychologist who knows that what he himself see as elliptical is to be accounted for by the particular circumstances under which he himself sees it. Philosophy does not have a "truer" account of nature than does Science; but it has the explicit recognition, which is not essentially part of Science itself, that the idea of nature itself is partly constituted by the characteristics of Scientific thought. Nor does Philosophy have privileged access to the world of concrete fact which is the unattainable object of History. It is rather the self-consciousness of the genuinely historical attitude which recognizes that it is itself a determining part of the object of inquiry. There is no implication that Philosophy is free error, but at least it is free from the *necessary* errors consequent for each of the other forms of experience on its failure to recognize the extent to which it has determined what it supposes itself to have found.

Such a failure of self-consciousness is what Collingwood refers to in distinguishing the "concrete thinking" of Philosophy from the error of "abstraction" which is imputed to all the other modes of experience; and it is, I think, all that he means. In the vocabulary of Hegel, from whom the terms have been borrowed, "abstract" means "partial" and "concrete" means "whole." For Hegel no theory is entirely false and no theory is entirely true, *except* that theory which shows the relation to each other within a single ("concrete") system of each partial or "abstract" theory. Collingwood has borrowed the terms but not all of their meanings or implications; he rejects, for instance, as "mere mythology" Hegel's notion of a "world-spirit" whose development appears in the evolution of human institutions and of nature itself. For Collingwood, the common characteristic of all forms of "abstract thinking" is the gratuitous assumption of a distinction between subject and object in which the latter is taken to be wholly different from and other than the former. "Concrete thinking" is the recognition

that subject and object "can only be distinctions which fall within one and the same whole, and . . . this whole can only be the infinite fact which is the absolute mind." And what holds for the subject-object distinction holds *mutatis mutandis* for other distinctions as well: condition and conditioned, ground and consequence, particular and universal, individual and society, determinism and indeterminism, "and in general every form of the two complementary abstractions one of which denies the whole to assert the part, while the other denies the part to assert the whole."

It would be too mild to say that philosophers today are suspicious of references to "absolutes" (not to mention those who equally suspect references to "minds"). And it cannot be denied that Collingwood is more prophetic than analytical in his section on Philosophy. But if the language is Hegel's, the voice sounds strangely like the accents of Locke; and if Collingwood permits himself a poetic license which in his later work he did not disavow and even undertook to defend, he clearly does not intend by "absolute mind" any frivolous hypostatization. Nor is it merely an "ideal concept," i.e., what mind could be if it were not so unfortunately what it is, nor yet is it a set of characteristics shared by all minds (such a description would obviously betray the abstractness of Science playing the psychologist). Collingwood never abandoned the view that mind "is what it does"; and "absolute mind" is therefore the historical record, with all its richness of difference, of human activity into which thought enters in any of its forms. So the record of "absolute mind" does not include knee-jerks, breathing, belches, and blinks (although it may include blushes and winks); but it does include, as for Hegel, works of art, religions, sciences, political and legal institutions, systems of philosophy, and so forth, and it is only through the construction of such external worlds that "mind can possibly come to that self-knowledge which is its end." It is in the history of these human worlds that mind discovers the *speculum mentis,* the mirror of the mind. "The absolute mind is an historical whole of which mind is a part," but a part, it is emphasized, which at the level of self-consciousness becomes a *different* part and therefore alters to a corresponding degree the whole itself.

2 THE DOCTRINE OF THE "CONCRETE UNIVERSAL," AND ITS CONSEQUENCES

Yet, "the absolute mind is not one stupendous whole! It lives in its entirety in every individual and every act of every individual, yet not indifferently, as triangularity is indifferently present in every triangle, but expressing itself in every individual uniquely and irreplaceably." This comes near to being an Orphic saying, yet its meaning is not open to arbitrary interpretation and can, I think, be illustrated from a major aspect, omitted in the summary so far, of the five forms of experience.

Several times Collingwood describes the object of History or Philosophy (but not of Science) as a whole whose parts repeat in their structure the plan of the whole. This is, in fact, a summary description of the difference between Science, History, and Philosophy: the objects of Science, which are abstract universals, are *not* wholes of which their instances are parts, nor do they stand to their instances as something whose structure is repeated in the instances. Presumably Collingwood means by this the well-known fact that the *concept* of circle (or the class of circles) is not circular—as the concept of man does not have a backbone. But whereas the object of Science is the abstract universal, the object of History is said to be the *concrete* universal, which is by definition a kind of whole whose essential characteristics are also characteristics of its parts. The difference between History and Philosophy, in brief, is that History cannot grasp this object and Philosophy can, because History does not recognize, and Philosophy does, that nothing can meet this specification except mind itself, embodied in or projected into its activities.

Now the objection to Collingwood at this point will be either that the notion of a concrete universal is too unclear to admit of reasonable dispute, or that it is clear enough but refers to nothing real. As we shall see, there is something to be said for the first objection; and after *Speculum Mentis* Collingwood dropped the Hegelian terminology of "organic whole" and "concrete universal." But he did not drop the nucleus of ideas which he was trying to express with this borrowed terminology, and they reappear in the *Essay on Philosophical Method* as the "overlap of classes" and the "scale of forms" and the principles associated with these ideas. One should at least not suppose that by "concrete universal" Collingwood (or anyone else) ever meant the abstract universal *plus* some conceptually undefinable and empirically unobservable added entity. "Abstract" and "concrete" are not two species of the common genus "universal," although the assumption that they are has vitiated almost all discussion of the issue and no doubt accounts for the fact that the issue has fallen into desuetude. But Collingwood never made this mistake. *Speculum Mentis* shows that he was aware from the beginning that the "concrete universal" is not a program for a new logic but is the leading idea of the *historical consciousness*; and as such it is the most important single strand which connects his earliest and last work. And it does so as one instance of its own meaning.

In *Religion and Philosophy,* Collingwood discussed and applied the idea of a whole whose structure is reduplicated in its parts, an idea which he regarded as identical with the so-called doctrine of "internal relations," i.e., the view that at least some entities are constituted entirely by their relations to other entities, as contrasted with the doctrine of "external relations" which holds that entities have some characteristics essentially, and independently of all other entities and their characteristics. So one finds Collingwood saying, "Every characteristic of the thing turns out to consist in a relation in which it stands to something else," and in a whole consisting of three parts, *x, y,* and *z,* "the inner nature of the part, *x,* then is entirely constituted by its relations to *y* and *z.*" Therefore, in such a whole, a part is simply one perspective of the whole: "the part is not added to other parts in order to make the whole, it is already in itself the whole, and the whole has other parts only in the sense that it can be looked at from other points of view, seen in other aspects. But in each aspect the whole is entirely present." A number of examples are adduced to support this apparently paradoxical view: a musical duet, which is not (conceivably) the *addition* of two independent parts but a single entity constituted by the relation between the parts; or a dramatic scene as the interplay of two or more characters; or the identity of a single personality throughout its thoughts and acts.

Now duets and dramas—aesthetic objects in general—are often adduced as examples of complex wholes which cannot be successfully analyzed as aggregates of independent parts. And Collingwood seems to have confused this kind of whole with the more special kind of whole (for which duets and dramas do not serve as examples) whose plan is reduplicated in each of its proper parts. It is significant that there is no mention anywhere in *Religion and Philosophy* of the "concrete universal," nor any mention of the latter after *Speculum Mentis*. Collingwood's route of thinking, I suggest, must have been something like the following: in *Religion and Philosophy* he regarded himself as an adversary of a contemporary philosophy of science which claimed the merits of science as its own. This philosophy of science was mechanistic and materialistic and its consequence was the denial to the human being of any authentic freedom or independent self-existence. In the course of defending these characteristics of human personality, Collingwood found himself distinguishing between the notion of *abstract identity* (e.g., the sense in which we say that all men are equal before the law) and that of *concrete unity* (e.g., the sense in which men may form a *Gemeinschaft* in virtue of having common although not identical interests). There can be a concrete unity of two things which are part of the same whole, but ordinarily one would not say that such parts are identical with each other. Yet by a priori argument Collingwood concluded that if a whole is to be "strictly" knowable, its parts must be not simply added to one another but interconnected in such a way that "each part is the whole." Hence in any "genuine" whole unity and identity are the same thing. And this is stated as a general doctrine or philosophical principle, although in fact it seems to be true only of the specific case of personality. Formally, it is an ad hoc argument; yet it is not unilluminating. What we mean by "personality" is clearly not some indwelling entity but a *pattern of behavior* such that no matter how we analyze or divide human behavior—whether into simple response as on psychological tests or into complex events such as the carrying through of an expedition or a business venture—there are distinguishable characteristics (e.g., aggressiveness, caution, imaginativeness, reflectiveness) which describe not only momentary responses but complex actions over time and in fact the *person* himself. It is still no doubt much too strong to say that "each part *is* the whole," but at the same time it clearly will not do to regard a personality as merely the aggregate or average of a person's responses over time. There *is* an identifiable patterning, and to say that each part is the whole is a mildly misleading way of calling attention to the fact that there is no *natural* way of dividing human action into units or further unanalyzable parts. No matter how we divide a human career, we must divide it into parts which have the characteristics observable in the whole or in other parts. And it is not then too strange to say that "each part [is] also in a sense the others," remembering what that sense is.

But by the time he found himself adapting this argument to his purposes in **Speculum Mentis,** Collingwood had found a new way of generalizing it. The idea of a whole whose parts are "identical" with it and with each other now appears, not as a logical or metaphysical principle, generalized to refer to "any really organic whole," but as the special object of *historical* consciousness.

It is as if, in the interim, Collingwood had read Kant's "Idea of a Universal History" and had adapted to his own use Kant's notion of a "universal history" which would "connect into something like *systematic* unity the great abstract of human actions that else seem a chaotic and incoherent *aggregate.*" The idea of a whole "identical" with its proper parts is reasonably applicable to the unity of personality simply because the unity of personality is an historical unity. So by the time of **Speculum Mentis** Collingwood could, as it were, provide a gloss to Kant's reference to the "systematic unity" of history by suggesting that what makes it systematic is not anything like the logical relations of a mathematical or conceptual system nor the theoretical relations of natural science but the dialectical relation, already explored, of whole and part.

To call the relation "dialectical" does not, of course, either explain or justify it. Negatively, it is an indication that it is not to be understood either by analogy to mechanical models, which Collingwood never accepted, or by analogy to the biological model of "organic unity," which in **Religion and Philosophy** he did accept. The conception of the self in **Speculum Mentis** is not (as a mechanist would interpret it) that it is stratified like the many Troys, each layer built upon the one below but isolated from it so that the activities of each city are supported by the rubber and shards of forgotten pasts. Nor is it (as an organicist would interpret it) a set of functions mutually related as ends and means, illustrated by the way in which the circulatory system returns to the digestive system in usable form the energy which the latter has converted. Rather the self is a *reflexive process* which takes into itself and retains, while it transforms, its own past experiences and activities. If a metaphor is wanted, its appropriate field is neither archaeology nor physiology but history, and its modality is not space but time. But the dialectic of experience is not really to be understood by metaphors, since metaphors are themselves extensions of its own meaning. It is not like anything more fundamental than itself; other things, less fundamental, are like it. The identification of *any* change as a *process* rather than as a sequence of states reflects the awareness by the self of itself as a process which incapsulates and transmutes its past in a way quite unlike an organism assimilating food or an avalanche taking into itself the objects in its path.

Whatever one thinks of the merits of the dialectic of whole and part, there can be no doubt that it comes very close to being the central idea the elucidation of which is the strand of continuity in the record of Collingwood's philosophical career. . . . [In] its various disguises, it solved some problems and started others. But since so far it has been stated very summarily and generally, it may not be out of place to observe that the application to history has an initial richness and plausibility which the generalized metaphysical version lacks. We cannot today think about history without some sort of essential, rather than merely chronological periodization. "Renaissance," "Enlightenment," "Feudalism," "Capitalism," even "Baroque," "Romantic," and other such designations are as indispensable as they are impossible to define precisely or to date sharply. An historical period is clearly neither merely the sum of its parts nor an entity which can be identified apart from them. It is, like national character or style in art, a partly but not completely analyzable pattern of complex form discernible in each of a wide range of instances. To say that "each part is the whole" means only that each *represents* the whole, that the Renaissance style is not Renaissance architecture plus Renaissance politics, and so on, but is wholly represented in any one of these (although we can see what is relevant in one only by comparing it with others), as all the elements of an artist's style can be identified in a single composition or painting (but only with other instances in mind).

3   THE DIALECTIC OF ETHICAL SYSTEMS

Now the little system of **Speculum Mentis** is itself self-exemplifying in this way. We have summarized Collingwood's discussion of Art, Religion, Science, History, and Philosophy as claims to knowledge or types of cognitive experience. But this is only part of what Collingwood means by "forms of consciousness"; they are also modes of action, or at least of the normative principles of action. So a practical ethics corresponds to each form of experience, and the connection between, say, Science as a mode of thought and Science as a mode of action is that each of these is a "part" in which the "whole" is fully exemplified. Thus they can be distinguished but not separated. And as each mode of thought is unstable and gives way to the next, or is true with respect to the mode it succeeds but is an error from the standpoint of its successor, so the corresponding systems of ethics go through a corresponding dialectical development.

To review this development from the beginning: Art is pure imagination, which makes no distinction between real and unreal and raises no questions about any relations among its self-contained objects. Now what sort of activity is analogous to this? It is hardly a guess: play, insofar as play is understood to be activity without ulterior ends and one which cannot be described as expedient or inexpedient, right or wrong. The question, of course, is not one of tactics or of rules. A move in chess may be expedient or inexpedient as a step toward checkmate, or legal or illegal according to the rules. But it is the activity of playing the game, *including* winning or losing, which is engaged in for its own sake. Chess as a livelihood, or as a way of making acquaintances, and so on, is of course not play at all. Nor should it now be any more difficult to identify the practical morality associated with Religion, remembering that this refers to the assertiveness of religious consciousness wholly without self-criticism: it could be nothing other than conventional morality, performances of all sorts which are chosen or avoided solely because they are or are not "done." Such a morality of propriety is, like the play of Art, capricious: it neither has nor claims justification. But it is a development from play, as assertion is from supposal, and differs from it by being *social*; conventional morality is to individual caprice as the creeds of Religion are to the free imagination of Art. Collingwood wisely remarks that even though conventional morality can only assert and not defend itself, mere rebellion against it is not an advance but a lapse into individual capriciousness.

What does represent the development beyond conventional morality (and is in fact the step taken by conventional moralists when conventions deteriorate and must be shored up by argument, viz., "Honesty is the best policy") is the utilitarian ethics appropriate to Science, which abstracts from the class of intentional actions their common element of purposiveness and calls it "utility." That utility is an abstraction can be seen if one remembers that the notion of a calculus is essential to utilitarianism; John Stuart Mill effectively abandoned utilitarianism in his defense of it by introducing the notion of qualitative, or incommensurable, differences among pleasures.

In general, as Science abstracts from the untidy concreteness of physical objects the measurable properties of mass, velocity, etc., so in the consideration of action it abstracts the concept of an action as such as well as the measurable properties of the effects of actions. This point is best brought out by the contrast between the abstract ethics of utility and the concrete ethics of duty appropriate to History; the latter ethics regards action not as a purely instrumental means to an end, with no value other than that derivative from the value of the end, but as something required in a specific situation, and needing no inherited justification from anything lying outside itself. But Collingwood argues that this account, like the others, will not suffice. An action is regarded as obligatory because it is demanded by the facts of the situation. Action may, however, alter the facts; and insofar as it does so, it is no answer to the question of how they *should* be altered that they are indeed thus and so. So the ethics of duty ("Historical ethics") is ambivalent; it says on the one hand that the will is autonomous, and on the other that the world of concrete fact lays upon it an obligation which is its duty. Hence the peculiarity of *law,* which is the embodiment of concrete ethics. Law achieves, unlike utilitarian ethics, the notion of responsibility, but enforces it from without; one obeys the law not because it is the law but because disobedience has predictable and painful consequences, and this attitude, needless to say, is a relapse into utilitarianism. Or again, the instability of "concrete ethics" is signified by the inescapable conflict between the claim of law and the claim of individual conscience. But this again (Collingwood claims) reveals a distinction between individual and society, which as an abstraction indicates that History has not yet fully emancipated itself from Science.

So as History is fulfilled only in Philosophy, the ethics of duty is fulfilled only in "absolute ethics," in which the distinction between individual and society disappears, and "the agent acts with full responsibility," the sense of compulsion by external law having disappeared. At this point Collingwood is at best programmatic and at worst filling out his a priori scheme. (The section on "Absolute Ethics" is the shortest in *Speculum Mentis,* less than two pages long.) He returned again and again to his classification of types of ethical theories, but in every later recapitulation the scheme culminates not with "Absolute Ethics" but with Duty. One must assume that in *Speculum Mentis* Collingwood felt that Hegel had spoken the last word; later he decided that Hegel had had one word too many.

4   THE UNRESOLVED PROBLEM OF *SPECULUM MENTIS*

The eloquence of Collingwood's eulogies to "absolute mind" and "absolute ethics" cannot conceal the fact that the stage of Philosophy, far from being the developed and comprehensive fulfillment of Art, Religion, Science, and History, seems, unlike these others, to have no positive content of its own; the great climax of the drama of development turns out to be nothing but the playwright stepping in front of the closed curtain to remind the audience of what it has already seen. But no transformation scene was advertised, and it is just Collingwood's point that Philosophy stands apart in having no special object or method of its own. It is in fact part of his objection to "aesthetic philosophy," "religious philosophy," "scientific philosophy," and "historical philosophy" that they commit the "error of conceiving philosophy as one specialized form of experience, instead of realizing that it is merely the self-consciousness of experience in general."

The record of the development from Art through History is itself the dialectical growth in thought's consciousness of itself; so one might say that it is Philosophy which fills up all the interstices of the series—or, since it is a dynamic series, Philosophy is the uneasiness with which each moment of thought backs into the next with its eye fixed unwaveringly on the last. *Speculum Mentis,* that is to say, is a philosophical book, and as such it must *exemplify* throughout what it may or may not illuminatingly describe in the final section as its own procedure. And this procedure, all things considered, is clearer and more cogent than the concluding description of Philosophy as the last term of the five-part series. It cannot be correct to say that Philosophy has no object: the whole of *Speculum Mentis* is a demonstration that the forms of consciousness, *including Philosophy itself,* and their relations to each other constitute the object of Philosophy. Nor can it be correct to say that Philosophy has no method: how are the features of a mode of experience identified and analyzed, for example, or the relation between one mode of experience and another discerned? The method of Philosophy at least must be the kind of thinking exemplified in the recapitulation of the series of modes of experience. Collingwood began *Speculum Mentis* with the "suspicion that a philosophy of this kind . . . is the only philosophy that can exist and that all other philosophies are included in it." But by the end of the argument there is generated an uneasy and unresolved tension between two different ways of viewing philosophy: one is that philosophy has its own province, which includes those of other forms of consciousness but is distinguishable from them, and the other is that philosophy is only the reflective self-awareness of any mode of experience, the bringing to explicit (i.e., *self-*) consciousness of principles, criteria or presuppositions normally implicit in the thought and action of that mode of experience.

Now if one recognizes this unsolved problem as the major issue of *Speculum Mentis,* it helps to account for many of the otherwise extraordinary passages in that book. They are neither uncontrolled flights of speculative imagination nor unabashed special pleading for the philosophical party of absolute idealism but attempts to elucidate the peculiar logic of a theory which is an instance of itself, to achieve a systematic comprehension of philosophy as it is described and philosophy as it is exemplified. But, more significantly, the whole series of Collingwood's books then falls into place as a continuing attempt to answer the unresolved question of *Speculum Mentis.*

To put this development in the briefest way, the *Essay on Philosophical Method* ignores the other forms of experience to elucidate a method claimed to be the special province of philosophy; it fulfills, or attempts to fulfill, what in *Speculum Mentis* is left as programatic, and provides a conceptual analysis of the concept of philosophy which in the earlier book is poetically expressed. The succeeding books, *The Idea of Nature, The Idea of History,* and *The Principles of Art,* are analyses of other forms of experience from the standpoint of philosophical reflection on them. In the *Essay on Philosophical Method,* Collingwood discusses philosophy but does not permit himself to think about the way in which his own discussion exemplifies it; in the

later applications, he exemplifies it but does not directly discuss it. Yet while attacking either half of the problem, the awareness of the other half persists. It was not until the *Essay on Metaphysics* that Collingwood attempted a synthesis which would illustrate that *coincidentia oppositorum* which, according to *Speculum Mentis,* is the living nature of thought itself.

The uneasy tension in *Speculum Mentis* between the claim of philosophy to be an independent (and the highest) form of experience and the conception of philosophy as the reflective self-consciousness of other forms of experience is itself a dialectical tension. The development of the former in abstraction from the latter results in the dialectic of concepts which is the subject of the *Essay on Philosophical Method*; the development of the latter in abstraction from the former results in the dialectic of mind which Collingwood had partially worked out even before the *Essay on Philosophical Method* but did not publish in explicit form (in *The New Leviathan*) until shortly before his death. The clue to understanding each is to see that it replicates the other, just as, in Collingwood's view, the "concrete universal" is a whole whose parts replicate the form of the whole and of each other; the later developments are intelligible only when they are seen to have a common dialectical form. The rather traditional defense in *Speculum Mentis* of the "concrete universal" is transformed by Collingwood into his theory of concepts as comprising a scale of forms . . . and into his theory of mind as constituted by levels of consciousness related to each other like the basic types of experience and concepts on a scale of forms. . . . Collingwood's ultimate dialectic of mind grows out of the dialectic of concepts, as that grows out of the dialectic of experience.

Lionel Rubinoff (essay date 1970)

SOURCE: "Philosophy and History: The Need for a Rapprochement," in *Collingwood and the Reform of Metaphysics: A Study in the Philosophy of Mind,* University of Toronto Press, 1970, pp. 3-34.

[*In the following excerpt, Rubinoff considers the relationship between Collingwood's views on history and philosophy.*]

1   THE PRIORITY OF HISTORY IN TWENTIETH-CENTURY THOUGHT

In 1938, a few years before his death, Collingwood characterized his life work as "in the main an attempt to bring about a *rapprochement* between philosophy and history." Indeed, his deep concern with history is evident from the very outset of his career. In 1919, for example, in his address to the Ruskin Centenary Conference, he argued that the main virtue of Ruskin's thought lay in its specifically historical character. In this essay, Collingwood characterized what he called "the historical habit of thought" as "the philosophy of the future";

it "aims at freedom and variety," and "its natural inclination is always towards tolerance". And in 1920 he expressed a similar conviction when he wrote, together with A. H. Hannay, in the preface to their translation of de Ruggiero's *Filosophia contemporanea,* that Italian philosophy is to be recommended to English readers because of its "penetrating study and exposition of history."

It was Collingwood's belief, lasting throughout his entire career, that historiography and philosophy of history had priority over other philosophical interests because history itself, the study of human affairs, had become the central preoccupation of the present age. The priority of historiography and philosophy of history in twentieth-century thought had, for Collingwood, a practical as well as a theoretical basis. Collingwood charged, in the *Autobiography,* that the first world war (including the Treaty of Versailles which concluded it) was a "war of unprecedented ferocity closed in a peace-settlement of unprecedented folly," an unprecedented triumph for natural science on the one hand and an unprecedented disgrace to the human intellect on the other hand. The contrast between success in controlling situations which were part of the physical world and failure to control situations in which human beings are elements, left an indelible mark on Collingwood's memory.

By 1937 the situation had become desperate. The dangers of any failure to control human situations were more serious than they had ever been before. Not only would such failure result in more and more widespread destruction as natural science added triumph after triumph, but the consequences would tend more and more to the destruction of whatever was good and reasonable in the civilized world. At such a time the academic bickerings of the philosophical sects struck Collingwood as an amusement for the foolish. There was really only one question for the serious philosopher to face: "what can we do to be saved from these present distresses?"

Collingwood's answer was that such a calamity could be avoided only through a proper understanding of the human mind. An attempt in this direction had been undertaken by both behaviouristic psychology and the positivistically conceived social sciences. But Collingwood regarded both of these enterprises as thoroughly misguided. Behaviourism and positivism treat human nature as though it were a mere species of nature proper, whereas a genuine science of mind must apprehend its object under the category of freedom. It was Collingwood's lifelong belief that the right way of investigating mind is by the methods of history. History is what the science of human nature professes to be. And it is only through history, therefore, that we can grasp the fact that human activity is free.

The problem is rendered all the more urgent when it is recognized that the historical thought which apprehends the fact of freedom is itself a necessary condition of the existence of that freedom. Historical self-knowledge, in other words, is a form of historical self-making; the

historical process "is a process in which man creates for himself this or that kind of human nature by recreating in his own thought the past to which he is heir." Historical knowledge is to be regarded, therefore, not simply as a luxury, or mere amusement of a mind at leisure from more pressing occupations, but as a prime duty, "whose discharge is essential to the maintenance, not only of any particular form or type of reason, but of reason itself." History, he wrote in **The New Leviathan** (1942), is the proper object of study for any man who has taken part in in the progress of human thought down to the present time; for it is in the world of history rather than in the world of nature that man finds the central problems he has to solve. Indeed, he wrote elsewhere, "history occupies in the world of to-day a position analogous to that occupied by physics in the time of Locke"; and just as the chief business of seventeenth-century philosophy was to reckon with seventeenth-century natural science, so, Collingwood contended, the chief business of twentieth-century philosophy is to reckon with twentieth-century history.

> As the seventeenth century needed a reasoned conviction that nature is intelligible and the problems of science in principle soluble, so the twentieth needs a reasoned conviction that human progress is possible and that the problems of moral and political life are in principle soluble. In both cases the need is one which only philosophy can supply. What is needed to-day is a philosophical reconsideration of the whole idea of progress or development, and especially its two main forms, 'evolution' in the world of nature and 'history' in the world of human affairs. What would correspond to the Renaissance conception of nature as a single intelligible system would be a philosophy showing that the human will is of a piece with nature in being genuinely creative; a *vera causa,* though singular in being consciously creative; that social and political institutions are creations of the human will, conserved by the same power which created them, and essentially plastic to its hand; and that therefore whatever evils they contain are in principle remediable. In short, the help which philosophy might give to our 'dissatisfied, anxious, apprehensive generation' would lie in a reasoned statement of the principle that there can be no evils in any human institution which human will cannot cure.

2 HISTORY AND THE SCIENCE OF HUMAN NATURE

The most significant feature of history, according to Collingwood, is the success with which it provides a basis for the unification of the various and diverse forms of human experience. On at least two occasions he cites with approval Hume's famous remark "that all the sciences have a relation, greater or less, to human nature . . . since they lie under the cognizance of man, and are judged of by their powers and faculties" (*Treatise*), and he gives every indication of further agreeing with Hume that "in pretending therefore to explain the principles of human nature, we in effect propose a compleat system of the sciences, built on a foundation almost entirely new, and the only one upon which they can stand with any security" (*Treatise*). Until recently, however, the attempt at a science of human nature failed because its method was distorted by the analogy of the natural sciences. This attempt at a naturalistically conceived science of human nature was part of the general programme of positivism, which, according to Collingwood, is founded on a philosophical error—the error of dogmatically assuming that all of the sciences are species of a common genus, and then proceeding to define the genus according to the differentia of only one of its species, the species of natural science. It was Collingwood's contention that the proposal of positivism, to investigate human nature by the methods of the natural sciences, has been successfully challenged by the counter claim that the right way of investigating mind is by the methods called historical.

In the *Idea of History* Collingwood insists that human nature is the concern of the philosophical and historical sciences only in so far as it is regarded as rational, that is to say, as an expression of mind. Other aspects of man, his body, his emotions, and anything that generally derives from his co-called animal nature (including the irrational), are more properly the concern of the natural sciences. In the *New Leviathan,* however, Collingwood seems to have transcended the mind-body dualism altogether and is now prepared to bring even the body under the sciences of mind. The concept of the historicity of embodied mind, which lies at the centre of the *New Leviathan,* is the culminating moment of Collingwood's philosophical achievements.

There is another source of Collingwood's tendency to characterize the sciences of mind as historical; namely, his lifelong rejection of the classical theory of metaphysics which defines reality as a permanent and eternal substance existing independently of its phenomenal appearances. He was therefore committed to repudiate all theories which presuppose the conception of mind or human nature as a fixed and unchanging substance: whether such theories take the form of the empirical study of attributes or the a priori study of essences. Neither reality in general nor mind in particular can be so defined. Reality is a "dialectical" process of change, and the *being* of mind, if it is to be found at all, is to be found only in its acts, as art, religion, science, history, morality, philosophy, and so on. Since such a study must necessarily be historical, it follows that Hume's proposal for the unity of science depends upon the possibility of establishing and maintaining an autonomous and self-justifying science of history whose methods are free from the domination of the natural sciences.

Thus, according to Collingwood, the task of twentieth-century philosophy is clear. It is to construct a critique of historical reason which will accomplish for the historical sciences what Kant's first critique has accomplished for the natural sciences: a critique which would answer the question, "How or under what conditions is historical knowledge possible?" It is with respect to this task that Collingwood urged the wise philosopher to "concentrate with all his might on the problems of history, at whatever cost, and so do his share in laying the foundations of the future."

3   PHILOSOPHY AND THE RAPPROCHEMENT BETWEEN THEORY AND PRACTICE

Collingwood's programme for the unity of science derives, then, from a profound need to lay the foundations for a new rapprochement between theory and practice. For Collingwood the main value of philosophy lies in its practical effects: a view which he identified with "the classical tradition in philosophy." "The philosophers of the classical tradition," he wrote, "were men who used their trained faculties of thinking in order to think about facts, and primarily of facts of practical importance in relation to the lives of their fellow-men." His interest in this rapprochement was a consequence of his steadily developing opposition to the principle of philosophical realism that *knowing makes no difference to the object known*. The opposite of this dogma seemed to Collingwood not only a truth, but a truth which, for the sake of one's integrity and efficacy as a practical agent, ought to be familiar to every human being: namely, that in our capacity as moral, political, or economic agents we live not only in a world of hard facts to which thoughts make no difference but in a world which is *essentially* one of thoughts. Which means, in other words, that a change in the moral, political, and economic theories generally accepted by society will result in a change in the very structure of that society itself, while a change in one's own personal theories will result in a change in one's relation to that society. In either case, the end result will be a change in the way we act.

Collingwood argued that the violation of the rapprochement between theory and practice implied by the principles of philosophical realism was one of the consequences of the disruption of the unity of the sciences which derived from the Renaissance concept of specialization. The motto of the Renaissance, regarding the relation of the sciences, was the principle that the secret of the well-being of each standpoint lay in mutual separation. Each science in its search for freedom demanded a complete separation from every other form of life; art for art's sake, truth for truth's sake, religion for religion's sake, and so on. The result of this trend of thought was that each science, in so far as it was cut off from the others, tended more and more to lead its followers into a desert where the world of human life was lost until finally the very motive for going on seemed to disappear altogether. Each tended to become a specialized activity pursued by specialists for the applause of specialists, useless to the rest of mankind and unsatisfying even to the specialist when he turned upon himself and asked why he was doing it.

This is the state of affairs which Collingwood believed his own generation to have reached: a state in which scholars, scientists, artists, and even philosophers "work only for themselves and their own kind in a vicious circle of academicism," with the result that they have lost contact not only with each other but with the public as well. "The producers and the consumers of spiritual wealth," he wrote, "are out of touch" Thus has the Renaissance search for abstract freedom come home to roost, in the form of a complete disruption of life. To-day, wrote Collingwood, "we can be as artistic, we can be as philosophical, we can be as religious as we please, but we cannot ever be men at all; we are wrecks and fragments of men, and we do not know where to take hold of life and how to begin looking for that happiness which we know we do not possess."

Against the radical pluralism of Renaissance thought Collingwood contended that the various forms of human activity were identical, that the theoretical moment of any experience had practical effects on that experience itself, and, in view of the unity of experience, on every other form of experience as well. He describes in his *Autobiography* how he set out to reconsider all the familiar topics and problems of morals, politics, and economics. There were, he held, no merely moral actions, no merely political actions, and no merely economic actions. Every action was moral, political, and economic. He even argued, with equal conviction, that scientific, historical, or philosophical thinking depends quite as much on moral qualities as on intellectual ones and that moral difficulties are to be overcome not by moral force alone but by clear thinking.

At the same time Collingwood realized that while the various forms of human activity could not be separated, neither is their identity a night in which all cows are black, a blind abstract identity which is indifferent to difference. "All such identities," he wrote, "are barren abstractions." On the contrary, he argued, the basis of the unity of the forms of experience is a concrete dialectical identity to which difference is essential and organic. "To assert the identity without the difference," he charged, "or the difference without the identity is to turn one's back on reality and amuse oneself with paradoxes." It was to the task of establishing the basis for such an identity that Collingwood devoted a great deal of his philosophical career and it was with the faith that this task could be accomplished that he proposed his remedy for the disease of his age.

> For we now recognize the nature of our disease. What is wrong with us is precisely the detachment of those forms of experience—art, religion, and the rest—from one another; and our cure can only be their reunion in a complete and undivided life. Our task is to seek for that life, to build up the conception of an activity which is at once art, and religion, and science, and the rest.

4   HISTORY AND THE PROBLEM OF HISTORICISM

Collingwood's emphasis on, and lifelong concern with, history has created the impression among most of his critics that as his thought developed he came closer and

closer to accepting a doctrine—hereafter referred to as 'radical historicism'—which he had originally repudiated: the doctrine, advanced by Croce, that philosophy is not only superseded but annihilated by history, and that philosophy, therefore, is nothing more than the methodological moment of history. Since Collingwood's relation to Croce as well as to other leading historicist thinkers is one of the main issues of [*Collingwood and the Reform of Metaphysics: A Study in the Philosophy of the Mind*], it would be advisable at this point to explain in some detail just what the doctrine of radical historicism asserts.

The core of this doctrine is well summed up in a famous declaration by the nineteenth-century philosopher York Von Wartenburg. Writing to Dilthey, Von Wartenburg declared with respect to the nature of philosophy, that "there is no genuine philosophizing which is not historical. The distinction between systematic philosophy and history of philosophy is in principle false." In Croce's philosophy this doctrine is given further support. "It is a curious fate," writes Croce, "that history should for a long time have been considered and treated as the most humble form of knowledge, while philosophy was considered the highest, and that now it not only is superior to philosophy but annihilates it." Thus Croce defines historicism as "the affirmation that life and reality are history and history alone."

> Every judgement is an historical judgement . . . Whatever it is that is being judged, is always an historical fact . . . Historical judgement is embodied even in the merest perception of the judging mind . . . historical judgement is not a variety of knowledge, but is knowledge itself; it is the form which completely fills and exhausts the field of knowing, leaving no room for anything else . . . Philosophy ceased to enjoy an autonomous existence because its claim to autonomy was founded upon its metaphysical character . . . that which has taken its place is history.

It follows from these statements that philosophy and history can no longer be regarded as either separate or distinct forms of experience. Their relation is one not simply of mutual interaction but of complete or immediate identity.

> The a priori synthesis which is the concreteness of the individual judgement and of definition is at the same time the concreteness of philosophy and of history. It is the formula of thought which by constituting itself qualifies intuition and constitutes history. History neither precedes philosophy nor philosophy history. They are both born in one act.

A parte subjecti, then, radical historicism may be properly defined as "the tendency to interpret the whole of reality, including what up to the romantic period had been conceived as absolute and unchanging human values including philosophy itself, in historical, that is to say, relative terms." *A parte objecti* it is "that standpoint which regards 'being in time' as the fundamental form of being, and all other forms of being as derived from it . . . which regards time as more important than space . . . which regards man as *animal historicum* . . . and which assumes that we cannot understand man's activities or his creations, like art, philosophy, religion, science, etc., except in their dependence on the flux of history."

Such definitions must be carefully distinguished, however, from a variety of other more popular ones which tend to provide misleading descriptions of historicism. Sir Karl Popper, for example, defines historicism as "an approach to the social sciences which assumes that *historical prediction* is their principal aim, and which assumes that this aim is attainable by discovering the 'rhythms' or the 'patterns', the 'laws' or the 'trends' that underlie the evolution of history," and on the basis of which we may therefore "prophesy the course of historical events." An equally misleading definition is given by Arnold Hauser, who defines historicism as "the doctrine that uncovers and stresses the unique and unrepeatable character of all historical events, but none the less asserts that everything historical is the manifestation of some superhuman and timeless principle." In this view, according to Hauser, "the individuals who build this world of time are just the servants of a world architect who is 'cunning' enough to play upon their impulses and interests . . . to give them a sense of freedom and creativity, whereas all the time they are only carrying out menial tasks for him." These definitions represent the two most common misunderstandings of historicism. In Popper's definition it is clear that historicism is confused with historical positivism, while Hauser's definition (intended, no doubt, as a description of Hegel's philosophy of history) is really about some kind of supernaturalism. But historicism, of whatever variety, is neither positivism nor supernaturalism; for historicism is committed to the very opposite of any view which sees history as the mere temporal expression of either natural or supernatural laws transcending the events of history themselves.

If radical historicism, then, as represented by Croce and as defined above, is in fact the doctrine which Collingwood himself eventually embraced, then his alleged rapprochement must certainly be judged a failure. For radical historicism gives to history precisely the same dogmatic status as positivism gives to science and is therefore open to the same criticisms. More importantly, radical historicism is a complete repudiation of Collingwood's lifelong campaign against all forms of abstract identity. Collingwood's own attitude to radical historicism (at least during the period 1916 to 1936) can be easily reconstructed from various passages in *Religion and Philosophy* (1916), **"Croce's Philosophy of History"** (1921), *Speculum Mentis* (1924), and **"Human Nature and Human History"** (1936). *Religion and Philosophy,* for example, is directed as much against the implications of radical historicism as against those of positivism and extreme empiricism.

In the first place Collingwood explicitly rejects the principle that to understand a thing we need only know its history and origin. This, together with his avowed commitment to the existence of transhistorical truths (such as the knowledge of God), is already a sufficient repudiation of radical historicism. "The attainment of any real truth," he writes, "is an event, doubtless in time, and capable of being catalogued in the chronologies of abstract history; but the truth itself is not historically circumscribed." Elsewhere, in the course of an important discussion of the concept of identity, he rejects all forms of abstract identity, such as pure "immanent pantheism," a doctrine which carries the same implications as radical historicism. Against this he considers another kind of identity which permits of identity in difference. Further evidence of Collingwood's rejection of historicism can be found in **"Croce's Philosophy of History,"** which is an uncompromising rejection of Croce's desertion of philosophy for history, and *Speculum Mentis* which characterizes all views which define the whole of knowledge in terms of only one of its species as cases of vicious dogmatism. And since, according to the argument of *Speculum Mentis,* historicism, scientism (i.e., positivism), realism, aestheticism, and theism all rest on the same set of presuppositions, the arguments against each are essentially the same. By accusing the later Collingwood of historicism, then, the critics are declaring that after 1936 (the period during which Collingwood is supposed to have undergone his radical conversion), he had come to adopt the very views which prior to 1936 he had explicitly repudiated.

It is my purpose . . . to take issue with any interpretation that charges Collingwood with having undergone a radical conversion to historicism (a view which will be hereafter referred to as "the radical conversion hypothesis"). It must be confessed, however, that the radical conversion hypothesis finds some support in the *apparent* change in emphasis which characterizes the development of Collingwood's thought from 1916 until 1941. Before developing in some detail my own interpretation of the growth of Collingwood's thought it would be advisable, therefore, not only to take an objective look at the "facts" themselves, but also to consider the major interpretations which have so far been placed upon those "facts."

Let us begin with a brief description and catalogue of the facts as revealed by a comprehensive but superficial reading of the texts. In *Religion and Philosophy,* published in 1916, Collingwood argued that history and philosophy were "the same thing." By this he meant simply that they have the same object, that they mutually presuppose each other, and that they are equally valid forms of knowledge. Precisely the same view is attributed to the relation between history and science in **"Are History and Science Different Kinds of Knowledge?"** (1922) In *Speculum Mentis* (1924) philosophy and history are still identified, but the identity is now characterized as "dialectical," with philosophy assuming ontological priority. *Speculum Mentis* is specifically described as "a New Treatise of Human Nature *philosophically* conceived" (italics mine), the aim of which is to enable us better to answer the question, "What shall we do to be saved from our present distress?"

The doctrine of the priority of philosophy over history, characteristic of the writings following *Speculum Mentis,* was asserted as part of a wider doctrine concerning the autonomy of philosophy in general. In **"Economics as a Philosophical Science"** (1925), for example, he distinguished clearly between philosophical studies of economic wealth and human conduct, and empirical studies of the same subject matters. And in **"The Nature and Aims of a Philosophy of History"** (1925) he specifically argues (as he does later in the *Idea of History*) that whereas the historian's thought is always of an object *other* than his own thinking, the philosopher's thought is knowledge of himself. If this view is applied specifically to the categorial relation between philosophy and history it follows that the philosophical act of thinking (and hence philosophy of history) is distinct from the actual act of historical thinking: a distinction which is explicitly affirmed in the introductory remarks to the *Idea of History* where history is described as "thought of the first degree" and philosophy as "thought of the second degree."

The most definitive expression of the autonomy of philosophy is given in *An Essay on Philosophical Method* (1933). The latter explores various aspects of the identity between philosophy and history; but in each case the identity is represented as "dialectical," and philosophy enjoys a clear-cut priority both in the order of knowledge and in the order of being. History, for example, is explicitly identified with philosophy in the sense that philosophy is conceived of as a system which itself develops in history. But, while the content of the system is progressively realized in history, the form or idea of it is transhistorical. Philosophy is also identified with history when both are defined as "categorical" judgments as opposed to the "hypothetical" judgments of natural science; philosophy is categorical universal while history is categorical singular. But again, the priority of philosophy is assured when (as in *Speculum Mentis*) the various forms of experience—art, religion, science, history, and philosophy—are placed on an overlapping scale of forms with philosophy at the summit: philosophy is not only implicit in all the other forms of experience but *is the act through which the implicit unity of the particular forms is rendered explicit.*

Beginning with the *Idea of History,* however, there appears to be a change of emphasis. It is true that the Introduction, written in 1936, continues to emphasize the priority of philosophy and its distinctness from history proper. But the main body of this work, written between 1936 and 1939, places more and more emphasis on history as the science of mind par excellence, and, according to his critics, it was precisely during this period that Collingwood is supposed to have changed his mind concerning the relation between history and philosophy. But the most telling evidence in support of Collingwood's change of attitude derives from the *Autobiography* (1939) and *An Essay on Metaphysics* (1940). In both works Collingwood argues for an identity between metaphysics and history based on a denial of the distinction between the purely historical question, What was so-and-so's answer to a particular question? and the purely philosophical question, Was he right? This newly conceived identity of the philosophical and the historical question is extended in the *Autobiography* to all branches of philosophy. And it is this apparent historicization of the whole of philosophy which suggests that philosophy has now been liquidated by being absorbed into history.

The *Principles of Art,* which appeared in 1938, does not at first sight appear to have any relevance to the question of Collingwood's conversion to historicism. But the *New Leviathan* (1942), Collingwood's last work, seems to favour the radical conversion hypothesis. Not only does the *New Leviathan* present history as the supreme object of study, but it presents itself explicitly as an historical account of man as mind, as a Treatise on Human Nature *historically* conceived, with the purpose of "deciding how to deal with the present attack on Civilization." And this, as we noted above, is precisely the problem which in 1924 was regarded as the fundamental one of philosophy.

It is clear then that throughout his entire career Collingwood repudiated any merely abstract separation of philosophy and history. Yet given this starting point at least two separate moves are possible. The first is the attempt to explicate the identity of philosophy and history in terms of the concept of a "dialectical *rapprochement.*" This means regarding history and philosophy as *distinct* but not *separate* forms on an overlapping scale: in the sense that the latter renders explicit what is implicit in the former. But the second possibility leads in the direction of radical historicism for which philosophy is totally subsumed under the category of history. It was Collingwood's own view that he had taken the first step while most of his critics have argued that he took the second.

A. J. M. Milne   (essay date 1972)

SOURCE: "Collingwood's Ethics and Political Theory," in *Critical Essays on the Philosophy of R. G. Collingwood,* edited by Michael Krausz, Oxford at the Clarendon Press, 1972, pp. 296-326.

[*In the following essay, Milne focuses on ethical and political ideas advanced in Collingwood's works.*]

Collingwood touched briefly on ethics in *Speculum Mentis* and in his *Autobiography* had some hard things to say about contemporary British politics. But it is to his last completed book, *The New Leviathan,* that we must go for a systematic exposition of his ideas in ethics and political theory. These ideas had apparently been maturing long before the writing of *The New Leviathan* was begun soon after the outbreak of the Second World War. In the Preface, speaking of his return to Oxford after the First World War, Collingwood wrote:

> It was now that I began to think out the fundamental ideas of the present book, thereafter revising and elaborating them year after year in experimental form, accumulating as time went on I will not say how many thousands of pages of manuscript on every problem of ethics and politics, and especially on the problems of history which bore on my subject; and imparting my results, when I seemed to reach any which were worth imparting, in lectures to my juniors and in manuscripts to such of my colleagues as seemed interested.

Collingwood describes *The New Leviathan* in the opening chapter as: 'an inquiry into civilization and the revolt against it which is the most conspicuous thing going on at the present time'. This inquiry is the context in which his ideas in ethics and political theory are expounded. He goes on:

> Civilization is a condition of communities; so to understand what civilization is, we must first understand what a community is. A community is a condition of man in which are included women and children; so to understand what a community is we must first understand what men are. This gives us the scheme of the present book: Part 1, an inquiry into man; Part 2, an inquiry into communities; Part 3, an inquiry into civilizations; and Part 4, an inquiry into revolts against civilization.

And he adds: 'About each subject we need to understand only so much as we need to understand what is to be said about the next'.

All this, like Collingwood's title, suggests that he is consciously following in the footsteps of Hobbes. That was certainly his intention. He had said in the Preface: 'My own book is best understood as an attempt to bring *The Leviathan* up-to-date in the light of the advances made since it was written, in history, psychology, and anthropology'. An essay might well be written about Collingwood's relation to Hobbes but that is not my purpose here. I shall confine myself to his leading ideas in ethics and political theory, and I shall discuss them under two heads: (A) Freedom and Practical Reason; and (B) The Body Politic. That means that I shall be concerned mainly with the latter part of Part 1 of *The New Leviathan* and with Part 2. But in a brief concluding section, C. Civilization, I shall have something to say about the later stages of Collingwood's enterprise. The thesis which I shall try to develop is briefly this. Collingwood's ideas in ethics and political theory need to be criticized, revised, and reformulated, if what is of value, and I think there is much of value, in his account of civilization is to stand.

Collingwood says that: 'Civilization is a thing of the mind and a community too is a thing of the mind'. An inquiry into civilization therefore belongs to what he calls 'the sciences of mind'. A discussion of his conception of sciences of mind and of their relation to the natural sciences would also need an essay to itself. Two things however need to be said about it here. The first is that for him psychology is not a science of mind but a natural science. The second, that what he is interested in is not the human mind at large but the modern European mind. 'Whatever I need to know about mind is about the modern European mind; for that is what has produced in itself the thing called modern European civilization, or civilization for short, and also the revolt against it'. I shall have something to say about this at the end of my essay, but at the outset it is enough to say that Collingwood is engaged in a conceptual inquiry of much the same sort that in the years since the Second World War has come to be regarded by many British and American philosophers as their main business. The concepts in which he is interested are those which he considers to lie at the centre of modern European thought and action in moral, social, and political contexts.

I have already said that my discussion of Collingwood's ethics and political theory will be critical. The kind of criticism in which I shall engage is best understood in terms of the Platonic distinction between 'eristic' and 'dialectic', a distinction which Collingwood himself appropriated and which plays a central role in his whole argument. 'What Plato calls an eristic discussion is one in which each party tries to prove that he was right and the other wrong. In a dialectical discussion you aim at showing that your own view is one with which your opponent really agrees even if at one time he denied it; or, conversely, that it was yourself and not your opponent who began by denying a view with which you really agree'. In eristic, there is disagreement, in dialectic, 'non-agreement', and the essence of the dialectical attitude is a 'constant endeavour to convert every occasion of non-agreement into an occasion of agreement'. There will be a number of occasions of non-agreement between Collingwood and myself in what follows, but I shall do my best to convert them into occasions of agreement.

(A) FREEDOM AND PRACTICAL REASON

1. According to Collingwood, men are not born free. They have to achieve freedom and this can be done only at a relatively advanced stage of mental development. What is achieved is freedom of the will. 'The freedom of the will is, positively, *freedom to choose; freedom to exercise a will;* and negatively *freedom from desire;* not the condition of having no desires but the condition of not being at their mercy'. If you are at their mercy, you can act from preference but not make choices. 'A man who prefers A. to B. does not choose at all; he suffers desire for A. and aversion towards B.: and goes where desire leads him'. Freedom, or freedom of the will, is achieved by an involuntary act of self-liberation. '*Lib-*

eration from what? From the dominance of desire. *Liberation to do what?* To make decisions'. If voluntary acts are those which issue from decisions, the act of self-liberation which makes voluntary acts possible cannot itself be a voluntary act. But while the act of self-liberation is involuntary, its occurrence is not inevitable. 'This achievement of free will marks the stage at which, in modern Europe, a man is supposed to reach intellectual maturity. If anything interferes with the course of his mental development, this step may never happen; he will then become a man who is incapable of growing up; perhaps a man who hates the thing (mental maturity) he does not possess'.

But the freedom of the will which any man can achieve is always a matter of degree. 'On certain questions and in certain circumstances an agent may be capable of decision, or free; on other questions or in other circumstances the same agent may be utterly unable to prevent a certain passion or a certain desire from taking charge'. Collingwood calls this breakdown of freedom 'a cracking of the will' and he adds: 'for any man, I suppose, there are conditions under which a crack of the will would happen'. Collingwood distinguishes between physical and mental force, and argues that when a man yields to mental force, he undergoes a crack of the will. 'When a man suffers force, *the origin of the force is always something within himself,* some irresistible emotion which makes him do something he does not intend to do'; and he goes on: 'If B. suffers force at the hands of A., it is A. who excites in B. this irresistible emotion'.

Choice is of the essence of freedom but choice in its simplest form is identical with caprice. Collingwood describes caprice as: 'Mere choice or mere decision, uncomplicated by any reason why it should be made in this way and not in that'. From this he concludes that a completely capricious act is a completely irrational act while a completely rational act is one from which all caprice has been eliminated. It follows that absence of caprice is the test of the rationality of action or of 'practical reason'. The greater the rationality the less the caprice and the greater the caprice the less the rationality. But what kinds of reason are there for choosing in one way rather than in another? What are the forms of practical reason? According to Collingwood, there are three. 'It is not because three is in my eyes a magical number; but I find that people talking about practical reason distinguish various types of it, and that these types, under inspection, resolve themselves into three falling in a certain order'. The three in ascending order of rationality are: Utility, Right, and Duty. Collingwood says that: 'On any occasion when a modern European answers the question: "Why did you do that?" he will answer: 1. "Because it is useful." 2. "Because it is right." 3. "Because it is my duty"'.

To do an act because it is useful is to do it as a means to an end. Utilitarian action therefore involves two decisions: one about the end and another about the means.

There has to be what Collingwood calls an 'ends plan' and a 'means plan'. The rationality of utilitarian action lies in: 'the abstract conformity of the means plan to the abstract specifications of the ends plan'. He calls both the ends plan and the means plan, 'indefinite individuals' and goes on: 'Everything except the conformity of these indefinite individuals to one another is, from the utilitarian point of view, irrational'. He says of an indefinite individual that it is 'required to satisfy certain specifications but free to vary so long as those specifications are satisfied'. What he has in mind seems to be this. The ends plan must specify a state of affairs in sufficient detail for it to be envisaged and brought about by human action. The means plan must specify a course of action in sufficient detail for it to be deliberately undertaken as a way of bringing about the state of affairs specified in the ends plan. The detail in each case is incomplete, being no more than is necessary for utilitarian action to get under way. With respect to the detail which it specifies, each plan is an individual plan. But with respect to what it leaves unspecified, each is indefinite or capricious. The unspecified details are free to vary, that is, are decided capriciously as action proceeds. Utility is therefore imperfectly rational owing to the element of caprice in both the ends plan and the means plan. It is also capricious in another way which Collingwood does not mention, although it is perhaps implicit in his account. This is in the decision about what state of affairs is to be the end for utilitarian action. So far as utility is concerned, there is no reason for choosing one end rather than another.

Right is the second form of practical reason. Collingwood contrasts it with utility. 'A thing is useful or the opposite in relation to the end it achieves; it is right or the opposite in relation to the rule it obeys'. Practical reason in the form of utility gives rise to utilitarian action. Practical reason in the form of right gives rise to regularian action. Collingwood says that: 'A man may, and often does, make rules solely for himself: this, indeed, is regularian action in its simplest form and unless we understand this we shall never understand the complex case in which a man makes rules for others to obey'. He says that a rule is a generalized purpose which he describes as: 'a purpose to do things of a certain kind on all occasions of a certain kind'. But 'a rule is only one part of a regularian action. There is also the decision to obey or disobey it'. Two kinds of decision are therefore involved in regularian action: decisions about what rules to obey; and decisions to obey them in situations which they cover. According to Collingwood, regularian action is infected with caprice although not to the same extent as utilitarian action. This is because 'a rule only specifies *some* act of a certain kind. The application of it to a given occasion bids me perform one, and only one, of the acts which would conform to its specifications. The acts which so conform may be many or few; which they are, depends not on the rule but on the circumstances; if they are many, I have got to choose between them, but the rule cannot tell me how. From the regularian point of view my choice between the alternatives is a matter of caprice'. So for that matter, although Collingwood does not mention it, is my initial decision about what rule to obey.

Duty is the third form of practical reason. According to Collingwood, duty is the discharging of an obligation which the agent has already incurred. His doctrine seems to be this. The incurring of an obligation is a free act. One chooses to give an undertaking to do something. Having given the undertaking one must then carry it out. This is what duty is: the carrying out of undertakings freely given, or the discharging of obligations freely incurred. Collingwood asks what is meant by the phrase 'his duty' when a man says that something is his duty and answers: 'A man's duty on a given occasion is that act which for him is both possible and necessary: the act which at the moment character and circumstance combine to make it inevitable, if he has a free will, that he should freely will to do'. Unlike utilitarian and regularian actions, 'dutiful' actions are definite individuals. Duty is in principle free from caprice. It is the only one of the three forms of practical reason which is completely rational. 'Any duty is a duty to do *this* act and only *this*, not *an act of this kind*'. But judgements about what one's duty is are never incorrigible. The most that a man can say is 'I have considered, X, Y and Z, as claimants for the title of my present duty; X is a better answer than Y, and Y than Z; but there may be a better answer than any which I have overlooked'.

2. In all this, there are a number of occasions of non-agreement between Collingwood and myself. To begin with his account of mental force: he says that what forces a man is always something within himself. This is not necessarily so. A man may yield to a threat not from panic, but because he judges it to be the lesser evil. His will does not crack. He makes a rational decision. Asked 'Why did you do that?' (for instance, hand over the money) his answer is: 'Because it was prudent.' *Pace* Collingwood, this is an answer in line with modern European ways of thinking and speaking. But although the man's action is rational, is it free? According to common sense: no, because it is done under constraint. According to Collingwood: yes, because he freely decides to yield. He might have resisted the threat. Both are partly right: Collingwood in that the man decides or wills to yield; common sense in that what he does in obeying whoever is threatening him is decided for him, not by him. He is obeying the will of another. The difficulty can be resolved if freedom is thought of in terms of 'self-determination', rather than merely in terms of 'will'. You are free to the extent that you determine your conduct for yourself. To the extent that it is determined for you, not by you, you are not free. This allows for different kinds and different degrees of freedom in a way that Collingwood's account does not. At the same time it preserves what is true in his account. A man who panics is not free. His action is determined by what he is afraid of. A man who acts from preference is free in the sense that he determines

his conduct. But a man who acts from a rational decision is free in a different and wider sense. He determines his conduct in the light of an assessment of the alternatives open to him. But more about this later.

Collingwood says that Right and Duty are different forms of practical reason. But in terms of his account, they are not really different. According to him, to say 'I did X because it was right', is to say: 'I did X because there is a rule which prescribes that X should be done.' To say 'I did X because it was my duty', is to say: 'I did X because I had freely undertaken to do it.' But why should I do what I have freely undertaken to do? Collingwood does not say, but there can be no doubt about the answer. Not to do so would be wrong. It would be to break the moral rule which says that people ought to keep their word. It follows that on Collingwood's account, Duty is a special case of Right. A duty is a certain kind of right act: namely an act of the kind which meets the requirements of the moral rule that people should always do what they have freely undertaken to do. This means that both the higher forms of practical reason are regularian in character. But Collingwood's account of regularian action is unsatisfactory. Although he distinguishes between 'willing the rule' and 'willing the particular act which obeys it', he does not seem to have grasped the significance of this distinction. 'Willing' or making a rule is not itself a case of regularian action: not, that is to say, a case of obeying a rule. Obeying a rule means deciding to do an act of the kind prescribed by it in a situation of the kind which it covers. You do not have to decide what to do. The rule tells you that. You only have to decide that you will do it. Making a rule means deciding what kind of situations are to be covered and what kind of act is to be done in them. You have to decide not only what is to be done, but when.

According to Collingwood, the simplest case of regularian action is that of a man making rules for himself. Making rules for others to obey is a 'more complex case'. This betrays his failure to grasp the significance of the distinction between making rules and obeying them. According to his own definition, in regularian action, acts are either right or wrong. They either obey or disobey a rule. But making a rule means deciding what rule to make and while this decision can be better or worse, it cannot be right or wrong. There cannot be a rule telling you what rule to make, although there can be a 'second-order' rule conferring on you authority to make one, but leaving it to you to decide what rule it should be. The simplest case of regularian action is that of obeying rules which you do not make but find already there. This begins early in life. A child learning to talk learns to obey linguistic rules. About the same time he begins learning how to behave which means learning to obey elementary rules of good manners and moral conduct. This priority of regularian action is logical as well as temporal. You must learn how to obey rules before you can make them either for yourself or for other people. The conclusion which follows is that the higher forms of practical reason are not regularian in character. They include the more sophisticated activity of making rules but this is not regularian. Regularian action properly so called belongs to a level below practical reason.

Collingwood arrived at the three forms of practical reason by considering how modern Europeans answer the question: 'Why did you do that?' He has neglected one kind of answer: 'I did it because it was prudent.' For instance, obeying the orders of a gunman. There is also another kind of answer he has not considered 'I did it because it was wise.' 'Why did you change your job?' 'For the sake of better prospects and more interesting work.' 'Why did you take up sailing?' 'Because it would add to my enjoyment of life.' It is wise for me to better my prospects and make my life more interesting and enjoyable. It is prudent for me to provide for my safety and security and avoid unnecessary danger. The common factor here is the idea of personal well-being. Modern Europeans think that it is rational for a man to act wisely and prudently because they think that it is rational for him to do what he can to maintain and develop his personal well-being. There are good reasons for this conviction. They lie in the fact that while circumstances play a large part in shaping the course of a man's life, he can himself influence it through his choices and decisions. What sort of life he has depends upon what he does in the face of the opportunities and limitations confronting him. He therefore has good reason to make the maintenance and development of his personal well-being a leading consideration in the determination of his conduct. If he does not concern himself with it, why should anyone else? If Collingwood had reflected on the meaning of acting wisely and prudently he might have seen that personal well-being is a form of practical reason. To say 'I did it because it was wise', or 'because it was prudent', is to say: 'I did it because in some way, it contributed to my personal well-being.'

Personal well-being must be distinguished from utility. Utility is a rational basis for the choice of means but so far as utility is concerned, the choice of ends is capricious. Personal well-being is a rational basis for the choice of ends. If a new job has better prospects and more interesting work, getting the job is a rational end of utilitarian action. But personal well-being is also relevant to the choice of means. A particular course of action may be expedient as a means, but tedious or dangerous. It may then be wise or prudent to find some other means, or, failing that, to abandon the end to which the tedious or dangerous course of action is the means. But this is not all. The perspective of utility is confined to action done as a means. The perspective of personal well-being is wider. It includes not only utilitarian action but leisure activities like sailing which are undertaken not as the means to further ends, but because they are interesting or enjoyable in themselves. As a form of practical reason, personal well-being is on a higher level than utility which is properly subordinate to it.

3. According to Collingwood, the third form of practical reason is Duty. But on his own showing, Duty is only a special case of Right. Doing my duty means obeying the moral rule that people should always do what they have freely undertaken to do. This is not an adequate account of duty, much less of the wider idea of morality. Consider the moral virtue of honesty. If there are any moral duties at all, there is certainly one to cultivate and practice this virtue. But it does not fit Collingwood's account of duty. My duty to be honest does not arise from any undertaking I have freely given. Rather it is presupposed in all such undertakings. Instead of: 'I ought to keep my word because I ought to be honest,' Collingwood is in effect maintaining: 'I ought to be honest because I ought to keep my word.' But why ought I to be honest? More generally: why does there have to be any morality at all? Collingwood ignores this question. But it must be answered if the claim that Duty is a form of practical reason is to be justified.

Morality has a rational basis in certain conditions necessary for human co-operation. People who co-operate together become dependent upon one another. Each must do his part if the common enterprise is not to break down. This means that there can be co-operation only if there is trust, and trust presupposes honesty. Other moral commitments besides honesty are also necessary. They include self-control, justice, and responsibility. A man who cannot control himself cannot be trusted. People who co-operate must deal justly with each other if destructive disputes are to be avoided. Each must be responsible to the rest for making the best contribution he can to the common enterprise. But is there an inescapable commitment to co-operation? Yes, if there is an inescapable commitment to social living, because co-operation is of the essence of social living. I can rationally reject the commitment to co-operation and therefore to morality only if I am prepared to withdraw from social living altogether. That means either committing suicide or becoming a hermit, if the latter is still a live option in the modern world. The answer to our question then is this; there has to be morality if there is to be social living, because without it there could be no co-operation and therefore no social living.

Self-control is the most elementary moral virtue. The duty to cultivate and practice it must be inculcated in early childhood because it is a necessary condition for any coherent activity: regularian and rational, moral and non-moral. Being honest means obeying certain rules: keeping your word, not lying, deceiving, or stealing. This suggests that over and above the elementary duty of self-control, morality is regularian in character. But justice and responsibility suggest that it is also something more. They are principles rather than merely rules. Acting on a principle involves deciding how best to implement it in the particular circumstances of a given situation: deciding what is most just or least unjust, having regard to all the interests involved; deciding how best to fulfil your responsibilities in the face of particular problems and exigencies. All this points to a distinction between two levels of moral development: a lower regularian level and a higher rational level. The lower level is that of childhood. Being moral consists of obeying established moral rules and in cases which these do not cover, or in which they conflict, relying on the guidance of parents or others to whose authority children are subject. The rational level is that of mature adult life. Being moral now means acting responsibly and justly, obeying moral rules in the spirit rather than the letter and, if doing so on a particular occasion is the lesser evil, breaking them. An important part of the process of growing up consists in making a gradual transition from the lower to the higher level. But there is nothing inevitable about this transition and, for most of us, it is never wholly completed.

At the lower level, morality is a form of regularian action, at the higher level a form of practical reason. But as a form of practical reason, it is best described as Social Morality. This brings out its rational basis. The drawback of the term 'duty' is that it is not confined to practical reason. There is a duty to act responsibly and also to act justly. But self-control and honesty are duties, and there is a general duty to obey moral rules. The question; 'Why did you do that?' can be answered in terms of social morality: 'I did it because it was the best way in which I could fulfil my responsibility', or: 'I did it because in the circumstances, it was more just than any alternative open to me.' It follows that, *pace* Collingwood, the three forms of practical reason are: Utility, Personal Well-Being, and Social Morality. Regularian action belongs to a level below practical reason but is an indispensable preparation for it and continues within it, being, however, subordinate to its requirements. To answer the question: 'Why did you do that?' by 'Because it was right', assumes that the rule which the right act obeys has a rational justification and that on the particular occasion there are no special circumstances which would justify breaking it.

Like personal well-being, social morality is a rational basis for the choice of ends in utilitarian action. 'It is my responsibility to see that the safety precautions are adequate.' 'If we are not to be unjust, we must give him a chance to state his case and make the necessary arrangements.' Social morality is also relevant to the choice of means. No matter how expedient an action may be, if it is unjust or socially irresponsible, it ought not to be chosen as a means. Social morality and personal well-being can sometimes conflict. There is no pre-established social harmony which guarantees that the maximum personal well-being of each is always and everywhere compatible with the maximum personal well-being of all. Acting responsibly or justly can sometimes mean personal sacrifice, hardship, or even death. When this happens, there are good reasons for giving priority to the demands of social morality. Not to do so would be to abandon the commitment entailed in social living. I am not entitled to the benefits of social living unless I am prepared to pay the price and the price is meeting the demands of social morality, not that social

morality and personal well-being are always in conflict. What is responsible and just is for the most part usually what is wise and prudent, but not invariably. The perspective of social morality is wider than that of personal well-being. It takes into account the nature and significance of the social dimension of human life. As a form of practical reason, it is on a higher level than personal well-being, which is properly subordinate to it.

According to Collingwood, a completely capricious act is completely irrational. He concludes from this that the less the caprice, the greater the rationality. Right is a higher form of practical reason than Utility, because it is less capricious. Duty is higher than Right, because in principle it is devoid of caprice altogether. But since Duty is only a special case of Right, and since his account of Right is vitiated by his failure to distinguish between regularian action properly so called, and the more sophisticated activity of making rules, his exposition of practical reason gets no further than Utility. I agree that a completely capricious act is completely irrational, or perhaps better, non-rational. I also agree that utility is infected with caprice, but what makes personal well-being a higher form of practical reason than utility is not that it is less capricious, although it is, but that its perspective is wider. The same is true of social morality in relation to personal well-being. One form of practical reason is higher than another, that is to say, because it embodies a better understanding of the character and conditions of human action. According to Collingwood, a rational act is always an individual act. But the point which seems to have eluded him is that in practical reason you have to deal with an individual situation, not as in regularian action merely with a situation of a particular kind. The problem is to decide what is most responsible, prudent, or expedient, in this situation now confronting you with its peculiar circumstances and features. A just or wise act is likely to contain elements of caprice. But that does not matter so long as they do not impair its justice or wisdom. A rational act must be as devoid of caprice as the situation being dealt with requires. It does not have to be a completely 'definite individual' but only as definite as is necessary for it to be responsible, wise, or expedient.

I suggested earlier that thinking of freedom in terms of self-determination, rather than merely in terms of will, brings out more clearly the sense in which freedom is a matter of degree. The relation of regularian action to practical reason bears this out. Regularian action is the first step towards the fuller self-determination involved in practical reason. A child who can follow rules is no longer completely dependent upon adults to tell him what to do. But he is still dependent on rules. He emancipates himself from this dependence and becomes more self-determining to the extent that, as he grows up, he becomes capable of acting in terms of practical reason. A man who is capable of pursuing his personal well-being wisely and prudently achieves personal freedom. Practical reason in the form of social morality is moral freedom. A man who acts responsibly and justly is self-determining as a moral agent. Finally, a brief word on dialectic and eristic. The thinking involved in regularian action is essentially eristical. A regularian act is either right or wrong. There is no room for discussion, for reconsideration and modification of decisions about what to do. The rule must be obeyed and that is the end of the matter. The thinking involved in practical reason is essentially dialectical. A rational act is better or worse, rather than simply right or wrong; for instance, more or less just, more or less prudent, more or less expedient. There is room for discussion, re-consideration, and revision of provisional decisions. The question is what would be the most responsible, the wisest, the most efficient course, and second thoughts are always possible. As we shall see later, this has a bearing on Collingwood's ideas about civilization.

(B) THE BODY POLITIC

1. Collingwood's theory of the body politic has two components: a theory of community and a theory of ruling. Of central importance in the theory of community is a distinction between a social and a non-social community. The theory of ruling is the key to this distinction. According to Collingwood: 'Ruling is either *immanent* or *transeunt*. It is immanent when that which rules, rules itself, the same thing being both agent and patient in respect of the same activity. It is transeunt when that which rules, rules something other than itself: when in respect of the same activity of ruling there is one thing which is agent, the ruler, and another thing which is patient, the ruled'. Immanent rule is an aspect of freedom. A free man rules himself. Those who have not yet reached the stage of freedom or who are incapable of reaching it, are incapable of immanent rule and, if they are to be ruled, must be subjected to transeunt rule at the hands of those who can exercise immanent rule over themselves. Transeunt rule is a form of mental force. It operates by means of reward and punishment. This is the basis for the distinction between a social and non-social community. A social community or society is made up of free persons and rules itself through the immanent rule of its members. A non-social community is made up of persons who, being not free and therefore incapable of immanent rule, have to be subjected to transeunt rule. But before saying more about this distinction, let us see what Collingwood's general theory of community is.

He says that: 'By a community I mean a state of affairs in which something is divided or shared by a number of human beings. This state of affairs I call the *Suum Cuique* of the community. What matters to the existence of a community is that it should have a suum cuique. Its taking one form rather than another makes no difference to the things being a community; though much to what kind of a community it is'. In addition to a *suum cuique,* something else is also necessary. 'Thus any community must have a home or place in which corporately it lives'. He goes on to say that: 'A community must be ruled if it is to exist'. This is because: 'A community depends for its existence on something which makes it a community and keeps it a community; that is, alots to its members their respective shares in whatever is divided between them, and causes them to remain faithful to this alotment: maintains the *suum cuique* which is the essence of its communal character. The establishment and maintainance of the *suum cuique* is called *ruling*'. The difference between a society or social community and a non-social community is that: 'A society is a *self-ruling* community. A non-social community needs for its existence to be ruled by something other than itself'.

What Collingwood has in mind can be seen in the case of the family. The parents, being adults, are in some measure free persons. They exercise immanent rule over themselves and maintain between them the life of the family as a social community. But for their children who are not yet free persons, the life of the family is the life of a non-social community. This non-social community of the 'Nursery' is kept in being by the parents who exercise transeunt rule over their children who are its members. Since all human beings begin life as children, all human beings begin by being members of non-social communities. They become fit for social life properly so called only when they develop mentally to the point of achieving freedom. Collingwood finds the key to social living in the idea of partnership. Becoming a free person means *inter alia* becoming capable of entering into partnerships with other free persons for the sake of carrying on joint activities with them. 'People become partners by deciding to behave like partners. A society or partnership is constituted by the social will of the partners, an act of free will whereby the person who thereby becomes a partner decides to take upon himself a share of the joint enterprise'. Partnerships or societies are originated and kept in being by the 'joint will' of the partners or members. There are as many forms of partnership or society as there are kinds of enterprise which free persons can undertake together. One distinction however, is of special importance for the theory of the body politic. 'This is a distinction between two kinds of enterprise, one intended to terminate within a length of time, planned to reach a conclusion at some definite period in the future; this I call a *temporary enterprise;* the other intended in Stevenson's words *to travel hopefully but not to arrive;* no time of termination being stated or implied; this I call a permanent enterprise. Every society is formed for the prosecution of some enterprise. Where it is a temporary enterprise, I call the society a temporary society; where permanent, a permanent society'. Two men going for a walk together constitute a temporary society. A society for studying the antiquities of a district is a permanent society.

According to Collingwood, a body politic is like a family 'writ large'. 'The simplest body politic differs from the simplest family only at one point. Each is divided into a social part and a non-social part; but whereas the family society is a temporary society, the political society is a permanent society'. The members of a body politic consist of two classes. 'The first class is a society and rules itself. Its members are *persons* or agents possessed of free will. It also rules the second class which is a community only because it is ruled. Members of the second class are devoid of free will'. He goes on: 'Let us call the first class the *Council* of the body politic; the second, its *Nursery*. It recruits the council by promotion from the nursery; it recruits the nursery by breeding babies and taking the consequences'. The body politic *qua* society is permanent because: 'In a body politic new babies are always being born; the nursery is always being replenished and the work of imposing order upon it is never concluded. Equally the work of establishing relations between it and the council is never concluded, nor the work of ordering the council itself, for that, too, is constantly being recruited'. The council is therefore faced with three never-ending tasks. It must define and maintain a way of life for itself, define and maintain a way of life for the nursery, and maintain the relation between itself and the nursery.

All this is summarized by Collingwood in three propositions which he calls the 'three laws of politics'. Of them he says: 'They are meant to hold good of every body politic without exception, irrespective of all differences between one kind and another. All good political practice is based on grasping them, and most bad political practice is based on failing to grasp them as rules of political activity'. They are normative, not descriptive laws, comparable in status to the laws of thought of traditional logic. The first law of politics is that: *'a body politic is divided into a ruling class and a ruled class.'* The second that: *'the barrier between the two classes is permeable in an upward direction.'* The third that: *'there is a correspondence between the ruler and the ruled* whereby the former become adapted to ruling these as distinct from other persons, and the latter to being ruled by these as distinct from other persons'. To this, however, he adds: 'But the third law also works inversely from the ruled class upwards and determines that whoever is to rule a certain people must rule them in a way in which they will let themselves be ruled'.

There are two other things in Collingwood's theory of the body politic about which a word must be said: his idea of political action, and of the 'dialectical' character of political life. Of the former he says: 'Political action pure and simple is will pure and simple; but differs from will as such in being, first, the joint will of a society, the rulers of a body politic; secondly, that will exercised immanently upon those who exercise it as the self-rule of that society; and thirdly, the same will exercised as force in transeunt rule over a non-social community, the ruled class of a body politic'. Political action, that is to say, is the action of free persons in their capacity as members of the council of a body politic not in their capacity as private persons. Like the action of an individual free man, political action can be capricious. It can also be rational in any one of the three forms of practical reason. Capricious political action is expressed in decrees. 'A decree is the simplest form of political

action because it represents the simplest form of will, namely caprice, transposed into the key of politics'. He goes on to say that political action in the form of Utility is 'policy', in the form of Right, it is 'Law', while in the form of Duty, it is what he calls 'Political Duty'. The trouble with this attempt to 'transpose practical reason into the key of politics' is that the defects of his account of practical reason reappear in his account of political action. But more about that later.

According to Collingwood: 'The world of politics is a dialectical world in which non-social communities (communities of men in what Hobbes called a "state of nature") turn into societies'. Whether or not he is right to interpret Hobbes in this way, what is there which is dialectical about this world of politics? The answer lies in his view of the body politic as a mixed community made up of a social and a non-social element. 'Such a community might be described by attending to the positive element as a society; by attending to the negative element as a non-social community; yet it might be one community which was being so described; the difference being only a difference in *point of view, a dialectical* difference'. The non-agreement between these points of view is converted into agreement when it is realized that the body politic is a mixed community, that it is always in process of becoming a society, and therefore ceasing to be a non-social community but that this process, because the nursery is always being replenished, never ceases. According to Collingwood, things whose existence is a process of transition from one state to another, a process which can never be completed and which never begins, but is always already under way, must be thought of in dialectical terms. To think of them eristically, that is as either being in the state from which they are turning or as being in the state into which they are turning, would be to fail to understand their nature. They are never wholly in either state but are always in the course of transition from one to the other, and this from of 'process' existence is best described as dialectical.

2. Collingwood regarded his theory of the body politic as an amendment to what he called the 'Classical Politics', that is, the political theories of Hobbes, Locke, and Rousseau. The amendment was the replacement of 'the doctrine of the State of Nature' in these theories by his theory of the non-social community. But there is also a clear Platonic strain in his theory of the body politic. A central thesis of *The Republic* is that those who are to rule others must first be able to rule themselves, and this is also the central thesis in Collingwood's theory. The resemblance between his ruled class and Plato's class of 'Producers' is obvious. So too is the resemblance between Collingwood's theory of mind and Plato's 'doctrine of the Soul'. But that is a matter which I cannot pursue here. Granted that those who are to rule others must first be able to rule themselves, is Collingwood's account of ruling in terms of the distinction between immanent and transeunt rule acceptable? I do not think that it is.

Immanent rule, like freedom, is a matter of degree. It is part and parcel of the capacity for self-determination. Its most elementary form is self-control which is a necessary condition for regularian action. For practical reason, something more than merely self-control is necessary, namely the ability to control and determine one's conduct in the light of purposes which have been freely chosen. Transeunt rule need not necessarily be a matter of force. People can and do obey rules which have been made by others for them, and which they could not have made for themselves, without having to be forced to do so. Civil law largely consists of such rules. People obey them for the most part because they recognize the need for them, although they could not have made them and do not understand in detail the particular reasons for their taking one form rather than another. Collingwood is maintaining that only those who can make rules for themselves can freely obey rules made by others, a view which repeats the error in his account of regularian action discussed in the last section.

All this has implications for his theory of the non-social community. Its members are said to be incapable of immanent rule and hence of freedom. They are at the mercy of their desires and passions, and act only from preference, not from choice. Could such people constitute a community at all? Any community must be a regularian community in the sense that its members must be capable of obeying rules and must therefore be capable of enough immanent rule to enable them to do so. They cannot therefore be wholly at the mercy of their desires and passions. No doubt there are cases, for instance a community of prisoners, in which the threat of force plays a large part in securing obedience. But the effective operation of such a threat presupposes some degree of prudence on the part of those who are threatened, not simply uncontrolled fear. According to Collingwood, non-social communities are always dependent on something else which rules them. In fact, he is not wholly consistent about this. In the course of his discussion of political action, he refers to international law as 'the customary law of a very ancient non-social community', and likens this customary law to the law of the Iceland of the Sagas. Presumably a community which maintains a customary law is not dependent on something else to rule it, and is best described as a regularian community. What would he say about the so-called 'traditional societies' studied by social anthropologists, that is tribal communities? These are regularian communities, or at least predominantly so. There may be the rudiments of practical reason in the form of utility, but little or nothing of free partnership or 'society' in his sense. Yet tribal communities are not dependent on something else for their existence. They maintain their own largely customary life from generation to generation. They can hardly be called non-social communities in his sense.

A tribal community may not be a social community, but it is a self-sufficient community in the sense of being sufficient for the maintenance of human life. Human life is and always has been carried on in self-sufficient communities. At different times and in different places these have taken very different forms. Tribes, kingdoms, city-states, the principalities and duchies of Medieval Europe, and the nation-states of the modern world, are instances. Collingwood's theory of the body politic is a theory of the essential characteristics which every self-sufficient community must possess. He is saying, in effect, that if a community is to be self-sufficient for human life, it must be a body politic. But as the case of a tribal community shows, he is wrong. A regularian community can be self-sufficient for human life. It does not have to be a social community as well. Moreover, since there can be no community without regularian action, every self-sufficient community must at least be a regularian community. But it need not be merely a regularian community, it can also be something more. It can become a social community to the extent that its adult members are able to make the transition from regularian to rational morality, that is, become capable of practical reason in the forms of personal well-being and social morality. After making this transition, they are still members of the self-sufficient community, but rational, not merely regularian members. They have become free persons and free moral agents in the sense of being self-determining in both capacities.

This suggests that something can be salvaged from Collingwood's theory of the body politic. The theory of the non-social community must go and be replaced by the theory of the regularian community, which unlike the non-social community, can be a self-sufficient community. But his theory of the social community based on the idea of partnership is compatible with the revised account of practical reason of the last section, and can be combined with the theory of the regularian community to yield a theory of the typical form of self-sufficient community in modern Europe: the nation-state. It is after all with modern Europe that he is primarily concerned. But while this is all right so far as it goes, there is another objection to be reckoned with. In what sense is this revised theory a theory of modern European bodies politic, as distinct from modern European self-sufficient communities? It may be acceptable as a theory of community and society, but in what respects, if any, can it be regarded as a political theory? The short answer is that with the removal of the theory of the non-social community, the political element, what I called earlier the Platonic strain, in his theory of the body politic has gone.

Modern European self-sufficient communities are political communities. They are not only nations but 'States'. Their political character comes from the institution of government. This institution is not essential to the existence of a self-sufficient community as such. Tribes have existed without it and it is absent from the Icelandic community of the Sagas. But it is clearly indispensable to modern European nations. Their ways of life would not be what they are without it. The key to its role lies in distinguishing between the 'public' and 'private' aspects of the ways of life of modern European nations. From one point of view, the life of a modern European nation is a life of 'private enterprise', not merely in economic activity, but in domestic and cultural spheres as well. It embraces many varieties of 'partnerships' in Collingwood's sense, or voluntary associations, undertaken by people who in some measure at least are free persons and free moral agents. But from another point of view it is a public life, that is a life subject to public regulation, supervision, and direction, the purpose of which is to establish and maintain conditions under which the members of the national community who may number many millions, can all of them participate in the life of private partnerships and voluntary associations. The role of government is to be the custodian of the public life of the nation. While this is only a hint of the complex character of the institution of government, it is enough to bring out the inadequacy of Collingwood's theory of the body politic as a theory of the modern European nation-state. His concept of the 'council' of the body politic throws no light on the distinction between 'public' and 'private'. To think of the body politic as a family 'writ large' is to miss the significance of the institution of government for the life of free partnership and voluntary association.

Of his three laws of politics, only the third contributes anything to the understanding of modern European political life. 'A people can only be governed in the way in which it will let itself be governed'. The first two turn on his distinction between the ruling class and the ruled. But this is only a distinction between those who are and those who are not capable of practical reason, a distinction which is a matter of degree, and which blurs the distinction between the public and private aspects of a nation's life. His account of political action fails to distinguish between political and social action. So far as 'transposing practical reason into the key of politics' is concerned, all that needs to be said is this. If the work of governing is to be well done, it must be in the hands of persons capable of practical reason in the form of social morality, that is, persons who can act responsibly and justly as 'custodians of the public interest', as well as wisely and prudently in determining in detail what must be done to promote it.

Collingwood argued that the world of politics is a dialectical world because a body politic is always in the course of a transition from being a non-social community to being a society. It is never wholly the one nor wholly the other. There is a sense in which this might be applied to the public and private aspects of the life of a modern European nation. Its life is never wholly private nor wholly public but always partly one and partly the other, and the line between the two is never fixed. But that is not all. There is another sense in which political life can be dialectical; when the form of government is democratic. However, more about that later. What is false in Collingwood's contention is that the life of a self-sufficient community is dialectical, simply

in virtue of its being a self-sufficient community. A tribal community with a predominantly regularian way of life is not in any meaningful sense always in the course of turning from one state into another. The fact that there is always a new generation in the course of growing up makes no difference. This is one of the most stable characteristics of the community. On the other hand, in a self-sufficient community like a modern European nation which is a social as well as a regularian community, the idea of a dialectical character is more plausible. Whether much is to be gained by thinking of modern European communities in this way is another question. Perhaps more important is the sense in which their lives are historical in character, that is, change from generation to generation through the cumulative and largely unforeseen actions in each generation. Collingwood would not have denied this, although he did not discuss it in *The New Leviathan*. But the matter cannot be pursued further here.

3. The Modern European Mind has produced 'the thing called Modern European Civilisation'. It has also produced the Modern Democratic State. While Collingwood has something to say about democracy and aristocracy in *The New Leviathan,* it is in connection with his doctrine of the ruling class in a body politic. He does not undertake any sort of examination of democracy as a form of government specially characteristic of Modern European Civilization. The omission is surprising in view of his declared intention to 'inquire into civilization and the revolt against it'. I shall try briefly to fill the gap. The modern democratic state, or 'Western Democracy', rests upon four main principles: the rule of law; representative government; constitutional opposition; and equality of citizenship. I do not say that these principles are fully implemented in self-professing Western democracies: far from it. But I think that thoughtful adherents of Western democracy would agree that they are morally committed to them. Let us look more closely at them.

The rule of law involves three things: the supremacy of law, that is, that legal obligations are paramount; equality before the law, that is the equal subjection of all including the government to the law, and the equal protection for all of the law; and freedom under the law, that is that where the law is silent, all are free to act according to their own volition. A representative government is one which is chosen from and accountable to a wider citizen body, this being secured by periodic free elections. Hence the necessity of the rule of law: electoral procedure must be provided for by law. But without the opportunity for choice and criticism, there can be no free elections: hence the necessity for constitutional opposition. The composition of the citizen body is determined by the fourth principle. Its membership must be co-extensive with the entire adult population. This guarantees not only 'one man, one vote', but the equal right of all to participate in politics. The principle of constitutional opposition means what it says. Opposition must be within the limits of the law. You are free to criticize and oppose the government of the day but not to undermine its authority to govern. This presupposes that the great majority of the citizen body had a clear practical understanding of the difference between opposition and rebellion. But they must not only understand the difference. They must be able and willing to act on it. That means acknowledging and fulfilling the paramount obligation to obey the law, and eschewing all forms of revolutionary political action.

Two preconditions are necessary for the successful working of democracy: one social, the other cultural. The social precondition is the absence of fundamental conflict. The members of the democratic body politic must be in broad agreement about the fundamental character of their way of life. It must not matter too much who wins the next election. People must be willing to accept the verdict of the ballot-box. Where this precondition is absent, for instance, in a self-sufficient community deeply and painfully divided along racial or religious lines, the best that can be managed is a government drawn from and accountable to the members of the dominant racial or religious group. Members of the subordinate group will be 'second-class citizens' whose voice can become effective only through revolutionary political action. The cultural precondition is a well-established and widespread tradition of discussion and argument, based on the recognition that to most questions there is more than one side, and that those who are on the opposite side are not for that reason either knaves or fools. This cultural precondition presupposes the social precondition. Both are necessary for the effective working of democracy.

In view of this, it is hardly surprising that democracy has taken root and lasted in only a minority of the nations of the modern world. It is only in Western Europe, North America, and Australasia that both the social and cultural preconditions are to be found. The majority of mankind have never known democracy, and for the foreseeable future will have to manage without it. It is not the best form of government if that means best for everyone always and everywhere. But there is no one form of government which is best in this sense. What is true, however, is that where the social and cultural preconditions are present, democracy is better than any other form of government. This is so for two reasons: one negative, the other positive. The negative reason is that democracy more than any other form of government takes account of and provides protection against human fallibility. It recognizes that no individual and no group has a monopoly of virtue or wisdom. The positive reason is that through the principles of constitutional opposition and equality of citizenship, democracy gives more scope and encouragement to more people to advance from regularian to rational morality than any other form of government. It enables practical reason 'to be transposed into the key of politics', which is another way of saying that it makes possible dialectical rather than merely eristical politics. Under a democratic form of government, occasions of political non-agreement have

at least a better chance of being converted into occasions of political agreement, instead of hardening into disagreement. To be fair to Collingwood, an understanding of this is implicit in his discussion of aristocracy and democracy although he did not relate it to an examination of the principles underlying democracy.

(C) CIVILIZATION

Collingwood distinguishes between the generic and the specific meaning of 'civilization'. According to the generic meaning: 'Civilization is a *process of approximation to an ideal state*. To civilize a thing is to impose on it or promote in it a process; a process of becoming; a process in something which we know to be a community; whereby it approximates nearer to an ideal state which I will call *civility* and recedes farther from its contradictory, an ideal state which I will call *barbarity*'. No community is ever simply barbarous, or completely civil. It is always in a condition of turning from the one into the other. To discover the specific meaning, it is necessary to determine the specific character of the process, to know what happens to a community as it becomes more civilized. Discussing the specific meaning, Collingwood says: 'According to the view I find expressed in books I have looked at, and in the mouths of persons I have questioned to find out what the thing called civilization is commonly thought to involve, civilization has something to do with the mutual relations of the members within a community; something to do with the relation of these members to the world of nature; and something to do with the relation between them and other human beings not being members of the same community'. The clue to what this something is, lies in the idea of civil behaviour.

'Behaving *civilly* to a man means respecting his feelings: abstaining from shocking him, annoying him, frightening him, or (briefly) arousing in him any passion or desire that might diminish his self-respect; that is, threatening his consciousness of freedom by making him feel that his power of choice is in danger of breaking down and passion or desire likely to take charge'. People who treat one another civilly act in a dialectical, not an eristical spirit. '*Being civilized* means living so far as possible, *dialectically,* that is, in constant endeavour to convert occasions of non-agreement into occasions of agreement.' What Collingwood means is clear. He is equating the process of civilization with the process by which a community becomes a social community. Civility equals sociality. 'Civilization is the process in a community by which the various members assert themselves as will; severally as individual will, corporately as social will (the two being inseparable)'. So far as relations with other communities are concerned, civilization means acting civilly towards their members. So far as the natural world is concerned, civilization means 'a spirit of intelligent exploitation'. This is possible only in a community whose members already treat one another civilly since that is necessary for development, conservation, and transmission of the knowledge and experience which is itself necessary for the intelligent exploitation of nature.

What about 'revolts against civilization', the fourth part of Collingwood's inquiry? It is important to distinguish between lack of civilization and the repudiation of civilization.

> I distinguish two ways of being uncivilized. I call them savagery and barbarism and distinguish them as follows. Savagery is a negative idea. It means not being civilized, and that is all. In practice, I need hardly say, there is no such thing as absolute savagery; there is only relative savagery, that is, being civilized up to a certain point and no more. By barbarism I mean hostility towards civilization; the effort, conscious, or unconscious, to become less civilized than you are, either in general or in some special way, and, so far as in you lies, to promote a similar change in others.

Relative savagery is equivalent to relative barbarity in his account of the generic meaning of civilization. Barbarism is the attempt to reverse the process of civilization and move back towards the ideal state of barbarity, and away from civility. It is the paradoxical attempt by members of a social community to revert to non-social community from which they have emerged, paradoxical because free persons are choosing to abandon freedom, choosing to give up choosing. Collingwood describes the will to barbarism as: 'a will to acquiesce in the chaotic rule of emotion, which it began by destroying. All it does is to assert itself as will and then deny itself as will'.

If my argument in this essay is sound, Collingwood's account of civilization needs amending. Civilization is a process which is undergone by a self-sufficient community. Such a community is always at the very least a regularian community. It becomes civilized to the extent that it becomes more than merely a regularian community, that is to the extent that practical reason, not merely regularian action, plays a part in its way of life. But practical reason means utility, personal well-being, and social morality. Collingwood's account of it gets no further than utility. The thinking involved in practical reason in terms of my revised version is dialectical, so Collingwood is right to say that 'being civilized means, so far as possible, living dialectically'. But he has failed to give a coherent account of how this manner of living is embodied in practical reason. To say that civilization is a process towards an ideal state of civility and away from an ideal state of barbarity is misleading. It fails to allow for the case of tribal communities which are not in any meaningful sense social communities, and which are untouched by civilization so far as the higher forms of practical reason are concerned. Finally, Collingwood's idea of the body politic leaves no room for a distinction between civilized and uncivilized forms of political life, since he is committed to holding that every self-sufficient community must be a body politic without

differentiating between the social and political aspects of its life. He has failed to see that democracy, because more than any other form of government it makes dialectical politics possible, is more civilized than any other form of government.

His conception of barbarism is really a conception of irrationality, as distinct from non-rationality and imperfect rationality. To what extent the historical examples of barbarism which he discusses in Part 4 of *The New Leviathan* are really examples of irrationality I am not competent to judge. But he is certainly right that irrationality, in the sense of the repudiation of practical reason by those who are capable of rational conduct, is a revolt against civilization. Whether he is right in contending that this always takes the form of 'acquiescing in the chaotic rule of emotion' is another matter. It may take the form of ideological commitment in the face of rational misgivings which are repressed or 'rationalized' away. It may take the form of a reaction against what Popper called 'the strain of civilization'. This might be described in Collingwood's terms as a relapse from dialectical into eristical thinking. Collingwood limited himself to revolts against civilization. Equally important is an inquiry into its 'strains' and into the obstacles which impede or arrest it. The social precondition for democracy, the absence of social conflict, is not something which can be created by good will. Dialectical thinking cannot end social divisions since it can flourish only where they are absent.

Collingwood regarded his inquiry into civilization as an essay in the science of mind. I suggested at the beginning of this essay that what he was engaged in was a conceptual inquiry of much the same sort as about a decade later were undertaken by many British and American philosophers. Both Collingwood and his postwar successors seemed to have thought of their task as essentially descriptive rather than critical. Collingwood was led to this conclusion by his ideas about the relation of philosophy to history, postwar philosophers by their views about philosophy and language. In the end perhaps these two views are not really different, since language is essentially a historical phenomenon. Be that as it may, a philosophical study of concepts which eschews criticism is failing to carry out its proper task. Not only 'What can be meant by . . . ?' but 'How should we think of . . . ?' concerns the philosopher. The defects in Collingwood's account of freedom and practical reason, and in his account of the body politic, stem as much from lack of critical appraisal as from incomplete descriptive analysis. But this is not the note on which to end. The impression given of *The New Leviathan* in this essay is misleading because of its concentration upon defects in certain parts of the argument. To do justice to the book as a whole would need more space than is available to me. In his autobiography Collingwood expressed his attitude towards potential critics by saying: 'Let them write, not about me, but about the subject'. The measure of his achievement in *The New Leviathan* is that if the subject is civilization and the writer a philosopher, he can hardly avoid writing about Collingwood.

David W. Black (essay date 1982)

SOURCE: "Collingwood on Corrupt Consciousness," in *The Journal of Aesthetics and Art Criticism,* Vol. XL, No. 4, Summer, 1982, pp. 395-400.

[*In the following essay, Black examines Collingwood's concept of "corrupt consciousness' and its relationship to his theory of art.*]

Taken at face value, Collingwood's theory of art seems to focus on an analysis of feeling. The work of art, in Collingwood's eyes, explicates the elements of sensibility by placing them in a self-conscious order. Such a theory of feeling is indeed fundamental to Collingwood's aesthetic; but he has an accompanying intent the purport of which is not fully revealed in his analysis of feeling. This second theory, which might be called a theory of the synthesis of feeling, is linked to the birth of perception itself. In his discussion of corrupt consciousness, Collingwood introduces what I believe to be a novel form of intelligibility. He suggests that the artwork maintains itself through a perceived relatedness that exists among the sensible qualities of the object. He presents a critique of perception itself by examining the internal relationships that generate the sensible side of our world.

In this way, Collingwood uncovers a pre-categorical, pre-conceptual order of meaning, an order of intelligibility that perhaps he himself does not fully understand. Collingwood's insight rests on his unique discovery that feeling, far from being chaotic, has a form of its own. This formal unity, which must be distinguished from a categorical synthesis, is a union not of concepts but of percepts. Collingwood's theory of corrupt consciousness is the catalyst that sets this principle of relation in motion.

I.

In his description of corrupt consciousness, Collingwood is intrigued by the following dilemma: Is there such a thing as brute sense? Or, are there only brutal interpretations of sense data? We tend to contrast our minds, our thoughts, and our conceptions with an objective sense world. There is little question that there are raw data in the world, but are these data constitutive factors in our sensible awareness of things? We find ourselves in confrontation with a world of objects. But to what extent do we ourselves fashion this sensible world? Do we sense what we cannot help but sense, or do we sense only what we have grown sensitive to? And, if one answers that sensibility is this latter, then one must ask how such a sensitivity is possible. Does this sensible maturity contrast with cognitive maturity? Does it suggest an alternative, noncognitive

means for mind to draw relations among the phenomena of its world?

Great art seems to generate a *new sensible given*; the genius somehow creates perception anew with each work he completes. But from where does this sensible given spring? What is it about sensibility that allows for creativity? The answers to these questions seem to lie, for Collingwood, in a principle of *sensible relatedness,* a notion that arises, I think, as an important parallel to expressiveness, a notion implicit in the banal untruth of a corrupt consciousness.

What, then, is corrupt consciousness? How does it turn corrupt? And what does it have to do with the notion of sensible relatedness and the pre-cognitive activity of mind? To deal with these questions is to deal with the dilemma of form. It must be remembered that, for Collingwood, every form present to consciousness carries with it an implicit emotional charge. These charges might be "sterilized" or ignored by consciousness but are, in this sense, not so much nonexistent as unrecognized. Collingwood claims that this sterilization of sensa is relatively absent in the perceptions of women, children, and artists; and that it is through the perceptions of these people that the public becomes aware of the emotive character of sensation. Yet, the sights and sounds of experience generate individual feelings, feelings that are peculiar to the forms in which they arise. The feeling is revealed in terms of the form and does not exist until the form arises. Hence the artist does not know what he is trying to express until he expresses it. To put it in Collingwood's words, "until a man has expressed his emotion, he does not yet know what emotion it is. The act of expressing it is therefore an exploration of his own emotions. He is trying to find out what these emotions are." Art thus produces original sensible forms but presupposes form itself as a fundamental given. Therefore, form must be distinguished from the mediation of form. The primary activity of "attention" must be distinguished from what Collingwood calls the "criteriological" activity of art. Quite simply, in order to answer the several questions that could be posed about corrupt consciousness, the corruption of consciousness must be distinguished from the birth of consciousness.

A corrupt consciousness is oblivious of its own nature. It fails in this regard to recognize something about the way in which it compares and relates feelings. A corrupt consciousness, for Collingwood, is thus bound up in its own lie. In contrast, awareness is born during the act of attention. Attention is the simplest act of consciousness. The consciousness that merely "attends" to feelings tells no lies because it makes no judgment. Through attention, consciousness sustains a feeling. But when corrupt, consciousness "disowns" the feeling it sustains; it refuses to believe that the feeling is its own. This latter act is far different from the former. In the act of attention, consciousness merely moves from the realm of sheer feeling to the awareness of form. However, in the act of corruption, consciousness works within the realm of form alone. It deals directly with the images at hand. Its action is directed against the image it is forming, not against the feeling implied by the image. When consciousness attends to a sensation, it simply pulls a sense datum into the purview of conscious life. Yet, in this act, consciousness merely holds on to the impression. It does nothing with it. It makes no claim about it. It simply retains it and fixes it before the mind. Collingwood describes the act of attending to a scarlet patch: "As I look, the red is actually fading; it is being obscured by the superimposition of its own after-image, which dulls the scarlet moment by moment. But by attending to the scarlet and neglecting everything else, I create a kind of compensation for this fading." Attention is the activity by which consciousness gains access to the sense world and is given, in Collingwood's words, "fair sight" of the perceptual object. Assuredly, this is the most basic of acts but it is nonetheless an act. It is that act which gathers together the data requisite for cognition.

Under conditions of corruption, a principle of relation is introduced. Consciousness now intervenes among the sensations it sustains. When consciousness "disowns" a feeling, it does more than merely ignore it; it actually mediates the relation of a particular to a whole. Consciousness is now involved in an act of judgment. If I disown a feeling, I judge that feeling to be alien to my consciousness, unrelated to my experience, disconnected from my state of affairs. I fail to see, through the comparison of perceptions, the interrelatedness of certain feelings. Therefore, the error I make about the feeling lies not in the attention process *per se,* not in the givenness of the feeling, but in the judgment I make about the feeling. When a feeling is mine and I claim that it is not, I am not failing to attend to the feeling for I *am* attending to it; it already stands before me. I err, simply in the fact that I fail to recognize the feeling as my own. I fail to see its relation to my perceived experience. This is not a failure, then, to attend to feelings; it is a failure to recognize them for what they are.

Attention is formational rather than transformational. When I attend to a feeling, Collingwood claims that I give it empirical form. Feelings at the psychical level are without form and receive only subconscious expression. Raw sensation is ungraspable, since it lacks formal expressiveness. A raw sensation is simply "felt" and, unless it is particularly powerful, there is no necessary need to sustain or attend to it. I can deal with it if I so desire, or I can ignore it and turn my attention to something else. Brute sensa, therefore, stand at the nether end of perception, as the implicit condition of empirical sensibility.

II.

To this point I have tried to show how Collingwood distinguishes form from feeling and how he separates the relation of form from both of these. Feeling is the passive surrender to sensation; form is the conscious

domination of raw sense; while the relation of form is the judgmental intervention among the images sustained by attentive consciousness. Collingwood has described these in his own way as: psychical experience, attention, and original expression. Thus, when dealing with form, consciousness is engaged in a relational act, an act which perceives an internal connectedness of form, an act which "mediates" perception. However, Collingwood claims that this relational act might take place abortively. One might attempt to mediate form and fail. I might remain frustrated in my effort to relate one image to another and, in effect, surrender a measure of my sensitivity. This success/failure relationship implies bipolarity. As Collingwood points out, one can succeed in one's attempt to deal with the image, or one can fail in this activity by creating a corrupt version of one's perceptual experience. There is, in other words, a right and a wrong way to imagine things.

Collingwood wants to claim that the artist, with each work he completes, creates a harmonious order of feeling by producing a coherent sensible form. When consciousness is corrupt, it denies this order of feeling; it attends to the order but does not "understand" it. In essence, a corrupt consciousness misinterprets its own interpretative activity. The activity of art is reflexive. The work of art makes an assertion about the way in which the human mind relates the disparate elements of sense. A corrupt consciousness is a consciousness replete with sense data, yet, frustrated in its efforts to set the data in a proper perceptual or imaginative order. As Collingwood points out, "the symptoms and consequences of a corrupt consciousness . . . are due not to functional disorder or to the impact of hostile forces upon the sufferer, but to its own self-mismanagement . . ."

It is not enough to claim that a corrupt consciousness simply directs attention away from some feeling it fears. It actually disavows knowledge of its feelings and misinforms itself; it fails to see that the relation it has drawn among images is inadequate or incomplete. If consciousness disowns a feeling which in point of fact is rightfully its own, its imaginative understanding of itself is incomplete and hence corrupt. It lies to itself by ommitting a truth.

Art fights corruption by constantly expanding our perceptual awareness. Art is perception in the act of discovering its own borders; it both refines and uncovers the limits of imaginative experience. Just as science maps the limits of cognitive understanding, art charts the geography of perception. With each work of art, a new aspect of this geography appears and a new dimension of perception is rendered concrete.

However, in order for this geography to appear, the awareness of sensible form must be shared. More than a private activity, this perceptual relatedness must appear as a *common* sensibility. It is important to remember that the artist does more than express his own feelings; he expresses the feelings of others as well. In an important passage, Collingwood states: "We know that the artist is expressing his emotions by the fact that he is enabling us to express ours. Here Collingwood claims that the sensible relatedness of things has an objective status: "If a poet expresses, for example, a certain kind of fear, the only hearers who can understand him are those capable of experiencing that kind of fear themselves." Collingwood wants to argue that a work of art is only a work of art when its meaning is, in some measure, shared. The particular meaning of a painting is not confined to the canvas alone; it is active and alive in the world, since it is shared through a culture's common perceptions. The work of art binds the sensibilities of the general public and the artist. Quite simply, the work provides a means for members of a common culture to communicate ideas that would otherwise be ineffable. Collingwood is clearly committed to such a view: "The aesthetic activity is an activity of thought in the form of consciousness, converting into imagination an experience which, apart from being so converted, is sensuous. This activity is a corporate activity belonging not to any one human being but to a community." To the extent that a work of art communicates anything, it must arise out of a common understanding.

This common understanding, since it is born in the act of perception, both requires and implies lawfulness. The order or relation of feelings is neither reckless nor ambiguous. It is concrete and precise. It is perspectival and uniform. We might say that consciousness generates its own law each time it intervenes among images. The perceptual world that consciousness makes for itself rests on its own activity. Given Collingwood's position, the work of art justifies itself, since it renders the common sense concrete.

III.

One might now ask: How is common sensibility shared? How are the internal elements of feeling externalized in the work of art? We know that, for Collingwood, corrupt consciousness evolves out of its own mismanaged activity and that this mismanagement is writ large in culture itself. Not only the artist, but his audience as well, share in the corruption of sensibility. If this is the case, and Collingwood insists that it is, then the work of art bears the burden of binding public taste with personal sensitivity. The real question, then, is how does the work of art, the created form, the external object, express anything? The answer to this question is already implied in the notion of sensible relatedness. If the work of art renders the common sense concrete, then the story must be told in the work itself. The expressive form and the feeling it expresses must be more than incidentally bound; they must be, in the final instance, identical.

Therefore, the possibility of common sense growing corrupt must rest on a *coherence* theory of expression. Given Collingwood's position, the development of corrupt consciousness cannot be understood apart from the internal harmony of sense elements in the self. Since, in

Collingwood's view, form and feeling arise together in sensation, the emotion expressed in a work of art is internal to the work and is identical to its form. A much less adequate view of Collingwood's theory is to say that it presents the work of art as a mere copy or transformation of some independent psychical feeling. Collingwood is quite careful to maintain that the work of art copies nothing. He insists that the artwork, being in this case the form, is in no measure independent of the feeling it conveys. "One cannot possibly decide that a certain emotion is one which for some reason it would be undesirable to express . . . unless one first becomes conscious of it; and doing this, as we saw, is somehow bound up with expressing it." As expressed feeling, the artwork is "lived" feeling. The artist strikes vitality into the world by generating the objective forms through which a culture shares its common sensitivity. Feeling cannot, in this sense, be drained from the work of art, since the shared perception of the work is the very essence of the feeling; indeed, it is even more than this, it is the feeling itself; it is the emotion in all its sum and substance. The emotion expressed in a work of art does not preexist in the psyche as such, but rather comes into form only *as* it is expressed.

This principle of coherence, wherein every element of a work is related to the whole that it helps sustain, is the principle on which the notion of corrupt consciousness depends. Consider a sequence of tones. As a first tone, tone A, is played and a second tone, tone B, follows in sequence, an immediate sense of bipolarity arises and an imaginative judgement is required. Either tone B is *appropriate* to A and expresses the feeling implicit in the sequence itself, or B is *inept* with respect to A and fails to add to the sequence, fails to cohere with respect to the whole. Tone B, in this second instance, works in a fashion that is counter-productive to the sequence. It fails with respect to a whole that is paradoxically incomplete. We know that tone B fails to complete the whole, since our idea of the whole arises during our attempt to express it. As Collingwood suggests, the act of creation, if it is genuine creation and not merely transformation, cannot be done by "imposing a new form on a pre-existing matter." Form and feeling condition one another; and it is this mutual act of conditioning that we call expression.

If we return to the sequence of tones and suppose that tone B arises as inept, consciousness can do one of two things. It can move on in its search for the appropriate or coherent tone, or it can deny that such a tone exists. It can continue its search for the proper tone or it can "give it up" and remain satisfied with what it has. This latter activity of giving up the search and denying that the appropriate tone exists is self-deception. The artist often compromises in such an instance and substitutes an inadequate or inappropriate tone in place of the tone he actually needs. A composer might say that "this chord is good enough" or "this harmony will suffice" when, in effect, he has settled for an inadequate version of the chord or a sentimental rendering of the harmony.

Instead of continuing its search for form, consciousness grows stagnant and repetitive, imitative and compromising. It has substituted correspondence for coherence, emulation for originality. A stagnant consciousness is a corrupt consciousness; it is a consciousness that forsakes the pursuit of the appropriate and remains satisfied with the everyday. A corrupt consciousness disowns certain truths of the imagination because such truths appear frightening and difficult to manage. It is a consciousness which, frustrated in its attempt to be original, convinces itself of the viability of the cliche.

IV.

I suggested at the outset of this paper that there is a sense in which the expressionistic interpretation of Collingwood's aesthetic is quite correct. I have maintained, however, that such an interpretation is naive unless it is read together with the coherence theory of form found in Collingwood's description of corrupt consciousness. Collingwood's theory of art does indeed incorporate both formal and expressionistic elements. His philosophy of art is as much a theory of feeling as it is of form. The question therefore remains: How can a work of art be both a copy and a genuinely original project? How is it that the work of art both transforms feelings and creates new feelings? Is this not a contradiction?

One must remember that, for Collingwood, consciousness is a process. He describes this process in terms of what he sees as a necessary "overlap" of classes. In the notions of feeling and form, we have two unique classes which overlap in that they are at once different and similar. Conscious or formal expression differs in degree from psychical expression, since it transforms or reshapes psychical feelings. But this difference in degree also constitutes a difference in kind. The emotion, once expressed at the conscious level, is no longer the same emotion. A feeling that is consciously expressed is inextricably bound to the form in which it arises. Hence it cannot arise or have any reality apart from this formal expression. The feeling is thus the same and not the same. Aesthetic feeling bears a relation to psychical feeling because it is "felt" as well as perceived. Yet, because the feeling is now "perceived" as well as felt, it differs not only in degree but in kind. The aesthetic feeling is transformed, as Collingwood sometimes claims; but it is transformed at the level of consciousness itself. In this sense, the feeling is not so much copied as formed anew. It is fashioned in terms of the formal activity of consciousness, in terms of the sensible relatedness mind perceives among things.

This notion of "overlap" is perhaps more clearly expressed in Collingwood's *Autobiography,* ". . . 'processes' are things which do not begin and end but turn into one another; and that if a process P1 turn into a process P2, there is no dividing line at which P1 stops and P2 begins; P1 never stops and P2 never begins, it has previously been going on in the earlier for P1." If one thinks of P1 as feeling and P2 as form in this schema, one has little trouble seeing why Collingwood's theory of art is at once expressionistic and formal. Feelings serve as a raw material for art because they serve as a raw material for mind. Psychical experience does not disappear with the intervention of consciousness; it simply appears in a new and different way. The feeling expressed by a work of art is new, since it reveals the feeling as a feeling that is related to the whole of imaginative experience. But this feeling is also transformed, since it never fully disappears when it is embraced at a different level.

I have stressed the notion of coherence in this paper, since it is *sensible relatedness* that makes the transformation of feeling possible. Expression in art is not so much the mimesis of feeling as the imaginative relation of feeling, a relation that differs both in degree and in kind from psychical reality. In this sense, creativity is not, nor can it ever be, the mere imitation of sensation. Creativity is not simply feeling; it is rather the impress of thought on feeling, a process that gives rise to the internal relatedness of sensible form.

John Grant   (essay date 1987)

SOURCE: "On Reading Collingwood's Principles of Art," in *The Journal of Aesthetics and Art Criticism,* Vol. XLVI, No. 2, Winter, 1987, pp. 239-48.

[*In the following essay, Grant finds that Collingwood's ideas concerning art significantly vary throughout the course of his treatise* The Principles of Art.]

Perhaps no work of English aesthetics in this century has been more disputed than Collingwood's **Principles of Art**. On one extreme it is insisted that Collingwood's chief and leading doctrine is that the work of art is something exclusively mental in nature, something whose physical and publicly accessible embodiment is aesthetically extraneous. On the other extreme, while it is granted that Collingwood believed the work of art to be something "mental," it is denied that he believed it to be something "exclusively" mental. Art, for Collingwood, it is held, is something which is "unintelligible" apart from physical and publicly accessible behavior.

The sharp divergence of opinion suggests what is true, i.e., that the text of the **Principles,** while enviable for its precocity, is rife with chaos and confusion. Yet regrettably it may also be thought to suggest what is false, that the controversy about what Collingwood meant is insoluble. Collingwood's thesis is obscured by frequent changes of mind, to be sure. But as I shall endeavor very shortly to show, the changes are not in every case indiscriminate and unwitting. We read in Book I that the work of art is something "(as we commonly say) 'existing in his [the artist's] head' and there only"; and in what has become the usual way of reading the **Prin-**

ciples, the trick has been to square this assertion with Collingwood's evident approbation in Books II and III for the doctrine that the work of art is in some sense a "bodily" and "publicly accessible" thing or activity. But this way of reading the *Principles,* I wish to insist, is entirely wrong. Whatever Collingwood's "definition" or "theory" of art, and however plausible or implausible that definition may be, it is most certainly not a definition that is stated in Book I. I wish now to examine this and other related assumptions.

I.

It is well known that Collingwood begins his famous work with the question, "What is art?" In his *Autobiography* Collingwood calls the question-form a "vague portmanteau-phrase covering a multitude of questions but not precisely expressing any of them." But in the *Principles* the question is immediately divided into two "stages." The purpose of the first stage, says Collingwood, is to "review the improper senses of the word 'art' . . . so that at the end of it we can say not only 'that and that and that are not art,' but also 'that is not art because it is pseudo-art of kind A' and 'that, because it is pseudo-art of kind B.'" The purpose of the second stage is to address "the problem of definition." "Definition," Collingwood particularly notes, "must come second, and not first, because no one can even try to define a term until he has satisfied himself that his own personal usage of it harmonizes with the common usage." "Definition," he goes on to say, "means defining one thing in terms of something else . . . ," "constructing . . . a 'theory' of something . . . ," and "having a clear idea of the thing" and "its relations to other things as well."

The avowed purpose of this strategy is first to settle on the sense or senses in which the word "art" is to be used and second, having done this, to investigate the nature of the activity to which "art" so defined refers. It is not immediately clear how "proper" and "improper" usages are to be distinguished or what sort of investigation into the nature of art Collingwood envisages. But for the present let us notice a distinction that we are likely to overlook. An attempt to state the meaning of a word, whether by description, stipulation, or some other method, is ordinarily called a "definition." By "definition" in other words we commonly mean the definition of *words,* and what Collingwood describes as settling on a proper usage of the word "art" we are inclined to think a "definition" of "art." But particular attention must be drawn to the fact that Collingwood himself uses the word "definition" in a different sense, not as a statement of the meaning of a word but as an investigation into the nature of the thing (activity, process, concept, word, etc.) to which a word may refer. Wherever ambiguity threatens, let us call definition in this sense "real definition," a definition whose purpose it is to state in one way or another—by a whole range of methods that philosophers do not always distinguish (analysis, synthesis, division, classification, etc.)—the nature of a thing. The

quite different activity of defining words we may call "verbal definition."

I shall have reason, very shortly, to modify and to make more precise this tentative description of the two stages into which Collingwood divides his answer to "What is art?" But setting aside for the moment this task, let us consider a much simpler matter: the precise locations in the text of the *Principles* of what I have defined in a preliminary way as Collingwood's "verbal" and "real" definitions of art. Alan Donagan's answer, which I take to be the generally accepted one (certainly it is the only explicit one), is that Collingwood's verbal definition, or account of "proper usage," consists of a brief history of the word "art" up to the present usage "in the modern European critical tradition" and comes in the introduction prior to Book I. What Collingwood calls his "definition" of art (and what I have called, tentatively, a "real" definition) is then presumed to begin at the outset of Book I.

This reading seems to me open to two objections, the second of which is fatal. First, the brevity of Collingwood's verbal definition, as Donagan construes it, is incompatible with Collingwood's declared purpose. Admittedly, an account of usage or verbal definition need not be a lengthy affair. It may consist for example of an arbitrary assignment of meaning or of a brief report of established usage. But Collingwood promises that his account of usage will tell us not merely in what senses the word "art" is and ought to be used, but also in what senses it ought not to be used and, most important, why. Contrary to Donagan, an account of "proper usage" for Collingwood consists not merely of a brief lexical or historical description of various usages, but of something else as well: a critical examination of the theory or theories of art that underlie these usages.

Now if Collingwood's account of usage is, in its nature, something that cannot be brief, then it seems unlikely that it can be contained in the brief space of Collingwood's introduction to the *Principles*. Indeed, Donagan shows himself aware of this. "Despite his historical narrative of how the aesthetic usage of the word 'art' emerged, he [Collingwood] did not explain how he discriminated that usage from its fellows." Donagan then devotes considerable space to supplying what he takes to be the missing explanation, an explanation which, evidently, he thinks implicit in what for him is Collingwood's "definition" of art in Book I. But here arises my second objection; for the assumption that Collingwood's account of usage is confined to the introduction prior to Book I and that his "definition" of art begins in Book I seems to me entirely dubious. No feature of the *Principles* has more entirely escaped notice than the one to which I am about to draw attention. The argument of Book I, I submit, is not Collingwood's attempt to construct a "definition" or "theory" of art, as virtually all Collingwood's readers have supposed, but nothing more nor less than the promised account of "proper usage" itself. The point is made frequently throughout Book I, but for reasons of space I shall cite only one instance of it.

> [W]e are still dealing with what are called questions of fact, or what in the first chapter were called questions of usage, not questions of theory. We shall not be trying to build up an argument which the reader is asked to examine and criticize, and accept if he finds no fatal flaw in it. . . . We shall be trying as best we can to remind ourselves of facts well known to us all: such facts as this, that on occasions of a certain kind we actually do use the word art or some kindred word to designate certain kinds of things. . . .

The work of constructing a "definition" or "theory" of art, in turn, comes not in Book I of the *Principles* but in Books II and III.

> The empirical and descriptive work of Book I left us with the conclusion that art proper, as distinct from amusement or magic, was (i) expressive (ii) imaginative. *Both these terms, however, awaited definition:* we might know how to apply them (that being a question of usage, or the ability to speak not so much English as the common tongue of European peoples), but we did not know to what theory concerning the thing so designated this application might commit us. It was to fill this gap in our knowledge that we went on to the analytical work of Book II. (italics mine).

Citing as conclusive evidence Collingwood's contention in Book I that the work of art is something made "in the mind, and there only," many writers, perhaps the majority, have defended what may be called the "Croce-Collingwood" interpretation of the *Principles*. But others, attempting to reconcile Books II and III with Book I, have insisted, on the contrary, that Collingwood specifically *denies* that art has no "bodily" and "publicly accessible" existence. "Assimilating Collingwood's views to those of Croce," writes one commentator, "runs the risk of seriously misreading *The Principles of Art* (and very likely Collingwood's major works as well)." But if what I have said is true, all such quibbles and disputes may be seen to rest, at least in part, on a premise that is demonstrably unwarranted; for if Book I is *not* a definition of art in the first place, it is obviously false to suppose that everything said in the later books needs to be shown to be compatible with Book I.

II.

The traditional reading of Collingwood's *Principles* may, however, be resurrected on another point. It will not have escaped the reader's notice that even if, as I have argued, what Collingwood calls his "definition" or "theory" of art does not come until Books II and III, Collingwood's actual strategy is quite different. For a theory *is* propounded in Book I, surely. An aesthetic doctrine—we may call it the "mental-only" doctrine—is implied more or less directly in Collingwood's analysis

of what he calls "proper usage." It is thus that the following commentators, for example, have written:

> We must appreciate that it is an essential feature of the Croce-Collingwood thesis that not only can the artist make works of art to himself, but that he may be in the situation in which he can only make works of art to himself.

> And—here is perhaps the most distinctive characteristics of the Croce-Collingwood theory—when the part process is completed in the artist's mind; when the final artistic intuition is present to his consciousness, the process of expression is also complete: for the intuition *is* the expression.

For evidence of what Wollheim and Hospers are saying it is only necessary to turn to Book I itself where, in spite of admitting, for example, the existence of "colours there in painting," Collingwood insists that all such "sensuous parts" do not exist "objectively" in the work of art, which is to say independently of a perceiving subject, but are always "imagined" or, as he is wont to say, "solely in the artist's head." Therefore, it may confidently be asserted, let us simply *assume* that Book I is a "definition" of art. Indeed, let us assume that it is a "definition" in precisely the sense that Collingwood himself defines the word "definition" in his *Essay on Philosophical Method,* that is to say, as a "real definition" as opposed to analysis of a word, term, or expression.

How should I reply to this way of reading Collingwood? Should I abandon my thesis that there is nonetheless a good reason for thinking Book I an account of usage as opposed to a "definition"? Certainly not. The distinction between Collingwood's account of usage in Book I and his definition of art in Books II and III, I suggest, may be cogently and faithfully reconstructed as a distinction between two species of *verbal* definition: one essentially restrictive and based on established critical usages, the other essentially nonrestrictive and based on established philosophical usage. Turning first to Collingwood's account of usage in Book I, the notoriously indefinite and confusing meaning of "art," Collingwood tells us, is not to be legislated according to a "private" rule, but is to be adopted by an analysis of conceptions underlying the word in established critical usage. We must, as Collingwood expresses it, settle on a meaning that both "fits onto common usage" and, at the same time, "clarifies" and "systematizes" ideas we already possess. Note, especially, that "clarification" and "systemization" mean, in this instance, arriving at a stipulation the application and logical consequences of which are at least clear (even if queried in Collingwood's later account) and which does not transgress the usage of art critics and other knowledgeable persons.

Proceeding in this way Collingwood ousts from the entangled set of usages of which the established critical usage of "art" consists what he calls the "distorting" idea that a work of art is something susceptible to an exhaustive analysis *per genus et differentiam* and adopts precisely the opposite idea, i.e., that art is something whose individuality defeats analysis in this sense. And all this is done, again, without at any point stepping outside of what is in Collingwood's view the realm of established critical usage. The argument of Book I may thus, to this extent, be likened to a disjunctive syllogism based on—or "restricted" to—various established usages of the word art. The syllogism begins with the disjunctive premise "we mean by 'art' in established critical usage one of two things—'craft' or 'expression.'" The craft alternative is then eliminated, leaving only one other established usage, that according to which art is "expression."

Now if this description of Book I is roughly true, then Donagan's explanation of what makes critical usage the "proper" usage for Collingwood cannot be correct. To be sure, Collingwood begins by assuming the existence of an established critical usage, as Donagan insists. But it is certainly false to say that he assumes such usage to be "aesthetically proper," leaving the way open, as it were, to construct (in Book I) what Donagan calls a "definition of the word 'art'" when it is used "aesthetically." Collingwood's approach is exactly the opposite: it is assumed, precisely, that critics are *not* exempt from the ambiguities and false implications that plague the common usage of "art." Only once various kinds of "art falsely so called" are "cleared away," Collingwood tells us, can the proper usage of the word art be brought to light. "We [critics and the like] are apt nowadays to think about most problems including those of art, in terms of economics or psychology," writes Collingwood, "and both ways of thinking tend to subsume the philosophy of art under the philosophy of craft. . . ." Old usages "cling to our minds like drowning men, and so jostle the present meaning that we can only distinguish it from them by the most careful analysis."

More important for present purposes, the foregoing brings clearly to light the distinction Collingwood means to draw between his account of usage in Book I and his definition of art in Books II and III. In contrast to the argument of Book I, the argument of Book II is, precisely, *unrestricted* by the established usage of critics and the like. The verbal and conceptual territory in which Book II operates, Collingwood tells us, is bounded only by established *philosophical* usage and conceptions.

> In Book II, therefore, I shall make a fresh start. I shall try to work out a theory of imagination and of its place in the structure of experience as a whole, by developing what has already been said about it by well-known philosophers. In doing this I shall make no use whatever of anything contained in Book I.

Indeed, in "developing what has already been said," Collingwood frequently has cause to go quite beyond the realm of established philosophical usage to stipulate entirely *new* meanings for old words and even to invent entirely new words. Thus the word "imagination" is wrenched from its established range of meanings in philosophy to denote an "act of attention" in which the momentary flux of immediate and undifferentiated sensation, "charged with emotion" is fixed long enough to form, for example, an idea of *this* particular grief, *this* particular warmth, *this* particular pain, and so on. Similarly, the word "language" is completely redefined to denote the "bodily expression of emotion" that accompanies all such acts of attention or "imagination." Last but not least, the term "psychical expression" is freshly minted to denote the "involuntary" and "wholly unconscious" bodily acts, the "distortions of the face" expressing "pain," "slackening of the muscles and cold pallor of the skin" expressing "fear," and so on, that are said to accompany the sentient being's immediate experience of sensuous flux.

Fortunately, I am under no obligation to unravel the intricacies of this elaborate homespun terminology. My purpose is merely to show that there is an obvious and legitimate distinction between Collingwood's account of "proper usage" and his "definition." The former, I suggest, aims at narrowing or "restricting" an established and already relatively specialized critical usage; the latter, at refining and even at altering established philosophical usage to the end of constructing a philosophical theory of art. There is no deadly rivalry between these "theories"; indeed, *neither* counts as Collingwood's definitive position. Book I identifies what is the established usage of "art," at least, what is that part of it for which no demonstrable falsehoods can be found; Book II analyzes the word from a philosophical perspective; Book III is then, as Collingwood puts it, the "union" of these. That is to say, it is an account of what, in light of philosophical analysis, the established usage of "art" *ought to* look like. Thus Book III, we may say, is a new, improved "theory" of art: not a "philosophical" theory exactly, but an attempt to provide, in light of philosophical analysis, a new conceptual underpinning for the work of artists, performers, and audiences in England "here and now." Essentially, then, established usages and conceptions undergo revision *twice*: first in Book I in which demonstrable falsehoods (vestiges of craft theory) are removed; second in Book III in which the philosophical implications of Book II are brought to bear. And it is the result of these revisions that counts as Collingwood's definitive theory. It is perhaps, more than anything else, I suggest, in failing to appreciate this fact that readers have fallen prey to the imprecision and ambiguity in Collingwood's use of the words "definition" and "theory" and have mistaken his account of usage in Book I for his "definition" or "theory" of art.

III.

The misconception to which I have called attention, however, is by no means fatal to traditional assumptions. For it will be insisted that even if Books II and III are independent of Collingwood's analysis of established usage in Book I, ultimately they serve merely to confirm and to perfect tendencies of thought already implicit in that analysis. The trump is the following passage from Book III.

> [A] work of art in the proper sense of that phrase is not an artifact, not a bodily or perceptible thing fabricated by the artist, but something existing solely in the artist's head. . . . No reader, I hope, has been inattentive enough to imagine that . . . this doctrine has been forgotten or denied.

This passage obviously lends considerable weight to the view that it is Collingwood's purpose to defend without possibility of appeal the "mental only" theory of art throughout the **Principles**. Against this, what have I to say in defense of my interpretation?

I should begin by noticing, quite apart from this passage, that I am not alone in the view that Collingwood changes his mind in Book III. "In Book III Collingwood quietly relinquished the sense of 'imaginary' in which an imaginary object exists only in the head," writes Donagan. But I should want to go further than Donagan here. I should want to say, first, by reference to Book II, not merely that the mental only line is "relinquished," but also that it is replaced by almost the contrary position. Art is "language," argues Collingwood in Books II and III, and "language" he particularly stresses is something which is "bodily" *in nature*.

> [L]anguage is simply bodily expression of emotion, dominated by thought in its primitive form as consciousness.

> Every kind of language is in this way a specialized form of bodily gesture, and in this sense it may be said that dance is the mother of all languages.

> [E]very kind or order of language (speech, gesture, and so forth) was an offshoot from an original language of total bodily gesture. . . . each one of us, whenever he expresses himself, is doing so with his whole body, and is thus actually talking in this "original" language of total bodily gesture.

And I should want to say, second, in reference to Book III, that far from being "quiet," the change is explicitly avowed in the following explicit criticism of Book I.

> On the theory of art propounded in this book, the audience seems at first sight to become inessential. It [the audience] seems to disappear altogether from the province of art as such. . . . If the implications of the expressive theory had been completely grasped in the case of the artist, there would have been no need to fall back on the technical theory in discussing his relation with his audience.

In Book I the process by which emotions are clarified and expressed is said to be an entirely *internal* affair: "a work of art may be completely created when it has been created as a thing whose only existence is in the artist's mind. . . ." "The actual making of the tune is something

that goes on in the head, and nowhere else. . . ." Its physical and publicly accessible counterpart is thus conceived of as something which is not the work of art, but merely something that conveys the work of art to the outside world by *standing for* it: "what is written or printed on the music paper is not the tune," we are told. "It is only something which when studied intelligently will enable others (or himself, when he has forgotten it) to construct the tune for themselves in their own heads." And since it is not necessary to the existence of a work of art that it be made public, the artist has an audience "only in so far as people hear him expressing himself, and understand what they hear him saying."

But all this changes in Book II and ipso facto in Collingwood's translation of the results of Book II into the more ordinary nomenclature of artists, performers, and audiences in Book III. The making of a work of art, says Collingwood, is a bodily activity from its inception. Art is language and language "simply bodily expression of emotion," "a specialized form of bodily gesture," and so on. There is no question of having to "externalize" it in order to make it publicly accessible. As Collingwood expresses it, there is no need "to fall back upon the technical theory" in order to explain how works of art are made publicly accessible. And elsewhere: "There is no question of 'externalizing' an inward experience which is complete in itself and by itself. There are two experiences, an inward and imaginative one called seeing and an outward or bodily one called painting, which in the painter's life are inseparable, and form one single and indivisible experience . . ."

Of course this hardly settles matters. Collingwood changes his mind to be sure. But what of the puzzling passage I cited at the outset? The fact of the matter is that it is precisely having asserted the "indivisibility" of the imaginative and the bodily experience that Collingwood goes on to insist that the mental-only doctrine from Book I has "not been forgotten or denied." Thus we should say not that Collingwood changes his mind in a manner that is conscious and deliberate but, quite the opposite, that he changes it in a manner that renders his theory inconsistent. Richard Wollheim writes:

> In book I of the **Principles of Art** Collingwood asserts that the work of art is something imaginary: it exists in, and only in, the artist's head or mind. In book III he denies that the relation of the audience is non-existent or inessential. Collingwood goes on to say that these two views—one an assertion, the other a denial—which jointly constitute his aesthetic, are not inconsistent: though superficially they might seem so.

But let us read further. The important question, Collingwood goes on to say, is whether the "solely" mental-only work may yet be "somehow necessarily connected" with the bodily work. And in the pages that follow, Collingwood reviews his *definition* of art (Book II) and is drawn ineluctably to the conclusion that there is indeed a "connection" and, what is more, that it is a connection in light of which the mental-only doctrine *cannot* be sustained.

> The work of artistic creation is *not* a work performed in any exclusive or complete fashion in the mind of the person whom we call the artist. That idea is a delusion bred of individualistic psychology together with a false view of the relation not so much between body and mind as between experience at the psychical level and experience at the level of thought. (italics mine)

Thus, significantly, Collingwood's attempt to resurrect the mental-only doctrine proves abortive. But more needs to be said than this, surely, lest Collingwood's argument should appear only more perversely erratic and irremediably inconsistent than before. Why, having defended throughout Book II the view that art is something bodily in nature, should Collingwood even contemplate the idea that it is something "solely" in the head? And why, having contemplated it, does he then abandon it?

The answer to the first question is this: that Collingwood's description of art as something both "bodily" and "inward" or "imaginative" in nature is equivocal, and equivocal in a way that lends superficial plausibility to the doctrine that the work of art exists "in the head." The "bodily" work and its "imaginative" counterpart, Collingwood insists, are "indivisible" and yet, curiously, are "two experiences," not one. The work of art, he says, is something that "exists solely in the head" and yet, at base, something that is "necessarily connected with" its bodily counterpart. Collingwood seems to want to have it both ways. He wants to say (and this is especially clear in the second example) that the "bodily" work is a necessary condition for the occurrence of the mental work but is not the mental work (or work of art proper) itself—an interpretation which echoes the doctrine of Book I. But he also wants to say something quite different: that far from belonging to two quite separate worlds, *res cogitans* and *res extensa,* the mental and bodily work are two aspects—the "psychical" and the "imaginative"—of one and the same thing—"experience"—a position that is consistent with Collingwood's definition of art in Book II.

Collingwood, I say, is not immediately aware of the difference between these two sorts of statements; and it is in this unfortunate context that the opportunity presents itself to suggest that there is yet a grain of truth in "common usage," a sense in which it is compatible with the philosophical work of Book II. Certainly there is such a sense. We should not identify the work of art with "fabrication" or mere physical exemplification; nor should we suppose that "imagination" is an activity in any sense directed towards an end which is known in advance, as in craft. These two things remain quite true in Book III, but they do not justify, obviously, the assertion that the work of art is something "solely" mental in nature.

But turning now to the second question, ultimately Collingwood is aware of an inconsistency in his position. As he expresses it, the idea that the work of art is something "solely" or "exclusively" mental implies "a false view of the relation not so much between body and mind as between experience at the psychical level and experience at the level of thought." The reference here is, of course, to the definition of art as "language" and, as such, as something intrinsically "sensuous" or "bodily." What is "sensuous" or "bodily" at the "psychical level"—our immediate experience of the world—Collingwood reminds us in Book III, is not "left behind," as it were, by the act of attention which makes us aware of it. Rather, the bodily component is retained at the higher "imaginative" level, but now in the form of "language" or "art." It is thus, I suggest, that we are urged to think of the work of art not as an amalgam or interaction of two separate worlds, the "mental" work existing in the artist's head and its exemplification existing somewhere else in an entirely distinct physical mode, but as a relationship holding between the "sensuous" and "imaginative" levels of experience, which in respect to their "matter," as Collingwood expresses it, are one and the same thing." We may say with Collingwood and, what is more, in agreement with Book I, that the work of art is "wholly and entirely imaginative," that it is something which is made "deliberately and responsibly" and yet without a plan. But as Collingwood ultimately stresses, this does not entitle us to say that it is something made "exclusively" in the head.

We continue to feel of course that a distinction between the mental and the physical is in some sense warranted—indeed Collingwood himself continues to suppose it—and it is by no means clear on Collingwood's monistic account of "experience" how this distinction is to be made, if at all. But I do not think my thesis is dented. The contention that Collingwood consciously and deliberately changes his mind about the mental-only doctrine of Book I is not, after all, incompatible with the fact that his new theory is not precisely worked out. Nor is it inconsistent with the fact that he initially sees a partial or superficial consistency between the provisional doctrine of Book I and the more definitive doctrine of Books II and III. To be sure, Collingwood may be justly criticized for being vague and imprecise and, as a result, for providing grist for the mills of numerous irreconcilable interpretations. But if my reading has warrant, in one important respect all these interpretations may be called into question. For it is clear that the dualistic tendency to see the mental and bodily aspects of the work of art as completely different entities is consciously and deliberately abandoned, and with it the doctrine that the work of art or imagination is something done exclusively in the head.

IV.

My account of Collingwood's argument may be thought open to one final objection. I have suggested that Collingwood rules out entirely the place of technique in art. But the opposite view is widely held. As one commentator expresses it: "Collingwood always stressed that technique was necessary to art, where technique is understood as the control which enables an artist to create exactly what he wants." Donagan advocates a qualified version of the view, saying that Collingwood believed craft to be "necessary" for the "best" art. This interpretation, I wish briefly to show, is undoubtedly false.

To be sure, Collingwood appears in his commentary on the theory of "poetic" or "artistic" technique to concede that technique or skill is, at the very least, a necessary condition of the best art if not, indeed, a necessary condition of any work of art "whatever." It should be clear on closer examination, however, that the matter is not quite as simple as this. When proponents of the theory of poetic technique say that craft or technique is necessary, what they are really saying, according to Collingwood, is two things. In one sense they are using the words "technique," "craft," and "skill" to mean a "directed process" or "an effort . . . directed upon a certain end," saying that *these* things are necessary to art. But in another sense, which in Collingwood's view they do not clearly distinguish from the latter, they mean to say that "craft" is an activity in which specific plans are laid out in advance and precisely followed, and that craft in *this* sense is necessary to art.

Now when Collingwood writes that it is quite true that craft or skill is a necessary condition of art, initially he does not say to which sense of the word craft he means to give his approval. And this perhaps has misled many readers. The key word "skill" in this context must be allowed "to pass for the moment unchallenged," he writes; and the assertion that "craft" is necessary, he says, is true, but "true" when "properly understood." But the matter is soon cleared up. Collingwood goes on to argue *against* the doctrine that craft or skill is necessary in the second sense, that is, as a means of achieving a specific end, and for the proposition that it is necessary in the first sense, that is to say, as an "effort" or "directed process" which is conscious and deliberate but *unplanned*. "What he [the artist] wants to say," Collingwood concludes, "is not present to him as an end towards which means have to be devised; . . ."

But further qualification needs to be made. Properly speaking, we are told, "craft," "technique," "skill," and the like are words which should not be used to refer to the "directed" but "unplanned" nature of art. The latter is "no doubt a thing worthy of our attention; but we are only frustrating our study of it in advance if we approach it in the determination to treat it as if it were the conscious working-out of means to the achievement of a conscious purpose, or in other words technique." "Technique" used in its proper sense must, in other words, refer to something which is planned. We are compelled to conclude, therefore, that "technique" in its proper sense, or "the control which enables an artist to create

exactly what he wants," is *not,* for Collingwood, a necessary condition of art.

But there is yet a further point in need of clarification. "[T]he description of the unwritten poem as an end to which his technique is a means is false," writes Collingwood, except in those instances where "the work of art is also a work of craft." Just as the joiner "knows the specifications of the table he is about to make" so the artist, where he is also a craftsman, we are told, knows the specifications of the work of art he is about to make. Collingwood seems to be admitting here the necessity of technique—at least in those cases where, as he puts it, "the work of art is also a work of craft." But we should examine this position more closely. Collingwood sharply distinguishes between "making" in the sense in which the craftsman makes, which he calls "fabricating," and "making" which is unique to the production of works of art. Making in the latter sense is not "fabricating" but "creating," that is, making without foreknowledge of the outcome or making which is "conscious and voluntary" but "non-technical." Now, to be sure, the artist who typically makes in the latter sense can also, if he is competent to do so, "make" in the quite different sense in which the craftsman does. But an artist who chooses to specify exactly how a work of art is to be made must be presumed, in Collingwood's view, already to have *created* it: "the artist has no idea what the experience is which demands expression until he has expressed it." Fabrication, or making in the sense in which the craftsman makes, therefore, is extraneous to "creating" and should on no account be thought necessary to it. No doubt things "created" can also be, in a manner of speaking, things "fabricated," but we must conclude that what makes such things the one, for Collingwood, is a separate matter from what makes them the other. "Expression," as Collingwood puts it, "is an activity of which there can be no technique."

Collingwood is open to criticism, no doubt, because we surely do use "craft," "technique," and like terms quite legitimately to refer to things which cannot be made according to exact specifications. This is obvious, for example, where the thing being made is a dugout canoe, an apple pie, or a leather shoe. No one tree, apple, or piece of leather is identical to any other; so we can never know precisely, that is, we can never specify exhaustively, what the end result of working with such material will be. We are very often compelled to revise our plans in midstream. But to return to the point at issue, if we feel such criticisms apt, it is only because Collingwood uses the word "technique" in a sense that obliges him precisely to deny that it is a necessary condition of art.

v.

In his *Essay on Philosophical Method,* Collingwood writes that philosophical thinking is a "dialectical process where the initial position is modified again and again as difficulties in it come to light." Certainly, we can say this much about the **Principles,** that having stated his position in a provisional way—before he has established the truth, adequacy, and relevance of its premises—Collingwood is later compelled to revise it. We read in Book I, for example, that "the actual making of the tune is (as we commonly say) something that goes on in his [the artist's] head and there only." But all this is revised in Book II, and it is not until Book III that we are given—again in the nomenclature of artists, audiences, and performers—what Collingwood thinks a definitive and practically applicable theory of art. There we read that the work of art is, precisely, *not* something that is "performed in any exclusive or complete fashion in the mind of the person whom we call the artist." It is to statements such as these, not to the argument of Book I, that readers who wish to understand Collingwood's "definition" or "theory" of art must give their unaccustomed attention.

Of course, above all else we should want to know whether Collingwood is right, a question that I have not here sought to address. But if my argument has warrant, most of the criticisms offered by critics against Collingwood's theory miss the mark, being not criticisms of his definitive position, but criticisms of the various tentative positions that precede it. To that extent my reading may be viewed as urging that the key question, whether Collingwood was right, be examined afresh.

Peter Lewis   (essay date 1989)

SOURCE: "Collingwood on Art and Fantasy," in *Philosophy,* Vol. LXIV, No. 250, October, 1989, pp. 547-56.

[*In the following essay, Lewis addresses the relationship between Collingwood's philosophy of art and concepts of psychoanalysis.*]

In *Art and Its Objects,* Richard Wollheim devotes considerable space to attacking a theory he calls the Croce-Collingwood Theory of Art. According to this theory, as Wollheim presents it, an artist's capacity to create works of art consists in his being able to elaborate images or intuitions in his own mind, irrespective of whether there is any means of publicly externalizing them in the form of paintings, poems, symphonies, etc. Wollheim argues, I think rightly, that this conception of artistic creation is absurd. But it can also be argued that neither Croce nor Collingwood ever espouses this absurd theory. I will not develop that argument in this paper; instead, I want to draw attention to an aspect of Wollheim's discussion which concerns the relations between Collingwood's aesthetic and concepts of psychoanalysis.

After demonstrating the absurdity of the Croce-Collingwood theory, Wollheim introduces Freud's comparison of the artist and the neurotic. Both the artist and the neurotic find substitute gratifications for their desires in fantasy; and yet, we are told, the neurotic is recognized by his continuing to remain in the world of his fantasy, whereas the artist, in Freud's words, 'finds a path back to reality'. Wollheim interprets Freud to mean by this that in making his work of art the artist renounces the immediate gratification of fantasy by making an object which 'can become a source of shared pleasure and consolation' for other people. And, Wollheim maintains, it is precisely this feature of art as renunciation which is totally denied by the Croce-Collingwood theory because it does not allow, except incidentally, for the artist's having to produce a work in a medium for an audience.

However apposite Wollheim's discussion may be to the so-called Croce-Collingwood theory, it is important to realize that it constitutes a grave injustice to the theory of art developed by Collingwood in *The Principles of Art.* For, as I hope to show, not only does Collingwood present his view of art as imagination by explicitly contrasting it with a view of art as fantasy, and in so doing highlights weaknesses in Freud's view of art; but he also attempts to explain how psychoanalytic concepts of fantasy, and such like, can be utilized to account for bad art within the framework of his own reinterpretation of traditional views of art as both disinterested and expressive. Moreover, though the articulation of these features of Collingwood's theory requires the denial of the absurd conception of artistic creation which Wollheim sketches, the fact that the fantasies of the neurotic are themselves elaborated within a medium which allows for the possibility of externalization demonstrates that that denial is not in itself sufficient to explain how art can involve the renunciation of fantasy.

I present Collingwood's ideas in two parts, the first concerning the distinction between art and non-art, the second concerning the distinction between good art and bad art.

I

In section 4 of Chapter 7, Collingwood draws a distinction between imagination proper and make-believe. The point of the distinction is that imagination is, while make-believe cannot be, constitutive of art proper; make-believe is constitutive of what Collingwood calls amusement art.

Collingwood has essentially two criteria for distinguishing imagination from make-believe: first, a relation to reality; second, a relation to desire.

Concerning the first relation, the relation to reality, Collingwood says, 'a make-believe situation can never be a real situation, and vice versa'; by contrast, 'imagination is indifferent to the distinction between the real and the unreal . . . the imagined object or situation or event is something which need not be real and need not be unreal . . .'

Concerning the second criterion, the relation to desire, Collingwood points out that there is usually a motive for any act of make-believe, viz. 'the desire for something which we would enjoy or possess if the make-believe were truth'; by contrast, 'imagination is indifferent . . . to the distinction between desire and aversion'.

Collingwood illustrates make-believe with the following example. 'If, being hungry, I "imagine" myself to be eating, this "bare imagination of a feast" is a make-believe situation which I may be said to create for myself imaginatively . . .' And he adds a few lines later, 'Dreaming consists to a great extent (some psychologists say altogether) of make-believe in which the dreamer's desires are thus satisfied; day-dreaming even more obviously so . . .'

He provides the following example of imagination proper. If, on looking out of a window, my view of the lawn is obscured by the window-frame, I may imagine 'the grass going on where [the] mullion hides it from my sight' and I may imagine 'a lawn-mower standing on that part of the lawn'. Now, Collingwood says, it so happens that 'the hidden part of the lawn is really there' just as I imagine it, but the lawn-mower is not really there. Nevertheless, according to Collingwood, 'I can detect nothing, either in the way in which I imagine the two things, or in the ways in which they respectively appear to my imagination, which at all corresponds to this distinction'.

It is evident from these two examples that make-believe is not, as Collingwood initially suggests, something distinct from imagination. The example of a make-believe feast is specified in terms of imaginatively creating a situation. So make-believe is a form of imagination. As Collingwood subsequently puts it, 'Make-believe presupposes imagination, and may be described as imagination operating in a peculiar way under the influence of peculiar forces'. By contrast, then, we can appreciate that what Collingwood calls imagination proper is simply visualizing, for example, an object or event or state of affairs, which may or may not actually exist, and attending to it without in any way considering whether it does or does not actually exist.

Since the imagination/make-believe distinction is the ground of the art/non-art distinction, we can see how Collingwood is re-presenting from the point of view of the creative artist the traditional notion of disinterestedness, taken by Kant and subsequent writers as a criterion of the aesthetic attitude. This strand in Collingwood's thought is displayed most clearly in his earlier essay **'Aesthetic'** in which he employs Edward Bullough's concept of psychical distance (or the principle of a psychological picture-frame, as Collingwood elucidates it) to explicate imagination as 'a kind of attitude towards objects in which we do not use the concepts of reality or unreality'. And this in turn helps to clarify a further point, that imagination is a state of mind which is achieved, and, once achieved, has to be preserved by an effort of will. For imagination is, as it were, always in danger of collapsing into make-believe, of succumbing to 'the influence of peculiar forces', the most potent of which is desire.

Not any case of imagination under the influence of desire will count as make-believe. Thus, in choosing a new pair of curtains for the bedroom, my wife might visualize how the curtains on display in the store would look when placed alongside the existing colour-scheme in the bedroom. Although prompted by desire, the desire to avoid a colour-clash, the aim of the imaginative project is accuracy or truth, which means that the content of the imaginative act is sensitive to beliefs about the real character of the objects which enter into the imagined state of affairs. In make-believe, however, imagination is dominated by, and not merely prompted by, desire. When I imagine myself taking on all-comers at snooker, eventually demolishing the opposition at the World Championships, any facts or beliefs which might interfere with the imaginary fulfilment of my desire for success are overlooked. Desire runs ahead of belief: objects and events are represented in imagination as I would have them be, rather than as they are or would be in reality. The content of the imaginative act is structured by desire. This is well described by Collingwood: 'Out of the numerous things which one imagines, some are chosen, whether consciously or unconsciously, to be imagined with peculiar completeness or vividness or tenacity, and others are repressed, because the first are things whose reality one desires, and the second things from whose reality one has an aversion. The result is make-believe, which is imagination acting under the censorship of desire; where desire means not the desire to imagine, nor even the desire to realize an imagined situation, but the desire that the situation imagined were real'.

Once again we see Collingwood re-presenting from the point of view of the creative individual the traditional requirement of the autonomy, as opposed to the heteronomy, of the judgment of taste. Hence, make-believe is the core of pseudo-art, rather than art proper, just because the resulting work of amusement art is manufactured in accordance with a preconceived and non-aesthetic end, viz. the arousal of emotion in the audience. 'It is', says Collingwood, 'the motive of all those sham works of art which provide their audiences or addicts with fantasies depicting a state of things in which their desires are satisfied'. And as confirmation he refers his readers to Hollywood.

It is in the light of Collingwood's re-working of traditional aesthetic notions that we can appreciate his criticism of psychoanalytic theories of art. Collingwood claims that '. . . the confusion between art and amusement has been both reflected and reinforced by a confusion between imagination and make-believe, which culminates in the attempt of the psychoanalysts to subsume artistic creation under their theory (certainly a true theory) of "fantasies" as make-believe gratifications of desire. This attempt is admirably successful so long as it deals with the art, falsely so-called, of the ordinary popular novel or film, but it could not conceivably be applied to art proper. When the attempt is made to base an aesthetic upon it (a thing which has happened lamentably often) the result is not an aesthetic but an anti-aesthetic'.

Although Collingwood does not here mention Freud by name, the reference to the 'ordinary popular novel' indicates that he might have been alluding to Freud's well-known paper, 'Creative Writers and Day-Dreaming'. For in that paper Freud begins his analysis of the creative or imaginative writer by concentrating not on 'the writers most highly esteemed by the critics, but [on] the less pretentious authors of novels, romances and short stories . . . [which] have the widest and most eager circle of readers of both sexes'. Their characteristic egocentricity ('each of [these stories] has a hero who is the centre of interest, for whom the writer tries to win our sympathy by every possible means and whom he seems to place under the protection of a special Providence') and unreality ('The fact that all the women in the novel invariably fall in love with the hero can hardly be looked on as a portrayal of reality') leads Freud to compare them with day-dreams and fantasies in which a person fulfils a wish that he cannot fulfil in real life, with the crucial difference that 'the writer softens the character of his egoistic day-dreams by altering and disguising it, and he bribes us by the purely formal—that is, aesthetic—yield of pleasure which he offers us in the presentation of his phantasies'.

There is without doubt a close correspondence between Collingwood's account of amusement art in terms of make-believe gratifications of desire and Freud's analysis of popular stories in terms of wish-fulfilling fantasy. And Collingwood appears to have been clearly aware of this. But, as the passage from *Principles of Art,* p. 138, quoted above, indicates, Collingwood disputes Freud's attempt to apply his analysis to the whole range of literature or to what Collingwood calls art proper. And, if you compare Ian Fleming's James Bond novels or Mills and Boon romances with, say, Henry James's *Portrait of a Lady* or Tolstoy's *Anna Karenina,* Collingwood's position is appealing. In the works by James and Tolstoy, there is a complexity in the imagined characters and situations, a sensitivity to details and attention to subtleties of motivation, which make them poor fuel for fantasies. The central characters in these stories cannot be regarded as heroes or heroines in the same way that James Bond is the hero of Ian Fleming's stories: instead of triumphing through disasters, they are, on the contrary, overwhelmed and broken.

Of course, Freud was aware of these obvious differences between different kinds of fiction. As he says, 'We are perfectly aware that very many imaginative writings are far removed from the model of the naive day-dream; and yet I cannot suppress the suspicion that even the most extreme deviations from that model could be linked with it through an uninterrupted series of transitional cases'. As an argument to persuade us that, in spite of their surface differences, literary art is essentially wish-fulfilling fantasy, this is far from convincing. A parallel argument would prove that red is essentially yellow or that night is essentially day. None the less, Freud's claim that we can conceive of a continuity of cases running from pulp fiction to literary works of art poses a challenge that Collingwood is compelled to confront. For Collingwood's distinction between imagination and make-believe, and the corresponding distinction between art proper and amusement art, is drawn in such a way as to exclude the possibility of a continuous series of transitional cases. If art is imagination as opposed to make-believe, and if imagination is *never* motivated by desire, whereas make-believe is *always* motivated by desire, then we should expect to find, not an uninterrupted series of transitional cases, but, somewhere within the series, a neat division where make-believe ends and art begins.

At any rate, the divergence of approach between Freud and Collingwood should now be clear. According to Freud's account (as set out in 'Creative Writers and Day-Dreaming'), the creative artist alters and disguises the character of his egoistic day-dreams, so-called literary works of art or great literature presumably requiring more extensive alterations and more ingenious disguises. While the artist renounces the purely private or personal pleasure of fantasizing, his work is essentially fantasy made public, institutionalized in the conventional trappings of art. This is unacceptable to Collingwood just for the reason that, in neglecting the distinction between imagination and make-believe or fantasy, it fails to acknowledge the depth of the artistic demand to renounce fantasy. According to Collingwood, art is liberation from fantasy. The artist proper, as opposed to the entertainer or amusement artist, attempts to free his imagination, and hence his work, from domination by selfish desires and personal obsessions, to eliminate the disfiguring influence of wish-fulfilment. Understood in this way, it is possible for Collingwood's theory to account for Freud's postulated series of transitional cases from pulp fiction to great literature. At one end of the series, we find the fiction of fantasy, escapist fiction, in which imagination is subordinate to desire; as we move along the series, we find a progressive diminution of the role of desire and a corresponding strengthening or enriching of the imaginative content, until we reach what Collingwood calls imagination proper, and what others, following Schopenhauer, call the impersonality of genius, manifested in the great works of literary art. For Collingwood, as for Iris Murdoch, one might say that 'art is an excellent analogy of morals or indeed that it is in this respect a case of morals'.

II

The artist proper renounces make-believe or fantasy. His imagination is, in Kant's phrase, allowed 'free play'; for it is constrained neither by a concern for substitute gratification of frustrated desire nor by considerations of the reality or unreality of its contents. He is not prohibited from drawing on or exhibiting his understanding, his knowledge and his beliefs of what people and things are like, and he is not restricted to visualizing, representing or thinking of actual people, events and situations. Indeed the artist's own desires and aversions, his fantasy life, can become the subject of his art, as in the work of Dostoyevsky, Kafka and Joyce. But in these cases the artist, and his audience, confronts rather than indulges his fantasies.

However, even though the artist strives to free his imagination from external interference, it seems that he must acknowledge some constraints if his imaginative project is not to be an arbitrary chaos. Collingwood proposes that the principle of organization is provided under the concept of the aesthetic. In his earlier writings, in *Speculum Mentis* and *Outlines of a Philosophy of Art,* Collingwood understood this to imply something like organic unity. Thus, for example, he says, 'A work of art, like any work of the spirit, must be a complete and coherent whole, systematic through and through, and built upon one consistent principle . . . a work of art [must be capable of being] *imagined* as a whole'. In *The Principles of Art* he understands the aesthetic to involve the expression of emotion: the imaginative content of a work is shaped and unified as the articulation of a distinctive emotional attitude or point of view (see Chapter 13, section 1). This poses no threat to aesthetic autonomy, since, on Collingwood's analysis, expression is an activity which does not require knowledge of an end which is foreseen and preconceived.

'What the artist is trying to do', says Collingwood, 'is to express a given emotion'. Good art, then, can be nothing less than successful expression, while bad art is failure in the attempt at expression. The difference between the bad artist and the amusement artist—the artist falsely so-called—is that the latter makes no attempt at imaginative expression, but instead uses his imagination as a means to the achievement of some preconceived end, such as substitute gratification of desire. In illustration of this distinction, one could perhaps cite the writings of Ian Fleming as opposed to those of John Le Carré. It is also, I think, just such a distinction which lies behind W. H. Auden's well-known remark that the novels of Raymond Chandler 'should be read and judged, not as escape literature, but as works of art'.

In Collingwood's theory, to express an emotion is to become conscious of it in the sense of clarifying it, making its constituent thoughts and feelings lucid and intelligible. A consciousness which at some point fails to 'grasp its own emotions' Collingwood calls a corrupt consciousness, corrupt in so far as failure to bring the emotion to consciousness involves duplicitously disowning it. Since, as we have seen, bad art is failure in the attempt to express emotion, it follows that 'corruption of consciousness is the same thing as bad art'.

Collingwood's combination of his theory of expression with his concept of a corrupt consciousness leads to all sorts of difficulties, though discussing them is not to my purpose now. What is more, it seems implausible to try to accommodate all that we are prepared to count as bad art by reference to bad faith in the artist; and it is perhaps significant that Collingwood provides not one example to illustrate his thesis. In concluding this paper, I would like to consider an example which suggests that Collingwood's concept of corruption of consciousness can help to explain one form that bad art can take.

Before coming to that, there is a further point pertinent to the theme of this paper. It is Collingwood's claim that what he describes as corruption of consciousness 'has already been described by psychologists in their own way' in such terminology as repression, projection, dissociation and fantasy-building. What is significant about this is just that, having previously rejected attempts to account for art in terms of psychoanalytic concepts, Collingwood incorporates such concepts into the articulation of his own final theory of art. And yet there is no inconsistency. On both occasions, the emphasis is the same, to reveal the artist's commitment to the renunciation of fantasy. The artistic endeavour as such is resistant to, and antithetical to, 'the familiar rat-runs of selfish day-dream': that is the point of the earlier discussion in Book One. But Collingwood recognizes—and this is the point of the later discussion in Book Three—that, in spite of the seriousness and sincerity of his artistic intentions, the artist is always liable to fail to realize those intentions for reasons having to do with the relations between his subject-matter and elements of his personal life.

The example I have chosen to illustrate Collingwood's view of bad art as corruption of consciousness is to be found in F. R. Leavis's analysis of George Eliot's novels. While applauding, and at the same time demonstrating, George Eliot's genius as a novelist, Leavis claims to detect a weakness which is exhibited in characters such as Maggie Tulliver in *The Mill on the Floss* and Dorothea Brooke in *Middlemarch*. Both exhibit a kind of soul-hunger, a yearning for knowledge, beauty and goodness. And both are depicted, at least initially, as emotionally confused and immature. But Leavis argues that the novelist shares the emotional vagueness of her characters. They are presented, he claims, with tender sympathy, but also 'with a remarkable absence of criticism. There *is,* somewhere, a discordance, a discrepancy, a failure to reduce things to a due relevance'. Representing as they do certain traits in George Eliot's own make-up, Leavis concludes that there is an element of self-idealization in their characterization and an element of self-indulgence, what Leavis interestingly calls 'day-dream self-indulgence'—'The emotional "fulness" represented by Dorothea depends for its exalting potency on an abeyance of intelligence and self-knowledge, and the situations offered by way of "objective correlative" have the day-dream relation to experience; they are generated by a need to soar above the indocile facts and conditions of the real world . . . In this kind of indulgence, complaisantly as she abandons herself to the current that is loosed, George Eliot's creative vitality has no part'.

Now one might, of course, dispute Leavis's criticism. Even so, it is as much the manner in which Leavis develops his objections, not simply their truth, which is relevant to seeing the object of his criticism as an instance of Collingwood's notion of bad art. Leavis reveals the weakness in the portrayal of Dorothea, for instance, by comparing her characterization with that of the other major figures in *Middlemarch*. The failure in expression is shown up against the backdrop of successful expression. As Leavis puts it, 'We have an alternation between the poised impersonal insight of a finely tempered wisdom and something like the emotional confusions and self-importance of adolescence'. George Eliot's failure, if that is what it is, is not incompetence. It is precisely the contrast between what George Eliot is capable of and what she ends up with in the portrayal of Dorothea that provokes the charge of corruption of consciousness. For Collingwood informs us that 'Corruptions of consciousness are always partial and temporary lapses in an activity which, on the whole, is successful in doing what it tries to do'. George Eliot evidently sets out to show us what a personality such as Dorothea's can be like in the same way that she explores Casaubon's deadly academicism, Rosamond's relentless egoism and Bulstrode's moral evasions. But, Leavis alleges, she fails to bring Dorothea into focus because she fails to clarify her own thoughts and feelings about this kind of yearning soul-hunger which is also an aspect of her own self.

Collingwood does not regard make-believe, or daydream fantasy, as bad in itself; as the heart of amusement art, it is bad when people come to feel that it is only make-believe which makes life worth living. But he does regard corruption of consciousness as harmful in itself. As the manifestation of self-deluding ignorance, it is the 'worst disease of mind', the 'true radix malorum'. Hence his conviction that art, good art, is not a luxury, for its discipline of imagination can deliver us from the fantasies of bad art.

W. Jan van der Dussen (essay date 1990)

SOURCE: "Collingwood and the Idea of Progress," in *History and Theory,* Vol. XXIX, No. 4, 1990, pp. 21-41.

[*In the following essay, van der Dussen examines Collingwood's view of the idea of progress as both epistemological and metaphysical in nature.*]

I

At the beginning of the chapter in his autobiography entitled "The Need for a Philosophy of History" Collingwood claims that two branches of philosophical inquiry need special attention. Besides epistemological problems related to historical knowledge he mentions in this connection "metaphysical problems, concerned with the nature of the historian's subject matter: the elucidation of terms like event, process, progress, civilization, and so forth" (*Aut,* 77). [In the text the following abbreviations are used for Collingwood's works: *EPM*: *An Essay on Philosophical Method*; *Aut*: *An Autobiography*; *EM*: *An Essay on Metaphysics*; *NL*: *The New Leviathan*; *IN*: *The Idea of Nature*; *IH*: *The Idea of History*. From *R. G. Collingwood: Essays in the Philosophy of History,* ed. W. Debbins (Austin, 1965): *CPH*: "Croce's Philosophy of History"; *SHC*: "Oswald Spengler and the Theory of Historical Cycles"; *THC*: "The Theory of Historical Cycles"; *PP*: "A Philosophy of Progress."]

Since Collingwood wrote these words, attention has been directed almost exclusively towards the epistemological aspects of history. It has become common to call this branch "critical" or "analytical" philosophy of history, as opposed to its "speculative" counterpart. It is striking, though, that the subjects dealt with by the latter do not correspond to the ones Collingwood mentions under the heading "metaphysical problems." For the usual questions discussed by speculative philosophy of history concern the possible patterns, mechanisms, or purpose of history and not the type of concepts Collingwood cites as examples. One can only wonder why Collingwood's admonition has not been taken to heart and why philosophers of history, on the rare occasions they were dealing with the object of historical study, have confined themselves to the "speculative" subjects mentioned before. For a conceptual analysis of the terms Collingwood mentions—and one could add to these concepts like contingency, unintended consequences, revolution, structure, culture, or nation— would certainly be of interest for a better understanding of the past.

Collingwood himself, however, had a keen interest in these metaphysical questions, and this is especially true of the concepts of process, progress, and civilization. Given the fact that they are also explicitly mentioned by Collingwood as examples of a special branch of the philosophy of history, it is surprising that they have almost completely escaped the notice of the many commentators on Collingwood's philosophy of history. An exception has been L. O. Mink, who has rightly brought to the fore the importance of the concept of process in Collingwood's philosophy of history. Though this doctrine is—in the words of Mink—a "recessive" one in *The Idea of History,* its significance is illustrated by the fact that Collingwood refers to it in his autobiography in connection with what he calls "my first principle of a philosophy of history" (*Aut,* 97). This principle was the idea, also expressed in *The Idea of History,* that the past is not dead, but in some sense living in the present. "At the time, I expressed this by saying," Collingwood remarks, "that history is concerned not with 'events' but with 'processes'; that 'processes' are things which do not begin and end but turn into one another" (*Aut,* 97-98). He developed his ideas on this subject at some length in 1920 in the essay **"Libellus de Generatione"** which "was primarily a study of the nature and implications of process or becoming" (*Aut,* 99); but unfortunately this essay is unavailable.

In addition to Collingwood's interest in certain "metaphysical problems" there is another reason for stressing their importance, which is that in both the "Preface" and "Introductory Lecture" of his **"Outlines of a Philosophy of History"** (the "Martouret essay" of 1928), Collingwood emphasizes that history *a parte subjecti* (epistemological or methodological problems) and history *a parte objecti* (metaphysical problems) are not only closely related, but are inseparable. This idea is based on the doctrine of the ideality of the past, which is the central theme of the Martouret essay. According to this doctrine the past should not be conceived as an objective reality, but as being intrinsically related to the thought of the historian. It was the error of the traditional "speculative" philosophers of history, in Collingwood's view (though he does not use the term), that they regarded the past as a special kind of reality with special characteristics. "But when the methodological view of the philosophy of history is combined with the doctrine of the ideality of history," Collingwood says, "all objection to a metaphysical philosophy of history vanishes. For the necessary forms and conditions of historical thought are now seen to determine the necessary forms and conditions of its object."

It is remarkable indeed to see Collingwood here advocating an idea that only lately has been put forward by philosophers of history such as Haskell Fain and Peter Munz, namely that instead of making the usual sharp distinction between "speculative" and "critical" philosophy of history we should conceive of them as mutually related. In cases like these—and other examples from the unpublished manuscripts could also be given—it is hard to avoid the conclusion that the course of the philosophy of history since the Second World War would have been different had Collingwood's manuscripts been known at an earlier date.

The fact that Collingwood considered history *a parte objecti* inseparable from history *a parte subjecti* does not mean that he was of the opinion that the traditional "speculative" philosophies of history should be seen as a valid enterprise. In addition to the fact that they viewed the past as an objective reality, their grand themes suffered, one could say, from violating what Collingwood called "the principle of the limited objective" (*NL,* 31.61).

An illustration of Collingwood's conception and treatment of metaphysical problems in the philosophy of history is provided by the course of lectures on the subject which he delivered during the first two terms of 1936. This course consisted of two parts: a "History of the Idea of History" and a "Metaphysical Epilegomena."

It has become famous, of course, because of its posthumous publication by T. M. Knox under the title *The Idea of History*. It is interesting to notice, here, that while Knox gave the second part the title "Epilegomena," Collingwood titled it "Metaphysical Epilegomena." In addition, Knox in two cases altered the titles of its subdivisions: Collingwood's "Re-enactment of past experience the essence of history" becomes Knox's "History as re-enactment of past experience," and Collingwood's "Progress" becomes Knox's "Progress as created by historical thinking."

The series of lectures under the title "Metaphysical Epilegomena" clearly illustrates how closely in Collingwood's opinion a typical "epistemological" subject like the re-enactment doctrine was intertwined with a "metaphysical" subject such as the idea of progress. (One might suggest that the reason why Knox altered the title of "Progress" and deleted the word "metaphysical" from the "Metaphysical Epilegomena" had to do with his differing conception of the "metaphysical").

II

The importance that Collingwood attached to the idea of progress can be gauged from the fact that he devotes a third of his space to the subject in the epilegomena to his course of lectures. It is also confirmed by the several articles he had already published which deal with the concept of progress: explicitly in **"A Philosophy of Progress"** (1929), and in some detail in **"Oswald Spengler and the Theory of Historical Cycles"** (1927), and especially **"The Theory of Historical Cycles"** (1927), while Croce's views on historical progress are criticized in **"Croce's Philosophy of History"** (1921).

It is not easy to come to grips with Collingwood's view of the idea of progress. It is less difficult, however, to find the reason for this. For the concept of progress is a typical example of a philosophical concept as elaborated in ***An Essay on Philosophical Method***. In that book Collingwood argues that the character of a philosophical concept is such that, unlike scientific or empirical concepts, no exhaustive definition of it can be provided. A philosophical concept is characterized by an overlap of its specific classes; these overlapping classes each embody the generic essence, but they make up a scale of forms differing from each other both in degree and kind and by opposition and distinction. A philosophical concept is therefore intrinsically unlimited in nature and "leaks or escapes" out of the limits characteristic of non-philosophical concepts (*EPM,* 35).

The ***Essay on Philosophical Method*** can be seen as a treatise in which Collingwood makes clear his ideas concerning the special characteristics of philosophical thought. As such it represents an intermediate stage between ***Speculum Mentis,*** published nine years previously, and his later works, the last of which to appear in his lifetime was *The New Leviathan,* published nine years later.

Though there are similarities as well as differences—both in form and content—between the philosophical studies Collingwood wrote between *Speculum Mentis* and *The New Leviathan,* one distinguishing feature remained constant: all of them are informed by a dialectical manner of thought. In *An Essay on Philosophical Method* the formal elements of this style of thought are worked out in a manner as brilliant as it is clear.

However, there is a problem in that the only explicit attempts made by Collingwood to apply the views expounded in the *Essay* to particular philosophical problems are to be found in his unpublished manuscripts. Thus, for example, in the **"Notes toward a Metaphysic"** (1933-1934) Collingwood deals with cosmological problems (especially those concerning the relation between matter, life, and mind), while in his lecture on **"Method and Metaphysics"** (1935) he deals with the concept of reality. In the published works, on the other hand, Collingwood rarely makes any explicit reference to the philosophical principles laid down in his *Essay.* These principles, however, are not only embedded in his works, but are also of value in the interpretation of them. This is clearly so in works such as *The Idea of Nature* or *The Idea of History,* and of those concepts, that of progress is a fine example.

III

In achieving an understanding of the way in which Collingwood conceives the concept of progress, one has always to bear in mind the way in which he understands other related concepts, for only in this way can the characteristics and specific problems related to the idea of progress be brought to the fore. I am thinking here in particular of the concepts of change, process, development, and evolution. One should further keep in mind the distinction Collingwood makes between nature and (human) history.

The difference between change and development or process (Collingwood in fact does not make a distinction between these terms) is based on the one between matter and life. In a case of change there is always a substratum x which is permanent and changes from one state into another, the cause being something from without. Water might be taken as an example. Though this exists in a solid, liquid, or gaseous state, its essence, Collingwood writes, "is represented by the formula H^2O," the variable in this case being "something extraneous to the generic essence" (*EPM,* 59).

In a development, however, "there is no substratum and no states of it, but always something turning into something else." This is typical of organic nature, and it was Aristotle who first worked this conception out. Collingwood is not always precise in his terminology, since he says of Aristotle that for him "nature as such

is process, growth, change" (*IN,* 82). After this he continues:

> This process is a development, i.e. the changing takes successive forms . . . in which each is the potentiality of its successor; but it is not what we call "evolution," because for Aristotle the kinds of change and of structure exhibited in the world of nature form an eternal repertory, and the items in the repertory are related logically, not temporally, among themselves. It follows that the change is in the last resort cyclical; circular movement is for him characteristic of the perfectly organic, not as for us of the inorganic. (*IN,* 82)

The same distinction is also made in *The Idea of History,* where Collingwood states that two views of natural process are possible: "that events in nature repeat one another specifically, the specific forms remaining constant through the diversity of their individual instances . . . , or that the specific forms themselves undergo change, new forms coming into existence by modification of the old. The second conception is what is meant by evolution" (*IH,* 321).

To use the language of *An Essay on Philosophical Method,* an evolutionary process differs both in degree and kind from a cyclical one. In Collingwood's view the idea of nature as an evolutionary process has been conceived since the end of the eighteenth century on the analogy of the study of human affairs, because by that time historians had begun to see history as a process instead of the succession of separate periods (*IN,* 9-10).

The theory of evolution itself had, especially following the appearance of Darwin's *Origin of Species,* an enormous influence on the study of history. As has been pointed out by, among others, Stephen Toulmin, this theory became popular mainly, however, in its vulgarized form as a doctrine of progression rather than as a theory concerning the descent of species as conceived by Darwin himself. Toulmin emphasizes that this progressive or "providential" conception of evolution got its inspiration from Lamarck and Herder and had little to do with Darwin's theory. It is doubtful whether Collingwood was conscious of this fact, since he says of Darwin that he "constantly used language implying teleology in organic nature" (*IN,* 135). He was, however, extremely critical of the naturalistic progressivism which was so popular during the nineteenth century: "In order to realize the lengths to which this dogma of progress was pushed, it is necessary to go slumming among the most unsavoury relics of third-rate historical work" (*IH,* 145).

On the other hand, Collingwood took the idea of a cosmic evolution seriously and even saw the concept of evolution as having passed through a biological and a cosmological phase (*IN,* 133). He was extremely interested in modern cosmological theories, in particular those propounded by Alexander and Whitehead. His extensive **"Notes toward a Metaphysic"** of 1933-

1934—on which *The Idea of Nature* is partly based—bears witness to this. In these notes Collingwood attempts, very much in the manner of Lloyd Morgan and J. C. Smuts, to develop a theory of "emergent evolution" from matter to life, mind and spirit, with a *nisus* as driving force.

Collingwood did not succeed in accomplishing a cosmological theory of his own. With hindsight there is no need for us to deplore this fact, nor to endorse Knox's opinion that by comparison with Alexander and Whitehead, Collingwood's "promise never became performance" (*IH,* xxii); for one important result of Collingwood's endeavors in this field has been his focus on the history of the idea of nature as expressed in the history of natural science. This view is at the present time more in vogue than cosmological theories, though Collingwood's own contribution to it is still hardly recognized.

Collingwood's study of modern cosmological theories had, however, another side effect which was of great importance in the development of his ideas. For though he agreed that nature should be seen as a process, he was unwilling to conclude from this that the distinction between natural and historical processes should be considered as superseded. When considering an historical process Collingwood always refers to the history of mind, that is, to the history of the human past. In his **"Notes toward a Metaphysic"** we see Collingwood already developing this view. Although he uses the term "spirit" where he was later to speak of "mind" or "thought," he maintains that:

> The life of the spirit is a history: i.e. not a process in which everything comes to be and passes away, but a process in which the past is conserved as an element in the present. The past is not merely a *pre*condition of the present but a condition of it. Whereas in nature the past *was* necessary in order that the present may *now* exist (e.g. there must have been an egg that there may now be a hen) the past being thus left behind when the present comes into being, in history, so far as this is real history and not mere time-sequence, the past conserves itself in the present, and the present could not be there unless it did.

In an historical series, Collingwood writes, the earlier continues with "accumulation or enrichment of the existent by the sum of its own past." "For mind in general," he then concludes, "this accumulation is called experience; for consciousness, it is called memory; for a social unity, it is called tradition; for knowledge, it is called history."

So an important result of Collingwood's examination of cosmological problems was the development of a clear distinction between natural and historical processes. This distinction pervades *The Idea of History*—all manifestations of naturalism or positivism being severely criticized in that book. The argument is represented in its most concise form in the essay **"Human Nature and Human History"** (*IH,* 205-231), which was first delivered as a lecture to the British Academy in 1936. In the draft of this essay Collingwood develops the argument point by point, a key part being the contention that not all processes are historical processes, as historical processes are rational and natural processes irrational. Then, implicitly making one of his rare references to the theory developed in *An Essay on Philosophical Method,* Collingwood remarks that in the relation between the natural and the historical "here, as elsewhere, there is an overlap of classes. *Man* occupies an ambiguous position. He stands with one foot in nature and one in history." The natural and irrational aspect includes "senses, instincts, impulses and in general the subject-matter of psychology," while the rational aspect includes "the intellect, will and their synonyms and implicates."

From the foregoing it may be concluded that Collingwood's views on history were partly derived from his study of natural processes, and the differences he saw between natural and historical processes. The essence of that difference lies in the fact that nature does not retain its own past in its development, while mind does: nature's past is dead, but mind's past is alive. In the draft of **"Human Nature and Human History"** Collingwood eloquently expresses this idea thus: "Nature ceases to be what it was in becoming what it is; the phases of its process fall outside one another. Mind, in becoming something new, also continues to be what it was; the stages of its development interpenetrate one another." This view fits in well, of course, with other well-known aspects of Collingwood's theory of history, such as the position that all history is the history of thought, or the re-enactment doctrine.

What are the implications of the foregoing for Collingwood's views on the concepts of development and process? Here we can use the theory of philosophical concepts elaborated in *An Essay on Philosophical Method* as a guide to answering the question. To do so requires that we understand a philosophical concept as constituting a scale of forms of overlapping classes differing both in degree and in kind and being related both by opposition and distinction.

We should, then, place the concept of change at the lowest end of the scale, it being characterized by the idea of a permanent substratum undergoing various changes caused from without. The next stage is the conception of nature as undergoing a cyclical and immanently caused development of both a logical and a spatial kind: from the temporal point of view it shows on the one hand no development, since the forms remain permanent, while on the other hand there is a development from the potential to the actual. Following this comes the concept of natural process or evolution, in which the forms themselves develop. Finally there is the idea of an historical process as the development of mind and rationality—the distinguishing feature of this conception being that in its development mind retains its past in its present.

In *An Essay on Philosophical Method* Collingwood elucidates the way in which overlap of classes is combined with the scale of forms. "Each term in the scale," he writes, "sums up the whole scale to that point" (*EPM,* 39), for it sees its own point of view as identical with the genus and denies the higher form. The higher form from its side includes the lower one except its denial of the higher form. Applied to the concept of process, this means that historical process as its highest form includes all the lower ones. So it is characterized by being a change, though without a permanent substratum, and of a logical, spatial, and temporal nature, immanently caused and—this being its own increment—retaining the past phases of its own development.

IV

Moving on to the concept of progress, one may observe as a preliminary that it includes the idea of development. It is development, however, of a specific type, which may be described by saying that a later phase is conceived as an improvement upon an earlier phase. As such it cannot be considered as just another increment on the scale of forms of the concept of development, for the concept of progress is also used within the sphere of natural development—although as previously remarked, this is the Lamarckian idea of a progressive evolution rather than the Darwinian theory.

Collingwood emphatically rejects the Lamarckian type of evolution: "The archaeopteryx may in fact have been an ancestor of the bird," he says, "but what entitles us to call the bird an improvement on the archaeopteryx? A bird is not a better archaeopteryx, but something different that has grown out of it. Each is trying to be itself" (*IH,* 322). He was also at times very critical of the idea of progress in history. For example, in 1921 he can be found criticizing Croce for his "vulgar optimism" and for seeing all history as "a change from the good to the better" (*CPH,* 16-17).

This was not, however, Collingwood's last word on the matter, since he later came back to the question on several occasions, developing rather different views. In this connection it should first of all be noted that he does not always use the concept of progress unambiguously. For though in his essay on the subject in *The Idea of History* Collingwood indeed rejects the idea of progress in nature in the sense of being a process of improving states, in a preceding passage he maintains that "in one sense, to call a natural process evolutionary is the same thing as calling it progressive" (*IH,* 321). He means by this that the modifications of the various forms of a natural process can only come into existence in a certain order: "In this sense of the word 'progress,' progressive only means orderly, that is, exhibiting order." In *The Idea of Nature* the term "progressive" is used in a simi-

lar sense, as for example when Collingwood comments: "where by progress I mean a change always leading to something new, with no necessary implication of betterment" (*IN,* 14). In his discussion of Kant in *The Idea of History* Collingwood even plainly states: "All history certainly shows progress, i.e. it is the development of something" (*IH,* 104).

It is obvious that in these cases the concept of progress is used in a wide sense, equating it with the idea of development as an orderly process. In that sense even natural evolution as conceived by Darwin can be seen as progressive. Collingwood did not dwell on this aspect and preferred to concentrate on the idea of historical process, which has, as we have seen, a rational nature. He considered it an achievement of the first order that in the eighteenth century history was conceived for the first time as making sense: "It had a plot. It revealed itself as something coherent, significant, intelligible," and he described this as "a genuine discovery" (**PP,** 111).

For Collingwood, seeing history as a plot means that it is conceived as a continuity consisting of the succession of problems confronting human beings and the various solutions found for them. "Now such a course of events may be truly called a progress," he maintains, "because it is a going forward; it has direction, everything in it proceeds out of what has gone before and could not have happened without the occurrence of its past" (**THC,** 86). He then continues: "But though history is in this sense a progress and nothing but a progress, it cannot be so in any other sense. No one of the phases through which it moves is any better, or any worse, than any of the others" (**THC,** 86-87). The reason given for this position is that each generation is confronted by unique situations giving rise to unique problems.

So we find Collingwood here using the concept of progress in two different ways: one in the sense of history as an orderly and rational process (a "going forward") and one in the sense of each phase of the historical process as an improvement on the last. Progress in the first sense is accepted by Collingwood and even thought necessary, while he rejects progress in the second sense—at least in the passages so far considered. Since progress in the second sense should be seen as its proper meaning, this is the sense on which we shall concentrate.

In order to assess the arguments developed by Collingwood concerning the idea of progress it is important to bear in mind certain relevant distinctions: such as, on the one hand, the distinction between history as an "objective" process and history as conceived by an historian; and on the other, the distinction between history seen "as a whole" and history seen only partially or under a certain aspect. Since Collingwood's essay on the idea of progress in *The Idea of History* was his latest explicit discussion of the subject, we will consider it first.

In this essay Collingwood discusses, and emphatically rejects, the conception of history as governed by a "law of progress"; for this idea is based, he argues, on the two false and contradictory assumptions of man's superiority to nature and his being subject to a supposed natural law (*IH,* 322-323). If there is anything like historical progress it should stand on its own merits and not as part of any kind of natural progress.

Progress is a process in which new forms are being developed, and Collingwood describes the idea of historical progress as "the coming into existence not merely of new actions or thoughts or situations belonging to the same specific type, but of new specific types," which should be conceived as improvements (*IH,* 324). As an example of such an improvement Collingwood asks us to consider a community of fish-eaters which develops a more efficient method of fishing, catching ten instead of five fish on an average day. He is reluctant to call this an "objective" improvement, since the older generation is inclined to consider changes such as these as a form of decadence, while the younger one will see it as progress. The important point here is the reason Collingwood supplies for the impossibility of comparing the two practices within the fisher-community. For the older generation will stick to the old method, thinking it better than the new, and this is not done "out of irrational prejudice," but "because the way of life which it knows and values is built round the old method, which is therefore certain to have social and religious associations that express the intimacy of its connexion with this way of life as a whole" (*IH,* 325).

The important distinction Collingwood makes here is that between change in respect of a certain activity within the fisher-community (namely catching more fish) and change related to its "way of life as a whole." Though one could claim, of course, that the first type of change can be seen only as an improvement, he is not willing to take this possibility seriously, since it is generally the case that improvements have unforeseen (and often negative) side effects or consequences and that it is precisely this which makes the idea of progress such a difficult one. Here one can only endorse Collingwood's position. A necessary condition of ascribing progress in any particular case is, therefore, that it is conceived as related to the whole of a community's way of life; and in order to do this it is also necessary that both ways of life are known "in the only way in which ways of life can be known: by actual experience, or by the sympathetic insight which may take its place for such a purpose" (*IH,* 325-326).

In discussing the problem of comparing two ways of life Collingwood deals first with the comparison made by the new generation, and then with a possible comparison made by an historian. "Experience shows," he says, "that nothing is harder than for a given generation in a changing society, which is living in a new way of its own, to enter sympathetically into the life of the last," and for this reason "the historical changes in a society's

way of life are very rarely conceived as progressive even by the generation that makes them" (*IH,* 326).

Though one can agree with the first part of this argument, its conclusion is doubtful. For it is certainly not shown by experience that a new generation only rarely conceives its accomplished changes as an improvement. On the contrary, rather the opposite will usually be the case and we will see that at other places Collingwood expresses this opinion also. It is quite another question, of course, whether a new generation has the *right* to conceive its accomplishments as an improvement. In order to have such a right, Collingwood argues, a person should know his society's past, that is, have historical knowledge of it; for only in this way can the merits of the old and new ways of life be compared. "In short," he concludes, "the revolutionary can only regard his revolution as a progress in so far as he is also an historian, genuinely re-enacting in his own historical thought the life he nevertheless rejects" (*IH,* 326).

Since it may be very difficult for a person of the new generation to have historical knowledge of the old way of life because of his or her lack of sympathy with it, Collingwood goes on to consider the possibility that an historian might function as a neutral judge; and this possibility he flatly rejects. What is required is a comparison of different "ways of life as a whole," and this is not possible: "the task of judging the value of a certain way of life taken in its entirety is an impossible task, because no such thing in its entirety is ever a possible object of historical knowledge" (*IH,* 327). The reason he gives is twofold, for, he says later, "there must be large tracts of its life for which he has either no data, or no data that he is in a position to interpret" (*IH,* 329).

However, Collingwood does not mention in this connection a more cogent argument which is relevant with regard to the conception of a way of life as a whole. Even if an historian had no lack of data and was in a position to interpret it faithfully, each way of life should be understood as a unity in which the various aspects are interrelated in a unique way. Though Collingwood is correct when he argues that one cannot speak of progress if certain problems are solved while the solutions to earlier problems are lost, it does not follow that where new problems are solved and the solutions to earlier problems retained we therefore have sufficient reason to assert that there has been progress. In particular, if we are comparing "ways of life as a whole," this being Collingwood's original focus, then the various aspects of a way of life—art, religion, science, technology, economy, and so on—need to be understood in their interrelation, and possible "real" progress in any one of these is a question of a different order.

This is not the only confusing element in Collingwood's discussion of the idea of progress. In the article **"The Theory of Historical Cycles"** he argues that no phase in history can be considered an improvement on an-

other, for in each phase "men found themselves confronted by a unique situation, which gave rise to a
unique problem, or the eternal problem in a unique
form" and "to live was to solve that problem, the condition of surviving until the problem changed"; and he
continues:

> So far as we can see history as a whole, that is
> how we see it; as a continuous development in
> which every phase consists of the solution of
> human problems set by the preceding phase. But
> that is only an ideal for the historian; that is
> what he knows history would look like if he could
> see it as a whole, which he never can. In point of
> fact, he can only see it in bits; he can only be
> acquainted with certain periods, and only com-
> petent in very small parts of those periods. (**THC,**
> 87)

The aspect dealt with here is not the one he takes as his
starting-point in *The Idea of History*; for the point at
issue here is whether or not it is possible to conceive
"history as a whole," which is a different question from
whether a "way of life as a whole" can be conceived: the
first concerns the historical process in its entirety conceived diachronically and the second a synchronic conception of a way of life in its entirety.

Collingwood's answer to the first question is clear: we
cannot conceive the historical process in its totality, but
only parts of it. He deals with this question in his discussion of the idea of historical cycles and argues that
the periods with which an historian is well acquainted
are seen as luminous and progressive, while the periods
with which the historian has little acquaintance are
considered dark, primitive, and irrational. This is the
background to the cyclical view of history which splits
the past up into disconnected episodes of rise and fall,
progress and decline (**SHC,** 74-75; **THC,** 87-89).

Though this argument is a cogent one, especially in
view of Collingwood's conception of the ideality of the
past (he does not object to the cyclical view as long as
the various periods are not seen as objective realities), it
is not related to the question of why a way of life as a
whole cannot be grasped by an historian. In fact the
latter question—which is crucial to an understanding of
the problem of progress—is not answered satisfactorily
at all. In *The Idea of History* it is raised and immediately skirted by using exactly the same argument as that
used above (*IH,* 327-328): but this argument, as we
have seen, is related to another question entirely.

Having used an irrelevant argument in addressing the
question of whether a way of life as a whole is conceivable, Collingwood nonetheless returns to the question
(albeit implicitly) when he develops the view that there
is one condition on which the idea of progress "can
represent a genuine thought": "The condition is that the
person who uses the word should use it in comparing
two historical periods or ways of life, both of which he
can understand historically, that is, with enough sympa-

thy and insight to reconstruct their experience for himself" (*IH,* 328-329). Here Collingwood explicitly equates
understanding an historical period with the understanding of a way of life, the possibility of the latter having
previously been in doubt. If for the moment we can
forego this problematic element, we find Collingwood
using three arguments for the impossibility of comparisons between two different historical periods being
made by historians. The first argument is that: "By re-
enacting the experience of either in his own mind he has
already accepted it as a thing to be judged by its own
standards: a form of life having its own problems, to be
judged by its success in solving those problems and no
others" (*IH,* 329). The second argument is that it cannot
be assumed that "two different ways of life were attempts to do one and the same thing," while the third
states that "it would be idle to ask whether any one
period of history taken as a whole showed a progress
over its predecessor. For the historian can never take
any period as a whole" (*IH,* 329). The reason given for
this last argument has already been mentioned (the historian has not enough data or is not in a position to
interpret certain data). But this argument is not consistent with what Collingwood maintains elsewhere, since,
for example, in his discussion of historical cycles, it is
at least not denied, and perhaps even implied, that an
historian is capable of understanding an historical period, the latter being equated with a way of life.

If we were to sum up our discussion of Collingwood's
treatment of the concept of historical progress, we have
to conclude that it shows a lack of consistency, for he
denies on the one hand that ways of life can be grasped,
while on the other he believes that historical periods
may be understood historically. It is nevertheless obvious that Collingwood denies the possibility that historical periods can be compared. The argument he gives is
that each period is to be characterized and judged in
terms of its own problems and the solutions it finds for
them, and that this does not allow comparisons to be
made. What is not satisfactory is that he does not properly discuss the basic problem of comparing the unique
interrelations between the various aspects within each
different period.

v

Collingwood's opinion that historical periods cannot be
compared is not his last word on the subject of progress,
but his ideas on the subject are varied and not always
easy to grasp. It is possible to distinguish four different
positions in Collingwood's attitude to the concept of
progress: a) It is dependent on a point of view; b) It is
meaningless; c) It is meaningful; d) It is necessary.

a) Collingwood's rejection of historical realism implies
that any suggestion of historical progress being conceived as an "objective phenomenon" is rejected accordingly. In this connection his usual reaction is to emphasize that not only the idea of progress, but also the idea
of decay, is dependent on the point of view taken up by

the historian. This emphasis is already to be found in his article of 1921 (long before his elaboration of the principle of the ideality of the past in the Martouret essay of 1928), in which Croce is criticized for his "transcendent attitude" of "asserting the existence of a criterion outside the historian's mind," which implies— at least in Croce's view—that history is seen as a purely progressive process. "A change that is really a progress seen from one end," Collingwood retorts, "is no less really a decadence, seen from the other. It is true to say that the decay of archery was the rise of firearms; but it is not less true to say that the rise of firearms was the decay of archery" (**CPH,** 16).

In **"The Theory of Historical Cycles"** the same argument is used, Collingwood this time also giving the "growth of the steamship" as an example, it being "the passing-away of that splendid thing, the sailing-ship" (**THC,** 81). He takes the same position with regard to periods, maintaining, as we have seen, that it is a lack of understanding or knowledge which makes an historian conceive a period as one of decay (**THC,** 81; **IH,** 164-165; 327-328) and he speaks in this connection of an "optical illusion" (**IH,** 328).

Although one cannot compare, in Collingwood's view, periods or aspects of periods in a neutral way, this does not imply that he considers such comparisons to be meaningless. They should be seen as only the expression of a certain point of view, and as long as this is realized Collingwood does not object to them. The cyclical view of history as alternating periods of progress and decay he even considers "a permanent feature of all historical thought." "But wherever it occurs," he adds, "it is incidental to a point of view. The cycle is the historian's field of vision at a given moment" (**SHC,** 75).

Collingwood does not yield, however, to the "cynical view" that it is only a "matter of taste" "whether you think the course of events is an upward or a downward course," depending "not on *it* but on *you*," with the implication "that our preferences are mere matters of chance or caprice" (**PP,** 109). For he believes that the concept of progress may indeed be used in a meaningful way. Before paying attention to this, however, we should first deal with the cases where Collingwood thinks this concept cannot be used meaningfully.

b) Collingwood is of the opinion that the concept of progress cannot be used in a meaningful way in the realms of art, happiness, and morality.

The reasons Collingwood gives for the impropriety of speaking of progress in art are threefold. The first is that "every phase of art has its own beauty, which it is idle to assess in terms of a scale of degrees" (**PP,** 110-111). So the various forms of art should apparently be seen as differing only in kind (one may here observe that in *An Essay on Philosophical Method* a different position is adopted). Using an argument that would return in *An Essay on Metaphysics* Collingwood main-

tains that asking whether there is progress or decadence in certain fields of art is a question that "does not arise" (**THC,** 82; **EM,** 26); for the various artists were not trying to do the same thing. Therefore, "if we take a single art and study two different phases of its development, we always find them differentiated by a difference of the ideal aimed at" (**THC,** 82). Of the various ideals it cannot be said that one is inherently better than another, for "a particular age has the task of realising beauty in a particular way" and therefore cannot be assessed "in terms of any other" (**PP,** 116). In *The Idea of History,* finally, Collingwood gives another argument for denying that progress in art is conceivable. For a work of art, he here maintains, "is the solution of a fresh problem which arises not out of a previous work of art but out of the artist's unreflective experience" and the flow of that experience "is not an historical process" (**IH,** 330).

The question whether human happiness has increased or decreased in the past is also considered meaningless (**PP,** 113). The reason given for this is that happiness cannot be measured and there is therefore no such thing as "the sum of human happiness": "Different ages find happiness in different things" and "the happiness of a peasant is not contained in the happiness of a millionaire," is the simple yet entirely adequate conclusion (**PP,** 114; **IH,** 330).

The reason that it is improper to speak of an increase in morality is that "a man's moral worth depends not on his circumstances, but on the way in which he confronts them" (**PP,** 115). Collingwood therefore particularly objects to the view that certain circumstances such as the abolition of slavery render those living under those circumstances morally more worthy than those who do not (**PP,** 115-116). The argument developed in this context is similar to the argument used in the discussion of the alleged intellectual superiority of Western civilization as against "primitive" civilizations, for here too Collingwood is of the opinion that "civilized man . . . mistakes the superiority of his tools for a superiority in himself."

As with art, so in *The Idea of History* a further argument is given for the denial of the possibility of progress in morality. For the latter is likewise seen as arising out of unreflective experience: "The course of our moral life is conditioned by the succession of our desires; and, though our desires change, they do not change historically" (**IH,** 330). As we shall later see, however, the possibility of moral progress conceived as expressed in institutions is left open.

So with regard to art, happiness, and morality we find Collingwood explicitly rejecting the idea that the concept of progress is applicable. In this connection it is worth noting that all three are typical of philosophical concepts in the sense developed in *An Essay on Philosophical Method*. Each of them exemplifies a certain dialectically conceived relation between its classes in the way discussed above. Although they show in this respect a conceptual development, Collingwood denies that there is any historical development, that is, a development in which they could be seen as forming a rational process. This position is a rather odd one, as histories of both art and morality are not only conceivable, but actually written: while one can endorse Collingwood's view that art and morality should be understood as, respectively, the expression of the ideals of a certain age and the confrontation of certain problems of a certain kind, this does not exclude the possibility that man is capable of retaining the experience of these expressions and confrontations from the past. The artistic and moral aspects of the past can therefore be understood as forming a living element of present art and morality.

Whether there can be progress in art or morality—let alone in happiness—is, of course, quite a different question. Though one can only endorse Collingwood's rejection, this does not mean that it is not possible to conceive of a history of them. With regard to art and morality the denial of this possibility is certainly wrong; although it should be added that they should be understood as the history of ideas of art and morality. Moreover, besides being the expression of the ideals of a certain age, art is also a part of that age and of its history; and the same is true of morality and the conditions in which it operates.

Although in *The Idea of History* Collingwood is of the opinion (as we will see) that progress in science is possible, in the manuscript called **"The Function of Metaphysics in Civilization"** (1937-1938) he is skeptical of the idea. This manuscript was written in preparation for *An Essay on Metaphysics* and it is here that the conception of metaphysics as a science of absolute presuppositions is developed for the first time. This conception is indeed relativistic and this is reflected in Collingwood's discussion in the manuscript of the question to what extent our science may be taken as superior to Greek science. He questions this alleged superiority in two ways. In the first place he points out that there is no real standard of comparison between them, though there exists a continuity and development. He suggests that Greek science has provided the spadework "preparing a soil out of which we moderns are winning our harvests." If this is the case, "is not the richness of these harvests a proof, not of our superiority to the ancients, but of the excellence of their pioneer work?"

In addition, he gives another, more fundamental argument for questioning the superiority of our science over Greek science. Deciding which of two things is better, he argues, implies the possibility of choosing between them; but we cannot be in a position to choose between our science and Greek science, and the question is therefore meaningless. He calls it "a nonsense question," because "to ask it presupposes the existence of a situation which does not exist."

In **"The Theory of Historical Cycles"** the idea of progress is also linked in a similar way to the possibility of practical choice, for Collingwood there makes the observation that the question whether we might prefer to live in a past period because we think it a better one "cannot arise" as a problem, since "the choice cannot be offered." He therefore says that in speaking of the past "we ought not to call it either better than the present or worse; for we are not called upon to choose it or to reject it, to like it or to dislike it, to approve it or to condemn it, but simply to accept it" (**THC,** 85). Comparison between historical periods is therefore considered to be both theoretically and practically meaningless.

c) "In its crudest form," Collingwood avers, "the idea of progress would imply that throughout history man has been working at the same problem, and has been solving it better and better" (**THC,** 84). The identity of a certain problem serves Collingwood as a criterion for the meaningful application of the concept of progress. The absence of such an identity also provides him with his reason for denying the possibility of progress in art or morality, both activities being responses to contingent problems.

There are, however, certain problems which Collingwood does regard as having a continuous historical identity and which therefore allow the possibility of progressive solution. An example is engineering. Discussing the preference one may have for Norman or Gothic buildings, he denies that this can be decided on rational grounds with regard to their aesthetic merits; but if judged by the standards of engineering, the transition from Norman to Gothic was "definitely an improvement": "The main purpose of the architect is to build; the Gothic architect built stronger and cheaper than the Norman" (**PP,** 110).

Things become rather more problematic when, later in the same article, Collingwood ascribes a similar "objective" improvement to the sphere of political life. Here he speaks of the individual being "progressively liberated . . . from the tyranny of custom and the crippling weight of a rigid political system" (**PP,** 119). He is apparently conscious of the possible weakness of this argument, since he goes on to add that "savages would think *our* political systems and social customs quite as oppressive and inimical to happiness as we think theirs." He escapes from this difficulty by claiming that the social and political institutions developed by us "suit *our* psychological structure," yielding by this move to a rather fundamental and irrationally based form of relativism. Anyhow, the increase in individual power is reflected in our society, according to Collingwood, in an institutional growth of political power. Both are closely interrelated in his view, and he reaches the conclusion that "The increase in the power of political institutions, which sometimes makes people fear for individual liberty, is thus one of the most certain proofs of human progress, and is both the effect and the cause of an increase in individual liberty itself" (**PP,** 119-120).

Similarly in *The Idea of History* societal progress is associated with institutional progress. This idea is strongly reminiscent of Hegel, especially as it is linked with the idea of moral progress: "Part of our moral life consists of coping with problems arising not out of our animal nature but out of our social institutions, and these are historical things, which create moral problems only in so far as they are already the expression of moral ideals" and in this sense "there is or may be moral progress" (*IH*, 330-331).

In the same essay on progress Collingwood maintains that science "is the simplest and most obvious case in which progress exists and is verifiable" (*IH*, 332). He contends that philosophy and religion may also be seen as progressing, but he makes two reservations: first, any solution to a group of problems should retain the already achieved solutions of past problems. Second, it is only by historical thought that progress can be established: "Whether it has actually occurred, and where and when and in what ways" (*IH*, 333). This means that progress cannot be postulated *a priori,* either generally or specifically, as has been done by so many progressivists in the past.

After this point there is a crucial shift in Collingwood's argument, for he now maintains that historical thought should not only *establish* whether there is any progress, but should *create* this progress as well: "For progress is not a mere fact to be discovered by historical thinking: it is only through historical thinking that it comes about at all" (*IH*, 333). The argument he uses to justify this conclusion is consistent with his view of history as a rational process. For we have seen that this process is characterized by retaining its past phases in its present. With regard to science this implies that at a certain phase achievements are kept "by the retention in the mind" and that this is the only way in which progress can take place (*IH*, 333).

Collingwood's argument is not only convincing, but also fully consistent with his general view of history, as outlined above: both the aspect of continuity and the rational nature of the historical process are emphasized. His position does not, however, appear to be consistent with the theory of absolute presuppositions as expounded in *An Essay on Metaphysics*. We might put it more bluntly: it flatly contradicts that theory, for according to the theory of absolute presuppositions it is exactly the *dis*continuity between the various fundamental principles which is most strongly emphasized. These principles are seen by Collingwood as merely succeeding each other throughout history without displaying any rational transition.

It is extremely difficult to conceive of any way in which Collingwood's theory of absolute presuppositions, with its implications of discontinuity, incommensurability, and irrational change, can be reconciled with his essay on progress in *The Idea of History,* in which he expresses directly contradictory views on the development of science. This contradiction can only be resolved, in my opinion, by keeping in mind the different context within which each argument was developed, and especially the different questions each was intended to answer.

An Essay on Metaphysics (written in 1938-1939) deals with Collingwood's conception of metaphysics. He was extremely concerned by attacks on metaphysics, the latest of which was expounded with great force and clarity by A. J. Ayer, and he was convinced that these attacks were based on misunderstandings concerning the nature of metaphysics. For this reason he decided to make his own contribution to the theory of metaphysics. His theory should not, it is important to note, be considered as an original theory of Collingwood's own making *within* metaphysics, but rather as a description of what metaphysics in his view had always been. This at least was his expressed intention. Metaphysics is and was, he claims, an historical science, that is, a science describing the absolute presuppositions of a certain time or culture. A metaphysician, therefore, should be a natural observer, who is not in a position to express judgment on the absolute presuppositions he surveys. This implies that any suggestion that any one system of absolute presuppositions is superior to any other is improper, and the possibility of progress in presuppositions is rejected accordingly. As science depends on a system of absolute presuppositions, the possibility of progress in science is also dismissed. As we have seen, Collingwood develops this argument explicitly in the manuscript **"The Function of Metaphysics in Civilization,"** coming to the conclusion that we do not have the right to consider our science better than Greek science.

The essay on progress in *The Idea of History* (written in 1936 and forming part of the lectures on the philosophy of history) deals with a completely different subject. Here the question is when and in what sense can the concept of progress be applied in a meaningful way. As we have seen, Collingwood is of the opinion that "ways of life as a whole" cannot be compared by an historian for the purposes of evaluation. One could draw a parallel between such "ways of life" and systems of absolute presuppositions in that both appear to be fundamental and all-embracing; and one could go on to conclude that ways of life and systems of absolute presuppositions cannot be judged by an historian, and accordingly cannot be seen as progressive. However, in discussing the possibility of scientific progress in *The Idea of History* Collingwood does not deal with the assessments made by historians, but those made by scientists themselves. Historical thought is therefore involved, but it is not the historical thought of *historians,* but that of *scientists*: "If Einstein makes an advance on Newton, he does it by knowing Newton's thought and retaining it within his own" (*IH*, 333). Collingwood therefore claims that in order to achieve scientific progress a scientist should be an historian of the subject he studies. Referring to Newton, Collingwood says: "It is only insofar as Einstein knows that theory, as a fact in the history of science, that he can make an advance upon it" (*IH,* 334).

In this case the past is not viewed, therefore, in the detached way of an historian, but as a participant in the—or better an—historical process. In this way scientists see themselves as participants in the latest stage within the history of science, as historians do within historiography and philosophers within philosophy.

This brings us to the final aspect of the concept of progress—its necessary nature.

d) Not only does Collingwood claim that in relation to certain aspects of the past the historian is justified in employing the concept of progress; he also considers that in relation to solving practical and theoretical problems it is necessary. These problems are always passed down from the past, and in order to be solved they have to be reconstructed and understood by historical thought. In this sense there is a real continuity between the past and the present, but Collingwood refers to it as a continuity "of a peculiar kind" (*IH,* 333).

What he means is what he refers to in his autobiography as the "incapsulation" of past thought within present thought. This means that present thought is not completely encompassed by the rethought thought of the past, but is conscious of the act of rethinking. In this way a distinction is made between the "primary series" of "real" life and the "secondary" series of the rethought thought of the past (*Aut,* 113). Collingwood furthermore holds the opinion that all thinking is critical thinking: "the thought which re-enacts past thoughts, therefore, criticizes them in re-enacting them" (*IH,* 216). It is this critical capacity which allows the possibility of progress, and this is what lies behind Collingwood's remarks when he says of the thought of Newton as re-enacted by Einstein, that it is "re-enacted here and now together with a development of itself that is partly constructive or positive and partly critical or negative" (*IH,* 334).

The necessary function of historical thought in solving present problems applies not only to theoretical but also to practical problems: having discussed Einstein's advance on Newton, Collingwood observes: "similarly with any other progress," giving the following example:

> If we want to abolish capitalism or war, and in doing so not only to destroy them but to bring into existence something better, we must begin by understanding them. . . . This understanding of the system we set out to supersede is a thing which we must retain throughout the work of superseding it, as a knowledge of the past conditioning our creation of the future. (*IH,* 334)

As we have already observed, it was Knox who gave the essay on progress in *The Idea of History* the title "Progress as created by historical thinking." Collingwood refers to this creative aspect only once, in

his statement that there is, besides determining whether progress has actually occurred, "one other thing for historical thought to do: namely to create this progress itself" (*IH,* 333). This statement should be interpreted to mean that historical thought is a necessary condition for any form of progress, since it is only from this that scientists, historians or philosophers can see their own work as an advancement. The idea of progress itself could then be understood as having the function of serving as a guiding principle in solving present problems. As such its position is similar to the regulative function of "ideas" in the Kantian sense (Kant's own *Idea for a Universal History* is a good example of this use). This is made clear by the way Collingwood concludes his article on **"A Philosophy of Progress"**:

The question whether, on the whole, history shows a progress can be answered, as we now see, by asking another question. Have you the courage of your convictions? If you have, if you regard the things which you are doing as things worth doing, then the course of history which has led to the doing of them is justified by its results, and its movement is a movement forward. (*PP,* 120)

The conception of progress as a necessary idea in guiding our actions is also to be found in Collingwood's discussion of the concept of civilization, for civilization is described in *The New Leviathan* as "a process of approximation to an ideal state" (*NL,* 34.5). And in his preparatory manuscript to that book he goes so far as to say that "civilization and the advancement of civilization are one and the same. The will to be civilized is identical with the will to become more civilized." In his Martouret essay Collingwood states similarly, though more explicitly, that "progress is universal because ideals are always progressively realised. A people which fails to realise a certain ideal is a people which does not regard that as an ideal."

That the concept of progress may serve as a guiding idea is also exemplified in Collingwood's work itself, when he closes his *Essay on Philosophical Method* by expressing the hope that through the methodological principles enunciated in that book "philosophy may . . . set its feet once more on the path of progress" (*EPM,* 226).

When the idea of progress plays such a crucial role in solving present theoretical and practical problems, it is also the task of the historian to reconstruct the idea as it was conceived in the past. Having stated in the passage quoted above from the Martouret essay that progress is to be seen as a necessary aspect of history *a parte objecti,* Collingwood therefore also goes on to express the same principle *a parte subjecti,* that is, as an historiographical principle. "Progress, then," he says, "is universal in the sense that a narrative of any particular historical period, as it proceeds, reveals more and more clearly the nature of that period's ideals; and it is by these ideals that it ought to be judged."

The concept of progress is an illustration, therefore, of Collingwood's principle that history *a parte objecti* and history *a parte subjecti* cannot be separated: the metaphysical questions and the epistemological questions are joined in a necessary unity. But this is not all: it has become clear that many of Collingwood's concerns are united in this principle—for example, the question of the relation between theory and practice. In his discussion of the idea of progress Collingwood raises many important issues and displays many brilliant insights, and for this reason alone is well worth our continuing attention.

Michael A. Kissell (essay date 1990)

SOURCE: "Progressive Traditionalism as the Spirit of Collingwood's Philosophy," in *History and Theory,* Vol. XXIX, No. 4, 1990, pp. 51-6.

[*In the following essay, Kissell characterizes Collingwood's thought as "progressive traditionalism" in the sense that it addresses both the changing phenomena of history and perennial issues of philosophy.*]

Thirty-two years ago when I began my dissertation on Collingwood's philosophy, the people around me said: "Who was he? Where did you dig him up and why, since nobody knows him?" As a young graduate student, I was philosophically very naive and educated in the spirit of dogmatically distorted Marxism, but I saw at once that in Collingwood's books there was an extraordinary clarity of thought, brilliant mastery of the English language, and carefully elaborated argumentation appealing to a human capacity for self-reflection rather than deduction from dogmatically asserted premises. These qualities I recognized before I could penetrate the philosophical meaning of his writings. But after three years of study the picture of Collingwood's philosophical system appeared before me for the first time. Initially I had no guidance and no help in understanding Collingwood's works except for several articles on the subject, including T. M. Knox's introductory remarks to *The Idea of History*—extremely valuable but not, as eventually became clear, altogether conclusive. The first major book on Collingwood, by Alan Donagan, was published in 1962, a year after my defense of my thesis.

Since that time much water has flowed under the bridge and now historical justice has been done to Collingwood's contribution to the philosophical thought of the twentieth century. There are, of course, remaining doubts about such matters as whether there is a basic unity to all his thought, growing out of the ideas developed in *Speculum Mentis,* or whether there were two distinct stages to his philosophical development. The former hypothesis is very attractive to a speculative mind, because it resolves apparent contradictions between certain assertions of Collingwood in the manner of Hegelian phenomenology—that is, by seeing them as partial embodiments of one and the same truth which

takes adequate form only at the end of its gradual unfolding. In such a case the contradictory statements which appear in Collingwood's different books can be interpreted as different stages of the argument, the contradictions being overcome in the final result of the thought-process. But I think this interpretative hypothesis is too beautiful to be true and the problem of the ambiguities and inconsistencies in Collingwood's thought remains.

Nevertheless, independently of the solution to this dilemma, there are certain leading ideas in the philosophy of Collingwood which in my opinion can be unmistakably identified. Selecting one for attention can be done on different grounds, one of which is practical importance—the intimate connection with the urgent needs of contemporary social life. On this criterion I choose the idea of progressive traditionalism as an expression of his basic social attitude, deeply rooted in the very core of his philosophy.

Progressive traditionalism is one of the manifestations or, to be more correct, one of the consequences of the basic program of rapprochement between philosophy and history. The methodological instrument of this rapprochement was dialectics. I wrote a special article on this topic which was not published for several years, and now I will take up only one of its ideas: that of cumulative change. Everybody knows that history means change, while philosophy—in the common opinion—deals with the eternal and immutable. Dialectics arose with the understanding of the fact that the eternal exists only by means of change and change becomes meaningful and intelligible only through participation in the eternal. The fusion of the two opposites and the attempt to explain their interrelation is the principal distinguishing feature of the Platonic tradition in the history of philosophy. This notion emerged at the beginning of Collingwood's philosophical career, as has been made clear in Henry Jones's remarks on Collingwood's "Truth and Contradiction." Jones says: "This is a version of the 'dialectic' of Plato and Hegel, and in a sense not new. But it is done in a fresh way: clear, frank, interesting, and somehow very 'taking'. . . . All the time he is showing the true nature of Philosophy, and finding that *movement, activity, process* is the living soul of all thinking and of all objects of thought."

I think this is a brilliant definition of the substantial content of all Collingwood's philosophical work. We can compare this definition with the authorized version by Collingwood himself in his 1935 article **"The Present Need of a Philosophy."** He writes:

> What is needed today is a philosophical reconsideration of the whole idea of progress or development, and especially its two main forms, "evolution" in the world of nature and "history" in the world of human affairs. . . . In short the help which philosophy might give . . . would lie in a reasoned statement of the principle that there

can be no evils in any human institution which human will cannot cure.

In these two citations we have evidence of the basic importance for Collingwood of the two ideas whose connection is given in the title of this article.

But the shortest way to the core of Collingwood's argument seems to be this: philosophy somehow deals with thought and thought is progressive by its very nature— of course if it is real thought aiming to be true, and not the product of the "corruption of consciousness." As Collingwood put it in *The Principles of Art,* philosophy in its dynamic aspect is "an attempt to think better," which implies a continuity amid changes. Tradition is the vehicle of cumulative changes. The logical structure of cumulative growth is explained by Collingwood in the notion of "scale of forms" elaborated in *An Essay on Philosophical Method* (1933).

Every form on the scale includes the totality of the previous ones plus a certain special quality which makes the form a new one and not a mere repetition of the former. Every higher form on a scale contains the solution of the problem posed by the previous phase. But there is no necessary or inevitable transition from the lower to the higher form, as in Hegelian dialectics. This peculiarity Collingwood has called "the Law of Chance," according to which the movement from the lower to the higher is not automatic (as in Hegel) but requires "the energy of mind." This energy is not always deployed; it may be absent, and then there is regression, simplification, and finally the fall of the civilization. This law has a practical and a theoretical side, as we know. Collingwood incessantly emphasized the primacy of the practical aspect of thought. "Thought exists for the sake of action. We try to understand ourselves and our world only in order that we may learn how to live." As we read also in *The New Leviathan*: "Thought is primarily practical."

Thus the scale of forms as the structure of practical action requires that the actor know the past in order to correct its faults and create the new which is better than the previously existing state of affairs. Hence the practical importance of historical knowledge for people of action, especially politicians. By historical knowledge we might think of something like "the old curiosity shop" where there are a lot of interesting and strange things absolutely unconnected with our present life and serving only for amusement. In Collingwoodian terms, this would be a "dead past" which by the special effort of real historians can be lifted to the state of a living past if the past things described are of real importance for the historians themselves.

Nevertheless this knowledge is theoretical because, as Collingwood says in his *Autobiography,* it is only "encapsulated" in the present and produces no light on it. For a person of action his or her knowledge of the past is interwoven in the structure of the action. This is a theme of the *Autobiography,* though one not fully developed in the book. But *The New Leviathan* takes the theme further by studying the problem of politics in a "civilized community." One of the most important statements in this treatise is as follows:

> Being civilized means living so far as possible dialectically, that is, in constant endeavour to convert every occasion of non-agreement into an occasion of agreement. A degree of force is inevitable in human life, but being civilized means cutting it down, and becoming more civilized means cutting it down still further.

The achievement of agreement implies the understanding of the Other, and this is typically the situation of re-enactment, which is at the core of Collingwood's theory of historical knowledge. I mean the necessity of re-enactment of others' thought from both sides in the process of communication in order to reach mutual understanding; and mutual understanding is the presupposition of common grounds of discourse, without which no consensus is possible. The achievement of agreement means self-correction of the two conflicting attitudes— an operation not altogether different from that of the theoretical thinking where we work to develop the past heritage in relation to the present conditions of the situation in science. In the sphere of theoretical reason just as in the sphere of the practical our first experience is with the hard facts of the "given."

But what is the given, the immediate data of theoretical thinking or practical activity? This is the principal question. The "given" is not isolated data—"sense data"— because these are abstractions of analytical thought. What we really encounter is a definite stage of the process, and in order to deal with it adequately we must re-create what was before. This is the encounter with tradition. We never begin with the beginning, but always continue, whether we know it or not. We are always at a certain point on the scale, which means the actual stage of social life or the present situation in the world of philosophy. The life of tradition is its creative re-enactment in response to the needs of an ever-changing life.

What is the tradition in philosophy to which Collingwood belongs? I think it is the tradition of the philosophy of self-consciousness in contrast to the so-called "realistic" approach focusing on stimuli from the external world. There are two approaches in the history of philosophy: from world to a person and from person to a world. Two types of philosophy are connected with them. The tradition I am speaking about is that which argues from a person to the larger world. Socrates, Descartes, and Husserl are the principal representatives of this tradition. *In interiore homine habitat veritas.* This famous dictum serves as a summary statement of the doctrine, which I believe we can call the genuine *philosophia perennis*—though of course not in a Thomistic sense. But the assertion now made raises a special problem with regard to the so-called historicism of Collingwood, which is often interpreted in the sense of extreme relativism. This relativistic interpretation is wrong, because it ignores the fact that Collingwoodian historicism was the philosophy of human nature with basic constants inherent in it. Among them reason was the first in importance. If there were no such constants progress would be impossible, since all points of reference would be absent.

According to Collingwood, there is an historical element of human activity too. Now I come to the very controversial "doctrine of absolute presuppositions." It is not possible here to discuss the doctrine as a whole; it is quite sufficient for me to note that only the existence of absolute presuppositions is absolute, not their concrete meanings, which are changeable in history. In my opinion, the term itself is not entirely appropriate, since "absolute" by definition excludes change. Absolutes cannot change themselves; change takes place only within them, with regard to separate fragments taken in relation to the whole. However, my purpose here is not to elaborate this point, so I may confine myself to observing that absolute presuppositions lying at the foundation of human civilization are the basic elements of tradition. They are conserved unchanged throughout centuries. When change does occur in this realm, it is the manifestation of a crisis in the whole fabric of human civilization.

Western civilization is based on the presupposition of Christianity, which in turn arose as a result of fundamental changes in the foundation of ancient Greco Roman culture. The vindication of this view is contained in *An Essay on Metaphysics,* where faith in a Christian God was propounded as the necessary presupposition of the operation of reason itself in its theoretical and practical aspects. In its theoretical aspect the presupposition led to faith in the rational order of nature by means of which science is possible. In its practical aspect the presupposition led to faith in a civilized way of life achieved by human reason in constant struggle with barbarism threatening the destruction of all that is genuinely human in society.

Thus philosophy is a systematic, theoretical form of self-consciousness of the tradition constituting the essence of the European way of life. Exercising its function, philosophy clarifies the ultimate constituents of our present epoch—features which remain disguised from the positivistic frame of mind, which is interested only in empirically verified relative and phenomenal factors. Philosophy also discovers "strains" in the very fabric of the historical form of human civilization. These "strains" are symptoms of crisis, of the grave social danger to come in the future. Philosophy indicates the deep processes in the underground which more and more appear on the surface as wars, revolutions, and dictatorial regimes annihilating basic human rights. But these processes are not fatal. The function of philosophy, appealing to the reason of humanity, is to understand in order to warn and to prevent. The progress of

philosophy lies in the increasing degree of understanding of the fate of absolute presuppositions and of the prospects of human civilization.

Of course, philosophy is too weak to neutralize these dangers by itself; but its announcement of basic values of the civilized way of life and of the "strains" in the latter contribute to the general struggle for the preservation and development of human relations on the earth. In 1937 Collingwood wrote:

> There is a pestilence abroad, and its symptoms in withered minds and paralysed wills are all around us. Most of our colleagues are its enthusiastic allies or its helpless victims, and I don't believe that controversial argument is the way to attack it. . . . Go on producing good stuff—not negative or controversial stuff, but meaty nourishing stuff— and drive them out of the field by showing that we can appeal over their heads to the people who need philosophy and will not be content with the sophisms of our friends.

What he was criticizing was the response of the prevailing school of British academic philosophy to the victorious spread of nazism and fascism. His colleagues were interested in the problems of language and the emerging nazism was so "unphilosophical" a problem. But it posed the problem of the very existence of all the principal institutions of European civilization, including philosophy as a free activity of human thinking. The vindication of the thesis which Collingwood elaborated in his last book, *The New Leviathan,* reminds us of the best work of his great compatriot who lived through the English Revolution and the first great European war in the modern epoch.

But to return to the problem previously mentioned: among the basic presuppositions of civilization there is one which brings philosophy into an intimate connection with religion. This is the presupposition of the ultimate rationality of the world as a whole. This ultimate rationality is unverifiable, and therefore is the product of faith. Thus reason itself, according to Collingwood, is "faith cultivating itself." Hence the importance of Christianity as an embodiment of this basic conviction. To a certain extent, the progress of European social and philosophical thought since the Middle Ages was the secularization of the Christian heritage. In the end this secularization turned against the Christian articles of faith themselves. This is the situation in which Collingwood took up his position of the defense of absolute presuppositions of civilization.

This is the meaning of his progressive traditionalism. It is "progressive" because thought is autonomous in its development, aiming to solve new problems engendered by life that is constantly in process. Philosophy is not *ancilla theologiae,* the handmaiden of theology, but it must sincerely recognize its own limits and roots. Mere change devoid of roots is the great danger, as the social experience of our century has demonstrated. Progress to be real must be not only new but better, including the real achievements of the past and not destroying them. Then it will be creative and a step beyond the old. This dialectic of progress and tradition is the secret of really successful and beneficial politics and the experience of revolutions, past and present, has verified this thesis. Now in my country we, for the most part, understand the necessity of conserving something of the old which is living if we are to create more satisfying social conditions.

Return to healthy traditions is one of the elements of Gorbachev's "new thinking." This return to tradition is manifested in our country in two respects: the age-old tradition of individual peasants' work, and the Russian Orthodox Church. Now we understand the significance of pluralism in the forms of property, especially in agriculture, and we recognize the importance of religious values, especially in situations of moral crisis. These traditions did not exhaust their creative élan. Why ought we to fight desperately against God? It would be better to fight together with those who have faith against the Devil—and the Devil is the spirit of war, destruction, oppression, and dishonest behavior in its infinite multifariousness. The cooperation of all people of good will leads to the amelioration of life; it changes the world for the better. It is deeply progressive, in contrast with the simple repetition of atheistic slogans.

Aggressive and ignorant atheism is not better than religious fanaticism, which even now is ready to kill in response to the orders of a leader. Now toleration must be not only for the atheists, as in the past, but also for the adherents of religion, who in certain countries are in the minority. Tolerance is a traditional philosophical value never outdated.

Collingwood's philosophy is especially pertinent, in my opinion, in his clear understanding of the spiritual heritage to be elaborated anew for each generation to come, in his reminding us of the great chain of thought uniting the ancient Greek past with our European present, and of our responsibility for preserving the very foundation of the civilized way of life, which is "law, order, prosperity, and peace."

FURTHER READING

Bibliography

Dreisbach, Christopher. *R. G. Collingwood: A Bibliographic Checklist.* Bowling Green, OH: Bowling Green State University, 1993, 139 p.
     Comprehensive bibliography of primary and secondary sources with brief annotations.

Taylor, Donald S. *R. G. Collingwood: A Bibliography—The Complete Manuscripts and Publications, Selected Secondary Writings, with Selective Annotation.* New York: Garland Publishing, Inc., 1988, 279 p.
     In-depth annotated bibliography of Collingwood's writings.

Criticism

Brown, Merle E. "R. G. Collingwood's Early Aesthetics: Art as Contradiction." In *Neo-Idealistic Aesthetics: Croce-Gentile-Collingwood*, pp. 182-207. Detroit, MI: Wayne State University, 1966.
     Critical analysis of Collingwood's aesthetic theory.

Buchdahl, G. "Has Collingwood Been Unfortunate in his Critics?" *The Australian Journal of Philosophy* 36, No. 2 (August 1958): 95-108.
     Attempts to vindicate Collingwood's statement that the historian "must re-enact the past in his own mind" in response to critics who may have misinterpreted it.

Cebik, L. B. "Collingwood: Action, Re-enactment, and Evidence." *The Philosophical Forum* II, No. 1 (Fall 1970): 68-89.
     Endeavors to separate Collingwood's theory of historical evidence from his "obfuscating notion of historical re-enactment."

Child, Arthur. "History as Imitation." *The Philosophical Quarterly* 2, No. 8 (July 1952): 193-207.
     Discusses history as a creative art of imitation, relating this notion to Collingwood's theory of the process of writing history.

Crossman, R. H. S. "When Lightning Struck the Ivory Tower—R. G. Collingwood." In *The Charm of Politics and Other Essays in Political Criticism*, pp. 105-109. New York: Harper & Brothers, 1958.
     Comments on the significance of the Spanish Revolution (1936-38) in shifting the focus of Collingwood's hitherto academic and intellectual view of history.

Dray, William. "Comments and Criticism—R. G. Collingwood on Reflective Thought." *The Journal of Philosophy* LVII, No. 5 (March 3, 1960): 157-63.
     Examines the levels of thought implied by Collingwood's main historical thesis: "the historian explains actions by discerning the thoughts of historical agents."

Krausz, Michael, ed. *Critical Essays on the Philosophy of R. G. Collingwood.* Oxford: Clarendon Press, 1972, 356 p.
     Collection of sixteen essays on Collingwood's views of history, metaphysics, ethics, aesthetics, and philosophic method.

Goldstein, Leon J. "Collingwood's Theory of Historical Knowing." *History and Theory: Studies in the Philosophy of History* IX, No. 1 (1970): 3-36.

Traces the development of Collingwood's theory of history, commenting on it as a rejection of philosophical realism and historical skepticism.

———. "The Idea of History as a Scale." *History and Theory: Studies in the Philosophy of History* XXIX, No. 4 (1990): 42-50.
    Critique of Collingwood's conception of history as a "logical development," as contained in *The Idea of History*.

Hepburn, R. W. "A Fresh Look at Collingwood." *The British Journal of Aesthetics* 3, No. 3 (July 1963): 259-61.
    Briefly examines the viability of Collingwood's aesthetic theory, describing it as one that acknowledges works of art both as "vehicles of communication" and as objective, autonomous creations.

Modood, Tariq. "The Later Collingwood's Alleged Historicism and Relativism." *Journal of the History of Philosophy* XXVII, No. 1 (January 1989): 101-25.
    Contends that "Collingwood's later views on philosophy are not an abandonment, but a critical modification of his earlier views."

Post, John Frederick. "A Defense of Collingwood's Theory of Presuppositions." *Inquiry* 8 (1965): 332-54.
    Reconstructs Collingwood's Theory of Presuppositions with the purpose of clarifying its theoretical strengths.

———. "Does Knowing Make a Difference to What Is Known?" *The Philosophical Quarterly* 15, No. 60 (July 1965): 220-28.
    Refutes Alan Donagan's suggestion that Collingwood's statement, "Knowing makes no difference to what is known," is inconsistent with his later philosophy.

Russell, Anthony F. *Logic, Philosophy, and History: A Study in the Philosophy of History Based on the Work of R. G. Collingwood.* Lanham, Md.: University Press of America, Inc., 1984, 527 p.
    Synthesis of Collingwood's conception of logical and philosophical inquiry as part of concrete historical thinking.

Salas, Charles G. "Collingwood's Historical Principles at Work." *History and Theory: Studies in the Philosophy of History* XXVI, No. 1 (1987): 53-71.
    Describes several practical examples of Collingwood's scientific method of historical study.

Smart, Harold R. "Croce and Collingwood: The Identification of Philosophy with History." In *Philosophy and Its History*, pp. 62-84. La Salle, Ill.: Open Court Publishing Company, 1962.
    Comparison of Benedotto Croce's and Collingwood's parallel philosophies of history.

Toynbee, Arnold J. "R. G. Collingwood's View of the Historian's Relation to the Objects That He Studies." In *A Study of History*, Volume IX, pp. 718-37. London: Oxford University Press, 1954.
    The eminent historian discusses Collingwood as a philosopher-historian and evaluates the merits of his reflective view of history.

V. I. Lenin

1870–1924

(Born Vladimir Ilyich Ulyanov) Russian political leader and theorist.

INTRODUCTION

The primary force behind the Russian Revolution, Lenin was a figure of enormous influence in twentieth-century politics and history. In his writings he claimed to be an orthodox Marxist, but in actuality he broke with his ideological predecessor Karl Marx on several key points. With his extreme emphasis on class struggle, Lenin believed that a workers' revolution could be created in the largely rural and agricultural nation of early twentieth-century Russia, in part contradicting Marx's theory that a nation must develop through a period of full industrial capitalism before a successful socialist revolution could occur. Lenin also differed with Marx and his collaborator Friedrich Engels, both of whom believed that workers in a capitalist system naturally inclined toward socialism. Lenin instead theorized that workers would acquire at most only "trade-union consciousness" and would need the assistance of an external party structure to achieve full socialism. Thus, as borne out by the actual events of history, Lenin is seen as instrumental in recasting the theories of Marx by organizing the Bolshevik Party and emphasizing its dictatorial leadership as a means of inciting the workers to revolution.

Biographical Information

Lenin was born on April 10, 1870, in Simbirsk. His mother was of middle-class German descent while his father was a provincial school-inspector who rose from humble origins to the level of nobility. As a child Lenin attended school at the Simbirsk Gymnasium between 1879 and 1887. In the year of his graduation his elder brother Aleksandr was executed for his involvement in the attempted assassination of Czar Alexander III. The incident contributed to Lenin's growing interest in revolutionary politics and led to his expulsion from the University of Kazan late in 1887. Later adopting the pen name Lenin in place of his own surname (Ulyanov), he began to deepen his political involvement with the Marxists in Russia, both writing on politics and continuing with his study of law as an external student of St. Petersburg University. He passed his examinations in 1891 and moved to St. Petersburg in 1893, but never practiced law. In 1895 Lenin was arrested for his political activities and imprisoned. Two years later he was exiled to Siberia, where he completed *Razvite kapitalizma v Rosii* (*The Development of Capitalism in Russia*). Released in 1900, he attempted to operate un-derground, but found this impossible, opting instead to leave Russia. In December of 1900, Lenin founded the Marxist political newspaper *Iskra* ("The Spark") in Munich as a mouthpiece for the movement. Three years later, amidst increasing factionalism among the revolutionaries, he formed the Bolshevik Party, which differed from the opposing Mensheviks on several party issues. Despite this factionalism, he continued to solidify his domination of the party over the next several years, although he failed to realize his revolutionary goals when he first returned to Russia in 1905. Only temporarily unsuccessful, he left his homeland once again in 1907, and in 1909 published an attack on his political opponents entitled *Materializm i empiriokrititsizm: Krit-ischeskiia zametki ob odnoi reaktsionnoi filosofii* (*Materialism and Empirio-Criticism: Critical Notes Concerning a Reactionary Philosophy*). The following years saw a revival of the Russian Worker's Union, as well as the commencement of World War I. In February of 1917, to Lenin's surprise, the Czarist regime in Russia was overthrown at Petrograd (formerly St. Petersburg) and a provisional government installed. Hearing of these events from abroad, Lenin immediately arranged his return to Russia. Several months later he delivered his *Aprel'skie tezisy* (*The April Conference*) attacking the new government. In October of the same year, the Bolsheviks seized power and installed Lenin as premier and head of the Soviet state. The following year Lenin negotiated the Treaty of Brest-Litovsk with Germany, agreeing to the German military demands in order so that he might better focus his energies on the burgeoning civil war in Russia, where open hostilities continued until 1922. Envisioning Russia as only the first European nation to undergo a worker's revolution, Lenin founded the Communist International in 1919 and unveiled his New Economic Policy (NEP) in 1921. The next year, however, he suffered a debilitating series of strokes, from which he never fully recovered. Lenin died on January 21, 1924. His embalmed body, the object of intense veneration until the collapse of the Soviet Union in 1989, was placed in the Mausoleum on Moscow's Red Square soon after his death.

Major Works

Most of Lenin's writings were either political essays intended to promote and justify the Russian Revolution or scathing invectives designed to weaken and destroy his political enemies. In *The Development of Capitalism in Russia* Lenin examined the contemporary economic state of Russia and observed that its industrial and agricultural progress proved that the nation was well on its way to capitalism and therefore becoming suitable for a future socialist revolution. Lenin's well-known 1902 book *Chto dielat'?: Nabolevshie voprosy nashego dvizheniia (What Is To Be Done?: Burning Questions of Our Movement)* is a invitation to political action and explains the need for a well-organized party structure to achieve the goal of revolution. *Materialism and Empirio-Criticism: Critical Notes Concerning a Reactionary Philosophy* is often considered Lenin's most cogent statement of his philosophy. Most western critics have observed, however, that the work is primarily a polemical assault against his critics. Lenin's *The April Conference* follows a similar vein as a highly charged denunciation of the provisional government formed in Petrograd during the February Revolution. In the pamphlet entitled *Imperializm, kak novieishii etap kaitalizma: populiarnyi ocherk (Imperialism, The Last Stage of Capitalism)* Lenin made his assessment of the significant roles that capitalism and imperialism played in bringing about the First World War. *Gosudarstvo i revoliutsiia: Uchenie marksizma o gosudarstvie i zadachi proletariata v revoliutsii (The State and Revolution)*, which was drafted just prior to the Bolshevik revolution in October 1917, and *Proletarskaia revoliutsiia i renegat Kautskii (The Proletarian Revolution and Kautsky the Renegade)* are seen as Lenin's theoretical and practical justifications for his creation of a "dictatorship of the proletariat."

PRINCIPAL WORKS

Ekonomicheskie etiudy: stat'i (nonfiction) 1899

Razvite kapitalizma v Rossii [The Development of Capitalism in Russia] (essay) 1899

Chto dielat'?: Nabolevshie voprosy nashego dvizheniia [What Is To Be Done?: Burning Questions of Our Movement] (nonfiction) 1902

K derevenskoi biednotie: ob'iasnenie dlia krest'ian, chego khotiat sotsial'demokraty (nonfiction) 1903

Shag vpered dva shaga nazad [published as "One Step Forward, Two Steps Back" in The Essentials of Lenin] (essay) 1904

Dve taktiti sotsial'demokratii v demokraticheskoi revoliutsii [Two Tactics of the Social-Democrats in the Democratic Revolution] (nonfiction) 1905

Materializm i empiriokrititsizm: Kritischeskiia zamietki ob odnoi reaktsionnoi filosofii [Materialism and Empirio-Criticism: Critical Notes Concerning a Reactionary Philosophy] (nonfiction) 1909

Imperializm, kak novieishii etap kaitalizma: populiarnyi ocherk [Imperialism: The Last Stage of Capitalism] (nonfiction) 1917

Iz istorii sotsial-demokraticheskoi agrarnoi programmy: Stat'i 1901-1906 (nonfiction) 1917

Novyia dannyia o zakonakh razvitiia kapitalizma v zemledielii. Vypusk l. Kapitalizm i zemledielie v

Soed. Shtatakh Ameriki [Capitalism and Agriculture in the United States of America] (nonfiction) 1917

Gosudarstvo i revoliutsiia: Uchenie marksizma o gosudarstvie i zadachi proletariata v revoliutsii [The State and Revolution] (nonfiction) 1918

Proletarskaia revoliutsiia i renegat Kautskii [The Proletarian Revolution and Kautsky the Renegade] (nonfiction) 1918

Detskaia bolezn' "levizny" v kommunizme ["Left Wing" Communism: An Infantile Disorder] (nonfiction) 1921

Sobranie sochinenii [Collected Works] (nonfiction, letters, and speeches) 1960-68

Aprel'skie tezisy [The April Conference] (essay) 1934

The Letters of Lenin (letters) 1937

Lenin on Language (nonfiction) 1983

Lenin's Struggle for a Revolutionary International: Documents, 1907-1916, The Preparatory Years (nonfiction) 1984

CRITICISM

M. W. Mikulak   (essay date 1963)

SOURCE: "Lenin on the 'Party' Nature of Science and Philosophy," in *Essays in Russian and Soviet History in Honour of Geroid Tanquary Robinson*, edited by John Shelton Curtiss, Columbia University Press, 1963, pp. 164-76.

[*In the following essay, Mikulak discusses Lenin's theory of the "partyness" of science and philosophy as evidenced in his* Materialism and Empirio-Criticism.]

The Soviet Communist *Concise Philosophical Dictionary* states: "Dialectical materialism teaches that philosophy, as all of science, appears to be class, party [in nature]." The idea that science and philosophy exhibit class or party characteristics is rather novel in the Western world, where one hardly considers these subjects as being bourgeois, capitalist or socialist in origin. Nonetheless, numerous examples can be found in Soviet publications having such labels according to the Marxist interpretation of the class development of society. In Russia, Lenin was chiefly responsible for spreading the teaching that science and philosophy are just as partisan as politics. Because much of Lenin's writing has the style of a war pamphleteer, it is difficult to present his ideas without revealing some of the background information pertinent to this study. Also, it must be realized that Lenin was not only writing during the period of world imperialism, as Soviet Communists refer to the stage of history around the time of the First World War, but it was a period of great upheaval in the world of physics. Classical physics, having its roots in the works of Galileo and Newton, was finally crumbling, and many individuals of professorial rank tried to revive it, bury it or modify it.

THE BACKGROUND OF THE CRISIS

One might say the crisis in classical physics went as far back as to Sir Isaac Newton's *Principia Mathematica,* where he expressed his belief in absolute, uniformly-flowing time and in absolute, motionless space that existed unchanged throughout the entire universe. His absolute time consisted of instants and his absolute space was composed of points. Into this framework Newton introduced particles of matter that occupied distinct points at given instants. And each particle had a mass that was able to exert forces on other particles in accordance with certain principles of nature developed by Newton. From the point of view of logic, the physics of Newton was faultless and appeared to account for all the observed *mechanical* facts known to science in the eighteenth century. From the point of view of philosophy, Newton's metaphysics was not very satisfactory. In his own lifetime, Leibnitz waged a consistent attack on the Newtonian absolute-space-time framework. Others, with a philosophic bent of mind, such as Berkeley, Hume, Kant, and Hegel, attempted to grapple with the problem of the nature and reality of space and time and came to no definite conclusions.

Toward the end of the nineteenth century, the most vigorous opponent of absolute time, space and motion was Ernst Mach, a Viennese physicist with a keen interest in epistemology. Mach realized, as many scientists of his day, that Newtonian physics was entirely inadequate in coping with the modern scientific discoveries of the latter part of the last century: the electromagnetic theory of light by Clerk Maxwell, the radioactivity of certain elements by Becquerel and Curie, the discovery by Thomson that the electron is a charged particle, and others. Instead of providing strict mathematico-scientific solutions to the pressing problems of physics, Ernst Mach offered philosophic arguments. His phenomenological theories emphasized the importance of experience based primarily on sensations or sense impressions (*Empfindungen*). A Zurich philosopher, Richard Avenarius, in many respects paralleled Mach. The chief work of Avenarius is *Kritik der reinen Erfahrung* and he called his doctrine empirio-criticism. He, as Mach, started with personal experience or sensations and attempted to evolve a system that could represent the many facets of reality regardless of the different human sources of the sense impressions. In effect, the Machian school of phenomenological theories denied the validity of the philosophical materialism inherent in Newtonian physics, and can be viewed as an attack on mechanical materialism in particular. Despite the fact that Mach anticipated some of Albert Einstein's results, the Machian school of philosophy passed into history once Einstein's special theory of relativity and Minkowski's four-dimensional space-time continuum accounted for the dual nature of space and motion, solving one of the crucial problems arising from classical physics. It was no longer necessary for the physicists to hide behind a facade of psychological-philosophical explanations that tended to avoid the real issues confronting the world of physics at the turn of this century.

LENIN'S MATERIALISM AND EMPIRIO-CRITICISM

Against this background of crisis appeared a collection of essays in 1908 under the heading of *Studies in the Philosophy of Marxism;* it was a symposium by Bazarov, Bogdanov, Lunacharskii, Berman, Helfond, Yushkevich and Suvorov. Some of the works appearing in this vein of study were Yushkevich's *Materialism and Critical Realism,* Berman's *Dialectics in the Light of the Modern Theory of Knowledge* and Valentinov's *The Philosophical Constructions of Marxism.* The intention of these writers, who regarded themselves as Marxists, was to revise the philosophic base of Marx and Engels so that it would harmonize with the then current trends in the field of epistemology. After scrutinizing the works of these Russian Marxists, Lenin set himself the task "to find out what was the stumbling block to these people who under the guise of Marxism are offering something incredibly muddled, confused and reactionary." In other words, Lenin was going to defend the materialism espoused by Marx and Engels against those Russian critics who sought to reconcile the revolutionary developments and discoveries of modern science with the breakdown of the materialism associated with classical physics. In May 1909, Lenin's critical commentaries on the "reactionary" philosophy appeared in print, entitled ***Materialism and Empirio-Criticism***.

Lenin followed Engels' division of philosophy into the two distinct and opposing camps of idealism and materialism. Consequently, it is important to note how these two divisions are defined by Lenin, for he placed the professional philosophers in one camp or the other. In discussing the "thing-in-itself" concept, Lenin stated that materialism rested on the belief that "objects in themselves" are capable of existence outside of the mind, but idealism is alleged to teach that objects cannot exist without the mind and are in essence "combinations of sensations." Furthermore, materialism requires that nature, and matter, be of primary importance and the spirit be regarded as of secondary significance. Idealism, on the contrary, reverses the importance of the spirit and matter, giving the spirit prime concern. Lenin wrote:

> Materialism, in full agreement with natural science, takes matter as primary and regards consciousness, thought, sensations as secondary, because in its well-defined form sensation is associated only with the higher forms of matter (organic matter), while "in the foundation of the structure of matter" one can only surmise the existence of a faculty akin to sensation.

At no time did Lenin deny the existence of sensations, but he did assert that sensations are the direct bridge between the external world and one's consciousness. He continued: "The sophism of idealist philosophy consists in the fact that it regards sensations as being not the connection between consciousness from the external world—not an image of the external phenomenon corresponding to the sensation, but the 'sole entity.'" To complete his argument against the idealist conception of sensation, Lenin analyzed its formation and concluded sensations are the result of matter stimulating our sense organs. Subsequently, matter has to be viewed as existing independently of sensations, and sensations, consciousness, and thought are the products of "matter organized in a particular way."

Having enunciated his clear-cut criteria for the idealist and the materialist trends in philosophy, it became an easy matter for Lenin to decide what trend his Russian Marxists supported. From the very beginning of his comments and critique, Lenin termed Bazarov, Yushkevich, Valentinov, Chernov, and their kind as Machians or opponents of materialism. Lenin accused the Russian empirio-criticists of "parroting the words of the reactionary professors on dialectical materialism without themselves knowing anything *either* of dialectics *or* of materialism." He pointed out that the Russian followers of the Viennese philosopher-physicist Ernst Mach and the Zurich philosopher Richard Avenarius failed to study the "idealist views" originally held by these two. The Russian Machists, according to Lenin, represented "their break with Marxism and their desertion to the camp of bourgeois philosophy as 'minor corrections' of Marxism!" Lenin declared the "thing-in-itself" problem is a "veritable *bête-noir*" with Bogdanov, Valentinov, Bazarov, Chernov, Berman and Yushkevich, who had denounced and abused this philosophic concept. It was at this point that Lenin made the observation that it was here "a division of the philosophers of Russian Machism according to political parties begins."

Because the Machian philosophy was having a devastating effect on the ideological outlook of certain Russian Marxists, Lenin devoted much space and effort to the substance and origin of Mach's views. He briefly summed up his opinion of Ernst Mach's philosophy as follows:

> The philosophy of the scientist Mach is to science what the kiss of the Christian Judas was to Christ. Mach likewise betrays science to the camp of philosophical idealism. Mach's renunciation of the natural-scientific materialism is a reactionary phenomenon in every respect. We saw this quite clearly when we spoke of the struggle of the "physical idealists" against the *majority* of the scientists who continue to maintain the standpoint of the old philosophy.

Lenin regarded Mach's views as idealist because the latter supported the thesis that sensation is primary and that bodies in the last analysis are "complexes of sensations." In asking the question whether nature existed prior to the coming of man, Lenin attempted to draw the logical conclusions of Machian philosophy: the non-existence of the environment without the presence of hu-

man sensations. He noticed this conclusion is avoided by Avenarius and considered his philosophy cowardly for exercising such elusiveness. Lenin developed the point that:

> No man at all educated or sound-minded doubts that the earth existed at a time when there *could not* have been any life on it, any sensation or any "central term," and consequently the whole theory of Mach and Avenarius, from which it follows that the earth is a complex of sensations ("bodies are complexes of sensations") or "complexes of elements in which the psychical and physical are identical," or "a counter-term of which the central term can never be equal to zero," is *philosophical obscurantism,* the carrying of subjective idealism to absurdity.

By a careful selection of quotations from the works of the Machian philosophers, Lenin sought to prove that their basic ideas stemmed from the arch-idealist, Bishop George Berkeley. He stated that Berkeley denied the absolute existence of objects (or things-in-themselves), but believed that only the collections of ideas, such as heat, colors, degrees of hardness or softness, taste, and so on, are available to us. Berkeley's philosophical opponents were those who thought that sensible objects existed without the mind. Then Lenin mentioned that "the 'new' discoveries of the Machians are the product of an outstanding ignorance of the history of the basic philosophical trends."

Finally, Lenin utilized a considerable amount of material from idealist and materialist writers who, in one way or another, judged the empirio-criticist philosophy to be idealist. He cited a comment by Diderot, of Encyclopedist fame, on Berkeley's collection of ideas or combination of sensations that illustrated the similarity of the criticisms leveled at Berkeley and those leveled at Mach by his opponents:

> Those philosophers are called *idealist* who, being conscious only of their existence and of the sensations which succeed each other within themselves, do not admit anything else. An extravagant system, which to my thinking, only the blind could have originated a system which, to the shame of the human intelligence and philosophy, is the most difficult to combat, although the most absurd of all.

Speaking of the English Machists, Lenin observed that they "*do not entertain even a shadow of doubt* as to the idealistic character of Mach's doctrine of space and time." However, the "would-be Russian Marxists" have found the materialism of Engels outmoded, but the outlook of the British Machist, Karl Pearson, for example, and the "muddled idealist," Mach, as being worthy of consideration because of their modernity. Lenin scored the point that only the Russian Marxists have failed to notice the idealist character of Machian philosophy. He quoted the comments of E. T. Dixon, a geometrician, on *The Grammar of Science,* written by the "Machian"

Pearson, to prove to the Russian Marxists how naively they accepted the Machian "philosophical muddle as the 'philosophy of natural science.'" Then Lenin presented the anti-Machian views of the German physicist, L. Boltzmann, and concluded that "this physicist rightly ridicules the supposedly 'new' 'phenomenalist view of Mach and Co. as the old absurdity of philosophical subjective idealism." And Lenin introduced the opinion of Eduard von Hartmann on Mach's philosophy that it is a "mixture (Nichtunterscheidung) of naive realism and absolute illusionism." He labeled von Hartmann "a consistent idealist and consistent reactionary in philosophy, *who sympathises with the Machians' fight against materialism*. . . ."

LENIN'S CONCEPT OF PARTYNESS

While no systematic and thorough exposition by Lenin can be found on the partyness or partisanship of science and philosophy, it is still possible to construct his concept on this subject matter from many scattered statements appearing principally in ***Materialism and Empirio-Criticism***. It was Lenin's purpose to deal with the basic trends of the various schools in physics and their relationship to the "rebirth of philosophical idealism." Nonetheless, the one glaring and inescapable fact that arises from Lenin's exposé of the empirio-criticists is that the Marxist philosophical world consists of the two distinct and irreconcilable camps of idealism and materialism. In this dichotomy the idealists are the villains, the reactionary forces composed mainly of bourgeois philosophers, theologians and professors. On the other side of the fence are the heroes of the new world, the materialists, who represent the progressive forces of mankind. Moreover, Lenin believed this dichotomy had existed over two thousand years, from Plato and Democritus to Mach and the materialists.

Lenin asked "whether there are parties generally in philosophy, and what is meant by non-partisanship in philosophy." He turned to Mach and Avenarius and examined their school from the point of view of parties in philosophy:

> Oh, these gentlemen *boast* of their non-partisanship, and if they have an antipodes, it is the *materialist* . . . and *only* the materialist. A red thread that runs through *all* the writings of *all* the Machians is the stupid claim to have "risen above" materialism and idealism, to have transcended this "absolute" antithesis; but *in fact* the whole fraternity are *continually* sliding into idealism and are conducting a steady and incessant struggle against materialism. The subtle epistemological crotchets of a man like Avenarius are but professorial inventions, an attempt to form a small philosophical sect "of his own"; but, *as a matter of fact,* in the general circumstances of the struggle of ideas and trends in modern society, the *objective* part played by these epistemological artifices is in every case the same, namely, to clear the way for idealism and fideism, and to

serve them faithfully. . . . It is the misfortune of the Russian Machians, who undertook to "reconcile" Machism with Marxism, that they trusted the reactionary professors of philosophy and as a result slipped down an inclined plane. . . . *Not a single one* of these professors, who are capable of making very valuable contributions in the special fields of chemistry, history, or physics, *can be trusted one iota* when it comes to philosophy. Why? For the same reason that *not a single* professor of political economy, who may be capable of very valuable contributions in the field of factual and specialised investigations, can be trusted *one iota* when it comes to the general theory of political economy. For in modern society the latter is as much a *partisan* science as is *epistemology*. Taken as a whole, the professors of economics are nothing but learned salesmen of the capitalist class, while the professors of philosophy are learned salesmen of the theologians.

Therefore, according to Lenin, the two major *parties* in philosophy are idealism and materialism. To those who claim impartiality in philosophy, Lenin contemptuously said of them: "Non-partisanship in philosophy is only wretchedly masked servility to idealism and fideism." And Lenin found himself in complete agreement with Joseph Dietzgen's opinion of the "middle party":

> Just as parties in politics are more and more becoming divided into two camps . . . so science too is being divided into two general classes (Generalklassen): metaphysicians on the one hand, and physicists, or materialists, on the other. . . . If we compare the two parties respectively to solid and liquid, between them there is a mush.

Even though Lenin did not concentrate on the party nature of science as much as on the party nature of philosophy, nonetheless he maintained the idea "that science is non-partisan in the struggle of materialism against idealism and religion is a favourite idea not only of Mach but of all modern bourgeois professors. . . ." Nowhere did he state that such-and-such established laws of physics, biology or chemistry are idealist or materialist. When he does attempt to discuss the serious technical aspects of science, especially the concept of Newtonian absolute time and space, his lack of technical training becomes apparent. What Lenin stressed time and time again was that there is a very definite connection between the crisis of modern physics and the emergence of physical idealism, which in Lenin's eyes meant "that one school of natural scientists in one branch of natural science has slid into a reactionary philosophy. . . ."

Not only do science and philosophy exhibit party characteristics in the Leninist world, but they also contain class elements. As an illustration of this feature, Lenin utilized the example of Ernst Haeckel's *The Riddle of the Universe* and its effects on the intellectuals who were idealistically or theologically inclined. Haeckel was no socialist and renounced the appellation of materialist. Despite this, Lenin said in reference to him: "He *ridicules all* idealist—more broadly, all peculiarly philosophical—artifices from the standpoint of natural science, *without even permitting the idea* that any other theory of knowledge but *natural-scientific materialism* is possible." The significance of Haeckel's book, Lenin indicated, was that it exposed the "*partisan character* of philosophy in modern society and, on the other, the true social significance of the struggle of materialism against idealism and agnosticism." *The Riddle of the Universe* became "a weapon in the class struggle," and tremendous abuse was heaped upon Ernst Haeckel by the theologians and the "official professors of philosophy." Lenin concluded that the denunciations of Haeckel by the idealists proved the existence of "the class nature of modern society and its class ideological tendencies."

Respecting the empirio-criticist school of philosophy, Lenin said that it must be understood as the "struggle of parties in philosophy, a struggle which in the last analysis reflects the tendencies and ideology of the antagonistic classes in modern society." And by 1913, Lenin continued to stress the class aspects of science even more strongly than in *Materialism and Empirio-Criticism*:

> In one way or another, *all* official and liberal science *defends* wage slavery, whereas Marxism has declared relentless war on wage slavery. To expect science to be impartial in a wage-slave society is as silly and naive as to expect impartiality from manufacturers on the question whether workers' wages should be increased by decreasing the profits of capital.

The Leninist concept of partyness in science and philosophy is based on the simple premise that philosophy, and its relation with science, can be divided into two principal factions. As long as the class background was not introduced into the materialist-idealist division, Lenin had little difficulty categorizing his professional philosophers and professors into one party or the other. Once we turn to his statements on the class features of science and philosophy, there is often a lack of strong supporting evidence and detailed analysis that would provide a workable framework for studying these features. For example, according to the Leninist world outlook, how would the writer Ernst Haeckel be classified? He admitted his antimaterialist and anti-socialist stand and yet was able to present an impressive attack on philosophical idealism. In the case of the Russian Marxists, these individuals supported the Marxist theory of the economic development of society and yet flirted with the idealist philosophic camp. From the class interpretation of science and philosophy, where do they fit in the bourgeois-socialist dichotomy?

Lenin, despite his references to the "class struggle," actually focused his attention on the struggle of *atheistic* materialism against *fideist* idealism. One serious objection Lenin had to Lunacharskii, Bazarov, and the other Russian Marxists, was that they were trying to reconcile Marxism with religion, a trend that gained popularity in Russia under Stolypin. Lenin also noted it was the theo-

logians who waged a bitter campaign against Haeckel's natural-scientific materialism. And what separated the materialists, Marx, Engels, Dietzgen, from the Machists, in Lenin's estimation, were their respective attitudes toward religion. Repeatedly Lenin linked the term *fideism* with the idealist philosophers. Originally, he had used the expression *popovshchina* (meaning priest-lore, clericalism) instead of fideism, but strict Tsarist censorship compelled him to use the milder term. Perhaps one reason Lenin never presented a thorough analysis of the class interpretation of science and philosophy was that he probably was more conscious of the influence of religion on the mass of Russian people and therefore saw the class conflict, at least on the philosophic plane, as essentially conflict for or against religion. Certainly, in tsarist Russia, it would have been difficult to sell Marxism to the Russian peasantry and workers without Christ or without the sign of the cross.

Looking toward the future, Lenin, in one of his last articles, **"On the Significance of Militant Materialism,"** emphasized that Communist revolutionaries must defend Marxism and materialism. He suggested that their chief organ, *Under the Banner of Marxism,* should be a powerful exponent of atheism. And he warned that they should be aware of the "reactionary" philosophical schools circulating throughout Europe at that time and that special attention be given to Einstein's theory of relativity from the philosophic viewpoint. And lastly, the weapon to be used against bourgeois ideas is Marxist dialectical materialism. This might well have been Lenin's last will and testament to the Soviet Communist philosophers.

LENINIST PARTYNESS AFTER LENIN

How seriously did the Soviet Communists embrace Lenin's teaching on the partyness of science and philosophy? Did they regard this teaching of fundamental importance or just a whimsy?

Soon after Lenin left the Soviet scene, the Soviet Communist philosophers began purging the Soviet state of the Menshevist idealist school. V. Adoratskii attributed the following characteristics to this school:

> . . . the severance of theory from practice; the denial of the party nature of philosophy; professorial, contemplative "objectiveness"; failure to appreciate Lenin as a materialist and dialectician; failure to appreciate Lenin's contributions to the development of dialectical materialism; the disguise of non-Marxian and idealistic views by Marxian phraseology; priggish "scholarliness" which is totally unjustified because this ostensible "scholarliness" is not backed by any practical work or by a positivistic study of the subject.

The net result of the purge conducted by the Soviet Communist philosophers was that *dialectical* materialism became the official philosophy of the Soviet state. Moreover, Lenin's works, teachings and dictums were treated with the sacredness accorded the Holy Writ. In 1934, a collection of essays appeared, honoring the twenty-fifth anniversary of the initial release of *Materialism and Empirio-Criticism*. It was impossible not to note the two basic themes that were repeatedly stressed by the Soviet philosophers: the partisan nature of philosophy and the struggle for dialectical materialism as the world outlook of the revolutionary proletariat. One contributing writer stated that the first thing Lenin taught was: "If the history of class societies is the history of class struggles, then the history of philosophy is the history of the class struggles in philosophy." In more recent times, the Soviet dialectical materialist, P. Belov, credited Lenin for developing the history of philosophy as a science, for discussing the partisanship of philosophy and the resultant struggles, for revealing the bond between philosophy and the natural sciences, and for exposing the reactionary content of bourgeois philosophy in the epoch of imperialism.

The concept of partisanship in philosophy and science is not a sterile, theoretical idea in Soviet Russia. In the postwar years, Leninist partyness became an important cornerstone of Soviet Communist policy. A. V. Vostrikov wrote that the principle of partyness is a sharp weapon in the fight for communism and, in accordance with the decisions of the Central Committee of the Communist Party, should be used to wage a decisive struggle against bourgeois ideology and culture. A side effect of this policy was the examination of a Soviet textbook, *History of Western European Philosophy,* written by G. F. Alexandrov. Andrei A. Zhdanov, who was responsible for investigating the inadequacies of this text, made the following report:

> Comrade Alexandrov finds it possible to say something good about almost every philosopher of the past. The more eminent the bourgeois philosopher, the greater the flattery that is offered him. All of this shows that Comrade Alexandrov, perhaps unknowingly, is himself a captive of bourgeois historians, who proceed from the assumption that every philosopher is first of all an associate of the profession, and only secondarily an opponent. Such conceptions, if they should take hold among us, would inevitably lead to objectivism, to subservience to bourgeois philosophers and exaggeration of their services, toward depriving our philosophy of its militant offensive spirit. And that would mean a departure from the basic principle of materialism—its principle of direction, its partyness.

Zhdanov not only attacked the failings in Soviet philosophy, but he declared that "contemporary bourgeois science supplies clericalism, supplies fideism with new arguments which must be mercilessly exposed." The application of the party principle was most evident in the field of Soviet genetics. Before a large audience of biologists at the Lenin All-Union Academy of Agricultural Sciences, Academician Lysenko said in his opening remarks:

> A sharp controversy, which has divided biologists into irreconcilable camps, has thus flared up over the old question: *can characters and properties acquired by the vegetable and animal organisms in the course of their life be inherited?* In other words, whether qualitative variations of the nature of vegetable and animal organisms depend on the nature of the conditions of life which act upon the living body, upon the organisms.

> The Michurin teaching, which is in essence materialist and dialectical, proves by facts that such dependence does exist.

> The Mendelist-Morganist teaching, which in essence is metaphysical and idealist, denies the existence of such dependency, though it can cite no evidence to prove its point.

Following the pattern established by Lysenko, the Leningrad Section of the All-Union Astronomical-Geodetic Society organized its own conference for the expressed purpose of studying the ideological questions as they pertain to astronomy. The bourgeois concepts in astronomy were noted, discussed and condemned by this body of Soviet scientists.

Even the area of contemporary physics was not above criticism from the Leninist partisan approach. The Russian lecturer and dialectical materialist, M. Omel'yanovskii, reviewed the conflict between the materialist and idealist tendencies in modern physics and stated that the progress of physics in the twentieth century can be properly understood and explained only in the light of dialectical materialism. And Andrei A. Zhdanov, while examining the philosophic front during the sessions on Alexandrov's textbook, had a few words to say about bourgeois physics: "The Kantian subterfuges of latter-day bourgeois atomic physicists lead them to deductions on the 'free will' of the electron and to attempts to represent matters as only some combination of waves and other such nonsense."

The number of Soviet articles, pamphlets and books concerned directly or indirectly with Lenin's concept of the partyness of science and philosophy is enormous. Though Lenin's contribution on the partisan character of philosophy and science is neither original nor profound, nonetheless this concept is given considerable weight by the Soviet Communist Party. In no other modern nation can one find the tremendous influence of philosophical thinking on the progress of the natural sciences as in the Soviet Union. This perhaps is the most outstanding development of Leninist partyness for the present generation of Soviet intellectuals.

Stefan Morawski (essay date 1965)

SOURCE: "Lenin as a Literary Theorist," in *Science and Society,* Vol. XXIX, No. 1, Winter, 1965, pp. 2-25.

[*In the following essay, Morawski explicates Lenin's writings on art and literature.*]

Lenin's statements on literature do not constitute a system. We know that Lenin was not an esthetician, and that he never concerned himself for any long period with literary theory and criticism. Like Marx, however, he was very much interested in literature and art. Lunacharsky's reminiscences contain the following typical story. One night in 1905, at a colleague's house, Lenin picked up some popular books on the history of art. The next morning he told Lunacharsky that he had been up all night reading those books, and sighed: "What a wonderful field for a Marxist! Alas, I shall never be able to go into it."

Lenin was not an esthetician, but that does not mean that there is no Leninist esthetics. His philosophical works contain methodological directives, on the basis of which a Leninist esthetics could obviously be erected; the effort has already been made, and more than once.

It is not our purpose here to analyze what Lenin's esthetics might be said to be on the basis of his writings on philosophy and other topics. We shall confine ourselves to what Lenin wrote directly on literature and art. These utterances fall into three classes. First, there are his theoretical and critical remarks on a given writer or given literary works; then, his esthetic tastes, which he expressed occasionally in connection with other questions, and as a rule in connection with their social consequences; thirdly, his directives in the field of cultural policy, dating from the last years of his life and dealing with problems of the propagation of education and culture.

The question of his esthetic tastes is peripheral as compared to the other two categories, and yet essential for discussion of them. The fact is that those tastes were limited. He gave the first place to realistic literature, naturalistic painting of the second half of the nineteenth century, and emotionalist music, basing himself primarily on Russian works. However, he never made his personal tastes directives in the field of cultural policy. To a certain extent they influenced the scope and character of his remarks on literary criticism, if only in that he selected certain works and writers; at bottom, however, his choice was due to immediate political questions.

Because of the wealth of materials and the complex nature of the questions, the problems of modern art and of directives in cultural policy require special analysis. Our discussion will relate to the remarks of Lenin on criticism and theory, chiefly dating from 1905-1911, e.g., his discussion of Tolstoy and the article *On Party Organization and Party Literature*. It will be necessary further to recall and make use of some later utterances dating from 1914, 1919, 1921, which are important supplements to the materials from the earlier period. The pieces on Tolstoy were written in 1908-1911. There

are six of them, published in various party journals, from *Proletarii* and *Sotsialdemokrat* to *Zvezda*. The article *On Party Organization and Party Literature* appeared in the party journal *Novaya Zhizn* at the end of 1905. Before discussing them, it should be emphasized that there is a certain fragmentation in Marxist esthetics; its line of development is constantly being broken, and its fundamental theses are formulated anew at need, for a second or a third time. For example, Lenin did not have available to him a complete collection of the statements of Marx and Engels on art and literature. The first work of this kind appeared in 1937 in the Soviet Union, edited by Lifshits. If Lenin arrived at similar conclusions, the explanation is to be found in the method of Marxism, which led in that direction.

We now propose to discuss Lenin's articles on Tolstoy, but in order to see what Lenin accomplished, we must first take note of the historical background, starting with pre-Leninist efforts in the field of Marxist esthetics. This esthetics had various roots, the beginnings of which can be traced to the seventeenth century. One of its sources are the discussions of historicism deriving from Vico, Winckelmann and Herder and summed up in the work of Hegel, as well as the investigations into the typical, the individual and the general, which occur in classical German esthetics from Baumgarten to Hegel and his followers. Another source are the concepts of useful art and the democratization of esthetic thought that developed primarily in the first thirty years of the nineteenth century, as well as considerations on the social function of the work of art (chiefly literary), i.e., the French tradition going from Diderot and Mercier to the school of the "doctrinaires."

It is a striking fact that to a certain extent Marxist esthetics absorbed these basic problems of the first half of the nineteenth century, postulating a many-sided interpretation of the work of art: genetic, mimetic and functional. Genetic: it aims at explaining the work in the context of definite historical causes and conditions; mimetic: it considers the cognitive value of the art work; functional: it deals with the way in which works of art are perceived, what social class (group) it serves. The basic analysis in Marxist esthetic studies is a sociological analysis in the sense that the emphasis is on a class (ideological) interpretation of the art work; the outcomes, to be sure, vary. Furthermore, this sociological point of view does not, according to the guiding principles of Marxist esthetics, exhaust the analysis of an art work.

An assertion of the class character of a given work appears to be a simple matter but actual investigation shows that it entails a very complex and often controversial interpretation. If it is asserted that a work of art by X or Y is linked to a given class, this is usually taken to mean that the writer is a representative (conscious or unconscious) of just that class. But we must examine how that happens; we must show that the fact that an artist represents a given class occurs either always or only sometimes. Such facts certainly exist. Marx and Engels, in many analyses on the basis of concrete examples, demonstrated that, and how, a given writer was linked with a given social class. Further analysis of this phenomenon, however, soon showed that this sort of simple functional dependence is not always present. For example, Lessing, Diderot and Hogarth support it, but the situation is different with Sterne and Watteau, say. The former came from and belonged to the petty bourgeoisie and represented it directly in their works; the latter were not determined by their class origin, and their ideological allegiances were a matter of some complexity. In the Marxist view, being born into a class is only a tentative indication. The essential factor is the ideological posture of the creator. It was soon found that analyzing this phenomenon requires prudence. In Marx's *Eighteenth Brumaire* we encounter a thesis that opened new horizons in sociological analysis. This is the well-known passage on the "shopkeepers" and their literary representatives. The latter are in a different social situation and are set apart from the former by their education, but still there is a certain parallelism in their views. The writer does not entirely "represent" (that is, express the way of perceiving, feeling and understanding the world) his own class or social group exclusively; he may have his origin in one class and be close to another ideologically: a related one or even a hostile one. He may even, as has often happened, express the ideology of more than one class, thereby manifesting the vagueness of his own view of the world, as well as the conflicts characteristic of the entire environment around him.

This is the line of another classical interpretation, which points out that the literal thesis of the artist as representing a class is only one among a number of possibilities: we refer to Engels' statements on Goethe. Goethe's internal contradictions, i.e. his Philistinism and his Olympian attitude (as with Schiller—radicalism along with escape from the world) describe not only himself but also his historical period. In Engels' interpretation, Goethe represents the contradictions of the Germany of his time. Now, the contradictions of an entire society can be explained by means of analysis of the literary texts and not by analysis of the artist's biography or his ideology taken by itself. It has to be kept in mind that artists, who are rarely fully aware of their ideological position *sensu stricto,* but most often react vigorously to psycho-sociological phenomena (myths, tabus, general sentiment, uncrystallized social trends, moral searchings, etc.) have by the very nature of their profession gone beyond the "one-class" point of view. One instance is the Romantics, who were against the entire world of the society of their time. They attacked both the defenders of official, bourgeois art and the supporters of republican-socialist art of revolt. A. Cassagne has given an excellent picture of their historical and theoretical adventures in his *La thèorie de l'art pour l'art en France* (1905, Pt. I) and derived from their positions the subsequent conception of "art for art's sake." Soon after, Plekhanov (*Art and Social Life,* 1912,

Secs. 1 and 2) showed that the "above-classes" posture of the Romantics was, to a great extent, specious.

Still another aspect of the sociological analysis was brought out by Engels' analysis of Balzac, in a letter written to Minna Kautsky in 1885. Balzac had pro-feudal sympathies, and yet what he presented in the *Human Comedy* was an affirmation of the ineluctable triumph of the bourgeoisie. The case of Balzac, Engels says, exhibits the internal collision between what may be called the objective truth of the work, that is, its artistic-cognitive content, and the writer's philosophy. Note that in the statements by Marx and Engels two meanings must be distinguished for the terms used synonymously by them, "world view" and "ideology." In one acceptation, a world view is a system of concepts or judgments (commentary by the author, in whatever form) explicitly stated in the literary work; in the other sense, it is the entire set of artistic judgments contained in the work, or a cognitive generalization that can be derived from the conflicts, figures, contents, etc. that are presented. We do not mean the philosophical effects, the function of the work in question, which are linked with the varying reception of the work, but what is called its objective message. By the last concept, a rather nebulous one, is meant the view of the world presented by the very structure of the work, i.e. the construction of the content, the hierarchy of themes and figures, the outcome of the whole, etc. Obviously, different works are unequivocal (or ambivalent) in varying degrees; greater ambivalence enables them to have philosophical influence even in opposing directions. This fact, however, does not deny the existence of that "objective message" that has to be studied and analyzed. More than that, this procedure is the only effectual one. Accordingly, of the two senses of "world view" mentioned, the second is the essential one for esthetic analysis. Among the factors it takes into account is the fact that the artist so often depicts inter-class conflicts (i.e. real contradictions, as they appear at the given historical epoch) not directly from the position of a single class but somehow "from within." From within—that is, from the position of a sensitive, intelligent and conscientious observer, on whom not so much the passion of the combatant, as the facts themselves, impose the side to take and consequently the position on some class-determined vector.

In the analyses of Marx and Engels, therefore, there occurs, in addition to the genetic aspect, the mimetic aspect, that is to say, the inquiry into the way in which the work reflects reality, whether it depicts the typical traits of the given individuality and the given society, or distorts or simply ignores those traits.

In the next phase of Marxist esthetics, running parallel to the sociologizing conceptions of the second half of the nineteenth century, Mehring and Plekhanov, its main representatives, narrowed and simplified analysis of the literary work. Plekhanov, for example, reduced it to socio-biographical interpretation; that is, he asked to what class the author in question belonged and what political ideology he showed. Mehring, in a discussion with Hauptmann, the author of *The Weavers,* applied essentially the same line of interpretation. That is, he measured the value of the work not by its cognitive-artistic value but by the political ideology of the writer. In a different but equally simplified manner, Plekhanov explained the case of Leo Tolstoy. Tolstoy, according to him, is a count, always and everywhere, in all his works. Plekhanov adds, however, that the working class likes him because of his moralistic position. He recognized the artistic genius of Tolstoy, of course, but the starting point, basis and main result of his analysis were Tolstoy's sectarian views, explained in relation to his origin and class position.

Lenin was familiar with Plekhanov's articles and accepted them, as is shown by his letter to Gorky dated January 3, 1911. It should be asked, however, what it was that he agreed with; actually, Lenin's analysis was essentially a polemic against Plekhanov's conception. Lenin shared the opinion that Tolstoy's work exhibits the contradictions between the artist and the thinker, and he accepted the attack on Tolstoyanism which he viewed as a rival ideology to Marxism. He explained the problem differently from Plekhanov, however. Before going into his discussion, we consider some other interpretations made at that time, to which Lenin reacted immediately. After Tolstoy's dramatic death at Astapovo station, all the newspapers set about discussing his philosophy. The theme was taken up by the government organs (*Russkoe Znamya, Novoe Vremya, Rech*) as well, which after years of applause for the 1901 excommunication (over *Resurrection*) suddenly discovered that Tolstoy was a great seeker after God, the conscience of his times. While these Black Hundred or Kadet journals confined themselves to commonplaces, the articles of Nevyadomsky and Bazarov in *Nasha Zarya,* the organ of the Menshevik-Liquidators, said on the one hand that Tolstoy's views represented the flabby Russian intelligentsia, and on the other that his world view was a great monolith, a great philosophical synthesis based on the conception of nonresistance to evil. It is noteworthy, in this connection, that all the above interpretations dealt with Tolstoy's ideological preachments, not with the artistic-cognitive value of his works.

The equivalent put forth by Plekhanov was socio-biographical, whereas the authors mentioned proposed the following substitutes: sociological (but with the intelligentsia taking the place of the rural nobility) and philosophico-religious-moral. The first of these, as in Plekhanov's version, at least linked Tolstoy's philosophy to a definite class or social group. Bazarov advanced the thesis of Tolstoy as the conscience of the "sprawling" intelligentsia, and used the thesis only as a propedaeutic to abstract considerations on Tolstoy as the ideologue of the conscience of all humanity. Thus, this interpretation, confined to philosophy and ethics, had an idealist character, similar to the one that prevailed in the school of *Literaturgeschichte als Geistesgeschichte.*

Lenin polemicized against both the idealist conception and over-simplification in interpretation based on materialistic principles. The methodological polemic does not emerge clearly in his remarks, but can be deduced from them. Even more apparent are the political motives that led Lenin to speak out on this matter.

In November 1910, workers and students in St. Petersburg demonstrated in the streets against the tsarist regime, in honor of the memory of Tolstoy. Lenin called attention to the fact, as evidence that the problem of Tolstoy was and is taken as a highly political one. Merely comparing the opinions stated in the various journals showed that against the background of Tolstoy (or by means of him) opposing political positions clashed, along with contradictory theoretical conceptions.

Lenin presented a conception that may be described as an attempt to return to Marx's standpoint. In the first place, he considered Tolstoy (and this was a stroke of genius) as the representative of the peasant masses. He started from the proposition that the works of the great writer were a reflection of the bourgeois revolution in Russia during the period 1861-1904, after the emancipation of the serfs but before the 1905 revolution, in which the proletariat was already the protagonist. In the period in question Russia went through its "birth pangs" and became a modern state. The peasantry, the basic mass of the society of the time, was in mutiny against the government, the church and the process of "primary accumulation." This protest was a manifestation of pain and despair, at the same time. The peasantry was unable to cope with the situation of the times; keenly aware of all the torments of the transition, it was still incapable of any constructive way out. At most there were regrets for the old patriarchal system, or dreams of some new religion that would bring about universal justice on earth. In his works Tolstoy exhibited these contradictions, latent in the Russian peasantry. In September 1908, in an article entitled ***Tolstoy as a Mirror of the Russian Revolution,*** Lenin said:

> On the one hand, an artist of genius, the creator not only of unrivaled pictures of Russian life but of works belonging in the first rank of world literature. On the other hand, the great landowner mad for Christ. On the one hand, the magnificent, powerful, immediate, frank protest against social hypocrisy and falsehood; on the other, the "Tolstoyan," i.e., the worn-out, hysterical sniveler known as the Russian intellectual, who beats his breast and bears public witness: "I am abject, I am revolting, but I am engaged in moral self-improvement, I do not eat meat and I nourish myself on rice cutlets." On the one hand, a merciless criticism of capitalist exploitation, an unmasking of the violence of the government, the comedy of government justice and administration, an exposure of the full depth of the contradiction between the growth of wealth and the achievements of civilization and the growth of poverty,

barbarism and suffering by the mass of workers; on the other hand—the insanely bigoted cry of "nonresistance to evil." On the one hand, the soberest realism, the tearing off of every mask; on the other, the propaganda of one of the worst things in the world, namely religion.

Later Lenin explained these contradictions: "Tolstoy is great as expressing the ideas and attitudes that formed in the minds of millions in the mass of Russian peasantry at the time of the advancing bourgeois revolution in Russia. Tolstoy is original in that his views, taken as a whole, express the very special character of our revolution as a *peasant* bourgeois revolution. From this point of view the contradictions in Tolstoy's views are an accurate reflection of the contradictory conditions under which the historical action of the peasantry in our revolution took place."

In the first three articles, in which Lenin spoke of these contradictions, he stressed the fact that they were present both in the system of Tolstoy's views and in the very structure of his works, i.e., in their artistic-cognitive content. He thus went beyond what Plekhanov had done. The opinions of Natasha Rostov, Pyotr Bezukhov or Konstanty Levin had been interpreted as opinions of the author, without relation to the environment presented in the stories. Lenin called attention to the peasantry presented in Tolstoy's works and to the fact that the author, despite an occasional opinion placed in the mouths of aristocrats, took the position of the "naive peasant" and expressed their psychology in his criticism.

This was a subtle analysis. In the case of great works, such as Tolstoy's, the artist cannot be treated as the representative of (or as expressing the interests of) merely his own class. Tolstoy represented all of the reality of the time, bringing out its internal contradictions. Thus, analysis from the mimetic point of view dominates the narrowly conceived genetic analysis. The gnoseological equivalent (obviously, artistic knowledge differs from scientific) prevails over the sociological equivalent. The decisive factor in interpreting the "world view" of the work is its immanent content and not the "bare" ideology of the writer, which often derives directly from his class origin. This procedure obviously does not exclude the question of the class genesis of the work. There the genetic and mimetic analyses are closely interwoven. In the case of Lenin's remarks on Tolstoy, this is immediately evident. The class point of view appears precisely by means of the parallel between the views of the writer and those of the peasant masses. This was brought out clearly by Lunacharsky in the discussion mentioned above.

In the other three articles, the functional analysis dominates, especially in **Tolstoy and the Struggle of the Proletariat** (December 1910). There, the accent is on the system of conceptions, on the ideology per se, rather than on the artistic-cognitive content. In the January

1911 article **L. N. Tolstoy and His Epoch,** the critic was interested in *Lucerna, Anna Karenina* and the *Kreutzer Sonata* chiefly for the philosophical theses presented there. Lenin dealt almost exclusively with the way in which Tolstoy's works were received by the working class, and what they give that class. Obviously, he did not doubt that Tolstoy's works were of permanent value. He often repeated, as we see from the reminiscences of Gorky and Krupskaya, that there was no other writer to compare with Tolstoy. But in 1911 Tolstoy interested him not only as artist, as mirror of a past epoch, but also as a thinker, as educator of the working and peasant masses. On this Lenin reacted just as Plekhanov had. Tolstoy is not the teacher of life, as the liberals assert, Lenin wrote, but "by penetrating into the works of Leo Tolstoy the Russian working class knows its enemies better; and by analyzing the doctrine of Tolstoy, the entire Russian people will be able to realize where the weakness lay that had prevented it from carrying its emancipation through to completion. And this has to be realized in order to go forward."

Thus, Tolstoy's doctrine, although so critical of Tsarism, yet so utopian and so reactionary in its principles, must be rejected by the proletariat where it harms the socialist movement.

The functional analysis, it will be seen, is far from being complete here. At this point, Lenin was not interested in the way Tolstoy was received by various social groups but, what was most important, in the reception of the artistic-cognitive content of his works. The analysis confined itself to an investigation of the class function of Tolstoy's philosophy at the given historical moment. By and large, it was a political point of view. If that were all that Lenin had to say, it would not have gone beyond the interpretation that Mehring made of Hauptmann. But Lenin gave a well-rounded point of view; for that reason, his interpretation was and is of extreme interest. At that time Lenin was the only person in the Marxist movement capable of giving such an analysis, since only in his philosophical work was there a well-developed theory of "reflection," one aspect of which was the mimetic analysis. The interesting thing is not merely that Lenin went back to the propositions of Marx, but above all that it was a true analysis, that is, that it corresponded to the artistic-cognitive and *sensu stricto* ideological content of what Tolstoy wrote. We know that with *Anna Karenina* (1870-1877) there was a turning point in his writing. As early as in *A Landowner's Morning* and *Polikushka,* in the 1860's, he was already taking the peasant's view. In *Three Deaths* the coachman dies calmly, like a peasant, with dignity, in harmony with nature. Closer to Tolstoy the individualist, as Plekhanov always referred to him, was the agitated, dramatic death of the aristocratic woman, but the reader is touched by Fyodor, rather than by her. Mention should also be made here of the figures of Platon Karataev, Karp and Vlas in *War and Peace,* representing the peasant masses, the personification of their (fatalistic) wisdom and their patriotism. Identical themes can be traced in the *Power of Darkness* and *Master and Servant*. Along with the peasant way of looking at things went a bitter criticism of the system, which is already to be seen in *Anna Karenina* but reaches its peak in *Resurrection* and Tolstoy's journalism (*Confession, The Kingdom of Heaven Is Within Us, I Can Not Remain Silent*). However, the critical attitude was blurred by the "new" religion that *inter alia* prevented the great writer from understanding the social and political situation of the time.

In *Resurrection* Tolstoy described the populists (*Narodniki*) with warm sympathy, but Kondratyev, the worker, reading Marx, is treated with ironic condescension. The same attitude recurred in the story *Divine and Human* (1905). Thus, Lenin's interpretation brought out the essential, intrinsic cleavage in Tolstoy's work, and remains to this day the basis for discussions of theoreticians and critics.

Not long ago, J. Vidmar (a Yugoslav critic) and M. Lifshits (a Soviet writer on esthetics) engaged in polemics on this subject, namely, the relation of philosophy or world view to artistic truth. Vidmar held, using Tolstoy as his example, that there is a contradiction between what the writer represents (which is a permanent value) and what he thinks of reality (which is an ideological illusion and has only transitory value). Lifshits in reply showed—and tellingly—that the contradictions in Tolstoy's works were both artistic and philosophical. The cleavage is apparent in the writer's whole point of view, and his artistic turbidities are a parallel to it, or rather a reflection of it. Even if we grant that Lifshits is correct in this case, it is not quite true that this is always so. A number of articles in the Soviet Union recently have pointed out that there is always a concordance between a writer's world view and the artistic-cognitive content of his work. E. M. Khrapchenko, in a discussion entitled "World View and Creative Work" (in *Problemy teorii literatury, shornik statei*), polemicizes not only against such contemporary writers on esthetics as Lukacs and Nedoshyvin but essentially against Engels as well, asserting categorically that a false philosophy inevitably leads to artistic-cognitive failures, viz., to an unrealistic picture of reality. Engels had expressly stated (see his letter to Margaret Harkness of April 1888) that Balzac was a realist, despite his legitimist views.

There is no doubt that creative work is dependent on the world view, but the assertion that there must be a concordance between them is something else again. What is meant by the world view in this connection is not quite clear. Khrapchenko means by it "the ensemble of views . . . on natural and social phenomena," as contrasted with the "artistic method," i.e., the embodiment of general views in the fabric of the narrative. Lifshits means by a view of life, apparently, the "artistic method," i.e., the ideas contained in the work, derived from its guiding themes. Between the writer's world view (in Khrapchenko's sense) and his creative work, a contradiction can certainly arise. Prior to socialist realism, at least,

this was endemic with respect to many outstanding works. If we take the meaning that Lifshits gives to the concept of "world view," there too we find a conflict within the artistic fabric itself; but this is a case of less frequent occurrence.

In Lenin also we find, outside his articles on Tolstoy, a methodological criterion for interpreting literature that stands in contradiction to the apodictic verdicts of Khrapchenko and his colleagues. Lenin asserted that the philosophy of the artist, as a system of concepts or judgments, may be in glaring contradiction with the artistic truth contained in the work in question, and that in that case the essential thing for literary criticism is what the artist presents, not what he thinks. In a letter to Gorky dated February 25, 1908 (a very grave period, with inner-party disputes and efforts to win the writer over to the Bolshevist side), Lenin said: "In my opinion, the writer can gain a great deal from any reading in philosophy that he does. I agree fully and unconditionally that all kinds of books are needed for our work as writers and that starting from *that* kind of view [Lenin had in mind empiriomonism—S. M.], from one's own artistic experimentation and *even from idealist philosophy,* it is possible to arrive at conclusions that are of great value to the party. . . ."

This was written with reference to Gorky's *Mother,* which Lenin considered to be a party novel. The statement is significant, but usually goes unnoticed by commentators. It was not, as some would have it, merely an occasional remark, bound up with the needs of the moment and the tactics of the fight to win Gorky. A similar interpretation is to be found in Lenin's remarks in 1921 on a book by A. Averchenko (a White emigré in Paris), *Twelve Knives in the Revolution's Back.* Lenin pointed out how vividly it presents the atmosphere of the Russia of the landowners and industrialists. We cite the conclusion of the article:

> In the last story, *Fragments of an Exploded World,* we find a former senator in the Crimea, at Sevastopol—"he had been rich, generous, well-connected," "now he was working as a day laborer in an artillery magazine, unloading and sorting shells"—and a former manager of "huge steel mills, which counted as the largest in the Viborg district. Now he is a clerk in a commission agency and recently has even acquired some skill in evaluating second-hand ladies' coats and children's plush teddy bears, left for sale."
>
> The two old timers recall the good old days, the sunsets in St. Petersburg, the streets, the theaters and, of course, the visits to the "Little Bear," "Vienna" and "Little Yaroslav," etc. Their reminiscences are broken into by cries: "What did we do to them? Whom did we interfere with? . . . What harm did that do them? . . . What have they done to Russia?"
>
> Arkadii Averchenko cannot understand why. The workers and peasants, apparently, had no trouble

in understanding why, and do not need any explanations.

Some of the stories deserve reprinting, in my opinion. Ability has to be supported.

The eloquence of this way of interpretation is obvious. Lenin is defending the "objective truth" of Averchenko's book. The writer is seething with hatred of the Soviet Union, but by writing the truth about himself and his class he undermines his own philosophy. Hence, the artistic-cognitive is the decisive factor in literary criticism, although, of course, not the only one.

If what we have said is correct, then the analysis of M. Merleau-Ponty in his *Les aventures de la dialectique . . .* is incorrect, according to which Lukacs contrasted his interpretation of realism to the narrow, purely ideological method proposed by Lenin. The position of Merleau-Ponty *contradicts* the historical facts concerning Lukacs' theory of realism as set forth in his *Geschichte und Klassenbewusstsein* (1923), alleged to deviate from "Leninist orthodoxy." Actually, Lukacs, with Lifshits and others, defended realism, in the sense of Lenin's propositions and on the basis of them, during the 1930's.

Lenin's position on objective truth is in line with other marginal remarks of his on the characteristic nature of literature and art. A complete presentation of these theses of Lenin would call for a reconstruction on my part of a view he expressed in only fragmentary form. Since I would like to avoid any such procedure, Lenin's ideas are given directly here, even though in a rather disconnected way. I feel that this is preferable, as being closely linked to the materials presented up to now.

In 1914 Lenin got from Inessa Armand a book by Winnichenko entitled *The Commandments of the Fathers.* He did not like the book because it was a "collection of the merest horrors." Obviously, said Lenin, crimes occur, diseases, pathological phenomena, etc. However, representing the world only in that version is a false method. In this judgment there was implicit an anti-naturalistic program. The cognitive value of literature is not constituted by realia taken independently of any generalization, and still less by realia subordinated to a false, superficial generalization. Accordingly, it is impossible to defend the artistic and cognitive value of a work of art merely by the plea that facts like those described "simply occur in real life." Lenin, although he did not write on realism as Marx and Engels did, went in the same direction. In a letter to Inessa Armand dated January 24, 1915 on the subject of free love, he pointed out *inter alia* that a story is based on an individual instance, a unique situation and individual characters, in whom and through whom, however, typical traits are manifested. These ideas are in a way a theoretical commentary on his articles on Tolstoy, the remarks in his 1908 letter to Gorky and his ironical evaluation of Averchenko's book. Everywhere, the leitmotiv is the problem of artistic truth.

Following up Lenin's suggestions concerning the nature of art, they can be carried still further. In reading Feuerbach's lectures on *The Essence of Religion,* Lenin noted with approval the statement that "Art does not require that its works be regarded as reality." Here we approach the limits of legitimate interpretations of Lenin's text. It appears, however, that it is possible, in the context of the analysis presented hitherto, to state Lenin's thought as leading to the recognition of the relative autonomy of the work of art. This is justified by the methodological considerations scattered in his *Philosophical Notebooks* concerning the relative independence of the various spheres of social consciousness. In a certain sense we are authorized to do this by the dialectical genius of Lenin, between the thesis of the politically immediate function of the work of art and the investigation of its rights, which are internal but obviously not autarkic. But this puts us once more at the threshold of reconstructing Lenin's esthetics on our own account. We must, therefore, return to the task we set ourselves at the outset: an analysis of what Lenin himself said; we proceed to a second problem: the party nature of the literary work.

This is a problem that should be treated along with the previous one, since it is directly connected with it. The artist, consciously or unconsciously, in dealing with a given theme and reflecting reality truly or falsely, always assumes some party position or other. However, with a view to an orderly exposition of Lenin's theses and the need for clarifying the terms, it seems desirable to divide the problem. The problem of the party nature of literature was posed by Lenin in the 1905 article cited above. Since the term is understood in differing ways, we must distinguish three meanings contained in Lenin's text. Lenin himself never made this *distinguo,* but consciously, i.e., for polemical reasons, used the three meanings, stressing what he had in mind in the given context.

The central meaning of the adjective "party" relates to *belonging to an organization.* The author of the article assigns the literary man the same kind of position as any other member of the party. There is nothing surprising in the fact that this problem appeared in Lenin's time, when the party of the Bolshevik type took form and established itself. Artists and literary men expected that they would be in some sense *legibus soluti* (above the law). Lenin pointed out with emphasis, both in the furious struggles within the Social Democratic movement and in the battle with enemies outside it, that party discipline is the same for everyone.

In another sense, "party nature" is the same as *committed in idea.* That is, anyone who commits himself in idea, or is in any sense tendentious, has thereby chosen some party. In this sense, the individualistic writer is likewise a partisan, if he takes his abstract and specious independence from any considerations as his creed and contrasts himself to the frankly engaged writer.

The third basic meaning of the adjective "party" is that of *being committed on the side of the proletariat, on the side of socialism*. The artist who is partisan in this sense need not necessarily be linked to a party organizationally. In this sense, "party-ness" is the same as what is currently defined as a revolutionary attitude.

Lenin's propositions have Marxist tradition behind them. After 1848, in connection with the discussion with Heine and Freiligrath, the problem was raised by Marx and Engels in the *Neue Rheinische Zeitung*. Marx gave the concept of "party-ness" the last of the above meanings. Later, in his correspondence with Freiligrath in 1860, he stated that a party writer is one who declares himself on the side of communism, without necessarily being a member of the Communist League. This theme was taken up by Mehring at the end of the century; he distinguished proletarian writing (the first sense) from party writing (third sense). If a shift in definition took place in Lenin, this was due to clearly political causes. Accordingly, it is in order to describe the situation in which the article appeared at that time.

In 1904 and 1905 the opinion was expressed in some party newspapers and in milieux connected with them, that socialism could be consistent with decadentism. Minsky, in the *Proletarii* and *Novaya Zhizn*, put forth the slogan of tolerance for the hyperindividualism of creative individuals. Representatives of the modernism of the time came forward with similar slogans. One magazine, *Polarnaya Zvezda*, wrote in a statement of policy: "In our philosophico-political world view, we start from the premise that the individual is the vehicle and the creator of all spiritual values. For us, individuality is sacred, in and of itself. In that sense, we are absolute individualists." This was written by S. Frank, but identical ideas were advocated by Bryusov, Merezhkovsky and Berdyaev. An editorial in the magazine *Zolotoe Runo* (which succeeded *Mir Iskusstva*, the organ of the symbolists) asserted that the times were perilous, since the bloody social conflicts were intruding on the fringes of art as an eternal value. The platform of the magazine proclaimed the following as truths: "Art is eternal, art is not bound to anything that is transitory. . . . Art is something unique, the spirit is unique in its source. Art is symbolic, since it always bears within itself a symbol, i.e., that which is eternal, and rejects that which is transitory. Art is free, since it arises from inspiration." Bryusov and Berdyaev protested that they could only recognize socialist ideas to the extent that socialism respects the basic principle of their world view: the unconditional independence of the artist.

The opinions of the Russian symbolists were a reflection of French Symbolism and Parnassism. At its base is the Romantic theory of art, derived from Novalis and F. Schlegel, according to which the artist is a Brahmin. (At the same time, a trend in Romanticism stressed the social obligations of the artist, e.g., Shelley in *Defence of Poetry*.) This apolitical tendency in Romanticism was inherited by the representatives of the idea of "art for art's sake." Baudelaire wrote, in the *Hymne:* "Que tu viennes du Ciel ou de l'Enfer, qu'importe, o Beauté." Flaubert thought: "Aimons-nous en l'art comme les mystiques s'aiment en Dieu" (*Correspondance*, Vol. II, 1983). The Goncourts wrote in their *Journal* in 1886 that only "pure literature" is a matter of life and death. And we are continually coming across statements in their writings concerning the eternality of the "truly beautiful," the independence of the artist, his superiority and disdain towards his clients and customers. Baudelaire wrote about Poe, and Gautier about Baudelaire, that the glory of the poet is his holding himself aloof from utopians, philanthropists, socialists, etc. Flaubert, speaking for all estheticizing poets, declared that "la morale de l'art consiste dans sa beauté même" (*Correspondance*, Vol. III).

But there is an important historical difference between the representatives of "art for art's sake" and Bryusov and Berdyaev. The former revolted against the bourgeois and petty-bourgeois Philistine, hostile to all ambitious art (cf. Marx's statements in Vol. I, of the *Theories of Surplus Value*). The Russian Decadents were not attacking the "bourgeois" alone, but also, and perhaps at that time mainly, the masses of the people in hopes of a new art that would open up horizons hitherto closed to them. The artists' fear of the masses dates from late Romanticism (cf. Heine's preface to the French edition of *Lutetia*) and continues down to the time of Benois and Merezhkovsky. In 1912, Roger Fry gave it symptomatic expression in his essay on *Art and Socialism*, read at the Fabian Society. But the antagonist of the poets in the 1840's and 1850's was a different one from that of the early twentieth century. At the earlier epoch, socialism was a "specter," while in Lenin's time it was a real, fertile historical force. It could be regarded as such from the point of view of the artists as well.

But not everybody at the time accepted the Decadent ideas. F. Makovsky and V. Stasov attacked by the Symbolists, appealing to the civic conscience of the creative, but their voices were regarded as outdated. Writers and critics linked with the social democracy carried most of the weight of the polemics. Their articles preceded Lenin's statements, e.g., Plekhanov's discussion of eighteenth-century French drama and French painting and his article on the proletarian movement and bourgeois art. Then there was Lunacharsky's article on "Marxism and Esthetics" in Number 9-10 of *Pravda*, and Maxim Gorky wrote his "Remarks on the Petty Bourgeois" in *Novaya Zhizn*. These articles asserted the social nature of art, demonstrated its class origin, content and function, attacked formalism for its absence of ideas, laid the foundations of a Marxist esthetics, lined up behind the proletariat in their struggle for social emancipation (and cultural revolution), exposed the fetishism of the eternal, absolutely beautiful and artistic individualism, showing its petty-bourgeois source. This was the background of Lenin's article on ***Party Organi-***

zation and Party Literature. His first basic thesis asserted that "literature must be a part of the general cause of the proletariat, a 'gear' in the single, solid, massive mechanism of social democracy powered by the entire conscious avant-garde of the working class." Lenin added at once that every comparison limps, and reinforced the assertion above in the following manner: "There is no doubt that literature is the last thing in the world to lend itself to mechanical leveling and uniformity, to the subjection of the minority by the majority. There is no doubt that in this field great freedom must be assured to individual initiative and personal inclinations, great freedom of thought and fantasy, form and content."

This fundamental thesis was aimed in a definite direction, at Minsky and his supporters. But it is an important fact, which will have to be returned to, that Lenin, in formulating a pointed political postulate, did not overlook the problem of the nature of art.

Another fundamental thesis of the article was addressed to Berdyaev, Benois, etc. Lenin punctured the declamations of the Decadent writers concerning absolute freedom. He said: "Now this absolute freedom is a bourgeois, i.e., an anarchist phrase (for anarchism as a philosophy is the bourgeois world view turned inside out). It is impossible to live in a society and be free from society. The freedom of the bourgeois writer, painter or actress is only masked (or hypocritically concealed) dependence on the purse, on bribery, on fees."

This conclusion led further, to a proposition going beyond the framework of literature organically linked to the party. Lenin interpreted freedom of art as follows: "Literature will be free to the extent that new forces are recruited into its ranks, not for personal advantage or a career, but for the idea of socialism and sympathy for the working people. Literature will be free when it serves, not the jaded heroine, not the bored and pudgy 'top ten thousand,' but the millions, the tens of millions of working people, who are the flower of the nation, its power, its future."

Thus, he appealed to all artists to whom the people's cause was dear to take part in the struggle for social justice. It was an appeal for realistic and optimistic creativity, oriented toward the future. Lunacharsky supported these theses in an article on "Problems of Social Democratic Artistic Creativity" in the magazine *Vestnik Zhizni* (1907, No. 1). Bryusov and Berdyaev answered him, defending anarchism as the indispensable attitude of the artist, and inspiration ("the mystic principle") as the source of creative process. The discussion continued, and is still going on, as we know.

We return to what Lenin said, in order to bring out the extraordinary scope of his view of the problem raised here. Lenin accented the importance of the ideas of the creative work, and fought for a direct bond between the artist and the party. These were natural arguments to

occur in the writings of the leader of a political party that shaped the history of the twentieth century. But Lenin also stressed the special nature of the work of the writer. This motif, by no means a sensational one, is linked with the fact that the statement was earlier than his conception of artistic truth, and with his later declarations. Lenin's struggle to win Gorky over to the communist view was at the same time a constant struggle not to interfere in any way with this creative writing. Lenin continually stressed that Gorky's personal authentic view of reality was a priceless gift for the party. In just the same way he defended Demian Bedny; but he held it against him, and the fact is symptomatic, that he sometimes merely repeated what the party had already established and society already knew. In Gorky's reminiscences we read that Lenin, without questioning the agitational value of Demian's works, added: "He is crude, he follows the reader, whereas what is needed is always to be a little ahead."

Thus, Lenin expected from the writer a *personal position, an individual penetration into reality, a treatment of problems and positions that the party, perhaps, had not yet got to*. Lenin was for the artistic individuality disclosing its own truth and going along with the party in its daily work; he was against excrescences of individualism.

Lenin's statements on the party quality of literature justify, as I see it, the following generalizations. Absolute freedom of the artist is an illusory freedom. Artistic work is inevitably entangled in the ideological battle. Conscious choice is always better than unconscious commitment. And in our time, there is no possible choice that is more humanistic than alliance with the people struggling for a communist society. What that alliance will be like is, another matter. It may be party writing in the sense of the public advocacy of communist ideas; but it may also be an approach to those ideas via categorical criticism of the capitalist system.

Developing these ideas of Lenin's, we could also say that this alliance may appear in creative work that directly attacks the central problems of ideas of our times, but it may also take the form of active participation in the process of democratization of esthetic culture (e.g., in the sphere of architecture and the applied arts). The alleged absolute independence of the artist is a fictional freedom; true freedom is every development and extension of esthetic values that are valuable from the point of view of the cultural needs of socialist society. Conscious commitment to the battle for socialism, with varying emotional coefficients and varying intellectual orientation, is always at the same time a battle for artistic de-alienation. The artist then not only communicates his own truths to others, but also gets truths from them, which lays a common foundation and makes it possible for everyone to determine his "place on earth." The artist who arrives in his own way at the world view that the communist party represents, not only has the right constantly to orient himself in the world, always to seek to reject the false and assert the truth, but simply feels that as an inner necessity. This applies as well, or rather, primarily, to the artist who is a member of a party. He is bound by the same party discipline as any other person, but he is also bound, as is every party intellectual, every creator, to independent thought and the expression of his own view of reality. The party gives him a vote of confidence, *inter alia,* for the reason that he has enriched socialist culture by his individual vision, as Gorky did with his *Mother.* Lenin learned that lesson in the case of the great presocialist writers, including Tolstoy. They were discoverers of truths, and not agents carrying out preestablished orders. Socialist writers continued and are continuing that attitude, which is partisan through and through.

It is a striking fact that Lenin, a politician and revolutionary of great genius, an outstanding philosopher and economist, also showed some outstanding traits in his literary criticism. This is a case of the irradiation of genius, since those *disjecta membra* that the materials I have cited represent indicate clearly that this was a field of knowledge with which Lenin occupied himself only marginally, either for political motives, and immediate ones at that, or out of fondness for certain writers and certain works. In other cases he made his judgments only as occasional remarks, not attaching any particular importance to them and certainly never expecting that his tastes or casual criticisms would ever become a palimpsest from which the outlines of a Leninist esthetics would be derived.

Lenin's return to postulates established at one time by Marx and Engels, with which he was never acquainted, is a very significant fact, but what is most interesting to us is his dialectical view of artistic problems. In what he says, the work and the creator always appear in relation to social, political, party matters, and at the same time he endows them with relative autonomy. Such is this rich heritage, despite the meagerness of the theses. Today's Marxist esthetics tries to take up the heritage of Lenin, opposing on the one hand simplifications that reduce the work of art to a product of the given social situation, and on the other hand, conceptions that divorce literature and art from their social basis.

In conclusion, I should like to call attention to two qualities of Lenin that appeared in his esthetic writings as in everything he did: his genius and his modesty. Not being a specialist in matters of art and esthetics (a fact which he recognized) he submitted to the decisions of experts. At the same time, as a politician and a philosopher, he put forth ideas and suggestions that laid a foundation for the specialists. In his work as a literary critic, Lenin showed two conjoined qualities that characterized him as a man, a leader of the Bolshevik party and a scholar—revolutionary make-up and humanism.

Arnold Toynbee (essay date 1970)

SOURCE: "A Centenary View of Lenin," in *International Affairs,* Vol. XXXXVI, No. 3, July, 1970, pp. 490-500.

[*In the following essay, Toynbee explains why Lenin remains one of the most important twentieth-century historical figures despite the failure of communism.*]

Everyone has been speaking or writing of Lenin recently, and there is very little that I can add.

I will start with the obvious: Lenin is one of the few people in our lifetime who has been recognised within his own lifetime as being a figure of first-class importance in world history. By 'world history', of course, I mean the tail-end of world history, just the last 5,000 years during which there have been records of people. No doubt there were as many other distinguished and able people in every branch of life in the first million years, but we do not have any record of them. But even to be as distinguished among people in the last 5,000 years as to be world-famous in your lifetime is quite an achievement.

Let us think for a moment of other people who have had the same immediate success. One thinks, first of all, of political people, and above all, conquerors, people like Alexander, or Caesar, or the Emperor Constantine the Great. They were world-famous—at least famous at our end of the Old World, on our side of the Old World—in their own lifetime. And they had Chinese counterparts who, I expect, when China becomes the dominant nation in the world in the next fifty or a hundred years, will be household words in the whole world, as Caesar and Alexander are in the West today. These Chinese names are not household words at present. They will be, but I will not mention them yet.

What other kinds of immediately world-famous people can one think of? There have been some religious leaders. In our world, of course, Luther and Calvin, who were so shocking that they immediately became famous in this tiny Western Europe. Some of the greater religious leaders did not become famous in their own lifetimes. The Buddha was the son of a small king, heir to a kingdom if he had chosen to be that, and he had the entrée to the bigger kings round about him (in Bihar and that part of India), so he was known socially, so to speak, to the great of his time. I doubt if any of the kings who received him because he was his father's son took him seriously as going to be *the* Buddha, the founder of one of the religions or philosophies which was going to have the majority of mankind for its adherents. Jesus, of course, was certainly not famous in His own lifetime. There is hardly any record of His existence by contemporary—or even later—Greek or Roman historians. Mohammed went into politics (and politics is the quick way, especially politics conducted by war, to immediate fame), yet Mohammed just missed being world-famous in his own lifetime. Just before he died, after he had conquered Arabia, he wrote to the Roman and Persian emperors, saying: 'Accept Islam, or else'. And they thought this an awful joke. Of course, six years later they did not think it a joke at all, either of them, but by that time Mohammed was dead, so he just missed it.

Then, if you think of artists who have become world famous in their own lifetimes, I suppose the Renaissance Italians who are known by their Christian names, Michelangelo, Leonardo, Raphael, and so on, must have been famous in their own lifetime, though only within our small Western world.

What of the scientists, Western scientists, who have become quickly famous? I suppose Copernicus was famous in his own lifetime; certainly Galileo was, and certainly Newton was, and certainly Darwin. When you say just 'Darwin', everyone knows that, out of all the Charles Darwins, you mean that particular one. That is real fame! Of course, Darwin was shocking, like Luther and Calvin, and this is one quick way to fame.

But, coming back to our generation, I can really think of only one other person who became immediately famous in his own lifetime, and that is Einstein. Lenin and Einstein, a curious pair: the supreme political leader, and the supreme thinker. Einstein, of course, is in that series that begins with Copernicus and Galileo. On second thoughts, I can think of two more: Freud and Hitler. But even now I have only four.

Of course, there may be people now living who are at present completely obscure, but who may become world-famous posthumously. I have mentioned Jesus. Mendel in the 19th century is another case. No one really knew about Mendel when he was abbot of a monastery, in Moravia. Then suddenly his work was discovered thirty or forty years after his death, and now anyone who has a glimmering of knowledge of science knows Mendel's name.

. . . . .

Now I have starred Lenin—I have put him with Einstein and Freud and Hitler as one of four people who became world famous in our time. So let us see if we can debunk him. That is always a healthy exercise. I say at once that I do not think we can debunk Lenin, but we can have a try.

So, first question: Has Lenin really changed the course of Russian history? Has not Lenin's revolution merely reproduced the previous Imperial Russian régime in a more extreme form—more authoritarian, more autocratic, more ruthless, but still unmistakably Muscovite? Is he not (a French analogy) like Napoleon? Did not Lenin outdo Peter the Great in the way Napoleon outdid Louis XIV? Napoleon did what some of the ministers of the *Ancien Régime* dreamed of doing but could not do,

and Napoleon achieved it. And is not Lenin like that, as compared with, say, Nicholas I? I think that is true, but I also think it is not the last word.

Then, economics: Lenin said something like—I can't remember the exact words—'Socialism is electrification'. A very striking phrase. But, in this forceful imposition on Russia of modern Western technology, was not Lenin just continuing, in Peter the Great's high-handed way, the bout of Western technology that Peter had started before the close of the 17th century? I think that is true, but, again, it is not the last word about Lenin.

Then, Lenin might claim to have transformed a nation of peasants into a nation of urban industrial workers. That is quite true, but this was happening at high speed in Russia before the First World War and before the Bolshevik Revolution of 1917. Russia's immediate pre-First World War economic development has, I think, been rather obscured by the fact that Russia gave such a poor technological performance in the First World War. It was poor compared with the contemporary performance in the First World War of Germany and the Western allies. But, compared to Russia's recent past, Russia's economic development—the growth of industries, the growth of urban population—during the twenty-five or thirty years before 1914 was terrific. So, has Lenin really done more than speed up things which were already going strong before he had a chance of taking control of Russia? In fact, did not the First World War, and the Russian Revolution, and the Civil War after that, merely retard a process that might have gone faster if Lenin had not intervened? Can Lenin therefore really be given credit for the resumption of Russia's pre-war industrialisation? Was he perhaps a retarding factor?

Again, industrialisation and urbanisation were not just a Russian phenomenon. In Russia these things had been done relatively late and had been relatively feeble. But this movement had started in Britain more than a century before 1870, the year in which Lenin was born. Was not Lenin merely the local instrument of an impersonal technological and social revolution that has been worldwide, and that did not begin or end either with Russia or with Lenin? Again, that is true, I think, but it does not dispose of Lenin.

. . . . .

So I am going to say why I think that Lenin is, all the same, an historic figure, and why I think that debunking, though one can do it rather plausibly, does not finish him off. I am going to say why I think he remains as big as before. I think that, whether we like it or not, Lenin's career is maybe 'the wave of the future'—a grim thought, but I think it may be true. Yet even if his career were just to miss being 'the wave of the future', it would certainly have come near enough to being that to ensure for Lenin his place as an historic figure. It is now more than half a century since Lenin seized power in Russia in 1917; already we can begin to see Lenin's career in perspective. We can see its effect on world history so far.

Now, I suggest three reasons why Lenin is—at least, so it seems to me—historic, whatever may be going to happen in the future to confirm or diminish his position. I think I see three things that Lenin stands for, or symbolises, or is posthumously working for.

First of all, the repudiation of the modern Western middle-class way of life and attitude to life, except (and this is a big exception) for technology and for the background and basis of technology in science.

Second, the revival of an intolerant, dogmatic, religious faith. Because Communism *is* a religion, and a religion of a particular family; it is religion of the Jewish-Christian-Muslim family, call it the Judaic family if you like. It is very thinly disguised. God—He is there as 'Historical Necessity'; the Chosen People—they are there as 'the Proletariat'. The millennium—that is there as 'the withering of the state'; the heathen raging furiously against Zion and not being able to prevail—that is in the Communist doctrine about the pre-destined fate of the capitalist world.

Of course Communism—Marxism—was invented in the Western world; it was invented by two Westerners from the Rhineland, one of whom spent most of his life in the British Museum Reading Room, and the other as manager of a small factory in Manchester in order to support Marx—I am talking of the amiable and disinterested Engels. Communism could have been invented only in the Western part of the world. It is inconceivable, I think, that Marxism could have been invented either in the Indian part of the world or in the East Asian part. It could not have been invented, either, in the pre-Christian Graeco-Roman world, which was much more like present-day India and Eastern Asia than like the post-Christian and post-Muslim western end of the Old World.

These are two things which make Lenin historic. The third thing is the belief in the need for, and in the legitimacy of, dictatorship. Let me enlarge a little on these three points about Lenin, because I think they are important in trying to estimate his place in history.

The repudiation of modern Western civilisation. In 1870 our Western middle-class civilisation was dominant in the world. Its enemies, as well as its friends, assumed that it had come to stay, in fact that this was 'the wave of the future'. You can establish certain conventional dates for the beginning of modern Western civilisation. You might say that the military date is the failure of the second Turkish siege of Vienna in 1682-83. After that, until the First World War and until the Russian Revolution, the Western civilisation had no formidable enemies in the world to face. It was dominant. Or you

might take, on a political plane, 'the Glorious Revolution' in this country in 1688. Or, on the intellectual and cultural plane, which is really more important, you might take the foundation of the Royal Society in 1660 or the 'Battle of the Books' in the latter part of the 17th century, the triumph of the idea that, after all, the Ancients were not oracles for ever, and that the Moderns had gone beyond the Ancients and had something to say which the Ancients did not know.

Those things together make the beginning of the Modern Age, I think, and they all happened in the latter part of the 17th century. Notice that Peter the Great of Russia was converted to modern Western civilisation just at that time, at the end of the 17th century. Notice also that Saint Vladímir, the Christianiser of Russia, was the first person to impose an ideology on Russia by force. Vladímir was converted to Eastern Orthodox Christianity when the Byzantine Empire was apparently on top of the world. It is rather interesting that it was *apparently,* but not really. It had a crash almost immediately afterwards, just as our Western civilisation had a crash, immediately after Lenin's career, as a result of the cumulative effect of the two world wars.

Now Lenin repudiated and challenged modern Western civilisation at a time when this seemed, to ordinary reason, unassailable. The West's dominance lasted from Peter's conversion to Lenin's challenge. You might say that, each time, it was a Russian who decided when the dominance of the West should begin (Peter decided that) and when it should end (Vladímir Ulyanov, the *new* Vladímir, decided that).

Now, since Lenin's death, on January 21, 1924, this challenge that Lenin initiated has grown. The external challenge to the West was delivered at first just by Russia. That was not new, because Peter the Great had challenged the West by adopting Western weapons as long ago as the end of the 17th century. But now we have China, Vietnam, Cuba, the liquidation of the Western colonial empires, Black Power in the United States, race conflict in this country—the challenge to white Western dominance has grown. Many non-Western peoples, of course, have rebelled against the West, against the West's military, political and cultural domination, in order to westernise their way of life voluntarily. That was Peter's reaction. That was the Meiji Revolution's reaction in Japan. It was also Atatürk's reaction in Turkey; and Communist Russia might involuntarily go the same way, because the compulsive power of technology is tremendous. If you do not adopt the latest modern technology, you fall behind in the race for power; if you do adopt it, then, as a consequence, you have to adopt dozens of other things besides, and the westernising process runs away with you.

A more significant revolt against modern Western civilisation is the internal revolt. I am not talking just about the hippies, who are perhaps exhibitionists, or about the militant students, who are, after all, a smallish minority. I am thinking, first of all, of the non-militant students who are rejecting the profit-motive and are opting for non-remunerative, or not very remunerative, liberal professions. This is the real portent, I think, in the United States today. And it is amusing to think that Lenin would—at least, so I believe—have disapproved, first of all, of the anti-technology movement; and, secondly, he would certainly have disapproved of the students being free to choose their careers (though Lenin himself, of course, chose his career freely, because he was brought up in a relatively liberal society; for even 19th-century Tsarism was a relatively free society). Lenin would also have disapproved of industrial workers using their trades-union organisation as a weapon in a free-for-all free-enterprise scramble for the fruits of technology. He recognised that the peasantry in Russia were potential capitalists and free enterprisers, and that is why he rejected any reliance on them and broke, over this, with the social revolutionaries. But he did not recognise that the industrial workers were going to go the same way.

Then, the revival of an intolerant, dogmatic religious faith. Lenin's religious career shows, I think, how difficult it is to jump clear of the cultural tradition of the society in which one has been born and brought up. Russia has been converted forcibly three times so far: by the first Vladímir to Eastern Orthodox Byzantine Christianity; by Peter to modern Western civilisation; and by Lenin to Communism, which is a modern Western rejection of modern Western civilisation.

Communism rejects two of the things which, to our minds, have been at the root of modern Western civilisation since the close of the 17th century, religious toleration and scientific open-mindedness. I suppose these are two facets of the same attitude of mind. Now, I think the first of those conversions—the conversion of Russia by Vladímir to Orthodox Eastern Christianity—has been by far the most important of the three, and I think it has continued to govern Russia's *Weltanschauung* through all her superficial metamorphoses since then. It was not for nothing that Lenin's Christian name was Vladímir.

This notion of Eastern Orthodoxy starts very early. The Greeks were civilised, the Romans were barbarians (though they conquered the Greeks). Greek Christianity, that was the orthodox form of Christianity. Western Christianity, that was deviationist. Catholicism and Protestantism—an Eastern Orthodox Christian cannot see the difference between them; to him they are both equally deviationist. Both have the same aberration in the creed. Now today Marxism, though Western, is orthodox for Russians and liberalism is heterodox. Russian Marxism is ultra-orthodox, but Western Marxism is just a capitulation to liberalism; it is not really Marxism at all.

Now Lenin's rejection of the Mensheviks, of the German revisionists and of the Second International re-

minds me of the Russians' rejection of the Ecclesiastical Union of Florence in 1439. You remember that, at that time, the Metropolitan of the Russian Church was a Greek. He came back from the Council of Florence to Russia with the Act of Union in his pocket, and the Russians kicked him out, saying 'We're not standing for this. We're the real Orthodox. You Greeks can come to terms with the schismatic Western Latins if you like, but not we'. This is very much like Lenin's attitude towards Western Marxists—'These degenerate Western Marxists'.

I think that in all ages since about the year 1,000—Vladímir was converted in 989—Russia has been Orthodox in her own eyes, and from this it follows inevitably that all the rest of the world ought to follow Russia's interpretation of Orthodoxy, or else it will be convicting itself of being heterodox. Russia is always the sole depository and citadel of the new faith. Lenin, I think, could not have repudiated Orthodox Christianity (he was brought up as a child as an ordinary Russian Orthodox Christian), if he had not replaced Orthodox Christianity by orthodox Marxism. I do not think he could have been just a sceptic or a scientific researcher with an open mind, as his elder brother, Alexander, was. Lenin believed, I think sincerely and unquestioningly, in the dogmas of Communism. But he believed in these dogmas as interpreted by Lenin. To Lenin, non-Leninist Marxism was anathema, perhaps even more anathema than non-Marxism or even than anti-Marxism.

This reminds me of a passage in Herzen's Memoirs. In this passage Herzen is standing on the Swiss Frontier in 1848 watching the failed West European revolutionaries streaming across the frontier into Switzerland for asylum. And Herzen comments: 'These miserable Western revolutionaries. Of course they have failed, the half-hearted creatures. When we make *our* revolution in Russia, we will show them what a real revolution is.' Herzen died in 1870, the year in which Lenin was born, but already he had foreseen what Lenin was going to do.

Lenin did not overlap chronologically as a grown-up person either with Herzen or with Marx. Marx died in 1883; Engels died in 1895, I think, and I have seen it said that Lenin quotes Engels rather more than Marx—Engels being a nearer contemporary is more real to him. Lenin was 25 when Engels died. I do not know whether he had already begun to read Marxist writings.

Then, thirdly, there is the belief in, and the need for, and the legitimacy of, dictatorship. And here I fear that Lenin's career may indeed be 'the wave of the future', though I hate to say so. Dictatorship has often been accepted as a lesser evil than anarchy in times of very revolutionary change; and majority rule by secret ballot, free speech, and free thought are, after all, spiritual luxuries, characteristic of times when life is relatively tranquil and secure. Today the human race is in the throes of the urban industrial revolution, the greatest revolution in human history since the agricultural revolution which was made about 8,000 or 10,000 years ago; and even lesser revolutions have produced dictatorships.

Russia is in the Roman tradition of revolutionary dictatorship. The Roman imperial office was always a revolutionary institution, never a constitutional one. Anyone could become Roman Emperor who had the ruthlessness, the ability, and the energy to force his way to the top, and, once he had done so, he was consecrated by having seized power. That goes through all the history of the Roman Empire and the Byzantine Empire, and, though dynasties in Russia have lasted rather longer than they did in the Roman and Byzantine Empires, I think there has always been this revolutionary aspect of autocracy in Russia too. This is why, unhappily, I think that Lenin's career might be 'the wave of the future', because I think that the conditions in the whole world today are pretty like the condition of Russia in Lenin's lifetime. We have world-wide anarchy today—nationalism, racialism, inflation, sabotage of all kinds, the generation-war, the revolt of the under-dog, the pollution of the natural environment by technology. Any one of those things is enough to hoist a dictator into power, and we have them all. So the world, I fear, is ripe for ruthless dictators, self-righteous and therefore self-confident, because a dictator believes himself to be the sole possessor of the orthodox faith and the sole agent for making orthodoxy prevail, and of course orthodoxy ought to be made to prevail. That is what the Roman Emperor Theodosius I thought when, at the end of the 4th century, he rammed Christianity down the throats of the non-Christian majority of the population of the Roman Empire.

So is not Lenin's career a trial trip for a coming world dictatorship?

. . . . .

Let me conclude with a word or two about Lenin's personality and career. The great thing about his beginning, I think, is that he had a very normal middle-class family background and upbringing. His father was an efficient and devoted civil servant who spread primary schools in the Simbirsk province, a rather outlying province of European Russia. What is interesting is that Lenin's father did not question the Imperial régime, and it did not question him. What he was doing really, in spreading primary education, was an extremely revolutionary act, but he was rewarded for it by being ennobled. Lenin was thus technically a noble.

Psychologists tell us that the things that change your inborn character, that warp it or develop it, are things that happen very early. Now, nothing bad or upsetting happened to Lenin very early. When his brother Alexander was put to death, Lenin was 17. I am sure this influenced Lenin's career, but I doubt whether it changed his character or personality at that age. I suspect that Lenin would have been what he was and that he would have done what he did, even if his brother,

instead of being put to death, had lived on, leading a peaceful life as a biologist or even as a monk—Alexander Ulyanov was rather monk-like in character. Indeed, he was a characteristic representative of one type of Russian hero, the non-violent martyr. The prototypes are the two princely saints Borís and Gleb, who were too proud to fight and who voluntarily gave themselves up to be put to death though they were the rightful heirs to the throne. I fancy that Alexander's fate confirmed Lenin's intention not himself to go like a lamb to the slaughter, as his brother had done, but to be Machiavelli's 'prophet armed', which is what he became. Of course Lenin suffered very unfairly for his brother's condemnation. He was banned from the university; he was not allowed to have a proper higher education. He was exiled to Siberia. A monstrous injustice and a grievance, but would not Lenin have been a revolutionary even if he had not been penalised? Was not his whole generation going to be revolutionary? After the reaction that had followed the assassination of Alexander II, was not revolution in the air in Russia in Lenin's time?

Personal life? All I will say about that is that I do not think any of the Communist leaders had time for much personal life, especially sexual life. They were rather Victorian about that, I think, not hypocritical Victorians, but *bona fide* ones.

Lenin's self-confidence is the astonishing thing about his personality. What was at the root of his self-confidence? As he was technically an aristocrat, one might think it was the same sort of self-confidence as the late Lord Russell had or the present Lord Salisbury has. A British aristocrat, when he has come to the conclusion that he is right, will back his opinion against the world. Perhaps the rest of us, if we are moved strongly by our conscience, may do the same, but we can do it only with agony. The British aristocrat does it effortlessly and painlessly. Now Lenin did it effortlessly and painlessly. And I think there may have been a touch in him of the late Lord Russell or the present Lord Salisbury. But I think the main part of his self-confidence came, not from his rather recent aristocratic label, but from religious conviction. I think this is more probable. If you are convinced that you know for certain what is true and right, say Marxism, and if you are also convinced that you alone know exactly what is true and right, this conviction will give you the self-confidence to defy the world single-handed whether you are an aristocrat or not. I think that in Lenin there was something of the late Lord Russell, but I feel that there was very much more of St. Paul.

When I read about Lenin's time in exile, when he muscled his way in among much older and more distinguished Russian revolutionaries, it reminds me of the second part of the Acts of the Apostles. Here is James, the brother of the Lord and the hereditary head of the Christian community, and here is Peter, the doyen of the Apostles, and Paul comes muscling in and says, 'I am an apostle, too', and they had to accept him. They say, 'But you represent nothing', and he says, 'You are wrong. I represent the majority of the population of the Roman Empire, whom I am going to convert, and you represent only a small sect of Jews'. In that critical vote in 1903, when the Bolsheviks and the Mensheviks split, there was a stage, I think, at which Lenin's party was actually the minority, but of course he called his party the majority party, the Bolshevik party. And the interesting thing is that the others became identified as being the minority, which of course is fatal for anyone. Lenin could put that over. This is very like St. Paul.

I think that self-identification with a cause is probably necessary if one's will to power, and we all have the will to power in some form, is to be uninhibited, to be total, to be devoted, ascetic and ruthless—here comes St. Paul again. Unless you can identify your personal will to power with a supra-personal cause, you cannot have the face to fight for your will to power. You have got to be unaware of the difference between your will to power and your cause.

The Russians in exile all adopted pseudonyms, and of course there was a matter-of-fact reason for this; they wanted to evade the secret police. But remember that monks, when they take their vows, adopt a new name as a symbol that they are starting a new life, and I think that, in these funny pseudonyms that Lenin and Trotsky and Stalin all adopted, there is an element of this monkish devotion which was a very strong spiritual force in the Russia in which Lenin grew up.

Finally, one word about the types of Russian revolutionary. I have mentioned the Borís and Gleb type which was represented by Lenin's elder brother Alexander. Then there is the Bazarov type, represented by the hero of Turgenev's *Fathers and Sons,* a revolutionary thinker who comes to a dead end, for whom suicide is the only way out. It is said that Lenin's favourite 19th-century Russian novelist was Turgenev, not Dostoyevsky. Dostoyevsky came too near to the bone, perhaps. Anyway, Lenin was not going to be a Bazarov; he was not going to come to a dead end and commit suicide; he was going to get through—as he did. Then there is the silly type in Dostoyevsky's *The Possessed,* the figure of fun, Stefan Trofimovich, a very common type among Russian revolutionaries abroad. That is why Lenin could knock most of them down like ninepins. Then there is the ruthless, practical type—Stefan Trofimovich's son, Piotr Stefanovich, the sinister hero of *The Possessed.* There is a lot of Lenin in Piotr Stefanovich. I do not think that Lenin was cynical through and through; I think he was cynical about the means he used, but not cynical about his ends. Dostoyevsky leaves you thinking that Piotr Stefanovich was cynical about everything. All the same, I think you can learn a good deal about Lenin from Dostoyevsky's portrayal of Stefan Trofimovich. You can also admire Dostoyevsky's amazing prescience in foreseeing what was coming a generation or two generations ahead of the event.

Lewis S. Feuer (essay date 1971)

SOURCE: "Between Fantasy and Reality: Lenin as a Philosopher and a Social Scientist," in *Lenin and Leninism: State, Law, and Society,* edited by Bernard W. Eissenstat, Lexington Books, 1971, pp. 59-79.

[*In the following essay, Feuer argues that Lenin's philosophical beliefs vacillated between sober materialism and utopian fantasy.*]

"'We ought to dream!' I wrote these words and got scared," Lenin said in his famous factional pamphlet *What Is to Be Done?* published in 1902. He dreamed of a centralized revolutionary organization in which "Social-Democratic Zheliabovs" would emerge; then he would dare say, a socialist Archimedes moving the social universe with an organizational lever: "'Give us an organization of revolutionists, and we shall overturn the whole of Russia!'" But inevitably, he wondered whether "a Marxist has any right at all to dream." Was his dream a fantasy like that which had moved Zheliabov to assassinate a czar? Was he enthralled by an illusion that a few bold revolutionists could open the way to a remaking of society and humanity? Was his choice of Zheliabov as a hero-model one which indicated Lenin's own fear that in his dream he was losing his hold on reality? He pondered what the connection between dream and reality should be, and this problem never left him all his life. He wrote that he would conceal himself "behind the back of Pisarev: 'There are differences and differences,' wrote Pisarev concerning the question of the difference between dreams and reality. 'My dream may run ahead of the natural progress of events or may fly off at a tangent in a direction to which no natural progress of events will ever succeed. . . . Divergence between dreams and reality causes no harm if only the person dreaming believes seriously in his dream, . . . and if, generally speaking, he works conscientiously for the achievement of his fantasies. If there is some connection between dreams and life then all is well!'"

More than a decade later, living in exile in Switzerland, with the world at war, his own movement shattered, Lenin was moved to think again: had fantasy penetrated his Marxist science? He immersed himself in the study of Hegelian texts and classical philosophy, seeking an answer to his life-problem. Then he confided boldly to his notebook that all human thought partakes of fantasy:

> The approach of the (human) mind to a particular thing, the taking of a copy (equal a concept) of it *is not* a simple, immediate act, a dead mirroring, but one which is complex, split into two, zig-zag-like, which *includes in it* the possibility of the flight of fantasy from life; more than that: the possibility of the *transformation* (moreover, an unnoticeable transformation, of which man is unaware) of the abstract concept, idea, into a *fantasy* (in letzter Instanz equal God). For even the simplest generalisation, in the most elementary general idea ('table' in general) *there*

is a certain bit of fantasy. (Vice versa: it would be stupid to deny the role of fantasy, even in the strictest science: *cf.* Pisarev on useful dreaming, as an impulse *to* work, and on empty day-dreaming).

This tension between fantasy and reality is probably the underlying theme of Lenin's work as a philosopher as well as his approach to social science. A man's philosophy and methodology are the outcome of his deepest strivings and anxieties. Lenin, as we shall see, in his lifetime alternated between two philosophies. At the outset, he endeavored to cling fast to reality; he was a simple materialist, ridiculing the dialectic of Hegel as virtual nonsense, and so hardheaded toward the sentimental "flabby" intellectuals that he reveled in the prospect of an authoritarian bureaucracy. When he brooded in solitary retreat during the First World War, however, he thrust reality away from him and allowed himself to yield to the solace of Utopian fantasy. Then he wrote that he was the only Marxist alive; he professed to find a master key to existence in the Hegelian triads; he saw the apocalyptic end of imperialism as a chapter in human history, and the virtual end of all bureaucracy within twenty-four hours after the triumph of the revolution. The materialist and social factualist became the metaphysician and Utopian. This oscillation between extremes remains embedded in Lenin's legacy to the intellectual life of the Soviet Union.

Lenin's first philosophical writing was part of his first book, published in 1894, entitled *What the "Friends of the People" Are and How They Fight the Social Democrats*. Like all his writing, it was polemical in character; Lenin was never impelled to study a subject for love of it; it was all part of a fight. In this case, Lenin was replying especially to the distinguished thinker of the elder generation, Nikolai Mikhailovsky, who had criticized the so-called dialectical method of Marx and Engels. What Lenin did was to reject dialectical materialism in favor of "scientific materialism." At the age of twenty-four, as a young revolutionary agitator, Lenin found the dialectic a lot of residual verbal nonsense. Anyone who reads the description of the dialectical method given by Marx in *Capital,* he wrote, "will see that the Hegelian triads are not even mentioned, and that it all amounts to regarding social evolution as the development of social-economic formations as a process of natural history." When Marx described what he meant by the dialectical method, asked Lenin, was there "even a single word, about triads, trichotomies, the unimpeachableness of the dialectical process, and suchlike nonsense . . . ?" In effect, says Lenin, Marx's use of the word "dialectic" had become vestigial. "No other role remains for the triads than as a lid and a skin ('I coquetted with the modes of expression peculiar to Hegel,' Marx says in the Preface), in which only philistines could be interested." To coquette with phrases is scarcely the mark of a serious passion, even a philosophical one. Marx derived his prediction of the downfall of the capitalist order from a study of its facts

and trends, not from triadic formulae, says Lenin, and what he coquettishly called the dialectical method was "nothing more nor less than the scientific method in sociology. . . ."

This then was Lenin at the outset of his career, a self-confident scientific materialist, a believer in a complete "determinism, which establishes the necessity of human acts and rejects the absurd fable about free will," ridiculing the "subjective method" in sociology, rejecting any notion that psychological variables, intellectual, sexual, have any independent causal efficacy in history. The ensuing years brought a bitter party factionalism; the choice of comrades for Lenin was translated into a rejection of comrades. Peter Struve, Julius Martov, George Plekhanov; towards all of them Lenin had a strong emotional attachment, so emotional that he would be embarrassed by his own feelings. And toward all of them he disciplined himself in accordance with his avowal of the primacy of politics for a rupture of relations, disciplining himself to transmute love into hatred. It was as if Lenin had a compulsive need to turn this weakness of his into a hatred, to harden himself. When he broke with the father of Russian Marxism, George Plekhanov, whom he revered, he wrote a document [**"How the *Spark* was Nearly Extinguished"**] which was poignant in the agony of its self-revelation:

> We walked, bursting with indignation. . . . His (Plekhanov's) behavior was insulting to such a degree that one could not help suspecting him of harboring 'unclean' thoughts about ourselves. . . . He tramples us underfoot, etc. . . . My 'infatuation' with Plekhanov disappeared as if by magic, and I felt offended and embittered to the highest degree. Never, never in my life, have I regarded any other man with such sincere respect and veneration. I have never stood before any man with such 'humility' as I stood before him, and never before have I been so brutally 'spurned'. We were actually spurned. We were scared like little children when grown-ups threaten to leave them, and when we funked (shame!) we were unceremoniously brushed aside in the most incredible manner.
>
> Such mixed, heavy, confused feelings. It was a real drama; the complete abandonment of a thing which for years we had tended like a favorite child. . . . And all because we were formerly enamoured with Plekanov. . . . Young comrades 'court' an old comrade out of the great love they bear for him—and suddenly he injects into this love an atmosphere of intrigue! He compels us to feel not as younger brothers, but as fools to be led by the nose, pawns to be moved at will. . . . An enamoured youth receives from the object of his love a bitter lesson: To regard all persons 'without sentiment'; to keep a stone in one's sling. Many more thoughts of an equally bitter nature did we give utterance to that night. . . . Blinded by our love, we had actually behaved like *slaves*. To be a slave is humiliating, and the sense of shame we felt was magnified a hundredfold by

the fact that 'he himself had forced us to realize how humiliating our position was.'

Is it I, the fervent worshipper of Plekhanov, who am now filled with bitter thoughts about him? Is it I, with clenched teeth, and a devilish chill at the heart, hurling cold and bitter words at him in announcing what is almost our 'breaking off of relations'? Perhaps it is only an ugly dream?

Indeed, so profoundly moved was I that at times I thought I would burst into tears . . . On the surface everything appeared as if nothing had happened; the apparatus must continue to work as it worked before. But we felt an internal twinge—instead of friendly relations, dry, business-like relations prevailed, we were always to be on guard, on the principle: *Si vis pacem, para bellum*.

II

Statesmen—Balfour, Smuts, Clemenceau—have not infrequently written philosophical works, but invariably they have been written as postpolitical reflections on the meaning of things. Lenin is the only man in history who wrote an epistemological book as part of his tactical plan to defeat another faction within his party. The book has one thesis, that materialism, defined as the belief in the reality of the external physical world, is the only ideology to which a true revolutionist, scientist, or man of common sense can subscribe. Sometimes he confuses this meaning of materialism as physical realism with materialism in two other senses, one, the notion that "nature is the sole reality," that supernatural entities don't exist, and the other, an evolutionary sense, in which materialism means that physical entities preceded the existence of mental ones. The villains of Lenin's book are the philosophical idealists and their ilk, from Bishop Berkeley to the physicist Ernst Mach, who dare to affirm that we can meaningfully speak only of observable elements. The book has more invective per page than any work written in the history of philosophy, and indeed, if one were to ask what its philosophical method was, we might say: usually the method of invective. Nonetheless, Bertrand Russell wrote a comparatively benign estimate of it, in 1934, to be sure, at a time during the depression when he was more sympathetic to Bolshevism.

While I do not think that materialism can be *proved,* I think Lenin is right in saying that it is not *dis*proved by modern physics. Since his time, and largely as a reaction against his success, respectable physicists have moved further and further from materialism, and it is naturally supposed, by themselves and by the general public, that it is physics which has caused this movement. I agree with Lenin that no substantially new argument has emerged since the time of Berkeley, with one exception.

This one exception Russell oddly enough found in the instrumentalist theory, which he attributed to Marx, that "truth" is a practical rather than a theoretical conception.

How shall we appraise Lenin's argument, and why was it that any departure from materialism struck him as a deviation and heresy, making its proponent a fit candidate for excommunication?

Lenin himself acknowledges: "by no proofs, or syllogisms, or definitions would it be possible to refute the solipsist." Then what shall be done with the person who says with Fichte: "the world is my sensation" (or with Wittgenstein in our time: "I am my world")? "Any healthy person," writes Lenin, "who is not an inmate of an insane asylum, or in the school of idealist philosophers" holds to "'naive realism'," a belief which "consists in this, that he believes reality, the environment and the things in it, to exist independently of his perception." The mental health, the sanity of the party, seem to Lenin to be at stake with the philosophical issue of materialism, "a problem concerning the confidence of man in the evidence of his sense-organs." Materialism, he insists, is "the instinctive viewpoint held by humanity which accepts the existence of the outer world independently of the mind." Those philosophies which purport to explicate a nonspatial, nontemporal existence are "products of a diseased mind." Nor will Lenin admit of any departure from the definition of truth as correspondence to fact. He is impatient with empiricists and pragmatists who speak of truth as an "organizing form of human experience," or who try to translate "the objective character of the physical world" as its "inter-subjectively verified" status. For, says Lenin, there are all sorts of ways for organizing human experience; every culture, as we would say, is a socially endorsed form for organizing human experience. And for the majority of mankind, Lenin observes, "house goblins and wood demons" are part of a "socially organized experience"; if so, then to say they exist is "truth," if all "truth" means is its employment to organize human experience.

What perturbs Lenin is that every definition of truth, other than as simple correspondence to fact, somehow loosens man's hold on reality. Every other definition refuses to acknowledge that the person does really get to know something about the existent world; every other definition concedes that the world given to us in perception may still be a phantom, a stage-play, an illusion. Every other definition of truth, by its very departure from the criterion of correspondence, introduces into itself an "alienation" of man from reality, as the current phrase goes. As Lenin states it, the idealist philosopher takes sensation not as a connection with the external world "but as a screen, as a wall which separates the mind from the outer world." The empiricists, Lenin protests, "do not sufficiently trust the evidence of our sense-organs." The Kantians likewise say, "that the thing exists in itself, but is unknowable." And the final test of the "absurdity" of a philosophy is that it leads one toward solipsism, toward the view that "the world is my sensation."

Lenin expounds what philosophers call a "copy theory of knowledge"; "sensations," he writes, are "the true copy of the objective world." A sound scientific theory, he holds, is "a copy, as an approximate reflection of objective reality." Scientific truth is founded on "a reality which is copied, photographed, and reflected by our sensations." Among revisionist Marxists today, especially the group of young Yugoslav philosophers associated with the magazine *Praxis,* Lenin's theory of sensation has been especially under attack. It is charged that Lenin's view that sensation provides a reflection of reality is the epistemological source of Stalinism. Lenin did, of course, insist that "human practice," which had eventuated in man's domination over nature, "is a result of an accurate objective 'reflection' within the mind of man." Although the science of any given historical period is only a relative approximation to the truth, still, said Lenin, each approximation does incorporate more of that absolute truth: "but it is unconditionally true that this picture reflects an objectively existing model."

The revisionist Marxists, however, seem to me to have fallen into the Leninist fallacy in reverse; their argument that Lenin's theory of reflection is the foundation for Stalinism seems to me to be based on misconceptions concerning the relation of philosophy to politics. The *Praxis* philosophers argue that Stalinism was founded on the notion that the correct theory in social science was a "reflection" of the inevitable line of development; therefore, it would be sound practice to compel everybody to follow that line of development; the Communist party, as scientific Marxists, would enunciate the correct line. Instead, say the *Praxis* philosophers, there are alternative lines of possible development, and the decision as to which will be actualized rests on the involvement, the engagement, of human actors who make their own history. The "truth" is not a "reflection" of a preexistent or predetermined reality but rather something which is created in human decision which shapes, constructs, and reconstructs reality rather than "reflects" it.

We might undertake to reply to the revisionists on Lenin's behalf. We would say: the revisionists are not really discussing the definition of truth; they are arguing against sociological determinism. The revisionists are arguing that the basic laws of sociology do not have a determinist form but that rather they are characterized, as far as predictable outcomes of systems are concerned, by domains of indeterminacy; hence, the initial states of a given social system, together with the laws of social science, never provide one with both the necessary and sufficient conditions of the emergent social state; the unpredictable role of human involvement and choice among indeterminate alternatives must be taken into account.

Let us assume that this revisionist standpoint is true. Still, it will be clear that it in no way challenges Lenin's conception of truth as correspondence to fact, or sensation as reflection of external reality. For the objective truth will now be regarded as stated by laws which provide for indeterminate domains; a principle of sociological indeterminacy will be the objective truth rather than sociological determinism. In either case, we shall be accepting as our criterion for scientific decision the crucial status of sensations as "reflecting" the objective state of things. The sociological indeterminist defends his standpoint just as much as the determinist by appealing to perceptions as reports or reflections of external reality. He avers, for instance, that perceived acts of human intervention are necessary to social outcomes, but he accepts the veracity, at least provisionally, of his perceptions, or sensations. There have been many naive realists who were democrats; and I do not think their democratic politics were inconsistent with their reflectional epistemology. The Yugoslav revisionists, like Lenin, like Stalin, have drawn too close a relationship between philosophy and politics, even though in their case, their concern is with an underpinning for more liberal values; they remain ideologists.

III

What strikes the reader as strange is the vehemence which possesses Lenin when he discusses this issue of the reality of the external world. He avails himself of Russian literary resources to ridicule the empiricists—Valentinov is like Gogol's *Petrushka,* Chernov is like Voroshilov in Turgenev's *Smoke,* others call forth Gogol's Inspector-General, the philosopher Avenarius is like Turgenev's rascal. For the great philosopher-physicist Ernst Mach, Lenin rises or stoops to the most demagogic invective: "The philosophy of Mach, the scientist, is to science what the kiss of Judas is to Christ. Mach betrays science into the hands of freedom. . . ." It would have been of no avail to point out that Mach was a stubborn anticlerical all his life. But Lenin seems himself as the Christ whom the empiricists are betraying. Nor would it have availed to observe that Mach had been, even before Lenin was born, a pioneer in the advocacy of socialistic reforms. Here was simply for Lenin a most menacing heresy, comparable to that of Judas Iscariot, subtly gnawing away at the heart of his doctrine.

The German Socialists, the French Socialists, the Italian Socialists, the American Socialists, scarcely attached any political importance to philosophical materialism. Jaurès, the great French leader, was drawn to Kantian ethical idealism, as were even such German leftists as Karl Liebknecht and Kurt Eisner. In America, the leftist organ *The International Socialist Review* was enthusiastic for the philosophy of Ernst Mach. And to Mach, the world owes the imperishable debt for the inspiration his philosophy gave to the young student in Zürich, Albert Einstein. For Einstein, partaking much of Machian ideas, especially under the stimulus of his student friend, Friedrich Adler, who was both a Marxist and a Machian, was guided to the critique of absolute space and time as unobservable entities. The theory of relativity was largely conceived under the influence of Machian emotions and a Machian frame of mind, trying to expel from one's physical theory whatever was not translatable into an observer's experiences. To Lenin, however, the philosophy of Ernst Mach signified a veritable threat to his sanity.

Indeed it is such highly personal psychological reasons rather than anything political or sociological which explain why Lenin attached so much importance to his materialism. Often enough, Lenin gave indications that he kept guard over an unstable personality, threatened by the fear of illusion, the fear of a commitment to an unreal world. Lenin's older sister told, for instance, how shaken Lenin was when he read Chekhov's short story *Ward No. 6*: "'Volodya summed up its effect on him in these words: 'When I finished reading this story last night, I felt positively afraid. I just could not remain in my room but had to get up and go out. I had the feeling that I, too, was locked up in Ward No. 6.' That had happened late at night when we had all gone to our rooms and some were even asleep, and he had nobody to talk to. Those words lifted a veil from his state of mind. . . .'" This was in the winter of 1892 in Samara. Chekhov's story was being published in a periodical, and Lenin was writing his first major work, *What the "Friends of the People" Are*; he was already a Marxist, and condescending towards the idealistic Narodniks of the older generation who were his neighbors. And in the midst of his materialistic philosophizing, the veil lifts, and he is filled with anxiety. Chekhov's story tells of an understanding reflective physician, who is in charge of a mental asylum; then through the intrigues of an assistant, he himself is declared insane. He finds himself then at the mercy of the brutal caretaker, Nikita, who beats him cruelly; the sane man has patronized the sadistic forces which misuse him, and declare him insane. He has lived in illusion; death ends his torment and insoluble problems. No wonder Lenin had the feeling that he too was locked in Ward No. 6, this strange prophetic dream was far more accurate than the Utopian declamation of *The State and Revolution*, for in the Soviet society the sane writers today find themselves thrust into insane asylums, a practice Stalin initiated and Nitika continued; thus the Soviet dialectic reached its new high stage, the rational transformed into the irrational.

Seeking to exorcise an inner anxiety of illusion, the fear that perhaps his Marxist learning was an exercise in fantasy, in myth, Lenin responded with an over-determination of his materialism. Leon Trotsky reports that when he first met Lenin, the latter was indeed drawn to Machian doctrines. But now he exorcised the Machian and the solipsist within himself. He especially polemicized against Dr. A. A. Bogdanov, a disciple of Mach, who together with Lenin had for a few years led the Bolshevik party. But now Bogdanov was leading a faction opposed to Lenin. Bogdanov, a remarkably exploratory and clear-thinking mind, was also given to

psychoanalyzing his contemporaries' philosophical divagations. He thus exerted his art on both the idealist Berdyaev, whom Lenin scorned, and on Lenin himself. Whenever Bogdanov would see Berdyaev, the latter tells, he "kept on asking all sorts of odd questions, such as, How did I feel in the morning? How did I sleep? What was my reaction to this or that? It eventually emerged that in his view my philosophical tendencies were evidence of an impending psychic disorder, and he, being by profession a psychiatrist, wanted to discover how far the process had gone." Bogdanov similarly indicated many years later what he thought was the root-source of Lenin's materialism: "'as a doctor, I concluded that Lenin occasionally suffered from a mental condition and displayed symptoms of abnormality.'"

We might call the fear that one's avowed goals are an illusion the "revolutionary anxiety." Since he is putting himself against the established norms and values of society, the "revolutionary anxiety" arises in moments of doubt; the phrases, the clichés, the programs, the manifestoes, suddenly acquire a hollow ring. The safeguarding of his materialism was a kind of defence mechanism against the revolutionary anxiety. Otherwise Lenin could have reacted mildly against empiricist and solipsist views, regarding them as men of common sense do as rather paradoxical intellectual standpoints, but scarcely looking upon their exponents as Judases, or ideological plotters. Lenin is so eager to confute the scientific standpoint of Ernst Mach that he allows himself to embark upon a polemic against the principle of economy in scientific logic, the principle which advises us to choose the simplest hypothesis among those which conform to the facts. Lenin queries challengingly: wouldn't it then be more "economical" to accept the hypothesis that the atom is indivisible rather than that it is composed of "positive and negative electrons"? Lenin's mistake is evident: he interprets the principle of economy as asserting that the world is simple; the principle does nothing of the sort: it tells you that, no matter how simple or complex the constitution of nature may be, you as a scientist will work with the simplest hypothesis which explains the facts. The hypothesis that the atom is indivisible was dropped not because it was simple but because it couldn't explain the experimental facts which such scientists as J. J. Thomson and Ernest Rutherford had adduced. Lenin's materialist defence mechanism, however, struck out wildly against whatever awakened his revolutionary anxiety. He struck out against the principle of relativity: "Another cause of 'idealistic physics' is the principle of *relativity*, the relativity of science, a principle which in a period of bankruptcy of old theories, imposes itself with special force upon physicists. . . ." No wonder that when Einstein's friend, Friedrich Adler, read Lenin's book, he said all that Lenin had proved, apart from his patient capacity to write a big book, was that he knew nothing about the subject. Einstein himself, in later years, wrote limericks about the stupidities of dialectical materialism. But Lenin's anxiety and defence mechanism was transmitted into the psyches of generations of Soviet students.

Lenin, moreover, as a simple nineteenth-century Russian materialist misconceived the relation of philosophy to the sciences, indeed, we should rather say, the relation of *philosophies* to the sciences. For this relationship is not unlike that between the philosophies and the arts. As Lenin wrote Gorky in 1908: "an artist can draw much that is useful to him from any philosophy." Similarly, different scientists have drawn inspiration in their work, models, analogues and motivations from the most diverse philosophies. In one mood, Einstein drew inspiration and guidance from Mach's empiricism; in another mood, he was doing work in the spirit of a follower of Boltzmann's atomism. Niels Bohr was somehow guided in his philosophy as a scientist, in his principle of complementarity, by a devotion to Kierkegaard and the pluralistic conciliation of his teacher Höffding. Heisenberg drew sustenance from Plato's *Timaeus.* Different philosophies are indications of different themes in the universe; none of them is controlling; and part of the life of science, the source of its vitality, is their unending alternation.

Many pages of Lenin's **Materialism and Empirio-Criticism** are strewn with invective against educators and professors. These reactionaries, he writes, aim "to implant in the high school students the spirit of idealism"; the opponent of materialism is a "police officer in a professorial chair"; "the bourgeois professors have a right to receive their salaries from reactionary governments," because they defend medieval, transcendental absurdities. "Not a single professor," he writes, even the most eminent physicists and chemists, "can be trusted even so far as a single word when it comes to philosophy. . . . [T]he professors of philosophy are scientific salesmen of theology." Why was Lenin's materialism so polemically oriented against these academics? The answer suggests itself in the facts of Lenin's own evolution from religion to materialism. Lenin's father, Ilya Nikolayevich, as Krupskaya tells us, "even though he was a teacher of physics and a meteorologist, believed in God until the end of his life. The fact that his sons had abandoned religion caused him anxiety." When the father complained to a friend "that his children were bad church attenders," the friend suggested: "Give them the stick, don't spare it." "Upon hearing this Ilyich, burning with indignation, decided to break with religion; he rushed into the garden, took off the cross that he wore around his neck, and threw it away." All this happened when Lenin was fourteen or fifteen years old.

From Lenin's standpoint, his father, the teacher of physics, the director of primary schools, the religious believer, was another police officer in the guise of an educator. The curious bitterness against academics seems to have been a recurring reenactment of Lenin's rebellion against his father's authority and religious devotion. Throughout his life he was tearing the cross from around his neck; his materialism always retained the polemical cast because it was for him less a scientific standpoint than the projection of a fixated emotion of generational rebellion.

Lenin's materialism always remained invested with emotions for overcoming feminine, or unmanly, weakness, for proving his toughness. The reactionary professors, he wrote, were succumbing to "the kisses" of the idealists and pragmatists, and were allowing themselves to be "nailed" to a pillory; these were "shameful things"; the professors in advanced capitalist countries were living in "concubinage"; the empiricists entwined all the idealistic weaknesses into a "chinese braid," this symbol of femininity, which Feuerbach had once cut off. Mach's "elements" were a "fig-leaf" for his idealism; kisses, concubines, fig-leaves, and Chinese braids, such were the metaphors for the emotional determinants of Lenin's materialism.

If Lenin indeed had followed his own suggestions that solipsism and idealism cannot be logically refuted but only psychologically analyzed, he would then have been led as well to examine the psychological basis of his own doctrine. But he could never engage in such self-scrutiny. His notion that philosophies have political consequences would have largely collapsed, for the basis of philosophies lies much more in temperament, as William James saw, than in political affiliation. But just as Lenin shrank from the subjectivist ingredient in sociology, he suppressed the suggestion of its relevance in philosophical decision. For what Lenin would have feared above all was self-knowledge of the unconscious determinants of his own materialistic dogmatism. Then the neurotic anxieties, fears, and cruelties which led to his materialistic over-affirmation would have come to view.

IV

Meanwhile, Lenin struggled with his neurosis. His nerves for years previously used to afflict him with physical inflammations and complete sleeplessness. The later years of emigration were especially hard; comrades became insane and committed suicide. "Another year or two of life in this atmosphere of squabbling and emigrant tragedy would have meant heading for a breakdown," wrote Lenin's wife. Fortunately for his sanity, the years of reaction were followed by revolutionary upsurge. Years earlier, after a series of squabbles which had led to the suicide of a famous student leader, Lenin wrote to his sister: "You'd better not wish any comrades from the intellectuals on me. . . ." "The worst thing about exile is these 'exile episodes.'" He had shaped and fashioned his personality to stamp out affections. "Friendship is friendship and work is work," Lenin would say, "and on this account the necessity for war will not disappear," as he would obliterate a friendship from his life. From the time of his adolescence he regarded Turgenev's short story *Andrei Kolosov* as the last word on love and sincerity. "He felt that Turgenev showed here, absolutely correctly and in a few lines, how to understand properly what is rather pompously called the 'sanctity' of love. He often told me that his views on this question were exactly the same as those expressed by Turgenev in *Andrei Kolosov*. 'These', he used to say, 'are not vulgar bourgeois views on the relations between men and women, but real, revolutionary ones.'" The story deals with a rather cold, calculating young man who without any compunction breaks with a girl who no longer pleases him. Evidently what pleased Lenin in the story was the hero's refusal to allow considerations of personal loyalty to sway him. When he saw Tolstoi's *The Living Corpse,* the rest of the audience sympathized with the character of the deserted wife in the play; Lenin sympathized with the deserting husband, and wanted to see the play again. Lenin tried to emulate such models, but the effort in his case involved terrific emotional strains. Krupskaya, his wife, was, according to Bernard Shaw, one of the two ugliest women in Europe. Lenin evidently could not bring himself to leave her when he loved another woman. But in more trivial matters he could more successfully fashion his character to ideological requirements. He found chess tremendously absorbing, but it impinged on the revolution; he gave it up. Skating, hunting, the study of Latin—all were eliminated from the revolutionist's life. He feared that music might deprive him of his capacity to be ruthless.

Such was Lenin's project for self-formation, to repress whatever spontaneous impulses and affections seemed inconsistent with the revolutionist's calling. When so much aggression is directed against one's self, the unconscious protests; a perpetual frustration of impulse and emotion always brings in its train a feeling of unreality; life loses its savor, and consists of a rehearsal of assigned lines in a play rather than a spontaneous partaking of life. The vehement reiteration of his materialism as a party tenet was proportional to his own feelings of unreality; he had to assure himself philosophically of an existence which his self-punitive actions were negating into nonexistence.

During the years of the World War, according to his closest coworker at that time, Gregory Zinoview, Lenin "seemed to have changed even in his appearance." Living in the poorest quarter of Zurich, "in the house of a shoemaker, in a sort of garret, his hatred of the bourgeoisie became sharp like a dagger." "Many, who knew him before," wrote Zinoview, "were surprised at the change which had taken place in him since the war." The shock of the collapse of the Second International had taken its toll. "The honor of the proletariat demanded that a war against this war be fought to a finish," and the "imperialist bandits" forever destroyed.

v

During the miserable years of exile, the temptation of the total absorption into dreams waxed stronger. Krupskaya tells: "During those very hard years of emigration, concerning which Ilyich always spoke with a feeling of sadness. . . , during those years he dreamed and dreamed," taking heart as a desperate person does from the chance good cheer of others more prosaically miserable, from a French charwoman singing: "Mais

votre coeur—vous ne l'ayez jamais," or from a Parisian café singer, with whom one evening he dreamed together of world revolution, or during sleepless nights reading the poems of Verhaeren. When Inessa Armand and her daughter would visit him, Krupskaya narrates, "Ilyich liked to indulge in day-dreaming in their presence." The dream always beckoned to a dialectical logic in which there were qualitative leaps to a reality transfigured. But it was precisely this dialectical logic which could tempt one into a qualitative leap beyond reality to the unreal, to fantasies in which one lost one's last moorings with the physical and social worlds. During the distress and isolation of the World War years, Lenin was converted to *dialectical* materialism.

From the triads and trichotomies which he had ridiculed in 1892 as a young scientific Marxist, Lenin in sombre isolation derived instead now a curious consolation, like an old believer falling back on new readings of sacred texts. He even wrote an "aphorism" in which he exulted in his solitary devotion: "It is impossible completely to understand Marx's *Capital,* and especially its first chapter, without having thoroughly studied and understood the *whole* of Hegel's Logic. Consequently, half a century later none of the Marxists understood Marx!!" At last he was the ultimate sectarian, the only one in the world in half a century who had divined the master's message; the mantle was his. Marx had in his maturity playfully belittled his coquetterie with Hegelian phrases; for Lenin the coquetterie became a passionate obsession: "Hegel actually *proved* that logical forms and laws are not an empty shell, but the *reflection* of the objective world," he wrote, then perturbed by his own flight to fantasy, he qualified it to "a brilliant guess." He invented more dialectical aphorisms: "*Dialectics* is the teaching which shows how *Opposites* can be and how they happen to be (how they become) *identical.* . . ." It was a Freudian dream world in which negation ceases to exist, the fantasy projected into a "logic" all its own. Without the Hegelian dialectic, the conception of development would be "lifeless, pale and dry"; the dialectic would make it "living," full of "self-movement," with "leaps." The vocabulary of this Hegelian conversion had the peculiar accents of a man of declining virility finding in the Hegelian words a kind of metaphysical restorative. And then he found in the Hegelian idealism itself the ultimate justification of revolution; the subjective will would create its own world, would posit the revolution itself. What was the meaning of "practice in the theory of knowledge"? Lenin said: "Alias: Man's consciousness not only reflects the objective world, but creates it." He indeed now preferred Hegel's theology to Huxley's agnosticism: "this philosophical idealism, openly, 'seriously' leading to God is more honest than modern agnosticism with its hypocrisy and cowardice. He called, in his loneliness, for a metaphysics to sustain his fantasy, to give assurance to his will to revolution. A few years before he had berated Gorky for venturing even to think of God as a class-name for human ethical strivings. "Is not God-building the worst form of self-castigation? Everyone engaged in building *God* . . .

castigates himself in the worst possible way, because instead of occupying himself with 'deeds' he indulges in self-contemplation." The God-builder was then for Lenin a philosophical masochist of the worst kind. Now however, in 1916, it was the scientific agnostic, with his perpetual demand for evidence, who most aroused Lenin's ire.

VI

It was during the war years, when Lenin's immersion in Hegelian dialectic was deepest, that he wrote the two works of social science for which he is most famous, ***Imperialism: The Highest Stage of Capitalism*** and ***The State and Revolution***. Here the power of fantasy was superimposed on the facts; the fantasy, which Lenin regarded as inherent in every generalization, took possession; dialectic indeed became the logic of projected fantasy. There were no longer realistic studies such as his youthful ***The Development of Capitalism in Russia***. Instead, Lenin found himself borne not by scientific prediction but by dialectical prophecy.

Lenin's thesis was imperialism in its economic nature was "moribund capitalism." The "destructive characteristics of imperialism" he wrote "compel us to define it as parasitic or decaying capitalism"; it was capitalism at "its highest historical stage of development," on "the eve of the socialist revolution." Now here was dialectical method at its highest. For imperialism, as historians have documented, has been a universal theme in the world's history. The Egyptians, Babylonians, Assyrians, Greeks, and Romans had their imperialism; feudal Europe had its imperialism in the Crusades; the Arabs had their Moslem imperialism; the nomadic Tartars had their imperial state, while the sea-faring Scandinavians went forth in their Viking imperialism. The French Revolution brought into being a revolutionary imperialism. Far from imperialism today being the last stage of capitalism, it seems today to be a second or third stage of socialism. The Czechs today complain of a Soviet military and economic exploitation, while Fidel Castro charged in 1966 that Communist China was exhibiting toward his country "the worst methods of piracy, oppression, and filibusterism" that had characterized "the imperialist states." He said it all came down to the "fundamental question for the peoples: whether in the world of tomorrow the powerful nations can assume the right to blackmail, extort, pressure, attack, and strangle small peoples. . . ."

Lenin, of course, was well aware that imperialism had been a recurrent, cross-systemic phenomenon. He was determined, however, to look at reality dialectically, to see all that he hated perish with capitalist society, and to see humanity making a qualitative leap into a new society in which imperialism would vanish together with the state and bureaucracy. He therefore was under an emotional compulsion to define imperialism in such a way so that it would end with capitalism. Nothing is so certain as a tautology, and Lenin was removing the question of imperialism in postcapitalist and pre-capitalist societies from the empirical domain simply by linking it through a definition necessarily to capitalism. So Lenin wrote:

> [I]mperialism existed before this latest stage of capitalism, and even before capitalism. Rome founded on slavery, pursued a colonial policy and achieved imperialism. But 'general' arguments about imperialism, which ignore, or put into the background the fundamental difference of social-economic systems, inevitably degenerate into absolutely empty banalities, or into grandiloquent expressions like 'Greater Rome and Greater Britain'.

Thus Lenin defends his definition of imperialism as specific to modern capitalism, his well-known definition of imperialism as involving the dominance of monopolies in production, the merger of bank capital with industrial capital, the export of capital, the formation of international monopolies, and the territorial division of the whole world among the greatest capitalist powers.

There are considerable doubts concerning the actuality of the specific traits which Lenin insisted were characteristic of imperialism. Foreign investment was in Britain and the United States primarily financed through a re-investment of profits, and involved a very small net outflow of capital. Tsarist Russia embarked on imperialist ventures though it had no surplus capital for export; the French colonies as a whole imported more in their trade than they exported; the average annual return on the invested capital in such major imperialist ventures as the Witwatersrand mines did not exceed 4.1 percent; British economy was not characterized by a merger between financial and industrial capital; critics in the colonies complained that imperialist countries didn't export enough capital to make for the development of industry. But all such specific criticisms, however, are minor when compared to the major methodological distortion in Lenin's perspective on imperialism.

For Lenin argues that "general" arguments about imperialism must degenerate into banalities. By the same token, one might have argued that Newton's general arguments about the gravitational attraction of all masses, or Einstein's arguments concerning all frames of reference, all observers, were "banalities" or "tautologies." A Leninist would have held that the specific differences between the moon's motion and that of the planets were the only kinds of subjects that could be fruitfully studied. Indeed, the Aristotelian resistance to Galileo's logic of mechanics had precisely something of this character. Lenin, in other words, failed utterly to appreciate the significance of general laws of science. And the reason why he so failed is that the element of fantasy possessed him when he confronted basic social realities. His emotions wanted to decree the end of imperialism as the consequence of the end of capitalism; his imperious revolutionary will wanted to annihilate imperialism; therefore, by a verbal sleight-of-hand he stipulated that imperialism could exist only under modern capitalism. He projected a whole evolutionary sequence of historical stages into a choice in the use of words obedient to his emotions. When Yugoslav, Polish, Soviet, Chinese, and Cuban Marxists, therefore, have tried to speak about the imperialist activities of Communist countries, they have found themselves stammering because of their Leninist inhibitions. To talk plainly of a Soviet or Communist or Socialist imperialism violated the binding rules of their Leninist political grammar; they struggled vainly with all sorts of equivalents. But to speak of "great-power chauvinism" is even more grandiloquent than the expressions such as "Greater Rome" which Lenin disliked. The dialectical tenet with its qualitative leap into the end of imperialism was a fantasy which simply could not be translated into reality.

Lenin wrote his *Imperialism* in Zürich, Switzerland, in the spring of 1916. Then came the March Revolution of 1917. The time for transposing fantasy into reality had come, and he dared not miss it. All sorts of fantastic schemes rushed through his mind. His sister Marya writes: "But how to get back? One fantastic plan after another was conceived by Lenin, but they were all impracticable. He spent sleepless nights worrying how to get away from Switzerland. In desperation he decided to act the part of a deaf-mute who had a Swedish passport. . . ." He asked an intermediary "to find a Swede who looked like Lenin." The intermediary, Ganetsky, wrote: "When I read the letter, I realized how depressed Lenin was, but all the same I had to laugh at this grotesque plan." Even Krupskaya acknowledges: "His nights were spent building the most improbable plans. We could fly over by plane. But such an idea could only be thought of in a waking dream. Put into words, its unreality became at once obvious." Then a proposal of his former friend Martov that they secure passage through Germany brought Lenin back to Russia.

During the months of August and September, 1917, while in hiding, and awaiting with growing impatience the seizure of power by his party, Lenin wrote his celebrated pamphlet *The State and Revolution*. It is a Utopia written in the language of social science, a melange of impassioned, unrestrained projective dreams together with harsh insistence on the necessity for violence in revolution. He never completed the pamphlet, for the October events intervened: "It is more pleasant and useful to go through the 'experience of the revolution' than to write about it." Again dialectical logic, with its schema of qualitative leap into the new world, with its negation of all that was repressive in the bourgeois society, provided Lenin with the formalism appropriate to his fantasy. Given the economic groundwork prepared by capitalism, universal literacy, the discipline of the workers, then, wrote Lenin, "it is perfectly possible, within twenty-four hours after the overthrow of the capitalists and bureaucrats, to replace them, in the control of production and distribution, in the business of

control of labor and products, by the armed workers, by the whole people in arms." This was a prophecy which never fulfilled itself; the "twenty-four hours" have been dilated into more than a half-century, but the time-coefficient is always expanded with added clauses and auxiliary variables. Accounting and control, predicted Lenin, will have been so simplified by capitalism so that its techniques will be "within the reach of anybody who can read and write and knows the first four rules of arithmetic." Then, said Lenin, bureaucracy will begin to "wither away." The antagonism between mental and physical labor will vanish, and with it, the economic basis of the state. While denying that Bolsheviks are Utopians, indulging in "dreams" of how to eliminate all administration, still Lenin insists, "within twenty-four hours" after the revolution, the managerial functions will be taken over by average city dwellers and performed for workingmen's wages.

Were Lenin's predictions ever founded on more than projective fantasy? Had he made any study of the procedures of accounting and management? Had he made any effort to learn the facts of industrial psychology, or to come to terms with the views of elites and the distribution of abilities enunciated by such sociologists as Michels and Pareto? The amazing thing is that Lenin, for all his training as a statistical sociologist, simply yielded to fantasy. If, as Lenin said in 1916, every generalization contains an element of fantasy, then we might say that some generalizations contain far more fantasy than others; we might even devise a "fantasy-fact" ratio for generalizations, and state the proportion of fantasy-projection in relation to verifiable fact in the construction of hypotheses. And Lenin would now have rated very high indeed in his "fantasy-fact ratio."

Curiously, in his early manhood, in 1902, Lenin had ridiculed those who raised an outcry against bureaucracy. In those days he thought that only flabby intellectuals wanted to dispense with bureaucracy. The average worker, Lenin insisted, realized that bureaucracy is a technological necessity. The proletarian who has gone through the school of the factory, wrote Lenin, who knows the function of "the factory as a means of organization" can teach the unstable, bourgeois intellectuals the necessity of bureaucracy. Those who railed "against people being transformed into 'wheels and cogs'" were raising a "tragi-comical outcry" against the workings of the division of labor. The distinction between orthodoxy and revisionism, wrote Lenin, is the counterpart of that between bureaucracy versus democracy. He chose bureaucracy; those who rejected it, he argued, suffered from some psychological ailment: "There is a close psychological connection between this hatred of discipline and that incessant nagging note of *injury* which is to be detected in all the writings of all opportunists today." Whatever this psychological ailment, Lenin himself in 1917 wrote pages of fantasy which went far beyond the ones written by those whom he had derided in 1902. The dialectical fantasy had superseded the method of social science.

VII

Persons who dwell in a world of political fantasy are apt to be characterized by great cruelty. For the very component which impels one to reject reality and to reach for a surrogate world is one of some deep, underlying frustration; and frustration, if it expresses itself in fantasy, is also laden with aggression against whomever seems to counterpose himself against that fantasy. Indeed, the fantasy itself can provide the formula needed for justifying aggression and presenting one's cruelties as historically justified. Certainly, the greatest of Lenin's contemporaries, among those who knew him, felt this ingredient of cruelty in Lenin's personality. Bertrand Russell in 1920 found him "dictatorial," and "embodied theory," with a "rather grim" laugh, lacking in "psychological imagination," and despising many people. Lenin, he wrote retrospectively, was a "narrow-minded fanatic and cheap cynic." "When I met Lenin, I had much less impression of a great man than I had expected; my most vivid impressions were of bigotry and Mongolian cruelty. . . . His guffaw at the thought of those massacred made my blood run cold." Maxim Gorky, who had known Lenin for many years, wrote from St. Petersburg in the midst of the revolution that Lenin "has no pity for the mass of the people . . . Lenin does not know the people . . . The working classes are to Lenin what minerals are to the metallurgist." Lenin, according to Gorky, was a Russian nobleman with his distinctive psychological traits, prepared to incite the working class to outrages against innocent people, and deeming himself as authorized "in performing with the Russian people a cruel experiment." Leon Trotsky in 1903 said that Lenin was a "party disorganizer," a would-be "dictator" whose conception of socialism was that of a "barracks regime." The gifted and idealistic Rosa Luxemburg thought there was a "Tartar-Mongolian savagery" about Lenin and his followers. The Utopian fantasy and the materialist harshness were a curious joint product, the two polarities of a personality racked with aggressions, toward self, toward others.

Lenin's materialist doctrine was absorbed into the official Soviet ideology, and its absolutism became an official tenet. The famous *Short History of the Communist Party,* to which Stalin lent his name, enunciated as canonical text: "Marxist philosophical materialism holds that the world and its laws are fully knowable, . . . and that there are no things in the world which are unknowable. . . ." This is a large philosophical commitment to demand of every Bolshevik. A more reflective, or postideological philosopher would say: Consider the two contradictory propositions, first: there are no things in the world which are unknowable, and second: there are some things in the world which are unknowable.

The postideological philosopher would say further: how could we possibly verify either of these two alternative contradictory propositions? For even if it happened that all things in the world taken distributively were knowable, we should still never be able to know whether we had sampled or enumerated all things; and if, on the other hand, there were something in the world which was unknowable, how would we possibly know it? When Lenin writes: "beyond the 'physical,' beyond the external world, with which everyone is familiar, there can be nothing," the agnostic responds: what manner of proof can there possibly be for such a proposition? It lies in the indeterminate domain.

In short, unless some emotion weights the scale, and inclines us to one alternative or the other, the philosopher without ideology acknowledges that we have here a pair of indeterminate alternatives, and that under such circumstances, an agnostic standpoint is justified. Lenin, on the other hand, endeavoring to contain his own propensity to fantasy, does so by overdetermining the indeterminate; he proclaims a materialism which is hard, dogmatic, and mandatory. That is why the new generation of dissidents in the Soviet Union, looking for a liberation from the thought-ways and emotional patterns of institutionalized harshness, of socialized sadism, have begun to turn toward philosophical idealism.

As the centenary of Lenin's birth is observed, the estimate of his life and work will be largely influenced by the pronouncement of the Central Committee of the Soviet Communist Party: "Lenin was the first thinker of the century who saw the achievements of natural science in his time as the beginning of an immense scientific revolution, who was able to disclose and to generalize in philosophical terms the revolutionary meaning of the fundamental discoveries made by the great explorers of nature." This is precisely the kind of statement which places fetters on the minds of the Soviet people, their students, their scientists. For Lenin more than any other thinker in this century contributed to the retardation of scientific inquiry. In the name of his narrow-minded materialism he rejected both Einstein's principle of relativity and Freud's psychoanalysis. His writings on imperialism and the state have deprived Soviet students of the intellectual tools which they need for analyzing their own society. In the measure in which his name is exalted as the first scientist of the century, in that proportion the society which he founded shows that its thinking still remains infantile, enthralled by ideology rather than guided by science. The Russian intellectual liberation is only now beginning.

Rodney Barfield   (essay date 1971)

SOURCE: "Lenin's Utopianism: *State and Revolution,*" in *Slavic Review,* Vol. 30, No. 1, March, 1971, pp. 45-56.

[*In the following essay, Barfield contends that* State and Revolution *is Lenin's credo on human nature, and as such should not be dismissed as mere utopianism, as many critics have done.*]

General histories give little credence to the utopian side of Lenin's revolutionary thought, especially in relation to his only formal utopian work, *State and Revolution*. Most histories pass off that book as an "intellectual deviation" resulting from Lenin's "revolutionary fever" of 1917 or as a piece of political opportunism, while offering *What Is To Be Done?* as the statement of orthodox Leninism. In keeping with the tone of *What Is To Be Done?* Lenin is generally portrayed as the political realist par excellence, a pragmatist of the first order, a "hard-nosed" strategist confined by neither intellectual theories (not even Marxism) nor human emotions. This neat and simple formula is most convenient in attributing the success of the November Revolution to Lenin's talents for organization and political astuteness.

This one-dimensional interpretation of Lenin has been more or less accepted by most historians without serious question; there has been, consequently, little study of the relation of *State and Revolution* to Lenin's revolutionary thought. Robert V. Daniels has stated the standard evaluation of the work in his article "The State and Revolution: A Case Study in the Genesis and Transformation of Communist Ideology." He compares *State and Revolution* with *What Is To Be Done?*, pointing up the disparity between the ideas and the attitudes displayed in the two works. He first stresses the predominant position given to the party vis-à-vis the masses in *What Is To Be Done?* and its essential role of revolutionary organization; to this he contrasts the minor role accorded the party and its organizational work in *State and Revolution*. That is, to prove the "uniqueness" of *State and Revolution*, Daniels shows how the work deviates from the ideas and attitudes expressed in *What Is To Be Done?*, which is supposed to represent the "true" Lenin or orthodox Leninism. It would then follow that since *State and Revolution* does not adhere to the concepts of *What Is To Be Done?*, it is obviously an aberration.

Such a comparison misses much of the intent of *State and Revolution*. *What Is To Be Done?* is a practical, revolutionary guide designed as a blueprint to be applied to the Russian situation in 1902; *State and Revolution* is a theoretical work looking into the future, a sort of prophecy that attempts to depict the new socialist order, the future utopia. It was not intended by its author to be achieved in his own lifetime; it was a "revolution" for the next generation, for the generation that would wage the successful socialist revolution. It was, according to Trotsky, to be Lenin's "secret last will and testament."

The general sympathy for Daniels's interpretation is quite understandable, since *State and Revolution* does appear, on the surface, to be completely antithetic to the spirit and program of most of Lenin's best-known works, and especially to the nature of his actual policies. One is immediately impressed in reading *State and Revolution* with the dominant role assigned to the proletarian masses, as opposed to the role of the party, in the coming revolution, and with its role in the process of constructing the new socialist society—with the emphasis on the *spontaneous* abilities of the working class

and with the minimal attention given to organization and discipline. The hard-line elitist approach to revolution, which constitutes a major theme of *What Is To Be Done?* and is an essential element of Leninism, gives way to spontaneous, anarchistic tendencies in *State and Revolution*; careful planning and organizing by the vanguard gives way to impatient, idealistic improvisation. The proletariat is not only to assume direction of the revolution; it is also expected to transport Russia from a semifeudal agrarian society to a socialist society in one great sweep, a feat reminiscent of the *narodnik* schemes which envisioned by-passing the capitalist stage of economic development and moving directly to a socialist society. Whereas Lenin had argued earlier that full capitalist development must precede socialism and had branded the *narodnik* "leap across the centuries" as utopian, in *State and Revolution* he put forward his own utopian "leap" but tried to eliminate it from the ranks of utopian schemes by providing for a brief period of transition from capitalism to communism. He admitted that it would be impossible to destroy all officialdom at one blow—that would be utopian. But to break up the old bureaucratic machinery and replace it with a new and different apparatus, an apparatus that would gradually "wither away" as its functions were replaced by the "natural" cooperation of all members of society—that was not utopian. . . .

Lenin's conception of the new society, of the "new age" as expressed in *State and Revolution,* was based in large part on Marx's historically dubious interpretation of the Paris Commune of 1871, found in Marx's *Civil War in France.* Marx described the ill-fated Commune as the "first manifestation of the real proletarian revolution." This description was essentially an idealized picture of the Communards smashing the old bureaucratic apparatus and replacing it with a new representative and democratic officialdom, an officialdom composed of working-class elements. The proletarian nature of the Commune government was to be ensured by direct democracy and the right of immediate recall. In a similar vein Lenin described the new society in *State and Revolution* as a universal bureaucracy in which the business of operating the state and the economy would be the task of every citizen. His defense of this anarchistic state of affairs was that the capitalist system had reduced the functions of state and economy to such simple operations of "registration, filing, and checking" that they could be performed by every literature citizen. Every citizen would thus be responsible for "running the state and the economy"; and he would perform these duties for "workingmen's wages." This universal bureaucracy would prevent the development of a professional, elitist bureaucratic system. It would be organized much like the postal system with a standard wage scale and would be under the control and direction of the "armed proletariat."

The transition period between the old and the new bureaucratic systems would be devoted to suppressing the old exploiters and to destroying every remnant of the old state machinery. This initial phase of the transition would introduce the "first" or "lower" stage of Communist society. The lower stage would involve the abolition of the standing army, which would be replaced by the armed masses; the abolition of all private property, which would be replaced by the social ownership of all property and the means of economic production; the election of all "officials" by direct vote, subject to immediate recall.

The higher stage of Communist society would witness the "withering away of the state." In order to explain away the existence of the state in the new order, Lenin invoked Hegel's law of "transformation of quantity into quality." That is, capitalist democracy, which employed the state apparatus as a special instrument to suppress the masses of the people, would be transformed into "proletarian democracy," something that would no longer be a state "in the accepted sense of the word." The lower stage of communism would not do away with all injustice and inequality, Lenin explained, but it would prevent human exploitation because all of the means of economic production would be held in common ownership by society. In fact, the lower stage of communism essentially amounted to the implementation of a complete socialist economy laced with a few anarchistic political decorations.

The higher stage of communism involved more than economics and politics; it was especially concerned with the social and psychological outlook of the population. This stage would be achieved only after the masses subordinated individual desires to the interests of the whole society, only after man's competitive instincts were transformed into a spirit of voluntary cooperation. When this stage of social harmony had been reached, society would witness the "withering away of the state," the "special functions of a special stratum" having become the everyday tasks of every citizen. The universal bureaucracy of bookkeepers, technicians, and managers would have become commonplace by this time. This was the stage at which every citizen would perform to the limits of his ability but receive merely according to his needs. Lenin sincerely believed that if man could become accustomed to observing what he termed the "fundamental rules of social life," then his labor would be so pleasant and productive that he would *naturally* work to the best of his capabilities without demanding personal material profit and that all social antagonism would consequently disappear. There would be such an abundance of goods within the economy that competition between individuals would be superfluous; everyone would have everything he would ever need. These citizens of the "new age" would naturally understand that profit was not a reward for individual talent but a reward for the general character of collective cooperation.

Such is the simplistic and utopian nature of *State and Revolution*. Yet regardless of how unrelated these naïve notions might appear to be to Lenin's practical activities, it is quite amiss to neglect the work because it is

"not serious." Such interpretations have resulted, at least in part, from the tendency of historians to associate *State and Revolution* with the Lenin of post-March 1917, that is, with the period of Lenin's revolutionary career when he made a pronounced shift to the left in his revolutionary tactics and thought. It is practically beyond dispute that Lenin was considerably affected by the successes of the 1917 revolutions and that his political judgment during that year was more than a little determined by these events. Post-March 1917 and the early months of 1918 clearly represent a period when Lenin moved furthest from the attitudes that we generally describe as Leninist, from the attitudes of *What Is To Be Done?*

To classify *State and Revolution* as simply a product of this revolutionary period, which is the usual method of treating it, is to mistake its motivation and to suggest that it is "un-Leninist" and not to be taken seriously; it is to suggest that the work was written by a Lenin who was "inebriated by revolutionary fever." This chronology is not explicitly outlined, but is rather implied by historians who apparently have not considered it important to distinguish between when the work was researched and essentially completed and when it was written. Daniels, for example, says: "*State and Revolution* is a work conforming neither to Lenin's previous thought nor to his subsequent practice. It stands as a monument to its author's intellectual deviation during the year of revolution, 1917." This statement implies that the work was conceived during the revolutionary period; it ignores the fact that the book was essentially completed before the March Revolution, at a time when Lenin was very pessimistic about the prospects of a revolution in his own lifetime.

Louis Fischer has made the implication even more forceful: "Despite its plethora of Marx-Engels terminology and quotations, the Lenin book is an aberrant intellectual enterprise, a fanciful exercise for so rock-hard a man, as un-Leninist as the mask he wore and the false name he bore in hiding while writing it." If *State and Revolution* is included in the revolutionary period, a period during which Lenin did experience a decided shift to the left and during which the new Bolshevik government issued a number of anarchistic decrees, it is quite logical to interpret the book as either an emotionally charged intellectual aberration or a propaganda piece designed to gain popular support for the Bolshevik cause. If, however, the work is placed in its proper chronology—that is, before the March Revolution—it becomes apparent that the interpretations cited above are quite inadequate.

It is usually overlooked that Lenin put together the materials for *State and Revolution* during the months of December 1916 through February 1917. While engaged in his research he had no inkling that Russia was on the verge of revolution. The nation was, it is true, experiencing a number of strikes and riots due to the breakdown of transportation and the economy, but these complications were nothing new to the wobbling tsarist regime. Few of Russia's revolutionaries anticipated revolution in 1917, and Lenin was no exception. It is against this pessimistic background that the ideas and attitudes expressed in *State and Revolution* must be viewed, since the bulk of the notes used in the actual writing of the work (entitled "Marxism on the State") are dated January and February 1917.

The fact that *State and Revolution* was essentially completed before the revolutionary period is substantiated by Lenin himself. A full month before he received the news of the March Revolution, he wrote to Alexandra Kollontai that he was "preparing (have almost got the material ready) an article on the question of the attitude of Marxism to the state." The letter was dated February 17, 1917. The article was, of course, *State and Revolution*. It was not until a month after his letter to Kollontai that Lenin learned of the Revolution, at which time he put aside the manuscript and devoted all of his efforts to returning to Russia. It was another month before he was successful in reaching his native land. He had left the manuscript in Stockholm. After finally arriving in Russia, he was too absorbed with organizing the Bolsheviks and attacking the Provisional Government to concern himself with the book. Yet shortly after the July Demonstrations, which prompted the government to outlaw the Bolsheviks, Lenin wrote to L. B. Kamenev, "If they do me in, I ask you to publish my notebook: 'Marxism on the State' (it got left behind in Stockholm). . . . I think that it could be published after a week's work."

Lenin's letter to Kollontai in February noting that the work was almost completed, the ensuing months during which the manuscript remained in Stockholm, and Lenin's letter to Kamenev in July stating that the book could be put into shape for publication with a week's work all indicate that *State and Revolution* was essentially completed before Lenin learned of the March Revolution. It is therefore a distortion of facts to imply that the work is a product of Lenin's "revolutionary fever" during the months of revolution, and consequently an "intellectual deviation." His concern that the work be published even if he should be killed would also indicate that he considered it to be more than a mere piece of political propaganda.

If *State and Revolution* is divorced from the revolutionary period and viewed as a theoretical work written for the future, a work intended to be Lenin's "last will and testament," consisting of ideas which were formulated not in the heat of revolution but in the cool detachment of the Zurich Library, then there is sufficient reason to interpret it as representing an integral part of the whole of Lenin's revolutionary thought and personal make-up. The book may then be viewed as a serious revelation of the end to which Lenin had devoted his life.

Lenin's research into the nature of the future state undoubtedly helped him to clarify his own position on the subject. It would seem that he had always felt a sympathy for the ideas expounded in *State and Revolution* but had never really categorized them in his mind or tried to weave them into any sort of coherent system. This process of defining his vague feelings about the nature of the new society can be traced through his changing attitude toward Nikolai Bukharin and Karl Kautsky. Lenin in fact took up the question of the nature of the state in response to certain "anarchistic" and "reformist" articles concerned with that question. L. B. Kamenev noted in *Leninskii sbornik* that it was precisely because of Bukharin's article "Der imperialistische Raubstaat" that Lenin began writing *State and Revolution*. Yet the final product hardly mentions Bukharin but includes a full chapter of invective against Kautsky. In the process of defining his feelings about the new society Lenin discovered that his position was much closer to Bukharin's leftism than to Kautsky's more realistic and moderate position. In the letter to Kollontai mentioned above, Lenin wrote that he had "come to conclusions which are even sharper against Kautsky than against Bukharin," and in a letter to Inessa Armand he wrote that he had arrived at conclusions *"much more* against Kautsky than against N. I. Bukharin (who, however, is not right all the same, though nearer to the truth than Kautsky)."

Kautsky had raised some very disturbing questions about the nature of the future socialist state, especially concerning bureaucracy and centralization—two of the very points on which Lenin's theory of the new state later broke down. Kautsky's conclusions were nothing less than a refutation of violent revolution and of Lenin's belief that the new state would eliminate coercion and social antagonism. Kautsky argued that "never, under any condition" could a proletarian revolution destroy state power; the most that it could hope to accomplish would be to shift the forces of power within the state from the hands of the bourgeoisie to the hands of the proletariat. In applying this assessment to Germany, he urged the German Social Democratic Party to capture state power by gaining a majority in parliament and making parliament the head of the government.

Kautsky's analysis epitomized Marxist "revisionism," that "bourgeois illness" which Lenin considered the greatest threat to the revolution. As he became increasingly opposed to Kautsky's views, he drew closer to Bukharin's leftist position. What he had described as Bukharin's "exceptional stupidities" in December 1916 had become "little mistakes" by February 1917. In fact, by February 1917 Lenin was prepared to publish Bukharin's article, which he had previously rejected, along with his own article on the state.

This same shift of emphasis is revealed in Lenin's research notes on *State and Revolution*. His initial research in August 1916 was concerned solely with refuting Bukharin's article on the state. The title of the work then was **"Notes on the Article of N. I. Bukharin 'On the Theory of the Imperialistic State'"**. In December 1916 he was still concerned with answering Bukharin, his research at that time being entitled **"Remarks on the Article of N. I. Bukharin 'The Imperialistic Robber State'"**. But his comprehensive notebook, which formed the basis of the book *State and Revolution* and which was compiled in January and February 1917 as "Marxism on the State," not only omitted Bukharin from the title but also omitted any criticism of him from the text, substituting an attack on Kautsky instead.

This revision of notes occurred long before Lenin learned of the March Revolution. Other than this revealing change of emphasis, the work written in August and September of 1917 and published in 1918 as *State and Revolution* is essentially the same work that was compiled in January and February of 1917 as "Marxism on the State." That is to say that Lenin did not change his views on the nature of the new society in the final draft of the book even though the final product was written during the revolutionary period. Furthermore, it is obvious from his letters to Kollontai and Armand that he was not excited over some novel discovery in his research on the nature of the state; his findings merely confirmed his ideas on the subject. The mention of his research in these letters is almost casual and would seem to indicate that the ideas expressed in *State and Revolution* were not strangers to his mind but were an integral part of his revolutionary outlook and had been vaguely formulated long before the eventful year of 1917.

The utopian notions voiced in *State and Revolution* were neither new nor alien to Lenin's intellectual and emotional outlook. It did not require the revolutionary excitement of 1917 to inspire him to produce such a work. From the very beginnings of his conversion to the ranks of the revolutionaries he had contemplated nothing less than the complete transformation of Russian society and even of the world. That transformation was not to be limited to the political, social, and economic aspects of society but would also include the psychological outlook of mankind. That is what *State and Revolution* is about—the harmonious new age that would emerge after the existing artificial psychological outlook of man had been redirected and man had returned to his "natural" state of "observing the fundamental rules of society."

The means described by Lenin for achieving the new harmonious age, however, constitute something of a paradox not only in his revolutionary thought but also within his work *State and Revolution*. How can an orderly and effective society be constructed out of the anarchistic proposals suggested in *State and Revolution*—destruction of the state, abolition of the army and police, the affairs of the entire society and economy placed in the hands of the masses? This represented no paradox for Lenin. He believed, as did his predecessors Chernyshevsky and Marx, that the state was actually the creator of anarchy and disorder, of "unnatural competition" and coercion, and that if the state and its exploitative economic system were destroyed, man would re-

turn to his "natural" inclinations of unselfish cooperation and voluntary social organization. Once man had returned to his natural state of observing the "fundamental rules" of social existence, there would be no functions left for the state to perform, no need for police, army, or government bureaucracy. The few national functions could be performed by all of the citizens working in harmony with one another and for the good of all.

The General Will would reconcile any and all conflicts between the individual and society and between individuals.

The inspiration behind these utopian notions was not revolutionary emotionalism. These attitudes were always a part of Lenin's intellectual and emotional make-up. They seem to have emerged in some sort of concrete form with his study of Chernyshevsky's *What Is To Be Done?* around 1887 and to have developed with his study of Marxism. That inspiration received its fullest expression in *State and Revolution*, a work compiled in the sober confines of the Zurich Library. Rather than being the product of revolutionary optimism, the material in *State and Revolution* was put together at a time when Lenin doubted that his generation would live to witness the "decisive battles of this coming revolution." He believed that it would be the youth of that day who would wage the victorious proletarian revolution. This assessment was made by him on January 22, 1917, little more than a month before the March Revolution. And it was for the youth, for future generations, and "for the sake of his own inner confidence," that Lenin was working over the problem of the nature of the new society.

The fact that *State and Revolution* is Lenin's only major utopian work makes it readily susceptible to charges of insincerity and deviation. Before 1917 he had been occupied almost exclusively with preparing the party and the proletariat for their roles in the "inevitable" revolution and especially with developing the effectiveness of the "vanguard." Even after the March Revolution he did not abandon these tasks, but he was not concerned with these efforts in *State and Revolution*, because that work did not apply to 1917. But even though it is Lenin's only formal work dealing with the nature of the new society, the ideas and attitudes contained in it may be found scattered throughout his earlier writings. The same unrestrained optimism and unbounded confidence in the inevitable development of proletarian class consciousness (that is, that the proletariat were *instinctively* Marxists) found in *State and Revolution* is quite in evidence in his *What the "Friends of the People" Are and How They Fight the Social Democrats,* published in 1894. Here can be found the same implicit faith in the innate intelligence and ability of the Russian worker and the same insistence that the revolution will not settle for a mere change in the political system but will bring about a complete regeneration of man. There is the same belief that the revolution will be a universal enterprise that will usher in a new historical era. The work also gives one something of the warm enthusiasm that Lenin felt for the "innocent," though duped, working masses: "When its [the working class] advanced representatives have mastered the ideas of scientific socialism, the idea of the historical role of the Russian worker, when these ideas become widespread, and when stable organizations are formed among the workers to transform the workers' present sporadic economic war into conscious class struggle—then the Russian WORKER, rising at the head of all the democratic elements, will overthrow absolutism and lead the RUSSIAN PROLETARIAT (side by side with the proletariat of ALL COUNTRIES) *along the straight road of open political struggle to* THE VICTORIOUS COMMUNIST REVOLUTION."

Lenin takes this unbounded faith in the revolutionary energies and abilities of the masses so far as to defend the "peasant socialists" of the 1860s and 1870s against the attacks of the contemporary *narodniki,* who often ridiculed the idealism of the early socialists: "*Faith in a special order, in the communal system of Russian life*— hence *faith in the possibility of a peasant socialist revolution*—that is what inspired them and roused dozens and hundreds of people to wage a heroic struggle against the government. And you, you cannot reproach the Social Democrats with failing to appreciate the immense historical services of these, the finest people of their day, with failing to respect their memory profoundly. But I ask you, where is that faith now? It has vanished." Vanished? It had apparently found new life in Lenin's revolutionary thought. In this instance he proudly acknowledged Russian Social Democracy's debt to the idealists of the 1860s and 1870s and also anticipated his future tactical contribution to Marxism which would call for a revolutionary alliance between peasantry and proletariat.

This same idealism, these same utopian notions are also present in Lenin's work **"To the Rural Poor,"** published in 1903, which likewise shows his early concern with the peasantry as a revolutionary force and as an important element in the new society. It may be instructive to compare **"To the Rural Poor"** with *State and Revolution,* noting especially the emphasis of both on primitive democracy, voluntary cooperation, and the absence of social antagonisms in the new society. From **"To the Rural Poor":**

> When the working class has defeated the entire bourgeoisie, it will take the land away from the big proprietors and introduce *cooperative farming* on the big estates, so that the workers will farm the land together, in common, and freely elect delegates to manage the farms. They will have all kinds of labor-saving machines, and work in shifts for not more than eight (or even six) hours a day. . . . There will then be no struggle for money between the big and the small farmer; there will be no working for hire for others; all workers will work for themselves, all improvements in methods of production and all machines will benefit the workers

themselves and help to make their work easier, improve their standard of living.

From *State and Revolution:*

> The state will be able to wither away completely when society adopts the rule: "From each according to his ability, to each according to his needs," that is, when people have become so accustomed to observing the fundamental rules of social intercourse and when their labor has become so productive that they will voluntarily work according to their ability. "The narrow horizon of bourgeois right," which compels one to calculate with the heartlessness of a Shylock whether one has worked half an hour more than somebody else, whether one is not getting less pay than somebody else—this narrow horizon will then be crossed. There will be no need for society, in distributing products, to regulate the quantity to be received by each; each will take freely "according to his needs."

So even in the 1890s and early 1900s, no less than in 1917, Lenin envisioned a society of voluntary toil and mutual self-sacrifice; even then he dreamed of a society free from social antagonism; even then he was concerned with ending the competitive struggle for wealth, with abolishing wage labor, and with creating a completely harmonious society, one in which the oppressive power of government would be unnecessary. He simply reiterated these ideals in *State and Revolution* when he wrote that in the new society men would voluntarily work to the best of their ability and receive according to their needs. "The suppression of the standing army, and the substitution for it of the armed people" in *State and Revolution* was advocated by the same Lenin who in 1903 demanded that "the standing army be abolished and that a militia be established in its stead, that all the people be armed." Yet no one has pointed to *What the "Friends of the People" Are* or *"To the Rural Poor"* as utopian works or intellectual deviations.

Why are these and many other of Lenin's writings which are based on the same utopian premises neglected in the treatment of his revolutionary thought? Do not the same elements of utopianism exist in the works cited above as are present in *State and Revolution*—those elements that have caused that work to be labeled an aberration? His belief in the innate intelligence of the masses, his idealization of the common man, and his conviction of the inevitable dawning of a new historical era of universal harmony are the basis of his entire revolutionary career and are the foundation upon which much of his writing rests.

Errors of political judgment resulting from his utopianism are especially in evidence during the 1905 and 1917 revolutions, when Lenin astonished even some of his most loyal disciples with his radical pronouncements and tactics. During the 1905 Revolution he wrote that the working class "is free of the cowardice, the hypocritical half-heartedness that is characteristic of the bourgeoisie as a class." He endowed the Russian worker with all the attributes characteristic of Chernyshevsky's "new people" who were supposed to herald the "new age": "Revolutions are the festivals of the oppressed and the exploited. At no other time are the masses of the people in a position to come forward so actively as creators of a new social order as at a time of revolution. At such times the people are capable of performing miracles. . ."

In 1917 Lenin dated the political maturity of the Russian masses from the 1905 Revolution:

> Prior to January 22, 1905, the revolutionary party of Russia consisted of a small group of people, and the reformists of those days . . . derisively called us a "sect." . . . Within a few months, however, the picture changed completely. The hundreds of revolutionary Social Democrats "suddenly" grew into thousands; the thousands became the leaders of between two and three million proletarians. The proletarian struggle produced widespread ferment, other revolutionary movements among the peasant masses, fifty to a hundred million strong; the peasant movement had its reverberations in the army and led to soldiers' revolts, to armed clashes between one section of the army and another. In this manner a colossal country, with a population of 130,000,000, went into the revolution; in this way dormant Russia was transformed into a Russia of revolutionary proletariat and a revolutionary people.

The 1905 Revolution had accomplished, Lenin believed, what even Bolshevik leadership could not achieve with its agitation and propaganda and organization. The revolution had divested the masses of their false attachments and had revealed their "natural" inclinations toward Marxism. The masses had generated a "fighting energy *a hundred times greater* than in ordinary, peaceful times," an energy directed against capitalism and in favor of socialism.

The revolutions of 1905 and 1917 were potent stimulants to Lenin's optimism and confirmed his fundamental utopian notions. They justified the "hope and faith" that he had always had in the masses and supported his assumptions about the nature of mankind. He was more concerned with mass radicalism than he was with the "objective stages" of capitalist development or with any of the other Marxist requirements for revolution. This optimism in turn affected his political judgment and tactics—revealed in 1905 by his sudden demands for an open party including the masses of workers, and in 1917 by his anarchistic decrees which presupposed communism to be "just around the corner."

While it would certainly be a distortion to offer *State and Revolution* as the basic statement of Lenin's political philosophy, it would be equally erroneous to dismiss it as a "fanciful exercise," as erroneous as to dismiss the implications of *What Is To Be Done?* simply out of sympathy for the ideals of *State and Revolution,* as

many of Lenin's followers and sympathizers did. *State and Revolution* does represent his fundamental philosophy of man, his inner convictions on human nature, his ideals for a more humane world.

Rufus W. Mathewson, Jr. (essay date 1975)

SOURCE: "Lenin and Gorky: The Turning Point," in *The Positive Hero in Russian Literature,* second edition, Stanford University Press, 1975, pp. 156-76.

[*In the following essay, Mathewson argues that Lenin's article* Party Organization and Party Literature *and Maxim Gorky's novel* Mother *together ushered in a new era in Russian thinking that revolved around Soviet literary ideals.*]

No fewer than six attitudes toward literature, some of them contradictory, have been discerned in Lenin's writings. Soviet critics have had to make the most of these disparate views, stressing one at the expense of the others, but never moving beyond them. Although, taken together, they indicate that Lenin sensed the fundamental antitheses between the Russian classical writers and the radical critics, his most consistent emphasis was functional, and his contribution to the utilitarian tradition is his declaration of the principle of outright political partisanship in literature. The most severely functionalist document in the Leninist heritage is his article *Party Organization and Party Literature,* published in November, 1905, which since 1932 has underlain all major efforts to subjugate literature to political interests.

Many critics have questioned its significance on the grounds that it is so much a product of local circumstances that it had little influence at the time it was written, and less in later years. Others have said that when he used the word *literature* he was talking about the Party press, not about imaginative writing. Still others have challenged his credentials as a literary critic and have discredited the article on those grounds.

Of course, in an atmosphere where the uses of the past are confined to a selective, Talmudic referral to authority, ideas are validated differently than they are when their evolution is undirected and their worth established in competition with other ideas. Lenin's article is important for the literary future because it was Lenin who wrote it, and because of the immense authority it gained in the USSR. When the accredited contributors to a society's stock of wisdom are so limited in number, any theoretical redefinition by a major prophet like Lenin may take on a lasting magnitude out of all proportion to its intrinsic worth.

The question of the ambiguity of the meaning of *literature* may be set aside here with the observation that, although the Russian word means both journalism and belles-lettres, the mere existence of uncertainty about Lenin's intentions is the most revealing point of all.

Judging from several comments Lenin made on works of fiction it is quite clear that, when he was in his "functionalist" mood, he in fact made *no* distinction between the two kinds of *literature*. As to the range of the article's applicability, since we are not concerned with its "correctness" as a guide to Soviet literary policy, we note only that extravagant emphasis has been placed on it in modern times, most notably by Zhdanov in 1946. But, considered with respect to the continuity of the utilitarian tradition, the article has great significance. Even at his most tactical, Lenin was seldom unaware of theoretical matters, and the article may be read, despite all qualifications, as the most sweeping statement of the contempt for literature inherent in Soviet Marxism. There are familiar echoes from the Russian past, too, in Lenin's concept of literary partisanship, although here it is given a narrowness and rigidity of statement that even the radical democrats stopped short of. The article takes on added significance from the fact that it contains some recognition of the delicacy and complexity of the literary process, stemming, no doubt, from Lenin's intelligentsia background. Even in this inhospitable atmosphere the opposition to the utilitarian trend receives reluctant recognition. At one moment Lenin seems to propose that the best of the two traditions be fused, but he makes no serious effort in the end to resolve the fundamental contradiction between them.

The emergence of the Party and its press from underground illegality late in 1905 provided the local occasion for the article, which poses the strategic question: now that the Party press has passed the "cursed time of Aesopian language, of literary servility, of slavish language, of intellectual serfdom," what use shall be made of the new freedom? Lenin's answer touches on so many of the permanent issues from the Russian past, his testament is so authoritative, so characteristic of recent Soviet thought on these matters, that it deserves intensive analysis.

The first statement of his thesis is in absolute terms:

> Literature must become permeated with Party spirit. To counterbalance bourgeois morals, the bourgeois entrepreneurial and huckstering press, to counterbalance bourgeois literary careerism and individualism, "noble anarchism," and the pursuit of profits—the socialist proletariat must advance the principle of Party literature, must develop this principle, and must establish it in reality to the fullest degree possible.

Lenin leaves no doubt that this principle is entirely a function of political concerns. The degree of subordination it demands of literature is, perhaps, unprecedented, short of certain anarchist prescriptions for the abolition of the written word.

> In what does this principle of Party literature consist? Not only that for the socialist proletariat the practice of literature must not be a source of profit for persons and groups, but that, in general,

it must not be an individual matter, independent of the whole proletarian cause. Down with non-Party writers! Down with superman writers! Literature must become a part of the general proletarian cause, the flywheel and screw of a single whole, of the great social-democratic mechanism, set in motion by the conscious vanguard of the entire working class. Literature must become a part of organized, systematic, unified Social Democratic Party work.

After this, there would seem to be little left to say. But Lenin anticipates the rebuttal he knows his opinions will provoke:

> There will be . . . hysterical members of the intelligentsia, who will raise a howl to the effect that such a comparison belittles, benumbs, "bureaucratizes" the free struggle of ideas, freedom of criticism, freedom of literary creation, and so on and so on. The fact of the matter is that such howls would only be an expression of bourgeois-intelligentsia individualism. There is no argument that literature, less than anything else, will yield to mechanical alignment, to leveling, to the supremacy of the majority over the minority. There is no argument . . . that the guarantee of the greatest range of personal initiative, of individual inclination, the range of thought and fantasy, of form and content, is unconditionally necessary. All this is indisputable.

There echo in this candid summary of the intelligentsia's probable objections the principal arguments made by Turgenev, Tolstoy, Chekhov, and others in defense of the free practice of their craft. Yet the original thesis still stands. He sees no contradiction in stating that

> literature must certainly and necessarily become indissolubly connected with other parts of Social Democratic Party work. . . . The organized socialist proletariat must look after all this work, control all of it, introduce into all its work, without a single exception, the living stream of the living proletarian cause.

With this point established, Lenin remains responsive to the Hegelian rhythm, nevertheless, and endeavors to resolve the two propositions in a kind of synthesis. The problem is essentially an administrative one, he seems to say, and needs only patient attention to it by all concerned:

> We are far from the idea of preaching any kind of uniform system, or solution to the problem by means of a few resolutions. No schematism can be considered in this area. . . . The point is that our entire Party . . . should be aware of this new problem, should state it clearly, and should undertake everywhere to solve it. Emerging from the captivity of feudal censorship, we do not want to go and will not go into the captivity of bourgeois-huckstering literary relations. We wish to form, and we will form, a free press not only

in the police sense, but also in the sense of freedom from careerism . . . also in the sense of freedom from bourgeois-anarchistic individualism.

In the second half of this passage (from the word "Emerging. . ."), and in the swift transition between the two parts of it, we are able to distinguish the essential *non sequitur* in all subsequent Soviet thinking about art—the deceptive key-change, the illegitimate merging of incommensurable orders of thought. Up to this point Lenin has been concerned primarily with the opposition between freedom and control as it concerns the functioning Party artist. Then suddenly, without warning, he has translated this antithesis into the terms of the unrelated *political* opposition between the bourgeoisie and the proletariat. With his transvalued definition of freedom he reaches the peak of his intellectual sleight of hand. For if we follow him to the end of his list of the negative freedoms it is impossible to avoid the conclusion that "freedom from . . . bourgeois-anarchistic individualism" is, in essence, freedom from every right and privilege the artist has demanded for himself since ancient Greece, that it is, indeed, freedom from freedom itself. Bourgeois freedom is slavery; proletarian "control" is freedom.

But Lenin was not satisfied with this formulation of the problem. In his new version, however, he amplifies the specious key-change and uses it to carry him triumphantly out of the otherwise insoluble dilemma. He begins by restating the original antithesis in very similar terms. Continuing his argument from the remark about "bourgeois-anarchistic individualism," he observes defensively:

> The last words will seem to be a paradox or a joke on the readers. What! Some member of the intelligentsia, a passionate partisan of freedom will shout, What! You want the subordination to the collective of such a fine individual matter as literary creation! You want the workers to decide questions of science, philosophy, aesthetics, by a majority vote! You deny the absolute freedom of absolutely individualistic intellectual creation!

> Calm yourselves, gentlemen! In the first place we are considering Party literature and its submission to Party control. Each is free to write and speak as he pleases without the slightest limitation.

It would appear then that all was well. Lenin recognizes the right of all writers who chafe at Party discipline to remove themselves from it and to write as they please. But he has approached the crux of the issue between the needs of the artist and the needs of an absolutist political group. In 1905 he could dispose of it with a pluralist solution, because there was no need at this time for him to face all the consequences of holding political power. If the opposition between these needs is absolute, Lenin felt free to say in 1905, let each go his own way. But there is a new note in his next formulation of the polarity between artist and revolutionary. He suggests that

the freedom of choice he has just granted the writer is, itself, spurious; that this is a freedom only to write irresponsibly or dishonestly:

> Every free union, among them the Party, is free to dismiss those members who make use of the Party label to preach anti-Party views. Freedom of speech must be complete. I am obliged to concede to you, in the name of freedom of speech, the full right to shout, to lie, and to write as you please. But you are obliged to concede to me in the name of the freedom of unions, the right to exclude or to break with people who talk this way and that way. The Party is a voluntary union which inevitably would disintegrate ideologically and then materially if it did not cleanse itself of members who preach anti-Party views.

At this point there is a note of plain suspicion of the freely judging intellectual, but on the whole it is a reasonable statement of a more or less gentlemanly stand-off, a reasonable statement for any political leader to make to freely committed followers. Though we know now that it is a provisional arrangement, one would think that it might have served as a final comment on the matter as things stood in 1905. Not so. Lenin is not content with this: the note of partisanship must be struck again, and the original thesis must be reestablished in its purity. The conflict between the classes is again superimposed on the issue of control versus freedom. His crude for or-against morality rearranges the elements of the argument in such a way that all virtue and the only valid freedom are found to reside in the proletarian cause. By the same token, the freedom Lenin has just granted the dissident artist is found to be false, nothing but a mask for the "free" writer's status as a kept hireling of the class enemy.

> Mister bourgeois individualists, we must tell you that your talk about absolute freedom is only hypocrisy. In a society based on the power of money, in a society where the mass of workers begs and a handful of the rich live like parasites, there cannot be real genuine freedom. Are you free of your bourgeois publisher, mister writer? from your bourgeois public which demands framed pornographic pictures from you. . . ? Actually this absolute freedom is a bourgeois or an anarchist phrase. . . . It is impossible to live in a society and be free of that society. The freedom of the bourgeois writer, artist, actress is only a masked dependence on the money bag, on bribes, on banknotes.

Lenin has abandoned all efforts to analyze the knottiest problem of all, and has retreated inside the political certainty that all who cannot be persuaded to be with you are unavoidably and implacably against you. All men are reducible in moral terms to their class allegiances, and their creative product can only be judged in those terms. At this point Lenin might have permitted himself the honesty Tolstoy showed when he faced the bitter fact that art and social change are, in a final sense, incompatible activities, and that if the latter is to gain absolute ascendancy, the former must be considered expendable. But Lenin wanted it both ways, and in the following pronouncement, with its sudden reversal of hitherto accepted meanings, there is a fateful setting of the future course of the Russian literary tradition. Socialists, he says, will unmask the "hypocritically free" literature of the bourgeoisie and will set against it "a truly free literature *openly* connected with the proletariat":

> This will be a free literature because not profit or career, but the idea of socialism and a sympathy for toilers will win over more and more new forces to its ranks. This will be a free literature because it will serve not a sated heroine, not the boring "upper ten thousand" suffering from obesity, but the millions and tens of millions of toilers, who make up the flower of the country, its strength, its future. This will be a free literature impregnating the most recent word of humanity's revolutionary thought with the experience . . . of the socialist proletariat. . . .

> To work, then, comrades! Before us is a difficult and new but great and noble task—the organization of a broad, many-sided diverse literature in close connection with the Social Democratic workers' meetings. All Social Democratic literature must become permeated with Party spirit . . . only then will Social Democratic literature . . . know how to carry out its duty, only then will it know how even in the framework of bourgeois society to tear itself loose from bourgeois slavery and to merge with the truly advanced . . . revolutionary class.

We have already noted the deceptive altering of the terms of the discussion. In a sense it proceeds out of the arrogance of the political revolutionary who insists—who, indeed, must insist—that his "made" universe contains not a portion of the truth or of virtue, but the whole of it, including the only meaningful definitions of freedom, and the only formula for creating a truly great literature. But this formula rests on the major fallacy in Soviet Marxian thinking about art: that art's worth is coterminous with its ideological value.

Much of the Soviet future is forecast in the final passage. First, there is the familiar idea that a "free," and presumably a great, literature, will express those qualities only through service to an idea and to the needs of the suffering masses. There is, in addition, the *mystique* of the *narod,* "the flower of the country, its strength, its future," the same *narod* which was, as Lenin repeatedly observed, such poor human material for social change that it had to be harnessed into a relationship of parental control so harsh that it was to require the indefinite suspension of many of the rights, privileges, and amenities of the most advanced civilizations. There is, too, the orientation toward the future, toward *should be* and *shall be,* conceived as the end of a long upward process of education, in which literature will be assigned a major share of the task of propagating healthy, correct, energizing ideas. Through the entire article runs the

certainty that this will be best accomplished through "controls," exercised in the name of politically conceived goals.

On the level of theory, whether or not he realized it, Lenin has completed the encirclement of the free intellect. He has accomplished it simply by extending the ethical imperative of revolutionary Marxism to the artist, with no allowance made for his professional needs. The fact that there is no formal barrier in Marxian theory to the assertion of a principle of conscription may now be translated into that other more ominous formula that neither Chernyshevsky, nor Lenin, nor, with few exceptions, the later Communist theorists have had the honesty or the perspicacity to admit, namely, that when the needs of revolution collide with the needs of art, the latter will always be denied.

In his thinking about art, Lenin has made an absolute choice within two sets of polar opposites that were isolated in the examination of Marxist theory. In the first place, he has clearly chosen future-oriented agitation over scientific investigation, and he has placed overwhelming emphasis on the harsh, one-sided command of interim revolutionary ethics as against the generous vision of man as a versatile, creative, many-sided creature—a vision implicit in the long-range Marxian perspective. Lenin is predictable in these choices since they are, part and parcel of his pioneering changes of emphasis within the whole world of Marxism. He was a changer, not an interpreter, of the world, and, drastic as his emphasis was, the conclusions he drew in this article are not in the end surprising. But we must note, since he is unwilling to do it, the disastrous consequences for the poet or the philosopher in the advocacy of a standard of political efficacy as the ultimate measure of truth.

Lenin's article may be said to mark the junction of the two principal currents of the Russian revolutionary tradition as it is concerned with imaginative literature. The waters are muddy, it is true, and Lenin makes no explicit acknowledgment here of his dependence on the Russian radical democrats, but their accent is unmistakable in the article, particularly in the final prescription for a socialist literature. The concepts of service to an idea and to the masses, of orienting art always toward a better future, and of educating men explicitly in their social responsibilities are nowhere to be found in the classical Marxist writings on art. Since they have been present in the Russian tradition since Belinsky, there is every reason to attribute them to Lenin's native inheritance, to Chernyshevsky, above all. Finally, Lenin has made an unequivocal choice within another crucial set of polarities, this time not Marxist but indigenous, that of knowledge versus political utility as the principal end of literature, as these ideas were developed in the mid-nineteenth-century debate in Russia.

At the risk of imposing too great a symmetry on very complex material, it is possible to outline the general terms of the merger between Marxism and radical democratic thought, as it affects literature. The complicated apparatus of Marxian determinism, with its claims to confirmation in the process of history and in nature itself, with its documented analysis of social injustice, and its proposals for action (as Lenin derived them from Marx and Engels), all replaced or supplemented the vaguer notions of "progress," "natural truth," and the rudimentary critique of social decay in the thinking of the Russians. Both bodies of ideas rested on the concept of an upward moving, dialectically operated universe, which the partisans of both had learned from Hegel. Brought together, as they were, by this shared belief, radical democratic ideas about literature seem to have survived the Marxian reinforcement to their assumptions, without fundamental change. There was, after all, a vacuum in classical Marxism on the matter of literature's role during the epoch of transition, which the Russian utilitarian theories were perfectly designed to fill. The wonder is that it took Soviet theorists so long to recognize the jigsaw neatness with which they fit together. Of course, early Soviet critics came into disturbing contact with the contrary, that is, the classical, or anti-utilitarian, trend in Marx's and Engels's remarks on art. Some of the critics may have been spellbound by the belittling designation, "pre-Marxist," which Plekhanov and others placed on the Russian radicals' ideas. Others may have inherited scruples from the classical past about controlling art and the artist as drastically as Chernyshevsky proposed. In any case, it was not until after 1932 that the prerevolutionary critics rose to a position of influence on a level with Marx and Engels. By 1946 they seemed to have gained absolute ascendancy. When the grand merger had been effected it became clear that the binding force between them was the supremacy of the activist, political ethic in both set of ideas.

Hegel to the contrary, history does not often organize itself into the form of dramatic tragedy. But if I may borrow the analogy, this moment (1905) deserves to be seen as one climax (albeit a hidden one) in the dramatic contest between the two factions within the Russian literary tradition, the moment of a fatal reversal of direction for the affairs of the protagonist, here thought of as the ideas of the classical tradition. Although it took years for this to become apparent, all else that follows is, in a sense, a denouement. The climactic moment was not apparent to the actors, but Lenin's article, together with Gorky's *Mother,* the novel that appeared a short time later as if to illustrate his doctrine, marks a watershed in the history of Russian thought. If these two documents announced the beginning of a new tradition, as postwar Soviet critics claimed, they also contained a veiled death sentence for the old. It may be that the sentence will not be carried out in the end, but for the trained ear in 1946 Zhdanov's "Report" had the ring of an epitaph.

II

Gorky had written to Chekhov as early as 1900: "The time has come when the heroic is required." Gorky felt this generalized need throughout his creative life: he found dignity and defiance, tenderness and courage, wisdom and saintliness in the lower depths of Russian life. His lifelong moral quest took the form of a search for heroes. He seems to have projected his own intense, almost virginal, sense of moral purity outward into the crowds he moved through, in a constant search for the men whose strength, humility, and independence he could admire. His searchlight picked them out of the most unexpected places. His gallery of heroes is varied and colorful—tramps, thieves, prostitutes, hermits, smugglers—and, although it is always threatened by sentimentalism, few of the portraits are blurred by the playing down of compensating vices, or by minimizing the filth, corruption, or despair that framed the reflected glint of virtue. In the tension of these contrasts, Gorky's notes of human affirmation establish their veracity. The function of these unlikely heroes was a simple one: to provide reassurance that man's dignity survived all vicissitudes, that there was hope. Nilovna, the heroine of his novel *Mother,* described the nourishing effects of contemplating virtue in others, in the broad, extrapolitical terms that characterize most of Gorky's own search:

> She knew men who had emancipated themselves from greed and evil; she understood that if there were more such people, the dark, incomprehensible, and awful face of life would become more kindly and simple, better and brighter.

He did not limit his search to a single class, or look for a single set of admirable qualities through the range of castes and classes in Imperial Russia. He found a successful tragic design, for example, in the career of the energetic, self-made bourgeois who was destroyed by the wealth he had accumulated. In his autobiography he tended to celebrate all kinds of dissenters, from the Old Believers to the most extreme elements of the revolutionary movement. When his quest centered momentarily on the rising Social Democratic Labor Party in the first decade of the twentieth century, and his long, uneven affiliation with that movement began, the generative force of a new kind of literature was created. It did not matter that *Mother,* the single novel he devoted to this theme, had no sequel, or that he shied away from the treatment of revolutionary political virtue in fiction in later years. The novel's publication in 1907 crystallized and gave literary expression to the fateful tendencies Lenin's article promised. The dangers that are forecast by this event may be summarized as the substitution of a programmatic, declamatory optimism for the undogmatic exploration of human life and suffering which had been the major preoccupation of the classical writers. The new novel promised, as Chernyshevsky had done in his novel, a way to end suffering. The issue of the positive hero becomes central again and is, according to the faction that welcomed the changes *Mother* initiated in Russian writing, the element that most solidly links the past with what is to come. In the novel's Bolshevik hero, Pavel Vlasov, we are told that Gorky continues the tradition of classical revolutionary-democratic literature, which created a series of freedom-loving heroes . . . but at the same time includes in it completely new material [so that] the image of Pavel Vlasov is the ancestor of the gallery of heroic images in Soviet literature: of Ostrovsky's Pavel Korchagin, the heroes of Fadeev's *Young Guard,* and a number of others.

Mother contains two formulas often found in later Soviet fiction: the conversion of the innocent, the ignorant, or the misled to a richer life of participation in the forward movement of society; and the more important pattern of emblematic political heroism in the face of terrible obstacles. The first theme is embodied in the figure of the mother, whose life is transformed by affiliation with the revolutionary movement, and the second in the grim figure of her son, Pavel. Actually the two themes are interwoven, with Pavel acting as the principal agent in restoring his mother to a life of dignity and purpose. This relationship also illustrates the kind of inspiriting effect the image of Pavel is intended to have on the sympathetic reader.

Pavel's inspirational value derives from the moral qualities he displays and the kind of purposeful activity in which he displays them. When courage, endurance, strength of will are exercised in certain kinds of tactically "correct" political behavior, during the May Day parade, for example, it is always a calculated effect he aims for. His later defiance of the Tsarist court reflects a public, not a private, emotion in the sense that it is not a personal defense, but an occasion to instruct the masses in the workings of the hateful system. Pavel acts on this, and on all other occasions, out of two supplementary kinds of knowledge that make up class consciousness: the abstract generalizations about society learned from his precious books, plus the documentation of working-class misery which is daily before his eyes. Thus equipped with emotion and knowledge, Pavel goes forth to permanent battle with the status quo.

This, at least, is the way we are asked to read the novel. It may be read quite differently, however. The novel's conflict is posed between moral absolutes and the writer's attitude toward the conflict is not that of an observer but of a partisan who is, himself, engaged in the bitter class warfare. In this rigid opposition there is no opportunity for the emblematic good man to move in the area between good and evil, or to be involved with, tempted by, or overcome from within by evil. He may reproach himself for lacking the endurance he needs to carry out the tasks history has set for him. He may search his soul to find the courage he needs. He may examine the reasons which brought him to his exposed position. But he will not question the position itself. Evil is tangible and external, and all man's resources are needed to combat it. Since, according to the formula in *Mother,* the good man is the most distant from evil, he cannot yield to it without forfeiting his position in the novel's moral hierarchy. Pavel's revolutionary colleague, the Ukrainian, Andrei Nakhodka, asks a question which is vital for the revolutionary and suggests at the same time a fruitful approach for the writer to the tensions of revolutionary activity. After he has confessed to the murder of a police spy, he asks, in effect, what crimes he will commit in the name of the revolution, what violations of his private moral code are permissible (or bearable) for the dedicated man. But Nakhodka is too weak, too susceptible. He is a good-hearted follower, but not the leader Pavel is. In Pavel's eyes such questions have a certain validity, but they do not really concern *him,* and can always be resolved in the terms of his political-moral absolutes.

But the ease with which he does resolve them seriously challenges his adequacy as a literary portrait. He is, among other things, a fanatical moralizer and prophet. It may be argued that these qualities have been forced on him by the stringencies of his situation, or that they are inevitable costs of his kind of life. In any case they are there—we know because Gorky, perhaps unwittingly, shows them to us—to be accounted for, overcome, or read into any final assessment of his human worth. At the very least they are barriers to awareness, if not to action. By failing to record his hero's limitations fully Gorky has provided grounds for seriously questioning his human and literary judgment in this matter.

The politicalizing of Pavel's emotions is very nearly complete. The following rapture is brought on by uttering the introductory word "Comrade" to a crowd of listening factory hands:

> When Pavel had thrown out the word to which he was meant to attach a deep and significant meaning, his throat contracted in a sharp spasm of the joy of fight. He was seized with the invincible desire to give himself up to the strength of his faith, to throw his heart to the people. His heart kindled with the dream of truth.

Despite the extravagantly bad writing and the hints of psychological imbalance, this passage, together with many others like it, is important because it describes the deepest emotional satisfaction of the political man. When his mother argues that he should not expose himself to danger by carrying the banner in the May Day parade, Pavel answers: "I must do it! Please understand me! It is my happiness." She is silent, and he continues in the vein of his grand political passion, hinting now at a taste for martyrdom: "You oughtn't to be grieved. You ought to rejoice. When are we going to have mothers who will rejoice in sending their children even to death?" Told by his mother that she speaks out of love for him, he answers: "There is a love that interferes with a man's very life," and then, later, "I want no love, I want no friendship which gets between my feet and holds me back." When Nakhodka, whose humane awareness is in inverse proportion to his political effectiveness, reproaches him for his harshness, and for acting the hero in front of his helpless mother, Gorky the writer has brought to light a legitimate conflict of values.

Pavel's pomposity, rigidity, and fixity of purpose, with their suggestions of sublimation and megalomania, are predictable consequences of his personality and of his way of life, as given. But Gorky the propagandist betrays his persuasive insight, a few moments later, by extracting a quick apology from Pavel. For the rest of the novel the insight is forgotten. Gorky's uncritical approval of Pavel is unmistakable as the latter grows into the most effective political leader in the area. Finally, when Pavel rises to speak at his trial, "A party man, I recognize only the court of my party and will not speak here in my defense," he has become in his own eyes the selfless incarnation of the public cause, without doubts, hesitations, or concern for personal loss, and Gorky, having surrendered his control over the character, can only agree.

The matter of tension between private and public life appears constantly, but it is resolved with one exception in favor of the latter. Sacrifice and suffering are often mentioned but seldom shown, and never explored to any depth. Consider the example of the design for marriage which Pavel's wife outlines to his mother:

> He's free at any moment. I am his comrade—a wife, of course. But the conditions of his work are such that for years and years I cannot regard our bond as the usual one, like that of others. It will be hard, I know it, to part with him; but, of course, I'll manage to. He knows that I'm not capable of regarding a man as my possession. . . . I love him very much and he me . . . we will enrich each other by all in our power; and if necessary we will part as friends.

Gorky records this solemnly, without irony, or any sense that it is any less than what will be accomplished. The two women sit enclosed in each other's arms: "It was quiet, melancholy and warm."

Nikolai, another revolutionary, whose marriage was broken up by the exigencies of exile and underground conspiracy, rationalized his loss in harsher terms:

> Family life always diminishes the energy of a revolutionary. Children must be maintained in security, and there's the need to work for one's bread. The revolutionist ought without cease to develop every iota of his energy; he must deepen and broaden it; but this demands time. He must always be at hand, because we—the working men—are called by the logic of history, to destroy the old world, to create a new life. . . . No revolutionist can attach himself to an individual—work through life side by side with another individual—without distorting his faith; and we must never forget our aim is not little conquests, but only complete victory!

Only once does raw human experience force its way through the web of political rationalization. Nakhodka's anguish at his casual blow which turned out to be an act of murder bespeaks real inner conflict. He knows the conventional terms in which the crime can be justified, and he recites them with an air of conviction:

> It so happens that we sometimes must abhor a certain person in order to hasten the time when it will be possible only to take delight in one another. You must destroy those who hinder the progress of life, who sell human beings for money in order to buy quiet or esteem for themselves. . . . If it happens sometimes that I am compelled to take their stick into my hands, what am I going to do then? Why I am going to take it, of course, I will not decline.

He has the right, even the duty, to act in that way. But this explanation is only "logic," he says, it has nothing to say to the conscience:

> I go against logic for once. I do not need your logic now. I know that blood can bring no results, I know that thin blood is barren, fruitless. . . . But I take the sin upon myself, I'll kill if I see a need for it. I speak only for myself, mind you. My crime dies with me. It will not remain a blot upon the future. It will sully no one but myself— no one but myself.

The crime which is justifiable in public terms is nevertheless unacceptable to Nakhodka's moral sensibility. It is the most terrible and destructive act of self-renunciation the revolutionary can be asked to carry out, even though he believes, as he does it, that it is in the name of the time when "free men will walk on the earth" and "life will be one great service to man":

> In your forward march it sometimes chances that you must go against your very self. You must be able to give up every thing—your heart and all. To give your life, to die for the cause—that's simple. Give more! Give that which is dearer to you than your life. . . . I will tear my heart out, if necessary, and will trample it with my own feet.

Despite the congealed rhetoric, this is intelligible moral utterance, exposing grounds for the deepest division between the individual and his cause, including permanent banishment from the Utopia to come. One need not agree with his definition of the dilemma to see in this the germ of genuine tragic conflict, the real drama of the revolution's honorable casualties. Gorky does not develop it further. Pavel, who, with his mother, remains in the center of the stage, understands and sympathizes: "Andrei won't forgive himself soon," he says, "if he'll forgive himself at all." But he reduces it again to the comforting blacks and whites of the political morality which Andrei has for a moment seen through:

> He killed a man unwittingly. He feels disgusted, ashamed, sick. . . . But they kill off thousands calmly, without a qualm, without a shudder of the heart. They kill with pleasure and with delight.

And then, true to the basic cadence of the book, Pavel dissolves his doubts in the strain of political evangelism that disfigures so much of the novel. Addressing his troubled mother, he says:

> If you felt the abomination of it all, the disgrace and rottenness, you would understand our truth; you would then perceive how great it is, how glorious.

With this the mother's doubts are set at rest, and the episode is ended. Gorky's optimism, at this time, about the revolutionary's capacity to endure hardship of all kinds, without moral damage, is summed up in some observations that the mother, by now a hardened revolutionary, makes to a comrade:

> There's a great deal of hardship, you know. People suffer; they are beaten, cruelly beaten, and everyone is oppressed and watched. They hide, live like monks, and many joys are closed to them, it's very hard. And when you look at them well you see that the hard things, the evil and difficult, are around them on the outside, and not within.

But even by the most ungenerous estimate, the virtues of monks do not contain Gorky's sense of human possibilities. It was this fact, perhaps, that prevented his ever again attempting a large-scale fictional treatment of the revolutionary movement.

We are confronted here with problems already made familiar to us by *What Is to Be Done?* The hardheaded visionaries of *Mother,* like the self-confident new men in Chernyshevsky's novel, have their minds fixed firmly on the emergent future. They are struggling to forward a trend which, they are convinced, is both inevitable and infinitely preferable to the unbearable present. Gorky makes no attempt to hide his own partisanship in this contest. Completely identified with his protagonists, he is as committed as they are to the overthrow of life as it is, in the name of a compelling vision of life as it should be. But the question again arises: how can the conflict between future and present be dramatized within the confines of the realistic novel? Apart from the many "utopian" speculations in the novel, the desirability of the future can be suggested only indirectly, through the intensity of the characters' dedication to it. Otherwise the affirmative case must be set forth in declamatory assertions by the hero or his lieutenants. In spite of the endless, florid talk about the better world their personal struggle brings closer, what these men are fighting against is always more vividly realized than what they are fighting for. Their anger is thus better motivated than their invincible optimism. In a novel of repeated tactical defeats this assurance is communicated only by defiant speeches.

The source of their optimism is a political truth founded upon abstractions. That the historical force championed by Pavel and his comrades is somehow benign is an assumption outside the novel which may or may not be accepted by the reader. Gorky's abandonment of a more traditional novelist's vantage for overt political commitment, therefore, prejudices any claims the novel may have to universal interest. The novel of open political partisanship can be acceptable only to like-minded readers. The only possibility of reaching a more indifferent audience rests in the acceptability or credibility of the human material—above all, of the hero—in the novel. And we have seen, I think, that the partisan blight has effectively neutralized his (or their) appeal.

The general difficulties we have indicated—involvement with the future, motivation by doctrine, and this writer's close identification with his heroes and with their cause—have one marked effect on the texture of the novel: it is shaped, down to the smallest technical details, by the spirit of political evangelism. It is not only that the climax of the novel is declamatory (Pavel's speech before the court), or that all the characters' actions and utterances are shaped by political considerations. The dialogue often resembles a verbal exchange of newspaper editorials, written in the turgid rhetoric which also disfigures Gorky's pamphleteering. The expository passages, the dramatic passages, the physical descriptions of the characters and of nature are likewise permeated with evangelism. As the mother goes down under the strangling fingers of the police spy at the novel's end she shouts a slogan, "You will not drown the truth in seas of blood." When Pavel has overcome her doubts about the essential justice of Nakhodka's act of homicide, "The mother arose agitated, full of a desire to fuse her heart into the heart of her son, into one burning, flaming torch." Class virtue manifests itself in the bodies, postures, faces, above all in the eyes of the characters. The eyes of the class enemy are muddy, bleared, or shifty, but, in the midst of his courtroom speech, "Pavel smiled, and the generous fire of his blue eyes blazed forth more brilliantly." At times Gorky comes very close to self-parody: "You'd better put on something; it's cold," one character remarks; and the other answers, "There's a fire inside of me." This is not simply bad writing but a striking example of the fusion of form and content. At the heart of the matter is Gorky's total partisanship. Under its influence all literary and human truth—even the truth of the physical universe—becomes subordinated to a single dogmatic view of political truth.

The history of this novel's reputation is voluminous. We may note only the major trend here: what was at first, in the opinion of critics, a very questionable piece of work is now considered the foundation of socialist realism. Lenin at his most functionalist is reported by Gorky to have told him while it was still in proofs:

> Yes, I should hurry up with it, such a book is needed, for many of the workers who take part in the revolutionary movement do so unconsciously, chaotically, and it would be very useful to them to read *Mother*. "The very book for the moment."

Gorky's biographer in English reports that Gorky himself was extremely displeased with it: "Gorky . . . has come to agree with most of his critics, namely, that the novel suffers from weakness of characterization and too obvious didacticism." His critics included many authoritative Soviet voices in the 1920s. Plekhanov and others found the novel schematic, sentimental, didactic, and ideologically false. The reversal of this generally held verdict coincided with the promulgation of socialist realism in 1932, with all that this meant for the setting of new standards of literary judgments on the leading personages in the novel. I. Bespalov's article on Gorky in the *Literary Encyclopedia* (1929) has this to say:

> Most vividly developed in *Mother* are the mother, Andrei Nakhodka, and Rybin. Pavel is presented schematically and somewhat bookishly.

In later judgments Andrei's and Pavel's positions are generally reversed. The Ukrainian is seen as a loyal, if fallible, lieutenant, but Pavel is the "first among equals." Timofeev's textbook for secondary schools notes Pavel's resemblance to Chernyshevsky's Rakhmetov, and praises his image as the incarnation of Bolshevik virtue. He is endowed with "will, intelligence," and "firmness of character." These traits in turn sustain his chief political attribute: "clarity of goal, readiness to surmount all obstacles for the achievement of this goal." This judgment echoes scores of others, which find in Pavel a point of junction of the old and the new, the first successful image of the positive Bolshevik hero, and the first successful solution of all attendant creative problems. At the heart of these opinions is the assumption that the contemplation of Pavel's image by the reader will stimulate him to emulate the hero's actions and thoughts, and coincidentally to respect Pavel's position as a representative of Communist leadership.

Gorky knew that his approach to literature implied important departures from classical realism. In his letter to Chekhov about the need for "the heroic," Gorky exposed some of the thinking that underlay this demand:

> So there you go, doing away with realism. And I am extremely glad. So be it! And to hell with it! . . . Everyone wants things that are exciting and brilliant so that it won't be like life, you see, but superior to life, better, more beautiful. Present-day literature must definitely begin to color life and as soon as it does this, life itself will acquire color. That is to say, people will live faster, more brilliantly.

The "realism" that must give way to the "heroic" was neutral, he felt, hopeless, and rooted in the present, in life as it is; the "heroic" that was to replace it was not escapist, but functional, in that it was to quicken and change men's lives and set them in motion toward an unspecified vision of life as it should be. On the single occasion when this general feeling was translated into political myth-making, he invested the "color" and the promise in Pavel and the other Bolsheviks. This lapse has been seized upon and made the theoretical basis of

"socialist romanticism," the ingredient of socialist realism which directs the writer not to a general heightening of experience as Gorky originally intended, but to the celebration of the emergent future exactly as it is defined in the Party program and in the five-year plans. This is the obligatory step beyond the present, beyond reality, beyond realism, and beyond the empirical truth that the figure of the Soviet hero must express. Pavel Vlasov is valued as an *ideological* portrait; made up of hope, doctrine, and tendency as much as he is of flesh and blood. Thus the grounds for doubting his human validity are built into the very basis of the theory he stands on.

In a sense, Gorky and Lenin collaborated in this first demonstration of Soviet literary partisanship. Perhaps in Lenin's, certainly in Gorky's, case, it did not represent their only or their final thought on literature. But it set an example of the extreme prescriptive potential in Soviet Marxism, which, even at that time, had the critical inheritance of the Russian radical tradition solidly grafted onto it. It has provided primary documentation ever since for the most extreme applications of this theory to Soviet writing.

Nina Tumarkin (essay date 1981)

SOURCE: "Religion, Bolshevism, and the Origins of the Lenin Cult," in *The Russian Review,* Vol. 40, No. 1, January, 1981, pp. 35-46.

[*In the following essay, Tumarkin examines the cult of Lenin that sprang up in Russia after the leader's death.*]

In 1925, one year after Lenin's death, a story, called "Clever Lenin," circulated among the peasants of the Viatka countryside. One day, it begins, Lenin was leafing through books and newspapers and in every one found writings about himself. "Why should we fear the Entente and America when we have Vladimir Il'ich, who goes by the name of Lenin?" Lenin worried about how his country would fare without him, so he sent for the finest Soviet doctor and explained that he wanted to appear to die but remain alive. "We will put you not in a grave," replied the doctor, "but in a spacious room, and we will cover you with glass so no one can poke you with his fingers."

And so, soon after, Lenin's death was announced. People wept and moaned: "What will become of us now? The British and French will attack us." But Kalinin consoled the people, urging them to stop weeping and start working. They put Lenin into a shed called a mausoleum and put a guard at the door.

One day, two, a week, and then a month passed and Lenin grew tired of lying under the glass. One night he slipped out the back door of the mausoleum and went to the Kremlin, where the commissars met. He entered just after a meeting and asked two janitors, who had been listening through the door, what they had heard. "Did they mention Lenin?" he queried. "What a question. 'Look,' they say, 'Lenin died but we now have almost twice as many communists. Now let the Entente dare make a peep.'" Lenin returned to the mausoleum and lay down under the glass feeling satisfied.

The next night he went to a factory. He asked the workers whether they were Party members. "Before Lenin's death we did not belong to the Party," they replied, "but now we are communists, we are Leninists." Lenin was very pleased.

On the third night he journeyed to a remote village. In one hut a light was still burning. "Can one rest here a little?" asked Lenin. "Come on in," came the reply. Lenin entered and was astonished. No icons. Red posters and portraits everywhere. "Are you not Christians?" he queried. "We are citizens, Comrade. This is a reading room and here is the Lenin Corner." "And how does the peasant fare?" "Not very well, but things are improving."

Lenin left the hut filled with joy, lay down in the mausoleum feeling reassured, and has been sleeping for many days now. He will probably awaken soon. What a joy that will be! Words cannot relate it, ink cannot describe it.

"Clever Lenin" displays elements of the classic Russian folk tale, such as the hero on a quest who undertakes three journeys. It also contains references to some of the most salient aspects of the early Lenin cult. The plot revolves around the idea that by 1924 Lenin had become such a powerful personification of Soviet authority that he worried about the sources of his nation's strength after his death. In fact, Lenin *had* become an important symbol of legitimacy beginning with the Civil War years, and Party leaders *did* worry bout the consequences of his disappearance from political life after his massive stroke of March 9, 1923. Those aspects of the Lenin cult that derived from the Agitation and Propaganda agencies of the Party and government—the Lenin Institute, the first Lenin museums, the Lenin Corner, the elevation of Leninism to the status of holy writ—were developed in 1923 in response to this concern and reached national proportions after Lenin's death in January 1924. "Clever Lenin" emphasizes three features of the cult that captured the popular imagination in 1924: the Lenin enrollment, the Lenin Corner, and most important, the embalmed body of Lenin on display in the newly constructed mausoleum. The underlying theme of the tale is that Lenin's death was merely illusory: Lenin lives.

The fact that these significant features of the cult of Lenin appear in a simple folk tale indicates that much of the form and inspiration for that cult derived from the traditional culture of the Russian peasant. In particular the belief that Lenin was alive despite his apparent death was evident in a variety of popular stories: an Uzbek tale of 1925 described Lenin as wandering in the

mountains searching for truth, and in 1926 a village correspondent from the northern Caucasus reported a local legend which held that "Lenin lives, but he secretly walks the earth and watches over Soviet power . . ." and that another person had been buried in his place. These stories of Lenin's life after apparent death resemble the famous legend widely current in the decade following the death of Alexander I in 1825, which maintained that Alexander was not dead, that he had chosen to wander the Russian land disguised as the hermit Fedor Kuzmich, and that the corpse sent to St. Petersburg from Taganrog was that of a sailor.

The uniformity of fantasy surrounding the deaths of the two Russian rulers indicates that although the deaths of Alexander and Lenin were separated by almost exactly a century, with a major revolution intervening, the Russian peasantry remained consistent in its political attitudes. The emotional power as well as the structural form of the Lenin cult derived, in part, from the peasant propensity to personify centralized political power and revere it in the person of the tsar, the "naive monarchism" eloquently discussed by Daniel Field in *Rebels in the Name of the Tsar*. A similar spontaneous popular veneration for Lenin which began during his lifetime was organized and promoted by the Communist Party and government during Lenin's illness and after his death to help mobilize and socialize the population. The success of the Lenin cult as a stabilizing and legitimizing force in Soviet political life is due in some measure to the extent to which its contours were shaped by traditional peasant culture.

But the power of the cult owes even more to its religious form and content. The Lenin Corner was derived from the icon or "red" corner, and Lenin's body, displayed as a holy relic, has been, paradoxically, the most evocative symbol of Lenin's immortality. The peasant tale just recounted indicates how the embalming could inspire the belief that his death had been merely illusory. From the moment of Lenin's death, the assertions of his immortality became the central emotional focus of his cult. "All around us, everywhere, Lenin is completely with us" was the slogan emblazoned on the banner of the Petrograd delegation to Lenin's funeral. Similar slogans filled the press of Moscow and Petrograd during the frenzied "mourning week" between Lenin's death and funeral. "He has not died and will never die!" read one; "Lenin is dead. Long live Lenin!" trumpeted another. Such declarations of Lenin's immortality have remained to the present day an integral part of the cult of Lenin, as attested by the ubiquitous banners and posters which read: "Lenin is more alive than the living!" and, from Maiakovskii's poem "Komsomol'skaia," published shortly after Lenin's death, the famous lines: "Lenin—lived. / Lenin—lives. / Lenin—will live."

How did religion come to play such a significant role in a Soviet political institution of primary importance? One explanation locates this link in the person of Stalin. Isaac Deutscher, and E. H. Carr following him, point to

Stalin's training at the Tiflis theological seminary as the main source of the religious cast to the Lenin cult so evident in the immediate aftermath of his death. Marxism, in order to survive in Russia, had to accommodate to that nation's "spiritual climate," argues Deutscher, and the former seminarian from Georgia showed his skill in this regard during the week of funerary rituals that followed Lenin's death, and particularly in the famous "oath" speech that Stalin delivered to the Second Congress of Soviets on the eve of Lenin's funeral. In this speech Stalin enumerated Lenin's "commandments" and swore to fulfill them in the name of the Communist Party, indicating, to Deutscher, his own unique blend of Marxism and Orthodoxy and, to Leonard Schapiro, his determination to lead the cult in order to secure his own position as Lenin's heir.

Robert C. Tucker, in *Stalin as Revolutionary,* maintains that Deutscher's emphasis on Stalin's role in the creation of the Lenin cult is misplaced and posits instead the leader-centered orientation of Bolshevism from its inception, its original resemblance to a religion with Lenin as a charismatic leader.

Links between religion and Bolshevism and religion and the Lenin cult do exist apart from Stalin and apart from the reverence for Lenin as leader which may have characterized his revolutionary following. These links are provided by three Bolsheviks who valued the spiritual, who were actively engaged with religion at the beginning of this century, and who, upon Lenin's death, became imaginative contributors to the most mystical aspects of the Lenin cult. They directed his funeral, the construction of his mausoleum, and the preservation of his body. The three men were V. D. Bonch-Bruevich, from 1917 to 1920 the Administrative Secretary of the Council of People's Commissars; Anatolii Lunacharskii, the erudite Commissar of Enlightenment; and Leonid Krasin, a man of energy, imagination, and talent, a diplomat and, at the time of Lenin's death, Commissar of Foreign Trade. Each of them was chosen by the presidium of the Central Executive Committee to oversee some important aspect of the cult of Lenin's body.

The man who measured that body for its coffin, who arranged Lenin's funeral, who selected his resting place in Red Square, and who chose as the inscription over the first crypt containing the leader's body the one word "LENIN," was V. D. Bonch-Bruevich, a man who had a deep understanding of Russian religious enthusiasm. He was designated a member of the Funeral Commission formed by the Central Executive Committee on January 22, 1924, and chaired by Feliks Dzerzhinskii. As Secretary of the Sovnarkom, Bonch-Bruevich had been in charge of Lenin's public image, making many of the arrangements for the portraits, sculptures, photographs and movies depicting the leader during the brief period of his active rule.

For three decades a student of Russian sectarianism, Bonch-Bruevich understood what Lenin did and could

mean to the Russian multitudes who had looked to the revolution with the vision of a new world consisting of old hopes realized. He was a Social Democrat who was fascinated by the history of Russian evangelical sects, and had had ties in the nineties both with Tolstoians in Swiss emigration and with Plekhanov (also in Swiss emigration), who shared his interest in religious movements. In 1899 Bonch-Bruevich had his first experience of living among sectarians when he travelled to Canada with the Dukhobors who were setting up a colony in that country. Not long afterwards, V. D. Bonch-Bruevich put his talents and knowledge to work for the Social Democrats by editing in Geneva a publication called *Rassvet* (Dawn) which was subtitled "A Social-Democratic Leaflet for Sectarians." Its function was to explain Marxism to Russian sectarians in concepts and language that they would find comprehensible and compelling. *Rassvet* began publication in 1904 as a response to a resolution passed by the 1903 Congress of Social Democrats, which stated that political activity among sectarians was to be intensified.

Twenty years later, when Lenin died, it was undoubtedly Bonch-Bruevich's sensitivity to Russian religion that gave him the requisite knowledge to organize the intense, dramatic, yet simple funeral rites that carried the nation through its gravest crisis since the Kronstadt rebellion, and that set the tone and, to a certain extent, the format for the extensive Lenin cult that immediately became entrenched in Soviet political behavior.

But Bonch-Bruevich, who was opposed to the idea of mummifying Lenin on the grounds that the leader himself had wanted a simple burial or cremation, did not supervise the preservation of Lenin's body. That job was entrusted to an Executive Troika of the Funeral Commission appointed one week after Lenin's funeral. The Troika consisted of Viacheslav Molotov, its nominal chairman, the rising Party functionary who was destined for a career of prominence under Stalin; A. S. Enukidze, Secretary of the Congress of Soviets' Central Executive Committee; and Leonid Krasin, who had been brought into the Funeral Commission five days earlier, on January 29, 1924. It was Krasin who supervised and reported on the tasks with which the Troika was charged. These included the design and construction of a wooden mausoleum and a sarcophagus to hold the body, the regulation and distribution of sculptures, pictures, and monuments to Lenin, and the preservation of his body. Krasin knew a great deal about modern art, and his taste dictated the choice of A. V. Schusev's design for the wooden mausoleum and Konstantin Mel'nikov's plans for an oak-lidded sarcophagus, both the winners of design competitions. An engineer by training, Krasin busied himself with the construction of a refrigeration unit which was to circulate cold air into the sarcophagus in order to maintain the body intact.

But within a month of Lenin's funeral, his body began to decay (in the words of the Commission report, *"vremia delalo svoe delo"*) and Professors V. P. Vorob'ev, an anatomist, and B. I. Zbarskii, a biochemist, were summoned in mid-March 1924 to repair the damage and devise a new technique of preservation—a task which they completed in four months. Two weeks after they had begun their labors, the Funeral Commission was renamed the Commission for the Immortalization of the Memory of V. I. Ul'ianov (Lenin), and later that year elaborate plans were begun to replace the newly constructed wooden mausoleum with a permanent one made of stone. Heading this effort was the Commissar of Enlightenment, Anatolii Lunacharskii.

The roots of Krasin's and Lunacharskii's impulses as cult creators date back to the first years of the twentieth century, when they were intensely involved in a search for spiritual regeneration that crystallized among the Bolsheviks in a movement known as "god-building" (*bogostroitel'stvo*). Maksim Gor'kii was the most prominent literary exponent of the movement, and its main theorist was the young Lunacharskii.

Lunacharskii became a revolutionary very early, at the age of fifteen. In 1892, at seventeen, he left Russia for Zurich where he studied philosophy with the "empirocriticist" Richard Avenarius and then moved to Paris. In 1898 he went to Moscow where he became a member of a Social-Democratic group, was arrested shortly thereafter and exiled to Kaluga for a brief period, and then to Vologda. In Vologda he argued with Berdiaev (at the time still a Marxist, after a fashion) whom he had met years before in Kiev, befriended V. A. Bazarov and the philosopher A. A. Bogdanov (Malinovskii), and married Bogdanov's sister.

Lunacharskii's interests tended toward the philosophical and the aesthetic. In exile his energies were in large part devoted to studying religion and myth; in later years he was to refer to himself as a "poet of the revolution." Following Bogdanov, at the time the most prominent Bolshevik within Russia, Lunacharskii joined the Bolshevik faction of the Russian Social-Democratic Party and in 1904, not long after the termination of his exile, he once again left the country for Europe, this time to work with Lenin who came to Paris to meet him.

Lunacharskii was passionately interested in art, but *as a Marxist* (he was careful to point out) he was also concerned with religion. For Lunacharskii, religion was the key to the realization of human potential, and socialism was bound to shape a new religion, one which would be totally humanistic. Marxist religious faith was to be a faith in future man, man unfettered by the shackles of class and individualism. In 1904 he first articulated his vision of a socialist religion; it was a deification of human potential:

> The faith of an active human being is a faith in mankind of the future; his religion is a combination of the feelings and thoughts which make him a participant in the life of mankind and a link in that chain which extends up to the super-

man . . . to a perfected organism. . . . If the essence of any life is self-preservation, then a life of beauty, goodness, and truth is self-realization.

At the end of the following year, Lunacharskii returned to Russia to work on the Bolshevik newspaper *Novaia zhizn'*, edited by Bogdanov and Gor'kii. After another arrest and a six-month imprisonment, Lunacharskii set about organizing conferences in St. Petersburg institutions of higher learning (suddenly open as forums during the 1905 Revolution), including an assignment on the history of religion. Soon afterwards he emigrated once again to Italy, and there wrote his two-volume work in which he expounded his theory of God-building, *Religion and Socialism* (1908-11).

Lunacharskii called Karl Marx one of Judaism's "precious gifts to mankind," along with Isaiah, Christ, St. Paul, and Spinoza. Feuerbach and then Marx "helped human consciousness to become human religion." Lunacharskii was deeply impressed by Feuerbach's *Essence of Christianity* and felt that its author had caught the heart of religion, unlike Plekhanov, who had caught "only its clothing." Lunacharskii understood that while the Bolsheviks emphasized the creative powers of the human will, rejecting Plekhanov's more traditionally deterministic view of history, their philosophy was no different from Plekhanov's arid rationalism. If Marx had bid his followers to *change* the world, they could accomplish this only as a result of the religious impulse, for religion was the emotional bond that linked human beings together. And religion provided the only prism through which the world could be understood, for "religion is enthusiasm and 'without enthusiasm it is not given to people to create anything great'." Bolshevism was to create a new religion, with a God who was human, who was all future humanity. "Scientific socialism," Lunacharskii wrote in 1907, "is the most religious of all religions, and the true Social Democrat is the most deeply religious of all human beings." The future of mankind was cause for boundless optimism, for mankind will evolve into a species unimaginably superior to what it is today. When we consider the wonder of human genius, when we witness "the miracle of the victory of human reason and will over nature," Lunacharskii remarked, "do we not feel how the god born between the ox and the donkey is becoming strong?"

Lunacharskii's eschatology promised a universal "development of the human spirit into an All-Spirit" (*Vsedusha*). This he called the process of "god-building," and the "greatest and most decisive act" in that process was to be revolution. The Marxist religion was even destined to overcome death, in Lunacharskii's view, through its capacity to link human beings to future generations, through man's perception of "the universal connectedness of life, of the all-life (*vsezhizn'*) which triumphs even in death."

Victory over death was a particularly important theme for Lunacharskii's friend, brother-in-law, and fellow proponent of god-building, A. A. Bogdanov. Bogdanov saw god-building as the creation of a living community of people which would transcend individualism and achieve immortality. He believed, furthermore, that transfusions of the blood could achieve eternal life, and eventually brought about his own death in 1928 by conducting transfusion experiments on himself.

Bogdanov is best known for having provoked Lenin's angry book, *Materialism and Empiriocriticism* (1909) which attacked him not for his religious views, but for his "tectological" epistemology which indicated that reality was dependent on our perception of it and was not absolute and independent. But between Bogdanov and Lenin the fight was intensely political as well. At the time of the split between the Mensheviks and Bolsheviks Bogdanov became the most important representative of Lenin's views in Russia while Lenin himself remained in emigration. Not long afterwards, between 1907 and 1910, Bogdanov was the leader of a powerful Bolshevik group that was influenced by syndicalism, inspired by the ideas of god-building and, above all, not centered around Lenin. Lunacharskii, Gor'kii, V. A. Bazarov, and I. I. Skvortsov-Stepanov, the future editor of *Izvestiia,* were part of this circle. And so was Leonid Krasin.

Krasin had been won over by Bogdanov's faith in physical immortality and may have been influenced, as well, by N. F. Federov, librarian of the Rumiantsev Museum in Moscow, who combined a faith in Christ with faith in human community and the miracle-working powers of technology and saw as the realizable goal of mankind the physical resurrection of the flesh. Leonid Krasin shared these philosophers' faith in the future possibility of physical resurrection. In 1931, the Old Bolshevik, M. S. Ol'minskii, wrote that Krasin had been a follower of Bogdanov and had returned to the fold only in 1918. In 1921, Ol'minskii continued, Krasin publicly preached his belief in the resurrection of the dead. It was at the funeral of L. Ia. Karpov that Krasin said:

> I am certain that the time will come when science will become all-powerful, that it will be able to recreate a deceased organism. I am certain that the time will come when one will be able to use the elements of a person's life to recreate the physical person. And I am certain that when that time will come, when the liberation of mankind, using all the might of science and technology, the strength and capacity of which we cannot now imagine, will be able to resurrect great historical figures—and I am certain that when that time will come, among the great figures will be our comrade, Lev Iakovlevich.

Three years later Krasin took charge of the preservation of Lenin's body. If Lev Iakovlevich was worthy of resurrection, was not Vladimir Il'ich even more worthy? It is more than likely that Krasin believed Lenin should be preserved intact *for his eventual resurrection.*

Is the system Krasin originally designed to keep Lenin's corpse intact, simple refrigeration without a vacuum to protect the body from mold, revealing of a mystical faith in the physical immortality of great figures? Did Krasin believe, perhaps, that Lenin's body, like that of an Orthodox saint, would not decay? Is that why he wrote, in February 1924 that the permanent Lenin Mausoleum was to surpass Mecca and Jerusalem in its human significance?

We cannot say, but in any event we know that shortly after Lenin's funeral Krasin was invited to join the Funeral Commission, and Konstantin Mel'nikov, the architect who won the competition organized by Krasin for the design of a sarcophagus for the body, later said that the "general idea" of permanently preserving and displaying Lenin's body originated with Leonid Krasin. Mel'nikov himself, says his biographer, S. Frederick Starr, looked to his art to overcome death, and saw the crystalline design of his sarcophagus as symbolic of eternity, as an affirmation of Lenin's immortality. Mel'nikov apparently had in mind the story of Sleeping Beauty, who was brought back to life by the kiss of a prince. "Who, then, is the Prince who will steal through the oaken door of Lenin's mausoleum in order to bring the sleeper back to life? It is, of course, the revolutionary Russian people, who possess the power of resurrection and will exercise it by endowing their leader with immortality."

In 1919 Lunacharskii obliquely reiterated his earlier commitment to god-building. Although in 1923 he supported anti-religious activities and wrote that "belief in personal immortality . . ." was a "'peasant belief no intelligent person could take seriously," it seems evident that Lunacharskii remained a god-builder. For the very next year, together with Krasin, he threw himself in the work of deifying Lenin. Lunacharskii's elegy on the day of Lenin's funeral is filled with the fervor and imagery of a religious zealot:

> After the passage of 100 years, the world will long since have known a new bright order. And people, looking back, will not have known an era more exalted, more holy, than the days of that Russian revolution which began the world revolution. And for this reason they will not have known a human figure who inspired more veneration, love and devotion than the figure, not only of a prophet, not only of a sage of the new communist world, but of its creator, its champion, its martyr (*muchenik*), . . . for Vladimir Il'ich . . . totally destroyed his gigantic brain . . . by his excessive superhuman, enormous work. . .
>
> We have seen Man, man with a capital letter. . . In him . . . are concentrated rays of light and heat. . . .

But Lunacharskii's real effort to immortalize Lenin as genius and Creator came in the autumn of 1924 when he took charge of the competition for the design of a permanent mausoleum of stone that would enshrine Lenin forever. Should we not assume that for Lunacharskii and Krasin it was the ardent religious striving of their earlier days, their god-building, which, finding a logical channel for expression, stirred them to help shape a cult of Lenin?

The god-building movement had emerged in Russia at the turn of the century, as part of a wide-ranging apocalyptic mood that pervaded many sectors of the intelligentsia from Vladimir Solov'ev and Federov to Andrei Belyi and Aleksandr Blok. In his famous poem "The Twelve" (1918) Blok anticipated that revolution would mean the Second Coming:

> With gentle step upon the snow,
> Through a pearly snowy cloud,
> In a white crown of roses—
> Marches in front—Jesus Christ.

And what event is more germane to the Second Coming than the resurrection of the flesh?

The immortalization of Lenin—*samyi chelovechnyi chelovek*—was a true deification of man. This Promethean impulse is implicit in Marxism which claims that conscious and free men will be the creators of a new world and is implicit as well in the Russian revolutionary tradition which was alternately fused with a faith in the greatness of the Russian *narod* and in the revolutionaries themselves, who were to transform Russia and, ultimately, the world according to a vision of equality. Marxism, Russian revolutionary thinking, and profound apocalyptic stirrings all help to explain the emergence of the god-building movement. It is an irony of history that the god-builders acted to deify human genius in the person of Lenin, for whom all religion was anathema and god-building was particularly repugnant, and that Lenin should have become, by the efforts of some of his oldest friends, the Man-God of Communism.

Paul N. Siegel (essay date 1984)

SOURCE: "Solzhenitsyn's Portrait of Lenin," in *CLIO*, Vol. 14, No. 1, 1984, pp. 1-13.

[*In the following essay, Siegel concludes that Alexander Solzhenitsyn's portrayal of Lenin in* Lenin in Zurich *bears little resemblance to the personality of the historical Lenin.*]

Alexander Solzhenitsyn's portrait of Lenin in *Lenin in Zurich,* which consists of chapters drawn from three volumes of his work in progress, is of interest in itself, in the light it casts on the historical accuracy of his project, whose avowed purpose is the correction of widespread misconceptions concerning the Russian revolution, and in its unwitting revelations about its author.

While using the methods of the literary artist, which permit him to enter his characters' heads, Solzhenitsyn emphasizes in an author's note that his fictional Lenin's "choice of words" and "way of thinking and acting" are drawn from a study of Lenin's works. In a BBC interview he stated: "I gathered every grain of information I could, every detail, and my only aim was to re-create him alive, as he was." Solzhenitsyn's portrait of Lenin is, therefore, to be judged for its historical authenticity as well as its artistry. It is primarily with the former that this paper will be concerned.

In his portrait of Stalin in *The First Circle* Solzhenitsyn, in cutting the towering figure of the Stalin of Stalinist myth-making down to size, showed him to be a human being at ironic variance with the image, a human being whose traits of character, as Gary Kern stated in an excellent analysis, were historically documented in Roy Medvedev's *Let History Judge*. In his portrait of Lenin Solzhenitsyn is concerned with destroying the Stalinist myth of Lenin as an all-wise god-like person incapable of making mistakes like ordinary men, a myth Stalin manufactured in order that he might proclaim himself the equally infallible successor of this god. But in dealing with a man further away in time Solzhenitsyn permitted his hatred of Bolshevism to cause him to draw a portrait that flies in the face of the consensus of scholarly opinion, of the historical record, and of the testimony of those who knew him well, including his enemies.

Leonard Schapiro's statement of the three character traits of Lenin "so generally accepted" by scholars who have gone through the literature on Lenin "that it is unlikely that they will ever be seriously challenged" furnishes an excellent means of judging Solzhenitsyn's portrait, in which each of these traits is replaced by another opposed to it. Schapiro was a leading historian well-known for his hostility to Bolshevism; his essay appeared in a book published in association with the right-wing Hoover Institution on War, Revolution, and Peace; the publisher of the book was Praeger, which at that time was receiving secret subsidies from the CIA to publish scholarly anti-Communist books. His appraisal of Lenin is not, therefore, at all sympathetic, but, since Schapiro was a responsible scholar, in giving the irreducible minimum on Lenin on which scholars agree, he is accurate.

The first of these traits, says Schapiro, is "Lenin's complete dedication to revolution, and the consequent subordination by him of his personal life to the cause for which he was prepared to sacrifice everything or any one. . . . The second generally accepted characteristic follows from the first: his kindliness on many occasions to individuals, coupled with ruthlessness on other occasions, to the same or different individuals. It simply depended on whether the 'cause' was involved or not. . . . The third characteristic of Lenin which all scholars would now accept was his complete lack of personal vanity or ambition."

This utter lack of vanity and ambition—attested to among others by Arthur Ransome, the *Manchester*

Guardian correspondent who had ready access to Lenin, by Pavel Axelrod and Angelica Balabanoff, close associates who became antagonists of his, and by Anatoly Lunacharsky, the Bolshevik leader whose *Revolutionary Silhouettes* objectively presented the strengths and weakness of the major figures of Bolshevism—is at sharp variance with Solzhenitsyn's Lenin, with the constant preening of himself on his ability and the constant looking down with scorn upon others. When, for instance, he is in despair, he ruminates: "All his incomparable abilities (appreciated now by everyone in the party, but he set a truer and still higher value on them), all his quickwittedness, his penetration, his grasp, his uselessly clear understanding of world events, had failed to bring him not only political victory but even the position of a member of Parliament in toyland, like Grimn [a swiss Social-Democratic leader]. Or that of a successful lawyer (though he would hate to be a lawyer—he had lost every case in Samara). Or even that of a journalist. Just because he had been born in accursed Russia." The self-satisfaction over the recognition he has achieved but the hunger for a still greater recognition, the loving elaboration of his self-proclaimed "incomparable abilities," the secret envy of the bourgeois careerists he outwardly despises, the blaming of his own failures upon his country—this is effective self-revelation, but not the self-revelation of one bearing any semblance to the Lenin who scholars agree was lacking in vanity and ambition.

When Alexander Parvus, the Russo-German Social-Democrat who supported Germany during the war, whom Solzhenitsyn presents as the real leader of the 1905 revolution and a corrupt genius whose superiority to himself as a theoretician and a man of action Lenin enviously recognizes in the inner recesses of his being, proposes that they form an alliance to make a Russian revolution with German money, Lenin rejects the idea because he does not want to be superseded. "Oh yes," he thinks, "I understand your Plan! You will emerge as the unifier of all the party groups. Add to that your financial power and your theoretical talent, and there you are—leader of a unified party and of the Second Revolution? Not again?!" Thus the revolution to which Lenin has dedicated his life is seen to be really a projection of his own ego, something which he will not sacrifice his own leadership role to attain. This is not the Lenin who scholars agree would have sacrificed everything for the revolution.

Looking with scorn at those about him, not only at his opponents but at his associates, whom Solzhenitsyn portrays as rogues Lenin despises but cynically uses, Lenin gives loose in his speech and in his thoughts to a constant stream of vituperation. The historical Lenin, it is well known, did not adhere to the "my respected opponent" manner of parliamentary debate in his polemics and made use of invectives such as "philistine," "renegade," and "servant of the bourgeoisie" in demolishing his opponents. Solzhenitsyn uses some of the epithets Lenin did and adds some choice ones of his own ("piss-poor slobbering pseudo-socialists," "little shit," "snot-nosed guttersnipes"). The unremitting flow of vituperation without a single kind word for anyone is indicative of both venomousness and coarseness. Although the correspondence of the real Lenin, as Scha-piro observes, "shows his concern for the personal welfare of bolsheviks and their families even at his busiest time," there is no hint of this in Solzhenitsyn.

Lenin, says Solzhenitsyn in an authorial comment, "never forgave a mistake. No matter who made it, he would remember as long as he lived." But Bukharin, in his letter "To a Future Generation of Party Leaders" which he had his wife memorize shortly before he was arrested by Stalin, spoke of Lenin's magnanimity toward those who had been mistaken: "If, more than once, I was mistaken about the methods of building socialism, let posterity judge me no more harshly than Vladimir Il'ich." Gorky, reminiscing on Lenin, exclaimed, "But how many times, in his judgment of people, whom he had yesterday criticized and 'pulled to bits,' did I clearly hear the note of genuine wonder before the talents and moral steadfastness of these people. . . ."

The historical Lenin, moreover, continued to recognize and pay tribute to the past accomplishments of those who became and remained his greatest political enemies. He insisted that Plekhanov, toward whom Solzhenitsyn's Lenin is full of bitter hatred, and Kautsky, whose picture Solzhenitsyn's Lenin states he cannot look at without retching as though he were swallowing a frog, be published in full and studied. He wrote an obituary for the Left Social-Revolutionist P. P. Prosh'ian, who had participated in the S-R insurrection against the Soviet government, in which he said, "Comrade Prosh'ian did more before July, 1918, to strengthen the Soviet regime than he did in July, 1918, to damage it." Lenin's wife Krupskaya tells of how, after he broke with his intimate associate Martov, he eagerly welcomed every position Martov took which he considered worthy of a revolutionist, and of how when he was struggling with his fatal illness he remarked sadly, "They say Martov is dying too." None of this is compatible with the Lenin of Solzhenitsyn's portrait.

Solzhenitsyn's Lenin not only regards both his political enemies and his associates with hatred and contempt; he regards everyone with hatred and contempt: peasants ("as obtuse as peasants the world over"), workers ("the workers had swarmed like ants out of their holes and into legal bodies," disregarding the Bolsheviks), women ("silly bitches"), young people ("these little piglets . . . were . . . so very sure of themselves, so ready to take over the leadership at any moment"). Above all, he despises the Russian people. "Why was he born in that uncouth country?" he asks himself. "Just because a quarter of his blood was Russian [Solzhenitsyn refers to Lenin throughout as an 'Asiatic'], fate had hitched him to the ramshackle Russian rattletrap. A quarter of his blood, but nothing in his character, his will, his inclinations made him kin to that slovenly, slapdash, eternally drunken country."

The real Lenin, however, was not at all contemptuous of ordinary people, talking easily with them and learning from what they had to say. This is attested to not only by Trotsky and Gorky, but by Balabanoff, who writes, "The desire to learn from others was characteristic of him. . . . He would ask peasants about agricultural matters. . . . He did not do it to attract attention or cause sensation, but rather unobtrusively." A number of accounts tell of Lenin visiting a Soviet art school, where he got into an animated exchange with two dozen students, who defended the futurist movement in art and literature against him. Lenin was delighted by the spirit of the youngsters and at the conclusion of the controversy good-naturedly joked that he would go home, read up on the subject, and then come back to defeat them in debate.

The historical Lenin was opposed to the party leadership granting itself special favors. Solzhenitsyn, however, has him make cavalier use of party funds, disbursing them freely to his favorites and stingily to others. "Find somebody to look after the children, we'll pay the expenses out of party funds," he tells Inessa Armand, urging her to attend an international congress, and in the next moment he thinks of how his associate Hanecki is not going because of his demand for expenses at a time when "party funds must be used carefully." But the real Lenin did not have such control of the money for functionaries' living expenses, and he himself was at times in dire need in his exile. "Lenin's personal finances were stretched," says Robert H. McNeal in his biography of Krupskaya, "and he implored the editors of *Pravda* to pay for Nadezhda's [Krupskaya's] operation. . . . but they must have let him down, for the request was repeated soon afterwards. . . ."

Tamara Deutscher in her *Not by Politics Alone . . . The Other Lenin* has a letter from Lenin to the office manager of the Council of People's Commissars officially reprimanding him for having raised Lenin's salary from 500 rubles a month to 800 rubles a month contrary to the decision of the Council, of which Lenin was chairperson. In a letter to the Library of the Rumyantsev Museum requesting permission to borrow certain books, Lenin wrote in 1920: "If, according to the rules, reference publications are not issued for home use, could not one get them for an evening, for the night, when the Library is closed. *I will return them by the morning*" (Lenin's emphasis).

Lenin's unbending dedication to the revolution and to revolutionary principles was a source of strength to him as a leader. Another source of strength, says Schapiro, was the combination of his lack of vanity and his "unwavering conviction" that "in any matter in dispute, he alone had the right answer." Solzhenitsyn's Lenin, however, despite his overweening vanity, is haunted by inner doubts. "His self-confidence had failed him [in

1905], and Lenin had skulked through the revolution in a daze. . . . It took years for the ribs dented by Parvus to straighten out again, for Lenin to regain his assurance that he, too, was of some use to the world." But the ribs dented by Parvus were not really straightened out. In 1916, when Parvus boasts to him of having sunk a battleship in 1905, Lenin thinks of himself that he can write, give lectures, influence young leftists, polemicize, but "there was only one thing he was incapable of—*action*."

His very insecurity makes Solzhenitsyn's Lenin incapable of admitting any error of judgment. "Yes, I made a mistake," he thinks to himself. "I was shortsighted, I wasn't bold enough. (But you must not talk like that even to your closest supporter, or you may rob him of his faith in his leader.)" The real Lenin, however, who believed that theory can never keep pace with changing reality, not infrequently admitted in retrospect to having erred. Especially was this true at the end of his life when he saw the growth of bureaucracy and of indifference to the rights and needs of the national minorities, to which he felt he had not paid sufficient attention. "In his statements, speeches, and notes made in the last period of his activity expressions such as 'the fault is mine,' 'I must correct another mistake of mine,' 'I am to blame,' are repeated several times," says Deutscher, quoting from documents in her book.

Beset by secret doubts he cannot voice, made irritable by people, exhausting himself in feverish activity, whose value he often questions to himself, Solzhenitsyn's Lenin is a jangle of nerves. Calmed for a moment as he walks along the bank of a Swiss lake, "he realized how hard-pressed and harassed he normally was." But Lunacharsky says of the Lenin he knew that, although at times he drove himself to exhaustion, he knew how to relax so that he emerged from his rest "freshened and ready for the fray again." "In the worst moments that he and I lived through together, Lenin was unshakeably calm and as ready as ever to break into cheerful laughter." The aged Boris Souvarine, one of the founders of the French Communist party, who knew Lenin well and came to be a strong anti-Bolshevik, is astounded at the feverishness of Solzhenitsyn's Lenin. "Day and night, even in response to the smallest thing, Lenin seems to be whirling. In all this we do not recognize the real Lenin and his habitual self-control."

The readiness to break into cheerful laughter of which Lunacharsky speaks is alien to Solzhenitsyn's Lenin. "Lenin often wore a mocking look," says Solzhenitsyn, "but very rarely smiled." On the occasions he does smile it is a "crooked little grin—suspicious, shrewd, derisory." When it occurs to Hanecki that Lenin's appearance is such that he might readily be taken for a Russian spy, he "wanted to tease him about it, but he knew that Lenin couldn't take a joke, and refrained."

But one of the distinctive characteristics of the real-life Lenin was his gaiety of disposition, which did not permit him to stand on false dignity. Arthur Ransome said of him, "I tried to think of any other man of his caliber who had a similar joyous temperament. I could think of none." Gorky said, "I have never met a man who could laugh so infectiously as Lenin." Trotsky described Lenin as "always . . . even-tempered and gay" and spoke of his "famous laughter." He told of how Lenin, in presiding over small committees, conducted the meetings in an efficient manner but sometimes, especially towards the end of a long, hard session, would be provoked to laughter by something that had amused him. "He tried to control himself as long as he could, but finally he would burst out with a peal of laughter which infected all the others."

Far from being unduly sensitive, he was ready to laugh at himself. N. Valentinov, an associate of Lenin's early in the century who later broke with him politically, related how on a picnic he observed that Lenin, instead of making a sandwich for himself, rapidly cut off pieces of bread, egg, and sausage and, with the nimble dexterity characteristic of him, popped them successively into his mouth. Valentinov commented on this, comparing Lenin's dexterity with the dexterity with which a character in Tolstoy's *War and Peace* put on his leggings. Instead of taking offense, Lenin found the comparison amusing. "His laughter was so infectious that Krupskaya also started to laugh at the sight of him; then I joined in too." There is no thin-skinned sensitivity here.

Solzhenitsyn's egocentric, dour Lenin, incapable of human warmth and geniality and hating every one, is utterly indifferent to others' suffering. He gleefully reads the figures on Russia's enormous war casualties, seeing them as evidence of the doom of the Tsarist regime. The climactic presentation of his indifference to suffering comes at the end of the first chapter of *Lenin in Zurich,* Chapter 22 in *August 1914* Lenin is at a parapet in a railroad station when a hospital train comes in. The dying are fearfully regarded by a crowd of people come to see if their dear ones are on the train, and the wounded are joyfully embraced. As Lenin surveys the scene, he has no thought for the emotions of the crowd: in a kind of demonic frenzy, he has been seized by the inspiration for his slogan "Convert the war into civil war!" a civil war "without quarter" that "will bring all the governments of Europe down in ruins!!!" "Daily, hourly, wherever you may be—*protest* angrily and uncompromisingly against this war! But . . . ! (The dialectic essence of the situation.) But . . . will it to continue! See that it does not stop short! That it drags on and is *transformed!* A war *like this one* must not be fumbled, must not be wasted. Such a war is a gift from history!"

Remarkably, Lenin is made responsible for the continuation of the war. He will "will it to continue." How can he, however great his will power, achieve this extraordinary feat? Earlier he had thought to himself, "You must find channels for negotiations, covertly reassure yourself that if difficulties arise in Russia and she starts suing for peace, Germany will not agree to peace talks,

will not abandon the Russian revolutionaries to the whim of fate." The unknown emigré will somehow influence the German government not to free itself from one front in a two-front war in order not to "abandon the Russian revolutionaries." This simply does not make sense.

Not only is the responsibility for the war foisted from the warring governments upon Lenin, but the bloodiness of the Russian civil war is attributed to the bloodthirstiness of Lenin. The White forces and the allied governments who supported them are absolved of all responsibility. Lenin's denunciations of the war are dismissed as mere verbiage to mask his sinister design. He is incapable of genuine moral indignation.

Lenin undoubtedly was, as Schapiro says, ruthless in the defense of the revolution. The question is, however, whether Lenin was like a humane surgeon who cuts off a limb to save a life or like the Nazi doctors who engaged in cruel experimentation without any regard for their concentration-camp victims. How one judges his acts will depend in good part upon one's own politics. Many who condemn such measures as holding hostages subject to execution to break the opposing side's will or executing the Tsar's children to deprive the monarchists of a rallying-point do not feel the same way about the fire-bombing of Dresden or the atom bombing of Hiroshima and Nagasaki in World War II, which killed innumerably more innocent people. But however one regards his actions, serious scholars do not find Lenin to have been the totally unfeeling person Solzhenitsyn makes him out to be.

Thus Bertram D. Wolfe, an ex-leader of the American Communist party who became Chief of the Ideological Advisory Staff of the Voice of America, said of Gorky's *Lenin* that it revealed his "faithfulness to himself as artist and observer of his subject." But Gorky, a long-time friend of Lenin's who attacked him sharply for the severity of his measures during the Civil War but who came to feel that they were necessary, depicted Lenin as keenly sympathetic toward the oppressed. "In a country where the inevitability of suffering is recommended as the universal road to the 'salvation of the soul,'" wrote the author of *The Lower Depths,* himself so sensitive to human misery, "I never met, I do not know a man who hated, loathed and despised human unhappiness, grief, and suffering as strongly and deeply as Lenin did."

Thus too Peter Reddaway, co-editor with Leonard Schapiro of *Lenin: The Man, The Theorist, The Leader,* while speaking of the "fanaticism" of Lenin's "revolutionary morality," speaks also of "the human side of Lenin, which he had to keep so rigidly under control. This is the Lenin of whom Lepeshinsky said: 'He possesses a remarkably tender soul, not lacking, I would say, even a certain sentimentality'; who rebuked Bogdanov with the words: 'Marxism does not deny, but, on the contrary, affirms the healthy enjoyment of life given by nature, love and so on'; who, as a youth, suddenly saw he must not become a farmer because 'my relations with the peasants are becoming abnormal'; who could not shoot a fox because 'really she was so beautiful'; who told Gorky: 'It is high time for you to realize that politics are a dirty business'; and who said in E. Zozulya's presence: 'O happy time, when there will be less politics.'"

The traits which Solzhenitsyn gives Lenin—vanity, ambition, envy, coarseness, unforgivingness, a sense of inferiority (at least, with regard to Parvus), readiness to use and dispense special privileges, readiness to take personal offense, unwillingness to admit mistakes, indifference to others' suffering—are, interestingly enough, those that he gives to Stalin in *The First Circle* and that were indeed part of Stalin's character. Solzhenitsyn regards Stalin as the legitimate political heir of Lenin, and this opinion is reflected in his projecting the personal traits of the heir upon his predecessor.

There is another person besides Stalin who, without Solzhenitsyn being aware of it, acted as a model for Solzhenitsyn's portrait of Lenin, a surprising one—Solzhenitsyn himself. Working in the very Zurich in which Lenin had worked, with the same object of undermining the Russian government, Solzhenitsyn unconsciously identified Lenin with himself. Just as his Lenin believes himself to be "the infallible interpreter" of a "compelling power which manifested itself through him," so Solzhenitsyn in his self-revelatory *The Oak and the Calf* marvels at his own ability to "hold out single-handed, yes, and fork over mountains of work" and exclaims: "Where do I get the strength? From what miraculous source?" He answers himself some pages later: "How wise and powerful is thy guiding hand, O Lord!" Even the style of Lenin's interior monologues is similar to that of Solzhenitsyn's memoir, making free use of parenthetical interjections, italics, and exclamation points to convey febrile excitement. Lenin's confrontation with Parvus, in which each of them seeks to penetrate the mask of the other, resembles Solzhenitsyn's confrontation with his former wife, who he is convinced is now a KGB agent.

Solzhenitsyn regards himself as alone in knowing how to combat the present Russian regime. Of the efforts of other dissidents he is scornful. He regards the "soft" Tvardovsky, the editor through whom he had been published, in much the same way that his Lenin regards the Mensheviks. He attacks the Medvedev brothers harshly as agents of the regime.

Just as Solzhenitsyn's Lenin is contemptuous of the Russian people, so Solzhenitsyn in one passage is contemptuous of them: "We spent ourselves in one unrestrained outburst in 1917, and then we *hurried* to submit. We submitted with *pleasure!* . . . We purely and simply *deserved* everything that happened afterward." Just as Lenin rejoices in World War I as an opportunity for revolution, so Solzhenitsyn relates how he longed in prison camp for the United States to use its monopoly of the atomic bomb to start a new war against the Soviet Union: "World war might bring us a speedier death . . . or it just might bring freedom. In either case, deliverance would be much nearer than the end of a twenty-five year sentence." Just as his Lenin was ready to serve the Kaiser against Russia, so Solzhenitsyn praises and justifies the Red Army soldiers who turned traitor and fought in the ranks of Hitler's army, himself making the explicit comparison: "Came the time when weapons were put in the hands of these people, should they have . . . allowed Bolshevism to outlive itself . . . ? . . . No, the natural thing was to copy the methods of Bolshevism itself: it had eaten into the body of a Russia sapped by the First World War, and it must be defeated at a similar moment in the Second."

Solzhenitsyn's portrait of Lenin, then, has many of the traits of Stalin and is also in part an unconscious mirror image of Solzhenitsyn himself. It bears little resemblance to the historical Lenin.

Alfred B. Evans   (essay date 1987)

SOURCE: "Rereading Lenin's *State and Revolution,*" in *Slavic Review,* Vol. 46, No. 1, Spring, 1987, pp. 1-19.

[*In the following essay, Evans argues that Lenin's* State and Revolution *is not antithetical to the rest of Lenin's work, as most critics contend, but rather that the "tension between the polarities of value in Lenin's thought" would later become an integral part of Soviet politics.*]

State and Revolution has long seemed to be the most puzzling of Lenin's written works. The traditional view among western scholars has regarded *State and Revolution* as a utopian fantasy that is completely out of character with the rest of Lenin's thought. The most prominent exponent of that viewpoint is Robert V. Daniels, who, in an influential article published in 1953, asserted that the ideas of *State and Revolution* were "permeated with an idealistic, almost utopian spirit." and who in a later work described *State and Revolution* as an "argument for utopian anarchism" and a treatise in "revolutionary utopianism." Similar comments have been offered by a number of other authors. Alfred Meyer, though not dealing in detail with *State and Revolution* in his brilliant review of Lenin's thought, regards the essay as a reflection of the "dream of the 'commune state'" expressed in Lenin's statements from early 1917 through the first few months of 1918. Adam Ulam refers to *State and Revolution* as "almost a straightforward profession of anarchism." All those authorities agree that the themes found in *State and Revolution* are strikingly inconsistent with the elitism, realism, and authoritarianism that permeated Lenin's other writings, before and after the publication of *State and Revolution,* and that guided him in practice as the leader of the Bolshevik party and the Soviet state. Deniels contends that "*State and Revolution* is a work conforming neither to Lenin's previous thought nor to his subsequent practice.

It stands as a monument to its author's intellectual deviation during the year of revolution, 1917." Louis Fischer calls *State and Revolution* an "aberrant intellectual enterprise, a fanciful exercise for so rockhard a man, as un-Leninist as the mask he wore and the false name he bore in hiding while writing it." According to Ulam, "no work could be more *un*-representative of its author's political philosophy and his general frame of mind than this one by Lenin." Viewed in that manner, *State and Revolution* is an anomaly, an instance of un-Leninist Leninism, and the question that inevitably is posed is why Lenin wrote an essay that is said to be very sharply at variance with the general tone and direction of his thought. Answers to that question differ considerably among the authors just cited, but the most common explanation for the utopianism of *State and Revolution* is that in 1917 the collapse of the tsarist regime, the upsurge of mass militancy and radicalism in Russia, and the rapid improvement of the prospects for a successful proletarian revolution aroused Lenin's optimism as never before and encouraged him to shift toward sympathy with the aspirations of Left Bolsheviks. Lenin, in that perspective, was so caught up in the revolutionary mood of 1917 that he was virtually intoxicated with optimism. Most of the proponents of that school of thought, however, see Lenin as sobering up when assuming the responsibility of exercising power and as discarding the dreams of *State and Revolution* when his authoritarianism reasserted itself increasingly from the spring of 1918 on.

Another school of thought, more frequently heard from in recent years, denies that *State and Revolution* represents a fundamental deviation from the general line of Lenin's thought. That revisionist interpretation of the place of *State and Revolution* among Lenin's works was expressed most emphatically in an article by Rodney Barfield in [*Slavic Review*] in 1971. Barfield agrees that Lenin's approach in *State and Revolution* "gives way to spontaneous, anarchistic tendencies," that the essay promises an "anarchistic state of affairs," and that it is filled with "utopian notions" and "anarchistic proposals." Barfield, however, sees Lenin's major treatise on the state as a "theoretical work looking into the future," a model of future socialist society that was, on the level of abstract theory, not incongruent with Lenin's general outlook. "*State and Revolution* does represent his fundamental philosophy of man, his inner conviction of human nature, his ideals for a more humane world." Barfield argues that both hard-nosed realism and utopian idealism were inherent elements of Lenin's values and expectations throughout his political career. Rolf Theen also charges that the interpretation of *State and Revolution* as an aberration or a daydream "fails to recognize . . . that underneath Lenin's pragmatism as a revolutionary there was always a powerful utopian vision." Though the essay,

> with its anarchistic tendencies, its emphasis on the spontaneous abilities and key role of the masses in the construction of the new society, as

well as its concomitant de-emphasis of discipline and organization . . . seems to be the perfect antithesis of the elitist and managerial approach to revolution which constitutes the central theme of *What Is To Be Done?*,

Theen contends that "the disparity is only superficial," because Lenin's essay on the state was "not as much concerned with the practical politics of the immediate present as with the theoretical exposition of the future society under socialism," and revealed Lenin's belief in "the ultimate rationality and perfectibility of man." A distinctly different position is taken by Neil Harding, who says that Lenin's writings of 1917 on political organization were not intended as an abstract, theoretical projection for the new society of the remote future but were meant to furnish "a coherent set of guidelines which would guide socialists in the practical task of establishing a socialist society." Harding, like other authors, describes *State and Revolution* as advocating the dominance of unrestrained, spontaneous mass initiative. That essay was a "project to dissolve the state and to inaugurate mass self-administration," a "vision of genuine direct democracy and genuine freedom," and a model of "radical direct democracy," which "necessarily entailed the broadest diffusion of authority and power to a multiplicity of self-acting organizations of the popular mass, its animating principles being camaraderie and spontaneous self-organization." Yet Harding rejects the view that *State and Revolution* was a pipe dream inconsistent with Lenin's writing before 1917, since he sees Lenin as primarily a somewhat idealistic theorist rather than a pragmatic political leader, and as innocent of the accusation of Jacobinism, at least until later in his life.

The focus of disagreement among commentators on *State and Revolution* has been the relationship between that essay and the rest of Lenin's thought and writings. There has been general agreement, however, that the content of *State and Revolution* is utopian in the sense of discarding the concern with elites, centralization, and hierarchy that is a prominent feature of many of Lenin's other works and endorsing a virtually unstructured, semi-anarchist system of rule by the autonomous popular masses. If that were indeed the content of Lenin's vision of socialism in *State and Revolution,* the essay would be something of an anomaly; reconciling that vision with the rest of Lenin's writings on politics and society would be difficult. It is the argument of this article, however, that *State and Revolution* has been misinterpreted in most of the scholarly literature on Lenin's thought. *State and Revolution* is simply not the utopian, quasi-anarchistic expression of hostility to authority and blind faith in the masses that it is usually made out to be. The essay does represent the high watermark of Lenin's optimism concerning the merits of mass initiative in building the new society, but elitism, hierarchy, and centralization are by no means absent from Lenin's picture of socialist society. In 1917 he did not in theory or practice throw all caution to the winds and stake everything on the unsullied wisdom of the masses. Lenin's essay was vulnerable to the charge of being unrealistic, not because he failed to allow for authority from above, but because he expected centralized planning and guidance to be easily compatible with enthusiastic initiative from below. Yet Lenin may have had good practical reasons for appearing at the time to be overly optimistic on that issue. The reexamination of *State and Revolution* in this article will proceed through two steps. The first is a description of the purposes Lenin sought to achieve in that essay, as shown by contextual evidence as well as statements in *State and Revolution* itself. The second step will be an analysis of the details of Lenin's remarks on the structure and operation of the institutions of the future socialist society, as discerned through a careful rereading of *State and Revolution* and reference to his other relevant works of 1917.

Before dealing with the purposes and content of *State and Revolution,* however, it will be worthwhile to review briefly the circumstances of its writing and publication. Recent scholarship has established that most of Lenin's preliminary work on *State and Revolution* preceded the February Revolution. There is some evidence that Lenin had shown particular interest in questions concerning the role and significance of the state in 1915 and 1916, yet other problems clearly preoccupied him more until the later part of 1916. Lenin's intensive reexamination of Marxist thought on the state was stimulated by Nikolai Bukharin, who in July 1916 submitted an essay, "Towards a Theory of the Imperialist State," for inclusion in a series edited by Lenin. The essay was rejected by Lenin, who bluntly informed Bukharin that it was ill-formed and erroneous in its treatment of political matters. Bukharin published another version of the article, titled "The Imperialist Pirate State," in *Jugend-Internationale* in December 1916. Lenin responded with a piece in *Sbornik Sotsial-Demokrata,* published in the same month, in which he again repudiated Bukharin's position and revealed that he hoped to compose an article of his own on the state. Lenin then "set to work" in the Zurich Library, as Nadezhda Krupskaia reported, "rereading all that Marx and Engels had written on the state and making notes on their work." He was absorbed in that theoretical effort during January and February of 1917, still expressing the intention of producing an "article" on "the attitude of Marxism to the state." In the course of his studies of early 1917, he arrived at conclusions that signified a virtual reconciliation with Bukharin. Lenin's notes from January and February 1917 were written in a notebook with a blue cover, bearing the title "Marxism on the State." Those notes, consisting of extensive quotations from Marx, Engels, and later socialist authors, along with Lenin's comments, set forth the essence of the argument that later was to be elaborated in *State and Revolution.* The principal themes of Lenin's major essay on the state were derived from his review of theoretical writings before the Russian Revolution of February 1917.

After the fall of the Romanov dynasty, Lenin's return to Russia and his involvement in revolutionary activity forced him to set aside theoretical endeavors. In July 1917, when Lenin fled Petrograd to avoid arrest, he left a note imploring Lev Kamenev to publish his notes on Marxism and the state if he were "bumped off." Finding himself alive and well in hiding near Razliv, Lenin was able to obtain the delivery of his blue notebook from Stockholm, where it had been left during his return to Russia. His labors at transforming his notes into a finished work continued in Finland in August and September. In the fall of 1917, Lenin planned to publish *State and Revolution* under a pseudonym, to avoid confiscation of the book by the Provisional Government. As the work was not published until January 1918, that subterfuge proved unnecessary. A second edition of *State and Revolution* was published in 1919 with the inclusion of only one additional section by Lenin and without the chapter on the experience of the Russian revolutions of 1905 and 1917 that Lenin had planned to add. The circumstances of the preparation and printing of *State and Revolution* indicate clearly that the main ideas in the essay took shape before February 1917 but that in the heat of revolutionary political activity, Lenin retained a keen interest in the completion and dissemination of his theoretical arguments on the relation of Marxists to the state.

Lenin's primary objective in *State and Revolution* was not the description of the state in the future socialist society, though he did turn to that subject in extensive passages of his essay. His primary objective is easily identified. Lenin opened the essay with the complaint that since Marx's death, his teachings had been distorted by the bourgeoisie and the "opportunists" within the labor movement. "In these circumstances, in view of the unprecedentedly widespread distortion of Marxism, our prime task is to *re-establish* what Marx really taught on the subject of the state." Lenin aimed to define the doctrinal orthodoxy of Marxism concerning the proper relationship of the proletariat toward the state. The principal theme of *State and Revolution,* supported by lengthy quotations from Marx and Engels, is that the working class cannot take over the existing bourgeois state for its own use but must smash (*razbit'*) the bourgeois state and replace it with a new one. "Marx's idea is that the working class must *break up, smash* the 'ready-made state machinery,' and not confine itself merely to laying hold of it." Lenin insisted that the imperative of destruction of the bourgeois state was of central importance for Marxism. "The necessity of systematically imbuing the masses with *this* and precisely this view of violent revolution lies at the root of the *entire* theory of Marx and Engels." But why did Lenin elevate the principle of destruction of the bourgeois state to the status of the key test of Marxist orthodoxy?

State and Revolution represented Lenin's bid to claim the mantle of international leadership in the interpretation of the teachings of Marx and Engels. The essay, like many others written by Lenin, had a polemical character; its chief target was the most prominent theoretician of German social democracy, Karl Kautsky.

Since Engels's death in 1895, Kautsky had been generally recognized as the world's leading exponent of Marxist theory. Lenin acknowledged in 1917 that Kautsky had been "the most outstanding authority" and the "best-known leader of the Second International." After the outbreak of World War I, however, Kautsky's adoption of a position of compromise on Germany's military efforts had outraged Lenin and prompted him to try to discredit Kautsky in the eyes of the world's Marxists. During the war, Lenin had adopted the aim of forming a new, genuinely radical international organization of Marxist parties. He urged impatiently, "our Party must not wait, but must immediately *found* a Third International." Lenin expected to be among the leaders of the new International. He sought to demonstrate that Kautsky, the most respected theoretician of the old International, had made errors of fundamental importance in the interpretation of Marxism.

Several pieces of evidence indicate that Kautsky was the chief target of Lenin's polemic in *State and Revolution*. Each of Lenin's letters of early 1917 that mentioned that he was writing an essay on the state noted that he was singling out Kautsky for criticism. He wrote to Aleksandra Kollontai in February 1917 that

> I am preparing (have almost got the material ready) an article on the question of the attitude of Marxism toward the state. I have come to conclusions more sharply against Kautsky, than against Bukharin. . . . The question is extremely important; Bukharin is much better than Kautsky, but Bukharin's mistakes may *ruin* this "just cause" in the struggle with Kautskyism.

Later in the same month, in a letter to Inessa Armand reporting on his study of Marxist views on the state, Lenin said.

> I . . . have come, it seems to me, to very interesting and important conclusions *much more* against Kautsky than against N. Iv. Bukharin (who, however, is still not right, although closer to the truth than Kautsky). I would terribly like to write of that: to publish No. 4 of the "Collection Social-Democrat" with Bukharin's article and my analysis of his small mistakes and Kautksy's big lies and vulgarization of Marxism.

When writing Armand again several days later, Lenin referred to the debate between Anton Pannekoek and Kautsky that would be reviewed in *State and Revolution:* "I have read Pannekoek's discussion in 'Neue Zeit' (1912) with Kautsky: Kautsky is an arch-villain, and Pannekoek is *almost* right; he only is guilty of *inaccuracies* and slight mistakes. Kautsky is the acme of opportunism." Lenin's correspondence revealed that his analysis of Marx's writings on the state was closely tied to the attack on Kautsky. In addition Kautsky was the only author other than Marx and Engels to whom major sections of Lenin's notes of January and February 1917, "Marxism on the State," were devoted.

The text of *State and Revolution* itself makes it clear that Lenin sought in that essay to demolish Kautsky's position among international Marxists. In the preface to that work, after asserting that "the struggle to free the working people from the influence of the bourgeoisie . . . is impossible without a struggle against opportunist prejudices concerning the state," Lenin adds that "we deal especially with the one who is chiefly responsible for these distortions, Karl Kautsky." In the first section of the essay following the preface, after complaining of the "doctoring" of Marxism and explaining that his prime task is to reestablish "what Marx really taught on the subject of the state," Lenin says that the inclusion of long excerpts from the works of Marx and Engels is necessary to present the views of the founders of scientific socialism "and so that their distortion by the 'Kautskyism' now prevailing may be documented and clearly demonstrated." The text of *State and Revolution* consists of six sections, of which the first five are devoted to quotations from Marx and Engels with commentary by Lenin, while the sixth deals with errors in the presentation of Marxist views on the state by the "opportunists." It is striking that, though Lenin finished writing his major work on the state while he was in Russia and Finland, during some of the most turbulent months of revolution in Russia, he pays little attention to Russian political figures in the course of the essay. He deigns to attack most spokesmen for other Russian parties and factions only briefly and in passing. He does devote one separate, but rather short, subdivision of the sixth section of *State and Revolution* to the criticism of one of Plekhanov's pamphlets. At the time Plekhanov was far more important as a theoretician of world Marxism than as a leader of any organized group of Russian socialists. Lenin attacked Plekhanov and engaged in a much longer polemic against Kautsky in the last section of *State and Revolution,* in order to attempt to damage the prestige of the intellectual leaders of the centrist forces within international Marxism.

The theoreticians of the Marxist "center" had gained great esteem as defenders of orthodox Marxism during debate with the revisionists in the early 1900s. Lenin's reexamination of passages on the state in the works of Marx and Engels in Zurich had clarified his own thinking on the bourgeois state and the proletarian revolution and, also, convinced him that he had found a point of strategic vulnerability in the position of the centrists, the most prominent of whom was Kautsky. Lenin felt he was now able to document a major deviation from Marx's precepts in Kautsky's writings. The point of attack was well chosen, for, though in actuality Kautsky was generally much more in accordance with the letter of Marx's doctrines than was Lenin, the centrists were, from the viewpoint of orthodox Marxism, most open to criticism on the grounds of their lack of enthusiasm for the traumatic and disruptive ordeal of the proletarian revolution. While being careful to postpone the consideration of the specific form of that future revolution, Kautsky had inched very close to forecasting the peaceful assumption of power within the state by a parliamentary majority of socialist deputies. Lenin tried to prove that the possibility of attaining control over the bourgeois state by constitutional means had been rejected by Marx (a dubious, one-sided interpretation of Marx's statements on the subject) and that Marx had insisted on violent revolution against the bourgeois state as the only possible means of instituting socialism. In the initial stages of his work on **State and Revolution,** during late 1916 and early 1917, Lenin evidently hoped that his reestablishment of the revolutionary essence of Marx's teachings on the state would serve as the basis for demonstrating the unrevolutionary character of the Marxist center, dethroning Kautsky from the status of a world-renowned disciple of Marx, and greatly enhancing his own reputation among international Marxists as an authority on the theory of scientific socialism.

The aims of discrediting Kautsky and winning recognition as the leading representative of the leftist tendency in world Marxism had not been abandoned by Lenin upon his return to Russia in April of 1917, as the international orientation of **State and Revolution** implies and that essay's focus on Kautsky's deviation demonstrates. **State and Revolution** is written in general terms, with its precepts applicable to any country (or at least any major power in Europe or North America) and not only to Russia. The completion of a theoretical essay on the state gained added value in relation to Russian events and conditions, so much so that Lenin considered it worthwhile to spend a great deal of time writing a lengthy theoretical treatise, even while in hiding in August and September of 1917 but still in close touch with the Bolsheviks in Petrograd and earnestly attempting to provide direction for his party. The constant theme of Lenin's speeches and writings since shortly after the February Revolution had been the necessity of renouncing all support for the Provisional Government and prodding the soviets toward the assumption of power. To show that Marx had repudiated parliamentarism as the means of the ultimate realization of socialism and had insisted on the destruction of the bourgeois state would offer a theoretical justification for the forcible elimination of the Provisional Government, help bring an end to the doubts and hesitation of many of Lenin's fellow Bolsheviks, and perhaps instill in the masses greater confidence in their capacity to make a revolution.

If the reformists were open to the accusation of excessive caution, Lenin was vulnerable to the charge of being unrealistic. How could it be possible to replace the entire organization of the existing state, virtually at once, with a new government by untutored and untested workers? In order to make a convincing argument for the destruction of the bourgeois state, Lenin had to persuade his audience that he offered a workable alternative. The urgency of his task of persuasion increased after February 1917, as the possibility of winning power in Russia presented itself and as informed political figures voiced their skepticism concerning the capacity of the Bolsheviks and their followers—or any other politi-

cal force—to handle the seemingly intractable problems facing Russia at the time. Daniel Tarschys has observed astutely that "a successful political platform is no cautious prognosis of what a party is likely to do but a partisan message advertising its hopes and strengths, moderately exaggerative, both suggestive enough to raise expectations and sober enough not to kill them by appearance of unreliability." If the Bolsheviks took power in Russia or leftist Marxists gained the upper hand in any other European nation, they could be expected to rely on the strengths, not of parliamentary experience or administrative skills, but of the energy and enthusiasm of their working-class adherents. **State and Revolution** asserts the superiority of the virtues of the working class; the new type of state will not merely equal but surpass the rule of the bourgeoisie in the quality of its performance. Here Lenin presses home the thesis of *proletarian competence*; as Tarschys puts it, "Lenin sought to demonstrate that the whole proletariat could govern." That thesis was vital to Lenin's argument but was subsidiary to his main theme of the necessity of smashing the bourgeois state.

In general rhetoric, Lenin does seem to endorse direct rule by the workers in the new society. His strongest language on that point comes in his first discussion in **State and Revolution** of the arrangements that will replace the bourgeois state that had been smashed by the revolution. According to Lenin, "instead of the special institutions of a privileged minority (privileged officialdom, the chiefs of the standing army), the majority itself can directly fulfill all these functions." He also argues that, since those performing the functions of suppressing the bourgeoisie and crushing their resistance will be the majority of the population, the need for the exercise of coercion by the state will immediately diminish, and "in this sense, the state *begins to wither away*." He confidently predicts that the majority will be able to suppress the remnants of the exploiting classes "even with a very simple 'machine,' almost without a 'machine,' without a special apparatus, by the simple *organization of the armed people*." Lenin affirms that the withering away of the state will find its result in the stateless communist society, when

> freed from capitalist slavery, from the untold horrors, savagery, absurdities and infamies of capitalist exploitation, people will gradually *become accustomed* to observing the elementary rules of social intercourse that have been known for centuries and repeated for thousands of years in all copy-book maxims. They will become accustomed to observing them without force, without coercion, without subordination, *without the special apparatus for coercion called the state.*

Much in the language of Lenin's essay gives a superficial impression of sympathy with the aspirations of anarcho-syndicalists, and the substance of his discussion of the proletarian revolution and the higher phase of communism does genuinely draw on elements of anarchism.

In *State and Revolution,* the word *anarchism,* in the sense of the endorsement of an outburst of violence by the masses for the destruction of political authority, pertains to the period of proletarian revolution and to the smashing of the bourgeois state. That sort of anarchism was to be left behind in the next stage, in which Lenin expected the reconstitution of authority under the rule of proletariat. Later in 1917 he distinguished between the stages of destruction and rebuilding of authority:

> So long as it is an instrument of violence exercised by the bourgeoisie against the proletariat, the proletariat can have only one slogan: *destruction* of the state. But when the state will be a proletarian state, when it will be an instrument of violence exercised by the proletariat against the bourgeoisie, we shall be fully and unreservedly in favor of a strong state power and of centralism.

Lenin argued that the movement from capitalism to full communism would be impossible without a period of transition, which he referred to as socialism or the first phase of communism, and that the state in that period would be the dictatorship of the proletariat. There can be no doubt that he wanted the dictatorship of the proletariat to exercise authority for the purposes of the suppression of resistance by the bourgeoisie, the construction of a new system of economic organization, and the supervision of the operation of the economy. The crucial question is, what structuring of authority in the political system of socialist society did Lenin envision?

At no point in *State and Revolution* or in any of his other writings did Lenin advocate the direct exercise of authority by the workers in the sense of the transfer of control over each productive enterprise to the workers within it, acting independently of the state and exerting their authority through a trade union or factory committee. Lenin's hope was not for a system of self-governing syndicates or communes. *State and Revolution* presents a picture of a "commune-state" only in the sense that Lenin's ideal was derived from Marx's description of the political arrangements of the Paris Commune in *The Civil War in France.* The notion of dispersing power among autonomous communes or regional bodies did not appeal to Lenin, who claimed that "there is not a trace of federalism in Marx's . . . observations on the experience of the commune" and asserted that "Marx was a centralist." Lenin was prepared to favor communes only as a transitional form, in the course of transforming private property into nationalized property.

> Now if the proletariat and the poor peasants take state power into their own hands, organize themselves quite freely into communes, and *unite* the action of all communes in striking at capital, in crushing the resistance of the capitalists, and in transferring the privately owned railways, factories, land, and so on to the *entire* nation, to the whole of society, won't that be centralism?

His hopes for the future of local organs of self-government by the workers were summarized by his reference to "the voluntary fusion of the proletarian communes." It is indicative of Lenin's position that in *State and Revolution* he touched on the subject of federalism or local autonomy only in discussions of bourgeois republics and of temporary arrangements during the beginning of socialism. The decentralization of authority did not play a great role in his vision of the fully developed dictatorship of the proletariat, as indicated by Lenin's observation that "centralism is possible both with the old and the new state machine" and by his statement, quoted earlier, that the proletariat needs "a centralized organization of force."

If by the rule of the workers and peasants Lenin did not mean a system akin to anarcho-syndicalism or anarchistic communalism, what did he mean? *State and Revolution* makes it clear that popular rule is to be realized in two ways. First, the workers and peasants will elect representatives to councils, or soviets, to which the government administration will be responsible. In late 1916 and early 1917, his study of Marx's writings on the state had encouraged Lenin to arrive at a more positive assessment of the value of the soviets, which had appeared in Russia during 1905, leading him to identify those bodies with the type of proletarian rule suggested by Marx's review of the experience of the Paris Commune. Lenin was thus theoretically well prepared to respond to the news of the February 1917 Revolution in Russia with the demand that power be transferred to the soviets. Both before and after his return to Russia, he repeatedly stressed that the soviets could be the embodiment of proletarian democracy, which, he insisted, would be markedly superior to bourgeois democracy. *State and Revolution* is quite consistent with Lenin's other works of 1917 calling for the concentration of power in the soviets. The crucial place of those bodies in Lenin's scheme is indicated by the fact that he equates the *"organization of the armed people"* with "the Soviets of Workers' and Soldiers' Deputies." He foresees the subordination of the executive departments of government, as well as all economic organizations, to the soviets. Lenin admits that "we cannot imagine democracy, even proletarian democracy, without representative institutions," though he adds, "we can and *must* imagine democracy without parliamentarism." The parliamentarism that inspired Lenin's disgust was that of bourgeois parliaments, which in his estimation were tainted by ineffectuality and corruption and misrepresented the interests of the working class. The means of destruction of that subculture of parliamentarism, according to Lenin, in addition to the stroke of expropriation that would eliminate the basis of the existence of the capitalist class, would be the abolition of the division between legislative and executive officials. That proposal, drawn directly from Marx's *The Civil War in France,* would have required that all members of the soviets discharge executive as well as legislative duties. Lenin argues that the result would have been "the conversion of the representative institutions from talking shops into 'working' bodies." Though Lenin repudiated the style of parliamentarism in bourgeois democracy and foresaw a significant expansion of the responsibility of elected representatives, his model of the socialist state was in essence a model of proletarian parliamentary democracy.

In addition to the control of executive organs by elected representatives, Lenin advocated a second means for realizing rule by the majority of the people: a high degree of direct popular participation in politics. The workers and peasants would elect representatives to the soviets, which is also to say that the laborers would choose major executive officials, with the stipulation that all such officials would be subject to recall by their constituents. In addition, all members of the laboring majority would frequently take their turns in carrying out the work of administration. Lenin promises that in socialism "the *mass* of the population will rise to taking an *independent* part, not only in voting and elections, *but also in the everyday administration of the state.*" Those whom Lenin labels as bureaucrats in the old order will be replaced en masse by workers and peasants. In his view, capitalism has created the prerequisites for widespread mass participation in bureaucratic work, through the achievement of universal literacy in the more economically developed countries and by accustoming the workers to the functioning of large complex bureaucratic organizations. Lenin contends that the duties of bureaucrats in advanced capitalist systems have been progressively simplified "and can be reduced to such exceedingly simple functions of registration, filing, and checking that they can easily be performed by every literate person." He goes so far as to say that the competence of bureaucrats requires no more than "supervising and recording, knowledge of the four rules of arithmetic, and issuing appropriate receipts." Offering another suggestion drawn from Marx's summary of the measures taken by the Paris Commune, Lenin specifies that under socialism the wages of the highest state officials will not exceed those of an ordinary worker. The regular rotation of all members of the laboring classes in and out of administrative positions will contribute to the withering away of the state by acquainting all with the principles enforced in supervisory roles and eventually making it possible for citizens to manage society without being subjected to coercion. "Under socialism *all* will govern in turn and soon will become accustomed to no one governing." Participatory bureaucracy will provide training for social self-administration.

It should be noted, however, that in Lenin's view bureaucracy would still exist in socialism, though it would be transformed to serve the interests of the workers rather than those of the capitalists. He admits that "abolishing the bureaucracy at once, everywhere and completely is out of the question" and espouses the replacement of the old bureaucracy with a new one. The pattern of hierarchical organization will persist within socialism. "We are not utopians. We do not 'dream' of dispensing *at once* with all administration, with all subordination." The rationale for the destruction of the old bureaucratic apparatus is not the rejection of the necessity of bureaucratic organization as such but, rather, is the complaint of the isolation of privileged officials from the masses, the association of the old bureaucrats with the interests of the bourgeoisie, and the consequent unfitness of the established administration to carry out the will of the proletariat. It was not the bureaucratic model of organization but the staff of bourgeois bureaucrats who would be replaced during the socialist revolution.

Lenin divides the employees of the capitalist state into two categories and foresees a different fate for each group. In the first category are those whom Lenin regards as "bureaucrats," the "foremen and accountants" who perform the tasks of supervision, calculation, and reporting and who will be replaced by proletarians. "It is quite possible, after the overthrow of the capitalists and the bureaucrats, to proceed immediately, overnight, to replace them in the *control* over production and distribution, in the work of *keeping account* of labor and products, by the armed workers, by the whole of the armed population." The second category of employees of the bourgeois state consists of "technicians of all sorts, types, and degrees," who will be retained by the dictatorship of the proletariat.

> The question of control and accounting should not be confused with the question of the scientifically trained staff of engineers, agronomists and so on. These gentlemen are working today in obedience to the wishes of the capitalists, and will work even better tomorrow in obedience to the wishes of the armed workers.

Lenin implicitly recognizes that the technical expertise that is vital for the performance of many specialized tasks cannot be readily acquired by the workers. He further assumes that technical knowledge is a flexible tool that may be used in the service of one or another set of class interests and political objectives. Thus even in September 1917 Lenin was prepared to allow the employment of bourgeois specialists by the proletarian state. In **"Can the Bolsheviks Retain State Power?"** which Lenin finished writing at the beginning of October 1917, he even indicated that for some time after the revolution the technical experts would receive wages higher than those of the average workers; "in all probability we shall introduce complete wage equality only gradually and shall pay these specialists higher salaries during the transition period." In that way Lenin sought to reconcile the values of expertise and popular control.

Just as Lenin differentiated between bureaucrats and technicians, he also distinguished between the structure of the state and the organization of production. According to Lenin, the state arises out of class struggle and performs the function of oppressing one class on behalf of another. Lenin defines the state primarily in terms of the exercise of coercion and identifies the state largely with coercive organs. State power "consists of special bodies of armed men having prisons, etc., at their command." Or as Lenin said in April 1917 in **"The Tasks** of the Proletariat in Our Revolution," "the state in the proper sense is the command over the masses by detachments of armed men, separated from the people." The state in the proper sense, or the apparatus of coercion, would be destroyed by the proletarian revolution and superseded by the dictatorship of the armed workers. The economic organizations created by capitalism would not be destroyed by the workers but would be taken over intact. "*We*, the workers, shall organize large-scale production on the basis of what capitalism has already created." Lenin was to expand on that theme in **"Can the Bolsheviks Retain State Power?"**

> In addition to the chiefly "oppressive" apparatus—the standing army, the police and the bureaucracy—the modern state possesses an apparatus which has extremely close connections with the banks and syndicates. . . . This apparatus must not, and should not, be smashed. It must be wrested from the control of the capitalists; . . . it must be *subordinated* to the proletarian Soviets; it must be expanded and made more comprehensive, and nationwide. And this *can* be done by utilizing the achievements already made by large scale capitalism.

In that same essay of September and October 1917, Lenin even held out the prospect that, in the course of subjecting the banks and syndicates to the control of the soviets, the employees of the capitalist enterprises would not be replaced. "We can 'lay hold of' and 'set in motion' this 'state apparatus' at one stroke, by a single decree, because the actual work of bookkeeping, control, registering, accounting and counting is performed by *employees,* the majority of whom themselves lead a proletarian or semi-proletarian existence." The growth of state capitalism, the consolidation of production by large trusts and syndicates, and the increasing bureaucratization of economic organizations were positive steps in preparing the way for socialism.

The workers' state would further concentrate control over production and distribution. In *State and Revolution* Lenin agrees with a statement that the postal service furnishes the example for a socialist economic system. "To organize the *whole* economy on the lines of the postal service . . . this is our immediate aim." Lenin prescribes "the conversion of *all* citizens into workers and other employees of *one* huge 'syndicate'," a single integrated economic machine on the scale of the entire nation. Workers' control over production will be realized, not through the fragmentation of capitalist monopolies into small, autonomous units, but through the combination of all enterprises into a single syndicate under the control of the elected soviets. It seems implicit that, since the pattern of economic organization in socialism will be that of state capitalism on a vast scale, the organization of production will be centralized and hierarchical. Indeed, Lenin leaves little doubt as to that conclusion when he refers with approval to Engels's rejection of the possibility of operating organizations combining the cooperative endeavors of substantial

numbers of people without the exercise of authority. "Take a factory, a railway, a ship on the high seas, said Engels; is it not clear that not one of these complex technical establishments, based on the use of machinery and systematic coordination of many people, could function without a certain amount of subordination and, consequently, without a certain amount of authority or power?" Lenin later observes that

> as far as the supposedly necessary "bureaucratic" organization is concerned, there is no difference whatever between a railway and any other enterprise in large-scale machine industry, any factory, large store, or large-scale capitalist agricultural enterprise. The technique of all these enterprises makes absolutely imperative the strictest discipline, the utmost precision on the part of everyone in carrying out his alloted task.

The organization of economic activity in socialism will be bureaucratic in the sense of including hierarchy and specialization but will not give birth to a privileged stratum of officials, because it will be responsible to the workers through the soviets. Lenin argues that the necessity of bureaucratic organization is derived from the technical imperative of coordinating people in the use of complex interrelated machines. For the working class to operate the productive machinery accumulated by capitalism, the hierarchical command of people engaged in production must survive the socialist revolution and be taken advantage of by the proletariat.

Lenin's acceptance of the bourgeois models of bureaucratic and economic organization even leads him into astonishing equivocation on his main thesis—the necessity of utterly destroying the bourgeois state. He observes that the first phase of communism will preserve "bourgeois right" in the distribution of products, in the form of the reward according to labor that Marx described as the principle governing distribution in the period of transition inaugurated by the proletarian revolution. Lenin reasons that bourgeois right presumes the existence of the bourgeois state, as the apparatus that will enforce compliance with reward on the basis of labor. He concludes that "in communism there remains for a certain time not only bourgeois right, but even the bourgeois state—without the bourgeoisie." It could be argued that Lenin is speaking figuratively on this point and that by the bourgeois state that persists in socialism he means only a state enforcing principles reflecting bourgeois values. In a later section of *State and Revolution,* however, Lenin seems to allow the possibility of the literal preservation of the previously existing departments of government. He quotes with disapproval Kautsky's statement that none of the ministries in a bourgeois state could be eliminated (since, Kautsky implies, all perform necessary functions). Lenin accuses Kautsky of displaying a "superstitious reverence" for ministries, which, according to Lenin, might be replaced by "committees of specialists" under the supervision of the soviets. He then offers the opinion that "the point is not at all whether 'ministries' will remain or whether 'committees of specialists' or some other bodies will be set up; that is quite immaterial." Lenin immediately reasserts his demand for the destruction of the old state machine, but that slogan has been robbed of much of its force by his expression of indifference as to whether government ministries will survive the workers' revolution. Lenin's call for the "destruction" or "smashing" of the "machine" of the bourgeois state reveals a feature often found in *State and Revolution*: the use of colorful language that creates a vivid impression but is metaphorical in content and therefore subject to ambiguity. In view of this admission of the possible persistence of ministries from existing governments, one plausible interpretation of Lenin's words could be that by the wholesale replacement of the old state apparatus with a new one he simply means the assumption of power by soviets of workers' and peasants' deputies. At any rate, that objective certainly is the heart of his program.

While *State and Revolution* repeatedly calls for the transfer of power to the soviets, it mentions only in one sentence the functions that the Leninist party will perform in proletarian democracy. That single sentence, however, has exceptionally rich political implications:

> By educating the workers' party, Marxism educates the vanguard of the proletariat, capable of assuming power and *leading the whole people* to socialism, of directing and organizing the new system, of being the teacher, the guide, the leader of all the working and exploited people in organizing their social life without the bourgeoisie and against the bourgeoisie.

Lenin refers to the party as the vanguard of the proletariat and ascribes to it the functions of teaching, leading, guiding, directing, and organizing the laboring people in socialism. Though Lenin provides no further discussion of the relationship of the governing party to the other agencies of proletarian dictatorship, he furnishes in capsule form a clear endorsement of what is now recognized as the principle of the guiding and directing role of the Communist party in Soviet society. Implicit in that principle is the distinction, which Lenin chose not to emphasize in *State and Revolution,* between the level of class consciousness of the vanguard and that of the less-sophisticated majority of workers.

Lenin's description of the dictatorship of the proletariat pertains to socialism or the first phase of communist society. He emphasizes that the state will wither away as society moves into the higher phase, in which the potential of communism will be fully realized. Lenin's depiction of full communism may appropriately be described as pervaded with anarchism. In predicting that the state would be abolished in the higher phase of communism, however, Lenin was only repeating Marx's well-known ideas. All Marxists are anarchists as far as their ultimate goals are concerned, but Lenin was careful to avoid promising the imminent attainment of complete communism. He shows awareness of the distance that

must be traveled in order to reach that goal, admitting that "politically, the distinction between the first, or lower, and the higher phase of communism will in time probably be enormous" and acknowledging that "by what stages, by means of what practical measures humanity will proceed to this supreme aim we do not and cannot know." By mentioning "stages" of transition to full communism, Lenin hints at the prospect of prolonged change through indirect means.

In *State and Revolution,* Lenin's forecasts for the withering away of the state are hedged with caution. He does argue that the state will *begin* to wither away at once with the beginning of socialism, in the sense that, because the majority will for the first time exercise coercion over a relatively small minority, less coercion will be necessary to protect the new relations of production. Lenin, however, is careful not to be very optimistic or specific with regard to the pace of the disappearance of the state or the eventual culmination of that process. He says that "clearly, there can be no question of specifying the moment of the *future* withering away, the more so since it will obviously be a lengthy process." While he promises that the need for the state will diminish as excesses in the conduct of individuals decrease, he adds that "we do not know how quickly and in what succession, but we do know that they will wither away." Arguing that the complete elimination of the state will presume the "gigantic development of productive forces" and the overcoming of the distinction between mental and physical labor, he concludes that "how rapidly this development will proceed . . . we do not and cannot know." What follows is Lenin's strongest and most explicit urging of caution in expectations for the abolition of the state.

> Therefore we are correct only to speak of the inevitable withering away of the state, emphasizing the protracted nature of that process and its dependence on the rapidity of development of the *higher phase* of communism, and leaving the question of the time required for, or the concrete forms of, the withering away quite open, because there is *no* material for answering such questions.

Lenin was content to postpone the elimination of the state to the indefinite future. After the Bolshevik Revolution, he became even more aware of the difficulty of dispensing with coercion. His only later addition to *State and Revolution* consisted of a section stressing that the dictatorship of the proletariat would be necessary for the "entire *historical period*" separating capitalism from the classless society. Even before the revolution, in his most extensive work on the state, Lenin's insistence on building a strong, disciplined proletariat dictatorship sharply distinguished him from the anarchists.

State and Revolution is conventionally described as an essay in which Lenin abandoned himself to quasi-anarchistic utopianism. Though the primary objective of that work was to discredit Karl Kautsky and other centrist leaders of international Marxism, it does reflect Lenin's enthusiasm in 1917 for the prospective benefits of rule by the proletariat. When Lenin speaks of the direct rule by the masses, however, he has in mind, not an anarcho-syndicalist form of workers' control of industry, but the replacement of bourgeois parliaments by soviets elected by the workers and the institution of widespread participation by laboring people in public administration. He is careful to indicate that neither of those changes will be incompatible with the preservation of hierarchical patterns of authority in government and the economy. In Lenin's model of the socialist state, authority will be centralized, bureaucracy will execute decisions of policy, and experts will still be indispensable in administration. In the economy, the units of organization inherited from capitalism will be further enlarged and control of them will be further centralized, as all enterprises will be combined into one enormous, nationwide syndicate subordinated to the highest organs of state power. The disappearance of the coercive aspects of government will be postponed to the indefinite and evidently remote future, while the necessity of a hierarchical structuring of economic institutions may never be transcended. All the organizations of workers and technicians in the new society will be guided by a vanguard party with higher knowledge of the goal of socialism and the means of its attainment. The political system of socialism discovered through a careful examination of Lenin's own words in *State and Revolution* is far removed from the hopes and ideals of anarchism. Lenin considered the anarchistic impulse toward the destruction of authority to be a positive factor only in the stage of smashing the bourgeois state, as a means of clearing the way for the establishment of an authoritative dictatorship of the proletariat.

Though Lenin's major work on the state has become historically important as political theory, it is so filled with ambiguities, equivocations, and inconsistencies that it is difficult to take it seriously as a theoretical contribution. Its numerous inconsistencies reflect its nature as a mixture of polemic, platform, and program but also more fundamentally betray the tension between contradictory themes simultaneously advanced by Lenin. The source of that tension is not, as is usually thought, a contradiction between the anarchistic rejection of authority and the Leninist acceptance of it. Lenin sees the proletarian revolution as a revolt not against authority in general but against the bourgeois state, and thus he repudiates the dominance of the interests of the capitalist class while importing into his plan the bourgeois model of bureaucracy. The underlying contradiction in *State and Revolution* is that between the themes of democracy and hierarchy. While warmly endorsing the virtues of willing and energetic mass initiative in the construction of the new society, Lenin readily agrees with Engels's thesis concerning the technical necessity of a hierarchical structure in all complex organizations. Revolutionary mass participation will be guided by hierarchical institutions, which will be coordinated by a

party whose members share a special vision of the future.

To describe Lenin as simply a cynical authoritarian or a revolutionary idealist would not do justice to the complexity and ambiguity of his thought, which was characterized by the interplay of apparently contradictory values. The themes of popular initiative and elite direction are not confined to *State and Revolution* but occur in all of Lenin's works. The relative emphasis on each varied, according to time and circumstance. In 1917 Lenin chose to stress the advantages of mass participation in elections and administration, but without relinquishing his conviction of the desirability of economic centralization, state bureaucracy, and party guidance of the political system. The solution to the apparent contradiction in *State and Revolution* was Lenin's assumption that in the approaching revolutionary situation the wishes of the masses and the decisions of the elite would be fully compatible; there would be a historically determined coincidence of spontaneity and consciousness. It would not be long before events in Soviet Russia would prove that assumption to be unrealistic, but the tension between the polarities of value in Lenin's thought of 1917 became a lasting part of the ideological heritage of Soviet communism.

Paul Le Blanc (essay date 1990)

SOURCE: "Introduction: Authentic Leninism," in *Lenin and the Revolutionary Party,* Humanities Press International, Inc., 1990, pp. 1-13.

[*In the following essay, Le Blanc contends the core of pure Leninism is the revolutionary Bolshevik movement.*]

Vladimir Ilyich Lenin was the foremost leader of the world's first working-class socialist revolution, which swept Russia in 1917 and continues to reverberate down to our own time. People throughout the world—longing for an end to injustice, war, and oppression—have looked hopefully to the example of the Russian Bolsheviks and to the ideas of Lenin as a guide for liberation struggles and social change in their own countries. As another leader of the Bolshevik Revolution, Leon Trotsky, explained: "The main work of Lenin's life was the organization of a party capable of carrying through the October revolution and of directing the construction of Socialism." Because of this, revolutionary-minded men and women have given special attention to Lenin's views on the revolutionary party.

With the triumph of the Bolshevik Revolution, Lenin and his comrades turned their attention to the task of helping revolutionaries in other countries mobilize the workers and the oppressed for the purpose of overthrowing capitalism on a global scale to establish a worldwide cooperative commonwealth in which, as Marx and Engels had written in the *Communist Manifesto,* "the free development of each is the condition for the free development of all." Renaming their own organization the Communist party, the Bolsheviks established the Communist International in 1919 in order to advance this expansive goal.

Millions of people—from a rich variety of cultures, traditions and experiences—responded to the revolutionary appeal of Bolshevism and the Communist International. One of these was James P. Cannon, a veteran of the American Socialist party's left wing and of the militant and colorful Industrial Workers of the World (IWW). Cannon helped to found the American Communist party in 1919, and he was one of its central leaders until his expulsion in 1928 as the Communist International became increasingly bureaucratized. Yet he never abandoned his revolutionary convictions, and in a remarkable essay written in the 1960s continued to affirm:

> The greatest contribution to the arsenal of Marxism since the death of Engels in 1895 was Lenin's conception of the vanguard party as the organizer and director of the proletarian revolution. That celebrated theory of organization was not, as some contend, simply a product of the special Russian conditions of his time and restricted to them. It is deep-rooted in two of the weightiest realities of the twentieth century: the *actuality* of the workers' struggle for the conquest of power, and the *necessity* of creating a leadership capable of carrying it through to the end.
>
> Recognizing that our epoch was characterized by imperialist wars, proletarian revolutions, and colonial uprisings, Lenin deliberately set out at the beginning of this century to form a party able to turn such cataclysmic events to the advantage of socialism. The triumph of the Bolsheviks in the upheavals of 1917, and the durability of the Soviet Union they established, attested to Lenin's foresight and the merits of his methods of organization. His party stands out as the unsurpassed prototype of what a democratic and centralized leadership of the workers, true to Marxist principles and applying them with courage and skill, can be and do.

These perceptions have been shared by innumerable workers and peasants and students and intellectuals of every continent. They consider themselves Leninists because they are animated by "the categorical imperative to overthrow all conditions in which man is a debased, enslaved, neglected, contemptible being." They are Leninists because they are committed, in a very real and practical way, to replacing the tyranny of capitalism with a *socialism* in which the immense economic resources of society will be the common property of all people, democratically controlled in order to ensure that the free development of each person can be possible.

1. WHAT LENINISM IS NOT

Lenin's ideas on the revolutionary party have been greatly distorted by many different kinds of people. It may be useful to survey some of these interpretations.

From the triumph of the Bolshevik Revolution down to the present, liberal and conservative ideologists of the capitalist status quo have utilized immense resources to spread the notion that Lenin and his works—especially his concept of the revolutionary party—constitute a hideous threat to law, order, simple human decency, and Western civilization. One of the clearest expositions of this viewpoint was offered by the late director of the Federal Bureau of Investigation, J. Edgar Hoover. In *Masters of Deceit,* the FBI chief gave this explanation to millions of frightened readers: "Lenin conceived of the Party as a vehicle of revolution. . . . The Party must be a small, tightly controlled, deeply loyal group. Fanaticism, not members, was the key. Members must live, eat, breathe, and dream revolution. They must lie, cheat, and murder if the Party was to be served. Discipline must be rigid. No deviations could be permitted. If an individual falters, he must be ousted. Revolutions cannot be won by clean hands or in white shirts; only by blood, sweat and the burning torch. . . . The skill of Lenin cannot be overestimated. He introduced into human relations a new dimension of evil and depravity not surpassed by Genghis Khan or Attila. His concept of Party supremacy, girded by ruthless and ironclad discipline, gave communism a fanaticism and an immorality that shocked Western civilization."

This basic interpretation is also offered—frequently in a more sophisticated and scholarly form—by many influential academics and intellectuals who are engaged in the defense of "Western civilization." Essential components of that civilization are a myriad "unavoidable" inequalities and "regrettable" injustices, not to mention the immense power of the big corporations and, of course, the aggressively procapitalist thrust of U.S. foreign policy. Although undoubtedly sincere, many of these ideologists have like J. Edgar Hoover, been in the pay of the U.S. government or have been conscious participants in government-controlled or corporate-funded operations designed to generate and spread anti-radical, anti-revolutionary propaganda. They are not objective commentators—they have an axe to grind. And yet their biased interpretations have a substantial impact among many who do not share their particular commitments to U.S. corporate-government power.

Other powerful distortions emanate from a quite different source—the Communist movement itself. Many people drawn to it over the years have absorbed interpretations of Lenin's ideas that have little to do with the experience of the Bolsheviks as, in the years leading up to 1917, they grew into a revolutionary party. Instead, these individuals have been trained in more rigid and stilted conceptions that became dominant particularly after Lenin's death, in 1924. Such conceptions gained currency as a rising bureaucratic layer, led by Joseph Stalin, sought to consolidate its control and privileges within the Union of Soviet Socialist Republics from the 1920s onward. The "Leninism" fashioned in this period assumed dominance among revolutionary-minded activists, but it proved to be more useful for enhancing the authority of the new ruling group in the Soviet Union than for duplicating the successes of the Bolsheviks for the peoples of other countries.

A shrewd and somewhat cynical observer in the Soviet Union during this period was *New York Times* correspondent Walter Duranty, who was sympathetic to Stalin—though with a decidedly nonrevolutionary detachment. He noted that a growing number of old Bolsheviks "were showing signs of restiveness, partly because they saw that Stalinism was progressing from Leninism (as Leninism had progressed from Marxism) towards a form and development of its own, partly because they were jealous and alarmed by Stalin's growing predominance." Duranty wrote as follows: "When Lenin died what ignorant mortal could know whether Stalin or Trotsky was the chosen son? Only results could prove that. . . . Stalin rose and Trotsky fell; therefore Stalin, inevitably, was right and Trotsky wrong. . . . Stalin deserved his victory because he was the strongest, and because his policies were most fitted to the Russian character and folkways in that they established Asiatic absolutism and put the interests of Russian Socialism before those of international Socialism."

Stalin portrayed his "progression from Leninism," however, as nothing more nor less than the most uncompromising defense of Leninist principles. At Lenin's funeral, he religiously intoned: "Leaving us, comrade Lenin enjoined on us to hold high and keep pure the great calling of member of the party. We vow to thee, comrade Lenin, that we will with honor fulfill this thy commandment. Leaving us, comrade Lenin enjoined on us to keep the unity of our party as the apple of our eye. We vow to thee, comrade Lenin, that we will with honor fulfill this thy commandment. . . . Leaving us, comrade Lenin enjoined on us loyalty to the principles of the Communist International. We vow to thee, comrade Lenin, that we will not spare our lives to strengthen and extend the union of the toilers of the whole world—the Communist International." Instead, Stalin sought to destroy politically (and, eventually, physically) all Communists—including most of Lenin's closest comrades—who challenged his authority, to drive out of the Communist party of the Soviet Union and Communist parties throughout the world all who were unprepared to abandon the "old Leninism" of the Bolsheviks' heroic period, and to subordinate the revolutionary aspirations of parties belonging to the Communist International to narrowly defined foreign policy considerations of the Soviet Union. He went so far as to formally dissolve the Communist International during World War II in order to reassure his wartime capitalist allies. Yet a typical, even obligatory, comment by Communist ideologists while such things were happening was that "the Party is training its cadres in Bolshevik ideological intransigence, is rallying its ranks still more closely around its Leninist Central Committee, around its leader and teacher, Comrade Stalin." Communists throughout the world were lectured that "a study of the history of the Bolshevik Party is impossible without a knowledge of the chief works of its founder and leader, Lenin, and of his best disciple, Stalin, who is continuing his work."

The organizational norms propagated in this period, peppered with fragments from Lenin quoted out of context, stressed "the Bolshevik conception of the Party as a monolithic whole." This was elaborated for the world Communist movement in such works as *Lenin's Teachings About the Party,* by Stalinist ideologist V. Sorin, and circulated widely throughout the Communist International in the early 1930s. Excerpts from that work are quite revealing:

> The Party is governed by leaders. If the Party is the vanguard of the working class then the leaders are the advanced post of this vanguard. . . . The special feature of the Communist Party is its strictest discipline, i.e., the unconditional and exact observance by all members of the Party of all directives coming from their Party organizations. . . . The Party must be sure that each of its members will do what the Party tells him even if he disagrees with it. . . . Discipline, firm and unrelenting, is necessary not only during the period of underground work and struggle against Tsarism, not only during civil war, but even during peaceful times. . . . The stricter the discipline, the stronger the Party, the more dangerous is it to the capitalists.

Such follow-the-leader conceptions of Leninism helped to overcome the danger of a critical-minded revolutionary membership questioning the policies developed by the Stalinist leadership of the Communist movement. But they had little in common with the organization that actually made the world's first socialist revolution. These conceptions continue to influence would-be Leninists of our own time, however. The pamphlet *Lenin's Teachings About the Party,* for example, was reprinted in the 1970s by former "new left" activists who, influenced by the Chinese and Vietnamese revolutions, believed that "a new communist party is essential for the revolutionary movement in the United States." Revolutionary-minded people throughout the world have mistaken such distortions for genuine Leninism.

Attentive readers may have noticed that the anti-Communist and the Stalinist descriptions of the Leninist party have much in common. Sometimes they are blended together, as in the case of Wolfgang Leonhard, a Stalinist functionary and instructor at the Karl Marx Political Academy of the German Communist party who defected from East Germany in 1949 and became a critical commentator on Communist affairs. Leonhard refrained from adopting the bitterly reactionary orientation of many who went through similar breaks, continuing to identify with what he calls humanist Marxism. Yet he offers the following as an objective description: "Instead of a democratically organized body representing the interests of all workers who engaged in free discussion, Lenin's doctrine of the Party now envisaged an elite led by professional revolutionaries, organized on the principle of democratic centralism, with restricted freedom of discussion, and making great demands on Party members, who must operate in unity and with closed ranks in order to lead the working class." Not surprisingly, many revolutionary-minded people have concluded that if this is Leninism, then Leninism is not for them.

Within the broadly defined socialist movement there is a particularly influential source for the notion that Leninism is basically authoritarian. This is the moderate-socialist current of post-1917 Social Democracy, many of whose spokespersons refer to themselves as "democratic socialists" in order to distinguish themselves from "authoritarian Communism." They tend to perceive democracy as electoral politics within a capitalist framework, to favor the implementation of reform legislation as a means for gradually eliminating the evils of capitalism, and to recognize a kinship with Lenin's moderate-socialist rivals in Russia. In many countries they can boast of mass parties (for example, the Labor party in Britain, the Socialist party in France, the Social Democratic party in Germany), which have sometimes taken office and implemented positive social reforms but have never even attempted to overthrow capitalism. Their current orientation in the United States, as Michael Harrington, of Democratic Socialists of America (DSA), has put it, holds that "the American social democracy" is an "invisible mass movement" consisting of the liberal-labor alliance in the Democratic party with its "ranging program for the democratization of the economy and the society." It is natural that the adherents of this position would find intolerable Lenin's "dogmatic" insistence that it is impossible to peacefully and gradually reform capitalism out of existence. They are inclined to echo, with varying degrees of sophistication, the interpretation articulated for many years within DSA's predecessor, the Socialist Party of America, when it was led by Norman Thomas. Thomas portrayed Leninism as "an authoritarian dogmatism which boasts that it is scientific." In 1931 he explained that Lenin's party was "organized with military discipline, exacting an unquestioning obedience from its members worthy of the order of Jesus." Twenty years later he continued to explain: "In Lenin's theory the Party was to be a dedicated group bent on serving the interests of the workers and the peasants, which it understood better than the masses themselves." Asserting that Stalin's policies were a continuation of the Leninist commitment to "the eventual world-wide triumph of communism," Thomas wrote that Stalin "emphasized Lenin's use of any tactics, including unbounded deceit and violence, to achieve that result." This interpretation of Leninism—remarkably similar, in important ways, to those offered by apologists for Stalinism, on the one hand, and for capitalism, on the other—is widely propagated even by formerly new-left adherents of "democratic socialism" who are not inclined to share Norman Thomas's support for U.S. Cold War policies.

Recently there has evolved another source from which a distorted interpretation of Leninism has arisen. Among new Western scholars studying the history of the Soviet Union, there is an innovative current that, while yielding some valuable new research, has also begun to fashion what Sheila Fitzpatrick has delicately termed "a less judgemental approach" to the Stalin era. Quite similar in temperament and in some of their perceptions to such earlier admirers of Stalin as Walter Duranty, these scholars are also inclined to be somewhat more aloof. "There was a wildly impractical and utopian streak in a great deal of Bolshevik thinking," writes Fitzpatrick. She adds the following, however: "No doubt all successful revolutions have this characteristic: the revolutionaries must always be driven by enthusiasm and irrational hope, since they would otherwise make the common-sense judgement that the risks and costs of revolution outweigh the possible benefits." Fleetingly entertaining the question "of whether in some cosmic sense it was all worthwhile," she draws back with the warning that this is "dangerous ground for historians," who should restrict themselves simply to determining "what seems to have happened and how it fits together."

From this standpoint, Fitzpatrick dispassionately summarizes the Russian Revolution's meaning as "terror, progress and upward mobility." By "upward mobility" she means the many thousands of workers who rose above their class to get relatively good and high-status jobs in the massive postrevolutionary bureaucracy (which she sees as a perversely nuts-and-bolts realization of the revolutionary socialist goal of working-class rule). By "progress" she presumably means the leap forward into industrialization and modernization, the elimination of the backward and inefficient semifeudal and tsarist order, the establishment (despite bureaucratic distortions) of a planned economy, the great strides in spreading education and health care to all, and so forth. And by "terror" she means the disruption and destruction of millions of lives, the violence against and coercion of peasants and workers during the "revolution from above" of collectivization and industrialization under Stalin, the purges and labor camps, and other authoritarian measures. Fitzpatrick asserts that there were "important elements of continuity linking Stalin's revolution with Lenin's," and that one element of this continuity was that "Stalin used Leninist methods against his opponents." (Here one is again reminded of Duranty, who wrote: "Stalin is no less of a Marxist than Lenin, who never allowed his Marxism to blind him to the needs of expediency. . . . When Lenin began a fight, whether the weapons were words or bullets, he showed no mercy to his opponents." Stalin was thus following Lenin in "the brutality of purpose which drove through to its goal regardless of sacrifice and suffering.")

This approach has obvious implications for how one interprets the nature of the Leninist party. Fitzpatrick suggests that "Lenin's dislike of looser mass organizations allowing greater diversity and spontaneity was not purely expedient but reflected a natural authoritarian bent," adding that "Lenin usually insisted on having his own way." She characterizes the Bolshevik party in this way: "It was a party with authoritarian tendencies, one that had always had a strong leader—even, according to Lenin's opponents, a dictatorial one. Party discipline and unity had always been stressed. Before 1917, Bolsheviks who disagreed with Lenin on any important issue usually left the party. In the period 1917-20, Lenin had to deal with dissent and even organized dissident factions within the party, but he seems to have regarded this as an abnormal and irritating situation, and finally took decisive steps to change it."

We will see that this interpretation does not correspond to historical realities. More insightful historians argue that the common thesis of a Lenin-Stalin continuity "rests upon a series of dubious formulations, concepts, and interpretations and . . . whatever its insights, it obscures more than it illuminates," as Stephen Cohen has put it. E. H. Carr has attempted to demonstrate the fundamental discontinuity with this argument:

> The *Communist Manifesto* recognized the role of leadership exercised by Communists as the only full class-conscious members of the proletariat and of proletarian parties. But it was a condition of the proletarian revolution that Communist consciousness should spread to a majority of the workers. . . . Lenin's conception of the party as the vanguard of the class contained *elitist* elements absent from Marx's writings and was the product of a period when political writers were turning their attention more and more to the problem of *elites*. The party was to lead and inspire the mass of workers; its own membership was to remain small and select. It would, however, be an error to suppose that Lenin regarded the revolution as the work of a minority. The task of leading the masses was not, properly understood, a task of indoctrination, of creating a consciousness that was not there, but of evoking a latent consciousness; and this latent consciousness of the masses was an essential condition of revolution. Lenin emphatically did not believe in revolution from above. . . . After Lenin's death, Lenin's successors lacked the capacity or the patience to evoke that measure of mass consciousness and mass support that Lenin had had behind him in the period of the revolution and the Civil War and took the short cut—always the temptation that lies in wait for an elite—of imposing their will, by measures of increasingly naked force, on the mass of the population and on the mass of the party. . . . The need, with which Lenin wrestled and which Stalin contemptuously dismissed, of reconciling elite leadership with mass democracy has emerged as a key problem in the Soviet Union today.

This general approach, regardless of imperfections one might find in Carr's specific formulations, captures important aspects of the historical reality that allow a fundamentally different and more perceptive approach to the question of the Bolshevik party's actual organizational structure and functioning. Thus, Moshe Lewin recounts the following:

Leninism, one of the Russian versions of Marxism, developed by Lenin, was shared by the Bolsheviks who had acquired their ideological formation before the revolution and who maintained an open-mindedness, an institutional flexibility in pursuing the struggle of ideas in particular, but not exclusively in the areas of strategy and tactics that made up the core of Leninism. It is important to recall that bolshevism had gone through quite a number of internal debates before 1917, that it had functioned in a multiparty environment, especially after the revolution of 1905, and even after the takeover of power, until 1920. Starting with the revolution of February 1917, in particular, and until the prohibition of factions by the Tenth Party Congress in March 1921, various wings and tendencies, opposing factions and platforms presented before and during the congresses [of the party], coexisted within the party; these were not only tolerated but were actually used as widely accepted *modus operandi* [procedure].

This authentic Leninism—qualitatively different from the grotesque distortions of Leninism that are so widely circulated—will be the subject of the present study.

2. A LIVING ORGANISM AND PHASES OF DEVELOPMENT

Like any living organism, the Bolshevik organization was characterized by a particular set of tensions *within* itself as well as *between* it and the larger social reality. These tensions gave it a vibrancy and generated growth, causing the organization to go through quite different phases of development. The organization cannot be adequately understood as a revolutionary force unless it is understood in this way. Lenin's views on the revolutionary party, which reflected and were part of this evolution, must likewise not be approached as if they were a finished and self-contained schema. The Leninist conception of the party is animated by certain essential principles and a definite methodological approach; there is an underlying continuity in Lenin's organizational perspectives from the 1890s up to 1917 and beyond. At the same time, there are important shifts in Lenin's thought, flowing from an accumulation of experience and also reflecting changes in the context of the Bolsheviks' activity.

A potential problem, even among revolutionaries who recognize a distinction between authentic Leninism and Stalinism, is a failure to grasp this dialectical aspect of Leninism. Leninist organizational principles are seen as an established organizational schema. This schema typically involves a constricting organizational tightness that supposedly constitutes "Leninist centralism and party discipline." It is something that "Leninist" leaders sometimes attempt to superimpose on the membership, often inflexibly, regardless of the actual situation. This is contrary to Lenin's own method, and it has often had destructive consequences for left-wing groups that glorify an abstract (and therefore non-Leninist) "Leninism." It may be appropriate for the consolidation of a small sectarian group, but it short-circuits the process of building a working-class party capable of leading a successful struggle for socialism.

The present study seeks to recover the actual meaning of Leninist organizational principles by locating them in the specific history of Russia's revolutionary socialist movement. Initially, the organized expression of this movement was the Russian Social Democratic Labor party (RSDLP), and especially its Bolshevik faction from 1903 to 1912; then it was concentrated in the independent Bolshevik party, which became the Russian Communist party after 1917. Within this context, the Leninist organizational perspective can be said to have gone through six phases of development from 1900 to 1923.

1. *1900-1904.* Lenin and other Marxists struggle to establish the RSDLP around the revolutionary program and centralized organizational concepts expounded in the newspaper *Iskra.* The Iskraists and the RSDLP split into bitterly counterposed majority/minority (Bolshevik/Menshevik) factions, with Lenin's Blosheviks advancing the most consistently centralist and uncompromisingly revolutionary orientation. In this period, however, the RSDLP consists mostly of radicalized intellectuals; it has a small minority of workers and a very weak base in the proletariat.

2. *1905-1906.* The revolutionary upsurge of 1905 catches both Bolshevik and Menshevik factions by surprise. Both factions are swept along by the revolutionary enthusiasm of the workers. Lenin's centralism is tempered by the understanding that looser and more democratic norms can help root the RSDLP in a dramatically radicalizing working class. A convergence of Bolshevik and Menshevik orientations and factions appears to be in process.

3. *1907-1912.* The defeat of the revolutionary wave and a triumphant reaction destroy the RSDLP mass base within Russia. The new situation reverses the convergence of Bolshevik and Menshevik factions as a fundamental programmatic difference, already visible in 1905, pulls the two factions apart. In the struggle to overthrow tsarist absolutism, the Mensheviks put greatest weight on an alliance of the working class with the "progressive" bourgeoisie, while the Bolsheviks counterpose to this a revolutionary alliance of the workers and the peasants. Among the Mensheviks an increasingly strong impulse develops to liquidate the revolutionary workers' party into reformist labor organizations. Among the Bolsheviks an ultraleft sectarian impulse arises, which threatens to draw them into an abstentionist course in the face of opportunities to participate in the actual class struggle. Lenin conducts a bitter war against both liquidators and abstentionists. He drives the latter out of the Bolshevik faction and attempts to drive the former out of the RSDLP altogether. Many nonliquidationist Mensheviks and even some nonabstentionist Bolsheviks fear that Lenin is being too "hard," and they seek "conciliation" with both liquidators and abstentionists in order to preserve the unity of the RSDLP. Lenin forces a decisive organizational split, constituting his faction as a separate party—the Russian Social Democratic Labor party (Bolsheviks).

4. *1912-1914.* The Bolshevik party, unified on the basis of a revolutionary class-struggle program, outstrips the incohesive and squabbling remnants of the non-Bolshevik RSDLP—particularly in the face of a dramatic new wave of working-class militancy.

5. *1914-1917.* The eruption of the First World War diverts the rising wave of militancy into patriotic hysteria and slaughter. The Bolsheviks and the minority of Menshevik-Internationalists vehemently oppose the Russian war effort and are savagely repressed. The reformist and pro-war majority of the Mensheviks are able to assume a dominant position in the workers' movement.

6. *1917-1923.* The devastation of the First World War has a profoundly radicalizing impact on the Russian masses, and the severely weakened tsarist regime is overthrown by a spontaneous revolutionary upsurge. In the new and volatile situation, the reformist and vacillating Mensheviks are once again outstripped by the Bolshevik party, which is able to lead the masses forward to a socialist revolution. The effects of war, civil war, and foreign blockades and interventions result in economic collapse and disintegration of the working class as a political force. The Bolsheviks feel compelled to adopt increasingly restrictive measures, in Russia as a whole and within their own party, while waiting for a revolutionary socialist triumph in the industrially advanced West that will end the desperate isolation of their impoverished and bleeding country.

This highly condensed sketch of the six phases of "Leninism under Lenin" does little more than suggest the shifting contexts within which Lenin's various (and sometimes seemingly contradictory) statements on the organizational question can be understood. There are obvious general points that must be kept in mind regarding the situation in tsarist Russia—the economic backwardness, the predominance in population of the peasantry, the peculiarities of Russian capitalist development, and the repressiveness of tsarist absolutism. This last factor, above all, compelled Russian revolutionaries to develop organizational forms that would be consistent with the realities of underground work and exile politics. There is much in all of this that necessitated the incorporation into the "Leninism of Lenin" of qualities that—at least at this point—have little immediate relevance to the situation of revolutionaries functioning in different contexts (for example, what are sometimes termed "advanced capitalist democracies").

Certain aspects of the Leninist organizational orientation, however, have universal applicability. One is the absolute primacy of the revolutionary program—the principles, general analysis, goals, and strategic and tactical orientation that can lead the class struggle to a revolutionary socialist conclusion. Another is the concept of the revolutionary vanguard party, made up only of activists committed to the revolutionary program. Such a party doesn't attempt to embrace into its ranks the entire working class, but rather seeks to interact with the working class in order to influence it in a revolutionary direction. (Obviously, in order to do this the vanguard party must be predominantly working-class in composition—but these must be revolutionary working-class activists.) Finally, organizational centralism and organizational democracy must be combined in such a way that makes the vanguard party most effective in applying the revolutionary program to living reality. Given the complex, dynamic, and ever-changing character of reality, it is necessary to be flexible in determining the weight to be given to democracy and centralism in different situations and in different periods.

To be true to Lenin's method, revolutionaries must be prepared to apply this orientation creatively to their own specific and changing situations, and to be as innovative as Lenin was from one period to another. . . .

FURTHER READING

Bibliography

Egan, David R. and Egan, Melinda A. *V. I. Lenin: An Annotated Bibliography of English-language Sources to 1980*. Metuchen, N. J.: The Scarecrow Press, Inc., 1982, 482 p.

> Bibliography of secondary sources on Lenin organized by subject.

Biography

Clark, Ronald W. *Lenin: The Man Behind the Mask*. London: Faber and Faber, 1988, 564 p.

> Attempts to reveal the influence of Lenin's private and public personas.

Conquest, Robert. *Lenin*. London: Fontana, 1972, 142 p.

> Political and historical analysis of Lenin's rise to power and subsequent influence as head of the Bolshevik Party.

Fischer, Louis. *The Life of Lenin*. New York: Harper & Row, 1964, 703 p.

> Lengthy biography focused on the historical stages in Lenin's life.

Pomper, Philip. *Lenin, Trotsky, and Stalin: The Intelligentsia and Power*. New York: Columbia University Press, 1990, 446 p.

> "Psychobiographical" study of the three major political figures in early twentieth-century Russian history.

Theen, Rolf H. W. *Lenin: Genesis and Development of a Revolutionary*. Philadelphia: J. B. Lippincott Company, 1973, 194 p.

> Biography with a primary focus on the years 1887 to 1900, emphasizing Lenin as a revolutionary, a theoretician, and a political leader.

Warth, Robert D. *Lenin*. New York: Twayne Publishers, 1973, 198 p.

> Intended as an objective survey of Lenin's life.

Criticism

Baranov, Vadim. "Revolution and Art." *Soviet Literature*, No. 11 (1988): 125-27

> Discusses Lenin's view of the artist's role as part of the Russian Revolution.

Copleston, Frederick C. "Marxism in Imperial Russia (2): Lenin." In *Philosophy in Russia: From Herzen to Lenin and Berdyaev*, pp. 284-312. Tunbridge Wells, Kent: Search Press, Ltd., 1986.

> Includes a survey of Lenin's philosophy and a brief biography of his life to 1917.

Daniels, Robert V. "Lenin and the Russian Revolutionary Tradition." *Harvard Slavic Studies* 4 (1957): 339-53.

> Argues that, rather than being an orthodox Marxist as he claimed, Lenin "radically transformed" the philosophy he inherited from Marx.

Feuer, Lewis S. "Lenin's Fantasy: The Interpretation of a Russian Revolutionary Dream." *Encounter* XXXV, No. 6 (December 1970): 23-35.

> Examines the tension between reality and fantasy in Lenin's thought, and its ramifications for his ideological doctrines.

Gerson, Lennard D, ed. *Lenin and the Twentieth Century: A Bertram D. Wolfe Retrospective*. Stanford, Calif.: Hoover Institution Press, 1984, 216 p.

> Collection of biographical, political, and historical essays on Lenin.

Harding, Neil. *Lenin's Political Thought, Volume 1: Theory and Practice in the Democratic Revolution* and *Volume 2: Theory and Practice in the Socialist Revolution*. London: Macmillan Press, Ltd., 1977-81, 747 p.

> Observes the theoretical underpinnings of the Leninist revolution.

Keep, John. "Lenin's Letters As a Historical Source." *The Russian Review* 30, No. 1 (January 1971): 33-42.

> Investigates the historical usefulness of Lenin's correspondence as it appears in his collected works.

Lomunov, Konstantin. "Lenin and Tolstoy." *Soviet Literature*, No. 10 (1983): 136-40.

> Notes the significance of Lenin's *Lev Tolstoy as a Mirror of the Russian Revolution* for understanding the latter writer.

Luck, David. "A Psycholinguistic Approach to Leader Personality: Imagery of Aggression, Sex, and Death in Lenin and Stalin." *Soviet Studies* XXX, No. 4 (October 1978): 491-515.
    Compares the symbolism employed in the words of Lenin and Stalin, based upon a Freudian psycho-analysis of both.

Meyer, Alfred G. *Leninism*. New York: Frederick A. Praeger, 1957, 324 p.
    Survey of Lenin's thought and the philosophy of Leninism that it spawned.

Polan, A. J. *Lenin and the End of Politics*. Berkeley: University of Californian Press, 1984, 229p.
    Discusses Leninism as an inherited form of Marxism centered around the "commune-state."

Schapiro, Leonard. "Lenin's Contribution to Politics." *The Political Quarterly* 35, No. 1 (January-March 1964): 9-22.
    Analysis of Lenin as revolutionary thinker, utopian philosopher, and " the originator of modern total-itarianism."

Tucker, Robert C., ed. *The Lenin Anthology*. New York: W. W. Norton & Company, 1975, 764 p.
    Collection of Lenin's political writings and letters, preceded by an introduction describing his role in the Russian Revolution.

Tumarkin, Nina. *Lenin Lives!: The Lenin Cult in Soviet Russia*. Cambridge, Mass.: Harvard University Press, 1983, 315 p.
    Explores the development of the Lenin Cult in the 1920s as part of early Soviet history.

Utechin, S. V. "Who Taught Lenin?" *Twentieth Century* 168, No. 1001 (July 1960): 8-16.
    Examines the influence of N. P. Ogarev's philosophy on that of Lenin.

Williams, Robert C. *The Other Bolsheviks: Lenin and His Critics, 1904-1914*. Bloomington: Indiana University Press, 1986, 233 p.
    Discusses Bolshevism as dominated by Leninism and as a multifaceted movement unto itself.

Additional coverage of Lenin's life and career is available in the following source published by Gale Research: *Contemporary Authors,* vol. 121.

Rachilde

1860–1953

(Born Marguerite Eymery) French novelist, short story writer, dramatist, biographer, autobiographer, and critic.

INTRODUCTION

Rachilde is considered an important figure in the fin-de-siècle French Decadent movement. Characterized in public life by her male dress, and habit of calling herself a "man of letters," Rachilde tittilated readers with frequent depictions of unconventional sexuality, including gender inversion, androgyny, and homoeroticism. Her most well-known novel, *Monsieur Vénus* (1884), is a meditation on the nature of sexual desire from the female perspective.

Biographical Information

Rachilde was born near Périgueux in southwestern France. Her mother was the daughter of a successful publisher, while her father was the illegitimate son of an aristocrat and a colonel in the French army. As a child Rachilde's relationship with her mother was strained, and she often felt the harsh disappointment of her father, who made it clear that he would have rather had a son. Informally educated in her parent's home, she was allowed to peruse the works of her grandfather's library, where she discovered the works of the Marquis de Sade. In her youth she turned to writing as a form of imaginative escapism, producing her first novel at the age of sixteen. She moved to Paris in 1878 to begin her career as a writer. Once there she adopted the name Rachilde and applied for permission from the French authorities to dress as a man in public. She published her first novel *Madame de sans-Dieu* that same year. In 1884 she won immediate notoriety with the publication of her fifth book *Monsieur Vénus*. The work, because of its frank and iconoclastic depiction of sexuality, was almost immediately banned in neighboring Belgium under charges of pornography, quickly earning her the appellation "Mademoiselle Baudelaire." By the late 1890s, Rachilde's weekly salons in Paris had become well known, and in 1889 she married Alfred Vallette. The following year, the couple began publication of *Mercure de France*, a journal devoted to promoting the literary works of the Symbolists and Decadents. Rachilde contributed short stories to the periodical (later collected and published separately under the title *Le démon de l'absurde* in 1894), and wrote regular reviews for it until 1914. After World War I she continued to produce novels as well as a handful of nonfiction works, most notably her biography *Alfred Jarry; ou, le Surmâle de lettres* (1928). By this time, however, she

was experiencing somewhat failing health and had taken to collaborating with other authors on many of her novels. In 1935 her husband died, leaving her with little money. She continued to write well into her eighties, producing her final work, the autobiographical *Quand j'étais jeune*, in 1947. She died at the age of 93 in 1953.

Major Works

The vast majority of Rachilde's writings were novels in the Decadent style. Among her early novels, *Monsieur Vénus* is typical in its emphasis on passion and sexuality from a female point of view. In this work Rachilde inverts the gender roles of master and mistress by allowing its heroine, Raoule de Vénérande, to take a working-class man as her lover. After his violent death in a duel, however, she withdraws from society and succumbs to a pathological depression. Several works that followed dramatized similar themes. *La Marquise de Sade* (1887) is a psychological study of Mary Barbe and her burgeoning sadism. Androgyny and gender ambiguity are the motifs of *Madame Adonis* (1888), in which the recently married Louise Bartau falls in love with a enigmatic woman whom she believes to be a man. The heroine of *Le Jongleuse* (1900) forsakes all men, choosing instead a Greek vase as the object of her amorous desires. The varied manifestations of sexual deviance are evident in a host of Rachilde's later novels, including studies of incest (*Les hors nature*, 1897), erotic obsession (*L'heure sexuelle*, 1898), and pedophilia (*La souris japonaise*, 1921). In her dramatic works Rachilde often employed symbolism to explore deeply hidden emotions or to develop a social critique. In *Madame la Mort*, first performed in 1891, a young man's thoughts of suicide are personified as Madame Death, who vies with his living girlfriend for his love. *Le vendeur de soleil*, originally staged in 1894, criticizes the inability of the bourgeoisie to appreciate natural beauty, as its protagonist attempts to sell indifferent passers-by a glimpse at the setting sun. Of her nonfictional works, Rachilde's essay *Pourquoi je ne suis pas féministe* (1928), is among the most telling. Semi-autobiographical in format, it describes her thoughts on relations between the sexes and explains the sources of her often misogynistic writings.

Critical Reception

Rachilde achieved considerable celebrity in her lifetime, in large part due to the publication of *Monsieur Vénus* and the charges of immorality it elicited. Her fame grew with the production of several plays in the 1890s and her many contributions to the *Mercure de France* into the early twentieth century. After the First World War, how-

however, her popularity declined as her Decadent novels—no longer in vogue—began to take on a bleaker and more cynical tone, and her strong female protagonists were replaced by mysterious and brooding male figures. Rachilde is little known outside of France and Belgium; only a few of her novels, including *Monsieur Vénus* and *Le jongleuse* (*The Juggler*), have been translated into English. Nevertheless, Rachilde, although typically appreciated for the role she played in the French Decadent movement, has most recently attracted the attention of critics for her nascent Modernism, as well as for her exploration of sexual politics and changing gender roles.

PRINCIPAL WORKS

Madame de sans-Dieu (novel) 1878
Monsieur de la nouveauté (novel) 1880
La Femme du 199e régiment (novel) 1881
Histoires bêtes pour amuser les petits enfants d'espirit (short stories) 1884
Monsieur Vénus (novel) 1884
Nono (novel) 1885
Queue de poisson (novel) 1885
À mort (novel) 1886
La virginité de Diane (novel) 1886
La Marquise de Sade (novel) 1887
Le tiroir de Mimi-Corail (novel) 1887
Madame Adonis (novel) 1888
Minette (novel) 1889
Le mordu (novel) 1889
Les oubliés: L'homme roux, filles de neige (novel) 1889
La sanglante ironie (novel) 1891
Théâtre: Madame la mort. Le vendeur de soleil. La voix du sang (dramas) 1891
L'animale (novel) 1893
Le démon de l'absurde (short stories) 1894
La princesse des ténèbres (novel) 1896
Les hors nature (novel) 1897
L'heure sexuelle (novel) 1898
La tour d'amour (novel) 1899
Contes et nouvelles, suivis du Théâtre (short stories, novellas, and dramas) 1900
La jongleuse [*The Juggler*] (novel) 1900
L'imitation de la mort (novel) 1903
Le dessous (novel) 1904
Le meneur de louves (novel) 1905
Son printemps (novel) 1912
La délivrance (novel) 1915
La terre qui rit (novel) 1917
La découverte de l'Amérique (novel) 1919
La maison vierge (novel) 1920
La souris japonaise (novel) 1921
Le grand Saigneur (novel) 1922
L'Hôtel du grand veneur (novel) 1922
Le château des deux amants (novel) 1923

Le parc du mystère [with Homen-Christo] (novel) 1923
La haine amoureuse (novel) 1924
Le Théâtres des bêtes (short stories) 1926
Refaire l'amour (novel) 1927
Alfred Jarry; ou, Le surmâle de lettres (biography) 1928
Madame de Lydone, assassin (novel) 1928
Pourquoi je ne suis pas féministe (essay) 1928
Le prisonnier [with André David] (novel) 1928
La femme aux mains d'ivoire (novel) 1929
Portraits d'hommes (biography) 1929
L'homme aux bras de féu (novel) 1930
Notre-Dame des Rats (novel) 1931
Les voluptés imprévues (novel) 1931
L'amazone rouge (novel) 1932
Jeux d'artifices (novel) 1932
La femme Dieu (novel) 1934
Mon étrange plaisir (novel) 1934
Les accords perdus (novel) 1937
L'autre Crime (novel) 1937
La fille inconnue (novel) 1938
Pour la lumière (novel) 1938
L'anneau de Saturne (novel) 1939
Face à la peur (novel) 1942
Duvet d'ange (novel) 1943
Quand j'étais jeune (autobiography) 1947

CRITICISM

Daniel Gerould (essay date 1983)

SOURCE: "Madame Rachilde: 'Man' of Letters," in *Performing Arts Journal*, Vol. 7, No. 1, 1983, pp. 117-22.

[*In the following essay, Gerould presents an overview of Rachilde's literary works, including several of her best-known plays.*]

One of the most colorful and appealing figures in Parisian artistic and literary circles at the turn of the century—a period rich in flamboyant characters—was Marguerite Eymery, wife of Alfred Vallette (founder of the magazine *Mercure de France*) but known to her readers and fellow writers by her pen name Rachilde. Author of dozens of novels with provocative titles (*The Marquise de Sade, The Sexual Hour*) that dealt with bizarre sexual fantasies, she was condemned by respectable bourgeois society as a monster and hounded by the police as a pornographer, but revered by the literary world for her generosity in recognizing and encouraging new talent. The guardian angel of Lugné-Poe's Théâtre de l'Oeuvre, Rachilde played a crucial role in advancing the cause of symbolist drama, herself contributing several of the earliest French plays in that new mode. As Alfred Jarry's closest friend and associate, she was instrumental in seeing that Lugné-Poe staged *Ubu Roi.* At a time when there were almost no women writers of any note in France, Rachilde was accepted as an intellectual equal by her peers. Maeterlinck, Verlaine, Mallarmé, Huysmans, and Remy de Gourmont, among many others, praised her talent and commented on the originality of her work.

Rachilde was also celebrated for her beauty, her enigmatic charm, her disconcerting wit. Sonnets were written about her greenish, cat-like eyes. Maurice Barrès nicknamed her Mademoiselle Baudelaire. According to Jean Lorrain, she was "very pale . . . rather thin, frail, with extremely small hands . . . and eyes—such eyes! Wide, wide, made heavy by unbelievable lashes, and clear as water." Her pallor, grave expression, inner fire, and outrageous imagination made Rachilde a perfect *fin-de-siècle* persona. Her career actually spanned almost an entire century. As an aspiring young teenage writer, she met Victor Hugo and received his blessing; when she died in 1953, *Waiting for Godot* was already playing at the Théâtre de Babylone.

Born in 1860 in Périgord (truffle country in Southwestern France), daughter of an army officer and, on her mother's side, descended from a Grand Inquisitor of Spain, Rachilde grew up in an isolated, bleak environment, cultivating the life of the imagination and obsessed with uncanny things. "She had always been improper," Barrès reports; "When she was still very young—erratic, generous, full of strange enthusiasms—she frightened her parents." She began writing stories at the age of twelve and was soon publishing them in local papers under various pseudonyms. By fifteen she had read the Marquis de Sade. Independent, emancipated, good at sports and handy with sword and pistol, Rachilde excelled in a world of men.

In 1878, the eighteen-year-old author came to Paris and began working as a journalist, writing for *L'Ecole des Femmes,* the first French women's magazine, directed by one of her cousins, where her first novels were published. At this point, given her limited financial resources, Rachilde decided to dress as a man in order to save money on clothes and also to facilitate her getting around Paris more easily as a reporter. She cut her hair short and sold her long tresses to Prince Romuald Gédroye, Grand Chamberlain of the Emperor Alexander II of Russia. On her visiting card she called herself: *homme de letters* (man of letters) and adopted the pseudonym Rachilde, supposedly the name of a medieval Swedish nobleman who spoke to her at a table-rapping seance.

In 1884, at the age of twenty-four, Rachilde achieved her first great success when a Belgian publisher brought out her decadent erotic novel, *Monsieur Venus,* whose virile and sadistic heroine, Raoule de Vénérande, keeps a pretty but stupid young working-class man as her mistress and systematically humiliates and torments him by turning him into a useless love object. After his

death, Raoule keeps a wax statue of her late lover, adorned with certain real parts—teeth, nails, and hair—taken from the corpse. With its shocking inversions of accepted sex roles and its advocacy of the androgynous ideal (long before it became fashionable in symbolist circles), *Monsieur Venus* caused an immense scandal, not the least of all because it was written by an innocent-looking young lady who dressed as a man. Declared obscene, the book was prosecuted in Belgium where the court sentenced Rachilde to a large fine and two years in jail, punishment which the author avoided by not crossing the French-Belgian border. When the Parisian police came searching for copies, Rachilde was obliged to hide her stock of *Monsieur Venus* at the apartment of her friend Jean Moréas, a symbolist poet then in vogue. Because of Raoule de Vénérande and her curious predilections, Rachilde was even accused of having invented a new vice; whereupon Verlaine declared, "Ah, my dear child. If you have invented a new vice, you would be the benefactor of mankind."

Outspoken and passionate in defense of her literary comrades, particularly the weak and helpless, the author of *Monsieur Venus* won the respect of artists and writers by her loyalty, courage, and good humor. When Paul Verlaine, sick and battered, was evicted by his landlord and without a place to stay, Rachilde moved out of her apartment, turned it over to the ailing poet, and took care of him. Verlaine later dedicated a poem to this strange creature whom he called a diabolic angel or an angelic devil.

In 1889 Rachilde married Alfred Vallette. Within a year they had a daughter and started the *Mercure de France,* which soon became the principal literary magazine for the symbolists as well as a major publishing house, continuing to flourish until after World War II. An avid reader, Rachilde reviewed all new fiction and was quick to discover and support new talent (she was one of the first to recognize Colette's genius). The *Mercure de France* receptions that the Vallettes held every Tuesday in their home provided opportunities for young artists—among them Gide, Valéry, Ravel—to meet their elders and launch their careers. When he came to France in 1891, Oscar Wilde, who had received ideas for *The Picture of Dorian Gray* from *Monsieur Venus,* went to the *Mercure de France* to meet Rachilde, who—he was surprised to find—was not a demon, but a quite normal human being. At his trial in London four years later, Wilde's liking for *Monsieur Venus* was cited as evidence of his depravity; after his sentencing, Rachilde was one of the few to speak publicly in Wilde's favor. During Aubrey Beardsley's visit to Paris in 1897, it was Rachilde who took him under her wing and introduced him to the French artistic world; the descriptions in her *Marquise de Sade* are very similar in spirit to Beardsley's drawings.

The most famous of the Vallette's proteges was Alfred Jarry, who was a close friend of both husband and wife from the moment he first came to the *Mercure de*

France in 1893 (making his debut, according to Rachilde, "like a wild animal entering the ring") until his death at the age of thirty-four in 1907. The Vallettes championed Jarry, published his works, and cared for him in his last poverty-stricken years. Not only did Rachilde keep Lugné-Poe firm in his resolve to produce *Ubu Roi* when he started to lose his nerve, she also shouted down the screaming demonstrators on the tumultuous opening night and told them to keep quiet.

Jarry's most revealing correspondence is addressed to Rachilde, and her book of affectionate reminiscences about their friendship, *Alfred Jarry, or The Supermale of Lettres* (1928), is a primary source of information about the author of *Ubu Roi*. Only the scurrilous Paul Leautaud, who worked at the *Mercure de France* and disliked Rachilde, implied—despite Jarry's homosexual tendencies—that the two were lovers. In fact, Rachilde was happily married to Vallette and led a conventional life. She and Jarry, whom she always addressed as "Père Ubu," were similar in temperament, endowed with the same peculiar sense of fantasy and humor, and they quite naturally found each other the best of companions. As a deadpan joker, Rachilde was able to rival and even best "Père Ubu." One day tired of hearing Jarry's boasting about his Gargantuan eating and drinking exploits, Rachilde proposed a raw-meat-eating contest and sent for two uncooked mutton chops, which they were to devour, fat and all, garnished only with pickles. Equipped with a strong stomach as well as mind, Rachilde methodically demolished her chop, drinking only her customary glass of water (she was a teetotaller), whereas "Père Ubu," even guzzling large quantities of his beloved absinthe, was unable to gag down the raw meat and left the table hastily overcome by a queasy feeling—although five years later he persuaded the gullible Guillaume Apollinaire (not a native-born Frenchman and therefore more easily hoaxed) that he lived exclusively on a diet of uncooked mutton. Not only gifted at Jarryesque horseplay, Rachilde could even write like Jarry if she was willing to make the effort. As the result of a bet between the two, she wrote Chapter VIII, La Peur chez l'amour (Fear's Visit to Love), of Jarry's *L'Amour en visites* (*The Visits of Love*) (1898) and did it so well that it has always been accepted until very recently as Jarry's.

Rachilde's own perverse and ghoulish fiction has often been said to be in bad taste, but in those pre-Freudian days by dealing with deviant sexual behavior (incest, homosexuality, bestiality) and violating deeply felt taboos, she was able to explore the unconscious and extend the boundaries of what could be treated in literature. Drawing upon themes and techniques from the decadent aesthetic, symbolism, and naturalism (movements which co-existed in the last two decades of the nineteenth century), Rachilde created novels and stories which are eclectic and highly personal, although essentially realistic studies in abnormal psychology and sexual psychopathology. As an artist she was obsessed with dreams and death, cruelty and the erotic. In his preface to *The Demon of the Absurd* (the collection of plays and fiction containing *The Crystal Spider*), Marcel Schwob points out that Rachilde penetrates—beyond cause and effect and the perceptible—into a realm of mysterious relationships and signs: "Rachilde's brain is equipped with antennae . . . With these delicate filaments, which extend her mental grasp, she scents death in the midst of love, the obscene in the midst of the normal, terror in the midst of peace and quiet. Like a cat on the watch, her ears prick up, and she hears the little mouse of death gnawing away at the wall, at our thoughts, at our flesh. And she stretches out her paw voluptuously to play with the little mouse of mortality."

Rachilde's plays, which include both grotesque comedy and horror drama, were frequently produced in small avant-garde theatres during the early 1890s. Her first work for the stage, the one-act anti-bourgeois satire, *Call of the Blood,* was given at the opening evening of Paul Fort's new symbolist-oriented Theatre d'Art in 1890, although it could equally as well have been appropriate for a program at the naturalistic Théâtre Libre. *Call of the Blood* presents the cozy after-dinner conversation of an idiotically self-satisfied middle class couple who remain indifferent to screams for help coming from someone in the street and congratulate themselves on being safe inside their apartment; only when the bloodied victim staggers through the door do they perceive that it was their own son who was being murdered under their window. Her second play, the three-act *Madame Death* (Gaugin did a frontispiece for the book edition), was given at Théâtre d'Art the following year. Called a cerebral drama by the author, the second "symbolist" act takes us inside the dying brain of the hero, a disgruntled artist who has committed suicide in the first act by smoking a poisoned cigar.

The Crystal Spider, with Lugné-Poe himself playing the role of Terror-Stricken, was presented in 1894 during the first season of the Théâtre de l'Oeuvre and was shown on tour in Copenhagen, Christiania, and Antwerp. In combining the twin symbolist themes of mirror and the double, *The Crystal Spider* reveals the influence of Edgar Allan Poe, so prevalent in France at the time via Baudelaire's translations. Rachilde conceives the fantastic not as a matter of supernatural agency, but of neurotic behavior, and probes the fears and anxieties of the hero who is suffering from catoptromania (obsession with mirrors). The shattered mirror becomes an image of how flaws in the personality determine where it will split under stress, as Freud will indicate a few years later, using the same basic metaphor: "If we throw a crystal to the floor, it breaks; but not into haphazard pieces. It comes apart along its lines of cleavage into fragments whose boundaries, though they were invisible, were predetermined by the crystal's structure."

The one-act *Salesman of the Sun,* given at the Théâtre de la Rive Gauche in 1894, was one of Rachilde's best known plays. It deals with an imaginative but down-and-out street vendor, who having no other wares left sells passers-by a view of the sun setting over the Seine. Translated into Russian, *Salesman of the Sun* was on Meyerhold's list for production at the Theatre Studio in 1905-6, but was not given in Moscow until 1920 (with a different director). *At the Sign of the Eagle,* written in 1928 but unperformed, is a one-act comedy in which Rachilde supposes that Napoleon has escaped to America when a look-alike takes his place and is sent off to Saint-Helena, and now the man of destiny runs an inn in Philadelphia. During the nineteen thirties Rachilde had three new plays staged, two of these at the Grand Guignol, a fitting theatre for an author whose works reveled in the morbid and the macabre. The last of these productions, in 1938, was a version of one of Rachilde's first novels, *The Tower of Love,* a powerful study of human solitude written in 1899, and now adapted for the stage in collaboration with Marcelle Maurette, a highly talented woman playwright of the younger generation.

Jennifer Birkett   (essay date 1986)

SOURCE: "'La Marquise de Sade': Rachilde (Marguerite Eymery) 1860-1953," in *The Sins of the Fathers: Decadence in France 1870-1914,* Quartet Books, 1986, pp. 159-89.

[In the following essay, Birkett provides a psychological interpretation of Rachilde's works.]

Woman's place, for the writers and artists of the decadence, was inside the work of art, as an image to fix the male imagination. If Rachilde, almost alone of women writers of her period, was accepted into the Club des Hydropathes and Le Chat Noir, patronized by Victor Hugo and Barbey d'Aurevilly, approved by the misogynists Huysmans and Léon Bloy, and befriended by Verlaine, Jean Lorrain, Catulle Mendès, Laurent Tailhade and Camille Lemonnier, this had much to do with her willingness to play and play up to the decadent stereotypes. Squeezing every possible thrill from her autocratic, sadistic heroines, casually dismissing effeminate and inept anti-heroes to madness and death, she nevertheless respected the limits of the images allotted her—Salome and Scheherazade, but never Herodias. She is the real-life counterpart of Clara, heroine of Octave Mirbeau's bitter satire on decadence, *Le Jardin des supplices,* maker, vehicle and victim of other people's dreams, whose function is to reproduce the values of a world with no energy of its own. For admirers and reviewers, she embodied all the contradictions of Baudelaire's women: animal and goddess, ingenuous infant and perverse adult. Albert Samain wrote sonnets to 'her eyes iced with green', and 'the 'enigmatic cat locked in the woman's form', observing 'The marquise's fine teeth / Crunch endlessly on exquisite caramel', as she savoured 'The voluptuous pleasure of being no man's conquest'. Camille Lemonnier, in an article in the *Mercure de France* (February 1891), reprinted as preface to her novel, *La Sanglante Ironie,*

savoured the blend of physical innocence and intellectual corruption which, he said, made her young heroines so much more vulnerable than Barbey's mature *Diaboliques:*

> Neurotic, their senses precociously aroused by the ferment of heredity, sick of an excess of reverie that delivers them to man already initiate and deflowered, they take on a kind of ingenuous perversity, and as long as they can they remain, in their subtle spiritual corruption, girls who have dabbled in sin but postpone its bodily embrace.

Like her male contemporaries, Rachilde found a market and packaged herself for it. Like them too, she paraded an ironic self-awareness that turned her concessions to the market into contempt, proclaiming her independence by caricaturing the parts she was forced to play. She boasts in her memoirs (*Quand j'étais jeune,* 1947) of going to the *bal des Quatz-z-Arts* in 1885 with Jean Lorrain, she in a short white spotted muslin dress, socks, baby shoes and a blue satin belt, he in a pink tunic and panther-skin cache-sexe he had got from a wrestler in Marseilles. The man's suit she wore to shock the Latin Quarter was a statement of intent, like the eighteenth-century marquise's costume for which she exchanged it to confuse and intrigue a staid suitor, her future husband and future editor of the *Mercure de France,* Alfred Vallette. But these carnival costumes, like the flamboyant gestures of her writing, have no alternative, more authentic, identity beneath them to justify the bravado. These masks, like Ensor's, are also the real face. In her pamphlet of 1928, explaining *Pourquoi je ne suis pas feministe,* Rachilde joined her claim to be an independent individual, an enemy of all groups, to an unrecognized and deeply rooted social conservatism: 'I have always acted as an individual, never dreaming of founding a new society or upsetting the one that existed.' She confesses to insecurities that are exactly those of her male contemporaries, the difference being that in her case the origins lie in gender. She knew, she wrote, that masculine privileges would have been useful in her struggle for financial survival and a career of her own, but she had no right to them: like all women, she said, she was neurotic and had no self-confidence. As the publisher's notice for her pamphlet observed, the celebrated artist spoke with the voice of 'the French middle class, faithful as ever to time-honoured experience and an entire tradition'.

In her pamphlet, Rachilde blamed her own contempt for women on her mother. All the family money came from her mother's side, from a radical anti-Bonapartist newspaper that Rachilde's grandfather had edited. The mother encouraged her daughter to despise her father, and at the same time did her best to frustrate her ambition to be a writer. In her autobiography, Rachilde describes, in contrast, her devotion to her father, commander of the cavalry regiment which covered Bazaine's retreat to Metz in 1870 and illegitimate son of an aristocratic family, with whom, Rachilde decided, her preferred allegiance lay.

From childhood, Rachilde was caught in multiple inse-curities. She identified herself twice over with defeated causes: the aristocratic tradition, and a father whose authority was in dispute. She had no desire to be iden-tified with her mother, the usurper, daughter of a radi-cal, challenging every kind of established order. And yet, her mother's strong-minded example was always there, to point out the weaknesses and failure on her father's side, and life was further complicated by her father's undisguised regret that the daughter had not been a son.

It is out of these divided and confused loyalties that Rachilde puts her creative imagination at the service of male masochistic fantasies, acting out the temporary triumph of the vengeful female and the humiliating overthrow of the male—subject to the reinstatement of paternal power in the last act. Like Baudelaire, she plays all the roles in the fantasy, which becomes her own, both executioner and victim.

For all their anarchic pretensions, Rachilde's rebellions never took her far outside the family circle. She gave plays and patronage to Paul Fort's Symbolist Théâtre de l'Art, founded in 1890; her pleasure in shocking the sensibilities of respectable theatregoers was greater than her understanding of some of the plays. She wrote for the anarchist and later Dreyfusard *Revue blanche,* but took care to mark her distance from its editorial policy. Her defence there of Oscar Wilde in 1896 ('Questions brûlantes'), was chiefly a defence of Lord Alfred Dou-glas, in the chaste name of romantic love, echoing the self-justifications Douglas had just published in the *Mercure.* When the literary anarchist Laurent Tailhade was caught in the blast of a real bomb in the café Foyot, she and Vallette drove to the scene of the accident to find their friend, and defended him against the jubilant sneers of the right-wing press; but five years later, Tailhade took her to task in a letter for drifting to the side of reaction, concluding hopefully: 'basically, you're on our side; the Triumph of the Republic, just, true, fraternal, is the triumph of all independent people. You'll support it—despite yourself, out of your love of independence and beauty' (20 November 1899). Rachilde was *not* on his side, though her 'love of inde-pendence and beauty' like those of other decadent con-temporaries were of considerable help to a Republic that was more conservative than Tailhade recognized, dis-placing as they did more fundamental political issues.

To some extent, Rachilde's own writing acknowledges and deprecates its conservatism. Among the many mediocre works she poured on to the market, certain texts indicate her awareness of the closed nature of decadent ideology, and of the destructive readings of social and personal relationships that its images rein-force. But this awareness leads to no search for alterna-tives. On the contrary, it locks her more firmly into the same symbolic patterns, and into a self-lacerating pessi-mism which finally turned to despair—particularly after the First World War, with its irrefutable evidence of the bankruptcy of the father-figures on whom she de-pended.

Rachilde's obsession with a fantasy of female power has led to considerable misinterpretation of her work by modern feminists, who repeat, in a different language, the appropriations to which she was subjected by the male reviewers and readers of her own day. The author of the introduction to the 1982 reprint of *La Jongleuse* (Editions des femmes) argues on the evidence of its domineering and sadistic heroine that Rachilde writes 'to proclaim that woman had the right to love in her own way and to remain mistress of her own fate', and that she is 'despite her reservations about feminism in 1900, an effective writer who by her verbal and imagi-native powers must be inscribed in the ranks of those whose aim is to furnish other women with the means to their own freedom'. This is a novel in which woman indiscriminately hands on misery to woman, as well as man, and where no one is free. At best, Rachilde's writing stirs the reader to uneasy awareness of the ugly implications of contemporary fantasies. At worst, it re-inforces the fantasies, making fear and guilt an integral part of their pleasure.

Marcel Schwob's preface to her collected short stories (*Le Démon de l'Absurde,* 1894) is still the most percep-tive assessment of her work. Rachilde is not Scheheza-zade but Cassandra, enclosed in her own prophecies of doom, unconscious of their real meaning, but fixing accurately and intuitively on the tiny signs of inexpress-ible, imminent disaster:

> This is the same obscure ability to make con-nections that sets death at the end of sexual desire, that invokes the obscenity of plump little hands, that brings a blurred edge of sadness to a spring landscape with its branches of flowering almond . . . With those delicate filaments that extend her intelligence, she sniffs the scent of death in love, obscenity in healthiness, terror in calm and silence. Like an alert cat, she pricks her ears and hears the little mouse of death gnawing away at walls, thoughts and flesh. And she stretches out a voluptuous paw to play with the little mortal creature.

Rachilde's first successful novel, *Monsieur Vénus,* sub-titled 'a materialist novel' and dedicated 'To physical beauty', was greeted on publication in Brussels in 1884 with a fine of 2,000 francs and a two-year prison sen-tence. For the French edition of 1889, Rachilde begged a preface from Maurice Barrès. The preface assured the book's success, but defeated its purpose. Barrès turned the would-be female subject back into object, humiliat-ing the humiliator, with his invitation to readers to be titillated by Rachilde's motives for creating a heroine who exploited men in the ways men usually exploit women. In these fantasies of a twenty-year-old virgin, the blend of innocence and vicious sophistication was 'one of the most mysterious riddles I know, mysterious as crime, genius, or infant madness, with elements of all three'. In Barrès' view, the novel had no ethical, psychological or artistic merit. Its author was a typical young woman, writing out of animal instinct, 'for her own sexual thrills'. To the perverse spectacle of Rachilde's own sexual naïveté was added the pleasure of seeing her heroine suffer, modern woman punished for her cold arrogance. Finally, Barrès reduced the distinctive female problem to one more manifestation of 'our' decadence:

> The sickness of our age, to which we must constantly revert, and which **Monsieur Vénus** shows us in woman taking one of its most interesting forms, is one of nervous fatigue taken to excess and a hitherto unknown arrogance. This book is the first to point out the strange forms it brings to the sensibility of passion.

The fashionable decor of Raoule de Vénérande's bedroom mirrors her adolescent sexuality, repressed and perverted by the bigoted aunt who brought her up. The walls, draped in red damask, are covered with weapons and licentious paintings; a bed of black ebony, loaded with cushions, reeks of heavy oriental perfume. Besieged by suitors of wealth and breeding equal to her own, she keeps an ironic distance. A marriageable—and marketable—virgin has power over men; a married woman does not. Unwilling to surrender to men of her own class, she turns instead to a man she plucks out of the city poor, with all the good looks and subservience that traditionally draw upper-class men to their female servants. Jacques Silvert is an untalented painter, earning a scanty living making artificial flowers. Raoule sizes him up like a prostitute: 'very dark red hair, almost tawny; a slightly stocky torso on jutting haunches, straight legs, slim ankles'. He has damp, beseeching, doggy eyes; he is young; he smells of fried potatoes. His harpy of a sister is quick to become his pimp.

Raoule's pleasure in Jacques is in seeing how much humiliation he will accept. Apparently there are no limits. She sets him up in his own studio, where she wanders in and out as she likes; he rebels at the intrusion, and then gives in. She watches him take a bath; he suspects she's watching but daren't challenge her. She gives him hashish, watches him under the influence of the drug, and makes love to him while he lies powerless, 'arousing terrifying ecstasies, with such exquisite skill that pleasure constantly rekindled at the moment of exhaustion'. He becomes the mistress, referred to as 'she', and she visits him in men's clothing. She confides her experiment to de Raittolbe, one of her suitors, declaring modern women have no intention of reproducing an aristocracy whose time is done, and see no point in giving pleasure they don't share to men who don't know how to make love. De Raittolbe, who should have been shocked, is simply entertained.

Jacques is gradually reduced to a passivity which he learns to enjoy. Raoule beats him, demands increasingly effeminate behaviour, and imposes on him 'degrading habits'. De Raittolbe too thrashes him, irritated eventu-

ally by such flagrant betrayal of masculine authority. Raoule, rightly suspecting the beginnings of homosexual attraction, falls furiously on Jacques' bleeding body, tearing off his bandages:

> . . . she bit his marbled flesh, squeezed it in handfuls, scratched it with her sharp nails. She ruthlessly deflowered all those wonderful charms that had once given her mystical, ecstatic happiness.
>
> Jacques writhed and squirmed, his blood flowing out through the deep gashes that Raoule pulled wider, in a refinement of sadistic pleasure.

She marries him, as much to keep her possession safe from her male rival as to flout convention.

The men at her wedding, like de Raittolbe, find themselves coveting the bridegroom. On the wedding night, Jacques' transformation and Raoule's discomfiture are complete; he bursts into tears because she isn't a man. One night shortly afterwards, he tries to seduce de Raittolbe, who resists, but the final result is a duel in which Jacques inevitably dies. Raittolbe, who genuinely loved him, mourns the boy, while Raoule is still more interested in possessing a property of her own. In the penultimate chapter, she works mysteriously over the corpse with a pair of gilt pincers, a velvet-covered hammer and solid silver scissors. In the last pages, her bedroom has become a shrine for a wax figure of Jacques. The hair, eyelashes, chest hair, teeth and nails are all natural, and a spring in the figure's mouth automatically presses open its things. The figure is an anatomical masterpiece, made by a German.

The images are ludicrous, and the text in one sense scarcely justifies more than one reading, since it relies for its effects on surprise and shock, which are not reusable commodities. What holds the reader is the sense of being introduced into a highly private but real world. Partly this comes from the intensely sensuous and idiosyncratic detail of Rachilde's observations and descriptions. But mostly it comes from the clarity with which she sets out the exploitative patterns in the relationship of men and women on which fantasy and reality are both structured, and the frustrating impossibility of breaking them. The *femme froide* is a social construct, the only part given to an independent woman to play. But even the *femme froide,* trying to play executioner, is forced back into the role of victim. Everything she invents for herself is recuperated for men's pleasure. And without their support—be it de Raittolbe's amused approval or the German craftsman's skill—she can neither rebel effectively, nor sustain her own fantasies.

For Rachilde, class is the insurmountable barrier which must always prevent change in women's condition. With Jacques, Raoule came closest to disrupting her world, first by taking a paid lover to challenge the sanctity of family order, and secondly in marrying him, to bring disorder inside the closed circle. This particular outsider was doubly dangerous, introducing sexual ambivalence into a hierarchy built on rigorous gender as well as class distinctions. The aristocratic de Raittolbe's response—to kill the destructive element—was a logical one. But Raoule, who shares Rachilde's own faith in hierarchy, was never more than half-hearted in her challenge to order. Her chosen instrument from the people, mindless and malleable as the wax doll he became, was no match for the men of her own world. Her retreat into her bedroom with her toy makes surrender an integral part of her fantasy of revolt—surrender made palatable by redoubling her sadistic cruelties against a totally powerless Jacques.

La Marquise de Sade (1887) performs precisely the same self-castrating movement against would-be castrating woman. The symbolism is as heavy as that of **Monsieur Vénus,** and the scenes of torture and sexual licence equally morbid and violent, but the fantasy moves in a more realistic setting, with a detailed analysis of the domestic, social and political circumstances that construct the female sadist. The opening scene at the abattoir, where Mary walks daily with her aunt, between the military parade ground and the cemetery, to fetch the pint of blood prescribed for her anaemic mother, actualizes the hostility and hatred in the child's environment, which adults conspire to conceal. Mary's formative trauma is the accidental sight of the slaughtered bull, dying in slow agony and splattering her with blood. She wakes from her collapse to see the anxious, fatherly face of the butcher bending over her. Growing up is the progression from this initial, shocking confrontation with the father who loves and kills, through states of indifference, masochism and passive resistance to vengeful violence. The counterpart of the butcher and the bull in Mary's adult life is her lover, her husband's illegitimate son, Paul, whose nose bleeds copiously over her dress at their first meeting, and later, with her encouragement, over her feet. She pricks him with hairpins, tattoos her name on his flesh, and longs to tear him to pieces, like a dove, or the kitten she had as a child, that grown-ups pulled to bits.

The moral and physical violence that Mary's family practises on her is returned by the child with interest to family, lovers and society at large. She is neglected by her dying mother, and brutalized by a beloved father. When her mother dies giving birth to a son, she competes unsuccessfully with her baby brother and her father's new mistress. Her first chance for revenge comes when a drunken nurse overlays the baby in bed; she watches without intervening, enjoying the power of irresponsibility. After her father's death in the Franco-Prussian War, she falls to the care of a misogynist uncle, who proposes to send her to a convent. At this point, the silent victim makes her first protest: 'I'm in the way, because I'm not a boy!' Intrigued by her resistance, her uncle takes an interest, and begins to educate her. Her initiation into anatomy becomes an initiation into debauch. She connives at his advances, which leave her technically a virgin, and him vulnerable to her

blackmail; from this moment, the victim of sexuality begins to reverse her role.

Marriage with a rich, ageing libertine is an escape into a lesser domestic dependence. She threatens to poison her husband if he tries to force her to have children. She is a mistress, not a wife, prepared on occasion to indulge all his desires, at a price. She stages a humiliating confrontation between him and her lover, his bastard son. Maddened by her perversity, poisoned by the aphrodisiacs she feeds him, exhausted by the mistresses she sends him, her husband dies of what the doctor calls 'a strange case of satyriasis'. Discovering she has poisoned his father, Paul leaves her in disgust, literally tearing himself away from her claws and teeth.

Mary is both victim and heroine, greater than her circumstances and the men around her, a daughter of the Roman decadence forced to live through 'their' pale imitation. She is an admirable monster, a robust carnivore, a salamander untouched by the flames of modern neurosis, a vampire:

> . . . she lived on others' nerves, not her own, sucking the brains of everyone around her with the exquisite pleasure of a mind that can analyse to a degree the value of others' infamies and will frankly confess to regretting its cruelties, since so many of its chosen dishes are in such doubtful taste.

The ethics Barrès complained were missing from **Monsieur Vénus** appear here, and they are his own, the 'cult of the ego' which he made the watchword of the Third Republic. If force is its own justification, then Mary has every qualification for preying on the weak—physical vigour, intellectual strength, and a powerful ego. She has no alternative occupation. Only politics attracts her, and politics, she knows, is closed to a woman who will not be satisfied with a supporting role. In her eyes, the world is too corrupt to be worth saving. She roams Paris at night in a restless quest for blood and strong emotions, in the company of her most recent suitor, chosen for 'the freshness of his complexion'. The vampire images decay into sadistic reveries: 'Sometimes a new wound would rise hideous from the city mists, and she would touch it with a raging finger, probing it with pleasure that erupted in shafts of irony'.

She stays in cheap hotels in the hope of seeing a murder, but never does; she avidly leans over balconies to watch fights in squalid dancehalls, surrounded by the unspoken contempt of her gigolo escorts. Her fantasies finally settle on a band of male transvestites being propositioned by a group of young aristocrats, all useless to society. One of these would be an ideal victim:

> Her nostrils dilated behind the velvet of her mask. She would take an ideal pleasure in the death agony of one of these men, incapable of defending himself against a woman. One spring night, she would toss her handkerchief into this heap of

animals for sale, bring him home, cover him with her jewels, wind him round with her laces, intoxicate him with her best wines and then, asking nothing in exchange but his repulsive life, tie him with satin ribbons to her antique bed and kill him with pins glowing red from the fire.

A subtle plan . . . that she wouldn't, perhaps, carry out, but would brighten her thoughts on her many dark days.

What restrains her from challenging man's indefensible claim to privilege is the risk of laying herself open to a jury that might misconstrue her act as a crime of passion. The 'true female from the era of the Earth's primitive fire' could never fall in love with 'one of these sexless creatures', 'fallen males'. Mary locks herself into a dream of murder she will never realize. The story comes full circle, closing in a bar at La Villette by the slaughterhouses, where she mingles with the butchers' apprentices, pretending to have the same lung complaint as her mother, so that, like them, she can mix her wine with blood. She is a vampire and a beast of prey, but also a sick woman and a pathetic child:

With her pallid face, wrapped in her marten furs, half little girl craving forbidden fruit, half lioness yielding to instinct, she slipped in among those people, held out her cup like them, drank with a delicate enjoyment concealed by a tubercular mask.

Unlike her usual escorts, the apprentices respect and pity her. There is an unspoken parallel between her 'strange mystic desire' to murder the weak males of her own class, and the slaughter of the butchers' victims; it brings Mary on to the fringes of the fathers' potent world. She enjoys their warmth, company, bad language, and the smell of blood from the open slaughterhouse door. But she drives away hermetically sealed from their reality in her furs and her carriage. She has nothing in common with workers. Dreams of destruction are enough. The novel hints darkly at the forces that could be unleashed by a misused woman, combining her animal vitality with that of the working people, and loosing it on a corrupt ruling class. It also swears its author would never dream of lowering herself to such levels, and reassures the reader that she *will* be good.

With its own limits abjectly stated, Rachilde's hatred is displaced from men to women. Paul's contemptuous abandonment of Mary had been quite justified, anticipating a conclusion in which the heroine, with only her own resentment to add to her husband's money and status, accepted again the marginalization she had suffered as a child. In *Nono* (1885), the poor young secretary whose adoration is mercilessly exploited by the General's daughter Renée, mistress of a duke, turns out to have a dignity, purity and nobility that puts the woman to shame. He goes to the guillotine on her behalf; she dies in madness at the moment the guillotine falls; and her father stands by Nono's bier to renounce his daughter and adopt the dead boy's family in her

place. In *Madame la Mort,* Rachilde's three-act symbolist drama staged at the Théâtre d'Art in March 1891, all the sympathy is for men, whose dreams can only be cast in empty or morbid female images. The wealthy hero, a morphine addict, tired of life, commits suicide by smoking a poisoned cigar. In the central dream sequence, Life and Death compete to win him. Life is Lucie, his treacherous mistress, who in the last act inherits his fortune. He prefers Death, the unknown woman who promises peace.

In the two other plays Rachilde wrote for Paul Fort, *Le Vendeur du soleil* and *La Voix du sang,* men are again the centre: the anarchist poet, whose lyrical tongue seduces the crowd and subverts the State, and the son stabbed in the street outside his home, while his screams go unrecognized and ignored by his parents, secure in their middle-class complacency.

In her preface to the collected edition of her three plays (1891), she noted the tremendous success of Shelley's *Cenci,* which had been Fort's second production, but makes no reference at all to his Beatrice, the heroine who incarnates almost all her own fantasies. And yet Camille de Sainte-Croix' review in *La Bataille,* included in her book's Appendix, spelled out the significance of this 'parricide for freedom', who murdered her incestuous father for revenge and for the public good, to expose the unholy alliance of dying powers—religion and aristocracy—by which the young are kept from their inheritance. Perhaps the answer is there: Rachilde would approve Beatrice's vengeful violence, but not her politics.

La Sanglante Ironie (1891) also takes a hero faced with a choice between Life, the Whore who deceives and cheats, and Death, the cold, consoling Mother. This novel, however, makes it clear that this set of symbols and choices is no more than the self-justifications of a particular narrator, constructed by a particular historical situation. The narrative has an analytical dimension that deconstructs the processes of male fantasy, and criticizes some of its definitions. At the same time, male authority is shown as more than fantasy. The narrator is a murderer, and his two female victims are dead before his text begins; their death, in fact, is the pretext of his writing.

The irony of the title lies partly in his discovery that death and prison are for him true freedom. It lies also in Rachilde's awareness that her exposure of the murderous violence on which male privilege rests is futile. As for Beatrice, death is the reward of opposition.

The narrator speaks from prison, and from experience, to explain that the desire to kill is a natural one. He has 'the cult of Death', an unknown, dreamy country, figured by a cool, elegant woman in a floating ash-coloured gown, with silky white hair, who offers no welcome, but a calm, neutral embrace.

Death is the aristocratic mother he never knew, and the place in aristocratic society that life has denied him. The son of a gentleman too proud to let him go to school with peasants and too poor to afford any but the cheapest of tutors, he is ridiculed and stoned by peasants' children whose freedom and vitality he envies. The woman he thought was his mother is his father's servant and mistress, dirty, stupid and unfaithful, whom he watches one night on the kitchen table with his tutor. Her liaison with his father shuts the family out of local aristocratic society. The boy inherits all the worst of the aristocratic tradition—arrogance, weakness, neurosis—and is cut off from the vigour of the peasantry. He knows them only as enemies, usurpers and thieves. When the Franco-Prussian War breaks out, he finds he would rather kill French peasants than Prussians.

Like Rachilde, he loves the father who has ruined his life. He adopts his aristocratic cult of blood and vengeance. When he murders a rival, or later his mistress, he is exercising in the private domain—the only one left to him—rights he has been told are traditionally his. The 'simple man's view' of national politics he gives from his cell are the clichés of post-1870 monarchism. War is a necessary 'periodic bleeding of nations'. The lilies of feudal France, which flourished before the Americas were discovered and before Europe decayed, were pure because they 'grew from a crimson compost . . . In their day, the blessed day of noble massacres, our country was more picturesque, less neurotic, healthier. Blood freely shed is what makes bodies healthy, and to retain an excess of blood generates corruption'. His health was too poor for him to join the army, to his father's disgust.

The symbol of his hopeless longing to 'return' to his aristocratic home is the still, lonely pool in the hills, surrounded by lilies, reeds and dragonflies, where he spent idyllic childhood hours, his only companions a wildcat and a snake. This Eden is forever unattainable, locked in the lost past, with his dead mother. All that is left for the present is the animal violence.

Denied his political and social heritage, he tries to carve an identity out of sexual relationships. He tries to marry Grangille, the illegitimate daughter of the local doctor, thinking she will make a submissive wife. Aware he has no future, Grangille makes use of him to get to Paris, but has no intention of saddling herself with his dead weight. In Paris, he finds Jeanne Simeon, his cousin's wife, an attractive blonde, dying of slow paralysis. Jeanne represents the sterile fascination of the aristocratic world—a dead past that resists all his necrophiliac desire to reclaim it. At her insistence, he enters her mother's tomb, and experiences a morbid thrill, as if he were violating his own dead mother.

Sexually and politically, he is caught between two extremes: peasant and princess, and life and death. Neither satisfies; he is determined to hold on to both; and in reality, neither is for him. Jeanne dies of shock and

grief on hearing of her rival, and he himself stabs Grangille, as she turns to leave him for a grocer.

He waits now in the limbo of prison, the figure of the decadent condition, desiring death but clinging to life. The impotence that was originally the fault of circumstances is now his by choice. Compared to the women, imprisoned in the roles of paralysed wife or bastard daughter, his limitations were far fewer. He used his relative freedom to choose death for all three.

Rachilde's best work consists of the short stories that appeared in the early 1890s, first in the early issues of the *Mercure de France,* and then in the collection *Le Démon de l'Absurde* (1894). In these, she explored the role of tradition, highlighting the burden and the restrictions which the cultural inheritance places on the present. Traditional ways of seeing—in the form of images, symbols or values—can produce dangerous constructions of reality, of which both men and women are victims. Like Lorrain or de Gourmont, she shows desire caught, repressed, or glamorized in the distorting mirror of learned perceptions, turning into fantasies that terrorize and destroy their originator.

In these tales, her writing is more sensuous. Woman is the fertile force of Nature, not vampire but serpent, set against the crabbed and confining conventions of man's authority. But reviewers who saw her as 'rehabilitating the flesh' (Camille Mauclair, *Mercure de France,* May 1893) were mistaken. In all her stories, the denying power of social and religious law still imbues pleasure, however intense, with a sense of guilt. 'Les Vendanges de Sodome' and 'La Panthère' (first published in March and October 1893) show how the voluptuous natural forms of sensuous and sensual life are constricted, crushed and perverted by the language of prejudice. These misperceptions are the result of a tragic blindness that pushes the destroyers into the pit along with their victims.

'Les Vendanges de Sodome' opens with images of rampant fecundity: the earth smoking under a red dawn sun, and a vine with 'leaves of blood and gold', heavy with giant fermenting grapes like huge black eyes, coiling convulsive tendrils over the ground, 'imploring arms stretching to the sun, in a delirium of suffering, all the guilty delight of Paradise'. Red, gold, black, green and silver, the brilliantly coloured symbol of all the ambiguous energy of female sexuality, the vine is the only living point in the Judaean landscape, except for a few sparse twisted figs and the distant bone-white stone town of Sodom. From the town comes a procession of young men to pick the grapes, led by a bony, twisted, old man, and trailed by a pretty youth. On the instructions of the old man, 'the sovereign image of eternal death', the pickers strip the vine, and 'angrily' trample the grapes into wine.

While they are asleep, a woman approaches, earth-spirit, fairy Melusine, faun and Virgin, clothed in her own awesome natural beauty:

She was thin, pale-necked and covered from head to foot in red, downy hairs, which seemed like clothing of spotless linen embroidered with golden stars; her brow against the blue of the sky was smooth and polished as a dazzling swordblade; her hair swept the earth, gathering to itself the rustling yellowing leaves; her heels, round like peaches, hardly touched the ground, and her step had a gay animal spring; but the two nipples on her breasts were black, a burnt, frightening black.

Having eaten the leftover grapes from the boy's basket, she creeps alongside him like a serpent and her 'impure fingers lay claim to his flesh'. He wakes with a sigh of pleasure that turns into a scream as consciousness returns and brings the men running. The woman is one of the wives and daughters ('gulfs of lust') banished from Sodom to die in the desert or flee to Gomorrah, so that the men's strength can be saved for the harvest. The men denounce her as a thief, and a seductress. The child's accusation is more complex, blaming her for the fascination and fear with which he contemplates sexuality, in his enforced ignorance: 'I never knew you, because I never wanted to!' Stoned, splattered with blood, she writhes into the vine and crawls to hide in the grape-vat. They trample her underfoot with the grapes, 'while from the miraculous black globules gleaming like rolling eyes flickered a glance with the ultimate curse'. That evening, drunk on 'the dreadful poisoned liquor of love', in a hellish moonlit landscape, 'the men of Sodom for the first time committed the sin against nature in the arms of their young brother Sineus, whose sweet shoulder had the scent of honey'.

The story has a crude but vigorous message. The law of the Jewish Father protects the interests of the impotent old men who impose it. It destroys women, and it destroys its own male children. Repression poisons the source of life.

The same theme reappears in **'Volupté'**, dedicated to Camille Mauclair. Two adolescents sitting on the edge of a forest pool, on the threshold of sexuality, are looking for a language from their own experience to describe the paradoxical identity of intense pleasure and intense pain. They find instead familiar images, expressing the traditional relationship of man and woman. She recalls the scent of hyacinths, the sensation of drops of water falling on the nape of the neck, and the image of the dying Christ. His images are of violation and penetration, longing to scrape his nails along smooth, glassy surfaces, or cutting his own finger with a razor.

She is afraid to let him touch her breasts, but allows him instead to drink the reflection of her face in the pool. Even fantasy is not safe. After he has drunk, leaning over the water, she sees at the bottom a real woman's dead face, with mouth wide-open. Unable to communicate the horror of what she sees, or draw back from the edge, she faints, and he carries her home.

There is no way out of the trap of tradition. In **'Le Piège à revenant'**, the enterprising son of a family who inherit a haunted mansion digs a trap to catch the spectre and then falls in it, spending the night wrapped in the terrors of the tradition he thought he could abolish.

The trick of these stories is to manufacture pleasure out of the knowledge that women are victims, by signalling their connivance with the executioners. In every case—wine-vat, pool, or pit—the source of death and fear, which is often also the source of nourishment and refreshment, is a female image. The guilt of being the transmitter of a poisoned tradition becomes part of the pleasure of the text.

'La Panthère' describes how the victim comes to cross to the side of the murderers. Hoisted from her underground cage into the centre of a circus to tear Christian captives to pieces, the young, elegant panther sits gravely licking her genitals. She ignores the men dying on the crosses, just as she ignored the spoiled, spiced meats served in her cage to excite her. She bites at last into the flesh of a dead elephant and sits eating it delicately. She has known freedom, and she intends 'to show her good breeding in the presence of appetites less natural than her own'. She 'whimsically declares herself for the weaker party', only to discover the price of virtue. She is attacked with dogs, spears and arrows; patricians and people fling stones, fruit, coins and jewels. Back in her cage, she is starved and tormented. The jailer burns out one of her eyes, and then leaves her to dream of her lost freedom. When the jailer's compassionate daughter comes into the cage with meat and fresh water the divine panther has turned into a demon. Suffering leaves no room for morality, or discrimination, only the blind desire for revenge:

> Then the panther lifted herself on to her haunches, which fortunately were still supple, shrank into herself, so as not to frighten the child, stared at her a moment with her twin luminous eyes, that suddenly turned into deep gulfs of shadow, and leapt straight at her throat and strangled her . . .

In their attribution of blame for the pain and suffering in her world, Rachilde's stories hit out wildly, in contradictory directions. This seems particularly true of those which first appeared in the enlarged collection of 1900. In **'La Mort d'Antinoüs'**, it is the patriarchy's web of blood and corruption that demands the sacrifice of the young. Decaying, dying authorities convince themselves of their potency by destroying a future they cannot share. The ageing Emperor Hadrian, in a fever of terror from the omens of death he has seen on the battlefield, still loves his favourite slave, the ephebe Antinoüs, whom he had once decreed a god; but jealous of his youth, and fearful of losing him, he turns on him with an unwitting curse.

Elsewhere, civilization is the destroyer. Florence is ravaged by plague, and only one man, a prince, left alive, with nothing to eat but the billowing roses sprung from the victims' dead bodies. The prince dies of a surfeit of poisoned roses ('**Le Mortis**'). In '**La Buveuse du sang**', an incantatory prose-poem dedicated to Jean Lorrain, it is not civilization but Nature herself, in the form of the moon, who, like the Emperor Hadrian, decrees and thrives on death. Woman is the victim of her own sexuality. A young girl dreams of being kissed by the honey mouth of the red moon: 'the laughing moon, that drinks women's blood'. Under a pale moon wreathed in bridal mist the girl is raped and 'the moon sniggers on . . . a fiery flower that lives on women's blood'. Under a crescent moon, a thin spur signifying crime and death, the woman, beside herself with frenzy, strangles her new-born baby. The moon shines on victorious, pure as a wax taper.

'**Le Tueur de grenouilles**', far from being a 'rehabilitation of the flesh' blames female sexuality for men's perversion. Toniot was beaten by his naked mother, afraid he would betray her nightly visits to her lover in the forest. As he watched them making love in the dark, sexual pleasure for him became a complex blend of revenge, excitement, fear, jealousy and contempt:

> He won't forget what he sees, it's too funny! He sees a big white frog, yes, that's it, those wonderfully flexible thighs, open arms, precise, elastic, stretching limbs, so pale they look like silver! . . . He'll see that all his life, inside, in that very image, like a poisoned spring, with its sweet, painful reflections.

The frogs he catches and puts in a bag made from his mother's old nightdress wave their legs like 'girls being raped' and he skins and eats them with erotic precision, deflowering and devouring his treacherous mother:

> Kneeling before the heap of tiny corpses he undresses them, removes the double ring of their golden eyes, lifts off their pretty green satin dresses, their sweet white velvet pants. It all slides off in a heap like dolls' clothes, and all that's left are the naked little thighs, very pale, nervously shivering, trembling . . .
>
> And there is a strange flame in the man's staring eyes, a gleam of desire or hate . . .

But more often, for Rachilde, woman's 'crime' is not example but collusion, reflecting for man, uncritically, the image of his desire. *L'Araignée de cristal,* which was staged by Lugné-Poë at the Théâtre de l'Oeuvre, is a short dialogue between son and devoted mother, in a darkening house. The language is convoluted as both try to avoid admitting guilt; Rachilde is adept at exposing decadent evasions. The son demands, he knows, the impossible: that 'blind women might sometimes appreciate the frightening situation they create for men who can see, even if only in the darkness'. What the son sees in women are his own impossible desires of shameful secrets, and these ensnare him like the mirrors men use to catch skylarks:

> Have you seen of a winter's morning the birds wheeling over the sparkling trap, thinking it a miraculous heap of silver oats or golden corn? Have you seen them falling one by one out of the sky . . . There's the mirror for skylarks and the mirror for catching men, that stands waiting at every dangerous corner in their dark existence, which will watch them die with their brows stuck to its icy enigmatic crystal . . .

He traces his hatred for mirrors back to the traumatic moment that marked his passage from child to adult—from infant dependency on the mother, to acknowledgement of the father's superior power, and the roles and responsibilities he must accept to function as an adult male in society. A ten-year-old schoolboy, writing his lessons in the shabby summerhouse, he found himself gazing absently into an old full-length mirror. In the stains in the glass he deciphered fluid, shifting images of waterlilies, and ghosts with streaming, slimy hair. He drifted into a reverie characterized as 'a muddy lake', 'dead water', 'this sleepy atmosphere'. The torpid, cloudy reflection in the glass of his own childish unselfconsciousness was broken into by a speck that became a spreading star-crack, a white spider, then a crab with a silver shell:

> . . . its head starred with dazzling spikes, its claws stretching and stretching over my head, lost in thought, it overran my brow, split my temples, consumed my eyes, gradually erased my image, sliced off my head . . . sucked out my brain!

The glass shattered and he fainted, coming round to find the gardener with his drill who had been fixing a nail on the other side of the wall.

What the mirror fixed was the violation of his unselfconscious existence by the power of the father, pushing him roughly out of formless, maternal dream into a world shaped by patriarchal authority and intentions and forcing him to accept it as his own. The mirror also fixed his fainting, his sense of impotence before that alien father. In mirrors now he sees that self he first saw as victim and failure, and so he hates them. Women too mirror his double and contradictory desire to be both passive dreamer and active authority. They don't see the cracks in the image, but he does. All unknowing, their reflections confront him with his inadequacy.

His mother responds, in the only way she can, by mirroring his terrors, and demanding that he go out (as his father would have, she says) to fetch the lamps to drive away the gathering darkness. He too is frightened of the dark, but he obeys. In the hall, he falls on her long looking-glass, and cuts his throat.

The mirror scene in de Gourmont's *Sixtine* was a brave assertion of the hero's ability to force his own patterns of desire on the world outside. When that hero, and others, failed in their intentions, the fault was always in a world that fell short of their desire. What Rachilde is saying is that the fault is in men, or rather, in the present generation of men who lack their fathers' power. Until they change, there will be no change. There can certainly be no initiative from women, who are even more deeply marked with that formative dependency. The mother will see her son's throat cut before she will make a new beginning. And when his throat is cut, she is left sitting in the dark.

There is considerable distance between Rachilde's versions of the female challenge and those of the emergent feminist movement, which she became aware of in the 1890s when male journalist colleagues took up the 'Woman Question'.

The radicalism of the women's movement at this time was more feared than actual, but the fear was still considerable. It was given striking expression in Strindberg's *Miss Julie,* premiered at the Théâtre Libre in February 1893. Louis Dumur, theatre critic of the *Mercure de France,* wrote a lengthy review in the March edition, drawing on Strindberg's Preface to explain the social implications of the play.

There is little in Strindberg's polemic that is not already anticipated by Rachilde's **Monsieur Vénus**. Dumur described a 'battle of castes' in which an aristocratic heiress, degenerate representative of a vanishing society, sells herself to a servant who 'aspires to rise, and carries in him the sap of future victories'. Julie acts in the name of a specious principle of female emancipation which in Strindberg's view is no more than egoism and fevered instinct. She is 'a half-woman, a man-hater', who learns the hard way that women are incurably weak by nature and training, and that outside the security of conventional duties and responsibilities offered by present society, there is nothing for them. If she joins forces with servants against masters, the servants will destroy her first.

On the first page of its January 1895 issue, the *Revue blanche* featured a translation of Strindberg's essay 'On the Inferiority of Woman'. Strindberg proposed arguments from evolutionary science to demonstrate woman's physical inferiority, which he equated with the negro's, or the child's. She had less grey matter than men, and her sense-perceptions were poorer. Natural incapacity, not lack of opportunity, was her problem. The tasks she was generally allowed to perform—drawing, music, or taking telegrams—were usually badly done. Her social inferiority was the result of her physical handicaps (menstruation and menopause), and of the division of labour in modern society, which was no more than the logical product of natural differences between the sexes. There was no reason to concede 'noisy' and 'raving' female demands for emancipation. Women could only merit it by working harder, which, Strindberg concluded with some satisfaction, was impossible given the present (natural) division of labour. As for the vote, there was no reason why inferiors of either sex should have it.

The *Revue blanche* was one of the few journals to run both sides of the feminist controversy. With a few ex-

ceptions, the voices countering Strindberg's authoritative pseudo-science were those of the occultists, using, more often than not, the language of their decadent origins. Paul Adam gave a positive account of the feminist congress of 1896, where most of the delegates, vociferously upholding family order, had demanded more jobs for women; only the radical Paule Mink, he thought, understood that the real task was to attack the values of patriarchy. In 1895, in his *Chronique des moeurs,* he had already included a lightly erotic, ironic piece on the dilemma of girls caught between changing notions of what women should be. A father who taunts his shy daughter for her unwillingness to say frankly how she reacts to the tale of *Sleeping Beauty* throws her out of the room in panic when she obeys: 'I thought of hot lips touching my own, hands clawing at my trembling breast, a whole body penetrating me with its odour, its vigour, its life . . . I thought of nakedness . . .' Jules Bois' lyrical account of the 'War of the Sexes', rewriting his mentor, John Stuart Mill, found supporting evidence for feminist complaints in the history of 'man's constant, relentless oppression [of woman] through the centuries'. For Bois, both partners now take a perverse pleasure in woman's enslavement. She submits to the role of prostitute in exchange for a continuous supply of fresh golden chains. Men set the fruits of their labour at her feet, while she in return generates bloodshed, lies and rivalry. Man owns the world, but woman owns man, through his passions; both need liberation.

In contrast, Rachilde's contribution to the arguments of 1896 ('Questions brûlantes') is a retreat into platitude. She refuses to take seriously any of the issues contemporaries are wasting their time on. She pictures herself sitting in the literary 'fun train', just an 'old lady who likes reading', lost in her book, ignoring both the changing landscapes and the travelling companions she despises for their readiness to take sides on voguish questions.

The only *real* burning question of the day, she claims, is the eternal question: whether Love is finished. The fashionable 'emancipatress', 'the ludicrous lady swelling with pamphlets', clouds this fundamental point with her prattle of free love, hygiene, sex education, and sexual harassment in factories. (German and American feminists are intelligent, if dull. French feminists are merely persistent.)

She claims that any woman who likes can be free, and that freedom is not a question of votes or party politics. Her free woman is a wife who is proud to confess an adulterous affair to her husband. The freedom to love is what matters most, and her admiration goes to Lord Alfred Douglas for braving convention and declaring his love for Oscar Wilde (which she is convinced is platonic). Outside her flamboyant fictions, Rachilde's sentiments are robustly bourgeois, slipping away from major problems with maudlin sentimentality.

Forced to state her position in plain language, Rachilde is banal and conventional. The more conservative she becomes in reality, the more wildly perverted are her fictions. *Les Hors nature* (1897) is the drama of a repressed homosexual relationship between two brothers, Paul-Eric and Jacques Reutler de Ferzen, of whom the first, and younger, resembles his French mother and the second his Prussian father. The characterization is curious, implying on Rachilde's part a covert admiration for Prussian authoritarianism, which no patriot (however frustrated she might be by the democratic degeneracy of her country) could openly admit. Repressed homosexual desire becomes a symbol of the guilt-ridden, impossible longing of French weakness to be consumed by Prussian strength; decadent masochism finds its appropriate political form.

Paul-Eric is corrupt, effeminate, sadistic, self-indulgently sensual, and wholly dependent on his brother for survival. Reutler, the Prussian, is harsh but upright, and devoted to Paul, who despises him. His rigid brutality is the result of his determination to hide the extent of his feeling for Paul, afraid of playing Hadrian to his brother's Antinoüs. Self-control is his watchword. He intends to be 'master in his own house', to 'make nature no more than the setting of my will'. The product of his repressed desire is a sadism that inevitably destroys them both: 'Death is the highest expression of my sensuality'.

Woman plays two supporting parts. She is first the medium through which the two opponents express their differences, and second the bringer of welcome death. Marie is an incendiary, found hiding in the brambles after setting the village church on fire, and taken in as a servant. When Reutler beats Paul for cutting off her hair, he feels the same thrill of perverse possession as Marie watching the church blaze, frustrated by being denied possession of her God. Destruction, Reutler acknowledges, is the only way out of the impasse, and he admires Marie's courage: 'Sometimes, it would be so good to blow up the world or set fire to the heavens . . . Really, that servant has breeding!' By setting fire to the house, releasing all three of them from an untenable situation, Marie at last becomes part of the family. As the flames lick into the boudoir where Paul lies dead, strangled by Reutler to save him from the pain of slow suffocation, Marie can acknowledge Reutler as master of the house, and he can call her 'sister'.

The clearer the political commentary in Rachilde's work, the more marked is its pessimism. The house of tradition disappears in purifying flames, or stands decaying at the centre of eternal 'natural' cycles of desire and frustration. *La Tour d' Amour* (1899), the ancient Breton lighthouse Ar-men, is the monster of a tradition outwardly sound and powerful, inwardly full of decay, madness, cruelty and death, to which its victims cling; the alternative is to be swamped by the sea.

By tradition, maintaining the lighthouse is man's work. The narrative centre is the young keeper, held to his post by principle—a sense of moral and patriotic responsibility—and also by economic necessity. He needs a job; he has no alternative. The rafts of corpses who drift past the rock are all men. Women stay safe at home. But men are not too much to be pitied. The lighthouse is a refuge as well as a responsibility. With all its stresses, it is better than the unknown: 'When you've been a long time in the same place, you get to love the place where you're suffering. It's more natural than to go out looking for happiness'.

The rules of the system—systematic isolation—make it impossible to look for happiness elsewhere. The keeper thought he had found a fiancée on one brief visit ashore, but she moved away during his long spell of duty. He is left with unsatisfied desires which turn to violence. He knifes the whore who accosts him, as her image fuses, in a drunken mist, with those of the drowned women who in his fantasies drift past the lighthouse. There comes a point in this system when all its participants really want is death.

All his anger at the limitations of his world is turned into sexual resentment, directed against women. He identifies with his lighthouse, united with it by 'a necessary evil: the evil of living for yourself'. He imagines it locked in sexual struggle with the moon and the sea. He watches in bitter envy one night as the moon, 'the great virgin', sailing high and seemingly free above the constraints of his own life, is embraced by the yearning arms of the lighthouse, 'the monster emerging from the darkness', and 'devours' it. The moon is an animal, shadowed and scarred every month, her face marked with the mouth that consumes men's mind and will. She floats on, and the lighthouse is quenched by dawn: 'human destiny is to burn out on one spot', to see eternally reiterated the evidence of its own futility.

The sea too is an image of woman and of life, cradling and consoling in her treacherous, murderous arms. She taunts the lighthouse like a mad whore:

> . . . flaunting her nakedness to her very entrails. The whore swelled like a belly, then caved in, flattened out, parting her green thighs; and in the lantern-light you saw things that made you want to turn away. But she began again, her hair flowing wild, in disarray, in fits of love or madness. She knew the watchers belonged to her. It was all in the family . . .

The sea also taunts the young man with an image of impossible freedom:

> The waves rose and fell, plump and opulent in a wealth of silk and jewels that insulted our poverty. Oh, the whore, the whores! All those little pussycat purrs, mad lioness screams, actresses dancing, and then in the end the torrents of blood and tears, streaming all round, and never tainting *them*. And their loveliness comes from all that freedom that men, prisoners of their own desire, can only admire from afar!

The young man's dreams of revenge are tame in comparison with those of his senior, who has kept the lighthouse for twenty years. The old man rows out to sea for the pleasure of putting two bullets into a drowned woman. He keeps the head of a rich young virgin, only two days drowned, locked away in the lighthouse in a bottle of spirits, its long hair streaming over the sides. The young man's initial horror and disgust develops into respect and finally collusion. When his mentor dies, he lives for weeks with the stinking corpse until the next supply ship arrives. When it comes, he accepts without demur the old man's job.

Men's power, the narrative suggests, may be limited, but within those limits it must be recognized as absolute. Since the world cannot be changed for the better, the lighthouse must be preserved. It must be accepted that in the lighthouse there is no room for living women. For the storm to be held off, women must let themselves be traduced to morbid fantasies.

After the Gothic self-denials of *La Tour d'Amour, La Jongleuse* (1900) is a welcome contrast, with its account of the satisfaction women can extract from their decadent roles. Yet even here, the illusion of women's all-sufficiency—Mother, Whore and Dream, Mary, Salome and Beatrice—is shown to be hollow at the centre.

The novel shows how women are defined by appearances, required to produce themselves through dress, decor and social rites and ritual as objects of pleasure for men. Women who are aware of this can juggle with men's fantasies as a means to power.

The text makes it plain these are sharp knives to play with, and they can cut; to challenge sadistic authority in its own language is a mistake. The ending shows the heroine, Eliante, forced to kill herself to preserve the fantasies, and with them the illusion that she, the Mother, is all-powerful. Rachilde writes her death as a perverse triumph that does indeed make Eliante the focus of all hearts and minds for eternity. But death is a poor kind of triumph, and the whole narrative, despite itself, throws up constant doubts and challenges. Who, it asks, does Eliante's play-acting really serve?

By choosing irony and parody rather than refusal, Eliante reinforces and internalizes the values she claims to reject. The centre of her house, her own bedroom, is furnished like a shrine with the erotic and exotic objects her husband brought back from his voyages to the East. Smoky light drifts through the topaz windows on to walls covered with skins and weapons set on cloth of gold, a red Turkish carpet, black furniture inlaid with iron, gold and mother-of-pearl, and—symbol of sexuality repressed and perverted—a marble statue of a black Eros with emerald eyes, set at the foot of the bed, his bow, hand and left arm cut off. These exotica, stolen from colonies she claims to despise by a husband she claims to have hated, represent all her identity and all her charm; she has nothing of her own.

Costume—masquerade—is the centre of the novel. Three distinct moments enact the same female fantasy that power can be won by pretending vulnerability. Men are to be fascinated with a display of sexuality that concedes nothing, forcing them into the spectator's role.

Eliante makes her first appearance in a sheath of watered black silk that gleams like metal, face blank white, hair flattened to blend with the lines of her dress. At first sight, the gown emphasizes her weakness; she is 'draped in thick shadow, apparently impenetrable mystery, rising high up her neck, tight, almost choking round her throat'. But it is also a 'snakeskin'; her long gloves fall into snakelike folds, and her veins run like little blue vipers under her white flesh. The dress is a snare. Her glance in the mirror at the foot of the stairs is not for her own image but that of the mesmerized Léon. She entangles him in his embarrassment as he treads accidentally on her train, almost pulling off the 'chaste sheath', and closes the trap with tantalizing fetishistic glimpses:

> . . . feet, lightly shod, edged with skin soft as her gloves, dark and naked in lacy stockings . . . eyes, dark and naked under a silky fringe of furry strands. The man halted, hypnotized, catching his breath.

In this costume, she makes Léon watch her make love with the Greek amphora in her bedroom, a kind of rape of an ideal phallus that she has created, and which he could never match. It was already an exquisite work of art when unearthed from its ancient site, but Eliante has improved it by removing all traces of the handles that stuck out and spoiled its harmonious lines, polished and scented it and set it on a carefully lit pedestal, throwing her favourite ring inside as an offering—a parody of the way men reshape and decorate women to suit their own idea of Beauty. Rachilde's imagery for Eliante's masturbation is blatant, down to the streaming 'starlight' from her eyes:

> Eliante, now poised over the neck of the white amphora, stretched up from nape to heels . . . Without a single indecent gesture, her arms chastely crossed over the slender form, neither girl nor youth, she clenched her fingers a little, in complete silence, and then the man saw her closed eyes part, her lips half open, and starlight pour from the white of her eyes and the bright enamel of her teeth; a slight tremor ran through her body—a ripple creasing the mysterious waves of her silk dress—and she gave a little imperceptible groan of pleasure, the authentic breath of the orgasmic spasm.

> Either this was the ultimate, splendid, manifestation of love, the true God descending to the temple, or the spectator had before him the most extraordinary actress, an artist who had transcended the limits of art's possibilities.

He was dazzled, charmed and indignant. 'It's shocking! To do that . . . in front of me . . . without me . . . No, it's abominable!'

Eliante's performance flatters Léon with this privileged glimpse of her hidden self-sufficiency, and leaves him disposed to see the same threat to his masculinity in more common forms of female exhibitionism. When she appears in the juggler's costume at Missie's white ball, he recognizes the contempt beneath her apparent anxiety to please her audience. Her close-fitting leotard, powdered clown's wig topped with a diamond butterfly, and velvet mask leave nothing visible but her red mouth 'between brackets . . . on a black and white page!' With its blatant framing of the symbol of sexual availability, it pretends she is like all women, mere performers, offered on the open market. But Eliante has no intention of parting with the merchandise. The professional's trick that brings the act to a triumphant finale is to catch the last falling knife apparently in her breast—in reality, in a small concealed pocket. The costume has a life-preserver built in for the wearer with the skill to use it. Playing with others' desire feeds her own pleasure, and confirms her self-sufficiency:

> [Léon] saw only too well that she wasn't juggling in his honour, or their honour, but for her own amusement. You could feel the vibration inside her of another blade, simultaneously treacherous and passive. She was innocently, absolutely amused by the original sensations of pleasure she procured for them, and at the same time she needed the sharp desire of those eyes aimed at her, the whole vibrating atmosphere charged with the electricity of passion.

> Léon knew how that would end off-stage! . . . She would go on playing, vibrating with the pure metallic vibration of her knives, a steel blade tempered in the fires of passion, scornful of real flesh and blood, using only her own black sheath!

Her Spanish dancer costume is a parody of female self-denigration, an ironic 'confession' that all women are cheap, and that she, now that she is growing old, is herself one of the cheapest. She wears the whore's version of the costume, that pushes her breasts into prominence and splits open at the back to reveal her shoulders; she adds a red flower (a 'blood-coloured kiss') and crude make-up that underlines the savage contrast between ageing face and athletic body: 'The eyes blackened with kohl were too big, too dark, casting a shadow over the rest, and the mouth, slashed with red, invoked a feeling of pain, like the sight of a surgical wound'. The dance is another masturbatory exercise, vibrating to her castanets, her own clicking heels and a demonic inner fever. It ends according to tradition, with the dancer 'dead' on the ground, covered in a black shawl. Eliante adds her own individual touch, reappearing from the 'wings' with a pot of red make-up thrown over her bodice, to kill the dancer off. Younger women are entering the picture, and Eliante is forced to compete through increasingly flamboyant disguises. Her downfall is grotesquely, tragi-

cally inevitable. The more the merchandise depreciates, the more risk there is of the buyer finally realizing that the market is, and always has been, his.

Eliante's fears of depreciation are linked to her knowledge of how completely she has made herself over into the image of man's dream. She tells Léon that she never loved her husband, 'and today is the first time I fear him, for your sake, because all he is now is what he's left behind in me. I am and shall always perhaps remain his humble servant, or yours . . . what can I give you that hasn't belonged to him?'. All she can give is the sexual identity that her husband has formed. She has two secrets, both his gifts, which symbolize that sexuality: perverse, glamorous, cruel and corrupting.

The first is a case of double-sided Chinese figurines, ivory divinity on one side, wax mortal on the other, locked in an obscene embrace, and all carved with her face. The key ornament is the crown of pleasure, made of men and women entwined in the dragon chimera of passion:

> . . . the eternal dragon who represents all things . . . a mouth filled with flames, bloody eyes, golden claws and wings studded with rubies. His immense prehensile ringed tail fulfils all natural, supernatural and social functions. Men and Women are studded with his precious jewels. Temples are lit by his brightness and for him, lanterns hang humbly before shops!

Patriarchal power controls its subjects with the illusion that sexual desire, shaped in its own monstrous, glamorous image, is the centre of existence, snaring them in its shiny coils, and through its seductions dictating every aspect of their daily life. Eliante's face is now part of the chain, and she is no more than an instrument for handing on the patriarchal tradition.

Her second secret is the trunk of costumes that dictates in advance the parts she can play. Her most useful role is the maternal one. She shows her costumes off to Léon, or gives them away to Missie and her friends, again handing on the corrupt tradition. The Mother, like the goddesses on the figurines, has all the appearance of power as long as she concedes her essential subjection:

> I'm not cruel, wicked, or even arrogant in the modern style. I humiliate myself as and when it pleases people. At a sign from the children who come up to me (and all men who come up to me, curious or tyrants, are just children); I juggle to amuse them, and if they cry, I rock them to sleep with pretty stories. I must be forgiven for being . . . happy. No one will ever know I carry inside the great source of illuminating fire, the fire of saints, martyrs, and great courtesans, not those who are paid for, but those who pay for their right to be respected, by inspiring love! I want . . . to be happy all by myself, arms crossed firmly over my breasts, thighs tightly sealed, smiling like a virgin at Communion.

Could you teach me anything better, dear little children, with your undignified shaking and trembling like puppets all hanging on the same string? It's my hand that holds the right end of the string!

Eliante hands on the tradition that passion is all that matters, and passion means domination: ' . . . to be truly passionate you must have a heart nearer the Devil than God, that is, be an arrogant man or woman . . . dreaming of infinity!' The text makes it clear that the dream of divine self-sufficiency can never be fulfilled; but implanting it in others is power in itself. Léon, and Eliante's niece Missie, both students, belong to a generation learning different ideas. Eliante intervenes to deride Missie's desire for independence:

> . . . born in middle-class suburbia, slightly bourgeoise, contentious, intoxicated by her new freedom, a raw beginner at everything, working haphazardly, piling up vulgarized information in the back of her mind so she can make her own vulgar deductions, to no great profit, so thirsty for pleasure, comfort and frills that she never remembers to wash her hands before she grabs; to be brief, always saying it takes very little to satisfy her— the little our grandmothers would have thought was a fortune.

In Rachilde's book, Missie is certainly a contemptible creature, feminist because it is the fashion; smoker, cyclist, and would-be bluestocking. Ironically, it was Eliante's husband who decided Missie should be educated. Eliante is certain she might otherwise have made of her a good wife or a witty courtesan. As it is, she makes sure Missie will never change the form of men's dreams. The girl she finally pushes into bed and marriage with Léon is someone for whom no partner could feel anything but contempt; and Eliante's suicide secures her own place as the unattainable ideal of which Missie will always fall short.

Eliante's is something of a Pyrrhic victory. She may have marked Léon's life with her dream-image, but Missie has the reality. Ironically, her aristocratic delusion of her own freedom and power is the instrument that has set up and will sustain one more part of the middle-class world it so despises. Eliante herself is completely caught up in that world. She may have been the daughter of a marquise, but she was orphaned by the Franco-Prussian War. When she married, she accepted responsibility not for children of her own but for her husband's family. That marriage itself, made for money, turned her from heroine to commodity. The last, unexpected discovery of Rachilde's text is the corruption of her aristocratic ideal by the values of the market. The queens of decadent mythology earn their keep by glamorizing the union of the primary-school teacher and the doctor.

Le Meneur de louves (1905), another attempt to glamorize simultaneously heroic rebellion and submission to order, is set in the completely different context of France's first struggles from barbarism to national identity. In this romance, self-denial is a moral and patriotic duty. Princesses and common people, united in revolt, are both shown as victims of injustice, and repositories of energy that could tear the new, weak nation apart. Princess Basine was raped and beaten by her father's soldiers, on the orders of her stepmother, Queen Fredegund. Like the she-wolves of the title, driven by starvation to attack cities, her own survival is at stake. The young Church struggling to unite the warring Franks is already corrupt, and rules by deceit and superstition. In Basine's army is a nun walled up for twenty years in her convent, whose stinking, rotten flesh is a living indictment of ecclesiastical power. But the alternative to the rule of the Church is anarchy, which Rachilde no longer condones: in 1905, the threat of revolution is too great. The nun is pitiful, but also ugly, vicious, and too broken to be of use. The starving wolf has to be destroyed for the general good. Basine's thirst for justice is rewritten as a bloody obsession with revenge, which leads to the sack of the countryside and the deaths of children. Harog the wolftamer, who raised his rabble army to avenge her, bewitched by her beauty, finally forces her to submit to the Church and ask for forgiveness.

Le Meneur de louves is one of Rachilde's last attempts to play the rebellious young barbarian. In later works, as Rachilde feels herself increasingly part of an order not merely under threat but displaced, she aligns herself completely with the dying kings.

The First World War gave her fresh images for the conflicts inside Byzantium. A set of new moral and technological values challenged outdated hierarchy, at the same time as the war's bloody horror gave a new lease of life to the old monsters. What she draws is the impossibility of concessions to the new world: the old order is dead, but must be defended at all costs.

Le Grand Saigneur (1922), with its title pun on *seigneur/saigneur*, 'Lord' and 'Bloodletter', brings the Marquis de Pontcroix back from presumed death in the trenches to renew the vampire traditions of his family. He discovers Marie, the daughter of poor working-class parents, who is acquiring a reputation as a major young painter, and takes her to his gloomy Breton stronghold to marry her, murdering her brother, who opposes the match. The belated discovery that Marie is not a virgin means marriage with her—a union between equals— will not save the marquis. Instead, he demands the right to survive by drinking her blood, which Marie, in her guilt, concedes. She is saved at the last minute by discovering evidence that he is her brother's murderer, and so more guilty than she is. In this curious competition for the cleanest conscience, the marquis finally scoops the pool by shooting himself, having first provided apparent proofs of his innocence. He becomes a vampire on Marie's world for eternity, a tragic hero unjustly accused.

The novel writes a general exculpation of the aristocracy. Admittedly, they were vampires, liars and destroyers. But the fault lay with history, and with their opponents. If the people had been better, aristocracy could have ruled with them; if Marie had been a virgin, there would have been a marriage, and no need for blood.

Corrupting the generation that will inherit is again the theme of *Madame de Lydone, assassin* (1928). The white-haired old lady, dressed in her favourite costume of eighteenth-century marquise, charms her nephew Gaston, an airman back from the front, with the manners, morals and decor of the past. In contrast to the stark devastation he has seen from his plane, she offers a haven of peace. Together the ill-matched couple think they might build a new life. But when she takes him back to her home village in the forêt d'Argonne, the dream-world she had promised him, the war has wiped it out.

Even before then, Gaston's dreams are filled with warnings of the impossibility of their love, with nightmare images of his plane sucked from the air by a mysterious, devouring monster which turns into his mistress's crippled dwarf servant. The creature's twisted relationship with Madame de Lydone—pity and exploitation on one side, devotion and resentment on the other—figures the contradictory relationship between rulers and dependants that pre-empts all hope of collaboration. The dwarf attempts to murder his mistress out of jealousy, and she shoots him in self-defence. They die together, leaving Gaston with the debilitating memory of a passion he will always believe could have restored meaning to his life. Yet the truth is that the two generations and ways of life are irreconcilable. Madame de Lydone herself, looking at the ruins of her village, had called for revenge, not forgiveness; forgiveness only brings the same mistakes again.

Rachilde's last novels are contradictory. The recognize, more than many contemporaries, the destructive nature of the old patriarchal order, but their chief focus remains the tragedy of its passing and the belief that nothing better can take its place. François de Valerne, the last of his line (*Les Voluptés imprévues,* 1931), sternly puritanical, strong-minded, strong-willed, and growing old, has chosen an heir for his wealth and his way of life. Lucien Girard, the type of the post-war generation, is the child of failure. His father, a rich coalmerchant, came home from the war disillusioned and ruined. His employer is a communist deputy, whose eagerness for equality is for Rachilde the cult of mediocrity, and whose belief is that France was ruined by the egoistic, imperialist values Valerne represents.

In this novel, Rachilde's traditionalism has a clearly extreme edge. Lucien's world is café society, artificial, spineless, superficial and discordant, surrendering human dignity to the basest of animal instincts. To the delight of the café, Valerne rolls up his white gloves and rams them down the throat of a bawling negro singer,

the symbol of the animality that dominates this world. Lucien, like his friends, is glad to be woken from the 'spell' of the music. But he is fundamentally unsympathetic to Valerne's values, however attractive the old man's fortune might be. Valerne's castle, at the end of a long damp drive, surrounded by ivy-wreathed oaks, is too antiquated to hold his frivolous attention, and he does not feel enough gratitude to his benefactor to endure his company for even a few days. Chafing at the old man's oppressiveness, he reveals that he is a homosexual, and Valerne collapses with a heart attack. Lucien inherits both castle and fortune, and all that the text can promise by way of justice is that great ancestral homes have been known to collapse on unworthy heirs.

Rachilde's work, for all its melodrama and its unevenness, is an important account of the possession and perversion of power in the years of the decadence, and the symbolic and instrumental role that women played. She is no feminist. From the beginning, she accepts dependency on men as the price of existence, and writes to extend dependency, glamorizing submission and painting the pleasures of self-delusion. She draws the political consequences of the unequal sexual relationships she prefers, and their interconnection. Hierarchy, authority and strong leadership are the principles by which she lives, dreamed into situations where their inappropriateness and ineffectiveness is increasingly obvious.

As a result, it is the death motif that predominates in her writing. The lighthouse that encloses the old man's rotting body and the young woman's head is the grotesque symbol of dying power: rigid order that kills the life it was built to sustain. Stifling the energy of the negro, handing over his wealth to Lucien's self-confessed weakness, Valerne deliberately chooses ruin.

In the end, all power drains into the decor. The old man's hoarded capital and ancestral mansion are left to wreak havoc in the weak hands of the future. In Rachilde's work, decadence makes the clearest confession of its own impotence. We do not live, or make history; our symbols do it for us.

Melanie C. Hawthorne (essay date 1987)

SOURCE: "Monsieur Venus: A Critique of Gender Roles," in *Nineteenth-Century French Studies,* Vol. XVI, Nos. 1 & 2, Fall, 1987 & Winter, 1988, pp. 162-79.

[*In the following essay, Hawthorne argues that Rachilde's literary portrayal of gender roles lends her works a greater interest and relevance than they are usually accorded.*]

A review of recent Modern Language Association Bibliographies reveals that most nineteenth-century French women prose fiction writers have received little critical attention. (The exceptions are, of course, Madame de Staël and George Sand.) Those who have been considered (Hortense Allart and Louise Colet, for example) have not been validated as writers, but rather considered in the context of their relationships with important men. This dearth of information may seem surprising to those familiar with the Anglo-American tradition, marked by the time and effort invested in the researching and recovery of a lost tradition of female writers.

This archaeological phase of feminist scholarship has resulted in a large body of primary and secondary material that now serves as the foundation for endeavors seeking to develop new critical theories and perspectives that inform the feminist study of literature. Perhaps paradoxically, the dominant mythological metaphor of the Anglo-American tradition would seem to be given by Freud: the discovery of some previously unsuspected rich tradition pre-existing the known one is "like the discovery, in another field, of the Minoan-Mycenaean civilization behind the civilization of Greece." [Sigmund Freud, *Female Sexuality*] Freud was, of course, referring to female sexuality, but the simile seems particularly apt in the domain of literature. Knowledge of that recovered tradition cannot help but reshape our conceptualization of the present one.

It is curious, then, that there has been no analogous phase in the French feminist tradition. There, theories seem rather to have sprung fully formed from the head of Jove. As Barthes has pointed out, "what is amazing in the myth of Minerva is not that the goddess sprang from her father's head but that she emerged 'tall and strong,' already fully armed and fully developed." [Roland Barthes, *S/Z*] This study attempts to tell something of the possible gestation period of this French literary Minerva, by focussing on the work of a nineteenth-century French author. Such a belated archaeological excavation can illustrate some critical perspectives that have recently been articulated within feminist scholarship, as well as serve to re-introduce a text which deserves to be more widely known.

Rachilde was the pseudonym of Marguerite Eymery Vallette. Her works are often cited as illustrations of the decadent novel, containing examples of most of the features associated with the decadent period: over-stimulated sensitivity trying to escape from boredom and banality through a constant search for new sensations in the form of mysticism, drugs, and sexual experimentation. However, her works are seldom given serious critical attention. For example, Jean Pierrot, in *The Decadent Imagination, 1880-1900,* dismisses her literary career as "built to a large extent on descriptions of monstrous and deviant sexual behavior, to the great outrage of the public and the astonishment of those who knew her personally." He evidently prefers to think of her as "[t]he product of a perfectly respectable background, happily married to Vallette, the editor of the *Mercure de France,* and accustomed to playing hostess." Her works are not widely read today, which is not surprising given this reduction of her work to the fantasies of a bored but conventional housewife. A more discriminating assessment of her work shows that her novels have contemporary relevance beyond the titillation often thought to be their sole asset.

In undertaking the re-assessment, it is necessary to be aware that looking for buried subversive treasures has been a prevalent mode of feminist reading. In some instances, it is claimed that subversion shows up in what are patently the most conservative texts. The feeling that such treasure hunts are motivated by some hope of gain or by wish-fulfillment makes such enterprises suspect and the sugar-coated subversions hard to swallow. For example, there is some gratification in thinking that even while Charlotte Brontë seemed to be affirming the values of romantic love and marriage, she was actually expressing feminist concerns about female autonomy, authority, and economic independence. It is reassuring to hear Kristeva affirm that obscenity is the return of the maternal semiotic, a sort of "amniotic semiotic," [Julie Kristeva, "From One Identity to an Other"] but such a celebration of disruptive codes seems inappropriate to the victim of verbal abuse.

This problem of discerning subversion points to a need within feminist criticism for understanding what textual conditions will support subversive readings. It is unlikely that authorial intent will provide a very good measure of subversive content for all kinds of reasons (unconscious intentions, lack of extant documentation concerning intentions), but this study will present some textual features as well as some aspects of reception which tell something about the politics of reading.

Rachilde's works appeared at a time when feminism was establishing itself in a serious way for the first time in France. In 1881, the Ferry government passed a series of laws that guaranteed the freedom of assembly and freedom of the press, laws whose effects were significant for feminism. The continuous censorship and repression that had dominated French politics had hitherto stifled any sustained feminist efforts at organizing. Towards the end of the century, however, the liberal measures introduced by the Third Republic contributed to the creation of an environment more receptive to feminism, as Claire Moses has demonstrated.

Rachilde's ***Monsieur Vénus*** was published in 1889. Given the context of public acceptance of feminism as legitimate discourse (that is to say, while not widely supported, it was at least no longer completely suppressed), this novel can be read as a (not so) sugar-coated subversion, a critique of gender roles made possible by the permissiveness of decadence and made palatable by its fictional form. At the level both of the plot and of the symbolic code, it involves the inversion of gender roles and illustrates what might happen if women were to enjoy the kinds of privilege usually accorded to men.

When considering the way in which *Monsieur Vénus* has been received and assessed, it is clear that the critique contained in the role reversal has been repressed. Besides being characterized as "perverse," a trait it shares with other decadent novels, this text has repeatedly received attention because of the "signature." This response is characteristic of what Mary Ellmann has named "phallic criticism." She notes that male critics of women's texts inevitably become preoccupied by the gender of the author:

> Books by women are treated as though they themselves were women, and criticism embarks, at its happiest, upon an intellectual measuring of busts and hips. [Mary Ellmann, *Thinking About Women*]

Such preoccupation with literary vital statistics effectively distracts from consideration of the text itself.

Jean Pierrot has already furnished one example of this tendency to discount the text; another is the preface written by Maurice Barrès to the current, 1977, Flammarion edition of the text. He treats the novel like a physical extension of the author, as "un prolongement de sa vie." He finds the book "abominable" and yet he experiences a certain attraction to it:

> Ce qui est tout à fait délicat dans la perversité de ce livre, c'est qu'il a été écrit par une jeune fille de vingt ans.

The perversion is "delicate," an adjective that at once both feminizes and domesticates the threat of non-conformity. It appears that for Barrès the attraction stems from the tension between the presumed sexual innocence of the author ("une jeune fille") and the sexual knowledge expressed in the text:

> . . . toute cette frénésie tendre et méchante, et ces formes d'amour qui sentent la mort, sont l'œuvre d'une enfant, de l'enfant la plus douce et la plus retirée! Voilà qui est d'un charme extrême pour les véritables dandys. Ce vice savant éclatant dans le rêve d'une vierge, c'est un des problèmes les plus mystérieux que je sache, mystérieux comme le crime, le génie ou la folie d'un enfant, et tenant de tous les trois.

From this it is clear that the novel is merely a medium of communication between author and (male) reader and that the gratification for the reader is not to be found in the pleasure of the text itself, but rather in some speculation as to its provenance. Thus, when Barrès suggests "qu'on regarde cet ouvrage comme une anatomie," it is clear that his interest extends beyond the body of the text. (Such misogynistic concerns are not limited by time and place. As recently as 1981, a preface to Rachilde's *La Jongleuse* displays the same characteristics.)

Such interest in the authorship has in some ways served as a digression from consideration of *Monsieur Vénus* itself, a defense against the subversive theme of the role reversal it offers. This narrative presents predominantly one "perversion." It is not necrophilia, it is not sadism, it is not bestiality. The perversion of this novel, which readers found so shocking, is love: "un amour tout neuf" to be precise. The main protagonist of the novel, Raoule de Vénérande, confides to her friend Monsieur de Raittolbe, "je suis amoureux." Hearing that the adjective remains in the masculine, Raittolbe assumes that this indicates that the relationship is a lesbian one, but Raoule is offended by such a suggestion:

> —Vous vous trompez, monsieur de Raittolbe: être Sapho, ce serait être tout le monde!

This claim that "to be Sapho [sic] is to be everyone" is ambiguous. In the context of decadent literature, it is clear that the theme of homosexuality (though not lesbianism) was commonplace, and thus the return to romantic heterosexuality was—at least temporarily—a novelty. But the remark has the added significance that (arguably) Raoule's proposal is more a threat to the status quo of a sex/gender system than conventional (if it can be so called) homosexuality. Instead, the new form of love which Raoule claims to have invented consists of a role reversal: she plans to take a male mistress whom she will "keep" as would a man of her social rank. Her justification for this departure is that she is tired of giving, but not sharing, pleasure in conventional relationships:

> . . . brutalité ou impuissance. Tel est le dilemme. Les brutaux exaspèrent, les impuissants avilissent et *ils* sont, les uns et les autres, si pressés de jouir, qu'*ils* oublient de nous donner, à nous, leurs victimes, le seul aphrodisiaque qui puisse les rendre heureux en nous rendant heureuses: l'*Amour*! . . .

Tired of being restricted to a choice between brutality and impotence, this frontal attack on the egocentric nature of male sexuality clearly represents an attempt to change the terms of sexual politics. This, then, is the great "perversion" of the novel: the "usurpation" of the male role by a female, and it is this threat which makes the novel simultaneously attractive and repulsive to the likes of Barrès, those who exorcise the threat by reminding themselves that this text is only, after all, "le rêve d'une vierge."

The role reversals carry over into the onomastic level of the text. Raoule's name is derived from a boy's name (Raoul), but the "e" ending marks it as feminized, stressing the gender ambiguity. Her last name (Vénérande), again grammatically connoting femininity with the mute "e" ending, appears to combine both the name of Venus—goddess of love and part of the novel's title—and the noun "veneration." The form of the name suggests the Latin gerundive which clearly places Raoule in the position of "she who is to be venerated." That Raoule is Monsieur Vénus can also be seen from the quotation above. She champions love—one source of sensation scorned by other decadent writers—and refers to it as an aphrodisiac, a word derived from "Aphrodite," the Greek name for the goddess of love known to the Romans as Venus. It is clear, too, that Raoule is not only the passive object of veneration, but the active party in the pursuit, since the name "Vénérande" also carries connotations of hunting ("la vénerie" is the art of hunting). The gender ambiguity is preserved in the title by the masculine address "Monsieur," which here reflects the fact that, due to the role reversal, Raoule comes to occupy a social position coded as masculine.

As might be expected, this role reversal operates to the general disadvantage of the "mistress," Jacques Silvert, who although financially secure, finds that he gradually loses his autonomy. A wretched artist and flowermaker, Jacques is coded as feminine from his very first appearance in the text:

> Autour de son torse, sur la blouse flottante, courait en spirale une guirlande de roses, des roses fort larges de satin chair velouté de grenat, qui lui passaient entre les jambes, filaient jusqu'aux épaules et venaient s'enrouler au col. A sa droite se dressait une gerbe de giroflées des murailles, et, à sa gauche, une touffe de violettes.

Surrounded by flowers and vegetation, Jacques appears to be caught mid-metamorphosis, like some latter-day Adonis, who was mortally wounded while hunting, and was changed into an anemone by Aphrodite. The comparison with Adonis is not only visual. Onomastically, too, Jacques is semi-vegetable. His name "Silvert" evokes the name "Sylvie" which comes from the Latin "silva" meaning "wood" or "forest." This sylvan connotation combines with the second syllable "vert" ("green") to reinforce the image of Jacques as a blossoming shrub or tree.

The floral images mark Jacques with femininity at his very first encounter both with Raoule and with the reader. When the former asks to speak to Marie Silvert, Jacques responds "pour le moment, Marie Silvert, c'est moi," thereby assuming a female identity within the linguistic code also. This gender confusion is even carried into the implicit visual codes of the text, where Jacques' androgynous physical characteristics add to the ambiguity:

> La main assez large, la voix boudeuse et les cheveux plantés drus étaient en lui les seuls indices révélateurs du sexe.

Numerous other references stress his vulnerability and girlish features and characteristics.

Raoule assumes the corresponding male lead to Jacques' supporting actress role. She is constantly referred to with masculine markers in the linguistic code, not only in the interview with Raittolbe cited above and in the title of the novel, but also in numerous other situations

and by other people. Her aunt, notably, refers to her as "mon neveu" ("my nephew") throughout. The clothing code also situates Raoule as male, with her man's clothes and Turkish cigarettes, while Jacques is often portrayed wearing women's blouses.

Of course, the switch in role carries with it a consequent change of status. Thus, although Jacques remains biologically male, when he assumes a female gender role, he loses power while Raoule gains it. She seems to control the terms of their interactions as well as being the sexual aggressor. Once again, their first encounter provides an illustration. Raoule remarks that Jacques has a strange profession, to which he replies, "ça n'empêche pas d'être un homme." With "une hardiesse ironique" Raoule observes, "je m'en aperçois." At the same time that she acknowledges Jacques' gender on the symbolic level, within the linguistic code, she usurps the male-marked place of the speaker who, as sexual aggressor, uses innuendo and *double entendre*.

Raoule's access to this level of privilege is facilitated by her class position. As a member of the aristocratic elite, her power is shored up by authority and economic advantage. Jacques, on the other hand, is clearly of working class origin, as evidenced by his occupation of flowermaker.

Although ***Monsieur Vénus*** depicts relationships affected by class position, the text does not challenge the class structure in the same way that it critiques gender. There are numerous examples in the novel of power conferred by class privilege. To begin with, the most obvious example is that Raoule has the financial resources to live out her fantasies.

The circumstances of Jacques' death are even more revealing of this textual blindspot. Jacques becomes so accustomed to his feminized role that when he engages in the adulterous affair, he offers his attentions to another man rather than a woman. Tipped off one evening by Marie Silvert, Raoule finds Jacques, dressed as a woman, in Raittolbe's bedroom. Raoule—presumably as the offended party—decides that in order to avoid public scandal the situation must be decided by a duel. Curiously, although Jacques is feminized elsewhere, Raoule assumes that he will take the traditional male role of duelist when honor is at stake. As she leaves, Raoule whispers to Raittolbe that it will be a duel to the death.

Both men are clearly being manipulated by Raoule in this matter, but Jacques, as a member of the working class, is immediately at even more of a disadvantage. He has had little or no training and practice at fencing (Raittolbe's choice of arms), and his seconds are equally inexperienced. Not surprisingly, he loses the duel and his life.

The point of Jacques' social disadvantage is made even clearer when the reader learns that the duel was conducted incorrectly. Raittolbe's seconds are troubled by this:

> —Vous n'avez pas remarqué, dit l'un des témoins du baron, lorsque la voiture se fut éloignée, emportant le cadavre, vous n'avez pas remarqué que Raittolbe, malgré son désespoir, a oublié de lui tendre la main?
>
> —Oui, d'ailleurs, ce duel a été aussi incorrect que possible . . . j'en suis navré pour notre ami.

They agree privately that the duel was improperly conducted. Personal opinion, however, is set aside in the face of class loyalty, and Raittolbe's seconds defend their friend to the inexperienced seconds of the deceased Jacques: "nous affirmons que M. de Raittolbe s'est parfaitement conduit." It is clear from this juxtaposition of comments that Raittolbe (and by extension Raoule) is shielded from censure by his class position.

This advantage is not challenged by the narrative. Indeed, the class structure is affirmed by the presentation of Raoule's "double," Marie Silvert. Marie is the only character to present a critique of the class system. Her critique is not limited to her own personal situation, but has far-reaching social implications. Remarking on how her brother Jacques' involvement with Raoule has changed his attitudes towards the aristocracy, she comments:

> Ah! les ouvriers pauvres ne feraient pas souvent des révolutions s'ils connaissaient mieux les femmes de la haute!

She recognizes the political power of sexuality and, in particular, the way it can be used as a recuperative force. In general, her understanding is not sophisticated, especially at the level of manipulation of the symbolic codes, and it is obvious that her commitment is to her class rather than to her gender. Nevertheless, because she possesses some degree of class consciousness, she is the character best suited to offer an indictment of the situation.

Any critique she makes at the level of content, however, is undercut at the narrative level by her positioning as a negative force in the plot development. As Jacques' sister, she benefits directly from the interest which Raoule shows in Jacques, both in the financial sense and also in terms of gaining power and influence. She exploits this position to the fullest. At times she appears to be orchestrating the entire relationship in order to derive personal gain. She wants to make an advantageous marriage and sees Raoule as a social contact to put her in touch with the right candidates. Failing this, she will continue to exercise her profession as prostitute (presented uncritically as a vice in the text), in which case she will still be in contact with rich potential clients.

In this way, the text presents any interest in changing class structure as yet another example of self-interest on the part of a wholly dislikable person. Marie seems to have no redeeming qualities whatsoever, and appears quite capable of literally selling her own brother for private gain. Ironically, although her name evokes virginity, purity, and self-sacrifice, Marie Silvert seems closer to Eve—the source of evil—than the redemptive Mary, and in damning her character, the text also appears to damn the social reforms put forth in her voice.

By neutralizing the threat of such social disruption, the structure of class privilege is consolidated. Before concluding, however, that ***Monsieur Vénus*** must be irredeemably reactionary, the connection of class to gender should be considered. It is clear that class privilege is a prerequisite to Raoule's autonomy. In the nineteenth century, a woman could aspire to independence only through her economic and class status. More importantly, however, and more significant for its contemporary relevance, the text is suggesting that only those who already have some degree of power (in this instance, economic and class-related) are in a position to make any other changes in the system.

It is because Raoule already has privilege in one power structure—that of class—that she can have an impact on a related structure, that of gender. It is evident that Raoule gains a considerable amount of autonomy and power through her decision to occupy male-marked positions within the symbolic code. She speaks from the position of power in sexual encounters and is in a position to command the behavior of others. In one scene, Raoule agrees to sleep with Jacques on condition that he *not* be her "amant" or (male) lover:

> —Tu seras mon esclave, Jacques, si l'on peut appeler esclavage l'abandon délicieux que tu me feras de ton corps.

When Jacques sulks at this proposition, Raoule traps him by a clever manipulation of the symbolic code in which Jacques is in a female position:

> —Pardon! murmura-t-elle, moi, j'oubliais que tu es une petite femme capricieuse qui a le droit, *chez elle,* de me torturer. Allons! . . . je ferai ce que tu voudras. . . .

In this exchange, Jacques is excused from taking a female role in sex on the grounds that he is a capricious female, an excuse which undermines his position at the same time as it appears to uphold it. When they retire to the bedroom, Raoule follows up this symbolic advantage by remaining sexually unresponsive until Jacques, "brisé de voluptés désespérantes," concedes and resigns himself to do whatever Raoule wants. Thus Raoule never needs to resort to overt force to get her own way: so long as she is a man, symbolically if not literally, she can control virtually any situation.

This is partially because, as for many other decadent characters, cerebral activity is a substitute for spontaneous action, and gender is nothing if not cerebral. Particularly in the sexual realm, which is where many questions of gender relations are worked out in this novel, Raoule enjoys a freedom and autonomy which derive from her ability to take care of her own needs. While it is suggested that she retains her control of Jacques by not letting him give her sexual gratification (consonant with her beliefs cited above concerning the inequality of gender roles in giving/sharing pleasure), she nevertheless lowers her guard when alone and able to contemplate the imaginary possibilities, fantasies of which she is in complete control.

The role reversals of this text make possible a number of challenges to male power structures. One scene in particular suggests the existence of a female gaze, a structure which would open up the possibility of analyzing and theorizing female subjectivity within patriarchal culture. The scene is a reworking of the story of Susanna and the Elders, which, as Mary Garrard has remarked, has been used extensively within the history of Western art as a pretext for representing the female nude in a sexually provocative way. John Berger locates the source of eroticism in the fact that the female subject of the painting is "naked as the spectator sees her." [John Berger, *Ways of Seeing*] This visual code constitutes the male as unselfconscious actor/ looker, and the female as object/victim of the look, aware of being looked at, and somehow complicit in treating herself as object. ***Monsieur Vénus*** contains an important episode in which the dynamics of the gaze are reversed. As in the story of Susanna and the Elders, bathing is the central activity. Raoule leads Jacques to the bathroom:

> —Enfermez-vous . . . Nous causerons á travers la portière.
>
> En effet, ils causèrent, chacum derrière le rideau du cabinet, lui pataugeant dans l'eau qu'il trouvait froide, le bain ayant été préparé avant leur arrivée; elle, riant de ses inepties.
>
> —Mais souvenez-vous donc que je suis un garçon, moi, disait-elle, un artiste que ma tante appelle son neveu . . . et que j'agis pour Jacques Silvert comme un camarade d'enfance. . . .

The role reversal is clear. Jacques is the one bathing, made vulnerable by his nakedness, while Raoule— who reminds both Jacques and the reader of the fact that she is occupying male-marked positions—remains clothed. Jacques at first relates to Raoule on an equal footing, as though he and Raoule were both men:

> Jacques tâtonnait. Après tout, le grand monde devait être plus libre que celui qu'il connaissait.
>
> Et, s'enhardissant, il émettait des réflexions polissonnes, lui demandant si elle ne le regardait pas, car ça le gênerait, naturellement. . . .
>
> Il lui fit des confidences. . . .

At first, like Susanna, he is not aware of being watched. Gradually, however, Jacques becomes uncomfortable with the situation, and begins to experience shame in connection with his body:

> Enfin, il y eut un fracas dans la baignoire.
>
> —J'en ai assez! déclara-til, troublé subitement par la honte de lui devoir aussi la propreté de son corps.
>
> Il chercha un linge et resta ruisselant, les bras en l'air. Il lui sembla qu'on froissait le rideau.
>
> —Vous savez, *monsieur* de Vénérande, dit-il d'un ton boudeur, même entre hommes ce n'est pas convenable . . . Vous regardez! Je vous demande si vous seriez content d'être à ma place.

Clearly, at this stage, Jacques still perceives the interaction as being "between men" but he evidently begins to sense an inequality in the relationship when he sees the curtain move. The rhetorical question draws attention to the fact that there is a difference in the experience of the looker and the object of that look.

The question highlights the fact that a most unusual inversion has taken place. For in some sense, Raoule does know what it is to be in Jacques' position and is not at all content with it. By reversing the situation, Raoule uses the dynamics of looking as a means of empowerment. She objectifies Jacques, and the more he becomes aware of being the object of the gaze, and the longer he remains complicit, the more Raoule has control:

> Clouée au sol, derrière le rideau, Mlle de Vénérande le voyait sans avoir besoin de se déranger. Les lueurs douces de la bougie tombaient mollement sur ces chairs blondes, toutes duvetées comme la peau d'une pêche. Il était tourné tourné vers le fond du cabinet et jouait le principal rôle d'une des scènes de Voltaire, que raconte en détail une courtisane nommée Bouche-Vermeille.
>
> Digne de la Vénus Callipyge, cette chute de reins où la ligne de l'épine dorsale fuyait dans un méplat voluptueux et se redressait, ferme, grasse, en deux contours adorables, avait l'aspect d'une sphère de Paros aux transparences d'ambre. Les cuisses, un peu moins fortes que des cuisses de femme, possédaient pourtant une rondeur solide qui effaçait leur sexe. Les mollets, placés haut, semblaient retrousser tout le buste, et cette impertinence d'un corps paraissant s'ignorer n'en était que plus piquante. Le talon, cambré, ne portait que sur un point imperceptible, tant il était rond.

Despite Jacques' appeal to the fraternity of the situation, addressing Raoule as "*monsieur* de Vénérande," the narrative here stresses that the occupier of the subject position is female, a "mademoiselle." The narrative depicts the scene from her point of view, presenting Jacques' body like the inanimate subject of a still life, in terms of lines, contours, and lighting. Jacques is even compared to a peach, an image which stresses his vulnerability, while intensifying the objectification. The fact that Jacques appears unaware of his role adds to Raoule's delight. The fact that this unselfconsciousness is only apparent is stressed: the "impertinence d'un corps *paraissant s'ignorer* n'en était que plus piquante" (emphasis added). As noted earlier, for the object of the look to be complicit in the objectification, he or she must somehow consent to be an object in order to confirm the power of the subject/looker.

Having asserted this symbolic advantage, Raoule consolidates her control by invoking other codes, notably by acting "imperiously," infantilizing Jacques, and controlling discourse:

> Elle écarta la draperie d'un mouvement impérieux. Jacques Silvert finissant à peine de s'éponger le corps.
>
> —Enfant, sais-tu que tu es merveilleux? lui dit-elle avec une cynique franchise.
>
> Le jeune homme poussa un cri de stupeur, ramenant son peignoir. Ensuite, navré, tout pâle de honte, il le laissa glisser passivement, car il comprenait, le pauvre.

Raoule reveals her presence to Jacques, forcing him to acknowledge his role as object of the gaze and reasserting the function of the look as constituting relationships of power. The victory is consummated by Jacques' gesture of defeat: pale with shame, he "passively" lets his bathrobe slip off, "for he understood."

It would seem from this episode that the gaze is by no means definitely male. Yet there are certain features of the text which make this a problematic conclusion. The text has operated throughout with a clear separation of biological sex and gender and has investigated a gender role inversion. To conclude from the scene above that the gaze is not male is to miss the fact that, although Raoule is biologically female and Jacques male, within the context of **Monsieur Vénus,** Raoule is actually occupying a male-marked position and Jacques a female one. A much more complicated dynamic is thereby set up in this "Susanna" scene. As the looker, Raoule would seem to occupy the more privileged, powerful position, and yet, because she is a *female* occupying this male space, she is still vulnerable. The threat comes specifically from the masculinity of the person looked at.

As Raoule contemplates Jacques, his masculinity reasserts itself in the visual code:

> Les deux coudes des bras allongés avaient deux trous roses. Entre la coupure de l'aisselle, et beaucoup plus bas que cette coupure, dépassaient quelques frisons d'or s'ébouriffant. Jacques Silvert disait vrai, il en avait partout. Il se serait trompé, par exemple, en jurant que cela seul témoignait de sa virilité.

Confronted with this evidence of biological maleness, Raoule literally retreats and clenches her hands. She feels that she is the prisoner, structured by the visual code instead of structuring: "J'ai cru le prendre, il s'empare de moi." Momentarily, the privileged subject position is challenged by the confusion of sex and gender, and it is only by repeating that Jacques is "une jeune fille" that Raoule regains her control of the situation and experiences the symbolic victory described above.

This ambivalence illustrates the problematic nature of the gaze. On the one hand, by occupying a male-marked space, Raoule becomes male. Gender is not a biological category, but a matter of symbolic positioning. However, if this is the case, Raoule's symbolic position of power is being undercut. For in the context of Western tradition (an iconographic one, admittedly, but one clearly evoked in this text), Raoule is occupying a position that has come to be coded as and associated with a male perspective. Raoule's example suggests that a biological female can occupy the male-marked position of subject of the gaze, but this merely seems to confirm the fact that the gaze is male. This subversive strategy gives temporary access to power, but it would seem to confirm the difficulties of imagining or locating a female gaze.

As Berger has noted, the voyeurism of the look is experienced as a pleasurable on two levels: the looker within the text and the looker at the text. If the gaze is problematic for the looker within the text, it is even more complicated for the looker at the text, that is, the reader. To the extent that Raoule's position, as the text repeatedly emphasizes, is symbolically male, the same dynamics of position would seem to constitute the reader as male through the act of reading, regardless of biological sex. The novel is narrated in the third person; thus the reader (an "I") experiences Raoule as an other, a "she." This means that in scenes such as the reworking of the Susanna theme cited above, there is a sense in which the reader is watching Raoule watch Jacques, a sequence in which the former becomes the object of the literary gaze of the reader. Although there is a hint of subversion here, particularly in the demonstration that gender is a matter of construction not biology, the promise is not lived up to and the correlation between masculinity and dominance in the symbolic code is reinforced.

This is not the only disappointment of a text which attempts to challenge male authority (in both senses of the word). Raoule's desire to scandalize extends so far as to make her marry Jacques, thinking that the introduction of such a social outsider into her aristocratic circle would add another dimension of intrigue to her experiment with new love. This backfires, since it instead serves to normalize and neutralize the disruption which her affair with Jacques hitherto represented. Her aunt, sole surviving relative, finally retires to a convent, uttering a curse which indeed leaves the house like a tomb. Raoule finds that her new role begins to dictate her behavior and rather than changing the nature of the unique position she occupies, she becomes marked by it. She starts to have fits of jealousy and sadism. She is so convinced by her own act that she begins to think that other men are trying to seduce Jacques. Once she begins to lose control of herself, other powers gradually also slip away. Jacques, who has become accustomed to Raoule's sexually controlling behavior, is distressed to find out that she can no longer maintain the illusion:

> Raoule, tu n'es donc pas un homme? tu ne peux donc pas être un homme?
>
> Et le sanglot des illusions détruites, pour toujours mortes, monta de ses flancs à sa gorge.

Jacques' lament that Raoule is no longer a man summarizes the problem that she now faces: the erosion of the power she had gained through the manipulation of the symbolic code. Monsieur Vénus has become Madame Silvert. Raoule discovers that the symbolic institution of marriage now seems to control her, prescribing behavior that was unthinkable for Raoule de Vénérande.

In the latter part of the novel, metaphors of death and morbidity become more prevalent, creating an atmosphere which announces the end of the drama as it reflects Raoule's decline into a pathetic recluse, alienated in the French (madness) and the English senses of the word. This decline is accompanied by the re-emergence of what Christian Berg calls "le côté moralisateur de ce soi-disant roman 'scandaleux.'" [Christian Berg, "Huysmans et l'Antiphysis"] Beneath the experimental surface is a reactionary current that must be confronted by the subversive treasure hunter, a current that re-asserts "natural" values in opposition to the social constructionist philosophy Raoule has embodied. At the end of the novel, she inhabits a mausoleum—a walled-up bedroom with a secret entrance:

> La nuit, une femme vêtue de deuil, quelquefois un jeune homme en habit noir, ouvrent cette porte.
>
> Ils viennent s'agenouiller près du lit, et, lorsqu'ils ont longtemps contemplé les formes merveilleuses de la statue de cire, ils l'enlacent, la baisent aux lèvres. Un ressort, disposé à l'intérieur des flancs, correspond à la bouche et l'anime.

This blue chamber contains a macabre figure, typical of decadent literature: a wax mannequin with rubber skin, adorned with human hair, teeth, and nails "ripped from a corpse." Its mouth is animated by a hidden spring. This ending brings the narrative to complete closure. The ambiguity concerning the nocturnal visitors hardly hides the fact that the visitor is merely Raoule in different disguises. (The reader knows it was not uncommon for her to dress up as a man.) Here, however, even dressed as a man, she does not wield power. She has, instead, become pathetic. The ending makes it clear that, although in life Jacques had little control over Raoule, in death he is a powerful, if morbid influence. The way in which Raoule worships his remains is tinged

with the religious fervor which characterized her aunt, particularly since the shrine, pagan though it may be, seems to contain relics which are preserved like those of a saint or martyr.

The implausibility of this ending (indeed of the entire plot) might be taken to justify the phallocritical judgments that the text should not be taken seriously as a novel. Barrès argues that such implausibilities are signs of the author's immaturity, again focussing on the author rather than on the text itself which has a limited appeal: "Dans toute son œuvre, qui aujourd'hui est considérable, Rachilde n'a guère fait que se raconter soi-même." Barrès views the novel as thinly disguised autobiography. By doing so, he avoids the need to address the narrative strategies of the text and to read the ending as anything other than immature embellishment. While dismissing the novel's fictional status, Barrès himself does, however, concede that the result is still a very unusual text. "*Monsieur Vénus* décrit l'âme d'une jeune fille *très singulière*" (emphasis added). Rachilde's mentality is of interest to "tous ceux qui aiment le rare," and her novel is testimony of "un état d'âme très particulier."

Nancy Miller has suggested that these two qualities of implausibility (or non-verisimilitude) and singularity are linked to the way female signatures have historically been read. Miller finds that one of the characteristics of women's writing has been that their narratives often contain breaks with convention that are misperceived as implausibilities or singularities, and she traces these implausibilities to power fantasies:

> The repressed content, I think, would be, not erotic impulses, but an impulse to power: a fantasy of power that would revise the social grammar in which women are never defined as subjects; a fantasy of power that disdains a sexual exchange in which women can participate only as objects of circulation. [Nancy Miller, "Emphasis Added: Plots and Plausibilities in Women's Fiction"]

This passage lends itself as a very apt summary of the plot of *Monsieur Vénus,* where the question of female subjectivity and the relations of sexual exchange are explored in depth. However, Miller goes on to suggest that women express their desires differently to men in texts. Rather than pursuing their fantasy and moving towards the object of desire, women instead preserve the fantasy intact by avoiding any attempt to "translate" it into reality. She cites the example of Mme de Clèves who "leaves the court not to flee passion but to preserve it," and to preserve it on her own terms, that is, as a fantasy:

> The daydream, then, is both the stuff of fairy tales ("Someday my prince will come") and their rewriting ("Someday my prince will come, but we will not live happily ever after"). The princess refuses to marry the duke, however, not because she does not want to live happily ever after, but because she does.

Raoule de Vénérande, though not a princess, is an aristocrat. In a role reversal of the fairy tale where the prince falls in love with the beautiful peasant girl, Raoule chooses as her princely object of desire the sylvan Jacques.

Unlike Mme de Clèves, Raoule does believe in the possibility of a happy ending and pursues her "bride," confident that the revision of social grammar effected by the gender ambiguities and reversals creates the conditions for the inscription of woman as subject of discourse. The strategy fails, however, with the consequences already noted. By attempting to inscribe her fantasy in reality, Raoule is reabsorbed into the dominant discourse.

Monsieur Vénus represents, then, a not entirely successful attempt at subversion by challenging phallocratic discourse and the structures of signification that mark male terms as positive and that exclude female subjectivity. While offering some insights into possible ways of manipulating the symbolic codes governing social interaction, the text could not maintain the subversive "thrust," and the closure of the text brings the reader back to a confrontation of female powerlessness. By the final chapter, Raoule has been totally effaced as a presence. Her name no longer appears in the text, and while the gender ambiguity lingers on in the personae of the nocturnal visitors, Raoule herself is no more than a pronoun.

Robert E. Ziegler   (essay date 1987)

SOURCE: "The Suicide of 'La Comedienne' in Rachilde's *La Jongleuse*," in *Continental, Latin-American and Francophone Women Writers,* edited by Eunice Myers and Ginette Adamson, University Press of America, 1987, pp. 55-61.

[In the following essay, Ziegler analyzes the implications of the sadistic behavior of Rachilde's female protagonists, focusing on the novel The Juggler.*]*

Swords and daggers, bayonets and scalpels: all the pointed instruments men use for invading others' bodies are appropriated by the women characters in the novels of Rachilde. In the evolution of "l'amour compliqué" [Maurice Barrès, Preface, *Monsieur Vénus*] that Barrès sees emerging in these works, the men are stripped of masculinity and weapons. They become vulnerable and sexless while the women turn into predators and warriors. Indeed, one need only consult Praz's list of "Belles dames sans merci," figures like Huysmans' Madame de Chantelouve or Clara, the torture-loving nymphomaniac in Mirbeau's *Le Jardin des supplices,* to realize how frequently such characters appear in "fin-de-siècle" fiction. In this respect, Rachilde's works differ little from the writings of her contemporaries. Still, her novels which show the conjugation of aggressiveness and female sexuality deserve attention, not just

because they examine from a woman's standpoint the same questions dealt with by her peers, but because they point out the result of such a view of domination, sex and love, show it leading to a kind of suicide, the extinction of all feelings for another and, finally, for oneself.

Born in 1860, Rachilde, née Marguerite Eymery, emerged as a prolific writer whose works appeared well into the present century. Friend to the notorious Jean Lorrain, candidate for the affections of Catulle Mendès, later wife of Alfred Vallette, editor of *Le Mercure de France,* Rachilde took pains to cultivate the image of her eccentricity. Yet there can be no doubt it was in her fiction, not in her life, that she advanced her boldest thoughts, there that she explored as few had done before her "ces formes d'amour qui sentent la mort" (Barrès).

Monsieur Vénus, La Marquise de Sade, La Jongleuse: In these three novels by Rachilde, texts which Claude Dauphine regards as "les véritables jalons de l'oeuvre," one can see at once the author's changing attitude toward the conflict between the sexes. From the experiment with transvestism, the chaste voluptuousness of Raoule de Vénérande, who keeps her pretty boyfriend in a sumptuous apartment and lavishes on him gifts of hashish, clothes and flowers, to Eliante Donalger, the juggler of knives who kills herself with one of them to preserve her passion's purity, one sees in Rachilde's works the emergence of a death-dedicated love, one that does more than fight against the dominion of "les phallocrates" but that submerges sexuality in a true "pulsion de mort."

It is primarily in *La Jongleuse* (1900), the last of these three novels, that the ultimately suicidal nature of these characters' pursuits, the consequence of love's repudiation, at last becomes apparent. Earlier in *Monsieur Vénus,* Raoule had mentioned that women looked on love divorced from its expression as the greatest aphrodisiac. The same holds true for Eliante, who sees love not as Eros, the binding of the two attracted partners in a union that transcends them, but as the enhancement of the individual who feels that love within her. There is no focusing of consciousness on that which one desires and an attendant sense of emptiness until one merges with it. Love does not entail a yearning for its object. For Eliante it is not a future- or goal-oriented feeling, but is rather more inclusive. "Je suis réellement amoureuse de tout ce qui est beau, bon, me paraît un absolu . . . ," she says. "Mais ce n'est pas le but, le plaisir; c'est une manière d'être." Instead of joining with the being on whom attention narrows, the loving person takes in everything, enjoys an environmental fullness. "J'ai le dégoût de l'union," she says. "Je n'y découvre aucune plénitude voluptueuse. Pour que ma chair s'émeuve et conçoive l'infini de plaisir, je n'ai pas besoin de chercher un sexe à l'objet de mon amour" (*La Jongleuse*).

From this standpoint the love she feels for Léon Reille, the man who would possess her, is but one increment of the total emotional charge that ties her to the world. For Eliante, the more indiscriminate the love, the greater is the range of objects to which it may attach. Thus the alabaster vase she bought in Tunis can affect her with its symmetry, its human shape and beauty, can bring her to a climax as much as can a lover whose inconstancy she fears. As Léon watches her be overcome by flattering her urn—"ce fut plutôt une risée plissant l'onde mystérieuse de sa robe de soie—et elle eut un petit râle de joie imperceptible, le souffle même du spasme" (*La Jongleuse*)—he reacts with outraged disbelief at this assault on his male ego. "Il fut ébloui, ravi, indigne.—C'est scandaleux! Là . . . devant moi . . . sans moi? Non, c'est abominable! Il se jeta sur elle, ivre d'une colère folle.—Comédienne! Abominable comédienne!" (*La Jongleuse*). But of course the truth of Eliante's orgasm is really no pretense, no performance meant to embarrass him and wound his vanity. Yet he is right in calling her an actress, not because the reactions she expresses are simulated, false, but because Eliante is usually more intent on acting out her feelings than sharing them with him and risking their dilution: "je vous ai donné ce que je peux *montrer* d'amour à un homme," as she pointedly remarks (*La Jongleuse*).

In this cult of love where Eliante is priestess, it is unimportant what triggers the emotion, the words and acts through which it is expressed. Eliante's amphora, her collection of erotic Chinese carvings, even her idealized impression of Léon, function simultaneously as many things. They are the sensual/esthetic forms that arouse the love she values, they are that through which her love must pass to be further sublimated and that which, through their shape, their words or the figures they depict, confirms the beliefs she holds most dear. For this reason what Eliante brings to her sanctuary-bedroom must act as object of devotion, medium and testimonial all at once. Léon imagines it is his person that stirs this love inside her and that at length she must respond with the surrender of her body. He has failed to realize that once Eliante identifies him as a disciple of love's god, it no longer matters whether he is there with her or not. His effect on her has been assimilated into her religion of the beautiful, so that his continued presence is merely a redundance. As a performer, Eliante is her own most valued audience; what she is in love with is the chance to elaborate on her own self-created myth. Eliante, more than Raoule de Vénérande and Mary Barde in *La Marquise de Sade,* is completely self-sufficient. Apart from her perverted husband, who had died some time before, she uses men as reiterations of her own views on love.

One way to understand more clearly the evolution of Rachilde's heroines is by examining the meaning of the knife/sword/dagger imagery that occurs in many of her texts. In *La Jongleuse,* the function of these figures is even more important, since the title of the book alludes to juggling with knives, one of which kills Eliante as she lets it plunge into her chest. With its deadly point, its ability to pierce, the danger that the knife holds out is often reinforced, but in the early pages of the book,

the woman is referred to as a weapon that is usually kept sheathed, concealed inside "sa robe noire, cette gaine satinée presque métallique" (*La Jongleuse*). The clothed body of the woman is like her gloved hand—"la femme étira le bout de ses gants, ce qui lui ajoutait des griffes pointues" (*La Jongleuse*)—in that the lethal power both represent is latent. Still Léon Reille looks on Eliante and hopes that underneath, inside its envelope, he will find an instrument of pleasure, not destruction.

On one occasion, he learns from Eliante how she had learned in Java the art of juggling with daggers, a skill she put to use for performing at the teas she held for her niece Missie and her friends. These performances meant more to her than mere parlor room amusements: they allowed her to define herself before an audience comprised of men as well as girls. As she stood exposed in her maillot before male onlookers entranced "devant la *forme* non déguisée" (*La Jongleuse*), she would catch and then release again the knives so rapidly, that in motion they created an invisible but cutting wall that separated her from others. A dialectic of interdiction and desire, the act consisted of an implied seduction, invitation or offering of self and a withdrawal, denial or retraction of the promise. Thus Léon saw her "séparée de sa famille, de la société, du monde entier . . . par l'énigme de sa comédie perpétuelle" (*La Jongleuse*). In addition, Eliante's performances are narcissistic ones, not designed to entertain admirers, but to please and flatter her with her power to attract, her ability to magnetize the love, the look and the attention of her audience. Everything becomes a knife, a point, a blade: the whetting of the appetite, the hunger of the men transfixed by watching Eliante, their pointed gaze, and the cold inflexibility of "la jongleuse," "lame d'acier trempée aux feux des passions" (*La Jongleuse*), who is tempered against the emergence of emotions that might weaken her. Eliante loves no one, nothing but her philosophy of love. So to protect herself against the awakening of undesired feelings, she redirects her energy away from people who might touch her into an assessment of her reaction to them, excluding them as causes in favor of effects. Earlier the aggressiveness of Mary Barbe had made her look outside for victims. Only with a realization that the object of her hate might be an aspect of herself could her anger be internalized and the path to suicide from self-involvement be eventually described. This is the course that Eliante will follow, one based on denying any hold that others have on her, on withdrawing affect from those who make her feel, and investing it instead in an awareness of those feelings. Steel blade, "dédaigneuse de sang et de chair, n'usant plus que son propre fourreau noir" (*La Jongleuse*), she does not assume the male penetrating role, but over time destroys herself through a simple lack of contact with another but herself.

Through the accentuation of her ornamental beauty, her virtue and devotion to her niece, Eliante in many ways resembles "les créatures relatives" of whom Francoise Basch has written. Yet she does not couple her attractiveness with docility, or obedience to men. Rather she manipulates them for amusement, juggles them like knives. She lives to feel their glances that are sharpened by desire. She exposes herself to them but is never in real danger. Yet she does fear growing older and not feeling others' looks, fears relinquishing the status of "prêtresse d'Eros" and being forced to take the role of "mendiante d'amour" (*La Jongleuse*). As much as she would like to see herself as an independent woman, not a creation or composite of men's opinions of her, it is only by attracting their admiration that she feels herself alive. At the same time she must detach herself from others, owe them nothing lest the autonomy she covets be all but forfeited. "On n'est libre qu'en tuant tout le monde . . . ," she says (*La Jongleuse*). Freed from obligation, from the need to interact, she must also forego love as the means to be complete. First she is the dagger and its sheath, then the wound it opens up and finally the knife and her own dead body in which her weapon is embedded.

All the characters in Rachilde try to overcome the ascendancy of men: Raoule through an esthetic neutering of her boyfriend Jacques Silvert; Mary Barbe through attacks with hairpins, poison gases; and Eliante through a sleight of hand dissociation of sexuality and love. Still, concealed beneath their declaration of "la haine de la force mâle" (Barrès), is less a belief in women's self-acceptance than a flight from the spontaneous, the unpredictable and free. They are drawn to what is mechanical, highly structured, and recoil from emotions that make them give up self-control. Their ambition is to follow Raoule de Vénérande in making men wax robots that cannot challenge them to grow. What they deny is that women are reactors, their range of choices limited by their need to answer men, so they insist on leading, taking the initiative themselves. As the man is made an object, becomes "un être insexué," the threat he posed is neutralized. Thus Rachilde's women characters define their strategies, their goals in terms of an absence of constraint. They destroy what repels or frightens them, but do not know, cannot attain, what it is they truly want. Once Raoule makes Jacques Silvert her property or "thing," once Mary Barbe does away with the men that she despises, the objectives that were negative are effectively achieved. The tyrants are thrown down; the masters are destroyed and the woman's self as object is liquidated, too. Disconnected from the men who impose on her a role, Eliante is relieved of her old "en-soi" existence and can say to Léon Reille: "Je suis déjà morte" (*La Jongleuse*). But if there is no future to create free of their lovers' domination, their lives will not be purposeful, nor their identities self-defined. They flee the image-prisons they were sent to by their men, kill off the factitious selves they felt had stifled them. Yet they run the risk of finding underneath an empty center where no real self is hidden. Léon Reille wonders whether the "comédienne"'s many masks may in fact be covering the absence of a face. And so when he believes she has finally acquiesced, he learns the woman he has conquered was never really there. Through a last trick,

Eliante makes use of Missie as a stand-in in her bed, so when Léon awakes in the arms of the wrong woman, he sees Eliante juggling for the last time with her "cinq glaives de douleur" (*La Jongleuse*), sees her about to become a victim of her most beloved performance. In death, for Eliante, there is no revelation, no disclosure of who she really is. "La femme glissa en arrière. Un flot pourpre noya le masque pâle . . . son dernier fard . . ." (*La Jongleuse*).

At the end these "Belles dames sans merci" show less mercy toward themselves. They begin by captivating men with their mystery and looks, bewitching and ensnaring them so they can make them into slaves. Their purpose in attracting them is, in fact, to give them nothing. The seduction is an unkept promise whose object is frustration. Yet the greater their self-loathing, the more violent their revenge. Mary Barbe will make men bleed to eradicate self-doubt, will commit sadistic acts from a lack of self-esteem. These characters are committed to eliminating men as well as that part of their own psyche that was willing to submit. But with the removal of the self that once had taken part, that had collaborated in their initial degradation, they find there is still no buried truth, no sense of authenticity. They don their attitudes like the masks of Eliante, masks directed at an audience that is meant to be misled. Yet without the onlookers to be duped, they die to their old roles. They have no knowledge of themselves or who they really want to be, so the obsolescence of their anger, their resentment and their shame leaves them directionless and empty, with lives that have no point. With no hate to motivate them, they have nothing more to do, except mourn a useless past which had left them so embittered, had turned them into monsters, half-crazed recluses, and which in time would lead to suicide, make them victims of themselves.

Melanie C. Hawthorne (essay date 1989)

SOURCE: "The Social Construction of Sexuality in Three Novels by Rachilde," in *Michigan Romance Studies,* Vol. 9, 1989, pp. 49-59.

[*In the following essay, Hawthorne regards Rachilde as a novelist whose works presented a view of human sexuality that was in opposition to the dominant psychological and medical theories of the late nineteenth century.*]

In his multi-volume work on the history of sexuality, Michel Foucault explains how, with the rise of capitalism, sexuality passes from action to discourse: the energy previously invested *in* action is transformed into discourse *about* action. One of the resulting intersections of power, sexuality, and knowledge is what Foucault calls *scientia sexualis,* a system in which "le sexe [a] été constitué comme un enjeu de vérité," a system which "ours" is the only culture to have elaborated.

The emergence of the discourse of *scientia sexualis* has been charted even more specifically by feminist historians such as Lillian Faderman and Judith Walkowitz. They have analyzed in particular the shifts in discourse of the nineteenth century (a period also privileged by Foucault), and the concomitant development of a form of medical discourse which structured contemporary ideology about sexuality. But while Foucault emphasizes the *continuity* of sexual discourse (while shifting from religious to medico-scientific, the discourse continues to depend upon the mechanism of confession), feminist historians stress the *changing* role of *scientia sexualis* in shaping and maintaining systems of male dominance. While Foucault argues that the shift in sexual discourse from sin to pathology continues to function as confession, feminists note that the shift had the effect of handing the policing of female sexuality over to the newly constituted medical profession. The historical evidence combines with cross-cultural, anthropological evidence to suggest that the concept of "natural" sex is an ideological one produced by discourse. Since human beings always exist in a context where culture mediates and shapes nature, sexuality is socially constructed.

The second half of the nineteenth century, in particular, has been the focus of much attention, since the well-documented rise of *scientia sexualis* at that time created the discursive legacy which has dominated the twentieth century. Lillian Faderman, for example, points to the fact that the most well-known sexologists were all intellectually active during this period. She cites the work of Carl von Westphal, who published one particularly influential article in 1869, as well as his disciples Richard von Krafft-Ebing (whose *Psychopathia Sexualis* was published in 1882) and Havelock Ellis (whose *Studies in the Psychology of Sex: Sexual Inversion* was published in 1897).

In documenting the emergence of this discourse in the nineteenth century, however, it is easy to overlook the existence of resistance to such ideological domination by the medical profession. Since dissenters ultimately lost the ideological battle for control over discourse, their voices have been subsequently silenced or ignored. It is only now, when the emergence of sexology as a form of scientific discourse is viewed as a historically specific phenomenon, that such opposition can be read. One voice opposing the dominant discourse is that of the novelist Rachilde, who, in several of her novels, describes the way forms of sexual expression are determined by various social factors, rather than by innate "natural" instincts. The three novels to be discussed here, all published in the last quarter of the nineteenth century, focus on this issue: *Monsieur Vénus* (published in 1884, and subtitled "roman matérialiste"), *La Marquise de Sade* (1887), and *La Jongleuse* (1900). In two of these three novels, the medical profession is explicitly represented by one of the characters acting as a spokesperson. In all three novels, the central character referred to in the title is a heroine who demonstrates what others consider "deviant" sexual behavior.

The focus in *Monsieur Vénus,* the first, and perhaps best known, of these three novels, is on gender roles, rather than specifically on sex roles as in the later texts. Since sex roles represent an important part of gender identity, however, the themes of this novel overlap considerably with those of *La Marquise de Sade*. Like the "Marquise", the heroine of *Monsieur Vénus,* Raoule de Vénérande, embodies the female counterpart to a male type. In general, literature offers numerous examples of aristocrats who choose sexual partners from inferior social classes (a relationship which often entails a form of exploitation), but in most instances, the aristocrats are male and their "victims" are female. Rachilde reverses this dynamic, presenting a heroine who dares to choose a working class man as her "mistress." In this respect, Rachilde's novel treats a constellation of issues subsequently explored separately in other novels. Raoule de Vénérande is the predecessor of many well-known literary figures, including the heroine of D.H. Lawrence's *Lady Chatterley's Lover,* whose adultery is in large part censured because it involves the socially inadmissible attraction of a domestic servant; and Proust's Swann, ostracized because he not only falls in love outside his class, but also because he marries outside it. Society tolerates, and at times condones, sexual relationships which transgress class boundaries, but love is another matter. In *Monsieur Vénus,* the defiant heroine seems in control only until she formalizes her unusual relationship through marriage, when suddenly things begin to go wrong.

Monsieur Vénus also illustrates the double standard which judges men's and women's sexuality differently. The novel depicts—and elicits—society's condemnation of a woman who behaves in the same way as the men of her social class. Raoule de Vénérande chooses as her lover a working-class flower-maker, Jacques Silvert. There is an extreme power imbalance in the relationship, with Raoule as the dominant partner, with the result that the relationship, as well as Rachilde's novel, has been viewed as deviant. Raoule's "masculine" behavior is censured, despite the fact that it occurs in the context of a romantic, heterosexual love relationship which in many respects is quite conventional. The novel itself has been judged as dangerous and pornographic. Thus, readers have fallen into the trap set by Rachilde: in upholding the double standard she describes, they find themselves shocked by romantic love, thereby illustrating the ways in which the rendering of sexuality into discourse is culturally mediated, and the appearance of naturalness or deviance can be manipulated.

In *La Marquise de Sade* (1887), as the title suggests, the dominant theme is the association between love, sexual pleasure, and pain. The title implies a straightforward case of sadism, yet sadism is a relatively minor theme of the novel. In fact, the mature—i.e., sadistic—sexual experiences of the heroine, Mary Barbe, occupy a small proportion of the novel as a whole (less than one third). Moreover, the nature of her sadism is quite tame when compared with, say, that of the Marquis de Sade to whom she is explicitly compared by the novel's title. She falls in love with a man who bleeds easily, and as the affair grows more passionate, she enjoys scratching him to provoke further bleeding. Her pleasure may certainly appear distasteful, but hardly approaches the levels of torture associated with sadism, and the novel presents her predilection as the natural outgrowth of her socialization rather than as a perversion.

The narrative consists of an account of Mary's childhood, and explains how her forms of sexual expression have been shaped by material circumstances. Very simply, Mary is an unwanted child, and her life consists of the experience of pain and suffering at the hands of others who supposedly love her, such as her mother and father; the message that love entails the physical and mental suffering of the loved one is established early on. One scene, in particular, at the beginning of the novel encapsulates this message and becomes a measurement of all subsequent experience. For health reasons, Mary's mother must drink fresh blood every day, a remedy prescribed by her doctor (the medical profession is frequently portrayed as inhumane in this novel). As a child, Mary accompanies her aunt on a trip to the slaughter-house. She is shielded from the true purpose of the visit, and is told instead that they are going to collect milk. When Mary accidentally witnesses the slow, agonizing death of the bull, slaughtered to provide "milk" for her mother, the trauma cements for Mary the association of love (expressed through maternal fluids of milk and blood) and the necessity of suffering and death. The later death of her mother in childbirth reinforces the association, summarized by the inscription carved on Mary's antique bed, which she reads over and over again: "aimer, c'est souffrir."

This motto recurs as the leitmotif of Mary's childhood and adolescence. She is orphaned when her father is killed in the Franco-Prussian war, and goes to live with her uncle, the doctor who had saved her baby brother but allowed her mother to die. A gynecologist, Célestin Barbe nevertheless admits that he does not like women, and that his profession is a way of limiting his interaction with them to "simples relations hygiéniques." At first he wants nothing to do with Mary, and like the madwoman in the attic, she is confined to certain areas of the house where she will be out of the way. But when she demonstrates the ability to be as dispassionate in her view of medicine as her uncle, he adopts her as disciple and token male, and shares with her his medical knowledge, which, since he is a gynecologist, consists mainly of the pathology of female sexuality. Thus Mary and her uncle "causaient comme deux hommes du même âge en choisissant des sujets à faire dresser les cheveux d'une demoiselle à marier." Mary ultimately rejects her uncle, together with his proposal of marriage, choosing instead a financially advantageous marriage with an older man whom she does not love, and beginning an affair with his illegitimate son, Paul. Only in the last two chapters of the novel does her sadism become aggressive: she tattoos Paul, whips her husband, brands his mistress,

poisons her husband, and bites Paul, who leaves her when he realizes she has become a murderer. Throughout the novel, she has enacted the lesson which crystallized in the slaughterhouse of her youth, that to love is to suffer, and that the objects of love are the ones who suffer most. The final scene completes the cycle begun in her youth: the lonely Mary is contemplating future murders while seated in a slaughterhouse bar.

Mary's story might have been subtitled "a case history," and might have been the kind of confession referred to by Foucault, and recorded by a pathologist or a psychoanalyst. In the hands of a novelist such as Rachilde, however, the narrative does not focus on the clinical symptoms of Mary's behavior, but instead offers insight into the protagonist's perspective. The novel, with no pretense of objectivity, reveals how Mary learns the meaning of love from certain experiences, which she then imitates. The medical profession may blame Mary while overlooking her abusive and selfish family, but the reader is able to see how the supposedly "normal" family and the so-called "deviant" daughter in fact exhibit the same patterns of behavior.

Like *Monsieur Vénus* and *La Marquise de Sade, La Jongleuse* (1900) focusses on apparent sexual deviance. Once again, the theme is approached through family structure. Mary Barbe's family of origin was highly dysfunctional; her mother's constant illness, her father's preference for a son, his military career, which necessitated frequent moves, and the alcoholism of her aunt combined to destabilize the family unit. After becoming an orphan, Mary lived with her bachelor uncle, a socially inept and incestuously-inclined recluse. This family structure is echoed in *Monsieur Vénus,* where Raoule is raised by a religious aunt who constantly refers to her as "my nephew." In *La Jongleuse,* we see little of the early childhood of the main protagonist, Eliante, but her family structure is evidently quite unusual. She lives with a deaf diplomat brother-in-law, and her niece Missie. Once again, parents seem conspicuously absent, while the uncle/aunt-nephew/niece relationship is privileged, with the focus this time on the aunt, rather than on the niece as in the previous two works. Eliante is also a widow; thus *La Jongleuse* differs from the previous two novels in that Eliante's story begins—in some ways—where the stories of Mary Barbe and Raoule de Vénérande end. While Eliante is an adult when the novel begins, the presence of her adolescent niece, Missie, provides an additional opportunity for Rachilde to depict the socialization process at work in a secondary character.

In all three cases, the absence of strong parental figures could be cited as a cause of the subsequent sexual abnormalities of the heroines, but such a reading overlooks a crucial point: the abnormality of these heroines is in fact very slight, and might not be labelled as deviant at all in a male character. Mary Barbe is not much of a sadist, and Raoule de Vénérande is quite conventional, preferring heterosexual romance in the context of monogamous marriage to any perversion. Eliante Donalger, for her part, enjoys an independence unusual for women of her time, and chooses casual sexual relationships with men younger than herself (further evidence of the double standard, since such behavior would be unremarkable in her male fictional counterpart).

In both *Monsieur Vénus* and *La Marquise de Sade,* Rachilde depicts but does not comment directly on the construction of sexuality. In *La Jongleuse,* however, this theory is made explicit, for Eliante's "perversion" is that her most enduring sexual relationship is with an inanimate object—a Greek vase—as she explains to a young student she picks up at a party. The student, Léon Reille, is a medical student, a professional affiliation which positions him as the symbolic representative of scientific discourse. When Eliante shows him her Greek amphora, he speaks for the medical establishment in condemning Eliante and labelling her sexual pleasure as deviant. Eliante articulates a different point of view, and traps Léon in the same kind of double bind Rachilde so skillfully deployed in *Monsieur Vénus.* Eliante allows herself to become sexually aroused by the vase in Léon's presence, thereby putting him in the role of third person observer of an intimate scene. Léon protests: "C'est scandaleux! Lá . . . devant moi . . . sans moi? Non, c'est abominable!" The reactions, summarized in his hesitation between "devant moi" and "sans moi," together with the uncertainty conveyed by the question mark after the latter, and the final judgment "c'est abominable," reveal the workings of the double bind. On the one hand, Léon wishes to deny that a vase can be a sexual partner, but if this is so, then there is no basis for jealousy. To admit his outrage and sense of exclusion is to undermine his own discourse: jealousy implies there is something to be jealous of. But Léon can hardly acknowledge that his rival is a Greek vase without confronting certain questions which, in the medical sexual discourse of late nineteenth century, had no place.

The dynamic of the double bind, then, already functions to alert the reader to the failure of *scientia sexualis* to establish a coherent ideology that would resist challenges. In addition, however, Rachilde also provides an example of such an alternative discourse of sexuality, making Eliante the spokesperson, albeit an amateur one, for the theory of social construction. She states the principles behind her preference for Greek vases in terms which point to the role of cultural mediation in determining sexual behavior. Eliante claims that her sexual pleasure does not necessarily depend upon human contact, and she states:

> Pour que ma chair s'émeuve et conçoive l'infini
> du plaisir, je n'ai pas besoin de chercher un sexe
> à l'objet de mon amour!

This is one logical corollary of the theory of the social construction of sexuality: the sex object is not endowed with some quality which makes it inherently, naturally, sexually appealing. Instead, it is the cultural lens imposed by society which defines certain objects or actions as sexual. If, as historians and anthropologists have claimed, the definition of "natural" sexuality varies cross-culturally and historically, then sex-appeal must indeed be in the eye of the beholder. The conclusion, to use Carole Vance's formulation, is that "the most important sexual organ in humans is located between the ears."

In practice, it may not be that individuals can manipulate sexual discourse. The fictional world of Rachilde, however, allows such speculation, and sexuality can be deconstructed and reconstructed in new forms with as much ease as a child's building set. Individuals, such as Mary Barbe and Raoule de Vénérande, learn certain patterns of sexual response that are "natural" for them, thereby undermining the possibility of a single, exclusive definition of natural behavior. Admittedly, the heroines of the three texts discussed here come to a bad end: Mary Barbe is a murderer, Raoule de Vénérande a reclusive necrophile, and Eliante Donalger commits suicide (though "joyfully," in the words of the author). These bleak conclusions suggest that the radical potential of oppositional fiction was limited, and could not sustain itself without leading to self-destruction. But such embryonic speculation opens the doors to the invention of new, experimental, perhaps liberating forms of sexual expression. In the age of AIDS this may be a matter of survival, but even on a purely representational level, Rachilde's novels have a role in demonstrating the existence of opposition and alternatives to the hegemony of medical discourse. Today, when the smooth ideological surface of *scientia sexualis* has begun to crack, Rachilde's experimental voice can better be heard and appreciated.

Melanie C. Hawthorne (essay date 1990)

SOURCE: Introduction to *The Juggler* by Rachilde, translated by Melanie C. Hawthorne, Rutgers University Press, 1990, pp. xi-xxix.

[In the following essay, Hawthorne focuses on Rachilde's thematic and technical innovations in her novel The Juggler.*]*

The novelist Rachilde (Marguerite Eymery Vallette) became an instant success in French literary circles when, at the age of twenty-four, she published her fourth novel, *Monsieur Vénus* (1884). Her celebrity stemmed in large part from the public condemnation of the book: it was published by Brancart in Brussels, where it was immediately declared pornographic. Copies of the book were seized, and Rachilde was condemned to two years in prison and a fine of two thousand francs. She prudently chose to remain instead in Paris, where the sentence offered a passport to notoriety. Maurice Barrès dubbed her "Mademoiselle Baudelaire," while Jules Barbey d'Aurevilly averred, "A pornographer, granted . . . but such a distinguished one!" A more measured, but no less fêted, response came from the poet Paul Verlaine. Responding to the heroine's claim to have discovered a new form of perversion, Verlaine retorted that if indeed Rachilde had succeeded in inventing a new vice, she would have been the benefactor of society. Whatever the subversive nature of **Monsieur Vénus** (and the debate goes on), the impact of the novel guaranteed Rachilde a faithful following. For several decades, a generation of readers and writers greeted each of her publications with enthusiasm.

Her early success can be attributed both to her independent spirit, enhanced by an unusual upbringing, and to her early apprenticeship to writing and determination to make it her career.

Rachilde was born Marguerite Eymery on 11 February 1860, at her family's home just outside the town of Périgueux in southwest France. Her provincial origins subsequently exercised great influence on her life and work. Although she lived in Paris from the age of twenty-one until her death in 1953 at the age of ninety-three, she never lost the ability to see society through the eyes of a "provincial," an outsider. (The present example, **The Juggler,** is no exception: the heroine is a creole whose marked difference sets her apart from the rest of society, and enables her to comment with detachment on Parisian high society.)

The atmosphere of the family home at Le Cros, together with family lore, gave Rachilde a highly developed sense of the gothic. The name "Cros," for example, was dialect for "hole," and Rachilde's description reveals how aptly the name fits:

> Le Cros was a damp estate around which grew too many periwinkles, too much ivy, too much Virginia creeper, too many weeping willows and too many truffles. In front of the house was a pond full of frogs; at the back there were farms filled with not very legitimate but very dirty babies. In the garden the damp prevented the strawberries from ripening, the radishes were eaten by some beast we could never see, and if the cows ever wandered into this garden, their milk dried up. The cherry jam was blue—moldy a fortnight after it was made; on the other hand, wild oats were everywhere, tossing their heads with the insolence of a queen's aigrette.

This monstrous and fantastic experience of nature is explicitly recalled in the preface to the autobiographical novel **A Mort [To the Death]**, but it is also evident throughout Rachilde's work, in her extravagant descriptive style, as well as her dramatic awareness of the dark and hidden powers of nature. With this vision as background, family lore also placed more active and tangible forces on the stage of Rachilde's imagination. Popular local legend maintained that the family turned into werewolves once a year because one of the ancestors had left the priesthood. Rachilde's arrival in the world on a night when the wind raged and owls screeched only

added to these rumors, giving her an early and personal connection with the sinister forces that would figure so prominently in her writing.

Rachilde's father, the illegitimate son of an aristocrat, became a career army officer, and her mother, a talented musician, was the daughter of a successful newspaper editor. She remained their only child, a fact which was to have the greatest significance on her development. Her father had desperately wanted a son, and thus her early years, and arguably her entire life, became an unending attempt to compensate her father for this disappointment and gain his approval. Rachilde began learning to ride when she was four, and later participated in hunts, even though she sympathized more with the hunted than with the hunters, all in an effort to please.

Her need to gain her father's approval was evidently an ambivalent one, however, for at the same time that she courted his benevolence on horseback, she turned to a hobby sure to draw his disapproval: writing. At first, the activity was a clandestine one, conducted by moonlight. Later, her stories were published anonymously in local newspapers. Although writing and journalism were Rachilde's legacies from her maternal grandparents, such an activity could only irritate her father, who referred to writers as "plumitifs," making the predilection for the pen rather than the sword sound like some kind of ailment. At first, he remained ignorant of his daughter's defiance, and would sometimes read her stories aloud, censoring the parts he found too daring, unaware that the author was seated next to him. Later, he would take pride in the young reporter riding at his side and preparing accounts of military manoeuvres, but his pride stemmed in no small part from the fact that she was mistaken for a boy by the commanding general.

At fourteen, Rachilde was engaged by her parents to an officer of her father's acquaintance. But the prospective match filled her with such antipathy that she revolted against her parents' will and threw herself in the frog-infested pond. Whether this action was a serious attempt at suicide, or whether the gesture was meant to convey, melodramatically, her strong resistance remains unclear, but the action made her parents realize that their daughter was now strong-willed and independent enough that she had outgrown their control. The engagement was broken off, and Rachilde turned once again to writing, this time more openly and committedly, as a means of self-expression. She was encouraged by a letter she received from the legendary Victor Hugo, and set her sights on Paris. Such a goal was not irrational: for a writer to succeed, he or she could not remain in the provinces. At the same time, however, this career was one of the few available choices that would justify moving so far away from home. Rachilde's willful and independent spirit, formed by childhood experience, nurtured by an unstructured, private education, and forced into premature responsibility by her mother's increasing mental instability, could only flourish at a distance from her immediate family.

At first, her visits to Paris were temporary and chaperoned (her mother, independently wealthy, maintained an apartment there). Thanks to the connections of a cousin, she was able to place her stories in Paris magazines and made several useful acquaintances and connections, among them writers and other society figures such as the actress Sarah Bernhardt. When she turned twenty-one, Rachilde moved definitively to Paris (by now with her father's blessing), and set up her own apartment in the Rue des Ecoles. During this period, she assumed the pseudonym she came to be known by for the rest of her life. When she had first used the name, she claimed it was that of a Swedish gentleman who had contacted her through a seance, but she later admitted that this fabrication had been for her credulous parents' benefit; it was, in fact, a name of her own invention.

Wishing to remain independent of her parents, Rachilde supported herself by her writing, gruelling work since it involved not only producing the stories, but taking them round from publisher to publisher in order to place them and collect the small sum they could bring. The latent hostilities with her mother emerged more clearly at this time, as the unstable Madame Eymery attempted to undercut her daughter's career. Word reached Rachilde of a rumor that she was not the author of the works she was selling, a serious charge since no editor wanted to get involved in cases of possible plagiarism. Finally she asked a sympathetic editor for a description of the person spreading the rumors. She recognized the verbal portrait as her own mother. Whether out of malice, or because of her increasing madness, Madame Eymery appeared to believe the story about the Swedish gentleman, and thus informed all who would listen that the stories were not really her daughter's own work.

In her memoirs, Rachilde dismisses this anecdote philosophically, with an indulgence and forbearance bred of time. While she acknowledged maternal disappointment, she never discusses her anger at her mother. There is ample evidence from her fiction, however, that her rage went deep. There are few maternal figures, and those that exist are weak and selfish, unable or unwilling to parent their offspring adequately. In *The Juggler,* for example, there are no mothers, and maternal relationships exist instead in surrogate relationships: between aunt and niece (a favored configuration in Rachilde's work) and between mistress and servant.

Rachilde's struggle to escape entirely from the family triangle succeeded with *Monsieur Vénus.* After this success, her future as a writer was assured. She continued to produce approximately one book a year for the next sixty years (her last publication was in 1947). Although she would never again have the kind of *succès de scandale* afforded by *Monsieur Vénus,* she steadily accumulated an impressive list of novels, many of which

received wide acclaim, including *La Marquise de Sade* (Monnier, 1887); *Madame Adonis* (Monnier, 1888), a companion piece to *Monsieur Vénus*; a collection of stories entitled *Le Démon de l'absurde, The Demon of the Absurd* (Mercure de France, 1894); and *La Tour d'amour, The Tower of Love* (Mercure de France, 1899), a horror story of madness and perversion set in a Breton lighthouse.

Rachilde continued to write and publish with almost obsessional regularity, and enjoyed continued success in the pre-World War I years (for example with the historical novel, *Le Meneur de louves, The Wolftamer*, in 1905), but the rise of the surrealist star gradually eclipsed her popularity, and her later work failed to earn her the wide support of a new generation of readers. Thus, *The Juggler (La Jongleuse),* first published by the Mercure de France in 1900 (the year of Nietzsche's death), represents the culmination of the fertile and prolific period of Rachilde's career spanning the years from 1884 until 1900. The novel stands out as the consummation of the themes that preoccupied her in the last two decades of the nineteenth century, as well as an expression of a remarkable social philosophy far ahead of its time (Eliante, the heroine of *The Juggler,* even refers to it as a "religion," in chapter 4). Witty, dramatic and profound, *The Juggler* is at once one of Rachilde's most carefully constructed novels, a simultaneous expression and parody of Decadence, and a meditation on female power, desire, and sexuality.

In this respect, *The Juggler* continues the established and important genre in French literature of works that analyze sexual politics. It can be compared, for example, to novels such as *Dangerous Liaisons* in its exploration through an epistolary exchange of the meaning of love and passion, as well as other libertine themes. The relationship between the principal characters Eliante and Leon is a dangerous liaison, indeed, for both parties, and Eliante's debt to the figure of a Marquis is not only the literal debt of daughter to parent, but the literary debt to a precursor. Eliante in turn becomes a precursor to others. With her hair worn in the style of a helmet, she is a *guerillère avant la lettre,* and a champion of women's independence. She expresses common themes of women's experience, such as the requirement that they hide their intelligence (chapter 3), the difficulty of maintaining platonic friendships and the fear that when women do act on sexual attractions, they lose men's respect (chapter 1).

The innovations of *The Juggler* are not only thematic, however, but also formal. The symbolist movement with which Rachilde was associated challenged the dominance of realism and naturalism in the novel and thus set the stage (to use one of *The Juggler*'s most pervasive metaphors) for twentieth-century experimentation. *The Juggler,* therefore, stands like the figure of Janus on the highway of prose development: on the one hand the novel turns in recognition to the past, but on the other it also looks boldly to the future.

At the turn of the century, when *The Juggler* was written and published, Rachilde's reputation was at its zenith. In 1889, she had married Alfred Vallette, and one year after, the celebrated review *Mercure de France* was born, along with their daughter. Rachilde's role in the appearance of the latter has never been questioned, but her role in the former has been underplayed or even entirely overlooked. Her name and reputation were extremely important factors in attracting contributors and readers, and thus in underwriting the success of the review. To her contemporaries, her role was evident, if not explicit. As well as acting as regular contributor and reviewer, she was the famous hostess of a Tuesday salon at the office of the *Mercure de France* that attracted the foremost literary figures of the Symbolist movement, along with international celebrities and up-and-coming writers.

One such guest was the young Colette, whose first in the famous series of "Claudine" novels, *Claudine à l'école, Claudine at School*, was published in the same year as *The Juggler*. Rachilde's close friendship with Colette's ex-husband Willy has clouded and obscured the nature of her relations with Colette, thought to be somewhat strained by rivalry and veiled hostility. More recently, however, it has been suggested not only that Rachilde was among the first to credit Colette, not Willy, as the true author of the Claudine stories, but also that she supported Colette both emotionally and financially.

Rachilde is certainly known to have been generous and supportive to another of her friends, also a regular guest at her salon, the young writer Alfred Jarry. The Vallettes supported Jarry throughout his brief life (he died in 1907 at the age of thirty-four), and in addition to material support, Rachilde in particular also offered less tangible gifts: she was one of Jarry's closest friends during his lifetime, and was instrumental in arranging for his play *Ubu Roi* to be performed at the Théâtre de l'Oeuvre in 1896, a performance which placed Jarry among the founders of modern drama. After his death, Rachilde contributed many anecdotes to the Jarry mythology. She wrote only one book of non-fiction devoted to a single author: her memoirs of the literary "superman" entitled *Alfred Jarry; ou, Le surmâle de lettres* (Grasset, 1928).

The extent to which Jarry and Rachilde influenced each other has never been fully studied, discussion having focused rather on the question of whether or not they were lovers, but *The Juggler* suggests some important points of comparison. Rachilde displays the same enjoyment of word play, in the form of puns and deformities, that characterizes Jarry's work, and shares his love of absurdity. She also shared his keen dramatic sense, and had had several plays performed before she came to write *The Juggler*. It is no coincidence that the heroine of this novel, Eliante, should be named after a character from Molière's *The Misanthrope*. The same elements that brought success in her plays—her memorable characters and a sense of timing—are apparent in her fictional works. Yet theatricality is more than a theme, it is an essential element of *The Juggler*. Not only is the novel permeated with the vocabulary of the theatre, but with the brief exceptions of the opening scene and the excursion to Leon's apartment, all the action is set in the heroine Eliante's house, with its two wings: the public world of receptions and parties approached via the courtyard, and the intimate world of Eliante's rooms approached via the garden. Not only do the two wings of the house correspond to the wings of the theatre, they even carry the nineteenth-century names for those two sides: "côté cour" (courtyard side) and "côté jardin (garden side)."

Thanks to this theatrical model, *The Juggler* is one of Rachilde's most carefully constructed novels. As a rule, she wrote rapidly and impetuously, revising little, and many of her novels suffer as a consequence. Indeed, the first version of *The Juggler*, in 1900, is decidedly inferior to the later, revised edition. . . . When rewriting, Rachilde eliminated one entire chapter . . . in which Eliante and Leon attend a performance of *Othello*. Formally, this cut simplifies the structure of the novel, preserving the unity of place (with the exceptions noted above). The excision further preserves the surprise of the ending by removing hints and suggestions that point too obviously to the conclusion. In other chapters, almost nothing has been added, and only an occasional word changed, but much has been omitted, and for the better. The rewriting removed repetitions and qualifications that either became redundant or else reduced Rachilde's delightfully suggestive ambiguity by answering the text's own rhetorical questions. The revisions leave the characteristic understatements intact, and allow a more active role for the reader, as was Rachilde's intention. Thus, *The Juggler* gained a remarkably coherent structure that gives shape to the sometimes effusive prose. Based on a complex yet regular pattern, the chapters alternate correspondence with dramatic personal confrontations. These interactions further alternate in their setting between the intimate scenes when characters enter via the garden, and social acts with entrance via the courtyard. All Leon's visits are clearly identified as occurring via one or the other of these entrances, which announce the tenor of the subsequent action.

In this domestic theatre, Eliante is the star performer: she juggles, she dances, and Leon continually accuses her of being an actress. The curtain falls at the end of each dramatic encounter (as Leon explicitly notes in chapter 1), and the plot confirms the hypothesis offered by Leon in chapter 3 with regard to the play they are about to see (a *mise en abyme* of the novel itself): a comedy that will become a drama toward the end.

The effect is not only to animate the plot and display Rachilde's considerable dramatic talent, but also to make the reader complicit as spectator, cast in the same role as Leon, constantly compelled to watch. Rachilde's theatre of passions evokes the drama of a courtroom where the audience-jury is called upon to pass judgement, or the spectacle of an amphitheatre in which hysterics performed like vaudeville acts for the edification of medical students. For every witch, there must be an inquisitor, for every hysteric, a doctor, as Catherine Clément notes in her study of witches and hysterics, "The Guilty One." Those who fall outside the symbolic order—"neurotics, ecstatics, outsiders, carnies, drifters, jugglers and acrobats" in Clément's text, or pathological cases, buffoons and histrions according to Eliante—are dangerously mobile unless locked into their symbolic position on the margins by the participation of the spectator. While Clément describes the Italian dance ritual of the tarantella, Eliante, in the final chapter of *The Juggler,* dances a no less symbolic and equally cathartic cure for symbolic illness in a flamenco which hypnotizes the spectator (Leon) and lures him into the web of the black widow (Eliante) for the last act. How appropriate that Eliante's blend of sorcery and hysteria in *The Juggler* should be situated in 1897, the year, as Clément notes, in which Freud recognized the similarities between the behavior of witches and the hysterics he was treating.

Eliante finally escapes from this circle of speculation in a manner readers often find at best ambiguous, at worst unequivocally defeatist. But as Nancy K. Miller has noted, the economy of female desire is often misread, and if Miller cites the example of the Princesse de Clèves, who refuses to marry the man she loves in an act of self-affirmation traditionally misinterpreted as self-sacrifice, the resemblance of Eliante to this paradigmatic character has not gone unnoticed. Like the Princesse de Clèves, Eliante realizes that the only way to preserve her ideal is to refrain from implementing it, and thus her last act is committed "with a supernatural joy."

This interpretation opens the way for a fuller appreciation of the social analysis set forth in *The Juggler,* an analysis which marks Rachilde's departure from Decadence and her links to other modern writers. She had experimented with themes of perversion in previous novels, but in *The Juggler* the experiment is accompanied by a hypothesis. Rachilde had been groping toward insights about love and sexual desire, but in fragmented fashion; *The Juggler* presents them for the first time integrated into one unified theory. As in earlier novels, she imagines a rather eccentric perversion with which to endow her heroine, a perversion intended to shock the bourgeois, but also a further variable in a series of experiments concerning the nature of love. Eliante Donalger is in love with a Greek amphora. The choice of an inanimate entity as love object marks an important breakthrough in this series. The vase can be sufficiently anthropomorphized that it escapes simple categorization as a form of fetishism, but remains sufficiently inhuman that it avoids preconceived notions about perversions such as necrophilia. The vase further remains gender unspecific, so that the nature of the anthropomorphism

escapes definition as either heterosexual or homosexual. Thanks to the grammatical gendering of nouns in French, the vase remains both "*une* urne" and "*un* vase"; as Eliante notes, it can be referred to as both "he" and "she," depending on the antecedent noun. This ambiguity is deliberately preserved and exploited by Eliante to illustrate not an androgyny predicated upon the recombination of two opposite sexes as in traditional definitions, but an inclusive bisexuality based on, in the words of Hélène Cixous, "the nonexclusion of difference."

In the amphora, Rachilde furthermore finds the perfect foil to illustrate the protean possibilities of human sexual expression, a theory for which Eliante becomes the spokesperson. Not only does she not need to look for a sex organ in the object of her desire, but she does not need human contact at all to obtain satisfaction. The "bisexuality" of Eliante's desire comprises not only gender difference; it defends the love of nonhuman objects as a natural extension of the insight that beauty is in the brain of the beholder, as maintained by her namesake. By laying bare the role of thought and imagination in human desire, Rachilde anticipates radically different theories of human sexuality, going against the grain of her contemporaries in the then burgeoning field of psychology.

Her insight goes one step further than this important recognition, however, for Rachilde further entrusts the policing of ideologically determined sex roles to the embryonic medical profession in the person of the medical student Leon Reille. Rachilde's dislike of doctors is a recurrent theme in her work (and a further link to the theatre of Molière), but in *The Juggler* the problem becomes specific. Leon not only invokes the threats used to maintain traditional sexual behavior (for example, he claims in chapter 6 that Eliante will be afflicted with St. Vitus's dance and general paralysis), he believes her cure lies in acceptance of "normal" sexual relations. He interprets her resistance to his sexual advances not as legitimate expression of autonomy, but as a desire to be raped, just as Freud would interpret his patients' accounts of resistance to incest as a fantasized desire to seduce and be seduced. Where outright threats fail, more subtle social control mechanisms can be deployed, as Eliante recognizes. The labelling of an expression of ecstasy, of *jouissance,* which exceeds the bounds of discourse, as a "pathological case" turns female desire into a form of deviance, a problem which appears to require a cure.

Studies of nineteenth- and twentieth-century history, in particular of the role of the medical profession in defining sexuality, confirm Rachilde's vision in less humorous and more sinister detail. Eliante's perception of the role of the mental health profession in demarcating the boundaries of deviance is also prophetic in anticipating the central role of female desire in subsequent theory, particularly in her answer to the as-yet-unasked question, "what do women want?" They do not know, suggests Eliante, perhaps failing only to add, as Lacan later would, "and they cannot know."

The Juggler also demonstrates the degree to which Rachilde is aware of the role of sexual difference in the construction of meaning. For Eliante, and perhaps for Rachilde, men and women speak different languages. The voice—and name—of the father are internalized here, but it is precisely from this paternal prohibition that Eliante escapes in her role of hysterical juggling witch in order to speak from a different source: women write, without knowing why, just as they cry. Cixous suggests that women write from the body using milk and blood; she might well have added tears, the invisible fluid of women's marginal status with which women write in *The Juggler*. Not "the madwoman in the attic"—though a creole nevertheless—Eliante's response to the masculine appropriation of the pen is not anxiety, but an escape to a different way of signifying, one which remains invisible to those who cannot read the body. Although Eliante does not know how to write, she knows how to sign, and thus she is a juggler not only in the literal sense, but also in the older and more general sense of *jongleur*, "a troubadour," not just one who entertains with dancing and acrobatics, but one who tells stories, who "finds"—and signs—them.

The implicit attack on phallogocentrism includes more than just a critique of the inscription of the feminine in discourse; it also illustrates the absence of fixed meaning in language through the treatment of origins. Not only do Eliante's origins remain obscure, the origins of communication itself are irretrievable in *The Juggler*. The structure of the novel relies partly on an exchange of letters, but the model for this exchange, while not denied, is no longer available. The parable of the lost letter in chapter 8 (and described as her obsession in chapter 10) tells the story of Eliante's first love letter. Like all discourse viewed through the prism of postmodernism, including the confessions Eliante prepared with her classmates in the convent, the letter never fails to recall what one does not mean to say. Between sender and receiver, however, the letter fell into the sea and therefore never reached its destination. Perhaps, though, this was for the best, since the words were not hers to begin with, but literally a *translation* from those of her black other, and thus a collaborative inscription in black and white that would nevertheless remain unreadable. This reintegration of binary opposites is a mitigating factor to be set against the overt racism of the text. There can be no doubt that Rachilde was as racist as she was misogynist and misanthropic, and she does not hesitate to invoke the negative stereotypes that were all too acceptable in her own time. But the personal relationship between Eliante and Ninaude, as well as their literary collaboration, enacts a reconciliation between black and white by presenting difference as a generative force.

These themes have only become readable in Rachilde's work since the development of postmodernism has chal-

lenged the place of a unified subject at the center of discourse. Although *The Juggler* went through several editions, Rachilde's contemporaries saw little of this vision in her work, and dismissed her literary contributions prematurely. While she continued to write and publish widely after World War I, she became increasingly viewed as an eccentric has-been. She maintained contact with other writers, but these were mostly young protégés with whom she collaborated, not those perceived as expanding the horizons of literature. In her later life she became isolated, lonely and poor, most unlike the independently wealthy and aristocratic widows of her fiction. Her writing turned toward memoirs, and she ventured into (for her) previously unexplored genres such as poetry. She died in her apartment at the *Mercure de France* on 4 April 1953. Her passing was noted in the major newspapers, such as *Le Monde,* but caused barely a ripple in the literary world. Rachilde's life was both too long and too short: she lived long enough to experience a decline in her popularity and a neglect of her work. She did not live long enough, however, to witness the revival of interest and the appreciation of a new generation of readers that is her due.

Ben Fisher   (essay date 1991)

SOURCE: "The Companion and the Dream: Delirium in Rachilde and Jarry," in *Romance Studies,* No. 18, Summer, 1991, pp. 33-41.

[*In the following essay, Fisher examines depictions of delirium in Rachilde's* La princesse des ténèbres *and Alfred Jarry's* Les jours et les nuits, *claiming that these works illustrate a view of dream-states differing from the theories advanced by Sigmund Freud in his* Interpretation of Dreams.]

It is inevitable that discussion of the dream in literature, and particularly over the last hundred years, tends to focus on Freud and the relevance of Freudian interpretation. The mark of Freud upon twentieth-century thought is in fact so great that other reflections on the dream are often forgotten. This article discusses two French novels of the 1890s, Rachilde's *La Princesse des ténèbres* and Alfred Jarry's *Les Jours et les nuits,* which belong to the period leading up to the publication of *Die Traumdeutung* (1900) and illustrate an approach to the literary dream which is distinct from Freudian attitudes, and has identifiable links with the native thought of the time. The novels also merit joint discussion on the grounds of the high level of intertextuality that exists between them. Jarry and Rachilde were close friends— indeed Jarry paid Rachilde the compliment of selecting her novel for the library of his Dr. Faustroll in the first manuscript version of *Gestes et Opinions du Docteur Faustroll, pataphysicien,* and praised it further in an article written for *La Plume* in 1903. *Les Jours et les nuits* and *La Princesse des ténèbres* share an approach to consciousness and delirium that makes for a fine practical example of the cult of textual mystery so dear to the Symbolist circles in which Rachilde and Jarry moved. At the same time, these works represent the apogee of the writing of delirium in both novelists, who subsequently moved away from their shared ground in opposing directions.

Jarry, a figure of diverse and extensive reading, and with contacts in virtually all the important Symbolist circles of the 1890s, often serves as a useful indicator of the writings fashionable among the members of these circles. In the matter of philosophical influences his literary connections are, however, less important than the influence of his schoolmasters. At the Lycée de Rennes, where his physics master embodied the nascent figure of Ubu, another master freely expounded the writings of Nietzsche, not even available in French at that time, and at the Lycée Henri IV in Paris Jarry was an attentive pupil of Henri Bergson, who was in the habit of developing his own thoughts while teaching. Jarry's notes from these lessons apparently survive. Anne Clancier, in a lecture given at Cerisy-la-Salle in 1981, has debated the question 'Jarry avait-il lu Freud?', without ultimately answering the question as posed; nowhere in Jarry can the presence of Freud be precisely located. Yet in the period prior to 1900 when he was producing his most distinctive work, Jarry became one of the most sustained illustrators in French literature of altered states of consciousness—the interface between life and the dream. The environment of thought in which he does this is non-Freudian (or equally, pre-Freudian), and his work at this time also shows the strong influence of Rachilde, a greater practical influence on his work than many care to admit. The links are nowhere closer than between *La Princesse des ténèbres* and *Les Jours et les nuits*.

It is hard to imagine a less fashionable French author than Rachilde (1860-1953). Born Marguerite Eymery, she married author and publisher Alfred Vallette after making an independent entry on to the literary scene, and together the couple were the driving force behind the *Mercure de France*, founded in 1890 and rapidly developed into the major social and artistic focus of late Symbolism. Rachilde tried her hand at various literary forms, but found her major success with the novel. There is no denying that much of her popularity rested on the *risqué* subject matter of certain of her writings, which often deal with taboo subjects such as homosexuality (*Les Hors-Nature*, 1897) and sexual inversion—the very titles of *Monsieur Vénus, Madame Adonis* and *La Marquise de Sade* are intended to shock, before one even reaches their narratives. These works do not stray into the cheaply pornographic *veine grivoise*, but their licentious associations have for some reason given rise to a widespread assumption that they are unfit for serious study. Their author's status has sunk accordingly. Also, while being for her contemporaries the most prominent woman writer of the *Belle Epoque*, Rachilde is unsuited to the mainstream feminist critique that has rescued many women writers from neglect—indeed she was noted for her pamphlet *Pourquoi je ne suis pas*

féministe, published in 1928. Nor has she been well treated by those who have promoted Jarry since the Second World War: indeed in recent years the highly respected Jarryist Noël Arnaud has chosen to launch a blistering and excessively partisan attack on Rachilde's biography of Jarry, *Alfred Jarry ou le Surmâle de lettres*. Rachilde was also an influential critic, through her reviews of novels and other prose in the *Mercure de France,* and her popular *mardis* at the *Mercure*'s premises, first in the Rue de l'Echaudé St-Germain, and later the Rue de Conde, were a major focus for the avant-grade around the turn of the century.

A fertile imagination and the great speed at which she wrote combined to make Rachilde's output of novels dauntingly large, yet most texts are hard to find today. Her current reputation is largely based on the few novels now in print, usually her urbanely bloodthirsty earlier novels *Monsieur Vénus* and *La Marquise de Sade,* which are far from being representative of her whole work. *La Princesse des ténèbres* is one of her many novels that have fallen into neglect; indeed it has yet to see its second edition. It chronicles the declining health and growing delirium of Madeleine Deslandes, an innocent, withdrawn provincial girl who in the course of the novel marries an upright and sympathetic local doctor, Edmond Sellier. The heroine's maiden name indicates the morose mood of the region where the novel is set, in tune with her frame of mind. It is relatively simple to spot literary inspirations in Rachilde, all the more so given that they often involve Sacher-Masoch's *Venus im Pelz;* here, the shadow of *Madame Bovary* is unmistakable, with a suitably ethereal slant to suit the fashion of the 1890s. Thus the doctor is not in fact Madeleine's true love; she undergoes a series of visions in which she meets the mysterious Hunter, who is quite patently the Devil. His identity is never explicitly stated, but lies not very deep between the lines—there is even a coy reference to the devil as he appears in a German play that Jarry was attempting to promote in translation at the time. Passion grows more intense at each of Hunter's meetings with the heroine, who is ignorant of his identity—and with this growing passion there is a proportional decline in her health. Hunter asks her to keep herself for him alone on her wedding night, and it is strongly implied that her pregnancy results from their encounter on that night. After her husband has diagnosed her as suffering from lycanthropy (the form of madness commonly associated with the appearance of werewolves), she miscarries, imagining that Hunter has asked for the baby in order to feed it to his dog. Before long she dies, possessed by near-constant visions of Hunter. The plot shows particularly deft handling of tension between the Present and the Beyond, and it is only in the final pages that the illusory nature of Madeleine's encounters with Hunter is clarified; the shock is genuine and strong for the first-time reader.

This form of tension between the Present and the Beyond is reflected in Jarry's *Les Jours et les nuits,* published in 1897 but started in 1895, the year of *La*

Princesse des ténèbres. It is a novel whose exterior is drawn from life, with many identifiable echoes of Jarry's own military service and of his revulsion at the brutality of military life. These aspects naturally invite comparison with Georges Darien's *Biribi,* selected by Jarry for the first draft of Dr. Faustroll's library along with *La Princesse,* but the influence of this brutally frank account of Army penal companies in Tunisia is distinct from the plot and psychology of *Les Jours et les nuits,* which are governed by notions of delirium, displaying here a considerable debt to Rachilde. It goes without saying that there is also much that is original and peculiar to Jarry, who creates a projection of himself in Sengle, the hero of the novel.

Les Jours et les nuits is subtitled 'Roman d'un déserteur', and its fascination lies in the strange desertion from the army that Sengle performs. He deserts from within; both from within the army and from within himself. By counterfeiting illness—though it cannot be unequivocally stated that Sengle has no real medical problems, his demobilisation being nominally on account of heart problems—he quickly becomes an internee of his barracks' hospital, as did Jarry during his own service, and finds a physically comfortable life as a patient while awaiting his *réforme.* His comfort is, however, tempered by observation of the gruesome, ignorant cruelty of the hospital and its inhabitants. The initial parallel with Rachilde emerges in Sengle's inner evasion. The precisely detailed, matter-of-fact world that he inhabits in civilian life fades as he enters the military world, and the dream begins. Sengle briefly imagines an escape to Belgium, lulled in his reverie by a repetitive 'Le train roula vers des Amiens et des Lille . . .', and from this point on the specificity of Sengle's world is lost. More often than not it is hard for the reader to distinguish reality from dream—and it is precisely so for the character also. This point of shared experience is the real key to following Jarry's novels, all of which are commonly held to be more 'difficult' than they need be. Sengle is moved into a world where the dream takes over—in other words, into a state of delirium.

Delirium invites medical attention, but that to which it is submitted by Rachilde and Jarry is strictly pre-Freudian, as it involves no attempt at psychoanalysis. Madeleine Deslandes is treated little differently from any stereotyped sickly young wife, excepting her husband's diagnosis of her lycanthropy, which (even admitting a *fin-de-siècle* taste for Petrus Borel) is so Gothic as to court ridicule, even without considering its technical inaccuracy. Sengle's treatment in the Rabelaisian *cour des Miracles* of the army hospital is hopelessly incapable of addressing his mental disturbance. The psychological aspects of Sengle's malady, explored in greater depth than the psyche of Rachilde's heroine, confirm links between these novels and Bergson, Jarry's schoolmaster. Like Freud, Bergson saw the dream as a symptom, but he allied himself with those who saw its details as symptoms of physical rather than mental illness. This

ties in with the narrative of *La Princesse des ténèbres,* where there is a simple and direct correlation between delirium and physical illness. *Les Jours et les nuits* is a more complicated case, just as Jarry is a more complicated writer than Rachilde, and hinges on a more tangible parallel with Bergson, many of whose theories Jarry had heard long before their publication, in the classrooms of the Lycée Henri IV. Sengle is a writer, and here is Bergson on dreams and writing, working from the example of Robert Louis Stevenson:

> [. . .] vous verrez que l'auteur a cønnu, pendant une certaine partie de sa vie, un état psychologique où il lui était difficile de savoir s'il dormait ou s'il veillait. Je crois, en effet, que lorsque l'esprit crée, lorsqu'il donne l'effort que réclame la composition d'une œuvre ou la solution d'un problème, il n'y a pas sommeil.

This is precisely Sengle's state of mind. He makes no distinction between unpleasant reality and the world into which he deserts, and after a certain point cannot distinguish day from night—hence the title of the novel. His own literary creation takes the form of a dream book:

> Sengle construisait ses littératures, curieusement et précisément équilibrées, par des sommeils d'une quinzaine de bonnes heures, après manger et boire; et éjaculait en une écriture de quelque méchante demi-heure le résultat. [. . .] Des professeurs de philosophie chantent que cette similitude aux productions naturelles est du Chef-d'œuvre.

Sengle understands his dreamer's power as his own way of controlling the world (he also has a degree of magnetism over physical objects), and from this develops the first clear version of Jarry's pseudo-science of 'la pataphysique', a way of viewing, grasping and manipulating the world which he would develop explicitly in *Faustroll,* and implicity in *L'Amour absolu* and *Le Surmâle.*

The blending of illusion with reality follows the same pattern as in *La Princesse des ténèbres:* an imperfectly delineated setting, the onset of illness, real or affected, and a specific symptom prominent in both novels, namely visions of a companion figure. In Rachilde's novel it is Hunter, the masterful and diabolical lover, and in Jarry's it is the shadowy figure of Sengle's younger brother, Valens. The presence of a brother does not challenge either the equivalence with a lover figure or the value of the self-projection by Jarry, who had only an elder sister; it has been demonstrated that Valens is a fond echo of homosexual lovers from Jarry's life, so both conditions are satisfied. The hazy indications of incestuous feelings (but not acts) in the novel point the way to Jarry's later depiction of them in *L'Amour absolu.* Just as Hunter represents the perverse ideal of Madeleine's illusory passion, Valens represents not only a physical ideal—his beauty is constantly stressed—but also an idealized image of the brothers' childhood, indivisible from more adult games played together. At the opening of the novel the brothers are with two women:

> La chambre et ceux qui étaient dans la chambre et leurs actes furent les mêmes les autres heures de la nuit, Sengle et Valens répondant peu aux filles parce qu'ils pouvaient plus intelligemment parler entre eux, et ne parlant pas entre eux parce qu'ils se comprenaient assez d'être ensemble.

Sengle speaks little in the novel, and Valens, whether present or remembered, not at all. Shortly before Jarry declares Sengle to have genuine medical concerns, he causes him to doubt the very existence of his brother. Even photographs fail to convey an impression of him as Sengle retreats from the memory of the palpably real Valens towards the memory of his ideal. Divisions between Sengle and others become blurred, even at the grammatical level of the agreement of verbs, as Alain Verjat has demonstrated. Sengle consciously absorbs the vaporous ideal of his sibling into his own being, and through this act of will compounds his delirium still further. Dream and reality meet, and clash:

> Et Sengle, amoureux du Souvenir de Soi, avait besoin d'un ami vivant et visible, parce qu'il n'avait aucun souvenir de Soi, étant dépourvu de toute mémoire. Il avait essayé de réaliser en soi ce souvenir de Soi en coupant sa légère moustache et endurant de son corps une méticuleuse épilation grecque; mais il s'aperçut qu'il risquait d'avoir l'air d'une tapette et non d'un petit garçon. Et surtout il était très nécessaire qu'il demeurât ce que Valens allait devenir, jusqu'au malheureux jour où la différence de deux ans et demi n'étant plus visible, ils se confondraient trop jumeaux.

Sengle's first decision to report sick comes immediately after the lengthy reflection on the metaphysics of love of which this is a part. In Rachilde's novel, the appearance of Hunter is governed by parallel emotional stress; Madeleine finds herself able to summon him when she is being put under pressure to marry Edmond Sellier. Thus, at the outset, both Hunter and Valens have for their unmistakably real companions the same status as the lonely child's invisible friend: someone who is conveniently available when wanted, absent when not, but above all who responds to a deep-seated need that palpable company cannot fulfil. In Sengle it is a need for a completion of his self, which would cancel out weaknesses and add to perceived strengths, such as physical beauty. In Madeleine, it is the need for both an extrovert lover and an escape from provincial monotony. The two protagonists meet parallel ends, in which the companion figures are prominent and are no longer under control: Madeleine dies and Sengle is reduced to a vegetable state by being hit on the head by a lump of plaster, after obtaining his release from the army; this imbecility is in Jarry's terms a fate worse than death, which for the author of *Faustroll* is a highly fluid concept. Both characters meet their obliteration through a state of delirium. Madeleine's death is closely associated with

strong sensory impressions of Hunter, whose very appearance becomes confused:

> Ses chaussures étaient poudreuses, tellement poudreuses qu'elles se confondaient avec le sable des allées du jardin, et qu'aussi, planté droit, sans pieds, on pouvait le croire ondulant au-dessus du sol, émanant de la terre, mais ne la foulant pas.

Hunter is drifting out of the frame of Madeleine's imagination, and is a world away from the more realistic figure she first encountered. Similarly, Sengle loses his impression of his brother; at the time Valens will be entering military life in his turn, he finds himself staring at a plaster moulding above him on the wall; in it he develops a vision of Valens, which he stands on a table to kiss. The plaster falls, the table tips up under Sengle's feet, and the damage is done: 'Et Sengle tâtonnait dans la nuit vers son Soi disparu comme le cœur d'une bombe, la bouche sur son meurtre'.

Both of these extended dreams lead to oblivion, through the process of self-delusion that leads the dreamer away from an undesirable reality into a delirium where the products of the imagination are as real, and indeed more destructive, than the contents of the real-world environment. The tension between the two sides lies in the division that the reader is able to perceive but which is veiled within the mind of the central characters, which is all the stronger as the novels are inherently biased towards the spiritual depiction of their central figures. Thus, Rachilde's heroine is unable to perceive her own growing illness, in fact she perceives quite the reverse, namely a growing strength in her relationship with Hunter, and on the earthly level of much of the narration, she becomes an uneasy, slightly pathetic figure for the reader as a result. Her proto-existentialist speech of self-definition on her deathbed only adds to the tragedy of her delusions. As one might expect, the situation in Jarry's novel is very much more involved, with the complications of his oblique manner of discourse and his added imposition on Sengle of other, artificial sources of hallucination. These have been ably discussed by Henri Béhar, and so require no discussion here. The ability of Sengle to create further states of hallucination, mainly through drugs, is a side issue to the main psychological progress of the novel, and in fact these hallucinations themselves constitute a temporary means of escape from another, more fundamental escape that is already under way and threatens the very identification of the hero.

The central delusion of the two figures, although self-generated, is involuntary, unlike Sengle's escape into hashish. Its onset stands as that of an illness, and thus attracts medical attention—in case of *La Princesse des ténèbres* the love and later the professional attentions of a doctor, in *Les Jours et les nuits* the life of a hospital patient, even if that hospital is alternately lax and inhuman. For medicine only exacerbates the illness, reinforcing the internal value of the companion—Madeleine reacts against her doctor to rely more and more on

Hunter, and the cures Sengle undergoes create obsessions, poisoning his mind to the point where he sends cultures of scarlet fever to his distant, beloved brother, intended to make him ill enough to avoid military service. Sengle's true illness has advanced to the point where it feeds itself and generates more sickness, until he sees a solution only in the crippling of a healthy brother. The illness is thus becoming perceptible from the outside—in other words, it is developing symptoms, and is therefore open to treatment. However, Sengle loses his reason before any treatment can appear; the medical notions are subservient to the tragic slant common in Jarry's novels, and indeed in those of Rachilde.

The Bergsonian concept of the dream was never as fully developed as the Freudian version, and it is if anything even more dated. It is impossible to say whether the delirium in the two novels discussed above is intended to be specifically Bergsonian, as Jarry's notes from his lessons remain unavailable, and any thoughts of Bergson's direct influence on Jarry or, at second hand, his friend Rachilde, can only be conjecture. However, the importance of the blurring of dream and life highlighted by Bergson fits easily into the intensely anti-realist streak of the general Symbolist aesthetic, and in these works, produced at the heart of one of the primary Symbolist *milieux*, the *Mercure de France* circle, we see notably sustained examples of literary delirium. The companion figures introduce statement rather than escapism; the difficulty of human relationships that governs the disaffected sadism of Rachilde's early novels, and would equally govern the rejection of affection in Jarry's *L'Amour en visites,* is developed into attempts to create the complete personality, with the internal generation of the vital figure of *l'Autre.* Yet the companion, as we have found, triggers delirium and ultimately invokes oblivion; tragedy is internalized by this effect, and is thus hard to analyse from outside. Through these self-contained figures, the Symbolist cult of difficulty becomes more than a decorative trope, and paints a cold portrait of the imaginative human as an endangered species.

The portrayal of tragic delirium is only sustained within the span of these particular novels, as the authors' stances rapidly drew apart. For Jarry, the pataphysical powers of Sengle define a central and unique direction for his subsequent work, leading directly to *Faustroll.* Rachilde, however, always suspicious of the abstruseness that characterizes Jarry's work, moved slowly away from writing about delirium, and we may note as a stage on that journey *L'Heure sexuelle* (1898), which, in a re-drafting, replaced *La Princesse des ténèbres* as Jarry's selection for Dr. Faustroll's library. *L'Heure sexuelle* relates the life and hallucinations of a novelist, Louis Rogès, who is obsessed with the figure of Cleopatra and attempts to project it on to a prostitute. He seeks to be 'celui qui va tuer le rêve', and he does so by trying to live out the dream with the prostitute, Léonie, whose unsuitability for the rôle of Cleopatra is the source not only of humour but also of an affirmation

that dreams cannot govern life—or at least not a life which is not destined for a tragic end, like those of Madeleine Deslandes and Sengle. For Rachilde, a way out has developed, and the therapy of the dream can be used as an antidote—whereas for Jarry the experiment of delirium points the way to still deeper alterations of the psyche, and to the constant reaching for the mysteries of the Self and the Beyond that is the hallmark of his novels.

Melanie C. Hawthorne (essay date 1992)

SOURCE: "To the Lighthouse: Fictions of Masculine Identity in Rachilde's *La Tour d'Amour,*" in *L'Esprit Createur,* Vol. 32, No. 4, Winter, 1992, pp. 41-51.

[*In the following essay, Hawthorne interprets Rachilde's novel* La tour d'amour *as an allegory of the author's place as a woman writing in a literary world dominated by men.*]

"Is a pen a metaphorical penis?" asked Gilbert and Gubar in their study of women writers, [*The Madwoman in the Attic: The Woman Writer and the Nineteenth-century Literary Imagination*] encapsulating the question of the role of gender in women's writing in the nineteenth century. The cultural assumption of a link between writing and gender explains in part the difficulties women had to overcome in order to write. But Gilbert and Gubar's study focused on British women writers; when turning to the French context, the question must be more nuanced. For one thing, the French nineteenth-century novel is not dominated by women in the same way as its British equivalent. As Joan DeJean writes [In *Tender Geographies: Women and the Origins of the Novel in France*]: "in the nineteenth century, when both the novel and English women's writing reach what from today's perspective is considered their fullest expression, the French female literary presence is, with an occasional exception, most notably that of George Sand, at its nadir." Naomi Schor has suggested that, in part, this relative paucity of women writers is related to the dominance of realism, a genre inimical to women's voices. What is striking, however, is that despite hostile cultural assumptions and psychological handicaps, women did write, continuously and prolifically, throughout the century. Like their British counterparts, they also inscribed their "anxiety of influence," the ambivalence they faced when taking up the pen, as well as reflecting the cultural assumptions about gender and writing.

Gender cannot be divorced from authorship in the history of nineteenth-century French literature. To the extent that writing was a male prerogative, women who wrote were anomalies and subject to various social penalties. The cultural prescription of maleness had several consequences for women writers. Women disguised themselves as men in a number of different registers in order to write: they put on a male mask in public by using male pseudonyms, for example; or they assumed a male appearance by cross-dressing; they proclaimed a hidden male essence despite a female appearance by claiming or acknowledging "virile" qualities in their writing. The history of this male identification is far from monolithic in the nineteenth century, however, and women appropriated different aspects of male roles at different times. The various issues at stake can be illustrated by the examination of one moment in the career of the writer Rachilde, a moment which offers a rich and complex inscription of what Hélène Cixous has called the "coming to writing." [*"Coming to Writing" and other Essays*] By placing this fin-de-siècle example in the context of the nineteenth century as a whole, I hope to show both some recurrent features of the pattern as well as those particular to this case.

Rachilde's life encompassed many of the issues that were paradigmatic for French women writers of the nineteenth century. She accepted the unspoken assumption that writing was a masculine activity, and set about fitting that mold. She adopted male pseudonyms to authorize her writing, cross-dressed during the launch of her literary career, and announced on her visiting cards that she was an "homme de lettres." At first glance, her coming to writing, then, appears to have been mediated by the paternal, the "nom-du-père"; however, Rachilde's case also suggests that writing could be a *defiance* of paternal authority. Women writers may adopt a male persona to rival their fathers, not to imitate them, to oppose rather than reaffirm patriarchal power.

For some women writers, such as Marie Dumas and Judith Gautier, the association of writing with the paternal is a given, but for others, fathers offered different influences, forces that shaped their writing but not as role models. Two examples, one from the beginning of the nineteenth century and one from the end, together form something resembling parentheses enclosing the experience of nineteenth-century women. Germaine de Staël idealized her father, Jacques Necker, but he did not approve of women writing and had already persuaded his wife to give up her literary pretensions. He ridiculed his daughter, mockingly referring to her as Monsieur de Sainte-Ecritoire (a name combining both female and male elements). For de Staël, then, writing entailed an ambivalence, since it involved disloyalty to an ideal. She acted out this internalized ambivalence by continuing to write, but in discomfort: she wrote standing at the mantelpiece so that her father would have the impression she could be doing nothing serious. Even after her father's death in 1804, she continued to integrate writing and her social duties as hostess:

> the Countess de Boigne records [Staël] never did have a study for work and wrote by placing a little writing case of green morocco containing her work and correspondence on her knees, carrying it from room to room, often surrounded by people. [Gutwirth, *Madame de Staël, Novelist: The Emergence of the Artist as Woman*]

(As an aside, this provides an extraordinary counterpart to the case of Jane Austen, doing a very similar thing at around the same time, just across the English Channel.) In these conditions, de Staël produced her most famous novel, *Corinne,* several hundred pages in length. The novel concerns a woman writer, but as Joan DeJean has pointed out, we never see Corinne writing, although we learn that she has published several books. It was only after both the death of her father and when the success of this work confirmed her as a writer that Staël considered buying a desk. She confided to her cousin: "I would really like to have a big desk; it seems to me I have the right to one now" (quoted in Gutwirth).

Closing the nineteenth century is the example of a contemporary and friend of Rachilde, Colette. Colette's father, a retired sea captain, did not discourage writing, on the contrary, he indirectly promoted it by serving as a kind of model himself, although what kind of model will become evident. After failing in business, he spent much of his time writing in his study, which also happened to be a good way to avoid facing the family. When he died, bound copies of his works, which bore titles like "My Campaigns" and "The Lessons of 1870," were found on his shelves. Upon examination, however, it was discovered that every one of them was blank. As though in answer to the implicit questions he asked in his titles—what *were* his campaigns, and what *did* he learn in 1870—he seems to have inscribed his failure in a most spectacular way. This image of male authorial impotence, the inability to stain the sheets of the page with the seminal mark of phallic potency, may have been liberating to Colette, who, as a woman writer, confronted what Susan Gubar has called the "blank page of female creativity." In contrast to the inhibiting effect Staël's father must have had, Colette inherited an image of male writing as a somewhat fraudulent endeavor, an effort which pretended to much seriousness but amounted to nothing, the products of which could easily be written over in a female hand. Despite the difference between these two cases, of Staël and Colette, it is clearly the father who mediates the "coming to writing," but not through identification.

This is no less true in Rachilde's case, though the story takes yet a different configuration. Although Rachilde, like Staël, idealized her father and craved his approval, she began her defiance much sooner. She took up writing in the full knowledge that it would offend him, since, although her mother's family were journalists, her father referred to writers as "des plumitifs," or scribblers (morphology manages to make the French word sound more pathological, however). At first Rachilde published her work anonymously in local newspapers, but her father provided a kind of mirror in which Rachilde was able to catch the reflections of her identity as a writer. Her father would read aloud her own stories from the newspaper to her, not suspecting that she was the author, since they were printed anonymously. This situation is unusual enough, but to complicate matters, he would censor the parts of the stories he found too daring. One can only speculate as to the effect this must have had on Rachilde's work, in which the desire to "épater le bourgeois" is so pronounced.

Part of the reason women adopted male pseudonyms was to create for themselves a public authorial persona which facilitated their writing, not so much because it presented a male, and therefore acceptable, mask to the public, but because it split, for them, the functions of reader and writer within their own psyche in a way that duplicated the received gender norms: men as writer, women as reader. Kathryn Crecelius has described this stage in the evolution from Aurore Dupin to George Sand, and claims that Aurore became her own narratee, while delegating the writing to her alter ego, George. Rachilde is split in the same way in this situation, recreating the dynamics that reigned in the family room when her father would return her won creations to her but in modified form. Rachilde, the writer, sent out her work into the public sphere, while Marguerite listened to those creations through the paternal filter.

This split is taken even further in another episode she recounts in her memoirs, **Quand j'étais jeune**. One day, when she was doing the rounds of the reviews and newspapers trying to place stories, an editor told her of a rumor that was circulating. According to this rumor, she was not really the author of the work she supplied. Obviously, no reputable editor would touch a case of plagiarism, so the rumor was seriously impairing her ability to earn a living. Rachilde asked the sympathetic editor for a description of the person who was spreading the rumor, and recognized in the verbal portrait she received her own mother. Madame Eymery had believed too well her daughter's explanation of her writing: that a Swedish nobleman named Rachilde dictated stories during seances. She bought the story, so to speak, and was making sure that no one else would buy her daughter's stories. The fiction that Rachilde wove with the intention of legitimizing her writing worked too well. The distinction between the masculine author and the female medium who merely acts as a form of transmission replicated social norms in a way that was too convincing. Rather than enabling, it temporarily blocked her ability to reach the reading public. Rachilde's reaction, an unconscious one no doubt, was to reassert her masculinity. At this period, she was wearing men's clothes anyway and had cut her hair short; and this was when she had visiting cards printed that read "Rachilde, homme de lettres." Thereafter, she made this public persona her own, private identity for the rest of her life: Marguerite completely disappeared, as it were, and Rachilde took her place at all times. She often referred to herself in the masculine, and she became known simply as Rachilde to everyone, including friends.

Nowhere, however, does Rachilde try to explain why her mother tried to sabotage her writing career in this act of passive aggression. She chose instead to see this incident as further evidence of her mother's mental illness, which, in some ways, of course, it was. But this maternal betrayal raises questions not only about Rachilde's place in her family of origin, but also about the family into which she sought adoption, the family of writers. In particular, Rachilde's very deep sense of maternal betrayal is a response not only to her biological mother, but to her literary foremothers. Her position within the family romance replicates her position within the family of "romanciers," or novelists; in both cases, she felt inadequately mothered.

A reading of one of Rachilde's novels that uses metaphors of family and the relationship to parents provides an allegorical view of Rachilde's link to reading and writing. The novel describes *la venue à l'écriture* of a writer and the ways in which authority—in both senses of the word—is mediated by maternal and paternal—or patriarchal—forces. This novel is **La Tour d'amour**, first published in 1899, and at one time Rachilde's favorite work. The narrative, a story of apprenticeship in a lighthouse, describes a process of integration into a pseudo-family, which suggests simultaneously the personal issues faced by Rachilde in her biological family of origin and the larger problems of a woman writer seeking adoption into a patriarchal family as an author with authority. The novel pits phallic power against "the eternal feminine," and describes the misfortune, or "malheur," of Jean Maleux, who is appointed as second lighthouse keeper to assist, and eventually succeed, the head keeper Mathurin Barnabas.

The novel is somewhat unusual for this period of Rachilde's fiction in having a first-person narrator. This narrator speaks, then, in the masculine, just as Rachilde herself spoke and wrote of herself in the masculine (though at this period she no longer cross-dressed). Given her father's desire for a male child and his disappointment that Marguerite, his only offspring, turned out to be a girl, Rachilde's assumption of a male identity as part of her lifelong quest for her father's approval appears overdetermined. Rachilde's description of her father as "un héros de roman" reveals the extent to which she also recognized the overlap between the "family romance" and its fictional reworkings.

The narrative voice of **La Tour d'amour** therefore has autobiographical overtones, and appears to weave biographical facts into a story of literary identity. At the opening of the novel, Jean accepts a posting to the lonely lighthouse because it represents "une maison." He further assumes the placement will make him master in his own home: "On était casé, son maître dans une propriété de l'état, un endroit respectable où qu'on serait tranquille." In assuming his "position" in life, Jean expects to attain a mastery sanctioned by the laws of the State, a placement that will bring respect, the destiny of both the *pater familias* and the male literary master.

The lighthouse is an exclusively male environment, and the two lighthouse keepers form bonds in a stereotypically bachelor atmosphere. They eat out of cans because there is no woman to cook for them: "Point de soupe, puisque point de cuisinière dans la maison" observes Jean. Jean's first gesture of appropriation of this new space is to place a pin-up above his bed. His companion Mathurin has the disgusting habits of throwing garbage on the floor and relieving himself against the door, as well as sleeping with his boots on and not washing his clothes.

The adoption process that takes place in this environment repeats the process Rachilde underwent both in earning her father's approval and in asserting her place in the literary tradition. As Jean sets off to take up his post, he is reminded of his new responsibilities and responds: "Bien, quoi, on sera un homme." The response, with the emphasis not on being but becoming, not a present but a future state, is the same response acted out by Rachilde. To please her father, she let herself be raised as a boy, to become a man; to please her literary peers, she became an "homme de lettres." Like both the female child Marguerite and the apprentice writer Rachilde, Jean Maleux, the "malheureux," finds that earning approval will not be the matter of course he had assumed. Having nearly drowned in reaching the lighthouse, Jean feels he has earned a warm reception: "rapport à mon entrée dans cette maison, la mienne un peu, je me croyais des droits à une bienvenue plus cordiale." Rachilde's entry into the world was no doubt greeted with the same indifference by her father; she certainly received the message as a young child that, as a girl, she was not entitled to a warm reception into the family. Like Rachilde before her father, Jean faces the cold indifference of Mathurin, who goes to bed without offering either a glass of rum or a word of advice, leaving the exhausted Jean the first night shift. Mathurin's indifference extends to the point that he duplicates Jean's work as though he were not even there. Jean thinks him a brute, but he no more renounces his intentions of overcoming the initial rejection, together with Mathurin's more explicit "anxiety of influence" that Jean will betray him, than Rachilde abandoned her plans to earn her father's approval and become a writer.

Lest there be any doubt, the masculinity of this "home" is underscored by the obviously phallic symbolism of the lighthouse itself. On first catching sight of it, Jean is impressed by its size: "Juché sur une roche où on ne devait pas pouvoir mettre les pieds, jadis, il tenait par miracle, si gros, si long, qu'on se sentait de l'orgueil pour la force de l'homme qui l'avait conçu." Its aspirations to transcendent signification lead to divine rivalry:

> Le phare se dressait, énorme, tendu comme une menace vers les cieux, s'érigeait, colossal, dans la direction de cette gueule d'ombre, de cette noire fêlure de la clarté céleste, car il y était attiré par le suprême devoir d'être aussi grand que Dieu.

This lighthouse, standing on a rock abandoned by God, is named Ar-Men, which means "on the rock" in Breton, its very name hinting at the incantation ("amen: ainsi soit-il") our men Jean and Mathurin implicitly intone as they reaffirm its power.

If the lighthouse is "Lui," its counterpart, "Elle," is the sea, the eternal feminine, the dangerous, engulfing female element kept in check by "MM. les ingénieurs" and the massive power of the lighthouse. The sea, source of darkness and death, is constantly compared to female figures. The waves are whores with green thighs in undulating waves of silk teasing the men imprisoned in the lighthouse, furies screaming and frothing at the mouth and biting at the lighthouse, and most especially suffocating mothers: "on leur confie sa destinée, et elles vous noient entre leurs seins mouvants."

Along with the valorization of the paternal, then, there is a corresponding rejection of the maternal. Rachilde bitterly acknowledged the disappointment she experienced in maternal relationships in *Pourquoi je ne suis pas féministe:*

> Je n'ai jamais eu confiance dans les femmes, l'éternel féminin m'ayant trompé d'abord sous le masque maternel et je n'ai pas plus confiance en moi. J'ai toujours regretté de ne pas être un homme, non point que je prise davantage l'autre moitié de l'humanité mais parce qu'obligée, par devoir ou par goût, de vivre comme un homme, de porter seule tout le plus lourd du fardeau de la vie pendant ma jeunesse, il eût été préférable d'en avoir au moins les privilèges sinon les apparences.

This account of maternal failure, written with hindsight when Rachilde was 68 years old, disingenuously fuses two situations from her youth: her childhood, when the burden was not that of material security, but of psychic survival in the face of a distant father and a mentally unstable mother who left her "with no confidence" in herself; and her early writing career, when the burden was to survive as a writer in spite of the lack of literary foremothers who, like her own biological mother, failed to provide for her, leaving her to "live like a man," a male author seeking the approval of a patriarchal male tradition.

Choosing not to take shore leaves, Jean rejects the sea and the feminine in order to earn Mathurin's respect and become a man. Jean is unable to completely repress the feminine, however. Just as the salt water seeps into every crevice of the lighthouse, Jean is haunted by images of women, from the ghostly feminine appearance of Mathurin and the eerie voice of a siren, to dreams of a former companion, Zuléma, which prove dangerous distractions from his duty. His relationships with women become the stuff of nostalgia and dream. Particularly in his fantasized recollections of Zuléma, the repressed feminine returns with uncanny echoes in the refrain to a series of comparisons: "comme les chats!" The slang meaning reinscribes the repressed knowledge of the mother's genitals and of sexual difference, echoed in the other uncanny manifestations of the feminine in the lighthouse.

Jean attempts to control these troubling irruptions by seeking a legitimate wife, but after a disappointing brief affair with a young girl named Marie, who has the maternal promise of a Madonna, but the sexual nature of a Magdalene, Jean begins to share Mathurin's perspective that the only good woman is a dead one. These are the only ones who will not deceive, the French word for this being "tromper," the very word Rachilde used to describe the failure of the eternal feminine behind the maternal mask.

Jean's disappointment at his own failure to control the dangerous feminine element by taming it through marriage fuels his hostility towards women. His disappointment turns to rage when the precarious sense of masculine identity so carefully constructed is challenged by a confrontation with a corpse. Mathurin has preserved the head of a drowned woman, which Jean finally discovers hidden in the lighthouse. Jean sees the head floating in a jar as though looking at an "étroit miroir de verre," and is horrified to discover not the illusory but satisfying image of a coherent—and male—identity, but "une autre tête que la [sienne] qui [le] regardait!" Expecting to see a man in the mirror, he instead sees a woman, "un jeune visage de femme contemplant la mer de ses yeux pleins de larmes . . ."

This confrontation with unacceptable reality culminates in an act of violence on his next shore leave. Drunk and still burning from Marie's rejection, Jean is leaving a bar in a dark alley, when a woman accosts him, calling him "petit homme," and throwing herself upon him in an octopus-like embrace. Jean stabs her with his knife, then declares "Ben, quoi? J'ai tué la mer." He claims to have killed the sea, but both through the symbolic associations of the sea itself, and through the homonym, in French, of "mer" (sea) and "mère" (mother), his rage and apparent triumph are also over that other feminine element, the maternal.

This cathartic act of erasure is not the end of the story, however, either literally or figuratively. Mathurin eventually dies, and Jean takes over as head keeper of the lighthouse, carrying on the tradition set by his adopted father and vowing never to set foot on land again. But there is one important digression from Mathurin's footsteps. The older man's identification with the phallic lighthouse had led to cultural sterility: Mathurin had *forgotten* how to read and write. Fearing the same fate, Jean has written his own account of events, creating the book the reader holds. The act is one of disloyalty, as it reveals the sordid details of a story Jean was resolved never to tell, but it remains the only protection against losing access to the symbolic code of language.

Rachilde, too, is "disloyal to civilization," inscribing the story of her paternal identification, her rage at the dis-

appointment of the feminine, and her struggle as a woman to become part of a literary family. Like Jean, who "knows neither mother nor grandmother," Rachilde knew no literary foremothers. Her education had been unsupervised, with the result that she educated herself by reading in her grandfather's library. This was liberating in the sense that she had access to Voltaire and Sade and others who developed her critical spirit, but it left her ignorant of the existence of women writers. Since Rachilde grew up at the end of the Second Empire, before the educational reforms of the Third Republic imposed a standard education for all, there was no formal education to fill the lacuna or impose an awareness of tradition. The loi Camille Sée, which provided for *lycées* and *collèges* for girls, was enacted in 1880, the year Rachilde turned twenty. She thus narrowly missed the shaping forces that formal education, for better or worse, would bring. Thus, in order to reconcile herself to a father who neglected his "métier de père" and a male literary tradition that excluded her, Rachilde rejects the disappointing feminine and forges an adoptive identification with the phallic in an attempt to speak against her culturally prescribed silence.

Like Jean, who wants Mathurin to "authorize" his marriage, Rachilde seeks an impossible reconciliation as a woman writer between the "madwoman" of female identity in the sea and the "père-version" she must confront in her adopted family in the lighthouse. Her example shows that the assumption of a male identity is far more than a simplistic imitation of father figures for women writers. In the fin-de-siècle period, after the collapse of realism with its constricting codes of representation, imaginative inscriptions of women's authorial anxiety begin to emerge. *La Tour d'amour* offers one such example, and challenges the reader to see a more complex process at work in the ways women writers picked up the pen in nineteenth-century France.

Renee A. Kingcaid (essay date 1992)

SOURCE: "The Epithalamic Horror: Displacement in Rachilde," in *Neurosis and Narrative: The Decadent Short Fiction of Proust, Lorrain, and Rachilde,* Southern Illinois University Press, 1992, pp. 111-44.

[*In the following essay, Kingcaid argues that the world of Rachilde's literary works is symbolic of the functions of women's bodies, especially the female reproductive system.*]

To be a woman writer at the turn of the century, Rachilde maintained, was to assume an unenviable personality. Rachilde's preface to her 1888 *Madame Adonis* assures that the "woman of letters" commits herself to "a god-awful career, the most god-awful career possible." Engaged in by women, this career "is immoral, meaning that it ruins one good marriage in twenty, produces illegitimate children under the specious pretext of excess cerebral activity, leads to unnatural vices for the same reason . . . disrupts the harmony of the household, stains the fingers, and bugs the hell out of magazine publishers."

Rachilde wrote this preface to counter a personal attack by the press. It seems that the author of *Monsieur Vénus,* whose masculine garb and provocative novels had already earned her considerable notoriety, had actually slapped a journalist, producing cries of outrage against her lack of feminine decorum. If she lacks feminine decorum, Rachilde responds, this is because she was either not enough, or too much, of a woman to abide by conventional notions of gender: "So I am a dog of letters," the preface continues, "to my great regret, an hysteric of letters, and lest one think I merit neither this excessive honor nor this indignity . . . I am an androgyne of letters."

The experience of the female body underlies Rachilde's fiction in the same way it does the preface to *Madame Adonis.* For a woman, the preface suggests, writing is a corporeal experience: it stains the fingers, produces bastard "children," ruins the sexual relationship between husband and wife. Moreover, it is physically demanding and can result in physical damage:

> It takes on average one year to write a good novel, six months to write a passable one, three months to write a bad one . . . those who write them in a month and a half, like my fellow women writers, belong to the category of hysterics. . . . During the different honeymoons of the *authoress* with her novel, she no longer converses, she takes on the air of a constipated hen, no longer combs her hair, horrible detail, has indigestion and nightmares, or else she scratches her lover.

This description is all the more apt for its representation of Rachilde's own writing habits, which recall the *condition seconde* theory of hysteria. Cranking out her annual novel in a thirty-day frenzy of writing, Rachilde impressed her friend Paul Léautaud as a woman possessed, as one of those writers "whose literary talent comes chiefly from a type of instinct, from an impulsive force that makes them write in a sort of delirium" (qtd. in Dauphiné, *Rachilde*). Clearly the urgency of her writing places her in her own "category of hysterics," all the more so that the thirty-day writing cycle is a lunar or menstrual cycle as well. Further bodily effects may result from the finished product of the woman writer. Because the woman of letters writes from what she knows, Rachilde's preface assures, "unsavory rumors are expelled from the shadows, [and] the vindictive woman always uses them to inform Paul that Caroline is cheating on him, to which Jacques . . . is obliged to respond by a duel to the death."

Claude Dauphiné gives the role of the body its due in Rachilde's life and career. Dauphiné attributes a hysterical paralysis that Rachilde suffered at the start of her career in the early 1880s to a libido at war with itself. Caught between the sexual aberrations she was describing in her works, the bourgeois respectability (despite the male garb) of her personal life as a young woman living alone in Paris, and the amorous attention being paid her by Catulle Mendés, Rachilde "had clearly what we would call a nervous breakdown that resulted in a temporary paralysis of her legs." It was only after a retreat from Paris to her native Périgord that Rachilde reconciled these competing expressions of desire. Her compromise solution is found, once again, in the preface to *Madame Adonis,* which announces a defiant justification of Rachilde's works by "life": "I wrote some stories.—They are hardly edifying. In that they resemble life. That is even the only contact that they have with life, it seems to me." Her books themselves, conduits of desire, are in turn desirable objects: they sell and people read them, since "all the critics in the world do not prevent an author from being read if the public likes that author."

The author-public relationship as Rachilde defines it carries strong overtones of promiscuity. Rachilde brags in her defense that "ten thousand readers" can read her without knowing her, as opposed to the handful of journalists who know and critique her personally but who do not read her. This defense recalls the reasons Rachilde had given earlier in her argument for why impecunious women may choose to become writers; it is an alternative to forthrightly selling one's body for cash or, only slightly better, for marriage:

> General rule: one is wrong to be a woman of letters.
> There is always something better to do.
> For some, prostitution, society's hygiene.
> For others, a husband.

In *Writing and the Body,* Gabriel Josipovici relates the sense of impotence attaching to language as expression of the body in literature. The body is seen as a discourse opposed to writing; it is that which cannot be said in words. Thus Josipovici asks, "Why this sense of a word that would make all the difference? Why this feeling that words are incapable of expressing the emotions of the body? Why this desire to write and the simultaneous sense that the desire has only to surface to be frustrated?"

The inadequacy of words to express the lived existence of the body opposes the very premise of Freud's "talking cure" at the same time that it acknowledges with him the semiotics of the hysterical body. The long-running antagonism between Freud and Dora can be understood as an opposition of this rational discourse to the prerational or irrational discourse of the body. It is, in other words, an antagonism between secondary and primary processes. Fresh from the insights of *The Interpretation of Dreams,* Freud made it a point of honor in the Dora case to interpret as figurative the least gesture, the least refusal, the least dream image shared by his often reticent patient. Indeed, as he states in his preface to the case, its title was originally "Dreams and Hysteria," for it seemed to me particularly well-adapted for showing how dream-interpretation is woven into the history of a treatment and how it can become a means of filling in amnesias and elucidating symptoms. . . . I must once more insist . . . that a thorough investigation of the problems of dreams is an indispensable prerequisite for any comprehension of the mental processes in hysteria and the other psychoneuroses.

As is well known, Freud's interpretations in the case are so aggressively couched in a language of triumph that Dora's *nos* are unhesitatingly understood as yesses and her objections routinely and authoritatively dismissed as concessions made by her unconscious to the principles of the analysis. Thus Freud explains:

> The "No" uttered by a patient after a repressed thought has been presented to his conscious perception for the first time does no more than register the existence of a repression and its severity; it acts, as it were, as a gauge of the repression's strength. If this "No," instead of being regarded as the expression of an impartial judgment (of which, indeed, the patient is incapable), is ignored, and if work is continued, the first evidence soon begins to appear that in such a case "No" signifies the desired "Yes."

The *yes,* of course, is desired by the analyst, who needs it to confirm the accuracy of his theories of repression and transference. If, however, Freud has to pronounce his treatment of Dora unsuccessful and call her case study a "fragment," it is a failure not only because, as he says, he failed to recognize the impact of transference on the analysis. The analysis also fails because Dora refuses to give up her privileges as a female body. She comes and goes as she pleases; she keeps to her own rituals of place and time; she is attuned to the sexual processes in ways that mystify Freud. As numerous critics have pointed out, Dora is smart enough to figure out the use the men around her (including Freud) have devised for her body: she is to be given to Herr K. in place of Frau K. so that her father and Frau K. can peacefully continue their liaison.

Consequently, the Dora case reveals nothing so much as Freud's attempts to make his (rational) language keep up with the (prerational) physical body as Dora knows and lives it. Having asserted in the *Studies on Hysteria* the happy coincidence between narrative coherence and the cure of the troubled psyche, Freud is obliged in his famous case study to keep changing the plot: first Dora is adjudged to be in love with Herr K., then with her father, then with Frau K., then with her childhood self, and finally, as Freud allows in his discussion of transference, with Freud himself. Dora's body, in other words, *chooses* hysteria by refusing the entrapment into language that Freud's scientific positivism would propose as its cure. *She* will choose whom *she* will love; in the detective game she plays with Freud, she changes her secrets so often and so skillfully that the louder

Freud's claim to understand her, the more hollow that claim rings out.

Dora abruptly ends her analysis by physically removing herself from the field: she stops coming to see Freud. She thereby asserts the superiority of her body, free of the snares of analytic discourse: Freud has not *pronounced* her cured. She reappears at the very end of the study, however; many years have passed since Freud has last seen her and she has married. In one sense, then, the men—Freud, Herr K., and Dora's father—have triumphed: Dora has ultimately submitted to the demand that she marry. The fact of the marriage makes Dora a "whole" body, consistent with Freud's demand that the body acquiesce to sexual gratification in order to be considered "healthy." That refrain is by now a familiar one: "I should without question consider a person hysterical in whom an occasion for sexual excitement elicited feelings that were preponderantly or exclusively unpleasurable".

But there is no word from Dora on this arrangement, second best in the eyes of the men, but an arrangement nevertheless. It is precisely Dora's silence, however, that preserves her bodily autonomy: no one is to know for sure whether her acceptance of the marital relationship was the right "answer" to the "hysteria" of her initial refusals. The plethora of commentaries on Dora's case are in large part grounded in this silence, in this suspension of the mystery of the body. Octave Mannoni cleverly and revealingly imagines Dora clinging to hysteria as an experience lived by the physical body opposed to the body of rational or scientific commentaries. The first chapter of Mannoni's *Fictions freudiennes* has an outraged Dora responding to her reading of Freud's "Fragment of an Analysis" in a letter to Frau K.:

> You see, if I wrote to the *Monatschrift* to give *my* version (it would be justified from a *scientific* point of view that I should have my say as well), in the first place they wouldn't publish it, and second they would surely find in it the proof that I am an hysteric. I might very well be an hysteric; what I particularly don't like is that they would say it's not up to me to judge! It's possible that I suffer from a "minor hysteria." So what? You see, up till now they had no use for hysteria. It had to have some purpose. Now that's done: now hysteria is popular, it's a research topic for professors. Do you think that makes things any better?

That the female body is *by nature* a hysterical body is one of the unexamined assumptions of Simone de Beauvoir's classic work on the feminine experience, *The Second Sex*. Launching the first salvos in the feminist attack on Freud, de Beauvoir objects to the psychoanalytic definition that understands female sexuality as a deviation from the male. "Freud never showed much concern with the destiny of woman," she observes correctly; "it is clear that he simply adapted his account from that of the destiny of man, with slight modifications." Accordingly, for de Beauvoir the processes of libidinal reinvestment required by woman's "two distinct erotic systems" (the clitoral and the vaginal) is an open invitation to dysfunction: "There is only one genital stage for man [the phallic], but there are two for woman; she runs a much greater risk of not reaching the end of her sexual evolution, of remaining at the infantile stage and thus of developing neuroses."

While de Beauvoir purports to disabuse her readers of Freud's view of woman, which she judges to be reductive and reifying, she nevertheless shows herself to be quite taken with the neurotic manifestations of female sexual development gone awry. It is not function but dysfunction that interests de Beauvoir; while *The Second Sex* treats the hysterical body as an explainable, changeable, product of culture, that body within the work still resists language in the way that Dora resisted Freud. Irrecuperable by language, the ambiguities of the body are the unrecognized conditions for meaning in *The Second Sex*. The missing body undermines de Beauvoir's social argument and reimposes the structure of hysteria on a discourse intended to conform in spirit and in style with rational (male) scientific discourse.

De Beauvoir fills her landmark essay with case studies of women chronically unable to reconcile their experience of themselves with their experience of their bodies. She quotes, for instance, Isadora Duncan's account of her first sexual experience in *My Life*:

> I, too, was aroused and dizzy, while an irresistible longing to press him closer and closer surged in me, until one night, losing all control and falling into a fury, he carried me to the sofa. Frightened but ecstatic and crying out in pain, I was initiated into the act of love. I confess that my first impressions were a horrible fright and an atrocious pain, as if someone had torn out several of my teeth at once; but a great pity for what he seemed to be suffering prevented me from running away from what was at first sheer mutilation and torture. . . . Next day what was at that time no more than a painful experience for me continued amidst my martyred cries and tears. I felt as if I were being mangled. (Qtd. in de Beauvoir)

Though literary intent informs much of this overwritten description, de Beauvoir presents it quite literally as evidence of the crisis of sexual union, "even when quite voluntary." For more pedestrian examples, she borrows amply from the files of the psychoanalyst Wilhelm Stekel to illustrate the drama of the female body, as in this example of an unhappy bride-to-be:

> When Stekel met her, she suffered from vomiting, took morphine every evening, flew into rages, refused to bathe, took her meals in bed, remained shut up in her room. She was engaged and claimed to be deeply in love with her fiancé. She admitted to Stekel that she had given herself to him. . . . Later, she said that she had had no pleasure in the act: that she now recalled his kisses with

repugnance and that is the source of her vomiting. It was discovered that in fact she had given herself to him to punish her mother, whom she did not feel loved her enough: as a child, she used to spy upon her parents at night for fear that they would give her a brother or sister; she adored her mother. "And now she was to get married, leave her father's house, abandon her parents' bedroom? it was impossible." She gained weight, scratched and mutilated her hands, fell stupid, fell ill, tried to offend her fiancé in every possible way. The doctor cured her but she begged her mother to call off the marriage: "She wanted to stay at home forever, to stay a child." Her mother insisted that she marry. A week before her wedding day they found her dead in her bed: she had shot herself.

For de Beauvoir the female body is hysterical to the measure that it is discursive. If the female body is radically different from the male, it is so because the female gives bodily expression to the hesitations and conflicts of the psyche or, to be more consistent with de Beauvoir's ontological vocabulary, to the ambiguities inherent in woman's sense of her being-in-the-world. The reluctant fiancée engaged in self-destructive behavior, the wife who turns frigid to punish a husband's infidelity, the mother-to-be experiencing morning sickness, or the woman-child suffering the pain of her first menstrual period—all these unfortunates who populate de Beauvoir's essay are acting in accordance with Freud's theory of hysteria. In other words, the hysterical body wills and wills not, knows and yet does not know. The psychic disorders traceable to the onset of menstruation express the girl's refusal of womanhood even as she ardently desires to leave behind the world of childhood; the adolescent who provokes and then flees men's advances both fears and longs for sexual experience; the wife whose frigidity originates in a disappointing wedding night wishes and does not wish to accept the reality of her married state.

Sexuality is always a crisis for the women of *The Second Sex*. In de Beauvoir's view, the forces of nature that assure the perpetuation of the species guarantee that woman's body is never wholly and completely her own. "Woman, like man," writes de Beauvoir, "*is* her body; but her body is something other than herself." "From puberty to menopause woman is the theater of a play that unfolds within her and in which she is not personally concerned." For most of her life, woman in de Beauvoir's view remains a stranger to the obscure forces of nature churning and burning within her.

It is hardly contemporary, and more than a little disheartening, to consider with de Beauvoir that the physical ailments accompanying the female reproductive cycle demonstrate "the revolt of the organism against the invading species." In fact, feminism has battled mightily to have the physical discomforts occasioned by the female reproductive cycle—from menstrual cramps to morning sickness to postpartum depression—recognized by the medical community as biologically "real" and not hysterically "made-up" phenomena. To take but the latter example, Carol Dix points out in *The New Mother Syndrome* that postpartum depression was considered by the medical profession as simply the manifestation of latent neurosis in new mothers rather than as a disorder with biochemical as well as psychical components. Only in 1984, she notes, did the *Journal of the American Medical Association* report that postpartum depression had not been included in the computer classifications of the *Diagnostic and Statistical Manual of Mental Disorders*.

Attempting to repudiate Freud, *The Second Sex* in fact follows his lead from hysteria to rational discourse. Hysteria must be "trappable" by language for de Beauvoir in much the same way as it must be for Freud. De Beauvoir's ability to tolerate the antithetical nature of hysteria—its will and will not—is countered by her desire to avoid impugning the existentialist values of choice and becoming that *The Second Sex* spells out for both men and women. Hysteria as a simultaneous willing and unwilling cannot be carried too far in de Beauvoir, for fear of giving the lie to the existentialist quest. For de Beauvoir, psychoanalysis is wrong because it is determinist; as she states in *The Second Sex,* "Replacing value with authority, choice with drive, psychoanalysis offers an *Ersatz,* a substitute, for morality—the concept of normality." Therefore, women must not be shown to be entirely determined by authority, inaccessible unconscious pulsations and the norm of standard behavior; rather, they must, and this is de Beauvoir's contention, have been forced into their corners by society's preconceptions of their place. *Hysteria* is limited to mean only the way in which woman's body translates the psychical into the physical; it is not irremediable. Given optimum social and economic conditions, even the hysterical woman will eventually conquer her right to her own choices and desires. The hysteric's inability to choose between competing desires is not an inborn trait of womanhood; it is for de Beauvoir a double bind imposed on women by a patriarchal society obsessed with interpreting women's bodies from the cultural (ad)vantage point of the male.

Yet hysteria in *The Second Sex* continues to oppose language to the body as two separate registers of semiotic experience. De Beauvoir's silent debt to Freud belies her attempts to comprehend woman's body fully within a superior, authoritarian discourse. Something important remains not said—and this is the body itself. De Beauvoir's own female body is repressed in the work to become the site of the unsayable; the authoritarian assertions "I have seen," "I have read," and "I have known" by which she introduces her examples and validates her conclusions limit her presence in the work strictly to that of a witness. This is intentional; she means to testify to the general experience of womankind. But it is indeed curious that de Beauvoir is never in her own right a corporeal source of female experience. Unlike Freud, who uses a number of his own dreams to buttress *The Interpretation of Dreams,* de

Beauvoir never once counts herself as one of the women in *The Second Sex*. As Mary Evans suggests in *Simone de Beauvoir: A Feminist Mandarin,*

> de Beauvoir's entry into feminism—or at any rate the arousal in her of something approaching a consciousness of the specificity of the female condition—occurred in a cerebral way that becomes apparent in the early pages of *The Second Sex*. Having experienced no disadvantages or difficulties in her own life that she could relate to her own sex, and having received a considerable amount of help and support from a man in her chosen vocation, de Beauvoir's attitude to women suggests a lack of engagement with and experience of the subjectivity of femininity.

Imposing a cerebral distance between her own body, held in reserve outside the limits of her discourse, and the hysterical female body that she describes but does not inhabit, de Beauvoir opposes the willed coherence of her discourse to the radical incoherence of the hysterical body she takes as her subject. Again, Evans notes de Beauvoir's refusal of feminine experience lived within a female body:

> [De Beauvoir's] uncritical belief in what she describes as rationality, her negation and denial of various forms of female experience, and her tacit assumption that paid work and contraception are the two keys to the absolute freedom of womankind, all suggest a set of values that place a major importance on living like a childless, rather singular, employed man. Indeed, a reading of *A Very Easy Death* and de Beauvoir's novels could lead to the conclusion that de Beauvoir's message to her readers is dominated by her view that to live like a traditional woman is to invite unhappiness—far better to live like a traditional man.

Determining the extent to which the female body does or does not "return" in de Beauvoir's novels, and particularly in her journals, exceeds the range of the present discussion. What is most useful for Rachilde in *The Second Sex* is the light it shines retrospectively on the novelist's perception of hysteria and the body. Where de Beauvoir would repress hysteria (like Freud) by describing it, Rachilde understands (like Dora) that hysteria is a discourse that must be allowed its say. As the (primary process) incoherence that challenges (secondary process) logic, hysteria is resolutely the domain of the feminine.

Rachilde's codes of feminine hysteria oppose the male to the female not as model to incomplete (castrated) copy but as sign systems whose aesthetic coherence actually depends on their relationship to the female, ultimately maternal, body. For Rachilde as for de Beauvoir, the female body is prey to alienating forces, to the debilitating work of nature that underlies and undermines the conventional appearance of the blushing bride or the bourgeois housewife. Rachilde, however, fully accepts this body as one that both wills and wills not. Under the pressure of the rational discourse by which the body would make contact with the world, metonymy allows Rachilde to preserve the unsayability of the body (its opposition to discourse as a separate register of experience) and to sublimate the internal divisions of that body into the devices of narrative. By an all-encompassing process of displacement, the universe in Rachilde becomes a vast metonymy for the female reproductive functions, bodily functions that are the very source of desire and meaning.

DESCRIPTION AND DISPLACEMENT: "*THE HARVESTS OF SODOM*" AND "*THE MORTIS*"

Rachilde claimed to prefer **Monsieur Vénus** to all her other novels. In the preface to **Madame Adonis,** she calls it a "work that I do not disavow and that I prefer to my other works, since mothers always prefer their hump-backed sons to their upright ones." The breathless quality of **Monsieur Vénus** is created by a profusion of loosely motivated episodes and a constant switching of genders through which the author drives home the perversity of Raoule de Vénérande's masculine love for the feminized Jacques Silvert.

The opening pages of **Monsieur Vénus** thus furnish a splendid example of the workings of displacement in Rachilde. As Raoule de Vénérande enters the dingy attic apartment of the florist Marie Silvert, her senses are assailed simultaneously by the unpleasant smell of apples cooking on the stove and by the sight of the exceptionally beautiful Jacques Silvert, half-covered by the artificial roses he is making at the single table in the room. The point of the scene is to establish as rapidly as possible the intense and contradictory passion Raoule is about to conceive for the young Jacques. The onset of this passion is marked, however, not by Raoule's responses to Jacques himself but by the changes in her response to the odor of the apples. At the beginning, she is categorical: "No odor was more repulsive to her than that of apples"; five pages later, however, "Mlle de Vénérande imagined that she could perhaps eat one of those apples without too much disgust".

The connection between the florist and the apples is metonymic in nature. It is based on the golden reddishness of the silken chest hairs alluringly displayed beneath Jacques's half-open shirt. The color that he shares with the apples forms the implicit connection between him and the (classically forbidden) fruit. This displacement of Raoule's pleasure from Silvert's body onto the apples is more than just a clever artistic device allowing Rachilde to engage in a steamy description of the first moments of an unusual passion. The combination of disgust and pleasure with which Raoule reacts to the apples, the "without too much disgust" with which she tempers her desire to taste them, announce the sexual ambiguity that will characterize her future relationship with Jacques: she will be the man, he will be the mistress, and their affair (whose consummation remains in doubt throughout the novel) will be governed by a single

"thought in common: the destruction of their sex" ("pensée commune: la destruction de leur sexe").

The displacement of Raoule's pleasure/disgust from Jacques to the apples preserves the ambiguities of female desire without violating its reserve. Because Raoule is a divided body, because neither attraction nor repulsion is a more "true" sexual response in hysteria, Rachilde preserves in this scene the unsayability of the hysterical body. If that body's *yes* and *no* are equivalent, there is no way to express the body in rational discourse based on the ability to distinguish, precisely, between *yes* and *no*, between that which is and that which is not. Rachilde makes this unsayability, this inability to distinguish, a determinant of the plot. Unlike the changing plot of the Dora case, which can be read as a constant frustration for Freud, Rachilde's plot is a mise-en-scène of her characters' sexual ambiguities. Rachilde is free, as it were, to keep tossing the coin between the competing couples of desire and disgust, male and female. Each successive chapter of **Monsieur Vénus** is based on whichever side of the coin turns up: Raoule as desiring male or disgusted female, Jacques as desiring female or disgusted male, and so on. It is for this reason, perhaps, that Maurice Barrès suggests so enthusiastically in his preface to the novel that "[Rachilde's] creations have a whiff of death about them". When Jacques is killed in a duel arranged by Raoule, it is impossible to determine which combination of male/female traits has been eliminated. The remaining complementary body, Raoule's, is thus properly left unsayable, corresponding to Rachilde's vague hint in the closing pages that Raoule's body has finally found its (necrophiliac) match in this corpse of indeterminate sexuality.

A similar process of metonymy in the short story **"The Harvests of Sodom" ("Les vendanges de Sodome"),** from the 1894 **Demon of Absurdity (Démon de l'absurde),** functions again both as stylistic device and as figuration of the unsayable female body. In this story, the body is represented only to be destroyed. Metonymy both announces this process of physical destruction and introduces the displacement of the female reproductive processes onto the world beyond the body that characterizes description and plot in much of Rachilde's short fiction. Moreover, the physical destruction of the female body is presented in this story as its very condition of meaning.

The plot of the story is relatively simple. The males of Sodom leave the city early in the morning to begin the grape harvest, the major agricultural task to which they devote their entire year's worth of saved-up physical energy. During their midday siesta, the men are furtively joined by a naked woman, who eats all the grapes from the basket of the youngest and most comely of the males, Sinéus, and then stretches out next to him in a none-too-subtle attempt at seduction. Her advances to Sinéus, however, awaken the entire group, who, furious at her attempts to divert their virile forces from the harvest, stone her to death. In her death agony, the woman crawls into the vat in which the men have been stomping the grapes: it is in her description of this moment that Rachilde pulls out the stops on metonymy:

> She made herself small, very small, crawled, humbly serpentine, slipped into the vat where the must was fermenting, and, pulling around herself heaps of crushed grapes, she remained inert, *adding to the blood of the grapes all the exquisite wine of her veins*. While she was still in agony, they climbed down into the barrel and *trampled her underfoot*, while there sprang *from the prodigious black fruits that seemed like so many rolling eyes,* a gaze of supreme malediction. (my emphasis)

The annihilation of the woman's body is her commingling with the forces of nature and the earth. Her blood is now wine, the wine is her blood, the grapes the men stomp by stomping her stare back at them with the curse reflected in her eyes. From the men's point of view, the annihilation of the female body is only to the good: they so consecrate their entire physical forces to the harvest that all women have long been banished from the city. The destruction of the woman's body at the end of the story responds to this unanimous repudiation of female desire:

> They all surrounded the woman. She was one of these wanderers, skulking around in search of love, that the wise men of Sodom had banished from their city. In a just and formidable anger, certain men of God had joined together to rid themselves of these demented women, who were haunted from dusk till dawn by hankerings after immoral pleasures. Sentencing themselves virilely to several years of chastity so as not to waste their best energies during the harvest on these abysses of sensual pleasure that were the daughters of Sodom, keeping only mothers in labor and old women, they had banished even their wives, even their sisters.

Yet by their entry into nature at the moment of the woman's death, female desire and the female body itself circumvent the interdiction imposed by the men. As Rachilde displaces desire from the body onto the surrounding natural environment, her model and vocabulary are the specifically female ones of the reproductive processes. Her description of the grapevines on the morning of the harvest at the beginning of the story both announces the future commingling of the wine and the woman's body and participates in an elaborately overdone metaphor of rampant sexuality, gestation, and birth.

> At this dawn, the earth was steaming like a vat filled with an infernal must, and the vine, in the center of the immense plain, gleamed red under an already ferocious rising sun, a purple sun coiffed with glowing embers that began already to ferment the enormous clusters whose grapes, supernaturally large, took on the reflections of rolling eyes, sprung completely black from their

orbits. . . . Like an overly fertile beast, who must not be held down by any restraint in the painful hours of her multiple births, [the vine] rolled against the earth in frightful convulsions, throwing out furious bursts of garlands, imploring arms raised toward the sun, seeming both to suffer and to be ecstatic with a guilty yet heavenly joy, while her overheated marrow overflowed from her, flooding her with a dew of thick tears. She gave birth anywhere she could to these prodigious fruits of a shining, velvety brown, mysterious blossoming of the mortal bitumen, which they recalled by their sooty hue, their shade of satanic sugar distilled in the violence of a volcano.

The description introduces to the story the unsettling ambiguity toward sexuality that makes up the "epithalamic horror," or the desire and fear of coupling in Rachilde. The displacements effected by her descriptive passages determine her plot: the result of the woman's death is that the men of Sodom, refreshing themselves with deep draughts of the wine into which she has been crushed, turn to each other in the first orgy of homosexual activity that would give their town its irrevocable notoriety. Thus, even as the story moves from a kind of universal parturition to the sterility of homosexual copulation, desire undoes the men's will to chastity by the very agent that the refusal of desire was intended to serve: the wine, which begins and ends as a metonymy of the female body.

In this way, the unsayable body becomes the condition of meaning. The "Sodom" of the title is not the Sodom of the reader's expectation *until* the elaborate physical and semiotic displacements of the story have been completed. It is only after the men drink the woman/wine that they invent homosexuality. Displaced from the city, then, woman inflicts her sexuality on nature and thus denatures desire among the men who once thought to disown her.

Rachilde repeats some of this descriptive technique, and much of this sexual displacement, in "The *Mortis,*" a short story from the 1900 collection *Stories (Contes et nouvelles)*. In this story, the female body appears not only in the feminized description of nature but also within the contradictions between the surface appearance of things and the seething world beneath them that strongly recall the alienation of woman from her body that is one of de Beauvoir's most frequently sounded themes.

"The *Mortis*" begins in similar fashion to **"The Harvests of Sodom."** An elaborate description of the natural setting precedes the entrance of the human protagonists. In this case, there is only one protagonist, Count Sebastiani Ceccaldo-Rossi, who is not only the "last survivor of the powerful house of Ceccaldo-Rossi" ("dernier survivant de la puissante maison Ceccaldo-Rossi") but also the last survivor of the plague in fourteenth-century Florence. Tormented by hunger, the Count ventures out of the relative safety of his palace into the nightmare world of the city, overgrown now not with massively "parturient" grapevines but with monstrously reproductive roses.

There are no women in "**The *Mortis***"; they have been finished off long before, in the early days of the plague, and are alluded to only in retrospect.

> No woman walked through the city, and rummaging through the heaps of putrefying bodies in the public squares, you would not have exhumed the least little scrap of a skirt. The women had disappeared, leaving no memory of their grace. Had they left perhaps from the very beginning of the scourge? Had they been the very first to die perhaps—of fear—before the plague?

Once again the feminine has been displaced onto the natural world; female desire is metonymically described through the profusion of flowers that cover the dying city as both a raging copulation and a superimposition of beauty on corruption. The result is a grotesque reunion of contradictions, simultaneously exalting and repudiating female desire. The flowers of domestic gardens, for example, are described as passionate women escaping from their familial restraints. "Crazy about their bodies, scrambling up the iron grillwork, overflowing their bronze urns, dropping down from gilded balconies," they are among the first to participate in the universal nuptials, to "break their last ties to their patrician class to unite themselves with the vagabond [flowers] in monstrous nuptials". At the same time, however, this vast fornication has a seamy underside: the wildly rampant flowers are "on fire with forbidden perfumes, seasoned by the human compost heap" from which they take their nourishment.

Thus the silent earth seethes with sexual processes. It is, however, not only by their vocabulary that Rachilde feminizes the descriptions of the earth in this story. Her marked discordances between surface appearance and underside reality are also displacements of the absent female body, paradigmatic site of division and ambiguity.

Through a wildly overwrought and unabashedly sexual vocabulary Rachilde describes the flowers, and in particular the over-grown roses, as participants in a vast cycle of fornication and birthing. The sustained fever pitch of this prolonged description is perhaps its most remarkable quality:

> In the amorous fire of a June sky, along the still-white steps of staircases falling in ruin toward an Arno that had become almost black, [the] most savage [flowers], warriors already accustomed to obstacles, mounted the assault against the city. . . . the wind of revolt entwined branches to branches, wove garlands, hung crowns of flowers, raised arches of triumph, sang the epithalamion in the middle of the great silence of death.
>
> The roses, mouths of embers, flames of flesh, licking against the incorruptibility of the marble surfaces, splashed the long pure columns up to the very top with stains red as wine, purple as blood, and that at night, made round signs, extravasating in brown, marking the skin of the pale monuments with violet shadows, like the traces of fingers deeply inserted. The roses, on all tonalities, from saffron to the dregs of wine, from furious scarlet to the hues of the tender limbs of newborns, screamed out their deliverance. They were mouths tirelessly open, clamoring cries that one surmised without seeing. They shook, above the open graves, their heavy buds feverishly anxious to bloom, buboes filled to bursting with sap, ready to explode in spurts of pus, and the horrible threat was accomplished in torrents of inebriating odors, violent and exasperated like screams. . . .
>
> A clinging type [of rose] having penetrated the bell tower, having thrown in through the rib of an arch, the forest of its ferocious thorns, clung to the length of a rope, made it sway beneath the weight of its young heads, and when the one hundredth [rose] bloomed, full of dew, a chalice heavy with tears, the rope stiffened, shook . . . one could hear the sound of a bell: the roses were tolling the tocsin! To the fire of the amorous sky was joined the furnace of their passionate odors.

Rachilde could hardly be more explicit in her evocation of sexual processes through this insistent vocabulary of grasping and clinging, of invasion and introduction, of climaxes offered or refused, or of sensual avidity represented in the nourishment of the roses likened to newborns, their mouths constantly open for nourishment from the *boutons*—which means both "nipples" and "flower buds"—to which yet other roses are compared.

Perhaps less evident, but equally evocative of female sexuality, is the split in the passage between the surface of the scene and its interior turmoil. The surface calm, beneath which churn the independent forces of nature, suggests the alienation of woman within her own female body. Rachilde's ingenuity is to represent this division between surface and interior by a nearly impossible sensual contrast in which the wind is said to "sing the epithalamion in the middle of the great silence of death." A chanted wedding hymn, noise is equated with sexuality while silence remains associated with death; the difficult simultaneity transforms the silent surface of the printed page into the silent surface of the earth or, by extension, into the silent surface of the female body beneath which nature boils.

The result is a frenetic synaesthesia in the rest of the passage that oscillates constantly from the perceptible to the surmised, from the calm to the turbulent, from the cold indifference of death to the procreative demands of female sexuality. The best example of this synaesthetic frenzy equates hearing with sight: the newborn roses scream out their deliverance, in "cries one surmised without *seeing*" (emphasis added). What is not seen is open to question: it could be the roses, but it is more likely their cries. Finally, the roses that toll the tocsin reunite the two strains of displacement in the story: the displacement of the female body onto nature, and the displacement of sensual processes within the description of nature once it has been feminized. This climactic moment is brought about by the blossoming of the one-hundredth rose in a long chain of roses. At this point the hidden noise of the sexual body rises to the audible surface of the text: Rachilde means for the reader to hear the tocsin ringing. However, that noise is itself immediately displaced onto yet another combination of senses. The sentence that follows veers off into sight and smell and frames the entire description by the imagery it repeats from the opening phrase: "To the fire of the amorous sky was added the furnace of their passionate odors."

The ringing of the tocsin by the twined and interlacing roses announces the ultimate symptom of the neurotic repulsion-attraction complex of feminine sexuality at work in the dénouement of *Monsieur Vénus:* the conviction that sex and death are one. A commonplace in Decadent fiction, the connection between sex and death is particularly evident in much of Rachilde's work. Raoule de Vénérande, as we have seen, cannot fully indulge her ambiguous desire for Jacques until he is dead; in *Madame Adonis,* the restless libertin/libertine Marcelle Desambres (disguised as her brother Marcel) provokes her own murder at the hands of her male lover Louis, who is also the husband of her female lover, Louise. The mirror images of this novel announce a willful confusion of male and female desire, the better to repudiate sexual intercourse in a single murderous act, itself highly sexualized: Louis plunges a dagger into Marcelle/Marcel's breast. The point, once again, is not that one or the other of the poles of heterosexuality be eliminated. Rachilde's concern is instead that the unsayable body enter, however tenuously, into representation through the negation of its potential and shifting opposites.

A negative expression of desire, the sex-death complex is the entire premise of *"The Mortis."* The grotesquely "natural" couplings that celebrate sexuality as the perverse vitality poured out by the plague, the promiscuous flowers, the marriage of noise and silence, and the jarringly synaesthetic mode of Rachilde's descriptions are all part of this complex. The roses carry the brunt of the association, first by their vocabulary—their *boutons* (nipples for nourishment) are also *boubons* (buboes, or pustules of poison)—and second by their definitive role in the plot. It is exactly this confusion between nourishment and poison that finishes off the Count: having gorged himself on rose petals, he dies.

Sebastiani's extended death scene at the end of the story is characterized by elaborate metonymy and displaced sexuality. The figure of the male introduces a discordant, if fleeting, note of innocence into the plague-ridden and female-dominated nature of the story: yielding to the oppressive heat of the afternoon and falsely reassured by the absence of any other living being in the

city, the Count undoes the elaborate armor he had donned for protection and appears "naked like the divine bambino sprung from the loins of the Virgin Mary". This sudden reference to virgin birth makes it abundantly clear that Sebastiani does not fit into the monstrously procreative world that surrounds him; like Jacques Silvert in *Monsieur Vénus* or the youngest brother in **"The Harvests of Sodom,"** his innocence, perceived as such by the marauding female, seals his doom. It does not help his case that Sebastiani is maladroit in handling the one eminently masculine feature remaining to him in his unprotected state—his sword. As he raises his sword to protect his face, Rachilde imagines that the roses, "new women's heads decorating the balconies of Florence, seemed to shiver with modesty and lean over curiously". In this way their petals, which Sebastiani gathers on the tip of his sword and consumes, can literally feed him to death.

The desperate frenzy of Sebastiani's meal of roses quickly deprives him of his innocence; by the time he has tasted the first petals, he is no longer the "divine bambino" but lithe as the *couleuvre,* or serpent, that now fully belongs to this perverse Eden. Under these conditions, the female body, round and nourishing, benefits from a series of displacements onto food and drink. Their metonymies determined now by color and shape, the flourishing roses are simultaneously breast and pustule, fruit and fountain in a long stretch of indirect discourse by which Sebastiani consecrates his union with the feminized nature around him:

> Flowers, flowers, and still more flowers! . . . If lemons and oranges were lacking, there were yellow roses! If the pomegranates and the melons never ripened, there were purple roses, red roses, pink roses! And if Asti wine did not run in rivers, this year of misfortune, one could breathe its suave and sparkling foam in the delicate aroma of the very smallest white roses, whose buds cracked like nuts beneath one's teeth!

Thus the roses represent the Fatal Woman, in whose embrace is death. Yet there is one more displacement in the story. This final trick of narrative displacement in **"The Mortis"** has to do with the place of the narrator or, more accurately, with her nonplace. Most of the **"The Mortis"** is recounted in the omniscient third person. The final pages, however, which recount Sebastiani's solitary procession through the decaying city, introduce a discordantly subjective voice that solemnly pronounces of the scene, "It was very beautiful" ("C'était très beau").

The voice is clearly not Sebastiani's; he remains dissociated from the text's point of view until the moment of his sexual union with the flowers, expressed in his poisonous banquet of roses/fruits/breasts. The sudden subjective statement is repeated before the reprise of the objective description: "but along the deserted streets it was even more beautiful". The statement makes it impossible to situate clearly the narrative voice in the story. It has been displaced from its objective or omniscient center to an indeterminate margin of incoherence that can apparently change at will. Thus, if woman's *body* is, by displacement, everywhere in nature, woman's *voice*—that of the "hysteric of letters" who wrote the story—is everywhere and nowhere: it is in nature and in the city, inside and outside the earth, above and within the narration, ultimately ready to pass judgment on the perverse fecundity of the universalized female body, of which it also pronounces, "It was very beautiful."

In this way, Rachilde realizes more fully the process of meaning at work in **"The Harvests of Sodom."** Her displacements of the female body join with the displacement of the female voice to stake out in **"The *Mortis*"** a claim to discourse beyond that of either language or the body taken independently of each other. Refusing to reduce the body to language or language to the body, Rachilde asserts the privilege of hysteria as a source and condition of narrative. Epithalamic horror in Rachilde is thus not only a refusal of sex. It is also the series of displacement of female body and voice that keeps the linguistically indomitable body beyond the reach of the discourse of reason.

NO END IN SIGHT? MOTHER'S BODY AND ONE LAST FROG

Limitless displacement, we recall, is the foundation of metonymy in the Lacanian scheme. A group of three stories from Rachilde's **Stories** and **The Demon of the Absurd** center the experience of displacement on the loss of the maternal body. Each of these three stories—**"The Hermetic Chateau"** ("Le château hermétique"), **"The Tooth"** ("La dent"), and **"The Frog Killer"** ("Le tueur de grenouilles")—thus depends on the experience of the incest prohibition to initiate desire for the maternal body. In other words, the maternal body becomes desirable only when it is prohibited; indeed, it is desirable by virtue of being prohibited. For Rachilde, this condition of desire entails a shift in the nature of the displacement we have seen inflicted on the female body: if the body is banished from culture in these stories as it is in **"The Harvests of Sodom"** and **"The Mortis,"** its entry into nature is not an automatic compensation. Rather, it is the simultaneous relationship of the body to nature *and* culture that stimulates Rachilde's reflections on desire and posits the conditions of meaning in the stories.

Of the three stories, **"The Hermetic Chateau"** offers perhaps the clearest representation of the creation of desire by the incest prohibition; in this story, the maternal body, emblematic in the hermetically sealed, unapproachable castle of the title, belongs both to nature and to culture. It thus doubly alienates the desire it inspires or discourages, depending on whether it is considered from the point of view of nature—which suggests in remembrance of the primordial mother-child union that one *ought* to be able to attain it—or culture—which resolutely forbids even so much as the attempt.

Visiting in Franche-Comté, the narrator of the story resolves to visit a ruined chateau he perceives at the top of one of the surrounding peaks—despite the insistence of his hosts that the chateau does not really exist, that it is merely a mirage created by the sun at certain moments of the day. He nevertheless persuades his friend Téard to accompany him on an excursion to the chateau, which they never reach. Their journey, moreover, is fraught with mishaps: their descent from the peak is one accident after another, and they arrive at the picnic site where Madame Téard, the friend's mother, awaits them with the unhappy news that all of their provisions have been lost.

Tempted by nature and yet forbidden by law, one cannot return to the original mother-child union. So the narrator's adventure is inscribed within a series of examples of other persons longing for that undefined yet acutely felt "elsewhere" (of the mother's body) of which they have only remnants of consciousness, but where they know they would be at home. The first of these persons was, the first-person narrator recounts,

> a peasant woman of the Limousin, very poor, a bit crazy, whose principal monomania consisted of an eternal need of locomotion. She dreamed of a place where she would have been *better,* where she ought to have *always* lived, and since she had no knowledge of this place that, for all she knew, existed nowhere else than in her head, she used to repeat as an ejaculation: "Ah, how unhappy they are, those people who have no home!" (**Contes**; Rachilde's emphasis)

The second, despite her superior sanity and social status, is no less obsessed with the appeal of the enigmatic "elsewhere":

> The other, a Countess de Beaumont-Landry, was hardly crazy, but she spent days dreaming about the *house of her dreams,* and this house did not represent for her a sentimental phase of her youth: it was *really, sincerely,* a dwelling built somewhere. . . . No paintings or engravings could give her any more precise indications, but she knew that that house was *over there* and that her place, coddled society lady that she was, was laid out for her in this modest place of rest. (Rachilde's emphasis)

This sense of eternal displacement is praised by the narrator in terms that seem a displacement of Rachilde's own style; instead of Rachilde, one might now be reading Baudelaire, Verlaine, or Jean Lorrain, as her narrator inquires, "If there is the *sister soul,* whom one seeks through all the disappointments and crimes of love, could there not also be the *brother country,* without which one is not happy in life, one cannot obtain a peaceful end?" (Rachilde's emphasis). The narrator goes on to speculate that the longed-for *là-bas*—"over there," or "elsewhere"—is also the place of one's very own predestined tomb, encountered with great joy but on rare occasions. Far more frequently, it remains elusive: "Often, also, in ecstasy before this country, we see it suddenly back away, melt away, fade away. It flees from us, abandons us, and for a reason we shall never know, for undoubtedly, *it is too frightening,* we divine that we will not reach it, that this promised land will be eternally kept away from us" (Rachilde's emphasis).

As we have noted, this prospect of irrecuperable exile from the mother's body, worded as banishment from the ideal house, country, or tomb, is nearly pure Lacanian metonymy, expressing the eternally receding displacement of desire. The miragelike nature of the chateau to which the narrator aspires, however (it is seen most clearly when he is farthest from it, and it disappears as he approaches), clearly posits nature and culture as complicitous in the inspiration of desire. Culture is the only condition by which nature can be perceived, or in terms of the protagonist's quest for the maternal body, desire is desire only when it is most clearly opposed to its object by the irremediable barrier of the incest prohibition.

The incest taboo first appears in the story by the comparison of the "elsewhere" with a sister soul or a brother country; the intimacy thus implied is tempting—the narrator considers it a "natural" desire—but is it obviously limited by the cultural prohibition against desiring one's sister or brother. As the narrator's personal "elsewhere," the chateau remains out of reach for exactly the same reason; the incest prohibition is that "too frightening reason" imposed by culture, which renders his attempted return to the mother's body not only impossible but both pleasing (because "natural") and horrible (because forbidden) to contemplate. Thus the experience of the chateau is a paradoxically "real chimera"; the oxymoron expresses the impossibility of return to the original object of desire, experienced and lost before the advent of any language that could have preserved it as integral and unambiguous: "And here is what I want to relate *in all sincerity,*" he writes, "about one of these chimerical countries that I *in all reality* found along my route" (Rachilde's emphasis).

The foregone impossibility of the return condemns the narrator to the wandering and constant deviations that are not only the plot of the story (the impossibility of reaching the chateau) but, once again, part and parcel of Rachilde's descriptions. The chateau is said to be one with the rock from which it looms; its imposing, unconstructed aspect contrasts sharply with the cultivated countryside before it; it opposes the picture-postcard Swiss village complete with its "unpretentious bell tower, rounded off like an aspergillum, and the vineyard, with its smattering of peasants in smocks and women in bright skirts." Constructed and unconstructed, natural and yet a fact of culture, the chateau, like the mother's body, resists all attempts to penetrate it. The narrator's urgent desire to "enter the chateau that I saw and that *existed* because I *had seen it!*" (Rachilde's emphasis) is opposed to his desperate observation that he had before him only "the rock, still the

rock, shining, sweating, without a crack, without a hole." Thus the two adventurers encounter the inevitability of the eternal displacement as they turn round and round the rock-chateau, increasingly aware that *"it was always farther away than we thought"* (Rachilde's emphasis) and that "we kept going astray, in spite of ourselves."

There is a second maternal figure in the story, however: Madame Téard, the mother of the narrator's companion. If the chateau figures as the natural mother to whom one is lured *because* of the incest taboo, Madame Téard is the cultural mother strictly circumscribed by this prohibition. There is no thought of scaling *her* in the story; in fact, this "exquisite, sensible old woman" ("exquise vieille femme raisonnable") cannot even imagine the chateau-mirage. "For my part, . . . I have often tried to make out the chateau," she explains to the narrator, "and I have not been able to distinguish the least little turret!" Whatever "natural" mother there is about her Rachilde promptly undermines: charged with providing the picnic food for the excursion, Madame Téard has to give up her nourishing role when she allows the provisions to be stolen by a wild dog. Her role as the mother prohibited by culture is clearly the more important. Not only does she not see the chateau, but she repeats the incest prohibition in the brief story she tells of a previous failure to conquer the chateau. Attempting to dissuade the narrator (and her own son!) from their quest, she tells of

> a draftee who had talked about getting some buzzard eggs out of their nest, up there, before joining his regiment, and since he was drunk the morning he attempted the ascent, he fell head over heels from your famous chateau back down to his cottage. If he did not find the buzzard eggs, he nonetheless found the police station when reporting for duty, because the simpleton had been laid up and had missed the first roll call.

The point of Madame Téard's story is the punishment inflicted on the witless soldier for his silly belief that he could actually scale the maternal chateau. In the narrator's failure to do the same, repression becomes the single most important determinant of his desire. As the group is safely dining at home on the evening of the expedition, the mirage reappears to the narrator more clearly and more alluringly than ever before. "Over there . . . over there," the narrator writes, "a diabolical play of purple lights, of violet shadows, brought back the ruins of the feudal castle. I made out more clearly than ever the dungeons, the rampart walk, the crenelles; and more formidably than ever, there rose, in the blood of the dying day, the *Hermetic Chateau,* the unknown homeland to which my heart was drawn." It is only by consenting to its loss that the narrator can clearly apprehend the ultimate and unobtainable object of his desire; it is only through his acquiescence to the *here* of culture that his vision of an elsewhere, of a contradictory *over there* of an inaccessible nostalgia, is restored to him, allowing him—in fact condemning him—to continue to exist in prey to a state of desire.

In contrast to the impenetrable female surfaces of **"The Hermetic Chateau,"** **"The Tooth"** opens up feminine space. But it does so in order to destroy it as an object of desire. Here the physical disintegration of the female, expressed as the sudden loss of a tooth, is experienced as sexual horror and proximity to death. Instead of the unscalable surface of the maternal body withheld by the incest taboo and thus made an object of desire, the heroine of **"The Tooth"** is a fissured being for whom no place exists any longer within culture.

"The Tooth" brings the internal warring forces of the female body to bear on the previously intact surface. Losing a tooth as she bites into a pistachio, the heroine, Bichette, is both revolted and incredulous. "Eaten away, but for how long? Attacked by what?" she asks in panic. "At first that caused her no suffering," the narration continues, "and now she finds herself plunged into one of those despairs that are no less terrible for lasting only one day: from now on she has a flaw!" (**Demon**).

The newfound flaw is replete with sexual connotations: the lost tooth leaves a hole in the mouth that the victim's tongue will incessantly probe, and the tooth itself is reminiscent of Jean Lorrain's decapitated heads: it is a "little corpse" ("petite morte") in itself, "crowned by a dark border at the broken end." The new opening "on the side, just behind the smile" turns the heroine's mouth into a sort of powerless *vagina edentula* within which there echoes the refrain, "You are no longer whole!" The yawning gap, moreover, is experienced as "a door just opened onto her thoughts, and she will no longer be able to keep back certain words which will spring, against her will, out of her mouth."

The heroine's empty mouth is a gap that will not be filled precisely because it is so openly offered. With nothing to prohibit desire, it has nothing to provoke it either. Even God no longer desires Bichette. For years, it had been her practice to avoid sleeping with her husband on the nights before she was to take Communion, thereby preserving all of her libidinal energy for the encounter with the sacred. After losing her tooth, however, she is horrified to discover that she can barely swallow the Host:

> she feels, she *sees* that God has paused. . . . He is not used to this yet, and is caught on a corner, next to the little breach! . . . In a panic she leaves the Holy Table, wishing sacrilegiously to spit in spite of her fervor. . . . Then, with a brutal thrust of her tongue, she detaches [the Host] and it is immediately swallowed; God disappears, is swallowed up as if he were afraid, after seeing. (Rachilde's emphasis)

From the single gap opened in the body by the loss of the tooth, there flow simultaneously life, language, and the sexual power to fascinate. Significantly, the image

of a chateau reappears in **"The Tooth"** to compare Bichette not to the impregnable façade of **"The Hermetic Chateau"** but to all that is open and openly decrepit, well past its sexual prime: "she has suddenly, poor woman, the totally absurd vision of a ruined chateau she had contemplated long ago, on her wedding trip. Yes . . . she perceives the tower, over there, a tower sporting at its summit a crenelated crown and that stands out against the storm clouds as the uneven jawline of an outsized aged woman."

Bichette ends up burying her fallen tooth in the ground, like the "little corpse" she has felt it to be. The dirt remaining beneath her fingernails after this operation suggests that she is somehow between nature and culture: too openly available to be defended by the incest prohibition, she is no longer desirable. Unlike the façade of the "hermetic chateau," there is no barrier of repression that would place Bichette on either side of the nature/culture opposition.

Because this barrier is, in the Lacanian scheme, the necessary precondition for language, Bichette's loss of sexuality is also a loss of her power over language. In **"The Hermetic Chateau,"** the narrator complains that the right word, had he only known it, might have breeched the impenetrable castle, with its "mute, blind façade, the threatening façade par excellence, the hermetic façade." However, Téard "assured me we would not have the last word on this damnable rock." In **"The Tooth,"** Bichette's exclusion from language is made evident by a series of puns on the word *tooth* itself, which her damaged body forces her not to "get."

To understand a pun is to demonstrate one's familiarity with the symbolic functions of language. A pun on *tooth,* for example, depends on the listener's knowing that there may be more than just physical teeth involved; thus, the pun shows language functioning at yet another remove from the physical experience of the body. Bichette's sense of her body, however, exacerbated by the loss of her tooth, prevents her from recognizing this symbolic distance and obliges her to take the puns literally. So, as the gap in her dentition prevents her from laughing, "it is already so long past, that time when she could laugh unrestrainedly"—literally, "with all her teeth" ("c'est déjà tellement loin, l'heure où elle riait de toutes ses dents"). A second pun by her husband is more serious, throwing her into a nervous convulsion by evoking the exact opposite of her loss. Her husband uses the French expression "garder une dent," or "to keep a tooth" (for "to hold a grudge"), to describe his running quarrel with a neighbor.

With Bichette, Rachilde seems to be asking whether it is possible to be just a body with no symbolic function attaching to it. Missing a tooth, Bichette's body does not figure anything; it will not be long until the rest of it follows the tooth into dust. In this way, the story is almost the exact opposite of the last one to be considered here: **"The Frog Killer,"** in which the maternal body is imagined to be accessible only through excess of symbolic function grafted on it. Thus the latter story picks up where **"The Tooth"** leaves off in the meditation on the role of the pun in the differentiation of the body from language: in **"The Frog Killer,"** the misperception of figurative language becomes a perverse solution to the prohibition of desire for the mother by crudely identifying the mother with the metaphor.

First, however, a word about the genders of *frog.* Jean Lorrain's bullfrog was most often given as the masculine noun *crapaud;* Rachilde prefers the feminine *grenouille* for the story that occupies in her collection the same privileged place of horror that "The Mask" does in Lorrain's. The biological differences between these two types of frogs is less significant than the gender difference. If Rachilde opts for the feminine, she does so evidently because her frog is destined to represent the body of the mother, figuratively raped (as a body and as a figure of speech) in **"The Frog Killer"** as a symbolic refusal of the incest prohibition. The destruction of the maternal body becomes here the dream of an impossible language, of a language that would venture beyond metonymy in an effort to establish consistency with the original, nurturing body. As the incest prohibition, however, installs signification by repressing the desire for the mother, the violation of the primordial cultural taboo sets language at odds with culture, creating an illusory, parodic coincidence of the body, language, and desire whose power to shock is no less compelling than that of Lorrain's blinded and bloody *crapaud.*

The Toniot family—composed of Toniot *père,* his spouse, and Toniot *fils*—is depicted from the outset as extracultural if not anticultural. They are poor and isolated; they live outside the bounds of the city; Toniot *père* makes their living by trapping without a permit. As for Toniot *fils,* the protagonist of the story: "He lived like an animal, going, coming, eating, sleeping, saying nothing" (**Contes**). In fact, the animal to which he is compared is none other than the frog, scion of the male version that so tormented Lorrain. Beating him for having surprised her illicit sexual activity, Toniot's mother curses him as the "seed of a bullfrog" ("graine de crapaud"). The term, still in the masculine, is further associated with the childish penis that the adolescent Toniot protects from his mother's blows:

> Squatting on his sheet, checking for injuries on his little burning limbs that will have turned blue by morning, the boy contemplated the female with an air of suffering curiosity, protecting his little sex with his left hand, for he well suspected that if she hit him there again that would be the end of his *little bullfrog,* who would give a little squeak and be dead. (Rachilde's emphasis)

The comparison of Toniot *fils* to the frog is the beginning of the morbid pun on which the plot of the story and the son's paradoxically anticultural discourse will

be based. Before this, however, the woman, all-powerful over her son, also holds the power of language. She complains that her husband refuses to speak to her and that he has passed on to their son this eminently male legacy of mutism: "he gave her a son," the narrator explains, "and she would have preferred a daughter, that is, an ally, an accomplice, a more supple creature capable of appreciating all the vapid phrases that escape from mouths driven to exasperation by days of rain." The incomprehensibility of her men makes them "wicked," the woman laments to one of her few rare visitors, "so wicked, Madame, that they flap their beaks without ever saying anything!"

The language barrier between mother and son gives rise to the serious misinterpretations from which the story proceeds. For Toniot *fils,* the problem is to discern figurative from literal language. Concerned that someone has been stealing onions from their garden at night, Toniot *fils* resolves to "surveiller leurs oignons," that is, to "watch over their onions." His literal use of the figurative expression for "to mind someone's business" (in French, "to watch over their onions") blinds him to the fact that *no one* is stealing these particular onions: his mother has been giving them away to her lover, a voluble salesman, in exchange for his linguistic and sexual favors. The child's most serious misapprehension, however, confuses the literal and the figurative uses of the word *frog*—this time, the feminine, maternal *grenouille*—to the point of losing all reference to the real. As Toniot *fils* attempts to track down the onion thief in the middle of the night, he discovers instead his mother in the arms of the salesman, looking very much indeed like a frog: "What he sees, oh, he'll never forget it now, because it's too funny! He sees a great white frog, yes, that's it, that marvelous flexibility of the open thighs and arms, that precise and elastic stretching of limbs so pale they appear to be silver."

Sexual and linguistic acculturation—the repression of desire that would have, in Lacan, granted him access to the symbolic exchange of language—would have permitted Toniot *fils* to recognize his mother in the figurative *grenouille* thus seen exercising in the moonlight. Instead, his desire, unbound by culture, causes him to take quite literally the figurative *frog.* As a result, his entire experience becomes suffused by the figurative, henceforth to be misunderstood as the "real": "Now, he understands why they call him a bullfrog, it's because he really is the son of a [mother] frog."

Toniot *père* kills the mother-frog in a fit of jealous rage and is arrested and imprisoned for his crime. In his absence, Toniot *fils* accedes to the place of the stubbornly silent hunter, beyond the bounds of the city and its civilization. More important, however, his confusion between the literal and the figurative places him squarely outside the bounds of language. Unable to distinguish the maternal body from the frog, for example, he even wonders why murder should be considered a crime: "Dang!" he reflects, "there are so many more . . .

frogs than men, anyone can see that" (Rachilde's emphasis).

As the title predicts, Toniot *fils* becomes a killer of frogs in his own right. Each frog killed repeats the crime of the mother's sexuality that both attracts and repels her son. This time, however, it is the son who is in control; access to the maternal body is freely granted by the frogs, but only on condition that the mother remain always and everywhere a perverted figure of speech. For it is undeniable that Toniot *fils* can attract the frog-body as much as it attracts him. Time after time, he throws out his bait, "a little scrap of red sheet as long as a woman's tongue," only to discover

> there they are falling all over themselves, the poor little monsters, just to look at the red tongue the man is sticking out at them from the tip of his goddammed string. It is the chimera's tongue of fire! They fascinated [him], these charmers, little sirens, and now in his turn, he fascinates them. The stick comes up, the string whips through space, and one hears an atrocious cry of a bird being plucked alive. The frog, overly curious, is seized by the double bait that, from afar, looks like an anchor of safety. She flails her little hind legs like the legs of a girl being raped.

As the rape metaphor continues, so does the sense of freedom, clearly related to sexual liberty and pleasure, enjoyed by Toniot *fils*:

> No, no longer can anyone prevent him from eating his fill, from living. He is free.

> Kneeling before the pile of little corpses, he undresses them, takes out the double ring of their golden eyes, takes off their pretty green satin dresses, their adorable white velvet panties. All that slides off pell-mell like doll's clothes, and all that remains are the little naked thighs, very pale, shaken with nervous spasms.

The voyeuristic slowness of this ending description accounts in large part for the lurid chill it evokes. Horror, as we saw with Lorrain's *crapaud,* poisoning the waters from which the young boy drank, is not only a matter of the unexpected; it is a creation of deliberate pacing as well. Thus this particular strip is clearly a tease. In this sensational prelude to rape, the actions may be presented as successive, but they do not constitute a syntagm or progress through a plot line so much as they repeat each other, sounding so many carefully crafted synonyms for violation.

This could bring us back to the return of the repressed in Lorrain's *crapaud,* except for one simple thing: Rachilde's motherly *grenouille* shows us that Toniot *fils* has never known the initial repression that would have permitted culturally acceptable language, separated mother from son and the maternal body from the figurative frog. Thus Toniot *fils's* discourse of desire is most chilling for the depths of incoherence that open up beneath it, careening downward to the origins of the primary process itself. Imagining itself exactly coextensive with the maternal body, this discourse does indeed bring to an end the shifts and displacements that so plagued the protagonists of the preceding stories. But it does so at a horrible price. The mother's body must be made to subsist indefinitely as a misinterpreted figure of speech—"mother" most fully available as a metaphor taken literally.

In *Feminist Novelists of the Belle Epoque,* Jennifer Waelti-Walters observes that "energy is certainly not lacking in Rachilde's novels, and plausibility is not a concern. [Her novels] are deliberately nightmarish parodies of male and female attitudes toward sexuality and marriage." What is implausible in **"The Frog Killer"**—and thus source of its power to shock—is the very language it uses; its parodic intent is directed not toward such higher "forms" of sexual expression as object choices and marriage but toward the very foundation of desire. Toniot *fils* will not give up the mother, even if—or especially if?—that refusal denies him access to culture. Can it be really so bad to continually misinterpret one's metaphors, or is such misinterpretation always in some sense a rape, a forcing of the sexual boundaries by which culture and language strive to keep desire in check?

An antisocial parody of the mother-child relationship, the discourse of Toniot *fils* can be read only as a parody of language. Denying the support of language in the experience of repression, **"The Frog Killer"** dreams of a paradoxically anticultural language, a language perched constantly, for want of repression, on the brink of its self-annihilation. This language is the discourse of reason turned exactly on its head—trump card, perhaps, of the "hysteric of letters" who would have sensed, given the chance, that Dora had no choice but to simply slither away.

Will L. McLendon (essay date 1992)

SOURCE: "Rachilde: Fin de siècle Perspective on Perversities," in *Modernity and Revolution in Late Nineteenth-Century France,* edited by Barbara T. Cooper and Mary Donaldson-Evans, University of Delaware Press, 1992, pp. 52-64.

[*In the following essay, McLendon perceives what is usually considered perverted behavior in Rachilde's fictional works as an indirect means used by the author to protest oppressive social conventions and institutions of her time.*]

So far from constituting a threat to "good" moral values of the *belle époque,* the offbeat French novel of the 1880s and 1890s, often subtitled "Parisian Manners" or even "Foreign Manners" and regularly kept under surveillance by the civil and literary police concerned about its depravity, actually promulgated a message and an ethic founded to a great extent on those very values it appeared to bring under attack. Bourgeois life during the Third Republic had done a rather good job of hiding its seamier side beneath the dignity of bearded faces and the amplitude of feminine attire. Certain novelists such as Oscar Méténier, Dubut de La Forest, Jean Lorrain, and the young Rachilde devoted considerable talent and energy to peeling off these false beards and pulling up those skirts a bit further than was deemed permissible. The images of this lovely society that have come down to us through Nadar's legacy of charming photographs and Gustave Caillebotte's and Jean Beraud's meticulous canvases have been somewhat impugned—raped, some might say—by these iconoclastic novelists and a host of even lesser-known colleagues.

The rehabilitation of Jean Lorrain's work has gotten well underway over the past fifteen years or so, primarily because of the efforts of the late Philippe Jullian and those of Pierre Kyria, Christian Berg, and Michel Desbrall, among others. It now appears to be the turn of his contemporary and faithful friend, Rachilde. Since 1984, a number of major studies of this author have come from Claude Dauphine, Micheline Besnard-Coursodon, Robert Ziegler, and Melanie Hawthorne, all of them decisively underscoring a shift in critical approach characterized by rigorous and sustained objectivity. From these nevertheless diverse evaluations a common premise emerges: that readers, especially males, should guard against jumping to the conclusion that the stratagems of Rachilde's protagonists are perverse. A person such as Raoule de Vénérande, heroine or hero, as one may choose to think, of the novel *Monsieur Vénus,* or another such as Mary Barbe, the "Marquise de Sade" of the novel by the same name, are likely to seem perverse if the reader refuses to understand that their attitudes and actions reveal, in the final analysis, that Western society has almost always adopted a double standard in judging human conduct. The person who begins to think and act in a manner fitting the stereotype of the opposite sex may seem perverse for having dared tamper with prevailing standards. What is true for many of Rachilde's most "shocking" female characters also holds true for a man such as Paul-Eric de Fertzen, one of the major characters of her novel *Les Hors-nature,* whom Huysmans, in an unpublished letter to Rachilde, described as *"une sirène dextrement campée"* ("a skillfully presented siren"). But the question is a much broader one; far from being limited to patterns of dress and physical mannerisms, the reversal of traditionally recognized male and female roles extends to intellectual attitudes and to reasoning, two realms in which much more serious reader disorientation is likely to occur.

Until very recently, literary critics have almost universally relegated Rachilde's work to the backwaters of modern French letters. In his history of French literature published just after World War II and seven years before Rachilde's death, Henri Clouard pigeonholed her in the *"coin des démoniaques"* ("the demonics' corner"). As Melanie Hawthorne has rightly pointed out in her article on gender roles in *Monsieur Vénus,* the scorn that critics have heaped upon Rachilde even in very recent times is almost invariably based upon the erroneous perception that her novels are little more than gratuitous descriptions of monstrous sexual deviations. Maurice Barrès, writing, presumably in way of promotion, the preface to the first French edition of *Monsieur Vénus* in 1889, had the dubious honor of being the first to shunt critics off in this direction. Our perspective one hundred years later allows for a somewhat more objective appraisal of the alleged perversities which we see as the radical means adopted by Rachilde to condemn what she perceived as equally monstrous abuses of women's rights, the principles of patriotism, honor, marriage, and a host of other cornerstones of French and Western civilization. By enthralling—or disgusting—us with the excesses of her heroes and heroines, Rachilde deftly suggests, and without being in the least didactic, that these "monsters" of hers have been produced not so much by bourgeois principles as by the shameless perversion of these values by men and women who proclaim themselves to be the defenders of the nation, women's honor, the family, and so forth. The more outrageous the abuse seems to Rachilde the more she ups the ante by inventing characters and aberrations that for her time were definitely beyond the pale.

In her novels published between 1880 and 1900, Marguerite Eymery, writing under the pseudonym Rachilde as well as the anagram of this pseudonym, Jean *de Chilra,* applied her talents to the parody, not so much of bourgeois values as of their abuse at the hands of a vicious and hypocritical society. With such slaps in society's face as *Monsieur Vénus* (1884), *La Marquise de Sade* (1887), and *Les Hors-nature* (1897), Rachilde espoused both feminist and homosexual causes, as well as the cause of "honest" people, supposing there were any. Love, country, conjugal fidelity, maternity, and paternity are targets of Rachilde's satire only to the extent that these values have been flouted by hosts of such preposterous puppets as those exemplified by the regiment under the command of Mary Barbe's father on the eve of the Franco-Prussian war; or by heads of families who parade their conjugal infidelity before others; or by parents who are incapable of setting for their children the example of a united and loving couple. The dearth of real parents is underscored by the large number of orphans, semi-orphans, and bastards in Rachilde's early novels. Raoule de Vénérande, the heroine of *Monsieur Vénus,* is without parents; and the precociously cruel young woman labeled the "Marquise de Sade" (Mary Barbe) is the legitimate fruit of a union so corrupted by hypocrisy and irresponsibility that she grows up very much on her own. Her painful childhood is little more than the uninterrupted observation of the cruelty, pettiness, and duplicity of adults. Continually uprooted by the clocklike reassignments of her father's regiment, the child will come to know but a single important emotional anchor, and that is her innocent but already sadistic love for a poor working-class boy who is, of course, a real orphan. After this helter-skelter upbringing, completely devoid of parental affection, Mary is at length emancipated by the death of her parents and married at the age of eighteen to a Parisian aristocrat, a fast-living baron who at forty thinks he has had enough of the company of money-grubbing courtesans. On their wedding night, the young baroness loses no time avenging herself of her father's lack of affection and innumerable despicable actions; she informs her husband that she will never love him, nor will she grant him the hope of a legitimate heir:

> Oh, I have some strange theories, but you must resign yourself to them, Sir. It so happens that I don't care to create others who will suffer some day as I've suffered. . . . As for this God-given maternity bestowed on every girl who surrenders to her husband, well, I exhaust its tremendous tenderness at the sacred moment that leaves us still free *not* to procreate, free *not* to bestow death while bestowing life, free to exempt from filth and despair one who has done nothing to merit such fate. Let me put it to you cynically: I don't choose to be a mother, first of all because I don't want to suffer, and next because I don't wish to cause suffering.

Having taken such a position, she quickly adopts imperious attitudes towards everyone about her and gains authority over some, including an elderly uncle who had been her guardian before her marriage. This distinguished Parisian scientist and professor of medicine will opt for suicide as a result of the carefully dosed torture administered by his former charge who had applied herself first to seducing her uncle, then to rejecting him disdainfully.

In Mary Barbe's protest against a phallocratic society, a dual goal rapidly becomes apparent: first, to wreak vengeance on the male of the species; second, to cast off all bonds of servitude or any attitude perceived as such. According to the novelistic focus Rachilde proposes, the reader is expected to take Mary Barbe as the real victim, who in turn makes victims of her own in the name of all women. The author generally chooses as the butt of ridicule pompous, even stupid men wholly lacking the finesse of sentiment and tormented intelligence with which she so generously endows her heroines. The Marquise de Sade indeed triumphs, but over male creatures so naive and abject that her victory scarcely deserves that name. The tactics in this one-sided struggle are the very ones that had been employed by young Mary's cat Minoute, who scratched and drew her little mistress's blood. Robert Ziegler, in his study of this novel, has underscored the importance of the cat's claws which allow for "cutting, scratching, stabbing [that] can be done more surreptitiously." The mores of this supposedly domesticated animal, preserving as they do a certain savagery, admirably sum up the case of Mary Barbe.

As for the imbrication of bourgeois values in all these diabolical arts, it would be difficult to cite a better ex-

ample than the love affair of Raoule de Vénérande and Jacques Silvert in ***Monsieur Vénus***. As Besnard-Coursodon has rightly observed: *"Non seulement la 'normalité' hétérosexuelle est effacée"* ("not only is heterosexual 'normality' wiped out")—since Raoule plays the man's role and Jacques the woman's—but homosexuality too is *"dépassée par la perversion, qui est complète . . . [et] qui rétablit l'apparence d'un couple 'normal' [minant] en fait la norme de la nature"* ("exceeded by perversion, which is complete . . . [and] which restores the appearance of a 'normal' couple, thus in fact [subverting] nature's norm"). It should be added, however, that the very fact that Rachilde is aiming here at an appearance of normality, even in parody, brings us back to a kind of bourgeois equilibrium, since the two roles *are* reversed. Heterosexuality of a sort is indeed preserved, but at what a price! The self-criticism implied in the very nature of parody, since it allows for reinterpretation of what it has itself proposed, would seem to apply here, as in other "outrageous" situations concocted by Rachilde. By attacking abuse with abuse she underscores one of the tenets of Decadence.

Mary Barbe, at the opposite pole from Raoule de Vénérande and in a less dramatic way, joins forces with bourgeois values through her almost total lack of visible revolt against appearances and ritual. She does *not* flaunt her incestuous liaison with her husband's bastard son; she *does* go into mourning for her elderly uncle whom she has effectively pushed into suicide—she always takes into account what other people will say, just as any submissive woman of her day would do. This feline-woman relishes her cruel pleasures all the more that they remain secret ones. By pursuing a line of conduct that is the opposite of Raoule de Vénérande's, by dissimulating her true feelings and motives, this young Marquise de Sade actually seems, to those who know her only superficially, to be very much like the bourgeois and aristocratic women for whom she actually harbors nothing but scorn. In the true tradition of the bourgeois who desire nothing more than to distinguish themselves from other bourgeois, Mary Barbe gives this somewhat ironic turn of the screw by striving to make her mendacious conformity the *sine qua non* of her secret revolt. The transvestite note that creeps into several scenes of **La Marquise de Sade** is a much more obvious theme in ***Monsieur Vénus*** and **Les Hors-nature**. As is the case in many of Jean Lorrain's novels, transvestism, so far from being an exceptional element, is rather the expression of a tendency which in *fin-de-siècle* literature approached something like an artistic fashion. *"Fin de siècle, fin de sexe"* ("end of century, end of sex") Jean Lorrain cynically opined. His brash quip at least has the merit of suggesting quite succinctly the sacrifices to an aesthetic mode that d'Annunzio and Debussy, among others, were prepared to make in their *Martyre de Saint-Sébastien*, incarnated not by a man but by a bosomless, boyish Ida Rubenstein. Similar sacrifices at the same altar were frequently and willingly performed by Richard Strauss, whose predilection for mezzo-sopranos in men's garb is confirmed in some of his finest operas, such as *Der Rosenkavalier* (in which there is even travesty of disguise in the first and third acts), *Arabella,* and *Ariadne auf Naxos.* In passing, let us not forget the example of Sarah Bernhardt as the Aiglon or as Pierrot. Paintings of this period frequently follow a similar course in the frail personages of indeterminate sex who preside, often with hieratic gestures, over the melancholy or cataclysmic scenes conceived by Odilon Redon and Gustave Moreau. Joséphin Péladan also adds a pseudoscientific note with his dissertations on the androgyne. But in all his theoretical poses, Sâr Péladan seems more attuned to asexuality than to bisexuality. And that is precisely one of the messages that Jean Lorrain was attempting to convey with his stinging rejoinder: *"Fin de siècle, fin de sexe."* He doubtless also had in mind other more popular and more concrete manifestations of sexual indecision and confusion: for example, masked balls, carnival, and the ever more brazen exhibitionism of the Miss Sacripants that Proust would soon describe in studying aspects of Odette de Crécy and her kind, such as Lucie Delarue-Mardrus, Romaine Brooks, Colette, and the famous "amazone" Natalie Clifford Barney.

The other side of the coin in matters of disguise shows the effigies of such characters as Adelsward de Fersen, the hero of a future novel by Roger Peyrefitte, *L'Exilé de Capri;* vaporous Pierre Lotis; and many another Baron de Charlus bent on putting the dogs on the wrong scent. As literary subjects, the coin was to prove to be worth its weight in gold in the closing years of the nineteenth century. And Rachilde, more resolutely and earlier than most, set about exploiting this vein of gold, or perhaps of quicksilver, more properly speaking. Indeed, well before Jung she seized on the importance of the symbolism of Mercurius, creating as she did a menagerie of intriguing monsters, all of whom possess that antinomian dual nature that Jung has analyzed as basic to Mercurius and in which the masculine and the feminine elements undergo strange metamorphoses. In a Jungian archetypal reading of the three Rachilde novels previously mentioned, one is impressed by the manner in which she exploits the Mercurius symbol, whether consciously or otherwise. The fundamental dualism of the principal characters stands out first and foremost, followed by their interdependence and the role reversibility of each of the members of the three couples in question.

It will be recalled that in **Monsieur Vénus** the couple is composed of an imperious young woman with masculine bearing, Raoule de Vénérande, and the all-too-handsome Jacques Silvert, whom she seduces, subjugates and effectively turns into her "mistress." In **La Marquise de Sade,** Mary Barbe, after having married a baron whom she proceeds to tame on their wedding night, as we have seen, loses no time seducing his bastard son, a young medical student. She quickly reduces the latter to near total dependency, playing with him and his emotions like a cat with a mouse. For his willpower and ambition she substitutes and imposes incestuous pleasures that she seasons with sadistic and vampiric condiments. His whole existence is soon circumscribed by the sphere of satisfaction of their sexual appetites. *Femme fatale* if ever there was one, Mary Barbe uses her fingernails like a cat's claws to exact their toll in the couple's caresses. In her secret, nocturnal visits to the apartment where she keeps her male victim—reversing once again the more prevalent arrangement—her thirst for his blood truly designates her as the incarnation of the "Sirène repue" ("Satiated Siren") depicted by the turn-of-the-century artist Gustav Adolphe Mossa.

Finally in **Les Hors-nature** the couple in question is composed of the two brothers, Reutler and Paul-Eric de Fertzen. Like his father a Prussian, Reutler has been striving all his life to repress his homosexual tendencies through total abstinence. He is tall, well-built, and of a very sober demeanor. On the other hand, his younger brother, Paul-Eric, who was born in France during the 1870 war, has inherited the fragile beauty of their French mother, who died in childbirth. Realizing quite early that Paul-Eric's temperament is much too feminine, the elder brother devotes his life and their considerable fortune to educating Paul-Eric in what he takes to be the "proper" manner, that is to say he throws the adolescent boy into the arms of Parisian courtesans and Egerias with the expectation of remedying his lack of virile attributes. But through the bewilderingly improbable developments of this drama, the younger brother's true nature remains unshaken and in the end wins out over such paltry remedies. He becomes more effeminate with each passing day. Reutler, himself the victim of his double betrayal of nature, is forced to recognize that his own punishment is to have fallen hopelessly in love with his brother. Much like Raoule de Vénérande and Mary Barbe, Reutler has up to this point always associated the concept of true love with abstinence. This man—whose firmness of purpose and manner and whose self-denial holds others at bay—could well subscribe tacitly to the motto carved over Mary Barbe's bed: *"Aimer, c'est souffrir"* ("To love is to suffer"). But Reutler goes further still, and, in the final expression of his overpowering and desperate love for his brother, effectively transforms the motto into: *"Aimer, c'est mourir"* ("To love is to die"). Everything exacerbates the awkward situation which for too long a time has prevailed between the brothers in their strange and estranged existence in the lonely family castle; to go on living in this way under the same roof is out of the question, as is a return to Paris and its follies. For this improbable and chaste couple with their dreams of the impossible only one solution remains, and that is to disappear in an apotheosis worthy of *Die Götterdämmerung,* the conflagration of their isolated Valhalla. In a letter to Rachilde, Huysmans dubs this denouement *"sardanapalesque";* then, in a rather long and flattering enumeration of the qualities he discovers in this novel, he warmly congratulates the author on having created such a character as Reutler: *"Car celui-là vous l'avez animé d'une sorte de souffle mystérieux et d'une grandeur épique . . . il reste inoubliable, avec son air* *souffrant, son rictus, ses yeux d'eau noire, toute l'énigme de son orgueil. Il emporte tout dans son sillage car il apparaît comme inconnu avant vous, comme jamais vu"* ("for you have endowed this character with a kind of mysterious breath and an epic grandeur . . . he is unforgettable with his suffering attitude, his gaping grin, his liquid black eyes, and the whole enigma of his pride. He sweeps aside everything in his path; he appears like something that was unknown before you, like something never seen before"). A most flattering comment, to be sure, but not quite exact. A similar love that "sweeps aside everything in its path" can be found in a previous novel by Rachilde, entitled, as it happens, *A Mort* (1886). The heroine, Berthe Soirès, attempts as Reutler does, to reinvent love, is overwhelmed by her superhuman effort, wastes away and dies in a kind of *Liebestod*.

In choosing to give the protagonists of *Les Hors-nature* the names Reutler and Paul-Eric de Fertzen, Rachilde seems to allude somewhat obliquely to the many rebuffs and disappointments suffered by her contemporary, count Adelsward de Fersen, a most celebrated example of the "bric-à-brac gréco-préraphaélitico modern' style"—Cocteau *dixit*—that provided cocktail conversation topics and tabloid "scoops" around the turn of the century. Jean Lorrain, too, had a nose for such game and was obviously fascinated by it, as evidenced in several of his journalistic pieces and short stories that beat around the subject of Adelsward de Fersen's life style without, however, quite daring to tackle the matter of homosexuality directly. The same timidity did not keep him from treating the subject of lesbianism, as evidenced in his novel *Maison pour dames,* a story whose intrigue hinges on the competition for a literary prize to be awarded to a woman poet and on the recruitment procedures used to attract applicants. Again because of a dual standard working in reverse, as it were, and for once to the woman's advantage, can we really be surprised that the intrepid Rachilde, the same young woman that Lorrain addresses in a letter as *"Chère Hermaphrodite"* (Dear Hermaphrodite") approaches the subject of homosexuality with relative ease in *Les Hors-nature*? From the beginning of her appearance on the literary scene she had resolutely decided to throw off her provincial origin and to hitch her wagon to the Parisian star. Claude Dauphine has expressed it most forcefully: *"Cette intrusion de 'La Fille aux yeux d'or' chez 'Eugénie Grandet' est révélatrice de l'optique de Rachilde: plutôt Sodome et Gomorrhe qu'une sous-préfecture. Hors de Paris, point de vie!"* ("This intrusion of 'The Girl with the Golden Eyes' into Eugenie Grandet's domain is revealing of Rachilde optics: Better to be in Sodom and Gomorrah than in some provincial backwater. Outside of Paris, nothing doing!")

Equivocal dualism, interdependence, reversibility of gender roles: these are the three characteristics associated in these three novels of Rachilde with sensual and physical love, as is the spirit Mercurius in his metaphysical and incorporeal sense. Jung tells us that "for

the alchemists, as we know not only from the ancient but also from the later writers, Mercurius as the arcane substance had a more or less secret connection with the goddess of love" and that in certain representations "Aphrodite appears with a vessel from the mouth of which pours a ceaseless stream of quicksilver." Other aspects of this spirit emphasized by Jung and that are striking in Rachilde's protagonists are a "many-sided, changeable, and deceitful" nature and the fact that this spirit "enjoys equally the company of the good and the wicked."

As a woman writer, then, Rachilde could doubtless afford to treat a subject such as *Les Hors-nature,* if not with impunity then at least without too much fear of reprisal from a certain literate public, the very one that showed far less tolerance of Jean Lorrain's sallies onto the same terrain. And Rachilde's relatively more favorable treatment was due not solely to the fact that she was a woman, but was in even larger part due to the narrative voice she adopts, permitting preservation of a certain distance and objectivity, two advantages that Jean Lorrain's much more personal style is surely lacking, his *La Maison Philibert* being a prime example. The exceptional adventures of the two de Fertzen brothers in *Les Hors-nature* may astound or intrigue us; they can not move us, let alone give the illusion of real events, as do Lorrain's novels. It is precisely this detachment and this hypothetical bent that allowed Rachilde to tackle broad matters of human behavior in general, and of sexuality in particular, without bringing down storms of critical invective as Lorrain did. Among her many merits as a novelist, more recognition is due her for having dared to put her finger squarely on an area of widespread medical error in the late nineteenth century, one that caused endless problems for such individuals as the young André Gide and for Marcel Proust throughout his life: *"La névrose, la monomanie? Cela n'existe qu'en faisant dévier une creature de sa ligne."* ("Neurosis and monomania? They come about only by causing a creature to deviate from its bent"), she wrote in *Les Hors-nature.* It is understood here that the bent is homosexuality; in Reutler de Fertzen's case without a trace of effeminate mannerism, in that of his brother, exaggerated effeminacy. Reutler finally grasps, but much too late, the fact that from the outset he should have accepted his own nature as well as his brother's, without attempting to "correct" them. *"N'est-il pas bien plus contre la nature,"* he says, *"de résister désespérément à ses instincts?"* ("Is it not much more unnatural to resist desperately one's instincts?"). An affirmative answer to his question is given in dramatic fashion through the disastrous events recorded in the final pages of this novel.

Margaret Bruzelius (essay date 1993)

SOURCE: "'En el Profundo Espejo del Deseo': Delmira Agustini, Rachilde, and the Vampire," in *Revista Hispanica Moderna: Columbia University Hispanic Studies,* Vol. XLVI, No. 1, 1993, pp. 51-63.

[In the following essay, Bruzelius examines the figure of the vampiric female as portrayed in the works of Rachilde and Uruguayan author Delmira Augustini.]

I have been faithful to thee,
Cynara, in my fashion.

E. DOWSON

The nineteenth century fascination with the *femme fatale* may have reached its apogee in the figure of the Vampire—that marble white, silent woman with luxuriant hair, heavy lidded eyes and blood red lips. Her nocturnal invasion of the daylight world of patriarchal propriety is invoked by artists who wish to escape the deadly trammels of the bourgeoisie (Baudelaire, Swinburne), by those who wish to reaffirm its primacy (Bram Stoker), and by those who cannot make up their minds (Coleridge, who could never finish Christabel). Of course, the history of the "belle dame sans merci" is an old and dishonorable one, and there are many fatal women who are not vampires. [Mario Praz's chapter entitled "La Belle Dame Sans Merci" in *The Romantic Agony* is a useful survey of this type of female character. Although he is not particularly interested in stressing the vampiric aspect of these women, a reading of this chapter makes clear how often the image comes up. For example, in his celebrated description of the Mona Lisa Pater writes: "She is older that the rocks among which she sits; like the vampire, she has been dead many times, and learned the secrets of the grave . . ." (quoted in Praz). It is interesting to note that Praz himself calls this female cliché a type and goes on to compare it to a disease: "A type is like a neuralgic area. Some chronic ailment has created a zone of weakened resistance, and whenever an analogous phenomenon makes itself felt it immediately confines itself to this predisposed area . . ." (Praz). His chapter on Sade calls forth no similar medical analogies. From a feminist perspective Nina Auerbach's *Woman and the Demon* is equally useful, although limited to English authors, and I am deeply indebted to her approach. Bram Dijkstra's *Idols of Perversity, Fantasies of Feminine Evil in Fin-de-Siècle Culture* is an exhaustive recent survey of the iconography of the fatal woman.] Nevertheless, the female vampire seems to enshrine the attributes of the fatal woman, and her continuing fascination may be seen in the fact that Bram Stoker's *Dracula* has never been out of print since 1897, when it was first published.

Although the nightmare fantasy of the power of the female incarnated in the vampire marks the entire nineteenth century, it is most closely associated with the tradition stretching from Poe through Baudelaire to the French and English decadents. This group of *poètes maudites* includes few women, and in fact it is hard to imagine a woman writer identifying herself with a written legacy in which the female is so unequivocally identified with silence, the literary equivalent of death. Yet within this tradition two women—Rachilde (Mme. Marguerite de la Vallette) in France and Delmira Agustini

in Uruguay—managed to create a niche for themselves. Rachilde wrote titillating novels for about fifty years, moving from the immense success of her early work, *M. Vénus*, to a rather pathetic old age in which newer crimes supplanted her rather retro transgressions. [Rachilde's first successful novel, *M. Vénus* was published in 1884. She continued to write at a great pace throughout her long life (apparently about one novel a year). According to Claude Dauphiné, whose maddening *Rachilde, femme des letters 1900* is the most recent work on Rachilde, her last novel, *Duvet d'Ange*, was published in 1942, although she published a collection of poems in 1945. Rachilde lived by her pen throughout her life, working as a novelist and also as a journalist at the *Mercure de France*. She died in Paris in 1953, at the age of 93.] Agustini, in her much briefer career, took the version of decadence offered her by Modernismo, especially as represented by Rubén Darío, and used it to create extraordinarily intense poetry of explicitly sexual female desire. It is perhaps unfair to compare the poet Agustini, whose best work continues to speak with electrifying energy, to an irretrievably dated prose writer such as Rachilde. But both women were able to write within the decadent tradition by taking the image of the vampiric fatal woman and using to create a parodic written persona. It is this ironic, distancing yet complicit stance which allows them to write as women within a tradition which seems by its nature to exclude women writers.

In using the motion of parody to describe these writers' engagement with their tradition I do not mean to suggest that their work is limited to humorous ridicule of the masters. This essay follows the lead of Linda Hutcheon's *A Theory of Parody* in choosing to emphasize parody as "extended repetition with critical, ironic difference." Hutcheon sees parody as a fundamental mode of modern aesthetics, and wishes to reclaim the genre from its association with amusing but "minor" work. For her, the artist's use of parody is an ironic appropriation whose *ethos* (defined as "the ruling intended response achieved by a literary text") is not limited to satire or ridicule but can evoke the entire range of human emotion. Within this context, Rachilde and Agustini can be seen as engaged in a fundamentally parodic process which plays on the fact that they are women writers, identified as women on the title pages of their books, writing within a tradition in which women are fatal, brooding creatures who don't say much. By using the image of the vampire woman, whose horror for the male world consists precisely in the fact that she freely expresses not only desire (Darling, let's go to Bloomingdale's) but specifically sexual desire (Darling, let's make love), they are able to create themselves as fatal women who talk. At the beginning of a modern aesthetic which Hutcheon sees as permeated by the idea of parody, Rachilde and Agustini can be read as early experimenters not only in their distanced appropriation of texts but also in their inversion of traditional sex roles.

The vampire image that both Rachilde and Agustini parody in different ways deserves some further exploration, before their uses of it are examined. The canonical expression of the female vampire is undoubtedly Bram Stoker's *Dracula* [I make no attempt to argue that Stoker directly influenced these two writers, and indeed in Rachilde's case it would be impossible, as *M. Vénus* (1884) predates *Dracula* (1897) by thirteen years. I use it as the clearest expression of a tradition that had been building for many years. James Twitchell, in his book *The Living Dead, A Study of the Vampire in Romantic Literature* has examined the recurrence of vampires (both male and female) in English romantic literature beginning with "The Rime of the Ancient Mariner." Stoker's most immediate predecessor is Sheridan LeFanu, in *Carmilla* (1871).], although many other writers have created both male and female vampires. Stoker's novel contains two heroines, Lucy Westenra and Mina Harker, both of whom are bitten by Dracula. Lucy dies and becomes a vampire but Mina is saved by Van Helsing, the scientist hero of the book who drives Dracula out of England and eventually kills him in Transylvania. As Christopher Craft points out, [in "'Kiss me with Those Red Lips': Gender and Inversion in Bram Stoker's *Dracula*,"] the novel is divided into three stages: the first, set in Transylvania, where the threat is exposed and Jonathan Harker experiences the intense sexual attraction/repulsion Dracula exerts; the second, in which the count moves to England, takes over Lucy and begins to feed on Mina; and the last, in which he is driven out of England and finally destroyed. Within the sexual economy of *Dracula,* vampirism seems to represent the threat of a free-floating sexual drive and a concomitant desire for total possession which exists unrestrained by any social proprieties and few physical ones. [Naturally, these limitations are not those associated with normal flesh and blood. The vampire's physical constraints, in addition to his well-known aversion to garlic and the cross, include such things as an inability to enter any place where he has not been invited, and the fact that he can only cross water at the slack or flood of the tide. Dracula himself seems to be able to transform himself into various creatures in order to roam from his tomb during the day, but the female vampires are not shown to share this capacity, at least in Stoker.] This sexual energy threatens the men of the novel precisely because it is not limited to traditional heterosexual exchange. Craft points out that Jonathan Harker's initial brush with vampirism, in his interrupted seduction in Transylvania by the three weird sisters who surround Dracula, is not only an inversion of the traditional proprieties of sexual behavior in which the male pursues and the female is pursued, but also a deviated display of the homo-erotic desire which the Count has for Harker. Dracula interrupts the seduction by erupting into the room in which it takes place and driving back the females declaring, "How dare you touch him, any of you? how dare you cast eyes on him when I had forbidden it? Back, I tell you all! This man belongs to me!" [Even Dracula cannot control his female troops all that well; they attempt here to take away his vital link to England in the person of Harker, and immediately after Dracula's outburst quoted above, one

of them says, "You yourself never loved; you never love!" The Count's reply to this confirms the homo-erotic content of his first statement: "Then the Count turned, after looking at my face attentively, and said in a soft whisper:—'Yes, I too can love; you yourselves can tell it from the past. Is it not so?'"] Dracula's invasion of London is seen as a nightmare vision of undifferentiated sexual desire undermining the great city: "he might, among its teeming millions . . . create a new and ever widening circle of semi-demons to batten on the helpless."

When the Count does move to England, the infection he carries is represented only as a threat to pure English women: on their own soil the band of men who combat Dracula feel no desire for him. But the horror with which the proper gentlemen of Stoker's tale receive the infection of their women with Dracula's greedy desire suggests the depth of threat they perceive in unlicensed—and uncontrollable—female desire. Their counter-attack against the one woman who is fatally infected, Lucy, astonishes in its ferocity. In the castle seduction scene Harker speaks of his "wicked" desire and the vampire's "animal" qualities. This theme is taken up by Seward in his description of Lucy as vampire: "[her] sweetness was turned to adamantine, heartless cruelty, and [her] purity to voluptuous wantonness. . . . When Lucy—I call the thing that was before us Lucy because it bore her shape—saw us she drew back with an angry snarl, such as a cat gives when taken unawares. . . . As she looked, her eyes blazed with unholy light, and the face became wreathed with a voluptuous smile. With a careless motion, she flung to the ground, callous as a devil, the child that up to now she had clutched strenuously to her breast, growling over it as a dog growls over a bone." Lucy is a thing, a cat, a devil, a dog. Seward's loving description of the stake used to kill the she-devil is token enough of the strength of his revulsion: "A round wooden stake, some two and a half or three inches thick and about three feet long. One end of it was hardened by charring in the fire, and was sharpened to a fine point. With this stake came a heavy hammer. . . . To me, a doctor's preparation for work of any kind are stimulating and bracing . . ." And his lingering insistence on Lucy's second death makes quite clear the price that must be paid for transgressing sexual laws: "Arthur place the point over the heart, and as I looked I could see its dint in the white flesh. Then he struck with all his might. The Thing in the coffin writhed; and a hideous, blood-curdling screech came from the opened red lips [no wonder]. The body shook and quivered and twisted in wild contortions; the sharp white teeth champed together till the lips were cut and the mouth was smeared with a crimson foam. But Arthur never faltered." The cure for vampirism has more than a tinge of homeopathy about it: the original Dracula was known as Vlad the Impaler, and the infection he carries is cured by similar impalement.

The sadism of Seward's description of Lucy's destruction (one can see why he describes the preparations as "stimulating and bracing") suggests his subliminal awareness that the "thing" that is Lucy may not at all regret her transformation, that the "doctor's work" is not cure but revenge. For beneath the fascination/repulsion exhibited by the proper Victorians for the female vampire's sexual voracity lies another fear: the fear that their women may actually desire to be infected. It is clear that at least part of Lucy wishes to be bitten, that she enjoys Dracula's embrace. [As Carol A. Senf points out ("'Dracula': Stoker's Response to the New Woman") even Mina succumbs momentarily to the pull of Dracula's seduction, and insists on calling herself "Unclean" until she is cleansed of her pollution at his death.] For though the female vampire can only be quickened to life by the bite of another's desire, once she is "nosferatu" or undead, she becomes able not only to speak, but also to express desire freely, to move out of her house—the tomb—at night, unaccompanied, to provide for herself, and to disguise herself easily. In other words, she gains a freedom entirely unknown to her living sisters. Moreover, although dead, these women are not even cut off from the possibility of generation, for they can breed new vampires, not through the laborious process of gestation but through their simultaneously fatal and reviving kiss/bite. And though they must obey Dracula, he, like many another seducer of maidens, has little interest in them once they can no longer provide him with blood, and leaves them to their own devices. [While in Transylvania Dracula seems to be compelled to provide food for his three female companions. In the seduction scene quoted above he gives them a sack: "'Are we to have nothing tonight?' said one of them, with a low laugh, as she pointed to the bag which he had thrown on the floor, and which moved as though there were some living thing within it . . . If my ears did not deceive me there was a gasp and a low wail, as of a half-smothered child. The women closed round . . ." However, in England he appears to be ready to leave Lucy to fend for herself. For Stoker, the sexual eagerness these women display seems inextricably linked to cruelty to children.]

Both Rachilde and Agustini clearly perceive and respond to the vampire's freedom. While the men of Stoker's tale keep emphasizing the fact that the vampires are cut off from God's grace, for writers firmly entrenched in the tradition of "poètes maudites" damnation may simply be the price one pays for writing. And the female vampire, unlike many other fatal women, is firmly associated with the ability to speak, to seduce with language—to write. Only at the moment of becoming a vampire (of human death) can Lucy speak her desire clearly, when she says to her fiance, "Arthur! Oh, my love, I am so glad you have come! Kiss me!" (at this point Van Helsing hurls him across the room to protect him from harm). And in her appearance later as a vampire, it is not only the fact that a child is "flung to the ground" with "a callous motion," that horrifies the men, it is also Lucy's open attempt to speak and show desire: "[s]he still advanced . . . and with a languorous, voluptuous grace, said:—'Come to me, Arthur. Leave these

others and come to me. My arms are hungry for you. Come, and we can rest together. Come, my husband, come!' There was something diabolically sweet in her tones." When Rachilde creates Raoule, the demi-vierge who keeps a male mistress, she produces a female vampire, not one in thrall to a higher power, but one who is herself Dracula. And Augustini creates a poetic persona as a monstrous female, a revenant who summons the male she desires from the grave.

Rachilde's *M. Vénus* tells the story of Raoule de la Vénérande, last scion of a noble house, who falls in love with the brother of her *fleuriste*, Jacques Silvert, who himself makes flowers, although he calls himself a painter. Overwhelmed by her desire for him, she establishes him in an ornately decorated atelier. She gradually comes to dominate and feminize him entirely, so that he wears robes and nighties, and she comes to make love to him dressed in male attire. After some struggle, he ceases even to wish to make love to her in what one might call the "normal" way and insists on her treating him as a woman. Raoule contrives to introduce him into society, and finally marries him. After the marriage Jacques becomes attracted to another man, de Raittolbe, and makes an attempt to seduce him in his female dress. Raoule, on discovering this intrigue, contrives to have de Raittolbe fight a duel with Jacques, who is killed. The story ends with Raoule a recluse in her ancestral mansion, where she has created a shrine to her dead lover. He lies, like Sleeping Beauty, a wax figure adorned with the real finger nails of Jacques: "Sur la couche en forme de conque . . . repose un mannequin de cire revêtu d'un épiderme de caoutchouc transparent. Les cheveux roux, les cils blonds, le duvet d'or de la poitrine sont naturels; les dents qui ornent la bouche, les ongles des mains et des pieds ont été arrachés à un cadavre. [It is clear from an earlier passage that the cadaver is Jacques'.] Les yeux en émail ont un adorable regard" (*M. Vénus*). [A brief glance at Dijkstra's illustrations in *Idols of Perversity* will suggest the extraordinary popularity of images of dead women in Rachilde's era. In light of this iconography, Jacques' apotheosis as a wax statue—a sort of stationary Lady of Shallott—is another dig at the fin-de-siècle identification of woman and death.]

Although Rachilde's novel clearly revels in its parodic reversal of the conventions of romantic tales, little has changed except for the sex of the seducer and the seduced. One example of the prose used to describe Jacques' enticing male beauty will establish the genre in and against which Rachilde is working: "Les lueurs douces . . . tombaient mollement sur ses chairs blondes, toutes duvetées comme la peau d'une pêche. . . . Digne de la Vénus Callipyge, cette chute de reins où la ligne de l'épine dorsale fuyait dans un méplat voluptueux et se redressait, ferme, grasse, en deux contours adorables . . ." Jacques is described throughout as blonde and gold, stupid, a bit pudgy ("grasse"), and after a brief period of unease, completely submissive; in short, the perfect woman.

Raoule, on the other hand, has many of the standard traits of the fatal, "other" woman. Her suitor, de Raittolbe, calls her "un agréable monstre," adding "l'étude du fauve n'a de charmes réels qu'en Algérie." She has driven all her lovers either mad or off on distant travels (one has gone off to Norway "[pour] essayer des réfrigérants". But she also shares a great deal with Dracula: she is pale, dark-haired, black eyed, and imperious: "Merveilleusement tracés, les sourcils avaient une tendance marquée à se rejoindre dans le pli impérieux d'une volonté constante. Les lèvres [étainet] minces . . . [l]es cheveux étaient bruns . . . et concuraient au parfait ovale d'un visage teinté de ce bistre italien qui pâlit aux lumières. Très noirs, avec des reflets métalliques sous de longs cils recourbés, les yeux devenaient deux braises quand la passion les alluma." In contrast to Jacques, who looks as edible as a peach, Raoule is drawn in dark lines, her eyebrows are marked, her face has a brown tint, and her eyes have a metallic glint that turns to red, just as Dracula's eyes also glare red. [These are some of Dracula's traits, from Harker's first description: "His face was a strong . . . aquiline . . . his eyebrows were very massive, almost meeting over the nose . . . The general effect was of extraordinary pallor" (*Dracula*).] She wears dark, almost masculine clothes with military trim: . . . vêtue d'un fourreau de drap noir à queue tortueuse, tout passementé de brandebourgs. Aucun bijou . . . ne scintillait porur égayer ce costume presque masculin." Although she is an urban creature, she lives, like Dracula, in a dark and ancient ancestral mansion. And like him, she also is marked as the last descendent of an ancient line; she can have no "natural" issue.

Although Raoule and Dracula share the inevitable similarity of figures generated in the horror tradition inaugurated by Poe, Rachilde explicitly invokes the vampire in the central scene of Jacques' sexual submission. Raoule is compared to a monster, and Jacques' downfall is sealed with a bite/kiss as was Lucy's: "Raoule l'embrassait sur ses cheveux d'or . . . voulant lui insuffler sa passion monstre. . . . Ses lèvres impérieuses lui firent courber la tête en avant, et derrière la nuque elle le mordit à plein bouche." Jacques' resistance to her "passion monstre" is to attempt one last time to assert his masculine way to make love, but Raoule's body then becomes like that of a dead woman: "Lorsqu'il l'embrassa, il lui semblait qu'un corps de marbre glissait entre les draps; il eut la sensation désagréable d'un frôlement de bête morte . . ." Like Dracula, Raoule is both dead and alive, animal and human ("un frôlement de bête morte"). Only when Jacques gives in entirely, "fais de moi ce que tu voudras à présent . . ." does she use her "science maudite" and fall on him with her "flancs gonflés d'ardeurs sauvages." [In a later scene, when Raoule sees that Jacques has been beaten by de Raittolbe, she again bites Jacques, but this scene of sadism seems included in order that all the bases of perversion are touched "pour épater les bourgeois." The final intrigue, in which Jacques attempts to seduce de Raittolbe, suggests that Raoule has awakened in him not a desire for her, but for a "real man." As in *Dracula*

there is a strong homo-erotic attraction between the two men. After wounding Jacques, de Raittolbe kneels down and sucks his wound (apparently to draw out the blood), but the sexual overtones are unmistakable. And in an earlier scene he is almost overcome by seeing Jacques naked, and calls him "Eros lui-même."] She is the evil genius, and he is her toy, her "thing," as Lucy is Dracula's. Finally, like a vampire, Raoule creates her own "undead," the effigy of Jacques in wax. In his secret tomb she comes to mourn him, dressed sometimes as a man, sometimes as a woman. She retains a capacity to transform herself, and a limited capacity to transform him into a semblance of a living being, for the dummy is equipped with a special spring which animates its mouth when Raoule kisses it: "Un ressort, disposé à l'intérieur des flancs[!], correspond à la bouche et l'anime."

The delicious horror with which Rachilde's book was received—it was banned in Belgium and an investigation of Rachilde was begun by judicial authorities in Paris—stems not only from the fact that sex roles in it are reversed, but that this reversal is accomplished by a woman protagonist imagined by a woman author. Rachilde was accused of having invented a "new vice," (which prompted Verlaine to remark: "Ah! ma chère enfant, si vous aviez inventé un vice de plus, vous seriez un bienfaiteur de l'humanité!" (quoted in Dauphiné)). Rachilde fueled the suspicion that the novel was autobiographic by wearing male dress (although all the surviving photographs of her that I have seen show her in simply cut dresses), cropping her long hair and having a calling card printed with the legend "Rachilde, homme de lettres." But, as Maurice Barrès points out ("Mademoiselle Baudelaire," *Chroniques,* Feb, 1887), Rachilde's sexual vapourings have something of a schoolgirl quality, "on dirait une petite fille qui fume la pipe en peinturlant avec soin les images d'Epinal." Her work has dated because its "perversité cérébrale" (to quote Barrès again) consists in merely inverting all the "shocking" literary conventions of her day, conventions which we no longer share.

Rachilde's effort to create a parodic inversion of the genres of romantic fiction and of the vampiric fatal woman finds an echo in the work of Agustini. Agustini may have read *M. Vénus,* as she and the circle of writers she knew were familiar with the writing of French decadence, and a "decadent" *sucés de scandale* like *M. Vénus* may well have been in circulation among her friends. Whether Agustini have read *M. Vénus* or not, she would have known something about Rachilde, as Rubén Dario, the champion of Modernismo, had included her—the lone woman—in his book *Los Raros* (publ. 1896), a collection of essays on the figures that either influenced or belonged to decadent/symbolist circles in Paris. Darío's description of Rachilde can be read as a blueprint for the literary *femme fatale*. He begins: "Trato de una mujer extraña y escabrosa, de un espíritu único esfingamente solitario . . . de un "caso" curiosísimo y turbador . . . satánica flor de decadencia picantemente perfumada, misteriosa y hechicera y mala como un pecado" (*Los Raros*). Throughout Darío's essay author and work are conflated: Rachilde's novels are always read as the work of a woman—a devotée of the Eleusinian mysteries or a Vestal Virgin. Darío's descriptions of Raoule and of Rachilde echo each other. Raoule is "una especie de mademoiselle Des Esseintes . . . de la familia de Nerón, y de aquel legendario y terrible Gilles de Laval . . . un amante vampirizada." Rachilde is described as a virgin whose dreams are possessed by the devil in a lurid passage:

> Imaginaos el dulce y puro sueño de una virgen, lleno de blandura, de delicadeza, de suavidad, una fiesta eucarística, una pascua de lirios y de cisnes. Entonces un diablo—Behemot quizá—, el mismo de Tamar, el mismo de Halagabal, el mismo de las posesas de Lodun, el mismo de Sade, el mismo de las misas negras, aparece. Y en aquel sueño casto y blanco hace brotar la roja flora de las aberraciones sexuales, los extractos y aromas que atraen a incubos y sucubos, las visiones locas de incógnitos y desoladores vicios, los besos ponzoñosos y embrujados, el crepúsculo misterioso en que se juntan y confunden el amor, el dolor y la muerte.

> La virgen tentada o poseída por el Maligno, escribe las visiones de sus sueños. De ahí estos libros . . .

If Raoule belongs to Nero and Gilles de Laval (the original Bluebeard), Darío associates Rachilde with Tamar, Halagabal, the black mass and the Marquis de Sade!

Darío's description of Rachilde is of importance only as a succinct statement of the image of a woman writer as *femme fatale,* as demon, as possessed by the devil—an image that Agustini herself certainly played up to. The fervid abandon with which Darío festoons his paragraph with incubi and sucubi, mysterious crepuscular sins, death, dreams, pain and love are echoed in Agustini's own summoning of her phantom lover. The telling difference is, of course, the sex of the writer. Darío can easily fit Rachilde into a tradition of fatal woman and dismiss her writing as the devil speaking *through* her; Agustini, like Rachilde, must create herself as the fatal woman who speaks. Darío may been able to fool himself that Rachilde wrote in an hypnotic trance; Agustini could permit herself no such illusion.

Agustini published three books in her lifetime, *El Libro Blanco* (1907), *Cantos de la Mañana* (1910), and *Los Cálices Vacíos* (1913). [After a brief marriage, Agustini was divorced from her husband, who murdered her in July, 1914.] In her poetry she constructs a female voice which gradually frees itself to express female sexual desire. Where Rachilde's novels are limited by her inability to do more than directly invert the clichés of her time, Agustini's enthusiastic adoption of the persona of the vampire lover infuses the shopworn images of the symbolists with new life. Her work is saturated with the image of the fatal woman, the dreamer possessed, but

with the essential, and inherently parodic, difference that this fatal woman is not the creation of male desire and fear, but of a female desire that authorizes itself. Agustini's astonishing accomplishment is to create her own voice solely through manipulation of the standard bric-à-brac of the decadent movement—antique statues, swans, lakes, moonlight, Salomé, the sphinx—all the familiar paraphernalia of the symbolists and decadents gain new life as the fatal woman herself, the "poetisa/pitonisa" summons them.

Agustini first sketches her stance as the poet/vampire who summons up the object of her desire in "Misterio: Ven . . ." from *El Libro Blanco* (*Poesías Completas,* 81, all further cites from this edition): "Ven, oye, yo te evoco, / extraño amado de mi musa extraña, / ven, tú, el que meces los enigmas hondos / en el vibrar de las pupilas cálidas." Here the woman speaks and commands her demon lover to appear, "Come, listen, I conjure you." The poet's word brings her lover back from the grave: "Ven, tú, el que imprimes un solemne ritmo / al parpadeo de la tumba helada . . . el poeta abrumador, que pulsas / la lira del silencio." The muse/incubus who will respond to the vampire's call will seal the fate of both with a kiss; the penetrating kiss of the vampire: "Ven . . . acércate más . . . clava en mis labios / tus fríos labios de ámbar." This kiss brings with it the standard enervation of the touch of the vampire, and the knowledge of "dark sins": "¡Guste yo en ellos el sabor ignoto / de la esencia enervante de tu alma! . . ."

In this early poem Agustini clearly suggests the qualities of the female voice that she seeks to create. Both she and the lover she summons share vampiric qualities, especially in their unappeasable sexual thirst. Agustini accepts the fact that the possibilities of this desire are limited by the clichés of the genre: desire exists as a night-time event brought into being in a dream; for her, a sunlit sexual encounter remains impossible. Moreover, a daylit lover would destroy the poet herself, whose voice depends on the spectral nature of her sexual encounters. In a later poem "¡Oh Tú!" Agustini conjures up a vision of this impossible sunlit encounter. The poem begins by describing the poet in her melancholy tower, "Yo vivía en la torre inclinada / de la Melancolía . . ." The tower is furnished with the standard claptrap of fatal places: dampness, spiders and an owl, "Las arañas del tedio, las arañas más grises, / en silencio y en gris tejían y tejían. / ¡Oh, la húmeda torre, / llena de la presencia / siniestra de un gran búho." It incubates a large, infertile egg—the poet?—whose eyes strain outward, "Eternamente incuba un gran huevo infecundo, / incrustadas las raras pupilas más allá." In its confines the poet "inclinada a mí misma" ("la torre inclinada") contemplates the abyss "yo temblaba / del horror de mi sima." [The play on cima/sima occurs several times in Agustini, as if to emphasize the inherently paradoxical nature of her enterprise.]

Having set the stage, in the last stanza the poet invokes her lover as in "Visión" except that here he appears to be real, at least initially: "¡Oh Tú que me arrancaste a la torre más fuerte!" But this vision of liberation stumbles as the poet goes on not only to suggest that this sunlit Tú can never exist, but also that she would not wish to be liberated: "¡Tú que en mí todo puedes, / en mí debes ser Dios!" The use of *deber* suggests not only must, but should, with the implication that lover might not be god. This uncertainty is reinforced by Agustini's subsequent use of the future in describing herself: "Soy el cáliz brillante que colmarás, Señor," as if to place the moment of fulfilling liberation in some indefinate future day of jubilee; we have by this time abandoned the *Tú* who pulled the poet out of her melancholy tower. Even this postponed, conditional liberation is described in oxymoronic terms as "el Bien que hace mal" to the poet who is both "caída y erguida." [Of course Agustini is also playing with the traditional oxymoronic language of mystic Christianity.] The image used for the poet, a lily at the feet of the god is not an image of empowerment but of total powerlessness. The poem ends by equating even the dream of a sunlit embrace with sin: "Perdón, perdón si peco alguna vez, soñando / que me abrazas con alas, ¡todo mío! en el Sol . . ." For Agustini, the embrace of the sunlit god contained in her allusion to the fertile, sunlit story of Leda and the swan ("me abrazas con alas") has become a sin against the voice which she has adopted. The poet remains within her tower as the poem trails off into an ellipsis, the suspension of the expressible.

Perhaps the strongest expression of the vampiric encounter is contained in "Visión". As in "Misterio: ven . . ." the poet imagines herself in a vampiric embrace, with the demon she has summoned brooding over her and this encounter also ends in failure—the buffet of the winged lover is never felt. The poem exists only as the expression of desire: fulfillment, the moment when the poet leaves the tower, equals silence. "Visión" begins with a question, as the poet is unable to distinguish waking from dreaming: "¿Acaso fue en un marco de ilusión, / o en el profundo espejo del deseo, / o fue divina y simplemente en vida / que yo te vi velar mi sueñe la otra noche?" The lover is evoked not in the sunlit terms of "¡Oh Tú!" but as a grotesque midnight growth, a giant mushroom, a being that is neither dead nor alive: "taciturno a mi lado apareciste / como un hongo gigante, muerto y vivo." In an incantatory, repetitive passage the poet evokes the demon lover looming over the sleeping poet as if to feed on her in the same way that Dracula looms over the sleeping Lucy: "the inclinabas a mí . . . como a la copa de cristal de un lago / . . . como un enfermo / de la vida a los opios infallibles." In an inversion of the Christian sacrament that brings life (Take, eat, this is my body . . .) the phantom yearns toward the sleeper "como el creyente / a la oblea de cielo de la hostia . . ." The following three line interjection, "—Gota de nieve con sabor de estrellas / que alimenta los lirios de la Carne, / chispa de Dios que estrella los espíritus—" describes not only the host but the sleeping poet as well, since they are identified as

the objects of desire of the phantom (who is himself dreamed by the poet). In the final two comparisons of this incantatory passage, the phantom realizes that only the sleeper can bring him to life, "Te inclinabas a mí como si fuera / mi cuerpo la inicial de tu destino / en la página oscura de mi lecho" and that through her he can achieve transcendence, "te inclinabas a mí como al milagro / de una ventana abierta al más allá."

The poet answers her invocation of male desire looming over the recumbent female with a vision of herself as serpent: "Y era mi mirada una culebra . . . y era me deseo una culebra" as if to equate sight and desire. The lover is white, he is "cisne" and "la estatua de lirios de tu cuerpo," while the poet is a snake gliding in the shadow, "glisando entre los riscos de la sombra . . ." The identification of woman, especially sexually desirous woman, with the snake, is, of course, an ancient image and one that would be well-known to Agustini, as she demonstrates in another poem where she overtly identifies herself with the triumphant and desiring snake ("Serpentina," which begins, "En mis sueños de amor ¡yo soy serpiente!" Here Agustini authorizes herself as a fatal woman, as lamia, to express her desire, and indeed the link of sexual desire to writing is clear not only in the image of the lover who sees in the poet "la inicial de tu destino / en la página oscura de me lecho" but in the image of printing used to describe their union, "Toda tu vida se imprimió en mi vida . . ." It is Agustini who writes, who is the black snake of letters on the white page of the lover's body.

But this vision of marking and interpenetration ends in failure. The embrace of the poet and her lover is never realized as Agustini again evokes the image of Leda and the swan in her failed encounter:

> Yo esperaba suspensa el aletazo
> del abrazo magnífico; un abrazo
> de cuatro brazos que la gloria viste
> de fiebre y de milagro, ¡será un vuelo!
> Y pueden ser los hechizados brazos
> cuatro raíces de una raza nueva.

The returned embrace "un abrazo de cuatro brazos" can be imagined, but not experienced; it remains in the future tense, "será un vuelo." Nevertheless, although the new race cannot appear, the poet remains in control of her phantom lover, for as she explores the failure of her desire she opens the eyes of her lover to determine the cause of her failure: "te abrí los ojos como un alma, vi / ¡que te hacías atrás y te envolvías / en yo no sé qué pliegue inmenso de la sombra!" And in fact the returned gaze of the phantom is the sign of the necessary failure, for when the lover has eyes of his own (before he has been a mushroom, a tower, a willow, a looming, but eyeless presence) he is no longer the mirror of Agustini's desire, "el profundo espejo del deseo," but a living entity whose opaqueness escapes the poet's desire to possess and be possessed. When she sees his eyes, even if she herself opens them, the lover disappears into an immense fold of darkness.

The sense of a vampiric encounter in these poems is inescapable. But in her conflation of the image of the dark lover who is associated with bats and night with the story of the god/swan of Leda, Agustini has written the female answer to the swan written by Darío and the French symbolists and given a parodic twist to the image of the fatal woman. She uses the same technique in her adoption of the figure of Salomé, another popular representative of the fatal woman. As in her use of the image of the vampire and of Leda, Salomé exists in her texts as a submerged theme, one of the monsters in the lake that stands for the poet's vision of herself: "el cristal de las aguas dormidas / refleja un dios o un monstruo" ("La Ruptura"). In "Lo Inefable" Agustini's poetic voice again asserts the half-dead, half-alive posture of the vampire and ends by invoking the desire of Salomé for the head of the man she loved. The poet begins by asserting her strangeness, she is neither dead, not alive: "Yo muero extrañamente . . . No me mata la vida, / no me mata la Muerte, no me mata el Amor." She is being killed by a thought which cannot express itself, "muero de un pensamiento mudo como una herida." This "pensamiento inmenso" like a monstrous pregnancy, has taken over the poet's life and is devouring her, "devorando alma y carne" and can never come to fruition "no alcanza a dar flor." Agustini again invokes the vampire as she compares this thought to a seed nailed to her entrails by a bite, "trágica simiente / clavada en las entrañas como un diente feroz!" And as always with Agustini, the poem ends in a vision expressed in the future tense of possibility highly mediated by doubt: "Pero arrancarla un día en una flor que abriera / milagrosa, inviolable . . . ¡Ah, más grande no fuera / tener entre las manos la cabeza de Dios!" Salomé, of course, received for her dancing the head of John the Baptist, God's representative. Agustini suggests here not only that the price to pay for the "miraculous, inviolable" flower is damnation but in the phrase "más grande no fuera," that this resolution is impossible.

Agustini's effort to appropriate the fatal woman, the vampire, Salomé as expressions of her own desire end always in failure: the daylit embrace of Leda and the swan can not exist for her. In a short untitled poem which begins "La intensa realidad de un sueño lúgubre" she makes clear the dilemma on which her poetic voice is based. As so often in her poetry, the poem begins by invoking a dream moment of total yearning, total possession:

> La intensa realidad de un sueño lúgubre
> puso en mis manos tu cabeza muerta;
> yo la apresaba como hambriento buitre . . .
> y con más alma que en la Vida, trémula,
> ¡le sonreía como nadie nunca! . . .
> ¡Era tan mía cuando estaba muerta!

The poet holds her lover's dead head which she clutches with the voraciousness of a vulture. She has more life in her dream than she has in life, and can smile as no one else can. This is a dream of total possession, and total frustration, since the poet can only hold part of the lover, even in dream he escapes her. The second verse makes clear the defeat of the dreamer:

> Hoy he visto en la Vida, bella, impávida,
> como un triunfo estatuario, tu cabeza.
> Más frío me dio así que en el idilio
> fúnebre aquél, al estrecharla muerta . . .
> ¡Y así la lloro hasta agotar mi vida . . .
> así tan viva cuando me es ajena!

The head (still unattached to a body) is now seen in life as untouchable, as lifeless as a statue. As it gains in life, it recedes from the poet, and she is left to weep in an agony of hopeless desire.

Agustini entitled the last group of verses published in her lifetime *Los Cálices Vacíos*. This negative image of the empty flower, which as we have seen in "¡Oh, Tú!" can never be filled, suggests the limitation inherent in Agustini's stance toward her tradition. For although she was able to use the stereotypical image of the *femme fatale* to create her own voice, the limitation of the parodic is its essential conservatism; Agustini was never able to imagine a new way to express desire. Barrès unkind remark about Rachilde, "on dirait une petite fille qui fume la pipe en peintulant" can be applied to Agustini as well. She is able to give Lucy a voice of her own, she has written desire on the white body of the lover she conjures up, she is both the vampire and the bitten. But she is nevertheless caught in an image of female desire as fatality which is limited by a fundamental aridity. Perhaps, had she lived, she would have been able to move beyond Lucy, beyond Salomé into the sunlit world which she could perceive, but not write.

Elaine Showalter   (essay date 1995)

SOURCE: "Decadent Queen," in *The Times Literary Supplement*, No. 4813, June 30, 1995, pp. 5-6.

[*In the following essay, Showalter discusses the dominant themes in Rachilde's works.*]

In **"Grape-Gatherers of Sodom"**, a remarkable story about the genesis of homosexuality published in 1894, the French writer Rachilde displayed the perverse tastes and sensuous prose style that had won her the nickname "Mademoiselle Baudelaire". Out of the walled town of Sodom comes a procession of male grape-pickers led by a stern patriarch. As they rest in the vineyard, the men are approached by a naked girl, her breasts burned black by the sun, who seductively twines about their sleeping bodies. She is one of the wives and daughters who have been condemned as temptresses by the priests, and driven into the desert. "I am thirsty", the woman cries, and the men look knowingly at one another: "Oh yes! It was evident to them all that she had a thirst in her!". At the patriarch's command, they stone her to death, and she falls writhing into the vat of grapes where her blood mingles with the wine. That night, the Sodomites fill their cups, and commit for the first time their eponymous "sin against nature".

This lurid parable (translated in Brian Stableford's *Dedalus Book of Decadence,* 1992) also conveys the negative and contradictory nature of Rachilde's sexual politics. Homosexuality, she appears to say, is the product of a murderous patriarchal misogyny; but on the other hand, women are poisonous *femmes fatales,* whose sexuality threatens male spirituality, genius, and transcendence. As the only women writer admitted to the literary men's club which dominated the Parisian cultural scene of the 1880s and 90s, Rachilde balanced feminist ambitions with decadent attitudes. Enormously productive—she wrote over sixty books—editor, *saloniste,* mentor of Jarry and Colette, defender of Dreyfus and Wilde, Rachilde was a major figure in *fin-desiècle* culture, and a reappraisal of her work is long overdue. These three English paperback translations of Rachilde's best-known novels, **Monsieur Venus, La Marquise de Sade,** and **La Jongleuse,** should spark a revival of this controversial writer. Her novels reverse the gender roles in French decadent writing, and carry their fantasies to sadistic extremes. Acting out elaborate rituals of sexual revenge against patriarchal conventions, her cruel heroines dominate, torment, corrupt and even embalm their lovers.

According to Jennifer Birkett, who has a brilliant chapter on Rachilde in her study of French decadence, *The Sins of the Fathers* (1986), she owed her success to "her willingness to play and play up the decadent stereotypes" and to put her imagination "at the service of male masochistic fantasies". None the less, Rachilde stands out as the only woman who successfully contested the theories which the decadent avant-garde used against female artists. Baudelaire and Wilde described the decadent dandy as the product of supreme artifice, opposed to all that is merely biological and material. Often called the Queen of the Decadents, Rachilde might also have been called the queen of the fetishists. She both pandered to and parodied decadent sensibility, using its symbols to work out a narrative logic of female fetishism, its sources in religious ritual and anthropology, and its relation to women's sado-masochism, ornamentation, commodification and art. Freudian theory links fetishism to the castration complex; female fetishism would represent an especially desperate effort of denial and compensation.

But the fetishism of Rachilde's heroines is always connected to the female body. Her women cross-dress or wear painfully tight dresses that make them look like insects, snakes, or flowers. They inhabit rooms that resemble the interior of the body, design piquant combinations of cuisine, collect eroticized objects that mirror themselves and combine the obsessions of the decadent artist with the domestic skills of conventional femininity. Whereas Huysmans's Des Esseintes in *A Rebours* gives a funeral banquet in memory of his lost virility, with a black menu of turtle soup, rye bread, olives,

caviar, liquorice and chocolate, Eliante, the heroine of Rachilde's novel **The Juggler,** slyly serves her lover a dish of poached eggs on a purée of brains. Eggs over brains—the woman's recipe; brains over eggs would be the choice of the man. It is woman's biological capacity to create that gives her the edge in the sexual struggle.

Rachilde's career was as daring as her fiction. Her real name was Marguerite Eymery, and she was born in 1860 at Le Cros in the Perigord, the only child of a cavalry officer—who was himself the illegitimate son of a marquis—and an intellectual bourgeoise mother. As a child, she struggled hopelessly to please her father, who wanted a son to hunt and ride with him; although he detested writers, whom he scornfully called *plumitifs,* she started to write very young and took advantage of the family's neglect by reading voraciously in her grandfather's library, where she encountered Voltaire and Sade.

When the family attempted to marry her off at the age of fourteen to a middle-aged army officer, she attempted suicide, flinging herself into the frog pond. The engagement was called off, and writing became more and more the centre of her life. Under the androgynous pseudonym "Rachilde", which she claimed had come to her from a sixteenth-century Swedish medium in a seance, she began to publish stories in local newspapers. At fifteen, she sent a story with a request for advice to Victor Hugo, who responded with a brief but encouraging note: "Remerciements et applaudissements. Courage, Mademoiselle".

Rachilde immediately left for Paris, where she moved into literary circles at Le Chat Noir, the Café de l'Avenir and the Théâtre des Arts. There was no shortage of women writers on the scene—as one wit remarked, "there are so many women of letters today that you can't find a housekeeper"—but Rachilde quickly stood out. Often cross-dressing, calling herself "Rachilde, Homme des Lettres", she was accepted by the masculine society of "Les Hydropathes" (so called because they never drank water). The Symbolist poet and novelist Jean Lorrain described her as "a studious schoolgirl . . . with tiny restless hands and the earnest profile of a Greek youth or a young Frenchman in love". They were a striking couple at the masquerade artists's ball, he in a pink tunic and leopard-skin *cache-sexe,* she in baby shoes and a short dress.

In 1884, Rachilde published her first great *succès de scandale,* **Monsieur Venus.** Printed in Brussels, the novel was immediately seized as pornography, and she was sentenced to two years imprisonment (if she ever entered Belgium), and a fine of 2,000 francs. The novel shocked and impressed her contemporaries. "Pornography, of course", Barbey d'Aurevilly remarked, "but so distinguished!" In Raoule de Vénérande, Rachilde created a notorious decadent heroine, an aristocratic Amazon who sets out to enslave, effeminize and corrupt a working-class man, and to savour every variation of sexual perversity, even necrophilia. Indeed, Wilde had originally considered calling the poisonous book which corrupts Dorian Gray *Le Secret de Raoul*. Raoule insists on playing the male role with her "mistress", Jacques Silvert, in a sadistic liaison which reaches consummation when he is killed in a duel. With hammer, scissors and pincers, she removes his hair, teeth and nails, and has them placed in a wax dummy. Jacques literally becomes "monsieur Venus"—a fetishized male version of the "anatomical Venus" used in European medical faculties to teach doctors about the female body. At night, sometimes dressed as a woman, sometimes as a man, Raoule comes to admire the mannequin: "A spring set inside the lower body is connected to the mouth and makes it move."

Rachilde returned to, and explained, this bizarre image of a mechanized body in *The Marquise de Sade* (1887), a partly autobiographical *Bildungsroman* that explores the development of a sadistic personality in a girl warped and embittered by a misogynist society. As a lonely child neglected by her parents, Mary Barbe learns that boys are worshipped while girls are despised. By the age of ten, she already lives out violent fantasies of power: "In the stories she made up for herself, Mary usually had a little slave, half boy, half angel, who loved her very much and as a matter of honour would put up with a multitude of grotesque tortures. The feelings around these chimerical travels were always unbelievably violent, in inverse ratio to the icy calm of her real actions. She would slaughter young Indians wholesale while she was quietly scalloping a handkerchief or counting embroidery stitches." Indeed, Rachilde observes, such violent dreams are common among unloved and neglected children. "There are more little girls or little boys making up stories than one would think: some of them have a cretinous look which distresses their parents, while others have the self-satisfied expression of studious children stuffed with their lessons."

As an orphaned adolescent, Mary goes to live with a reclusive uncle who is a scientist. Summoned for the first time to his office, she sees "an anatomical Venus . . . stretched asleep in a corner above the library, banished there like some discarded doll". The mannequin becomes both her image for the objectification of women and her instrument of revenge. If the female body is seen by men as a case to be pried open, or a painted shell to be admired, women's best protection is to turn themselves into automatons, to construct a glossy carapace. Mary uses her intelligence and sexuality to control her uncle, persuading him to teach her all he knows about geology, anatomy and chemistry, and finally convincing him to instruct her about sex. "When Mary did not grasp something he would explain it, choosing technical terms in preference to an erotic vocabulary, and soon this virgin was as experienced as a long-married woman." The anatomical Venus, "that marvellous and mechanically obscene precious thing", becomes a figure of Mary herself.

When she marries a wealthy baron, Mary uses her expertise to defend herself, explaining on her wedding night that she hates men, does not wish to bear a child and will poison him if he attempts to force her. Instead, she initiates a sado-masochistic relationship with her husband's illegitimate son, the student Paul Riche. At the end of the novel, she has destroyed both men, and is still seeking her male equal: "Where was the fearsome male she needed, she, a female whose mettle was that of a lioness? . . . He was either extinct or to come." At a transvestite ball, she is struck by the beauty and variety of the men, "better dressed than the women, in more striking colours and more costly fabrics . . . there were Watteau pastorals studded with flowers from bosom to toe and solidly corseted like dolls' waists, and several in Attic peplums with cameos; many wore picture-book outfits, slender as can be in Empire-style crinolines." Excited and repelled, she fantasizes about killing one of the men in sadistic ritual: "an exquisite plan . . . one which she would perhaps never carry out, but would brighten her thoughts through many a dull day".

La Marquise de Sade is a unique text in nineteenth-century women's writing, combining the realistic structure of a Victorian women's novel like *Jane Eyre* or *The Mill on the Floss* with the pornographic and the surreal. It was Rachilde's most intense and transgressive speculation on the psychodynamics of female perversion. In 1889, she married the writer Alfred Vallette, and the next year they produced a child, Gabrielle, and jointly revived the review *Mercure de France*. Its first issue included contributions from Mallarmé, Rémy de Gourmont and Villiers de l'Isle-Adam. Rachilde continued to play an active role in French literary life, as a writer, playwright and mentor of the young Alfred Jarry. Among her admirers were Wilde and Beardsley, who attended her Tuesday salon in the rue des Ecoles when they were in Paris. Rachilde managed to charm the dissolute, eccentric, radical and hedonistic artists of her day without succumbing to disorder herself. She remained happily married to Vallette, and became well known as someone who never danced, drank, or took more drugs than an occasional taste of hashish mixed with apricot jam.

The Juggler (1900), regarded by many critics as Rachilde's best novel, contains many of the elements of her earlier work, but represents a different, more disillusioned phase. The decadent heroine is still a glamorous "painted doll" in a tight, metallic dress, her hair a "sharp-edged helmet"; she is still dominant, capricious, aloof; still expert in exotic sexual and culinary techniques; but she is ageing and giving way to the New Woman, the practical feminist of the twentieth century who lacks mystery and art. Eliante is a dancer who juggles with knives, in a metaphor for the risky play with sex roles that continues in this book. The Creole widow of a sea captain, she lives alone with her egg-shaped bed, collections of spices, pornographic ivory idols and oriental robes. Although Leon, the medical student she picks up at the theatre, is fascinated by her,

her desires are completely fetishistic; she loves an exquisite alabaster urn and can achieve orgasm only in contemplating it. Eliante calls herself "a free recluse", an "emancipated nun", who must remain celibate and pour her passion into the objects that surround her.

In contrast to Eliante is her niece Missie, the cigarette-smoking, gauche, outspoken woman of the future: "a little coarse, quarrelsome, drunk on her recent freedom, new at everything, working at random, and piling up popularizers in the bottom of her memory to vulgarize more without much gain". Eliante sees femininity as a commodity which the new century will market like clothes in the department stores; Missie is the symbol of a future when "the grace of woman . . . may be recognized as a public utility and be socialized to the point of becoming a banal article, a bazaar object. . . . One will find types of tender or amusing women with millions of copies like the creations of the big . . . *fashion stores* where it is always the same thing." But after seducing Leon into marriage with Missie, Eliante kills herself in her final juggling performance.

The Juggler is the bitter-sweet tale of the older woman who loses or yields a younger man to a woman of his own age, a romantic triangle which has been a staple of twentieth-century French narrative from Colette's *Chéri* to Eric Rohmer's film *Ma Nuit Chez Maud*. Rachilde had accurately foreseen her own decline in the face of a younger generation. Although she continued to publish novels and plays, her moment had passed. She feuded with the Surrealists over their blatant sexism, while her 1928 polemic, *Pourquoi je ne suis pas feministe,* alienated other radical women writers who might have supported her. When she died in 1953 at the age of ninety-four, Rachilde had been virtually forgotten.

Now rediscovered in Britain, Rachilde provokes much debate over her standing as a feminist writer. Clearly Rachilde cannot be easily assimilated into the feminist canon; she is a disturbing writer who celebrates the destructive and mechanized trappings of hyper-femininity while denouncing feminism and its interventions in the real world. But the discussion of her relation to feminism obscures the originality and distinction of her work, and perhaps has kept it from receiving the full critical attention it deserves. Like Wilde, Rachilde speaks to and about the glittering psychopathologies of the *fin de siècle;* she ought to be a writer whose time has come.

FURTHER READING

Lukacher, Maryline. "'Mademoiselle Baudelaire': Rachilde and the Sexual Difference." In *Maternal Fictions: Stendhal, Sand, Rachilde, and Bataille*, pp. 109-69. Durham, N. C.: Duke University Press, 1994.
    Feminist, psychoanalytic readings of Rachilde's *Monsieur Vénus, La Marquise de Sade*, and *Le meneur de louves.*

Waelti-Walters, Jennifer. "Perversion and Social Criticism." In *Feminist Novelists of the Belle Epoque: Love as a Lifestyle*, pp. 156-73. Bloomington: Indiana University Press, 1990.
    Discusses Rachilde's presentation of sexual deviance in her novels as a critique of nineteenth-century bourgeois morality.

Zeigler, Robert. "Rachilde and 'l'amour compliqué'." In *Atlantis: A Women's Studies Journal* 11, No. 2 (Spring 1986): 115-24.
    Links qualities of aggressive female sexuality in Rachilde's novels, *Monsieur Vénus, La Marquise de Sade*, and *La jongleuse*, to the suicidal proclivity of her heroines.

Additional coverage of Rachilde's life and career is contained in the following source published by Gale Research: *Dictionary of Literary Biography,* vol. 123.

Twentieth-Century Literary Criticism

Cumulative Indexes
Volumes 1-67

How to Use This Index

The main references

Calvino, Italo
1923-1985.....CLC 5, 8, 11, 22, 33, 39,
73; SSC 3

list all author entries in the following Gale Literary Criticism series:

BLC = *Black Literature Criticism*
CLC = *Contemporary Literary Criticism*
CLR = *Children's Literature Review*
CMLC = *Classical and Medieval Literature Criticism*
DA = *DISCovering Authors*
DC = *Drama Criticism*
HLC = *Hispanic Literature Criticism*
LC = *Literature Criticism from 1400 to 1800*
NCLC = *Nineteenth-Century Literature Criticism*
PC = *Poetry Criticism*
SSC = *Short Story Criticism*
TCLC = *Twentieth-Century Literary Criticism*
WLC = *World Literature Criticism, 1500 to the Present*

The cross-references

See also CANR 23; CA 85-88;
obituary CA 116

list all author entries in the following Gale biographical and literary sources:

AAYA = *Authors & Artists for Young Adults*
AITN = *Authors in the News*
BEST = *Bestsellers*
BW = *Black Writers*
CA = *Contemporary Authors*
CAAS = *Contemporary Authors Autobiography Series*
CABS = *Contemporary Authors Bibliographical Series*
CANR = *Contemporary Authors New Revision Series*
CAP = *Contemporary Authors Permanent Series*
CDALB = *Concise Dictionary of American Literary Biography*
CDBLB = *Concise Dictionary of British Literary Biography*
DLB = *Dictionary of Literary Biography*
DLBD = *Dictionary of Literary Biography Documentary Series*
DLBY = *Dictionary of Literary Biography Yearbook*
HW = *Hispanic Writers*
JRDA = *Junior DISCovering Authors*
MAICYA = *Major Authors and Illustrators for Children and Young Adults*
MTCW = *Major 20th-Century Writers*
NNAL = *Native North American Literature*
SAAS = *Something about the Author Autobiography Series*
SATA = *Something about the Author*
YABC = *Yesterday's Authors of Books for Children*

Literary Criticism Series
Cumulative Author Index

A. E. . . . . TCLC 3, 10
See also Russell, George William

Abasiyanik, Sait Faik   1906-1954
See Sait Faik
See also CA 123

Abbey, Edward   1927-1989 . . . . . . CLC 36, 59
See also CA 45-48; 128; CANR 2, 41

Abbott, Lee K(ittredge)   1947- . . . . . . CLC 48
See also CA 124; CANR 51; DLB 130

Abe, Kobo
1924-1993 . . . . CLC 8, 22, 53, 81;
DAM NOV
See also CA 65-68; 140; CANR 24; MTCW

Abelard, Peter   c. 1079-c. 1142 . . . CMLC 11
See also DLB 115

Abell, Kjeld   1901-1961. . . . . CLC 15
See also CA 111

Abish, Walter   1931- . . . . CLC 22
See also CA 101; CANR 37; DLB 130

Abrahams, Peter (Henry)   1919- . . . . . CLC 4
See also BW 1; CA 57-60; CANR 26;
DLB 117; MTCW

Abrams, M(eyer) H(oward)   1912- . . . CLC 24
See also CA 57-60; CANR 13, 33; DLB 67

Abse, Dannie
1923- . . . CLC 7, 29; DAB; DAM POET
See also CA 53-56; CAAS 1; CANR 4, 46;
DLB 27

Achebe, (Albert) Chinua(lumogu)
1930- . . . . . CLC 1, 3, 5, 7, 11, 26, 51, 75;
BLC; DA; DAB; DAC; DAM MST,
MULT, NOV; WLC
See also AAYA 15; BW 2; CA 1-4R;
CANR 6, 26, 47; CLR 20; DLB 117;
MAICYA; MTCW; SATA 40;
SATA-Brief 38

Acker, Kathy   1948- . . . . CLC 45
See also CA 117; 122; CANR 55

Ackroyd, Peter   1949- . . . . CLC 34, 52
See also CA 123; 127; CANR 51; DLB 155;
INT 127

Acorn, Milton   1923- . . . . CLC 15; DAC
See also CA 103; DLB 53; INT 103

Adamov, Arthur
1908-1970 . . . . CLC 4, 25; DAM DRAM
See also CA 17-18; 25-28R; CAP 2; MTCW

Adams, Alice (Boyd)   1926- . . . CLC 6, 13, 46
See also CA 81-84; CANR 26, 53;
DLBY 86; INT CANR-26; MTCW

Adams, Andy   1859-1935. . . . . TCLC 56
See also YABC 1

Adams, Douglas (Noel)
1952- . . . . CLC 27, 60; DAM POP
See also AAYA 4; BEST 89:3; CA 106;
CANR 34; DLBY 83; JRDA

Adams, Francis   1862-1893 . . . . NCLC 33

Adams, Henry (Brooks)
1838-1918 . . . . . . TCLC 4, 52; DA; DAB;
DAC; DAM MST
See also CA 104; 133; DLB 12, 47

Adams, Richard (George)
1920- . . . . CLC 4, 5, 18; DAM NOV
See also AAYA 16; AITN 1, 2; CA 49-52;
CANR 3, 35; CLR 20; JRDA; MAICYA;
MTCW; SATA 7, 69

Adamson, Joy(-Friederike Victoria)
1910-1980 . . . . CLC 17
See also CA 69-72; 93-96; CANR 22;
MTCW; SATA 11; SATA-Obit 22

Adcock, Fleur   1934- . . . . CLC 41
See also CA 25-28R; CAAS 23; CANR 11,
34; DLB 40

Addams, Charles (Samuel)
1912-1988 . . . . CLC 30
See also CA 61-64; 126; CANR 12

Addison, Joseph   1672-1719 . . . . LC 18
See also CDBLB 1660-1789; DLB 101

Adler, Alfred (F.)   1870-1937 . . . . . . TCLC 61
See also CA 119

Adler, C(arole) S(chwerdtfeger)
1932- . . . . CLC 35
See also AAYA 4; CA 89-92; CANR 19,
40; JRDA; MAICYA; SAAS 15;
SATA 26, 63

Adler, Renata   1938- . . . . CLC 8, 31
See also CA 49-52; CANR 5, 22, 52;
MTCW

Ady, Endre   1877-1919 . . . . TCLC 11
See also CA 107

Aeschylus
525B.C.-456B.C. . . . . CMLC 11; DA;
DAB; DAC; DAM DRAM, MST

Afton, Effie
See Harper, Frances Ellen Watkins

Agapida, Fray Antonio
See Irving, Washington

Agee, James (Rufus)
1909-1955 . . . . TCLC 1, 19; DAM NOV
See also AITN 1; CA 108; 148;
CDALB 1941-1968; DLB 2, 26, 152

Aghill, Gordon
See Silverberg, Robert

Agnon, S(hmuel) Y(osef Halevi)
1888-1970 . . . . CLC 4, 8, 14
See also CA 17-18; 25-28R; CAP 2; MTCW

Agrippa von Nettesheim, Henry Cornelius
1486-1535 . . . . LC 27

Aherne, Owen
See Cassill, R(onald) V(erlin)

Ai   1947- . . . . CLC 4, 14, 69
See also CA 85-88; CAAS 13; DLB 120

Aickman, Robert (Fordyce)
1914-1981 . . . . CLC 57
See also CA 5-8R; CANR 3

Aiken, Conrad (Potter)
1889-1973 . . . . CLC 1, 3, 5, 10, 52;
DAM NOV, POET; SSC 9
See also CA 5-8R; 45-48; CANR 4;
CDALB 1929-1941; DLB 9, 45, 102;
MTCW; SATA 3, 30

Aiken, Joan (Delano)   1924- . . . . CLC 35
See also AAYA 1; CA 9-12R; CANR 4, 23,
34; CLR 1, 19; DLB 161; JRDA;
MAICYA; MTCW; SAAS 1; SATA 2,
30, 73

Ainsworth, William Harrison
1805-1882 . . . . NCLC 13
See also DLB 21; SATA 24

Aitmatov, Chingiz (Torekulovich)
1928- . . . . CLC 71
See also CA 103; CANR 38; MTCW;
SATA 56

Akers, Floyd
See Baum, L(yman) Frank

Akhmadulina, Bella Akhatovna
1937- . . . . CLC 53; DAM POET
See also CA 65-68

Akhmatova, Anna
1888-1966 . . . . CLC 11, 25, 64;
DAM POET; PC 2
See also CA 19-20; 25-28R; CANR 35;
CAP 1; MTCW

Aksakov, Sergei Timofeyvich
1791-1859 . . . . NCLC 2

Aksenov, Vassily
See Aksyonov, Vassily (Pavlovich)

Aksyonov, Vassily (Pavlovich)
1932- . . . . CLC 22, 37
See also CA 53-56; CANR 12, 48

Akutagawa Ryunosuke
1892-1927 . . . . TCLC 16
See also CA 117

Alain   1868-1951 . . . . TCLC 41

Alain-Fournier . . . . TCLC 6
See also Fournier, Henri Alban
See also DLB 65

Alarcon, Pedro Antonio de
1833-1891 . . . . NCLC 1

Alas (y Urena), Leopoldo (Enrique Garcia)
1852-1901 . . . . TCLC 29
See also CA 113; 131; HW

Albee, Edward (Franklin III)
1928- . . . . . . CLC 1, 2, 3, 5, 9, 11, 13, 25,
53, 86; DA; DAB; DAC; DAM DRAM,
MST; WLC
See also AITN 1; CA 5-8R; CABS 3;
CANR 8, 54; CDALB 1941-1968; DLB 7;
INT CANR-8; MTCW

Alberti, Rafael   1902- . . . . CLC 7
See also CA 85-88; DLB 108

Albert the Great   1200(?)-1280 . . . . CMLC 16
See also DLB 115

Alcala-Galiano, Juan Valera y
See Valera y Alcala-Galiano, Juan

Alcott, Amos Bronson 1799-1888 . . **NCLC 1**
See also DLB 1

Alcott, Louisa May
1832-1888 . . . . . **NCLC 6, 58; DA; DAB;**
DAC; DAM MST, NOV; WLC
See also CDALB 1865-1917; CLR 1, 38;
DLB 1, 42, 79; DLBD 14; JRDA;
MAICYA; YABC 1

Aldanov, M. A.
See Aldanov, Mark (Alexandrovich)

Aldanov, Mark (Alexandrovich)
1886(?)-1957 . . . . **TCLC 23**
See also CA 118

Aldington, Richard 1892-1962. . . . . . **CLC 49**
See also CA 85-88; CANR 45; DLB 20, 36,
100, 149

Aldiss, Brian W(ilson)
1925- . . . . **CLC 5, 14, 40; DAM NOV**
See also CA 5-8R; CAAS 2; CANR 5, 28;
DLB 14; MTCW; SATA 34

Alegria, Claribel
1924- . . . . **CLC 75; DAM MULT**
See also CA 131; CAAS 15; DLB 145; HW

Alegria, Fernando 1918-. . . . . **CLC 57**
See also CA 9-12R; CANR 5, 32; HW

Aleichem, Sholom . . . . **TCLC 1, 35**
See also Rabinovitch, Sholem

Aleixandre, Vicente
1898-1984 . . . . **CLC 9, 36; DAM POET;**
PC 15
See also CA 85-88; 114; CANR 26;
DLB 108; HW; MTCW

Alepoudelis, Odysseus
See Elytis, Odysseus

Aleshkovsky, Joseph 1929-
See Aleshkovsky, Yuz
See also CA 121; 128

Aleshkovsky, Yuz . . . . **CLC 44**
See also Aleshkovsky, Joseph

Alexander, Lloyd (Chudley) 1924- . . **CLC 35**
See also AAYA 1; CA 1-4R; CANR 1, 24,
38, 55; CLR 1, 5; DLB 52; JRDA;
MAICYA; MTCW; SAAS 19; SATA 3,
49, 81

Alexie, Sherman (Joseph, Jr.)
1966- . . . . **CLC 96; DAM MULT**
See also CA 138; NNAL

Alfau, Felipe 1902-. . . . . **CLC 66**
See also CA 137

Alger, Horatio, Jr. 1832-1899. . . . . **NCLC 8**
See also DLB 42; SATA 16

Algren, Nelson 1909-1981 . . . . **CLC 4, 10, 33**
See also CA 13-16R; 103; CANR 20;
CDALB 1941-1968; DLB 9; DLBY 81,
82; MTCW

Ali, Ahmed 1910- . . . . **CLC 69**
See also CA 25-28R; CANR 15, 34

Alighieri, Dante 1265-1321 . . . . **CMLC 3, 18**

Allan, John B.
See Westlake, Donald E(dwin)

Allen, Edward 1948-. . . . . **CLC 59**

Allen, Paula Gunn
1939- . . . . **CLC 84; DAM MULT**
See also CA 112; 143; NNAL

Allen, Roland
See Ayckbourn, Alan

Allen, Sarah A.
See Hopkins, Pauline Elizabeth

Allen, Woody
1935- . . . . **CLC 16, 52; DAM POP**
See also AAYA 10; CA 33-36R; CANR 27,
38; DLB 44; MTCW

Allende, Isabel
1942- . . . . **CLC 39, 57, 97; DAM MULT,**
NOV; HLC
See also AAYA 18; CA 125; 130;
CANR 51; DLB 145; HW; INT 130;
MTCW

Alleyn, Ellen
See Rossetti, Christina (Georgina)

Allingham, Margery (Louise)
1904-1966 . . . . **CLC 19**
See also CA 5-8R; 25-28R; CANR 4;
DLB 77; MTCW

Allingham, William 1824-1889 . . . **NCLC 25**
See also DLB 35

Allison, Dorothy E. 1949- . . . . **CLC 78**
See also CA 140

Allston, Washington 1779-1843. . . . **NCLC 2**
See also DLB 1

Almedingen, E. M. . . . . **CLC 12**
See also Almedingen, Martha Edith von
See also SATA 3

Almedingen, Martha Edith von 1898-1971
See Almedingen, E. M.
See also CA 1-4R; CANR 1

Almqvist, Carl Jonas Love
1793-1866 . . . . **NCLC 42**

Alonso, Damaso 1898-1990 . . . . **CLC 14**
See also CA 110; 131; 130; DLB 108; HW

Alov
See Gogol, Nikolai (Vasilyevich)

Alta 1942-. . . . . **CLC 19**
See also CA 57-60

Alter, Robert B(ernard) 1935-. . . . . . **CLC 34**
See also CA 49-52; CANR 1, 47

Alther, Lisa 1944-. . . . . **CLC 7, 41**
See also CA 65-68; CANR 12, 30, 51;
MTCW

Altman, Robert 1925-. . . . . **CLC 16**
See also CA 73-76; CANR 43

Alvarez, A(lfred) 1929-. . . . . **CLC 5, 13**
See also CA 1-4R; CANR 3, 33; DLB 14,
40

Alvarez, Alejandro Rodriguez 1903-1965
See Casona, Alejandro
See also CA 131; 93-96; HW

Alvarez, Julia 1950-. . . . . **CLC 93**
See also CA 147

Alvaro, Corrado 1896-1956 . . . . **TCLC 60**

Amado, Jorge
1912- . . . . **CLC 13, 40; DAM MULT,**
NOV; HLC
See also CA 77-80; CANR 35; DLB 113;
MTCW

Ambler, Eric 1909-. . . . . **CLC 4, 6, 9**
See also CA 9-12R; CANR 7, 38; DLB 77;
MTCW

Amichai, Yehuda 1924- . . . . . . **CLC 9, 22, 57**
See also CA 85-88; CANR 46; MTCW

Amiel, Henri Frederic 1821-1881 . . **NCLC 4**

Amis, Kingsley (William)
1922-1995 . . . . . **CLC 1, 2, 3, 5, 8, 13, 40,**
44; DA; DAB; DAC; DAM MST, NOV
See also AITN 2; CA 9-12R; 150; CANR 8,
28, 54; CDBLB 1945-1960; DLB 15, 27,
100, 139; INT CANR-8; MTCW

Amis, Martin (Louis)
1949- . . . . **CLC 4, 9, 38, 62**
See also BEST 90:3; CA 65-68; CANR 8,
27, 54; DLB 14; INT CANR-27

Ammons, A(rchie) R(andolph)
1926- . . . . **CLC 2, 3, 5, 8, 9, 25, 57;**
DAM POET; PC 16
See also AITN 1; CA 9-12R; CANR 6, 36,
51; DLB 5, 165; MTCW

Amo, Tauraatua i
See Adams, Henry (Brooks)

Anand, Mulk Raj
1905- . . . . **CLC 23, 93; DAM NOV**
See also CA 65-68; CANR 32; MTCW

Anatol
See Schnitzler, Arthur

Anaya, Rudolfo A(lfonso)
1937- . . . . **CLC 23; DAM MULT, NOV;**
HLC
See also CA 45-48; CAAS 4; CANR 1, 32,
51; DLB 82; HW 1; MTCW

Andersen, Hans Christian
1805-1875 . . . . **NCLC 7; DA; DAB;**
DAC; DAM MST, POP; SSC 6; WLC
See also CLR 6; MAICYA; YABC 1

Anderson, C. Farley
See Mencken, H(enry) L(ouis); Nathan,
George Jean

Anderson, Jessica (Margaret) Queale
. . . . **CLC 37**
See also CA 9-12R; CANR 4

Anderson, Jon (Victor)
1940- . . . . **CLC 9; DAM POET**
See also CA 25-28R; CANR 20

Anderson, Lindsay (Gordon)
1923-1994 . . . . **CLC 20**
See also CA 125; 128; 146

Anderson, Maxwell
1888-1959 . . . . . . **TCLC 2; DAM DRAM**
See also CA 105; 152; DLB 7

Anderson, Poul (William) 1926- . . . . **CLC 15**
See also AAYA 5; CA 1-4R; CAAS 2;
CANR 2, 15, 34; DLB 8; INT CANR-15;
MTCW; SATA 90; SATA-Brief 39

Anderson, Robert (Woodruff)
1917- . . . . **CLC 23; DAM DRAM**
See also AITN 1; CA 21-24R; CANR 32;
DLB 7

Anderson, Sherwood
1876-1941 . . . . **TCLC 1, 10, 24; DA;**
DAB; DAC; DAM MST, NOV; SSC 1;
WLC
See also CA 104; 121; CDALB 1917-1929;
DLB 4, 9, 86; DLBD 1; MTCW

Andier, Pierre
See Desnos, Robert

Andouard
See Giraudoux, (Hippolyte) Jean

Andrade, Carlos Drummond de . . . . . . **CLC 18**
See also Drummond de Andrade, Carlos

Andrade, Mario de   1893-1945 . . . . . **TCLC 43**

Andreae, Johann V(alentin)
1586-1654 . . . . **LC 32**
See also DLB 164

Andreas-Salome, Lou   1861-1937 . . . **TCLC 56**
See also DLB 66

Andrewes, Lancelot   1555-1626 . . . . **LC 5**
See also DLB 151, 172

Andrews, Cicily Fairfield
See West, Rebecca

Andrews, Elton V.
See Pohl, Frederik

Andreyev, Leonid (Nikolaevich)
1871-1919 . . . . **TCLC 3**
See also CA 104

Andric, Ivo   1892-1975 . . . . **CLC 8**
See also CA 81-84; 57-60; CANR 43;
DLB 147; MTCW

Angelique, Pierre
See Bataille, Georges

Angell, Roger   1920- . . . . **CLC 26**
See also CA 57-60; CANR 13, 44; DLB 171

Angelou, Maya
1928- . . . . **CLC 12, 35, 64, 77; BLC; DA;
DAB; DAC; DAM MST, MULT, POET,
POP**
See also AAYA 7; BW 2; CA 65-68;
CANR 19, 42; DLB 38; MTCW;
SATA 49

Annensky, Innokenty Fyodorovich
1856-1909 . . . . **TCLC 14**
See also CA 110

Anon, Charles Robert
See Pessoa, Fernando (Antonio Nogueira)

Anouilh, Jean (Marie Lucien Pierre)
1910-1987 . . . . . . **CLC 1, 3, 8, 13, 40, 50;
DAM DRAM**
See also CA 17-20R; 123; CANR 32;
MTCW

Anthony, Florence
See Ai

Anthony, John
See Ciardi, John (Anthony)

Anthony, Peter
See Shaffer, Anthony (Joshua); Shaffer,
Peter (Levin)

Anthony, Piers   1934- . . **CLC 35; DAM POP**
See also AAYA 11; CA 21-24R; CANR 28;
DLB 8; MTCW; SAAS 22; SATA 84

Antoine, Marc
See Proust, (Valentin-Louis-George-Eugene-)
Marcel

Antoninus, Brother
See Everson, William (Oliver)

Antonioni, Michelangelo   1912- . . . . . **CLC 20**
See also CA 73-76; CANR 45

Antschel, Paul   1920-1970
See Celan, Paul
See also CA 85-88; CANR 33; MTCW

Anwar, Chairil   1922-1949 . . . . **TCLC 22**
See also CA 121

Apollinaire, Guillaume
1880-1918 . . . . **TCLC 3, 8, 51;
DAM POET; PC 7**
See also Kostrowitzki, Wilhelm Apollinaris
de
See also CA 152

Appelfeld, Aharon   1932- . . . . **CLC 23, 47**
See also CA 112; 133

Apple, Max (Isaac)   1941- . . . . **CLC 9, 33**
See also CA 81-84; CANR 19, 54; DLB 130

Appleman, Philip (Dean)   1926- . . . . . **CLC 51**
See also CA 13-16R; CAAS 18; CANR 6,
29

Appleton, Lawrence
See Lovecraft, H(oward) P(hillips)

Apteryx
See Eliot, T(homas) S(tearns)

Apuleius, (Lucius Madaurensis)
125(?)-175(?) . . . . **CMLC 1**

Aquin, Hubert   1929-1977 . . . . **CLC 15**
See also CA 105; DLB 53

Aragon, Louis
1897-1982 . . . . . **CLC 3, 22; DAM NOV,
POET**
See also CA 69-72; 108; CANR 28;
DLB 72; MTCW

Arany, Janos   1817-1882 . . . . **NCLC 34**

Arbuthnot, John   1667-1735 . . . . **LC 1**
See also DLB 101

Archer, Herbert Winslow
See Mencken, H(enry) L(ouis)

Archer, Jeffrey (Howard)
1940- . . . . **CLC 28; DAM POP**
See also AAYA 16; BEST 89:3; CA 77-80;
CANR 22, 52; INT CANR-22

Archer, Jules   1915- . . . . **CLC 12**
See also CA 9-12R; CANR 6; SAAS 5;
SATA 4, 85

Archer, Lee
See Ellison, Harlan (Jay)

Arden, John
1930- . . . . . **CLC 6, 13, 15; DAM DRAM**
See also CA 13-16R; CAAS 4; CANR 31;
DLB 13; MTCW

Arenas, Reinaldo
1943-1990 . . . . . . **CLC 41; DAM MULT;
HLC**
See also CA 124; 128; 133; DLB 145; HW

Arendt, Hannah   1906-1975 . . . . **CLC 66**
See also CA 17-20R; 61-64; CANR 26;
MTCW

Aretino, Pietro   1492-1556 . . . . **LC 12**

Arghezi, Tudor . . . . **CLC 80**
See also Theodorescu, Ion N.

Arguedas, Jose Maria
1911-1969 . . . . **CLC 10, 18**
See also CA 89-92; DLB 113; HW

Argueta, Manlio   1936- . . . . **CLC 31**
See also CA 131; DLB 145; HW

Ariosto, Ludovico   1474-1533 . . . . **LC 6**

Aristides
See Epstein, Joseph

Aristophanes
450B.C.-385B.C. . . . . **CMLC 4; DA;
DAB; DAC; DAM DRAM, MST; DC 2**

Arlt, Roberto (Godofredo Christophersen)
1900-1942 . . . . . **TCLC 29; DAM MULT;
HLC**
See also CA 123; 131; HW

Armah, Ayi Kwei
1939- . . . . **CLC 5, 33; BLC;
DAM MULT, POET**
See also BW 1; CA 61-64; CANR 21;
DLB 117; MTCW

Armatrading, Joan   1950- . . . . **CLC 17**
See also CA 114

Arnette, Robert
See Silverberg, Robert

Arnim, Achim von (Ludwig Joachim von
Arnim)   1781-1831 . . . . **NCLC 5**
See also DLB 90

Arnim, Bettina von   1785-1859 . . . . **NCLC 38**
See also DLB 90

Arnold, Matthew
1822-1888 . . . . . **NCLC 6, 29; DA; DAB;
DAC; DAM MST, POET; PC 5; WLC**
See also CDBLB 1832-1890; DLB 32, 57

Arnold, Thomas   1795-1842 . . . . . . **NCLC 18**
See also DLB 55

Arnow, Harriette (Louisa) Simpson
1908-1986 . . . . **CLC 2, 7, 18**
See also CA 9-12R; 118; CANR 14; DLB 6;
MTCW; SATA 42; SATA-Obit 47

Arp, Hans
See Arp, Jean

Arp, Jean   1887-1966 . . . . **CLC 5**
See also CA 81-84; 25-28R; CANR 42

Arrabal
See Arrabal, Fernando

Arrabal, Fernando   1932- . . . **CLC 2, 9, 18, 58**
See also CA 9-12R; CANR 15

Arrick, Fran . . . . **CLC 30**
See also Gaberman, Judie Angell

Artaud, Antonin (Marie Joseph)
1896-1948 . . . **TCLC 3, 36; DAM DRAM**
See also CA 104; 149

Arthur, Ruth M(abel)   1905-1979 . . . . **CLC 12**
See also CA 9-12R; 85-88; CANR 4;
SATA 7, 26

Artsybashev, Mikhail (Petrovich)
1878-1927 . . . . **TCLC 31**

Arundel, Honor (Morfydd)
1919-1973 . . . . **CLC 17**
See also CA 21-22; 41-44R; CAP 2;
CLR 35; SATA 4; SATA-Obit 24

Asch, Sholem   1880-1957 . . . . **TCLC 3**
See also CA 105

Ash, Shalom
See Asch, Sholem

Ashbery, John (Lawrence)
1927- . . . . . . **CLC 2, 3, 4, 6, 9, 13, 15, 25,
41, 77; DAM POET**
See also CA 5-8R; CANR 9, 37; DLB 5,
165; DLBY 81; INT CANR-9; MTCW

Ashdown, Clifford
See Freeman, R(ichard) Austin

Ashe, Gordon
See Creasey, John

Ashton-Warner, Sylvia (Constance)
1908-1984 .... **CLC 19**
See also CA 69-72; 112; CANR 29; MTCW

Asimov, Isaac
1920-1992 ...... **CLC 1, 3, 9, 19, 26, 76,**
92; DAM POP
See also AAYA 13; BEST 90:2; CA 1-4R;
137; CANR 2, 19, 36; CLR 12; DLB 8;
DLBY 92; INT CANR-19; JRDA;
MAICYA; MTCW; SATA 1, 26, 74

Assis, Joaquim Maria Machado de
See Machado de Assis, Joaquim Maria

Astley, Thea (Beatrice May)
1925- .... **CLC 41**
See also CA 65-68; CANR 11, 43

Aston, James
See White, T(erence) H(anbury)

Asturias, Miguel Angel
1899-1974 .... **CLC 3, 8, 13;**
DAM MULT, NOV; HLC
See also CA 25-28; 49-52; CANR 32;
CAP 2; DLB 113; HW; MTCW

Atares, Carlos Saura
See Saura (Atares), Carlos

Atheling, William
See Pound, Ezra (Weston Loomis)

Atheling, William, Jr.
See Blish, James (Benjamin)

Atherton, Gertrude (Franklin Horn)
1857-1948 .... **TCLC 2**
See also CA 104; DLB 9, 78

Atherton, Lucius
See Masters, Edgar Lee

Atkins, Jack
See Harris, Mark

Attaway, William (Alexander)
1911-1986 .... **CLC 92; BLC;**
DAM MULT
See also BW 2; CA 143; DLB 76

Atticus
See Fleming, Ian (Lancaster)

Atwood, Margaret (Eleanor)
1939- ..... **CLC 2, 3, 4, 8, 13, 15, 25, 44,**
84; DA; DAB; DAC; DAM MST, NOV,
POET; PC 8; SSC 2; WLC
See also AAYA 12; BEST 89:2; CA 49-52;
CANR 3, 24, 33; DLB 53;
INT CANR-24; MTCW; SATA 50

Aubigny, Pierre d'
See Mencken, H(enry) L(ouis)

Aubin, Penelope 1685-1731(?) .... **LC 9**
See also DLB 39

Auchincloss, Louis (Stanton)
1917- .... **CLC 4, 6, 9, 18, 45;**
DAM NOV; SSC 22
See also CA 1-4R; CANR 6, 29, 55; DLB 2;
DLBY 80; INT CANR-29; MTCW

Auden, W(ystan) H(ugh)
1907-1973 ...... **CLC 1, 2, 3, 4, 6, 9, 11,**
14, 43; DA; DAB; DAC; DAM DRAM,
MST, POET; PC 1; WLC
See also AAYA 18; CA 9-12R; 45-48;
CANR 5; CDBLB 1914-1945; DLB 10,
20; MTCW

Audiberti, Jacques
1900-1965 ...... **CLC 38; DAM DRAM**
See also CA 25-28R

Audubon, John James
1785-1851 .... **NCLC 47**

Auel, Jean M(arie)
1936- .... **CLC 31; DAM POP**
See also AAYA 7; BEST 90:4; CA 103;
CANR 21; INT CANR-21

Auerbach, Erich 1892-1957 ...... **TCLC 43**
See also CA 118

Augier, Emile 1820-1889 .... **NCLC 31**

August, John
See De Voto, Bernard (Augustine)

Augustine, St. 354-430 ...... **CMLC 6; DAB**

Aurelius
See Bourne, Randolph S(illiman)

Aurobindo, Sri 1872-1950 .... **TCLC 63**

Austen, Jane
1775-1817 ..... **NCLC 1, 13, 19, 33, 51;**
DA; DAB; DAC; DAM MST, NOV;
WLC
See also AAYA 19; CDBLB 1789-1832;
DLB 116

Auster, Paul 1947- .... **CLC 47**
See also CA 69-72; CANR 23, 52

Austin, Frank
See Faust, Frederick (Schiller)

Austin, Mary (Hunter)
1868-1934 .... **TCLC 25**
See also CA 109; DLB 9, 78

Autran Dourado, Waldomiro
See Dourado, (Waldomiro Freitas) Autran

Averroes 1126-1198 .... **CMLC 7**
See also DLB 115

Avicenna 980-1037 .... **CMLC 16**
See also DLB 115

Avison, Margaret
1918- .... **CLC 2, 4, 97; DAC;**
DAM POET
See also CA 17-20R; DLB 53; MTCW

Axton, David
See Koontz, Dean R(ay)

Ayckbourn, Alan
1939- ...... **CLC 5, 8, 18, 33, 74; DAB;**
DAM DRAM
See also CA 21-24R; CANR 31; DLB 13;
MTCW

Aydy, Catherine
See Tennant, Emma (Christina)

Ayme, Marcel (Andre) 1902-1967 ... **CLC 11**
See also CA 89-92; CLR 25; DLB 72

Ayrton, Michael 1921-1975 .... **CLC 7**
See also CA 5-8R; 61-64; CANR 9, 21

Azorin .... **CLC 11**
See also Martinez Ruiz, Jose

Azuela, Mariano
1873-1952 ..... **TCLC 3; DAM MULT;**
HLC
See also CA 104; 131; HW; MTCW

Baastad, Babbis Friis
See Friis-Baastad, Babbis Ellinor

Bab
See Gilbert, W(illiam) S(chwenck)

Babbis, Eleanor
See Friis-Baastad, Babbis Ellinor

Babel, Isaak (Emmanuilovich)
1894-1941(?) ...... **TCLC 2, 13; SSC 16**
See also CA 104

Babits, Mihaly 1883-1941 .... **TCLC 14**
See also CA 114

Babur 1483-1530 .... **LC 18**

Bacchelli, Riccardo 1891-1985 ..... **CLC 19**
See also CA 29-32R; 117

Bach, Richard (David)
1936- ...... **CLC 14; DAM NOV, POP**
See also AITN 1; BEST 89:2; CA 9-12R;
CANR 18; MTCW; SATA 13

Bachman, Richard
See King, Stephen (Edwin)

Bachmann, Ingeborg 1926-1973..... **CLC 69**
See also CA 93-96; 45-48; DLB 85

Bacon, Francis 1561-1626 .... **LC 18, 32**
See also CDBLB Before 1660; DLB 151

Bacon, Roger 1214(?)-1292 ...... **CMLC 14**
See also DLB 115

Bacovia, George .... **TCLC 24**
See also Vasiliu, Gheorghe

Badanes, Jerome 1937- .... **CLC 59**

Bagehot, Walter 1826-1877 ...... **NCLC 10**
See also DLB 55

Bagnold, Enid
1889-1981 ...... **CLC 25; DAM DRAM**
See also CA 5-8R; 103; CANR 5, 40;
DLB 13, 160; MAICYA; SATA 1, 25

Bagritsky, Eduard 1895-1934 ..... **TCLC 60**

Bagrjana, Elisaveta
See Belcheva, Elisaveta

Bagryana, Elisaveta .... **CLC 10**
See also Belcheva, Elisaveta
See also DLB 147

Bailey, Paul 1937- .... **CLC 45**
See also CA 21-24R; CANR 16; DLB 14

Baillie, Joanna 1762-1851 .... **NCLC 2**
See also DLB 93

Bainbridge, Beryl (Margaret)
1933- .... **CLC 4, 5, 8, 10, 14, 18, 22, 62;**
DAM NOV
See also CA 21-24R; CANR 24, 55;
DLB 14; MTCW

Baker, Elliott 1922- .... **CLC 8**
See also CA 45-48; CANR 2

Baker, Nicholson
1957- .... **CLC 61; DAM POP**
See also CA 135

Baker, Ray Stannard 1870-1946 ... **TCLC 47**
See also CA 118

Baker, Russell (Wayne) 1925- ...... **CLC 31**
See also BEST 89:4; CA 57-60; CANR 11,
41; MTCW

Bakhtin, M.
See Bakhtin, Mikhail Mikhailovich

Bakhtin, M. M.
See Bakhtin, Mikhail Mikhailovich

Bakhtin, Mikhail
See Bakhtin, Mikhail Mikhailovich

Bakhtin, Mikhail Mikhailovich
1895-1975 .... **CLC 83**
See also CA 128; 113

Bakshi, Ralph 1938(?)-............ **CLC 26**
See also CA 112; 138

Bakunin, Mikhail (Alexandrovich)
1814-1876 .... **NCLC 25, 58**

Baldwin, James (Arthur)
1924-1987 ...... **CLC 1, 2, 3, 4, 5, 8, 13,
15, 17, 42, 50, 67, 90; BLC; DA; DAB;
DAC; DAM MST, MULT, NOV, POP;
DC 1; SSC 10; WLC**
See also AAYA 4; BW 1; CA 1-4R; 124;
CABS 1; CANR 3, 24;
CDALB 1941-1968; DLB 2, 7, 33;
DLBY 87; MTCW; SATA 9;
SATA-Obit 54

Ballard, J(ames) G(raham)
1930- .... **CLC 3, 6, 14, 36; DAM NOV,
POP; SSC 1**
See also AAYA 3; CA 5-8R; CANR 15, 39;
DLB 14; MTCW

Balmont, Konstantin (Dmitriyevich)
1867-1943 .... **TCLC 11**
See also CA 109

Balzac, Honore de
1799-1850 .... **NCLC 5, 35, 53; DA;
DAB; DAC; DAM MST, NOV; SSC 5;
WLC**
See also DLB 119

Bambara, Toni Cade
1939-1995 ...... **CLC 19, 88; BLC; DA;
DAC; DAM MST, MULT**
See also AAYA 5; BW 2; CA 29-32R; 150;
CANR 24, 49; DLB 38; MTCW

Bamdad, A.
See Shamlu, Ahmad

Banat, D. R.
See Bradbury, Ray (Douglas)

Bancroft, Laura
See Baum, L(yman) Frank

Banim, John 1798-1842 .... **NCLC 13**
See also DLB 116, 158, 159

Banim, Michael 1796-1874 ...... **NCLC 13**
See also DLB 158, 159

Banks, Iain
See Banks, Iain M(enzies)

Banks, Iain M(enzies) 1954- .... **CLC 34**
See also CA 123; 128; INT 128

Banks, Lynne Reid .... **CLC 23**
See also Reid Banks, Lynne
See also AAYA 6

Banks, Russell 1940- .... **CLC 37, 72**
See also CA 65-68; CAAS 15; CANR 19,
52; DLB 130

Banville, John 1945-............. **CLC 46**
See also CA 117; 128; DLB 14; INT 128

Banville, Theodore (Faullain) de
1832-1891 .... **NCLC 9**

Baraka, Amiri
1934- .... **CLC 1, 2, 3, 5, 10, 14, 33;
BLC; DA; DAC; DAM MST, MULT,
POET, POP; DC 6; PC 4**
See also Jones, LeRoi
See also BW 2; CA 21-24R; CABS 3;
CANR 27, 38; CDALB 1941-1968;
DLB 5, 7, 16, 38; DLBD 8; MTCW

Barbauld, Anna Laetitia
1743-1825 .... **NCLC 50**
See also DLB 107, 109, 142, 158

Barbellion, W. N. P................ **TCLC 24**
See also Cummings, Bruce F(rederick)

Barbera, Jack (Vincent) 1945-...... **CLC 44**
See also CA 110; CANR 45

Barbey d'Aurevilly, Jules Amedee
1808-1889 .... **NCLC 1; SSC 17**
See also DLB 119

Barbusse, Henri 1873-1935 .... **TCLC 5**
See also CA 105; DLB 65

Barclay, Bill
See Moorcock, Michael (John)

Barclay, William Ewert
See Moorcock, Michael (John)

Barea, Arturo 1897-1957 .... **TCLC 14**
See also CA 111

Barfoot, Joan 1946-.............. **CLC 18**
See also CA 105

Baring, Maurice 1874-1945 .... **TCLC 8**
See also CA 105; DLB 34

Barker, Clive 1952- ... **CLC 52; DAM POP**
See also AAYA 10; BEST 90:3; CA 121;
129; INT 129; MTCW

Barker, George Granville
1913-1991 ..... **CLC 8, 48; DAM POET**
See also CA 9-12R; 135; CANR 7, 38;
DLB 20; MTCW

Barker, Harley Granville
See Granville-Barker, Harley
See also DLB 10

Barker, Howard 1946-............ **CLC 37**
See also CA 102; DLB 13

Barker, Pat(ricia) 1943-........ **CLC 32, 94**
See also CA 117; 122; CANR 50; INT 122

Barlow, Joel 1754-1812 .... **NCLC 23**
See also DLB 37

Barnard, Mary (Ethel) 1909-....... **CLC 48**
See also CA 21-22; CAP 2

Barnes, Djuna
1892-1982 ... **CLC 3, 4, 8, 11, 29; SSC 3**
See also CA 9-12R; 107; CANR 16, 55;
DLB 4, 9, 45; MTCW

Barnes, Julian (Patrick)
1946-................... **CLC 42; DAB**
See also CA 102; CANR 19, 54; DLBY 93

Barnes, Peter 1931- .... **CLC 5, 56**
See also CA 65-68; CAAS 12; CANR 33,
34; DLB 13; MTCW

Baroja (y Nessi), Pio
1872-1956 .... **TCLC 8; HLC**
See also CA 104

Baron, David
See Pinter, Harold

Baron Corvo
See Rolfe, Frederick (William Serafino
Austin Lewis Mary)

Barondess, Sue K(aufman)
1926-1977 .... **CLC 8**
See also Kaufman, Sue
See also CA 1-4R; 69-72; CANR 1

Baron de Teive
See Pessoa, Fernando (Antonio Nogueira)

Barres, Maurice 1862-1923 .... **TCLC 47**
See also DLB 123

Barreto, Afonso Henrique de Lima
See Lima Barreto, Afonso Henrique de

Barrett, (Roger) Syd 1946- ...... **CLC 35**

Barrett, William (Christopher)
1913-1992 .... **CLC 27**
See also CA 13-16R; 139; CANR 11;
INT CANR-11

Barrie, J(ames) M(atthew)
1860-1937 .... **TCLC 2; DAB;
DAM DRAM**
See also CA 104; 136; CDBLB 1890-1914;
CLR 16; DLB 10, 141, 156; MAICYA;
YABC 1

Barrington, Michael
See Moorcock, Michael (John)

Barrol, Grady
See Bograd, Larry

Barry, Mike
See Malzberg, Barry N(athaniel)

Barry, Philip 1896-1949......... **TCLC 11**
See also CA 109; DLB 7

Bart, Andre Schwarz
See Schwarz-Bart, Andre

Barth, John (Simmons)
1930-...... **CLC 1, 2, 3, 5, 7, 9, 10, 14,
27, 51, 89; DAM NOV; SSC 10**
See also AITN 1, 2; CA 1-4R; CABS 1;
CANR 5, 23, 49; DLB 2; MTCW

Barthelme, Donald
1931-1989 ...... **CLC 1, 2, 3, 5, 6, 8, 13,
23, 46, 59; DAM NOV; SSC 2**
See also CA 21-24R; 129; CANR 20;
DLB 2; DLBY 80, 89; MTCW; SATA 7;
SATA-Obit 62

Barthelme, Frederick 1943-........ **CLC 36**
See also CA 114; 122; DLBY 85; INT 122

Barthes, Roland (Gerard)
1915-1980 .... **CLC 24, 83**
See also CA 130; 97-100; MTCW

Barzun, Jacques (Martin) 1907- .... **CLC 51**
See also CA 61-64; CANR 22

Bashevis, Isaac
See Singer, Isaac Bashevis

Bashkirtseff, Marie 1859-1884 ... **NCLC 27**

Basho
See Matsuo Basho

Bass, Kingsley B., Jr.
See Bullins, Ed

Bass, Rick 1958-................. **CLC 79**
See also CA 126; CANR 53

Bassani, Giorgio 1916-............ **CLC 9**
See also CA 65-68; CANR 33; DLB 128;
MTCW

Bastos, Augusto (Antonio) Roa
See Roa Bastos, Augusto (Antonio)

Bataille, Georges 1897-1962 .... **CLC 29**
See also CA 101; 89-92

Bates, H(erbert) E(rnest)
1905-1974 .... **CLC 46; DAB;**
DAM POP; SSC 10
See also CA 93-96; 45-48; CANR 34;
DLB 162; MTCW

Bauchart
See Camus, Albert

Baudelaire, Charles
1821-1867 .... **NCLC 6, 29, 55; DA;**
DAB; DAC; DAM MST, POET; PC 1;
SSC 18; WLC

Baudrillard, Jean 1929- .... **CLC 60**

Baum, L(yman) Frank 1856-1919 ... **TCLC 7**
See also CA 108; 133; CLR 15; DLB 22;
JRDA; MAICYA; MTCW; SATA 18

Baum, Louis F.
See Baum, L(yman) Frank

Baumbach, Jonathan 1933- ...... **CLC 6, 23**
See also CA 13-16R; CAAS 5; CANR 12;
DLBY 80; INT CANR-12; MTCW

Bausch, Richard (Carl) 1945- ...... **CLC 51**
See also CA 101; CAAS 14; CANR 43;
DLB 130

Baxter, Charles
1947- .... **CLC 45, 78; DAM POP**
See also CA 57-60; CANR 40; DLB 130

Baxter, George Owen
See Faust, Frederick (Schiller)

Baxter, James K(eir) 1926-1972 .... **CLC 14**
See also CA 77-80

Baxter, John
See Hunt, E(verette) Howard, (Jr.)

Bayer, Sylvia
See Glassco, John

Baynton, Barbara 1857-1929 ...... **TCLC 57**

Beagle, Peter S(oyer) 1939- .... **CLC 7**
See also CA 9-12R; CANR 4, 51;
DLBY 80; INT CANR-4; SATA 60

Bean, Normal
See Burroughs, Edgar Rice

Beard, Charles A(ustin)
1874-1948 .... **TCLC 15**
See also CA 115; DLB 17; SATA 18

Beardsley, Aubrey 1872-1898 ..... **NCLC 6**

Beattie, Ann
1947- .... **CLC 8, 13, 18, 40, 63;**
DAM NOV, POP; SSC 11
See also BEST 90:2; CA 81-84; CANR 53;
DLBY 82; MTCW

Beattie, James 1735-1803 .... **NCLC 25**
See also DLB 109

Beauchamp, Kathleen Mansfield 1888-1923
See Mansfield, Katherine
See also CA 104; 134; DA; DAC;
DAM MST

Beaumarchais, Pierre-Augustin Caron de
1732-1799 .... **DC 4**
See also DAM DRAM

Beaumont, Francis
1584(?)-1616 .... **LC 33; DC 6**
See also CDBLB Before 1660; DLB 58, 121

Beauvoir, Simone (Lucie Ernestine Marie
Bertrand) de
1908-1986 .... **CLC 1, 2, 4, 8, 14, 31, 44,**
50, 71; DA; DAB; DAC; DAM MST,
NOV; WLC
See also CA 9-12R; 118; CANR 28;
DLB 72; DLBY 86; MTCW

Becker, Carl 1873-1945 .... **TCLC 63:**
See also DLB 17

Becker, Jurek 1937-............ **CLC 7, 19**
See also CA 85-88; DLB 75

Becker, Walter 1950-............. **CLC 26**

Beckett, Samuel (Barclay)
1906-1989 ...... **CLC 1, 2, 3, 4, 6, 9, 10,**
11, 14, 18, 29, 57, 59, 83; DA; DAB;
DAC; DAM DRAM, MST, NOV;
SSC 16; WLC
See also CA 5-8R; 130; CANR 33;
CDBLB 1945-1960; DLB 13, 15;
DLBY 90; MTCW

Beckford, William 1760-1844 .... **NCLC 16**
See also DLB 39

Beckman, Gunnel 1910-........... **CLC 26**
See also CA 33-36R; CANR 15; CLR 25;
MAICYA; SAAS 9; SATA 6

Becque, Henri 1837-1899........ **NCLC 3**

Beddoes, Thomas Lovell
1803-1849 .... **NCLC 3**
See also DLB 96

Bedford, Donald F.
See Fearing, Kenneth (Flexner)

Beecher, Catharine Esther
1800-1878 .... **NCLC 30**
See also DLB 1

Beecher, John 1904-1980.......... **CLC 6**
See also AITN 1; CA 5-8R; 105; CANR 8

Beer, Johann 1655-1700............. **LC 5**
See also DLB 168

Beer, Patricia 1924-............... **CLC 58**
See also CA 61-64; CANR 13, 46; DLB 40

Beerbohm, Henry Maximilian
1872-1956 .... **TCLC 1, 24**
See also CA 104; DLB 34, 100

Beerbohm, Max
See Beerbohm, Henry Maximilian

Beer-Hofmann, Richard
1866-1945 .... **TCLC 60**
See also DLB 81

Begiebing, Robert J(ohn) 1946-..... **CLC 70**
See also CA 122; CANR 40

Behan, Brendan
1923-1964 .... **CLC 1, 8, 11, 15, 79;**
DAM DRAM
See also CA 73-76; CANR 33;
CDBLB 1945-1960; DLB 13; MTCW

Behn, Aphra
1640(?)-1689 ...... **LC 1, 30; DA; DAB;**
DAC; DAM DRAM, MST, NOV,
POET; DC 4; PC 13; WLC
See also DLB 39, 80, 131

Behrman, S(amuel) N(athaniel)
1893-1973 .... **CLC 40**
See also CA 13-16; 45-48; CAP 1; DLB 7,
44

Belasco, David 1853-1931 .... **TCLC 3**
See also CA 104; DLB 7

Belcheva, Elisaveta 1893- .... **CLC 10**
See also Bagryana, Elisaveta

Beldone, Phil "Cheech"
See Ellison, Harlan (Jay)

Beleno
See Azuela, Mariano

Belinski, Vissarion Grigoryevich
1811-1848 .... **NCLC 5**

Belitt, Ben 1911-................. **CLC 22**
See also CA 13-16R; CAAS 4; CANR 7;
DLB 5

Bell, Gertrude 1868-1926........ **TCLC 67**
See also DLB 174

Bell, James Madison
1826-1902 .... **TCLC 43; BLC;**
DAM MULT
See also BW 1; CA 122; 124; DLB 50

Bell, Madison Smartt 1957-........ **CLC 41**
See also CA 111; CANR 28, 54

Bell, Marvin (Hartley)
1937- .... **CLC 8, 31; DAM POET**
See also CA 21-24R; CAAS 14; DLB 5;
MTCW

Bell, W. L. D.
See Mencken, H(enry) L(ouis)

Bellamy, Atwood C.
See Mencken, H(enry) L(ouis)

Bellamy, Edward 1850-1898 ...... **NCLC 4**
See also DLB 12

Bellin, Edward J.
See Kuttner, Henry

Belloc, (Joseph) Hilaire (Pierre)
1870-1953 ... **TCLC 7, 18; DAM POET**
See also CA 106; 152; DLB 19, 100, 141,
174; YABC 1

Belloc, Joseph Peter Rene Hilaire
See Belloc, (Joseph) Hilaire (Pierre)

Belloc, Joseph Pierre Hilaire
See Belloc, (Joseph) Hilaire (Pierre)

Belloc, M. A.
See Lowndes, Marie Adelaide (Belloc)

Bellow, Saul
1915- .... **CLC 1, 2, 3, 6, 8, 10, 13, 15,**
25, 33, 34, 63, 79; DA; DAB; DAC;
DAM MST, NOV, POP; SSC 14; WLC
See also AITN 2; BEST 89:3; CA 5-8R;
CABS 1; CANR 29, 53;
CDALB 1941-1968; DLB 2, 28; DLBD 3;
DLBY 82; MTCW

Belser, Reimond Karel Maria de 1929-
See Ruyslinck, Ward
See also CA 152

Bely, Andrey .... **TCLC 7; PC 11**
See also Bugayev, Boris Nikolayevich

Benary, Margot
See Benary-Isbert, Margot

Benary-Isbert, Margot   1889-1979 . . . **CLC 12**
See also CA 5-8R; 89-92; CANR 4;
CLR 12; MAICYA; SATA 2;
SATA-Obit 21

Benavente (y Martinez), Jacinto
1866-1954 . . . . . **TCLC 3; DAM DRAM,
MULT**
See also CA 106; 131; HW; MTCW

Benchley, Peter (Bradford)
1940- . . . . . **CLC 4, 8; DAM NOV, POP**
See also AAYA 14; AITN 2; CA 17-20R;
CANR 12, 35; MTCW; SATA 3, 89

Benchley, Robert (Charles)
1889-1945 . . . . **TCLC 1, 55**
See also CA 105; 153; DLB 11

Benda, Julien   1867-1956 . . . . **TCLC 60**
See also CA 120

Benedict, Ruth   1887-1948 . . . . **TCLC 60**

Benedikt, Michael   1935- . . . . **CLC 4, 14**
See also CA 13-16R; CANR 7; DLB 5

Benet, Juan   1927-. . . . . **CLC 28**
See also CA 143

Benet, Stephen Vincent
1898-1943 . . . . . . **TCLC 7; DAM POET;
SSC 10**
See also CA 104; 152; DLB 4, 48, 102;
YABC 1

Benet, William Rose
1886-1950 . . . . . . **TCLC 28; DAM POET**
See also CA 118; 152; DLB 45

Benford, Gregory (Albert)   1941-. . . **CLC 52**
See also CA 69-72; CANR 12, 24, 49;
DLBY 82

Bengtsson, Frans (Gunnar)
1894-1954 . . . . **TCLC 48**

Benjamin, David
See Slavitt, David R(ytman)

Benjamin, Lois
See Gould, Lois

Benjamin, Walter   1892-1940 . . . . . **TCLC 39**

Benn, Gottfried   1886-1956. . . . . **TCLC 3**
See also CA 106; 153; DLB 56

Bennett, Alan
1934- . . . **CLC 45, 77; DAB; DAM MST**
See also CA 103; CANR 35, 55; MTCW

Bennett, (Enoch) Arnold
1867-1931 . . . . **TCLC 5, 20**
See also CA 106; CDBLB 1890-1914;
DLB 10, 34, 98, 135

Bennett, Elizabeth
See Mitchell, Margaret (Munnerlyn)

Bennett, George Harold   1930-
See Bennett, Hal
See also BW 1; CA 97-100

Bennett, Hal . . . . **CLC 5**
See also Bennett, George Harold
See also DLB 33

Bennett, Jay   1912-. . . . . **CLC 35**
See also AAYA 10; CA 69-72; CANR 11,
42; JRDA; SAAS 4; SATA 41, 87;
SATA-Brief 27

Bennett, Louise (Simone)
1919- . . . . . **CLC 28; BLC; DAM MULT**
See also BW 2; CA 151; DLB 117

Benson, E(dward) F(rederic)
1867-1940 . . . . **TCLC 27**
See also CA 114; DLB 135, 153

Benson, Jackson J.   1930-. . . . . **CLC 34**
See also CA 25-28R; DLB 111

Benson, Sally   1900-1972 . . . . **CLC 17**
See also CA 19-20; 37-40R; CAP 1;
SATA 1, 35; SATA-Obit 27

Benson, Stella   1892-1933. . . . . **TCLC 17**
See also CA 117; DLB 36, 162

Bentham, Jeremy   1748-1832 . . . . . **NCLC 38**
See also DLB 107, 158

Bentley, E(dmund) C(lerihew)
1875-1956 . . . . **TCLC 12**
See also CA 108; DLB 70

Bentley, Eric (Russell)   1916-. . . . . . **CLC 24**
See also CA 5-8R; CANR 6; INT CANR-6

Beranger, Pierre Jean de
1780-1857 . . . . **NCLC 34**

Berdyaev, Nicolas
See Berdyaev, Nikolai (Aleksandrovich)

Berdyaev, Nikolai (Aleksandrovich)
1874-1948 . . . . **TCLC 67**
See also CA 120

Berendt, John (Lawrence)   1939-. . . . **CLC 86**
See also CA 146

Berger, Colonel
See Malraux, (Georges-)Andre

Berger, John (Peter)   1926- . . . . . . **CLC 2, 19**
See also CA 81-84; CANR 51; DLB 14

Berger, Melvin H.   1927- . . . . **CLC 12**
See also CA 5-8R; CANR 4; CLR 32;
SAAS 2; SATA 5, 88

Berger, Thomas (Louis)
1924- . . . . **CLC 3, 5, 8, 11, 18, 38;
DAM NOV**
See also CA 1-4R; CANR 5, 28, 51; DLB 2;
DLBY 80; INT CANR-28; MTCW

Bergman, (Ernst) Ingmar
1918- . . . . **CLC 16, 72**
See also CA 81-84; CANR 33

Bergson, Henri   1859-1941 . . . . **TCLC 32**

Bergstein, Eleanor   1938- . . . . **CLC 4**
See also CA 53-56; CANR 5

Berkoff, Steven   1937-. . . . . **CLC 56**
See also CA 104

Bermant, Chaim (Icyk)   1929- . . . . . . **CLC 40**
See also CA 57-60; CANR 6, 31

Bern, Victoria
See Fisher, M(ary) F(rances) K(ennedy)

Bernanos, (Paul Louis) Georges
1888-1948 . . . . **TCLC 3**
See also CA 104; 130; DLB 72

Bernard, April   1956- . . . . **CLC 59**
See also CA 131

Berne, Victoria
See Fisher, M(ary) F(rances) K(ennedy)

Bernhard, Thomas
1931-1989 . . . . **CLC 3, 32, 61**
See also CA 85-88; 127; CANR 32;
DLB 85, 124; MTCW

Berriault, Gina   1926- . . . . **CLC 54**
See also CA 116; 129; DLB 130

Berrigan, Daniel   1921-. . . . . **CLC 4**
See also CA 33-36R; CAAS 1; CANR 11,
43; DLB 5

Berrigan, Edmund Joseph Michael, Jr.
1934-1983
See Berrigan, Ted
See also CA 61-64; 110; CANR 14

Berrigan, Ted. . . . . **CLC 37**
See also Berrigan, Edmund Joseph Michael,
Jr.
See also DLB 5, 169

Berry, Charles Edward Anderson   1931-
See Berry, Chuck
See also CA 115

Berry, Chuck . . . . **CLC 17**
See also Berry, Charles Edward Anderson

Berry, Jonas
See Ashbery, John (Lawrence)

Berry, Wendell (Erdman)
1934- . . . . **CLC 4, 6, 8, 27, 46;
DAM POET**
See also AITN 1; CA 73-76; CANR 50;
DLB 5, 6

Berryman, John
1914-1972 . . . . . . **CLC 1, 2, 3, 4, 6, 8, 10,
13, 25, 62; DAM POET**
See also CA 13-16; 33-36R; CABS 2;
CANR 35; CAP 1; CDALB 1941-1968;
DLB 48; MTCW

Bertolucci, Bernardo   1940- . . . . **CLC 16**
See also CA 106

Bertrand, Aloysius   1807-1841 . . . . **NCLC 31**

Bertran de Born   c. 1140-1215 . . . . . **CMLC 5**

Besant, Annie (Wood)   1847-1933 . . . **TCLC 9**
See also CA 105

Bessie, Alvah   1904-1985. . . . . **CLC 23**
See also CA 5-8R; 116; CANR 2; DLB 26

Bethlen, T. D.
See Silverberg, Robert

Beti, Mongo . . . . **CLC 27; BLC; DAM MULT**
See also Biyidi, Alexandre

Betjeman, John
1906-1984 . . . . **CLC 2, 6, 10, 34, 43;
DAB; DAM MST, POET**
See also CA 9-12R; 112; CANR 33;
CDBLB 1945-1960; DLB 20; DLBY 84;
MTCW

Bettelheim, Bruno   1903-1990 . . . . . . **CLC 79**
See also CA 81-84; 131; CANR 23; MTCW

Betti, Ugo   1892-1953 . . . . **TCLC 5**
See also CA 104

Betts, Doris (Waugh)   1932-. . . . **CLC 3, 6, 28**
See also CA 13-16R; CANR 9; DLBY 82;
INT CANR-9

Bevan, Alistair
See Roberts, Keith (John Kingston)

Bialik, Chaim Nachman
1873-1934 . . . . **TCLC 25**

Bickerstaff, Isaac
See Swift, Jonathan

Bidart, Frank   1939- . . . . **CLC 33**
See also CA 140

Bienek, Horst   1930-. . . . . **CLC 7, 11**
See also CA 73-76; DLB 75

Bierce, Ambrose (Gwinett)
1842-1914(?) ...... **TCLC 1, 7, 44; DA;**
DAC; DAM MST; SSC 9; WLC
See also CA 104; 139; CDALB 1865-1917;
DLB 11, 12, 23, 71, 74

Biggers, Earl Derr 1884-1933 ..... **TCLC 65**
See also CA 108; 153

Billings, Josh
See Shaw, Henry Wheeler

Billington, (Lady) Rachel (Mary)
1942- .... **CLC 43**
See also AITN 2; CA 33-36R; CANR 44

Binyon, T(imothy) J(ohn) 1936- .... **CLC 34**
See also CA 111; CANR 28

Bioy Casares, Adolfo
1914- .... **CLC 4, 8, 13, 88;**
DAM MULT; HLC; SSC 17
See also CA 29-32R; CANR 19, 43;
DLB 113; HW; MTCW

Bird, Cordwainer
See Ellison, Harlan (Jay)

Bird, Robert Montgomery
1806-1854 .... **NCLC 1**

Birney, (Alfred) Earle
1904- .... **CLC 1, 4, 6, 11; DAC;**
DAM MST, POET
See also CA 1-4R; CANR 5, 20; DLB 88;
MTCW

Bishop, Elizabeth
1911-1979 ...... **CLC 1, 4, 9, 13, 15, 32;**
DA; DAC; DAM MST, POET; PC 3
See also CA 5-8R; 89-92; CABS 2;
CANR 26; CDALB 1968-1988; DLB 5,
169; MTCW; SATA-Obit 24

Bishop, John 1935- .... **CLC 10**
See also CA 105

Bissett, Bill 1939- .... **CLC 18; PC 14**
See also CA 69-72; CAAS 19; CANR 15;
DLB 53; MTCW

Bitov, Andrei (Georgievich) 1937- ... **CLC 57**
See also CA 142

Biyidi, Alexandre 1932-
See Beti, Mongo
See also BW 1; CA 114; 124; MTCW

Bjarme, Brynjolf
See Ibsen, Henrik (Johan)

Bjornson, Bjornstjerne (Martinius)
1832-1910 .... **TCLC 7, 37**
See also CA 104

Black, Robert
See Holdstock, Robert P.

Blackburn, Paul 1926-1971 ...... **CLC 9, 43**
See also CA 81-84; 33-36R; CANR 34;
DLB 16; DLBY 81

Black Elk
1863-1950 ..... **TCLC 33; DAM MULT**
See also CA 144; NNAL

Black Hobart
See Sanders, (James) Ed(ward)

Blacklin, Malcolm
See Chambers, Aidan

Blackmore, R(ichard) D(oddridge)
1825-1900 .... **TCLC 27**
See also CA 120; DLB 18

Blackmur, R(ichard) P(almer)
1904-1965 .... **CLC 2, 24**
See also CA 11-12; 25-28R; CAP 1; DLB 63

Black Tarantula, The
See Acker, Kathy

Blackwood, Algernon (Henry)
1869-1951 .... **TCLC 5**
See also CA 105; 150; DLB 153, 156

Blackwood, Caroline 1931-1996 ... **CLC 6, 9**
See also CA 85-88; 151; CANR 32;
DLB 14; MTCW

Blade, Alexander
See Hamilton, Edmond; Silverberg, Robert

Blaga, Lucian 1895-1961 .... **CLC 75**

Blair, Eric (Arthur) 1903-1950
See Orwell, George
See also CA 104; 132; DA; DAB; DAC;
DAM MST, NOV; MTCW; SATA 29

Blais, Marie-Claire
1939- .... **CLC 2, 4, 6, 13, 22; DAC;**
DAM MST
See also CA 21-24R; CAAS 4; CANR 38;
DLB 53; MTCW

Blaise, Clark 1940- .... **CLC 29**
See also AITN 2; CA 53-56; CAAS 3;
CANR 5; DLB 53

Blake, Nicholas
See Day Lewis, C(ecil)
See also DLB 77

Blake, William
1757-1827 .... **NCLC 13, 37, 57; DA;**
DAB; DAC; DAM MST, POET; PC 12;
WLC
See also CDBLB 1789-1832; DLB 93, 163;
MAICYA; SATA 30

Blake, William J(ames) 1894-1969 ... **PC 12**
See also CA 5-8R; 25-28R

Blasco Ibanez, Vicente
1867-1928 .... **TCLC 12; DAM NOV**
See also CA 110; 131; HW; MTCW

Blatty, William Peter
1928- .... **CLC 2; DAM POP**
See also CA 5-8R; CANR 9

Bleeck, Oliver
See Thomas, Ross (Elmore)

Blessing, Lee 1949- .... **CLC 54**

Blish, James (Benjamin)
1921-1975 .... **CLC 14**
See also CA 1-4R; 57-60; CANR 3; DLB 8;
MTCW; SATA 66

Bliss, Reginald
See Wells, H(erbert) G(eorge)

Blixen, Karen (Christentze Dinesen)
1885-1962
See Dinesen, Isak
See also CA 25-28; CANR 22, 50; CAP 2;
MTCW; SATA 44

Bloch, Robert (Albert) 1917-1994 ... **CLC 33**
See also CA 5-8R; 146; CAAS 20; CANR 5;
DLB 44; INT CANR-5; SATA 12;
SATA-Obit 82

Blok, Alexander (Alexandrovich)
1880-1921 .... **TCLC 5**
See also CA 104

Blom, Jan
See Breytenbach, Breyten

Bloom, Harold 1930- .... **CLC 24**
See also CA 13-16R; CANR 39; DLB 67

Bloomfield, Aurelius
See Bourne, Randolph S(illiman)

Blount, Roy (Alton), Jr. 1941- ..... **CLC 38**
See also CA 53-56; CANR 10, 28;
INT CANR-28; MTCW

Bloy, Leon 1846-1917............ **TCLC 22**
See also CA 121; DLB 123

Blume, Judy (Sussman)
1938- ... **CLC 12, 30; DAM NOV, POP**
See also AAYA 3; CA 29-32R; CANR 13,
37; CLR 2, 15; DLB 52; JRDA;
MAICYA; MTCW; SATA 2, 31, 79

Blunden, Edmund (Charles)
1896-1974 .... **CLC 2, 56**
See also CA 17-18; 45-48; CANR 54;
CAP 2; DLB 20, 100, 155; MTCW

Bly, Robert (Elwood)
1926- .... **CLC 1, 2, 5, 10, 15, 38;**
DAM POET
See also CA 5-8R; CANR 41; DLB 5;
MTCW

Boas, Franz 1858-1942........... **TCLC 56**
See also CA 115

Bobette
See Simenon, Georges (Jacques Christian)

Boccaccio, Giovanni
1313-1375 .... **CMLC 13; SSC 10**

Bochco, Steven 1943- .... **CLC 35**
See also AAYA 11; CA 124; 138

Bodenheim, Maxwell 1892-1954 ... **TCLC 44**
See also CA 110; DLB 9, 45

Bodker, Cecil 1927- .... **CLC 21**
See also CA 73-76; CANR 13, 44; CLR 23;
MAICYA; SATA 14

Boell, Heinrich (Theodor)
1917-1985 ... **CLC 2, 3, 6, 9, 11, 15, 27,**
32, 72; DA; DAB; DAC; DAM MST,
NOV; SSC 23; WLC
See also CA 21-24R; 116; CANR 24;
DLB 69; DLBY 85; MTCW

Boerne, Alfred
See Doeblin, Alfred

Boethius 480(?)-524(?) .... **CMLC 15**
See also DLB 115

Bogan, Louise
1897-1970 .... **CLC 4, 39, 46, 93;**
DAM POET; PC 12
See also CA 73-76; 25-28R; CANR 33;
DLB 45, 169; MTCW

Bogarde, Dirk .... **CLC 19**
See also Van Den Bogarde, Derek Jules
Gaspard Ulric Niven
See also DLB 14

Bogosian, Eric 1953- .... **CLC 45**
See also CA 138

Bograd, Larry 1953- .... **CLC 35**
See also CA 93-96; SAAS 21; SATA 33, 89

Boiardo, Matteo Maria 1441-1494 .... **LC 6**

Boileau-Despreaux, Nicolas
1636-1711 .... **LC 3**

Bojer, Johan 1872-1959......... **TCLC 64**

Boland, Eavan (Aisling)
1944- . . . . **CLC 40, 67; DAM POET**
See also CA 143; DLB 40

Bolt, Lee
See Faust, Frederick (Schiller)

Bolt, Robert (Oxton)
1924-1995 . . . . . . **CLC 14; DAM DRAM**
See also CA 17-20R; 147; CANR 35;
DLB 13; MTCW

Bombet, Louis-Alexandre-Cesar
See Stendhal

Bomkauf
See Kaufman, Bob (Garnell)

Bonaventura. . . . . **NCLC 35**
See also DLB 90

Bond, Edward
1934- . . . **CLC 4, 6, 13, 23; DAM DRAM**
See also CA 25-28R; CANR 38; DLB 13;
MTCW

Bonham, Frank 1914-1989. . . . . **CLC 12**
See also AAYA 1; CA 9-12R; CANR 4, 36;
JRDA; MAICYA; SAAS 3; SATA 1, 49;
SATA-Obit 62

Bonnefoy, Yves
1923- . . . . . . **CLC 9, 15, 58; DAM MST,
POET**
See also CA 85-88; CANR 33; MTCW

Bontemps, Arna(ud Wendell)
1902-1973 . . . . **CLC 1, 18; BLC;
DAM MULT, NOV, POET**
See also BW 1; CA 1-4R; 41-44R; CANR 4,
35; CLR 6; DLB 48, 51; JRDA;
MAICYA; MTCW; SATA 2, 44;
SATA-Obit 24

Booth, Martin 1944-. . . . . **CLC 13**
See also CA 93-96; CAAS 2

Booth, Philip 1925-. . . . . **CLC 23**
See also CA 5-8R; CANR 5; DLBY 82

Booth, Wayne C(layson) 1921- . . . . . **CLC 24**
See also CA 1-4R; CAAS 5; CANR 3, 43;
DLB 67

Borchert, Wolfgang 1921-1947 . . . . . **TCLC 5**
See also CA 104; DLB 69, 124

Borel, Petrus 1809-1859. . . . . **NCLC 41**

Borges, Jorge Luis
1899-1986 . . . **CLC 1, 2, 3, 4, 6, 8, 9, 10,
13, 19, 44, 48, 83; DA; DAB; DAC;
DAM MST, MULT; HLC; SSC 4; WLC**
See also AAYA 19; CA 21-24R; CANR 19,
33; DLB 113; DLBY 86; HW; MTCW

Borowski, Tadeusz 1922-1951. . . . . . **TCLC 9**
See also CA 106

Borrow, George (Henry)
1803-1881 . . . . **NCLC 9**
See also DLB 21, 55, 166

Bosman, Herman Charles
1905-1951 . . . . **TCLC 49**

Bosschere, Jean de 1878(?)-1953. . . **TCLC 19**
See also CA 115

Boswell, James
1740-1795 . . . . . . **LC 4; DA; DAB; DAC;
DAM MST; WLC**
See also CDBLB 1660-1789; DLB 104, 142

Bottoms, David 1949-. . . . . **CLC 53**
See also CA 105; CANR 22; DLB 120;
DLBY 83

Boucicault, Dion 1820-1890. . . . . . **NCLC 41**

Boucolon, Maryse 1937(?)-
See Conde, Maryse
See also CA 110; CANR 30, 53

Bourget, Paul (Charles Joseph)
1852-1935 . . . . **TCLC 12**
See also CA 107; DLB 123

Bourjaily, Vance (Nye) 1922- . . . . **CLC 8, 62**
See also CA 1-4R; CAAS 1; CANR 2;
DLB 2, 143

Bourne, Randolph S(illiman)
1886-1918 . . . . **TCLC 16**
See also CA 117; DLB 63

Bova, Ben(jamin William) 1932-. . . . **CLC 45**
See also AAYA 16; CA 5-8R; CAAS 18;
CANR 11; CLR 3; DLBY 81;
INT CANR-11; MAICYA; MTCW;
SATA 6, 68

Bowen, Elizabeth (Dorothea Cole)
1899-1973 . . . . . . **CLC 1, 3, 6, 11, 15, 22;
DAM NOV; SSC 3**
See also CA 17-18; 41-44R; CANR 35;
CAP 2; CDBLB 1945-1960; DLB 15, 162;
MTCW

Bowering, George 1935-. . . . . **CLC 15, 47**
See also CA 21-24R; CAAS 16; CANR 10;
DLB 53

Bowering, Marilyn R(uthe) 1949-. . . **CLC 32**
See also CA 101; CANR 49

Bowers, Edgar 1924- . . . . **CLC 9**
See also CA 5-8R; CANR 24; DLB 5

Bowie, David. . . . . **CLC 17**
See also Jones, David Robert

Bowles, Jane (Sydney)
1917-1973 . . . . **CLC 3, 68**
See also CA 19-20; 41-44R; CAP 2

Bowles, Paul (Frederick)
1910- . . . . **CLC 1, 2, 19, 53; SSC 3**
See also CA 1-4R; CAAS 1; CANR 1, 19,
50; DLB 5, 6; MTCW

Box, Edgar
See Vidal, Gore

Boyd, Nancy
See Millay, Edna St. Vincent

Boyd, William 1952-. . . . . **CLC 28, 53, 70**
See also CA 114; 120; CANR 51

Boyle, Kay
1902-1992 . . . . . **CLC 1, 5, 19, 58; SSC 5**
See also CA 13-16R; 140; CAAS 1;
CANR 29; DLB 4, 9, 48, 86; DLBY 93;
MTCW

Boyle, Mark
See Kienzle, William X(avier)

Boyle, Patrick 1905-1982. . . . . **CLC 19**
See also CA 127

Boyle, T. C. 1948-
See Boyle, T(homas) Coraghessan

Boyle, T(homas) Coraghessan
1948- . . . . . **CLC 36, 55, 90; DAM POP;
SSC 16**
See also BEST 90:4; CA 120; CANR 44;
DLBY 86

Boz
See Dickens, Charles (John Huffam)

Brackenridge, Hugh Henry
1748-1816 . . . . **NCLC 7**
See also DLB 11, 37

Bradbury, Edward P.
See Moorcock, Michael (John)

Bradbury, Malcolm (Stanley)
1932- . . . . **CLC 32, 61; DAM NOV**
See also CA 1-4R; CANR 1, 33; DLB 14;
MTCW

Bradbury, Ray (Douglas)
1920- . . . . **CLC 1, 3, 10, 15, 42; DA;
DAB; DAC; DAM MST, NOV, POP;
WLC**
See also AAYA 15; AITN 1, 2; CA 1-4R;
CANR 2, 30; CDALB 1968-1988; DLB 2,
8; INT CANR-30; MTCW; SATA 11, 64

Bradford, Gamaliel 1863-1932. . . . . **TCLC 36**
See also DLB 17

Bradley, David (Henry, Jr.)
1950- . . . . . **CLC 23; BLC; DAM MULT**
See also BW 1; CA 104; CANR 26; DLB 33

Bradley, John Ed(mund, Jr.)
1958- . . . . **CLC 55**
See also CA 139

Bradley, Marion Zimmer
1930- . . . . **CLC 30; DAM POP**
See also AAYA 9; CA 57-60; CAAS 10;
CANR 7, 31, 51; DLB 8; MTCW;
SATA 90

Bradstreet, Anne
1612(?)-1672 . . . . . . **LC 4, 30; DA; DAC;
DAM MST, POET; PC 10**
See also CDALB 1640-1865; DLB 24

Brady, Joan 1939- . . . . **CLC 86**
See also CA 141

Bragg, Melvyn 1939-. . . . . **CLC 10**
See also BEST 89:3; CA 57-60; CANR 10,
48; DLB 14

Braine, John (Gerard)
1922-1986 . . . . **CLC 1, 3, 41**
See also CA 1-4R; 120; CANR 1, 33;
CDBLB 1945-1960; DLB 15; DLBY 86;
MTCW

Brammer, William 1930(?)-1978 . . . . **CLC 31**
See also CA 77-80

Brancati, Vitaliano 1907-1954. . . . . **TCLC 12**
See also CA 109

Brancato, Robin F(idler) 1936-. . . . . **CLC 35**
See also AAYA 9; CA 69-72; CANR 11,
45; CLR 32; JRDA; SAAS 9; SATA 23

Brand, Max
See Faust, Frederick (Schiller)

Brand, Millen 1906-1980. . . . . **CLC 7**
See also CA 21-24R; 97-100

Branden, Barbara . . . . **CLC 44**
See also CA 148

Brandes, Georg (Morris Cohen)
1842-1927 . . . . **TCLC 10**
See also CA 105

Brandys, Kazimierz 1916-. . . . . **CLC 62**

Branley, Franklyn M(ansfield)
1915- . . . . **CLC 21**
See also CA 33-36R; CANR 14, 39;
CLR 13; MAICYA; SAAS 16; SATA 4,
68

Brathwaite, Edward Kamau
1930- . . . . **CLC 11; DAM POET**
See also BW 2; CA 25-28R; CANR 11, 26,
47; DLB 125

Brautigan, Richard (Gary)
1935-1984 . . . . **CLC 1, 3, 5, 9, 12, 34, 42;**
DAM NOV
See also CA 53-56; 113; CANR 34; DLB 2,
5; DLBY 80, 84; MTCW; SATA 56

Brave Bird, Mary 1953-
See Crow Dog, Mary
See also NNAL

Braverman, Kate 1950- . . . . **CLC 67**
See also CA 89-92

Brecht, Bertolt
1898-1956 . . . . . . **TCLC 1, 6, 13, 35; DA;**
DAB; DAC; DAM DRAM, MST; DC 3;
WLC
See also CA 104; 133; DLB 56, 124; MTCW

Brecht, Eugen Berthold Friedrich
See Brecht, Bertolt

Bremer, Fredrika 1801-1865 . . . . . **NCLC 11**

Brennan, Christopher John
1870-1932 . . . . **TCLC 17**
See also CA 117

Brennan, Maeve 1917- . . . . **CLC 5**
See also CA 81-84

Brentano, Clemens (Maria)
1778-1842 . . . . **NCLC 1**
See also DLB 90

Brent of Bin Bin
See Franklin, (Stella Maraia Sarah) Miles

Brenton, Howard 1942- . . . . **CLC 31**
See also CA 69-72; CANR 33; DLB 13;
MTCW

Breslin, James 1930-
See Breslin, Jimmy
See also CA 73-76; CANR 31; DAM NOV;
MTCW

Breslin, Jimmy . . . . **CLC 4, 43**
See also Breslin, James
See also AITN 1

Bresson, Robert 1901- . . . . **CLC 16**
See also CA 110; CANR 49

Breton, Andre
1896-1966 . . . . . **CLC 2, 9, 15, 54; PC 15**
See also CA 19-20; 25-28R; CANR 40;
CAP 2; DLB 65; MTCW

Breytenbach, Breyten
1939(?)- . . . . **CLC 23, 37; DAM POET**
See also CA 113; 129

Bridgers, Sue Ellen 1942- . . . . **CLC 26**
See also AAYA 8; CA 65-68; CANR 11,
36; CLR 18; DLB 52; JRDA; MAICYA;
SAAS 1; SATA 22, 90

Bridges, Robert (Seymour)
1844-1930 . . . . **TCLC 1; DAM POET**
See also CA 104; 152; CDBLB 1890-1914;
DLB 19, 98

Bridie, James . . . . **TCLC 3**
See also Mavor, Osborne Henry
See also DLB 10

Brin, David 1950- . . . . **CLC 34**
See also CA 102; CANR 24;
INT CANR-24; SATA 65

Brink, Andre (Philippus)
1935- . . . . **CLC 18, 36**
See also CA 104; CANR 39; INT 103;
MTCW

Brinsmead, H(esba) F(ay) 1922- . . . . **CLC 21**
See also CA 21-24R; CANR 10; MAICYA;
SAAS 5; SATA 18, 78

Brittain, Vera (Mary)
1893(?)-1970 . . . . **CLC 23**
See also CA 13-16; 25-28R; CAP 1; MTCW

Broch, Hermann 1886-1951 . . . . . . **TCLC 20**
See also CA 117; DLB 85, 124

Brock, Rose
See Hansen, Joseph

Brodkey, Harold (Roy) 1930-1996 . . **CLC 56**
See also CA 111; 151; DLB 130

Brodsky, Iosif Alexandrovich 1940-1996
See Brodsky, Joseph
See also AITN 1; CA 41-44R; 151;
CANR 37; DAM POET; MTCW

Brodsky, Joseph . . **CLC 4, 6, 13, 36, 50; PC 9**
See also Brodsky, Iosif Alexandrovich

Brodsky, Michael Mark 1948- . . . . . **CLC 19**
See also CA 102; CANR 18, 41

Bromell, Henry 1947- . . . . **CLC 5**
See also CA 53-56; CANR 9

Bromfield, Louis (Brucker)
1896-1956 . . . . **TCLC 11**
See also CA 107; DLB 4, 9, 86

Broner, E(sther) M(asserman)
1930- . . . . **CLC 19**
See also CA 17-20R; CANR 8, 25; DLB 28

Bronk, William 1918- . . . . **CLC 10**
See also CA 89-92; CANR 23; DLB 165

Bronstein, Lev Davidovich
See Trotsky, Leon

Bronte, Anne 1820-1849 . . . . **NCLC 4**
See also DLB 21

Bronte, Charlotte
1816-1855 . . . . . **NCLC 3, 8, 33, 58; DA;**
DAB; DAC; DAM MST, NOV; WLC
See also AAYA 17; CDBLB 1832-1890;
DLB 21, 159

Bronte, Emily (Jane)
1818-1848 . . . . **NCLC 16, 35; DA; DAB;**
DAC; DAM MST, NOV, POET; PC 8;
WLC
See also AAYA 17; CDBLB 1832-1890;
DLB 21, 32

Brooke, Frances 1724-1789 . . . . **LC 6**
See also DLB 39, 99

Brooke, Henry 1703(?)-1783 . . . . **LC 1**
See also DLB 39

Brooke, Rupert (Chawner)
1887-1915 . . . . **TCLC 2, 7; DA; DAB;**
DAC; DAM MST, POET; WLC
See also CA 104; 132; CDBLB 1914-1945;
DLB 19; MTCW

Brooke-Haven, P.
See Wodehouse, P(elham) G(renville)

Brooke-Rose, Christine 1926- . . . . . . **CLC 40**
See also CA 13-16R; DLB 14

Brookner, Anita
1928- . . . . **CLC 32, 34, 51; DAB;**
DAM POP
See also CA 114; 120; CANR 37; DLBY 87;
MTCW

Brooks, Cleanth 1906-1994 . . . . . **CLC 24, 86**
See also CA 17-20R; 145; CANR 33, 35;
DLB 63; DLBY 94; INT CANR-35;
MTCW

Brooks, George
See Baum, L(yman) Frank

Brooks, Gwendolyn
1917- . . . . . . **CLC 1, 2, 4, 5, 15, 49; BLC;**
DA; DAC; DAM MST, MULT, POET;
PC 7; WLC
See also AITN 1; BW 2; CA 1-4R;
CANR 1, 27, 52; CDALB 1941-1968;
CLR 27; DLB 5, 76, 165; MTCW;
SATA 6

Brooks, Mel . . . . **CLC 12**
See also Kaminsky, Melvin
See also AAYA 13; DLB 26

Brooks, Peter 1938- . . . . **CLC 34**
See also CA 45-48; CANR 1

Brooks, Van Wyck 1886-1963 . . . . . . **CLC 29**
See also CA 1-4R; CANR 6; DLB 45, 63,
103

Brophy, Brigid (Antonia)
1929-1995 . . . . **CLC 6, 11, 29**
See also CA 5-8R; 149; CAAS 4; CANR 25,
53; DLB 14; MTCW

Brosman, Catharine Savage 1934- . . . . **CLC 9**
See also CA 61-64; CANR 21, 46

Brother Antoninus
See Everson, William (Oliver)

Broughton, T(homas) Alan 1936- . . . **CLC 19**
See also CA 45-48; CANR 2, 23, 48

Broumas, Olga 1949- . . . . **CLC 10, 73**
See also CA 85-88; CANR 20

Brown, Charles Brockden
1771-1810 . . . . **NCLC 22**
See also CDALB 1640-1865; DLB 37, 59,
73

Brown, Christy 1932-1981 . . . . **CLC 63**
See also CA 105; 104; DLB 14

Brown, Claude
1937- . . . . . **CLC 30; BLC; DAM MULT**
See also AAYA 7; BW 1; CA 73-76

Brown, Dee (Alexander)
1908- . . . . **CLC 18, 47; DAM POP**
See also CA 13-16R; CAAS 6; CANR 11,
45; DLBY 80; MTCW; SATA 5

Brown, George
See Wertmueller, Lina

Brown, George Douglas
1869-1902 . . . . **TCLC 28**

Brown, George Mackay
1921-1996 . . . . **CLC 5, 48**
See also CA 21-24R; 151; CAAS 6;
CANR 12, 37; DLB 14, 27, 139; MTCW;
SATA 35

Brown, (William) Larry 1951-...... **CLC 73**
See also CA 130; 134; INT 133

Brown, Moses
See Barrett, William (Christopher)

Brown, Rita Mae
1944-..... **CLC 18, 43, 79; DAM NOV,
POP**
See also CA 45-48; CANR 2, 11, 35;
INT CANR-11; MTCW

Brown, Roderick (Langmere) Haig-
See Haig-Brown, Roderick (Langmere)

Brown, Rosellen 1939-........... **CLC 32**
See also CA 77-80; CAAS 10; CANR 14, 44

Brown, Sterling Allen
1901-1989 .... **CLC 1, 23, 59; BLC;
DAM MULT, POET**
See also BW 1; CA 85-88; 127; CANR 26;
DLB 48, 51, 63; MTCW

Brown, Will
See Ainsworth, William Harrison

Brown, William Wells
1813-1884 .... **NCLC 2; BLC;
DAM MULT; DC 1**
See also DLB 3, 50

Browne, (Clyde) Jackson 1948(?)-... **CLC 21**
See also CA 120

Browning, Elizabeth Barrett
1806-1861 ..... **NCLC 1, 16; DA; DAB;
DAC; DAM MST, POET; PC 6; WLC**
See also CDBLB 1832-1890; DLB 32

Browning, Robert
1812-1889 .... **NCLC 19; DA; DAB;
DAC; DAM MST, POET; PC 2**
See also CDBLB 1832-1890; DLB 32, 163;
YABC 1

Browning, Tod 1882-1962 .... **CLC 16**
See also CA 141; 117

Brownson, Orestes (Augustus)
1803-1876 .... **NCLC 50**

Bruccoli, Matthew J(oseph) 1931-.. **CLC 34**
See also CA 9-12R; CANR 7; DLB 103

Bruce, Lenny.................... **CLC 21**
See also Schneider, Leonard Alfred

Bruin, John
See Brutus, Dennis

Brulard, Henri
See Stendhal

Brulls, Christian
See Simenon, Georges (Jacques Christian)

Brunner, John (Kilian Houston)
1934-1995 ...... **CLC 8, 10; DAM POP**
See also CA 1-4R; 149; CAAS 8; CANR 2,
37; MTCW

Bruno, Giordano 1548-1600........ **LC 27**

Brutus, Dennis
1924-..... **CLC 43; BLC; DAM MULT,
POET**
See also BW 2; CA 49-52; CAAS 14;
CANR 2, 27, 42; DLB 117

Bryan, C(ourtlandt) D(ixon) B(arnes)
1936-...................... **CLC 29**
See also CA 73-76; CANR 13;
INT CANR-13

Bryan, Michael
See Moore, Brian

Bryant, William Cullen
1794-1878 ..... **NCLC 6, 46; DA; DAB;
DAC; DAM MST, POET**
See also CDALB 1640-1865; DLB 3, 43, 59

Bryusov, Valery Yakovlevich
1873-1924 .... **TCLC 10**
See also CA 107

Buchan, John
1875-1940 .... **TCLC 41; DAB;
DAM POP**
See also CA 108; 145; DLB 34, 70, 156;
YABC 2

Buchanan, George 1506-1582 .... **LC 4**

Buchheim, Lothar-Guenther 1918-... **CLC 6**
See also CA 85-88

Buchner, (Karl) Georg
1813-1837 .... **NCLC 26**

Buchwald, Art(hur) 1925-........... **CLC 33**
See also AITN 1; CA 5-8R; CANR 21;
MTCW; SATA 10

Buck, Pearl S(ydenstricker)
1892-1973 .... **CLC 7, 11, 18; DA; DAB;
DAC; DAM MST, NOV**
See also AITN 1; CA 1-4R; 41-44R;
CANR 1, 34; DLB 9, 102; MTCW;
SATA 1, 25

Buckler, Ernest
1908-1984 .. **CLC 13; DAC; DAM MST**
See also CA 11-12; 114; CAP 1; DLB 68;
SATA 47

Buckley, Vincent (Thomas)
1925-1988 .... **CLC 57**
See also CA 101

Buckley, William F(rank), Jr.
1925-....... **CLC 7, 18, 37; DAM POP**
See also AITN 1; CA 1-4R; CANR 1, 24,
53; DLB 137; DLBY 80; INT CANR-24;
MTCW

Buechner, (Carl) Frederick
1926-........ **CLC 2, 4, 6, 9; DAM NOV**
See also CA 13-16R; CANR 11, 39;
DLBY 80; INT CANR-11; MTCW

Buell, John (Edward) 1927-........ **CLC 10**
See also CA 1-4R; DLB 53

Buero Vallejo, Antonio 1916-... **CLC 15, 46**
See also CA 106; CANR 24, 49; HW;
MTCW

Bufalino, Gesualdo 1920(?)-........ **CLC 74**

Bugayev, Boris Nikolayevich 1880-1934
See Bely, Andrey
See also CA 104

Bukowski, Charles
1920-1994 .... **CLC 2, 5, 9, 41, 82;
DAM NOV, POET**
See also CA 17-20R; 144; CANR 40;
DLB 5, 130, 169; MTCW

Bulgakov, Mikhail (Afanas'evich)
1891-1940 .... **TCLC 2, 16;
DAM DRAM, NOV; SSC 18**
See also CA 105; 152

Bulgya, Alexander Alexandrovich
1901-1956 .... **TCLC 53**
See also Fadeyev, Alexander
See also CA 117

Bullins, Ed
1935-.............. **CLC 1, 5, 7; BLC;
DAM DRAM, MULT; DC 6**
See also BW 2; CA 49-52; CAAS 16;
CANR 24, 46; DLB 7, 38; MTCW

Bulwer-Lytton, Edward (George Earle Lytton)
1803-1873 .... **NCLC 1, 45**
See also DLB 21

Bunin, Ivan Alexeyevich
1870-1953 .... **TCLC 6; SSC 5**
See also CA 104

Bunting, Basil
1900-1985 .... **CLC 10, 39, 47;
DAM POET**
See also CA 53-56; 115; CANR 7; DLB 20

Bunuel, Luis
1900-1983 .... **CLC 16, 80;
DAM MULT; HLC**
See also CA 101; 110; CANR 32; HW

Bunyan, John
1628-1688 ...... **LC 4; DA; DAB; DAC;
DAM MST; WLC**
See also CDBLB 1660-1789; DLB 39

Burckhardt, Jacob (Christoph)
1818-1897 .... **NCLC 49**

Burford, Eleanor
See Hibbert, Eleanor Alice Burford

Burgess, Anthony
. **CLC 1, 2, 4, 5, 8, 10, 13, 15, 22, 40, 62,
81, 94; DAB**
See also Wilson, John (Anthony) Burgess
See also AITN 1; CDBLB 1960 to Present;
DLB 14

Burke, Edmund
1729(?)-1797 .... **LC 7; DA; DAB; DAC;
DAM MST; WLC**
See also DLB 104

Burke, Kenneth (Duva)
1897-1993 .... **CLC 2, 24**
See also CA 5-8R; 143; CANR 39; DLB 45,
63; MTCW

Burke, Leda
See Garnett, David

Burke, Ralph
See Silverberg, Robert

Burke, Thomas 1886-1945 .... **TCLC 63**
See also CA 113

Burney, Fanny 1752-1840 .... **NCLC 12, 54**
See also DLB 39

Burns, Robert 1759-1796............ **PC 6**
See also CDBLB 1789-1832; DA; DAB;
DAC; DAM MST, POET; DLB 109;
WLC

Burns, Tex
See L'Amour, Louis (Dearborn)

Burnshaw, Stanley 1906-..... **CLC 3, 13, 44**
See also CA 9-12R; DLB 48

Burr, Anne 1937-................. **CLC 6**
See also CA 25-28R

Burroughs, Edgar Rice
1875-1950 .... **TCLC 2, 32; DAM NOV**
See also AAYA 11; CA 104; 132; DLB 8;
MTCW; SATA 41

Burroughs, William S(eward)
1914- .... **CLC 1, 2, 5, 15, 22, 42, 75;**
DA; DAB; DAC; DAM MST, NOV,
POP; WLC
See also AITN 2; CA 9-12R; CANR 20, 52;
DLB 2, 8, 16, 152; DLBY 81; MTCW

Burton, Richard F. 1821-1890.... **NCLC 42**
See also DLB 55

Busch, Frederick 1941- ... **CLC 7, 10, 18, 47**
See also CA 33-36R; CAAS 1; CANR 45;
DLB 6

Bush, Ronald 1946- .... **CLC 34**
See also CA 136

Bustos, F(rancisco)
See Borges, Jorge Luis

Bustos Domecq, H(onorio)
See Bioy Casares, Adolfo; Borges, Jorge
Luis

Butler, Octavia E(stelle)
1947- ..... **CLC 38; DAM MULT, POP**
See also AAYA 18; BW 2; CA 73-76;
CANR 12, 24, 38; DLB 33; MTCW;
SATA 84

Butler, Robert Olen (Jr.)
1945- .... **CLC 81; DAM POP**
See also CA 112; DLB 173; INT 112

Butler, Samuel 1612-1680 .... **LC 16**
See also DLB 101, 126

Butler, Samuel
1835-1902 ...... **TCLC 1, 33; DA; DAB;**
DAC; DAM MST, NOV; WLC
See also CA 143; CDBLB 1890-1914;
DLB 18, 57, 174

Butler, Walter C.
See Faust, Frederick (Schiller)

Butor, Michel (Marie Francois)
1926- .... **CLC 1, 3, 8, 11, 15**
See also CA 9-12R; CANR 33; DLB 83;
MTCW

Buzo, Alexander (John) 1944-...... **CLC 61**
See also CA 97-100; CANR 17, 39

Buzzati, Dino 1906-1972 .... **CLC 36**
See also CA 33-36R

Byars, Betsy (Cromer) 1928-....... **CLC 35**
See also AAYA 19; CA 33-36R; CANR 18,
36; CLR 1, 16; DLB 52; INT CANR-18;
JRDA; MAICYA; MTCW; SAAS 1;
SATA 4, 46, 80

Byatt, A(ntonia) S(usan Drabble)
1936- ... **CLC 19, 65; DAM NOV, POP**
See also CA 13-16R; CANR 13, 33, 50;
DLB 14; MTCW

Byrne, David 1952-.............. **CLC 26**
See also CA 127

Byrne, John Keyes 1926-
See Leonard, Hugh
See also CA 102; INT 102

Byron, George Gordon (Noel)
1788-1824 ..... **NCLC 2, 12; DA; DAB;**
DAC; DAM MST, POET; PC 16; WLC
See also CDBLB 1789-1832; DLB 96, 110

Byron, Robert 1905-1941........ **TCLC 67**

C. 3. 3.
See Wilde, Oscar (Fingal O'Flahertie Wills)

Caballero, Fernan 1796-1877..... **NCLC 10**

Cabell, Branch
See Cabell, James Branch

Cabell, James Branch 1879-1958 ... **TCLC 6**
See also CA 105; 152; DLB 9, 78

Cable, George Washington
1844-1925 .... **TCLC 4; SSC 4**
See also CA 104; DLB 12, 74; DLBD 13

Cabral de Melo Neto, Joao
1920- .... **CLC 76; DAM MULT**
See also CA 151

Cabrera Infante, G(uillermo)
1929- ..... **CLC 5, 25, 45; DAM MULT;**
HLC
See also CA 85-88; CANR 29; DLB 113;
HW; MTCW

Cade, Toni
See Bambara, Toni Cade

Cadmus and Harmonia
See Buchan, John

Caedmon fl. 658-680............. **CMLC 7**
See also DLB 146

Caeiro, Alberto
See Pessoa, Fernando (Antonio Nogueira)

Cage, John (Milton, Jr.) 1912- ..... **CLC 41**
See also CA 13-16R; CANR 9;
INT CANR-9

Cain, G.
See Cabrera Infante, G(uillermo)

Cain, Guillermo
See Cabrera Infante, G(uillermo)

Cain, James M(allahan)
1892-1977 .... **CLC 3, 11, 28**
See also AITN 1; CA 17-20R; 73-76;
CANR 8, 34; MTCW

Caine, Mark
See Raphael, Frederic (Michael)

Calasso, Roberto 1941- .... **CLC 81**
See also CA 143

Calderon de la Barca, Pedro
1600-1681 .... **LC 23; DC 3**

Caldwell, Erskine (Preston)
1903-1987 .... **CLC 1, 8, 14, 50, 60;**
DAM NOV; SSC 19
See also AITN 1; CA 1-4R; 121; CAAS 1;
CANR 2, 33; DLB 9, 86; MTCW

Caldwell, (Janet Miriam) Taylor (Holland)
1900-1985 .... **CLC 2, 28, 39;**
DAM NOV, POP
See also CA 5-8R; 116; CANR 5

Calhoun, John Caldwell
1782-1850 .... **NCLC 15**
See also DLB 3

Calisher, Hortense
1911- ..... **CLC 2, 4, 8, 38; DAM NOV;**
SSC 15
See also CA 1-4R; CANR 1, 22; DLB 2;
INT CANR-22; MTCW

Callaghan, Morley Edward
1903-1990 ..... **CLC 3, 14, 41, 65; DAC;**
DAM MST
See also CA 9-12R; 132; CANR 33;
DLB 68; MTCW

Callimachus
c. 305B.C.-c. 240B.C........ **CMLC 18**

Calvino, Italo
1923-1985 ..... **CLC 5, 8, 11, 22, 33, 39,**
73; DAM NOV; SSC 3
See also CA 85-88; 116; CANR 23; MTCW

Cameron, Carey 1952-............ **CLC 59**
See also CA 135

Cameron, Peter 1959-............. **CLC 44**
See also CA 125; CANR 50

Campana, Dino 1885-1932........ **TCLC 20**
See also CA 117; DLB 114

Campanella, Tommaso 1568-1639.... **LC 32**

Campbell, John W(ood, Jr.)
1910-1971 .... **CLC 32**
See also CA 21-22; 29-32R; CANR 34;
CAP 2; DLB 8; MTCW

Campbell, Joseph 1904-1987....... **CLC 69**
See also AAYA 3; BEST 89:2; CA 1-4R;
124; CANR 3, 28; MTCW

Campbell, Maria 1940-...... **CLC 85; DAC**
See also CA 102; CANR 54; NNAL

Campbell, (John) Ramsey
1946- .... **CLC 42; SSC 19**
See also CA 57-60; CANR 7; INT CANR-7

Campbell, (Ignatius) Roy (Dunnachie)
1901-1957 .... **TCLC 5**
See also CA 104; DLB 20

Campbell, Thomas 1777-1844 .... **NCLC 19**
See also DLB 93; 144

Campbell, Wilfred................. TCLC 9
See also Campbell, William

Campbell, William 1858(?)-1918
See Campbell, Wilfred
See also CA 106; DLB 92

Campion, Jane................... CLC 95
See also CA 138

Campos, Alvaro de
See Pessoa, Fernando (Antonio Nogueira)

Camus, Albert
1913-1960 .... **CLC 1, 2, 4, 9, 11, 14, 32,**
63, 69; DA; DAB; DAC; DAM DRAM,
MST, NOV; DC 2; SSC 9; WLC
See also CA 89-92; DLB 72; MTCW

Canby, Vincent 1924-............. **CLC 13**
See also CA 81-84

Cancale
See Desnos, Robert

Canetti, Elias
1905-1994 .... **CLC 3, 14, 25, 75, 86**
See also CA 21-24R; 146; CANR 23;
DLB 85, 124; MTCW

Canin, Ethan 1960-.............. **CLC 55**
See also CA 131; 135

Cannon, Curt
See Hunter, Evan

Cape, Judith
See Page, P(atricia) K(athleen)

Capek, Karel
1890-1938 ...... **TCLC 6, 37; DA; DAB;**
DAC; DAM DRAM, MST, NOV; DC 1;
WLC
See also CA 104; 140

Capote, Truman
1924-1984 . . . . . . **CLC 1, 3, 8, 13, 19, 34, 38, 58; DA; DAB; DAC; DAM MST, NOV, POP; SSC 2; WLC**
See also CA 5-8R; 113; CANR 18; CDALB 1941-1968; DLB 2; DLBY 80, 84; MTCW

Capra, Frank 1897-1991. . . . . **CLC 16**
See also CA 61-64; 135

Caputo, Philip 1941-. . . . . **CLC 32**
See also CA 73-76; CANR 40

Card, Orson Scott
1951- . . . . . . **CLC 44, 47, 50; DAM POP**
See also AAYA 11; CA 102; CANR 27, 47; INT CANR-27; MTCW; SATA 83

Cardenal, Ernesto
1925- . . . . **CLC 31; DAM MULT, POET; HLC**
See also CA 49-52; CANR 2, 32; HW; MTCW

Cardozo, Benjamin N(athan)
1870-1938 . . . . **TCLC 65**
See also CA 117

Carducci, Giosue 1835-1907. . . . . . **TCLC 32**

Carew, Thomas 1595(?)-1640. . . . . . . **LC 13**
See also DLB 126

Carey, Ernestine Gilbreth 1908- . . . . **CLC 17**
See also CA 5-8R; SATA 2

Carey, Peter 1943-. . . . . **CLC 40, 55, 96**
See also CA 123; 127; CANR 53; INT 127; MTCW

Carleton, William 1794-1869. . . . . . **NCLC 3**
See also DLB 159

Carlisle, Henry (Coffin) 1926-. . . . . . **CLC 33**
See also CA 13-16R; CANR 15

Carlsen, Chris
See Holdstock, Robert P.

Carlson, Ron(ald F.) 1947-. . . . . **CLC 54**
See also CA 105; CANR 27

Carlyle, Thomas
1795-1881 . . . . **NCLC 22; DA; DAB; DAC; DAM MST**
See also CDBLB 1789-1832; DLB 55; 144

Carman, (William) Bliss
1861-1929 . . . . **TCLC 7; DAC**
See also CA 104; 152; DLB 92

Carnegie, Dale 1888-1955 . . . . **TCLC 53**

Carossa, Hans 1878-1956. . . . . **TCLC 48**
See also DLB 66

Carpenter, Don(ald Richard)
1931-1995 . . . . **CLC 41**
See also CA 45-48; 149; CANR 1

Carpentier (y Valmont), Alejo
1904-1980 . . . . **CLC 8, 11, 38; DAM MULT; HLC**
See also CA 65-68; 97-100; CANR 11; DLB 113; HW

Carr, Caleb 1955(?)-. . . . . **CLC 86**
See also CA 147

Carr, Emily 1871-1945. . . . . **TCLC 32**
See also DLB 68

Carr, John Dickson 1906-1977 . . . . . . **CLC 3**
See also CA 49-52; 69-72; CANR 3, 33; MTCW

Carr, Philippa
See Hibbert, Eleanor Alice Burford

Carr, Virginia Spencer 1929-. . . . . . . **CLC 34**
See also CA 61-64; DLB 111

Carrere, Emmanuel 1957- . . . . **CLC 89**

Carrier, Roch
1937- . . . **CLC 13, 78; DAC; DAM MST**
See also CA 130; DLB 53

Carroll, James P. 1943(?)-. . . . . **CLC 38**
See also CA 81-84

Carroll, Jim 1951- . . . . **CLC 35**
See also AAYA 17; CA 45-48; CANR 42

Carroll, Lewis . . . . **NCLC 2, 53; WLC**
See also Dodgson, Charles Lutwidge
See also CDBLB 1832-1890; CLR 2, 18; DLB 18, 163; JRDA

Carroll, Paul Vincent 1900-1968. . . . **CLC 10**
See also CA 9-12R; 25-28R; DLB 10

Carruth, Hayden
1921- . . . . . . **CLC 4, 7, 10, 18, 84; PC 10**
See also CA 9-12R; CANR 4, 38; DLB 5, 165; INT CANR-4; MTCW; SATA 47

Carson, Rachel Louise
1907-1964 . . . . **CLC 71; DAM POP**
See also CA 77-80; CANR 35; MTCW; SATA 23

Carter, Angela (Olive)
1940-1992 . . . . . . **CLC 5, 41, 76; SSC 13**
See also CA 53-56; 136; CANR 12, 36; DLB 14; MTCW; SATA 66; SATA-Obit 70

Carter, Nick
See Smith, Martin Cruz

Carver, Raymond
1938-1988 . . . . **CLC 22, 36, 53, 55; DAM NOV; SSC 8**
See also CA 33-36R; 126; CANR 17, 34; DLB 130; DLBY 84, 88; MTCW

Cary, Elizabeth, Lady Falkland
1585-1639 . . . . **LC 30**

Cary, (Arthur) Joyce (Lunel)
1888-1957 . . . . **TCLC 1, 29**
See also CA 104; CDBLB 1914-1945; DLB 15, 100

Casanova de Seingalt, Giovanni Jacopo
1725-1798 . . . . **LC 13**

Casares, Adolfo Bioy
See Bioy Casares, Adolfo

Casely-Hayford, J(oseph) E(phraim)
1866-1930 . . . . **TCLC 24; BLC; DAM MULT**
See also BW 2; CA 123; 152

Casey, John (Dudley) 1939-. . . . . **CLC 59**
See also BEST 90:2; CA 69-72; CANR 23

Casey, Michael 1947-. . . . . **CLC 2**
See also CA 65-68; DLB 5

Casey, Patrick
See Thurman, Wallace (Henry)

Casey, Warren (Peter) 1935-1988 . . . **CLC 12**
See also CA 101; 127; INT 101

Casona, Alejandro. . . . . **CLC 49**
See also Alvarez, Alejandro Rodriguez

Cassavetes, John 1929-1989. . . . . **CLC 20**
See also CA 85-88; 127

Cassill, R(onald) V(erlin) 1919-. . . **CLC 4, 23**
See also CA 9-12R; CAAS 1; CANR 7, 45; DLB 6

Cassirer, Ernst 1874-1945 . . . . **TCLC 61**

Cassity, (Allen) Turner 1929- . . . . **CLC 6, 42**
See also CA 17-20R; CAAS 8; CANR 11; DLB 105

Castaneda, Carlos 1931(?)-. . . . . **CLC 12**
See also CA 25-28R; CANR 32; HW; MTCW

Castedo, Elena 1937-. . . . . **CLC 65**
See also CA 132

Castedo-Ellerman, Elena
See Castedo, Elena

Castellanos, Rosario
1925-1974 . . . . . . **CLC 66; DAM MULT; HLC**
See also CA 131; 53-56; DLB 113; HW

Castelvetro, Lodovico 1505-1571. . . . . **LC 12**

Castiglione, Baldassare 1478-1529 . . . **LC 12**

Castle, Robert
See Hamilton, Edmond

Castro, Guillen de 1569-1631. . . . . . . **LC 19**

Castro, Rosalia de
1837-1885 . . . . . . **NCLC 3; DAM MULT**

Cather, Willa
See Cather, Willa Sibert

Cather, Willa Sibert
1873-1947 . . . . **TCLC 1, 11, 31; DA; DAB; DAC; DAM MST, NOV; SSC 2; WLC**
See also CA 104; 128; CDALB 1865-1917; DLB 9, 54, 78; DLBD 1; MTCW; SATA 30

Catton, (Charles) Bruce
1899-1978 . . . . **CLC 35**
See also AITN 1; CA 5-8R; 81-84; CANR 7; DLB 17; SATA 2; SATA-Obit 24

Catullus c. 84B.C.-c. 54B.C. . . . . . **CMLC 18**

Cauldwell, Frank
See King, Francis (Henry)

Caunitz, William J. 1933-1996 . . . . . **CLC 34**
See also BEST 89:3; CA 125; 130; 152; INT 130

Causley, Charles (Stanley) 1917-. . . . . **CLC 7**
See also CA 9-12R; CANR 5, 35; CLR 30; DLB 27; MTCW; SATA 3, 66

Caute, David 1936-. . . . **CLC 29; DAM NOV**
See also CA 1-4R; CAAS 4; CANR 1, 33; DLB 14

Cavafy, C(onstantine) P(eter)
1863-1933 . . . . **TCLC 2, 7; DAM POET**
See also Kavafis, Konstantinos Petrou
See also CA 148

Cavallo, Evelyn
See Spark, Muriel (Sarah)

Cavanna, Betty . . . . **CLC 12**
See also Harrison, Elizabeth Cavanna
See also JRDA; MAICYA; SAAS 4; SATA 1, 30

Cavendish, Margaret Lucas
1623-1673 . . . . **LC 30**
See also DLB 131

Caxton, William   1421(?)-1491(?) . . . . . **LC 17**
See also DLB 170

Cayrol, Jean 1911- . . . . **CLC 11**
See also CA 89-92; DLB 83

Cela, Camilo Jose
    1916- . . . . . **CLC 4, 13, 59; DAM MULT;**
                              HLC
See also BEST 90:2; CA 21-24R; CAAS 10;
   CANR 21, 32; DLBY 89; HW; MTCW

Celan, Paul . . . . . . **CLC 10, 19, 53, 82; PC 10**
See also Antschel, Paul
See also DLB 69

Celine, Louis-Ferdinand
. . . . **CLC 1, 3, 4, 7, 9, 15, 47**
See also Destouches, Louis-Ferdinand
See also DLB 72

Cellini, Benvenuto 1500-1571 . . . . **LC 7**

Cendrars, Blaise . . . . **CLC 18**
See also Sauser-Hall, Frederic

Cernuda (y Bidon), Luis
    1902-1963 . . . . **CLC 54; DAM POET**
See also CA 131; 89-92; DLB 134; HW

Cervantes (Saavedra), Miguel de
    1547-1616 . . . . **LC 6, 23; DA; DAB;**
    DAC; DAM MST, NOV; SSC 12; WLC

Cesaire, Aime (Fernand)
    1913- . . . . **CLC 19, 32; BLC;**
               DAM MULT, POET
See also BW 2; CA 65-68; CANR 24, 43;
   MTCW

Chabon, Michael 1963- . . . . **CLC 55**
See also CA 139

Chabrol, Claude 1930- . . . . **CLC 16**
See also CA 110

Challans, Mary 1905-1983
See Renault, Mary
See also CA 81-84; 111; SATA 23;
   SATA-Obit 36

Challis, George
See Faust, Frederick (Schiller)

Chambers, Aidan 1934- . . . . **CLC 35**
See also CA 25-28R; CANR 12, 31; JRDA;
   MAICYA; SAAS 12; SATA 1, 69

Chambers, James 1948-
See Cliff, Jimmy
See also CA 124

Chambers, Jessie
See Lawrence, D(avid) H(erbert Richards)

Chambers, Robert W. 1865-1933 . . . **TCLC 41**

Chandler, Raymond (Thornton)
    1888-1959 . . . . **TCLC 1, 7; SSC 23**
See also CA 104; 129; CDALB 1929-1941;
   DLBD 6; MTCW

Chang, Jung 1952- . . . . **CLC 71**
See also CA 142

Channing, William Ellery
    1780-1842 . . . . **NCLC 17**
See also DLB 1, 59

Chaplin, Charles Spencer
    1889-1977 . . . . **CLC 16**
See also Chaplin, Charlie
See also CA 81-84; 73-76

Chaplin, Charlie
See Chaplin, Charles Spencer
See also DLB 44

Chapman, George
    1559(?)-1634 . . . . . **LC 22; DAM DRAM**
See also DLB 62, 121

Chapman, Graham 1941-1989 . . . . . . **CLC 21**
See also Monty Python
See also CA 116; 129; CANR 35

Chapman, John Jay 1862-1933 . . . . . **TCLC 7**
See also CA 104

Chapman, Lee
See Bradley, Marion Zimmer

Chapman, Walker
See Silverberg, Robert

Chappell, Fred (Davis) 1936- . . . . **CLC 40, 78**
See also CA 5-8R; CAAS 4; CANR 8, 33;
   DLB 6, 105

Char, Rene(-Emile)
    1907-1988 . . . . **CLC 9, 11, 14, 55;**
                     DAM POET
See also CA 13-16R; 124; CANR 32;
   MTCW

Charby, Jay
See Ellison, Harlan (Jay)

Chardin, Pierre Teilhard de
See Teilhard de Chardin, (Marie Joseph)
   Pierre

Charles I 1600-1649 . . . . **LC 13**

Charyn, Jerome 1937- . . . . **CLC 5, 8, 18**
See also CA 5-8R; CAAS 1; CANR 7;
   DLBY 83; MTCW

Chase, Mary (Coyle) 1907-1981 . . . . . . **DC 1**
See also CA 77-80; 105; SATA 17;
   SATA-Obit 29

Chase, Mary Ellen 1887-1973 . . . . . . **CLC 2**
See also CA 13-16; 41-44R; CAP 1;
   SATA 10

Chase, Nicholas
See Hyde, Anthony

Chateaubriand, Francois Rene de
    1768-1848 . . . . **NCLC 3**
See also DLB 119

Chatterje, Sarat Chandra 1876-1936(?)
See Chatterji, Saratchandra
See also CA 109

Chatterji, Bankim Chandra
    1838-1894 . . . . **NCLC 19**

Chatterji, Saratchandra . . . . **TCLC 13**
See also Chatterje, Sarat Chandra

Chatterton, Thomas
    1752-1770 . . . . **LC 3; DAM POET**
See also DLB 109

Chatwin, (Charles) Bruce
    1940-1989 . . **CLC 28, 57, 59; DAM POP**
See also AAYA 4; BEST 90:1; CA 85-88;
   127

Chaucer, Daniel
See Ford, Ford Madox

Chaucer, Geoffrey
    1340(?)-1400 . . . . **LC 17; DA; DAB;**
    DAC; DAM MST, POET
See also CDBLB Before 1660; DLB 146

Chaviaras, Strates 1935-
See Haviaras, Stratis
See also CA 105

Chayefsky, Paddy . . . . **CLC 23**
See also Chayefsky, Sidney
See also DLB 7, 44; DLBY 81

Chayefsky, Sidney 1923-1981
See Chayefsky, Paddy
See also CA 9-12R; 104; CANR 18;
   DAM DRAM

Chedid, Andree 1920- . . . . **CLC 47**
See also CA 145

Cheever, John
    1912-1982 . . . . . . **CLC 3, 7, 8, 11, 15, 25,**
    64; DA; DAB; DAC; DAM MST, NOV,
    POP; SSC 1; WLC
See also CA 5-8R; 106; CABS 1; CANR 5,
   27; CDALB 1941-1968; DLB 2, 102;
   DLBY 80, 82; INT CANR-5; MTCW

Cheever, Susan 1943- . . . . **CLC 18, 48**
See also CA 103; CANR 27, 51; DLBY 82;
   INT CANR-27

Chekhonte, Antosha
See Chekhov, Anton (Pavlovich)

Chekhov, Anton (Pavlovich)
    1860-1904 . . . . . **TCLC 3, 10, 31, 55; DA;**
    DAB; DAC; DAM DRAM, MST; SSC 2;
    WLC
See also CA 104; 124; SATA 90

Chernyshevsky, Nikolay Gavrilovich
    1828-1889 . . . . **NCLC 1**

Cherry, Carolyn Janice 1942-
See Cherryh, C. J.
See also CA 65-68; CANR 10

Cherryh, C. J. . . . . **CLC 35**
See also Cherry, Carolyn Janice
See also DLBY 80

Chesnutt, Charles W(addell)
    1858-1932 . . . . **TCLC 5, 39; BLC;**
    DAM MULT; SSC 7
See also BW 1; CA 106; 125; DLB 12, 50,
   78; MTCW

Chester, Alfred 1929(?)-1971 . . . . **CLC 49**
See also CA 33-36R; DLB 130

Chesterton, G(ilbert) K(eith)
    1874-1936 . . . . **TCLC 1, 6, 64;**
    DAM NOV, POET; SSC 1
See also CA 104; 132; CDBLB 1914-1945;
   DLB 10, 19, 34, 70, 98, 149; MTCW;
   SATA 27

Chiang Pin-chin 1904-1986
See Ding Ling
See also CA 118

Ch'ien Chung-shu 1910- . . . . **CLC 22**
See also CA 130; MTCW

Child, L. Maria
See Child, Lydia Maria

Child, Lydia Maria 1802-1880 . . . . **NCLC 6**
See also DLB 1, 74; SATA 67

Child, Mrs.
See Child, Lydia Maria

Child, Philip 1898-1978 . . . . **CLC 19, 68**
See also CA 13-14; CAP 1; SATA 47

Childers, (Robert) Erskine
    1870-1922 . . . . **TCLC 65**
See also CA 113; 153; DLB 70

Childress, Alice
    1920-1994 .... **CLC 12, 15, 86, 96; BLC;**
        DAM DRAM, MULT, NOV; DC 4
    See also AAYA 8; BW 2; CA 45-48; 146;
    CANR 3, 27, 50; CLR 14; DLB 7, 38;
    JRDA; MAICYA; MTCW; SATA 7, 48,
    81

Chislett, (Margaret) Anne 1943- .... **CLC 34**
    See also CA 151

Chitty, Thomas Willes 1926- .... **CLC 11**
    See also Hinde, Thomas
    See also CA 5-8R

Chivers, Thomas Holley
    1809-1858 .... **NCLC 49**
    See also DLB 3

Chomette, Rene Lucien 1898-1981
    See Clair, Rene
    See also CA 103

Chopin, Kate
    .... **TCLC 5, 14; DA; DAB; SSC 8**
    See also Chopin, Katherine
    See also CDALB 1865-1917; DLB 12, 78

Chopin, Katherine 1851-1904
    See Chopin, Kate
    See also CA 104; 122; DAC; DAM MST,
    NOV

Chretien de Troyes
    c. 12th cent. - .... **CMLC 10**

Christie
    See Ichikawa, Kon

Christie, Agatha (Mary Clarissa)
    1890-1976 ...... **CLC 1, 6, 8, 12, 39, 48;**
        DAB; DAC; DAM NOV
    See also AAYA 9; AITN 1, 2; CA 17-20R;
    61-64; CANR 10, 37; CDBLB 1914-1945;
    DLB 13, 77; MTCW; SATA 36

Christie, (Ann) Philippa
    See Pearce, Philippa
    See also CA 5-8R; CANR 4

Christine de Pizan 1365(?)-1431(?) .... **LC 9**

Chubb, Elmer
    See Masters, Edgar Lee

Chulkov, Mikhail Dmitrievich
    1743-1792 .... **LC 2**
    See also DLB 150

Churchill, Caryl 1938- ... **CLC 31, 55; DC 5**
    See also CA 102; CANR 22, 46; DLB 13;
    MTCW

Churchill, Charles 1731-1764 .... **LC 3**
    See also DLB 109

Chute, Carolyn 1947- .... **CLC 39**
    See also CA 123

Ciardi, John (Anthony)
    1916-1986 .... **CLC 10, 40, 44;**
        DAM POET
    See also CA 5-8R; 118; CAAS 2; CANR 5,
    33; CLR 19; DLB 5; DLBY 86;
    INT CANR-5; MAICYA; MTCW;
    SATA 1, 65; SATA-Obit 46

Cicero, Marcus Tullius
    106B.C.-43B.C. .... **CMLC 3**

Cimino, Michael 1943- .... **CLC 16**
    See also CA 105

Cioran, E(mil) M. 1911-1995 .... **CLC 64**
    See also CA 25-28R; 149

Cisneros, Sandra
    1954- ..... **CLC 69; DAM MULT; HLC**
    See also AAYA 9; CA 131; DLB 122, 152;
    HW

Cixous, Helene 1937- .... **CLC 92**
    See also CA 126; CANR 55; DLB 83;
    MTCW

Clair, Rene .... **CLC 20**
    See also Chomette, Rene Lucien

Clampitt, Amy 1920-1994 .... **CLC 32**
    See also CA 110; 146; CANR 29; DLB 105

Clancy, Thomas L., Jr. 1947-
    See Clancy, Tom
    See also CA 125; 131; INT 131; MTCW

Clancy, Tom ..... **CLC 45; DAM NOV, POP**
    See also Clancy, Thomas L., Jr.
    See also AAYA 9; BEST 89:1, 90:1

Clare, John
    1793-1864 .... **NCLC 9; DAB;**
        DAM POET
    See also DLB 55, 96

Clarin
    See Alas (y Urena), Leopoldo (Enrique
    Garcia)

Clark, Al C.
    See Goines, Donald

Clark, (Robert) Brian 1932- .... **CLC 29**
    See also CA 41-44R

Clark, Curt
    See Westlake, Donald E(dwin)

Clark, Eleanor 1913-1996 .... **CLC 5, 19**
    See also CA 9-12R; 151; CANR 41; DLB 6

Clark, J. P.
    See Clark, John Pepper
    See also DLB 117

Clark, John Pepper
    1935- .... **CLC 38; BLC; DAM DRAM,**
        MULT; DC 5
    See also Clark, J. P.
    See also BW 1; CA 65-68; CANR 16

Clark, M. R.
    See Clark, Mavis Thorpe

Clark, Mavis Thorpe 1909- .... **CLC 12**
    See also CA 57-60; CANR 8, 37; CLR 30;
    MAICYA; SAAS 5; SATA 8, 74

Clark, Walter Van Tilburg
    1909-1971 .... **CLC 28**
    See also CA 9-12R; 33-36R; DLB 9;
    SATA 8

Clarke, Arthur C(harles)
    1917- .... **CLC 1, 4, 13, 18, 35;**
        DAM POP; SSC 3
    See also AAYA 4; CA 1-4R; CANR 2, 28,
    55; JRDA; MAICYA; MTCW; SATA 13,
    70

Clarke, Austin
    1896-1974 ...... **CLC 6, 9; DAM POET**
    See also CA 29-32; 49-52; CAP 2; DLB 10,
    20

Clarke, Austin C(hesterfield)
    1934- .... **CLC 8, 53; BLC; DAC;**
        DAM MULT
    See also BW 1; CA 25-28R; CAAS 16;
    CANR 14, 32; DLB 53, 125

Clarke, Gillian 1937- .... **CLC 61**
    See also CA 106; DLB 40

Clarke, Marcus (Andrew Hislop)
    1846-1881 .... **NCLC 19**

Clarke, Shirley 1925- .... **CLC 16**

Clash, The
    See Headon, (Nicky) Topper; Jones, Mick;
    Simonon, Paul; Strummer, Joe

Claudel, Paul (Louis Charles Marie)
    1868-1955 .... **TCLC 2, 10**
    See also CA 104

Clavell, James (duMaresq)
    1925-1994 .... **CLC 6, 25, 87;**
        DAM NOV, POP
    See also CA 25-28R; 146; CANR 26, 48;
    MTCW

Cleaver, (Leroy) Eldridge
    1935- ..... **CLC 30; BLC; DAM MULT**
    See also BW 1; CA 21-24R; CANR 16

Cleese, John (Marwood) 1939- ..... **CLC 21**
    See also Monty Python
    See also CA 112; 116; CANR 35; MTCW

Cleishbotham, Jebediah
    See Scott, Walter

Cleland, John 1710-1789 .... **LC 2**
    See also DLB 39

Clemens, Samuel Langhorne 1835-1910
    See Twain, Mark
    See also CA 104; 135; CDALB 1865-1917;
    DA; DAB; DAC; DAM MST, NOV;
    DLB 11, 12, 23, 64, 74; JRDA;
    MAICYA; YABC 2

Cleophil
    See Congreve, William

Clerihew, E.
    See Bentley, E(dmund) C(lerihew)

Clerk, N. W.
    See Lewis, C(live) S(taples)

Cliff, Jimmy .... **CLC 21**
    See also Chambers, James

Clifton, (Thelma) Lucille
    1936- .... **CLC 19, 66; BLC;**
        DAM MULT, POET
    See also BW 2; CA 49-52; CANR 2, 24, 42;
    CLR 5; DLB 5, 41; MAICYA; MTCW;
    SATA 20, 69

Clinton, Dirk
    See Silverberg, Robert

Clough, Arthur Hugh 1819-1861 .. **NCLC 27**
    See also DLB 32

Clutha, Janet Paterson Frame 1924-
    See Frame, Janet
    See also CA 1-4R; CANR 2, 36; MTCW

Clyne, Terence
    See Blatty, William Peter

Cobalt, Martin
    See Mayne, William (James Carter)

Cobbett, William 1763-1835 ..... **NCLC 49**
    See also DLB 43, 107, 158

Coburn, D(onald) L(ee) 1938- ...... **CLC 10**
    See also CA 89-92

Cocteau, Jean (Maurice Eugene Clement)
    1889-1963 .... **CLC 1, 8, 15, 16, 43; DA;**
        DAB; DAC; DAM DRAM, MST, NOV;
        WLC
    See also CA 25-28; CANR 40; CAP 2;
    DLB 65; MTCW

Codrescu, Andrei
1946- . . . . **CLC 46; DAM POET**
See also CA 33-36R; CAAS 19; CANR 13,
34, 53

Coe, Max
See Bourne, Randolph S(illiman)

Coe, Tucker
See Westlake, Donald E(dwin)

Coetzee, J(ohn) M(ichael)
1940- . . . . . . **CLC 23, 33, 66; DAM NOV**
See also CA 77-80; CANR 41, 54; MTCW

Coffey, Brian
See Koontz, Dean R(ay)

Cohan, George M. 1878-1942 . . . . . **TCLC 60**

Cohen, Arthur A(llen)
1928-1986 . . . . **CLC 7, 31**
See also CA 1-4R; 120; CANR 1, 17, 42;
DLB 28

Cohen, Leonard (Norman)
1934- . . . . **CLC 3, 38; DAC; DAM MST**
See also CA 21-24R; CANR 14; DLB 53;
MTCW

Cohen, Matt 1942- . . . . **CLC 19; DAC**
See also CA 61-64; CAAS 18; CANR 40;
DLB 53

Cohen-Solal, Annie 19(?)- . . . . **CLC 50**

Colegate, Isabel 1931- . . . . **CLC 36**
See also CA 17-20R; CANR 8, 22; DLB 14;
INT CANR-22; MTCW

Coleman, Emmett
See Reed, Ishmael

Coleridge, Samuel Taylor
1772-1834 . . . . . **NCLC 9, 54; DA; DAB;
DAC; DAM MST, POET; PC 11; WLC**
See also CDBLB 1789-1832; DLB 93, 107

Coleridge, Sara 1802-1852 . . . . **NCLC 31**

Coles, Don 1928- . . . . **CLC 46**
See also CA 115; CANR 38

Colette, (Sidonie-Gabrielle)
1873-1954 . . . . **TCLC 1, 5, 16;
DAM NOV; SSC 10**
See also CA 104; 131; DLB 65; MTCW

Collett, (Jacobine) Camilla (Wergeland)
1813-1895 . . . . **NCLC 22**

Collier, Christopher 1930- . . . . **CLC 30**
See also AAYA 13; CA 33-36R; CANR 13,
33; JRDA; MAICYA; SATA 16, 70

Collier, James L(incoln)
1928- . . . . **CLC 30; DAM POP**
See also AAYA 13; CA 9-12R; CANR 4,
33; CLR 3; JRDA; MAICYA; SAAS 21;
SATA 8, 70

Collier, Jeremy 1650-1726 . . . . **LC 6**

Collier, John 1901-1980 . . . . **SSC 19**
See also CA 65-68; 97-100; CANR 10;
DLB 77

Collingwood, R(obin) G(eorge)
1889(?)-1943 . . . . **TCLC 67**
See also CA 117

Collins, Hunt
See Hunter, Evan

Collins, Linda 1931- . . . . **CLC 44**
See also CA 125

Collins, (William) Wilkie
1824-1889 . . . . **NCLC 1, 18**
See also CDBLB 1832-1890; DLB 18, 70,
159

Collins, William
1721-1759 . . . . **LC 4; DAM POET**
See also DLB 109

Collodi, Carlo 1826-1890 . . . . **NCLC 54**
See also Lorenzini, Carlo
See also CLR 5

Colman, George
See Glassco, John

Colt, Winchester Remington
See Hubbard, L(afayette) Ron(ald)

Colter, Cyrus 1910- . . . . **CLC 58**
See also BW 1; CA 65-68; CANR 10;
DLB 33

Colton, James
See Hansen, Joseph

Colum, Padraic 1881-1972 . . . . **CLC 28**
See also CA 73-76; 33-36R; CANR 35;
CLR 36; MAICYA; MTCW; SATA 15

Colvin, James
See Moorcock, Michael (John)

Colwin, Laurie (E.)
1944-1992 . . . . **CLC 5, 13, 23, 84**
See also CA 89-92; 139; CANR 20, 46;
DLBY 80; MTCW

Comfort, Alex(ander)
1920- . . . . **CLC 7; DAM POP**
See also CA 1-4R; CANR 1, 45

Comfort, Montgomery
See Campbell, (John) Ramsey

Compton-Burnett, I(vy)
1884(?)-1969 . . . . . . **CLC 1, 3, 10, 15, 34;
DAM NOV**
See also CA 1-4R; 25-28R; CANR 4;
DLB 36; MTCW

Comstock, Anthony 1844-1915 . . . . **TCLC 13**
See also CA 110

Comte, Auguste 1798-1857 . . . . **NCLC 54**

Conan Doyle, Arthur
See Doyle, Arthur Conan

Conde, Maryse
1937- . . . . **CLC 52, 92; DAM MULT**
See also Boucolon, Maryse
See also BW 2

Condillac, Etienne Bonnot de
1714-1780 . . . . **LC 26**

Condon, Richard (Thomas)
1915-1996 . . . . **CLC 4, 6, 8, 10, 45;
DAM NOV**
See also BEST 90:3; CA 1-4R; 151;
CAAS 1; CANR 2, 23; INT CANR-23;
MTCW

Confucius
551B.C.-479B.C. . . . . **CMLC 19; DA;
DAB; DAC; DAM MST**

Congreve, William
1670-1729 . . . . **LC 5, 21; DA; DAB;
DAC; DAM DRAM, MST, POET;
DC 2; WLC**
See also CDBLB 1660-1789; DLB 39, 84

Connell, Evan S(helby), Jr.
1924- . . . . **CLC 4, 6, 45; DAM NOV**
See also AAYA 7; CA 1-4R; CAAS 2;
CANR 2, 39; DLB 2; DLBY 81; MTCW

Connelly, Marc(us Cook)
1890-1980 . . . . **CLC 7**
See also CA 85-88; 102; CANR 30; DLB 7;
DLBY 80; SATA-Obit 25

Connor, Ralph . . . . **TCLC 31**
See also Gordon, Charles William
See also DLB 92

Conrad, Joseph
1857-1924 . . . . **TCLC 1, 6, 13, 25, 43, 57;
DA; DAB; DAC; DAM MST, NOV;
SSC 9; WLC**
See also CA 104; 131; CDBLB 1890-1914;
DLB 10, 34, 98, 156; MTCW; SATA 27

Conrad, Robert Arnold
See Hart, Moss

Conroy, Pat
1945- . . . **CLC 30, 74; DAM NOV, POP**
See also AAYA 8; AITN 1; CA 85-88;
CANR 24, 53; DLB 6; MTCW

Constant (de Rebecque), (Henri) Benjamin
1767-1830 . . . . **NCLC 6**
See also DLB 119

Conybeare, Charles Augustus
See Eliot, T(homas) S(tearns)

Cook, Michael 1933- . . . . **CLC 58**
See also CA 93-96; DLB 53

Cook, Robin 1940- . . . . **CLC 14; DAM POP**
See also BEST 90:2; CA 108; 111;
CANR 41; INT 111

Cook, Roy
See Silverberg, Robert

Cooke, Elizabeth 1948- . . . . **CLC 55**
See also CA 129

Cooke, John Esten 1830-1886 . . . . . **NCLC 5**
See also DLB 3

Cooke, John Estes
See Baum, L(yman) Frank

Cooke, M. E.
See Creasey, John

Cooke, Margaret
See Creasey, John

Cook-Lynn, Elizabeth
1930- . . . . **CLC 93; DAM MULT**
See also CA 133; NNAL

Cooney, Ray . . . . **CLC 62**

Cooper, Douglas 1960- . . . . **CLC 86**

Cooper, Henry St. John
See Creasey, John

Cooper, J. California
. . . . **CLC 56; DAM MULT**
See also AAYA 12; BW 1; CA 125;
CANR 55

Cooper, James Fenimore
1789-1851 . . . . **NCLC 1, 27, 54**
See also CDALB 1640-1865; DLB 3;
SATA 19

Coover, Robert (Lowell)
1932- . . . . **CLC 3, 7, 15, 32, 46, 87;
DAM NOV; SSC 15**
See also CA 45-48; CANR 3, 37; DLB 2;
DLBY 81; MTCW

Copeland, Stewart (Armstrong)
1952- . . . . **CLC 26**

Coppard, A(lfred) E(dgar)
1878-1957 . . . . **TCLC 5; SSC 21**
See also CA 114; DLB 162; YABC 1

Coppee, Francois 1842-1908 . . . . . **TCLC 25**

Coppola, Francis Ford 1939- . . . . **CLC 16**
See also CA 77-80; CANR 40; DLB 44

Corbiere, Tristan 1845-1875 . . . . . **NCLC 43**

Corcoran, Barbara 1911- . . . . **CLC 17**
See also AAYA 14; CA 21-24R; CAAS 2;
CANR 11, 28, 48; DLB 52; JRDA;
SAAS 20; SATA 3, 77

Cordelier, Maurice
See Giraudoux, (Hippolyte) Jean

Corelli, Marie 1855-1924 . . . . **TCLC 51**
See also Mackay, Mary
See also DLB 34, 156

Corman, Cid . . . . **CLC 9**
See also Corman, Sidney
See also CAAS 2; DLB 5

Corman, Sidney 1924-
See Corman, Cid
See also CA 85-88; CANR 44; DAM POET

Cormier, Robert (Edmund)
1925- . . . . **CLC 12, 30; DA; DAB; DAC;
DAM MST, NOV**
See also AAYA 3, 19; CA 1-4R; CANR 5,
23; CDALB 1968-1988; CLR 12; DLB 52;
INT CANR-23; JRDA; MAICYA;
MTCW; SATA 10, 45, 83

Corn, Alfred (DeWitt III) 1943- . . . . **CLC 33**
See also CA 104; CAAS 25; CANR 44;
DLB 120; DLBY 80

Corneille, Pierre
1606-1684 . . . . **LC 28; DAB; DAM MST**

Cornwell, David (John Moore)
1931- . . . . **CLC 9, 15; DAM POP**
See also le Carre, John
See also CA 5-8R; CANR 13, 33; MTCW

Corso, (Nunzio) Gregory 1930- . . . **CLC 1, 11**
See also CA 5-8R; CANR 41; DLB 5, 16;
MTCW

Cortazar, Julio
1914-1984 . . . . . . **CLC 2, 3, 5, 10, 13, 15,
33, 34, 92; DAM MULT, NOV; HLC;
SSC 7**
See also CA 21-24R; CANR 12, 32;
DLB 113; HW; MTCW

CORTES, HERNAN 1484-1547 . . . . . **LC 31**

Corwin, Cecil
See Kornbluth, C(yril) M.

Cosic, Dobrica 1921- . . . . **CLC 14**
See also CA 122; 138

Costain, Thomas B(ertram)
1885-1965 . . . . **CLC 30**
See also CA 5-8R; 25-28R; DLB 9

Costantini, Humberto
1924(?)-1987 . . . . **CLC 49**
See also CA 131; 122; HW

Costello, Elvis 1955- . . . . **CLC 21**

Cotter, Joseph Seamon Sr.
1861-1949 . . . . **TCLC 28; BLC;
DAM MULT**
See also BW 1; CA 124; DLB 50

Couch, Arthur Thomas Quiller
See Quiller-Couch, Arthur Thomas

Coulton, James
See Hansen, Joseph

Couperus, Louis (Marie Anne)
1863-1923 . . . . **TCLC 15**
See also CA 115

Coupland, Douglas
1961- . . . . **CLC 85; DAC; DAM POP**
See also CA 142

Court, Wesli
See Turco, Lewis (Putnam)

Courtenay, Bryce 1933- . . . . **CLC 59**
See also CA 138

Courtney, Robert
See Ellison, Harlan (Jay)

Cousteau, Jacques-Yves 1910- . . . . . . **CLC 30**
See also CA 65-68; CANR 15; MTCW;
SATA 38

Coward, Noel (Peirce)
1899-1973 . . . . **CLC 1, 9, 29, 51;
DAM DRAM**
See also AITN 1; CA 17-18; 41-44R;
CANR 35; CAP 2; CDBLB 1914-1945;
DLB 10; MTCW

Cowley, Malcolm 1898-1989 . . . . **CLC 39**
See also CA 5-8R; 128; CANR 3, 55;
DLB 4, 48; DLBY 81, 89; MTCW

Cowper, William
1731-1800 . . . . . . **NCLC 8; DAM POET**
See also DLB 104, 109

Cox, William Trevor
1928- . . . . **CLC 9, 14, 71; DAM NOV**
See also Trevor, William
See also CA 9-12R; CANR 4, 37, 55;
DLB 14; INT CANR-37; MTCW

Coyne, P. J.
See Masters, Hilary

Cozzens, James Gould
1903-1978 . . . . **CLC 1, 4, 11, 92**
See also CA 9-12R; 81-84; CANR 19;
CDALB 1941-1968; DLB 9; DLBD 2;
DLBY 84; MTCW

Crabbe, George 1754-1832 . . . . . . **NCLC 26**
See also DLB 93

Craddock, Charles Egbert
See Murfree, Mary Noailles

Craig, A. A.
See Anderson, Poul (William)

Craik, Dinah Maria (Mulock)
1826-1887 . . . . **NCLC 38**
See also DLB 35, 163; MAICYA; SATA 34

Cram, Ralph Adams 1863-1942 . . . . **TCLC 45**

Crane, (Harold) Hart
1899-1932 . . . . **TCLC 2, 5; DA; DAB;
DAC; DAM MST, POET; PC 3; WLC**
See also CA 104; 127; CDALB 1917-1929;
DLB 4, 48; MTCW

Crane, R(onald) S(almon)
1886-1967 . . . . **CLC 27**
See also CA 85-88; DLB 63

Crane, Stephen (Townley)
1871-1900 . . . . . . **TCLC 11, 17, 32; DA;
DAB; DAC; DAM MST, NOV, POET;
SSC 7; WLC**
See also CA 109; 140; CDALB 1865-1917;
DLB 12, 54, 78; YABC 2

Crase, Douglas 1944- . . . . **CLC 58**
See also CA 106

Crashaw, Richard 1612(?)-1649 . . . . . . **LC 24**
See also DLB 126

Craven, Margaret
1901-1980 . . . . **CLC 17; DAC**
See also CA 103

Crawford, F(rancis) Marion
1854-1909 . . . . **TCLC 10**
See also CA 107; DLB 71

Crawford, Isabella Valancy
1850-1887 . . . . **NCLC 12**
See also DLB 92

Crayon, Geoffrey
See Irving, Washington

Creasey, John 1908-1973 . . . . **CLC 11**
See also CA 5-8R; 41-44R; CANR 8;
DLB 77; MTCW

Crebillon, Claude Prosper Jolyot de (fils)
1707-1777 . . . . **LC 28**

Credo
See Creasey, John

Creeley, Robert (White)
1926- . . . . . **CLC 1, 2, 4, 8, 11, 15, 36, 78;
DAM POET**
See also CA 1-4R; CAAS 10; CANR 23, 43;
DLB 5, 16, 169; MTCW

Crews, Harry (Eugene)
1935- . . . . **CLC 6, 23, 49**
See also AITN 1; CA 25-28R; CANR 20;
DLB 6, 143; MTCW

Crichton, (John) Michael
1942- . . . . **CLC 2, 6, 54, 90; DAM NOV,
POP**
See also AAYA 10; AITN 2; CA 25-28R;
CANR 13, 40, 54; DLBY 81;
INT CANR-13; JRDA; MTCW; SATA 9,
88

Crispin, Edmund . . . . **CLC 22**
See also Montgomery, (Robert) Bruce
See also DLB 87

Cristofer, Michael
1945(?)- . . . . **CLC 28; DAM DRAM**
See also CA 110; 152; DLB 7

Croce, Benedetto 1866-1952 . . . . . . **TCLC 37**
See also CA 120

Crockett, David 1786-1836 . . . . **NCLC 8**
See also DLB 3, 11

Crockett, Davy
See Crockett, David

Crofts, Freeman Wills
1879-1957 . . . . **TCLC 55**
See also CA 115; DLB 77

Croker, John Wilson 1780-1857 . . **NCLC 10**
See also DLB 110

Crommelynck, Fernand 1885-1970 . . **CLC 75**
See also CA 89-92

Cronin, A(rchibald) J(oseph)
    1896-1981 .... CLC 32
    See also CA 1-4R; 102; CANR 5; SATA 47;
    SATA-Obit 25

Cross, Amanda
    See Heilbrun, Carolyn G(old)

Crothers, Rachel   1878(?)-1958..... TCLC 19
    See also CA 113; DLB 7

Croves, Hal
    See Traven, B.

Crow Dog, Mary .... CLC 93
    See also Brave Bird, Mary

Crowfield, Christopher
    See Stowe, Harriet (Elizabeth) Beecher

Crowley, Aleister................. TCLC 7
    See also Crowley, Edward Alexander

Crowley, Edward Alexander   1875-1947
    See Crowley, Aleister
    See also CA 104

Crowley, John   1942-............. CLC 57
    See also CA 61-64; CANR 43; DLBY 82;
    SATA 65

Crud
    See Crumb, R(obert)

Crumarums
    See Crumb, R(obert)

Crumb, R(obert)   1943-............ CLC 17
    See also CA 106

Crumbum
    See Crumb, R(obert)

Crumski
    See Crumb, R(obert)

Crum the Bum
    See Crumb, R(obert)

Crunk
    See Crumb, R(obert)

Crustt
    See Crumb, R(obert)

Cryer, Gretchen (Kiger)   1935-...... CLC 21
    See also CA 114; 123

Csath, Geza   1887-1919........... TCLC 13
    See also CA 111

Cudlip, David   1933-............. CLC 34

Cullen, Countee
    1903-1946 ...... TCLC 4, 37; BLC; DA;
                DAC; DAM MST, MULT, POET
    See also BW 1; CA 108; 124;
    CDALB 1917-1929; DLB 4, 48, 51;
    MTCW; SATA 18

Cum, R.
    See Crumb, R(obert)

Cummings, Bruce F(rederick)   1889-1919
    See Barbellion, W. N. P.
    See also CA 123

Cummings, E(dward) E(stlin)
    1894-1962 ...... CLC 1, 3, 8, 12, 15, 68;
                DA; DAB; DAC; DAM MST, POET;
                             PC 5; WLC 2
    See also CA 73-76; CANR 31;
    CDALB 1929-1941; DLB 4, 48; MTCW

Cunha, Euclides (Rodrigues Pimenta) da
    1866-1909 .... TCLC 24
    See also CA 123

Cunningham, E. V.
    See Fast, Howard (Melvin)

Cunningham, J(ames) V(incent)
    1911-1985 .... CLC 3, 31
    See also CA 1-4R; 115; CANR 1; DLB 5

Cunningham, Julia (Woolfolk)
    1916- .... CLC 12
    See also CA 9-12R; CANR 4, 19, 36;
    JRDA; MAICYA; SAAS 2; SATA 1, 26

Cunningham, Michael   1952- .... CLC 34
    See also CA 136

Cunninghame Graham, R(obert) B(ontine)
    1852-1936 .... TCLC 19
    See also Graham, R(obert) B(ontine)
    Cunninghame
    See also CA 119; DLB 98

Currie, Ellen   19(?)-.............. CLC 44

Curtin, Philip
    See Lowndes, Marie Adelaide (Belloc)

Curtis, Price
    See Ellison, Harlan (Jay)

Cutrate, Joe
    See Spiegelman, Art

Czaczkes, Shmuel Yosef
    See Agnon, S(hmuel) Y(osef Halevi)

Dabrowska, Maria (Szumska)
    1889-1965 .... CLC 15
    See also CA 106

Dabydeen, David   1955- .... CLC 34
    See also BW 1; CA 125

Dacey, Philip   1939- .... CLC 51
    See also CA 37-40R; CAAS 17; CANR 14,
    32; DLB 105

Dagerman, Stig (Halvard)
    1923-1954 .... TCLC 17
    See also CA 117

Dahl, Roald
    1916-1990 ...... CLC 1, 6, 18, 79; DAB;
                DAC; DAM MST, NOV, POP
    See also AAYA 15; CA 1-4R; 133;
    CANR 6, 32, 37; CLR 1, 7, 41; DLB 139;
    JRDA; MAICYA; MTCW; SATA 1, 26,
    73; SATA-Obit 65

Dahlberg, Edward   1900-1977... CLC 1, 7, 14
    See also CA 9-12R; 69-72; CANR 31;
    DLB 48; MTCW

Dale, Colin..................... TCLC 18
    See also Lawrence, T(homas) E(dward)

Dale, George E.
    See Asimov, Isaac

Daly, Elizabeth   1878-1967........ CLC 52
    See also CA 23-24; 25-28R; CAP 2

Daly, Maureen   1921-............. CLC 17
    See also AAYA 5; CANR 37; JRDA;
    MAICYA; SAAS 1; SATA 2

Damas, Leon-Gontran   1912-1978 ... CLC 84
    See also BW 1; CA 125; 73-76

Dana, Richard Henry Sr.
    1787-1879 .... NCLC 53

Daniel, Samuel   1562(?)-1619........ LC 24
    See also DLB 62

Daniels, Brett
    See Adler, Renata

Dannay, Frederic
    1905-1982 .... CLC 11; DAM POP
    See also Queen, Ellery
    See also CA 1-4R; 107; CANR 1, 39;
    DLB 137; MTCW

D'Annunzio, Gabriele
    1863-1938 .... TCLC 6, 40
    See also CA 104

Danois, N. le
    See Gourmont, Remy (-Marie-Charles) de

d'Antibes, Germain
    See Simenon, Georges (Jacques Christian)

Danticat, Edwidge   1969- .... CLC 94
    See also CA 152

Danvers, Dennis   1947-............ CLC 70

Danziger, Paula   1944- .... CLC 21
    See also AAYA 4; CA 112; 115; CANR 37;
    CLR 20; JRDA; MAICYA; SATA 36,
    63; SATA-Brief 30

Da Ponte, Lorenzo   1749-1838.... NCLC 50

Dario, Ruben
    1867-1916 ..... TCLC 4; DAM MULT;
                            HLC; PC 15
    See also CA 131; HW; MTCW

Darley, George   1795-1846........ NCLC 2
    See also DLB 96

Darwin, Charles   1809-1882 ...... NCLC 57
    See also DLB 57, 166

Daryush, Elizabeth   1887-1977.... CLC 6, 19
    See also CA 49-52; CANR 3; DLB 20

Dashwood, Edmee Elizabeth Monica de la
        Pasture   1890-1943
    See Delafield, E. M.
    See also CA 119

Daudet, (Louis Marie) Alphonse
    1840-1897 .... NCLC 1
    See also DLB 123

Daumal, Rene   1908-1944........ TCLC 14
    See also CA 114

Davenport, Guy (Mattison, Jr.)
    1927-.......... CLC 6, 14, 38; SSC 16
    See also CA 33-36R; CANR 23; DLB 130

Davidson, Avram   1923-
    See Queen, Ellery
    See also CA 101; CANR 26; DLB 8

Davidson, Donald (Grady)
    1893-1968 .... CLC 2, 13, 19
    See also CA 5-8R; 25-28R; CANR 4;
    DLB 45

Davidson, Hugh
    See Hamilton, Edmond

Davidson, John   1857-1909........ TCLC 24
    See also CA 118; DLB 19

Davidson, Sara   1943-............. CLC 9
    See also CA 81-84; CANR 44

Davie, Donald (Alfred)
    1922-1995 .... CLC 5, 8, 10, 31
    See also CA 1-4R; 149; CAAS 3; CANR 1,
    44; DLB 27; MTCW

Davies, Ray(mond Douglas)   1944- .. CLC 21
    See also CA 116; 146

Davies, Rhys   1903-1978........... CLC 23
    See also CA 9-12R; 81-84; CANR 4;
    DLB 139

Davies, (William) Robertson
1913-1995 ..... **CLC 2, 7, 13, 25, 42, 75,**
91; DA; DAB; DAC; DAM MST, NOV,
POP; WLC
See also BEST 89:2; CA 33-36R; 150;
CANR 17, 42; DLB 68; INT CANR-17;
MTCW

Davies, W(illiam) H(enry)
1871-1940 .... **TCLC 5**
See also CA 104; DLB 19, 174

Davies, Walter C.
See Kornbluth, C(yril) M.

Davis, Angela (Yvonne)
1944- .... **CLC 77; DAM MULT**
See also BW 2; CA 57-60; CANR 10

Davis, B. Lynch
See Bioy Casares, Adolfo; Borges, Jorge
Luis

Davis, Gordon
See Hunt, E(verette) Howard, (Jr.)

Davis, Harold Lenoir 1896-1960.... **CLC 49**
See also CA 89-92; DLB 9

Davis, Rebecca (Blaine) Harding
1831-1910 .... **TCLC 6**
See also CA 104; DLB 74

Davis, Richard Harding
1864-1916 .... **TCLC 24**
See also CA 114; DLB 12, 23, 78, 79;
DLBD 13

Davison, Frank Dalby 1893-1970 ... **CLC 15**
See also CA 116

Davison, Lawrence H.
See Lawrence, D(avid) H(erbert Richards)

Davison, Peter (Hubert) 1928- ..... **CLC 28**
See also CA 9-12R; CAAS 4; CANR 3, 43;
DLB 5

Davys, Mary 1674-1732............. **LC 1**
See also DLB 39

Dawson, Fielding 1930- .... **CLC 6**
See also CA 85-88; DLB 130

Dawson, Peter
See Faust, Frederick (Schiller)

Day, Clarence (Shepard, Jr.)
1874-1935 .... **TCLC 25**
See also CA 108; DLB 11

Day, Thomas 1748-1789............. **LC 1**
See also DLB 39; YABC 1

Day Lewis, C(ecil)
1904-1972 .... **CLC 1, 6, 10;**
DAM POET; PC 11
See also Blake, Nicholas
See also CA 13-16; 33-36R; CANR 34;
CAP 1; DLB 15, 20; MTCW

Dazai, Osamu .... **TCLC 11**
See also Tsushima, Shuji

de Andrade, Carlos Drummond
See Drummond de Andrade, Carlos

Deane, Norman
See Creasey, John

de Beauvoir, Simone (Lucie Ernestine Marie
Bertrand)
See Beauvoir, Simone (Lucie Ernestine
Marie Bertrand) de

de Brissac, Malcolm
See Dickinson, Peter (Malcolm)

de Chardin, Pierre Teilhard
See Teilhard de Chardin, (Marie Joseph)
Pierre

Dee, John 1527-1608 .... **LC 20**

Deer, Sandra 1940-............... **CLC 45**

De Ferrari, Gabriella 1941-........ **CLC 65**
See also CA 146

Defoe, Daniel
1660(?)-1731 .... **LC 1; DA; DAB; DAC;**
DAM MST, NOV; WLC
See also CDBLB 1660-1789; DLB 39, 95,
101; JRDA; MAICYA; SATA 22

de Gourmont, Remy(-Marie-Charles)
See Gourmont, Remy (-Marie-Charles) de

de Hartog, Jan 1914-............. **CLC 19**
See also CA 1-4R; CANR 1

de Hostos, E. M.
See Hostos (y Bonilla), Eugenio Maria de

de Hostos, Eugenio M.
See Hostos (y Bonilla), Eugenio Maria de

Deighton, Len .... **CLC 4, 7, 22, 46**
See also Deighton, Leonard Cyril
See also AAYA 6; BEST 89:2;
CDBLB 1960 to Present; DLB 87

Deighton, Leonard Cyril 1929-
See Deighton, Len
See also CA 9-12R; CANR 19, 33;
DAM NOV, POP; MTCW

Dekker, Thomas
1572(?)-1632 ..... **LC 22; DAM DRAM**
See also CDBLB Before 1660; DLB 62, 172

Delafield, E. M. 1890-1943 ...... **TCLC 61**
See also Dashwood, Edmee Elizabeth
Monica de la Pasture
See also DLB 34

de la Mare, Walter (John)
1873-1956 .... **TCLC 4, 53; DAB; DAC;**
DAM MST, POET; SSC 14; WLC
See also CDBLB 1914-1945; CLR 23;
DLB 162; SATA 16

Delaney, Franey
See O'Hara, John (Henry)

Delaney, Shelagh
1939- .... **CLC 29; DAM DRAM**
See also CA 17-20R; CANR 30;
CDBLB 1960 to Present; DLB 13;
MTCW

Delany, Mary (Granville Pendarves)
1700-1788 .... **LC 12**

Delany, Samuel R(ay, Jr.)
1942- .... **CLC 8, 14, 38; BLC;**
DAM MULT
See also BW 2; CA 81-84; CANR 27, 43;
DLB 8, 33; MTCW

De La Ramee, (Marie) Louise 1839-1908
See Ouida
See also SATA 20

de la Roche, Mazo 1879-1961 ...... **CLC 14**
See also CA 85-88; CANR 30; DLB 68;
SATA 64

Delbanco, Nicholas (Franklin)
1942- .... **CLC 6, 13**
See also CA 17-20R; CAAS 2; CANR 29,
55; DLB 6

del Castillo, Michel 1933- .... **CLC 38**
See also CA 109

Deledda, Grazia (Cosima)
1875(?)-1936 .... **TCLC 23**
See also CA 123

Delibes, Miguel .... **CLC 8, 18**
See also Delibes Setien, Miguel

Delibes Setien, Miguel 1920-
See Delibes, Miguel
See also CA 45-48; CANR 1, 32; HW;
MTCW

DeLillo, Don
1936- ..... **CLC 8, 10, 13, 27, 39, 54, 76;**
DAM NOV, POP
See also BEST 89:1; CA 81-84; CANR 21;
DLB 6, 173; MTCW

de Lisser, H. G.
See De Lisser, Herbert George
See also DLB 117

De Lisser, Herbert George
1878-1944 .... **TCLC 12**
See also de Lisser, H. G.
See also BW 2; CA 109; 152

Deloria, Vine (Victor), Jr.
1933- .... **CLC 21; DAM MULT**
See also CA 53-56; CANR 5, 20, 48;
MTCW; NNAL; SATA 21

Del Vecchio, John M(ichael)
1947- .... **CLC 29**
See also CA 110; DLBD 9

de Man, Paul (Adolph Michel)
1919-1983 .... **CLC 55**
See also CA 128; 111; DLB 67; MTCW

De Marinis, Rick 1934-........... **CLC 54**
See also CA 57-60; CAAS 24; CANR 9, 25,
50

Dembry, R. Emmet
See Murfree, Mary Noailles

Demby, William
1922- ..... **CLC 53; BLC; DAM MULT**
See also BW 1; CA 81-84; DLB 33

Demijohn, Thom
See Disch, Thomas M(ichael)

de Montherlant, Henry (Milon)
See Montherlant, Henry (Milon) de

Demosthenes 384B.C.-322B.C. .... **CMLC 13**

de Natale, Francine
See Malzberg, Barry N(athaniel)

Denby, Edwin (Orr) 1903-1983..... **CLC 48**
See also CA 138; 110

Denis, Julio
See Cortazar, Julio

Denmark, Harrison
See Zelazny, Roger (Joseph)

Dennis, John 1658-1734........... **LC 11**
See also DLB 101

Dennis, Nigel (Forbes) 1912-1989.... **CLC 8**
See also CA 25-28R; 129; DLB 13, 15;
MTCW

De Palma, Brian (Russell) 1940-.... **CLC 20**
See also CA 109

De Quincey, Thomas 1785-1859 ... **NCLC 4**
See also CDBLB 1789-1832; DLB 110; 144

Deren, Eleanora 1908(?)-1961
　　See Deren, Maya
　　See also CA 111

Deren, Maya . . . . **CLC 16**
　　See also Deren, Eleanora

Derleth, August (William)
　　1909-1971 . . . . **CLC 31**
　　See also CA 1-4R; 29-32R; CANR 4;
　　DLB 9; SATA 5

Der Nister 1884-1950 . . . . **TCLC 56**

de Routisie, Albert
　　See Aragon, Louis

Derrida, Jacques 1930- . . . . **CLC 24, 87**
　　See also CA 124; 127

Derry Down Derry
　　See Lear, Edward

Dersonnes, Jacques
　　See Simenon, Georges (Jacques Christian)

Desai, Anita
　　1937- . . . . **CLC 19, 37, 97; DAB;**
　　　　　　　　　　　　　　　　　DAM NOV
　　See also CA 81-84; CANR 33, 53; MTCW;
　　SATA 63

de Saint-Luc, Jean
　　See Glassco, John

de Saint Roman, Arnaud
　　See Aragon, Louis

Descartes, Rene 1596-1650 . . . . . . **LC 20, 35**

De Sica, Vittorio 1901(?)-1974 . . . . . **CLC 20**
　　See also CA 117

Desnos, Robert 1900-1945 . . . . **TCLC 22**
　　See also CA 121; 151

Destouches, Louis-Ferdinand
　　1894-1961 . . . . **CLC 9, 15**
　　See also Celine, Louis-Ferdinand
　　See also CA 85-88; CANR 28; MTCW

Deutsch, Babette 1895-1982 . . . . . . **CLC 18**
　　See also CA 1-4R; 108; CANR 4; DLB 45;
　　SATA 1; SATA-Obit 33

Devenant, William 1606-1649 . . . . **LC 13**

Devkota, Laxmiprasad
　　1909-1959 . . . . **TCLC 23**
　　See also CA 123

De Voto, Bernard (Augustine)
　　1897-1955 . . . . **TCLC 29**
　　See also CA 113; DLB 9

De Vries, Peter
　　1910-1993 . . . . **CLC 1, 2, 3, 7, 10, 28, 46;**
　　　　　　　　　　　　　　　　　　DAM NOV
　　See also CA 17-20R; 142; CANR 41;
　　DLB 6; DLBY 82; MTCW

Dexter, John
　　See Bradley, Marion Zimmer

Dexter, Martin
　　See Faust, Frederick (Schiller)

Dexter, Pete
　　1943- . . . . **CLC 34, 55; DAM POP**
　　See also BEST 89:2; CA 127; 131; INT 131;
　　MTCW

Diamano, Silmang
　　See Senghor, Leopold Sedar

Diamond, Neil 1941- . . . . **CLC 30**
　　See also CA 108

Diaz del Castillo, Bernal 1496-1584 . . **LC 31**

di Bassetto, Corno
　　See Shaw, George Bernard

Dick, Philip K(indred)
　　1928-1982 . . . . **CLC 10, 30, 72;**
　　　　　　　　　　　　　　　　DAM NOV, POP
　　See also CA 49-52; 106; CANR 2, 16;
　　DLB 8; MTCW

Dickens, Charles (John Huffam)
　　1812-1870 . . . . . . **NCLC 3, 8, 18, 26, 37,**
　　　　50; DA; DAB; DAC; DAM MST, NOV;
　　　　　　　　　　　　　　　　SSC 17; WLC
　　See also CDBLB 1832-1890; DLB 21, 55,
　　70, 159, 166; JRDA; MAICYA; SATA 15

Dickey, James (Lafayette)
　　1923- . . . . **CLC 1, 2, 4, 7, 10, 15, 47;**
　　　　　　　　　　　　DAM NOV, POET, POP
　　See also AITN 1, 2; CA 9-12R; CABS 2;
　　CANR 10, 48; CDALB 1968-1988;
　　DLB 5; DLBD 7; DLBY 82, 93;
　　INT CANR-10; MTCW

Dickey, William 1928-1994 . . . . . **CLC 3, 28**
　　See also CA 9-12R; 145; CANR 24; DLB 5

Dickinson, Charles 1951- . . . . **CLC 49**
　　See also CA 128

Dickinson, Emily (Elizabeth)
　　1830-1886 . . . . **NCLC 21; DA; DAB;**
　　　　　DAC; DAM MST, POET; PC 1; WLC
　　See also CDALB 1865-1917; DLB 1;
　　SATA 29

Dickinson, Peter (Malcolm)
　　1927- . . . . **CLC 12, 35**
　　See also AAYA 9; CA 41-44R; CANR 31;
　　CLR 29; DLB 87, 161; JRDA; MAICYA;
　　SATA 5, 62

Dickson, Carr
　　See Carr, John Dickson

Dickson, Carter
　　See Carr, John Dickson

Diderot, Denis 1713-1784 . . . . **LC 26**

Didion, Joan
　　1934- . . **CLC 1, 3, 8, 14, 32; DAM NOV**
　　See also AITN 1; CA 5-8R; CANR 14, 52;
　　CDALB 1968-1988; DLB 2, 173;
　　DLBY 81, 86; MTCW

Dietrich, Robert
　　See Hunt, E(verette) Howard, (Jr.)

Dillard, Annie
　　1945- . . . . **CLC 9, 60; DAM NOV**
　　See also AAYA 6; CA 49-52; CANR 3, 43;
　　DLBY 80; MTCW; SATA 10

Dillard, R(ichard) H(enry) W(ilde)
　　1937- . . . . **CLC 5**
　　See also CA 21-24R; CAAS 7; CANR 10;
　　DLB 5

Dillon, Eilis 1920-1994 . . . . **CLC 17**
　　See also CA 9-12R; 147; CAAS 3; CANR 4,
　　38; CLR 26; MAICYA; SATA 2, 74;
　　SATA-Obit 83

Dimont, Penelope
　　See Mortimer, Penelope (Ruth)

Dinesen, Isak . . . . **CLC 10, 29, 95; SSC 7**
　　See also Blixen, Karen (Christentze
　　Dinesen)

Ding Ling . . . . **CLC 68**
　　See also Chiang Pin-chin

Disch, Thomas M(ichael) 1940- . . . **CLC 7, 36**
　　See also AAYA 17; CA 21-24R; CAAS 4;
　　CANR 17, 36, 54; CLR 18; DLB 8;
　　MAICYA; MTCW; SAAS 15; SATA 54

Disch, Tom
　　See Disch, Thomas M(ichael)

d'Isly, Georges
　　See Simenon, Georges (Jacques Christian)

Disraeli, Benjamin 1804-1881 . . **NCLC 2, 39**
　　See also DLB 21, 55

Ditcum, Steve
　　See Crumb, R(obert)

Dixon, Paige
　　See Corcoran, Barbara

Dixon, Stephen 1936- . . . . . **CLC 52; SSC 16**
　　See also CA 89-92; CANR 17, 40, 54;
　　DLB 130

Dobell, Sydney Thompson
　　1824-1874 . . . . **NCLC 43**
　　See also DLB 32

Doblin, Alfred . . . . **TCLC 13**
　　See also Doeblin, Alfred

Dobrolyubov, Nikolai Alexandrovich
　　1836-1861 . . . . **NCLC 5**

Dobyns, Stephen 1941- . . . . **CLC 37**
　　See also CA 45-48; CANR 2, 18

Doctorow, E(dgar) L(aurence)
　　1931- . . . . . **CLC 6, 11, 15, 18, 37, 44, 65;**
　　　　　　　　　　　　　　　　DAM NOV, POP
　　See also AITN 2; BEST 89:3; CA 45-48;
　　CANR 2, 33, 51; CDALB 1968-1988;
　　DLB 2, 28, 173; DLBY 80; MTCW

Dodgson, Charles Lutwidge 1832-1898
　　See Carroll, Lewis
　　See also CLR 2; DA; DAB; DAC;
　　DAM MST, NOV, POET; MAICYA;
　　YABC 2

Dodson, Owen (Vincent)
　　1914-1983 . . . . **CLC 79; BLC;**
　　　　　　　　　　　　　　　　　　DAM MULT
　　See also BW 1; CA 65-68; 110; CANR 24;
　　DLB 76

Doeblin, Alfred 1878-1957 . . . . **TCLC 13**
　　See also Doblin, Alfred
　　See also CA 110; 141; DLB 66

Doerr, Harriet 1910- . . . . **CLC 34**
　　See also CA 117; 122; CANR 47; INT 122

Domecq, H(onorio) Bustos
　　See Bioy Casares, Adolfo; Borges, Jorge
　　Luis

Domini, Rey
　　See Lorde, Audre (Geraldine)

Dominique
　　See Proust, (Valentin-Louis-George-Eugene-)
　　Marcel

Don, A
　　See Stephen, Leslie

Donaldson, Stephen R.
　　1947- . . . . **CLC 46; DAM POP**
　　See also CA 89-92; CANR 13, 55;
　　INT CANR-13

Donleavy, J(ames) P(atrick)
　　1926- . . . . **CLC 1, 4, 6, 10, 45**
　　See also AITN 2; CA 9-12R; CANR 24, 49;
　　DLB 6, 173; INT CANR-24; MTCW

Donne, John
1572-1631 .... **LC 10, 24; DA; DAB;
DAC; DAM MST, POET; PC 1**
See also CDBLB Before 1660; DLB 121,
151

Donnell, David 1939(?)- .... **CLC 34**

Donoghue, P. S.
See Hunt, E(verette) Howard, (Jr.)

Donoso (Yanez), Jose
1924- .... **CLC 4, 8, 11, 32;
DAM MULT; HLC**
See also CA 81-84; CANR 32; DLB 113;
HW; MTCW

Donovan, John 1928-1992 .... **CLC 35**
See also CA 97-100; 137; CLR 3;
MAICYA; SATA 72; SATA-Brief 29

Don Roberto
See Cunninghame Graham, R(obert)
B(ontine)

Doolittle, Hilda
1886-1961 ..... **CLC 3, 8, 14, 31, 34, 73;
DA; DAC; DAM MST, POET; PC 5;
WLC**
See also H. D.
See also CA 97-100; CANR 35; DLB 4, 45;
MTCW

Dorfman, Ariel
1942- .... **CLC 48, 77; DAM MULT;
HLC**
See also CA 124; 130; HW; INT 130

Dorn, Edward (Merton) 1929-... **CLC 10, 18**
See also CA 93-96; CANR 42; DLB 5;
INT 93-96

Dorsan, Luc
See Simenon, Georges (Jacques Christian)

Dorsange, Jean
See Simenon, Georges (Jacques Christian)

Dos Passos, John (Roderigo)
1896-1970 ...... **CLC 1, 4, 8, 11, 15, 25,
34, 82; DA; DAB; DAC; DAM MST,
NOV; WLC**
See also CA 1-4R; 29-32R; CANR 3;
CDALB 1929-1941; DLB 4, 9; DLBD 1;
MTCW

Dossage, Jean
See Simenon, Georges (Jacques Christian)

Dostoevsky, Fedor Mikhailovich
1821-1881 ...... **NCLC 2, 7, 21, 33, 43;
DA; DAB; DAC; DAM MST, NOV;
SSC 2; WLC**

Doughty, Charles M(ontagu)
1843-1926 .... **TCLC 27**
See also CA 115; DLB 19, 57, 174

Douglas, Ellen .... **CLC 73**
See also Haxton, Josephine Ayres;
Williamson, Ellen Douglas

Douglas, Gavin 1475(?)-1522 .... **LC 20**

Douglas, Keith 1920-1944 .... **TCLC 40**
See also DLB 27

Douglas, Leonard
See Bradbury, Ray (Douglas)

Douglas, Michael
See Crichton, (John) Michael

Douglass, Frederick
1817(?)-1895 .... **NCLC 7, 55; BLC; DA;
DAC; DAM MST, MULT; WLC**
See also CDALB 1640-1865; DLB 1, 43, 50,
79; SATA 29

Dourado, (Waldomiro Freitas) Autran
1926- .... **CLC 23, 60**
See also CA 25-28R; CANR 34

Dourado, Waldomiro Autran
See Dourado, (Waldomiro Freitas) Autran

Dove, Rita (Frances)
1952- .... **CLC 50, 81; DAM MULT,
POET; PC 6**
See also BW 2; CA 109; CAAS 19;
CANR 27, 42; DLB 120

Dowell, Coleman 1925-1985 .... **CLC 60**
See also CA 25-28R; 117; CANR 10;
DLB 130

Dowson, Ernest (Christopher)
1867-1900 .... **TCLC 4**
See also CA 105; 150; DLB 19, 135

Doyle, A. Conan
See Doyle, Arthur Conan

Doyle, Arthur Conan
1859-1930 .... **TCLC 7; DA; DAB;
DAC; DAM MST, NOV; SSC 12; WLC**
See also AAYA 14; CA 104; 122;
CDBLB 1890-1914; DLB 18, 70, 156;
MTCW; SATA 24

Doyle, Conan
See Doyle, Arthur Conan

Doyle, John
See Graves, Robert (von Ranke)

Doyle, Roddy 1958(?)- .... **CLC 81**
See also AAYA 14; CA 143

Doyle, Sir A. Conan
See Doyle, Arthur Conan

Doyle, Sir Arthur Conan
See Doyle, Arthur Conan

Dr. A
See Asimov, Isaac; Silverstein, Alvin

Drabble, Margaret
1939- .... **CLC 2, 3, 5, 8, 10, 22, 53;
DAB; DAC; DAM MST, NOV, POP**
See also CA 13-16R; CANR 18, 35;
CDBLB 1960 to Present; DLB 14, 155;
MTCW; SATA 48

Drapier, M. B.
See Swift, Jonathan

Drayham, James
See Mencken, H(enry) L(ouis)

Drayton, Michael 1563-1631 .... **LC 8**

Dreadstone, Carl
See Campbell, (John) Ramsey

Dreiser, Theodore (Herman Albert)
1871-1945 .... **TCLC 10, 18, 35; DA;
DAC; DAM MST, NOV; WLC**
See also CA 106; 132; CDALB 1865-1917;
DLB 9, 12, 102, 137; DLBD 1; MTCW

Drexler, Rosalyn 1926- .... **CLC 2, 6**
See also CA 81-84

Dreyer, Carl Theodor 1889-1968 .... **CLC 16**
See also CA 116

Drieu la Rochelle, Pierre(-Eugene)
1893-1945 .... **TCLC 21**
See also CA 117; DLB 72

Drinkwater, John 1882-1937 ...... **TCLC 57**
See also CA 109; 149; DLB 10, 19, 149

Drop Shot
See Cable, George Washington

Droste-Hulshoff, Annette Freiin von
1797-1848 .... **NCLC 3**
See also DLB 133

Drummond, Walter
See Silverberg, Robert

Drummond, William Henry
1854-1907 .... **TCLC 25**
See also DLB 92

Drummond de Andrade, Carlos
1902-1987 .... **CLC 18**
See also Andrade, Carlos Drummond de
See also CA 132; 123

Drury, Allen (Stuart) 1918- .... **CLC 37**
See also CA 57-60; CANR 18, 52;
INT CANR-18

Dryden, John
1631-1700 .... **LC 3, 21; DA; DAB;
DAC; DAM DRAM, MST, POET;
DC 3; WLC**
See also CDBLB 1660-1789; DLB 80, 101,
131

Duberman, Martin 1930- .... **CLC 8**
See also CA 1-4R; CANR 2

Dubie, Norman (Evans) 1945- ...... **CLC 36**
See also CA 69-72; CANR 12; DLB 120

Du Bois, W(illiam) E(dward) B(urghardt)
1868-1963 ...... **CLC 1, 2, 13, 64, 96;
BLC; DA; DAC; DAM MST, MULT,
NOV; WLC**
See also BW 1; CA 85-88; CANR 34;
CDALB 1865-1917; DLB 47, 50, 91;
MTCW; SATA 42

Dubus, Andre
1936- .... **CLC 13, 36, 97; SSC 15**
See also CA 21-24R; CANR 17; DLB 130;
INT CANR-17

Duca Minimo
See D'Annunzio, Gabriele

Ducharme, Rejean 1941- .... **CLC 74**
See also DLB 60

Duclos, Charles Pinot 1704-1772 ..... **LC 1**

Dudek, Louis 1918- .... **CLC 11, 19**
See also CA 45-48; CAAS 14; CANR 1;
DLB 88

Duerrenmatt, Friedrich
1921-1990 ...... **CLC 1, 4, 8, 11, 15, 43;
DAM DRAM**
See also CA 17-20R; CANR 33; DLB 69,
124; MTCW

Duffy, Bruce (?)- .... **CLC 50**

Duffy, Maureen 1933- .... **CLC 37**
See also CA 25-28R; CANR 33; DLB 14;
MTCW

Dugan, Alan 1923- .... **CLC 2, 6**
See also CA 81-84; DLB 5

du Gard, Roger Martin
See Martin du Gard, Roger

Duhamel, Georges 1884-1966 .... **CLC 8**
See also CA 81-84; 25-28R; CANR 35;
DLB 65; MTCW

Dujardin, Edouard (Emile Louis)
1861-1949 .... **TCLC 13**
See also CA 109; DLB 123

Dumas, Alexandre (Davy de la Pailleterie)
1802-1870 .... **NCLC 11; DA; DAB;**
DAC; DAM MST, NOV; WLC
See also DLB 119; SATA 18

Dumas, Alexandre
1824-1895 .... **NCLC 9; DC 1**

Dumas, Claudine
See Malzberg, Barry N(athaniel)

Dumas, Henry L. 1934-1968 ..... **CLC 6, 62**
See also BW 1; CA 85-88; DLB 41

du Maurier, Daphne
1907-1989 .... **CLC 6, 11, 59; DAB;**
DAC; DAM MST, POP; SSC 18
See also CA 5-8R; 128; CANR 6, 55;
MTCW; SATA 27; SATA-Obit 60

Dunbar, Paul Laurence
1872-1906 ...... **TCLC 2, 12; BLC; DA;**
DAC; DAM MST, MULT, POET; PC 5;
SSC 8; WLC
See also BW 1; CA 104; 124;
CDALB 1865-1917; DLB 50, 54, 78;
SATA 34

Dunbar, William 1460(?)-1530(?) .... **LC 20**
See also DLB 132, 146

Duncan, Lois 1934-............... **CLC 26**
See also AAYA 4; CA 1-4R; CANR 2, 23,
36; CLR 29; JRDA; MAICYA; SAAS 2;
SATA 1, 36, 75

Duncan, Robert (Edward)
1919-1988 .... **CLC 1, 2, 4, 7, 15, 41, 55;**
DAM POET; PC 2
See also CA 9-12R; 124; CANR 28; DLB 5,
16; MTCW

Duncan, Sara Jeannette
1861-1922 .... **TCLC 60**
See also DLB 92

Dunlap, William 1766-1839 .... **NCLC 2**
See also DLB 30, 37, 59

Dunn, Douglas (Eaglesham)
1942-..................... **CLC 6, 40**
See also CA 45-48; CANR 2, 33; DLB 40;
MTCW

Dunn, Katherine (Karen) 1945-..... **CLC 71**
See also CA 33-36R

Dunn, Stephen 1939- .... **CLC 36**
See also CA 33-36R; CANR 12, 48, 53;
DLB 105

Dunne, Finley Peter 1867-1936.... **TCLC 28**
See also CA 108; DLB 11, 23

Dunne, John Gregory 1932-........ **CLC 28**
See also CA 25-28R; CANR 14, 50;
DLBY 80

Dunsany, Edward John Moreton Drax
Plunkett 1878-1957
See Dunsany, Lord
See also CA 104; 148; DLB 10

Dunsany, Lord................. **TCLC 2, 59**
See also Dunsany, Edward John Moreton
Drax Plunkett
See also DLB 77, 153, 156

du Perry, Jean
See Simenon, Georges (Jacques Christian)

Durang, Christopher (Ferdinand)
1949- .... **CLC 27, 38**
See also CA 105; CANR 50

Duras, Marguerite
1914-1996 .. **CLC 3, 6, 11, 20, 34, 40, 68**
See also CA 25-28R; 151; CANR 50;
DLB 83; MTCW

Durban, (Rosa) Pam 1947-........ **CLC 39**
See also CA 123

Durcan, Paul
1944- .... **CLC 43, 70; DAM POET**
See also CA 134

Durkheim, Emile 1858-1917 ...... **TCLC 55**

Durrell, Lawrence (George)
1912-1990 .... **CLC 1, 4, 6, 8, 13, 27, 41;**
DAM NOV
See also CA 9-12R; 132; CANR 40;
CDBLB 1945-1960; DLB 15, 27;
DLBY 90; MTCW

Durrenmatt, Friedrich
See Duerrenmatt, Friedrich

Dutt, Toru 1856-1877........... **NCLC 29**

Dwight, Timothy 1752-1817...... **NCLC 13**
See also DLB 37

Dworkin, Andrea 1946- .... **CLC 43**
See also CA 77-80; CAAS 21; CANR 16,
39; INT CANR-16; MTCW

Dwyer, Deanna
See Koontz, Dean R(ay)

Dwyer, K. R.
See Koontz, Dean R(ay)

Dylan, Bob 1941-...... **CLC 3, 4, 6, 12, 77**
See also CA 41-44R; DLB 16

Eagleton, Terence (Francis) 1943-
See Eagleton, Terry
See also CA 57-60; CANR 7, 23; MTCW

Eagleton, Terry .... **CLC 63**
See also Eagleton, Terence (Francis)

Early, Jack
See Scoppettone, Sandra

East, Michael
See West, Morris L(anglo)

Eastaway, Edward
See Thomas, (Philip) Edward

Eastlake, William (Derry) 1917-..... **CLC 8**
See also CA 5-8R; CAAS 1; CANR 5;
DLB 6; INT CANR-5

Eastman, Charles A(lexander)
1858-1939 ..... **TCLC 55; DAM MULT**
See also NNAL; YABC 1

Eberhart, Richard (Ghormley)
1904- .. **CLC 3, 11, 19, 56; DAM POET**
See also CA 1-4R; CANR 2;
CDALB 1941-1968; DLB 48; MTCW

Eberstadt, Fernanda 1960-........ **CLC 39**
See also CA 136

Echegaray (y Eizaguirre), Jose (Maria Waldo)
1832-1916 .... **TCLC 4**
See also CA 104; CANR 32; HW; MTCW

Echeverria, (Jose) Esteban (Antonino)
1805-1851 .... **NCLC 18**

Echo
See Proust, (Valentin-Louis-George-Eugene-)
Marcel

Eckert, Allan W. 1931- .... **CLC 17**
See also AAYA 18; CA 13-16R; CANR 14,
45; INT CANR-14; SAAS 21; SATA 29;
SATA-Brief 27

Eckhart, Meister 1260(?)-1328(?) .. **CMLC 9**
See also DLB 115

Eckmar, F. R.
See de Hartog, Jan

Eco, Umberto
1932- ... **CLC 28, 60; DAM NOV, POP**
See also BEST 90:1; CA 77-80; CANR 12,
33, 55; MTCW

Eddison, E(ric) R(ucker)
1882-1945 .... **TCLC 15**
See also CA 109

Edel, (Joseph) Leon 1907-...... **CLC 29, 34**
See also CA 1-4R; CANR 1, 22; DLB 103;
INT CANR-22

Eden, Emily 1797-1869 .... **NCLC 10**

Edgar, David
1948- .... **CLC 42; DAM DRAM**
See also CA 57-60; CANR 12; DLB 13;
MTCW

Edgerton, Clyde (Carlyle) 1944- .... **CLC 39**
See also AAYA 17; CA 118; 134; INT 134

Edgeworth, Maria 1768-1849... **NCLC 1, 51**
See also DLB 116, 159, 163; SATA 21

Edmonds, Paul
See Kuttner, Henry

Edmonds, Walter D(umaux) 1903- .. **CLC 35**
See also CA 5-8R; CANR 2; DLB 9;
MAICYA; SAAS 4; SATA 1, 27

Edmondson, Wallace
See Ellison, Harlan (Jay)

Edson, Russell.................... **CLC 13**
See also CA 33-36R

Edwards, Bronwen Elizabeth
See Rose, Wendy

Edwards, G(erald) B(asil)
1899-1976 .... **CLC 25**
See also CA 110

Edwards, Gus 1939-.............. **CLC 43**
See also CA 108; INT 108

Edwards, Jonathan
1703-1758 .... **LC 7; DA; DAC;**
DAM MST
See also DLB 24

Efron, Marina Ivanovna Tsvetaeva
See Tsvetaeva (Efron), Marina (Ivanovna)

Ehle, John (Marsden, Jr.) 1925-.... **CLC 27**
See also CA 9-12R

Ehrenbourg, Ilya (Grigoryevich)
See Ehrenburg, Ilya (Grigoryevich)

Ehrenburg, Ilya (Grigoryevich)
1891-1967 .... **CLC 18, 34, 62**
See also CA 102; 25-28R

Ehrenburg, Ilyo (Grigoryevich)
See Ehrenburg, Ilya (Grigoryevich)

Eich, Guenter 1907-1972 .... **CLC 15**
See also CA 111; 93-96; DLB 69, 124

Eichendorff, Joseph Freiherr von
　　1788-1857 .... NCLC 8
　　See also DLB 90

Eigner, Larry..................... CLC 9
　　See also Eigner, Laurence (Joel)
　　See also CAAS 23; DLB 5

Eigner, Laurence (Joel)　1927-1996
　　See Eigner, Larry
　　See also CA 9-12R; 151; CANR 6

Einstein, Albert　1879-1955 .... TCLC 65
　　See also CA 121; 133; MTCW

Eiseley, Loren Corey　1907-1977..... CLC 7
　　See also AAYA 5; CA 1-4R; 73-76;
　　CANR 6

Eisenstadt, Jill　1963- .... CLC 50
　　See also CA 140

Eisenstein, Sergei (Mikhailovich)
　　1898-1948 .... TCLC 57
　　See also CA 114; 149

Eisner, Simon
　　See Kornbluth, C(yril) M.

Ekeloef, (Bengt) Gunnar
　　1907-1968 .... CLC 27; DAM POET
　　See also CA 123; 25-28R

Ekelof, (Bengt) Gunnar
　　See Ekeloef, (Bengt) Gunnar

Ekwensi, C. O. D.
　　See Ekwensi, Cyprian (Odiatu Duaka)

Ekwensi, Cyprian (Odiatu Duaka)
　　1921- ...... CLC 4; BLC; DAM MULT
　　See also BW 2; CA 29-32R; CANR 18, 42;
　　DLB 117; MTCW; SATA 66

Elaine......................... TCLC 18
　　See also Leverson, Ada

El Crummo
　　See Crumb, R(obert)

Elia
　　See Lamb, Charles

Eliade, Mircea　1907-1986 .... CLC 19
　　See also CA 65-68; 119; CANR 30; MTCW

Eliot, A. D.
　　See Jewett, (Theodora) Sarah Orne

Eliot, Alice
　　See Jewett, (Theodora) Sarah Orne

Eliot, Dan
　　See Silverberg, Robert

Eliot, George
　　1819-1880 ..... NCLC 4, 13, 23, 41, 49;
　　DA; DAB; DAC; DAM MST, NOV;
　　WLC
　　See also CDBLB 1832-1890; DLB 21, 35, 55

Eliot, John　1604-1690 .... LC 5
　　See also DLB 24

Eliot, T(homas) S(tearns)
　　1888-1965 ..... CLC 1, 2, 3, 6, 9, 10, 13,
　　15, 24, 34, 41, 55, 57; DA; DAB; DAC;
　　DAM DRAM, MST, POET; PC 5;
　　WLC 2
　　See also CA 5-8R; 25-28R; CANR 41;
　　CDALB 1929-1941; DLB 7, 10, 45, 63;
　　DLBY 88; MTCW

Elizabeth　1866-1941 .... TCLC 41

Elkin, Stanley L(awrence)
　　1930-1995 ..... CLC 4, 6, 9, 14, 27, 51,
　　91; DAM NOV, POP; SSC 12
　　See also CA 9-12R; 148; CANR 8, 46;
　　DLB 2, 28; DLBY 80; INT CANR-8;
　　MTCW

Elledge, Scott.................... CLC 34

Elliott, Don
　　See Silverberg, Robert

Elliott, George P(aul)　1918-1980..... CLC 2
　　See also CA 1-4R; 97-100; CANR 2

Elliott, Janice　1931- .... CLC 47
　　See also CA 13-16R; CANR 8, 29; DLB 14

Elliott, Sumner Locke　1917-1991 ... CLC 38
　　See also CA 5-8R; 134; CANR 2, 21

Elliott, William
　　See Bradbury, Ray (Douglas)

Ellis, A. E......................... CLC 7

Ellis, Alice Thomas................ CLC 40
　　See also Haycraft, Anna

Ellis, Bret Easton
　　1964- .... CLC 39, 71; DAM POP
　　See also AAYA 2; CA 118; 123; CANR 51;
　　INT 123

Ellis, (Henry) Havelock
　　1859-1939 .... TCLC 14
　　See also CA 109

Ellis, Landon
　　See Ellison, Harlan (Jay)

Ellis, Trey　1962-................. CLC 55
　　See also CA 146

Ellison, Harlan (Jay)
　　1934- ...... CLC 1, 13, 42; DAM POP;
　　SSC 14
　　See also CA 5-8R; CANR 5, 46; DLB 8;
　　INT CANR-5; MTCW

Ellison, Ralph (Waldo)
　　1914-1994 .... CLC 1, 3, 11, 54, 86;
　　BLC; DA; DAB; DAC; DAM MST,
　　MULT, NOV; WLC
　　See also AAYA 19; BW 1; CA 9-12R; 145;
　　CANR 24, 53; CDALB 1941-1968;
　　DLB 2, 76; DLBY 94; MTCW

Ellmann, Lucy (Elizabeth)　1956-.... CLC 61
　　See also CA 128

Ellmann, Richard (David)
　　1918-1987 .... CLC 50
　　See also BEST 89:2; CA 1-4R; 122;
　　CANR 2, 28; DLB 103; DLBY 87;
　　MTCW

Elman, Richard　1934-............. CLC 19
　　See also CA 17-20R; CAAS 3; CANR 47

Elron
　　See Hubbard, L(afayette) Ron(ald)

Eluard, Paul................... TCLC 7, 41
　　See also Grindel, Eugene

Elyot, Sir Thomas　1490(?)-1546 ..... LC 11

Elytis, Odysseus
　　1911-1996 .... CLC 15, 49; DAM POET
　　See also CA 102; 151; MTCW

Emecheta, (Florence Onye) Buchi
　　1944- .. CLC 14, 48; BLC; DAM MULT
　　See also BW 2; CA 81-84; CANR 27;
　　DLB 117; MTCW; SATA 66

Emerson, Ralph Waldo
　　1803-1882 ..... NCLC 1, 38; DA; DAB;
　　DAC; DAM MST, POET; WLC
　　See also CDALB 1640-1865; DLB 1, 59, 73

Eminescu, Mihail　1850-1889 ..... NCLC 33

Empson, William
　　1906-1984 .... CLC 3, 8, 19, 33, 34
　　See also CA 17-20R; 112; CANR 31;
　　DLB 20; MTCW

Enchi Fumiko (Ueda)　1905-1986.... CLC 31
　　See also CA 129; 121

Ende, Michael (Andreas Helmuth)
　　1929-1995 .... CLC 31
　　See also CA 118; 124; 149; CANR 36;
　　CLR 14; DLB 75; MAICYA; SATA 61;
　　SATA-Brief 42; SATA-Obit 86

Endo, Shusaku
　　1923-1996 .... CLC 7, 14, 19, 54;
　　DAM NOV
　　See also CA 29-32R; 153; CANR 21, 54;
　　MTCW

Engel, Marian　1933-1985.......... CLC 36
　　See also CA 25-28R; CANR 12; DLB 53;
　　INT CANR-12

Engelhardt, Frederick
　　See Hubbard, L(afayette) Ron(ald)

Enright, D(ennis) J(oseph)
　　1920- .... CLC 4, 8, 31
　　See also CA 1-4R; CANR 1, 42; DLB 27;
　　SATA 25

Enzensberger, Hans Magnus
　　1929-....................... CLC 43
　　See also CA 116; 119

Ephron, Nora　1941- .... CLC 17, 31
　　See also AITN 2; CA 65-68; CANR 12, 39

Epsilon
　　See Betjeman, John

Epstein, Daniel Mark　1948- .... CLC 7
　　See also CA 49-52; CANR 2, 53

Epstein, Jacob　1956- .... CLC 19
　　See also CA 114

Epstein, Joseph　1937-............. CLC 39
　　See also CA 112; 119; CANR 50

Epstein, Leslie　1938- .... CLC 27
　　See also CA 73-76; CAAS 12; CANR 23

Equiano, Olaudah
　　1745(?)-1797 .... LC 16; BLC;
　　DAM MULT
　　See also DLB 37, 50

Erasmus, Desiderius　1469(?)-1536.... LC 16

Erdman, Paul E(mil)　1932- .... CLC 25
　　See also AITN 1; CA 61-64; CANR 13, 43

Erdrich, Louise
　　1954- .... CLC 39, 54; DAM MULT,
　　NOV, POP
　　See also AAYA 10; BEST 89:1; CA 114;
　　CANR 41; DLB 152; MTCW; NNAL

Erenburg, Ilya (Grigoryevich)
　　See Ehrenburg, Ilya (Grigoryevich)

Erickson, Stephen Michael　1950-
　　See Erickson, Steve
　　See also CA 129

Erickson, Steve .... CLC 64
　　See also Erickson, Stephen Michael

Ericson, Walter
See Fast, Howard (Melvin)

Eriksson, Buntel
See Bergman, (Ernst) Ingmar

Ernaux, Annie   1940- . . . . **CLC 88**
See also CA 147

Eschenbach, Wolfram von
See Wolfram von Eschenbach

Eseki, Bruno
See Mphahlele, Ezekiel

Esenin, Sergei (Alexandrovich)
1895-1925 . . . . **TCLC 4**
See also CA 104

Eshleman, Clayton   1935- . . . . **CLC 7**
See also CA 33-36R; CAAS 6; DLB 5

Espriella, Don Manuel Alvarez
See Southey, Robert

Espriu, Salvador   1913-1985 . . . . **CLC 9**
See also CA 115; DLB 134

Espronceda, Jose de   1808-1842 . . . **NCLC 39**

Esse, James
See Stephens, James

Esterbrook, Tom
See Hubbard, L(afayette) Ron(ald)

Estleman, Loren D.
1952- . . . . . . **CLC 48; DAM NOV, POP**
See also CA 85-88; CANR 27;
INT CANR-27; MTCW

Eugenides, Jeffrey   1960(?)- . . . . **CLC 81**
See also CA 144

Euripides   c. 485B.C.-406B.C. . . . . **DC 4**
See also DA; DAB; DAC; DAM DRAM,
MST

Evan, Evin
See Faust, Frederick (Schiller)

Evans, Evan
See Faust, Frederick (Schiller)

Evans, Marian
See Eliot, George

Evans, Mary Ann
See Eliot, George

Evarts, Esther
See Benson, Sally

Everett, Percival L.   1956- . . . . **CLC 57**
See also BW 2; CA 129

Everson, R(onald) G(ilmour)
1903- . . . . **CLC 27**
See also CA 17-20R; DLB 88

Everson, William (Oliver)
1912-1994 . . . . **CLC 1, 5, 14**
See also CA 9-12R; 145; CANR 20; DLB 5,
16; MTCW

Evtushenko, Evgenii Aleksandrovich
See Yevtushenko, Yevgeny (Alexandrovich)

Ewart, Gavin (Buchanan)
1916-1995 . . . . **CLC 13, 46**
See also CA 89-92; 150; CANR 17, 46;
DLB 40; MTCW

Ewers, Hanns Heinz   1871-1943 . . . **TCLC 12**
See also CA 109; 149

Ewing, Frederick R.
See Sturgeon, Theodore (Hamilton)

Exley, Frederick (Earl)
1929-1992 . . . . **CLC 6, 11**
See also AITN 2; CA 81-84; 138; DLB 143;
DLBY 81

Eynhardt, Guillermo
See Quiroga, Horacio (Sylvestre)

Ezekiel, Nissim   1924- . . . . **CLC 61**
See also CA 61-64

Ezekiel, Tish O'Dowd   1943- . . . . **CLC 34**
See also CA 129

Fadeyev, A.
See Bulgya, Alexander Alexandrovich

Fadeyev, Alexander . . . . **TCLC 53**
See also Bulgya, Alexander Alexandrovich

Fagen, Donald   1948- . . . . **CLC 26**

Fainzilberg, Ilya Arnoldovich   1897-1937
See Ilf, Ilya
See also CA 120

Fair, Ronald L.   1932- . . . . **CLC 18**
See also BW 1; CA 69-72; CANR 25;
DLB 33

Fairbairns, Zoe (Ann)   1948- . . . . **CLC 32**
See also CA 103; CANR 21

Falco, Gian
See Papini, Giovanni

Falconer, James
See Kirkup, James

Falconer, Kenneth
See Kornbluth, C(yril) M.

Falkland, Samuel
See Heijermans, Herman

Fallaci, Oriana   1930- . . . . **CLC 11**
See also CA 77-80; CANR 15; MTCW

Faludy, George   1913- . . . . **CLC 42**
See also CA 21-24R

Faludy, Gyoergy
See Faludy, George

Fanon, Frantz
1925-1961 . . . . **CLC 74; BLC;**
DAM MULT
See also BW 1; CA 116; 89-92

Fanshawe, Ann   1625-1680 . . . . **LC 11**

Fante, John (Thomas)   1911-1983 . . . **CLC 60**
See also CA 69-72; 109; CANR 23;
DLB 130; DLBY 83

Farah, Nuruddin
1945- . . . . . **CLC 53; BLC; DAM MULT**
See also BW 2; CA 106; DLB 125

Fargue, Leon-Paul   1876(?)-1947 . . . **TCLC 11**
See also CA 109

Farigoule, Louis
See Romains, Jules

Farina, Richard   1936(?)-1966 . . . . **CLC 9**
See also CA 81-84; 25-28R

Farley, Walter (Lorimer)
1915-1989 . . . . **CLC 17**
See also CA 17-20R; CANR 8, 29; DLB 22;
JRDA; MAICYA; SATA 2, 43

Farmer, Philip Jose   1918- . . . . **CLC 1, 19**
See also CA 1-4R; CANR 4, 35; DLB 8;
MTCW

Farquhar, George
1677-1707 . . . . **LC 21; DAM DRAM**
See also DLB 84

Farrell, J(ames) G(ordon)
1935-1979 . . . . **CLC 6**
See also CA 73-76; 89-92; CANR 36;
DLB 14; MTCW

Farrell, James T(homas)
1904-1979 . . . . **CLC 1, 4, 8, 11, 66**
See also CA 5-8R; 89-92; CANR 9; DLB 4,
9, 86; DLBD 2; MTCW

Farren, Richard J.
See Betjeman, John

Farren, Richard M.
See Betjeman, John

Fassbinder, Rainer Werner
1946-1982 . . . . **CLC 20**
See also CA 93-96; 106; CANR 31

Fast, Howard (Melvin)
1914- . . . . **CLC 23; DAM NOV**
See also AAYA 16; CA 1-4R; CAAS 18;
CANR 1, 33, 54; DLB 9; INT CANR-33;
SATA 7

Faulcon, Robert
See Holdstock, Robert P.

Faulkner, William (Cuthbert)
1897-1962 . . . . . **CLC 1, 3, 6, 8, 9, 11, 14,
18, 28, 52, 68; DA; DAB; DAC;
DAM MST, NOV; SSC 1; WLC**
See also AAYA 7; CA 81-84; CANR 33;
CDALB 1929-1941; DLB 9, 11, 44, 102;
DLBD 2; DLBY 86; MTCW

Fauset, Jessie Redmon
1884(?)-1961 . . . . **CLC 19, 54; BLC;
DAM MULT**
See also BW 1; CA 109; DLB 51

Faust, Frederick (Schiller)
1892-1944(?) . . . . . **TCLC 49; DAM POP**
See also CA 108; 152

Faust, Irvin   1924- . . . . **CLC 8**
See also CA 33-36R; CANR 28; DLB 2, 28;
DLBY 80

Fawkes, Guy
See Benchley, Robert (Charles)

Fearing, Kenneth (Flexner)
1902-1961 . . . . **CLC 51**
See also CA 93-96; DLB 9

Fecamps, Elise
See Creasey, John

Federman, Raymond   1928- . . . . . . **CLC 6, 47**
See also CA 17-20R; CAAS 8; CANR 10,
43; DLBY 80

Federspiel, J(uerg) F.   1931- . . . . **CLC 42**
See also CA 146

Feiffer, Jules (Ralph)
1929- . . . . . . **CLC 2, 8, 64; DAM DRAM**
See also AAYA 3; CA 17-20R; CANR 30;
DLB 7, 44; INT CANR-30; MTCW;
SATA 8, 61

Feige, Hermann Albert Otto Maximilian
See Traven, B.

Feinberg, David B.   1956-1994 . . . . . . **CLC 59**
See also CA 135; 147

Feinstein, Elaine   1930- . . . . **CLC 36**
See also CA 69-72; CAAS 1; CANR 31;
DLB 14, 40; MTCW

Feldman, Irving (Mordecai)   1928- . . . . **CLC 7**
See also CA 1-4R; CANR 1; DLB 169

Fellini, Federico 1920-1993 . . . . . **CLC 16, 85**
See also CA 65-68; 143; CANR 33

Felsen, Henry Gregor 1916- . . . . **CLC 17**
See also CA 1-4R; CANR 1; SAAS 2;
SATA 1

Fenton, James Martin 1949- . . . . **CLC 32**
See also CA 102; DLB 40

Ferber, Edna 1887-1968 . . . . **CLC 18, 93**
See also AITN 1; CA 5-8R; 25-28R; DLB 9,
28, 86; MTCW; SATA 7

Ferguson, Helen
See Kavan, Anna

Ferguson, Samuel 1810-1886 . . . . . **NCLC 33**
See also DLB 32

Fergusson, Robert 1750-1774 . . . . **LC 29**
See also DLB 109

Ferling, Lawrence
See Ferlinghetti, Lawrence (Monsanto)

Ferlinghetti, Lawrence (Monsanto)
1919(?)- . . . . **CLC 2, 6, 10, 27;**
DAM POET; PC 1
See also CA 5-8R; CANR 3, 41;
CDALB 1941-1968; DLB 5, 16; MTCW

Fernandez, Vicente Garcia Huidobro
See Huidobro Fernandez, Vicente Garcia

Ferrer, Gabriel (Francisco Victor) Miro
See Miro (Ferrer), Gabriel (Francisco
Victor)

Ferrier, Susan (Edmonstone)
1782-1854 . . . . **NCLC 8**
See also DLB 116

Ferrigno, Robert 1948(?)- . . . . **CLC 65**
See also CA 140

Ferron, Jacques 1921-1985 . . . **CLC 94; DAC**
See also CA 117; 129; DLB 60

Feuchtwanger, Lion 1884-1958 . . . . . **TCLC 3**
See also CA 104; DLB 66

Feuillet, Octave 1821-1890 . . . . . . **NCLC 45**

Feydeau, Georges (Leon Jules Marie)
1862-1921 . . . . . **TCLC 22; DAM DRAM**
See also CA 113; 152

Ficino, Marsilio 1433-1499 . . . . **LC 12**

Fiedeler, Hans
See Doeblin, Alfred

Fiedler, Leslie A(aron)
1917- . . . . **CLC 4, 13, 24**
See also CA 9-12R; CANR 7; DLB 28, 67;
MTCW

Field, Andrew 1938- . . . . **CLC 44**
See also CA 97-100; CANR 25

Field, Eugene 1850-1895 . . . . **NCLC 3**
See also DLB 23, 42, 140; DLBD 13;
MAICYA; SATA 16

Field, Gans T.
See Wellman, Manly Wade

Field, Michael . . . . **TCLC 43**

Field, Peter
See Hobson, Laura Z(ametkin)

Fielding, Henry
1707-1754 . . . . . . **LC 1; DA; DAB; DAC;**
DAM DRAM, MST, NOV; WLC
See also CDBLB 1660-1789; DLB 39, 84,
101

Fielding, Sarah 1710-1768 . . . . **LC 1**
See also DLB 39

Fierstein, Harvey (Forbes)
1954- . . . . . **CLC 33; DAM DRAM, POP**
See also CA 123; 129

Figes, Eva 1932- . . . . **CLC 31**
See also CA 53-56; CANR 4, 44; DLB 14

Finch, Robert (Duer Claydon)
1900- . . . . **CLC 18**
See also CA 57-60; CANR 9, 24, 49;
DLB 88

Findley, Timothy
1930- . . . . . . **CLC 27; DAC; DAM MST**
See also CA 25-28R; CANR 12, 42;
DLB 53

Fink, William
See Mencken, H(enry) L(ouis)

Firbank, Louis 1942-
See Reed, Lou
See also CA 117

Firbank, (Arthur Annesley) Ronald
1886-1926 . . . . **TCLC 1**
See also CA 104; DLB 36

Fisher, M(ary) F(rances) K(ennedy)
1908-1992 . . . . **CLC 76, 87**
See also CA 77-80; 138; CANR 44

Fisher, Roy 1930- . . . . **CLC 25**
See also CA 81-84; CAAS 10; CANR 16;
DLB 40

Fisher, Rudolph
1897-1934 . . . . **TCLC 11; BLC;**
DAM MULT
See also BW 1; CA 107; 124; DLB 51, 102

Fisher, Vardis (Alvero) 1895-1968 . . . . **CLC 7**
See also CA 5-8R; 25-28R; DLB 9

Fiske, Tarleton
See Bloch, Robert (Albert)

Fitch, Clarke
See Sinclair, Upton (Beall)

Fitch, John IV
See Cormier, Robert (Edmund)

Fitzgerald, Captain Hugh
See Baum, L(yman) Frank

FitzGerald, Edward 1809-1883 . . . . **NCLC 9**
See also DLB 32

Fitzgerald, F(rancis) Scott (Key)
1896-1940 . . . . **TCLC 1, 6, 14, 28, 55;**
DA; DAB; DAC; DAM MST, NOV;
SSC 6; WLC
See also AITN 1; CA 110; 123;
CDALB 1917-1929; DLB 4, 9, 86;
DLBD 1; DLBY 81; MTCW

Fitzgerald, Penelope 1916- . . . **CLC 19, 51, 61**
See also CA 85-88; CAAS 10; DLB 14

Fitzgerald, Robert (Stuart)
1910-1985 . . . . **CLC 39**
See also CA 1-4R; 114; CANR 1; DLBY 80

FitzGerald, Robert D(avid)
1902-1987 . . . . **CLC 19**
See also CA 17-20R

Fitzgerald, Zelda (Sayre)
1900-1948 . . . . **TCLC 52**
See also CA 117; 126; DLBY 84

Flanagan, Thomas (James Bonner)
1923- . . . . **CLC 25, 52**
See also CA 108; CANR 55; DLBY 80;
INT 108; MTCW

Flaubert, Gustave
1821-1880 . . . . **NCLC 2, 10, 19; DA;**
DAB; DAC; DAM MST, NOV; SSC 11;
WLC
See also DLB 119

Flecker, Herman Elroy
See Flecker, (Herman) James Elroy

Flecker, (Herman) James Elroy
1884-1915 . . . . **TCLC 43**
See also CA 109; 150; DLB 10, 19

Fleming, Ian (Lancaster)
1908-1964 . . . . . . **CLC 3, 30; DAM POP**
See also CA 5-8R; CDBLB 1945-1960;
DLB 87; MTCW; SATA 9

Fleming, Thomas (James) 1927- . . . . **CLC 37**
See also CA 5-8R; CANR 10;
INT CANR-10; SATA 8

Fletcher, John 1579-1625 . . . . . . **LC 33; DC 6**
See also CDBLB Before 1660; DLB 58

Fletcher, John Gould 1886-1950 . . . **TCLC 35**
See also CA 107; DLB 4, 45

Fleur, Paul
See Pohl, Frederik

Flooglebuckle, Al
See Spiegelman, Art

Flying Officer X
See Bates, H(erbert) E(rnest)

Fo, Dario 1926- . . . . . **CLC 32; DAM DRAM**
See also CA 116; 128; MTCW

Fogarty, Jonathan Titulescu Esq.
See Farrell, James T(homas)

Folke, Will
See Bloch, Robert (Albert)

Follett, Ken(neth Martin)
1949- . . . . . . **CLC 18; DAM NOV, POP**
See also AAYA 6; BEST 89:4; CA 81-84;
CANR 13, 33, 54; DLB 87; DLBY 81;
INT CANR-33; MTCW

Fontane, Theodor 1819-1898 . . . . . **NCLC 26**
See also DLB 129

Foote, Horton
1916- . . . . **CLC 51, 91; DAM DRAM**
See also CA 73-76; CANR 34, 51; DLB 26;
INT CANR-34

Foote, Shelby
1916- . . . . . . **CLC 75; DAM NOV, POP**
See also CA 5-8R; CANR 3, 45; DLB 2, 17

Forbes, Esther 1891-1967 . . . . **CLC 12**
See also AAYA 17; CA 13-14; 25-28R;
CAP 1; CLR 27; DLB 22; JRDA;
MAICYA; SATA 2

Forche, Carolyn (Louise)
1950- . . . . **CLC 25, 83, 86; DAM POET;**
PC 10
See also CA 109; 117; CANR 50; DLB 5;
INT 117

Ford, Elbur
See Hibbert, Eleanor Alice Burford

Ford, Ford Madox
1873-1939 . . . . **TCLC 1, 15, 39, 57;**
DAM NOV
See also CA 104; 132; CDBLB 1914-1945;
DLB 162; MTCW

Ford, John 1895-1973 . . . . **CLC 16**
See also CA 45-48

Ford, Richard 1944- . . . . **CLC 46**
See also CA 69-72; CANR 11, 47

Ford, Webster
See Masters, Edgar Lee

Foreman, Richard 1937- . . . . **CLC 50**
See also CA 65-68; CANR 32

Forester, C(ecil) S(cott)
1899-1966 . . . . **CLC 35**
See also CA 73-76; 25-28R; SATA 13

Forez
See Mauriac, Francois (Charles)

Forman, James Douglas 1932- . . . . . . **CLC 21**
See also AAYA 17; CA 9-12R; CANR 4,
19, 42; JRDA; MAICYA; SATA 8, 70

Fornes, Maria Irene 1930- . . . . . . **CLC 39, 61**
See also CA 25-28R; CANR 28; DLB 7;
HW; INT CANR-28; MTCW

Forrest, Leon 1937- . . . . **CLC 4**
See also BW 2; CA 89-92; CAAS 7;
CANR 25, 52; DLB 33

Forster, E(dward) M(organ)
1879-1970 . . . . . **CLC 1, 2, 3, 4, 9, 10, 13,**
15, 22, 45, 77; DA; DAB; DAC;
DAM MST, NOV; WLC
See also AAYA 2; CA 13-14; 25-28R;
CANR 45; CAP 1; CDBLB 1914-1945;
DLB 34, 98, 162; DLBD 10; MTCW;
SATA 57

Forster, John 1812-1876 . . . . **NCLC 11**
See also DLB 144

Forsyth, Frederick
1938- . . **CLC 2, 5, 36; DAM NOV, POP**
See also BEST 89:4; CA 85-88; CANR 38;
DLB 87; MTCW

Forten, Charlotte L. . . . . **TCLC 16; BLC**
See also Grimke, Charlotte L(ottie) Forten
See also DLB 50

Foscolo, Ugo 1778-1827 . . . . **NCLC 8**

Fosse, Bob . . . . **CLC 20**
See also Fosse, Robert Louis

Fosse, Robert Louis 1927-1987
See Fosse, Bob
See also CA 110; 123

Foster, Stephen Collins
1826-1864 . . . . **NCLC 26**

Foucault, Michel
1926-1984 . . . . **CLC 31, 34, 69**
See also CA 105; 113; CANR 34; MTCW

Fouque, Friedrich (Heinrich Karl) de la Motte
1777-1843 . . . . **NCLC 2**
See also DLB 90

Fourier, Charles 1772-1837 . . . . . . **NCLC 51**

Fournier, Henri Alban 1886-1914
See Alain-Fournier
See also CA 104

Fournier, Pierre 1916- . . . . **CLC 11**
See also Gascar, Pierre
See also CA 89-92; CANR 16, 40

Fowles, John
1926- . . . . . **CLC 1, 2, 3, 4, 6, 9, 10, 15,**
33, 87; DAB; DAC; DAM MST
See also CA 5-8R; CANR 25; CDBLB 1960
to Present; DLB 14, 139; MTCW;
SATA 22

Fox, Paula 1923- . . . . **CLC 2, 8**
See also AAYA 3; CA 73-76; CANR 20,
36; CLR 1; DLB 52; JRDA; MAICYA;
MTCW; SATA 17, 60

Fox, William Price (Jr.) 1926- . . . . . **CLC 22**
See also CA 17-20R; CAAS 19; CANR 11;
DLB 2; DLBY 81

Foxe, John 1516(?)-1587 . . . . **LC 14**

Frame, Janet
1924- . . . . **CLC 2, 3, 6, 22, 66, 96**
See also Clutha, Janet Paterson Frame

France, Anatole . . . . **TCLC 9**
See also Thibault, Jacques Anatole Francois
See also DLB 123

Francis, Claude 19(?)- . . . . **CLC 50**

Francis, Dick
1920- . . . . **CLC 2, 22, 42; DAM POP**
See also AAYA 5; BEST 89:3; CA 5-8R;
CANR 9, 42; CDBLB 1960 to Present;
DLB 87; INT CANR-9; MTCW

Francis, Robert (Churchill)
1901-1987 . . . . **CLC 15**
See also CA 1-4R; 123; CANR 1

Frank, Anne(lies Marie)
1929-1945 . . . . **TCLC 17; DA; DAB;**
DAC; DAM MST; WLC
See also AAYA 12; CA 113; 133; MTCW;
SATA 87; SATA-Brief 42

Frank, Elizabeth 1945- . . . . **CLC 39**
See also CA 121; 126; INT 126

Frankl, Viktor E(mil) 1905- . . . . **CLC 93**
See also CA 65-68

Franklin, Benjamin
See Hasek, Jaroslav (Matej Frantisek)

Franklin, Benjamin
1706-1790 . . . . . **LC 25; DA; DAB; DAC;**
DAM MST
See also CDALB 1640-1865; DLB 24, 43,
73

Franklin, (Stella Maraia Sarah) Miles
1879-1954 . . . . **TCLC 7**
See also CA 104

Fraser, (Lady) Antonia (Pakenham)
1932- . . . . **CLC 32**
See also CA 85-88; CANR 44; MTCW;
SATA-Brief 32

Fraser, George MacDonald 1925- . . . . **CLC 7**
See also CA 45-48; CANR 2, 48

Fraser, Sylvia 1935- . . . . **CLC 64**
See also CA 45-48; CANR 1, 16

Frayn, Michael
1933- . . . . **CLC 3, 7, 31, 47;**
DAM DRAM, NOV
See also CA 5-8R; CANR 30; DLB 13, 14;
MTCW

Fraze, Candida (Merrill) 1945- . . . . . **CLC 50**
See also CA 126

Frazer, J(ames) G(eorge)
1854-1941 . . . . **TCLC 32**
See also CA 118

Frazer, Robert Caine
See Creasey, John

Frazer, Sir James George
See Frazer, J(ames) G(eorge)

Frazier, Ian 1951- . . . . **CLC 46**
See also CA 130; CANR 54

Frederic, Harold 1856-1898 . . . . . . **NCLC 10**
See also DLB 12, 23; DLBD 13

Frederick, John
See Faust, Frederick (Schiller)

Frederick the Great 1712-1786 . . . . . **LC 14**

Fredro, Aleksander 1793-1876 . . . . . **NCLC 8**

Freeling, Nicolas 1927- . . . . **CLC 38**
See also CA 49-52; CAAS 12; CANR 1, 17,
50; DLB 87

Freeman, Douglas Southall
1886-1953 . . . . **TCLC 11**
See also CA 109; DLB 17

Freeman, Judith 1946- . . . . **CLC 55**
See also CA 148

Freeman, Mary Eleanor Wilkins
1852-1930 . . . . **TCLC 9; SSC 1**
See also CA 106; DLB 12, 78

Freeman, R(ichard) Austin
1862-1943 . . . . **TCLC 21**
See also CA 113; DLB 70

French, Albert 1943- . . . . **CLC 86**

French, Marilyn
1929- . . . . **CLC 10, 18, 60;**
DAM DRAM, NOV, POP
See also CA 69-72; CANR 3, 31;
INT CANR-31; MTCW

French, Paul
See Asimov, Isaac

Freneau, Philip Morin 1752-1832 . . **NCLC 1**
See also DLB 37, 43

Freud, Sigmund 1856-1939 . . . . **TCLC 52**
See also CA 115; 133; MTCW

Friedan, Betty (Naomi) 1921- . . . . . . **CLC 74**
See also CA 65-68; CANR 18, 45; MTCW

Friedlander, Saul 1932- . . . . **CLC 90**
See also CA 117; 130

Friedman, B(ernard) H(arper)
1926- . . . . **CLC 7**
See also CA 1-4R; CANR 3, 48

Friedman, Bruce Jay 1930- . . . . **CLC 3, 5, 56**
See also CA 9-12R; CANR 25, 52; DLB 2,
28; INT CANR-25

Friel, Brian 1929- . . . . **CLC 5, 42, 59**
See also CA 21-24R; CANR 33; DLB 13;
MTCW

Friis-Baastad, Babbis Ellinor
1921-1970 . . . . **CLC 12**
See also CA 17-20R; 134; SATA 7

Frisch, Max (Rudolf)
1911-1991 . . . . . **CLC 3, 9, 14, 18, 32, 44;**
DAM DRAM, NOV
See also CA 85-88; 134; CANR 32;
DLB 69, 124; MTCW

Fromentin, Eugene (Samuel Auguste)
1820-1876 . . . . **NCLC 10**
See also DLB 123

Frost, Frederick
See Faust, Frederick (Schiller)

Frost, Robert (Lee)
1874-1963 .... **CLC 1, 3, 4, 9, 10, 13, 15, 26, 34, 44; DA; DAB; DAC; DAM MST, POET; PC 1; WLC**
See also CA 89-92; CANR 33;
CDALB 1917-1929; DLB 54; DLBD 7;
MTCW; SATA 14

Froude, James Anthony
1818-1894 .... **NCLC 43**
See also DLB 18, 57, 144

Froy, Herald
See Waterhouse, Keith (Spencer)

Fry, Christopher
1907- ..... **CLC 2, 10, 14; DAM DRAM**
See also CA 17-20R; CAAS 23; CANR 9,
30; DLB 13; MTCW; SATA 66

Frye, (Herman) Northrop
1912-1991 .... **CLC 24, 70**
See also CA 5-8R; 133; CANR 8, 37;
DLB 67, 68; MTCW

Fuchs, Daniel 1909-1993 .... **CLC 8, 22**
See also CA 81-84; 142; CAAS 5;
CANR 40; DLB 9, 26, 28; DLBY 93

Fuchs, Daniel 1934- .... **CLC 34**
See also CA 37-40R; CANR 14, 48

Fuentes, Carlos
1928- ...... **CLC 3, 8, 10, 13, 22, 41, 60; DA; DAB; DAC; DAM MST, MULT, NOV; HLC; WLC**
See also AAYA 4; AITN 2; CA 69-72;
CANR 10, 32; DLB 113; HW; MTCW

Fuentes, Gregorio Lopez y
See Lopez y Fuentes, Gregorio

Fugard, (Harold) Athol
1932- .... **CLC 5, 9, 14, 25, 40, 80; DAM DRAM; DC 3**
See also AAYA 17; CA 85-88; CANR 32,
54; MTCW

Fugard, Sheila 1932- .... **CLC 48**
See also CA 125

Fuller, Charles (H., Jr.)
1939- .... **CLC 25; BLC; DAM DRAM, MULT; DC 1**
See also BW 2; CA 108; 112; DLB 38;
INT 112; MTCW

Fuller, John (Leopold) 1937- ...... **CLC 62**
See also CA 21-24R; CANR 9, 44; DLB 40

Fuller, Margaret .... **NCLC 5, 50**
See also Ossoli, Sarah Margaret (Fuller
marchesa d')

Fuller, Roy (Broadbent)
1912-1991 .... **CLC 4, 28**
See also CA 5-8R; 135; CAAS 10;
CANR 53; DLB 15, 20; SATA 87

Fulton, Alice 1952- .... **CLC 52**
See also CA 116

Furphy, Joseph 1843-1912 .... **TCLC 25**

Fussell, Paul 1924- .... **CLC 74**
See also BEST 90:1; CA 17-20R; CANR 8,
21, 35; INT CANR-21; MTCW

Futabatei, Shimei 1864-1909 ..... **TCLC 44**

Futrelle, Jacques 1875-1912 ...... **TCLC 19**
See also CA 113

Gaboriau, Emile 1835-1873 ...... **NCLC 14**

Gadda, Carlo Emilio 1893-1973 .... **CLC 11**
See also CA 89-92

Gaddis, William
1922- ..... **CLC 1, 3, 6, 8, 10, 19, 43, 86**
See also CA 17-20R; CANR 21, 48; DLB 2;
MTCW

Gage, Walter
See Inge, William (Motter)

Gaines, Ernest J(ames)
1933- .... **CLC 3, 11, 18, 86; BLC; DAM MULT**
See also AAYA 18; AITN 1; BW 2;
CA 9-12R; CANR 6, 24, 42;
CDALB 1968-1988; DLB 2, 33, 152;
DLBY 80; MTCW; SATA 86

Gaitskill, Mary 1954- .... **CLC 69**
See also CA 128

Galdos, Benito Perez
See Perez Galdos, Benito

Gale, Zona
1874-1938 ...... **TCLC 7; DAM DRAM**
See also CA 105; 153; DLB 9, 78

Galeano, Eduardo (Hughes) 1940-... **CLC 72**
See also CA 29-32R; CANR 13, 32; HW

Galiano, Juan Valera y Alcala
See Valera y Alcala-Galiano, Juan

Gallagher, Tess
1943- .. **CLC 18, 63; DAM POET; PC 9**
See also CA 106; DLB 120

Gallant, Mavis
1922- .... **CLC 7, 18, 38; DAC; DAM MST; SSC 5**
See also CA 69-72; CANR 29; DLB 53;
MTCW

Gallant, Roy A(rthur) 1924- .... **CLC 17**
See also CA 5-8R; CANR 4, 29, 54;
CLR 30; MAICYA; SATA 4, 68

Gallico, Paul (William) 1897-1976 ... **CLC 2**
See also AITN 1; CA 5-8R; 69-72;
CANR 23; DLB 9, 171; MAICYA;
SATA 13

Gallo, Max Louis 1932- .... **CLC 95**
See also CA 85-88

Gallois, Lucien
See Desnos, Robert

Gallup, Ralph
See Whitemore, Hugh (John)

Galsworthy, John
1867-1933 ...... **TCLC 1, 45; DA; DAB; DAC; DAM DRAM, MST, NOV; SSC 22; WLC 2**
See also CA 104; 141; CDBLB 1890-1914;
DLB 10, 34, 98, 162

Galt, John 1779-1839 .... **NCLC 1**
See also DLB 99, 116, 159

Galvin, James 1951- .... **CLC 38**
See also CA 108; CANR 26

Gamboa, Federico 1864-1939 ..... **TCLC 36**

Gandhi, M. K.
See Gandhi, Mohandas Karamchand

Gandhi, Mahatma
See Gandhi, Mohandas Karamchand

Gandhi, Mohandas Karamchand
1869-1948 ..... **TCLC 59; DAM MULT**
See also CA 121; 132; MTCW

Gann, Ernest Kellogg 1910-1991.... **CLC 23**
See also AITN 1; CA 1-4R; 136; CANR 1

Garcia, Cristina 1958- .... **CLC 76**
See also CA 141

Garcia Lorca, Federico
1898-1936 ... **TCLC 1, 7, 49; DA; DAB; DAC; DAM DRAM, MST, MULT, POET; DC 2; HLC; PC 3; WLC**
See also CA 104; 131; DLB 108; HW;
MTCW

Garcia Marquez, Gabriel (Jose)
1928- ... **CLC 2, 3, 8, 10, 15, 27, 47, 55, 68; DA; DAB; DAC; DAM MST, MULT, NOV, POP; HLC; SSC 8; WLC**
See also AAYA 3; BEST 89:1, 90:4;
CA 33-36R; CANR 10, 28, 50; DLB 113;
HW; MTCW

Gard, Janice
See Latham, Jean Lee

Gard, Roger Martin du
See Martin du Gard, Roger

Gardam, Jane 1928- .... **CLC 43**
See also CA 49-52; CANR 2, 18, 33, 54;
CLR 12; DLB 14, 161; MAICYA;
MTCW; SAAS 9; SATA 39, 76;
SATA-Brief 28

Gardner, Herb(ert) 1934- .... **CLC 44**
See also CA 149

Gardner, John (Champlin), Jr.
1933-1982 ..... **CLC 2, 3, 5, 7, 8, 10, 18, 28, 34; DAM NOV, POP; SSC 7**
See also AITN 1; CA 65-68; 107;
CANR 33; DLB 2; DLBY 82; MTCW;
SATA 40; SATA-Obit 31

Gardner, John (Edmund)
1926- .... **CLC 30; DAM POP**
See also CA 103; CANR 15; MTCW

Gardner, Miriam
See Bradley, Marion Zimmer

Gardner, Noel
See Kuttner, Henry

Gardons, S. S.
See Snodgrass, W(illiam) D(e Witt)

Garfield, Leon 1921-1996.......... **CLC 12**
See also AAYA 8; CA 17-20R; 152;
CANR 38, 41; CLR 21; DLB 161; JRDA;
MAICYA; SATA 1, 32, 76;
SATA-Obit 90

Garland, (Hannibal) Hamlin
1860-1940 .... **TCLC 3; SSC 18**
See also CA 104; DLB 12, 71, 78

Garneau, (Hector de) Saint-Denys
1912-1943 .... **TCLC 13**
See also CA 111; DLB 88

Garner, Alan
1934- .... **CLC 17; DAB; DAM POP**
See also AAYA 18; CA 73-76; CANR 15;
CLR 20; DLB 161; MAICYA; MTCW;
SATA 18, 69

Garner, Hugh 1913-1979 .... **CLC 13**
See also CA 69-72; CANR 31; DLB 68

Garnett, David 1892-1981 .... **CLC 3**
See also CA 5-8R; 103; CANR 17; DLB 34

Garos, Stephanie
See Katz, Steve

Garrett, George (Palmer)
1929- . . . . **CLC 3, 11, 51**
See also CA 1-4R; CAAS 5; CANR 1, 42;
DLB 2, 5, 130, 152; DLBY 83

Garrick, David
1717-1779 . . . . **LC 15; DAM DRAM**
See also DLB 84

Garrigue, Jean 1914-1972 . . . . **CLC 2, 8**
See also CA 5-8R; 37-40R; CANR 20

Garrison, Frederick
See Sinclair, Upton (Beall)

Garth, Will
See Hamilton, Edmond; Kuttner, Henry

Garvey, Marcus (Moziah, Jr.)
1887-1940 . . . . **TCLC 41; BLC;
DAM MULT**
See also BW 1; CA 120; 124

Gary, Romain . . . . **CLC 25**
See also Kacew, Romain
See also DLB 83

Gascar, Pierre . . . . **CLC 11**
See also Fournier, Pierre

Gascoyne, David (Emery) 1916- . . . . **CLC 45**
See also CA 65-68; CANR 10, 28, 54;
DLB 20; MTCW

Gaskell, Elizabeth Cleghorn
1810-1865 . . **NCLC 5; DAB; DAM MST**
See also CDBLB 1832-1890; DLB 21, 144,
159

Gass, William H(oward)
1924- . . . **CLC 1, 2, 8, 11, 15, 39; SSC 12**
See also CA 17-20R; CANR 30; DLB 2;
MTCW

Gasset, Jose Ortega y
See Ortega y Gasset, Jose

Gates, Henry Louis, Jr.
1950- . . . . **CLC 65; DAM MULT**
See also BW 2; CA 109; CANR 25, 53;
DLB 67

Gautier, Theophile
1811-1872 . . . . . . **NCLC 1; DAM POET;
SSC 20**
See also DLB 119

Gawsworth, John
See Bates, H(erbert) E(rnest)

Gay, Oliver
See Gogarty, Oliver St. John

Gaye, Marvin (Penze) 1939-1984 . . . **CLC 26**
See also CA 112

Gebler, Carlo (Ernest) 1954- . . . . **CLC 39**
See also CA 119; 133

Gee, Maggie (Mary) 1948- . . . . **CLC 57**
See also CA 130

Gee, Maurice (Gough) 1931- . . . . **CLC 29**
See also CA 97-100; SATA 46

Gelbart, Larry (Simon) 1923- . . . **CLC 21, 61**
See also CA 73-76; CANR 45

Gelber, Jack 1932- . . . . **CLC 1, 6, 14, 79**
See also CA 1-4R; CANR 2; DLB 7

Gellhorn, Martha (Ellis) 1908- . . **CLC 14, 60**
See also CA 77-80; CANR 44; DLBY 82

Genet, Jean
1910-1986 . . . . . . **CLC 1, 2, 5, 10, 14, 44,
46; DAM DRAM**
See also CA 13-16R; CANR 18; DLB 72;
DLBY 86; MTCW

Gent, Peter 1942- . . . . **CLC 29**
See also AITN 1; CA 89-92; DLBY 82

Gentlewoman in New England, A
See Bradstreet, Anne

Gentlewoman in Those Parts, A
See Bradstreet, Anne

George, Jean Craighead 1919- . . . . . . **CLC 35**
See also AAYA 8; CA 5-8R; CANR 25;
CLR 1; DLB 52; JRDA; MAICYA;
SATA 2, 68

George, Stefan (Anton)
1868-1933 . . . . **TCLC 2, 14**
See also CA 104

Georges, Georges Martin
See Simenon, Georges (Jacques Christian)

Gerhardi, William Alexander
See Gerhardie, William Alexander

Gerhardie, William Alexander
1895-1977 . . . . **CLC 5**
See also CA 25-28R; 73-76; CANR 18;
DLB 36

Gerstler, Amy 1956- . . . . **CLC 70**
See also CA 146

Gertler, T. . . . . **CLC 34**
See also CA 116; 121; INT 121

gfgg . . . . **CLC XvXzc**

Ghalib . . . . **NCLC 39**
See also Ghalib, Hsadullah Khan

Ghalib, Hsadullah Khan 1797-1869
See Ghalib
See also DAM POET

Ghelderode, Michel de
1898-1962 . . . . **CLC 6, 11; DAM DRAM**
See also CA 85-88; CANR 40

Ghiselin, Brewster 1903- . . . . **CLC 23**
See also CA 13-16R; CAAS 10; CANR 13

Ghose, Zulfikar 1935- . . . . **CLC 42**
See also CA 65-68

Ghosh, Amitav 1956- . . . . **CLC 44**
See also CA 147

Giacosa, Giuseppe 1847-1906 . . . . . . **TCLC 7**
See also CA 104

Gibb, Lee
See Waterhouse, Keith (Spencer)

Gibbon, Lewis Grassic . . . . **TCLC 4**
See also Mitchell, James Leslie

Gibbons, Kaye
1960- . . . . **CLC 50, 88; DAM POP**
See also CA 151

Gibran, Kahlil
1883-1931 . . . . **TCLC 1, 9; DAM POET,
POP; PC 9**
See also CA 104; 150

Gibran, Khalil
See Gibran, Kahlil

Gibson, William
1914- . . . . **CLC 23; DA; DAB; DAC;
DAM DRAM, MST**
See also CA 9-12R; CANR 9, 42; DLB 7;
SATA 66

Gibson, William (Ford)
1948- . . . . **CLC 39, 63; DAM POP**
See also AAYA 12; CA 126; 133; CANR 52

Gide, Andre (Paul Guillaume)
1869-1951 . . . . **TCLC 5, 12, 36; DA;
DAB; DAC; DAM MST, NOV; SSC 13;
WLC**
See also CA 104; 124; DLB 65; MTCW

Gifford, Barry (Colby) 1946- . . . . **CLC 34**
See also CA 65-68; CANR 9, 30, 40

Gilbert, W(illiam) S(chwenck)
1836-1911 . . . . . **TCLC 3; DAM DRAM,
POET**
See also CA 104; SATA 36

Gilbreth, Frank B., Jr. 1911- . . . . **CLC 17**
See also CA 9-12R; SATA 2

Gilchrist, Ellen
1935- . . . . **CLC 34, 48; DAM POP;
SSC 14**
See also CA 113; 116; CANR 41; DLB 130;
MTCW

Giles, Molly 1942- . . . . **CLC 39**
See also CA 126

Gill, Patrick
See Creasey, John

Gilliam, Terry (Vance) 1940- . . . . **CLC 21**
See also Monty Python
See also AAYA 19; CA 108; 113;
CANR 35; INT 113

Gillian, Jerry
See Gilliam, Terry (Vance)

Gilliatt, Penelope (Ann Douglass)
1932-1993 . . . . **CLC 2, 10, 13, 53**
See also AITN 2; CA 13-16R; 141;
CANR 49; DLB 14

Gilman, Charlotte (Anna) Perkins (Stetson)
1860-1935 . . . . . . **TCLC 9, 37; SSC 13**
See also CA 106; 150

Gilmour, David 1949- . . . . **CLC 35**
See also CA 138, 147

Gilpin, William 1724-1804 . . . . **NCLC 30**

Gilray, J. D.
See Mencken, H(enry) L(ouis)

Gilroy, Frank D(aniel) 1925- . . . . **CLC 2**
See also CA 81-84; CANR 32; DLB 7

Ginsberg, Allen
1926- . . . . . . **CLC 1, 2, 3, 4, 6, 13, 36, 69;
DA; DAB; DAC; DAM MST, POET;
PC 4; WLC 3**
See also AITN 1; CA 1-4R; CANR 2, 41;
CDALB 1941-1968; DLB 5, 16, 169;
MTCW

Ginzburg, Natalia
1916-1991 . . . . **CLC 5, 11, 54, 70**
See also CA 85-88; 135; CANR 33; MTCW

Giono, Jean 1895-1970 . . . . **CLC 4, 11**
See also CA 45-48; 29-32R; CANR 2, 35;
DLB 72; MTCW

Giovanni, Nikki
1943- . . . . . . CLC 2, 4, 19, 64; BLC; DA;
DAB; DAC; DAM MST, MULT, POET
See also AITN 1; BW 2; CA 29-32R;
CAAS 6; CANR 18, 41; CLR 6; DLB 5,
41; INT CANR-18; MAICYA; MTCW;
SATA 24

Giovene, Andrea 1904- . . . . CLC 7
See also CA 85-88

Gippius, Zinaida (Nikolayevna) 1869-1945
See Hippius, Zinaida
See also CA 106

Giraudoux, (Hippolyte) Jean
1882-1944 . . . . TCLC 2, 7; DAM DRAM
See also CA 104; DLB 65

Gironella, Jose Maria 1917- . . . . CLC 11
See also CA 101

Gissing, George (Robert)
1857-1903 . . . . TCLC 3, 24, 47
See also CA 105; DLB 18, 135

Giurlani, Aldo
See Palazzeschi, Aldo

Gladkov, Fyodor (Vasilyevich)
1883-1958 . . . . TCLC 27

Glanville, Brian (Lester) 1931- . . . . . . CLC 6
See also CA 5-8R; CAAS 9; CANR 3;
DLB 15, 139; SATA 42

Glasgow, Ellen (Anderson Gholson)
1873(?)-1945 . . . . TCLC 2, 7
See also CA 104; DLB 9, 12

Glaspell, Susan (Keating)
1882(?)-1948 . . . . TCLC 55
See also CA 110; DLB 7, 9, 78; YABC 2

Glassco, John 1909-1981 . . . . CLC 9
See also CA 13-16R; 102; CANR 15;
DLB 68

Glasscock, Amnesia
See Steinbeck, John (Ernst)

Glasser, Ronald J. 1940(?)- . . . . CLC 37

Glassman, Joyce
See Johnson, Joyce

Glendinning, Victoria 1937- . . . . CLC 50
See also CA 120; 127; DLB 155

Glissant, Edouard
1928- . . . . CLC 10, 68; DAM MULT
See also CA 153

Gloag, Julian 1930- . . . . CLC 40
See also AITN 1; CA 65-68; CANR 10

Glowacki, Aleksander
See Prus, Boleslaw

Gluck, Louise (Elisabeth)
1943- . . . . CLC 7, 22, 44, 81;
DAM POET; PC 16
See also CA 33-36R; CANR 40; DLB 5

Gobineau, Joseph Arthur (Comte) de
1816-1882 . . . . NCLC 17
See also DLB 123

Godard, Jean-Luc 1930- . . . . CLC 20
See also CA 93-96

Godden, (Margaret) Rumer 1907- . . . CLC 53
See also AAYA 6; CA 5-8R; CANR 4, 27,
36, 55; CLR 20; DLB 161; MAICYA;
SAAS 12; SATA 3, 36

Godoy Alcayaga, Lucila 1889-1957
See Mistral, Gabriela
See also BW 2; CA 104; 131; DAM MULT;
HW; MTCW

Godwin, Gail (Kathleen)
1937- . . . . CLC 5, 8, 22, 31, 69;
DAM POP
See also CA 29-32R; CANR 15, 43; DLB 6;
INT CANR-15; MTCW

Godwin, William 1756-1836 . . . . . . NCLC 14
See also CDBLB 1789-1832; DLB 39, 104,
142, 158, 163

Goethe, Johann Wolfgang von
1749-1832 . . . . NCLC 4, 22, 34; DA;
DAB; DAC; DAM DRAM, MST,
POET; PC 5; WLC 3
See also DLB 94

Gogarty, Oliver St. John
1878-1957 . . . . TCLC 15
See also CA 109; 150; DLB 15, 19

Gogol, Nikolai (Vasilyevich)
1809-1852 . . . . NCLC 5, 15, 31; DA;
DAB; DAC; DAM DRAM, MST; DC 1;
SSC 4; WLC

Goines, Donald
1937(?)-1974 . . . . CLC 80; BLC;
DAM MULT, POP
See also AITN 1; BW 1; CA 124; 114;
DLB 33

Gold, Herbert 1924- . . . . CLC 4, 7, 14, 42
See also CA 9-12R; CANR 17, 45; DLB 2;
DLBY 81

Goldbarth, Albert 1948- . . . . CLC 5, 38
See also CA 53-56; CANR 6, 40; DLB 120

Goldberg, Anatol 1910-1982 . . . . CLC 34
See also CA 131; 117

Goldemberg, Isaac 1945- . . . . CLC 52
See also CA 69-72; CAAS 12; CANR 11,
32; HW

Golding, William (Gerald)
1911-1993 . . . . CLC 1, 2, 3, 8, 10, 17, 27,
58, 81; DA; DAB; DAC; DAM MST,
NOV; WLC
See also AAYA 5; CA 5-8R; 141;
CANR 13, 33, 54; CDBLB 1945-1960;
DLB 15, 100; MTCW

Goldman, Emma 1869-1940 . . . . . . TCLC 13
See also CA 110; 150

Goldman, Francisco 1955- . . . . CLC 76

Goldman, William (W.) 1931- . . . . CLC 1, 48
See also CA 9-12R; CANR 29; DLB 44

Goldmann, Lucien 1913-1970 . . . . . . CLC 24
See also CA 25-28; CAP 2

Goldoni, Carlo
1707-1793 . . . . LC 4; DAM DRAM

Goldsberry, Steven 1949- . . . . CLC 34
See also CA 131

Goldsmith, Oliver
1728-1774 . . . . . . LC 2; DA; DAB; DAC;
DAM DRAM, MST, NOV, POET;
WLC
See also CDBLB 1660-1789; DLB 39, 89,
104, 109, 142; SATA 26

Goldsmith, Peter
See Priestley, J(ohn) B(oynton)

Gombrowicz, Witold
1904-1969 . . . . CLC 4, 7, 11, 49;
DAM DRAM
See also CA 19-20; 25-28R; CAP 2

Gomez de la Serna, Ramon
1888-1963 . . . . CLC 9
See also CA 153; 116; HW

Goncharov, Ivan Alexandrovich
1812-1891 . . . . NCLC 1

Goncourt, Edmond (Louis Antoine Huot) de
1822-1896 . . . . NCLC 7
See also DLB 123

Goncourt, Jules (Alfred Huot) de
1830-1870 . . . . NCLC 7
See also DLB 123

Gontier, Fernande 19(?)- . . . . CLC 50

Goodman, Paul 1911-1972 . . . . CLC 1, 2, 4, 7
See also CA 19-20; 37-40R; CANR 34;
CAP 2; DLB 130; MTCW

Gordimer, Nadine
1923- . . . . CLC 3, 5, 7, 10, 18, 33, 51, 70;
DA; DAB; DAC; DAM MST, NOV;
SSC 17
See also CA 5-8R; CANR 3, 28;
INT CANR-28; MTCW

Gordon, Adam Lindsay
1833-1870 . . . . NCLC 21

Gordon, Caroline
1895-1981 . . . CLC 6, 13, 29, 83; SSC 15
See also CA 11-12; 103; CANR 36; CAP 1;
DLB 4, 9, 102; DLBY 81; MTCW

Gordon, Charles William 1860-1937
See Connor, Ralph
See also CA 109

Gordon, Mary (Catherine)
1949- . . . . CLC 13, 22
See also CA 102; CANR 44; DLB 6;
DLBY 81; INT 102; MTCW

Gordon, Sol 1923- . . . . CLC 26
See also CA 53-56; CANR 4; SATA 11

Gordone, Charles
1925-1995 . . . . . CLC 1, 4; DAM DRAM
See also BW 1; CA 93-96; 150; CANR 55;
DLB 7; INT 93-96; MTCW

Gorenko, Anna Andreevna
See Akhmatova, Anna

Gorky, Maxim . . . . TCLC 8; DAB; WLC
See also Peshkov, Alexei Maximovich

Goryan, Sirak
See Saroyan, William

Gosse, Edmund (William)
1849-1928 . . . . TCLC 28
See also CA 117; DLB 57, 144

Gotlieb, Phyllis Fay (Bloom)
1926- . . . . CLC 18
See also CA 13-16R; CANR 7; DLB 88

Gottesman, S. D.
See Kornbluth, C(yril) M.; Pohl, Frederik

Gottfried von Strassburg
fl. c. 1210- . . . . CMLC 10
See also DLB 138

Gould, Lois . . . . CLC 4, 10
See also CA 77-80; CANR 29; MTCW

Gourmont, Remy (-Marie-Charles) de
1858-1915 . . . . **TCLC 17**
See also CA 109; 150

Govier, Katherine 1948- . . . . **CLC 51**
See also CA 101; CANR 18, 40

Goyen, (Charles) William
1915-1983 . . . . **CLC 5, 8, 14, 40**
See also AITN 2; CA 5-8R; 110; CANR 6;
DLB 2; DLBY 83; INT CANR-6

Goytisolo, Juan
1931- . . . . . **CLC 5, 10, 23; DAM MULT;**
HLC
See also CA 85-88; CANR 32; HW; MTCW

Gozzano, Guido 1883-1916 . . . . **PC 10**
See also DLB 114

Gozzi, (Conte) Carlo 1720-1806 . . **NCLC 23**

Grabbe, Christian Dietrich
1801-1836 . . . . **NCLC 2**
See also DLB 133

Grace, Patricia 1937- . . . . **CLC 56**

Gracian y Morales, Baltasar
1601-1658 . . . . **LC 15**

Gracq, Julien . . . . **CLC 11, 48**
See also Poirier, Louis
See also DLB 83

Grade, Chaim 1910-1982 . . . . **CLC 10**
See also CA 93-96; 107

Graduate of Oxford, A
See Ruskin, John

Graham, John
See Phillips, David Graham

Graham, Jorie 1951- . . . . **CLC 48**
See also CA 111; DLB 120

Graham, R(obert) B(ontine) Cunninghame
See Cunninghame Graham, R(obert)
B(ontine)
See also DLB 98, 135, 174

Graham, Robert
See Haldeman, Joe (William)

Graham, Tom
See Lewis, (Harry) Sinclair

Graham, W(illiam) S(ydney)
1918-1986 . . . . **CLC 29**
See also CA 73-76; 118; DLB 20

Graham, Winston (Mawdsley)
1910- . . . . **CLC 23**
See also CA 49-52; CANR 2, 22, 45;
DLB 77

Grahame, Kenneth
1859-1932 . . . . **TCLC 64; DAB**
See also CA 108; 136; CLR 5; DLB 34, 141;
MAICYA; YABC 1

Grant, Skeeter
See Spiegelman, Art

Granville-Barker, Harley
1877-1946 . . . . . . **TCLC 2; DAM DRAM**
See also Barker, Harley Granville
See also CA 104

Grass, Guenter (Wilhelm)
1927- . . . . . **CLC 1, 2, 4, 6, 11, 15, 22, 32,**
49, 88; DA; DAB; DAC; DAM MST,
NOV; WLC
See also CA 13-16R; CANR 20; DLB 75,
124; MTCW

Gratton, Thomas
See Hulme, T(homas) E(rnest)

Grau, Shirley Ann
1929- . . . . **CLC 4, 9; SSC 15**
See also CA 89-92; CANR 22; DLB 2;
INT CANR-22; MTCW

Gravel, Fern
See Hall, James Norman

Graver, Elizabeth 1964- . . . . **CLC 70**
See also CA 135

Graves, Richard Perceval 1945- . . . . **CLC 44**
See also CA 65-68; CANR 9, 26, 51

Graves, Robert (von Ranke)
1895-1985 . . . . . . **CLC 1, 2, 6, 11, 39, 44,**
45; DAB; DAC; DAM MST, POET;
PC 6
See also CA 5-8R; 117; CANR 5, 36;
CDBLB 1914-1945; DLB 20, 100;
DLBY 85; MTCW; SATA 45

Graves, Valerie
See Bradley, Marion Zimmer

Gray, Alasdair (James) 1934- . . . . . . **CLC 41**
See also CA 126; CANR 47; INT 126;
MTCW

Gray, Amlin 1946- . . . . **CLC 29**
See also CA 138

Gray, Francine du Plessix
1930- . . . . **CLC 22; DAM NOV**
See also BEST 90:3; CA 61-64; CAAS 2;
CANR 11, 33; INT CANR-11; MTCW

Gray, John (Henry) 1866-1934 . . . . **TCLC 19**
See also CA 119

Gray, Simon (James Holliday)
1936- . . . . **CLC 9, 14, 36**
See also AITN 1; CA 21-24R; CAAS 3;
CANR 32; DLB 13; MTCW

Gray, Spalding 1941- . . **CLC 49; DAM POP**
See also CA 128

Gray, Thomas
1716-1771 . . . . . . **LC 4; DA; DAB; DAC;**
DAM MST; PC 2; WLC
See also CDBLB 1660-1789; DLB 109

Grayson, David
See Baker, Ray Stannard

Grayson, Richard (A.) 1951- . . . . **CLC 38**
See also CA 85-88; CANR 14, 31

Greeley, Andrew M(oran)
1928- . . . . **CLC 28; DAM POP**
See also CA 5-8R; CAAS 7; CANR 7, 43;
MTCW

Green, Anna Katharine
1846-1935 . . . . **TCLC 63**
See also CA 112

Green, Brian
See Card, Orson Scott

Green, Hannah
See Greenberg, Joanne (Goldenberg)

Green, Hannah . . . . **CLC 3**
See also CA 73-76

Green, Henry 1905-1973 . . . . . **CLC 2, 13, 97**
See also Yorke, Henry Vincent
See also DLB 15

Green, Julian (Hartridge) 1900-
See Green, Julien
See also CA 21-24R; CANR 33; DLB 4, 72;
MTCW

Green, Julien . . . . **CLC 3, 11, 77**
See also Green, Julian (Hartridge)

Green, Paul (Eliot)
1894-1981 . . . . . . **CLC 25; DAM DRAM**
See also AITN 1; CA 5-8R; 103; CANR 3;
DLB 7, 9; DLBY 81

Greenberg, Ivan 1908-1973
See Rahv, Philip
See also CA 85-88

Greenberg, Joanne (Goldenberg)
1932- . . . . **CLC 7, 30**
See also AAYA 12; CA 5-8R; CANR 14,
32; SATA 25

Greenberg, Richard 1959(?)- . . . . **CLC 57**
See also CA 138

Greene, Bette 1934- . . . . **CLC 30**
See also AAYA 7; CA 53-56; CANR 4;
CLR 2; JRDA; MAICYA; SAAS 16;
SATA 8

Greene, Gael . . . . **CLC 8**
See also CA 13-16R; CANR 10

Greene, Graham
1904-1991 . . . . **CLC 1, 3, 6, 9, 14, 18, 27,**
37, 70, 72; DA; DAB; DAC; DAM MST,
NOV; WLC
See also AITN 2; CA 13-16R; 133;
CANR 35; CDBLB 1945-1960; DLB 13,
15, 77, 100, 162; DLBY 91; MTCW;
SATA 20

Greer, Richard
See Silverberg, Robert

Gregor, Arthur 1923- . . . . **CLC 9**
See also CA 25-28R; CAAS 10; CANR 11;
SATA 36

Gregor, Lee
See Pohl, Frederik

Gregory, Isabella Augusta (Persse)
1852-1932 . . . . **TCLC 1**
See also CA 104; DLB 10

Gregory, J. Dennis
See Williams, John A(lfred)

Grendon, Stephen
See Derleth, August (William)

Grenville, Kate 1950- . . . . **CLC 61**
See also CA 118; CANR 53

Grenville, Pelham
See Wodehouse, P(elham) G(renville)

Greve, Felix Paul (Berthold Friedrich)
1879-1948
See Grove, Frederick Philip
See also CA 104; 141; DAC; DAM MST

Grey, Zane
1872-1939 . . . . **TCLC 6; DAM POP**
See also CA 104; 132; DLB 9; MTCW

Grieg, (Johan) Nordahl (Brun)
1902-1943 . . . . **TCLC 10**
See also CA 107

Grieve, C(hristopher) M(urray)
1892-1978 . . . . **CLC 11, 19; DAM POET**
See also MacDiarmid, Hugh; Pteleon
See also CA 5-8R; 85-88; CANR 33;
MTCW

Griffin, Gerald 1803-1840 .... **NCLC 7**
See also DLB 159

Griffin, John Howard 1920-1980.... **CLC 68**
See also AITN 1; CA 1-4R; 101; CANR 2

Griffin, Peter 1942- .... **CLC 39**
See also CA 136

Griffiths, Trevor 1935-........ **CLC 13, 52**
See also CA 97-100; CANR 45; DLB 13

Grigson, Geoffrey (Edward Harvey)
1905-1985 .... **CLC 7, 39**
See also CA 25-28R; 118; CANR 20, 33;
DLB 27; MTCW

Grillparzer, Franz 1791-1872...... **NCLC 1**
See also DLB 133

Grimble, Reverend Charles James
See Eliot, T(homas) S(tearns)

Grimke, Charlotte L(ottie) Forten
1837(?)-1914
See Forten, Charlotte L.
See also BW 1; CA 117; 124; DAM MULT,
POET

Grimm, Jacob Ludwig Karl
1785-1863 .... **NCLC 3**
See also DLB 90; MAICYA; SATA 22

Grimm, Wilhelm Karl 1786-1859 .. **NCLC 3**
See also DLB 90; MAICYA; SATA 22

Grimmelshausen, Johann Jakob Christoffel
von 1621-1676 .... **LC 6**
See also DLB 168

Grindel, Eugene 1895-1952
See Eluard, Paul
See also CA 104

Grisham, John 1955- .. **CLC 84; DAM POP**
See also AAYA 14; CA 138; CANR 47

Grossman, David 1954- .... **CLC 67**
See also CA 138

Grossman, Vasily (Semenovich)
1905-1964 .... **CLC 41**
See also CA 124; 130; MTCW

Grove, Frederick Philip .... **TCLC 4**
See also Greve, Felix Paul (Berthold
Friedrich)
See also DLB 92

Grubb
See Crumb, R(obert)

Grumbach, Doris (Isaac)
1918- .... **CLC 13, 22, 64**
See also CA 5-8R; CAAS 2; CANR 9, 42;
INT CANR-9

Grundtvig, Nicolai Frederik Severin
1783-1872 .... **NCLC 1**

Grunge
See Crumb, R(obert)

Grunwald, Lisa 1959-............. **CLC 44**
See also CA 120

Guare, John
1938- .... **CLC 8, 14, 29, 67;
DAM DRAM**
See also CA 73-76; CANR 21; DLB 7;
MTCW

Gudjonsson, Halldor Kiljan 1902-
See Laxness, Halldor
See also CA 103

Guenter, Erich
See Eich, Guenter

Guest, Barbara 1920-............ **CLC 34**
See also CA 25-28R; CANR 11, 44; DLB 5

Guest, Judith (Ann)
1936- .... **CLC 8, 30; DAM NOV, POP**
See also AAYA 7; CA 77-80; CANR 15;
INT CANR-15; MTCW

Guevara, Che .... **CLC 87; HLC**
See also Guevara (Serna), Ernesto

Guevara (Serna), Ernesto 1928-1967
See Guevara, Che
See also CA 127; 111; DAM MULT; HW

Guild, Nicholas M. 1944-......... **CLC 33**
See also CA 93-96

Guillemin, Jacques
See Sartre, Jean-Paul

Guillen, Jorge
1893-1984 ...... **CLC 11; DAM MULT,
POET**
See also CA 89-92; 112; DLB 108; HW

Guillen, Nicolas (Cristobal)
1902-1989 .... **CLC 48, 79; BLC;
DAM MST, MULT, POET; HLC**
See also BW 2; CA 116; 125; 129; HW

Guillevic, (Eugene) 1907-......... **CLC 33**
See also CA 93-96

Guillois
See Desnos, Robert

Guillois, Valentin
See Desnos, Robert

Guiney, Louise Imogen
1861-1920 .... **TCLC 41**
See also DLB 54

Guiraldes, Ricardo (Guillermo)
1886-1927 .... **TCLC 39**
See also CA 131; HW; MTCW

Gumilev, Nikolai Stephanovich
1886-1921 .... **TCLC 60**

GuneSekera, Romesh.............. **CLC 91**

Gunn, Bill .... **CLC 5**
See also Gunn, William Harrison
See also DLB 38

Gunn, Thom(son William)
1929- .... **CLC 3, 6, 18, 32, 81;
DAM POET**
See also CA 17-20R; CANR 9, 33;
CDBLB 1960 to Present; DLB 27;
INT CANR-33; MTCW

Gunn, William Harrison 1934(?)-1989
See Gunn, Bill
See also AITN 1; BW 1; CA 13-16R; 128;
CANR 12, 25

Gunnars, Kristjana 1948-......... **CLC 69**
See also CA 113; DLB 60

Gurganus, Allan
1947- .... **CLC 70; DAM POP**
See also BEST 90:1; CA 135

Gurney, A(lbert) R(amsdell), Jr.
1930- .... **CLC 32, 50, 54; DAM DRAM**
See also CA 77-80; CANR 32

Gurney, Ivor (Bertie) 1890-1937 ... **TCLC 33**

Gurney, Peter
See Gurney, A(lbert) R(amsdell), Jr.

Guro, Elena 1877-1913.......... **TCLC 56**

Gustafson, Ralph (Barker) 1909-.... **CLC 36**
See also CA 21-24R; CANR 8, 45; DLB 88

Gut, Gom
See Simenon, Georges (Jacques Christian)

Guterson, David 1956-............ **CLC 91**
See also CA 132

Guthrie, A(lfred) B(ertram), Jr.
1901-1991 .... **CLC 23**
See also CA 57-60; 134; CANR 24; DLB 6;
SATA 62; SATA-Obit 67

Guthrie, Isobel
See Grieve, C(hristopher) M(urray)

Guthrie, Woodrow Wilson 1912-1967
See Guthrie, Woody
See also CA 113; 93-96

Guthrie, Woody................... **CLC 35**
See also Guthrie, Woodrow Wilson

Guy, Rosa (Cuthbert) 1928-........ **CLC 26**
See also AAYA 4; BW 2; CA 17-20R;
CANR 14, 34; CLR 13; DLB 33; JRDA;
MAICYA; SATA 14, 62

Gwendolyn
See Bennett, (Enoch) Arnold

H. D. .... **CLC 3, 8, 14, 31, 34, 73; PC 5**
See also Doolittle, Hilda

H. de V.
See Buchan, John

Haavikko, Paavo Juhani
1931-.................... **CLC 18, 34**
See also CA 106

Habbema, Koos
See Heijermans, Herman

Hacker, Marilyn
1942- .... **CLC 5, 9, 23, 72, 91;
DAM POET**
See also CA 77-80; DLB 120

Haggard, H(enry) Rider
1856-1925 .... **TCLC 11**
See also CA 108; 148; DLB 70, 156, 174;
SATA 16

Hagiosy, L.
See Larbaud, Valery (Nicolas)

Hagiwara Sakutaro 1886-1942 .... **TCLC 60**

Haig, Fenil
See Ford, Ford Madox

Haig-Brown, Roderick (Langmere)
1908-1976 .... **CLC 21**
See also CA 5-8R; 69-72; CANR 4, 38;
CLR 31; DLB 88; MAICYA; SATA 12

Hailey, Arthur
1920- .... **CLC 5; DAM NOV, POP**
See also AITN 2; BEST 90:3; CA 1-4R;
CANR 2, 36; DLB 88; DLBY 82; MTCW

Hailey, Elizabeth Forsythe 1938-... **CLC 40**
See also CA 93-96; CAAS 1; CANR 15, 48;
INT CANR-15

Haines, John (Meade) 1924-....... **CLC 58**
See also CA 17-20R; CANR 13, 34; DLB 5

Hakluyt, Richard 1552-1616 .... **LC 31**

Haldeman, Joe (William) 1943-..... **CLC 61**
See also CA 53-56; CAAS 25; CANR 6;
DLB 8; INT CANR-6

Haley, Alex(ander Murray Palmer)
1921-1992 .... **CLC 8, 12, 76; BLC; DA;**
DAB; DAC; DAM MST, MULT, POP
See also BW 2; CA 77-80; 136; DLB 38;
MTCW

Haliburton, Thomas Chandler
1796-1865 .... **NCLC 15**
See also DLB 11, 99

Hall, Donald (Andrew, Jr.)
1928- .. **CLC 1, 13, 37, 59; DAM POET**
See also CA 5-8R; CAAS 7; CANR 2, 44;
DLB 5; SATA 23

Hall, Frederic Sauser
See Sauser-Hall, Frederic

Hall, James
See Kuttner, Henry

Hall, James Norman 1887-1951 ... **TCLC 23**
See also CA 123; SATA 21

Hall, (Marguerite) Radclyffe
1886-1943 .... **TCLC 12**
See also CA 110; 150

Hall, Rodney 1935- .... **CLC 51**
See also CA 109

Halleck, Fitz-Greene 1790-1867 .. **NCLC 47**
See also DLB 3

Halliday, Michael
See Creasey, John

Halpern, Daniel 1945- .... **CLC 14**
See also CA 33-36R

Hamburger, Michael (Peter Leopold)
1924- .... **CLC 5, 14**
See also CA 5-8R; CAAS 4; CANR 2, 47;
DLB 27

Hamill, Pete 1935- .... **CLC 10**
See also CA 25-28R; CANR 18

Hamilton, Alexander
1755(?)-1804 .... **NCLC 49**
See also DLB 37

Hamilton, Clive
See Lewis, C(live) S(taples)

Hamilton, Edmond 1904-1977 .... **CLC 1**
See also CA 1-4R; CANR 3; DLB 8

Hamilton, Eugene (Jacob) Lee
See Lee-Hamilton, Eugene (Jacob)

Hamilton, Franklin
See Silverberg, Robert

Hamilton, Gail
See Corcoran, Barbara

Hamilton, Mollie
See Kaye, M(ary) M(argaret)

Hamilton, (Anthony Walter) Patrick
1904-1962 .... **CLC 51**
See also CA 113; DLB 10

Hamilton, Virginia
1936- .... **CLC 26; DAM MULT**
See also AAYA 2; BW 2; CA 25-28R;
CANR 20, 37; CLR 1, 11, 40; DLB 33,
52; INT CANR-20; JRDA; MAICYA;
MTCW; SATA 4, 56, 79

Hammett, (Samuel) Dashiell
1894-1961 .... **CLC 3, 5, 10, 19, 47;**
SSC 17
See also AITN 1; CA 81-84; CANR 42;
CDALB 1929-1941; DLBD 6; MTCW

Hammon, Jupiter
1711(?)-1800(?) .... **NCLC 5; BLC;**
DAM MULT, POET; PC 16
See also DLB 31, 50

Hammond, Keith
See Kuttner, Henry

Hamner, Earl (Henry), Jr. 1923- ... **CLC 12**
See also AITN 2; CA 73-76; DLB 6

Hampton, Christopher (James)
1946- .... **CLC 4**
See also CA 25-28R; DLB 13; MTCW

Hamsun, Knut .... **TCLC 2, 14, 49**
See also Pedersen, Knut

Handke, Peter
1942- .... **CLC 5, 8, 10, 15, 38;**
DAM DRAM, NOV
See also CA 77-80; CANR 33; DLB 85,
124; MTCW

Hanley, James 1901-1985 ... **CLC 3, 5, 8, 13**
See also CA 73-76; 117; CANR 36; MTCW

Hannah, Barry 1942- .... **CLC 23, 38, 90**
See also CA 108; 110; CANR 43; DLB 6;
INT 110; MTCW

Hannon, Ezra
See Hunter, Evan

Hansberry, Lorraine (Vivian)
1930-1965 ...... **CLC 17, 62; BLC; DA;**
DAB; DAC; DAM DRAM, MST,
MULT; DC 2
See also BW 1; CA 109; 25-28R; CABS 3;
CDALB 1941-1968; DLB 7, 38; MTCW

Hansen, Joseph 1923-............. **CLC 38**
See also CA 29-32R; CAAS 17; CANR 16,
44; INT CANR-16

Hansen, Martin A. 1909-1955..... **TCLC 32**

Hanson, Kenneth O(stlin) 1922- .... **CLC 13**
See also CA 53-56; CANR 7

Hardwick, Elizabeth
1916- .... **CLC 13; DAM NOV**
See also CA 5-8R; CANR 3, 32; DLB 6;
MTCW

Hardy, Thomas
1840-1928 ...... **TCLC 4, 10, 18, 32, 48,**
53; DA; DAB; DAC; DAM MST, NOV,
POET; PC 8; SSC 2; WLC
See also CA 104; 123; CDBLB 1890-1914;
DLB 18, 19, 135; MTCW

Hare, David 1947- .... **CLC 29, 58**
See also CA 97-100; CANR 39; DLB 13;
MTCW

Harford, Henry
See Hudson, W(illiam) H(enry)

Hargrave, Leonie
See Disch, Thomas M(ichael)

Harjo, Joy 1951- ... **CLC 83; DAM MULT**
See also CA 114; CANR 35; DLB 120;
NNAL

Harlan, Louis R(udolph) 1922- ..... **CLC 34**
See also CA 21-24R; CANR 25, 55

Harling, Robert 1951(?)- .... **CLC 53**
See also CA 147

Harmon, William (Ruth) 1938- ..... **CLC 38**
See also CA 33-36R; CANR 14, 32, 35;
SATA 65

Harper, F. E. W.
See Harper, Frances Ellen Watkins

Harper, Frances E. W.
See Harper, Frances Ellen Watkins

Harper, Frances E. Watkins
See Harper, Frances Ellen Watkins

Harper, Frances Ellen
See Harper, Frances Ellen Watkins

Harper, Frances Ellen Watkins
1825-1911 .... **TCLC 14; BLC;**
DAM MULT, POET
See also BW 1; CA 111; 125; DLB 50

Harper, Michael S(teven) 1938- .. **CLC 7, 22**
See also BW 1; CA 33-36R; CANR 24;
DLB 41

Harper, Mrs. F. E. W.
See Harper, Frances Ellen Watkins

Harris, Christie (Lucy) Irwin
1907- .... **CLC 12**
See also CA 5-8R; CANR 6; DLB 88;
JRDA; MAICYA; SAAS 10; SATA 6, 74

Harris, Frank 1856-1931 .... **TCLC 24**
See also CA 109; 150; DLB 156

Harris, George Washington
1814-1869 .... **NCLC 23**
See also DLB 3, 11

Harris, Joel Chandler
1848-1908 .... **TCLC 2; SSC 19**
See also CA 104; 137; DLB 11, 23, 42, 78,
91; MAICYA; YABC 1

Harris, John (Wyndham Parkes Lucas)
Beynon 1903-1969
See Wyndham, John
See also CA 102; 89-92

Harris, MacDonald .... **CLC 9**
See also Heiney, Donald (William)

Harris, Mark 1922- .... **CLC 19**
See also CA 5-8R; CAAS 3; CANR 2, 55;
DLB 2; DLBY 80

Harris, (Theodore) Wilson 1921-.... **CLC 25**
See also BW 2; CA 65-68; CAAS 16;
CANR 11, 27; DLB 117; MTCW

Harrison, Elizabeth Cavanna 1909-
See Cavanna, Betty
See also CA 9-12R; CANR 6, 27

Harrison, Harry (Max) 1925- ...... **CLC 42**
See also CA 1-4R; CANR 5, 21; DLB 8;
SATA 4

Harrison, James (Thomas)
1937- .... **CLC 6, 14, 33, 66; SSC 19**
See also CA 13-16R; CANR 8, 51;
DLBY 82; INT CANR-8

Harrison, Jim
See Harrison, James (Thomas)

Harrison, Kathryn 1961- .... **CLC 70**
See also CA 144

Harrison, Tony 1937- .... **CLC 43**
See also CA 65-68; CANR 44; DLB 40;
MTCW

Harriss, Will(ard Irvin) 1922- ...... **CLC 34**
See also CA 111

Harson, Sley
See Ellison, Harlan (Jay)

Hart, Ellis
See Ellison, Harlan (Jay)

Hart, Josephine
    1942(?)- .... **CLC 70; DAM POP**
    See also CA 138

Hart, Moss
    1904-1961 ...... **CLC 66; DAM DRAM**
    See also CA 109; 89-92; DLB 7

Harte, (Francis) Bret(t)
    1836(?)-1902 .... **TCLC 1, 25; DA; DAC;**
        DAM MST; SSC 8; WLC
    See also CA 104; 140; CDALB 1865-1917;
    DLB 12, 64, 74, 79; SATA 26

Hartley, L(eslie) P(oles)
    1895-1972 .... **CLC 2, 22**
    See also CA 45-48; 37-40R; CANR 33;
    DLB 15, 139; MTCW

Hartman, Geoffrey H.   1929-....... **CLC 27**
    See also CA 117; 125; DLB 67

Hartmann von Aue
    c. 1160-c. 1205 .... **CMLC 15**
    See also DLB 138

Hartmann von Aue   1170-1210.... **CMLC 15**

Haruf, Kent   1943- .... **CLC 34**
    See also CA 149

Harwood, Ronald
    1934- .... **CLC 32; DAM DRAM, MST**
    See also CA 1-4R; CANR 4, 55; DLB 13

Hasek, Jaroslav (Matej Frantisek)
    1883-1923 .... **TCLC 4**
    See also CA 104; 129; MTCW

Hass, Robert   1941-..... **CLC 18, 39; PC 16**
    See also CA 111; CANR 30, 50; DLB 105

Hastings, Hudson
    See Kuttner, Henry

Hastings, Selina. .... **CLC 44**

Hatteras, Amelia
    See Mencken, H(enry) L(ouis)

Hatteras, Owen .... **TCLC 18**
    See also Mencken, H(enry) L(ouis); Nathan,
    George Jean

Hauptmann, Gerhart (Johann Robert)
    1862-1946 ...... **TCLC 4; DAM DRAM**
    See also CA 104; 153; DLB 66, 118

Havel, Vaclav
    1936- .... **CLC 25, 58, 65;**
        DAM DRAM; DC 6
    See also CA 104; CANR 36; MTCW

Haviaras, Stratis .... **CLC 33**
    See also Chaviaras, Strates

Hawes, Stephen   1475(?)-1523(?) ..... **LC 17**

Hawkes, John (Clendennin Burne, Jr.)
    1925- ...... **CLC 1, 2, 3, 4, 7, 9, 14, 15,**
        27, 49
    See also CA 1-4R; CANR 2, 47; DLB 2, 7;
    DLBY 80; MTCW

Hawking, S. W.
    See Hawking, Stephen W(illiam)

Hawking, Stephen W(illiam)
    1942- .... **CLC 63**
    See also AAYA 13; BEST 89:1; CA 126;
    129; CANR 48

Hawthorne, Julian   1846-1934 ..... **TCLC 25**

Hawthorne, Nathaniel
    1804-1864 ...... **NCLC 39; DA; DAB;**
        DAC; DAM MST, NOV; SSC 3; WLC
    See also AAYA 18; CDALB 1640-1865;
    DLB 1, 74; YABC 2

Haxton, Josephine Ayres   1921-
    See Douglas, Ellen
    See also CA 115; CANR 41

Hayaseca y Eizaguirre, Jorge
    See Echegaray (y Eizaguirre), Jose (Maria
    Waldo)

Hayashi Fumiko   1904-1951....... **TCLC 27**

Haycraft, Anna
    See Ellis, Alice Thomas
    See also CA 122

Hayden, Robert E(arl)
    1913-1980 ...... **CLC 5, 9, 14, 37; BLC;**
        DA; DAC; DAM MST, MULT, POET;
        PC 6
    See also BW 1; CA 69-72; 97-100; CABS 2;
    CANR 24; CDALB 1941-1968; DLB 5,
    76; MTCW; SATA 19; SATA-Obit 26

Hayford, J(oseph) E(phraim) Casely
    See Casely-Hayford, J(oseph) E(phraim)

Hayman, Ronald   1932-............ **CLC 44**
    See also CA 25-28R; CANR 18, 50;
    DLB 155

Haywood, Eliza (Fowler)
    1693(?)-1756 .... **LC 1**

Hazlitt, William   1778-1830 ...... **NCLC 29**
    See also DLB 110, 158

Hazzard, Shirley   1931- .... **CLC 18**
    See also CA 9-12R; CANR 4; DLBY 82;
    MTCW

Head, Bessie
    1937-1986 .... **CLC 25, 67; BLC;**
        DAM MULT
    See also BW 2; CA 29-32R; 119; CANR 25;
    DLB 117; MTCW

Headon, (Nicky) Topper   1956(?)- ... **CLC 30**

Heaney, Seamus (Justin)
    1939- ...... **CLC 5, 7, 14, 25, 37, 74, 91;**
        DAB; DAM POET
    See also CA 85-88; CANR 25, 48;
    CDBLB 1960 to Present; DLB 40;
    DLBY 95; MTCW

Hearn, (Patricio) Lafcadio (Tessima Carlos)
    1850-1904 .... **TCLC 9**
    See also CA 105; DLB 12, 78

Hearne, Vicki   1946-.............. **CLC 56**
    See also CA 139

Hearon, Shelby   1931-............. **CLC 63**
    See also AITN 2; CA 25-28R; CANR 18,
    48

Heat-Moon, William Least......... **CLC 29**
    See also Trogdon, William (Lewis)
    See also AAYA 9

Hebbel, Friedrich
    1813-1863 .... **NCLC 43; DAM DRAM**
    See also DLB 129

Hebert, Anne
    1916- .... **CLC 4, 13, 29; DAC;**
        DAM MST, POET
    See also CA 85-88; DLB 68; MTCW

Hecht, Anthony (Evan)
    1923- ...... **CLC 8, 13, 19; DAM POET**
    See also CA 9-12R; CANR 6; DLB 5, 169

Hecht, Ben   1894-1964 .... **CLC 8**
    See also CA 85-88; DLB 7, 9, 25, 26, 28, 86

Hedayat, Sadeq   1903-1951........ **TCLC 21**
    See also CA 120

Hegel, Georg Wilhelm Friedrich
    1770-1831 .... **NCLC 46**
    See also DLB 90

Heidegger, Martin   1889-1976 ...... **CLC 24**
    See also CA 81-84; 65-68; CANR 34;
    MTCW

Heidenstam, (Carl Gustaf) Verner von
    1859-1940 .... **TCLC 5**
    See also CA 104

Heifner, Jack   1946-.............. **CLC 11**
    See also CA 105; CANR 47

Heijermans, Herman   1864-1924 ... **TCLC 24**
    See also CA 123

Heilbrun, Carolyn G(old)   1926-..... **CLC 25**
    See also CA 45-48; CANR 1, 28

Heine, Heinrich   1797-1856 .... **NCLC 4, 54**
    See also DLB 90

Heinemann, Larry (Curtiss)   1944- .. **CLC 50**
    See also CA 110; CAAS 21; CANR 31;
    DLBD 9; INT CANR-31

Heiney, Donald (William)   1921-1993
    See Harris, MacDonald
    See also CA 1-4R; 142; CANR 3

Heinlein, Robert A(nson)
    1907-1988 ...... **CLC 1, 3, 8, 14, 26, 55;**
        DAM POP
    See also AAYA 17; CA 1-4R; 125;
    CANR 1, 20, 53; DLB 8; JRDA;
    MAICYA; MTCW; SATA 9, 69;
    SATA-Obit 56

Helforth, John
    See Doolittle, Hilda

Hellenhofferu, Vojtech Kapristian z
    See Hasek, Jaroslav (Matej Frantisek)

Heller, Joseph
    1923- .... **CLC 1, 3, 5, 8, 11, 36, 63; DA;**
        DAB; DAC; DAM MST, NOV, POP;
        WLC
    See also AITN 1; CA 5-8R; CABS 1;
    CANR 8, 42; DLB 2, 28; DLBY 80;
    INT CANR-8; MTCW

Hellman, Lillian (Florence)
    1906-1984 ...... **CLC 2, 4, 8, 14, 18, 34,**
        44, 52; DAM DRAM; DC 1
    See also AITN 1, 2; CA 13-16R; 112;
    CANR 33; DLB 7; DLBY 84; MTCW

Helprin, Mark
    1947-.............. **CLC 7, 10, 22, 32;**
        DAM NOV, POP
    See also CA 81-84; CANR 47; DLBY 85;
    MTCW

Helvetius, Claude-Adrien
    1715-1771 .... **LC 26**

Helyar, Jane Penelope Josephine   1933-
    See Poole, Josephine
    See also CA 21-24R; CANR 10, 26;
    SATA 82

Hemans, Felicia   1793-1835 ...... **NCLC 29**
    See also DLB 96

Hemingway, Ernest (Miller)
1899-1961 .... **CLC 1, 3, 6, 8, 10, 13, 19,
30, 34, 39, 41, 44, 50, 61, 80; DA; DAB;
DAC; DAM MST, NOV; SSC 1; WLC**
See also AAYA 19; CA 77-80; CANR 34;
CDALB 1917-1929; DLB 4, 9, 102;
DLBD 1; DLBY 81, 87; MTCW

Hempel, Amy 1951- .... **CLC 39**
See also CA 118; 137

Henderson, F. C.
See Mencken, H(enry) L(ouis)

Henderson, Sylvia
See Ashton-Warner, Sylvia (Constance)

Henley, Beth .... **CLC 23; DC 6**
See also Henley, Elizabeth Becker
See also CABS 3; DLBY 86

Henley, Elizabeth Becker 1952-
See Henley, Beth
See also CA 107; CANR 32; DAM DRAM,
MST; MTCW

Henley, William Ernest
1849-1903 .... **TCLC 8**
See also CA 105; DLB 19

Hennissart, Martha
See Lathen, Emma
See also CA 85-88

Henry, O. .... **TCLC 1, 19; SSC 5; WLC**
See also Porter, William Sydney

Henry, Patrick 1736-1799 .... **LC 25**

Henryson, Robert 1430(?)-1506(?).... **LC 20**
See also DLB 146

Henry VIII 1491-1547 .... **LC 10**

Henschke, Alfred
See Klabund

Hentoff, Nat(han Irving) 1925- ..... **CLC 26**
See also AAYA 4; CA 1-4R; CAAS 6;
CANR 5, 25; CLR 1; INT CANR-25;
JRDA; MAICYA; SATA 42, 69;
SATA-Brief 27

Heppenstall, (John) Rayner
1911-1981 .... **CLC 10**
See also CA 1-4R; 103; CANR 29

Herbert, Frank (Patrick)
1920-1986 ...... **CLC 12, 23, 35, 44, 85;
DAM POP**
See also CA 53-56; 118; CANR 5, 43;
DLB 8; INT CANR-5; MTCW; SATA 9,
37; SATA-Obit 47

Herbert, George
1593-1633 .... **LC 24; DAB;
DAM POET; PC 4**
See also CDBLB Before 1660; DLB 126

Herbert, Zbigniew
1924- .... **CLC 9, 43; DAM POET**
See also CA 89-92; CANR 36; MTCW

Herbst, Josephine (Frey)
1897-1969 .... **CLC 34**
See also CA 5-8R; 25-28R; DLB 9

Hergesheimer, Joseph
1880-1954 .... **TCLC 11**
See also CA 109; DLB 102, 9

Herlihy, James Leo 1927-1993 ...... **CLC 6**
See also CA 1-4R; 143; CANR 2

Hermogenes fl. c. 175- .... **CMLC 6**

Hernandez, Jose 1834-1886 ...... **NCLC 17**

Herodotus c. 484B.C.-429B.C.... **CMLC 17**

Herrick, Robert
1591-1674 ..... **LC 13; DA; DAB; DAC;
DAM MST, POP; PC 9**
See also DLB 126

Herring, Guilles
See Somerville, Edith

Herriot, James
1916-1995 .... **CLC 12; DAM POP**
See also Wight, James Alfred
See also AAYA 1; CA 148; CANR 40;
SATA 86

Herrmann, Dorothy 1941- .... **CLC 44**
See also CA 107

Herrmann, Taffy
See Herrmann, Dorothy

Hersey, John (Richard)
1914-1993 .... **CLC 1, 2, 7, 9, 40, 81, 97;
DAM POP**
See also CA 17-20R; 140; CANR 33;
DLB 6; MTCW; SATA 25;
SATA-Obit 76

Herzen, Aleksandr Ivanovich
1812-1870 .... **NCLC 10**

Herzl, Theodor 1860-1904 .... **TCLC 36**

Herzog, Werner 1942- .... **CLC 16**
See also CA 89-92

Hesiod c. 8th cent. B.C.- .... **CMLC 5**

Hesse, Hermann
1877-1962 .... **CLC 1, 2, 3, 6, 11, 17, 25,
69; DA; DAB; DAC; DAM MST, NOV;
SSC 9; WLC**
See also CA 17-18; CAP 2; DLB 66;
MTCW; SATA 50

Hewes, Cady
See De Voto, Bernard (Augustine)

Heyen, William 1940- .... **CLC 13, 18**
See also CA 33-36R; CAAS 9; DLB 5

Heyerdahl, Thor 1914- .... **CLC 26**
See also CA 5-8R; CANR 5, 22; MTCW;
SATA 2, 52

Heym, Georg (Theodor Franz Arthur)
1887-1912 .... **TCLC 9**
See also CA 106

Heym, Stefan 1913- .... **CLC 41**
See also CA 9-12R; CANR 4; DLB 69

Heyse, Paul (Johann Ludwig von)
1830-1914 .... **TCLC 8**
See also CA 104; DLB 129

Heyward, (Edwin) DuBose
1885-1940 .... **TCLC 59**
See also CA 108; DLB 7, 9, 45; SATA 21

Hibbert, Eleanor Alice Burford
1906-1993 .... **CLC 7; DAM POP**
See also BEST 90:4; CA 17-20R; 140;
CANR 9, 28; SATA 2; SATA-Obit 74

Hichens, Robert S. 1864-1950 ..... **TCLC 64**
See also DLB 153

Higgins, George V(incent)
1939- .... **CLC 4, 7, 10, 18**
See also CA 77-80; CAAS 5; CANR 17, 51;
DLB 2; DLBY 81; INT CANR-17;
MTCW

Higginson, Thomas Wentworth
1823-1911 .... **TCLC 36**
See also DLB 1, 64

Highet, Helen
See MacInnes, Helen (Clark)

Highsmith, (Mary) Patricia
1921-1995 .... **CLC 2, 4, 14, 42;
DAM NOV, POP**
See also CA 1-4R; 147; CANR 1, 20, 48;
MTCW

Highwater, Jamake (Mamake)
1942(?)- .... **CLC 12**
See also AAYA 7; CA 65-68; CAAS 7;
CANR 10, 34; CLR 17; DLB 52;
DLBY 85; JRDA; MAICYA; SATA 32,
69; SATA-Brief 30

Highway, Tomson
1951- ..... **CLC 92; DAC; DAM MULT**
See also CA 151; NNAL

Higuchi, Ichiyo 1872-1896....... **NCLC 49**

Hijuelos, Oscar
1951- .... **CLC 65; DAM MULT, POP;
HLC**
See also BEST 90:1; CA 123; CANR 50;
DLB 145; HW

Hikmet, Nazim 1902(?)-1963....... **CLC 40**
See also CA 141; 93-96

Hildesheimer, Wolfgang
1916-1991 .... **CLC 49**
See also CA 101; 135; DLB 69, 124

Hill, Geoffrey (William)
1932- ... **CLC 5, 8, 18, 45; DAM POET**
See also CA 81-84; CANR 21;
CDBLB 1960 to Present; DLB 40;
MTCW

Hill, George Roy 1921- .... **CLC 26**
See also CA 110; 122

Hill, John
See Koontz, Dean R(ay)

Hill, Susan (Elizabeth)
1942- .. **CLC 4; DAB; DAM MST, NOV**
See also CA 33-36R; CANR 29; DLB 14,
139; MTCW

Hillerman, Tony
1925- .... **CLC 62; DAM POP**
See also AAYA 6; BEST 89:1; CA 29-32R;
CANR 21, 42; SATA 6

Hillesum, Etty 1914-1943 .... **TCLC 49**
See also CA 137

Hilliard, Noel (Harvey) 1929-...... **CLC 15**
See also CA 9-12R; CANR 7

Hillis, Rick 1956-................ **CLC 66**
See also CA 134

Hilton, James 1900-1954........ **TCLC 21**
See also CA 108; DLB 34, 77; SATA 34

Himes, Chester (Bomar)
1909-1984 .... **CLC 2, 4, 7, 18, 58; BLC;
DAM MULT**
See also BW 2; CA 25-28R; 114; CANR 22;
DLB 2, 76, 143; MTCW

Hinde, Thomas .... **CLC 6, 11**
See also Chitty, Thomas Willes

Hindin, Nathan
See Bloch, Robert (Albert)

Hine, (William) Daryl 1936- . . . . **CLC 15**
See also CA 1-4R; CAAS 15; CANR 1, 20;
DLB 60

Hinkson, Katharine Tynan
See Tynan, Katharine

Hinton, S(usan) E(loise)
1950- . . . . **CLC 30; DA; DAB; DAC;**
                                    DAM MST, NOV
See also AAYA 2; CA 81-84; CANR 32;
CLR 3, 23; JRDA; MAICYA; MTCW;
SATA 19, 58

Hippius, Zinaida . . . . **TCLC 9**
See also Gippius, Zinaida (Nikolayevna)

Hiraoka, Kimitake 1925-1970
See Mishima, Yukio
See also CA 97-100; 29-32R; DAM DRAM;
MTCW

Hirsch, E(ric) D(onald), Jr. 1928- . . . **CLC 79**
See also CA 25-28R; CANR 27, 51;
DLB 67; INT CANR-27; MTCW

Hirsch, Edward 1950- . . . . **CLC 31, 50**
See also CA 104; CANR 20, 42; DLB 120

Hitchcock, Alfred (Joseph)
1899-1980 . . . . **CLC 16**
See also CA 97-100; SATA 27;
SATA-Obit 24

Hitler, Adolf 1889-1945 . . . . **TCLC 53**
See also CA 117; 147

Hoagland, Edward 1932- . . . . **CLC 28**
See also CA 1-4R; CANR 2, 31; DLB 6;
SATA 51

Hoban, Russell (Conwell)
1925- . . . . **CLC 7, 25; DAM NOV**
See also CA 5-8R; CANR 23, 37; CLR 3;
DLB 52; MAICYA; MTCW; SATA 1,
40, 78

Hobbs, Perry
See Blackmur, R(ichard) P(almer)

Hobson, Laura Z(ametkin)
1900-1986 . . . . **CLC 7, 25**
See also CA 17-20R; 118; CANR 55;
DLB 28; SATA 52

Hochhuth, Rolf
1931- . . . . . **CLC 4, 11, 18; DAM DRAM**
See also CA 5-8R; CANR 33; DLB 124;
MTCW

Hochman, Sandra 1936- . . . . **CLC 3, 8**
See also CA 5-8R; DLB 5

Hochwaelder, Fritz
1911-1986 . . . . . . **CLC 36; DAM DRAM**
See also CA 29-32R; 120; CANR 42;
MTCW

Hochwalder, Fritz
See Hochwaelder, Fritz

Hocking, Mary (Eunice) 1921- . . . . . **CLC 13**
See also CA 101; CANR 18, 40

Hodgins, Jack 1938- . . . . **CLC 23**
See also CA 93-96; DLB 60

Hodgson, William Hope
1877(?)-1918 . . . . **TCLC 13**
See also CA 111; DLB 70, 153, 156

Hoeg, Peter 1957- . . . . **CLC 95**
See also CA 151

Hoffman, Alice
1952- . . . . **CLC 51; DAM NOV**
See also CA 77-80; CANR 34; MTCW

Hoffman, Daniel (Gerard)
1923- . . . . **CLC 6, 13, 23**
See also CA 1-4R; CANR 4; DLB 5

Hoffman, Stanley 1944- . . . . **CLC 5**
See also CA 77-80

Hoffman, William M(oses) 1939- . . . **CLC 40**
See also CA 57-60; CANR 11

Hoffmann, E(rnst) T(heodor) A(madeus)
1776-1822 . . . . **NCLC 2; SSC 13**
See also DLB 90; SATA 27

Hofmann, Gert 1931- . . . . **CLC 54**
See also CA 128

Hofmannsthal, Hugo von
1874-1929 . . . . **TCLC 11; DAM DRAM;**
                                                             DC 4
See also CA 106; 153; DLB 81, 118

Hogan, Linda
1947- . . . . **CLC 73; DAM MULT**
See also CA 120; CANR 45; NNAL

Hogarth, Charles
See Creasey, John

Hogarth, Emmett
See Polonsky, Abraham (Lincoln)

Hogg, James 1770-1835 . . . . **NCLC 4**
See also DLB 93, 116, 159

Holbach, Paul Henri Thiry Baron
1723-1789 . . . . **LC 14**

Holberg, Ludvig 1684-1754 . . . . **LC 6**

Holden, Ursula 1921- . . . . **CLC 18**
See also CA 101; CAAS 8; CANR 22

Holderlin, (Johann Christian) Friedrich
1770-1843 . . . . **NCLC 16; PC 4**

Holdstock, Robert
See Holdstock, Robert P.

Holdstock, Robert P. 1948- . . . . **CLC 39**
See also CA 131

Holland, Isabelle 1920- . . . . **CLC 21**
See also AAYA 11; CA 21-24R; CANR 10,
25, 47; JRDA; MAICYA; SATA 8, 70

Holland, Marcus
See Caldwell, (Janet Miriam) Taylor
(Holland)

Hollander, John 1929- . . . . . . **CLC 2, 5, 8, 14**
See also CA 1-4R; CANR 1, 52; DLB 5;
SATA 13

Hollander, Paul
See Silverberg, Robert

Holleran, Andrew 1943(?)- . . . . **CLC 38**
See also CA 144

Hollinghurst, Alan 1954- . . . . **CLC 55, 91**
See also CA 114

Hollis, Jim
See Summers, Hollis (Spurgeon, Jr.)

Holly, Buddy 1936-1959 . . . . **TCLC 65**

Holmes, John
See Souster, (Holmes) Raymond

Holmes, John Clellon 1926-1988 . . . . **CLC 56**
See also CA 9-12R; 125; CANR 4; DLB 16

Holmes, Oliver Wendell
1809-1894 . . . . **NCLC 14**
See also CDALB 1640-1865; DLB 1;
SATA 34

Holmes, Raymond
See Souster, (Holmes) Raymond

Holt, Victoria
See Hibbert, Eleanor Alice Burford

Holub, Miroslav 1923- . . . . **CLC 4**
See also CA 21-24R; CANR 10

Homer
c. 8th cent. B.C.- . . . . . **CMLC 1, 16; DA;**
                            DAB; DAC; DAM MST, POET

Honig, Edwin 1919- . . . . **CLC 33**
See also CA 5-8R; CAAS 8; CANR 4, 45;
DLB 5

Hood, Hugh (John Blagdon)
1928- . . . . **CLC 15, 28**
See also CA 49-52; CAAS 17; CANR 1, 33;
DLB 53

Hood, Thomas 1799-1845 . . . . **NCLC 16**
See also DLB 96

Hooker, (Peter) Jeremy 1941- . . . . . . **CLC 43**
See also CA 77-80; CANR 22; DLB 40

hooks, bell . . . . **CLC 94**
See also Watkins, Gloria

Hope, A(lec) D(erwent) 1907- . . . . **CLC 3, 51**
See also CA 21-24R; CANR 33; MTCW

Hope, Brian
See Creasey, John

Hope, Christopher (David Tully)
1944- . . . . **CLC 52**
See also CA 106; CANR 47; SATA 62

Hopkins, Gerard Manley
1844-1889 . . . . **NCLC 17; DA; DAB;**
          DAC; DAM MST, POET; PC 15; WLC
See also CDBLB 1890-1914; DLB 35, 57

Hopkins, John (Richard) 1931- . . . . . . **CLC 4**
See also CA 85-88

Hopkins, Pauline Elizabeth
1859-1930 . . . . **TCLC 28; BLC;**
                                                       DAM MULT
See also BW 2; CA 141; DLB 50

Hopkinson, Francis 1737-1791 . . . . . . **LC 25**
See also DLB 31

Hopley-Woolrich, Cornell George 1903-1968
See Woolrich, Cornell
See also CA 13-14; CAP 1

Horatio
See Proust, (Valentin-Louis-George-Eugene-)
Marcel

Horgan, Paul (George Vincent O'Shaughnessy)
1903-1995 . . . . . . **CLC 9, 53; DAM NOV**
See also CA 13-16R; 147; CANR 9, 35;
DLB 102; DLBY 85; INT CANR-9;
MTCW; SATA 13; SATA-Obit 84

Horn, Peter
See Kuttner, Henry

Hornem, Horace Esq.
See Byron, George Gordon (Noel)

Hornung, E(rnest) W(illiam)
1866-1921 . . . . **TCLC 59**
See also CA 108; DLB 70

Horovitz, Israel (Arthur)
  1939- . . . . **CLC 56; DAM DRAM**
  See also CA 33-36R; CANR 46; DLB 7

Horvath, Odon von
  See Horvath, Oedoen von
  See also DLB 85, 124

Horvath, Oedoen von 1901-1938. . . **TCLC 45**
  See also Horvath, Odon von
  See also CA 118

Horwitz, Julius 1920-1986. . . . . **CLC 14**
  See also CA 9-12R; 119; CANR 12

Hospital, Janette Turner 1942- . . . . . **CLC 42**
  See also CA 108; CANR 48

Hostos, E. M. de
  See Hostos (y Bonilla), Eugenio Maria de

Hostos, Eugenio M. de
  See Hostos (y Bonilla), Eugenio Maria de

Hostos, Eugenio Maria
  See Hostos (y Bonilla), Eugenio Maria de

Hostos (y Bonilla), Eugenio Maria de
  1839-1903 . . . . **TCLC 24**
  See also CA 123; 131; HW

Houdini
  See Lovecraft, H(oward) P(hillips)

Hougan, Carolyn 1943- . . . . **CLC 34**
  See also CA 139

Household, Geoffrey (Edward West)
  1900-1988 . . . . **CLC 11**
  See also CA 77-80; 126; DLB 87; SATA 14;
  SATA-Obit 59

Housman, A(lfred) E(dward)
  1859-1936 . . . . . . **TCLC 1, 10; DA; DAB;**
  DAC; DAM MST, POET; PC 2
  See also CA 104; 125; DLB 19; MTCW

Housman, Laurence 1865-1959 . . . . . **TCLC 7**
  See also CA 106; DLB 10; SATA 25

Howard, Elizabeth Jane 1923- . . . **CLC 7, 29**
  See also CA 5-8R; CANR 8

Howard, Maureen 1930- . . . . . **CLC 5, 14, 46**
  See also CA 53-56; CANR 31; DLBY 83;
  INT CANR-31; MTCW

Howard, Richard 1929- . . . . . . **CLC 7, 10, 47**
  See also AITN 1; CA 85-88; CANR 25;
  DLB 5; INT CANR-25

Howard, Robert Ervin 1906-1936 . . . **TCLC 8**
  See also CA 105

Howard, Warren F.
  See Pohl, Frederik

Howe, Fanny 1940- . . . . **CLC 47**
  See also CA 117; SATA-Brief 52

Howe, Irving 1920-1993 . . . . **CLC 85**
  See also CA 9-12R; 141; CANR 21, 50;
  DLB 67; MTCW

Howe, Julia Ward 1819-1910 . . . . . **TCLC 21**
  See also CA 117; DLB 1

Howe, Susan 1937- . . . . **CLC 72**
  See also DLB 120

Howe, Tina 1937- . . . . **CLC 48**
  See also CA 109

Howell, James 1594(?)-1666 . . . . **LC 13**
  See also DLB 151

Howells, W. D.
  See Howells, William Dean

Howells, William D.
  See Howells, William Dean

Howells, William Dean
  1837-1920 . . . . **TCLC 7, 17, 41**
  See also CA 104; 134; CDALB 1865-1917;
  DLB 12, 64, 74, 79

Howes, Barbara 1914-1996 . . . . **CLC 15**
  See also CA 9-12R; 151; CAAS 3;
  CANR 53; SATA 5

Hrabal, Bohumil 1914- . . . . **CLC 13, 67**
  See also CA 106; CAAS 12

Hsun, Lu
  See Lu Hsun

Hubbard, L(afayette) Ron(ald)
  1911-1986 . . . . **CLC 43; DAM POP**
  See also CA 77-80; 118; CANR 52

Huch, Ricarda (Octavia)
  1864-1947 . . . . **TCLC 13**
  See also CA 111; DLB 66

Huddle, David 1942- . . . . **CLC 49**
  See also CA 57-60; CAAS 20; DLB 130

Hudson, Jeffrey
  See Crichton, (John) Michael

Hudson, W(illiam) H(enry)
  1841-1922 . . . . **TCLC 29**
  See also CA 115; DLB 98, 153, 174;
  SATA 35

Hueffer, Ford Madox
  See Ford, Ford Madox

Hughart, Barry 1934- . . . . **CLC 39**
  See also CA 137

Hughes, Colin
  See Creasey, John

Hughes, David (John) 1930- . . . . **CLC 48**
  See also CA 116; 129; DLB 14

Hughes, Edward James
  See Hughes, Ted
  See also DAM MST, POET

Hughes, (James) Langston
  1902-1967 . . . . . **CLC 1, 5, 10, 15, 35, 44;**
  BLC; DA; DAB; DAC; DAM DRAM,
  MST, MULT, POET; DC 3; PC 1;
  SSC 6; WLC
  See also AAYA 12; BW 1; CA 1-4R;
  25-28R; CANR 1, 34; CDALB 1929-1941;
  CLR 17; DLB 4, 7, 48, 51, 86; JRDA;
  MAICYA; MTCW; SATA 4, 33

Hughes, Richard (Arthur Warren)
  1900-1976 . . . . . . **CLC 1, 11; DAM NOV**
  See also CA 5-8R; 65-68; CANR 4;
  DLB 15, 161; MTCW; SATA 8;
  SATA-Obit 25

Hughes, Ted
  1930- . . . . **CLC 2, 4, 9, 14, 37; DAB;**
  DAC; PC 7
  See also Hughes, Edward James
  See also CA 1-4R; CANR 1, 33; CLR 3;
  DLB 40, 161; MAICYA; MTCW;
  SATA 49; SATA-Brief 27

Hugo, Richard F(ranklin)
  1923-1982 . . . . **CLC 6, 18, 32;**
  DAM POET
  See also CA 49-52; 108; CANR 3; DLB 5

Hugo, Victor (Marie)
  1802-1885 . . . . **NCLC 3, 10, 21; DA;**
  DAB; DAC; DAM DRAM, MST, NOV,
  POET; WLC
  See also DLB 119; SATA 47

Huidobro, Vicente
  See Huidobro Fernandez, Vicente Garcia

Huidobro Fernandez, Vicente Garcia
  1893-1948 . . . . **TCLC 31**
  See also CA 131; HW

Hulme, Keri 1947- . . . . **CLC 39**
  See also CA 125; INT 125

Hulme, T(homas) E(rnest)
  1883-1917 . . . . **TCLC 21**
  See also CA 117; DLB 19

Hume, David 1711-1776. . . . . **LC 7**
  See also DLB 104

Humphrey, William 1924- . . . . **CLC 45**
  See also CA 77-80; DLB 6

Humphreys, Emyr Owen 1919- . . . . . **CLC 47**
  See also CA 5-8R; CANR 3, 24; DLB 15

Humphreys, Josephine 1945- . . . . **CLC 34, 57**
  See also CA 121; 127; INT 127

Huneker, James Gibbons
  1857-1921 . . . . **TCLC 65**
  See also DLB 71

Hungerford, Pixie
  See Brinsmead, H(esba) F(ay)

Hunt, E(verette) Howard, (Jr.)
  1918- . . . . **CLC 3**
  See also AITN 1; CA 45-48; CANR 2, 47

Hunt, Kyle
  See Creasey, John

Hunt, (James Henry) Leigh
  1784-1859 . . . . . . **NCLC 1; DAM POET**

Hunt, Marsha 1946- . . . . **CLC 70**
  See also BW 2; CA 143

Hunt, Violet 1866-1942 . . . . **TCLC 53**
  See also DLB 162

Hunter, E. Waldo
  See Sturgeon, Theodore (Hamilton)

Hunter, Evan
  1926- . . . . **CLC 11, 31; DAM POP**
  See also CA 5-8R; CANR 5, 38; DLBY 82;
  INT CANR-5; MTCW; SATA 25

Hunter, Kristin (Eggleston) 1931- . . . **CLC 35**
  See also AITN 1; BW 1; CA 13-16R;
  CANR 13; CLR 3; DLB 33;
  INT CANR-13; MAICYA; SAAS 10;
  SATA 12

Hunter, Mollie 1922- . . . . **CLC 21**
  See also McIlwraith, Maureen Mollie
  Hunter
  See also AAYA 13; CANR 37; CLR 25;
  DLB 161; JRDA; MAICYA; SAAS 7;
  SATA 54

Hunter, Robert (?)-1734. . . . . **LC 7**

Hurston, Zora Neale
  1903-1960 . . . . **CLC 7, 30, 61; BLC; DA;**
  DAC; DAM MST, MULT, NOV; SSC 4
  See also AAYA 15; BW 1; CA 85-88;
  DLB 51, 86; MTCW

Huston, John (Marcellus)
  1906-1987 . . . . **CLC 20**
  See also CA 73-76; 123; CANR 34; DLB 26

Hustvedt, Siri 1955-............ **CLC 76**
See also CA 137

Hutten, Ulrich von 1488-1523....... **LC 16**

Huxley, Aldous (Leonard)
1894-1963 ..... **CLC 1, 3, 4, 5, 8, 11, 18,**
35, 79; DA; DAB; DAC; DAM MST,
NOV; WLC
See also AAYA 11; CA 85-88; CANR 44;
CDBLB 1914-1945; DLB 36, 100, 162;
MTCW; SATA 63

Huysmans, Charles Marie Georges
1848-1907
See Huysmans, Joris-Karl
See also CA 104

Huysmans, Joris-Karl............. **TCLC 7**
See also Huysmans, Charles Marie Georges
See also DLB 123

Hwang, David Henry
1957-.... **CLC 55; DAM DRAM; DC 4**
See also CA 127; 132; INT 132

Hyde, Anthony 1946-............ **CLC 42**
See also CA 136

Hyde, Margaret O(ldroyd) 1917-... **CLC 21**
See also CA 1-4R; CANR 1, 36; CLR 23;
JRDA; MAICYA; SAAS 8; SATA 1, 42,
76

Hynes, James 1956(?)-........... **CLC 65**

Ian, Janis 1951- .... **CLC 21**
See also CA 105

Ibanez, Vicente Blasco
See Blasco Ibanez, Vicente

Ibarguengoitia, Jorge 1928-1983.... **CLC 37**
See also CA 124; 113; HW

Ibsen, Henrik (Johan)
1828-1906 .... **TCLC 2, 8, 16, 37, 52;**
DA; DAB; DAC; DAM DRAM, MST;
DC 2; WLC
See also CA 104; 141

Ibuse Masuji 1898-1993........... **CLC 22**
See also CA 127; 141

Ichikawa, Kon 1915-.............. **CLC 20**
See also CA 121

Idle, Eric 1943-................ **CLC 21**
See also Monty Python
See also CA 116; CANR 35

Ignatow, David 1914-...... **CLC 4, 7, 14, 40**
See also CA 9-12R; CAAS 3; CANR 31;
DLB 5

Ihimaera, Witi 1944- .... **CLC 46**
See also CA 77-80

Ilf, Ilya......................... **TCLC 21**
See also Fainzilberg, Ilya Arnoldovich

Illyes, Gyula 1902-1983........... **PC 16**
See also CA 114; 109

Immermann, Karl (Lebrecht)
1796-1840 .... **NCLC 4, 49**
See also DLB 133

Inclan, Ramon (Maria) del Valle
See Valle-Inclan, Ramon (Maria) del

Infante, G(uillermo) Cabrera
See Cabrera Infante, G(uillermo)

Ingalls, Rachel (Holmes) 1940-..... **CLC 42**
See also CA 123; 127

Ingamells, Rex 1913-1955 .... **TCLC 35**

Inge, William (Motter)
1913-1973 .. **CLC 1, 8, 19; DAM DRAM**
See also CA 9-12R; CDALB 1941-1968;
DLB 7; MTCW

Ingelow, Jean 1820-1897 .... **NCLC 39**
See also DLB 35, 163; SATA 33

Ingram, Willis J.
See Harris, Mark

Innaurato, Albert (F.) 1948(?)-... **CLC 21, 60**
See also CA 115; 122; INT 122

Innes, Michael
See Stewart, J(ohn) I(nnes) M(ackintosh)

Ionesco, Eugene
1909-1994 .... **CLC 1, 4, 6, 9, 11, 15, 41,**
86; DA; DAB; DAC; DAM DRAM,
MST; WLC
See also CA 9-12R; 144; CANR 55;
MTCW; SATA 7; SATA-Obit 79

Iqbal, Muhammad 1873-1938 ..... **TCLC 28**

Ireland, Patrick
See O'Doherty, Brian

Iron, Ralph
See Schreiner, Olive (Emilie Albertina)

Irving, John (Winslow)
1942-..... **CLC 13, 23, 38; DAM NOV,**
POP
See also AAYA 8; BEST 89:3; CA 25-28R;
CANR 28; DLB 6; DLBY 82; MTCW

Irving, Washington
1783-1859 ..... **NCLC 2, 19; DA; DAB;**
DAM MST; SSC 2; WLC
See also CDALB 1640-1865; DLB 3, 11, 30,
59, 73, 74; YABC 2

Irwin, P. K.
See Page, P(atricia) K(athleen)

Isaacs, Susan 1943- ... **CLC 32; DAM POP**
See also BEST 89:1; CA 89-92; CANR 20,
41; INT CANR-20; MTCW

Isherwood, Christopher (William Bradshaw)
1904-1986 .... **CLC 1, 9, 11, 14, 44;**
DAM DRAM, NOV
See also CA 13-16R; 117; CANR 35;
DLB 15; DLBY 86; MTCW

Ishiguro, Kazuo
1954-...... **CLC 27, 56, 59; DAM NOV**
See also BEST 90:2; CA 120; CANR 49;
MTCW

Ishikawa, Hakuhin
See Ishikawa, Takuboku

Ishikawa, Takuboku
1886(?)-1912 .... **TCLC 15;**
DAM POET; PC 10
See also CA 113; 153

Iskander, Fazil 1929-............. **CLC 47**
See also CA 102

Isler, Alan .... **CLC 91**

Ivan IV 1530-1584 .... **LC 17**

Ivanov, Vyacheslav Ivanovich
1866-1949 .... **TCLC 33**
See also CA 122

Ivask, Ivar Vidrik 1927-1992....... **CLC 14**
See also CA 37-40R; 139; CANR 24

Ives, Morgan
See Bradley, Marion Zimmer

J. R. S.
See Gogarty, Oliver St. John

Jabran, Kahlil
See Gibran, Kahlil

Jabran, Khalil
See Gibran, Kahlil

Jackson, Daniel
See Wingrove, David (John)

Jackson, Jesse 1908-1983 .... **CLC 12**
See also BW 1; CA 25-28R; 109; CANR 27;
CLR 28; MAICYA; SATA 2, 29;
SATA-Obit 48

Jackson, Laura (Riding) 1901-1991
See Riding, Laura
See also CA 65-68; 135; CANR 28; DLB 48

Jackson, Sam
See Trumbo, Dalton

Jackson, Sara
See Wingrove, David (John)

Jackson, Shirley
1919-1965 .... **CLC 11, 60, 87; DA;**
DAC; DAM MST; SSC 9; WLC
See also AAYA 9; CA 1-4R; 25-28R;
CANR 4, 52; CDALB 1941-1968; DLB 6;
SATA 2

Jacob, (Cyprien-)Max 1876-1944 ... **TCLC 6**
See also CA 104

Jacobs, Jim 1942-................ **CLC 12**
See also CA 97-100; INT 97-100

Jacobs, W(illiam) W(ymark)
1863-1943 .... **TCLC 22**
See also CA 121; DLB 135

Jacobsen, Jens Peter 1847-1885 .. **NCLC 34**

Jacobsen, Josephine 1908-........ **CLC 48**
See also CA 33-36R; CAAS 18; CANR 23,
48

Jacobson, Dan 1929- .... **CLC 4, 14**
See also CA 1-4R; CANR 2, 25; DLB 14;
MTCW

Jacqueline
See Carpentier (y Valmont), Alejo

Jagger, Mick 1944-.............. **CLC 17**

Jakes, John (William)
1932-...... **CLC 29; DAM NOV, POP**
See also BEST 89:4; CA 57-60; CANR 10,
43; DLBY 83; INT CANR-10; MTCW;
SATA 62

James, Andrew
See Kirkup, James

James, C(yril) L(ionel) R(obert)
1901-1989 .... **CLC 33**
See also BW 2; CA 117; 125; 128; DLB 125;
MTCW

James, Daniel (Lewis) 1911-1988
See Santiago, Danny
See also CA 125

James, Dynely
See Mayne, William (James Carter)

James, Henry Sr. 1811-1882 ..... **NCLC 53**

James, Henry
1843-1916 ...... **TCLC 2, 11, 24, 40, 47,**
64; DA; DAB; DAC; DAM MST, NOV;
SSC 8; WLC
See also CA 104; 132; CDALB 1865-1917;
DLB 12, 71, 74; DLBD 13; MTCW

James, M. R.
See James, Montague (Rhodes)
See also DLB 156

James, Montague (Rhodes)
1862-1936 . . . . **TCLC 6; SSC 16**
See also CA 104

James, P. D. . . . . **CLC 18, 46**
See also White, Phyllis Dorothy James
See also BEST 90:2; CDBLB 1960 to
Present; DLB 87

James, Philip
See Moorcock, Michael (John)

James, William 1842-1910 . . . . . **TCLC 15, 32**
See also CA 109

James I 1394-1437 . . . . **LC 20**

Jameson, Anna 1794-1860 . . . . . . **NCLC 43**
See also DLB 99, 166

Jami, Nur al-Din 'Abd al-Rahman
1414-1492 . . . . **LC 9**

Jandl, Ernst 1925- . . . . **CLC 34**

Janowitz, Tama
1957- . . . . **CLC 43; DAM POP**
See also CA 106; CANR 52

Japrisot, Sebastien 1931- . . . . **CLC 90**

Jarrell, Randall
1914-1965 . . . . **CLC 1, 2, 6, 9, 13, 49;**
DAM POET
See also CA 5-8R; 25-28R; CABS 2;
CANR 6, 34; CDALB 1941-1968; CLR 6;
DLB 48, 52; MAICYA; MTCW; SATA 7

Jarry, Alfred
1873-1907 . . . . **TCLC 2, 14;**
DAM DRAM; SSC 20
See also CA 104; 153

Jarvis, E. K.
See Bloch, Robert (Albert); Ellison, Harlan
(Jay); Silverberg, Robert

Jeake, Samuel, Jr.
See Aiken, Conrad (Potter)

Jean Paul 1763-1825 . . . . **NCLC 7**

Jefferies, (John) Richard
1848-1887 . . . . **NCLC 47**
See also DLB 98, 141; SATA 16

Jeffers, (John) Robinson
1887-1962 . . . . **CLC 2, 3, 11, 15, 54; DA;**
DAC; DAM MST, POET; WLC
See also CA 85-88; CANR 35;
CDALB 1917-1929; DLB 45; MTCW

Jefferson, Janet
See Mencken, H(enry) L(ouis)

Jefferson, Thomas 1743-1826 . . . . **NCLC 11**
See also CDALB 1640-1865; DLB 31

Jeffrey, Francis 1773-1850 . . . . **NCLC 33**
See also DLB 107

Jelakowitch, Ivan
See Heijermans, Herman

Jellicoe, (Patricia) Ann 1927- . . . . . . **CLC 27**
See also CA 85-88; DLB 13

Jen, Gish . . . . **CLC 70**
See also Jen, Lillian

Jen, Lillian 1956(?)-
See Jen, Gish
See also CA 135

Jenkins, (John) Robin 1912- . . . . . . **CLC 52**
See also CA 1-4R; CANR 1; DLB 14

Jennings, Elizabeth (Joan)
1926- . . . . **CLC 5, 14**
See also CA 61-64; CAAS 5; CANR 8, 39;
DLB 27; MTCW; SATA 66

Jennings, Waylon 1937- . . . . **CLC 21**

Jensen, Johannes V. 1873-1950 . . . . **TCLC 41**

Jensen, Laura (Linnea) 1948- . . . . . . **CLC 37**
See also CA 103

Jerome, Jerome K(lapka)
1859-1927 . . . . **TCLC 23**
See also CA 119; DLB 10, 34, 135

Jerrold, Douglas William
1803-1857 . . . . **NCLC 2**
See also DLB 158, 159

Jewett, (Theodora) Sarah Orne
1849-1909 . . . . **TCLC 1, 22; SSC 6**
See also CA 108; 127; DLB 12, 74;
SATA 15

Jewsbury, Geraldine (Endsor)
1812-1880 . . . . **NCLC 22**
See also DLB 21

Jhabvala, Ruth Prawer
1927- . . . . **CLC 4, 8, 29, 94; DAB;**
DAM NOV
See also CA 1-4R; CANR 2, 29, 51;
DLB 139; INT CANR-29; MTCW

Jibran, Kahlil
See Gibran, Kahlil

Jibran, Khalil
See Gibran, Kahlil

Jiles, Paulette 1943- . . . . **CLC 13, 58**
See also CA 101

Jimenez (Mantecon), Juan Ramon
1881-1958 . . . . . **TCLC 4; DAM MULT,**
POET; HLC; PC 7
See also CA 104; 131; DLB 134; HW;
MTCW

Jimenez, Ramon
See Jimenez (Mantecon), Juan Ramon

Jimenez Mantecon, Juan
See Jimenez (Mantecon), Juan Ramon

Joel, Billy . . . . **CLC 26**
See also Joel, William Martin

Joel, William Martin 1949-
See Joel, Billy
See also CA 108

John of the Cross, St. 1542-1591 . . . . **LC 18**

Johnson, B(ryan) S(tanley William)
1933-1973 . . . . **CLC 6, 9**
See also CA 9-12R; 53-56; CANR 9;
DLB 14, 40

Johnson, Benj. F. of Boo
See Riley, James Whitcomb

Johnson, Benjamin F. of Boo
See Riley, James Whitcomb

Johnson, Charles (Richard)
1948- . . . . **CLC 7, 51, 65; BLC;**
DAM MULT
See also BW 2; CA 116; CAAS 18;
CANR 42; DLB 33

Johnson, Denis 1949- . . . . **CLC 52**
See also CA 117; 121; DLB 120

Johnson, Diane 1934- . . . . **CLC 5, 13, 48**
See also CA 41-44R; CANR 17, 40;
DLBY 80; INT CANR-17; MTCW

Johnson, Eyvind (Olof Verner)
1900-1976 . . . . **CLC 14**
See also CA 73-76; 69-72; CANR 34

Johnson, J. R.
See James, C(yril) L(ionel) R(obert)

Johnson, James Weldon
1871-1938 . . . . **TCLC 3, 19; BLC;**
DAM MULT, POET
See also BW 1; CA 104; 125;
CDALB 1917-1929; CLR 32; DLB 51;
MTCW; SATA 31

Johnson, Joyce 1935- . . . . **CLC 58**
See also CA 125; 129

Johnson, Lionel (Pigot)
1867-1902 . . . . **TCLC 19**
See also CA 117; DLB 19

Johnson, Mel
See Malzberg, Barry N(athaniel)

Johnson, Pamela Hansford
1912-1981 . . . . **CLC 1, 7, 27**
See also CA 1-4R; 104; CANR 2, 28;
DLB 15; MTCW

Johnson, Samuel
1709-1784 . . . . . **LC 15; DA; DAB; DAC;**
DAM MST; WLC
See also CDBLB 1660-1789; DLB 39, 95,
104, 142

Johnson, Uwe
1934-1984 . . . . **CLC 5, 10, 15, 40**
See also CA 1-4R; 112; CANR 1, 39;
DLB 75; MTCW

Johnston, George (Benson) 1913- . . . **CLC 51**
See also CA 1-4R; CANR 5, 20; DLB 88

Johnston, Jennifer 1930- . . . . **CLC 7**
See also CA 85-88; DLB 14

Jolley, (Monica) Elizabeth
1923- . . . . **CLC 46; SSC 19**
See also CA 127; CAAS 13

Jones, Arthur Llewellyn 1863-1947
See Machen, Arthur
See also CA 104

Jones, D(ouglas) G(ordon) 1929- . . . . **CLC 10**
See also CA 29-32R; CANR 13; DLB 53

Jones, David (Michael)
1895-1974 . . . . **CLC 2, 4, 7, 13, 42**
See also CA 9-12R; 53-56; CANR 28;
CDBLB 1945-1960; DLB 20, 100; MTCW

Jones, David Robert 1947-
See Bowie, David
See also CA 103

Jones, Diana Wynne 1934- . . . . **CLC 26**
See also AAYA 12; CA 49-52; CANR 4,
26; CLR 23; DLB 161; JRDA; MAICYA;
SAAS 7; SATA 9, 70

Jones, Edward P. 1950- . . . . **CLC 76**
See also BW 2; CA 142

Jones, Gayl
1949- . . . . **CLC 6, 9; BLC; DAM MULT**
See also BW 2; CA 77-80; CANR 27;
DLB 33; MTCW

Jones, James 1921-1977 . . . . **CLC 1, 3, 10, 39**
See also AITN 1, 2; CA 1-4R; 69-72;
CANR 6; DLB 2, 143; MTCW

Jones, John J.
See Lovecraft, H(oward) P(hillips)

Jones, LeRoi . . . . **CLC 1, 2, 3, 5, 10, 14**
See also Baraka, Amiri

Jones, Louis B. . . . . **CLC 65**
See also CA 141

Jones, Madison (Percy, Jr.) 1925- . . . **CLC 4**
See also CA 13-16R; CAAS 11; CANR 7,
54; DLB 152

Jones, Mervyn 1922- . . . . **CLC 10, 52**
See also CA 45-48; CAAS 5; CANR 1;
MTCW

Jones, Mick 1956(?)- . . . . **CLC 30**

Jones, Nettie (Pearl) 1941- . . . . **CLC 34**
See also BW 2; CA 137; CAAS 20

Jones, Preston 1936-1979 . . . . **CLC 10**
See also CA 73-76; 89-92; DLB 7

Jones, Robert F(rancis) 1934- . . . . **CLC 7**
See also CA 49-52; CANR 2

Jones, Rod 1953- . . . . **CLC 50**
See also CA 128

Jones, Terence Graham Parry
1942- . . . . **CLC 21**
See also Jones, Terry; Monty Python
See also CA 112; 116; CANR 35; INT 116

Jones, Terry
See Jones, Terence Graham Parry
See also SATA 67; SATA-Brief 51

Jones, Thom 1945(?)- . . . . **CLC 81**

Jong, Erica
1942- . . . . **CLC 4, 6, 8, 18, 83;**
DAM NOV, POP
See also AITN 1; BEST 90:2; CA 73-76;
CANR 26, 52; DLB 2, 5, 28, 152;
INT CANR-26; MTCW

Jonson, Ben(jamin)
1572(?)-1637 . . . . . . **LC 6, 33; DA; DAB;**
DAC; DAM DRAM, MST, POET;
DC 4; WLC
See also CDBLB Before 1660; DLB 62, 121

Jordan, June
1936- . . . . . **CLC 5, 11, 23; DAM MULT,**
POET
See also AAYA 2; BW 2; CA 33-36R;
CANR 25; CLR 10; DLB 38; MAICYA;
MTCW; SATA 4

Jordan, Pat(rick M.) 1941- . . . . **CLC 37**
See also CA 33-36R

Jorgensen, Ivar
See Ellison, Harlan (Jay)

Jorgenson, Ivar
See Silverberg, Robert

Josephus, Flavius c. 37-100 . . . . . . **CMLC 13**

Josipovici, Gabriel 1940- . . . . **CLC 6, 43**
See also CA 37-40R; CAAS 8; CANR 47;
DLB 14

Joubert, Joseph 1754-1824 . . . . **NCLC 9**

Jouve, Pierre Jean 1887-1976 . . . . . . **CLC 47**
See also CA 65-68

Joyce, James (Augustine Aloysius)
1882-1941 . . . . **TCLC 3, 8, 16, 35, 52;**
DA; DAB; DAC; DAM MST, NOV,
POET; SSC 3; WLC
See also CA 104; 126; CDBLB 1914-1945;
DLB 10, 19, 36, 162; MTCW

Jozsef, Attila 1905-1937 . . . . **TCLC 22**
See also CA 116

Juana Ines de la Cruz 1651(?)-1695 . . . **LC 5**

Judd, Cyril
See Kornbluth, C(yril) M.; Pohl, Frederik

Julian of Norwich 1342(?)-1416(?) . . . . **LC 6**
See also DLB 146

Juniper, Alex
See Hospital, Janette Turner

Junius
See Luxemburg, Rosa

Just, Ward (Swift) 1935- . . . . **CLC 4, 27**
See also CA 25-28R; CANR 32;
INT CANR-32

Justice, Donald (Rodney)
1925- . . . . **CLC 6, 19; DAM POET**
See also CA 5-8R; CANR 26, 54;
DLBY 83; INT CANR-26

Juvenal c. 55-c. 127 . . . . **CMLC 8**

Juvenis
See Bourne, Randolph S(illiman)

Kacew, Romain 1914-1980
See Gary, Romain
See also CA 108; 102

Kadare, Ismail 1936- . . . . **CLC 52**

Kadohata, Cynthia . . . . **CLC 59**
See also CA 140

Kafka, Franz
1883-1924 . . . . **TCLC 2, 6, 13, 29, 47, 53;**
DA; DAB; DAC; DAM MST, NOV;
SSC 5; WLC
See also CA 105; 126; DLB 81; MTCW

Kahanovitsch, Pinkhes
See Der Nister

Kahn, Roger 1927- . . . . **CLC 30**
See also CA 25-28R; CANR 44; DLB 171;
SATA 37

Kain, Saul
See Sassoon, Siegfried (Lorraine)

Kaiser, Georg 1878-1945 . . . . **TCLC 9**
See also CA 106; DLB 124

Kaletski, Alexander 1946- . . . . **CLC 39**
See also CA 118; 143

Kalidasa fl. c. 400- . . . . **CMLC 9**

Kallman, Chester (Simon)
1921-1975 . . . . **CLC 2**
See also CA 45-48; 53-56; CANR 3

Kaminsky, Melvin 1926-
See Brooks, Mel
See also CA 65-68; CANR 16

Kaminsky, Stuart M(elvin) 1934- . . . **CLC 59**
See also CA 73-76; CANR 29, 53

Kane, Francis
See Robbins, Harold

Kane, Paul
See Simon, Paul (Frederick)

Kane, Wilson
See Bloch, Robert (Albert)

Kanin, Garson 1912- . . . . **CLC 22**
See also AITN 1; CA 5-8R; CANR 7;
DLB 7

Kaniuk, Yoram 1930- . . . . **CLC 19**
See also CA 134

Kant, Immanuel 1724-1804 . . . . . . **NCLC 27**
See also DLB 94

Kantor, MacKinlay 1904-1977 . . . . . . **CLC 7**
See also CA 61-64; 73-76; DLB 9, 102

Kaplan, David Michael 1946- . . . . . . **CLC 50**

Kaplan, James 1951- . . . . **CLC 59**
See also CA 135

Karageorge, Michael
See Anderson, Poul (William)

Karamzin, Nikolai Mikhailovich
1766-1826 . . . . **NCLC 3**
See also DLB 150

Karapanou, Margarita 1946- . . . . **CLC 13**
See also CA 101

Karinthy, Frigyes 1887-1938 . . . . . . **TCLC 47**

Karl, Frederick R(obert) 1927- . . . . . **CLC 34**
See also CA 5-8R; CANR 3, 44

Kastel, Warren
See Silverberg, Robert

Kataev, Evgeny Petrovich 1903-1942
See Petrov, Evgeny
See also CA 120

Kataphusin
See Ruskin, John

Katz, Steve 1935- . . . . **CLC 47**
See also CA 25-28R; CAAS 14; CANR 12;
DLBY 83

Kauffman, Janet 1945- . . . . **CLC 42**
See also CA 117; CANR 43; DLBY 86

Kaufman, Bob (Garnell)
1925-1986 . . . . **CLC 49**
See also BW 1; CA 41-44R; 118; CANR 22;
DLB 16, 41

Kaufman, George S.
1889-1961 . . . . . . **CLC 38; DAM DRAM**
See also CA 108; 93-96; DLB 7; INT 108

Kaufman, Sue . . . . **CLC 3, 8**
See also Barondess, Sue K(aufman)

Kavafis, Konstantinos Petrou 1863-1933
See Cavafy, C(onstantine) P(eter)
See also CA 104

Kavan, Anna 1901-1968 . . . . . . **CLC 5, 13, 82**
See also CA 5-8R; CANR 6; MTCW

Kavanagh, Dan
See Barnes, Julian (Patrick)

Kavanagh, Patrick (Joseph)
1904-1967 . . . . **CLC 22**
See also CA 123; 25-28R; DLB 15, 20;
MTCW

Kawabata, Yasunari
1899-1972 . . . . **CLC 2, 5, 9, 18;**
DAM MULT; SSC 17
See also CA 93-96; 33-36R

Kaye, M(ary) M(argaret) 1909- . . . . . **CLC 28**
See also CA 89-92; CANR 24; MTCW;
SATA 62

Kaye, Mollie
See Kaye, M(ary) M(argaret)

Kaye-Smith, Sheila 1887-1956 . . . . . **TCLC 20**
See also CA 118; DLB 36

Kaymor, Patrice Maguilene
See Senghor, Leopold Sedar

Kazan, Elia 1909- . . . . **CLC 6, 16, 63**
See also CA 21-24R; CANR 32

Kazantzakis, Nikos
1883(?)-1957 . . . . **TCLC 2, 5, 33**
See also CA 105; 132; MTCW

Kazin, Alfred 1915- . . . . **CLC 34, 38**
See also CA 1-4R; CAAS 7; CANR 1, 45;
DLB 67

Keane, Mary Nesta (Skrine) 1904-1996
See Keane, Molly
See also CA 108; 114; 151

Keane, Molly . . . . **CLC 31**
See also Keane, Mary Nesta (Skrine)
See also INT 114

Keates, Jonathan 19(?)- . . . . **CLC 34**

Keaton, Buster 1895-1966 . . . . **CLC 20**

Keats, John
1795-1821 . . . . NCLC 8; DA; DAB;
DAC; DAM MST, POET; PC 1; WLC
See also CDBLB 1789-1832; DLB 96, 110

Keene, Donald 1922- . . . . **CLC 34**
See also CA 1-4R; CANR 5

Keillor, Garrison . . . . **CLC 40**
See also Keillor, Gary (Edward)
See also AAYA 2; BEST 89:3; DLBY 87;
SATA 58

Keillor, Gary (Edward) 1942-
See Keillor, Garrison
See also CA 111; 117; CANR 36;
DAM POP; MTCW

Keith, Michael
See Hubbard, L(afayette) Ron(ald)

Keller, Gottfried 1819-1890 . . . . **NCLC 2**
See also DLB 129

Kellerman, Jonathan
1949- . . . . **CLC 44; DAM POP**
See also BEST 90:1; CA 106; CANR 29, 51;
INT CANR-29

Kelley, William Melvin 1937- . . . . . . **CLC 22**
See also BW 1; CA 77-80; CANR 27;
DLB 33

Kellogg, Marjorie 1922- . . . . **CLC 2**
See also CA 81-84

Kellow, Kathleen
See Hibbert, Eleanor Alice Burford

Kelly, M(ilton) T(erry) 1947- . . . . . . **CLC 55**
See also CA 97-100; CAAS 22; CANR 19,
43

Kelman, James 1946- . . . . **CLC 58, 86**
See also CA 148

Kemal, Yashar 1923- . . . . **CLC 14, 29**
See also CA 89-92; CANR 44

Kemble, Fanny 1809-1893 . . . . **NCLC 18**
See also DLB 32

Kemelman, Harry 1908- . . . . **CLC 2**
See also AITN 1; CA 9-12R; CANR 6;
DLB 28

Kempe, Margery 1373(?)-1440(?) . . . . . **LC 6**
See also DLB 146

Kempis, Thomas a 1380-1471 . . . . **LC 11**

Kendall, Henry 1839-1882 . . . . **NCLC 12**

Keneally, Thomas (Michael)
1935- . . . . . . **CLC 5, 8, 10, 14, 19, 27, 43;**
DAM NOV
See also CA 85-88; CANR 10, 50; MTCW

Kennedy, Adrienne (Lita)
1931- . . . . . **CLC 66; BLC; DAM MULT;**
DC 5
See also BW 2; CA 103; CAAS 20; CABS 3;
CANR 26, 53; DLB 38

Kennedy, John Pendleton
1795-1870 . . . . **NCLC 2**
See also DLB 3

Kennedy, Joseph Charles 1929-
See Kennedy, X. J.
See also CA 1-4R; CANR 4, 30, 40;
SATA 14, 86

Kennedy, William
1928- . . . **CLC 6, 28, 34, 53; DAM NOV**
See also AAYA 1; CA 85-88; CANR 14,
31; DLB 143; DLBY 85; INT CANR-31;
MTCW; SATA 57

Kennedy, X. J. . . . . **CLC 8, 42**
See also Kennedy, Joseph Charles
See also CAAS 9; CLR 27; DLB 5;
SAAS 22

Kenny, Maurice (Francis)
1929- . . . . **CLC 87; DAM MULT**
See also CA 144; CAAS 22; NNAL

Kent, Kelvin
See Kuttner, Henry

Kenton, Maxwell
See Southern, Terry

Kenyon, Robert O.
See Kuttner, Henry

Kerouac, Jack . . . . . **CLC 1, 2, 3, 5, 14, 29, 61**
See also Kerouac, Jean-Louis Lebris de
See also CDALB 1941-1968; DLB 2, 16;
DLBD 3; DLBY 95

Kerouac, Jean-Louis Lebris de 1922-1969
See Kerouac, Jack
See also AITN 1; CA 5-8R; 25-28R;
CANR 26, 54; DA; DAB; DAC;
DAM MST, NOV, POET, POP; MTCW;
WLC

Kerr, Jean 1923- . . . . **CLC 22**
See also CA 5-8R; CANR 7; INT CANR-7

Kerr, M. E. . . . . **CLC 12, 35**
See also Meaker, Marijane (Agnes)
See also AAYA 2; CLR 29; SAAS 1

Kerr, Robert . . . . **CLC 55**

Kerrigan, (Thomas) Anthony
1918- . . . . **CLC 4, 6**
See also CA 49-52; CAAS 11; CANR 4

Kerry, Lois
See Duncan, Lois

Kesey, Ken (Elton)
1935- . . . . . . **CLC 1, 3, 6, 11, 46, 64; DA;**
DAB; DAC; DAM MST, NOV, POP;
WLC
See also CA 1-4R; CANR 22, 38;
CDALB 1968-1988; DLB 2, 16; MTCW;
SATA 66

Kesselring, Joseph (Otto)
1902-1967 . . . . . **CLC 45; DAM DRAM,**
MST
See also CA 150

Kessler, Jascha (Frederick) 1929- . . . . **CLC 4**
See also CA 17-20R; CANR 8, 48

Kettelkamp, Larry (Dale) 1933- . . . . **CLC 12**
See also CA 29-32R; CANR 16; SAAS 3;
SATA 2

Key, Ellen 1849-1926 . . . . **TCLC 65**

Keyber, Conny
See Fielding, Henry

Keyes, Daniel
1927- . . . . **CLC 80; DA; DAC;**
DAM MST, NOV
See also CA 17-20R; CANR 10, 26, 54;
SATA 37

Keynes, John Maynard
1883-1946 . . . . **TCLC 64**
See also CA 114; DLBD 10

Khanshendel, Chiron
See Rose, Wendy

Khayyam, Omar
1048-1131 . . . . **CMLC 11; DAM POET;**
PC 8

Kherdian, David 1931- . . . . **CLC 6, 9**
See also CA 21-24R; CAAS 2; CANR 39;
CLR 24; JRDA; MAICYA; SATA 16, 74

Khlebnikov, Velimir . . . . **TCLC 20**
See also Khlebnikov, Viktor Vladimirovich

Khlebnikov, Viktor Vladimirovich 1885-1922
See Khlebnikov, Velimir
See also CA 117

Khodasevich, Vladislav (Felitsianovich)
1886-1939 . . . . **TCLC 15**
See also CA 115

Kielland, Alexander Lange
1849-1906 . . . . **TCLC 5**
See also CA 104

Kiely, Benedict 1919- . . . . **CLC 23, 43**
See also CA 1-4R; CANR 2; DLB 15

Kienzle, William X(avier)
1928- . . . . **CLC 25; DAM POP**
See also CA 93-96; CAAS 1; CANR 9, 31;
INT CANR-31; MTCW

Kierkegaard, Soren 1813-1855 . . . . **NCLC 34**

Killens, John Oliver 1916-1987 . . . . . **CLC 10**
See also BW 2; CA 77-80; 123; CAAS 2;
CANR 26; DLB 33

Killigrew, Anne 1660-1685 . . . . **LC 4**
See also DLB 131

Kim
See Simenon, Georges (Jacques Christian)

Kincaid, Jamaica
1949- . . . . **CLC 43, 68; BLC;**
DAM MULT, NOV
See also AAYA 13; BW 2; CA 125;
CANR 47; DLB 157

King, Francis (Henry)
1923- . . . . **CLC 8, 53; DAM NOV**
See also CA 1-4R; CANR 1, 33; DLB 15,
139; MTCW

King, Martin Luther, Jr.
1929-1968 . . . . **CLC 83; BLC; DA; DAB;**
DAC; DAM MST, MULT
See also BW 2; CA 25-28; CANR 27, 44;
CAP 2; MTCW; SATA 14

King, Stephen (Edwin)
1947- . . . . **CLC 12, 26, 37, 61;**
DAM NOV, POP; SSC 17
See also AAYA 1, 17; BEST 90:1;
CA 61-64; CANR 1, 30, 52; DLB 143;
DLBY 80; JRDA; MTCW; SATA 9, 55

King, Steve
See King, Stephen (Edwin)

King, Thomas
1943- . . . . . **CLC 89; DAC; DAM MULT**
See also CA 144; NNAL

Kingman, Lee . . . . **CLC 17**
See also Natti, (Mary) Lee
See also SAAS 3; SATA 1, 67

Kingsley, Charles 1819-1875 . . . . . **NCLC 35**
See also DLB 21, 32, 163; YABC 2

Kingsley, Sidney 1906-1995 . . . . **CLC 44**
See also CA 85-88; 147; DLB 7

Kingsolver, Barbara
1955- . . . . **CLC 55, 81; DAM POP**
See also AAYA 15; CA 129; 134; INT 134

Kingston, Maxine (Ting Ting) Hong
1940- . . . . **CLC 12, 19, 58; DAM MULT,**
NOV
See also AAYA 8; CA 69-72; CANR 13,
38; DLB 173; DLBY 80; INT CANR-13;
MTCW; SATA 53

Kinnell, Galway
1927- . . . . **CLC 1, 2, 3, 5, 13, 29**
See also CA 9-12R; CANR 10, 34; DLB 5;
DLBY 87; INT CANR-34; MTCW

Kinsella, Thomas 1928- . . . . **CLC 4, 19**
See also CA 17-20R; CANR 15; DLB 27;
MTCW

Kinsella, W(illiam) P(atrick)
1935- . . . . **CLC 27, 43; DAC;**
DAM NOV, POP
See also AAYA 7; CA 97-100; CAAS 7;
CANR 21, 35; INT CANR-21; MTCW

Kipling, (Joseph) Rudyard
1865-1936 . . . . . . **TCLC 8, 17; DA; DAB;**
DAC; DAM MST, POET; PC 3; SSC 5;
WLC
See also CA 105; 120; CANR 33;
CDBLB 1890-1914; CLR 39; DLB 19, 34,
141, 156; MAICYA; MTCW; YABC 2

Kirkup, James 1918- . . . . **CLC 1**
See also CA 1-4R; CAAS 4; CANR 2;
DLB 27; SATA 12

Kirkwood, James 1930(?)-1989 . . . . . . **CLC 9**
See also AITN 2; CA 1-4R; 128; CANR 6,
40

Kirshner, Sidney
See Kingsley, Sidney

Kis, Danilo 1935-1989 . . . . **CLC 57**
See also CA 109; 118; 129; MTCW

Kivi, Aleksis 1834-1872 . . . . **NCLC 30**

Kizer, Carolyn (Ashley)
1925- . . . . . **CLC 15, 39, 80; DAM POET**
See also CA 65-68; CAAS 5; CANR 24;
DLB 5, 169

Klabund 1890-1928 . . . . **TCLC 44**
See also DLB 66

Klappert, Peter 1942- . . . . **CLC 57**
See also CA 33-36R; DLB 5

Klein, A(braham) M(oses)
1909-1972 . . . . **CLC 19; DAB; DAC;**
DAM MST
See also CA 101; 37-40R; DLB 68

Klein, Norma 1938-1989 . . . . **CLC 30**
See also AAYA 2; CA 41-44R; 128;
CANR 15, 37; CLR 2, 19;
INT CANR-15; JRDA; MAICYA;
SAAS 1; SATA 7, 57

Klein, T(heodore) E(ibon) D(onald)
1947- . . . . **CLC 34**
See also CA 119; CANR 44

Kleist, Heinrich von
1777-1811 . . . . **NCLC 2, 37;**
DAM DRAM; SSC 22
See also DLB 90

Klima, Ivan 1931- . . . . . **CLC 56; DAM NOV**
See also CA 25-28R; CANR 17, 50

Klimentov, Andrei Platonovich 1899-1951
See Platonov, Andrei
See also CA 108

Klinger, Friedrich Maximilian von
1752-1831 . . . . **NCLC 1**
See also DLB 94

Klopstock, Friedrich Gottlieb
1724-1803 . . . . **NCLC 11**
See also DLB 97

Knebel, Fletcher 1911-1993 . . . . **CLC 14**
See also AITN 1; CA 1-4R; 140; CAAS 3;
CANR 1, 36; SATA 36; SATA-Obit 75

Knickerbocker, Diedrich
See Irving, Washington

Knight, Etheridge
1931-1991 . . . . **CLC 40; BLC;**
DAM POET; PC 14
See also BW 1; CA 21-24R; 133; CANR 23;
DLB 41

Knight, Sarah Kemble 1666-1727 . . . . . **LC 7**
See also DLB 24

Knister, Raymond 1899-1932 . . . . . . **TCLC 56**
See also DLB 68

Knowles, John
1926- . . . . . . **CLC 1, 4, 10, 26; DA; DAC;**
DAM MST, NOV
See also AAYA 10; CA 17-20R; CANR 40;
CDALB 1968-1988; DLB 6; MTCW;
SATA 8, 89

Knox, Calvin M.
See Silverberg, Robert

Knye, Cassandra
See Disch, Thomas M(ichael)

Koch, C(hristopher) J(ohn) 1932- . . . **CLC 42**
See also CA 127

Koch, Christopher
See Koch, C(hristopher) J(ohn)

Koch, Kenneth
1925- . . . . **CLC 5, 8, 44; DAM POET**
See also CA 1-4R; CANR 6, 36; DLB 5;
INT CANR-36; SATA 65

Kochanowski, Jan 1530-1584 . . . . **LC 10**

Kock, Charles Paul de
1794-1871 . . . . **NCLC 16**

Koda Shigeyuki 1867-1947
See Rohan, Koda
See also CA 121

Koestler, Arthur
1905-1983 . . . . **CLC 1, 3, 6, 8, 15, 33**
See also CA 1-4R; 109; CANR 1, 33;
CDBLB 1945-1960; DLBY 83; MTCW

Kogawa, Joy Nozomi
1935- . . . . . . **CLC 78; DAC; DAM MST,**
MULT
See also CA 101; CANR 19

Kohout, Pavel 1928- . . . . **CLC 13**
See also CA 45-48; CANR 3

Koizumi, Yakumo
See Hearn, (Patricio) Lafcadio (Tessima
Carlos)

Kolmar, Gertrud 1894-1943 . . . . **TCLC 40**

Komunyakaa, Yusef 1947- . . . . . . **CLC 86, 94**
See also CA 147; DLB 120

Konrad, George
See Konrad, Gyoergy

Konrad, Gyoergy 1933- . . . . . . **CLC 4, 10, 73**
See also CA 85-88

Konwicki, Tadeusz 1926- . . . . . **CLC 8, 28, 54**
See also CA 101; CAAS 9; CANR 39;
MTCW

Koontz, Dean R(ay)
1945- . . . . . . **CLC 78; DAM NOV, POP**
See also AAYA 9; BEST 89:3, 90:2;
CA 108; CANR 19, 36, 52; MTCW

Kopit, Arthur (Lee)
1937- . . . . . **CLC 1, 18, 33; DAM DRAM**
See also AITN 1; CA 81-84; CABS 3;
DLB 7; MTCW

Kops, Bernard 1926- . . . . **CLC 4**
See also CA 5-8R; DLB 13

Kornbluth, C(yril) M. 1923-1958 . . . . **TCLC 8**
See also CA 105; DLB 8

Korolenko, V. G.
See Korolenko, Vladimir Galaktionovich

Korolenko, Vladimir
See Korolenko, Vladimir Galaktionovich

Korolenko, Vladimir G.
See Korolenko, Vladimir Galaktionovich

Korolenko, Vladimir Galaktionovich
1853-1921 . . . . **TCLC 22**
See also CA 121

Korzybski, Alfred (Habdank Skarbek)
1879-1950 . . . . **TCLC 61**
See also CA 123

Kosinski, Jerzy (Nikodem)
1933-1991 . . . . **CLC 1, 2, 3, 6, 10, 15, 53,**
70; DAM NOV
See also CA 17-20R; 134; CANR 9, 46;
DLB 2; DLBY 82; MTCW

Kostelanetz, Richard (Cory) 1940- . . **CLC 28**
See also CA 13-16R; CAAS 8; CANR 38

Kostrowitzki, Wilhelm Apollinaris de
1880-1918
See Apollinaire, Guillaume
See also CA 104

Kotlowitz, Robert 1924- . . . . **CLC 4**
See also CA 33-36R; CANR 36

Kotzebue, August (Friedrich Ferdinand) von
1761-1819 . . . . **NCLC 25**
See also DLB 94

Kotzwinkle, William 1938- ... **CLC 5, 14, 35**
See also CA 45-48; CANR 3, 44; CLR 6;
DLB 173; MAICYA; SATA 24, 70

Kozol, Jonathan 1936- .... **CLC 17**
See also CA 61-64; CANR 16, 45

Kozoll, Michael 1940(?)- .... **CLC 35**

Kramer, Kathryn 19(?)- .... **CLC 34**

Kramer, Larry 1935- .. **CLC 42; DAM POP**
See also CA 124; 126

Krasicki, Ignacy 1735-1801 .... **NCLC 8**

Krasinski, Zygmunt 1812-1859 .... **NCLC 4**

Kraus, Karl 1874-1936 .... **TCLC 5**
See also CA 104; DLB 118

Kreve (Mickevicius), Vincas
1882-1954 .... **TCLC 27**

Kristeva, Julia 1941- .... **CLC 77**

Kristofferson, Kris 1936- .... **CLC 26**
See also CA 104

Krizanc, John 1956- .... **CLC 57**

Krleza, Miroslav 1893-1981 .... **CLC 8**
See also CA 97-100; 105; CANR 50;
DLB 147

Kroetsch, Robert
1927- .... **CLC 5, 23, 57; DAC;
DAM POET**
See also CA 17-20R; CANR 8, 38; DLB 53;
MTCW

Kroetz, Franz
See Kroetz, Franz Xaver

Kroetz, Franz Xaver 1946- .... **CLC 41**
See also CA 130

Kroker, Arthur 1945- .... **CLC 77**

Kropotkin, Peter (Aleksieevich)
1842-1921 .... **TCLC 36**
See also CA 119

Krotkov, Yuri 1917- .... **CLC 19**
See also CA 102

Krumb
See Crumb, R(obert)

Krumgold, Joseph (Quincy)
1908-1980 .... **CLC 12**
See also CA 9-12R; 101; CANR 7;
MAICYA; SATA 1, 48; SATA-Obit 23

Krumwitz
See Crumb, R(obert)

Krutch, Joseph Wood 1893-1970. ... **CLC 24**
See also CA 1-4R; 25-28R; CANR 4;
DLB 63

Krutzch, Gus
See Eliot, T(homas) S(tearns)

Krylov, Ivan Andreevich
1768(?)-1844 .... **NCLC 1**
See also DLB 150

Kubin, Alfred (Leopold Isidor)
1877-1959 .... **TCLC 23**
See also CA 112; 149; DLB 81

Kubrick, Stanley 1928- .... **CLC 16**
See also CA 81-84; CANR 33; DLB 26

Kumin, Maxine (Winokur)
1925- ..... **CLC 5, 13, 28; DAM POET;
PC 15**
See also AITN 2; CA 1-4R; CAAS 8;
CANR 1, 21; DLB 5; MTCW; SATA 12

Kundera, Milan
1929- .... **CLC 4, 9, 19, 32, 68;
DAM NOV**
See also AAYA 2; CA 85-88; CANR 19,
52; MTCW

Kunene, Mazisi (Raymond) 1930- ... **CLC 85**
See also BW 1; CA 125; DLB 117

Kunitz, Stanley (Jasspon)
1905- .... **CLC 6, 11, 14**
See also CA 41-44R; CANR 26; DLB 48;
INT CANR-26; MTCW

Kunze, Reiner 1933- .... **CLC 10**
See also CA 93-96; DLB 75

Kuprin, Aleksandr Ivanovich
1870-1938 .... **TCLC 5**
See also CA 104

Kureishi, Hanif 1954(?)- .... **CLC 64**
See also CA 139

Kurosawa, Akira
1910- .... **CLC 16; DAM MULT**
See also AAYA 11; CA 101; CANR 46

Kushner, Tony
1957(?)- .... **CLC 81; DAM DRAM**
See also CA 144

Kuttner, Henry 1915-1958 .... **TCLC 10**
See also CA 107; DLB 8

Kuzma, Greg 1944- .... **CLC 7**
See also CA 33-36R

Kuzmin, Mikhail 1872(?)-1936 .... **TCLC 40**

Kyd, Thomas
1558-1594 .... **LC 22; DAM DRAM;
DC 3**
See also DLB 62

Kyprianos, Iossif
See Samarakis, Antonis

La Bruyere, Jean de 1645-1696 ...... **LC 17**

Lacan, Jacques (Marie Emile)
1901-1981 .... **CLC 75**
See also CA 121; 104

Laclos, Pierre Ambroise Francois Choderlos
de 1741-1803 .... **NCLC 4**

Lacolere, Francois
See Aragon, Louis

La Colere, Francois
See Aragon, Louis

La Deshabilleuse
See Simenon, Georges (Jacques Christian)

Lady Gregory
See Gregory, Isabella Augusta (Persse)

Lady of Quality, A
See Bagnold, Enid

La Fayette, Marie (Madelaine Pioche de la
Vergne Comtes 1634-1693 .... **LC 2**

Lafayette, Rene
See Hubbard, L(afayette) Ron(ald)

Laforgue, Jules
1860-1887 .... **NCLC 5, 53; PC 14;
SSC 20**

Lagerkvist, Paer (Fabian)
1891-1974 .... **CLC 7, 10, 13, 54;
DAM DRAM, NOV**
See also Lagerkvist, Par
See also CA 85-88; 49-52; MTCW

Lagerkvist, Par .... **SSC 12**
See also Lagerkvist, Paer (Fabian)

Lagerloef, Selma (Ottiliana Lovisa)
1858-1940 .... **TCLC 4, 36**
See also Lagerlof, Selma (Ottiliana Lovisa)
See also CA 108; SATA 15

Lagerlof, Selma (Ottiliana Lovisa)
See Lagerloef, Selma (Ottiliana Lovisa)
See also CLR 7; SATA 15

La Guma, (Justin) Alex(ander)
1925-1985 .... **CLC 19; DAM NOV**
See also BW 1; CA 49-52; 118; CANR 25;
DLB 117; MTCW

Laidlaw, A. K.
See Grieve, C(hristopher) M(urray)

Lainez, Manuel Mujica
See Mujica Lainez, Manuel
See also HW

Laing, R(onald) D(avid)
1927-1989 .... **CLC 95**
See also CA 107; 129; CANR 34; MTCW

Lamartine, Alphonse (Marie Louis Prat) de
1790-1869 ..... **NCLC 11; DAM POET;
PC 16**

Lamb, Charles
1775-1834 .... **NCLC 10; DA; DAB;
DAC; DAM MST; WLC**
See also CDBLB 1789-1832; DLB 93, 107,
163; SATA 17

Lamb, Lady Caroline 1785-1828 .. **NCLC 38**
See also DLB 116

Lamming, George (William)
1927- .... **CLC 2, 4, 66; BLC;
DAM MULT**
See also BW 2; CA 85-88; CANR 26;
DLB 125; MTCW

L'Amour, Louis (Dearborn)
1908-1988 .... **CLC 25, 55; DAM NOV,
POP**
See also AAYA 16; AITN 2; BEST 89:2;
CA 1-4R; 125; CANR 3, 25, 40;
DLBY 80; MTCW

Lampedusa, Giuseppe (Tomasi) di ... **TCLC 13**
See also Tomasi di Lampedusa, Giuseppe

Lampman, Archibald 1861-1899 .. **NCLC 25**
See also DLB 92

Lancaster, Bruce 1896-1963 .... **CLC 36**
See also CA 9-10; CAP 1; SATA 9

Landau, Mark Alexandrovich
See Aldanov, Mark (Alexandrovich)

Landau-Aldanov, Mark Alexandrovich
See Aldanov, Mark (Alexandrovich)

Landis, Jerry
See Simon, Paul (Frederick)

Landis, John 1950- .... **CLC 26**
See also CA 112; 122

Landolfi, Tommaso 1908-1979 ... **CLC 11, 49**
See also CA 127; 117

Landon, Letitia Elizabeth
1802-1838 .... **NCLC 15**
See also DLB 96

Landor, Walter Savage
1775-1864 .... **NCLC 14**
See also DLB 93, 107

Landwirth, Heinz   1927-
See Lind, Jakov
See also CA 9-12R; CANR 7

Lane, Patrick
1939- . . . . **CLC 25; DAM POET**
See also CA 97-100; CANR 54; DLB 53;
INT 97-100

Lang, Andrew   1844-1912 . . . . **TCLC 16**
See also CA 114; 137; DLB 98, 141;
MAICYA; SATA 16

Lang, Fritz   1890-1976 . . . . **CLC 20**
See also CA 77-80; 69-72; CANR 30

Lange, John
See Crichton, (John) Michael

Langer, Elinor   1939- . . . . **CLC 34**
See also CA 121

Langland, William
1330(?)-1400(?) . . . . . . **LC 19; DA; DAB;
DAC; DAM MST, POET**
See also DLB 146

Langstaff, Launcelot
See Irving, Washington

Lanier, Sidney
1842-1881 . . . . . . **NCLC 6; DAM POET**
See also DLB 64; DLBD 13; MAICYA;
SATA 18

Lanyer, Aemilia   1569-1645 . . . . . . **LC 10, 30**
See also DLB 121

Lao Tzu . . . . **CMLC 7**

Lapine, James (Elliot)   1949- . . . . **CLC 39**
See also CA 123; 130; CANR 54; INT 130

Larbaud, Valery (Nicolas)
1881-1957 . . . . **TCLC 9**
See also CA 106; 152

Lardner, Ring
See Lardner, Ring(gold) W(ilmer)

Lardner, Ring W., Jr.
See Lardner, Ring(gold) W(ilmer)

Lardner, Ring(gold) W(ilmer)
1885-1933 . . . . **TCLC 2, 14**
See also CA 104; 131; CDALB 1917-1929;
DLB 11, 25, 86; MTCW

Laredo, Betty
See Codrescu, Andrei

Larkin, Maia
See Wojciechowska, Maia (Teresa)

Larkin, Philip (Arthur)
1922-1985 . . . . **CLC 3, 5, 8, 9, 13, 18, 33,
39, 64; DAB; DAM MST, POET**
See also CA 5-8R; 117; CANR 24;
CDBLB 1960 to Present; DLB 27;
MTCW

Larra (y Sanchez de Castro), Mariano Jose de
1809-1837 . . . . **NCLC 17**

Larsen, Eric   1941- . . . . **CLC 55**
See also CA 132

Larsen, Nella
1891-1964 . . . . **CLC 37; BLC;
DAM MULT**
See also BW 1; CA 125; DLB 51

Larson, Charles R(aymond)   1938- . . . **CLC 31**
See also CA 53-56; CANR 4

Las Casas, Bartolome de   1474-1566 . . **LC 31**

Lasker-Schueler, Else   1869-1945 . . **TCLC 57**
See also DLB 66, 124

Latham, Jean Lee   1902- . . . . **CLC 12**
See also AITN 1; CA 5-8R; CANR 7;
MAICYA; SATA 2, 68

Latham, Mavis
See Clark, Mavis Thorpe

Lathen, Emma . . . . **CLC 2**
See also Hennissart, Martha; Latsis, Mary
J(ane)

Lathrop, Francis
See Leiber, Fritz (Reuter, Jr.)

Latsis, Mary J(ane)
See Lathen, Emma
See also CA 85-88

Lattimore, Richmond (Alexander)
1906-1984 . . . . **CLC 3**
See also CA 1-4R; 112; CANR 1

Laughlin, James   1914- . . . . **CLC 49**
See also CA 21-24R; CAAS 22; CANR 9,
47; DLB 48

Laurence, (Jean) Margaret (Wemyss)
1926-1987 . . . . **CLC 3, 6, 13, 50, 62;
DAC; DAM MST; SSC 7**
See also CA 5-8R; 121; CANR 33; DLB 53;
MTCW; SATA-Obit 50

Laurent, Antoine   1952- . . . . **CLC 50**

Lauscher, Hermann
See Hesse, Hermann

Lautreamont, Comte de
1846-1870 . . . . **NCLC 12; SSC 14**

Laverty, Donald
See Blish, James (Benjamin)

Lavin, Mary   1912-1996 . . **CLC 4, 18; SSC 4**
See also CA 9-12R; 151; CANR 33;
DLB 15; MTCW

Lavond, Paul Dennis
See Kornbluth, C(yril) M.; Pohl, Frederik

Lawler, Raymond Evenor   1922- . . . . **CLC 58**
See also CA 103

Lawrence, D(avid) H(erbert Richards)
1885-1930 . . . . **TCLC 2, 9, 16, 33, 48, 61;
DA; DAB; DAC; DAM MST, NOV,
POET; SSC 4, 19; WLC**
See also CA 104; 121; CDBLB 1914-1945;
DLB 10, 19, 36, 98, 162; MTCW

Lawrence, T(homas) E(dward)
1888-1935 . . . . **TCLC 18**
See also Dale, Colin
See also CA 115

Lawrence of Arabia
See Lawrence, T(homas) E(dward)

Lawson, Henry (Archibald Hertzberg)
1867-1922 . . . . **TCLC 27; SSC 18**
See also CA 120

Lawton, Dennis
See Faust, Frederick (Schiller)

Laxness, Halldor . . . . **CLC 25**
See also Gudjonsson, Halldor Kiljan

Layamon   fl. c. 1200- . . . . **CMLC 10**
See also DLB 146

Laye, Camara
1928-1980 . . . . **CLC 4, 38; BLC;
DAM MULT**
See also BW 1; CA 85-88; 97-100;
CANR 25; MTCW

Layton, Irving (Peter)
1912- . . . . **CLC 2, 15; DAC; DAM MST,
POET**
See also CA 1-4R; CANR 2, 33, 43;
DLB 88; MTCW

Lazarus, Emma   1849-1887 . . . . **NCLC 8**

Lazarus, Felix
See Cable, George Washington

Lazarus, Henry
See Slavitt, David R(ytman)

Lea, Joan
See Neufeld, John (Arthur)

Leacock, Stephen (Butler)
1869-1944 . . **TCLC 2; DAC; DAM MST**
See also CA 104; 141; DLB 92

Lear, Edward   1812-1888 . . . . **NCLC 3**
See also CLR 1; DLB 32, 163, 166;
MAICYA; SATA 18

Lear, Norman (Milton)   1922- . . . . . . **CLC 12**
See also CA 73-76

Leavis, F(rank) R(aymond)
1895-1978 . . . . **CLC 24**
See also CA 21-24R; 77-80; CANR 44;
MTCW

Leavitt, David   1961- . . . **CLC 34; DAM POP**
See also CA 116; 122; CANR 50; DLB 130;
INT 122

Leblanc, Maurice (Marie Emile)
1864-1941 . . . . **TCLC 49**
See also CA 110

Lebowitz, Fran(ces Ann)
1951(?)- . . . . **CLC 11, 36**
See also CA 81-84; CANR 14;
INT CANR-14; MTCW

Lebrecht, Peter
See Tieck, (Johann) Ludwig

le Carre, John . . . . **CLC 3, 5, 9, 15, 28**
See also Cornwell, David (John Moore)
See also BEST 89:4; CDBLB 1960 to
Present; DLB 87

Le Clezio, J(ean) M(arie) G(ustave)
1940- . . . . **CLC 31**
See also CA 116; 128; DLB 83

Leconte de Lisle, Charles-Marie-Rene
1818-1894 . . . . **NCLC 29**

Le Coq, Monsieur
See Simenon, Georges (Jacques Christian)

Leduc, Violette   1907-1972 . . . . **CLC 22**
See also CA 13-14; 33-36R; CAP 1

Ledwidge, Francis   1887(?)-1917 . . . **TCLC 23**
See also CA 123; DLB 20

Lee, Andrea
1953- . . . . . **CLC 36; BLC; DAM MULT**
See also BW 1; CA 125

Lee, Andrew
See Auchincloss, Louis (Stanton)

Lee, Chang-rae   1965- . . . . **CLC 91**
See also CA 148

Lee, Don L. . . . . **CLC 2**
See also Madhubuti, Haki R.

Lee, George W(ashington)
1894-1976 .... **CLC 52; BLC;**
DAM MULT
See also BW 1; CA 125; DLB 51

Lee, (Nelle) Harper
1926- .... **CLC 12, 60; DA; DAB; DAC;**
DAM MST, NOV; WLC
See also AAYA 13; CA 13-16R; CANR 51;
CDALB 1941-1968; DLB 6; MTCW;
SATA 11

Lee, Helen Elaine 1959(?)- .... **CLC 86**
See also CA 148

Lee, Julian
See Latham, Jean Lee

Lee, Larry
See Lee, Lawrence

Lee, Laurie
1914- .... **CLC 90; DAB; DAM POP**
See also CA 77-80; CANR 33; DLB 27;
MTCW

Lee, Lawrence 1941-1990......... **CLC 34**
See also CA 131; CANR 43

Lee, Manfred B(ennington)
1905-1971 .... **CLC 11**
See also Queen, Ellery
See also CA 1-4R; 29-32R; CANR 2;
DLB 137

Lee, Stan 1922-................. **CLC 17**
See also AAYA 5; CA 108; 111; INT 111

Lee, Tanith 1947-................ **CLC 46**
See also AAYA 15; CA 37-40R; CANR 53;
SATA 8, 88

Lee, Vernon....................... TCLC 5
See also Paget, Violet
See also DLB 57, 153, 156, 174

Lee, William
See Burroughs, William S(eward)

Lee, Willy
See Burroughs, William S(eward)

Lee-Hamilton, Eugene (Jacob)
1845-1907 .... **TCLC 22**
See also CA 117

Leet, Judith 1935- .... **CLC 11**

Le Fanu, Joseph Sheridan
1814-1873 .... **NCLC 9, 58; DAM POP;**
SSC 14
See also DLB 21, 70, 159

Leffland, Ella 1931- .... **CLC 19**
See also CA 29-32R; CANR 35; DLBY 84;
INT CANR-35; SATA 65

Leger, Alexis
See Leger, (Marie-Rene Auguste) Alexis
Saint-Leger

Leger, (Marie-Rene Auguste) Alexis
Saint-Leger
1887-1975 .... **CLC 11; DAM POET**
See also Perse, St.-John
See also CA 13-16R; 61-64; CANR 43;
MTCW

Leger, Saintleger
See Leger, (Marie-Rene Auguste) Alexis
Saint-Leger

Le Guin, Ursula K(roeber)
1929- ...... **CLC 8, 13, 22, 45, 71; DAB;**
DAC; DAM MST, POP; SSC 12
See also AAYA 9; AITN 1; CA 21-24R;
CANR 9, 32, 52; CDALB 1968-1988;
CLR 3, 28; DLB 8, 52; INT CANR-32;
JRDA; MAICYA; MTCW; SATA 4, 52

Lehmann, Rosamond (Nina)
1901-1990 .... **CLC 5**
See also CA 77-80; 131; CANR 8; DLB 15

Leiber, Fritz (Reuter, Jr.)
1910-1992 .... **CLC 25**
See also CA 45-48; 139; CANR 2, 40;
DLB 8; MTCW; SATA 45;
SATA-Obit 73

Leibniz, Gottfried Wilhelm von
1646-1716 .... **LC 35**
See also DLB 168

Leimbach, Martha 1963-
See Leimbach, Marti
See also CA 130

Leimbach, Marti .... CLC 65
See also Leimbach, Martha

Leino, Eino .... TCLC 24
See also Loennbohm, Armas Eino Leopold

Leiris, Michel (Julien) 1901-1990 ... **CLC 61**
See also CA 119; 128; 132

Leithauser, Brad 1953-............. **CLC 27**
See also CA 107; CANR 27; DLB 120

Lelchuk, Alan 1938-............... **CLC 5**
See also CA 45-48; CAAS 20; CANR 1

Lem, Stanislaw 1921-........ **CLC 8, 15, 40**
See also CA 105; CAAS 1; CANR 32;
MTCW

Lemann, Nancy 1956-............. **CLC 39**
See also CA 118; 136

Lemonnier, (Antoine Louis) Camille
1844-1913 .... **TCLC 22**
See also CA 121

Lenau, Nikolaus 1802-1850 ...... **NCLC 16**

L'Engle, Madeleine (Camp Franklin)
1918- .... **CLC 12; DAM POP**
See also AAYA 1; AITN 2; CA 1-4R;
CANR 3, 21, 39; CLR 1, 14; DLB 52;
JRDA; MAICYA; MTCW; SAAS 15;
SATA 1, 27, 75

Lengyel, Jozsef 1896-1975......... **CLC 7**
See also CA 85-88; 57-60

Lenin 1870-1924
See Lenin, V. I.
See also CA 121

Lenin, V. I. .... TCLC 67
See also Lenin

Lennon, John (Ono)
1940-1980 .... **CLC 12, 35**
See also CA 102

Lennox, Charlotte Ramsay
1729(?)-1804 .... **NCLC 23**
See also DLB 39

Lentricchia, Frank (Jr.) 1940-...... **CLC 34**
See also CA 25-28R; CANR 19

Lenz, Siegfried 1926-............ **CLC 27**
See also CA 89-92; DLB 75

Leonard, Elmore (John, Jr.)
1925- ...... **CLC 28, 34, 71; DAM POP**
See also AITN 1; BEST 89:1, 90:4;
CA 81-84; CANR 12, 28, 53; DLB 173;
INT CANR-28; MTCW

Leonard, Hugh..................... CLC 19
See also Byrne, John Keyes
See also DLB 13

Leonov, Leonid (Maximovich)
1899-1994 .... **CLC 92; DAM NOV**
See also CA 129; MTCW

Leopardi, (Conte) Giacomo
1798-1837 .... **NCLC 22**

Le Reveler
See Artaud, Antonin (Marie Joseph)

Lerman, Eleanor 1952-............. **CLC 9**
See also CA 85-88

Lerman, Rhoda 1936-............. **CLC 56**
See also CA 49-52

Lermontov, Mikhail Yuryevich
1814-1841 .... **NCLC 47**

Leroux, Gaston 1868-1927........ **TCLC 25**
See also CA 108; 136; SATA 65

Lesage, Alain-Rene 1668-1747....... **LC 28**

Leskov, Nikolai (Semyonovich)
1831-1895 .... **NCLC 25**

Lessing, Doris (May)
1919- ..... **CLC 1, 2, 3, 6, 10, 15, 22, 40,**
94; DA; DAB; DAC; DAM MST, NOV;
SSC 6
See also CA 9-12R; CAAS 14; CANR 33,
54; CDBLB 1960 to Present; DLB 15,
139; DLBY 85; MTCW

Lessing, Gotthold Ephraim
1729-1781 .... **LC 8**
See also DLB 97

Lester, Richard 1932-............. **CLC 20**

Lever, Charles (James)
1806-1872 .... **NCLC 23**
See also DLB 21

Leverson, Ada 1865(?)-1936(?) .... **TCLC 18**
See also Elaine
See also CA 117; DLB 153

Levertov, Denise
1923- ...... **CLC 1, 2, 3, 5, 8, 15, 28, 66;**
DAM POET; PC 11
See also CA 1-4R; CAAS 19; CANR 3, 29,
50; DLB 5, 165; INT CANR-29; MTCW

Levi, Jonathan................... CLC 76

Levi, Peter (Chad Tigar) 1931-..... **CLC 41**
See also CA 5-8R; CANR 34; DLB 40

Levi, Primo
1919-1987 .... **CLC 37, 50; SSC 12**
See also CA 13-16R; 122; CANR 12, 33;
MTCW

Levin, Ira 1929- ..... **CLC 3, 6; DAM POP**
See also CA 21-24R; CANR 17, 44;
MTCW; SATA 66

Levin, Meyer
1905-1981 .... **CLC 7; DAM POP**
See also AITN 1; CA 9-12R; 104;
CANR 15; DLB 9, 28; DLBY 81;
SATA 21; SATA-Obit 27

Levine, Norman 1924- . . . . CLC 54
See also CA 73-76; CAAS 23; CANR 14;
DLB 88

Levine, Philip
1928- . . . . CLC 2, 4, 5, 9, 14, 33;
DAM POET
See also CA 9-12R; CANR 9, 37, 52;
DLB 5

Levinson, Deirdre 1931- . . . . CLC 49
See also CA 73-76

Levi-Strauss, Claude 1908- . . . . CLC 38
See also CA 1-4R; CANR 6, 32; MTCW

Levitin, Sonia (Wolff) 1934- . . . . CLC 17
See also AAYA 13; CA 29-32R; CANR 14,
32; JRDA; MAICYA; SAAS 2; SATA 4,
68

Levon, O. U.
See Kesey, Ken (Elton)

Lewes, George Henry
1817-1878 . . . . NCLC 25
See also DLB 55, 144

Lewis, Alun 1915-1944. . . . . TCLC 3
See also CA 104; DLB 20, 162

Lewis, C. Day
See Day Lewis, C(ecil)

Lewis, C(live) S(taples)
1898-1963 . . . . . CLC 1, 3, 6, 14, 27; DA;
DAB; DAC; DAM MST, NOV, POP;
WLC
See also AAYA 3; CA 81-84; CANR 33;
CDBLB 1945-1960; CLR 3, 27; DLB 15,
100, 160; JRDA; MAICYA; MTCW;
SATA 13

Lewis, Janet 1899- . . . . CLC 41
See also Winters, Janet Lewis
See also CA 9-12R; CANR 29; CAP 1;
DLBY 87

Lewis, Matthew Gregory
1775-1818 . . . . NCLC 11
See also DLB 39, 158

Lewis, (Harry) Sinclair
1885-1951 . . . . . TCLC 4, 13, 23, 39; DA;
DAB; DAC; DAM MST, NOV; WLC
See also CA 104; 133; CDALB 1917-1929;
DLB 9, 102; DLBD 1; MTCW

Lewis, (Percy) Wyndham
1884(?)-1957 . . . . TCLC 2, 9
See also CA 104; DLB 15

Lewisohn, Ludwig 1883-1955. . . . . . TCLC 19
See also CA 107; DLB 4, 9, 28, 102

Leyner, Mark 1956- . . . . CLC 92
See also CA 110; CANR 28, 53

Lezama Lima, Jose
1910-1976 . . . . CLC 4, 10; DAM MULT
See also CA 77-80; DLB 113; HW

L'Heureux, John (Clarke) 1934- . . . . CLC 52
See also CA 13-16R; CANR 23, 45

Liddell, C. H.
See Kuttner, Henry

Lie, Jonas (Lauritz Idemil)
1833-1908(?) . . . . TCLC 5
See also CA 115

Lieber, Joel 1937-1971. . . . . CLC 6
See also CA 73-76; 29-32R

Lieber, Stanley Martin
See Lee, Stan

Lieberman, Laurence (James)
1935- . . . . CLC 4, 36
See also CA 17-20R; CANR 8, 36

Lieksman, Anders
See Haavikko, Paavo Juhani

Li Fei-kan 1904-
See Pa Chin
See also CA 105

Lifton, Robert Jay 1926- . . . . CLC 67
See also CA 17-20R; CANR 27;
INT CANR-27; SATA 66

Lightfoot, Gordon 1938- . . . . CLC 26
See also CA 109

Lightman, Alan P. 1948- . . . . CLC 81
See also CA 141

Ligotti, Thomas (Robert)
1953- . . . . CLC 44; SSC 16
See also CA 123; CANR 49

Li Ho 791-817. . . . . PC 13

Liliencron, (Friedrich Adolf Axel) Detlev von
1844-1909 . . . . TCLC 18
See also CA 117

Lilly, William 1602-1681. . . . . LC 27

Lima, Jose Lezama
See Lezama Lima, Jose

Lima Barreto, Afonso Henrique de
1881-1922 . . . . TCLC 23
See also CA 117

Limonov, Edward 1944- . . . . CLC 67
See also CA 137

Lin, Frank
See Atherton, Gertrude (Franklin Horn)

Lincoln, Abraham 1809-1865. . . . . NCLC 18

Lind, Jakov . . . . CLC 1, 2, 4, 27, 82
See also Landwirth, Heinz
See also CAAS 4

Lindbergh, Anne (Spencer) Morrow
1906- . . . . CLC 82; DAM NOV
See also CA 17-20R; CANR 16; MTCW;
SATA 33

Lindsay, David 1878-1945. . . . . TCLC 15
See also CA 113

Lindsay, (Nicholas) Vachel
1879-1931 . . . . TCLC 17; DA; DAC;
DAM MST, POET; WLC
See also CA 114; 135; CDALB 1865-1917;
DLB 54; SATA 40

Linke-Poot
See Doeblin, Alfred

Linney, Romulus 1930- . . . . CLC 51
See also CA 1-4R; CANR 40, 44

Linton, Eliza Lynn 1822-1898. . . . NCLC 41
See also DLB 18

Li Po 701-763. . . . . CMLC 2

Lipsius, Justus 1547-1606 . . . . LC 16

Lipsyte, Robert (Michael)
1938- . . . . CLC 21; DA; DAC;
DAM MST, NOV
See also AAYA 7; CA 17-20R; CANR 8;
CLR 23; JRDA; MAICYA; SATA 5, 68

Lish, Gordon (Jay) 1934-. . CLC 45; SSC 18
See also CA 113; 117; DLB 130; INT 117

Lispector, Clarice 1925-1977. . . . . . CLC 43
See also CA 139; 116; DLB 113

Littell, Robert 1935(?)- . . . . CLC 42
See also CA 109; 112

Little, Malcolm 1925-1965
See Malcolm X
See also BW 1; CA 125; 111; DA; DAB;
DAC; DAM MST, MULT; MTCW

Littlewit, Humphrey Gent.
See Lovecraft, H(oward) P(hillips)

Litwos
See Sienkiewicz, Henryk (Adam Alexander
Pius)

Liu E 1857-1909. . . . . TCLC 15
See also CA 115

Lively, Penelope (Margaret)
1933- . . . . CLC 32, 50; DAM NOV
See also CA 41-44R; CANR 29; CLR 7;
DLB 14, 161; JRDA; MAICYA; MTCW;
SATA 7, 60

Livesay, Dorothy (Kathleen)
1909- . . . . CLC 4, 15, 79; DAC;
DAM MST, POET
See also AITN 2; CA 25-28R; CAAS 8;
CANR 36; DLB 68; MTCW

Livy c. 59B.C.-c. 17 . . . . CMLC 11

Lizardi, Jose Joaquin Fernandez de
1776-1827 . . . . NCLC 30

Llewellyn, Richard
See Llewellyn Lloyd, Richard Dafydd
Vivian
See also DLB 15

Llewellyn Lloyd, Richard Dafydd Vivian
1906-1983 . . . . CLC 7, 80
See also Llewellyn, Richard
See also CA 53-56; 111; CANR 7;
SATA 11; SATA-Obit 37

Llosa, (Jorge) Mario (Pedro) Vargas
See Vargas Llosa, (Jorge) Mario (Pedro)

Lloyd Webber, Andrew 1948-
See Webber, Andrew Lloyd
See also AAYA 1; CA 116; 149;
DAM DRAM; SATA 56

Llull, Ramon c. 1235-c. 1316. . . . . CMLC 12

Locke, Alain (Le Roy)
1886-1954 . . . . TCLC 43
See also BW 1; CA 106; 124; DLB 51

Locke, John 1632-1704 . . . . LC 7, 35
See also DLB 101

Locke-Elliott, Sumner
See Elliott, Sumner Locke

Lockhart, John Gibson
1794-1854 . . . . NCLC 6
See also DLB 110, 116, 144

Lodge, David (John)
1935- . . . . CLC 36; DAM POP
See also BEST 90:1; CA 17-20R; CANR 19,
53; DLB 14; INT CANR-19; MTCW

Loennbohm, Armas Eino Leopold 1878-1926
See Leino, Eino
See also CA 123

Loewinsohn, Ron(ald William)
1937- . . . . CLC 52
See also CA 25-28R

Logan, Jake
See Smith, Martin Cruz

Logan, John (Burton) 1923-1987..... **CLC 5**
See also CA 77-80; 124; CANR 45; DLB 5

Lo Kuan-chung 1330(?)-1400(?)...... **LC 12**

Lombard, Nap
See Johnson, Pamela Hansford

London, Jack.. **TCLC 9, 15, 39; SSC 4; WLC**
See also London, John Griffith
See also AAYA 13; AITN 2;
    CDALB 1865-1917; DLB 8, 12, 78;
    SATA 18

London, John Griffith 1876-1916
See London, Jack
See also CA 110; 119; DA; DAB; DAC;
    DAM MST, NOV; JRDA; MAICYA;
    MTCW

Long, Emmett
See Leonard, Elmore (John, Jr.)

Longbaugh, Harry
See Goldman, William (W.)

Longfellow, Henry Wadsworth
    1807-1882 ..... **NCLC 2, 45; DA; DAB;**
                    DAC; DAM MST, POET
See also CDALB 1640-1865; DLB 1, 59;
    SATA 19

Longley, Michael 1939-.......... **CLC 29**
See also CA 102; DLB 40

Longus fl. c. 2nd cent. - .... **CMLC 7**

Longway, A. Hugh
See Lang, Andrew

Lonnrot, Elias 1802-1884....... **NCLC 53**

Lopate, Phillip 1943- .... **CLC 29**
See also CA 97-100; DLBY 80; INT 97-100

Lopez Portillo (y Pacheco), Jose
    1920-....................... **CLC 46**
See also CA 129; HW

Lopez y Fuentes, Gregorio
    1897(?)-1966 .... **CLC 32**
See also CA 131; HW

Lorca, Federico Garcia
See Garcia Lorca, Federico

Lord, Bette Bao 1938- .... **CLC 23**
See also BEST 90:3; CA 107; CANR 41;
    INT 107; SATA 58

Lord Auch
See Bataille, Georges

Lord Byron
See Byron, George Gordon (Noel)

Lorde, Audre (Geraldine)
    1934-1992 .... **CLC 18, 71; BLC;**
                    DAM MULT, POET; PC 12
See also BW 1; CA 25-28R; 142; CANR 16,
    26, 46; DLB 41; MTCW

Lord Jeffrey
See Jeffrey, Francis

Lorenzini, Carlo 1826-1890
See Collodi, Carlo
See also MAICYA; SATA 29

Lorenzo, Heberto Padilla
See Padilla (Lorenzo), Heberto

Loris
See Hofmannsthal, Hugo von

Loti, Pierre .... **TCLC 11**
See also Viaud, (Louis Marie) Julien
See also DLB 123

Louie, David Wong 1954- .... **CLC 70**
See also CA 139

Louis, Father M.
See Merton, Thomas

Lovecraft, H(oward) P(hillips)
    1890-1937 .... **TCLC 4, 22; DAM POP;**
                    SSC 3
See also AAYA 14; CA 104; 133; MTCW

Lovelace, Earl 1935-............. **CLC 51**
See also BW 2; CA 77-80; CANR 41;
    DLB 125; MTCW

Lovelace, Richard 1618-1657....... **LC 24**
See also DLB 131

Lowell, Amy
    1874-1925 .... **TCLC 1, 8; DAM POET;**
                    PC 13
See also CA 104; 151; DLB 54, 140

Lowell, James Russell 1819-1891 .. **NCLC 2**
See also CDALB 1640-1865; DLB 1, 11, 64,
    79

Lowell, Robert (Traill Spence, Jr.)
    1917-1977 ... **CLC 1, 2, 3, 4, 5, 8, 9, 11,**
        15, 37; DA; DAB; DAC; DAM MST,
                    NOV; PC 3; WLC
See also CA 9-12R; 73-76; CABS 2;
    CANR 26; DLB 5, 169; MTCW

Lowndes, Marie Adelaide (Belloc)
    1868-1947 .... **TCLC 12**
See also CA 107; DLB 70

Lowry, (Clarence) Malcolm
    1909-1957 .... **TCLC 6, 40**
See also CA 105; 131; CDBLB 1945-1960;
    DLB 15; MTCW

Lowry, Mina Gertrude 1882-1966
See Loy, Mina
See also CA 113

Loxsmith, John
See Brunner, John (Kilian Houston)

Loy, Mina .... **CLC 28; DAM POET; PC 16**
See also Lowry, Mina Gertrude
See also DLB 4, 54

Loyson-Bridet
See Schwob, (Mayer Andre) Marcel

Lucas, Craig 1951-............... **CLC 64**
See also CA 137

Lucas, George 1944-............... **CLC 16**
See also AAYA 1; CA 77-80; CANR 30;
    SATA 56

Lucas, Hans
See Godard, Jean-Luc

Lucas, Victoria
See Plath, Sylvia

Ludlam, Charles 1943-1987 ..... **CLC 46, 50**
See also CA 85-88; 122

Ludlum, Robert
    1927- ... **CLC 22, 43; DAM NOV, POP**
See also AAYA 10; BEST 89:1, 90:3;
    CA 33-36R; CANR 25, 41; DLBY 82;
    MTCW

Ludwig, Ken................... **CLC 60**

Ludwig, Otto 1813-1865.......... **NCLC 4**
See also DLB 129

Lugones, Leopoldo 1874-1938 ..... **TCLC 15**
See also CA 116; 131; HW

Lu Hsun 1881-1936 ...... **TCLC 3; SSC 20**
See also Shu-Jen, Chou

Lukacs, George .... **CLC 24**
See also Lukacs, Gyorgy (Szegeny von)

Lukacs, Gyorgy (Szegeny von) 1885-1971
See Lukacs, George
See also CA 101; 29-32R

Luke, Peter (Ambrose Cyprian)
    1919-1995 .... **CLC 38**
See also CA 81-84; 147; DLB 13

Lunar, Dennis
See Mungo, Raymond

Lurie, Alison 1926-........ **CLC 4, 5, 18, 39**
See also CA 1-4R; CANR 2, 17, 50; DLB 2;
    MTCW; SATA 46

Lustig, Arnost 1926-.............. **CLC 56**
See also AAYA 3; CA 69-72; CANR 47;
    SATA 56

Luther, Martin 1483-1546.......... **LC 9**

Luxemburg, Rosa 1870(?)-1919.... **TCLC 63**
See also CA 118

Luzi, Mario 1914-................ **CLC 13**
See also CA 61-64; CANR 9; DLB 128

L'Ymagier
See Gourmont, Remy (-Marie-Charles) de

Lynch, B. Suarez
See Bioy Casares, Adolfo; Borges, Jorge
    Luis

Lynch, David (K.) 1946-.......... **CLC 66**
See also CA 124; 129

Lynch, James
See Andreyev, Leonid (Nikolaevich)

Lynch Davis, B.
See Bioy Casares, Adolfo; Borges, Jorge
    Luis

Lyndsay, Sir David 1490-1555 ...... **LC 20**

Lynn, Kenneth S(chuyler) 1923-.... **CLC 50**
See also CA 1-4R; CANR 3, 27

Lynx
See West, Rebecca

Lyons, Marcus
See Blish, James (Benjamin)

Lyre, Pinchbeck
See Sassoon, Siegfried (Lorraine)

Lytle, Andrew (Nelson) 1902-1995 .. **CLC 22**
See also CA 9-12R; 150; DLB 6; DLBY 95

Lyttelton, George 1709-1773........ **LC 10**

Maas, Peter 1929- .... **CLC 29**
See also CA 93-96; INT 93-96

Macaulay, Rose 1881-1958 ..... **TCLC 7, 44**
See also CA 104; DLB 36

Macaulay, Thomas Babington
    1800-1859 .... **NCLC 42**
See also CDBLB 1832-1890; DLB 32, 55

MacBeth, George (Mann)
    1932-1992 .... **CLC 2, 5, 9**
See also CA 25-28R; 136; DLB 40; MTCW;
    SATA 4; SATA-Obit 70

MacCaig, Norman (Alexander)
    1910- ..... **CLC 36; DAB; DAM POET**
See also CA 9-12R; CANR 3, 34; DLB 27

MacCarthy, (Sir Charles Otto) Desmond
1877-1952 . . . . **TCLC 36**

MacDiarmid, Hugh
. . . . **CLC 2, 4, 11, 19, 63; PC 9**
See also Grieve, C(hristopher) M(urray)
See also CDBLB 1945-1960; DLB 20

MacDonald, Anson
See Heinlein, Robert A(nson)

Macdonald, Cynthia 1928- . . . . . . **CLC 13, 19**
See also CA 49-52; CANR 4, 44; DLB 105

MacDonald, George 1824-1905 . . . . . **TCLC 9**
See also CA 106; 137; DLB 18, 163;
MAICYA; SATA 33

Macdonald, John
See Millar, Kenneth

MacDonald, John D(ann)
1916-1986 . . . . **CLC 3, 27, 44;**
                               DAM NOV, POP
See also CA 1-4R; 121; CANR 1, 19;
DLB 8; DLBY 86; MTCW

Macdonald, John Ross
See Millar, Kenneth

Macdonald, Ross . . . . . **CLC 1, 2, 3, 14, 34, 41**
See also Millar, Kenneth
See also DLBD 6

MacDougal, John
See Blish, James (Benjamin)

MacEwen, Gwendolyn (Margaret)
1941-1987 . . . . **CLC 13, 55**
See also CA 9-12R; 124; CANR 7, 22;
DLB 53; SATA 50; SATA-Obit 55

Macha, Karel Hynek 1810-1846 . . **NCLC 46**

Machado (y Ruiz), Antonio
1875-1939 . . . . **TCLC 3**
See also CA 104; DLB 108

Machado de Assis, Joaquim Maria
1839-1908 . . . . **TCLC 10; BLC**
See also CA 107; 153

Machen, Arthur . . . . **TCLC 4; SSC 20**
See also Jones, Arthur Llewellyn
See also DLB 36, 156

Machiavelli, Niccolo
1469-1527 . . . . . . **LC 8; DA; DAB; DAC;**
                     DAM MST

MacInnes, Colin 1914-1976 . . . . . . **CLC 4, 23**
See also CA 69-72; 65-68; CANR 21;
DLB 14; MTCW

MacInnes, Helen (Clark)
1907-1985 . . . . . **CLC 27, 39; DAM POP**
See also CA 1-4R; 117; CANR 1, 28;
DLB 87; MTCW; SATA 22;
SATA-Obit 44

Mackay, Mary 1855-1924
See Corelli, Marie
See also CA 118

Mackenzie, Compton (Edward Montague)
1883-1972 . . . . **CLC 18**
See also CA 21-22; 37-40R; CAP 2;
DLB 34, 100

Mackenzie, Henry 1745-1831 . . . . **NCLC 41**
See also DLB 39

Mackintosh, Elizabeth 1896(?)-1952
See Tey, Josephine
See also CA 110

MacLaren, James
See Grieve, C(hristopher) M(urray)

Mac Laverty, Bernard 1942- . . . . **CLC 31**
See also CA 116; 118; CANR 43; INT 118

MacLean, Alistair (Stuart)
1922-1987 . . . . **CLC 3, 13, 50, 63;**
                           DAM POP
See also CA 57-60; 121; CANR 28; MTCW;
SATA 23; SATA-Obit 50

Maclean, Norman (Fitzroy)
1902-1990 . . . . **CLC 78; DAM POP;**
                       SSC 13
See also CA 102; 132; CANR 49

MacLeish, Archibald
1892-1982 . . . . **CLC 3, 8, 14, 68;**
                            DAM POET
See also CA 9-12R; 106; CANR 33; DLB 4,
7, 45; DLBY 82; MTCW

MacLennan, (John) Hugh
1907-1990 . . . . **CLC 2, 14, 92; DAC;**
                       DAM MST
See also CA 5-8R; 142; CANR 33; DLB 68;
MTCW

MacLeod, Alistair
1936- . . . . . . **CLC 56; DAC; DAM MST**
See also CA 123; DLB 60

MacNeice, (Frederick) Louis
1907-1963 . . . . . . **CLC 1, 4, 10, 53; DAB;**
                      DAM POET
See also CA 85-88; DLB 10, 20; MTCW

MacNeill, Dand
See Fraser, George MacDonald

Macpherson, James 1736-1796 . . . . . . **LC 29**
See also DLB 109

Macpherson, (Jean) Jay 1931- . . . . . . **CLC 14**
See also CA 5-8R; DLB 53

MacShane, Frank 1927- . . . . **CLC 39**
See also CA 9-12R; CANR 3, 33; DLB 111

Macumber, Mari
See Sandoz, Mari(e Susette)

Madach, Imre 1823-1864 . . . . **NCLC 19**

Madden, (Jerry) David 1933- . . . . **CLC 5, 15**
See also CA 1-4R; CAAS 3; CANR 4, 45;
DLB 6; MTCW

Maddern, Al(an)
See Ellison, Harlan (Jay)

Madhubuti, Haki R.
1942- . . . . **CLC 6, 73; BLC;**
                               DAM MULT, POET; PC 5
See also Lee, Don L.
See also BW 2; CA 73-76; CANR 24, 51;
DLB 5, 41; DLBD 8

Maepenn, Hugh
See Kuttner, Henry

Maepenn, K. H.
See Kuttner, Henry

Maeterlinck, Maurice
1862-1949 . . . . . . **TCLC 3; DAM DRAM**
See also CA 104; 136; SATA 66

Maginn, William 1794-1842 . . . . **NCLC 8**
See also DLB 110, 159

Mahapatra, Jayanta
1928- . . . . **CLC 33; DAM MULT**
See also CA 73-76; CAAS 9; CANR 15, 33

Mahfouz, Naguib (Abdel Aziz Al-Sabilgi)
1911(?)-
See Mahfuz, Najib
See also BEST 89:2; CA 128; CANR 55;
DAM NOV; MTCW

Mahfuz, Najib . . . . **CLC 52, 55**
See also Mahfouz, Naguib (Abdel Aziz
Al-Sabilgi)
See also DLBY 88

Mahon, Derek 1941- . . . . **CLC 27**
See also CA 113; 128; DLB 40

Mailer, Norman
1923- . . . . . . **CLC 1, 2, 3, 4, 5, 8, 11, 14,**
               28, 39, 74; DA; DAB; DAC; DAM MST,
               NOV, POP
See also AITN 2; CA 9-12R; CABS 1;
CANR 28; CDALB 1968-1988; DLB 2,
16, 28; DLBD 3; DLBY 80, 83; MTCW

Maillet, Antonine 1929- . . . . . . **CLC 54; DAC**
See also CA 115; 120; CANR 46; DLB 60;
INT 120

Mais, Roger 1905-1955 . . . . **TCLC 8**
See also BW 1; CA 105; 124; DLB 125;
MTCW

Maistre, Joseph de 1753-1821 . . . . **NCLC 37**

Maitland, Frederic 1850-1906 . . . . . **TCLC 65**

Maitland, Sara (Louise) 1950- . . . . . . **CLC 49**
See also CA 69-72; CANR 13

Major, Clarence
1936- . . . . **CLC 3, 19, 48; BLC;**
                           DAM MULT
See also BW 2; CA 21-24R; CAAS 6;
CANR 13, 25, 53; DLB 33

Major, Kevin (Gerald)
1949- . . . . **CLC 26; DAC**
See also AAYA 16; CA 97-100; CANR 21,
38; CLR 11; DLB 60; INT CANR-21;
JRDA; MAICYA; SATA 32, 82

Maki, James
See Ozu, Yasujiro

Malabaila, Damiano
See Levi, Primo

Malamud, Bernard
1914-1986 . . . . . . **CLC 1, 2, 3, 5, 8, 9, 11,**
               18, 27, 44, 78, 85; DA; DAB; DAC;
               DAM MST, NOV, POP; SSC 15; WLC
See also AAYA 16; CA 5-8R; 118; CABS 1;
CANR 28; CDALB 1941-1968; DLB 2,
28, 152; DLBY 80, 86; MTCW

Malaparte, Curzio 1898-1957 . . . . . **TCLC 52**

Malcolm, Dan
See Silverberg, Robert

Malcolm X . . . . **CLC 82; BLC**
See also Little, Malcolm

Malherbe, Francois de 1555-1628 . . . . . **LC 5**

Mallarme, Stephane
1842-1898 . . . . **NCLC 4, 41;**
                                  DAM POET; PC 4

Mallet-Joris, Francoise 1930- . . . . . . **CLC 11**
See also CA 65-68; CANR 17; DLB 83

Malley, Ern
See McAuley, James Phillip

Mallowan, Agatha Christie
See Christie, Agatha (Mary Clarissa)

Maloff, Saul 1922- . . . . **CLC 5**
See also CA 33-36R

Malone, Louis
See MacNeice, (Frederick) Louis

Malone, Michael (Christopher)
1942- . . . . **CLC 43**
See also CA 77-80; CANR 14, 32

Malory, (Sir) Thomas
1410(?)-1471(?) . . . . . . **LC 11; DA; DAB;**
DAC; DAM MST
See also CDBLB Before 1660; DLB 146;
SATA 59; SATA-Brief 33

Malouf, (George Joseph) David
1934- . . . . **CLC 28, 86**
See also CA 124; CANR 50

Malraux, (Georges-)Andre
1901-1976 . . . . . . **CLC 1, 4, 9, 13, 15, 57;**
DAM NOV
See also CA 21-22; 69-72; CANR 34;
CAP 2; DLB 72; MTCW

Malzberg, Barry N(athaniel) 1939-. . . **CLC 7**
See also CA 61-64; CAAS 4; CANR 16;
DLB 8

Mamet, David (Alan)
1947- . . . . **CLC 9, 15, 34, 46, 91;**
DAM DRAM; DC 4
See also AAYA 3; CA 81-84; CABS 3;
CANR 15, 41; DLB 7; MTCW

Mamoulian, Rouben (Zachary)
1897-1987 . . . . **CLC 16**
See also CA 25-28R; 124

Mandelstam, Osip (Emilievich)
1891(?)-1938(?) . . . . . . **TCLC 2, 6; PC 14**
See also CA 104; 150

Mander, (Mary) Jane 1877-1949. . . **TCLC 31**

Mandeville, John fl. 1350- . . . . **CMLC 19**
See also DLB 146

Mandiargues, Andre Pieyre de. . . . . . **CLC 41**
See also Pieyre de Mandiargues, Andre
See also DLB 83

Mandrake, Ethel Belle
See Thurman, Wallace (Henry)

Mangan, James Clarence
1803-1849 . . . . **NCLC 27**

Maniere, J.-E.
See Giraudoux, (Hippolyte) Jean

Manley, (Mary) Delariviere
1672(?)-1724 . . . . **LC 1**
See also DLB 39, 80

Mann, Abel
See Creasey, John

Mann, (Luiz) Heinrich 1871-1950. . . **TCLC 9**
See also CA 106; DLB 66

Mann, (Paul) Thomas
1875-1955 . . . **TCLC 2, 8, 14, 21, 35, 44,**
60; DA; DAB; DAC; DAM MST, NOV;
SSC 5; WLC
See also CA 104; 128; DLB 66; MTCW

Mannheim, Karl 1893-1947 . . . . . . **TCLC 65**

Manning, David
See Faust, Frederick (Schiller)

Manning, Frederic 1887(?)-1935 . . . **TCLC 25**
See also CA 124

Manning, Olivia 1915-1980 . . . . . . **CLC 5, 19**
See also CA 5-8R; 101; CANR 29; MTCW

Mano, D. Keith 1942- . . . . **CLC 2, 10**
See also CA 25-28R; CAAS 6; CANR 26;
DLB 6

Mansfield, Katherine
. . **TCLC 2, 8, 39; DAB; SSC 9, 23; WLC**
See also Beauchamp, Kathleen Mansfield
See also DLB 162

Manso, Peter 1940- . . . . **CLC 39**
See also CA 29-32R; CANR 44

Mantecon, Juan Jimenez
See Jimenez (Mantecon), Juan Ramon

Manton, Peter
See Creasey, John

Man Without a Spleen, A
See Chekhov, Anton (Pavlovich)

Manzoni, Alessandro 1785-1873 . . **NCLC 29**

Mapu, Abraham (ben Jekutiel)
1808-1867 . . . . **NCLC 18**

Mara, Sally
See Queneau, Raymond

Marat, Jean Paul 1743-1793. . . . . . . **LC 10**

Marcel, Gabriel Honore
1889-1973 . . . . **CLC 15**
See also CA 102; 45-48; MTCW

Marchbanks, Samuel
See Davies, (William) Robertson

Marchi, Giacomo
See Bassani, Giorgio

Margulies, Donald. . . . . **CLC 76**

Marie de France c. 12th cent. -. . . . **CMLC 8**

Marie de l'Incarnation 1599-1672. . . . **LC 10**

Mariner, Scott
See Pohl, Frederik

Marinetti, Filippo Tommaso
1876-1944 . . . . **TCLC 10**
See also CA 107; DLB 114

Marivaux, Pierre Carlet de Chamblain de
1688-1763 . . . . **LC 4**

Markandaya, Kamala . . . . **CLC 8, 38**
See also Taylor, Kamala (Purnaiya)

Markfield, Wallace 1926-. . . . . **CLC 8**
See also CA 69-72; CAAS 3; DLB 2, 28

Markham, Edwin 1852-1940 . . . . . . **TCLC 47**
See also DLB 54

Markham, Robert
See Amis, Kingsley (William)

Marks, J
See Highwater, Jamake (Mamake)

Marks-Highwater, J
See Highwater, Jamake (Mamake)

Markson, David M(errill) 1927- . . . . **CLC 67**
See also CA 49-52; CANR 1

Marley, Bob. . . . . **CLC 17**
See also Marley, Robert Nesta

Marley, Robert Nesta 1945-1981
See Marley, Bob
See also CA 107; 103

Marlowe, Christopher
1564-1593 . . . . . **LC 22; DA; DAB; DAC;**
DAM DRAM, MST; DC 1; WLC
See also CDBLB Before 1660; DLB 62

Marlowe, Stephen 1928-
See Queen, Ellery
See also CA 13-16R; CANR 6, 55

Marmontel, Jean-Francois
1723-1799 . . . . **LC 2**

Marquand, John P(hillips)
1893-1960 . . . . **CLC 2, 10**
See also CA 85-88; DLB 9, 102

Marques, Rene
1919-1979 . . . . . . **CLC 96; DAM MULT;**
HLC
See also CA 97-100; 85-88; DLB 113; HW

Marquez, Gabriel (Jose) Garcia
See Garcia Marquez, Gabriel (Jose)

Marquis, Don(ald Robert Perry)
1878-1937 . . . . **TCLC 7**
See also CA 104; DLB 11, 25

Marric, J. J.
See Creasey, John

Marrow, Bernard
See Moore, Brian

Marryat, Frederick 1792-1848 . . . . **NCLC 3**
See also DLB 21, 163

Marsden, James
See Creasey, John

Marsh, (Edith) Ngaio
1899-1982 . . . . . . **CLC 7, 53; DAM POP**
See also CA 9-12R; CANR 6; DLB 77;
MTCW

Marshall, Garry 1934-. . . . . **CLC 17**
See also AAYA 3; CA 111; SATA 60

Marshall, Paule
1929- . . . . **CLC 27, 72; BLC;**
DAM MULT; SSC 3
See also BW 2; CA 77-80; CANR 25;
DLB 157; MTCW

Marsten, Richard
See Hunter, Evan

Marston, John
1576-1634 . . . . **LC 33; DAM DRAM**
See also DLB 58, 172

Martha, Henry
See Harris, Mark

Martial c. 40-c. 104 . . . . **PC 10**

Martin, Ken
See Hubbard, L(afayette) Ron(ald)

Martin, Richard
See Creasey, John

Martin, Steve 1945-. . . . . **CLC 30**
See also CA 97-100; CANR 30; MTCW

Martin, Valerie 1948-. . . . . **CLC 89**
See also BEST 90:2; CA 85-88; CANR 49

Martin, Violet Florence
1862-1915 . . . . **TCLC 51**

Martin, Webber
See Silverberg, Robert

Martindale, Patrick Victor
See White, Patrick (Victor Martindale)

Martin du Gard, Roger
1881-1958 . . . . **TCLC 24**
See also CA 118; DLB 65

Martineau, Harriet 1802-1876. . . . **NCLC 26**
See also DLB 21, 55, 159, 163, 166;
YABC 2

Martines, Julia
  See O'Faolain, Julia

Martinez, Jacinto Benavente y
  See Benavente (y Martinez), Jacinto

Martinez Ruiz, Jose 1873-1967
  See Azorin; Ruiz, Jose Martinez
  See also CA 93-96; HW

Martinez Sierra, Gregorio
  1881-1947 . . . . **TCLC 6**
  See also CA 115

Martinez Sierra, Maria (de la O'LeJarraga)
  1874-1974 . . . . **TCLC 6**
  See also CA 115

Martinsen, Martin
  See Follett, Ken(neth Martin)

Martinson, Harry (Edmund)
  1904-1978 . . . . **CLC 14**
  See also CA 77-80; CANR 34

Marut, Ret
  See Traven, B.

Marut, Robert
  See Traven, B.

Marvell, Andrew
  1621-1678 . . . . . . **LC 4; DA; DAB; DAC;**
        DAM MST, POET; PC 10; WLC
  See also CDBLB 1660-1789; DLB 131

Marx, Karl (Heinrich)
  1818-1883 . . . . **NCLC 17**
  See also DLB 129

Masaoka Shiki . . . . **TCLC 18**
  See also Masaoka Tsunenori

Masaoka Tsunenori 1867-1902
  See Masaoka Shiki
  See also CA 117

Masefield, John (Edward)
  1878-1967 . . . . **CLC 11, 47; DAM POET**
  See also CA 19-20; 25-28R; CANR 33;
        CAP 2; CDBLB 1890-1914; DLB 10, 19,
        153, 160; MTCW; SATA 19

Maso, Carole 19(?)- . . . . **CLC 44**

Mason, Bobbie Ann
  1940- . . . . **CLC 28, 43, 82; SSC 4**
  See also AAYA 5; CA 53-56; CANR 11,
        31; DLB 173; DLBY 87; INT CANR-31;
        MTCW

Mason, Ernst
  See Pohl, Frederik

Mason, Lee W.
  See Malzberg, Barry N(athaniel)

Mason, Nick 1945- . . . . **CLC 35**

Mason, Tally
  See Derleth, August (William)

Mass, William
  See Gibson, William

Masters, Edgar Lee
  1868-1950 . . . . . . **TCLC 2, 25; DA; DAC;**
        DAM MST, POET; PC 1
  See also CA 104; 133; CDALB 1865-1917;
        DLB 54; MTCW

Masters, Hilary 1928- . . . . **CLC 48**
  See also CA 25-28R; CANR 13, 47

Mastrosimone, William 19(?)- . . . . . . **CLC 36**

Mathe, Albert
  See Camus, Albert

Matheson, Richard Burton 1926- . . . **CLC 37**
  See also CA 97-100; DLB 8, 44; INT 97-100

Mathews, Harry 1930- . . . . **CLC 6, 52**
  See also CA 21-24R; CAAS 6; CANR 18,
        40

Mathews, John Joseph
  1894-1979 . . . . . **CLC 84; DAM MULT**
  See also CA 19-20; 142; CANR 45; CAP 2;
        NNAL

Mathias, Roland (Glyn) 1915- . . . . . . **CLC 45**
  See also CA 97-100; CANR 19, 41; DLB 27

Matsuo Basho 1644-1694 . . . . **PC 3**
  See also DAM POET

Mattheson, Rodney
  See Creasey, John

Matthews, Greg 1949- . . . . **CLC 45**
  See also CA 135

Matthews, William 1942- . . . . **CLC 40**
  See also CA 29-32R; CAAS 18; CANR 12;
        DLB 5

Matthias, John (Edward) 1941- . . . . . . **CLC 9**
  See also CA 33-36R

Matthiessen, Peter
  1927- . . . . **CLC 5, 7, 11, 32, 64;**
        DAM NOV
  See also AAYA 6; BEST 90:4; CA 9-12R;
        CANR 21, 50; DLB 6, 173; MTCW;
        SATA 27

Maturin, Charles Robert
  1780(?)-1824 . . . . **NCLC 6**

Matute (Ausejo), Ana Maria
  1925- . . . . **CLC 11**
  See also CA 89-92; MTCW

Maugham, W. S.
  See Maugham, W(illiam) Somerset

Maugham, W(illiam) Somerset
  1874-1965 . . . . **CLC 1, 11, 15, 67, 93;**
        DA; DAB; DAC; DAM DRAM, MST,
        NOV; SSC 8; WLC
  See also CA 5-8R; 25-28R; CANR 40;
        CDBLB 1914-1945; DLB 10, 36, 77, 100,
        162; MTCW; SATA 54

Maugham, William Somerset
  See Maugham, W(illiam) Somerset

Maupassant, (Henri Rene Albert) Guy de
  1850-1893 . . . . . **NCLC 1, 42; DA; DAB;**
        DAC; DAM MST; SSC 1; WLC
  See also DLB 123

Maupin, Armistead
  1944- . . . . **CLC 95; DAM POP**
  See also CA 125; 130; INT 130

Maurhut, Richard
  See Traven, B.

Mauriac, Claude 1914-1996 . . . . **CLC 9**
  See also CA 89-92; 152; DLB 83

Mauriac, Francois (Charles)
  1885-1970 . . . . **CLC 4, 9, 56**
  See also CA 25-28; CAP 2; DLB 65;
        MTCW

Mavor, Osborne Henry 1888-1951
  See Bridie, James
  See also CA 104

Maxwell, William (Keepers, Jr.)
  1908- . . . . **CLC 19**
  See also CA 93-96; CANR 54; DLBY 80;
        INT 93-96

May, Elaine 1932- . . . . **CLC 16**
  See also CA 124; 142; DLB 44

Mayakovski, Vladimir (Vladimirovich)
  1893-1930 . . . . **TCLC 4, 18**
  See also CA 104

Mayhew, Henry 1812-1887 . . . . . . **NCLC 31**
  See also DLB 18, 55

Mayle, Peter 1939(?)- . . . . **CLC 89**
  See also CA 139

Maynard, Joyce 1953- . . . . **CLC 23**
  See also CA 111; 129

Mayne, William (James Carter)
  1928- . . . . **CLC 12**
  See also CA 9-12R; CANR 37; CLR 25;
        JRDA; MAICYA; SAAS 11; SATA 6, 68

Mayo, Jim
  See L'Amour, Louis (Dearborn)

Maysles, Albert 1926- . . . . **CLC 16**
  See also CA 29-32R

Maysles, David 1932- . . . . **CLC 16**

Mazer, Norma Fox 1931- . . . . **CLC 26**
  See also AAYA 5; CA 69-72; CANR 12,
        32; CLR 23; JRDA; MAICYA; SAAS 1;
        SATA 24, 67

Mazzini, Guiseppe 1805-1872 . . . . **NCLC 34**

McAuley, James Phillip
  1917-1976 . . . . **CLC 45**
  See also CA 97-100

McBain, Ed
  See Hunter, Evan

McBrien, William Augustine
  1930- . . . . **CLC 44**
  See also CA 107

McCaffrey, Anne (Inez)
  1926- . . . . . . **CLC 17; DAM NOV, POP**
  See also AAYA 6; AITN 2; BEST 89:2;
        CA 25-28R; CANR 15, 35, 55; DLB 8;
        JRDA; MAICYA; MTCW; SAAS 11;
        SATA 8, 70

McCall, Nathan 1955(?)- . . . . **CLC 86**
  See also CA 146

McCann, Arthur
  See Campbell, John W(ood, Jr.)

McCann, Edson
  See Pohl, Frederik

McCarthy, Charles, Jr. 1933-
  See McCarthy, Cormac
  See also CANR 42; DAM POP

McCarthy, Cormac 1933- . . . . . **CLC 4, 57, 59**
  See also McCarthy, Charles, Jr.
  See also DLB 6, 143

McCarthy, Mary (Therese)
  1912-1989 . . . **CLC 1, 3, 5, 14, 24, 39, 59**
  See also CA 5-8R; 129; CANR 16, 50;
        DLB 2; DLBY 81; INT CANR-16;
        MTCW

McCartney, (James) Paul
  1942- . . . . **CLC 12, 35**
  See also CA 146

McCauley, Stephen (D.) 1955- . . . . . **CLC 50**
  See also CA 141

McClure, Michael (Thomas)
1932- .... **CLC 6, 10**
See also CA 21-24R; CANR 17, 46;
DLB 16

McCorkle, Jill (Collins) 1958-...... **CLC 51**
See also CA 121; DLBY 87

McCourt, James 1941-............ **CLC 5**
See also CA 57-60

McCoy, Horace (Stanley)
1897-1955 .... **TCLC 28**
See also CA 108; DLB 9

McCrae, John 1872-1918........ **TCLC 12**
See also CA 109; DLB 92

McCreigh, James
See Pohl, Frederik

McCullers, (Lula) Carson (Smith)
1917-1967 .... **CLC 1, 4, 10, 12, 48; DA;**
DAB; DAC; DAM MST, NOV; SSC 9;
WLC
See also CA 5-8R; 25-28R; CABS 1, 3;
CANR 18; CDALB 1941-1968; DLB 2, 7,
173; MTCW; SATA 27

McCulloch, John Tyler
See Burroughs, Edgar Rice

McCullough, Colleen
1938(?)-.... **CLC 27; DAM NOV, POP**
See also CA 81-84; CANR 17, 46; MTCW

McDermott, Alice 1953- .... **CLC 90**
See also CA 109; CANR 40

McElroy, Joseph 1930- .... **CLC 5, 47**
See also CA 17-20R

McEwan, Ian (Russell)
1948- .... **CLC 13, 66; DAM NOV**
See also BEST 90:4; CA 61-64; CANR 14,
41; DLB 14; MTCW

McFadden, David 1940-......... **CLC 48**
See also CA 104; DLB 60; INT 104

McFarland, Dennis 1950- .... **CLC 65**

McGahern, John
1934- .... **CLC 5, 9, 48; SSC 17**
See also CA 17-20R; CANR 29; DLB 14;
MTCW

McGinley, Patrick (Anthony)
1937- .... **CLC 41**
See also CA 120; 127; INT 127

McGinley, Phyllis 1905-1978 ...... **CLC 14**
See also CA 9-12R; 77-80; CANR 19;
DLB 11, 48; SATA 2, 44; SATA-Obit 24

McGinniss, Joe 1942-............. **CLC 32**
See also AITN 2; BEST 89:2; CA 25-28R;
CANR 26; INT CANR-26

McGivern, Maureen Daly
See Daly, Maureen

McGrath, Patrick 1950-........... **CLC 55**
See also CA 136

McGrath, Thomas (Matthew)
1916-1990 .... **CLC 28, 59; DAM POET**
See also CA 9-12R; 132; CANR 6, 33;
MTCW; SATA 41; SATA-Obit 66

McGuane, Thomas (Francis III)
1939-................ **CLC 3, 7, 18, 45**
See also AITN 2; CA 49-52; CANR 5, 24,
49; DLB 2; DLBY 80; INT CANR-24;
MTCW

McGuckian, Medbh
1950- .... **CLC 48; DAM POET**
See also CA 143; DLB 40

McHale, Tom 1942(?)-1982...... **CLC 3, 5**
See also AITN 1; CA 77-80; 106

McIlvanney, William 1936-........ **CLC 42**
See also CA 25-28R; DLB 14

McIlwraith, Maureen Mollie Hunter
See Hunter, Mollie
See also SATA 2

McInerney, Jay
1955- .... **CLC 34; DAM POP**
See also AAYA 18; CA 116; 123;
CANR 45; INT 123

McIntyre, Vonda N(eel) 1948- ..... **CLC 18**
See also CA 81-84; CANR 17, 34; MTCW

McKay, Claude
.... **TCLC 7, 41; BLC; DAB; PC 2**
See also McKay, Festus Claudius
See also DLB 4, 45, 51, 117

McKay, Festus Claudius 1889-1948
See McKay, Claude
See also BW 1; CA 104; 124; DA; DAC;
DAM MST, MULT, NOV, POET;
MTCW; WLC

McKuen, Rod 1933-............. **CLC 1, 3**
See also AITN 1; CA 41-44R; CANR 40

McLoughlin, R. B.
See Mencken, H(enry) L(ouis)

McLuhan, (Herbert) Marshall
1911-1980 .... **CLC 37, 83**
See also CA 9-12R; 102; CANR 12, 34;
DLB 88; INT CANR-12; MTCW

McMillan, Terry (L.)
1951- .... **CLC 50, 61; DAM MULT,**
NOV, POP
See also BW 2; CA 140

McMurtry, Larry (Jeff)
1936- .... **CLC 2, 3, 7, 11, 27, 44;**
DAM NOV, POP
See also AAYA 15; AITN 2; BEST 89:2;
CA 5-8R; CANR 19, 43;
CDALB 1968-1988; DLB 2, 143;
DLBY 80, 87; MTCW

McNally, T. M. 1961- .... **CLC 82**

McNally, Terrence
1939- ... **CLC 4, 7, 41, 91; DAM DRAM**
See also CA 45-48; CANR 2; DLB 7

McNamer, Deirdre 1950-......... **CLC 70**

McNeile, Herman Cyril 1888-1937
See Sapper
See also DLB 77

McNickle, (William) D'Arcy
1904-1977 ...... **CLC 89; DAM MULT**
See also CA 9-12R; 85-88; CANR 5, 45;
NNAL; SATA-Obit 22

McPhee, John (Angus) 1931- ...... **CLC 36**
See also BEST 90:1; CA 65-68; CANR 20,
46; MTCW

McPherson, James Alan
1943- .... **CLC 19, 77**
See also BW 1; CA 25-28R; CAAS 17;
CANR 24; DLB 38; MTCW

McPherson, William (Alexander)
1933- .... **CLC 34**
See also CA 69-72; CANR 28;
INT CANR-28

Mead, Margaret 1901-1978 .... **CLC 37**
See also AITN 1; CA 1-4R; 81-84;
CANR 4; MTCW; SATA-Obit 20

Meaker, Marijane (Agnes) 1927-
See Kerr, M. E.
See also CA 107; CANR 37; INT 107;
JRDA; MAICYA; MTCW; SATA 20, 61

Medoff, Mark (Howard)
1940- .... **CLC 6, 23; DAM DRAM**
See also AITN 1; CA 53-56; CANR 5;
DLB 7; INT CANR-5

Medvedev, P. N.
See Bakhtin, Mikhail Mikhailovich

Meged, Aharon
See Megged, Aharon

Meged, Aron
See Megged, Aharon

Megged, Aharon 1920-............ **CLC 9**
See also CA 49-52; CAAS 13; CANR 1

Mehta, Ved (Parkash) 1934-....... **CLC 37**
See also CA 1-4R; CANR 2, 23; MTCW

Melanter
See Blackmore, R(ichard) D(oddridge)

Melikow, Loris
See Hofmannsthal, Hugo von

Melmoth, Sebastian
See Wilde, Oscar (Fingal O'Flahertie Wills)

Meltzer, Milton 1915- .... **CLC 26**
See also AAYA 8; CA 13-16R; CANR 38;
CLR 13; DLB 61; JRDA; MAICYA;
SAAS 1; SATA 1, 50, 80

Melville, Herman
1819-1891 ..... **NCLC 3, 12, 29, 45, 49;**
DA; DAB; DAC; DAM MST, NOV;
SSC 1, 17; WLC
See also CDALB 1640-1865; DLB 3, 74;
SATA 59

Menander
c. 342B.C.-c. 292B.C........ **CMLC 9;**
DAM DRAM; DC 3

Mencken, H(enry) L(ouis)
1880-1956 .... **TCLC 13**
See also CA 105; 125; CDALB 1917-1929;
DLB 11, 29, 63, 137; MTCW

Mercer, David
1928-1980 .... **CLC 5; DAM DRAM**
See also CA 9-12R; 102; CANR 23;
DLB 13; MTCW

Merchant, Paul
See Ellison, Harlan (Jay)

Meredith, George
1828-1909 .. **TCLC 17, 43; DAM POET**
See also CA 117; 153; CDBLB 1832-1890;
DLB 18, 35, 57, 159

Meredith, William (Morris)
1919- .. **CLC 4, 13, 22, 55; DAM POET**
See also CA 9-12R; CAAS 14; CANR 6, 40;
DLB 5

Merezhkovsky, Dmitry Sergeyevich
1865-1941 .... **TCLC 29**

Merimee, Prosper
        1803-1870 . . . . **NCLC 6; SSC 7**
        See also DLB 119

Merkin, Daphne 1954- . . . . **CLC 44**
        See also CA 123

Merlin, Arthur
        See Blish, James (Benjamin)

Merrill, James (Ingram)
        1926-1995 . . . . **CLC 2, 3, 6, 8, 13, 18, 34,
                                                 91; DAM POET**
        See also CA 13-16R; 147; CANR 10, 49;
        DLB 5, 165; DLBY 85; INT CANR-10;
        MTCW

Merriman, Alex
        See Silverberg, Robert

Merritt, E. B.
        See Waddington, Miriam

Merton, Thomas
        1915-1968 . . **CLC 1, 3, 11, 34, 83; PC 10**
        See also CA 5-8R; 25-28R; CANR 22, 53;
        DLB 48; DLBY 81; MTCW

Merwin, W(illiam) S(tanley)
        1927- . . . . . . **CLC 1, 2, 3, 5, 8, 13, 18, 45,
                                                 88; DAM POET**
        See also CA 13-16R; CANR 15, 51; DLB 5,
        169; INT CANR-15; MTCW

Metcalf, John 1938- . . . . **CLC 37**
        See also CA 113; DLB 60

Metcalf, Suzanne
        See Baum, L(yman) Frank

Mew, Charlotte (Mary)
        1870-1928 . . . . **TCLC 8**
        See also CA 105; DLB 19, 135

Mewshaw, Michael 1943- . . . . **CLC 9**
        See also CA 53-56; CANR 7, 47; DLBY 80

Meyer, June
        See Jordan, June

Meyer, Lynn
        See Slavitt, David R(ytman)

Meyer-Meyrink, Gustav 1868-1932
        See Meyrink, Gustav
        See also CA 117

Meyers, Jeffrey 1939- . . . . **CLC 39**
        See also CA 73-76; CANR 54; DLB 111

Meynell, Alice (Christina Gertrude Thompson)
        1847-1922 . . . . **TCLC 6**
        See also CA 104; DLB 19, 98

Meyrink, Gustav . . . . **TCLC 21**
        See also Meyer-Meyrink, Gustav
        See also DLB 81

Michaels, Leonard
        1933- . . . . **CLC 6, 25; SSC 16**
        See also CA 61-64; CANR 21; DLB 130;
        MTCW

Michaux, Henri 1899-1984 . . . . . . **CLC 8, 19**
        See also CA 85-88; 114

Michelangelo 1475-1564 . . . . **LC 12**

Michelet, Jules 1798-1874 . . . . . . **NCLC 31**

Michener, James A(lbert)
        1907(?)- . . . . **CLC 1, 5, 11, 29, 60;
                                                 DAM NOV, POP**
        See also AITN 1; BEST 90:1; CA 5-8R;
        CANR 21, 45; DLB 6; MTCW

Mickiewicz, Adam 1798-1855 . . . . . **NCLC 3**

Middleton, Christopher 1926- . . . . . . **CLC 13**
        See also CA 13-16R; CANR 29, 54;
        DLB 40

Middleton, Richard (Barham)
        1882-1911 . . . . **TCLC 56**
        See also DLB 156

Middleton, Stanley 1919- . . . . **CLC 7, 38**
        See also CA 25-28R; CAAS 23; CANR 21,
        46; DLB 14

Middleton, Thomas
        1580-1627 . . . . **LC 33; DAM DRAM,
                                                 MST; DC 5**
        See also DLB 58

Migueis, Jose Rodrigues 1901- . . . . . **CLC 10**

Mikszath, Kalman 1847-1910 . . . . . **TCLC 31**

Miles, Josephine (Louise)
        1911-1985 . . . . **CLC 1, 2, 14, 34, 39;
                                                 DAM POET**
        See also CA 1-4R; 116; CANR 2, 55;
        DLB 48

Militant
        See Sandburg, Carl (August)

Mill, John Stuart 1806-1873 . . **NCLC 11, 58**
        See also CDBLB 1832-1890; DLB 55

Millar, Kenneth
        1915-1983 . . . . **CLC 14; DAM POP**
        See also Macdonald, Ross
        See also CA 9-12R; 110; CANR 16; DLB 2;
        DLBD 6; DLBY 83; MTCW

Millay, E. Vincent
        See Millay, Edna St. Vincent

Millay, Edna St. Vincent
        1892-1950 . . . . . . **TCLC 4, 49; DA; DAB;
                                                 DAC; DAM MST, POET; PC 6**
        See also CA 104; 130; CDALB 1917-1929;
        DLB 45; MTCW

Miller, Arthur
        1915- . . . . **CLC 1, 2, 6, 10, 15, 26, 47, 78;
                                                 DA; DAB; DAC; DAM DRAM, MST;
                                                 DC 1; WLC**
        See also AAYA 15; AITN 1; CA 1-4R;
        CABS 3; CANR 2, 30, 54;
        CDALB 1941-1968; DLB 7; MTCW

Miller, Henry (Valentine)
        1891-1980 . . . . **CLC 1, 2, 4, 9, 14, 43, 84;
                                                 DA; DAB; DAC; DAM MST, NOV;
                                                 WLC**
        See also CA 9-12R; 97-100; CANR 33;
        CDALB 1929-1941; DLB 4, 9; DLBY 80;
        MTCW

Miller, Jason 1939(?)- . . . . **CLC 2**
        See also AITN 1; CA 73-76; DLB 7

Miller, Sue 1943- . . . . . **CLC 44; DAM POP**
        See also BEST 90:3; CA 139; DLB 143

Miller, Walter M(ichael, Jr.)
        1923- . . . . **CLC 4, 30**
        See also CA 85-88; DLB 8

Millett, Kate 1934- . . . . **CLC 67**
        See also AITN 1; CA 73-76; CANR 32, 53;
        MTCW

Millhauser, Steven 1943- . . . . **CLC 21, 54**
        See also CA 110; 111; DLB 2; INT 111

Millin, Sarah Gertrude 1889-1968 . . **CLC 49**
        See also CA 102; 93-96

Milne, A(lan) A(lexander)
        1882-1956 . . . . **TCLC 6; DAB; DAC;
                                                 DAM MST**
        See also CA 104; 133; CLR 1, 26; DLB 10,
        77, 100, 160; MAICYA; MTCW;
        YABC 1

Milner, Ron(ald)
        1938- . . . . . **CLC 56; BLC; DAM MULT**
        See also AITN 1; BW 1; CA 73-76;
        CANR 24; DLB 38; MTCW

Milosz, Czeslaw
        1911- . . . . **CLC 5, 11, 22, 31, 56, 82;
                                                 DAM MST, POET; PC 8**
        See also CA 81-84; CANR 23, 51; MTCW

Milton, John
        1608-1674 . . . . . . **LC 9; DA; DAB; DAC;
                                                 DAM MST, POET; WLC**
        See also CDBLB 1660-1789; DLB 131, 151

Min, Anchee 1957- . . . . **CLC 86**
        See also CA 146

Minehaha, Cornelius
        See Wedekind, (Benjamin) Frank(lin)

Miner, Valerie 1947- . . . . **CLC 40**
        See also CA 97-100

Minimo, Duca
        See D'Annunzio, Gabriele

Minot, Susan 1956- . . . . **CLC 44**
        See also CA 134

Minus, Ed 1938- . . . . **CLC 39**

Miranda, Javier
        See Bioy Casares, Adolfo

Mirbeau, Octave 1848-1917 . . . . . . **TCLC 55**
        See also DLB 123

Miro (Ferrer), Gabriel (Francisco Victor)
        1879-1930 . . . . **TCLC 5**
        See also CA 104

Mishima, Yukio
        . . . . **CLC 2, 4, 6, 9, 27; DC 1; SSC 4**
        See also Hiraoka, Kimitake

Mistral, Frederic 1830-1914 . . . . . . **TCLC 51**
        See also CA 122

Mistral, Gabriela . . . . **TCLC 2; HLC**
        See also Godoy Alcayaga, Lucila

Mistry, Rohinton 1952- . . . . . . **CLC 71; DAC**
        See also CA 141

Mitchell, Clyde
        See Ellison, Harlan (Jay); Silverberg, Robert

Mitchell, James Leslie 1901-1935
        See Gibbon, Lewis Grassic
        See also CA 104; DLB 15

Mitchell, Joni 1943- . . . . **CLC 12**
        See also CA 112

Mitchell, Margaret (Munnerlyn)
        1900-1949 . . . . . . **TCLC 11; DAM NOV,
                                                 POP**
        See also CA 109; 125; CANR 55; DLB 9;
        MTCW

Mitchell, Peggy
        See Mitchell, Margaret (Munnerlyn)

Mitchell, S(ilas) Weir 1829-1914 . . **TCLC 36**

Mitchell, W(illiam) O(rmond)
        1914- . . . . . . **CLC 25; DAC; DAM MST**
        See also CA 77-80; CANR 15, 43; DLB 88

Mitford, Mary Russell 1787-1855.. **NCLC 4**
See also DLB 110, 116

Mitford, Nancy 1904-1973........ **CLC 44**
See also CA 9-12R

Miyamoto, Yuriko 1899-1951 ..... **TCLC 37**

Mo, Timothy (Peter) 1950(?)-...... **CLC 46**
See also CA 117; MTCW

Modarressi, Taghi (M.) 1931-...... **CLC 44**
See also CA 121; 134; INT 134

Modiano, Patrick (Jean) 1945-..... **CLC 18**
See also CA 85-88; CANR 17, 40; DLB 83

Moerck, Paal
See Roelvaag, O(le) E(dvart)

Mofolo, Thomas (Mokopu)
1875(?)-1948 .... **TCLC 22; BLC;**
DAM MULT
See also CA 121; 153

Mohr, Nicholasa
1935- ..... **CLC 12; DAM MULT; HLC**
See also AAYA 8; CA 49-52; CANR 1, 32;
CLR 22; DLB 145; HW; JRDA; SAAS 8;
SATA 8

Mojtabai, A(nn) G(race)
1938-................ **CLC 5, 9, 15, 29**
See also CA 85-88

Moliere
1622-1673 ..... **LC 28; DA; DAB; DAC;**
DAM DRAM, MST; WLC

Molin, Charles
See Mayne, William (James Carter)

Molnar, Ferenc
1878-1952 ..... **TCLC 20; DAM DRAM**
See also CA 109; 153

Momaday, N(avarre) Scott
1934- ..... **CLC 2, 19, 85, 95; DA; DAB;**
DAC; DAM MST, MULT, NOV, POP
See also AAYA 11; CA 25-28R; CANR 14,
34; DLB 143; INT CANR-14; MTCW;
NNAL; SATA 48; SATA-Brief 30

Monette, Paul 1945-1995.......... **CLC 82**
See also CA 139; 147

Monroe, Harriet 1860-1936...... **TCLC 12**
See also CA 109; DLB 54, 91

Monroe, Lyle
See Heinlein, Robert A(nson)

Montagu, Elizabeth 1917-........ **NCLC 7**
See also CA 9-12R

Montagu, Mary (Pierrepont) Wortley
1689-1762 .... **LC 9; PC 16**
See also DLB 95, 101

Montagu, W. H.
See Coleridge, Samuel Taylor

Montague, John (Patrick)
1929-..................... **CLC 13, 46**
See also CA 9-12R; CANR 9; DLB 40;
MTCW

Montaigne, Michel (Eyquem) de
1533-1592 ...... **LC 8; DA; DAB; DAC;**
DAM MST; WLC

Montale, Eugenio
1896-1981 .... **CLC 7, 9, 18; PC 13**
See also CA 17-20R; 104; CANR 30;
DLB 114; MTCW

Montesquieu, Charles-Louis de Secondat
1689-1755 .... **LC 7**

Montgomery, (Robert) Bruce 1921-1978
See Crispin, Edmund
See also CA 104

Montgomery, L(ucy) M(aud)
1874-1942 .... **TCLC 51; DAC;**
DAM MST
See also AAYA 12; CA 108; 137; CLR 8;
DLB 92; DLBD 14; JRDA; MAICYA;
YABC 1

Montgomery, Marion H., Jr. 1925-.. **CLC 7**
See also AITN 1; CA 1-4R; CANR 3, 48;
DLB 6

Montgomery, Max
See Davenport, Guy (Mattison, Jr.)

Montherlant, Henry (Milon) de
1896-1972 .... **CLC 8, 19; DAM DRAM**
See also CA 85-88; 37-40R; DLB 72;
MTCW

Monty Python
See Chapman, Graham; Cleese, John
(Marwood); Gilliam, Terry (Vance); Idle,
Eric; Jones, Terence Graham Parry; Palin,
Michael (Edward)
See also AAYA 7

Moodie, Susanna (Strickland)
1803-1885 .... **NCLC 14**
See also DLB 99

Mooney, Edward 1951-
See Mooney, Ted
See also CA 130

Mooney, Ted .... **CLC 25**
See also Mooney, Edward

Moorcock, Michael (John)
1939-.................. **CLC 5, 27, 58**
See also CA 45-48; CAAS 5; CANR 2, 17,
38; DLB 14; MTCW

Moore, Brian
1921-...... **CLC 1, 3, 5, 7, 8, 19, 32, 90;**
DAB; DAC; DAM MST
See also CA 1-4R; CANR 1, 25, 42; MTCW

Moore, Edward
See Muir, Edwin

Moore, George Augustus
1852-1933 .... **TCLC 7; SSC 19**
See also CA 104; DLB 10, 18, 57, 135

Moore, Lorrie .... **CLC 39, 45, 68**
See also Moore, Marie Lorena

Moore, Marianne (Craig)
1887-1972 .... **CLC 1, 2, 4, 8, 10, 13, 19,**
47; DA; DAB; DAC; DAM MST, POET;
PC 4
See also CA 1-4R; 33-36R; CANR 3;
CDALB 1929-1941; DLB 45; DLBD 7;
MTCW; SATA 20

Moore, Marie Lorena 1957-
See Moore, Lorrie
See also CA 116; CANR 39

Moore, Thomas 1779-1852........ **NCLC 6**
See also DLB 96, 144

Morand, Paul 1888-1976 .. **CLC 41; SSC 22**
See also CA 69-72; DLB 65

Morante, Elsa 1918-1985........ **CLC 8, 47**
See also CA 85-88; 117; CANR 35; MTCW

Moravia, Alberto....... **CLC 2, 7, 11, 27, 46**
See also Pincherle, Alberto

More, Hannah 1745-1833 .... **NCLC 27**
See also DLB 107, 109, 116, 158

More, Henry 1614-1687............. **LC 9**
See also DLB 126

More, Sir Thomas 1478-1535 .... **LC 10, 32**

Moreas, Jean...................... **TCLC 18**
See also Papadiamantopoulos, Johannes

Morgan, Berry 1919-.............. **CLC 6**
See also CA 49-52; DLB 6

Morgan, Claire
See Highsmith, (Mary) Patricia

Morgan, Edwin (George) 1920-..... **CLC 31**
See also CA 5-8R; CANR 3, 43; DLB 27

Morgan, (George) Frederick
1922-...................... **CLC 23**
See also CA 17-20R; CANR 21

Morgan, Harriet
See Mencken, H(enry) L(ouis)

Morgan, Jane
See Cooper, James Fenimore

Morgan, Janet 1945-............. **CLC 39**
See also CA 65-68

Morgan, Lady 1776(?)-1859...... **NCLC 29**
See also DLB 116, 158

Morgan, Robin 1941-.............. **CLC 2**
See also CA 69-72; CANR 29; MTCW;
SATA 80

Morgan, Scott
See Kuttner, Henry

Morgan, Seth 1949(?)-1990 .... **CLC 65**
See also CA 132

Morgenstern, Christian
1871-1914 .... **TCLC 8**
See also CA 105

Morgenstern, S.
See Goldman, William (W.)

Moricz, Zsigmond 1879-1942 ..... **TCLC 33**

Morike, Eduard (Friedrich)
1804-1875 .... **NCLC 10**
See also DLB 133

Mori Ogai .... **TCLC 14**
See also Mori Rintaro

Mori Rintaro 1862-1922
See Mori Ogai
See also CA 110

Moritz, Karl Philipp 1756-1793 ...... **LC 2**
See also DLB 94

Morland, Peter Henry
See Faust, Frederick (Schiller)

Morren, Theophil
See Hofmannsthal, Hugo von

Morris, Bill 1952-................ **CLC 76**

Morris, Julian
See West, Morris L(anglo)

Morris, Steveland Judkins 1950(?)-
See Wonder, Stevie
See also CA 111

Morris, William 1834-1896 .... **NCLC 4**
See also CDBLB 1832-1890; DLB 18, 35,
57, 156

Morris, Wright 1910-... **CLC 1, 3, 7, 18, 37**
See also CA 9-12R; CANR 21; DLB 2;
DLBY 81; MTCW

Morrison, Chloe Anthony Wofford
See Morrison, Toni

Morrison, James Douglas 1943-1971
See Morrison, Jim
See also CA 73-76; CANR 40

Morrison, Jim . . . . **CLC 17**
See also Morrison, James Douglas

Morrison, Toni
1931- . . . . **CLC 4, 10, 22, 55, 81, 87;
BLC; DA; DAB; DAC; DAM MST,
MULT, NOV, POP**
See also AAYA 1; BW 2; CA 29-32R;
CANR 27, 42; CDALB 1968-1988;
DLB 6, 33, 143; DLBY 81; MTCW;
SATA 57

Morrison, Van 1945- . . . . **CLC 21**
See also CA 116

Mortimer, John (Clifford)
1923- . . . . . . **CLC 28, 43; DAM DRAM,
POP**
See also CA 13-16R; CANR 21;
CDBLB 1960 to Present; DLB 13;
INT CANR-21; MTCW

Mortimer, Penelope (Ruth) 1918- . . . . **CLC 5**
See also CA 57-60; CANR 45

Morton, Anthony
See Creasey, John

Mosher, Howard Frank 1943- . . . . . . **CLC 62**
See also CA 139

Mosley, Nicholas 1923- . . . . **CLC 43, 70**
See also CA 69-72; CANR 41; DLB 14

Mosley, Walter
1952- . . . . . **CLC 97; DAM MULT, POP**
See also AAYA 17; BW 2; CA 142

Moss, Howard
1922-1987 . . . . **CLC 7, 14, 45, 50;
DAM POET**
See also CA 1-4R; 123; CANR 1, 44;
DLB 5

Mossgiel, Rab
See Burns, Robert

Motion, Andrew (Peter) 1952- . . . . . . **CLC 47**
See also CA 146; DLB 40

Motley, Willard (Francis)
1909-1965 . . . . **CLC 18**
See also BW 1; CA 117; 106; DLB 76, 143

Motoori, Norinaga 1730-1801 . . . . **NCLC 45**

Mott, Michael (Charles Alston)
1930- . . . . **CLC 15, 34**
See also CA 5-8R; CAAS 7; CANR 7, 29

Mountain Wolf Woman
1884-1960 . . . . **CLC 92**
See also CA 144; NNAL

Moure, Erin 1955- . . . . **CLC 88**
See also CA 113; DLB 60

Mowat, Farley (McGill)
1921- . . . . . . **CLC 26; DAC; DAM MST**
See also AAYA 1; CA 1-4R; CANR 4, 24,
42; CLR 20; DLB 68; INT CANAR-24;
JRDA; MAICYA; MTCW; SATA 3, 55

Moyers, Bill 1934- . . . . **CLC 74**
See also AITN 2; CA 61-64; CANR 31, 52

Mphahlele, Es'kia
See Mphahlele, Ezekiel
See also DLB 125

Mphahlele, Ezekiel
1919- . . . . . **CLC 25; BLC; DAM MULT**
See also Mphahlele, Es'kia
See also BW 2; CA 81-84; CANR 26

Mqhayi, S(amuel) E(dward) K(rune Loliwe)
1875-1945 . . . . **TCLC 25; BLC;
DAM MULT**
See also CA 153

Mrozek, Slawomir 1930- . . . . **CLC 3, 13**
See also CA 13-16R; CAAS 10; CANR 29;
MTCW

Mrs. Belloc-Lowndes
See Lowndes, Marie Adelaide (Belloc)

Mtwa, Percy (?)- . . . . **CLC 47**

Mueller, Lisel 1924- . . . . **CLC 13, 51**
See also CA 93-96; DLB 105

Muir, Edwin 1887-1959 . . . . **TCLC 2**
See also CA 104; DLB 20, 100

Muir, John 1838-1914 . . . . **TCLC 28**

Mujica Lainez, Manuel
1910-1984 . . . . **CLC 31**
See also Lainez, Manuel Mujica
See also CA 81-84; 112; CANR 32; HW

Mukherjee, Bharati
1940- . . . . **CLC 53; DAM NOV**
See also BEST 89:2; CA 107; CANR 45;
DLB 60; MTCW

Muldoon, Paul
1951- . . . . **CLC 32, 72; DAM POET**
See also CA 113; 129; CANR 52; DLB 40;
INT 129

Mulisch, Harry 1927- . . . . **CLC 42**
See also CA 9-12R; CANR 6, 26

Mull, Martin 1943- . . . . **CLC 17**
See also CA 105

Mulock, Dinah Maria
See Craik, Dinah Maria (Mulock)

Munford, Robert 1737(?)-1783 . . . . **LC 5**
See also DLB 31

Mungo, Raymond 1946- . . . . **CLC 72**
See also CA 49-52; CANR 2

Munro, Alice
1931- . . . . . . **CLC 6, 10, 19, 50, 95; DAC;
DAM MST, NOV; SSC 3**
See also AITN 2; CA 33-36R; CANR 33,
53; DLB 53; MTCW; SATA 29

Munro, H(ector) H(ugh) 1870-1916
See Saki
See also CA 104; 130; CDBLB 1890-1914;
DA; DAB; DAC; DAM MST, NOV;
DLB 34, 162; MTCW; WLC

Murasaki, Lady . . . . **CMLC 1**

Murdoch, (Jean) Iris
1919- . . . . . . **CLC 1, 2, 3, 4, 6, 8, 11, 15,
22, 31, 51; DAB; DAC; DAM MST,
NOV**
See also CA 13-16R; CANR 8, 43;
CDBLB 1960 to Present; DLB 14;
INT CANR-8; MTCW

Murfree, Mary Noailles
1850-1922 . . . . **SSC 22**
See also CA 122; DLB 12, 74

Murnau, Friedrich Wilhelm
See Plumpe, Friedrich Wilhelm

Murphy, Richard 1927- . . . . **CLC 41**
See also CA 29-32R; DLB 40

Murphy, Sylvia 1937- . . . . **CLC 34**
See also CA 121

Murphy, Thomas (Bernard) 1935- . . . **CLC 51**
See also CA 101

Murray, Albert L. 1916- . . . . **CLC 73**
See also BW 2; CA 49-52; CANR 26, 52;
DLB 38

Murray, Les(lie) A(llan)
1938- . . . . **CLC 40; DAM POET**
See also CA 21-24R; CANR 11, 27

Murry, J. Middleton
See Murry, John Middleton

Murry, John Middleton
1889-1957 . . . . **TCLC 16**
See also CA 118; DLB 149

Musgrave, Susan 1951- . . . . **CLC 13, 54**
See also CA 69-72; CANR 45

Musil, Robert (Edler von)
1880-1942 . . . . **TCLC 12; SSC 18**
See also CA 109; CANR 55; DLB 81, 124

Muske, Carol 1945- . . . . **CLC 90**
See also Muske-Dukes, Carol (Anne)

Muske-Dukes, Carol (Anne) 1945-
See Muske, Carol
See also CA 65-68; CANR 32

Musset, (Louis Charles) Alfred de
1810-1857 . . . . **NCLC 7**

My Brother's Brother
See Chekhov, Anton (Pavlovich)

Myers, L. H. 1881-1944 . . . . **TCLC 59**
See also DLB 15

Myers, Walter Dean
1937- . . . . . **CLC 35; BLC; DAM MULT,
NOV**
See also AAYA 4; BW 2; CA 33-36R;
CANR 20, 42; CLR 4, 16, 35; DLB 33;
INT CANR-20; JRDA; MAICYA;
SAAS 2; SATA 41, 71; SATA-Brief 27

Myers, Walter M.
See Myers, Walter Dean

Myles, Symon
See Follett, Ken(neth Martin)

Nabokov, Vladimir (Vladimirovich)
1899-1977 . . . . . **CLC 1, 2, 3, 6, 8, 11, 15,
23, 44, 46, 64; DA; DAB; DAC;
DAM MST, NOV; SSC 11; WLC**
See also CA 5-8R; 69-72; CANR 20;
CDALB 1941-1968; DLB 2; DLBD 3;
DLBY 80, 91; MTCW

Nagai Kafu . . . . **TCLC 51**
See also Nagai Sokichi

Nagai Sokichi 1879-1959
See Nagai Kafu
See also CA 117

Nagy, Laszlo 1925-1978 . . . . **CLC 7**
See also CA 129; 112

Naipaul, Shiva(dhar Srinivasa)
1945-1985 . . . . . **CLC 32, 39; DAM NOV**
See also CA 110; 112; 116; CANR 33;
DLB 157; DLBY 85; MTCW

Naipaul, V(idiadhar) S(urajprasad)
1932- .... **CLC 4, 7, 9, 13, 18, 37; DAB;**
DAC; DAM MST, NOV
See also CA 1-4R; CANR 1, 33, 51;
CDBLB 1960 to Present; DLB 125;
DLBY 85; MTCW

Nakos, Lilika 1899(?)- .... **CLC 29**

Narayan, R(asipuram) K(rishnaswami)
1906- .... **CLC 7, 28, 47; DAM NOV**
See also CA 81-84; CANR 33; MTCW;
SATA 62

Nash, (Frediric) Ogden
1902-1971 .... **CLC 23; DAM POET**
See also CA 13-14; 29-32R; CANR 34;
CAP 1; DLB 11; MAICYA; MTCW;
SATA 2, 46

Nathan, Daniel
See Dannay, Frederic

Nathan, George Jean 1882-1958 ... **TCLC 18**
See also Hatteras, Owen
See also CA 114; DLB 137

Natsume, Kinnosuke 1867-1916
See Natsume, Soseki
See also CA 104

Natsume, Soseki .... **TCLC 2, 10**
See also Natsume, Kinnosuke

Natti, (Mary) Lee 1919-
See Kingman, Lee
See also CA 5-8R; CANR 2

Naylor, Gloria
1950- ..... **CLC 28, 52; BLC; DA; DAC;**
DAM MST, MULT, NOV, POP
See also AAYA 6; BW 2; CA 107;
CANR 27, 51; DLB 173; MTCW

Neihardt, John Gneisenau
1881-1973 .... **CLC 32**
See also CA 13-14; CAP 1; DLB 9, 54

Nekrasov, Nikolai Alekseevich
1821-1878 .... **NCLC 11**

Nelligan, Emile 1879-1941 .... **TCLC 14**
See also CA 114; DLB 92

Nelson, Willie 1933- .... **CLC 17**
See also CA 107

Nemerov, Howard (Stanley)
1920-1991 .... **CLC 2, 6, 9, 36;**
DAM POET
See also CA 1-4R; 134; CABS 2; CANR 1,
27, 53; DLB 5, 6; DLBY 83;
INT CANR-27; MTCW

Neruda, Pablo
1904-1973 ..... **CLC 1, 2, 5, 7, 9, 28, 62;**
DA; DAB; DAC; DAM MST, MULT,
POET; HLC; PC 4; WLC
See also CA 19-20; 45-48; CAP 2; HW;
MTCW

Nerval, Gerard de
1808-1855 ..... **NCLC 1; PC 13; SSC 18**

Nervo, (Jose) Amado (Ruiz de)
1870-1919 .... **TCLC 11**
See also CA 109; 131; HW

Nessi, Pio Baroja y
See Baroja (y Nessi), Pio

Nestroy, Johann 1801-1862 ...... **NCLC 42**
See also DLB 133

Neufeld, John (Arthur) 1938- ...... **CLC 17**
See also AAYA 11; CA 25-28R; CANR 11,
37; MAICYA; SAAS 3; SATA 6, 81

Neville, Emily Cheney 1919- .... **CLC 12**
See also CA 5-8R; CANR 3, 37; JRDA;
MAICYA; SAAS 2; SATA 1

Newbound, Bernard Slade 1930-
See Slade, Bernard
See also CA 81-84; CANR 49;
DAM DRAM

Newby, P(ercy) H(oward)
1918- .... **CLC 2, 13; DAM NOV**
See also CA 5-8R; CANR 32; DLB 15;
MTCW

Newlove, Donald 1928- .... **CLC 6**
See also CA 29-32R; CANR 25

Newlove, John (Herbert) 1938- ..... **CLC 14**
See also CA 21-24R; CANR 9, 25

Newman, Charles 1938- .... **CLC 2, 8**
See also CA 21-24R

Newman, Edwin (Harold) 1919- .... **CLC 14**
See also AITN 1; CA 69-72; CANR 5

Newman, John Henry
1801-1890 .... **NCLC 38**
See also DLB 18, 32, 55

Newton, Suzanne 1936- .... **CLC 35**
See also CA 41-44R; CANR 14; JRDA;
SATA 5, 77

Nexo, Martin Andersen
1869-1954 .... **TCLC 43**

Nezval, Vitezslav 1900-1958 ...... **TCLC 44**
See also CA 123

Ng, Fae Myenne 1957(?)- .... **CLC 81**
See also CA 146

Ngema, Mbongeni 1955- .... **CLC 57**
See also BW 2; CA 143

Ngugi, James T(hiong'o) .... **CLC 3, 7, 13**
See also Ngugi wa Thiong'o

Ngugi wa Thiong'o
1938- ..... **CLC 36; BLC; DAM MULT,**
NOV
See also Ngugi, James T(hiong'o)
See also BW 2; CA 81-84; CANR 27;
DLB 125; MTCW

Nichol, B(arrie) P(hillip)
1944-1988 .... **CLC 18**
See also CA 53-56; DLB 53; SATA 66

Nichols, John (Treadwell) 1940- .... **CLC 38**
See also CA 9-12R; CAAS 2; CANR 6;
DLBY 82

Nichols, Leigh
See Koontz, Dean R(ay)

Nichols, Peter (Richard)
1927- .... **CLC 5, 36, 65**
See also CA 104; CANR 33; DLB 13;
MTCW

Nicolas, F. R. E.
See Freeling, Nicolas

Niedecker, Lorine
1903-1970 .... **CLC 10, 42; DAM POET**
See also CA 25-28; CAP 2; DLB 48

Nietzsche, Friedrich (Wilhelm)
1844-1900 .... **TCLC 10, 18, 55**
See also CA 107; 121; DLB 129

Nievo, Ippolito 1831-1861 .... **NCLC 22**

Nightingale, Anne Redmon 1943-
See Redmon, Anne
See also CA 103

Nik. T. O.
See Annensky, Innokenty Fyodorovich

Nin, Anais
1903-1977 ...... **CLC 1, 4, 8, 11, 14, 60;**
DAM NOV, POP; SSC 10
See also AITN 2; CA 13-16R; 69-72;
CANR 22, 53; DLB 2, 4, 152; MTCW

Nishiwaki, Junzaburo 1894-1982 .... **PC 15**
See also CA 107

Nissenson, Hugh 1933-........... **CLC 4, 9**
See also CA 17-20R; CANR 27; DLB 28

Niven, Larry .... **CLC 8**
See also Niven, Laurence Van Cott
See also DLB 8

Niven, Laurence Van Cott 1938-
See Niven, Larry
See also CA 21-24R; CAAS 12; CANR 14,
44; DAM POP; MTCW

Nixon, Agnes Eckhardt 1927-...... **CLC 21**
See also CA 110

Nizan, Paul 1905-1940.......... **TCLC 40**
See also DLB 72

Nkosi, Lewis
1936- ..... **CLC 45; BLC; DAM MULT**
See also BW 1; CA 65-68; CANR 27;
DLB 157

Nodier, (Jean) Charles (Emmanuel)
1780-1844 .... **NCLC 19**
See also DLB 119

Nolan, Christopher 1965-.......... **CLC 58**
See also CA 111

Noon, Jeff 1957-................. **CLC 91**
See also CA 148

Norden, Charles
See Durrell, Lawrence (George)

Nordhoff, Charles (Bernard)
1887-1947 .... **TCLC 23**
See also CA 108; DLB 9; SATA 23

Norfolk, Lawrence 1963-.......... **CLC 76**
See also CA 144

Norman, Marsha
1947- .... **CLC 28; DAM DRAM**
See also CA 105; CABS 3; CANR 41;
DLBY 84

Norris, Benjamin Franklin, Jr.
1870-1902 .... **TCLC 24**
See also Norris, Frank
See also CA 110

Norris, Frank
See Norris, Benjamin Franklin, Jr.
See also CDALB 1865-1917; DLB 12, 71

Norris, Leslie 1921-.............. **CLC 14**
See also CA 11-12; CANR 14; CAP 1;
DLB 27

North, Andrew
See Norton, Andre

North, Anthony
See Koontz, Dean R(ay)

North, Captain George
See Stevenson, Robert Louis (Balfour)

North, Milou
See Erdrich, Louise

Northrup, B. A.
    See Hubbard, L(afayette) Ron(ald)

North Staffs
    See Hulme, T(homas) E(rnest)

Norton, Alice Mary
    See Norton, Andre
    See also MAICYA; SATA 1, 43

Norton, Andre 1912- .... **CLC 12**
    See also Norton, Alice Mary
    See also AAYA 14; CA 1-4R; CANR 2, 31;
    DLB 8, 52; JRDA; MTCW

Norton, Caroline 1808-1877...... **NCLC 47**
    See also DLB 21, 159

Norway, Nevil Shute 1899-1960
    See Shute, Nevil
    See also CA 102; 93-96

Norwid, Cyprian Kamil
    1821-1883 .... **NCLC 17**

Nosille, Nabrah
    See Ellison, Harlan (Jay)

Nossack, Hans Erich 1901-1978 ..... **CLC 6**
    See also CA 93-96; 85-88; DLB 69

Nostradamus 1503-1566............ **LC 27**

Nosu, Chuji
    See Ozu, Yasujiro

Notenburg, Eleanora (Genrikhovna) von
    See Guro, Elena

Nova, Craig 1945-............. **CLC 7, 31**
    See also CA 45-48; CANR 2, 53

Novak, Joseph
    See Kosinski, Jerzy (Nikodem)

Novalis 1772-1801 .... **NCLC 13**
    See also DLB 90

Nowlan, Alden (Albert)
    1933-1983 .. **CLC 15; DAC; DAM MST**
    See also CA 9-12R; CANR 5; DLB 53

Noyes, Alfred 1880-1958 .... **TCLC 7**
    See also CA 104; DLB 20

Nunn, Kem 19(?)-............... **CLC 34**

Nye, Robert
    1939- .... **CLC 13, 42; DAM NOV**
    See also CA 33-36R; CANR 29; DLB 14;
    MTCW; SATA 6

Nyro, Laura 1947- .... **CLC 17**

Oates, Joyce Carol
    1938- ...... **CLC 1, 2, 3, 6, 9, 11, 15, 19,**
        33, 52; DA; DAB; DAC; DAM MST,
        NOV, POP; SSC 6; WLC
    See also AAYA 15; AITN 1; BEST 89:2;
        CA 5-8R; CANR 25, 45;
        CDALB 1968-1988; DLB 2, 5, 130;
        DLBY 81; INT CANR-25; MTCW

O'Brien, Darcy 1939-............. **CLC 11**
    See also CA 21-24R; CANR 8

O'Brien, E. G.
    See Clarke, Arthur C(harles)

O'Brien, Edna
    1936- .... **CLC 3, 5, 8, 13, 36, 65;**
        DAM NOV; SSC 10
    See also CA 1-4R; CANR 6, 41;
        CDBLB 1960 to Present; DLB 14;
        MTCW

O'Brien, Fitz-James 1828-1862... **NCLC 21**
    See also DLB 74

O'Brien, Flann........ **CLC 1, 4, 5, 7, 10, 47**
    See also O Nuallain, Brian

O'Brien, Richard 1942- .... **CLC 17**
    See also CA 124

O'Brien, Tim
    1946- .... **CLC 7, 19, 40; DAM POP**
    See also AAYA 16; CA 85-88; CANR 40;
        DLB 152; DLBD 9; DLBY 80

Obstfelder, Sigbjoern 1866-1900... **TCLC 23**
    See also CA 123

O'Casey, Sean
    1880-1964 ...... **CLC 1, 5, 9, 11, 15, 88;**
        DAB; DAC; DAM DRAM, MST
    See also CA 89-92; CDBLB 1914-1945;
        DLB 10; MTCW

O'Cathasaigh, Sean
    See O'Casey, Sean

Ochs, Phil 1940-1976............. **CLC 17**
    See also CA 65-68

O'Connor, Edwin (Greene)
    1918-1968 .... **CLC 14**
    See also CA 93-96; 25-28R

O'Connor, (Mary) Flannery
    1925-1964 .... **CLC 1, 2, 3, 6, 10, 13, 15,**
        21, 66; DA; DAB; DAC; DAM MST,
        NOV; SSC 1, 23; WLC
    See also AAYA 7; CA 1-4R; CANR 3, 41;
        CDALB 1941-1968; DLB 2, 152;
        DLBD 12; DLBY 80; MTCW

O'Connor, Frank.......... **CLC 23; SSC 5**
    See also O'Donovan, Michael John
    See also DLB 162

O'Dell, Scott 1898-1989........... **CLC 30**
    See also AAYA 3; CA 61-64; 129;
        CANR 12, 30; CLR 1, 16; DLB 52;
        JRDA; MAICYA; SATA 12, 60

Odets, Clifford
    1906-1963 ... **CLC 2, 28; DAM DRAM;**
        DC 6
    See also CA 85-88; DLB 7, 26; MTCW

O'Doherty, Brian 1934-........... **CLC 76**
    See also CA 105

O'Donnell, K. M.
    See Malzberg, Barry N(athaniel)

O'Donnell, Lawrence
    See Kuttner, Henry

O'Donovan, Michael John
    1903-1966 .... **CLC 14**
    See also O'Connor, Frank
    See also CA 93-96

Oe, Kenzaburo
    1935- ..... **CLC 10, 36, 86; DAM NOV;**
        SSC 20
    See also CA 97-100; CANR 36, 50;
        DLBY 94; MTCW

O'Faolain, Julia 1932-....... **CLC 6, 19, 47**
    See also CA 81-84; CAAS 2; CANR 12;
        DLB 14; MTCW

O'Faolain, Sean
    1900-1991 .... **CLC 1, 7, 14, 32, 70;**
        SSC 13
    See also CA 61-64; 134; CANR 12;
        DLB 15, 162; MTCW

O'Flaherty, Liam
    1896-1984 .... **CLC 5, 34; SSC 6**
    See also CA 101; 113; CANR 35; DLB 36,
        162; DLBY 84; MTCW

Ogilvy, Gavin
    See Barrie, J(ames) M(atthew)

O'Grady, Standish James
    1846-1928 .... **TCLC 5**
    See also CA 104

O'Grady, Timothy 1951- .... **CLC 59**
    See also CA 138

O'Hara, Frank
    1926-1966 .... **CLC 2, 5, 13, 78;**
        DAM POET
    See also CA 9-12R; 25-28R; CANR 33;
        DLB 5, 16; MTCW

O'Hara, John (Henry)
    1905-1970 ...... **CLC 1, 2, 3, 6, 11, 42;**
        DAM NOV; SSC 15
    See also CA 5-8R; 25-28R; CANR 31;
        CDALB 1929-1941; DLB 9, 86; DLBD 2;
        MTCW

O Hehir, Diana 1922- .... **CLC 41**
    See also CA 93-96

Okigbo, Christopher (Ifenayichukwu)
    1932-1967 .... **CLC 25, 84; BLC;**
        DAM MULT, POET; PC 7
    See also BW 1; CA 77-80; DLB 125;
        MTCW

Okri, Ben 1959- .... **CLC 87**
    See also BW 2; CA 130; 138; DLB 157;
        INT 138

Olds, Sharon
    1942- ..... **CLC 32, 39, 85; DAM POET**
    See also CA 101; CANR 18, 41; DLB 120

Oldstyle, Jonathan
    See Irving, Washington

Olesha, Yuri (Karlovich)
    1899-1960 .... **CLC 8**
    See also CA 85-88

Oliphant, Laurence
    1829(?)-1888 .... **NCLC 47**
    See also DLB 18, 166

Oliphant, Margaret (Oliphant Wilson)
    1828-1897 .... **NCLC 11**
    See also DLB 18, 159

Oliver, Mary 1935-............. **CLC 19, 34**
    See also CA 21-24R; CANR 9, 43; DLB 5

Olivier, Laurence (Kerr)
    1907-1989 .... **CLC 20**
    See also CA 111; 150; 129

Olsen, Tillie
    1913- ..... **CLC 4, 13; DA; DAB; DAC;**
        DAM MST; SSC 11
    See also CA 1-4R; CANR 1, 43; DLB 28;
        DLBY 80; MTCW

Olson, Charles (John)
    1910-1970 ..... **CLC 1, 2, 5, 6, 9, 11, 29;**
        DAM POET
    See also CA 13-16; 25-28R; CABS 2;
        CANR 35; CAP 1; DLB 5, 16; MTCW

Olson, Toby 1937- .... **CLC 28**
    See also CA 65-68; CANR 9, 31

Olyesha, Yuri
    See Olesha, Yuri (Karlovich)

Ondaatje, (Philip) Michael
1943- . . . . CLC 14, 29, 51, 76; DAB;
DAC; DAM MST
See also CA 77-80; CANR 42; DLB 60

Oneal, Elizabeth 1934-
See Oneal, Zibby
See also CA 106; CANR 28; MAICYA;
SATA 30, 82

Oneal, Zibby . . . . CLC 30
See also Oneal, Elizabeth
See also AAYA 5; CLR 13; JRDA

O'Neill, Eugene (Gladstone)
1888-1953 . . . . . . TCLC 1, 6, 27, 49; DA;
DAB; DAC; DAM DRAM, MST; WLC
See also AITN 1; CA 110; 132;
CDALB 1929-1941; DLB 7; MTCW

Onetti, Juan Carlos
1909-1994 . . . . CLC 7, 10; DAM MULT,
NOV; SSC 23
See also CA 85-88; 145; CANR 32;
DLB 113; HW; MTCW

O Nuallain, Brian 1911-1966
See O'Brien, Flann
See also CA 21-22; 25-28R; CAP 2

Oppen, George 1908-1984 . . . . CLC 7, 13, 34
See also CA 13-16R; 113; CANR 8; DLB 5,
165

Oppenheim, E(dward) Phillips
1866-1946 . . . . TCLC 45
See also CA 111; DLB 70

Origen c. 185-c. 254 . . . . CMLC 19

Orlovitz, Gil 1918-1973 . . . . CLC 22
See also CA 77-80; 45-48; DLB 2, 5

Orris
See Ingelow, Jean

Ortega y Gasset, Jose
1883-1955 . . . . . TCLC 9; DAM MULT;
HLC
See also CA 106; 130; HW; MTCW

Ortese, Anna Maria 1914- . . . . CLC 89

Ortiz, Simon J(oseph)
1941- . . . . CLC 45; DAM MULT, POET
See also CA 134; DLB 120; NNAL

Orton, Joe . . . . CLC 4, 13, 43; DC 3
See also Orton, John Kingsley
See also CDBLB 1960 to Present; DLB 13

Orton, John Kingsley 1933-1967
See Orton, Joe
See also CA 85-88; CANR 35;
DAM DRAM; MTCW

Orwell, George
. . . . . TCLC 2, 6, 15, 31, 51; DAB; WLC
See also Blair, Eric (Arthur)
See also CDBLB 1945-1960; DLB 15, 98

Osborne, David
See Silverberg, Robert

Osborne, George
See Silverberg, Robert

Osborne, John (James)
1929-1994 . . . . . CLC 1, 2, 5, 11, 45; DA;
DAB; DAC; DAM DRAM, MST; WLC
See also CA 13-16R; 147; CANR 21;
CDBLB 1945-1960; DLB 13; MTCW

Osborne, Lawrence 1958- . . . . CLC 50

Oshima, Nagisa 1932- . . . . CLC 20
See also CA 116; 121

Oskison, John Milton
1874-1947 . . . . . TCLC 35; DAM MULT
See also CA 144; NNAL

Ossoli, Sarah Margaret (Fuller marchesa d')
1810-1850
See Fuller, Margaret
See also SATA 25

Ostrovsky, Alexander
1823-1886 . . . . NCLC 30, 57

Otero, Blas de 1916-1979 . . . . CLC 11
See also CA 89-92; DLB 134

Otto, Whitney 1955- . . . . CLC 70
See also CA 140

Ouida . . . . TCLC 43
See also De La Ramee, (Marie) Louise
See also DLB 18, 156

Ousmane, Sembene 1923- . . . . CLC 66; BLC
See also BW 1; CA 117; 125; MTCW

Ovid
43B.C.-18(?) . . . CMLC 7; DAM POET;
PC 2

Owen, Hugh
See Faust, Frederick (Schiller)

Owen, Wilfred (Edward Salter)
1893-1918 . . . . . . TCLC 5, 27; DA; DAB;
DAC; DAM MST, POET; WLC
See also CA 104; 141; CDBLB 1914-1945;
DLB 20

Owens, Rochelle 1936- . . . . CLC 8
See also CA 17-20R; CAAS 2; CANR 39

Oz, Amos
1939- . . . . CLC 5, 8, 11, 27, 33, 54;
DAM NOV
See also CA 53-56; CANR 27, 47; MTCW

Ozick, Cynthia
1928- . . . . CLC 3, 7, 28, 62; DAM NOV,
POP; SSC 15
See also BEST 90:1; CA 17-20R; CANR 23;
DLB 28, 152; DLBY 82; INT CANR-23;
MTCW

Ozu, Yasujiro 1903-1963 . . . . CLC 16
See also CA 112

Pacheco, C.
See Pessoa, Fernando (Antonio Nogueira)

Pa Chin . . . . CLC 18
See also Li Fei-kan

Pack, Robert 1929- . . . . CLC 13
See also CA 1-4R; CANR 3, 44; DLB 5

Padgett, Lewis
See Kuttner, Henry

Padilla (Lorenzo), Heberto 1932- . . . CLC 38
See also AITN 1; CA 123; 131; HW

Page, Jimmy 1944- . . . . CLC 12

Page, Louise 1955- . . . . CLC 40
See also CA 140

Page, P(atricia) K(athleen)
1916- . . . . CLC 7, 18; DAC; DAM MST;
PC 12
See also CA 53-56; CANR 4, 22; DLB 68;
MTCW

Page, Thomas Nelson 1853-1922 . . . . SSC 23
See also CA 118; DLB 12, 78; DLBD 13

Paget, Violet 1856-1935
See Lee, Vernon
See also CA 104

Paget-Lowe, Henry
See Lovecraft, H(oward) P(hillips)

Paglia, Camille (Anna) 1947- . . . . . . CLC 68
See also CA 140

Paige, Richard
See Koontz, Dean R(ay)

Pakenham, Antonia
See Fraser, (Lady) Antonia (Pakenham)

Palamas, Kostes 1859-1943 . . . . TCLC 5
See also CA 105

Palazzeschi, Aldo 1885-1974 . . . . CLC 11
See also CA 89-92; 53-56; DLB 114

Paley, Grace
1922- . . . . CLC 4, 6, 37; DAM POP;
SSC 8
See also CA 25-28R; CANR 13, 46;
DLB 28; INT CANR-13; MTCW

Palin, Michael (Edward) 1943- . . . . . CLC 21
See also Monty Python
See also CA 107; CANR 35; SATA 67

Palliser, Charles 1947- . . . . CLC 65
See also CA 136

Palma, Ricardo 1833-1919 . . . . TCLC 29

Pancake, Breece Dexter 1952-1979
See Pancake, Breece D'J
See also CA 123; 109

Pancake, Breece D'J . . . . CLC 29
See also Pancake, Breece Dexter
See also DLB 130

Panko, Rudy
See Gogol, Nikolai (Vasilyevich)

Papadiamantis, Alexandros
1851-1911 . . . . TCLC 29

Papadiamantopoulos, Johannes 1856-1910
See Moreas, Jean
See also CA 117

Papini, Giovanni 1881-1956 . . . . TCLC 22
See also CA 121

Paracelsus 1493-1541 . . . . LC 14

Parasol, Peter
See Stevens, Wallace

Parfenie, Maria
See Codrescu, Andrei

Parini, Jay (Lee) 1948- . . . . CLC 54
See also CA 97-100; CAAS 16; CANR 32

Park, Jordan
See Kornbluth, C(yril) M.; Pohl, Frederik

Parker, Bert
See Ellison, Harlan (Jay)

Parker, Dorothy (Rothschild)
1893-1967 . . . . CLC 15, 68;
DAM POET; SSC 2
See also CA 19-20; 25-28R; CAP 2;
DLB 11, 45, 86; MTCW

Parker, Robert B(rown)
1932- . . . . . . CLC 27; DAM NOV, POP
See also BEST 89:4; CA 49-52; CANR 1,
26, 52; INT CANR-26; MTCW

Parkin, Frank 1940- . . . . CLC 43
See also CA 147

Parkman, Francis, Jr.
1823-1893 .... **NCLC 12**
See also DLB 1, 30

Parks, Gordon (Alexander Buchanan)
1912- ... **CLC 1, 16; BLC; DAM MULT**
See also AITN 2; BW 2; CA 41-44R;
CANR 26; DLB 33; SATA 8

Parnell, Thomas 1679-1718 .... **LC 3**
See also DLB 94

Parra, Nicanor
1914- ...... **CLC 2; DAM MULT; HLC**
See also CA 85-88; CANR 32; HW; MTCW

Parrish, Mary Frances
See Fisher, M(ary) F(rances) K(ennedy)

Parson
See Coleridge, Samuel Taylor

Parson Lot
See Kingsley, Charles

Partridge, Anthony
See Oppenheim, E(dward) Phillips

Pascal, Blaise 1623-1662 .... **LC 35**

Pascoli, Giovanni 1855-1912 ...... **TCLC 45**

Pasolini, Pier Paolo
1922-1975 .... **CLC 20, 37**
See also CA 93-96; 61-64; DLB 128;
MTCW

Pasquini
See Silone, Ignazio

Pastan, Linda (Olenik)
1932- .... **CLC 27; DAM POET**
See also CA 61-64; CANR 18, 40; DLB 5

Pasternak, Boris (Leonidovich)
1890-1960 ..... **CLC 7, 10, 18, 63; DA;
DAB; DAC; DAM MST, NOV, POET;
PC 6; WLC**
See also CA 127; 116; MTCW

Patchen, Kenneth
1911-1972 ... **CLC 1, 2, 18; DAM POET**
See also CA 1-4R; 33-36R; CANR 3, 35;
DLB 16, 48; MTCW

Pater, Walter (Horatio)
1839-1894 .... **NCLC 7**
See also CDBLB 1832-1890; DLB 57, 156

Paterson, A(ndrew) B(arton)
1864-1941 .... **TCLC 32**

Paterson, Katherine (Womeldorf)
1932- .... **CLC 12, 30**
See also AAYA 1; CA 21-24R; CANR 28;
CLR 7; DLB 52; JRDA; MAICYA;
MTCW; SATA 13, 53

Patmore, Coventry Kersey Dighton
1823-1896 .... **NCLC 9**
See also DLB 35, 98

Paton, Alan (Stewart)
1903-1988 ..... **CLC 4, 10, 25, 55; DA;
DAB; DAC; DAM MST, NOV; WLC**
See also CA 13-16; 125; CANR 22; CAP 1;
MTCW; SATA 11; SATA-Obit 56

Paton Walsh, Gillian 1937-
See Walsh, Jill Paton
See also CANR 38; JRDA; MAICYA;
SAAS 3; SATA 4, 72

Paulding, James Kirke 1778-1860 .. **NCLC 2**
See also DLB 3, 59, 74

Paulin, Thomas Neilson 1949-
See Paulin, Tom
See also CA 123; 128

Paulin, Tom .... **CLC 37**
See also Paulin, Thomas Neilson
See also DLB 40

Paustovsky, Konstantin (Georgievich)
1892-1968 .... **CLC 40**
See also CA 93-96; 25-28R

Pavese, Cesare
1908-1950 ..... **TCLC 3; PC 13; SSC 19**
See also CA 104; DLB 128

Pavic, Milorad 1929- .... **CLC 60**
See also CA 136

Payne, Alan
See Jakes, John (William)

Paz, Gil
See Lugones, Leopoldo

Paz, Octavio
1914- .... **CLC 3, 4, 6, 10, 19, 51, 65;
DA; DAB; DAC; DAM MST, MULT,
POET; HLC; PC 1; WLC**
See also CA 73-76; CANR 32; DLBY 90;
HW; MTCW

p'Bitek, Okot
1931-1982 .... **CLC 96; BLC;
DAM MULT**
See also BW 2; CA 124; 107; DLB 125;
MTCW

Peacock, Molly 1947- .... **CLC 60**
See also CA 103; CAAS 21; CANR 52;
DLB 120

Peacock, Thomas Love
1785-1866 .... **NCLC 22**
See also DLB 96, 116

Peake, Mervyn 1911-1968 ...... **CLC 7, 54**
See also CA 5-8R; 25-28R; CANR 3;
DLB 15, 160; MTCW; SATA 23

Pearce, Philippa .... **CLC 21**
See also Christie, (Ann) Philippa
See also CLR 9; DLB 161; MAICYA;
SATA 1, 67

Pearl, Eric
See Elman, Richard

Pearson, T(homas) R(eid) 1956- .... **CLC 39**
See also CA 120; 130; INT 130

Peck, Dale 1967- .... **CLC 81**
See also CA 146

Peck, John 1941- .... **CLC 3**
See also CA 49-52; CANR 3

Peck, Richard (Wayne) 1934- ...... **CLC 21**
See also AAYA 1; CA 85-88; CANR 19,
38; CLR 15; INT CANR-19; JRDA;
MAICYA; SAAS 2; SATA 18, 55

Peck, Robert Newton
1928- .. **CLC 17; DA; DAC; DAM MST**
See also AAYA 3; CA 81-84; CANR 31;
JRDA; MAICYA; SAAS 1; SATA 21, 62

Peckinpah, (David) Sam(uel)
1925-1984 .... **CLC 20**
See also CA 109; 114

Pedersen, Knut 1859-1952
See Hamsun, Knut
See also CA 104; 119; MTCW

Peeslake, Gaffer
See Durrell, Lawrence (George)

Peguy, Charles Pierre
1873-1914 .... **TCLC 10**
See also CA 107

Pena, Ramon del Valle y
See Valle-Inclan, Ramon (Maria) del

Pendennis, Arthur Esquir
See Thackeray, William Makepeace

Penn, William 1644-1718 .... **LC 25**
See also DLB 24

Pepys, Samuel
1633-1703 ..... **LC 11; DA; DAB; DAC;
DAM MST; WLC**
See also CDBLB 1660-1789; DLB 101

Percy, Walker
1916-1990 .... **CLC 2, 3, 6, 8, 14, 18, 47,
65; DAM NOV, POP**
See also CA 1-4R; 131; CANR 1, 23;
DLB 2; DLBY 80, 90; MTCW

Perec, Georges 1936-1982 .... **CLC 56**
See also CA 141; DLB 83

Pereda (y Sanchez de Porrua), Jose Maria de
1833-1906 .... **TCLC 16**
See also CA 117

Pereda y Porrua, Jose Maria de
See Pereda (y Sanchez de Porrua), Jose
Maria de

Peregoy, George Weems
See Mencken, H(enry) L(ouis)

Perelman, S(idney) J(oseph)
1904-1979 ...... **CLC 3, 5, 9, 15, 23, 44,
49; DAM DRAM**
See also AITN 1, 2; CA 73-76; 89-92;
CANR 18; DLB 11, 44; MTCW

Peret, Benjamin 1899-1959 .... **TCLC 20**
See also CA 117

Peretz, Isaac Loeb 1851(?)-1915 ... **TCLC 16**
See also CA 109

Peretz, Yitzhok Leibush
See Peretz, Isaac Loeb

Perez Galdos, Benito 1843-1920 ... **TCLC 27**
See also CA 125; 153; HW

Perrault, Charles 1628-1703 .... **LC 2**
See also MAICYA; SATA 25

Perry, Brighton
See Sherwood, Robert E(mmet)

Perse, St.-John .... **CLC 4, 11, 46**
See also Leger, (Marie-Rene Auguste) Alexis
Saint-Leger

Perutz, Leo 1882-1957 .... **TCLC 60**
See also DLB 81

Peseenz, Tulio F.
See Lopez y Fuentes, Gregorio

Pesetsky, Bette 1932- .... **CLC 28**
See also CA 133; DLB 130

Peshkov, Alexei Maximovich 1868-1936
See Gorky, Maxim
See also CA 105; 141; DA; DAC;
DAM DRAM, MST, NOV

Pessoa, Fernando (Antonio Nogueira)
1888-1935 .... **TCLC 27; HLC**
See also CA 125

Peterkin, Julia Mood 1880-1961.... **CLC 31**
See also CA 102; DLB 9

Peters, Joan K. 1945-.............. **CLC 39**

Peters, Robert L(ouis) 1924-........ **CLC 7**
See also CA 13-16R; CAAS 8; DLB 105

Petofi, Sandor 1823-1849........ **NCLC 21**

Petrakis, Harry Mark 1923-........ **CLC 3**
See also CA 9-12R; CANR 4, 30

Petrarch 1304-1374................ **PC 8**
See also DAM POET

Petrov, Evgeny .... **TCLC 21**
See also Kataev, Evgeny Petrovich

Petry, Ann (Lane) 1908- ...... **CLC 1, 7, 18**
See also BW 1; CA 5-8R; CAAS 6;
CANR 4, 46; CLR 12; DLB 76; JRDA;
MAICYA; MTCW; SATA 5

Petursson, Halligrimur 1614-1674 .... **LC 8**

Philips, Katherine 1632-1664....... **LC 30**
See also DLB 131

Philipson, Morris H. 1926-........ **CLC 53**
See also CA 1-4R; CANR 4

Phillips, Caryl
1958- .... **CLC 96; DAM MULT**
See also BW 2; CA 141; DLB 157

Phillips, David Graham
1867-1911 .... **TCLC 44**
See also CA 108; DLB 9, 12

Phillips, Jack
See Sandburg, Carl (August)

Phillips, Jayne Anne
1952- .... **CLC 15, 33; SSC 16**
See also CA 101; CANR 24, 50; DLBY 80;
INT CANR-24; MTCW

Phillips, Richard
See Dick, Philip K(indred)

Phillips, Robert (Schaeffer) 1938-... **CLC 28**
See also CA 17-20R; CAAS 13; CANR 8;
DLB 105

Phillips, Ward
See Lovecraft, H(oward) P(hillips)

Piccolo, Lucio 1901-1969.......... **CLC 13**
See also CA 97-100; DLB 114

Pickthall, Marjorie L(owry) C(hristie)
1883-1922 .... **TCLC 21**
See also CA 107; DLB 92

Pico della Mirandola, Giovanni
1463-1494 .... **LC 15**

Piercy, Marge
1936- .... **CLC 3, 6, 14, 18, 27, 62**
See also CA 21-24R; CAAS 1; CANR 13,
43; DLB 120; MTCW

Piers, Robert
See Anthony, Piers

Pieyre de Mandiargues, Andre 1909-1991
See Mandiargues, Andre Pieyre de
See also CA 103; 136; CANR 22

Pilnyak, Boris .... **TCLC 23**
See also Vogau, Boris Andreyevich

Pincherle, Alberto
1907-1990 ..... **CLC 11, 18; DAM NOV**
See also Moravia, Alberto
See also CA 25-28R; 132; CANR 33;
MTCW

Pinckney, Darryl 1953-.......... **CLC 76**
See also BW 2; CA 143

Pindar 518B.C.-446B.C......... **CMLC 12**

Pineda, Cecile 1942-............. **CLC 39**
See also CA 118

Pinero, Arthur Wing
1855-1934 ..... **TCLC 32; DAM DRAM**
See also CA 110; 153; DLB 10

Pinero, Miguel (Antonio Gomez)
1946-1988 .... **CLC 4, 55**
See also CA 61-64; 125; CANR 29; HW

Pinget, Robert 1919- .... **CLC 7, 13, 37**
See also CA 85-88; DLB 83

Pink Floyd
See Barrett, (Roger) Syd; Gilmour, David;
Mason, Nick; Waters, Roger; Wright,
Rick

Pinkney, Edward 1802-1828 ..... **NCLC 31**

Pinkwater, Daniel Manus 1941- ... **CLC 35**
See also Pinkwater, Manus
See also AAYA 1; CA 29-32R; CANR 12,
38; CLR 4; JRDA; MAICYA; SAAS 3;
SATA 46, 76

Pinkwater, Manus
See Pinkwater, Daniel Manus
See also SATA 8

Pinsky, Robert
1940- .. **CLC 9, 19, 38, 94; DAM POET**
See also CA 29-32R; CAAS 4; DLBY 82

Pinta, Harold
See Pinter, Harold

Pinter, Harold
1930- ..... **CLC 1, 3, 6, 9, 11, 15, 27, 58,
73; DA; DAB; DAC; DAM DRAM,
MST; WLC**
See also CA 5-8R; CANR 33; CDBLB 1960
to Present; DLB 13; MTCW

Piozzi, Hester Lynch (Thrale)
1741-1821 .... **NCLC 57**
See also DLB 104, 142

Pirandello, Luigi
1867-1936 ...... **TCLC 4, 29; DA; DAB;
DAC; DAM DRAM, MST; DC 5;
SSC 22; WLC**
See also CA 104; 153

Pirsig, Robert M(aynard)
1928- .... **CLC 4, 6, 73; DAM POP**
See also CA 53-56; CANR 42; MTCW;
SATA 39

Pisarev, Dmitry Ivanovich
1840-1868 .... **NCLC 25**

Pix, Mary (Griffith) 1666-1709...... **LC 8**
See also DLB 80

Pixerecourt, Guilbert de
1773-1844 .... **NCLC 39**

Plaidy, Jean
See Hibbert, Eleanor Alice Burford

Planche, James Robinson
1796-1880 .... **NCLC 42**

Plant, Robert 1948- .... **CLC 12**

Plante, David (Robert)
1940- .... **CLC 7, 23, 38; DAM NOV**
See also CA 37-40R; CANR 12, 36;
DLBY 83; INT CANR-12; MTCW

Plath, Sylvia
1932-1963 ..... **CLC 1, 2, 3, 5, 9, 11, 14,
17, 50, 51, 62; DA; DAB; DAC;
DAM MST, POET; PC 1; WLC**
See also AAYA 13; CA 19-20; CANR 34;
CAP 2; CDALB 1941-1968; DLB 5, 6,
152; MTCW

Plato
428(?)B.C.-348(?)B.C..... **CMLC 8; DA;
DAB; DAC; DAM MST**

Platonov, Andrei .... **TCLC 14**
See also Klimentov, Andrei Platonovich

Platt, Kin 1911- .... **CLC 26**
See also AAYA 11; CA 17-20R; CANR 11;
JRDA; SAAS 17; SATA 21, 86

Plautus c. 251B.C.-184B.C. .... **DC 6**

Plick et Plock
See Simenon, Georges (Jacques Christian)

Plimpton, George (Ames) 1927-.... **CLC 36**
See also AITN 1; CA 21-24R; CANR 32;
MTCW; SATA 10

Plomer, William Charles Franklin
1903-1973 .... **CLC 4, 8**
See also CA 21-22; CANR 34; CAP 2;
DLB 20, 162; MTCW; SATA 24

Plowman, Piers
See Kavanagh, Patrick (Joseph)

Plum, J.
See Wodehouse, P(elham) G(renville)

Plumly, Stanley (Ross) 1939- ...... **CLC 33**
See also CA 108; 110; DLB 5; INT 110

Plumpe, Friedrich Wilhelm
1888-1931 .... **TCLC 53**
See also CA 112

Poe, Edgar Allan
1809-1849 .... **NCLC 1, 16, 55; DA;
DAB; DAC; DAM MST, POET; PC 1;
SSC 1, 22; WLC**
See also AAYA 14; CDALB 1640-1865;
DLB 3, 59, 73, 74; SATA 23

Poet of Titchfield Street, The
See Pound, Ezra (Weston Loomis)

Pohl, Frederik 1919- .... **CLC 18**
See also CA 61-64; CAAS 1; CANR 11, 37;
DLB 8; INT CANR-11; MTCW;
SATA 24

Poirier, Louis 1910-
See Gracq, Julien
See also CA 122; 126

Poitier, Sidney 1927- .... **CLC 26**
See also BW 1; CA 117

Polanski, Roman 1933- .... **CLC 16**
See also CA 77-80

Poliakoff, Stephen 1952- .... **CLC 38**
See also CA 106; DLB 13

Police, The
See Copeland, Stewart (Armstrong);
Summers, Andrew James; Sumner,
Gordon Matthew

Polidori, John William
1795-1821 .... **NCLC 51**
See also DLB 116

Pollitt, Katha 1949- .... **CLC 28**
See also CA 120; 122; MTCW

Pollock, (Mary) Sharon
    1936- .... **CLC 50; DAC; DAM DRAM,**
                                          MST
    See also CA 141; DLB 60

Polo, Marco 1254-1324 .... **CMLC 15**

Polonsky, Abraham (Lincoln)
    1910- .... **CLC 92**
    See also CA 104; DLB 26; INT 104

Polybius c. 200B.C.-c. 118B.C.... **CMLC 17**

Pomerance, Bernard
    1940- .... **CLC 13; DAM DRAM**
    See also CA 101; CANR 49

Ponge, Francis (Jean Gaston Alfred)
    1899-1988 ..... **CLC 6, 18; DAM POET**
    See also CA 85-88; 126; CANR 40

Pontoppidan, Henrik 1857-1943 ... **TCLC 29**

Poole, Josephine .... **CLC 17**
    See also Helyar, Jane Penelope Josephine
    See also SAAS 2; SATA 5

Popa, Vasko 1922-1991 .... **CLC 19**
    See also CA 112; 148

Pope, Alexander
    1688-1744 ..... **LC 3; DA; DAB; DAC;**
                                DAM MST, POET; WLC
    See also CDBLB 1660-1789; DLB 95, 101

Porter, Connie (Rose) 1959(?)- ..... **CLC 70**
    See also BW 2; CA 142; SATA 81

Porter, Gene(va Grace) Stratton
    1863(?)-1924 .... **TCLC 21**
    See also CA 112

Porter, Katherine Anne
    1890-1980 ...... **CLC 1, 3, 7, 10, 13, 15,**
        27; DA; DAB; DAC; DAM MST, NOV;
                                          SSC 4
    See also AITN 2; CA 1-4R; 101; CANR 1;
        DLB 4, 9, 102; DLBD 12; DLBY 80;
        MTCW; SATA 39; SATA-Obit 23

Porter, Peter (Neville Frederick)
    1929- .... **CLC 5, 13, 33**
    See also CA 85-88; DLB 40

Porter, William Sydney 1862-1910
    See Henry, O.
    See also CA 104; 131; CDALB 1865-1917;
        DA; DAB; DAC; DAM MST; DLB 12,
        78, 79; MTCW; YABC 2

Portillo (y Pacheco), Jose Lopez
    See Lopez Portillo (y Pacheco), Jose

Post, Melville Davisson
    1869-1930 .... **TCLC 39**
    See also CA 110

Potok, Chaim
    1929- .... **CLC 2, 7, 14, 26; DAM NOV**
    See also AAYA 15; AITN 1, 2; CA 17-20R;
        CANR 19, 35; DLB 28, 152;
        INT CANR-19; MTCW; SATA 33

Potter, Beatrice
    See Webb, (Martha) Beatrice (Potter)
    See also MAICYA

Potter, Dennis (Christopher George)
    1935-1994 .... **CLC 58, 86**
    See also CA 107; 145; CANR 33; MTCW

Pound, Ezra (Weston Loomis)
    1885-1972 ...... **CLC 1, 2, 3, 4, 5, 7, 10,**
        13, 18, 34, 48, 50; DA; DAB; DAC;
                    DAM MST, POET; PC 4; WLC
    See also CA 5-8R; 37-40R; CANR 40;
        CDALB 1917-1929; DLB 4, 45, 63;
        MTCW

Povod, Reinaldo 1959-1994 .... **CLC 44**
    See also CA 136; 146

Powell, Adam Clayton, Jr.
    1908-1972 .... **CLC 89; BLC;**
                                          DAM MULT
    See also BW 1; CA 102; 33-36R

Powell, Anthony (Dymoke)
    1905- .... **CLC 1, 3, 7, 9, 10, 31**
    See also CA 1-4R; CANR 1, 32;
        CDBLB 1945-1960; DLB 15; MTCW

Powell, Dawn 1897-1965 .... **CLC 66**
    See also CA 5-8R

Powell, Padgett 1952-............. **CLC 34**
    See also CA 126

Power, Susan..................... **CLC 91**

Powers, J(ames) F(arl)
    1917- .... **CLC 1, 4, 8, 57; SSC 4**
    See also CA 1-4R; CANR 2; DLB 130;
        MTCW

Powers, John J(ames) 1945-
    See Powers, John R.
    See also CA 69-72

Powers, John R. .... **CLC 66**
    See also Powers, John J(ames)

Powers, Richard (S.) 1957- .... **CLC 93**
    See also CA 148

Pownall, David 1938-............. **CLC 10**
    See also CA 89-92; CAAS 18; CANR 49;
        DLB 14

Powys, John Cowper
    1872-1963 .... **CLC 7, 9, 15, 46**
    See also CA 85-88; DLB 15; MTCW

Powys, T(heodore) F(rancis)
    1875-1953 .... **TCLC 9**
    See also CA 106; DLB 36, 162

Prager, Emily 1952-............. **CLC 56**

Pratt, E(dwin) J(ohn)
    1883(?)-1964 .... **CLC 19; DAC;**
                                          DAM POET
    See also CA 141; 93-96; DLB 92

Premchand...................... **TCLC 21**
    See also Srivastava, Dhanpat Rai

Preussler, Otfried 1923-........... **CLC 17**
    See also CA 77-80; SATA 24

Prevert, Jacques (Henri Marie)
    1900-1977 .... **CLC 15**
    See also CA 77-80; 69-72; CANR 29;
        MTCW; SATA-Obit 30

Prevost, Abbe (Antoine Francois)
    1697-1763 .... **LC 1**

Price, (Edward) Reynolds
    1933- .... **CLC 3, 6, 13, 43, 50, 63;**
                                DAM NOV; SSC 22
    See also CA 1-4R; CANR 1, 37; DLB 2;
        INT CANR-37

Price, Richard 1949- .... **CLC 6, 12**
    See also CA 49-52; CANR 3; DLBY 81

Prichard, Katharine Susannah
    1883-1969 .... **CLC 46**
    See also CA 11-12; CANR 33; CAP 1;
        MTCW; SATA 66

Priestley, J(ohn) B(oynton)
    1894-1984 .... **CLC 2, 5, 9, 34;**
                                DAM DRAM, NOV
    See also CA 9-12R; 113; CANR 33;
        CDBLB 1914-1945; DLB 10, 34, 77, 100,
        139; DLBY 84; MTCW

Prince 1958(?)- .... **CLC 35**

Prince, F(rank) T(empleton) 1912- .. **CLC 22**
    See also CA 101; CANR 43; DLB 20

Prince Kropotkin
    See Kropotkin, Peter (Aleksieevich)

Prior, Matthew 1664-1721.......... **LC 4**
    See also DLB 95

Pritchard, William H(arrison)
    1932-..................... **CLC 34**
    See also CA 65-68; CANR 23; DLB 111

Pritchett, V(ictor) S(awdon)
    1900- .... **CLC 5, 13, 15, 41;**
                                DAM NOV; SSC 14
    See also CA 61-64; CANR 31; DLB 15,
        139; MTCW

Private 19022
    See Manning, Frederic

Probst, Mark 1925- .... **CLC 59**
    See also CA 130

Prokosch, Frederic 1908-1989.... **CLC 4, 48**
    See also CA 73-76; 128; DLB 48

Prophet, The
    See Dreiser, Theodore (Herman Albert)

Prose, Francine 1947-............. **CLC 45**
    See also CA 109; 112; CANR 46

Proudhon
    See Cunha, Euclides (Rodrigues Pimenta) da

Proulx, E. Annie 1935- .... **CLC 81**

Proust, (Valentin-Louis-George-Eugene-)
    Marcel
    1871-1922 .... **TCLC 7, 13, 33; DA;**
        DAB; DAC; DAM MST, NOV; WLC
    See also CA 104; 120; DLB 65; MTCW

Prowler, Harley
    See Masters, Edgar Lee

Prus, Boleslaw 1845-1912 .... **TCLC 48**

Pryor, Richard (Franklin Lenox Thomas)
    1940- .... **CLC 26**
    See also CA 122

Przybyszewski, Stanislaw
    1868-1927 .... **TCLC 36**
    See also DLB 66

Pteleon
    See Grieve, C(hristopher) M(urray)
    See also DAM POET

Puckett, Lute
    See Masters, Edgar Lee

Puig, Manuel
    1932-1990 .... **CLC 3, 5, 10, 28, 65;**
                                DAM MULT; HLC
    See also CA 45-48; CANR 2, 32; DLB 113;
        HW; MTCW

Purdy, Al(fred Wellington)
1918- . . . . CLC 3, 6, 14, 50; DAC;
DAM MST, POET
See also CA 81-84; CAAS 17; CANR 42;
DLB 88

Purdy, James (Amos)
1923- . . . . CLC 2, 4, 10, 28, 52
See also CA 33-36R; CAAS 1; CANR 19,
51; DLB 2; INT CANR-19; MTCW

Pure, Simon
See Swinnerton, Frank Arthur

Pushkin, Alexander (Sergeyevich)
1799-1837 . . . . . NCLC 3, 27; DA; DAB;
DAC; DAM DRAM, MST, POET;
PC 10; WLC
See also SATA 61

P'u Sung-ling 1640-1715 . . . . LC 3

Putnam, Arthur Lee
See Alger, Horatio, Jr.

Puzo, Mario
1920- . . . . . CLC 1, 2, 6, 36; DAM NOV,
POP
See also CA 65-68; CANR 4, 42; DLB 6;
MTCW

Pygge, Edward
See Barnes, Julian (Patrick)

Pym, Barbara (Mary Crampton)
1913-1980 . . . . CLC 13, 19, 37
See also CA 13-14; 97-100; CANR 13, 34;
CAP 1; DLB 14; DLBY 87; MTCW

Pynchon, Thomas (Ruggles, Jr.)
1937- . . . . . CLC 2, 3, 6, 9, 11, 18, 33, 62,
72; DA; DAB; DAC; DAM MST, NOV,
POP; SSC 14; WLC
See also BEST 90:2; CA 17-20R; CANR 22,
46; DLB 2, 173; MTCW

Qian Zhongshu
See Ch'ien Chung-shu

Qroll
See Dagerman, Stig (Halvard)

Quarrington, Paul (Lewis) 1953- . . . . CLC 65
See also CA 129

Quasimodo, Salvatore 1901-1968 . . . CLC 10
See also CA 13-16; 25-28R; CAP 1;
DLB 114; MTCW

Quay, Stephen 1947- . . . . CLC 95

Quay, The Brothers
See Quay, Stephen; Quay, Timothy

Quay, Timothy 1947- . . . . CLC 95

Queen, Ellery. . . . . CLC 3, 11
See also Dannay, Frederic; Davidson,
Avram; Lee, Manfred B(ennington);
Marlowe, Stephen; Sturgeon, Theodore
(Hamilton); Vance, John Holbrook

Queen, Ellery, Jr.
See Dannay, Frederic; Lee, Manfred
B(ennington)

Queneau, Raymond
1903-1976 . . . . CLC 2, 5, 10, 42
See also CA 77-80; 69-72; CANR 32;
DLB 72; MTCW

Quevedo, Francisco de 1580-1645 . . . . LC 23

Quiller-Couch, Arthur Thomas
1863-1944 . . . . TCLC 53
See also CA 118; DLB 135, 153

Quin, Ann (Marie) 1936-1973 . . . . . . CLC 6
See also CA 9-12R; 45-48; DLB 14

Quinn, Martin
See Smith, Martin Cruz

Quinn, Peter 1947- . . . . CLC 91

Quinn, Simon
See Smith, Martin Cruz

Quiroga, Horacio (Sylvestre)
1878-1937 . . . . . TCLC 20; DAM MULT;
HLC
See also CA 117; 131; HW; MTCW

Quoirez, Francoise 1935- . . . . CLC 9
See also Sagan, Francoise
See also CA 49-52; CANR 6, 39; MTCW

Raabe, Wilhelm 1831-1910 . . . . TCLC 45
See also DLB 129

Rabe, David (William)
1940- . . . . . . CLC 4, 8, 33; DAM DRAM
See also CA 85-88; CABS 3; DLB 7

Rabelais, Francois
1483-1553 . . . . . . LC 5; DA; DAB; DAC;
DAM MST; WLC

Rabinovitch, Sholem 1859-1916
See Aleichem, Sholom
See also CA 104

Rachilde 1860-1953 . . . . TCLC 67
See also DLB 123

Racine, Jean
1639-1699 . . . . LC 28; DAB; DAM MST

Radcliffe, Ann (Ward)
1764-1823 . . . . NCLC 6, 55
See also DLB 39

Radiguet, Raymond 1903-1923 . . . . TCLC 29
See also DLB 65

Radnoti, Miklos 1909-1944 . . . . TCLC 16
See also CA 118

Rado, James 1939- . . . . CLC 17
See also CA 105

Radvanyi, Netty 1900-1983
See Seghers, Anna
See also CA 85-88; 110

Rae, Ben
See Griffiths, Trevor

Raeburn, John (Hay) 1941- . . . . CLC 34
See also CA 57-60

Ragni, Gerome 1942-1991 . . . . CLC 17
See also CA 105; 134

Rahv, Philip 1908-1973 . . . . CLC 24
See also Greenberg, Ivan
See also DLB 137

Raine, Craig 1944- . . . . CLC 32
See also CA 108; CANR 29, 51; DLB 40

Raine, Kathleen (Jessie) 1908- . . . CLC 7, 45
See also CA 85-88; CANR 46; DLB 20;
MTCW

Rainis, Janis 1865-1929 . . . . TCLC 29

Rakosi, Carl. . . . . CLC 47
See also Rawley, Callman
See also CAAS 5

Raleigh, Richard
See Lovecraft, H(oward) P(hillips)

Raleigh, Sir Walter 1554(?)-1618 . . . . LC 31
See also CDBLB Before 1660; DLB 172

Rallentando, H. P.
See Sayers, Dorothy L(eigh)

Ramal, Walter
See de la Mare, Walter (John)

Ramon, Juan
See Jimenez (Mantecon), Juan Ramon

Ramos, Graciliano 1892-1953 . . . . . TCLC 32

Rampersad, Arnold 1941- . . . . CLC 44
See also BW 2; CA 127; 133; DLB 111;
INT 133

Rampling, Anne
See Rice, Anne

Ramsay, Allan 1684(?)-1758 . . . . LC 29
See also DLB 95

Ramuz, Charles-Ferdinand
1878-1947 . . . . TCLC 33

Rand, Ayn
1905-1982 . . . . . . CLC 3, 30, 44, 79; DA;
DAC; DAM MST, NOV, POP; WLC
See also AAYA 10; CA 13-16R; 105;
CANR 27; MTCW

Randall, Dudley (Felker)
1914- . . . . . . CLC 1; BLC; DAM MULT
See also BW 1; CA 25-28R; CANR 23;
DLB 41

Randall, Robert
See Silverberg, Robert

Ranger, Ken
See Creasey, John

Ransom, John Crowe
1888-1974 . . . . CLC 2, 4, 5, 11, 24;
DAM POET
See also CA 5-8R; 49-52; CANR 6, 34;
DLB 45, 63; MTCW

Rao, Raja 1909- . . . CLC 25, 56; DAM NOV
See also CA 73-76; CANR 51; MTCW

Raphael, Frederic (Michael)
1931- . . . . CLC 2, 14
See also CA 1-4R; CANR 1; DLB 14

Ratcliffe, James P.
See Mencken, H(enry) L(ouis)

Rathbone, Julian 1935- . . . . CLC 41
See also CA 101; CANR 34

Rattigan, Terence (Mervyn)
1911-1977 . . . . CLC 7; DAM DRAM
See also CA 85-88; 73-76;
CDBLB 1945-1960; DLB 13; MTCW

Ratushinskaya, Irina 1954- . . . . CLC 54
See also CA 129

Raven, Simon (Arthur Noel)
1927- . . . . CLC 14
See also CA 81-84

Rawley, Callman 1903-
See Rakosi, Carl
See also CA 21-24R; CANR 12, 32

Rawlings, Marjorie Kinnan
1896-1953 . . . . TCLC 4
See also CA 104; 137; DLB 9, 22, 102;
JRDA; MAICYA; YABC 1

Ray, Satyajit
1921-1992 . . . CLC 16, 76; DAM MULT
See also CA 114; 137

Read, Herbert Edward 1893-1968 . . . . CLC 4
See also CA 85-88; 25-28R; DLB 20, 149

Read, Piers Paul 1941- ...... **CLC 4, 10, 25**
See also CA 21-24R; CANR 38; DLB 14;
SATA 21

Reade, Charles 1814-1884 .... **NCLC 2**
See also DLB 21

Reade, Hamish
See Gray, Simon (James Holliday)

Reading, Peter 1946- .... **CLC 47**
See also CA 103; CANR 46; DLB 40

Reaney, James
1926- ...... **CLC 13; DAC; DAM MST**
See also CA 41-44R; CAAS 15; CANR 42;
DLB 68; SATA 43

Rebreanu, Liviu 1885-1944 .... **TCLC 28**

Rechy, John (Francisco)
1934- .... **CLC 1, 7, 14, 18;**
DAM MULT; HLC
See also CA 5-8R; CAAS 4; CANR 6, 32;
DLB 122; DLBY 82; HW; INT CANR-6

Redcam, Tom 1870-1933 .... **TCLC 25**

Reddin, Keith .... **CLC 67**

Redgrove, Peter (William)
1932- .... **CLC 6, 41**
See also CA 1-4R; CANR 3, 39; DLB 40

Redmon, Anne .... **CLC 22**
See also Nightingale, Anne Redmon
See also DLBY 86

Reed, Eliot
See Ambler, Eric

Reed, Ishmael
1938- .... **CLC 2, 3, 5, 6, 13, 32, 60;**
BLC; DAM MULT
See also BW 2; CA 21-24R; CANR 25, 48;
DLB 2, 5, 33, 169; DLBD 8; MTCW

Reed, John (Silas) 1887-1920 ...... **TCLC 9**
See also CA 106

Reed, Lou .... **CLC 21**
See also Firbank, Louis

Reeve, Clara 1729-1807 .... **NCLC 19**
See also DLB 39

Reich, Wilhelm 1897-1957 .... **TCLC 57**

Reid, Christopher (John) 1949- ..... **CLC 33**
See also CA 140; DLB 40

Reid, Desmond
See Moorcock, Michael (John)

Reid Banks, Lynne 1929-
See Banks, Lynne Reid
See also CA 1-4R; CANR 6, 22, 38;
CLR 24; JRDA; MAICYA; SATA 22, 75

Reilly, William K.
See Creasey, John

Reiner, Max
See Caldwell, (Janet Miriam) Taylor
(Holland)

Reis, Ricardo
See Pessoa, Fernando (Antonio Nogueira)

Remarque, Erich Maria
1898-1970 .... **CLC 21; DA; DAB; DAC;**
DAM MST, NOV
See also CA 77-80; 29-32R; DLB 56;
MTCW

Remizov, A.
See Remizov, Aleksei (Mikhailovich)

Remizov, A. M.
See Remizov, Aleksei (Mikhailovich)

Remizov, Aleksei (Mikhailovich)
1877-1957 .... **TCLC 27**
See also CA 125; 133

Renan, Joseph Ernest
1823-1892 .... **NCLC 26**

Renard, Jules 1864-1910 .... **TCLC 17**
See also CA 117

Renault, Mary .... **CLC 3, 11, 17**
See also Challans, Mary
See also DLBY 83

Rendell, Ruth (Barbara)
1930- .... **CLC 28, 48; DAM POP**
See also Vine, Barbara
See also CA 109; CANR 32, 52; DLB 87;
INT CANR-32; MTCW

Renoir, Jean 1894-1979 .... **CLC 20**
See also CA 129; 85-88

Resnais, Alain 1922- .... **CLC 16**

Reverdy, Pierre 1889-1960 .... **CLC 53**
See also CA 97-100; 89-92

Rexroth, Kenneth
1905-1982 ...... **CLC 1, 2, 6, 11, 22, 49;**
DAM POET
See also CA 5-8R; 107; CANR 14, 34;
CDALB 1941-1968; DLB 16, 48, 165;
DLBY 82; INT CANR-14; MTCW

Reyes, Alfonso 1889-1959 .... **TCLC 33**
See also CA 131; HW

Reyes y Basoalto, Ricardo Eliecer Neftali
See Neruda, Pablo

Reymont, Wladyslaw (Stanislaw)
1868(?)-1925 .... **TCLC 5**
See also CA 104

Reynolds, Jonathan 1942- .... **CLC 6, 38**
See also CA 65-68; CANR 28

Reynolds, Joshua 1723-1792 .... **LC 15**
See also DLB 104

Reynolds, Michael Shane 1937- .... **CLC 44**
See also CA 65-68; CANR 9

Reznikoff, Charles 1894-1976 .... **CLC 9**
See also CA 33-36; 61-64; CAP 2; DLB 28,
45

Rezzori (d'Arezzo), Gregor von
1914- .... **CLC 25**
See also CA 122; 136

Rhine, Richard
See Silverstein, Alvin

Rhodes, Eugene Manlove
1869-1934 .... **TCLC 53**

R'hoone
See Balzac, Honore de

Rhys, Jean
1890(?)-1979 .... **CLC 2, 4, 6, 14, 19, 51;**
DAM NOV; SSC 21
See also CA 25-28R; 85-88; CANR 35;
CDBLB 1945-1960; DLB 36, 117, 162;
MTCW

Ribeiro, Darcy 1922- .... **CLC 34**
See also CA 33-36R

Ribeiro, Joao Ubaldo (Osorio Pimentel)
1941- .... **CLC 10, 67**
See also CA 81-84

Ribman, Ronald (Burt) 1932- .... **CLC 7**
See also CA 21-24R; CANR 46

Ricci, Nino 1959- .... **CLC 70**
See also CA 137

Rice, Anne 1941- ..... **CLC 41; DAM POP**
See also AAYA 9; BEST 89:2; CA 65-68;
CANR 12, 36, 53

Rice, Elmer (Leopold)
1892-1967 .... **CLC 7, 49; DAM DRAM**
See also CA 21-22; 25-28R; CAP 2; DLB 4,
7; MTCW

Rice, Tim(othy Miles Bindon)
1944- .... **CLC 21**
See also CA 103; CANR 46

Rich, Adrienne (Cecile)
1929- .... **CLC 3, 6, 7, 11, 18, 36, 73, 76;**
DAM POET; PC 5
See also CA 9-12R; CANR 20, 53; DLB 5,
67; MTCW

Rich, Barbara
See Graves, Robert (von Ranke)

Rich, Robert
See Trumbo, Dalton

Richard, Keith .... **CLC 17**
See also Richards, Keith

Richards, David Adams
1950- .... **CLC 59; DAC**
See also CA 93-96; DLB 53

Richards, I(vor) A(rmstrong)
1893-1979 .... **CLC 14, 24**
See also CA 41-44R; 89-92; CANR 34;
DLB 27

Richards, Keith 1943-
See Richard, Keith
See also CA 107

Richardson, Anne
See Roiphe, Anne (Richardson)

Richardson, Dorothy Miller
1873-1957 .... **TCLC 3**
See also CA 104; DLB 36

Richardson, Ethel Florence (Lindesay)
1870-1946
See Richardson, Henry Handel
See also CA 105

Richardson, Henry Handel .... **TCLC 4**
See also Richardson, Ethel Florence
(Lindesay)

Richardson, John
1796-1852 .... **NCLC 55; DAC**
See also DLB 99

Richardson, Samuel
1689-1761 ...... **LC 1; DA; DAB; DAC;**
DAM MST, NOV; WLC
See also CDBLB 1660-1789; DLB 39

Richler, Mordecai
1931- .... **CLC 3, 5, 9, 13, 18, 46, 70;**
DAC; DAM MST, NOV
See also AITN 1; CA 65-68; CANR 31;
CLR 17; DLB 53; MAICYA; MTCW;
SATA 44; SATA-Brief 27

Richter, Conrad (Michael)
1890-1968 .... **CLC 30**
See also CA 5-8R; 25-28R; CANR 23;
DLB 9; MTCW; SATA 3

Ricostranza, Tom
See Ellis, Trey

Riddell, J. H. 1832-1906 .... **TCLC 40**

Riding, Laura. .... **CLC 3, 7**
See also Jackson, Laura (Riding)

Riefenstahl, Berta Helene Amalia 1902-
See Riefenstahl, Leni
See also CA 108

Riefenstahl, Leni .... **CLC 16**
See also Riefenstahl, Berta Helene Amalia

Riffe, Ernest
See Bergman, (Ernst) Ingmar

Riggs, (Rolla) Lynn
1899-1954 ..... **TCLC 56; DAM MULT**
See also CA 144; NNAL

Riley, James Whitcomb
1849-1916 ...... **TCLC 51; DAM POET**
See also CA 118; 137; MAICYA; SATA 17

Riley, Tex
See Creasey, John

Rilke, Rainer Maria
1875-1926 .... **TCLC 1, 6, 19;**
DAM POET; PC 2
See also CA 104; 132; DLB 81; MTCW

Rimbaud, (Jean Nicolas) Arthur
1854-1891 ..... **NCLC 4, 35; DA; DAB;**
DAC; DAM MST, POET; PC 3; WLC

Rinehart, Mary Roberts
1876-1958 .... **TCLC 52**
See also CA 108

Ringmaster, The
See Mencken, H(enry) L(ouis)

Ringwood, Gwen(dolyn Margaret) Pharis
1910-1984 .... **CLC 48**
See also CA 148; 112; DLB 88

Rio, Michel 19(?)- .... **CLC 43**

Ritsos, Giannes
See Ritsos, Yannis

Ritsos, Yannis 1909-1990 ..... **CLC 6, 13, 31**
See also CA 77-80; 133; CANR 39; MTCW

Ritter, Erika 1948(?)-............. **CLC 52**

Rivera, Jose Eustasio 1889-1928... **TCLC 35**
See also HW

Rivers, Conrad Kent 1933-1968...... **CLC 1**
See also BW 1; CA 85-88; DLB 41

Rivers, Elfrida
See Bradley, Marion Zimmer

Riverside, John
See Heinlein, Robert A(nson)

Rizal, Jose 1861-1896. .... **NCLC 27**

Roa Bastos, Augusto (Antonio)
1917- ..... **CLC 45; DAM MULT; HLC**
See also CA 131; DLB 113; HW

Robbe-Grillet, Alain
1922- ...... **CLC 1, 2, 4, 6, 8, 10, 14, 43**
See also CA 9-12R; CANR 33; DLB 83;
MTCW

Robbins, Harold
1916- .... **CLC 5; DAM NOV**
See also CA 73-76; CANR 26, 54; MTCW

Robbins, Thomas Eugene 1936-
See Robbins, Tom
See also CA 81-84; CANR 29; DAM NOV,
POP; MTCW

Robbins, Tom. .... **CLC 9, 32, 64**
See also Robbins, Thomas Eugene
See also BEST 90:3; DLBY 80

Robbins, Trina 1938- .... **CLC 21**
See also CA 128

Roberts, Charles G(eorge) D(ouglas)
1860-1943 .... **TCLC 8**
See also CA 105; CLR 33; DLB 92;
SATA 88; SATA-Brief 29

Roberts, Kate 1891-1985 .... **CLC 15**
See also CA 107; 116

Roberts, Keith (John Kingston)
1935- .... **CLC 14**
See also CA 25-28R; CANR 46

Roberts, Kenneth (Lewis)
1885-1957 .... **TCLC 23**
See also CA 109; DLB 9

Roberts, Michele (B.) 1949-........ **CLC 48**
See also CA 115

Robertson, Ellis
See Ellison, Harlan (Jay); Silverberg, Robert

Robertson, Thomas William
1829-1871 .... **NCLC 35; DAM DRAM**

Robinson, Edwin Arlington
1869-1935 .... **TCLC 5; DA; DAC;**
DAM MST, POET; PC 1
See also CA 104; 133; CDALB 1865-1917;
DLB 54; MTCW

Robinson, Henry Crabb
1775-1867 .... **NCLC 15**
See also DLB 107

Robinson, Jill 1936-............. **CLC 10**
See also CA 102; INT 102

Robinson, Kim Stanley 1952- ...... **CLC 34**
See also CA 126

Robinson, Lloyd
See Silverberg, Robert

Robinson, Marilynne 1944-........ **CLC 25**
See also CA 116

Robinson, Smokey. .... **CLC 21**
See also Robinson, William, Jr.

Robinson, William, Jr. 1940-
See Robinson, Smokey
See also CA 116

Robison, Mary 1949-............. **CLC 42**
See also CA 113; 116; DLB 130; INT 116

Rod, Edouard 1857-1910 .... **TCLC 52**

Roddenberry, Eugene Wesley 1921-1991
See Roddenberry, Gene
See also CA 110; 135; CANR 37; SATA 45;
SATA-Obit 69

Roddenberry, Gene .... **CLC 17**
See also Roddenberry, Eugene Wesley
See also AAYA 5; SATA-Obit 69

Rodgers, Mary 1931-............. **CLC 12**
See also CA 49-52; CANR 8; CLR 20;
INT CANR-8; JRDA; MAICYA;
SATA 8

Rodgers, W(illiam) R(obert)
1909-1969 .... **CLC 7**
See also CA 85-88; DLB 20

Rodman, Eric
See Silverberg, Robert

Rodman, Howard 1920(?)-1985..... **CLC 65**
See also CA 118

Rodman, Maia
See Wojciechowska, Maia (Teresa)

Rodriguez, Claudio 1934-......... **CLC 10**
See also DLB 134

Roelvaag, O(le) E(dvart)
1876-1931 .... **TCLC 17**
See also CA 117; DLB 9

Roethke, Theodore (Huebner)
1908-1963 ...... **CLC 1, 3, 8, 11, 19, 46;**
DAM POET; PC 15
See also CA 81-84; CABS 2;
CDALB 1941-1968; DLB 5; MTCW

Rogers, Thomas Hunton 1927- ..... **CLC 57**
See also CA 89-92; INT 89-92

Rogers, Will(iam Penn Adair)
1879-1935 ..... **TCLC 8; DAM MULT**
See also CA 105; 144; DLB 11; NNAL

Rogin, Gilbert 1929-.............. **CLC 18**
See also CA 65-68; CANR 15

Rohan, Koda .... **TCLC 22**
See also Koda Shigeyuki

Rohmer, Eric .... **CLC 16**
See also Scherer, Jean-Marie Maurice

Rohmer, Sax .... **TCLC 28**
See also Ward, Arthur Henry Sarsfield
See also DLB 70

Roiphe, Anne (Richardson)
1935- .... **CLC 3, 9**
See also CA 89-92; CANR 45; DLBY 80;
INT 89-92

Rojas, Fernando de 1465-1541 ...... **LC 23**

Rolfe, Frederick (William Serafino Austin
Lewis Mary) 1860-1913...... **TCLC 12**
See also CA 107; DLB 34, 156

Rolland, Romain 1866-1944........ **TCLC 23**
See also CA 118; DLB 65

Rolvaag, O(le) E(dvart)
See Roelvaag, O(le) E(dvart)

Romain Arnaud, Saint
See Aragon, Louis

Romains, Jules 1885-1972.......... **CLC 7**
See also CA 85-88; CANR 34; DLB 65;
MTCW

Romero, Jose Ruben 1890-1952 ... **TCLC 14**
See also CA 114; 131; HW

Ronsard, Pierre de
1524-1585 .... **LC 6; PC 11**

Rooke, Leon
1934- .... **CLC 25, 34; DAM POP**
See also CA 25-28R; CANR 23, 53

Roper, William 1498-1578.......... **LC 10**

Roquelaure, A. N.
See Rice, Anne

Rosa, Joao Guimaraes 1908-1967 ... **CLC 23**
See also CA 89-92; DLB 113

Rose, Wendy
1948- .... **CLC 85; DAM MULT; PC 13**
See also CA 53-56; CANR 5, 51; NNAL;
SATA 12

Rosen, Richard (Dean) 1949-....... **CLC 39**
See also CA 77-80; INT CANR-30

Rosenberg, Isaac 1890-1918. . . . . . . **TCLC 12**
See also CA 107; DLB 20

Rosenblatt, Joe . . . . **CLC 15**
See also Rosenblatt, Joseph

Rosenblatt, Joseph 1933-
See Rosenblatt, Joe
See also CA 89-92; INT 89-92

Rosenfeld, Samuel 1896-1963
See Tzara, Tristan
See also CA 89-92

Rosenstock, Sami
See Tzara, Tristan

Rosenstock, Samuel
See Tzara, Tristan

Rosenthal, M(acha) L(ouis)
1917-1996 . . . . **CLC 28**
See also CA 1-4R; 152; CAAS 6; CANR 4,
51; DLB 5; SATA 59

Ross, Barnaby
See Dannay, Frederic

Ross, Bernard L.
See Follett, Ken(neth Martin)

Ross, J. H.
See Lawrence, T(homas) E(dward)

Ross, Martin
See Martin, Violet Florence
See also DLB 135

Ross, (James) Sinclair
1908- . . . . . . **CLC 13; DAC; DAM MST**
See also CA 73-76; DLB 88

Rossetti, Christina (Georgina)
1830-1894 . . . . . **NCLC 2, 50; DA; DAB;**
DAC; DAM MST, POET; PC 7; WLC
See also DLB 35, 163; MAICYA; SATA 20

Rossetti, Dante Gabriel
1828-1882 . . . . **NCLC 4; DA; DAB;**
DAC; DAM MST, POET; WLC
See also CDBLB 1832-1890; DLB 35

Rossner, Judith (Perelman)
1935- . . . . **CLC 6, 9, 29**
See also AITN 2; BEST 90:3; CA 17-20R;
CANR 18, 51; DLB 6; INT CANR-18;
MTCW

Rostand, Edmond (Eugene Alexis)
1868-1918 . . . . . **TCLC 6, 37; DA; DAB;**
DAC; DAM DRAM, MST
See also CA 104; 126; MTCW

Roth, Henry 1906-1995 . . . . **CLC 2, 6, 11**
See also CA 11-12; 149; CANR 38; CAP 1;
DLB 28; MTCW

Roth, Joseph 1894-1939 . . . . **TCLC 33**
See also DLB 85

Roth, Philip (Milton)
1933- . . . . . . **CLC 1, 2, 3, 4, 6, 9, 15, 22,**
31, 47, 66, 86; DA; DAB; DAC;
DAM MST, NOV, POP; WLC
See also BEST 90:3; CA 1-4R; CANR 1, 22,
36; CDALB 1968-1988; DLB 2, 28, 173;
DLBY 82; MTCW

Rothenberg, Jerome 1931- . . . . **CLC 6, 57**
See also CA 45-48; CANR 1; DLB 5

Roumain, Jacques (Jean Baptiste)
1907-1944 . . . . **TCLC 19; BLC;**
DAM MULT
See also BW 1; CA 117; 125

Rourke, Constance (Mayfield)
1885-1941 . . . . **TCLC 12**
See also CA 107; YABC 1

Rousseau, Jean-Baptiste 1671-1741 . . . **LC 9**

Rousseau, Jean-Jacques
1712-1778 . . . . . **LC 14; DA; DAB; DAC;**
DAM MST; WLC

Roussel, Raymond 1877-1933 . . . . . **TCLC 20**
See also CA 117

Rovit, Earl (Herbert) 1927- . . . . **CLC 7**
See also CA 5-8R; CANR 12

Rowe, Nicholas 1674-1718 . . . . **LC 8**
See also DLB 84

Rowley, Ames Dorrance
See Lovecraft, H(oward) P(hillips)

Rowson, Susanna Haswell
1762(?)-1824 . . . . **NCLC 5**
See also DLB 37

Roy, Gabrielle
1909-1983 . . . . **CLC 10, 14; DAB; DAC;**
DAM MST
See also CA 53-56; 110; CANR 5; DLB 68;
MTCW

Rozewicz, Tadeusz
1921- . . . . **CLC 9, 23; DAM POET**
See also CA 108; CANR 36; MTCW

Ruark, Gibbons 1941- . . . . **CLC 3**
See also CA 33-36R; CAAS 23; CANR 14,
31; DLB 120

Rubens, Bernice (Ruth) 1923- . . . **CLC 19, 31**
See also CA 25-28R; CANR 33; DLB 14;
MTCW

Rubin, Harold
See Robbins, Harold

Rudkin, (James) David 1936- . . . . . . **CLC 14**
See also CA 89-92; DLB 13

Rudnik, Raphael 1933- . . . . **CLC 7**
See also CA 29-32R

Ruffian, M.
See Hasek, Jaroslav (Matej Frantisek)

Ruiz, Jose Martinez . . . . **CLC 11**
See also Martinez Ruiz, Jose

Rukeyser, Muriel
1913-1980 . . . . **CLC 6, 10, 15, 27;**
DAM POET; PC 12
See also CA 5-8R; 93-96; CANR 26;
DLB 48; MTCW; SATA-Obit 22

Rule, Jane (Vance) 1931- . . . . **CLC 27**
See also CA 25-28R; CAAS 18; CANR 12;
DLB 60

Rulfo, Juan
1918-1986 . . . . **CLC 8, 80; DAM MULT;**
HLC
See also CA 85-88; 118; CANR 26;
DLB 113; HW; MTCW

Runeberg, Johan 1804-1877 . . . . . . **NCLC 41**

Runyon, (Alfred) Damon
1884(?)-1946 . . . . **TCLC 10**
See also CA 107; DLB 11, 86, 171

Rush, Norman 1933- . . . . **CLC 44**
See also CA 121; 126; INT 126

Rushdie, (Ahmed) Salman
1947- . . . . . **CLC 23, 31, 55; DAB; DAC;**
DAM MST, NOV, POP
See also BEST 89:3; CA 108; 111;
CANR 33; INT 111; MTCW

Rushforth, Peter (Scott) 1945- . . . . . **CLC 19**
See also CA 101

Ruskin, John 1819-1900 . . . . **TCLC 63**
See also CA 114; 129; CDBLB 1832-1890;
DLB 55, 163; SATA 24

Russ, Joanna 1937- . . . . **CLC 15**
See also CA 25-28R; CANR 11, 31; DLB 8;
MTCW

Russell, George William 1867-1935
See A. E.
See also CA 104; 153; CDBLB 1890-1914;
DAM POET

Russell, (Henry) Ken(neth Alfred)
1927- . . . . **CLC 16**
See also CA 105

Russell, Willy 1947- . . . . **CLC 60**

Rutherford, Mark . . . . **TCLC 25**
See also White, William Hale
See also DLB 18

Ruyslinck, Ward 1929- . . . . **CLC 14**
See also Belser, Reimond Karel Maria de

Ryan, Cornelius (John) 1920-1974 . . . **CLC 7**
See also CA 69-72; 53-56; CANR 38

Ryan, Michael 1946- . . . . **CLC 65**
See also CA 49-52; DLBY 82

Rybakov, Anatoli (Naumovich)
1911- . . . . **CLC 23, 53**
See also CA 126; 135; SATA 79

Ryder, Jonathan
See Ludlum, Robert

Ryga, George
1932-1987 . . **CLC 14; DAC; DAM MST**
See also CA 101; 124; CANR 43; DLB 60

S. S.
See Sassoon, Siegfried (Lorraine)

Saba, Umberto 1883-1957 . . . . **TCLC 33**
See also CA 144; DLB 114

Sabatini, Rafael 1875-1950 . . . . **TCLC 47**

Sabato, Ernesto (R.)
1911- . . . . **CLC 10, 23; DAM MULT;**
HLC
See also CA 97-100; CANR 32; DLB 145;
HW; MTCW

Sacastru, Martin
See Bioy Casares, Adolfo

Sacher-Masoch, Leopold von
1836(?)-1895 . . . . **NCLC 31**

Sachs, Marilyn (Stickle) 1927- . . . . . **CLC 35**
See also AAYA 2; CA 17-20R; CANR 13,
47; CLR 2; JRDA; MAICYA; SAAS 2;
SATA 3, 68

Sachs, Nelly 1891-1970 . . . . **CLC 14**
See also CA 17-18; 25-28R; CAP 2

Sackler, Howard (Oliver)
1929-1982 . . . . **CLC 14**
See also CA 61-64; 108; CANR 30; DLB 7

Sacks, Oliver (Wolf) 1933- . . . . **CLC 67**
See also CA 53-56; CANR 28, 50;
INT CANR-28; MTCW

Sade, Donatien Alphonse Francois Comte
1740-1814 . . . . **NCLC 47**

Sadoff, Ira 1945- . . . . **CLC 9**
See also CA 53-56; CANR 5, 21; DLB 120

Saetone
See Camus, Albert

Safire, William 1929- . . . . **CLC 10**
See also CA 17-20R; CANR 31, 54

Sagan, Carl (Edward) 1934- . . . . **CLC 30**
See also AAYA 2; CA 25-28R; CANR 11, 36; MTCW; SATA 58

Sagan, Francoise . . . . **CLC 3, 6, 9, 17, 36**
See also Quoirez, Francoise
See also DLB 83

Sahgal, Nayantara (Pandit) 1927- . . . **CLC 41**
See also CA 9-12R; CANR 11

Saint, H(arry) F. 1941- . . . . **CLC 50**
See also CA 127

St. Aubin de Teran, Lisa 1953-
See Teran, Lisa St. Aubin de
See also CA 118; 126; INT 126

Sainte-Beuve, Charles Augustin
1804-1869 . . . . **NCLC 5**

Saint-Exupery, Antoine (Jean Baptiste Marie Roger) de
1900-1944 . . . . **TCLC 2, 56; DAM NOV; WLC**
See also CA 108; 132; CLR 10; DLB 72; MAICYA; MTCW; SATA 20

St. John, David
See Hunt, E(verette) Howard, (Jr.)

Saint-John Perse
See Leger, (Marie-Rene Auguste) Alexis Saint-Leger

Saintsbury, George (Edward Bateman)
1845-1933 . . . . **TCLC 31**
See also DLB 57, 149

Sait Faik . . . . **TCLC 23**
See also Abasiyanik, Sait Faik

Saki . . . . **TCLC 3; SSC 12**
See also Munro, H(ector) H(ugh)

Sala, George Augustus . . . . **NCLC 46**

Salama, Hannu 1936- . . . . **CLC 18**

Salamanca, J(ack) R(ichard)
1922- . . . . **CLC 4, 15**
See also CA 25-28R

Sale, J. Kirkpatrick
See Sale, Kirkpatrick

Sale, Kirkpatrick 1937- . . . . **CLC 68**
See also CA 13-16R; CANR 10

Salinas, Luis Omar
1937- . . . . . **CLC 90; DAM MULT; HLC**
See also CA 131; DLB 82; HW

Salinas (y Serrano), Pedro
1891(?)-1951 . . . . **TCLC 17**
See also CA 117; DLB 134

Salinger, J(erome) D(avid)
1919- . . . . . . **CLC 1, 3, 8, 12, 55, 56; DA; DAB; DAC; DAM MST, NOV, POP; SSC 2; WLC**
See also AAYA 2; CA 5-8R; CANR 39; CDALB 1941-1968; CLR 18; DLB 2, 102, 173; MAICYA; MTCW; SATA 67

Salisbury, John
See Caute, David

Salter, James 1925- . . . . **CLC 7, 52, 59**
See also CA 73-76; DLB 130

Saltus, Edgar (Everton)
1855-1921 . . . . **TCLC 8**
See also CA 105

Saltykov, Mikhail Evgrafovich
1826-1889 . . . . **NCLC 16**

Samarakis, Antonis 1919- . . . . **CLC 5**
See also CA 25-28R; CAAS 16; CANR 36

Sanchez, Florencio 1875-1910 . . . . . **TCLC 37**
See also CA 153; HW

Sanchez, Luis Rafael 1936- . . . . **CLC 23**
See also CA 128; DLB 145; HW

Sanchez, Sonia
1934- . . . . . . **CLC 5; BLC; DAM MULT; PC 9**
See also BW 2; CA 33-36R; CANR 24, 49; CLR 18; DLB 41; DLBD 8; MAICYA; MTCW; SATA 22

Sand, George
1804-1876 . . . . **NCLC 2, 42, 57; DA; DAB; DAC; DAM MST, NOV; WLC**
See also DLB 119

Sandburg, Carl (August)
1878-1967 . . . . **CLC 1, 4, 10, 15, 35; DA; DAB; DAC; DAM MST, POET; PC 2; WLC**
See also CA 5-8R; 25-28R; CANR 35; CDALB 1865-1917; DLB 17, 54; MAICYA; MTCW; SATA 8

Sandburg, Charles
See Sandburg, Carl (August)

Sandburg, Charles A.
See Sandburg, Carl (August)

Sanders, (James) Ed(ward) 1939- . . . **CLC 53**
See also CA 13-16R; CAAS 21; CANR 13, 44; DLB 16

Sanders, Lawrence
1920- . . . . **CLC 41; DAM POP**
See also BEST 89:4; CA 81-84; CANR 33; MTCW

Sanders, Noah
See Blount, Roy (Alton), Jr.

Sanders, Winston P.
See Anderson, Poul (William)

Sandoz, Mari(e Susette)
1896-1966 . . . . **CLC 28**
See also CA 1-4R; 25-28R; CANR 17; DLB 9; MTCW; SATA 5

Saner, Reg(inald Anthony) 1931- . . . . **CLC 9**
See also CA 65-68

Sannazaro, Jacopo 1456(?)-1530 . . . . . . **LC 8**

Sansom, William
1912-1976 . . . . . . **CLC 2, 6; DAM NOV; SSC 21**
See also CA 5-8R; 65-68; CANR 42; DLB 139; MTCW

Santayana, George 1863-1952 . . . . . **TCLC 40**
See also CA 115; DLB 54, 71; DLBD 13

Santiago, Danny . . . . **CLC 33**
See also James, Daniel (Lewis)
See also DLB 122

Santmyer, Helen Hoover
1895-1986 . . . . **CLC 33**
See also CA 1-4R; 118; CANR 15, 33; DLBY 84; MTCW

Santos, Bienvenido N(uqui)
1911-1996 . . . . . . **CLC 22; DAM MULT**
See also CA 101; 151; CANR 19, 46

Sapper . . . . **TCLC 44**
See also McNeile, Herman Cyril

Sappho
fl. 6th cent. B.C.- . . . . **CMLC 3; DAM POET; PC 5**

Sarduy, Severo 1937-1993 . . . . **CLC 6, 97**
See also CA 89-92; 142; DLB 113; HW

Sargeson, Frank 1903-1982 . . . . **CLC 31**
See also CA 25-28R; 106; CANR 38

Sarmiento, Felix Ruben Garcia
See Dario, Ruben

Saroyan, William
1908-1981 . . . . . **CLC 1, 8, 10, 29, 34, 56; DA; DAB; DAC; DAM DRAM, MST, NOV; SSC 21; WLC**
See also CA 5-8R; 103; CANR 30; DLB 7, 9, 86; DLBY 81; MTCW; SATA 23; SATA-Obit 24

Sarraute, Nathalie
1900- . . . . **CLC 1, 2, 4, 8, 10, 31, 80**
See also CA 9-12R; CANR 23; DLB 83; MTCW

Sarton, (Eleanor) May
1912-1995 . . . . **CLC 4, 14, 49, 91; DAM POET**
See also CA 1-4R; 149; CANR 1, 34; DLB 48; DLBY 81; INT CANR-34; MTCW; SATA 36; SATA-Obit 86

Sartre, Jean-Paul
1905-1980 . . . . **CLC 1, 4, 7, 9, 13, 18, 24, 44, 50, 52; DA; DAB; DAC; DAM DRAM, MST, NOV; DC 3; WLC**
See also CA 9-12R; 97-100; CANR 21; DLB 72; MTCW

Sassoon, Siegfried (Lorraine)
1886-1967 . . . . **CLC 36; DAB; DAM MST, NOV, POET; PC 12**
See also CA 104; 25-28R; CANR 36; DLB 20; MTCW

Satterfield, Charles
See Pohl, Frederik

Saul, John (W. III)
1942- . . . . **CLC 46; DAM NOV, POP**
See also AAYA 10; BEST 90:4; CA 81-84; CANR 16, 40

Saunders, Caleb
See Heinlein, Robert A(nson)

Saura (Atares), Carlos 1932- . . . . **CLC 20**
See also CA 114; 131; HW

Sauser-Hall, Frederic 1887-1961 . . . . **CLC 18**
See also Cendrars, Blaise
See also CA 102; 93-96; CANR 36; MTCW

Saussure, Ferdinand de
1857-1913 . . . . **TCLC 49**

Savage, Catharine
See Brosman, Catharine Savage

Savage, Thomas 1915- . . . . **CLC 40**
See also CA 126; 132; CAAS 15; INT 132

Savan, Glenn 19(?)- . . . . **CLC 50**

Sayers, Dorothy L(eigh)
1893-1957 ..... **TCLC 2, 15; DAM POP**
See also CA 104; 119; CDBLB 1914-1945;
DLB 10, 36, 77, 100; MTCW

Sayers, Valerie 1952-............. **CLC 50**
See also CA 134

Sayles, John (Thomas)
1950- .... **CLC 7, 10, 14**
See also CA 57-60; CANR 41; DLB 44

Scammell, Michael .... **CLC 34**

Scannell, Vernon 1922- .... **CLC 49**
See also CA 5-8R; CANR 8, 24; DLB 27;
SATA 59

Scarlett, Susan
See Streatfeild, (Mary) Noel

Schaeffer, Susan Fromberg
1941- .... **CLC 6, 11, 22**
See also CA 49-52; CANR 18; DLB 28;
MTCW; SATA 22

Schary, Jill
See Robinson, Jill

Schell, Jonathan 1943-............ **CLC 35**
See also CA 73-76; CANR 12

Schelling, Friedrich Wilhelm Joseph von
1775-1854 .... **NCLC 30**
See also DLB 90

Schendel, Arthur van 1874-1946 ... **TCLC 56**

Scherer, Jean-Marie Maurice 1920-
See Rohmer, Eric
See also CA 110

Schevill, James (Erwin) 1920-....... **CLC 7**
See also CA 5-8R; CAAS 12

Schiller, Friedrich
1759-1805 .... **NCLC 39; DAM DRAM**
See also DLB 94

Schisgal, Murray (Joseph) 1926-..... **CLC 6**
See also CA 21-24R; CANR 48

Schlee, Ann 1934-................ **CLC 35**
See also CA 101; CANR 29; SATA 44;
SATA-Brief 36

Schlegel, August Wilhelm von
1767-1845 .... **NCLC 15**
See also DLB 94

Schlegel, Friedrich 1772-1829 .... **NCLC 45**
See also DLB 90

Schlegel, Johann Elias (von)
1719(?)-1749 .... **LC 5**

Schlesinger, Arthur M(eier), Jr.
1917- .... **CLC 84**
See also AITN 1; CA 1-4R; CANR 1, 28;
DLB 17; INT CANR-28; MTCW;
SATA 61

Schmidt, Arno (Otto) 1914-1979.... **CLC 56**
See also CA 128; 109; DLB 69

Schmitz, Aron Hector 1861-1928
See Svevo, Italo
See also CA 104; 122; MTCW

Schnackenberg, Gjertrud 1953-..... **CLC 40**
See also CA 116; DLB 120

Schneider, Leonard Alfred 1925-1966
See Bruce, Lenny
See also CA 89-92

Schnitzler, Arthur
1862-1931 .... **TCLC 4; SSC 15**
See also CA 104; DLB 81, 118

Schopenhauer, Arthur
1788-1860 .... **NCLC 51**
See also DLB 90

Schor, Sandra (M.) 1932(?)-1990 ... **CLC 65**
See also CA 132

Schorer, Mark 1908-1977 .... **CLC 9**
See also CA 5-8R; 73-76; CANR 7;
DLB 103

Schrader, Paul (Joseph) 1946-...... **CLC 26**
See also CA 37-40R; CANR 41; DLB 44

Schreiner, Olive (Emilie Albertina)
1855-1920 .... **TCLC 9**
See also CA 105; DLB 18, 156

Schulberg, Budd (Wilson)
1914- .... **CLC 7, 48**
See also CA 25-28R; CANR 19; DLB 6, 26,
28; DLBY 81

Schulz, Bruno
1892-1942 .... **TCLC 5, 51; SSC 13**
See also CA 115; 123

Schulz, Charles M(onroe) 1922-.... **CLC 12**
See also CA 9-12R; CANR 6;
INT CANR-6; SATA 10

Schumacher, E(rnst) F(riedrich)
1911-1977 .... **CLC 80**
See also CA 81-84; 73-76; CANR 34

Schuyler, James Marcus
1923-1991 ..... **CLC 5, 23; DAM POET**
See also CA 101; 134; DLB 5, 169; INT 101

Schwartz, Delmore (David)
1913-1966 ... **CLC 2, 4, 10, 45, 87; PC 8**
See also CA 17-18; 25-28R; CANR 35;
CAP 2; DLB 28, 48; MTCW

Schwartz, Ernst
See Ozu, Yasujiro

Schwartz, John Burnham 1965- .... **CLC 59**
See also CA 132

Schwartz, Lynne Sharon 1939-..... **CLC 31**
See also CA 103; CANR 44

Schwartz, Muriel A.
See Eliot, T(homas) S(tearns)

Schwarz-Bart, Andre 1928-....... **CLC 2, 4**
See also CA 89-92

Schwarz-Bart, Simone 1938-........ **CLC 7**
See also BW 2; CA 97-100

Schwob, (Mayer Andre) Marcel
1867-1905 .... **TCLC 20**
See also CA 117; DLB 123

Sciascia, Leonardo
1921-1989 .... **CLC 8, 9, 41**
See also CA 85-88; 130; CANR 35; MTCW

Scoppettone, Sandra 1936-........ **CLC 26**
See also AAYA 11; CA 5-8R; CANR 41;
SATA 9

Scorsese, Martin 1942- .... **CLC 20, 89**
See also CA 110; 114; CANR 46

Scotland, Jay
See Jakes, John (William)

Scott, Duncan Campbell
1862-1947 .... **TCLC 6; DAC**
See also CA 104; 153; DLB 92

Scott, Evelyn 1893-1963.......... **CLC 43**
See also CA 104; 112; DLB 9, 48

Scott, F(rancis) R(eginald)
1899-1985 .... **CLC 22**
See also CA 101; 114; DLB 88; INT 101

Scott, Frank
See Scott, F(rancis) R(eginald)

Scott, Joanna 1960- .... **CLC 50**
See also CA 126; CANR 53

Scott, Paul (Mark) 1920-1978.... **CLC 9, 60**
See also CA 81-84; 77-80; CANR 33;
DLB 14; MTCW

Scott, Walter
1771-1832 .... **NCLC 15; DA; DAB;
DAC; DAM MST, NOV, POET; PC 13;
WLC**
See also CDBLB 1789-1832; DLB 93, 107,
116, 144, 159; YABC 2

Scribe, (Augustin) Eugene
1791-1861 .... **NCLC 16; DAM DRAM;
DC 5**

Scrum, R.
See Crumb, R(obert)

Scudery, Madeleine de 1607-1701..... **LC 2**

Scum
See Crumb, R(obert)

Scumbag, Little Bobby
See Crumb, R(obert)

Seabrook, John
See Hubbard, L(afayette) Ron(ald)

Sealy, I. Allan 1951- .... **CLC 55**

Search, Alexander
See Pessoa, Fernando (Antonio Nogueira)

Sebastian, Lee
See Silverberg, Robert

Sebastian Owl
See Thompson, Hunter S(tockton)

Sebestyen, Ouida 1924-........... **CLC 30**
See also AAYA 8; CA 107; CANR 40;
CLR 17; JRDA; MAICYA; SAAS 10;
SATA 39

Secundus, H. Scriblerus
See Fielding, Henry

Sedges, John
See Buck, Pearl S(ydenstricker)

Sedgwick, Catharine Maria
1789-1867 .... **NCLC 19**
See also DLB 1, 74

Seelye, John 1931-............... **CLC 7**

Seferiades, Giorgos Stylianou 1900-1971
See Seferis, George
See also CA 5-8R; 33-36R; CANR 5, 36;
MTCW

Seferis, George .... **CLC 5, 11**
See also Seferiades, Giorgos Stylianou

Segal, Erich (Wolf)
1937- .... **CLC 3, 10; DAM POP**
See also BEST 89:1; CA 25-28R; CANR 20,
36; DLBY 86; INT CANR-20; MTCW

Seger, Bob 1945-................ **CLC 35**

Seghers, Anna .... **CLC 7**
See also Radvanyi, Netty
See also DLB 69

Seidel, Frederick (Lewis) 1936- ..... **CLC 18**
See also CA 13-16R; CANR 8; DLBY 84

Seifert, Jaroslav
1901-1986 .... **CLC 34, 44, 93**
See also CA 127; MTCW

Sei Shonagon c. 966-1017(?) ...... **CMLC 6**

Selby, Hubert, Jr.
1928- .... **CLC 1, 2, 4, 8; SSC 20**
See also CA 13-16R; CANR 33; DLB 2

Selzer, Richard 1928- .... **CLC 74**
See also CA 65-68; CANR 14

Sembene, Ousmane
See Ousmane, Sembene

Senancour, Etienne Pivert de
1770-1846 .... **NCLC 16**
See also DLB 119

Sender, Ramon (Jose)
1902-1982 .. **CLC 8; DAM MULT; HLC**
See also CA 5-8R; 105; CANR 8; HW;
MTCW

Seneca, Lucius Annaeus
4B.C.-65. ..... **CMLC 6; DAM DRAM;
DC 5**

Senghor, Leopold Sedar
1906- ..... **CLC 54; BLC; DAM MULT,
POET**
See also BW 2; CA 116; 125; CANR 47;
MTCW

Serling, (Edward) Rod(man)
1924-1975 .... **CLC 30**
See also AAYA 14; AITN 1; CA 65-68;
57-60; DLB 26

Serna, Ramon Gomez de la
See Gomez de la Serna, Ramon

Serpieres
See Guillevic, (Eugene)

Service, Robert
See Service, Robert W(illiam)
See also DAB; DLB 92

Service, Robert W(illiam)
1874(?)-1958 ...... **TCLC 15; DA; DAC;
DAM MST, POET; WLC**
See also Service, Robert
See also CA 115; 140; SATA 20

Seth, Vikram
1952- .... **CLC 43, 90; DAM MULT**
See also CA 121; 127; CANR 50; DLB 120;
INT 127

Seton, Cynthia Propper
1926-1982 .... **CLC 27**
See also CA 5-8R; 108; CANR 7

Seton, Ernest (Evan) Thompson
1860-1946 .... **TCLC 31**
See also CA 109; DLB 92; DLBD 13;
JRDA; SATA 18

Seton-Thompson, Ernest
See Seton, Ernest (Evan) Thompson

Settle, Mary Lee 1918- .... **CLC 19, 61**
See also CA 89-92; CAAS 1; CANR 44;
DLB 6; INT 89-92

Seuphor, Michel
See Arp, Jean

Sevigne, Marie (de Rabutin-Chantal) Marquise
de 1626-1696 .... **LC 11**

Sexton, Anne (Harvey)
1928-1974 .... **CLC 2, 4, 6, 8, 10, 15, 53;
DA; DAB; DAC; DAM MST, POET;
PC 2; WLC**
See also CA 1-4R; 53-56; CABS 2;
CANR 3, 36; CDALB 1941-1968; DLB 5,
169; MTCW; SATA 10

Shaara, Michael (Joseph, Jr.)
1929-1988 .... **CLC 15; DAM POP**
See also AITN 1; CA 102; 125; CANR 52;
DLBY 83

Shackleton, C. C.
See Aldiss, Brian W(ilson)

Shacochis, Bob .... **CLC 39**
See also Shacochis, Robert G.

Shacochis, Robert G. 1951-
See Shacochis, Bob
See also CA 119; 124; INT 124

Shaffer, Anthony (Joshua)
1926- .... **CLC 19; DAM DRAM**
See also CA 110; 116; DLB 13

Shaffer, Peter (Levin)
1926- ...... **CLC 5, 14, 18, 37, 60; DAB;
DAM DRAM, MST**
See also CA 25-28R; CANR 25, 47;
CDBLB 1960 to Present; DLB 13;
MTCW

Shakey, Bernard
See Young, Neil

Shalamov, Varlam (Tikhonovich)
1907(?)-1982 .... **CLC 18**
See also CA 129; 105

Shamlu, Ahmad 1925- .... **CLC 10**

Shammas, Anton 1951- .... **CLC 55**

Shange, Ntozake
1948- .... **CLC 8, 25, 38, 74; BLC;
DAM DRAM, MULT; DC 3**
See also AAYA 9; BW 2; CA 85-88;
CABS 3; CANR 27, 48; DLB 38; MTCW

Shanley, John Patrick 1950- .... **CLC 75**
See also CA 128; 133

Shapcott, Thomas W(illiam) 1935- .. **CLC 38**
See also CA 69-72; CANR 49

Shapiro, Jane .... **CLC 76**

Shapiro, Karl (Jay) 1913- .. **CLC 4, 8, 15, 53**
See also CA 1-4R; CAAS 6; CANR 1, 36;
DLB 48; MTCW

Sharp, William 1855-1905 .... **TCLC 39**
See also DLB 156

Sharpe, Thomas Ridley 1928-
See Sharpe, Tom
See also CA 114; 122; INT 122

Sharpe, Tom .... **CLC 36**
See also Sharpe, Thomas Ridley
See also DLB 14

Shaw, Bernard .... **TCLC 45**
See also Shaw, George Bernard
See also BW 1

Shaw, G. Bernard
See Shaw, George Bernard

Shaw, George Bernard
1856-1950 ... **TCLC 3, 9, 21; DA; DAB;
DAC; DAM DRAM, MST; WLC**
See also Shaw, Bernard
See also CA 104; 128; CDBLB 1914-1945;
DLB 10, 57; MTCW

Shaw, Henry Wheeler
1818-1885 .... **NCLC 15**
See also DLB 11

Shaw, Irwin
1913-1984 .... **CLC 7, 23, 34;
DAM DRAM, POP**
See also AITN 1; CA 13-16R; 112;
CANR 21; CDALB 1941-1968; DLB 6,
102; DLBY 84; MTCW

Shaw, Robert 1927-1978 .... **CLC 5**
See also AITN 1; CA 1-4R; 81-84;
CANR 4; DLB 13, 14

Shaw, T. E.
See Lawrence, T(homas) E(dward)

Shawn, Wallace 1943- .... **CLC 41**
See also CA 112

Shea, Lisa 1953- .... **CLC 86**
See also CA 147

Sheed, Wilfrid (John Joseph)
1930- .... **CLC 2, 4, 10, 53**
See also CA 65-68; CANR 30; DLB 6;
MTCW

Sheldon, Alice Hastings Bradley
1915(?)-1987
See Tiptree, James, Jr.
See also CA 108; 122; CANR 34; INT 108;
MTCW

Sheldon, John
See Bloch, Robert (Albert)

Shelley, Mary Wollstonecraft (Godwin)
1797-1851 .... **NCLC 14; DA; DAB;
DAC; DAM MST, NOV; WLC**
See also CDBLB 1789-1832; DLB 110, 116,
159; SATA 29

Shelley, Percy Bysshe
1792-1822 .... **NCLC 18; DA; DAB;
DAC; DAM MST, POET; PC 14; WLC**
See also CDBLB 1789-1832; DLB 96, 110,
158

Shepard, Jim 1956- .... **CLC 36**
See also CA 137; SATA 90

Shepard, Lucius 1947- .... **CLC 34**
See also CA 128; 141

Shepard, Sam
1943- .... **CLC 4, 6, 17, 34, 41, 44;
DAM DRAM; DC 5**
See also AAYA 1; CA 69-72; CABS 3;
CANR 22; DLB 7; MTCW

Shepherd, Michael
See Ludlum, Robert

Sherburne, Zoa (Morin) 1912- ...... **CLC 30**
See also AAYA 13; CA 1-4R; CANR 3, 37;
MAICYA; SAAS 18; SATA 3

Sheridan, Frances 1724-1766 .... **LC 7**
See also DLB 39, 84

Sheridan, Richard Brinsley
1751-1816 .... **NCLC 5; DA; DAB;
DAC; DAM DRAM, MST; DC 1; WLC**
See also CDBLB 1660-1789; DLB 89

Sherman, Jonathan Marc .... **CLC 55**

Sherman, Martin 1941(?)- . . . . **CLC 19**
See also CA 116; 123

Sherwin, Judith Johnson 1936-. . . **CLC 7, 15**
See also CA 25-28R; CANR 34

Sherwood, Frances 1940-. . . . . **CLC 81**
See also CA 146

Sherwood, Robert E(mmet)
1896-1955 . . . . . . **TCLC 3; DAM DRAM**
See also CA 104; 153; DLB 7, 26

Shestov, Lev 1866-1938 . . . . **TCLC 56**

Shevchenko, Taras 1814-1861 . . . . **NCLC 54**

Shiel, M(atthew) P(hipps)
1865-1947 . . . . **TCLC 8**
See also CA 106; DLB 153

Shields, Carol 1935-. . . . . **CLC 91; DAC**
See also CA 81-84; CANR 51

Shields, David 1956-. . . . . **CLC 97**
See also CA 124; CANR 48

Shiga, Naoya 1883-1971. . . **CLC 33; SSC 23**
See also CA 101; 33-36R

Shilts, Randy 1951-1994 . . . . **CLC 85**
See also AAYA 19; CA 115; 127; 144;
CANR 45; INT 127

Shimazaki, Haruki 1872-1943
See Shimazaki Toson
See also CA 105; 134

Shimazaki Toson. . . . . **TCLC 5**
See also Shimazaki, Haruki

Sholokhov, Mikhail (Aleksandrovich)
1905-1984 . . . . **CLC 7, 15**
See also CA 101; 112; MTCW;
SATA-Obit 36

Shone, Patric
See Hanley, James

Shreve, Susan Richards 1939-. . . . . . **CLC 23**
See also CA 49-52; CAAS 5; CANR 5, 38;
MAICYA; SATA 46; SATA-Brief 41

Shue, Larry
1946-1985 . . . . . . **CLC 52; DAM DRAM**
See also CA 145; 117

Shu-Jen, Chou 1881-1936
See Lu Hsun
See also CA 104

Shulman, Alix Kates 1932- . . . . . . **CLC 2, 10**
See also CA 29-32R; CANR 43; SATA 7

Shuster, Joe 1914- . . . . **CLC 21**

Shute, Nevil. . . . . **CLC 30**
See also Norway, Nevil Shute

Shuttle, Penelope (Diane) 1947- . . . . . **CLC 7**
See also CA 93-96; CANR 39; DLB 14, 40

Sidney, Mary 1561-1621 . . . . **LC 19**

Sidney, Sir Philip
1554-1586 . . . . . **LC 19; DA; DAB; DAC;**
DAM MST, POET
See also CDBLB Before 1660; DLB 167

Siegel, Jerome 1914-1996 . . . . **CLC 21**
See also CA 116; 151

Siegel, Jerry
See Siegel, Jerome

Sienkiewicz, Henryk (Adam Alexander Pius)
1846-1916 . . . . **TCLC 3**
See also CA 104; 134

Sierra, Gregorio Martinez
See Martinez Sierra, Gregorio

Sierra, Maria (de la O'LeJarraga) Martinez
See Martinez Sierra, Maria (de la
O'LeJarraga)

Sigal, Clancy 1926-. . . . . **CLC 7**
See also CA 1-4R

Sigourney, Lydia Howard (Huntley)
1791-1865 . . . . **NCLC 21**
See also DLB 1, 42, 73

Siguenza y Gongora, Carlos de
1645-1700 . . . . **LC 8**

Sigurjonsson, Johann 1880-1919. . . **TCLC 27**

Sikelianos, Angelos 1884-1951 . . . . **TCLC 39**

Silkin, Jon 1930- . . . . **CLC 2, 6, 43**
See also CA 5-8R; CAAS 5; DLB 27

Silko, Leslie (Marmon)
1948- . . . . **CLC 23, 74; DA; DAC;**
DAM MST, MULT, POP
See also AAYA 14; CA 115; 122;
CANR 45; DLB 143; NNAL

Sillanpaa, Frans Eemil 1888-1964. . . **CLC 19**
See also CA 129; 93-96; MTCW

Sillitoe, Alan
1928- . . . . **CLC 1, 3, 6, 10, 19, 57**
See also AITN 1; CA 9-12R; CAAS 2;
CANR 8, 26; CDBLB 1960 to Present;
DLB 14, 139; MTCW; SATA 61

Silone, Ignazio 1900-1978 . . . . **CLC 4**
See also CA 25-28; 81-84; CANR 34;
CAP 2; MTCW

Silver, Joan Micklin 1935- . . . . **CLC 20**
See also CA 114; 121; INT 121

Silver, Nicholas
See Faust, Frederick (Schiller)

Silverberg, Robert
1935- . . . . **CLC 7; DAM POP**
See also CA 1-4R; CAAS 3; CANR 1, 20,
36; DLB 8; INT CANR-20; MAICYA;
MTCW; SATA 13

Silverstein, Alvin 1933-. . . . . **CLC 17**
See also CA 49-52; CANR 2; CLR 25;
JRDA; MAICYA; SATA 8, 69

Silverstein, Virginia B(arbara Opshelor)
1937-. . . . . **CLC 17**
See also CA 49-52; CANR 2; CLR 25;
JRDA; MAICYA; SATA 8, 69

Sim, Georges
See Simenon, Georges (Jacques Christian)

Simak, Clifford D(onald)
1904-1988 . . . . **CLC 1, 55**
See also CA 1-4R; 125; CANR 1, 35;
DLB 8; MTCW; SATA-Obit 56

Simenon, Georges (Jacques Christian)
1903-1989 . . . . . . **CLC 1, 2, 3, 8, 18, 47;**
DAM POP
See also CA 85-88; 129; CANR 35;
DLB 72; DLBY 89; MTCW

Simic, Charles
1938- . . . . **CLC 6, 9, 22, 49, 68;**
DAM POET
See also CA 29-32R; CAAS 4; CANR 12,
33, 52; DLB 105

Simmel, Georg 1858-1918 . . . . **TCLC 64**

Simmons, Charles (Paul) 1924-. . . . . **CLC 57**
See also CA 89-92; INT 89-92

Simmons, Dan 1948-. . . **CLC 44; DAM POP**
See also AAYA 16; CA 138; CANR 53

Simmons, James (Stewart Alexander)
1933-. . . . . **CLC 43**
See also CA 105; CAAS 21; DLB 40

Simms, William Gilmore
1806-1870 . . . . **NCLC 3**
See also DLB 3, 30, 59, 73

Simon, Carly 1945-. . . . . **CLC 26**
See also CA 105

Simon, Claude
1913- . . . . **CLC 4, 9, 15, 39; DAM NOV**
See also CA 89-92; CANR 33; DLB 83;
MTCW

Simon, (Marvin) Neil
1927- . . . . **CLC 6, 11, 31, 39, 70;**
DAM DRAM
See also AITN 1; CA 21-24R; CANR 26,
54; DLB 7; MTCW

Simon, Paul (Frederick) 1941(?)- . . . **CLC 17**
See also CA 116; 153

Simonon, Paul 1956(?)- . . . . **CLC 30**

Simpson, Harriette
See Arnow, Harriette (Louisa) Simpson

Simpson, Louis (Aston Marantz)
1923- . . . . **CLC 4, 7, 9, 32; DAM POET**
See also CA 1-4R; CAAS 4; CANR 1;
DLB 5; MTCW

Simpson, Mona (Elizabeth) 1957-. . . **CLC 44**
See also CA 122; 135

Simpson, N(orman) F(rederick)
1919-. . . . . **CLC 29**
See also CA 13-16R; DLB 13

Sinclair, Andrew (Annandale)
1935-. **CLC 2, 14**
See also CA 9-12R; CAAS 5; CANR 14, 38;
DLB 14; MTCW

Sinclair, Emil
See Hesse, Hermann

Sinclair, Iain 1943-. . . . . **CLC 76**
See also CA 132

Sinclair, Iain MacGregor
See Sinclair, Iain

Sinclair, Mary Amelia St. Clair 1865(?)-1946
See Sinclair, May
See also CA 104

Sinclair, May. . . . . **TCLC 3, 11**
See also Sinclair, Mary Amelia St. Clair
See also DLB 36, 135

Sinclair, Upton (Beall)
1878-1968 . . . . . . **CLC 1, 11, 15, 63; DA;**
DAB; DAC; DAM MST, NOV; WLC
See also CA 5-8R; 25-28R; CANR 7;
CDALB 1929-1941; DLB 9;
INT CANR-7; MTCW; SATA 9

Singer, Isaac
See Singer, Isaac Bashevis

Singer, Isaac Bashevis
    1904-1991 .... **CLC 1, 3, 6, 9, 11, 15, 23,
        38, 69; DA; DAB; DAC; DAM MST,
        NOV; SSC 3; WLC**
    See also AITN 1, 2; CA 1-4R; 134;
        CANR 1, 39; CDALB 1941-1968; CLR 1;
        DLB 6, 28, 52; DLBY 91; JRDA;
        MAICYA; MTCW; SATA 3, 27;
        SATA-Obit 68

Singer, Israel Joshua 1893-1944 ... **TCLC 33**

Singh, Khushwant 1915-.......... **CLC 11**
    See also CA 9-12R; CAAS 9; CANR 6

Sinjohn, John
    See Galsworthy, John

Sinyavsky, Andrei (Donatevich)
    1925- .... **CLC 8**
    See also CA 85-88

Sirin, V.
    See Nabokov, Vladimir (Vladimirovich)

Sissman, L(ouis) E(dward)
    1928-1976 .... **CLC 9, 18**
    See also CA 21-24R; 65-68; CANR 13;
        DLB 5

Sisson, C(harles) H(ubert) 1914-..... **CLC 8**
    See also CA 1-4R; CAAS 3; CANR 3, 48;
        DLB 27

Sitwell, Dame Edith
    1887-1964 .... **CLC 2, 9, 67;
        DAM POET; PC 3**
    See also CA 9-12R; CANR 35;
        CDBLB 1945-1960; DLB 20; MTCW

Sjoewall, Maj 1935-.............. **CLC 7**
    See also CA 65-68

Sjowall, Maj
    See Sjoewall, Maj

Skelton, Robin 1925-............. **CLC 13**
    See also AITN 2; CA 5-8R; CAAS 5;
        CANR 28; DLB 27, 53

Skolimowski, Jerzy 1938-......... **CLC 20**
    See also CA 128

Skram, Amalie (Bertha)
    1847-1905 .... **TCLC 25**

Skvorecky, Josef (Vaclav)
    1924- .... **CLC 15, 39, 69; DAC;
        DAM NOV**
    See also CA 61-64; CAAS 1; CANR 10, 34;
        MTCW

Slade, Bernard................ **CLC 11, 46**
    See also Newbound, Bernard Slade
    See also CAAS 9; DLB 53

Slaughter, Carolyn 1946-.......... **CLC 56**
    See also CA 85-88

Slaughter, Frank G(ill) 1908- ...... **CLC 29**
    See also AITN 2; CA 5-8R; CANR 5;
        INT CANR-5

Slavitt, David R(ytman) 1935-.... **CLC 5, 14**
    See also CA 21-24R; CAAS 3; CANR 41;
        DLB 5, 6

Slesinger, Tess 1905-1945 .... **TCLC 10**
    See also CA 107; DLB 102

Slessor, Kenneth 1901-1971........ **CLC 14**
    See also CA 102; 89-92

Slowacki, Juliusz 1809-1849 ..... **NCLC 15**

Smart, Christopher
    1722-1771 ... **LC 3; DAM POET; PC 13**
    See also DLB 109

Smart, Elizabeth 1913-1986........ **CLC 54**
    See also CA 81-84; 118; DLB 88

Smiley, Jane (Graves)
    1949- .... **CLC 53, 76; DAM POP**
    See also CA 104; CANR 30, 50;
        INT CANR-30

Smith, A(rthur) J(ames) M(arshall)
    1902-1980 .... **CLC 15; DAC**
    See also CA 1-4R; 102; CANR 4; DLB 88

Smith, Anna Deavere 1950-........ **CLC 86**
    See also CA 133

Smith, Betty (Wehner) 1896-1972... **CLC 19**
    See also CA 5-8R; 33-36R; DLBY 82;
        SATA 6

Smith, Charlotte (Turner)
    1749-1806 .... **NCLC 23**
    See also DLB 39, 109

Smith, Clark Ashton 1893-1961 .... **CLC 43**
    See also CA 143

Smith, Dave................... **CLC 22, 42**
    See also Smith, David (Jeddie)
    See also CAAS 7; DLB 5

Smith, David (Jeddie) 1942-
    See Smith, Dave
    See also CA 49-52; CANR 1; DAM POET

Smith, Florence Margaret 1902-1971
    See Smith, Stevie
    See also CA 17-18; 29-32R; CANR 35;
        CAP 2; DAM POET; MTCW

Smith, Iain Crichton 1928- .... **CLC 64**
    See also CA 21-24R; DLB 40, 139

Smith, John 1580(?)-1631 .... **LC 9**

Smith, Johnston
    See Crane, Stephen (Townley)

Smith, Joseph, Jr. 1805-1844 .... **NCLC 53**

Smith, Lee 1944-.............. **CLC 25, 73**
    See also CA 114; 119; CANR 46; DLB 143;
        DLBY 83; INT 119

Smith, Martin
    See Smith, Martin Cruz

Smith, Martin Cruz
    1942- ..... **CLC 25; DAM MULT, POP**
    See also BEST 89:4; CA 85-88; CANR 6,
        23, 43; INT CANR-23; NNAL

Smith, Mary-Ann Tirone 1944-..... **CLC 39**
    See also CA 118; 136

Smith, Patti 1946- .... **CLC 12**
    See also CA 93-96

Smith, Pauline (Urmson)
    1882-1959 .... **TCLC 25**

Smith, Rosamond
    See Oates, Joyce Carol

Smith, Sheila Kaye
    See Kaye-Smith, Sheila

Smith, Stevie....... **CLC 3, 8, 25, 44; PC 12**
    See also Smith, Florence Margaret
    See also DLB 20

Smith, Wilbur (Addison) 1933-..... **CLC 33**
    See also CA 13-16R; CANR 7, 46; MTCW

Smith, William Jay 1918- .... **CLC 6**
    See also CA 5-8R; CANR 44; DLB 5;
        MAICYA; SAAS 22; SATA 2, 68

Smith, Woodrow Wilson
    See Kuttner, Henry

Smolenskin, Peretz 1842-1885.... **NCLC 30**

Smollett, Tobias (George) 1721-1771 .. **LC 2**
    See also CDBLB 1660-1789; DLB 39, 104

Snodgrass, W(illiam) D(e Witt)
    1926- .... **CLC 2, 6, 10, 18, 68;
        DAM POET**
    See also CA 1-4R; CANR 6, 36; DLB 5;
        MTCW

Snow, C(harles) P(ercy)
    1905-1980 .... **CLC 1, 4, 6, 9, 13, 19;
        DAM NOV**
    See also CA 5-8R; 101; CANR 28;
        CDBLB 1945-1960; DLB 15, 77; MTCW

Snow, Frances Compton
    See Adams, Henry (Brooks)

Snyder, Gary (Sherman)
    1930- .. **CLC 1, 2, 5, 9, 32; DAM POET**
    See also CA 17-20R; CANR 30; DLB 5, 16,
        165

Snyder, Zilpha Keatley 1927-...... **CLC 17**
    See also AAYA 15; CA 9-12R; CANR 38;
        CLR 31; JRDA; MAICYA; SAAS 2;
        SATA 1, 28, 75

Soares, Bernardo
    See Pessoa, Fernando (Antonio Nogueira)

Sobh, A.
    See Shamlu, Ahmad

Sobol, Joshua.................... **CLC 60**

Soderberg, Hjalmar 1869-1941 .... **TCLC 39**

Sodergran, Edith (Irene)
    See Soedergran, Edith (Irene)

Soedergran, Edith (Irene)
    1892-1923 .... **TCLC 31**

Softly, Edgar
    See Lovecraft, H(oward) P(hillips)

Softly, Edward
    See Lovecraft, H(oward) P(hillips)

Sokolov, Raymond 1941-.......... **CLC 7**
    See also CA 85-88

Solo, Jay
    See Ellison, Harlan (Jay)

Sologub, Fyodor.................. **TCLC 9**
    See also Teternikov, Fyodor Kuzmich

Solomons, Ikey Esquir
    See Thackeray, William Makepeace

Solomos, Dionysios 1798-1857 ... **NCLC 15**

Solwoska, Mara
    See French, Marilyn

Solzhenitsyn, Aleksandr I(sayevich)
    1918- ...... **CLC 1, 2, 4, 7, 9, 10, 18, 26,
        34, 78; DA; DAB; DAC; DAM MST,
        NOV; WLC**
    See also AITN 1; CA 69-72; CANR 40;
        MTCW

Somers, Jane
    See Lessing, Doris (May)

Somerville, Edith 1858-1949 ...... **TCLC 51**
    See also DLB 135

Somerville & Ross
See Martin, Violet Florence; Somerville, Edith

Sommer, Scott 1951- . . . . **CLC 25**
See also CA 106

Sondheim, Stephen (Joshua)
1930- . . . . . . **CLC 30, 39; DAM DRAM**
See also AAYA 11; CA 103; CANR 47

Sontag, Susan
1933- . . . . **CLC 1, 2, 10, 13, 31;**
DAM POP
See also CA 17-20R; CANR 25, 51; DLB 2, 67; MTCW

Sophocles
496(?)B.C.-406(?)B.C. . . . . **CMLC 2; DA;**
DAB; DAC; DAM DRAM, MST; DC 1

Sordello 1189-1269 . . . . **CMLC 15**

Sorel, Julia
See Drexler, Rosalyn

Sorrentino, Gilbert
1929- . . . . **CLC 3, 7, 14, 22, 40**
See also CA 77-80; CANR 14, 33; DLB 5, 173; DLBY 80; INT CANR-14

Soto, Gary
1952- . . . . **CLC 32, 80; DAM MULT;**
HLC
See also AAYA 10; CA 119; 125; CANR 50; CLR 38; DLB 82; HW; INT 125; JRDA; SATA 80

Soupault, Philippe 1897-1990 . . . . . . **CLC 68**
See also CA 116; 147; 131

Souster, (Holmes) Raymond
1921- . . . **CLC 5, 14; DAC; DAM POET**
See also CA 13-16R; CAAS 14; CANR 13, 29, 53; DLB 88; SATA 63

Southern, Terry 1924(?)-1995 . . . . **CLC 7**
See also CA 1-4R; 150; CANR 1; DLB 2

Southey, Robert 1774-1843 . . . . **NCLC 8**
See also DLB 93, 107, 142; SATA 54

Southworth, Emma Dorothy Eliza Nevitte
1819-1899 . . . . **NCLC 26**

Souza, Ernest
See Scott, Evelyn

Soyinka, Wole
1934- . . . . **CLC 3, 5, 14, 36, 44; BLC;**
DA; DAB; DAC; DAM DRAM, MST,
MULT; DC 2; WLC
See also BW 2; CA 13-16R; CANR 27, 39; DLB 125; MTCW

Spackman, W(illiam) M(ode)
1905-1990 . . . . **CLC 46**
See also CA 81-84; 132

Spacks, Barry 1931- . . . . **CLC 14**
See also CA 29-32R; CANR 33; DLB 105

Spanidou, Irini 1946- . . . . **CLC 44**

Spark, Muriel (Sarah)
1918- . . . . . **CLC 2, 3, 5, 8, 13, 18, 40, 94;**
DAB; DAC; DAM MST, NOV; SSC 10
See also CA 5-8R; CANR 12, 36; CDBLB 1945-1960; DLB 15, 139; INT CANR-12; MTCW

Spaulding, Douglas
See Bradbury, Ray (Douglas)

Spaulding, Leonard
See Bradbury, Ray (Douglas)

Spence, J. A. D.
See Eliot, T(homas) S(tearns)

Spencer, Elizabeth 1921- . . . . **CLC 22**
See also CA 13-16R; CANR 32; DLB 6; MTCW; SATA 14

Spencer, Leonard G.
See Silverberg, Robert

Spencer, Scott 1945- . . . . **CLC 30**
See also CA 113; CANR 51; DLBY 86

Spender, Stephen (Harold)
1909-1995 . . . . . . **CLC 1, 2, 5, 10, 41, 91;**
DAM POET
See also CA 9-12R; 149; CANR 31, 54; CDBLB 1945-1960; DLB 20; MTCW

Spengler, Oswald (Arnold Gottfried)
1880-1936 . . . . **TCLC 25**
See also CA 118

Spenser, Edmund
1552(?)-1599 . . . . **LC 5; DA; DAB; DAC;**
DAM MST, POET; PC 8; WLC
See also CDBLB Before 1660; DLB 167

Spicer, Jack
1925-1965 . . . . **CLC 8, 18, 72;**
DAM POET
See also CA 85-88; DLB 5, 16

Spiegelman, Art 1948- . . . . **CLC 76**
See also AAYA 10; CA 125; CANR 41

Spielberg, Peter 1929- . . . . **CLC 6**
See also CA 5-8R; CANR 4, 48; DLBY 81

Spielberg, Steven 1947- . . . . **CLC 20**
See also AAYA 8; CA 77-80; CANR 32; SATA 32

Spillane, Frank Morrison 1918-
See Spillane, Mickey
See also CA 25-28R; CANR 28; MTCW; SATA 66

Spillane, Mickey . . . . **CLC 3, 13**
See also Spillane, Frank Morrison

Spinoza, Benedictus de 1632-1677 . . . . **LC 9**

Spinrad, Norman (Richard) 1940- . . . **CLC 46**
See also CA 37-40R; CAAS 19; CANR 20; DLB 8; INT CANR-20

Spitteler, Carl (Friedrich Georg)
1845-1924 . . . . **TCLC 12**
See also CA 109; DLB 129

Spivack, Kathleen (Romola Drucker)
1938- . . . . **CLC 6**
See also CA 49-52

Spoto, Donald 1941- . . . . **CLC 39**
See also CA 65-68; CANR 11

Springsteen, Bruce (F.) 1949- . . . . . . **CLC 17**
See also CA 111

Spurling, Hilary 1940- . . . . **CLC 34**
See also CA 104; CANR 25, 52

Spyker, John Howland
See Elman, Richard

Squires, (James) Radcliffe
1917-1993 . . . . **CLC 51**
See also CA 1-4R; 140; CANR 6, 21

Srivastava, Dhanpat Rai 1880(?)-1936
See Premchand
See also CA 118

Stacy, Donald
See Pohl, Frederik

Stael, Germaine de
See Stael-Holstein, Anne Louise Germaine Necker Baronn
See also DLB 119

Stael-Holstein, Anne Louise Germaine Necker Baronn 1766-1817 . . . . **NCLC 3**
See also Stael, Germaine de

Stafford, Jean 1915-1979 . . . **CLC 4, 7, 19, 68**
See also CA 1-4R; 85-88; CANR 3; DLB 2, 173; MTCW; SATA-Obit 22

Stafford, William (Edgar)
1914-1993 . . . **CLC 4, 7, 29; DAM POET**
See also CA 5-8R; 142; CAAS 3; CANR 5, 22; DLB 5; INT CANR-22

Staines, Trevor
See Brunner, John (Kilian Houston)

Stairs, Gordon
See Austin, Mary (Hunter)

Stannard, Martin 1947- . . . . **CLC 44**
See also CA 142; DLB 155

Stanton, Maura 1946- . . . . **CLC 9**
See also CA 89-92; CANR 15; DLB 120

Stanton, Schuyler
See Baum, L(yman) Frank

Stapledon, (William) Olaf
1886-1950 . . . . **TCLC 22**
See also CA 111; DLB 15

Starbuck, George (Edwin)
1931-1996 . . . . **CLC 53; DAM POET**
See also CA 21-24R; 153; CANR 23

Stark, Richard
See Westlake, Donald E(dwin)

Staunton, Schuyler
See Baum, L(yman) Frank

Stead, Christina (Ellen)
1902-1983 . . . . **CLC 2, 5, 8, 32, 80**
See also CA 13-16R; 109; CANR 33, 40; MTCW

Stead, William Thomas
1849-1912 . . . . **TCLC 48**

Steele, Richard 1672-1729 . . . . **LC 18**
See also CDBLB 1660-1789; DLB 84, 101

Steele, Timothy (Reid) 1948- . . . . **CLC 45**
See also CA 93-96; CANR 16, 50; DLB 120

Steffens, (Joseph) Lincoln
1866-1936 . . . . **TCLC 20**
See also CA 117

Stegner, Wallace (Earle)
1909-1993 . . . **CLC 9, 49, 81; DAM NOV**
See also AITN 1; BEST 90:3; CA 1-4R; 141; CAAS 9; CANR 1, 21, 46; DLB 9; DLBY 93; MTCW

Stein, Gertrude
1874-1946 . . . . . . **TCLC 1, 6, 28, 48; DA;**
DAB; DAC; DAM MST, NOV, POET;
WLC
See also CA 104; 132; CDALB 1917-1929; DLB 4, 54, 86; MTCW

Steinbeck, John (Ernst)
1902-1968 . . . . . **CLC 1, 5, 9, 13, 21, 34,**
45, 75; DA; DAB; DAC; DAM DRAM,
MST, NOV; SSC 11; WLC
See also AAYA 12; CA 1-4R; 25-28R; CANR 1, 35; CDALB 1929-1941; DLB 7, 9; DLBD 2; MTCW; SATA 9

Steinem, Gloria 1934-............. **CLC 63**
See also CA 53-56; CANR 28, 51; MTCW

Steiner, George
1929- .... **CLC 24; DAM NOV**
See also CA 73-76; CANR 31; DLB 67;
MTCW; SATA 62

Steiner, K. Leslie
See Delany, Samuel R(ay, Jr.)

Steiner, Rudolf 1861-1925........ **TCLC 13**
See also CA 107

Stendhal
1783-1842 .... **NCLC 23, 46; DA; DAB;**
DAC; DAM MST, NOV; WLC
See also DLB 119

Stephen, Leslie 1832-1904........ **TCLC 23**
See also CA 123; DLB 57, 144

Stephen, Sir Leslie
See Stephen, Leslie

Stephen, Virginia
See Woolf, (Adeline) Virginia

Stephens, James 1882(?)-1950...... **TCLC 4**
See also CA 104; DLB 19, 153, 162

Stephens, Reed
See Donaldson, Stephen R.

Steptoe, Lydia
See Barnes, Djuna

Sterchi, Beat 1949-............... **CLC 65**

Sterling, Brett
See Bradbury, Ray (Douglas); Hamilton,
Edmond

Sterling, Bruce 1954-............. **CLC 72**
See also CA 119; CANR 44

Sterling, George 1869-1926....... **TCLC 20**
See also CA 117; DLB 54

Stern, Gerald 1925- .... **CLC 40**
See also CA 81-84; CANR 28; DLB 105

Stern, Richard (Gustave) 1928-... **CLC 4, 39**
See also CA 1-4R; CANR 1, 25, 52;
DLBY 87; INT CANR-25

Sternberg, Josef von 1894-1969..... **CLC 20**
See also CA 81-84

Sterne, Laurence
1713-1768 ...... **LC 2; DA; DAB; DAC;**
DAM MST, NOV; WLC
See also CDBLB 1660-1789; DLB 39

Sternheim, (William Adolf) Carl
1878-1942 .... **TCLC 8**
See also CA 105; DLB 56, 118

Stevens, Mark 1951- .... **CLC 34**
See also CA 122

Stevens, Wallace
1879-1955 .... **TCLC 3, 12, 45; DA;**
DAB; DAC; DAM MST, POET; PC 6;
WLC
See also CA 104; 124; CDALB 1929-1941;
DLB 54; MTCW

Stevenson, Anne (Katharine)
1933- .... **CLC 7, 33**
See also CA 17-20R; CAAS 9; CANR 9, 33;
DLB 40; MTCW

Stevenson, Robert Louis (Balfour)
1850-1894 ..... **NCLC 5, 14; DA; DAB;**
DAC; DAM MST, NOV; SSC 11; WLC
See also CDBLB 1890-1914; CLR 10, 11;
DLB 18, 57, 141, 156, 174; DLBD 13;
JRDA; MAICYA; YABC 2

Stewart, J(ohn) I(nnes) M(ackintosh)
1906-1994 .... **CLC 7, 14, 32**
See also CA 85-88; 147; CAAS 3;
CANR 47; MTCW

Stewart, Mary (Florence Elinor)
1916- .... **CLC 7, 35; DAB**
See also CA 1-4R; CANR 1; SATA 12

Stewart, Mary Rainbow
See Stewart, Mary (Florence Elinor)

Stifle, June
See Campbell, Maria

Stifter, Adalbert 1805-1868...... **NCLC 41**
See also DLB 133

Still, James 1906-................ **CLC 49**
See also CA 65-68; CAAS 17; CANR 10,
26; DLB 9; SATA 29

Sting
See Sumner, Gordon Matthew

Stirling, Arthur
See Sinclair, Upton (Beall)

Stitt, Milan 1941-................ **CLC 29**
See also CA 69-72

Stockton, Francis Richard 1834-1902
See Stockton, Frank R.
See also CA 108; 137; MAICYA; SATA 44

Stockton, Frank R................ **TCLC 47**
See also Stockton, Francis Richard
See also DLB 42, 74; DLBD 13;
SATA-Brief 32

Stoddard, Charles
See Kuttner, Henry

Stoker, Abraham 1847-1912
See Stoker, Bram
See also CA 105; DA; DAC; DAM MST,
NOV; SATA 29

Stoker, Bram
1847-1912 .... **TCLC 8; DAB; WLC**
See also Stoker, Abraham
See also CA 150; CDBLB 1890-1914;
DLB 36, 70

Stolz, Mary (Slattery) 1920-....... **CLC 12**
See also AAYA 8; AITN 1; CA 5-8R;
CANR 13, 41; JRDA; MAICYA;
SAAS 3; SATA 10, 71

Stone, Irving
1903-1989 .... **CLC 7; DAM POP**
See also AITN 1; CA 1-4R; 129; CAAS 3;
CANR 1, 23; INT CANR-23; MTCW;
SATA 3; SATA-Obit 64

Stone, Oliver (William) 1946-...... **CLC 73**
See also AAYA 15; CA 110

Stone, Robert (Anthony)
1937-................ **CLC 5, 23, 42**
See also CA 85-88; CANR 23; DLB 152;
INT CANR-23; MTCW

Stone, Zachary
See Follett, Ken(neth Martin)

Stoppard, Tom
1937-...... **CLC 1, 3, 4, 5, 8, 15, 29, 34,**
63, 91; DA; DAB; DAC; DAM DRAM,
MST; DC 6; WLC
See also CA 81-84; CANR 39;
CDBLB 1960 to Present; DLB 13;
DLBY 85; MTCW

Storey, David (Malcolm)
1933- ..... **CLC 2, 4, 5, 8; DAM DRAM**
See also CA 81-84; CANR 36; DLB 13, 14;
MTCW

Storm, Hyemeyohsts
1935- .... **CLC 3; DAM MULT**
See also CA 81-84; CANR 45; NNAL

Storm, (Hans) Theodor (Woldsen)
1817-1888 .... **NCLC 1**

Storni, Alfonsina
1892-1938 ..... **TCLC 5; DAM MULT;**
HLC
See also CA 104; 131; HW

Stout, Rex (Todhunter) 1886-1975 ... **CLC 3**
See also AITN 2; CA 61-64

Stow, (Julian) Randolph 1935- .. **CLC 23, 48**
See also CA 13-16R; CANR 33; MTCW

Stowe, Harriet (Elizabeth) Beecher
1811-1896 ..... **NCLC 3, 50; DA; DAB;**
DAC; DAM MST, NOV; WLC
See also CDALB 1865-1917; DLB 1, 12, 42,
74; JRDA; MAICYA; YABC 1

Strachey, (Giles) Lytton
1880-1932 .... **TCLC 12**
See also CA 110; DLB 149; DLBD 10

Strand, Mark
1934- .. **CLC 6, 18, 41, 71; DAM POET**
See also CA 21-24R; CANR 40; DLB 5;
SATA 41

Straub, Peter (Francis)
1943- .... **CLC 28; DAM POP**
See also BEST 89:1; CA 85-88; CANR 28;
DLBY 84; MTCW

Strauss, Botho 1944-............. **CLC 22**
See also DLB 124

Streatfeild, (Mary) Noel
1895(?)-1986 .... **CLC 21**
See also CA 81-84; 120; CANR 31;
CLR 17; DLB 160; MAICYA; SATA 20;
SATA-Obit 48

Stribling, T(homas) S(igismund)
1881-1965 .... **CLC 23**
See also CA 107; DLB 9

Strindberg, (Johan) August
1849-1912 ..... **TCLC 1, 8, 21, 47; DA;**
DAB; DAC; DAM DRAM, MST; WLC
See also CA 104; 135

Stringer, Arthur 1874-1950....... **TCLC 37**
See also DLB 92

Stringer, David
See Roberts, Keith (John Kingston)

Strugatskii, Arkadii (Natanovich)
1925-1991 .... **CLC 27**
See also CA 106; 135

Strugatskii, Boris (Natanovich)
1933- .... **CLC 27**
See also CA 106

Strummer, Joe 1953(?)-.......... **CLC 30**

Stuart, Don A.
See Campbell, John W(ood, Jr.)

Stuart, Ian
See MacLean, Alistair (Stuart)

Stuart, Jesse (Hilton)
1906-1984 . . . . **CLC 1, 8, 11, 14, 34**
See also CA 5-8R; 112; CANR 31; DLB 9, 48, 102; DLBY 84; SATA 2; SATA-Obit 36

Sturgeon, Theodore (Hamilton)
1918-1985 . . . . **CLC 22, 39**
See also Queen, Ellery
See also CA 81-84; 116; CANR 32; DLB 8; DLBY 85; MTCW

Sturges, Preston 1898-1959 . . . . . . **TCLC 48**
See also CA 114; 149; DLB 26

Styron, William
1925- . . . . **CLC 1, 3, 5, 11, 15, 60; DAM NOV, POP**
See also BEST 90:4; CA 5-8R; CANR 6, 33; CDALB 1968-1988; DLB 2, 143; DLBY 80; INT CANR-6; MTCW

Suarez Lynch, B.
See Bioy Casares, Adolfo; Borges, Jorge Luis

Su Chien 1884-1918
See Su Man-shu
See also CA 123

Suckow, Ruth 1892-1960 . . . . **SSC 18**
See also CA 113; DLB 9, 102

Sudermann, Hermann 1857-1928 . . **TCLC 15**
See also CA 107; DLB 118

Sue, Eugene 1804-1857 . . . . **NCLC 1**
See also DLB 119

Sueskind, Patrick 1949- . . . . **CLC 44**
See also Suskind, Patrick

Sukenick, Ronald 1932- . . . . . **CLC 3, 4, 6, 48**
See also CA 25-28R; CAAS 8; CANR 32; DLB 173; DLBY 81

Suknaski, Andrew 1942- . . . . **CLC 19**
See also CA 101; DLB 53

Sullivan, Vernon
See Vian, Boris

Sully Prudhomme 1839-1907 . . . . . **TCLC 31**

Su Man-shu . . . . **TCLC 24**
See also Su Chien

Summerforest, Ivy B.
See Kirkup, James

Summers, Andrew James 1942- . . . . . **CLC 26**

Summers, Andy
See Summers, Andrew James

Summers, Hollis (Spurgeon, Jr.)
1916- . . . . **CLC 10**
See also CA 5-8R; CANR 3; DLB 6

Summers, (Alphonsus Joseph-Mary Augustus) Montague 1880-1948 . . . . **TCLC 16**
See also CA 118

Sumner, Gordon Matthew 1951- . . . . **CLC 26**

Surtees, Robert Smith
1803-1864 . . . . **NCLC 14**
See also DLB 21

Susann, Jacqueline 1921-1974 . . . . . . **CLC 3**
See also AITN 1; CA 65-68; 53-56; MTCW

Su Shih 1036-1101 . . . . **CMLC 15**

Suskind, Patrick
See Sueskind, Patrick
See also CA 145

Sutcliff, Rosemary
1920-1992 . . . . **CLC 26; DAB; DAC; DAM MST, POP**
See also AAYA 10; CA 5-8R; 139; CANR 37; CLR 1, 37; JRDA; MAICYA; SATA 6, 44, 78; SATA-Obit 73

Sutro, Alfred 1863-1933 . . . . **TCLC 6**
See also CA 105; DLB 10

Sutton, Henry
See Slavitt, David R(ytman)

Svevo, Italo . . . . **TCLC 2, 35**
See also Schmitz, Aron Hector

Swados, Elizabeth (A.) 1951- . . . . **CLC 12**
See also CA 97-100; CANR 49; INT 97-100

Swados, Harvey 1920-1972 . . . . **CLC 5**
See also CA 5-8R; 37-40R; CANR 6; DLB 2

Swan, Gladys 1934- . . . . **CLC 69**
See also CA 101; CANR 17, 39

Swarthout, Glendon (Fred)
1918-1992 . . . . **CLC 35**
See also CA 1-4R; 139; CANR 1, 47; SATA 26

Sweet, Sarah C.
See Jewett, (Theodora) Sarah Orne

Swenson, May
1919-1989 . . . . **CLC 4, 14, 61; DA; DAB; DAC; DAM MST, POET; PC 14**
See also CA 5-8R; 130; CANR 36; DLB 5; MTCW; SATA 15

Swift, Augustus
See Lovecraft, H(oward) P(hillips)

Swift, Graham (Colin) 1949- . . . . **CLC 41, 88**
See also CA 117; 122; CANR 46

Swift, Jonathan
1667-1745 . . . . . . **LC 1; DA; DAB; DAC; DAM MST, NOV, POET; PC 9; WLC**
See also CDBLB 1660-1789; DLB 39, 95, 101; SATA 19

Swinburne, Algernon Charles
1837-1909 . . . . . . **TCLC 8, 36; DA; DAB; DAC; DAM MST, POET; WLC**
See also CA 105; 140; CDBLB 1832-1890; DLB 35, 57

Swinfen, Ann . . . . **CLC 34**

Swinnerton, Frank Arthur
1884-1982 . . . . **CLC 31**
See also CA 108; DLB 34

Swithen, John
See King, Stephen (Edwin)

Sylvia
See Ashton-Warner, Sylvia (Constance)

Symmes, Robert Edward
See Duncan, Robert (Edward)

Symonds, John Addington
1840-1893 . . . . **NCLC 34**
See also DLB 57, 144

Symons, Arthur 1865-1945 . . . . **TCLC 11**
See also CA 107; DLB 19, 57, 149

Symons, Julian (Gustave)
1912-1994 . . . . **CLC 2, 14, 32**
See also CA 49-52; 147; CAAS 3; CANR 3, 33; DLB 87, 155; DLBY 92; MTCW

Synge, (Edmund) J(ohn) M(illington)
1871-1909 . . . . **TCLC 6, 37; DAM DRAM; DC 2**
See also CA 104; 141; CDBLB 1890-1914; DLB 10, 19

Syruc, J.
See Milosz, Czeslaw

Szirtes, George 1948- . . . . **CLC 46**
See also CA 109; CANR 27

Tabori, George 1914- . . . . **CLC 19**
See also CA 49-52; CANR 4

Tagore, Rabindranath
1861-1941 . . . . **TCLC 3, 53; DAM DRAM, POET; PC 8**
See also CA 104; 120; MTCW

Taine, Hippolyte Adolphe
1828-1893 . . . . **NCLC 15**

Talese, Gay 1932- . . . . **CLC 37**
See also AITN 1; CA 1-4R; CANR 9; INT CANR-9; MTCW

Tallent, Elizabeth (Ann) 1954- . . . . . **CLC 45**
See also CA 117; DLB 130

Tally, Ted 1952- . . . . **CLC 42**
See also CA 120; 124; INT 124

Tamayo y Baus, Manuel
1829-1898 . . . . **NCLC 1**

Tammsaare, A(nton) H(ansen)
1878-1940 . . . . **TCLC 27**

Tan, Amy (Ruth)
1952- . . . . **CLC 59; DAM MULT, NOV, POP**
See also AAYA 9; BEST 89:3; CA 136; CANR 54; DLB 173; SATA 75

Tandem, Felix
See Spitteler, Carl (Friedrich Georg)

Tanizaki, Jun'ichiro
1886-1965 . . . . . . **CLC 8, 14, 28; SSC 21**
See also CA 93-96; 25-28R

Tanner, William
See Amis, Kingsley (William)

Tao Lao
See Storni, Alfonsina

Tarassoff, Lev
See Troyat, Henri

Tarbell, Ida M(inerva)
1857-1944 . . . . **TCLC 40**
See also CA 122; DLB 47

Tarkington, (Newton) Booth
1869-1946 . . . . **TCLC 9**
See also CA 110; 143; DLB 9, 102; SATA 17

Tarkovsky, Andrei (Arsenyevich)
1932-1986 . . . . **CLC 75**
See also CA 127

Tartt, Donna 1964(?)- . . . . **CLC 76**
See also CA 142

Tasso, Torquato 1544-1595 . . . . **LC 5**

Tate, (John Orley) Allen
1899-1979 . . . . **CLC 2, 4, 6, 9, 11, 14, 24**
See also CA 5-8R; 85-88; CANR 32; DLB 4, 45, 63; MTCW

Tate, Ellalice
See Hibbert, Eleanor Alice Burford

Tate, James (Vincent) 1943- . . . **CLC 2, 6, 25**
See also CA 21-24R; CANR 29; DLB 5, 169

Tavel, Ronald 1940- . . . . **CLC 6**
See also CA 21-24R; CANR 33

Taylor, C(ecil) P(hilip) 1929-1981. . . **CLC 27**
See also CA 25-28R; 105; CANR 47

Taylor, Edward
1642(?)-1729 . . . . **LC 11; DA; DAB; DAC; DAM MST, POET**
See also DLB 24

Taylor, Eleanor Ross 1920- . . . . **CLC 5**
See also CA 81-84

Taylor, Elizabeth 1912-1975 . . . **CLC 2, 4, 29**
See also CA 13-16R; CANR 9; DLB 139; MTCW; SATA 13

Taylor, Henry (Splawn) 1942- . . . . . . **CLC 44**
See also CA 33-36R; CAAS 7; CANR 31; DLB 5

Taylor, Kamala (Purnaiya) 1924-
See Markandaya, Kamala
See also CA 77-80

Taylor, Mildred D. . . . . **CLC 21**
See also AAYA 10; BW 1; CA 85-88; CANR 25; CLR 9; DLB 52; JRDA; MAICYA; SAAS 5; SATA 15, 70

Taylor, Peter (Hillsman)
1917-1994 . . . . . **CLC 1, 4, 18, 37, 44, 50, 71; SSC 10**
See also CA 13-16R; 147; CANR 9, 50; DLBY 81, 94; INT CANR-9; MTCW

Taylor, Robert Lewis 1912- . . . . **CLC 14**
See also CA 1-4R; CANR 3; SATA 10

Tchekhov, Anton
See Chekhov, Anton (Pavlovich)

Teasdale, Sara 1884-1933. . . . . **TCLC 4**
See also CA 104; DLB 45; SATA 32

Tegner, Esaias 1782-1846. . . . . **NCLC 2**

Teilhard de Chardin, (Marie Joseph) Pierre
1881-1955 . . . . **TCLC 9**
See also CA 105

Temple, Ann
See Mortimer, Penelope (Ruth)

Tennant, Emma (Christina)
1937- . . . . **CLC 13, 52**
See also CA 65-68; CAAS 9; CANR 10, 38; DLB 14

Tenneshaw, S. M.
See Silverberg, Robert

Tennyson, Alfred
1809-1892 . . . . . . **NCLC 30; DA; DAB; DAC; DAM MST, POET; PC 6; WLC**
See also CDBLB 1832-1890; DLB 32

Teran, Lisa St. Aubin de . . . . **CLC 36**
See also St. Aubin de Teran, Lisa

Terence 195(?)B.C.-159B.C. . . . . . . **CMLC 14**

Teresa de Jesus, St. 1515-1582 . . . . . . **LC 18**

Terkel, Louis 1912-
See Terkel, Studs
See also CA 57-60; CANR 18, 45; MTCW

Terkel, Studs . . . . **CLC 38**
See also Terkel, Louis
See also AITN 1

Terry, C. V.
See Slaughter, Frank G(ill)

Terry, Megan 1932- . . . . **CLC 19**
See also CA 77-80; CABS 3; CANR 43; DLB 7

Tertz, Abram
See Sinyavsky, Andrei (Donatevich)

Tesich, Steve 1943(?)-1996. . . . . . **CLC 40, 69**
See also CA 105; 152; DLBY 83

Teternikov, Fyodor Kuzmich 1863-1927
See Sologub, Fyodor
See also CA 104

Tevis, Walter 1928-1984 . . . . **CLC 42**
See also CA 113

Tey, Josephine . . . . **TCLC 14**
See also Mackintosh, Elizabeth
See also DLB 77

Thackeray, William Makepeace
1811-1863 . . . . **NCLC 5, 14, 22, 43; DA; DAB; DAC; DAM MST, NOV; WLC**
See also CDBLB 1832-1890; DLB 21, 55, 159, 163; SATA 23

Thakura, Ravindranatha
See Tagore, Rabindranath

Tharoor, Shashi 1956- . . . . **CLC 70**
See also CA 141

Thelwell, Michael Miles 1939- . . . . . **CLC 22**
See also BW 2; CA 101

Theobald, Lewis, Jr.
See Lovecraft, H(oward) P(hillips)

Theodorescu, Ion N. 1880-1967
See Arghezi, Tudor
See also CA 116

Theriault, Yves
1915-1983 . . **CLC 79; DAC; DAM MST**
See also CA 102; DLB 88

Theroux, Alexander (Louis)
1939- . . . . **CLC 2, 25**
See also CA 85-88; CANR 20

Theroux, Paul (Edward)
1941- . . . . **CLC 5, 8, 11, 15, 28, 46; DAM POP**
See also BEST 89:4; CA 33-36R; CANR 20, 45; DLB 2; MTCW; SATA 44

Thesen, Sharon 1946- . . . . **CLC 56**

Thevenin, Denis
See Duhamel, Georges

Thibault, Jacques Anatole Francois
1844-1924
See France, Anatole
See also CA 106; 127; DAM NOV; MTCW

Thiele, Colin (Milton) 1920- . . . . **CLC 17**
See also CA 29-32R; CANR 12, 28, 53; CLR 27; MAICYA; SAAS 2; SATA 14, 72

Thomas, Audrey (Callahan)
1935- . . . . **CLC 7, 13, 37; SSC 20**
See also AITN 2; CA 21-24R; CAAS 19; CANR 36; DLB 60; MTCW

Thomas, D(onald) M(ichael)
1935- . . . . **CLC 13, 22, 31**
See also CA 61-64; CAAS 11; CANR 17, 45; CDBLB 1960 to Present; DLB 40; INT CANR-17; MTCW

Thomas, Dylan (Marlais)
1914-1953 . . . **TCLC 1, 8, 45; DA; DAB; DAC; DAM DRAM, MST, POET; PC 2; SSC 3; WLC**
See also CA 104; 120; CDBLB 1945-1960; DLB 13, 20, 139; MTCW; SATA 60

Thomas, (Philip) Edward
1878-1917 . . . . . . **TCLC 10; DAM POET**
See also CA 106; 153; DLB 19

Thomas, Joyce Carol 1938- . . . . **CLC 35**
See also AAYA 12; BW 2; CA 113; 116; CANR 48; CLR 19; DLB 33; INT 116; JRDA; MAICYA; MTCW; SAAS 7; SATA 40, 78

Thomas, Lewis 1913-1993 . . . . **CLC 35**
See also CA 85-88; 143; CANR 38; MTCW

Thomas, Paul
See Mann, (Paul) Thomas

Thomas, Piri 1928- . . . . **CLC 17**
See also CA 73-76; HW

Thomas, R(onald) S(tuart)
1913- . . . . **CLC 6, 13, 48; DAB; DAM POET**
See also CA 89-92; CAAS 4; CANR 30; CDBLB 1960 to Present; DLB 27; MTCW

Thomas, Ross (Elmore) 1926-1995 . . **CLC 39**
See also CA 33-36R; 150; CANR 22

Thompson, Francis Clegg
See Mencken, H(enry) L(ouis)

Thompson, Francis Joseph
1859-1907 . . . . **TCLC 4**
See also CA 104; CDBLB 1890-1914; DLB 19

Thompson, Hunter S(tockton)
1939- . . . . **CLC 9, 17, 40; DAM POP**
See also BEST 89:1; CA 17-20R; CANR 23, 46; MTCW

Thompson, James Myers
See Thompson, Jim (Myers)

Thompson, Jim (Myers)
1906-1977(?) . . . . **CLC 69**
See also CA 140

Thompson, Judith . . . . **CLC 39**

Thomson, James
1700-1748 . . . . . **LC 16, 29; DAM POET**
See also DLB 95

Thomson, James
1834-1882 . . . . . **NCLC 18; DAM POET**
See also DLB 35

Thoreau, Henry David
1817-1862 . . . . . **NCLC 7, 21; DA; DAB; DAC; DAM MST; WLC**
See also CDALB 1640-1865; DLB 1

Thornton, Hall
See Silverberg, Robert

Thucydides c. 455B.C.-399B.C. . . . . **CMLC 17**

Thurber, James (Grover)
1894-1961 .... CLC 5, 11, 25; DA; DAB;
DAC; DAM DRAM, MST, NOV; SSC 1
See also CA 73-76; CANR 17, 39;
CDALB 1929-1941; DLB 4, 11, 22, 102;
MAICYA; MTCW; SATA 13

Thurman, Wallace (Henry)
1902-1934 .... TCLC 6; BLC;
DAM MULT
See also BW 1; CA 104; 124; DLB 51

Ticheburn, Cheviot
See Ainsworth, William Harrison

Tieck, (Johann) Ludwig
1773-1853 .... NCLC 5, 46
See also DLB 90

Tiger, Derry
See Ellison, Harlan (Jay)

Tilghman, Christopher 1948(?)-..... CLC 65

Tillinghast, Richard (Williford)
1940- .... CLC 29
See also CA 29-32R; CAAS 23; CANR 26,
51

Timrod, Henry 1828-1867 .... NCLC 25
See also DLB 3

Tindall, Gillian 1938-.............. CLC 7
See also CA 21-24R; CANR 11

Tiptree, James, Jr. .... CLC 48, 50
See also Sheldon, Alice Hastings Bradley
See also DLB 8

Titmarsh, Michael Angelo
See Thackeray, William Makepeace

Tocqueville, Alexis (Charles Henri Maurice
Clerel Comte) 1805-1859 ..... NCLC 7

Tolkien, J(ohn) R(onald) R(euel)
1892-1973 .... CLC 1, 2, 3, 8, 12, 38;
DA; DAB; DAC; DAM MST, NOV,
POP; WLC
See also AAYA 10; AITN 1; CA 17-18;
45-48; CANR 36; CAP 2;
CDBLB 1914-1945; DLB 15, 160; JRDA;
MAICYA; MTCW; SATA 2, 32;
SATA-Obit 24

Toller, Ernst 1893-1939 .... TCLC 10
See also CA 107; DLB 124

Tolson, M. B.
See Tolson, Melvin B(eaunorus)

Tolson, Melvin B(eaunorus)
1898(?)-1966 .... CLC 36; BLC;
DAM MULT, POET
See also BW 1; CA 124; 89-92; DLB 48, 76

Tolstoi, Aleksei Nikolaevich
See Tolstoy, Alexey Nikolaevich

Tolstoy, Alexey Nikolaevich
1882-1945 .... TCLC 18
See also CA 107

Tolstoy, Count Leo
See Tolstoy, Leo (Nikolaevich)

Tolstoy, Leo (Nikolaevich)
1828-1910 ..... TCLC 4, 11, 17, 28, 44;
DA; DAB; DAC; DAM MST, NOV;
SSC 9; WLC
See also CA 104; 123; SATA 26

Tomasi di Lampedusa, Giuseppe 1896-1957
See Lampedusa, Giuseppe (Tomasi) di
See also CA 111

Tomlin, Lily...................... CLC 17
See also Tomlin, Mary Jean

Tomlin, Mary Jean 1939(?)-
See Tomlin, Lily
See also CA 117

Tomlinson, (Alfred) Charles
1927- .... CLC 2, 4, 6, 13, 45;
DAM POET
See also CA 5-8R; CANR 33; DLB 40

Tonson, Jacob
See Bennett, (Enoch) Arnold

Toole, John Kennedy
1937-1969 .... CLC 19, 64
See also CA 104; DLBY 81

Toomer, Jean
1894-1967 ...... CLC 1, 4, 13, 22; BLC;
DAM MULT; PC 7; SSC 1
See also BW 1; CA 85-88;
CDALB 1917-1929; DLB 45, 51; MTCW

Torley, Luke
See Blish, James (Benjamin)

Tornimparte, Alessandra
See Ginzburg, Natalia

Torre, Raoul della
See Mencken, H(enry) L(ouis)

Torrey, E(dwin) Fuller 1937-....... CLC 34
See also CA 119

Torsvan, Ben Traven
See Traven, B.

Torsvan, Benno Traven
See Traven, B.

Torsvan, Berick Traven
See Traven, B.

Torsvan, Berwick Traven
See Traven, B.

Torsvan, Bruno Traven
See Traven, B.

Torsvan, Traven
See Traven, B.

Tournier, Michel (Edouard)
1924- ....CLC 6, 23, 36, 95
See also CA 49-52; CANR 3, 36; DLB 83;
MTCW; SATA 23

Tournimparte, Alessandra
See Ginzburg, Natalia

Towers, Ivar
See Kornbluth, C(yril) M.

Towne, Robert (Burton) 1936(?)-.... CLC 87
See also CA 108; DLB 44

Townsend, Sue 1946-.. CLC 61; DAB; DAC
See also CA 119; 127; INT 127; MTCW;
SATA 55; SATA-Brief 48

Townshend, Peter (Dennis Blandford)
1945-..................... CLC 17, 42
See also CA 107

Tozzi, Federigo 1883-1920....... TCLC 31

Traill, Catharine Parr
1802-1899 .... NCLC 31
See also DLB 99

Trakl, Georg 1887-1914.......... TCLC 5
See also CA 104

Transtroemer, Tomas (Goesta)
1931- .... CLC 52, 65; DAM POET
See also CA 117; 129; CAAS 17

Transtromer, Tomas Gosta
See Transtroemer, Tomas (Goesta)

Traven, B. (?)-1969............. CLC 8, 11
See also CA 19-20; 25-28R; CAP 2; DLB 9,
56; MTCW

Treitel, Jonathan 1959- .... CLC 70

Tremain, Rose 1943-............. CLC 42
See also CA 97-100; CANR 44; DLB 14

Tremblay, Michel
1942-...... CLC 29; DAC; DAM MST
See also CA 116; 128; DLB 60; MTCW

Trevanian........................ CLC 29
See also Whitaker, Rod(ney)

Trevor, Glen
See Hilton, James

Trevor, William
1928-...... CLC 7, 9, 14, 25, 71; SSC 21
See also Cox, William Trevor
See also DLB 14, 139

Trifonov, Yuri (Valentinovich)
1925-1981 .... CLC 45
See also CA 126; 103; MTCW

Trilling, Lionel 1905-1975 .... CLC 9, 11, 24
See also CA 9-12R; 61-64; CANR 10;
DLB 28, 63; INT CANR-10; MTCW

Trimball, W. H.
See Mencken, H(enry) L(ouis)

Tristan
See Gomez de la Serna, Ramon

Tristram
See Housman, A(lfred) E(dward)

Trogdon, William (Lewis) 1939-
See Heat-Moon, William Least
See also CA 115; 119; CANR 47; INT 119

Trollope, Anthony
1815-1882 ..... NCLC 6, 33; DA; DAB;
DAC; DAM MST, NOV; WLC
See also CDBLB 1832-1890; DLB 21, 57,
159; SATA 22

Trollope, Frances 1779-1863 ..... NCLC 30
See also DLB 21, 166

Trotsky, Leon 1879-1940........ TCLC 22
See also CA 118

Trotter (Cockburn), Catharine
1679-1749 .... LC 8
See also DLB 84

Trout, Kilgore
See Farmer, Philip Jose

Trow, George W. S. 1943-........ CLC 52
See also CA 126

Troyat, Henri 1911-............. CLC 23
See also CA 45-48; CANR 2, 33; MTCW

Trudeau, G(arretson) B(eekman) 1948-
See Trudeau, Garry B.
See also CA 81-84; CANR 31; SATA 35

Trudeau, Garry B................. CLC 12
See also Trudeau, G(arretson) B(eekman)
See also AAYA 10; AITN 2

Truffaut, Francois 1932-1984....... CLC 20
See also CA 81-84; 113; CANR 34

Trumbo, Dalton 1905-1976 .... CLC 19
See also CA 21-24R; 69-72; CANR 10;
DLB 26

Trumbull, John 1750-1831...... NCLC 30
See also DLB 31

Trundlett, Helen B.
See Eliot, T(homas) S(tearns)

Tryon, Thomas
1926-1991 ..... CLC 3, 11; DAM POP
See also AITN 1; CA 29-32R; 135;
CANR 32; MTCW

Tryon, Tom
See Tryon, Thomas

Ts'ao Hsueh-ch'in 1715(?)-1763...... LC 1

Tsushima, Shuji 1909-1948
See Dazai, Osamu
See also CA 107

Tsvetaeva (Efron), Marina (Ivanovna)
1892-1941 .... TCLC 7, 35; PC 14
See also CA 104; 128; MTCW

Tuck, Lily 1938-................. CLC 70
See also CA 139

Tu Fu 712-770.................... PC 9
See also DAM MULT

Tunis, John R(oberts) 1889-1975 ... CLC 12
See also CA 61-64; DLB 22, 171; JRDA;
MAICYA; SATA 37; SATA-Brief 30

Tuohy, Frank.................... CLC 37
See also Tuohy, John Francis
See also DLB 14, 139

Tuohy, John Francis 1925-
See Tuohy, Frank
See also CA 5-8R; CANR 3, 47

Turco, Lewis (Putnam) 1934- ... CLC 11, 63
See also CA 13-16R; CAAS 22; CANR 24,
51; DLBY 84

Turgenev, Ivan
1818-1883 .... NCLC 21; DA; DAB;
DAC; DAM MST, NOV; SSC 7; WLC

Turgot, Anne-Robert-Jacques
1727-1781 .... LC 26

Turner, Frederick 1943-.......... CLC 48
See also CA 73-76; CAAS 10; CANR 12,
30; DLB 40

Tutu, Desmond M(pilo)
1931- ..... CLC 80; BLC; DAM MULT
See also BW 1; CA 125

Tutuola, Amos
1920- .... CLC 5, 14, 29; BLC;
DAM MULT
See also BW 2; CA 9-12R; CANR 27;
DLB 125; MTCW

Twain, Mark
..... TCLC 6, 12, 19, 36, 48, 59; SSC 6;
WLC
See also Clemens, Samuel Langhorne
See also DLB 11, 12, 23, 64, 74

Tyler, Anne
1941-........ CLC 7, 11, 18, 28, 44, 59;
DAM NOV, POP
See also AAYA 18; BEST 89:1; CA 9-12R;
CANR 11, 33, 53; DLB 6, 143; DLBY 82;
MTCW; SATA 7, 90

Tyler, Royall 1757-1826.......... NCLC 3
See also DLB 37

Tynan, Katharine 1861-1931 ...... TCLC 3
See also CA 104; DLB 153

Tyutchev, Fyodor 1803-1873 ..... NCLC 34

Tzara, Tristan
1896-1963 ...... CLC 47; DAM POET
See also Rosenfeld, Samuel; Rosenstock,
Sami; Rosenstock, Samuel
See also CA 153

Uhry, Alfred
1936- ..... CLC 55; DAM DRAM, POP
See also CA 127; 133; INT 133

Ulf, Haerved
See Strindberg, (Johan) August

Ulf, Harved
See Strindberg, (Johan) August

Ulibarri, Sabine R(eyes)
1919- .... CLC 83; DAM MULT
See also CA 131; DLB 82; HW

Unamuno (y Jugo), Miguel de
1864-1936 ... TCLC 2, 9; DAM MULT,
NOV; HLC; SSC 11
See also CA 104; 131; DLB 108; HW;
MTCW

Undercliffe, Errol
See Campbell, (John) Ramsey

Underwood, Miles
See Glassco, John

Undset, Sigrid
1882-1949 .... TCLC 3; DA; DAB;
DAC; DAM MST, NOV; WLC
See also CA 104; 129; MTCW

Ungaretti, Giuseppe
1888-1970 .... CLC 7, 11, 15
See also CA 19-20; 25-28R; CAP 2;
DLB 114

Unger, Douglas 1952-............. CLC 34
See also CA 130

Unsworth, Barry (Forster) 1930-.... CLC 76
See also CA 25-28R; CANR 30, 54

Updike, John (Hoyer)
1932- ...... CLC 1, 2, 3, 5, 7, 9, 13, 15,
23, 34, 43, 70; DA; DAB; DAC;
DAM MST, NOV, POET, POP;
SSC 13; WLC
See also CA 1-4R; CABS 1; CANR 4, 33,
51; CDALB 1968-1988; DLB 2, 5, 143;
DLBD 3; DLBY 80, 82; MTCW

Upshaw, Margaret Mitchell
See Mitchell, Margaret (Munnerlyn)

Upton, Mark
See Sanders, Lawrence

Urdang, Constance (Henriette)
1922-...................... CLC 47
See also CA 21-24R; CANR 9, 24

Uriel, Henry
See Faust, Frederick (Schiller)

Uris, Leon (Marcus)
1924- .... CLC 7, 32; DAM NOV, POP
See also AITN 1, 2; BEST 89:2; CA 1-4R;
CANR 1, 40; MTCW; SATA 49

Urmuz
See Codrescu. Andrei

Urquhart, Jane 1949-........ CLC 90; DAC
See also CA 113; CANR 32

Ustinov, Peter (Alexander) 1921-.... CLC 1
See also AITN 1; CA 13-16R; CANR 25,
51; DLB 13

Vaculik, Ludvik 1926-............. CLC 7
See also CA 53-56

Valdez, Luis (Miguel)
1940- ..... CLC 84; DAM MULT; HLC
See also CA 101; CANR 32; DLB 122; HW

Valenzuela, Luisa
1938- ... CLC 31; DAM MULT; SSC 14
See also CA 101; CANR 32; DLB 113; HW

Valera y Alcala-Galiano, Juan
1824-1905 .... TCLC 10
See also CA 106

Valery, (Ambroise) Paul (Toussaint Jules)
1871-1945 .... TCLC 4, 15;
DAM POET; PC 9
See also CA 104; 122; MTCW

Valle-Inclan, Ramon (Maria) del
1866-1936 ..... TCLC 5; DAM MULT;
HLC
See also CA 106; 153; DLB 134

Vallejo, Antonio Buero
See Buero Vallejo, Antonio

Vallejo, Cesar (Abraham)
1892-1938 .... TCLC 3, 56;
DAM MULT; HLC
See also CA 105; 153; HW

Vallette, Marguerite Eymery
See Rachilde

Valle Y Pena, Ramon del
See Valle-Inclan, Ramon (Maria) del

Van Ash, Cay 1918-.............. CLC 34

Vanbrugh, Sir John
1664-1726 .... LC 21; DAM DRAM
See also DLB 80

Van Campen, Karl
See Campbell, John W(ood, Jr.)

Vance, Gerald
See Silverberg, Robert

Vance, Jack..................... CLC 35
See also Vance, John Holbrook
See also DLB 8

Vance, John Holbrook 1916-
See Queen, Ellery; Vance, Jack
See also CA 29-32R; CANR 17; MTCW

Van Den Bogarde, Derek Jules Gaspard Ulric
Niven 1921-
See Bogarde, Dirk
See also CA 77-80

Vandenburgh, Jane .... CLC 59

Vanderhaeghe, Guy 1951-......... CLC 41
See also CA 113

van der Post, Laurens (Jan) 1906- ... CLC 5
See also CA 5-8R; CANR 35

van de Wetering, Janwillem 1931- .. CLC 47
See also CA 49-52; CANR 4

Van Dine, S. S.................. TCLC 23
See also Wright, Willard Huntington

Van Doren, Carl (Clinton)
1885-1950 .... TCLC 18
See also CA 111

Van Doren, Mark 1894-1972..... CLC 6, 10
See also CA 1-4R; 37-40R; CANR 3;
DLB 45; MTCW

Van Druten, John (William)
1901-1957 . . . . **TCLC 2**
See also CA 104; DLB 10

Van Duyn, Mona (Jane)
1921- . . . . **CLC 3, 7, 63; DAM POET**
See also CA 9-12R; CANR 7, 38; DLB 5

Van Dyne, Edith
See Baum, L(yman) Frank

van Itallie, Jean-Claude 1936- . . . . **CLC 3**
See also CA 45-48; CAAS 2; CANR 1, 48;
DLB 7

van Ostaijen, Paul 1896-1928 . . . . . **TCLC 33**

Van Peebles, Melvin
1932- . . . . **CLC 2, 20; DAM MULT**
See also BW 2; CA 85-88; CANR 27

Vansittart, Peter 1920- . . . . **CLC 42**
See also CA 1-4R; CANR 3, 49

Van Vechten, Carl 1880-1964 . . . . . . **CLC 33**
See also CA 89-92; DLB 4, 9, 51

Van Vogt, A(lfred) E(lton) 1912- . . . . . **CLC 1**
See also CA 21-24R; CANR 28; DLB 8;
SATA 14

Varda, Agnes 1928- . . . . **CLC 16**
See also CA 116; 122

Vargas Llosa, (Jorge) Mario (Pedro)
1936- . . . . **CLC 3, 6, 9, 10, 15, 31, 42, 85;**
DA; DAB; DAC; DAM MST, MULT,
NOV; HLC
See also CA 73-76; CANR 18, 32, 42;
DLB 145; HW; MTCW

Vasiliu, Gheorghe 1881-1957
See Bacovia, George
See also CA 123

Vassa, Gustavus
See Equiano, Olaudah

Vassilikos, Vassilis 1933- . . . . **CLC 4, 8**
See also CA 81-84

Vaughan, Henry 1621-1695 . . . . **LC 27**
See also DLB 131

Vaughn, Stephanie . . . . **CLC 62**

Vazov, Ivan (Minchov)
1850-1921 . . . . **TCLC 25**
See also CA 121; DLB 147

Veblen, Thorstein (Bunde)
1857-1929 . . . . **TCLC 31**
See also CA 115

Vega, Lope de 1562-1635 . . . . **LC 23**

Venison, Alfred
See Pound, Ezra (Weston Loomis)

Verdi, Marie de
See Mencken, H(enry) L(ouis)

Verdu, Matilde
See Cela, Camilo Jose

Verga, Giovanni (Carmelo)
1840-1922 . . . . **TCLC 3; SSC 21**
See also CA 104; 123

Vergil
70B.C.-19B.C. . . . . . **CMLC 9; DA; DAB;**
DAC; DAM MST, POET; PC 12

Verhaeren, Emile (Adolphe Gustave)
1855-1916 . . . . **TCLC 12**
See also CA 109

Verlaine, Paul (Marie)
1844-1896 . . . . **NCLC 2, 51;**
DAM POET; PC 2

Verne, Jules (Gabriel)
1828-1905 . . . . **TCLC 6, 52**
See also AAYA 16; CA 110; 131; DLB 123;
JRDA; MAICYA; SATA 21

Very, Jones 1813-1880 . . . . **NCLC 9**
See also DLB 1

Vesaas, Tarjei 1897-1970 . . . . **CLC 48**
See also CA 29-32R

Vialis, Gaston
See Simenon, Georges (Jacques Christian)

Vian, Boris 1920-1959 . . . . **TCLC 9**
See also CA 106; DLB 72

Viaud, (Louis Marie) Julien 1850-1923
See Loti, Pierre
See also CA 107

Vicar, Henry
See Felsen, Henry Gregor

Vicker, Angus
See Felsen, Henry Gregor

Vidal, Gore
1925- . . . . . **CLC 2, 4, 6, 8, 10, 22, 33, 72;**
DAM NOV, POP
See also AITN 1; BEST 90:2; CA 5-8R;
CANR 13, 45; DLB 6, 152;
INT CANR-13; MTCW

Viereck, Peter (Robert Edwin)
1916- . . . . **CLC 4**
See also CA 1-4R; CANR 1, 47; DLB 5

Vigny, Alfred (Victor) de
1797-1863 . . . . . . **NCLC 7; DAM POET**
See also DLB 119

Vilakazi, Benedict Wallet
1906-1947 . . . . **TCLC 37**

Villiers de l'Isle Adam, Jean Marie Mathias
Philippe Auguste Comte
1838-1889 . . . . **NCLC 3; SSC 14**
See also DLB 123

Villon, Francois 1431-1463(?) . . . . **PC 13**

Vinci, Leonardo da 1452-1519 . . . . . . **LC 12**

Vine, Barbara . . . . **CLC 50**
See also Rendell, Ruth (Barbara)
See also BEST 90:4

Vinge, Joan D(ennison) 1948- . . . . . . **CLC 30**
See also CA 93-96; SATA 36

Violis, G.
See Simenon, Georges (Jacques Christian)

Visconti, Luchino 1906-1976 . . . . **CLC 16**
See also CA 81-84; 65-68; CANR 39

Vittorini, Elio 1908-1966 . . . . . . **CLC 6, 9, 14**
See also CA 133; 25-28R

Vizinczey, Stephen 1933- . . . . **CLC 40**
See also CA 128; INT 128

Vliet, R(ussell) G(ordon)
1929-1984 . . . . **CLC 22**
See also CA 37-40R; 112; CANR 18

Vogau, Boris Andreyevich 1894-1937(?)
See Pilnyak, Boris
See also CA 123

Vogel, Paula A(nne) 1951- . . . . **CLC 76**
See also CA 108

Voight, Ellen Bryant 1943- . . . . **CLC 54**
See also CA 69-72; CANR 11, 29; DLB 120

Voigt, Cynthia 1942- . . . . **CLC 30**
See also AAYA 3; CA 106; CANR 18, 37,
40; CLR 13; INT CANR-18; JRDA;
MAICYA; SATA 48, 79; SATA-Brief 33

Voinovich, Vladimir (Nikolaevich)
1932- . . . . **CLC 10, 49**
See also CA 81-84; CAAS 12; CANR 33;
MTCW

Vollmann, William T.
1959- . . . . . . **CLC 89; DAM NOV, POP**
See also CA 134

Voloshinov, V. N.
See Bakhtin, Mikhail Mikhailovich

Voltaire
1694-1778 . . . . . **LC 14; DA; DAB; DAC;**
DAM DRAM, MST; SSC 12; WLC

von Daeniken, Erich 1935- . . . . **CLC 30**
See also AITN 1; CA 37-40R; CANR 17,
44

von Daniken, Erich
See von Daeniken, Erich

von Heidenstam, (Carl Gustaf) Verner
See Heidenstam, (Carl Gustaf) Verner von

von Heyse, Paul (Johann Ludwig)
See Heyse, Paul (Johann Ludwig von)

von Hofmannsthal, Hugo
See Hofmannsthal, Hugo von

von Horvath, Odon
See Horvath, Oedoen von

von Horvath, Oedoen
See Horvath, Oedoen von

von Liliencron, (Friedrich Adolf Axel) Detlev
See Liliencron, (Friedrich Adolf Axel)
Detlev von

Vonnegut, Kurt, Jr.
1922- . . . . . . **CLC 1, 2, 3, 4, 5, 8, 12, 22,**
40, 60; DA; DAB; DAC; DAM MST,
NOV, POP; SSC 8; WLC
See also AAYA 6; AITN 1; BEST 90:4;
CA 1-4R; CANR 1, 25, 49;
CDALB 1968-1988; DLB 2, 8, 152;
DLBD 3; DLBY 80; MTCW

Von Rachen, Kurt
See Hubbard, L(afayette) Ron(ald)

von Rezzori (d'Arezzo), Gregor
See Rezzori (d'Arezzo), Gregor von

von Sternberg, Josef
See Sternberg, Josef von

Vorster, Gordon 1924- . . . . **CLC 34**
See also CA 133

Vosce, Trudie
See Ozick, Cynthia

Voznesensky, Andrei (Andreievich)
1933- . . . . . . **CLC 1, 15, 57; DAM POET**
See also CA 89-92; CANR 37; MTCW

Waddington, Miriam 1917- . . . . **CLC 28**
See also CA 21-24R; CANR 12, 30;
DLB 68

Wagman, Fredrica 1937- . . . . **CLC 7**
See also CA 97-100; INT 97-100

Wagner, Richard 1813-1883 . . . . **NCLC 9**
See also DLB 129

Wagner-Martin, Linda 1936-...... **CLC 50**

Wagoner, David (Russell)
1926- .... **CLC 3, 5, 15**
See also CA 1-4R; CAAS 3; CANR 2;
DLB 5; SATA 14

Wah, Fred(erick James) 1939-...... **CLC 44**
See also CA 107; 141; DLB 60

Wahloo, Per 1926-1975 .... **CLC 7**
See also CA 61-64

Wahloo, Peter
See Wahloo, Per

Wain, John (Barrington)
1925-1994 .... **CLC 2, 11, 15, 46**
See also CA 5-8R; 145; CAAS 4; CANR 23,
54; CDBLB 1960 to Present; DLB 15, 27,
139, 155; MTCW

Wajda, Andrzej 1926-............ **CLC 16**
See also CA 102

Wakefield, Dan 1932-............. **CLC 7**
See also CA 21-24R; CAAS 7

Wakoski, Diane
1937- .... **CLC 2, 4, 7, 9, 11, 40;**
DAM POET; PC 15
See also CA 13-16R; CAAS 1; CANR 9;
DLB 5; INT CANR-9

Wakoski-Sherbell, Diane
See Wakoski, Diane

Walcott, Derek (Alton)
1930- .... **CLC 2, 4, 9, 14, 25, 42, 67, 76;**
BLC; DAB; DAC; DAM MST, MULT,
POET
See also BW 2; CA 89-92; CANR 26, 47;
DLB 117; DLBY 81; MTCW

Waldman, Anne 1945- .... **CLC 7**
See also CA 37-40R; CAAS 17; CANR 34;
DLB 16

Waldo, E. Hunter
See Sturgeon, Theodore (Hamilton)

Waldo, Edward Hamilton
See Sturgeon, Theodore (Hamilton)

Walker, Alice (Malsenior)
1944- .... **CLC 5, 6, 9, 19, 27, 46, 58;**
BLC; DA; DAB; DAC; DAM MST,
MULT, NOV, POET, POP; SSC 5
See also AAYA 3; BEST 89:4; BW 2;
CA 37-40R; CANR 9, 27, 49;
CDALB 1968-1988; DLB 6, 33, 143;
INT CANR-27; MTCW; SATA 31

Walker, David Harry 1911-1992.... **CLC 14**
See also CA 1-4R; 137; CANR 1; SATA 8;
SATA-Obit 71

Walker, Edward Joseph 1934-
See Walker, Ted
See also CA 21-24R; CANR 12, 28, 53

Walker, George F.
1947- .... **CLC 44, 61; DAB; DAC;**
DAM MST
See also CA 103; CANR 21, 43; DLB 60

Walker, Joseph A.
1935- .... **CLC 19; DAM DRAM, MST**
See also BW 1; CA 89-92; CANR 26;
DLB 38

Walker, Margaret (Abigail)
1915- .... **CLC 1, 6; BLC; DAM MULT**
See also BW 2; CA 73-76; CANR 26, 54;
DLB 76, 152; MTCW

Walker, Ted...................... **CLC 13**
See also Walker, Edward Joseph
See also DLB 40

Wallace, David Foster 1962-....... **CLC 50**
See also CA 132

Wallace, Dexter
See Masters, Edgar Lee

Wallace, (Richard Horatio) Edgar
1875-1932 .... **TCLC 57**
See also CA 115; DLB 70

Wallace, Irving
1916-1990 ..... **CLC 7, 13; DAM NOV,**
POP
See also AITN 1; CA 1-4R; 132; CAAS 1;
CANR 1, 27; INT CANR-27; MTCW

Wallant, Edward Lewis
1926-1962 .... **CLC 5, 10**
See also CA 1-4R; CANR 22; DLB 2, 28,
143; MTCW

Walley, Byron
See Card, Orson Scott

Walpole, Horace 1717-1797.......... **LC 2**
See also DLB 39, 104

Walpole, Hugh (Seymour)
1884-1941 .... **TCLC 5**
See also CA 104; DLB 34

Walser, Martin 1927-............ **CLC 27**
See also CA 57-60; CANR 8, 46; DLB 75,
124

Walser, Robert
1878-1956 .... **TCLC 18; SSC 20**
See also CA 118; DLB 66

Walsh, Jill Paton.................. **CLC 35**
See also Paton Walsh, Gillian
See also AAYA 11; CLR 2; DLB 161;
SAAS 3

Walter, Villiam Christian
See Andersen, Hans Christian

Wambaugh, Joseph (Aloysius, Jr.)
1937- .... **CLC 3, 18; DAM NOV, POP**
See also AITN 1; BEST 89:3; CA 33-36R;
CANR 42; DLB 6; DLBY 83; MTCW

Ward, Arthur Henry Sarsfield 1883-1959
See Rohmer, Sax
See also CA 108

Ward, Douglas Turner 1930-....... **CLC 19**
See also BW 1; CA 81-84; CANR 27;
DLB 7, 38

Ward, Mary Augusta
See Ward, Mrs. Humphry

Ward, Mrs. Humphry
1851-1920 .... **TCLC 55**
See also DLB 18

Ward, Peter
See Faust, Frederick (Schiller)

Warhol, Andy 1928(?)-1987....... **CLC 20**
See also AAYA 12; BEST 89:4; CA 89-92;
121; CANR 34

Warner, Francis (Robert le Plastrier)
1937- .... **CLC 14**
See also CA 53-56; CANR 11

Warner, Marina 1946-............ **CLC 59**
See also CA 65-68; CANR 21

Warner, Rex (Ernest) 1905-1986.... **CLC 45**
See also CA 89-92; 119; DLB 15

Warner, Susan (Bogert)
1819-1885 .... **NCLC 31**
See also DLB 3, 42

Warner, Sylvia (Constance) Ashton
See Ashton-Warner, Sylvia (Constance)

Warner, Sylvia Townsend
1893-1978 .... **CLC 7, 19; SSC 23**
See also CA 61-64; 77-80; CANR 16;
DLB 34, 139; MTCW

Warren, Mercy Otis 1728-1814... **NCLC 13**
See also DLB 31

Warren, Robert Penn
1905-1989 .... **CLC 1, 4, 6, 8, 10, 13, 18,**
39, 53, 59; DA; DAB; DAC; DAM MST,
NOV, POET; SSC 4; WLC
See also AITN 1; CA 13-16R; 129;
CANR 10, 47; CDALB 1968-1988;
DLB 2, 48, 152; DLBY 80, 89;
INT CANR-10; MTCW; SATA 46;
SATA-Obit 63

Warshofsky, Isaac
See Singer, Isaac Bashevis

Warton, Thomas
1728-1790 .... **LC 15; DAM POET**
See also DLB 104, 109

Waruk, Kona
See Harris, (Theodore) Wilson

Warung, Price 1855-1911........ **TCLC 45**

Warwick, Jarvis
See Garner, Hugh

Washington, Alex
See Harris, Mark

Washington, Booker T(aliaferro)
1856-1915 .... **TCLC 10; BLC;**
DAM MULT
See also BW 1; CA 114; 125; SATA 28

Washington, George 1732-1799...... **LC 25**
See also DLB 31

Wassermann, (Karl) Jakob
1873-1934 .... **TCLC 6**
See also CA 104; DLB 66

Wasserstein, Wendy
1950- .... **CLC 32, 59, 90;**
DAM DRAM; DC 4
See also CA 121; 129; CABS 3; CANR 53;
INT 129

Waterhouse, Keith (Spencer)
1929- .... **CLC 47**
See also CA 5-8R; CANR 38; DLB 13, 15;
MTCW

Waters, Frank (Joseph)
1902-1995 .... **CLC 88**
See also CA 5-8R; 149; CAAS 13; CANR 3,
18; DLBY 86

Waters, Roger 1944-.............. **CLC 35**

Watkins, Frances Ellen
See Harper, Frances Ellen Watkins

Watkins, Gerrold
See Malzberg, Barry N(athaniel)

Watkins, Gloria 1955(?)-
See hooks, bell
See also BW 2; CA 143

Watkins, Paul 1964-.............. **CLC 55**
See also CA 132

Watkins, Vernon Phillips
1906-1967 . . . . **CLC 43**
See also CA 9-10; 25-28R; CAP 1; DLB 20

Watson, Irving S.
See Mencken, H(enry) L(ouis)

Watson, John H.
See Farmer, Philip Jose

Watson, Richard F.
See Silverberg, Robert

Waugh, Auberon (Alexander) 1939- . . **CLC 7**
See also CA 45-48; CANR 6, 22; DLB 14

Waugh, Evelyn (Arthur St. John)
1903-1966 . . . . . . **CLC 1, 3, 8, 13, 19, 27,**
44; DA; DAB; DAC; DAM MST, NOV,
POP; WLC
See also CA 85-88; 25-28R; CANR 22;
CDBLB 1914-1945; DLB 15, 162; MTCW

Waugh, Harriet 1944- . . . . **CLC 6**
See also CA 85-88; CANR 22

Ways, C. R.
See Blount, Roy (Alton), Jr.

Waystaff, Simon
See Swift, Jonathan

Webb, (Martha) Beatrice (Potter)
1858-1943 . . . . **TCLC 22**
See also Potter, Beatrice
See also CA 117

Webb, Charles (Richard) 1939- . . . . . . **CLC 7**
See also CA 25-28R

Webb, James H(enry), Jr. 1946- . . . . **CLC 22**
See also CA 81-84

Webb, Mary (Gladys Meredith)
1881-1927 . . . . **TCLC 24**
See also CA 123; DLB 34

Webb, Mrs. Sidney
See Webb, (Martha) Beatrice (Potter)

Webb, Phyllis 1927- . . . . **CLC 18**
See also CA 104; CANR 23; DLB 53

Webb, Sidney (James)
1859-1947 . . . . **TCLC 22**
See also CA 117

Webber, Andrew Lloyd . . . . **CLC 21**
See also Lloyd Webber, Andrew

Weber, Lenora Mattingly
1895-1971 . . . . **CLC 12**
See also CA 19-20; 29-32R; CAP 1;
SATA 2; SATA-Obit 26

Webster, John
1579(?)-1634(?) . . . . . . **LC 33; DA; DAB;**
DAC; DAM DRAM, MST; DC 2; WLC
See also CDBLB Before 1660; DLB 58

Webster, Noah 1758-1843 . . . . **NCLC 30**

Wedekind, (Benjamin) Frank(lin)
1864-1918 . . . . . . **TCLC 7; DAM DRAM**
See also CA 104; 153; DLB 118

Weidman, Jerome 1913- . . . . **CLC 7**
See also AITN 2; CA 1-4R; CANR 1;
DLB 28

Weil, Simone (Adolphine)
1909-1943 . . . . **TCLC 23**
See also CA 117

Weinstein, Nathan
See West, Nathanael

Weinstein, Nathan von Wallenstein
See West, Nathanael

Weir, Peter (Lindsay) 1944- . . . . **CLC 20**
See also CA 113; 123

Weiss, Peter (Ulrich)
1916-1982 . . . . **CLC 3, 15, 51;**
DAM DRAM
See also CA 45-48; 106; CANR 3; DLB 69,
124

Weiss, Theodore (Russell)
1916- . . . . **CLC 3, 8, 14**
See also CA 9-12R; CAAS 2; CANR 46;
DLB 5

Welch, (Maurice) Denton
1915-1948 . . . . **TCLC 22**
See also CA 121; 148

Welch, James
1940- . . . . . **CLC 6, 14, 52; DAM MULT,**
POP
See also CA 85-88; CANR 42; NNAL

Weldon, Fay
1933- . . . . **CLC 6, 9, 11, 19, 36, 59;**
DAM POP
See also CA 21-24R; CANR 16, 46;
CDBLB 1960 to Present; DLB 14;
INT CANR-16; MTCW

Wellek, Rene 1903-1995 . . . . **CLC 28**
See also CA 5-8R; 150; CAAS 7; CANR 8;
DLB 63; INT CANR-8

Weller, Michael 1942- . . . . **CLC 10, 53**
See also CA 85-88

Weller, Paul 1958- . . . . **CLC 26**

Wellershoff, Dieter 1925- . . . . **CLC 46**
See also CA 89-92; CANR 16, 37

Welles, (George) Orson
1915-1985 . . . . **CLC 20, 80**
See also CA 93-96; 117

Wellman, Mac 1945- . . . . **CLC 65**

Wellman, Manly Wade 1903-1986 . . **CLC 49**
See also CA 1-4R; 118; CANR 6, 16, 44;
SATA 6; SATA-Obit 47

Wells, Carolyn 1869(?)-1942 . . . . . . **TCLC 35**
See also CA 113; DLB 11

Wells, H(erbert) G(eorge)
1866-1946 . . . . **TCLC 6, 12, 19; DA;**
DAB; DAC; DAM MST, NOV; SSC 6;
WLC
See also AAYA 18; CA 110; 121;
CDBLB 1914-1945; DLB 34, 70, 156;
MTCW; SATA 20

Wells, Rosemary 1943- . . . . **CLC 12**
See also AAYA 13; CA 85-88; CANR 48;
CLR 16; MAICYA; SAAS 1; SATA 18,
69

Welty, Eudora
1909- . . . . . . **CLC 1, 2, 5, 14, 22, 33; DA;**
DAB; DAC; DAM MST, NOV; SSC 1;
WLC
See also CA 9-12R; CABS 1; CANR 32;
CDALB 1941-1968; DLB 2, 102, 143;
DLBD 12; DLBY 87; MTCW

Wen I-to 1899-1946 . . . . **TCLC 28**

Wentworth, Robert
See Hamilton, Edmond

Werfel, Franz (V.) 1890-1945 . . . . . **TCLC 8**
See also CA 104; DLB 81, 124

Wergeland, Henrik Arnold
1808-1845 . . . . **NCLC 5**

Wersba, Barbara 1932- . . . . **CLC 30**
See also AAYA 2; CA 29-32R; CANR 16,
38; CLR 3; DLB 52; JRDA; MAICYA;
SAAS 2; SATA 1, 58

Wertmueller, Lina 1928- . . . . **CLC 16**
See also CA 97-100; CANR 39

Wescott, Glenway 1901-1987 . . . . **CLC 13**
See also CA 13-16R; 121; CANR 23;
DLB 4, 9, 102

Wesker, Arnold
1932- . . . . **CLC 3, 5, 42; DAB;**
DAM DRAM
See also CA 1-4R; CAAS 7; CANR 1, 33;
CDBLB 1960 to Present; DLB 13;
MTCW

Wesley, Richard (Errol) 1945- . . . . . . **CLC 7**
See also BW 1; CA 57-60; CANR 27;
DLB 38

Wessel, Johan Herman 1742-1785 . . . . **LC 7**

West, Anthony (Panther)
1914-1987 . . . . **CLC 50**
See also CA 45-48; 124; CANR 3, 19;
DLB 15

West, C. P.
See Wodehouse, P(elham) G(renville)

West, (Mary) Jessamyn
1902-1984 . . . . **CLC 7, 17**
See also CA 9-12R; 112; CANR 27; DLB 6;
DLBY 84; MTCW; SATA-Obit 37

West, Morris L(anglo) 1916- . . . . . **CLC 6, 33**
See also CA 5-8R; CANR 24, 49; MTCW

West, Nathanael
1903-1940 . . . . . **TCLC 1, 14, 44; SSC 16**
See also CA 104; 125; CDALB 1929-1941;
DLB 4, 9, 28; MTCW

West, Owen
See Koontz, Dean R(ay)

West, Paul 1930- . . . . **CLC 7, 14, 96**
See also CA 13-16R; CAAS 7; CANR 22,
53; DLB 14; INT CANR-22

West, Rebecca 1892-1983 . . **CLC 7, 9, 31, 50**
See also CA 5-8R; 109; CANR 19; DLB 36;
DLBY 83; MTCW

Westall, Robert (Atkinson)
1929-1993 . . . . **CLC 17**
See also AAYA 12; CA 69-72; 141;
CANR 18; CLR 13; JRDA; MAICYA;
SAAS 2; SATA 23, 69; SATA-Obit 75

Westlake, Donald E(dwin)
1933- . . . . **CLC 7, 33; DAM POP**
See also CA 17-20R; CAAS 13; CANR 16,
44; INT CANR-16

Westmacott, Mary
See Christie, Agatha (Mary Clarissa)

Weston, Allen
See Norton, Andre

Wetcheek, J. L.
See Feuchtwanger, Lion

Wetering, Janwillem van de
See van de Wetering, Janwillem

Wetherell, Elizabeth
See Warner, Susan (Bogert)

Whale, James 1889-1957 . . . . **TCLC 63**

Whalen, Philip 1923- . . . . **CLC 6, 29**
See also CA 9-12R; CANR 5, 39; DLB 16

Wharton, Edith (Newbold Jones)
1862-1937 . . . . . . **TCLC 3, 9, 27, 53; DA;**
DAB; DAC; DAM MST, NOV; SSC 6;
WLC
See also CA 104; 132; CDALB 1865-1917;
DLB 4, 9, 12, 78; DLBD 13; MTCW

Wharton, James
See Mencken, H(enry) L(ouis)

Wharton, William (a pseudonym)
. . . . **CLC 18, 37**
See also CA 93-96; DLBY 80; INT 93-96

Wheatley (Peters), Phillis
1754(?)-1784 . . . . **LC 3; BLC; DA; DAC;**
DAM MST, MULT, POET; PC 3; WLC
See also CDALB 1640-1865; DLB 31, 50

Wheelock, John Hall 1886-1978 . . . . **CLC 14**
See also CA 13-16R; 77-80; CANR 14;
DLB 45

White, E(lwyn) B(rooks)
1899-1985 . . **CLC 10, 34, 39; DAM POP**
See also AITN 2; CA 13-16R; 116;
CANR 16, 37; CLR 1, 21; DLB 11, 22;
MAICYA; MTCW; SATA 2, 29;
SATA-Obit 44

White, Edmund (Valentine III)
1940- . . . . **CLC 27; DAM POP**
See also AAYA 7; CA 45-48; CANR 3, 19,
36; MTCW

White, Patrick (Victor Martindale)
1912-1990 . . **CLC 3, 4, 5, 7, 9, 18, 65, 69**
See also CA 81-84; 132; CANR 43; MTCW

White, Phyllis Dorothy James 1920-
See James, P. D.
See also CA 21-24R; CANR 17, 43;
DAM POP; MTCW

White, T(erence) H(anbury)
1906-1964 . . . . **CLC 30**
See also CA 73-76; CANR 37; DLB 160;
JRDA; MAICYA; SATA 12

White, Terence de Vere
1912-1994 . . . . **CLC 49**
See also CA 49-52; 145; CANR 3

White, Walter F(rancis)
1893-1955 . . . . **TCLC 15**
See also White, Walter
See also BW 1; CA 115; 124; DLB 51

White, William Hale 1831-1913
See Rutherford, Mark
See also CA 121

Whitehead, E(dward) A(nthony)
1933- . . . . **CLC 5**
See also CA 65-68

Whitemore, Hugh (John) 1936- . . . . . **CLC 37**
See also CA 132; INT 132

Whitman, Sarah Helen (Power)
1803-1878 . . . . **NCLC 19**
See also DLB 1

Whitman, Walt(er)
1819-1892 . . . . . **NCLC 4, 31; DA; DAB;**
DAC; DAM MST, POET; PC 3; WLC
See also CDALB 1640-1865; DLB 3, 64;
SATA 20

Whitney, Phyllis A(yame)
1903- . . . . **CLC 42; DAM POP**
See also AITN 2; BEST 90:3; CA 1-4R;
CANR 3, 25, 38; JRDA; MAICYA;
SATA 1, 30

Whittemore, (Edward) Reed (Jr.)
1919- . . . . **CLC 4**
See also CA 9-12R; CAAS 8; CANR 4;
DLB 5

Whittier, John Greenleaf
1807-1892 . . . . **NCLC 8**
See also DLB 1

Whittlebot, Hernia
See Coward, Noel (Peirce)

Wicker, Thomas Grey 1926-
See Wicker, Tom
See also CA 65-68; CANR 21, 46

Wicker, Tom . . . . **CLC 7**
See also Wicker, Thomas Grey

Wideman, John Edgar
1941- . . . . **CLC 5, 34, 36, 67; BLC;**
DAM MULT
See also BW 2; CA 85-88; CANR 14, 42;
DLB 33, 143

Wiebe, Rudy (Henry)
1934- . . . . **CLC 6, 11, 14; DAC;**
DAM MST
See also CA 37-40R; CANR 42; DLB 60

Wieland, Christoph Martin
1733-1813 . . . . **NCLC 17**
See also DLB 97

Wiene, Robert 1881-1938 . . . . **TCLC 56**

Wieners, John 1934- . . . . **CLC 7**
See also CA 13-16R; DLB 16

Wiesel, Elie(zer)
1928- . . . . . . **CLC 3, 5, 11, 37; DA; DAB;**
DAC; DAM MST, NOV
See also AAYA 7; AITN 1; CA 5-8R;
CAAS 4; CANR 8, 40; DLB 83;
DLBY 87; INT CANR-8; MTCW;
SATA 56

Wiggins, Marianne 1947- . . . . **CLC 57**
See also BEST 89:3; CA 130

Wight, James Alfred 1916-
See Herriot, James
See also CA 77-80; SATA 55;
SATA-Brief 44

Wilbur, Richard (Purdy)
1921- . . . **CLC 3, 6, 9, 14, 53; DA; DAB;**
DAC; DAM MST, POET
See also CA 1-4R; CABS 2; CANR 2, 29;
DLB 5, 169; INT CANR-29; MTCW;
SATA 9

Wild, Peter 1940- . . . . **CLC 14**
See also CA 37-40R; DLB 5

Wilde, Oscar (Fingal O'Flahertie Wills)
1854(?)-1900 . . . . **TCLC 1, 8, 23, 41; DA;**
DAB; DAC; DAM DRAM, MST, NOV;
SSC 11; WLC
See also CA 104; 119; CDBLB 1890-1914;
DLB 10, 19, 34, 57, 141, 156; SATA 24

Wilder, Billy . . . . **CLC 20**
See also Wilder, Samuel
See also DLB 26

Wilder, Samuel 1906-
See Wilder, Billy
See also CA 89-92

Wilder, Thornton (Niven)
1897-1975 . . . . . . **CLC 1, 5, 6, 10, 15, 35,**
82; DA; DAB; DAC; DAM DRAM,
MST, NOV; DC 1; WLC
See also AITN 2; CA 13-16R; 61-64;
CANR 40; DLB 4, 7, 9; MTCW

Wilding, Michael 1942- . . . . **CLC 73**
See also CA 104; CANR 24, 49

Wiley, Richard 1944- . . . . **CLC 44**
See also CA 121; 129

Wilhelm, Kate . . . . **CLC 7**
See also Wilhelm, Katie Gertrude
See also CAAS 5; DLB 8; INT CANR-17

Wilhelm, Katie Gertrude 1928-
See Wilhelm, Kate
See also CA 37-40R; CANR 17, 36; MTCW

Wilkins, Mary
See Freeman, Mary Eleanor Wilkins

Willard, Nancy 1936- . . . . **CLC 7, 37**
See also CA 89-92; CANR 10, 39; CLR 5;
DLB 5, 52; MAICYA; MTCW;
SATA 37, 71; SATA-Brief 30

Williams, C(harles) K(enneth)
1936- . . . . **CLC 33, 56; DAM POET**
See also CA 37-40R; DLB 5

Williams, Charles
See Collier, James L(incoln)

Williams, Charles (Walter Stansby)
1886-1945 . . . . **TCLC 1, 11**
See also CA 104; DLB 100, 153

Williams, (George) Emlyn
1905-1987 . . . . . . **CLC 15; DAM DRAM**
See also CA 104; 123; CANR 36; DLB 10,
77; MTCW

Williams, Hugo 1942- . . . . **CLC 42**
See also CA 17-20R; CANR 45; DLB 40

Williams, J. Walker
See Wodehouse, P(elham) G(renville)

Williams, John A(lfred)
1925- . . . **CLC 5, 13; BLC; DAM MULT**
See also BW 2; CA 53-56; CAAS 3;
CANR 6, 26, 51; DLB 2, 33;
INT CANR-6

Williams, Jonathan (Chamberlain)
1929- . . . . **CLC 13**
See also CA 9-12R; CAAS 12; CANR 8;
DLB 5

Williams, Joy 1944- . . . . **CLC 31**
See also CA 41-44R; CANR 22, 48

Williams, Norman 1952- . . . . **CLC 39**
See also CA 118

Williams, Sherley Anne
1944- . . . . . **CLC 89; BLC; DAM MULT,**
POET
See also BW 2; CA 73-76; CANR 25;
DLB 41; INT CANR-25; SATA 78

Williams, Shirley
See Williams, Sherley Anne

Williams, Tennessee
1911-1983 . . . . . **CLC 1, 2, 5, 7, 8, 11, 15, 19, 30, 39, 45, 71; DA; DAB; DAC; DAM DRAM, MST; DC 4; WLC**
See also AITN 1, 2; CA 5-8R; 108; CABS 3; CANR 31; CDALB 1941-1968; DLB 7; DLBD 4; DLBY 83; MTCW

Williams, Thomas (Alonzo)
1926-1990 . . . . **CLC 14**
See also CA 1-4R; 132; CANR 2

Williams, William C.
See Williams, William Carlos

Williams, William Carlos
1883-1963 . . . . **CLC 1, 2, 5, 9, 13, 22, 42, 67; DA; DAB; DAC; DAM MST, POET; PC 7**
See also CA 89-92; CANR 34; CDALB 1917-1929; DLB 4, 16, 54, 86; MTCW

Williamson, David (Keith) 1942-. . . . **CLC 56**
See also CA 103; CANR 41

Williamson, Ellen Douglas 1905-1984
See Douglas, Ellen
See also CA 17-20R; 114; CANR 39

Williamson, Jack. . . . . **CLC 29**
See also Williamson, John Stewart
See also CAAS 8; DLB 8

Williamson, John Stewart 1908-
See Williamson, Jack
See also CA 17-20R; CANR 23

Willie, Frederick
See Lovecraft, H(oward) P(hillips)

Willingham, Calder (Baynard, Jr.)
1922-1995 . . . . **CLC 5, 51**
See also CA 5-8R; 147; CANR 3; DLB 2, 44; MTCW

Willis, Charles
See Clarke, Arthur C(harles)

Willy
See Colette, (Sidonie-Gabrielle)

Willy, Colette
See Colette, (Sidonie-Gabrielle)

Wilson, A(ndrew) N(orman) 1950- . . **CLC 33**
See also CA 112; 122; DLB 14, 155

Wilson, Angus (Frank Johnstone)
1913-1991 . . **CLC 2, 3, 5, 25, 34; SSC 21**
See also CA 5-8R; 134; CANR 21; DLB 15, 139, 155; MTCW

Wilson, August
1945- . . . . **CLC 39, 50, 63; BLC; DA; DAB; DAC; DAM DRAM, MST, MULT; DC 2**
See also AAYA 16; BW 2; CA 115; 122; CANR 42, 54; MTCW

Wilson, Brian 1942-. . . . . **CLC 12**

Wilson, Colin 1931- . . . . **CLC 3, 14**
See also CA 1-4R; CAAS 5; CANR 1, 22, 33; DLB 14; MTCW

Wilson, Dirk
See Pohl, Frederik

Wilson, Edmund
1895-1972 . . . . **CLC 1, 2, 3, 8, 24**
See also CA 1-4R; 37-40R; CANR 1, 46; DLB 63; MTCW

Wilson, Ethel Davis (Bryant)
1888(?)-1980 . . . . **CLC 13; DAC; DAM POET**
See also CA 102; DLB 68; MTCW

Wilson, John 1785-1854. . . . . **NCLC 5**

Wilson, John (Anthony) Burgess 1917-1993
See Burgess, Anthony
See also CA 1-4R; 143; CANR 2, 46; DAC; DAM NOV; MTCW

Wilson, Lanford
1937- . . . . . **CLC 7, 14, 36; DAM DRAM**
See also CA 17-20R; CABS 3; CANR 45; DLB 7

Wilson, Robert M. 1944-. . . . . **CLC 7, 9**
See also CA 49-52; CANR 2, 41; MTCW

Wilson, Robert McLiam 1964- . . . . . **CLC 59**
See also CA 132

Wilson, Sloan 1920-. . . . . **CLC 32**
See also CA 1-4R; CANR 1, 44

Wilson, Snoo 1948-. . . . . **CLC 33**
See also CA 69-72

Wilson, William S(mith) 1932- . . . . . **CLC 49**
See also CA 81-84

Winchilsea, Anne (Kingsmill) Finch Counte
1661-1720 . . . . **LC 3**

Windham, Basil
See Wodehouse, P(elham) G(renville)

Wingrove, David (John) 1954-. . . . . . **CLC 68**
See also CA 133

Winters, Janet Lewis . . . . **CLC 41**
See also Lewis, Janet
See also DLBY 87

Winters, (Arthur) Yvor
1900-1968 . . . . **CLC 4, 8, 32**
See also CA 11-12; 25-28R; CAP 1; DLB 48; MTCW

Winterson, Jeanette
1959- . . . . **CLC 64; DAM POP**
See also CA 136

Winthrop, John 1588-1649. . . . . **LC 31**
See also DLB 24, 30

Wiseman, Frederick 1930-. . . . . **CLC 20**

Wister, Owen 1860-1938 . . . . **TCLC 21**
See also CA 108; DLB 9, 78; SATA 62

Witkacy
See Witkiewicz, Stanislaw Ignacy

Witkiewicz, Stanislaw Ignacy
1885-1939 . . . . **TCLC 8**
See also CA 105

Wittgenstein, Ludwig (Josef Johann)
1889-1951 . . . . **TCLC 59**
See also CA 113

Wittig, Monique 1935(?)-. . . . . **CLC 22**
See also CA 116; 135; DLB 83

Wittlin, Jozef 1896-1976 . . . . **CLC 25**
See also CA 49-52; 65-68; CANR 3

Wodehouse, P(elham) G(renville)
1881-1975 . . . **CLC 1, 2, 5, 10, 22; DAB; DAC; DAM NOV; SSC 2**
See also AITN 2; CA 45-48; 57-60; CANR 3, 33; CDBLB 1914-1945; DLB 34, 162; MTCW; SATA 22

Woiwode, L.
See Woiwode, Larry (Alfred)

Woiwode, Larry (Alfred) 1941-. . . **CLC 6, 10**
See also CA 73-76; CANR 16; DLB 6; INT CANR-16

Wojciechowska, Maia (Teresa)
1927-. . . . . **CLC 26**
See also AAYA 8; CA 9-12R; CANR 4, 41; CLR 1; JRDA; MAICYA; SAAS 1; SATA 1, 28, 83

Wolf, Christa 1929- . . . . **CLC 14, 29, 58**
See also CA 85-88; CANR 45; DLB 75; MTCW

Wolfe, Gene (Rodman)
1931-. . . . . **CLC 25; DAM POP**
See also CA 57-60; CAAS 9; CANR 6, 32; DLB 8

Wolfe, George C. 1954-. . . . . **CLC 49**
See also CA 149

Wolfe, Thomas (Clayton)
1900-1938 . . . . . **TCLC 4, 13, 29, 61; DA; DAB; DAC; DAM MST, NOV; WLC**
See also CA 104; 132; CDALB 1929-1941; DLB 9, 102; DLBD 2; DLBY 85; MTCW

Wolfe, Thomas Kennerly, Jr. 1931-
See Wolfe, Tom
See also CA 13-16R; CANR 9, 33; DAM POP; INT CANR-9; MTCW

Wolfe, Tom . . . . **CLC 1, 2, 9, 15, 35, 51**
See also Wolfe, Thomas Kennerly, Jr.
See also AAYA 8; AITN 2; BEST 89:1; DLB 152

Wolff, Geoffrey (Ansell) 1937- . . . . . **CLC 41**
See also CA 29-32R; CANR 29, 43

Wolff, Sonia
See Levitin, Sonia (Wolff)

Wolff, Tobias (Jonathan Ansell)
1945-. . . . . **CLC 39, 64**
See also AAYA 16; BEST 90:2; CA 114; 117; CAAS 22; CANR 54; DLB 130; INT 117

Wolfram von Eschenbach
c. 1170-c. 1220 . . . . **CMLC 5**
See also DLB 138

Wolitzer, Hilma 1930-. . . . . **CLC 17**
See also CA 65-68; CANR 18, 40; INT CANR-18; SATA 31

Wollstonecraft, Mary 1759-1797. . . . . . **LC 5**
See also CDBLB 1789-1832; DLB 39, 104, 158

Wonder, Stevie . . . . **CLC 12**
See also Morris, Steveland Judkins

Wong, Jade Snow 1922-. . . . . **CLC 17**
See also CA 109

Woodcott, Keith
See Brunner, John (Kilian Houston)

Woodruff, Robert W.
See Mencken, H(enry) L(ouis)

Woolf, (Adeline) Virginia
1882-1941 . . . . **TCLC 1, 5, 20, 43, 56; DA; DAB; DAC; DAM MST, NOV; SSC 7; WLC**
See also CA 104; 130; CDBLB 1914-1945; DLB 36, 100, 162; DLBD 10; MTCW

Woollcott, Alexander (Humphreys)
1887-1943 . . . . **TCLC 5**
See also CA 105; DLB 29

Woolrich, Cornell 1903-1968....... **CLC 77**
See also Hopley-Woolrich, Cornell George

Wordsworth, Dorothy
1771-1855 .... **NCLC 25**
See also DLB 107

Wordsworth, William
1770-1850 .... **NCLC 12, 38; DA; DAB;
DAC; DAM MST, POET; PC 4; WLC**
See also CDBLB 1789-1832; DLB 93, 107

Wouk, Herman
1915- .. **CLC 1, 9, 38; DAM NOV, POP**
See also CA 5-8R; CANR 6, 33; DLBY 82;
INT CANR-6; MTCW

Wright, Charles (Penzel, Jr.)
1935- .... **CLC 6, 13, 28**
See also CA 29-32R; CAAS 7; CANR 23,
36; DLB 165; DLBY 82; MTCW

Wright, Charles Stevenson
1932- .... **CLC 49; BLC 3;
DAM MULT, POET**
See also BW 1; CA 9-12R; CANR 26;
DLB 33

Wright, Jack R.
See Harris, Mark

Wright, James (Arlington)
1927-1980 .... **CLC 3, 5, 10, 28;
DAM POET**
See also AITN 2; CA 49-52; 97-100;
CANR 4, 34; DLB 5, 169; MTCW

Wright, Judith (Arandell)
1915- .... **CLC 11, 53; PC 14**
See also CA 13-16R; CANR 31; MTCW;
SATA 14

Wright, L(aurali) R. 1939-........ **CLC 44**
See also CA 138

Wright, Richard (Nathaniel)
1908-1960 .... **CLC 1, 3, 4, 9, 14, 21, 48,
74; BLC; DA; DAB; DAC; DAM MST,
MULT, NOV; SSC 2; WLC**
See also AAYA 5; BW 1; CA 108;
CDALB 1929-1941; DLB 76, 102;
DLBD 2; MTCW

Wright, Richard B(ruce) 1937- ...... **CLC 6**
See also CA 85-88; DLB 53

Wright, Rick 1945-............... **CLC 35**

Wright, Rowland
See Wells, Carolyn

Wright, Stephen Caldwell 1946- .... **CLC 33**
See also BW 2

Wright, Willard Huntington 1888-1939
See Van Dine, S. S.
See also CA 115

Wright, William 1930-............ **CLC 44**
See also CA 53-56; CANR 7, 23

Wroth, LadyMary 1587-1653(?) ..... **LC 30**
See also DLB 121

Wu Ch'eng-en 1500(?)-1582(?)........ **LC 7**

Wu Ching-tzu 1701-1754 .... **LC 2**

Wurlitzer, Rudolph 1938(?)- ... **CLC 2, 4, 15**
See also CA 85-88; DLB 173

Wycherley, William
1641-1715 ..... **LC 8, 21; DAM DRAM**
See also CDBLB 1660-1789; DLB 80

Wylie, Elinor (Morton Hoyt)
1885-1928 .... **TCLC 8**
See also CA 105; DLB 9, 45

Wylie, Philip (Gordon) 1902-1971... **CLC 43**
See also CA 21-22; 33-36R; CAP 2; DLB 9

Wyndham, John.................. **CLC 19**
See also Harris, John (Wyndham Parkes
Lucas) Beynon

Wyss, Johann David Von
1743-1818 .... **NCLC 10**
See also JRDA; MAICYA; SATA 29;
SATA-Brief 27

Xenophon
c. 430B.C.-c. 354B.C......... **CMLC 17**

Yakumo Koizumi
See Hearn, (Patricio) Lafcadio (Tessima
Carlos)

Yanez, Jose Donoso
See Donoso (Yanez), Jose

Yanovsky, Basile S.
See Yanovsky, V(assily) S(emenovich)

Yanovsky, V(assily) S(emenovich)
1906-1989 .... **CLC 2, 18**
See also CA 97-100; 129

Yates, Richard 1926-1992 ..... **CLC 7, 8, 23**
See also CA 5-8R; 139; CANR 10, 43;
DLB 2; DLBY 81, 92; INT CANR-10

Yeats, W. B.
See Yeats, William Butler

Yeats, William Butler
1865-1939 ..... **TCLC 1, 11, 18, 31; DA;
DAB; DAC; DAM DRAM, MST,
POET; WLC**
See also CA 104; 127; CANR 45;
CDBLB 1890-1914; DLB 10, 19, 98, 156;
MTCW

Yehoshua, A(braham) B.
1936- .... **CLC 13, 31**
See also CA 33-36R; CANR 43

Yep, Laurence Michael 1948-...... **CLC 35**
See also AAYA 5; CA 49-52; CANR 1, 46;
CLR 3, 17; DLB 52; JRDA; MAICYA;
SATA 7, 69

Yerby, Frank G(arvin)
1916-1991 .... **CLC 1, 7, 22; BLC;
DAM MULT**
See also BW 1; CA 9-12R; 136; CANR 16,
52; DLB 76; INT CANR-16; MTCW

Yesenin, Sergei Alexandrovich
See Esenin, Sergei (Alexandrovich)

Yevtushenko, Yevgeny (Alexandrovich)
1933- .... **CLC 1, 3, 13, 26, 51;
DAM POET**
See also CA 81-84; CANR 33, 54; MTCW

Yezierska, Anzia 1885(?)-1970 ..... **CLC 46**
See also CA 126; 89-92; DLB 28; MTCW

Yglesias, Helen 1915-........... **CLC 7, 22**
See also CA 37-40R; CAAS 20; CANR 15;
INT CANR-15; MTCW

Yokomitsu Riichi 1898-1947 ...... **TCLC 47**

Yonge, Charlotte (Mary)
1823-1901 .... **TCLC 48**
See also CA 109; DLB 18, 163; SATA 17

York, Jeremy
See Creasey, John

York, Simon
See Heinlein, Robert A(nson)

Yorke, Henry Vincent 1905-1974 ... **CLC 13**
See also Green, Henry
See also CA 85-88; 49-52

Yosano Akiko 1878-1942 .. **TCLC 59; PC 11**

Yoshimoto, Banana .... **CLC 84**
See also Yoshimoto, Mahoko

Yoshimoto, Mahoko 1964-
See Yoshimoto, Banana
See also CA 144

Young, Al(bert James)
1939- ..... **CLC 19; BLC; DAM MULT**
See also BW 2; CA 29-32R; CANR 26;
DLB 33

Young, Andrew (John) 1885-1971.... **CLC 5**
See also CA 5-8R; CANR 7, 29

Young, Collier
See Bloch, Robert (Albert)

Young, Edward 1683-1765.......... **LC 3**
See also DLB 95

Young, Marguerite (Vivian)
1909-1995 .... **CLC 82**
See also CA 13-16; 150; CAP 1

Young, Neil 1945-............... **CLC 17**
See also CA 110

Young Bear, Ray A.
1950- .... **CLC 94; DAM MULT**
See also CA 146; NNAL

Yourcenar, Marguerite
1903-1987 .... **CLC 19, 38, 50, 87;
DAM NOV**
See also CA 69-72; CANR 23; DLB 72;
DLBY 88; MTCW

Yurick, Sol 1925-................. **CLC 6**
See also CA 13-16R; CANR 25

Zabolotskii, Nikolai Alekseevich
1903-1958 .... **TCLC 52**
See also CA 116

Zamiatin, Yevgenii
See Zamyatin, Evgeny Ivanovich

Zamora, Bernice (B. Ortiz)
1938- ..... **CLC 89; DAM MULT; HLC**
See also CA 151; DLB 82; HW

Zamyatin, Evgeny Ivanovich
1884-1937 .... **TCLC 8, 37**
See also CA 105

Zangwill, Israel 1864-1926........ **TCLC 16**
See also CA 109; DLB 10, 135

Zappa, Francis Vincent, Jr. 1940-1993
See Zappa, Frank
See also CA 108; 143

Zappa, Frank.................... **CLC 17**
See also Zappa, Francis Vincent, Jr.

Zaturenska, Marya 1902-1982.... **CLC 6, 11**
See also CA 13-16R; 105; CANR 22

Zelazny, Roger (Joseph)
1937-1995 .... **CLC 21**
See also AAYA 7; CA 21-24R; 148;
CANR 26; DLB 8; MTCW; SATA 57;
SATA-Brief 39

Zhdanov, Andrei A(lexandrovich)
1896-1948 .... **TCLC 18**
See also CA 117

Zhukovsky, Vasily 1783-1852 . . . . **NCLC 35**

Ziegenhagen, Eric . . . . **CLC 55**

Zimmer, Jill Schary
See Robinson, Jill

Zimmerman, Robert
See Dylan, Bob

Zindel, Paul
1936- . . . . . **CLC 6, 26; DA; DAB; DAC;
DAM DRAM, MST, NOV; DC 5**
See also AAYA 2; CA 73-76; CANR 31;
CLR 3; DLB 7, 52; JRDA; MAICYA;
MTCW; SATA 16, 58

Zinov'Ev, A. A.
See Zinoviev, Alexander (Aleksandrovich)

Zinoviev, Alexander (Aleksandrovich)
1922- . . . . **CLC 19**
See also CA 116; 133; CAAS 10

Zoilus
See Lovecraft, H(oward) P(hillips)

Zola, Emile (Edouard Charles Antoine)
1840-1902 . . . . . . **TCLC 1, 6, 21, 41; DA;
DAB; DAC; DAM MST, NOV; WLC**
See also CA 104; 138; DLB 123

Zoline, Pamela 1941- . . . . **CLC 62**

Zorrilla y Moral, Jose 1817-1893 . . **NCLC 6**

Zoshchenko, Mikhail (Mikhailovich)
1895-1958 . . . . **TCLC 15; SSC 15**
See also CA 115

Zuckmayer, Carl 1896-1977 . . . . **CLC 18**
See also CA 69-72; DLB 56, 124

Zuk, Georges
See Skelton, Robin

Zukofsky, Louis
1904-1978 . . . . **CLC 1, 2, 4, 7, 11, 18;
DAM POET; PC 11**
See also CA 9-12R; 77-80; CANR 39;
DLB 5, 165; MTCW

Zweig, Paul 1935-1984 . . . . **CLC 34, 42**
See also CA 85-88; 113

Zweig, Stefan 1881-1942 . . . . **TCLC 17**
See also CA 112; DLB 81, 118

Literary Criticism Series
Cumulative Topic Index

This index lists all topic entries in Gale's *Classical and Medieval Literature Criticism, Contemporary Literary Criticism, Literature Criticism from 1400 to 1800, Nineteenth-Century Literature Criticism,* and *Twentieth-Century Literary Criticism.*

Age of Johnson LC 15: 1-87
Johnson's London, 3-15
aesthetics of neoclassicism, 15-36
"age of prose and reason," 36-45
clubmen and bluestockings, 45-56
printing technology, 56-62
periodicals: "a map of busy life," 62-74
transition, 74-86

AIDS in Literature CLC 81: 365-416

American Abolitionism NCLC 44: 1-73
overviews, 2-26
abolitionist ideals, 26-46
the literature of abolitionism, 46-72

American Black Humor Fiction TCLC 54: 1-85
characteristics of black humor, 2-13
origins and development, 13-38
black humor distinguished from related literary trends, 38-60
black humor and society, 60-75
black humor reconsidered, 75-83

American Civil War in Literature NCLC 32: 1-109
overviews, 2-20
regional perspectives, 20-54
fiction popular during the war, 54-79
the historical novel, 79-108

American Frontier in Literature NCLC 28: 1-103
definitions, 2-12
development, 12-17
nonfiction writing about the frontier, 17-30
frontier fiction, 30-45
frontier protagonists, 45-66
portrayals of Native Americans, 66-86
feminist readings, 86-98

twentieth-century reaction against frontier literature, 98-100

American Humor Writing NCLC 52: 1-59
overviews, 2-12
the Old Southwest, 12-42
broader impacts, 42-5
women humorists, 45-58

American Popular Song, Golden Age of TCLC 42: 1-49
background and major figures, 2-34
the lyrics of popular songs, 34-47

American Proletarian Literature TCLC 54: 86-175
overviews, 87-95
American proletarian literature and the American Communist Party, 95-111
ideology and literary merit, 111-7
novels, 117-36
Gastonia, 136-48
drama, 148-54
journalism, 154-9
proletarian literature in the United States, 159-74

American Romanticism NCLC 44: 74-138
overviews, 74-84
sociopolitical influences, 84-104
Romanticism and the American frontier, 104-15
thematic concerns, 115-37

American Western Literature TCLC 46: 1-100
definition and development of American Western literature, 2-7
characteristics of the Western novel, 8-23
Westerns as history and fiction, 23-34
critical reception of American Western

literature, 34-41
the Western hero, 41-73
women in Western fiction, 73-91
later Western fiction, 91-9

Art and Literature TCLC 54: 176-248
overviews, 176-93
definitions, 193-219
influence of visual arts on literature, 219-31
spatial form in literature, 231-47

Arthurian Literature CMLC 10: 1-127
historical context and literary beginnings, 2-27
development of the legend through Malory, 27-64
development of the legend from Malory to the Victorian Age, 65-81
themes and motifs, 81-95
principal characters, 95-125

Arthurian Revival NCLC 36: 1-77
overviews, 2-12
Tennyson and his influence, 12-43
other leading figures, 43-73
the Arthurian legend in the visual arts, 73-6

Australian Literature TCLC 50: 1-94
origins and development, 2-21
characteristics of Australian literature, 21-33
historical and critical perspectives, 33-41
poetry, 41-58
fiction, 58-76
drama, 76-82
Aboriginal literature, 82-91

Beat Generation, Literature of the TCLC 42: 50-102

overviews, 51-9
the Beat generation as a social phenom-
    enon, 59-62
development, 62-5
Beat literature, 66-96
influence, 97-100

The Bell Curve Controversy CLC 91: 281-
330

Bildungsroman in Nineteenth-Century
Literature NCLC 20: 92-168
surveys, 93-113
in Germany, 113-40
in England, 140-56
female *Bildungsroman,* 156-67

Bloomsbury Group TCLC 34: 1-73
history and major figures, 2-13
definitions, 13-7
influences, 17-27
thought, 27-40
prose, 40-52
and literary criticism, 52-4
political ideals, 54-61
response to, 61-71

Bly, Robert, *Iron John: A Book about Men
and Men's Work* CLC 70: 414-62

The Book of J CLC 65: 289-311

Businessman in American Literature
TCLC 26: 1-48
portrayal of the businessman, 1-32
themes and techniques in business
    fiction, 32-47

Celtic Twilight
See **Irish Literary Renaissance**

Children's Literature, Nineteenth-Century
NCLC 52: 60-135
overviews, 61-72
moral tales, 72-89
fairy tales and fantasy, 90-119
making men/making women, 119-34

Civic Critics, Russian NCLC 20: 402-46
principal figures and background, 402-9
and Russian Nihilism, 410-6
aesthetic and critical views, 416-45

Colonial America: The Intellectual
Background LC 25: 1-98
overviews, 2-17
philosophy and politics, 17-31
early religious influences in Colonial
    America, 31-60
consequences of the Revolution, 60-78
religious influences in post-revolution-
    ary America, 78-87
colonial literary genres, 87-97

Colonialism in Victorian English Literature NCLC 56: 1-77
overviews, 2-34
colonialism and gender, 34-51
monsters and the occult, 51-76

Columbus, Christopher, Books on the
Quincentennial of His Arrival in the New
World CLC 70: 329-60

Comic Books TCLC 66: 1-139
historical and critical perspectives, 2-48
superheroes, 48-67
underground comix, 67-88
comic books and society, 88-122
adult comics and graphic novels, 122-36

Connecticut Wits NCLC 48: 1-95
general overviews, 2-40
major works, 40-76
intellectual context, 76-95

Crime in Literature TCLC 54: 249-307
evolution of the criminal figure in
    literature, 250-61
crime and society, 261-77
literary perspectives on crime and
    punishment, 277-88
writings by criminals, 288-306

Czechoslovakian Literature of the
Twentieth Century TCLC 42: 103-96
through World War II, 104-35
de-Stalinization, the Prague Spring, and
    contemporary literature, 135-72
Slovak literature, 172-85
Czech science fiction, 185-93

Dadaism TCLC 46: 101-71
background and major figures, 102-16
definitions, 116-26
manifestos and commentary by
    Dadaists, 126-40

theater and film, 140-58
nature and characteristics of Dadaist
    writing, 158-70

Darwinism and Literature NCLC 32: 110-
206
background, 110-31
direct responses to Darwin, 131-71
collateral effects of Darwinism, 171-205

de Man, Paul, Wartime Journalism of
CLC 55: 382-424

Detective Fiction, Nineteenth-Century
NCLC 36: 78-148
origins of the genre, 79-100
history of nineteenth-century detective
    fiction, 101-33
significance of nineteenth-century
    detective fiction, 133-46

Detective Fiction, Twentieth-Century
TCLC 38: 1-96
genesis and history of the detective
    story, 3-22
defining detective fiction, 22-32
evolution and varieties, 32-77
the appeal of detective fiction, 77-90

Disease and Literature TCLC 66: 140-283
overviews, 141-65
disease in nineteenth-century literature,
    165-81
tuberculosis and literature, 181-94
women and disease in literature, 194-
    221
plague literature, 221-53
AIDS in literature, 253-82

The Double in Nineteenth-Century
Literature NCLC 40: 1-95
genesis and development of the theme,
    2-15
the double and Romanticism, 16-27
sociological views, 27-52
psychological interpretations, 52-87
philosophical considerations, 87-95

Dramatic Realism NCLC 44: 139-202
overviews, 140-50
origins and definitions, 150-66
impact and influence, 166-93
realist drama and tragedy, 193-201

Electronic "Books": Hypertext and Hyperfiction CLC 86: 367-404
books vs. CD-ROMS, 367-76
hypertext and hyperfiction, 376-95
implications for publishing, libraries, and the public, 395-403

Eliot, T. S., Centenary of Birth CLC 55: 345-75

Elizabethan Drama LC 22: 140-240
origins and influences, 142-67
characteristics and conventions, 167-83
theatrical production, 184-200
histories, 200-12
comedy, 213-20
tragedy, 220-30

The Encyclopedists LC 26: 172-253
overviews, 173-210
intellectual background, 210-32
views on esthetics, 232-41
views on women, 241-52

English Caroline Literature LC 13: 221-307
background, 222-41
evolution and varieties, 241-62
the Cavalier mode, 262-75
court and society, 275-91
politics and religion, 291-306

English Decadent Literature of the 1890s NCLC 28: 104-200
fin de siècle: the Decadent period, 105-19
definitions, 120-37
major figures: "the tragic generation," 137-50
French literature and English literary Decadence, 150-7
themes, 157-61
poetry, 161-82
periodicals, 182-96

English Essay, Rise of the LC 18: 238-308
definitions and origins, 236-54
influence on the essay, 254-69
historical background, 269-78
the essay in the seventeenth century, 279-93
the essay in the eighteenth century, 293-307

English Mystery Cycle Dramas LC 34: 1-88
overviews, 1-27
the nature of dramatic performances, 27-42
the medieval worldview and the mystery cycles, 43-67
the doctrine of repentance and the mystery cycles, 67-76
the fall from grace in the mystery cycles, 76-88

English Romantic Poetry NCLC 28: 201-327
overviews and reputation, 202-37
major subjects and themes, 237-67
forms of Romantic poetry, 267-78
politics, society, and Romantic poetry, 278-99
philosophy, religion, and Romantic poetry, 299-324

Espionage Literature TCLC 50: 95-159
overviews, 96-113
espionage fiction/formula fiction, 113-26
spies in fact and fiction, 126-38
the female spy, 138-44
social and psychological perspectives, 144-58

European Romanticism NCLC 36: 149-284
definitions, 149-77
origins of the movement, 177-82
Romantic theory, 182-200
themes and techniques, 200-23
Romanticism in Germany, 223-39
Romanticism in France, 240-61
Romanticism in Italy, 261-4
Romanticism in Spain, 264-8
impact and legacy, 268-82

Existentialism and Literature TCLC 42: 197-268
overviews and definitions, 198-209
history and influences, 209-19
Existentialism critiqued and defended, 220-35
philosophical and religious perspectives, 235-41
Existentialist fiction and drama, 241-67

Familiar Essay NCLC 48: 96-211
definitions and origins, 97-130
overview of the genre, 130-43
elements of form and style, 143-59
elements of content, 159-73
the Cockneys: Hazlitt, Lamb, and Hunt, 173-91
status of the genre, 191-210

Feminism in the 1990s: Commentary on Works by Naomi Wolf, Susan Faludi, and Camille Paglia CLC 76: 377-415

Feminist Criticism in 1990 CLC 65: 312-60

Fifteenth-Century English Literature LC 17: 248-334
background, 249-72
poetry, 272-315
drama, 315-23
prose, 323-33

Film and Literature TCLC 38: 97-226
overviews, 97-119
film and theater, 119-34
film and the novel, 134-45
the art of the screenplay, 145-66
genre literature/genre film, 167-79
the writer and the film industry, 179-90
authors on film adaptations of their works, 190-200
fiction into film: comparative essays, 200-23

French Drama in the Age of Louis XIV LC 28: 94-185
overview, 95-127
tragedy, 127-46
comedy, 146-66
tragicomedy, 166-84

French Enlightenment LC 14: 81-145
the question of definition, 82-9
Le siècle des lumières, 89-94
women and the salons, 94-105
censorship, 105-15
the philosophy of reason, 115-31
influence and legacy, 131-44

French Realism NCLC 52: 136-216
origins and definitions, 137-70
issues and influence, 170-98
realism and representation, 198-215

Topic Index

French Revolution and English Literature
NCLC 40: 96-195
    history and theory, 96-123
    romantic poetry, 123-50
    the novel, 150-81
    drama, 181-92
    children's literature, 192-5

Futurism, Italian TCLC 42: 269-354
    principles and formative influences,
        271-9
    manifestos, 279-88
    literature, 288-303
    theater, 303-19
    art, 320-30
    music, 330-6
    architecture, 336-9
    and politics, 339-46
    reputation and significance, 346-51

Gaelic Revival
See **Irish Literary Renaissance**

**Gates, Henry Louis, Jr., and African-
American Literary Criticism** CLC 65:
361-405

Gay and Lesbian Literature CLC 76:
416-39

German Exile Literature TCLC 30: 1-
58
    the writer and the Nazi state, 1-10
    definition of, 10-4
    life in exile, 14-32
    surveys, 32-50
    Austrian literature in exile, 50-2
    German publishing in the United States,
        52-7

German Expressionism TCLC 34: 74-
160
    history and major figures, 76-85
    aesthetic theories, 85-109
    drama, 109-26
    poetry, 126-38
    film, 138-42
    painting, 142-7
    music, 147-53
    and politics, 153-8

***Glasnost* and Contemporary Soviet
Literature** CLC 59: 355-97

Gothic Novel NCLC 28: 328-402
    development and major works, 328-34
    definitions, 334-50
    themes and techniques, 350-78
    in America, 378-85
    in Scotland, 385-91
    influence and legacy, 391-400

Graphic Narratives CLC 86: 405-32
    history and overviews, 406-21
    the "Classics Illustrated" series, 421-2
    reviews of recent works, 422-32

Greek Historiography CMLC 17: 1-49

Harlem Renaissance TCLC 26: 49-125
    principal issues and figures, 50-67
    the literature and its audience, 67-74
    theme and technique in poetry, fiction,
        and drama, 74-115
    and American society, 115-21
    achievement and influence, 121-2

Havel, Václav, Playwright and President
CLC 65: 406-63

Historical Fiction, Nineteenth-Century
NCLC 48: 212-307
    definitions and characteristics, 213-36
    Victorian historical fiction, 236-65
    American historical fiction, 265-88
    realism in historical fiction, 288-306

**Holocaust and the Atomic Bomb: Fifty
Years Later** CLC 91: 331-82
    the Holocaust remembered, 333-52
    Anne Frank revisited, 352-62
    the atomic bomb and American memory,
        362-81

Holocaust Denial Literature TCLC 58: 1-
110
    overviews, 1-30
    Robert Faurisson and Noam Chomsky,
        30-52
    Holocaust denial literature in America,
        52-71
    library access to Holocaust denial
        literature, 72-5
    the authenticity of Anne Frank's diary,
        76-90
    David Irving and the "normalization" of
        Hitler, 90-109

Holocaust, Literature of the TCLC 42:
355-450
    historical overview, 357-61
    critical overview, 361-70
    diaries and memoirs, 370-95
    novels and short stories, 395-425
    poetry, 425-41
    drama, 441-8

**Homosexuality in Nineteenth-Century
Literature** NCLC 56: 78-182
    defining homosexuality, 80-111
    Greek love, 111-44
    trial and danger, 144-81

**Hungarian Literature of the Twentieth
Century** TCLC 26: 126-88
    surveys of, 126-47
    Nyugat and early twentieth-century
        literature, 147-56
    mid-century literature, 156-68
    and politics, 168-78
    since the 1956 revolt, 178-87

Indian Literature in English TCLC 54:
308-406
    overview, 309-13
    origins and major figures, 313-25
    the Indo-English novel, 325-55
    Indo-English poetry, 355-67
    Indo-English drama, 367-72
    critical perspectives on Indo-English
        literature, 372-80
    modern Indo-English literature, 380-9
    Indo-English authors on their work,
        389-404

Industrial Revolution in Literature, The
NCLC 56: 183-273
    historical and cultural perspectives, 184-
        201
    contemporary reactions to the machine,
        201-21
    themes and symbols in literature, 221-73

Irish Literary Renaissance TCLC 46: 172-
287
    overview, 173-83
    development and major figures, 184-202
    influence of Irish folklore and mythol-
        ogy, 202-22
    Irish poetry, 222-34
    Irish drama and the Abbey Theatre, 234-
        56
    Irish fiction, 256-86

Irish Nationalism and Literature NCLC 44: 203-73
    the Celtic element in literature, 203-19
    anti-Irish sentiment and the Celtic response, 219-34
    literary ideals in Ireland, 234-45
    literary expressions, 245-73

Italian Futurism
See **Futurism, Italian**

Italian Humanism LC 12: 205-77
    origins and early development, 206-18
    revival of classical letters, 218-23
    humanism and other philosophies, 224-39
    humanisms and humanists, 239-46
    the plastic arts, 246-57
    achievement and significance, 258-76

Jacobean Drama LC 33: 1-37
    the Jacobean worldview: an era of transition, 2-14
    the moral vision of Jacobean drama, 14-22
    Jacobean tragedy, 22-23
    the Jacobean masque, 23-36

Jewish-American Fiction TCLC 62: 1-181
    overviews, 2-24
    major figures, 24-48
    Jewish writers and American life, 48-78
    Jewish characters in American fiction, 78-108
    themes in Jewish-American fiction, 108-43
    Jewish-American women writers, 143-59
    the Holocaust and Jewish-American fiction, 159-81

Knickerbocker Group, The NCLC 56: 274-341
    overviews, 276-314
    Knickerbocker periodicals, 314-26
    writers and artists, 326-40

Lake Poets, The NCLC 52: 217-304
    characteristics of the Lake Poets and their works, 218-27
    literary influences and collaborations, 227-66
    defining and developing Romantic ideals, 266-84
    embracing Conservatism, 284-303

Larkin, Philip, Controversy CLC 81: 417-64

Latin American Literature, Twentieth-Century TCLC 58: 111-98
    historical and critical perspectives, 112-36
    the novel, 136-45
    the short story, 145-9
    drama, 149-60
    poetry, 160-7
    the writer and society, 167-86
    Native Americans in Latin American literature, 186-97

Madness in Twentieth-Century Literature TCLC 50: 160-225
    overviews, 161-71
    madness and the creative process, 171-86
    suicide, 186-91
    madness in American literature, 191-207
    madness in German literature, 207-13
    madness and feminist artists, 213-24

Metaphysical Poets LC 24: 356-439
    early definitions, 358-67
    surveys and overviews, 367-92
    cultural and social influences, 392-406
    stylistic and thematic variations, 407-38

Modern Essay, The TCLC 58: 199-273
    overview, 200-7
    the essay in the early twentieth century, 207-19
    characteristics of the modern essay, 219-32
    modern essayists, 232-45
    the essay as a literary genre, 245-73

Modern Japanese Literature TCLC 66: 284-389
    poetry, 285-305
    drama, 305-29
    fiction, 329-61
    western influences, 361-87

Muckraking Movement in American Journalism TCLC 34: 161-242
    development, principles, and major figures, 162-70
    publications, 170-9
    social and political ideas, 179-86
    targets, 186-208

    fiction, 208-19
    decline, 219-29
    impact and accomplishments, 229-40

Multiculturalism in Literature and Education CLC 70: 361-413

Music and Modern Literature TCLC 62: 182-329
    overviews, 182-211
    musical form/literary form, 211-32
    music in literature, 232-50
    the influence of music on literature, 250-73
    literature and popular music, 273-303
    jazz and poetry, 303-28

Native American Literature CLC 76: 440-76

Natural School, Russian NCLC 24: 205-40
    history and characteristics, 205-25
    contemporary criticism, 225-40

Naturalism NCLC 36: 285-382
    definitions and theories, 286-305
    critical debates on Naturalism, 305-16
    Naturalism in theater, 316-32
    European Naturalism, 332-61
    American Naturalism, 361-72
    the legacy of Naturalism, 372-81

Negritude TCLC 50: 226-361
    origins and evolution, 227-56
    definitions, 256-91
    Negritude in literature, 291-343
    Negritude reconsidered, 343-58

New Criticism TCLC 34: 243-318
    development and ideas, 244-70
    debate and defense, 270-99
    influence and legacy, 299-315

The New World in Renaissance Literature LC 31: 1-51
    overview, 1-18
    utopia vs. terror, 18-31
    explorers and Native Americans, 31-51

New York Intellectuals and *Partisan Review* TCLC 30: 117-98

development and major figures, 118-28
influence of Judaism, 128-39
Partisan Review, 139-57
literary philosophy and practice, 157-75
political philosophy, 175-87
achievement and significance, 187-97

The New Yorker TCLC 58: 274-357
overviews, 274-95
major figures, 295-304
New Yorker style, 304-33
fiction, journalism, and humor at *The
New Yorker,* 333-48
the new *New Yorker,* 348-56

Newgate Novel NCLC 24: 166-204
development of Newgate literature, 166-
73
Newgate Calendar, 173-7
Newgate fiction, 177-95
Newgate drama, 195-204

**Nigerian Literature of the Twentieth
Century** TCLC 30: 199-265
surveys of, 199-227
English language and African life, 227-45
politics and the Nigerian writer, 245-54
Nigerian writers and society, 255-62

Northern Humanism LC 16: 281-356
background, 282-305
precursor of the Reformation, 305-14
the Brethren of the Common Life, the
Devotio Moderna, and education,
314-40
the impact of printing, 340-56

Novel of Manners, The NCLC 56: 342-96
social and political order, 343-53
domestic order, 353-73
depictions of gender, 373-83
American novel of manners, the, 383-95

**Nuclear Literature: Writings and
Criticism in the Nuclear Age** TCLC 46:
288-390
overviews, 290-301
fiction, 301-35
poetry, 335-8
nuclear war in Russo-Japanese literature, 338-55
nuclear war and women writers, 355-67
the nuclear referent and literary
criticism, 367-88

Occultism in Modern Literature TCLC 50:
362-406
influence of occultism on literature,
363-72
occultism, literature, and society, 372-87
fiction, 387-96
drama, 396-405

**Opium and the Nineteenth-Century
Literary Imagination** NCLC 20: 250-301
original sources, 250-62
historical background, 262-71
and literary society, 271-9
and literary creativity, 279-300

Periodicals, Nineteenth-Century British
NCLC 24: 100-65
overviews, 100-30
in the Romantic Age, 130-41
in the Victorian era, 142-54
and the reviewer, 154-64

Plath, Sylvia, and the Nature of Biography
CLC 86: 433-62
the nature of biography, 433-52
reviews of *The Silent Woman,* 452-61

Polish Romanticism NCLC 52: 305-71
overviews, 306-26
major figures, 326-40
Polish Romantic drama, 340-62
influences, 362-71

Pre-Raphaelite Movement NCLC 20: 302-
401
overview, 302-4
genesis, 304-12
Germ and *Oxford and Cambridge
Magazine,* 312-20
Robert Buchanan and the "Fleshly
School of Poetry," 320-31
satires and parodies, 331-4
surveys, 334-51
aesthetics, 351-75
sister arts of poetry and painting, 375-94
influence, 394-9

Psychoanalysis and Literature TCLC 38:
227-338
overviews, 227-46
Freud on literature, 246-51
psychoanalytic views of the literary
process, 251-61
psychoanalytic theories of response to

literature, 261-88
psychoanalysis and literary criticism,
288-312
psychoanalysis as literature/literature
as psychoanalysis, 313-34

Rap Music CLC 76: 477-50

Renaissance Natural Philosophy LC 27:
201-87
cosmology, 201-28
astrology, 228-54
magic, 254-86

Restoration Drama LC 21: 184-275
general overviews, 185-230
Jeremy Collier stage controversy, 230-9
other critical interpretations, 240-75

Revising the Literary Canon CLC 81:
465-509

Robin Hood, Legend of LC 19: 205-58
origins and development of the Robin
Hood legend, 206-20
representations of Robin Hood, 220-44
Robin Hood as hero, 244-56

**Rushdie, Salman, *Satanic Verses* Contro-
versy** CLC 55: 214-63; 59: 404-56

Russian Nihilism NCLC 28: 403-47
definitions and overviews, 404-17
women and Nihilism, 417-27
literature as reform: the Civic Critics,
427-33
Nihilism and the Russian novel:
Turgenev and Dostoevsky, 433-47

Russian Thaw TCLC 26: 189-247
literary history of the period, 190-206
theoretical debate of socialist realism,
206-11
Novy Mir, 211-7
Literary Moscow, 217-24
Pasternak, *Zhivago,* and the Nobel
Prize, 224-7
poetry of liberation, 228-31
Brodsky trial and the end of the Thaw,
231-6
achievement and influence, 236-46

Salinger, J. D., Controversy Surrounding *In Search of J. D. Salinger* CLC 55: 325-44

Science Fiction, Nineteenth-Century NCLC 24: 241-306
    background, 242-50
    definitions of the genre, 251-6
    representative works and writers, 256-75
    themes and conventions, 276-305

Scottish Chaucerians LC 20: 363-412

Scottish Poetry, Eighteenth-Century LC 29: 95-167
    overviews, 96-114
    the Scottish Augustans, 114-28
    the Scots Vernacular Revival, 132-63
    Scottish poetry after Burns, 163-6

Sherlock Holmes Centenary TCLC 26: 248-310
    Doyle's life and the composition of the Holmes stories, 248-59
    life and character of Holmes, 259-78
    method, 278-9
    Holmes and the Victorian world, 279-92
    Sherlockian scholarship, 292-301
    Doyle and the development of the detective story, 301-7
    Holmes's continuing popularity, 307-9

Slave Narratives, American NCLC 20: 1-91
    background, 2-9
    overviews, 9-24
    contemporary responses, 24-7
    language, theme, and technique, 27-70
    historical authenticity, 70-5
    antecedents, 75-83
    role in development of Black American literature, 83-8

Spanish Civil War Literature TCLC 26: 311-85
    topics in, 312-33
    British and American literature, 333-59
    French literature, 359-62
    Spanish literature, 362-73
    German literature, 373-5
    political idealism and war literature, 375-83

Spanish Golden Age Literature LC 23: 262-332
    overviews, 263-81
    verse drama, 281-304
    prose fiction, 304-19
    lyric poetry, 319-31

Spasmodic School of Poetry NCLC 24: 307-52
    history and major figures, 307-21
    the Spasmodics on poetry, 321-7
    Firmilian and critical disfavor, 327-39
    theme and technique, 339-47
    influence, 347-51

Steinbeck, John, Fiftieth Anniversary of *The Grapes of Wrath* CLC 59: 311-54

Sturm und Drang NCLC 40: 196-276
    definitions, 197-238
    poetry and poetics, 238-58
    drama, 258-75

Supernatural Fiction in the Nineteenth Century NCLC 32: 207-87
    major figures and influences, 208-35
    the Victorian ghost story, 236-54
    the influence of science and occultism, 254-66
    supernatural fiction and society, 266-86

Supernatural Fiction, Modern TCLC 30: 59-116
    evolution and varieties, 60-74
    "decline" of the ghost story, 74-86
    as a literary genre, 86-92
    technique, 92-101
    nature and appeal, 101-15

Surrealism TCLC 30: 334-406
    history and formative influences, 335-43
    manifestos, 343-54
    philosophic, aesthetic, and political principles, 354-75
    poetry, 375-81
    novel, 381-6
    drama, 386-92
    film, 392-8
    painting and sculpture, 398-403
    achievement, 403-5

Symbolism, Russian TCLC 30: 266-333
    doctrines and major figures, 267-92

    theories, 293-8
    and French Symbolism, 298-310
    themes in poetry, 310-4
    theater, 314-20
    and the fine arts, 320-32

Symbolist Movement, French NCLC 20: 169-249
    background and characteristics, 170-86
    principles, 186-91
    attacked and defended, 191-7
    influences and predecessors, 197-211
    and Decadence, 211-6
    theater, 216-26
    prose, 226-33
    decline and influence, 233-47

Theater of the Absurd TCLC 38: 339-415
    "The Theater of the Absurd," 340-7
    major plays and playwrights, 347-58
    and the concept of the absurd, 358-86
    theatrical techniques, 386-94
    predecessors of, 394-402
    influence of, 402-13

Tin Pan Alley
See **American Popular Song, Golden Age of**

Transcendentalism, American NCLC 24: 1-99
    overviews, 3-23
    contemporary documents, 23-41
    theological aspects of, 42-52
    and social issues, 52-74
    literature of, 74-96

Travel Writing in the Nineteenth Century NCLC 44: 274-392
    the European grand tour, 275-303
    the Orient, 303-47
    North America, 347-91

Travel Writing in the Twentieth Century TCLC 30: 407-56
    conventions and traditions, 407-27
    and fiction writing, 427-43
    comparative essays on travel writers, 443-54

***Ulysses* and the Process of Textual Reconstruction** TCLC 26: 386-416
    evaluations of the new *Ulysses,* 386-94

editorial principles and procedures,
    394-401
theoretical issues, 401-16

Utopian Literature, Nineteenth-Century
NCLC 24: 353-473
    definitions, 354-74
    overviews, 374-88
    theory, 388-408
    communities, 409-26
    fiction, 426-53
    women and fiction, 454-71

Utopian Literature, Renaissance LC-32:
1-63
    overviews, 2-25
    classical background, 25-33
    utopia and the social contract, 33-9
    origins in mythology, 39-48
    utopia and the Renaissance country
        house, 48-52
    influence of millenarianism, 52-62

Vampire in Literature TCLC 46: 391-454
    origins and evolution, 392-412
    social and psychological perspectives,
        413-44
    vampire fiction and science fiction,
        445-53

Victorian Autobiography NCLC 40: 277-
363
    development and major characteristics,
        278-88
    themes and techniques, 289-313
    the autobiographical tendency in
        Victorian prose and poetry, 313-47
    Victorian women's autobiographies,
        347-62

Victorian Novel NCLC 32: 288-454
    development and major characteristics,
        290-310
    themes and techniques, 310-58
    social criticism in the Victorian novel,
        359-97
    urban and rural life in the Victorian
        novel, 397-406
    women in the Victorian novel, 406-25
    Mudie's Circulating Library, 425-34
    the late-Victorian novel, 434-51

Vietnam War in Literature and Film CLC
91: 383-437

overview, 384-8
prose, 388-412
film and drama, 412-24
poetry, 424-35

Vorticism TCLC 62: 330-426
    Wyndham Lewis and Vorticism, 330-8
    characteristics and principles of
        Vorticism, 338-65
    Lewis and Pound, 365-82
    Vorticist writing, 382-416
    Vorticist painting, 416-26

Women's Diaries, Nineteenth-Century
NCLC 48: 308-54
    overview, 308-13
    diary as history, 314-25
    sociology of diaries, 325-34
    diaries as psychological scholarship,
        334-43
    diary as autobiography, 343-8
    diary as literature, 348-53

Women Writers, Seventeenth-Century
LC 30: 2-58
    overview, 2-15
    women and education, 15-9
    women and autobiography, 19-31
    women's diaries, 31-9
    early feminists, 39-58

World War I Literature TCLC 34: 392-
486
    overview, 393-403
    English, 403-27
    German, 427-50
    American, 450-66
    French, 466-74
    and modern history, 474-82

Yellow Journalism NCLC 36: 383-456
    overviews, 384-96
    major figures, 396-413

Young Playwrights Festival
    1988–CLC 55: 376-81
    1989–CLC 59: 398-403
    1990–CLC 65: 444-8

Cumulative Nationality Index

AMERICAN

Adams, Andy **56**
Adams, Henry (Brooks) **4, 52**
Agee, James (Rufus) **1, 19**
Anderson, Maxwell **2**
Anderson, Sherwood **1, 10, 24**
Atherton, Gertrude (Franklin Horn) **2**
Austin, Mary (Hunter) **25**
Baker, Ray Stannard **47**
Barry, Philip **11**
Baum, L(yman) Frank **7**
Beard, Charles A(ustin) **15**
Becker, Carl **63:**
Belasco, David **3**
Bell, James Madison **43**
Benchley, Robert (Charles) **1, 55**
Benedict, Ruth **60**
Benet, Stephen Vincent **7**
Benet, William Rose **28**
Bierce, Ambrose (Gwinett) **1, 7, 44**
Biggers, Earl Derr **65**
Black Elk **33**
Boas, Franz **56**
Bodenheim, Maxwell **44**
Bourne, Randolph S(illiman) **16**
Bradford, Gamaliel **36**
Brennan, Christopher John **17**
Bromfield, Louis (Brucker) **11**
Burroughs, Edgar Rice **2, 32**
Cabell, James Branch **6**
Cable, George Washington **4**
Cardozo, Benjamin N(athan) **65**
Carnegie, Dale **53**
Cather, Willa Sibert **1, 11, 31**
Chambers, Robert W. **41**
Chandler, Raymond (Thornton) **1, 7**
Chapman, John Jay **7**
Chesnutt, Charles W(addell) **5, 39**
Chopin, Kate **5, 14**

Cohan, George M. **60**
Comstock, Anthony **13**
Cotter, Joseph Seamon Sr. **28**
Cram, Ralph Adams **45**
Crane, (Harold) Hart **2, 5**
Crane, Stephen (Townley) **11, 17, 32**
Crawford, F(rancis) Marion **10**
Crothers, Rachel **19**
Cullen, Countee **4, 37**
Davis, Rebecca (Blaine) Harding **6**
Davis, Richard Harding **24**
Day, Clarence (Shepard Jr.) **25**
De Voto, Bernard (Augustine) **29**
Dreiser, Theodore (Herman Albert) **10, 18, 35**
Dunbar, Paul Laurence **2, 12**
Dunne, Finley Peter **28**
Eastman, Charles A(lexander) **55**
Einstein, Albert **65**
Faust, Frederick (Schiller) **49**
Fisher, Rudolph **11**
Fitzgerald, F(rancis) Scott (Key) **1, 6, 14, 28, 55**
Fitzgerald, Zelda (Sayre) **52**
Flecker, (Herman) James Elroy **43**
Fletcher, John Gould **35**
Forten, Charlotte L. **16**
Freeman, Douglas Southall **11**
Freeman, Mary Eleanor Wilkins **9**
Futrelle, Jacques **19**
Gale, Zona **7**
Garland, (Hannibal) Hamlin **3**
Gilman, Charlotte (Anna) Perkins (Stetson) **9, 37**
Glasgow, Ellen (Anderson Gholson) **2, 7**
Glaspell, Susan **55**
Goldman, Emma **13**
Green, Anna Katharine **63**
Grey, Zane **6**

Guiney, Louise Imogen **41**
Hall, James Norman **23**
Harper, Frances Ellen Watkins **14**
Harris, Joel Chandler **2**
Harte, (Francis) Bret(t) **1, 25**
Hatteras, Owen **18**
Hawthorne, Julian **25**
Hearn, (Patricio) Lafcadio (Tessima Carlos) **9**
Henry, O. **1, 19**
Hergesheimer, Joseph **11**
Higginson, Thomas Wentworth **36**
Holly, Buddy **65**
Hopkins, Pauline Elizabeth **28**
Howard, Robert Ervin **8**
Howe, Julia Ward **21**
Howells, William Dean **7, 17, 41**
Huneker, James Gibbons **65**
James, Henry **2, 11, 24, 40, 47, 64**
James, William **15, 32**
Jewett, (Theodora) Sarah Orne **1, 22**
Johnson, James Weldon **3, 19**
Kornbluth, C(yril) M. **8**
Korzybski, Alfred (Habdank Skarbek) **61**
Kuttner, Henry **10**
Lardner, Ring(gold) W(ilmer) **2, 14**
Lewis, (Harry) Sinclair **4, 13, 23, 39**
Lewisohn, Ludwig **19**
Lindsay, (Nicholas) Vachel **17**
Locke, Alain (Le Roy) **43**
London, Jack **9, 15, 39**
Lovecraft, H(oward) P(hillips) **4, 22**
Lowell, Amy **1, 8**
Markham, Edwin **47**
Marquis, Don(ald Robert Perry) **7**
Masters, Edgar Lee **2, 25**
McCoy, Horace (Stanley) **28**
McKay, Claude **7, 41**
Mencken, H(enry) L(ouis) **13**

431

Millay, Edna St. Vincent   **4, 49**
Mitchell, Margaret (Munnerlyn)   **11**
Mitchell, S(ilas) Weir   **36**
Monroe, Harriet   **12**
Muir, John   **28**
Nathan, George Jean   **18**
Nordhoff, Charles (Bernard)   **23**
Norris, Benjamin Franklin Jr.   **24**
O'Neill, Eugene (Gladstone)   **1, 6, 27, 49**
Oskison, John Milton   **35**
Phillips, David Graham   **44**
Porter, Gene(va Grace) Stratton   **21**
Post, Melville Davisson   **39**
Rawlings, Marjorie Kinnan   **4**
Reed, John (Silas)   **9**
Reich, Wilhelm   **57**
Rhodes, Eugene Manlove   **53**
Riggs, (Rolla) Lynn   **56**
Riley, James Whitcomb   **51**
Rinehart, Mary Roberts   **52**
Roberts, Kenneth (Lewis)   **23**
Robinson, Edwin Arlington   **5**
Roelvaag, O(le) E(dvart)   **17**
Rogers, Will(iam Penn Adair)   **8**
Rourke, Constance (Mayfield)   **12**
Runyon, (Alfred) Damon   **10**
Saltus, Edgar (Everton)   **8**
Santayana, George   **40**
Sherwood, Robert E(mmet)   **3**
Slesinger, Tess   **10**
Steffens, (Joseph) Lincoln   **20**
Stein, Gertrude   **1, 6, 28, 48**
Sterling, George   **20**
Stevens, Wallace   **3, 12, 45**
Stockton, Frank R.   **47**
Sturges, Preston   **48**
Tarbell, Ida M(inerva)   **40**
Tarkington, (Newton) Booth   **9**
Teasdale, Sara   **4**
Thurman, Wallace (Henry)   **6**
Twain, Mark   **6, 12, 19, 36, 48, 59**
Van Dine, S. S.   **23**
Van Doren, Carl (Clinton)   **18**
Veblen, Thorstein (Bunde)   **31**
Washington, Booker T(aliaferro)   **10**
Wells, Carolyn   **35**
West, Nathanael   **1, 14, 44**
Whale, James   **63**
Wharton, Edith (Newbold Jones)   **3, 9, 27, 53**
White, Walter F(rancis)   **15**
Wister, Owen   **21**
Wolfe, Thomas (Clayton)   **4, 13, 29, 61**
Woollcott, Alexander (Humphreys)   **5**
Wylie, Elinor (Morton Hoyt)   **8**

ARGENTINIAN
Arlt, Roberto (Godofredo Christophersen)   **29**
Guiraldes, Ricardo (Guillermo)   **39**
Lugones, Leopoldo   **15**
Storni, Alfonsina   **5**

AUSTRALIAN
Baynton, Barbara   **57**
Franklin, (Stella Maraia Sarah) Miles   **7**
Furphy, Joseph   **25**
Ingamells, Rex   **35**
Lawson, Henry (Archibald Hertzberg)   **27**
Paterson, A(ndrew) B(arton)   **32**
Richardson, Henry Handel   **4**
Warung, Price   **45**

AUSTRIAN
Beer-Hofmann, Richard   **60**
Broch, Hermann   **20**
Freud, Sigmund   **52**
Hofmannsthal, Hugo von   **11**
Kafka, Franz   **2, 6, 13, 29, 47, 53**
Kraus, Karl   **5**
Kubin, Alfred (Leopold Isidor)   **23**
Meyrink, Gustav   **21**
Musil, Robert (Edler von)   **12**
Perutz, Leo   **60**
Roth, Joseph   **33**
Schnitzler, Arthur   **4**
Steiner, Rudolf   **13**
Trakl, Georg   **5**
Werfel, Franz (V.)   **8**
Zweig, Stefan   **17**

BELGIAN
Bosschere, Jean de   **19**
Lemonnier, (Antoine Louis) Camille   **22**
Maeterlinck, Maurice   **3**
van Ostaijen, Paul   **33**
Verhaeren, Emile (Adolphe Gustave)   **12**

BRAZILIAN
Andrade, Mario de   **43**
Cunha, Euclides (Rodrigues Pimenta) da   **24**
Lima Barreto, Afonso Henrique de   **23**
Machado de Assis, Joaquim Maria   **10**
Ramos, Graciliano   **32**

BULGARIAN
Vazov, Ivan (Minchov)   **25**

CANADIAN
Campbell, Wilfred   **9**
Carman, (William) Bliss   **7**
Carr, Emily   **32**
Connor, Ralph   **31**
Drummond, William Henry   **25**
Duncan, Sara Jeannette   **60**
Garneau, (Hector de) Saint-Denys   **13**
Grove, Frederick Philip   **4**
Knister, Raymond   **56**
Leacock, Stephen (Butler)   **2**
McCrae, John   **12**
Montgomery, L(ucy) M(aud)   **51**
Nelligan, Emile   **14**
Pickthall, Marjorie L(owry) C(hristie)   **21**
Roberts, Charles G(eorge) D(ouglas)   **8**
Scott, Duncan Campbell   **6**
Service, Robert W(illiam)   **15**
Seton, Ernest (Evan) Thompson   **31**
Stringer, Arthur   **37**

CHILEAN
Huidobro Fernandez, Vicente Garcia   **31**
Mistral, Gabriela   **2**

CHINESE
Liu E   **15**
Lu Hsun   **3**
Su Man-shu   **24**
Wen I-to   **28**

COLOMBIAN
Rivera, Jose Eustasio   **35**

CZECH
Capek, Karel   **6, 37**

Freud, Sigmund   **52**
Hasek, Jaroslav (Matej Frantisek)   **4**
Kafka, Franz   **2, 6, 13, 29, 47, 53**
Nezval, Vitezslav   **44**

DANISH
Brandes, Georg (Morris Cohen)   **10**
Hansen, Martin A.   **32**
Jensen, Johannes V.   **41**
Nexo, Martin Andersen   **43**
Pontoppidan, Henrik   **29**

DUTCH
Couperus, Louis (Marie Anne)   **15**
Frank, Anne(lies Marie)   **17**
Heijermans, Herman   **24**
Hillesum, Etty   **49**
Schendel, Arthur van   **56**

ENGLISH
Barbellion, W. N. P.   **24**
Baring, Maurice   **8**
Beerbohm, (Henry) Max(imilian)   **1, 24**
Bell, Gertrude   **67**
Belloc, (Joseph) Hilaire (Pierre Sebastien Rene Swanton)   **7, 18**
Bennett, (Enoch) Arnold   **5, 20**
Benson, E(dward) F(rederic)   **27**
Benson, Stella   **17**
Bentley, E(dmund) C(lerihew)   **12**
Besant, Annie (Wood)   **9**
Blackmore, R(ichard) D(oddridge)   **27**
Blackwood, Algernon (Henry)   **5**
Bridges, Robert (Seymour)   **1**
Brooke, Rupert (Chawner)   **2, 7**
Burke, Thomas   **63**
Butler, Samuel   **1, 33**
Byron, Robert   **67**
Chesterton, G(ilbert) K(eith)   **1, 6, 64**
Childers, (Robert) Erskine   **65**
Collingwood, R(obin) G(eorge)   **67**
Conrad, Joseph   **1, 6, 13, 25, 43, 57**
Coppard, A(lfred) E(dgar)   **5**
Corelli, Marie   **51**
Crofts, Freeman Wills   **55**
Crowley, Aleister   **7**
Dale, Colin   **18**
Delafield, E. M.   **61**
de la Mare, Walter (John)   **4, 53**
Doughty, Charles M(ontagu)   **27**
Douglas, Keith   **40**
Dowson, Ernest (Christopher)   **4**
Doyle, Arthur Conan   **7**
Drinkwater, John   **57**
Eddison, E(ric) R(ucker)   **15**
Elaine   **18**
Elizabeth   **41**
Ellis, (Henry) Havelock   **14**
Field, Michael   **43**
Firbank, (Arthur Annesley) Ronald   **1**
Ford, Ford Madox   **1, 15, 39, 57**
Freeman, R(ichard) Austin   **21**
Galsworthy, John   **1, 45**
Gilbert, W(illiam) S(chwenck)   **3**
Gissing, George (Robert)   **3, 24, 47**
Gosse, Edmund (William)   **28**
Grahame, Kenneth   **64**
Granville-Barker, Harley   **2**
Gray, John (Henry)   **19**
Gurney, Ivor (Bertie)   **33**
Haggard, H(enry) Rider   **11**
Hall, (Marguerite) Radclyffe   **12**

Hardy, Thomas   4, 10, 18, 32, 48, 53
Henley, William Ernest   8
Hichens, Robert S.   64
Hilton, James   21
Hodgson, William Hope   13
Housman, A(lfred) E(dward)   1, 10
Housman, Laurence   7
Hudson, W(illiam) H(enry)   29
Hulme, T(homas) E(rnest)   21
Hunt, Violet   53
Jacobs, W(illiam) W(ymark)   22
James, Montague (Rhodes)   6
Jerome, Jerome K(lapka)   23
Johnson, Lionel (Pigot)   19
Kaye-Smith, Sheila   20
Keynes, John Maynard   64
Kipling, (Joseph) Rudyard   8, 17
Lawrence, D(avid) H(erbert Richards)   2, 9, 16, 33, 48, 61
Lawrence, T(homas) E(dward)   18
Lee, Vernon   5
Lee-Hamilton, Eugene (Jacob)   22
Leverson, Ada   18
Lewis, (Percy) Wyndham   2, 9
Lindsay, David   15
Lowndes, Marie Adelaide (Belloc)   12
Lowry, (Clarence) Malcolm   6, 40
Macaulay, Rose   7, 44
MacCarthy, (Sir Charles Otto) Desmond   36
Maitland, Frederic   65
Manning, Frederic   25
Meredith, George   17, 43
Mew, Charlotte (Mary)   8
Meynell, Alice (Christina Gertrude Thompson)   6
Middleton, Richard (Barham)   56
Milne, A(lan) A(lexander)   6
Murry, John Middleton   16
Noyes, Alfred   7
Oppenheim, E(dward) Phillips   45
Orwell, George   2, 6, 15, 31, 51
Ouida   43
Owen, Wilfred (Edward Salter)   5, 27
Pinero, Arthur Wing   32
Powys, T(heodore) F(rancis)   9
Quiller-Couch, Arthur Thomas   53
Richardson, Dorothy Miller   3
Rohmer, Sax   28
Rolfe, Frederick (William Serafino Austin Lewis Mary)   12
Rosenberg, Isaac   12
Ruskin, John   20
Rutherford, Mark   25
Sabatini, Rafael   47
Saintsbury, George (Edward Bateman)   31
Saki   3
Sapper   44
Sayers, Dorothy L(eigh)   2, 15
Shiel, M(atthew) P(hipps)   8
Sinclair, May   3, 11
Stapledon, (William) Olaf   22
Stead, William Thomas   48
Stephen, Leslie   23
Strachey, (Giles) Lytton   12
Summers, (Alphonsus Joseph-Mary Augustus) Montague   16
Sutro, Alfred   6
Swinburne, Algernon Charles   8, 36
Symons, Arthur   11
Thomas, (Philip) Edward   10
Thompson, Francis Joseph   4

Van Druten, John (William)   2
Wallace, (Richard Horatio) Edgar   57
Walpole, Hugh (Seymour)   5
Ward, Mrs. Humphry   55
Warung, Price   45
Webb, (Martha) Beatrice (Potter)   22
Webb, Mary (Gladys Meredith)   24
Webb, Sidney (James)   22
Welch, (Maurice) Denton   22
Wells, H(erbert) G(eorge)   6, 12, 19
Williams, Charles (Walter Stansby)   1, 11
Woolf, (Adeline) Virginia   1, 5, 20, 43, 56
Yonge, Charlotte (Mary)   48
Zangwill, Israel   16

ESTONIAN
Tammsaare, A(nton) H(ansen)   27

FINNISH
Leino, Eino   24
Soedergran, Edith (Irene)   31

FRENCH
Alain   41
Alain-Fournier   6
Apollinaire, Guillaume   3, 8, 51
Artaud, Antonin (Marie Joseph)   3, 36
Barbusse, Henri   5
Barres, Maurice   47
Benda, Julien   60
Bergson, Henri   32
Bernanos, (Paul Louis) Georges   3
Bloy, Leon   22
Bourget, Paul (Charles Joseph)   12
Claudel, Paul (Louis Charles Marie)   2, 10
Colette, (Sidonie-Gabrielle)   1, 5, 16
Coppee, Francois   25
Daumal, Rene   14
Desnos, Robert   22
Drieu la Rochelle, Pierre(-Eugene)   21
Dujardin, Edouard (Emile Louis)   13
Durkheim, Emile   55
Eluard, Paul   7, 41
Fargue, Leon-Paul   11
Feydeau, Georges (Leon Jules Marie)   22
France, Anatole   9
Gide, Andre (Paul Guillaume)   5, 12, 36
Giraudoux, (Hippolyte) Jean   2, 7
Gourmont, Remy (-Marie-Charles) de   17
Huysmans, Joris-Karl   7
Jacob, (Cyprien-)Max   6
Jarry, Alfred   2, 14
Larbaud, Valery (Nicolas)   9
Leblanc, Maurice (Marie Emile)   49
Leroux, Gaston   25
Loti, Pierre   11
Martin du Gard, Roger   24
Mirbeau, Octave   55
Mistral, Frederic   51
Moreas, Jean   18
Nizan, Paul   40
Peguy, Charles Pierre   10
Peret, Benjamin   20
Proust, (Valentin-Louis-George-Eugene-) Marcel   7, 13, 33
Rachilde   67
Radiguet, Raymond   29
Renard, Jules   17
Rolland, Romain   23
Rostand, Edmond (Eugene Alexis)   6, 37
Roussel, Raymond   20

Saint-Exupery, Antoine (Jean Baptiste Marie Roger) de   2, 56
Schwob, (Mayer Andre) Marcel   20
Sully Prudhomme   31
Teilhard de Chardin, (Marie Joseph) Pierre   9
Valery, (Ambroise) Paul (Toussaint Jules)   4, 15
Verne, Jules (Gabriel)   6, 52
Vian, Boris   9
Weil, Simone (Adolphine)   23
Zola, Emile (Edouard Charles Antoine)   1, 6, 21, 41

GERMAN
Andreas-Salome, Lou   56
Auerbach, Erich   43
Benjamin, Walter   39
Benn, Gottfried   3
Borchert, Wolfgang   5
Brecht, Bertolt   1, 6, 13, 35
Carossa, Hans   48
Cassirer, Ernst   61
Doblin, Alfred   13
Doeblin, Alfred   13
Einstein, Albert   65
Ewers, Hanns Heinz   12
Feuchtwanger, Lion   3
George, Stefan (Anton)   2, 14
Hauptmann, Gerhart (Johann Robert)   4
Heym, Georg (Theodor Franz Arthur)   9
Heyse, Paul (Johann Ludwig von)   8
Hitler, Adolf   53
Huch, Ricarda (Octavia)   13
Kaiser, Georg   9
Klabund   44
Kolmar, Gertrud   40
Lasker-Schueler, Else   57
Liliencron, (Friedrich Adolf Axel) Detlev von   18
Luxemburg, Rosa   63
Mann, (Luiz) Heinrich   9
Mann, (Paul) Thomas   2, 8, 14, 21, 35, 44, 60
Mannheim, Karl   65
Morgenstern, Christian   8
Nietzsche, Friedrich (Wilhelm)   10, 18, 55
Plumpe, Friedrich Wilhelm   53
Raabe, Wilhelm   45
Rilke, Rainer Maria   1, 6, 19
Simmel, Georg   64
Spengler, Oswald (Arnold Gottfried)   25
Sternheim, (William Adolf) Carl   8
Sudermann, Hermann   15
Toller, Ernst   10
Wassermann, (Karl) Jakob   6
Wedekind, (Benjamin) Frank(lin)   7
Wiene, Robert   56

GHANIAN
Casely-Hayford, J(oseph) E(phraim)   24

GREEK
Cavafy, C(onstantine) P(eter)   2, 7
Kazantzakis, Nikos   2, 5, 33
Palamas, Kostes   5
Papadiamantis, Alexandros   29
Sikelianos, Angelos   39

HAITIAN
Roumain, Jacques (Jean Baptiste)   19

Nationality Index

HUNGARIAN
Ady, Endre **11**
Babits, Mihaly **14**
Csath, Geza **13**
Herzl, Theodor **36**
Horvath, Oedoen von **45**
Jozsef, Attila **22**
Karinthy, Frigyes **47**
Mikszath, Kalman **31**
Molnar, Ferenc **20**
Moricz, Zsigmond **33**
Radnoti, Miklos **16**

ICELANDIC
Sigurjonsson, Johann **27**

INDIAN
Aurobindo, Sri **63**
Chatterji, Saratchandra **13**
Gandhi, Mohandas Karamchand **59**
Iqbal, Muhammad **28**
Premchand **21**
Tagore, Rabindranath **3, 53**

INDONESIAN
Anwar, Chairil **22**

IRANIAN
Hedayat, Sadeq **21**

IRISH
Cary, (Arthur) Joyce (Lunel) **1, 29**
Dunsany, Lord **2, 59**
Gogarty, Oliver St. John **15**
Gregory, Isabella Augusta (Persse) **1**
Harris, Frank **24**
Joyce, James (Augustine Aloysius) **3, 8, 16, 35, 52**
Ledwidge, Francis **23**
Martin, Violet Florence **51**
Moore, George Augustus **7**
O'Grady, Standish James **5**
Riddell, J. H. **40**
Shaw, Bernard **45**
Shaw, George Bernard **3, 9, 21**
Somerville, Edith **51**
Stephens, James **4**
Stoker, Bram **8**
Synge, (Edmund) J(ohn) M(illington) **6, 37**
Tynan, Katharine **3**
Wilde, Oscar (Fingal O'Flahertie Wills) **1, 8, 23, 41**
Yeats, William Butler **1, 11, 18, 31**

ITALIAN
Alvaro, Corrado **60**
Betti, Ugo **5**
Brancati, Vitaliano **12**
Campana, Dino **20**
Carducci, Giosue **32**
Croce, Benedetto **37**
D'Annunzio, Gabriele **6, 40**
Deledda, Grazia (Cosima) **23**
Giacosa, Giuseppe **7**
Lampedusa, Giuseppe (Tomasi) di **13**
Malaparte, Curzio **52**
Marinetti, Filippo Tommaso **10**
Papini, Giovanni **22**
Pascoli, Giovanni **45**
Pavese, Cesare **3**
Pirandello, Luigi **4, 29**
Saba, Umberto **33**

Svevo, Italo **2, 35**
Tozzi, Federigo **31**
Verga, Giovanni (Carmelo) **3**

JAMAICAN
De Lisser, H(erbert) G(eorge) **12**
Garvey, Marcus (Moziah Jr.) **41**
Mais, Roger **8**
McKay, Claude **7, 41**
Redcam, Tom **25**

JAPANESE
Akutagawa, Ryunosuke **16**
Dazai, Osamu **11**
Futabatei, Shimei **44**
Hagiwara Sakutaro **60**
Hayashi Fumiko **27**
Ishikawa, Takuboku **15**
Masaoka Shiki **18**
Miyamoto, Yuriko **37**
Mori Ogai **14**
Nagai Kafu **51**
Natsume, Soseki **2, 10**
Rohan, Koda **22**
Shimazaki Toson **5**
Yokomitsu Riichi **47**
Yosano Akiko **59**

LATVIAN
Rainis, Janis **29**

LEBANESE
Gibran, Kahlil **1, 9**

LESOTHAN
Mofolo, Thomas (Mokopu) **22**

LITHUANIAN
Kreve (Mickevicius), Vincas **27**

MEXICAN
Azuela, Mariano **3**
Gamboa, Federico **36**
Nervo, (Jose) Amado (Ruiz de) **11**
Reyes, Alfonso **33**
Romero, Jose Ruben **14**

NEPALI
Devkota, Laxmiprasad **23**

NEW ZEALANDER
Mander, (Mary) Jane **31**
Mansfield, Katherine **2, 8, 39**

NICARAGUAN
Dario, Ruben **4**

NORWEGIAN
Bjornson, Bjornstjerne (Martinius) **7, 37**
Bojer, Johan **64**
Grieg, (Johan) Nordahl (Brun) **10**
Hamsun, Knut **2, 14, 49**
Ibsen, Henrik (Johan) **2, 8, 16, 37, 52**
Kielland, Alexander Lange **5**
Lie, Jonas (Lauritz Idemil) **5**
Obstfelder, Sigbjoern **23**
Skram, Amalie (Bertha) **25**
Undset, Sigrid **3**

PAKISTANI
Iqbal, Muhammad **28**

PERUVIAN
Palma, Ricardo **29**
Vallejo, Cesar (Abraham) **3, 56**

POLISH
Asch, Sholem **3**
Borowski, Tadeusz **9**
Conrad, Joseph **1, 6, 13, 25, 43, 57**
Peretz, Isaac Loeb **16**
Prus, Boleslaw **48**
Przybyszewski, Stanislaw **36**
Reymont, Wladyslaw (Stanislaw) **5**
Schulz, Bruno **5, 51**
Sienkiewicz, Henryk (Adam Alexander Pius) **3**
Singer, Israel Joshua **33**
Witkiewicz, Stanislaw Ignacy **8**

PORTUGUESE
Pessoa, Fernando (Antonio Nogueira) **27**

PUERTO RICAN
Hostos (y Bonilla), Eugenio Maria de **24**

ROMANIAN
Bacovia, George **24**
Rebreanu, Liviu **28**

RUSSIAN
Aldanov, Mark (Alexandrovich) **23**
Andreyev, Leonid (Nikolaevich) **3**
Annensky, Innokenty Fyodorovich **14**
Artsybashev, Mikhail (Petrovich) **31**
Babel, Isaak (Emmanuilovich) **2, 13**
Bagritsky, Eduard **60**
Balmont, Konstantin (Dmitriyevich) **11**
Bely, Andrey **7**
Berdyaev, Nikolai (Aleksandrovich) **67**
Blok, Alexander (Alexandrovich) **5**
Bryusov, Valery Yakovlevich **10**
Bulgakov, Mikhail (Afanas'evich) **2, 16**
Bulgya, Alexander Alexandrovich **53**
Bunin, Ivan Alexeyevich **6**
Chekhov, Anton (Pavlovich) **3, 10, 31, 55**
Der Nister **56**
Eisenstein, Sergei (Mikhailovich) **57**
Esenin, Sergei (Alexandrovich) **4**
Fadeyev, Alexander **53**
Gladkov, Fyodor (Vasilyevich) **27**
Gorky, Maxim **8**
Gumilev, Nikolai Stephanovich **60**
Guro, Elena **56**
Hippius, Zinaida **9**
Ilf, Ilya **21**
Ivanov, Vyacheslav Ivanovich **33**
Khlebnikov, Velimir **20**
Khodasevich, Vladislav (Felitsianovich) **15**
Korolenko, Vladimir Galaktionovich **22**
Kropotkin, Peter (Aleksieevich) **36**
Kuprin, Aleksandr Ivanovich **5**
Kuzmin, Mikhail **40**
Lenin, V. I. **67**
Mandelstam, Osip (Emilievich) **2, 6**
Mayakovski, Vladimir (Vladimirovich) **4, 18**
Merezhkovsky, Dmitry Sergeyevich **29**
Petrov, Evgeny **21**
Pilnyak, Boris **23**
Platonov, Andrei **14**
Remizov, Aleksei (Mikhailovich) **27**
Shestov, Lev **56**
Sologub, Fyodor **9**

Tolstoy, Alexey Nikolaevich **18**
Tolstoy, Leo (Nikolaevich) **4, 11, 17, 28, 44**
Trotsky, Leon **22**
Tsvetaeva (Efron), Marina (Ivanovna) **7, 35**
Zabolotskii, Nikolai Alekseevich **52**
Zamyatin, Evgeny Ivanovich **8, 37**
Zhdanov, Andrei A(lexandrovich) **18**
Zoshchenko, Mikhail (Mikhailovich) **15**

SCOTTISH
Barrie, J(ames) M(atthew) **2**
Bridie, James **3**
Brown, George Douglas **28**
Buchan, John **41**
Cunninghame Graham, R(obert) B(ontine) **19**
Davidson, John **24**
Frazer, J(ames) G(eorge) **32**
Gibbon, Lewis Grassic **4**
Lang, Andrew **16**
MacDonald, George **9**
Muir, Edwin **2**
Sharp, William **39**
Tey, Josephine **14**

SOUTH AFRICAN
Bosman, Herman Charles **49**
Campbell, (Ignatius) Roy (Dunnachie) **5**
Mqhayi, S(amuel) E(dward) K(rune Loliwe) **25**
Schreiner, Olive (Emilie Albertina) **9**
Smith, Pauline (Urmson) **25**
Vilakazi, Benedict Wallet **37**

SPANISH
Alas (y Urena), Leopoldo (Enrique Garcia) **29**
Barea, Arturo **14**
Baroja (y Nessi), Pio **8**
Benavente (y Martinez), Jacinto **3**
Blasco Ibanez, Vicente **12**
Echegaray (y Eizaguirre), Jose (Maria Waldo) **4**
Garcia Lorca, Federico **1, 7, 49**
Jimenez (Mantecon), Juan Ramon **4**
Machado (y Ruiz), Antonio **3**
Martinez Sierra, Gregorio **6**
Martinez Sierra, Maria (de la O'LeJarraga) **6**
Miro (Ferrer), Gabriel (Francisco Victor) **5**
Ortega y Gasset, Jose **9**
Pereda (y Sanchez de Porrua), Jose Maria de **16**
Perez Galdos, Benito **27**
Salinas (y Serrano), Pedro **17**
Unamuno (y Jugo), Miguel de **2, 9**
Valera y Alcala-Galiano, Juan **10**
Valle-Inclan, Ramon (Maria) del **5**

SWEDISH
Bengtsson, Frans (Gunnar) **48**
Dagerman, Stig (Halvard) **17**
Heidenstam, (Carl Gustaf) Verner von **5**
Key, Ellen **65**
Lagerloef, Selma (Ottiliana Lovisa) **4, 36**
Soderberg, Hjalmar **39**
Strindberg, (Johan) August **1, 8, 21, 47**

SWISS
Ramuz, Charles-Ferdinand **33**

Rod, Edouard **52**
Saussure, Ferdinand de **49**
Spitteler, Carl (Friedrich Georg) **12**
Walser, Robert **18**

SYRIAN
Gibran, Kahlil **1, 9**

TURKISH
Sait Faik **23**

UKRAINIAN
Aleichem, Sholom **1, 35**
Bialik, Chaim Nachman **25**

URUGUAYAN
Quiroga, Horacio (Sylvestre) **20**
Sanchez, Florencio **37**

WELSH
Davies, W(illiam) H(enry) **5**
Lewis, Alun **3**
Machen, Arthur **4**
Thomas, Dylan (Marlais) **1, 8, 45**

Nationality Index

TCLC VOL 67

ISBN 0-7876-1166-2

90000

9 780787 611668